The Persecution and Murder of the Jews, 1933–1945

The Persecution and Murder of the European Jews by Nazi Germany, 1933–1945

Series edited on behalf of the German Federal Archives, the Leibniz Institute for Contemporary History (IfZ), the Modern History Research Group at the Albert Ludwig University of Freiburg, and the Chair for East European History at the Freie Universität Berlin

In cooperation with Yad Vashem

Volume 12

edited by
Susanne Heim, Ulrich Herbert, Michael Hollmann, Horst Möller, Dieter Pohl, Simone Walther-von Jena, and Andreas Wirsching

English edition also edited by
Sybille Steinbacher

The Persecution and Murder of the European Jews by Nazi Germany, 1933–1945

Volume 12

Western and Northern Europe June 1942–1945

Executive Editors
Katja Happe, Barbara Lambauer, and Clemens Maier-Wolthausen, with Maja Peers

English-language edition prepared by
Elizabeth Harvey, Johannes Gamm, Georg Felix Harsch, Dorothy A. Mas, and Caroline Pearce

DE GRUYTER
OLDENBOURG

יד ושם
YAD VASHEM
THE WORLD HOLOCAUST REMEMBRANCE CENTER

THE INTERNATIONAL INSTITUTE FOR HOLOCAUST RESEARCH

ISBN 978-3-11-068332-5
e-ISBN (PDF) 978-3-11-068773-6
e-ISBN (EPUB) 978-3-11-068787-3

Library of Congress Control Number: 2021940464

Bibliographical information published by the Deutsche Nationalbibliothek
The Deutsche Nationalbibliothek lists this publication in the Deutsche Nationalbibliografie; detailed bibliographical information is available at http://dnb.dnb.de.

Typesetting: Meta Systems Publishing & Printservices GmbH, Wustermark
Cover and dust jacket: Frank Ortmann
Cartography: Peter Palm
Printing and binding: Beltz Bad Langensalza GmbH

www.degruyter.com

Contents

Foreword to the English Edition

The Persecution and Murder of the European Jews by Nazi Germany, 1933–1945 presents a broad range of primary sources in a scholarly edition. A total of sixteen English-language volumes will be published in this series, organized chronologically and according to region. The series places particular focus on the countries which had the highest Jewish populations before the outbreak of the Second World War, above all Poland and the occupied territories of the Soviet Union. The English-language edition reproduces all the materials in the German edition and has been adapted for an English-speaking readership. Apart from those originally written in English, all documents presented here have been translated from the language of the original source.

This volume, the twelfth in the series, covers the persecution of Jews in Norway, the Netherlands, Belgium, Luxembourg, and France from summer 1942 onwards. At that time deportations from Luxembourg and France had already begun, and they were imminent in the Netherlands, Belgium, and Norway. The preceding developments in these countries between 1940 and 1942 are covered in volume 5 of the series (published in 2021). The present volume additionally records the situation of the Jews in Denmark after June 1939, and documents the onset of persecution by the German occupiers in that country around August 1943. It covers developments across all these countries up until the end of the war, also including responses to liberation as it occurred in different parts of Western and Northern Europe.

The foreword to the first volume of the series details the criteria for the selection of the documents. These criteria can be summarized as follows. First, the sources used are written documents and, occasionally, transcribed audio recordings, dating from the period of Nazi rule between 1933 and 1945. The decision was taken not to include memoirs, reports, and judicial documents produced after 1945; however, the footnotes make extensive reference to such retrospective testimonies and historical accounts. Second, the documents shed light on the actions and reactions of people with differing backgrounds and convictions and in different places, and indicate their intentions, as well as the frequently limited options available to them. The volumes include a variety of document types such as official correspondence, private letters, diary entries, legal texts, newspaper articles, and the reports of foreign observers.

Key themes of this twelfth volume are the mass roundups of Jews, the seizure of Jewish property, confinement and conditions in internment and transit camps, forced labour, and the deportations to the East. The documents provide detailed insights into the role and collaboration of local administrations and police forces in the implementation of antisemitic measures. They illustrate the reactions of the Jewish and non-Jewish population to the escalating persecution, as well as actions taken by the resistance and attempts to flee or go into hiding. The sources included range from a letter from a female Nasjonal Samling activist to Vidkun Quisling calling for tougher antisemitic measures, the report by Werner Best on the roundup of Danish Jews in October 1943, a French Protestant pastor's description of conditions in the internment camp in Gurs, and diary entries by Jews imprisoned in Westerbork and facing deportation, to a report by a Jewish resistance organization in Belgium on actions taken to hide Jewish children. Events and developments are therefore presented from multiple perspectives. The arrangement of the documents by country highlights regional similarities and differences regarding the situation of the Jews at the time. A detailed index makes it possible to locate documents by theme.

The editors wish to thank the German Research Foundation (DFG) for its generous funding of the German and English-language projects. The English-language volumes are produced in cooperation with the Yad Vashem International Institute for Holocaust Research. The editors are also grateful to the large number of specialists and private individuals who provided the editors with advice and comments on sources and with information for the annotations, including biographical details for the people featured in the documents.

Kathleen Luft, Todd Brown, Simon Garnett, David Hill, Martin Pearce, and Allen G. Blunden translated the German documents for this twelfth volume in the series. Cathy Mulder translated the documents from Danish and Swedish, and the Norwegian translations were completed by John Kingmann. Rasmus Rønn and Christian Schmittwilken also worked on the translations from Scandinavian languages. The Dutch and Flemish documents were translated by Hilde ten Hacken. Rick Tazelaar provided additional assistance with these translations. Christine Baycroft, Daria Chernysheva, and Karine Zbinden translated the French documents. Yad Vashem provided translations from Yiddish and Hebrew: Rebecca Wolpe translated the Yiddish document and Naftali Greenwood translated the Hebrew documents. David Hill revised and adapted the texts of poems translated from German and Dutch. Rona Johnston Gordon, Alissa Jones Nelson, and Merle Read provided proofreading and copy-editing services. Peter Palm created and Giles Bennett advised on the maps, and Frank Ortmann designed the book jacket. Nora Huberty, Lea von der Hude, Ashley Kirspel, Priska Komaromi, Benedict Oldfield, Charlie Perris, Aliena Stürzer, Barbara Uchdorf, Lena Werner, and Max Zeterberg contributed to this volume as student assistants. The following people contributed to the original German volume as student assistants: Olav Bogen, Florian Brandenburg, Johannes Breit, Bjarte Bruland, Florian Danecke, Stefanie Haupt, Anne-Christin Klotz, Bernhard Lück, Anselm Meyer, Carolin Raabe, Miriam Schelp, Sarah Scherzer, Remigius Stachowiak and Barbara Wünnenberg. Romina Becker, Sarah Berger, Jean-Marc Dreyfus, Johannes Gamm, Ingo Loose, Andrea Löw, Sonja Schilcher, Gudrun Schroeter, and Maria Wilke worked on the original German volume in their capacity as research fellows and associates.

Despite all the care taken, occasional inaccuracies cannot be entirely avoided in a document collection on this scale. We would be grateful for any notifications to this effect. The address of the editorial board is: Leibniz Institute for Contemporary History, Edition 'The Persecution and Murder of the European Jews by Nazi Germany, 1933–1945', Finckensteinallee 85/87, 12205 Berlin, Germany.

Berlin/Munich/Freiburg/Klagenfurt/Jerusalem, May 2022

Editorial Preface

This document collection on the persecution and murder of the European Jews should be cited using the abbreviation PMJ. This citation style is also used in the work itself where there are cross references between the individual volumes. The documents are consecutively numbered, beginning anew with each volume. Accordingly, 'PMJ 1/200' refers to document number 200 in the first volume of this edition. The individual documents are presented as follows: title (in bold type), header, document, footnotes.

The titles have been formulated by the editor(s) of the respective volume and provide information on the date of origin of the document, its core message, author, and recipient(s). The header, placed underneath the title, is part of the document itself. It specifies the type of source (letter, draft law, minutes, and so on), the name of the author, the place of origin, the file reference (where applicable), remarks indicating confidential or classified status, and other special features of the document. The location of the ministries or other central agencies in Berlin at the time, for instance the Reich Security Main Office or the Chancellery of the Führer, is not cited. The header also contains details about the addressee and, where applicable, the date of the receipt stamp, and it concludes with the date of origin and reference to the stage of processing of the source, for instance 'draft', 'carbon copy', or 'copy'.

The header is followed by the document text. Salutations and valedictions are printed, though signatures are only included once, in the header. Instances of emphasis by the author in the original document are retained. Irrespective of the type of emphasis used in the original source (for example, underlined, spaced, bold, capitalized, or italicized), they always appear in italics in the printed version. Where necessary, additional particulars on the document are to be found in the footnotes. In order to enhance readability, letters and words are added in square brackets where they are missing in the original due to obvious mistakes, or where the meaning would otherwise be unclear in the translation.

Abbreviations are explained in the List of Abbreviations. Uncommon abbreviations, primarily from private correspondence, are explained in a footnote at the first mention in a given document.

Handwritten additions in typewritten originals have been adopted by the editors without further indication insofar as they are formal corrections and most probably inserted by the author. If the additions significantly alter the content – either by mitigating or radicalizing it – this is mentioned in the footnotes, and, if known, the author of the addition(s) is given.

As a rule, the documents are reproduced here in full. Documents are only abridged in exceptional cases where the original source was overly long, or where, in the case of the written records of meetings, Nazi policies relating to the persecution of Jews, or reactions to these policies, were only addressed within a single part of the proceedings. Any such abridgements are indicated by an ellipsis in square brackets; the contents of the omitted text are outlined in a footnote.

Documents within each section are presented in chronological order, except for a few cases where they are presented after the date of the event described. A number of descriptive texts written soon after the period covered, but nonetheless retrospectively, are classified according to the date of the events portrayed rather than the date of origin.

Where there is any uncertainty regarding the date of the documents or whether they constitute originals or copies, reference is made in the footnotes. The first footnote for each document, which is linked to the title, contains the location of the source and, insofar as it denotes an archive, the reference number, as well as the folio number(s) if available. Reference to copies of archival documents in research institutions and in the German Federal Archives in Berlin is always made if the original held at the location first mentioned was not consulted there. In the case of printed sources, for instance newspaper articles or legislative texts, this footnote contains standard bibliographical information. The documents in this series have been translated from the original source. If the source has already been published in a document collection on National Socialism or on the persecution of the Jews, reference is made to its first publication, alongside the original location of the source. The next footnote places the document into context and, where appropriate, mentions related discussions, the specific role of authors and recipients, and activities accompanying or immediately following its genesis. Subsequent footnotes provide additional information related to the theme of the document and the persons relevant to the content. They refer to other – published or unpublished – sources that contribute to historical contextualization.

The footnotes also point out individual features of the documents, for instance handwritten notes in the margin, underlining, or deletions, whether by the author or the recipient(s). Annotations and instructions for submission are referred to in the footnotes where the editors consider them to contain significant information. Where possible, the locations of the treaties, laws, and decrees cited in the source text are provided in the footnotes, while other documents are given with their archival reference number. If these details could not be ascertained, this is also noted.

Where biographical information is available on the senders and recipients of the documents, this is provided in the footnotes. The same applies to persons mentioned in the text if they play an active role in the events described. As a general rule, this information is given in the footnote inserted after the first mention of the name in question in the volume. Biographical information on a particular person can thus be retrieved easily via the index.

The short biographies draw on data found in reference works, scholarly literature, or the Central Database of Shoah Victims' Names established and run by Yad Vashem. In many cases additional information was retrieved by consulting personnel files and indexes, municipal and company archives, registry offices, restitution and denazification files, or specialists in the field. Indexes and files on persons from the Nazi era held in archives were also used, primarily those of the former Berlin Document Center and the Central Office of the Judicial Authorities of the Federal States for the Investigation of National Socialist Crimes (Zentrale Stelle der Landesjustizverwaltungen zur Aufklärung nationalsozialistischer Verbrechen) in Ludwigsburg, the latter now stored in the German Federal Archives. National archives and special archives on the Second World War and the persecution of the Jews in the respective countries were also consulted. Despite every effort, it has not always been possible to obtain complete biographical information. In such cases, the footnote in question contains only verified facts such as the year of birth. Where a person could not be identified, there is no footnote reference.

As a rule, in the titles, footnotes, and introduction inverted commas are not placed around terms that were commonplace in Nazi Germany, such as Führer, Jewish Council, or Aryanization, but German-language terms expressing ideological concepts of race, such as *Mischling*, are placed in italics. In line with the circumstances of the time, the terms 'Jew' and 'Jewish' are used for people who did not regard themselves as Jewish but were defined as such on the basis of racial legislation and thus subjected to persecution. References in the documents to the 'Gestapo', an acronym of the German GEheime STAatsPOlizei, and to the 'State Police' denote one and the same institution: the Secret State Police.

The glossary contains concise descriptions of key terms and concepts that are repeated on multiple occasions or are related to the events and developments described in the volume. All primary and secondary sources consulted are listed in the footnotes and bibliography. Where English-language versions of these sources are available, these are included. If a document has already been published in English translation but has been newly translated for this volume, this is indicated in a footnote.

In this volume, following the re-dating of document 184, the numbering of documents in the sequence from document 184 to document 188 has been changed from the original numbering in the German edition.

Note on the translation

British English is used in all translations into English. Where a document was originally written in British or American English, the spelling, grammar, and punctuation of the original have been retained, with silent correction of minor typographical or grammatical errors and insertions in square brackets to clarify the meaning if necessary.

The spelling, grammar, and punctuation of the translated documents broadly conform to the guidelines in *New Hart's Rules: The Oxford Style Guide* (2014). Accordingly, the ending -ize rather than -ise is preferred throughout.

SS, Wehrmacht, and certain other ranks are given in the original German, as are titles where there is no standard equivalent in English or where there may be confusion with contemporary usage. A table of military and police ranks is included as an appendix, along with English-language equivalents of these terms and an indication of their position in the National Socialist hierarchy. Administrative ranks and other terms have been left in the original language where there is no satisfactory equivalent in English. These terms are either explained in a footnote or, if they appear on multiple occasions, in the glossary.

After the Second World War, the Dutch language underwent a spelling reform to make orthography closer to actual pronunciation. The names of Dutch organizations and periodicals in this volume are spelt as they were prior to the spelling reform, for example Joodsche Raad rather than Joodse Raad for Jewish Council.

In the Netherlands, qualified lawyers use the title 'mr' (*meester der rechten*). To avoid confusion with the English word 'Mr', this term has not been included in the translated documents or footnotes, but the individual's status as a lawyer is noted. In Belgium, physicians and lawyers are awarded the title 'Dr' upon qualifying, but the title is not generally used for those holding a doctorate in another discipline. For this reason, 'Dr' is only used in the biographical footnotes if this is standard practice in the respective country.

All laws and institutions are translated into English in the documents. In the introduction and footnotes, foreign-language terms and expressions are added in brackets after the translation where this is considered important for understanding or context. The original spelling of foreign organizations is retained in the footnotes. The titles of published works not in the English language are not translated unless the work in question is of contextual or substantial relevance. If a foreign-language word or phrase appears in a document, this is retained in the translated text and its meaning explained in a footnote or, if necessary, the glossary.

Where the documents contain quotations from the Bible, the King James Version has been preferred, especially where the context is religious or ecclesiastical.

In order to avoid confusion between British and American English, dates are spelt out in the order day, month, and year. Foreign proper names are not italicized. Thus, names of institutions, organizations, and places are written in roman type in the footnotes, but legislation and conceptual terms are in italics.

In the titles, footnotes, and translated documents, place names are generally written according to the contemporary (English) name or the variant commonly used in scholarly literature on the period. This also applies to places that have since been renamed. The seat of government of the Netherlands is known both as The Hague and 's-Gravenhage. The translated documents follow usage in the original document, while the individual document titles and footnotes refer to The Hague. Belgian place names are given according to the language divisions within the country or standard usage in English (for example Brussels or Liège). The footnotes give place names in Flanders in Flemish with French in brackets, and places in Wallonia are presented in French with the Flemish name in brackets. Many places in Luxembourg have German, French, and/or Luxemburgish equivalents – for example, Esch a. d. Alzette (German); Esch-sur-Alzette (French); Esch-Uelzecht (Luxemburgish). The translated documents follow usage in the original. Alternative place names within each country are given in the index.

Diacritical marks in languages such as Czech and Polish are retained, with the exception of the names of the extermination camps in Eastern Europe, where they have been removed in order to emphasize that these camps were established by the German National Socialist regime. Language-specific characters such as the German ß (Eszett) for ss have also been retained.

Hebrew and Yiddish terms are described in the footnotes or glossary, along with any other words requiring explanation.

The term 'Israélite' (in French) as a designation for 'Jew' originated in 1808 in Napoleonic France and spread from there to German- and Dutch-speaking countries ('Israelit' and 'Israëliet' respectively), based on the notion that Jews should be defined as belonging to a faith – 'Mosaic' – rather than an ethnic entity, and intended as a means of integrating Jews into West European societies. In contemporary discourse the term 'Jew' often had a negative overtone. In France the term 'Jew' was reintroduced in official discourse after 1940, though the term 'Israélite' was not entirely abandoned – for instance, in the case of the Union générale des Israélites de France (UGIF). In Belgium, usage of the term 'Israélite'/'Israëliet' ceased with the establishment of the Association of Jews in Belgium (AJB/VJB) in 1941. In the Netherlands too, official usage of the term 'Israëliet' ceased shortly after the occupation but remained in the titles of Jewish organizations. The translated documents use the term 'Israelite' if this is in the original document. The exception is the Union générale des Israélites de France, which has been translated as the General Union of French Jews, as this has become the customary translation in scholarly literature.

Introduction

The yellow star worn to identify the Jewish population was introduced in Luxembourg in the summer of 1941 and in the rest of occupied Western Europe in the spring of 1942.[1] It not only made Jews immediately recognizable in public but also prepared the rest of the population for further anti-Jewish measures and was intended to deter them from approaching or assisting those who were marginalized in this way. From this perspective, the yellow star was both a mark of shame and a token of warning and intimidation. Moreover, for the German occupiers it served as a means of registering Jews and preparing for their deportation.

During the first eighteen months of the German occupation, policy towards the Jews in Western and Northern Europe was mostly decided upon by the German occupation administration in each country, which introduced the main elements of the policy that had already been tried out in the preceding years in Germany, annexed Austria, the Protectorate of Bohemia and Moravia, and Poland. The implementation of the policy differed depending on circumstances in each country. This situation began to change only as the Final Solution began to take shape as a European-wide objective. At the so-called Wannsee Conference on 20 January 1942, which was convened by Reinhard Heydrich, Chief of the Security Police and the SS Security Service (SD), the relevant departments were informed about the new direction adopted by the Reich Security Main Office (RSHA) with respect to the European Jews. Forced emigration of the Jews had come to an end, Heydrich explained in his introductory remarks, and was to be replaced by 'evacuation to the East', which had the Führer's approval. The written record of the meeting (the so-called Protocol) stated that 'In the course of the practical execution of the final solution, Europe will be combed through from west to east'.[2] The systematic murder of the Jews in occupied Eastern Europe had, however, already begun in the summer of 1941.

In the months following the Wannsee Conference, the German authorities in all the occupied countries of Western Europe began to prepare for the deportation of the Jews. An order issued in October 1941 had already banned Jews from emigrating from these countries.[3] The German occupying forces set up several extermination camps in occupied Poland from the end of 1941: after Kulmhof and Belzec followed Auschwitz, Sobibor, and Treblinka. The representatives of the Security Police and the SD in France, Belgium, and the Netherlands coordinated their actions at several meetings presided over by Adolf Eichmann, and on 11 June 1942 the decision was taken to begin the systematic deportation of

1 See PMJ 5/130, 193, 323, and 212.

2 The Protocol of the Wannsee Conference is published in Mark Roseman, *The Villa, the Lake, the Meeting: Wannsee and the Final Solution* (London: Penguin Books, 2003); the quotation here is on p. 129. See also Norbert Kampe and Peter Klein (eds.), *Die "Wannsee-Konferenz" am 20. Januar 1942: Eine Einführung* (Berlin: Metropol, 2017); Elke Gryglewski, Hans-Christian Rasch, and David Zolldan (eds.), *The Meeting at Wannsee and the Murder of the European Jews: Exhibition Catalogue*, trans. Caroline Pearce (Berlin: House of the Wannsee Conference, 2020 [German edn, 2020]); Hans-Christian Jasch and Christoph Kreutzmüller, *The Participants: The Men of the Wannsee Conference*, trans. Charlotte Kreutzmüller and Jane Paulick (New York: Berghahn, 2017 [German edn, 2017]); and Peter Longerich, *Wannseekonferenz: Der Weg zur 'Endlösung'* (Munich: Pantheon, 2016).

3 Letter from the Reich Security Main Office (Müller) on 23 Oct. 1941 to the representative of the Chief of the Security Police and the SD for Belgium and France: see PMJ 5/286.

Jews from these countries. Some 15,000 Jews were to be deported from the Netherlands, 10,000 from Belgium, and 100,000 from France. Due to local factors the number was subsequently reduced to 90,000: the number for France decreased to 40,000, the total for the Netherlands increased to 40,000, and the number for Belgium remained the same. The change in the number of deportations originally envisaged for France was a result of problems with transportation, which meant that fewer Jews could be deported within the intended time frame.

The Jews living in these three countries were successively concentrated in several cities, called up for labour or rounded up, and afterwards interned in transit camps: Drancy near Paris in France, the Dossin Barracks in the town of Mechelen in Belgium, and Westerbork in the east of the Netherlands. The majority of those initially affected were either stateless Jews or foreign nationals, including many who had fled from Germany, Austria, or Czechoslovakia. In the following months, however, the German authorities prevailed against the administrations in the Netherlands, Belgium, and France, and Jewish nationals of these countries were gradually included in the deportations. From the end of June 1942, transport trains ran regularly to the extermination camps.

The introduction to this volume provides separate accounts of developments in Norway, the Netherlands, Belgium, Luxembourg, and France for the period from the summer of 1942 to the weeks during which these countries were liberated. The phase from the outbreak of the war up until June 1942 is covered in the introduction to volume five of this series, although as Denmark is touched on only briefly in that earlier volume, the account below starts with a brief summary of the history of Jews in Denmark and an account of German occupation policy following the invasion of Denmark in the spring of 1940.

Denmark

The history of the Jews in Denmark began with the first writ of protection issued in 1619 by King Christian IV for Samuel Jachia, a Sephardic Jew. The king encouraged additional Sephardic Jews from Amsterdam and Hamburg to settle in Glückstadt, a Danish town at the time, and promised them freedom to practise their religion. For the time being, however, this dispensation applied solely to Glückstadt; permission to stay elsewhere in the country was given only to Jews who were in possession of a letter of safe conduct or had been granted individual privileges by the monarch. It was not until 1673 that Christian V gave a Jew from Hamburg the general entitlement to live in his kingdom,[4] with several Jewish communities established subsequently. The Jewish community in Copenhagen grew particularly rapidly and in the first half of the eighteenth century had some 2,500 members.

4 Per Katz, *Jøderne i Danmark i det 17. århundrede* (Copenhagen: Reitzel, 1981), pp. 16 and 70. On the history of the Jews in Denmark in general: Harald Jørgensen (ed.), *Indenfor murene: Jødisk liv i Danmark 1684–1984* (Copenhagen: Reitzel, 1984); Martin Schwarz Lausten, *Jews and Christians in Denmark: From the Middle Ages to Recent Times, ca. 1100–1948*, trans. Margaret Ryan Hellman (Boston: Brill, 2015 [Danish edn, 2007]); on their persecution and wartime experiences: Leni Yahil, *The Rescue of Danish Jewry: Test of a Democracy* (Philadelphia: Jewish Publication Society of America, 1969); Leo Goldberger (ed.), *The Rescue of the Danish Jews: Moral Courage under Stress* (New York: New York University Press, 1987); Sofie Lene Bak, *Nothing to Speak of: Wartime Experiences of the Danish Jews, 1943–1945* (Copenhagen: Danish Jewish Museum, 2013).

In 1814 Jews obtained the same civil rights as other Danes in most respects, although full equality came only with the changes to the constitution made in 1849. For the Danish population, and especially among the influential Lutheran clergy, the question of whether non-Christians could be part of the Danish people remained contentious for many years. Not least as a result of this controversy, Danish Jews felt significant pressure to acculturate. However, in Denmark too, assimilation and acculturation provided no protection from the so-called Hep-Hep riots, which spread from Germany in 1819. In Copenhagen the rioting led to the destruction of Jewish shops.[5] Despite such violent attacks, for a long time Denmark remained a relatively safe, if not particularly attractive, country for Jews. Between 1881 and the beginning of the First World War, some 12,000 East European Jews fleeing pogroms in the Russian Empire sought shelter in Denmark. Approximately 3,000 of them remained in Denmark permanently.[6] These new immigrants contributed significantly to the invigoration of Jewish religious and cultural life and to the upsurge in Jewish institutions.

A restrictive Danish refugee policy after 1933 had ensured that only few Jewish refugees from Germany and Austria found sanctuary in Denmark. An addendum made in 1934 to the Aliens Act of 1875 allowed the police to refuse entry to so-called undesirable foreigners. After the 'J-stamp' was introduced for the passports of German Jews in 1938, Denmark, like many other countries, adopted a policy of denying entry to those who could be assumed to have no intention of returning to their homeland. Despite the palpable mistrust and fear of a possible mass immigration, some German Jews were able to use Denmark as a stop on their journey into permanent exile.[7] There were 5,513 Jews living in Copenhagen on 1 January 1938.[8] At the time of the German invasion in the spring of 1940, approximately 1,000 German Jews were still in Denmark. In addition, approximately 380 young Jews were in Denmark undertaking agricultural training in preparation for emigration to Palestine, as well as approximately 250 children who were to travel on to Palestine as part of the Youth Aliyah programme (Doc. 1).[9]

On 9 April 1940 German troops crossed into Denmark and Norway. The primary aim of this invasion, known as Operation Weserübung, was to occupy the Norwegian ports. Additionally, the Germans hoped to secure the supply of iron ore from the Swedish town of Kiruna, which was shipped through the port of Narvik in Norway.

5 Yahil, *The Rescue of Danish Jewry*, pp. 7–9. For a detailed account of the individual riots, see Martin Schwarz Lausten, *Folkekirken og jøderne: Forholdet mellem kristne og jøder i Danmark fra 1849 til begyndelsen af det 20. århundrede* (Copenhagen: Anis, 2007).

6 Morten Thing, *De russiske jøder i København 1882–1943* (Copenhagen: Gyldendal, 2008), p. 33.

7 Sofie Lene Bak, *Dansk antisemitisme 1930–1945* (Copenhagen: Aschehoug, 2004), pp. 310–322; Hans Kirchhoff and Lone Rünitz, *Udsendt til Tyskland: Dansk flygtningepolitik under besættelsen* (Odense: Syddansk Universitetsforlag, 2007), pp. 41–43.

8 Lone Rünitz, *Danmark og de jødiske flygtninge 1933–1940: En bog om flygtninge og menneskerettigheder* (Copenhagen: Museum Tusculanum, 2000), p. 115.

9 Peretz Leshem, *Strasse zur Rettung: 1933–1939 aus Deutschland vertrieben – bereitet sich jüdische Jugend auf Palästina vor* (Tel Aviv: Verband der Freunde der Histadrut, 1973), pp. 28–29, 31–32; Hans Kirchhoff, *Et menneske uden pas er ikke noget menneske: Danmark i den internationale flygtningepolitik 1933–1939* (Odense: Syddansk Universitetsforlag, 2005), p. 157; Kirchhoff and Rünitz, *Udsendt til Tyskland*, p. 35.

Denmark's principal significance for the German Reich was as a supply base for operations in Norway, which had greater strategic importance for the war against Britain.[10]

Danish troops were powerless against the vastly superior Wehrmacht units. Military resistance ceased after only a few hours, and the Danish government conceded defeat on the day of the invasion. The so-called peaceful occupation meant that although Denmark was occupied, it was not officially at war with Germany.[11] The country retained its political institutions and a large degree of sovereignty. The Danish constitution remained in force; the king, the government, and the administration stayed in office. Denmark was intended to become a showcase for the Reich, demonstrating that loyal cooperation with the German occupiers could be beneficial for a country. In the spring of 1943, elections were even held to the national parliament, from which the Social Democrats emerged victorious. It was envisaged that, after the expected total victory of the German forces, Denmark might become part of the planned Greater Germanic Reich, although at the time the Nazi leadership only had very vague notions about such an entity.

The Reich Foreign Office handled Germany's relations with Denmark through diplomatic channels. Germany's interests were represented by the German envoy and career diplomat Cécil von Renthe-Fink, who served as the Reich plenipotentiary in negotiations with the Danish Ministry of Foreign Affairs. The four larger parties represented in the Danish parliament had banded together at the beginning of the occupation to form a national unity government, the political approach of which has been variously characterized as one of 'negotiation', 'adaptation, 'cooperation', or even 'collaboration'.[12] For most Danes, however, little changed in their daily life, which explains why the majority of the Danish people supported their government's policy over the next three years.[13]

Anti-Jewish sentiments and outright antisemitism were not widespread. They remained limited even after the National Socialists seized power in Germany and spread antisemitic propaganda via the Danish media. Most Jews living in Denmark initially experienced no new restrictions after the German invasion. Fearing persecution, some German émigrés fled from Denmark to Sweden before, during, or shortly after the German invasion. Among them was the playwright Bertolt Brecht, who had been living with

10 Richard Petrow, *The Bitter Years: The Invasion and Occupation of Denmark and Norway, April 1940–May 1945* (New York: William Morrow & Company, 1974), p. 33; Hans-Martin Ottmer, *'Weserübung': Der deutsche Angriff auf Dänemark und Norwegen im April 1940* (Munich: Oldenbourg, 1994); Jill Stephenson and John Gilmour (eds.), *Hitler's Scandinavian Legacy* (London: Bloomsbury, 2014).

11 Claus Bundgård Christensen et al., *Danmark besat: Krig og hverdag 1940–45* (Copenhagen: Høst, 2005), p. 111. For a summary of occupation policy in Denmark, see Therkel Stræde, 'Deutsche Besatzungspolitik in Dänemark 1940–1945', in Oliver von Wrochem (ed.), *Skandinavien im Zweiten Weltkrieg und die Rettungsaktion Weiße Busse: Ereignisse und Erinnerung* (Berlin: Metropol, 2012), pp. 21–30; and Ethan J. Hollander, *Hegemony and the Holocaust: State Power and Jewish Survival in Occupied Europe* (London: Palgrave Macmillan, 2017), p. 46.

12 Erich Thomsen, *Deutsche Besatzungspolitik in Dänemark, 1940–1945* (Düsseldorf: Bertelsmann, 1971), pp. 11–12; Søren Helstrup, 'Besættelsen 9. April 1940', in Hans Kirchhoff, John T. Lauridsen, and Aage Trommer (eds.), *Gads leksikon om dansk besættelsestid 1940–1945* (Copenhagen: GAD, 2002), pp. 42–47.

13 On Danish reactions to occupation and Jewish persecution, see Carsten Holbraad, *Danish Reactions to German Occupation: History and Historiography* (London: UCL Press, 2017).

his family in Svendborg, on the Danish coast, since 1933 and, despite the demands of the Danish National Socialists, had not been extradited to Germany. For its part, the German government demanded the extradition of a number of political refugees, some of whom were Jewish. However, in the period up until the autumn of 1942, when he was dismissed as plenipotentiary of the German Reich, Renthe-Fink did nothing that would have extended persecution to Danish Jews. Officially, he had no instructions to do so, although in January 1942 he had been advised verbally by Franz Rademacher, head of the Reich Foreign Office's section for Jewish affairs, that the German government wished to see the introduction of laws pertaining to Jews in Denmark (Doc. 3). Shortly afterwards Renthe-Fink expressed his disagreement, insisting that to do so would run counter to German interests in Denmark.[14] Unlike in Norway, where registration of the Jews had begun as early as the spring of 1940 with the order that they hand in their radios, in Denmark neither the occupiers nor the Danish authorities sought to register the Jews. The leaders of Copenhagen's Jewish Community were aware that the Danish policy of cooperation was their most important protection against persecution by the Germans. They therefore warned the members of the community against resistance or flight and urged them to do nothing to provoke the occupying power.[15] The Jewish Community continued to pursue this policy until the end of September 1943.

From the summer of 1942, discontent with the German occupation and the policy of cooperation adopted by the Danish government intensified noticeably. As a result of the entry of the United States into the war, Denmark's forced accession to the Anti-Comintern Pact, and the escalating activities of British intelligence in Denmark, individual groups, both left-wing and right-wing, began to engage in active resistance against the Germans. They distributed illegal newspapers and carried out the first acts of sabotage. As a result, Renthe-Fink was recalled and on 5 November 1942 replaced by SS-Obergruppenführer Werner Best. Best had earlier made his mark as Reinhard Heydrich's deputy during the setting up of the Security Police and the Reich Security Main Office, and as a member of the Military Commander in France's administrative staff during the establishment of the German occupation regime. He could be expected to adopt an iron fist in the model protectorate of Denmark as well. At the same time, Vilhelm Buhl, the unpopular prime minister, was replaced with Erik Scavenius, former minister of foreign affairs, from whom the Germans expected much smoother cooperation.[16]

14 Kirchhoff and Rünitz, *Udsendt til Tyskland*, pp. 73–81; Lone Rünitz, 'Danish Refugee Policy, 1933–1939', in Marc Dujardin (ed.), *Refugees from Nazi-Germany in West-European Border States, 1933–1939/1940: Similarities and Differences in Granting Asylum between European Liberal States and Societies. Causes and Consequences of the Distinct Refugee Politics in Europe in the 1930s* (Brussels: Koninklijke Vlaamse Academie van België voor Wetenschappen en Kunsten, 2004), pp. 55–60; Eckart Conze et al., *Das Amt und die Vergangenheit: Deutsche Diplomaten im Dritten Reich und in der Bundesrepublik* (Munich: Pantheon, 2010), p. 246.

15 Bent Blüdnikow, 'Stille diplomati og flygtningehjælp: Den jødiske menigheds ledelse 1933–1943', in Hans Sode-Madsen, *'Føreren har befalet!' Jødeaktionen oktober 1943* (Copenhagen: Samleren, 1993), pp. 137–173 and 155–156; Rasmus Jørgensen, *Deporteret: Beretningen om de danske kz-fanger* (Copenhagen: Jyllands-Postens Forlag, 2005), pp. 40–41.

16 Hans Kirchhoff, *Augustoprøret 1943: Samarbejdspolitikkens fald – Forudsætninger og forløb: En studie i kollaboration og modstand*, vol. 1 (Copenhagen: Gyldendal, 1979), pp. 48–72; Ulrich Herbert, *Best: Biographische Studien über Radikalismus, Weltanschauung und Vernunft 1903–1989* (Bonn: Dietz, 1996), pp. 323–342.

In practice, however, Best continued the policy of his predecessor, Renthe-Fink. At first, he too remained restrained in his approach to the Jews. Even as late as the beginning of 1943, he responded to a query from the Reich Foreign Office by proposing that the deportation of Jews from Denmark be ruled out for as long as its implementation would jeopardize the 'Danish model' of occupation. However, should the policy of cooperation come to an end for other reasons, Best noted, then one could also proceed with the deportation of the Jews. Three months later, Best reasserted this position, pointing to the Jews' limited influence in Denmark (Doc. 5). Both the Reich Foreign Office and Heinrich Himmler concurred. Mindful of Best's policy, at the end of June 1943 Himmler decided that 'measures concerning Jews' in Denmark should be avoided for the time being.[17]

However, the situation changed as a result of German military setbacks in the Soviet Union and southern Italy in 1943. Supported by the British Secret Service, communist resistance groups in particular intensified their activities in Denmark. Acts of sabotage and bomb attacks became more frequent. When the occupying authorities responded to a wave of strikes in August 1943[18] with calls for special courts and the death penalty, the Danish government resigned. As a result, in the same month the German occupiers declared a state of emergency and assumed complete control. Strikes were prohibited and summary courts martial introduced. To avoid losing all influence over the running of the country, the state secretaries in the various Danish ministries formed a provisional leadership, under the direction of Nils Svenningsen, state secretary of the Ministry of Foreign Affairs. Although they continued to be informally advised by members of the government that had resigned,[19] essentially the policy of cooperation, with its fiction of Danish sovereignty, had failed.

As a result, the main rationale for the earlier restraint towards the Jews also ceased to apply. On 8 September 1943 Best proposed to the Reich Foreign Office that the state of emergency be used as an opportunity to consider 'a solution to the Jewish question and Freemason question in Denmark', for which the German police forces in Denmark would need to be reinforced (Doc. 7). On 17 September, Hitler approved Best's proposal. The latter therefore requested that both Security Police and Order Police receive reinforcements, and also that ships be made available for the deportation of the Jews.[20]

The deportation did not proceed as planned. Rumours that anti-Jewish measures by the Germans were imminent had been circulating for some time, especially in Copenhagen. They were fuelled by the arrest of prominent members of the Jewish Community in late August 1943 (Doc. 6) and by the seizure of the community's files on 17 September 1943 (Doc. 8). When the additional German police units arrived in Copenhagen and made known the reason for their transfer from Norway, little doubt remained that the

17 Best to the Reich Foreign Office, 13 Jan. 1943, PA AA, R 100 864, fols. 45–47. Himmler's decision was communicated to Kaltenbrunner in Wagner's letter dated 30 June 1943, PA AA, R 100 864, fol. 87: see Herbert, *Best*, p. 362.

18 In August 1943 strikes took place in Odense and Esbjerg, which then spread to many other towns. The staff of large workplaces led the way, and soon there was large-scale unrest involving demonstrations and street battles with the German and Danish authorities.

19 Jørgen Hæstrup, *… til landets bedste: Hovedtræk af departementschefsstyrets virke 1943–1945*, vol. 1 (Copenhagen: Gyldendal, 1966), pp. 70–78.

20 Best to the Reich Foreign Office, no. 1094, 18 Sept. 1943, PA AA, R 100 864, fols. 101–102.

long-feared deportation of the Danish Jews was looming. As early as mid September some Jews began to prepare to flee and hid in the homes of non-Jewish friends, even though it was still unclear just when the deportation would begin.[21]

On his arrival in Copenhagen from Katowice on 20 September 1943, Rudolf Mildner, the new Senior Commander of the Security Police and the SD in Denmark, realized that word of the impending anti-Jewish measures had already spread throughout Denmark and that those who would be affected were prepared. Furthermore, the newly deployed German police forces lacked any local knowledge, while the Wehrmacht sought to avoid being involved in the unpopular measures and left the deportation of Danish Jews to the police and the SS (Doc. 9).

As a result, on 23 September the issue of the deportation was submitted to Hitler again, along with an indication of the possible consequences: rioting or general strikes could take place; a new constitutional government might not be viable; and the abdication of the king was a possibility. Hitler brushed aside these concerns and decided that, despite all objections, the deportation as proposed by Best was to be carried out.[22]

On 28 September, Best notified one of his associates, maritime expert Georg Ferdinand Duckwitz, of the date (1 October 1943) and time (10 p.m.) the arrests were to be carried out. Duckwitz conveyed this information to several leading Danish politicians with whom he was in contact. Hans Hedtoft Hansen, former chairman of the Social Democratic Party, took the details to Carl Henriques, chairman of the Jewish Community, who immediately spread the news to its members. In his sermon the next morning, Rabbi Marcus Melchior openly alerted those attending the service and urged them to go home and go into hiding.[23] Herbert Pundik, a schoolboy at the time, reported that he had been warned at school too: his headmaster had said to him and to several of his classmates, 'You had better hurry home. The Germans may be here at any moment.'[24] Pundik and his family escaped to Sweden. As rumours of impending arrests and the first escape attempts spread, a willingness to provide help also grew, extending throughout Danish society and into hospitals, municipal administrations, trade unions, and schools.

Already by this point the success of the planned mass arrests was uncertain, indeed unlikely. Best alerted the Reich Foreign Office by telegram and referred specifically to the 'rumours concerning the impending anti-Jewish operation', noting that these had 'arisen here immediately after the imposition of the state of emergency and have escalated to the point of panic'. He had tried to conceal the plan, he insisted, but without

21 Best to the Reich Foreign Office, no. 1162, 29 Sept. 1943, ibid., fols. 125–126; Yahil, *The Rescue of Danish Jewry*, pp. 216–217.

22 Ribbentrop memorandum, 23 Sept. 1943, *Akten zur deutschen auswärtigen Politik 1918–1945 [ADAP]*, series E: *1941–1945*, vol. 6: *1. Mai bis 30. September 1943* (Göttingen: Vandenhoeck & Ruprecht, 1974), no. 344.

23 Duckwitz was already aware of Best's plan but only now learned of the actual date: Hans Kirchhoff, *Den gode tysker: G. F. Duckwitz – De danske jøders redningsmand* (Copenhagen: Gyldendal, 2013), p. 171; Hans Kirchhoff, 'Endlösung over Danmark', in Hans Sode-Madsen (ed.), *I Hitler-Tysklands skygge: Dramaet om de danske jøder 1933–1945* (Copenhagen: Aschehoug, 2003), pp. 136–181, here p. 173.

24 Herbert Pundik, *In Denmark It Could Not Happen: The Flight of the Jews to Sweden* (Jerusalem: Gefen Publishing, 1998), p. 12.

success. Many Jews were no longer living in their homes, and, he warned, it was to be expected that the plan would be at least a partial failure.[25]

By the morning of 1 October, the preparations made by the occupiers were complete. After the SS had cut the telephone lines, the arrests began at 9 p.m. In an act of desperation, that same evening Svenningsen asked Best to at least refrain from deporting the Jews and to intern them in Denmark instead. This approach had proved successful when Danish communists were arrested – they had been taken to a Danish internment camp rather than to a German concentration camp. The chairman of the Jewish Community had acceded to this proposal, but Best refused. At the same time, the German Security Police ordered that apartment doors were not to be forced should the inhabitants fail to respond to ringing and knocking.[26] This directive was not always obeyed. According to their own records, the Germans arrested 284 persons in total (Doc. 18), although the actual number of deportees was 281; they were deported the following morning on two transports to Theresienstadt, where they arrived on 5 and 6 October 1943.[27] With additional Danish Jews deported on 13 October and 23 November, 470 persons in all were taken to Theresienstadt.[28]

Following the arrests, broad sections of the Danish population proved no longer willing to cooperate with the occupiers – protests ensued from all social and political circles. Trade unions and industrial associations wrote to Best, as did the student body of the University of Copenhagen, which declared that the persecution of the Danish Jews was 'utterly irreconcilable with the Danish way of thinking' (Doc. 17).

Following the temporary detention of the leaders of the Jewish Community in late August, a pastoral letter signed by the Bishop of Copenhagen on behalf of all bishops of Denmark was read out from pulpits everywhere on 3 October 1943. The letter stated that it was the 'duty of the Christian Church to protest wherever the Jews are persecuted on account of their race or religion'. It stated that Christians should not forget that Jesus was a Jew, and referred to the Old Testament as a sign of common ground between Christians and Jews. Moreover, it asserted that the persecution of the Jews was counter to the concept of loving one's neighbour and violated 'the Danish people's sense of justice' (Doc. 11). The pastoral letter was of great importance, because with this statement the church, the sole Danish authority still functioning nationwide, legitimated support for the Jews. The Freedom Council, formed after the August strikes and ensuing riots as a kind of coordinating committee for various resistance groups, also called upon Danes to help those who had gone into hiding.[29]

25 Best to the Reich Foreign Office, no. 1187, 1 Oct. 1943, PA AA, R 100 864, fol. 145. On the course of the operation and the organization of the mass escape, see Yahil, *The Rescue of Danish Jewry*, pp. 147–195 and 223–282, and Rasmus Kreth and Michael Mogensen, *Flugten til Sverige: Aktionen mod de danske jøder oktober 1943* (Copenhagen: Gyldendal, 1995).

26 Jørgensen, *Deporteret*, p. 42; Henrik Lundtofte, 'Den store undtagelse – Gestapo og jødeaktionen', in Sode-Madsen (ed.), *I Hitler-Tysklands skygge*, pp. 182–201, here p. 192.

27 For clarification of the figures, see Silvia Goldbaum Tarabini Fracapane, *The Jews of Denmark in the Holocaust: Life and Death in Theresienstadt Ghetto* (London: Routledge, 2021), pp. 364–365.

28 Ibid., p. 81.

29 Palle Andersen, *Det moralske dilemma: Den illegale presse og den tyske jødeaktion oktober 1943* (Esbjerg: Historisk Samling fra Besættelsestiden 1940–1945, 2003), p. 12; Martin Schwarz Lausten, *Jødesympati og jødehad i Folkekirken: Forholdet mellem kristne og jøder i Danmark fra begyndelsen af det 20. århundrede til 1948* (Copenhagen: Anis, 2007), pp. 382–386.

Many Danes now became involved in organizing a mass escape across the Sound to Sweden. The arrests and also the end of the policy of cooperation in August had triggered considerable disquiet in neighbouring Sweden. On 31 August 1943 Gösta Engzell, department head in the Swedish Ministry of Foreign Affairs, had authorized Gustaf von Dardel, the Swedish representative in Copenhagen, to issue Swedish passports to Danish Jews born in Sweden and to their families. A strategy already tested in Norway was thereby extended to Denmark. Believing the arrest of Jews in Denmark to be imminent, on 29 September the Swedish Ministry of Foreign Affairs instructed the Swedish ambassador in Berlin to inform the Germans of Sweden's disapproval. In Copenhagen, von Dardel informed Henriques, the chairman of the Jewish Community, that Jewish refugees would be able to enter Sweden. On 2 October 1943 the Swedish government made known via the news agency Tidningarnas Telegrambyrå that Sweden would accept all Danish Jews.[30] Word spread quickly, not only in Denmark but also worldwide, passed on by news correspondents (Doc. 16).

The first Jewish refugees had approached fishermen and organized their own escape, but now groups offering assistance formed spontaneously at the ports and increasingly banded together to manage the numbers seeking to flee. In Copenhagen many Jews were initially hidden in hospitals. Before the wave of arrests began, approximately 500 refugees had already reached Sweden. Between 1 and 10 October, more than 5,000 persons were saved. The flood of refugees then abated.[31]

Every trip across the Sound had to be paid for by the refugees or by those who helped them. Money was received by drivers who brought people to the coast and by Danish coastguard officials as protection money. Most of the money, however, went to fishermen, compensating them for their loss of earnings and their fuel costs and offsetting the risk that they might be arrested or have their ships confiscated. Some refugees found themselves required to pay the equivalent of a year's salary for their rescue, a sum that not everyone could afford. The first crossings therefore likely saved wealthier Jews, while others had to wait. When the pressure of numbers was greatest, a crossing cost 2,000 kroner; as the flood of refugees diminished, with more fishermen and helpers available and fewer Jews waiting to flee, the cost fell to just 500 kroner.[32]

The costs faced by poorer Jews were often borne by more prosperous refugees. In addition, many Danes contributed to collections in support of the refugees (Doc. 19). This fundraising took place both within rescue groups that were formed spontaneously and

30 Paul A. Levine, *From Indifference to Activism: Swedish Diplomacy and the Holocaust, 1938–1944* (Uppsala: Ubsaliensis S. Academiae, 1996), pp. 229 and 232–236; Kirchhoff, 'Endlösung over Danmark', p. 174.

31 Kreth and Mogensen, *Flugten til Sverige*, p. 46.

32 Michael Mogensen, 'October 1943 – The Rescue of the Danish Jews', in Mette Bastholm Jensen and Steven L. B. Jensen (eds.), *Denmark and the Holocaust* (Copenhagen: Danish Center for Holocaust and Genocide Studies, 2003), pp. 33–61, here p. 48; Kreth and Mogensen, *Flugten til Sverige*, p. 91; for an introduction to the various organizations, see Hermann Weiss, 'Die Rettung der Juden in Dänemark während der deutschen Besetzung 1940–1945', in Wolfgang Benz and Juliane Wetzel (eds.), *Solidarität und Hilfe für Juden während der NS-Zeit*, vol. 3: *Dänemark, Niederlande, Spanien, Portugal, Ungarn, Albanien, Weißrußland* (Berlin: Metropol, 1996), pp. 11–86, here pp. 56–63 and 69–78.

within the organized resistance movement. Belongings and assets that the refugees left behind were quickly safeguarded by the Danish authorities and protected from looting. A new service provided by the City of Copenhagen cooperated with the guarantors to whom fleeing owners had managed to entrust their assets and possessions (Docs. 12 and 24). In Sweden the refugees were looked after by the Danish embassy, state institutions, and, not least, local Jews.[33]

The vast majority of the Danish Jews were carried to safety across the Sound in small boats and ships; sometimes even rowing boats were put to use. In total some 600 to 700 crossings likely took place. The Swedish navy patrolled the coast in order to be able to come to the aid of the refugees if necessary. The German navy and the Danish coastguard remained passive and did not obstruct the mass escape. On shore the Wehrmacht and the Order Police took only limited action against those fleeing. Wehrmacht units carried out only a few roundups, and only in response to demands by the Gestapo. The German Security Police had to rely on their own personnel, who were in short supply and whose enthusiasm for the pursuit varied. Much depended on the zeal of individual Gestapo commanders. A disproportionately large number of Jews were arrested in the area around Helsingør that was supervised by SS-Hauptscharführer Hans Juhl, also known as 'Gestapo-Juhl'. Juhl was responsible for the largest single roundup after the wave of arrests on 1/2 October: during the night of 6/7 October, the Gestapo and Wehrmacht soldiers who had received orders to participate arrested eighty-six Jews who had hidden in a church in Gilleleje, north of Copenhagen.[34]

A combination of factors ensured that 95 per cent of the Jews living in Denmark were rescued. First, because they had been warned, most Jews managed to go into hiding before the arrests even began. Their numbers were not large, and as most of the Jews in Denmark lived in Copenhagen, word of the impending arrests reached them in time. Second, the moment was right for a mass flight. Part of the population had already been mobilized by the strikes, and Sweden was willing to accept those who fled. Many Danes viewed support for the rescue initiative as a way of demonstrating their hostility towards the German occupation. The nature of the occupation regime, more lenient in Denmark than in other occupied countries, also played a role, because the risk for those who provided help seemed smaller, and up to that point no member of the resistance movement in Denmark had been executed. In addition, organizational and communication structures within Danish society were still largely intact.

By contrast, the motivation for the actions taken by the Germans, and by the Reich plenipotentiary in particular, remains harder to construe. Since Mildner's arrival, he and Best had been convinced that the German police would only be able to catch a small number of Jews. That failure would make it necessary to keep combing the country to round up Jews and to patrol the Danish coast for weeks, if not months. It would thus be impossible to defuse the situation and to put an end to the state of emergency,

33 Per Møller and Knud Secher, *De danske flygtninge i Sverige* (Stockholm: Gyldendal, 1945), pp. 194–196; Mogensen, 'October 1943 – The Rescue of the Danish Jews', p. 41; Svante Hansson, *Flykt och överlevnad: Flyktingverksamhet i Mosaiska församlingen i Stockholm 1933–1950* (Stockholm: Hillelförlaget, 2004), pp. 254–262.

34 Mogensen, 'October 1943 – The Rescue of the Danish Jews', pp. 53–57.

even in the longer term, which would run counter not only to Best's own interests but also to Hitler's instructions. When Duckwitz (with or without Best's knowledge) informed the Danish resistance of the scheduled date for the arrests, the advance notice heightened panic among Danish Jews and accelerated the flight from Denmark that was already under way. As a result, the Jews left the country as soon as they possibly could. This, Best said later, had been his intention. During a confidential discussion on 2 October 1943, Best explained his actions to Franz-Alfred Six, a former department head at the Reich Security Main Office. Knowledge of the upcoming 'anti-Jewish operation' had led to outright panic in September, and therefore, he suggested, simply giving notice of the deportation had caused the Jews to leave the country.[35] In his report to the Reich Foreign Office, Best also presented the nocturnal raid as a success: 'Because the actual aim of the Jew operation in Denmark was to de-Jewify the country and not to carry out a headhunt that was as successful as possible, it must be noted that the Jew operation did achieve its aim' (Doc. 18). This assessment explains why, with the exception of the Gestapo chief in Helsingør mentioned above, the German occupying forces demonstrated little readiness to continue the pursuit of Jews after 2 October. The single operation was intended to be sufficient, with calm expected to return quickly thereafter.

Best continued to pursue this approach after the deportation. In a conversation with Adolf Eichmann in early November 1943, he was able to insist that the Jews deported from Denmark would remain in Theresienstadt and not be transported further, for instance to Auschwitz. The prisoners themselves were unaware of this decision. Johan Grün, 22 years old at the time, later reported: 'We had no idea that we were privileged and would not be put on a transport. We were perpetually nervous, especially when a new transport was being put together.'[36] In Theresienstadt the Jews were separated according to gender, and families were thus torn apart. For the Danish Jews, who had previously experienced few restrictions, the dreadful living conditions in the ghetto came as a shock. From February 1944 parcels were sent to the inmates through a private network working in close cooperation with the Danish Ministry for Social Affairs and the friends and relatives of the deportees. However, the German authorities had not granted permission for these shipments and rejected all requests for authorization from the Danish administration. The organizers of the shipments repeatedly wrote to sponsors stating that there was no guarantee that the parcels would arrive. It was only during the visit by the delegation of the International Red Cross and the Danish civil administration to Theresienstadt in June 1944 that the German authorities authorized the shipment of parcels to the Danish inmates. Even if they did receive parcels, the Danish prisoners still suffered from hunger, as Meier Munitz, one of the Danish Jews in Theresienstadt, covertly informed his relatives in Sweden. On 17 July 1944 Munitz signed a postcard, which had to pass censorship, with the words 'Your

35 Notes by Six for the state secretary, 25 Oct. 1943, PA AA, R 29 567, fols. 386–388.

36 Johan Grün, cited in Jørgensen, *Deporteret*, p. 53; Sode-Madsen, '"Her er livets lov egoisme": De danske jøder i Theresienstadt', in Sode-Madsen, *'Føreren har befalet!'*, pp. 174–219, here p. 192; corresponding telegram 1353 to the Reich Foreign Office, dated 3 Nov. 1943, with Best's report on the conversation the previous day, PA AA, R 100 865, fol. 26.

son, brother and brother-in-law Madsult'.[37] *Mads* is a common given name for Danish men, but *mad* is the Danish word for food, and *sult* means 'hunger'.

In February 1945 the Swedish Ministry of Foreign Affairs informed the Germans that Sweden was willing to admit Jewish prisoners from Germany.[38] This gave rise to the largest single relief effort for prisoners in German camps during the war, the Danish-Swedish rescue operation known as 'White Buses'. Approximately 15,000 people, including Danish prisoners held in the Theresienstadt ghetto, were evacuated to Sweden on buses during the final stages of the war and were thus saved from the death marches and killing operations carried out by the SS. The buses were manned by Swedish and Danish volunteers and operated under the auspices of the Red Cross (Doc. 27). Max Friediger, chief rabbi of Copenhagen, who had been forced to join the Council of Elders (Ältestenrat) in Theresienstadt, a body created by the SS, reported that at around 11 a.m. on 13 April a Czech office worker had rushed excitedly into his office to tell him that a Danish motor car was parked in front of the commandant's office. Friediger thought it was a joke until he was brought to the commandant shortly afterwards: 'He was sitting in his office with some higher SS ranks and an unknown gentleman. It was Dr Holm from Copenhagen! It was he who was the main speaker, and he informed me that the Danes were to come to Sweden.' Friediger was then sent to let all the Danish Jews know that they would be leaving that evening.[39]

On 15 April 1945 the Danish prisoners, more than 400 in total, began their journey from Theresienstadt through Denmark to Malmö. Of the Danish Jews who had been deported, fifty-three adults died, along with two infants born in Theresienstadt. At the end of May 1945, the first of the approximately 7,000 Jews who had been saved by fleeing to Sweden returned to Denmark.

Norway

For the German troops the occupation of Norway proved considerably more complex and involved much heavier losses than the occupation of Denmark. Attacks by the British navy sank many German warships, and in the first days after the German invasion, which took place on 9 April 1940, Norwegian and Allied infantry forces drove the German units into a substantial retreat. After the advance of the Wehrmacht into France, however, the Allies were forced to withdraw their troops from Norway and redeploy them to Western Europe. As a result the Norwegian armed forces capitulated, and Norway was occupied. The German number of casualties was substantial: approximately 3,000 men were killed in action and 1,500 were wounded; almost one third of the entire German navy was destroyed during the combat.

37 Postcards from Mendel Meier Munitz to Isak Notkin, dated 12 June 1944, and to Elieser Munitz, dated 17 July 1944, YVA, O.27/22. On the food shortages faced by Danish prisoners, see Hans Sode-Madsen, 'The Perfect Deception: The Danish Jews and Theresienstadt, 1940–1945', *Leo Baeck Institute Year Book*, 38 (1993), pp. 263–290, here pp. 275–280.

38 Sune Persson, *'Vi åker till Sverige': De vita bussarna 1945* (Rimbo: Fischer & Co, 2002), p. 123.

39 Max Friediger, *Theresienstadt* (Copenhagen: Clausen, 1946), pp. 135–137. For details of the negotiations and the rescue operation, see Hans Sode-Madsen, *Reddet fra Hitlers helvede: Danmark og de Hvide Busser 1941–45* (Copenhagen: Aschehoug, 2005).

After the Norwegian government and the king fled to Britain following the capitulation, Josef Terboven, Gauleiter of Essen, was appointed Reich commissioner for the occupied Norwegian territories. Like Denmark, Norway was intended to remain an independent state, with a view to its eventual inclusion in the Greater Germanic Reich. Terboven began by banning all democratic parties and by designating the fascist Nasjonal Samling party as representative of the interests of the state.[40]

For the approximately 2,100 Jewish Norwegians and Jewish refugees from Central Europe living in the country, little changed at first. That said, some Jews were prohibited from practising their profession, as was the case for psychiatrist Leo Eitinger, who had fled from Czechoslovakia to Norway in 1939 through Nansen Relief and now lost his position at the hospital in Bodø, in northern Norway (Doc. 51). With the German invasion of the Soviet Union in June 1941, however, the overall situation began to change noticeably. In northern Norway the Germans arrested all Jewish men, but in southern Norway only those who were stateless. In March 1942 Leo Eitinger, who was now living in hiding on Norway's western coast, was also arrested. Individual Jews fled across the Norwegian–Swedish border, but their number remained small, as most hoped that no additional persecution would follow or feared retaliatory measures against family members.[41] In addition, Norwegian Jewish refugees had occasionally been turned back at the border by Swedish officials (PMJ 5/17). From February 1942, on the orders of Heinrich Fehlis, Senior Commander of the Security Police and the SD in Norway, the passports and identity cards of Jews were marked with the word 'Jew'. In addition, Nasjonal Samling's Office for Statistics required all Jews to complete a questionnaire disclosing their financial circumstances, in preparation for their dispossession. In total, 1,417 persons provided the information requested; children were listed on their parents' questionnaires. On 12 March 1942 the puppet government under Vidkun Quisling that had been installed by Terboven restored the Norwegian Constitution's 'Jew clause', a passage that had been eliminated in 1851, forbidding Jews to enter the kingdom.[42]

At the Wannsee Conference in January 1942, the representative of the Reich Foreign Office, Martin Luther, had spoken out against including the Scandinavian countries in the policy of extermination. Over the course of the next few months, however, the attitude of the German decision makers changed. Count Helmuth James von Moltke, who

40 On the German occupation of Norway, see Hans-Dietrich Loock, *Quisling, Rosenberg und Terboven: Zur Vorgeschichte und Geschichte der nationalsozialistischen Revolution in Norwegen* (Stuttgart: Deutsche Verlags-Anstalt, 1970); Ole Kristian Grimnes, *Norge under okkupasjonen* (Oslo: Aschehoug, 1983); Robert Bohn, *Reichskommissariat Norwegen: 'Nationalsozialistische Neuordnung' und Kriegswirtschaft* (Munich: Oldenbourg, 2000); Johannes Andenaes, Olav Riste, and Magne Skodvin, *Norway and the Second World War* (Oslo: Tanum, 1966); Erik J. Friis, 'The Norwegian Government-in-Exile, 1940–45', in Carl F. Bayerschmidt and Erik J. Friis (eds.), *Scandinavian Studies: Essays Presented to Dr. Henry Goddard Leach on the Occasion of His Eighty-fifth Birthday* (Seattle: University of Washington Press, 1965), pp. 422–444; Hans Fredrik Dahl, *Quisling: A Study in Treachery* (Cambridge: Cambridge University Press, 1999); Petrow, *The Bitter Years*.

41 Karin Kvist Geverts, 'Ett främmande element i nationen: Svensk flyktingpolitik och de judiska flyktingarna 1938–1944', *Acta Universitatis Upsaliensis, Studia Historica Upsaliensa*, 233 (Uppsala: Universitetsbiblioteket, 2008), pp. 184–194.

42 See PMJ 5/14, 20, 21, and 23; Oskar Mendelsohn, *Jødenes historie i Norge gjennom 300 år* (Oslo: Universitetsforlaget, 1987), p. 56; and Oskar Mendelsohn, *The Persecution of the Norwegian Jews in WW II* (Oslo: Norges Hjemmefrontmuseum, 2000).

visited Norway in September 1942 on behalf of the Amt Ausland/Abwehr, the military intelligence agency of the Wehrmacht High Command (OKW), is said to have warned the resistance movement during his stay about the forthcoming deportations of Jews, although he could not give a specific date.[43] Statements made by Gestapo official Wilhelm Wagner after the war indicate that in the summer of 1942 the Reich Security Main Office suggested that the 'Jewish problem' in Norway also be addressed and resolved in accordance with the wishes of the Norwegian government.[44] For its part, the government was keen to show the Reich Commissioner that it was radically antisemitic. As a result of its dwindling popularity among Norwegians, the Quisling government had increasingly lost the confidence of the German authorities, and now it evidently sought to regain favour by taking a tough approach to the Jews.[45] From the beginning, the Norwegian authorities and the population were involved in the disenfranchisement and persecution of the Jews.

From late September 1942 there was an increase in the number of acts of sabotage and attacks on German institutions in northern Norway. In reprisal, on 6 October 1942 the occupying forces had ten people shot, one of whom was a Norwegian Jew. Simultaneously, a state of emergency was declared in Trondheim and the surrounding area, and by order of the Reich Commissioner the Norwegian police arrested thirty Jewish men, who were taken, along with non-Jewish hostages, to the camp at Falstad, north-east of Trondheim. While some Jews recognized that they were no longer safe and fled across the border to Sweden, others expected that the state of emergency would soon be lifted and hoped they would then cease to be in any immediate danger.[46] Among Nasjonal Samling supporters, however, the call for the 'final settlement' of the so-called Jewish question, which was to be 'radical and unsentimental', became louder (Doc. 29).

On 22 October 1942 a group of fleeing Norwegian Jews, accompanied by a member of the resistance who was helping with the escape, was travelling by train from Oslo to Halden. At the Swedish border, while the Norwegian Border Police was conducting a passenger check, shots were exchanged and a policeman was killed. The helper and two Jewish refugees managed to get away, but the other members of the group were arrested and taken to the prison camp at Grini. The Norwegian press, which had been brought under Nazi control, reported at length on the events because a harsh reaction by the Germans was anticipated. The *New York Times* also surmised as much (Doc. 30). On 25 October 1942 Gestapo official Wilhelm Wagner gave the order to have all male Jews aged fifteen and over arrested the following day; the head of the Norwegian State Police

43 Christhard Hoffmann, 'Fluchthilfe als Widerstand: Verfolgung und Rettung der Juden in Norwegen', in Wolfgang Benz and Juliane Wetzel (eds.), *Solidarität und Hilfe für Juden während der NS-Zeit*, vol. 1: *Polen, Rumänien, Griechenland, Luxemburg, Norwegen, Schweiz* (Berlin: Metropol, 1999), pp. 205–232, here p. 216; Klaus Alberts, *Theodor Steltzer: Szenarien seines Lebens. Eine Biographie* (Heide: Boyens, 2009), pp. 100–101.

44 Bjarte Bruland, *Forsøket på å tilintetgjøre jødene i Norge* (Bergen: B. Bruland, 1995), p. 58.

45 Hoffmann, 'Fluchthilfe als Widerstand', p. 209.

46 Mendelsohn, *Jødenes historie i Norge*, p. 74; Stein Ugelvik Larsen, Beatrice Sandberg and Volker Dahm, *Meldungen aus Norwegen 1940–1945: Die geheimen Lageberichte des Befehlshabers der Sicherheitspolizei und des SD in Norwegen*, vol. 1 (Munich: Oldenbourg, 2008), p. 846; Frode Sæland, *Herman Beckers krig: Historien om familien Becker og jødene i Rogaland under andre verdenskrig* (Oslo: Aschehoug, 2009), p. 139.

communicated the order to all police stations (Doc. 31). The Quisling government had created a legal basis for this operation by passing the Law on Preventive Detention on 24 October 1942. Jews were not specifically mentioned in this law, but it regulated the detention of persons accused of subversive activities. On the day the arrests were carried out, the Norwegian government issued an additional law under which all the assets of Norwegian and stateless Jews were expropriated and handed over to the public purse. Gold and silver jewellery items were immediately confiscated by Norwegian officials and placed at the disposal of the Reich Commissioner as a 'voluntary contribution for war-related expenditure'. Confiscated watches were handed over to the Wehrmacht.[47] The police delivered the confiscation orders to those they were arresting and their families. The eldest remaining member of each family had to report daily to the relevant police station. Any attempt to withhold property or to circumvent the obligation to report was subject to the severest penalties. The male Jews were first incarcerated in Bredtveit prison, and then in the internment camp at Berg, near Tønsberg.[48] Samuel Steinmann, nineteen years old at the time, described the camp, which was guarded by Norwegians and known as 'Quisling's chicken yard': 'The Berg internment camp was a brand new camp, which had not previously been used. We were housed in barracks that had only floors, walls and ceilings, no furnishings, no beds, no mattresses.'[49]

Reactions among Norwegians and the resistance movement to the actions taken against the Jews were not unequivocal. Two weeks after the arrests, the Norwegian bishops and the leaders of the sizeable Norwegian Free Church societies and organizations wrote a letter of protest to Quisling stating their opposition to the collaborationist government's law on the confiscation of property and to the discriminatory treatment of Jews under the law. 'By virtue of our calling', they had written, 'we thus exhort the secular authorities and declare in the name of Jesus Christ: stop the persecution of Jews and put a stop to the racial hatred which is being spread by the press in our country' (Doc. 34). The Norwegian National Socialists were unmoved by this exhortation. Members of the Nasjonal Samling party profited from the seizure of assets (Doc. 44). On 17 November 1942 the government issued the Law on the Compulsory Registration of Jews (Doc. 35), which determined who in Norway was regarded as a Jew. The term 'Jew' was defined more broadly than in the Nuremberg Laws, for it included *Mischlinge* of the second degree who belonged to a Jewish community.[50]

In retrospect, the relative inaction on the part of Norwegian resistance groups is surprising. Since the end of 1940 they had been organizing civil disobedience against the German occupying forces and their Norwegian henchmen. Increasingly large sections of the population had taken part in this struggle for hearts and minds, for example in the protests against the Nazification of the state church and of schoolteachers. However,

47 'Inndragning av jødisk eiendom i Norge under den 2. verdenskrig', *Norges offentlige utredninger* [NOU] 1997: 22 (Oslo: Statens forvaltningstjeneste statens trykning, 1997) [hereafter NOU, 1997], pp. 67–124, here p. 76.

48 Seizure order published in NOU, 1997, p. 171; Bjarte Bruland, *Det norske Holocaust: Forsøket på å tilintetgjøre de norske jødene* (Oslo: HL-senteret, 2008), p. 19.

49 Samuel Steinmann, cited in Jakob Lothe and Anette Storeide (eds.), *Tidsvitner: Fortellinger fra Auschwitz og Sachsenhausen* (Oslo: Gyldendal, 2006), p. 124.

50 Oskar Mendelsohn, 'Norwegen', in Wolfgang Benz (ed.), *Dimension des Völkermords: Die Zahl der jüdischen Opfer des Nationalsozialismus* (Munich: Oldenbourg, 1991), pp. 187–197, here p. 192.

the leaders of the resistance movement passively acquiesced in the registration of Jews in the spring of 1942 and in the arrests carried out that autumn.

On 25 November 1942 the Germans ordered the arrest of women and children as well as hospital patients, who had all been spared thus far. The next day, members of the Norwegian State Police, Criminal Police and riot police, together with Hird (the paramilitary troops of Nasjonal Samling), and the Germanic SS removed people, who were completely unprepared, from homes and hospitals and took them to the landing pier for the troopship *Donau* at the port of Oslo. Fehlis reported that evening that the *Donau* had put to sea, bound for Stettin, at 2.55 p.m. with 532 persons on board. Yet the perpetrators were still not content. Karl Marthinsen, head of the Norwegian State Police, complained in a report to Quisling that there had been too little time to arrest all the Jews. And, he noted, the order from Germany that partners in so-called mixed marriages be spared had meant extra effort and expense (Doc. 38).

The reason for the over-hasty nature of the operation may have been that shipping space had unexpectedly become available, a possibility supported by the fact that the Reich Security Main Office in Berlin was not informed of the deportations in advance. Like the head office of the Stettin Gestapo, the Reich Security Main Office received notice of the sudden availability of transport only a day before the *Donau* set sail (Doc. 36). Eichmann's section for Jewish affairs had very limited time to establish the rules for the deportation. In contrast to the Norwegian government, however, Berlin insisted that only Norwegian and stateless Jews be deported. Holders of British or American passports and citizens of countries that were neutral or allied with Germany were excluded, as were Jews living in mixed marriages (Doc. 37).

The fact that Norwegian personnel had carried out the arrests and the deportation gave hope to some of the prisoners, who, segregated by gender, were forced below deck on the *Donau*. According to Samuel Steinmann, some of those on board thought that things would turn out for them as they had for the Norwegian academics who had been arrested after the large waves of protest in March and April 1942: 'We sailed into the fjord and hoped in our hearts that we would be sent to northern Norway, to the Finnmark. That was where the teachers and clerics who were arrested previously had been sent, to labour camps.'[51] The next day, however, this hope foundered when the deportees realized that the transport was heading for Germany. On 30 November the *Donau* arrived in port at Stettin, from where the prisoners were taken by train directly to Auschwitz extermination camp. On 1 December 1942 the camp commandant, Rudolf Höss, confirmed the arrival of 532 Jews who had been deported from Norway on 25 November (Docs. 36 and 37). Most of them, including all the women and children, were murdered immediately.

Because the deportation was handled with unexpected speed, some deportees from more remote regions did not reach Oslo in time. Employees of the Norwegian Red Cross and railway staff may have deliberately delayed the transport. The detainees concerned were initially confined in Bredtveit prison, north-east of Oslo, until the second deportation of Norwegian Jews, which took 158 prisoners on the *Gotenland* to Stettin, departing on 25 February 1943. From there, they were taken first to Berlin and after a brief stay in

51 Samuel Steinmann, cited in Lothe and Storeide (eds.), *Tidsvitner: Fortellinger fra Auschwitz og Sachsenhausen*, p. 125.

Levetzowstraße assembly camp they were added to a transport to Auschwitz, which reached the extermination camp on the night of 2/3 March 1943.[52] Twenty-eight men deemed fit for work were taken to Monowitz camp; all the others were murdered straight away.[53] The psychiatrist Leo Eitinger was among the few survivors (Doc. 51). He returned to Norway after the war, undertook psychiatric work with concentration camp prisoners, and gained an international reputation in the field of trauma research.

After the deportation of the Norwegian Jews, the distribution of their property began, on the basis of the aforementioned law of 26 October 1942. Because the anti-Jewish regulations could be traced back to the Quisling government rather than the occupiers and because Norwegian officials had carried out the arrests, many Norwegians viewed the confiscations as legal. The Norwegian government set up a separate authority, the Liquidations Office, to administer the assets. The office appointed administrators for the homes that had had to be abandoned.[54] Household items and movable belongings were either sold at public auction or offered for sale to Norwegian volunteers in the Waffen SS (Doc. 44). Real estate, by contrast, was generally not sold, but instead managed by the Ministry of Finance.

Those Jews who had avoided arrest were clearly in mortal danger. A few non-Jewish Norwegians endeavoured to persuade the Norwegian authorities to defer action against their Jewish friends and acquaintances, but usually without success (Doc. 48). As had been the case during the first wave of arrests, in October 1942 a number of Norwegian policemen succeeded in warning a few individuals, who with the help of fellow Norwegians now went into hiding. Hospitals in particular came to the aid of many of those fleeing and in the first few days also provided a place to hide.[55] Aiding an escape in this way was dangerous, for on 12 October 1942 Reich Commissioner Terboven had threatened to impose the death penalty on those who were fleeing and their helpers. Nonetheless, after the arrests in October 1942 and the deportation the following month, more and more non-Jewish Norwegians attempted to save the remaining Jews and take them to neighbouring Sweden. Most Jews came from the area in and around Oslo. The Swedish border was only around 100 kilometres away, but it was guarded extremely closely. Until an opportunity to smuggle people across the border arose it was necessary to find safe places to hide and to procure food. However, the unexpected rush risked exposing the escape routes which had been set up earlier by the resistance movement. Moreover, in recent months roundups by the German authorities had markedly weakened the organized Norwegian resistance movement.[56]

52 Vera Komissar and Sverre M. Nyrønning, *På tross av alt. Julius Paltiel, norsk jøde i Auschwitz* (Oslo: Aschehoug, 1995), pp. 39 and 48. This was the so-called Osttransport 32 from Berlin, the second deportation transport after the so-called Factory Action (*Fabrikaktion*) in Berlin. Besides the 158 Norwegian Jews, there were 1,654 Jews from Berlin and elsewhere on this transport.

53 Sæland, *Herman Beckers krig*, p. 221.

54 NOU, 1997, p. 78.

55 Ragnar Ulstein, *Svensketrafikken*, vol. 1, *Flyktningar til Sverige 1940–43* (Oslo: Samlaget, 1974), p. 210; Berit Nøkleby, *Holdningskamp* (*Norge i krig: Fremmedåk og frihetskamp 1940–1945*, ed. Magne Skodvin, vol. 4) (Oslo: Aschehoug, 1986), p. 213.

56 On the escape routes and helpers, see Ragnar Ulstein, *Jødar på flukt* (Oslo: Det Norske Samlaget, 1995). On the Norwegian resistance movement in general, see Olav Riste and Berit Nøkleby, *Norway, 1940–45: The Resistance Movement* (Oslo: Aschehoug, 1994 [Norwegian edn, 1970]).

The most extensive rescue operation in Norway during the war was organized by a married couple, Alf and Gerd Pettersen. Together with their friends Rolf Syversen and Reidar Larsen, they took two truckloads of Jews to the border almost daily between December 1942 and February 1943, thereby saving the lives of several hundred people. The code name of this resistance group, Carl Fredriksens Transport, was an allusion to King Haakon VII of Norway, whose first names included 'Carl' and 'Fredrik'. Among those saved were fourteen children who had come to Norway from Czechoslovakia through Nansen Relief and had been accommodated in a home in Holbergsgate in Oslo.[57] On the evening of 25 November 1942, Sigrid Helliesen Lund, who was involved in Nansen Relief and refugee work, received a tip from an anonymous caller that there was to be another 'party' and 'the small parcels' were now also going to be picked up. Lund realized that this had to be a reference to the arrest of the children. Together with Nina Hasvold, the home's director, Caroline 'Nic' Waal, who was a child psychiatrist, and a number of others, she rescued the children by taking them to Sweden (Docs. 41 and 46).[58]

Most of those fleeing were first driven to the area near the border by helpers. Then, in groups led by guides, they had to undertake lengthy treks through the snow-covered mountain ranges and forests along the Swedish border, constantly at risk of falling into the hands of German patrols. Those who were less robust, who were often not equal to the exertions, were a particular hazard on these journeys, as were small children, whose cries could put the entire group at risk. Anna Rothschild and her 18-month-old daughter, Inger Lise, had remained in Norway after her husband managed to flee to Sweden during the first arrests of Jewish men. The person helping her to escape demanded that she leave her child behind. Looking back, she described her debilitation, fear, and weariness and, above all, the difficult decision as to what was to become of Inger Lise: 'Should I rip out my heart and leave her behind in Norway? Should I wait with her? Wait to be caught, deported, and possibly killed?'[59] On 4 December 1942 she finally managed to escape. Inger Lise was placed with a foster mother and smuggled into Sweden on 16 May 1943. In total, more than 1,000 Jews were saved by escape to neighbouring Sweden.

In Sweden, the 'anti-Jewish operation' in Norway had attracted great attention. The Swedish Ministry of Foreign Affairs had been quickly and thoroughly briefed about the events by its consul general in Oslo. Efforts were made in Stockholm to at least do something for Jews who had family connections with Sweden. At the same time, the Swedish Ministry of Foreign Affairs, which thus far had maintained a certain distance from Jewish refugees from Germany and Eastern Europe, came under public pressure as a result of the large number of enquiries made by Swedish relatives of the persecuted (Doc. 39). In early December 1942 Sweden offered to accept all Jews who had not yet been deported from Norway, but the German government rejected this proposal. Claes Westring, the Swedish consul general in Norway, attempted to save the remaining Jews there by issuing

57 Mendelsohn, *Jødenes historie i Norge*, p. 226; Mats Tangestuen, *Carl Fredriksens Transport: Krigens største redningsbragd* (Oslo: URO/KORO, 2012); Irene Levin, 'Det jødiske barnehjemmet og Nic Waal', *Tidsskrift for Norsk psykologforening*, vol. 46, no. 1 (2009), pp. 76–80.

58 In 2006 Yad Vashem honoured Hasvold, Waal, Lund, and other rescuers as Righteous Among the Nations.

59 Anna Rothschild, cited in Vera Komissar, *Nådetid: Norske Jøder på flukt* (Oslo: Aschehoug, 1992), p. 70.

Swedish identity papers liberally.[60] This course of action was supported by leading officials at the Ministry of Foreign Affairs and also by the minister of foreign affairs himself. However, by declining to recognize any citizenship acquired after 26 November 1942, the Germans effectively rejected the intervention by the Swedish Ministry of Foreign Affairs for those who had already been deported.[61] In October 1944, shortly before the end of the war, the fear that the Germans might still deport approximately sixty Jews in so-called mixed marriages who had been arrested but not yet deported led the Swedish consul general in Oslo to begin efforts to get these individuals to Sweden. After lengthy negotiations, the individuals concerned were allowed to leave Norway for Sweden as of 21 April 1945, prior to Germany's capitulation.[62]

In all, at least 772 Jews were deported from Norway, of whom just 34 survived. Together with those who were murdered in Norway or took their own lives, 764 Jews from Norway – almost half of the Jewish population – lost their lives.[63]

Netherlands

At the Wannsee Conference on 20 January 1942, Heydrich and his expert on Jewish affairs Adolf Eichmann estimated the number of Jews living in the Netherlands at 160,800. This number, based on the 1941 census of Jews in the Netherlands, also included *Mischlinge* of the first and second degree.[64] Initial figures for deportation that were agreed at meetings held up to 11 June 1942 set a total of 15,000, with deportations to start in July 1942. That figure was then revised dramatically upwards: in a letter dated 22 June 1942 to the Reich Foreign Office, Eichmann was already writing of deporting 40,000 Jews from the Netherlands.[65]

A few days later, on 26 June, SS-Hauptsturmführer Ferdinand aus der Fünten, head of the Central Office for Jewish Emigration in Amsterdam, informed the Jewish Council

60 Levine, *From Indifference to Activism*, pp. 136–138 and 145–146; Mendelsohn, 'Norwegen', p. 195; Steven Koblik, *The Stones Cry Out: Sweden's Response to the Persecution of the Jews, 1933–1945* (New York: Holocaust Library, 1988), p. 60.

61 Klas Åmark, *Att bo granne med ondskan: Sveriges förhållande till nazismen, Nazityskland og Förintelsen* (Stockholm: Albert Bonniers, 2011), pp. 536–554; Kvist Geverts, 'Ett främmande element i nationen', pp. 188–189.

62 Correspondence in Tôviyyā Friedman, *Dokumentensammlung über 'Die Deportierung der Juden aus Norwegen nach Auschwitz'* (Ramat Gan: City Council, 1963). Also see Hoffmann, 'Fluchthilfe als Widerstand', p. 230.

63 Bruland, *Det norske Holocaust*, p. 29.

64 See PMJ 5/90.

65 See PMJ 5/145. On the history of the occupation period in the Netherlands, see Werner Warmbrunn, *The Dutch under German Occupation, 1940–1945* (Stanford: Stanford University Press, 1963); L. de Jong, *Het Koninkrijk der Nederlanden in de Tweede Wereldoorlog*, 12 vols. (The Hague: Nijhoff, 1969–1986); Gerhard Hirschfeld, *Nazi Rule and Dutch Collaboration: The Netherlands under German Occupation, 1940–1945* (Oxford and New York: Berg, 1988); Hans Blom, *In de ban van goed en fout: Geschiedschrijving over de bezettingstijd in Nederland* (Amsterdam: Boom, 2007); Jennifer L. Foray, *Visions of Empire in the Nazi-Occupied Netherlands* (Cambridge: Cambridge University Press, 2014); Chris van der Heijden, *Grijs verleden: Nederland en de Tweede Wereldoorlog* (Amsterdam: Contact, 2001). On the deportation figures, see Christoph Kreutzmüller, 'Eichmanns Zahlen für die Niederlande', in Norbert Kampe und Peter Klein (eds.), *Die Wannsee-Konferenz am 20. Januar 1942 – Dokumente, Forschungsstand, Kontroversen* (Vienna: Böhlau, 2013), pp. 357–378.

(Joodsche Raad) that Jewish workers were to be called up for 'labour deployment in Germany'. The Central Office was to be in charge of the call-ups, while the Jewish Council was required to handle transport documentation and the declarations of assets submitted by those affected. After some hesitation and with grave reservations, the two chairmen of the Jewish Council, David Cohen and Abraham Asscher, declared themselves willing to cooperate. They were given various promises, supposedly as concessions: families would not be split up; only adults between eighteen and forty would be affected; postal traffic would be possible; and members of certain professions as well as employees of the Jewish Council would be exempt from labour deployment.[66]

On 5 July 1942 and in the days that followed, 4,000 persons summoned for labour deployment were told to report to the police-run transit camp at Westerbork, where they were to undergo medical examination. Enclosed with the summons was a list of the items of clothing allowed and a travel permit for the journey to Westerbork. Only a few people actually turned up after receiving a summons. The fear was too great, not least as rumours of a deportation to Poland had begun to circulate. When numbers at the assembly points failed to increase even after the Amsterdam police delivered written summons, on 14 July the German Order Police carried out raids in Amsterdam, taking more than 500 Jews hostage and threatening to send them to Mauthausen concentration camp if those who had been summoned continued to refuse to report. In the Netherlands, 'Mauthausen' had become synonymous with death ever since, in retaliation for the February Strike in 1941, Jewish men had been deported there and death notices for many of them were received just a few months later. This threat and a renewed appeal by the Jewish Council had an effect, and in the coming days many Amsterdam Jews obeyed the summons and were taken to Westerbork. On 15 July 1942 the first deportation train left from there, bringing 1,135 Jews to Auschwitz.[67] After a three-day train journey, several hundred deportees were immediately led into the gas chambers and murdered; the others were placed in the concentration camp. From then until the end of November 1942, deportation trains departed approximately twice a week and took a total of 36,084 Jews from Westerbork to Auschwitz.

66 NIOD, 182/1d. Minutes of the discussion between Ferdinand aus der Fünten and representatives of the Jewish Council, dated 26 June 1942. On the history of the persecution of the Jews in the Netherlands, see Jacques Presser, *Ondergang: De vervolging en verdelging van het Nederlandse Jodendom 1940–1945* (The Hague: Staatsuitgeverij, 1965) (abridged English edn: *Ashes in the Wind: The Destruction of Dutch Jewry*, trans. Arnold Pomerans [London: Souvenir Press, 2010]); Abel Herzberg, *Kroniek der Jodenvervolging, 1940–1945* (Amsterdam: Querido, 1985); Loe de Jong, *Jodenvervolging in Nederland 1940–1945*, 2 vols. (Amsterdam: Verbum and NIOD, 2018); de Jong, *Het Koninkrijk*, vols. 5–8; Bob Moore, *Victims and Survivors: The Nazi Persecution of the Jews in the Netherlands, 1940–1945* (London: Arnold, 1997); Jozeph Michman, Hartog Beem, and Dan Michman, *Pinkas: Geschiedenis van de joodse gemeenschap in Nederland* (Amsterdam: Contact, 1999); Peter Romijn et al., *The Persecution of the Jews in the Netherlands, 1940–1945: New Perspectives* (Amsterdam: Vossiuspers UvA, 2012); Frits Boterman, *Duitse daders: De Jodenvervolging en de nazificatie van Nederland (1940–1945)* (Amsterdam and Antwerp: Arbeiderspers, 2015); Katja Happe, *Viele falsche Hoffnungen: Judenverfolgung in den Niederlanden 1940–1945* (Paderborn: Ferdinand Schöningh, 2017). For comparison with France and Belgium, see Pim Griffioen and Ron Zeller, *Jodenvervolging in Nederland, Frankrijk en België: Overeenkomsten, verschillen, oorzaken* (Amsterdam: Boom, 2010), and Pim Griffioen and Ron Zeller, 'Comparing the persecution of the Jews in the Netherlands, France and Belgium, 1940–1945: Similarities, Differences, Causes', in Romijn et al., *The Persecution of the Jews in the Netherlands, 1940–1945: New Perspectives*, pp. 55–92.

67 NIOD, 182/1c. Minutes of the Jewish Council, 14 July 1942. The information on the deportation numbers is based on Gerhard Hirschfeld, 'Niederlande', in Benz (ed.), *Dimension des Völkermords*, pp. 137–165. List of deportees' names: *In Memoriam* (The Hague: Sdu Publishers, 1995).

Some of the Jews (among them Christian Jews) deported from Westerbork had been transferred here from Amersfoort police transit camp. Of the approximately 42,000 Jews deported to Auschwitz by February 1943, only a few dozen survived. However, some 3,400 Dutch (along with 1,200 Belgian and 5,000 French) Jews were taken off a few of the transports in Koźle (Upper Silesia) to undertake forced labour in local camps; of these, 875 survived, 185 of them Dutch Jews.[68]

Otto Bene, Reich Foreign Office representative in The Hague, noted the start of the deportations in his report to Berlin on 17 July 1942, in which he stated 'that the first two trains have set off without difficulties of any kind' (Doc. 60). Only a few weeks later, however, he was forced to concede that since learning what 'is implied by transport or labour deployment in the East', large numbers of Jews were evading deportation. 'Of the 2,000 summoned for this week', he reported, 'only around 400 turned up. Those who were summoned are no longer to be found in their apartments. There are therefore difficulties in filling the two trains' (Doc. 71).[69]

To ensure full use was made of the trains' capacity, the German authorities changed their approach. After written summonses had failed to yield the desired result, units of the German Order Police and Dutch police arrested Jews who had received these notifications at their homes and brought them, along with their luggage, to assembly points from where they were to travel to Westerbork.[70] This measure was facilitated by a regulation issued in late June 1942 by Hanns Albin Rauter, commissioner general for security, requiring Jews to remain in their homes between 8 p.m. and 6 a.m. (Doc. 53). The collection of people from their homes marked the beginning of a time of mounting anxiety for the Jews. The Jewish writer Sam Goudsmit described such evenings in his diary:

> So this evening again, thousands of Jews in Amsterdam, sitting together with narrowed eyes and the blood drained from their faces, waiting to find out if they will be allowed to sleep at home tonight or will be pounced upon at any moment, when the sound of the bell will cut straight through their heart, and they will have to leave their home behind forever. (Doc. 75)

68 The exact numbers have only recently been ascertained: see Herman van Rens and Annelies Wilms, *Tussenstation Cosel: Joodse mannen uit West-Europa naar dwangarbeiderskampen in Silezië, 1942–1945* (Hilversum: Verloren, 2020). For earlier studies, see L. Landsberger, A. de Haas, and K. Selowsky, *Auschwitz*, vol. 2: *De deportatietransporten van 15 juli tot en met 24 augustus 1942* (The Hague: Nederlandsche Roode Kruis, 1948); Danuta Czech, *Kalendarium der Ereignisse im Konzentrationslager Auschwitz-Birkenau, 1939–1945* (Reinbek: Rowohlt, 1989); de Jong, *Het Koninkrijk*, vol. 8/2: *Gevangenen en gedeporteerden*, p. 833.

69 For an attempt to assess the extent of the population's awareness of the persecution of the Jews, see Bart van der Boom, *'We weten niets van hun lot': Gewone Nederlanders en de Holocaust* (Amsterdam: Boom, 2012), and 'Ordinary Dutchmen and the Holocaust: A Summary of Findings', in Peter Romijn et al., *The Persecution of the Jews in the Netherlands, 1940–1945: New Perspectives*, pp. 29–55. Van der Boom's study and its methodology have been sharply criticized: see a summarizing overview in Christina Morina, 'The "bystander" in recent Dutch historiography', *German History*, 32:1 (2014), pp. 101–111.

70 Guus Meershoek, *Dienaren van het gezag: De Amsterdamse politie tijdens de bezetting* (Amsterdam: Van Gennep, 1999); Ad van Liempt and Jan H. Kompagnie (eds.), *Jodenjacht: De onthutsende rol van de Nederlandse politie in de Tweede Wereldoorlog* (Amsterdam: Balans, 2011); Marnix Croes, 'The Dutch Police Force and the Persecution of the Jews in the Netherlands during the German Occupation, 1940–1945', in Bruno De Wever, Herman Van Goethem, and Nico Wouters (eds.), *Local Government in Occupied Europe (1939–1945)* (Ghent: Academia Press, 2006), pp. 67–82.

After months of fear, German refugee Gerhard Durlacher ultimately perceived his arrest like 'a menacing but inevitable natural disaster'.[71]

The German authorities did not keep any of the promises they had made to the Jewish Council. Young children and the elderly were summoned, and letters or cards from Auschwitz forcibly written by the deportees upon arrival reached the Jewish Council only after several weeks, if at all. Only exemptions – or 'exemption stamps' (*Sperrstempel*) as they were termed in reference to the number stamped in the passport of the person exempted – promised relative protection from deportation. Employees of the Jewish Council and their families were exempt, as were members of certain occupational groups, such as diamond merchants or metal dealers, who were considered important to Germany's wartime economy.[72] In view of the opportunity for exemption, as well as the increasing workload, the number of employees at the Jewish Council rose rapidly, at times reaching 10,000. The council thus increasingly became a kind of 'state within the state',[73] responsible for every sphere of Jewish life, from social welfare and hospitals and schools to the cultural programme and efforts on behalf of those who had been selected for labour deployment. David Cohen adopted the maxim 'at least to retain the most important people for as long as possible' (Doc. 79). The scope for action by the Jewish Council was restricted, however, by German directives and orders. The council therefore no longer tended to lodge overarching protests and instead limited them to isolated cases. Its role as an instrument or compliant helper of the occupying forces was the cause of fierce controversy even during the occupation.[74] Employees who survived for some time under the protection of the Jewish Council, such as the writer Grete Weil, recalled its role with ambivalence:

> Today I feel guilt for having been part of the Jewish Council. No one knows what would have happened if it had not existed. […] But for me, it is not a guilt that casts a cloud over my life. I can only say that I would feel easier in my mind if I had not been a part of it.[75]

71 Gerhard Durlacher, *Stripes in the Sky* (London: Serpent's Tail, 1991), p. 28.

72 On the economic interests of the German occupiers in connection with the persecution of the Jews, see Martin Dean, *Robbing the Jews: The Confiscation of Jewish Property in the Holocaust, 1933–1945* (Cambridge: Cambridge University Press, 2010); Gerard Aalders, *Nazi Looting: The Plunder of Dutch Jewry during the Second World War* (Oxford: Berg, 2004); Christoph Kreutzmüller, *Händler und Handlungsgehilfen: Der Finanzplatz Amsterdam und die deutschen Großbanken (1918–1945)* (Stuttgart: Steiner, 2005); Christoph Kreutzmüller, 'Contested Dispossession: The Netherlands', in Christoph Kreutzmüller and Jonathan R. Zatlin (eds.), *Dispossession: Plundering German Jewry, 1933–1953* (Ann Arbor, MI: University of Michigan Press, 2020), pp. 216–235.

73 The 'state within the state' was Presser's heading for his chapter on the Jewish Council: see Presser, *Ondergang*, vol. 1, p. 214. On the number of employees, see ibid., p. 290.

74 Hans Knoop, *De Joodsche Raad: Het drama van Abraham Asscher en David Cohen* (Amsterdam: Elsevier, 1983); Willy Lindwer, *Het fatale dilemma: De Joodsche Raad voor Amsterdam 1941–1943* (The Hague: Sdu Uitgeverij Koninginnegracht, 1995); Johannes Houwink ten Cate, 'Die moralische Debatte über den Amsterdamer Judenrat', in Norbert Fasse, Johannes Houwink ten Cate, and Horst Lademacher (eds.), *Nationalsozialistische Herrschaft und Besatzungszeit: Historische Erfahrung und Verarbeitung aus niederländischer und deutscher Sicht* (Münster: Waxmann, 2000), pp. 211–216; Bernard Wasserstein, *The Ambiguity of Virtue: Gertrude van Tijn and the Fate of the Dutch Jews* (Cambridge, MA: Harvard University Press, 2014).

75 Grete Weil, cited in Dorlies Pollmann and Edith Laudowicz (eds.), *Weil ich das Leben liebe: Persönliches und Politisches aus dem Leben engagierter Frauen* (Cologne: Pahl-Rugenstein, 1981), p. 176.

The deportation of Jewish citizens, now a regular occurrence, provoked protest from various quarters. On 11 July 1942 the Christian churches of the Netherlands appealed to Reich Commissioner Arthur Seyss-Inquart in a telegram, requesting that the measure be cancelled. In particular, the churches intervened on behalf of those who had been baptized but were considered Jews according to National Socialist racial principles (Doc. 65). The churches obtained an exemption from the Reich Commissioner for those who had converted to Christianity and been baptized before January 1941. The telegram of protest was to have been read aloud in every church in the Netherlands on 26 July 1942, but Seyss-Inquart made the exemption for those who had been baptized conditional on the telegram not being read out. The Dutch Reformed Church complied, but the majority of the other churches did not. The Reich Commissioner now sought to undermine the solidarity of the Dutch churches by exempting Jews who had converted to Protestantism, while those baptized in the Catholic Church were deported as punishment for the reading out of the telegram. His attempts to play off the churches against each other proved unsuccessful, but overall Catholics of Jewish origin still had a much slighter chance of survival than non-Aryan Protestants (Doc. 69).

The illegal newspapers published in the Netherlands also took a stand against the deportations. *Het Parool* and other newspapers repeatedly addressed the horrific fate of the Jews and called upon the Dutch population to provide active help.[76] In August 1942 they even published a joint 'Manifesto on the Reintroduction of Slavery', in which they demanded: 'Protect the Jews wherever you can. Hide them, give them shelter and food, however hard it may be for you!' (Doc. 68). A two-page leaflet titled 'Netherlands, Wake Up' (*Nederland Ontwaakt*), dated 24 July 1942, reacted to the first transport from Amsterdam, stating that at Westerbork 'Jewish men were separated from their wives and deported in German livestock wagons with an unknown destination to their mass grave far beyond the German border … It must never be allowed for 120,000 Dutch Jews to be driven like animals to the slaughter.'[77]

Nonetheless, many Jews felt helpless and exposed. Jules Schelvis, one of the few survivors, described this sentiment retrospectively:

> What was most painful for us was the humiliation to which we were subjected. To be completely defenceless and unable to do anything to end this degrading state of affairs. Why was no one able to stop what happened to us? How could the world allow us, upright Dutch citizens, to be treated like dirt?[78]

The Dutch government in exile in London spoke out when the deportations began. On 25 July 1942 Prime Minister Gerbrandy declared on Radio Oranje, the Dutch-language programme of the British Broadcasting Corporation (BBC), that the implementation of these measures was 'in breach of the Dutch constitution, according to which all

76 See, for example, *Het Parool*, 14 July 1942, p. 1; no. 4, 25 July 1942, p. 3; and no. 42, 21 August 1942, p. 5; Madelon de Keizer, *Het Parool 1940–1945: Verzetsblad in oorlogstijd* (Amsterdam: Otto Cramwinckel, 1991).

77 NIOD, collection 556, box no. 40; Jewish Historical Museum, Amsterdam.

78 Jules Schelvis, *Er reed een trein naar Sobibor* (Hooghalen: Herinneringscentrum Kamp Westerbork, 2012), p. 36.

citizens are equal before the law' (Doc. 64). Overall, however, the Dutch government in exile did relatively little for the persecuted Jews in the Netherlands during the first few months. When David Cohen was asked by his acquaintance Meyer Sluijser what the government in exile had done for the Jews, he replied: 'My answer to that is short: Nothing.'[79]

By the beginning of 1942 the Germans had already interned more than 5,000 Jews in Dutch labour camps,[80] a measure that had originally been intended for the Dutch unemployed. In so doing, the occupation authorities had brought a section of the Dutch Jews under their control. At the end of September 1942 Rauter reported to Reichsführer-SS Heinrich Himmler on his further plans: 'We hope to reach a total of 8,000 Jews by 1 October. These 8,000 Jews have around 22,000 relatives throughout Holland. On 1 October the Werkverruiming [labour] camps will be occupied by me at a stroke, and on the same day the relatives outside the camps will be arrested' (Doc. 81).

Westerbork transit camp had been established as a central refugee camp back in the autumn of 1939. For this reason, Jewish refugees from Germany who had been interned there since the creation of the camp were at the top of the Jewish prisoner hierarchy even after Westerbork was taken over by the German occupation authorities in the summer of 1942. Konrad Gemmeker, a former policeman and employee of the Security Police, was in charge of the camp, which was guarded jointly by members of the German SS and the Dutch military police. The internal organization, however, was largely in Jewish hands. The 'long-term' camp inmates, as they were known, often held key positions and were able to make similarly favourable positions available to friends and acquaintances. Sometimes they were even able to influence who was included on transport lists. That ability fostered conflict within the camp between the German Jews and the Dutch Jews. According to Aad van As, a non-Jewish administrative official from the Westerbork municipality who dealt with both groups: 'The Jewish population in the camp resisted the idea that they should follow orders given by German Jewish émigrés on Dutch soil. For that is how it was seen. They were regarded as Germans, not as fellow Jews who suffered under the occupying forces in the same way.'[81]

The constant fear of deportation dominated life in Westerbork more than such internal conflict and all the hardships in the camp. Advantageous positions in the camp administration, at the hospital, or with the 'Westerbork Revue', the camp cabaret featuring well-known Jewish performers and musicians, provided only a temporary reprieve. Inmates repeatedly had to bid farewell to friends and relatives who were deported. As a nurse in Westerbork, Jeanne van den Berg-van Cleeff witnessed many transports: 'I had to take the people to the train, all the way to the railway wagon. Adults, children, and babies. The wagons were simply loaded up with those who were there.'[82]

79 David Cohen, *Voorzitter van de Joodse Raad: De herinneringen van David Cohen (1941–1943)*, ed. Erik Sommers (Zutphen: Walburg Pers, 2010), p. 205. On the role of the government in exile, see also Jord Schaap, *Het recht om te waarschuwen: Jodenvervolging en vernieuwing in de Radio Oranje-toespraken van Wilhelmina* (Groningen: Wolters-Noordhoff, 2005), and Onno Sinke, *Verzet vanuit de verte: De behoedzame koers van Radio Oranje* (Amsterdam: Augustus, 2009).

80 PMJ 5, p. 45.

81 Aad van As, *In het hol van de leeuw* (Hooghalen: Herinneringscentrum Kamp Westerbork, 2004), p. 67.

82 Anna Hájková, 'Das Polizeiliche Durchgangslager Westerbork', in Wolfgang Benz and Barbara Distel (eds.), *Terror im Westen: Nationalsozialistische Lager in den Niederlanden, Belgien und Lux-*

Besides Westerbork there were two other camps in the Netherlands in which Jews were interned over a lengthy period. In January 1943 the SS established Vught concentration camp, officially named KL Herzogenbusch due to its proximity to the town of 's-Hertogenbosch. In addition to non-Jews in protective custody, university students, and hostages, thousands of Jews were temporarily interned here. Many of them were forced to undertake hard physical labour as members of work squads and were mistreated (Doc. 108). Both Jews and non-Jews detailed to the Philips electrical company were lucky to start with. The work there was relatively tolerable, and both the company's management and its employees sought to alleviate the situation of the Jews (Doc. 144). However, the firm could prevent neither the departure of a transport with more than 1,000 Jews that travelled from Vught directly to Auschwitz in November 1943, nor the eventual deportation of the remaining Jewish inmates of the camp to Westerbork.[83] Those deported from Vught to Auschwitz survived there until January 1944, when approximately 300 men and 5 women were distributed among various labour camps and all the others were murdered. Only 53 persons from this deportation survived and returned to the Netherlands after their liberation.[84]

In what became the third transit camp in the Netherlands, at Barneveld, a small town in the province of Gelderland, several hundred intellectuals, artists, and otherwise well-known persons were interned in two small castles from December 1942. Reich Commissioner Seyss-Inquart had allowed Dutch secretaries general Karel Frederiks and Jan van Dam, who as the most senior ministry officials were in charge of the Dutch administration, to name around 500 Jews who were to be considered 'privileged' and thus exempted from deportation (Doc. 102). This status protected the inmates for less than a year. In September 1943 the camp was closed, and the internees were first sent to Westerbork and later deported to Theresienstadt. Henny Bing-Rudelsheim, a member of the so-called Barneveld Group, recalled the shock of learning that they would be deported from Westerbork to the East.[85] Bing-Rudelsheim survived, but many of her fellow sufferers were deported from Theresienstadt to Auschwitz and other camps, where they perished. Although the secretaries general had repeatedly protested against the treatment of the Jews during the first years of the occupation, barely anything was done to protect the Jews after the start of the deportations, with the exception of the granting of protected

emburg 1940–1945 (Berlin: Metropol, 2004), pp. 217–248; Nanda van der Zee, *Westerbork: Het doorgangskamp en zijn commandant* (Soesterberg: Aspekt, 2006); Jeanne van den Berg-van Cleeff, 'Verpleegster uit nood', in Guido Abuys and Dirk Mulder (eds.), *Genezen verklaard voor … Een ziekenhuis in kamp Westerbork, 1939–1945* (Hooghalen: Herinneringscentrum Kamp Westerbork, 2006), p. 36.

83 P. W. Klein and Justus van de Kamp, *Het Philips-Kommando in Kamp* Vught (Amsterdam: Contact, 2003); Hans de Vries, 'Konzentrationslager Herzogenbusch (Vught)', in Wolfgang Benz and Barbara Distel (eds.), *Der Ort des Terrors*, vol. 7: *Niederhagen/Wewelsburg, Lublin-Majdanek, Arbeitsdorf, Herzogenbusch (Vught), Bergen-Belsen, Mittelbau-Dora* (Munich: Beck, 2008), pp. 153–184.

84 An early post-war study by L. Landsberger, A. de Haas, and K. Selowsky, *Auschwitz*, vol. 4: *De deportatietransporten in 1943* (The Hague: Nederlandsche Roode Kruis, 1953), pp. 44 and 57–59, mentions 38 survivors (32 males and 6 females). However, new research indicates that the number of survivors was higher – 53: see Aline Pennewaard, 'Lists and Human Beings: The Deportation of Dutch Jewry, Viewed from Within and Without, 1942–1943,' PhD dissertation, University of Haifa (2021).

85 'Waar is zuster Henny?', in Abuys and Mulder, *Genezen verklaard voor …*, p. 61.

status to the Barneveld group. The 'exemptions' which many Jews hoped would protect them from deportation thus became increasingly important. At the same time, these exemptions provided the German authorities with a means of categorizing Jews and of treating particular groups in different ways and playing them off against each other. New exemption lists appeared repeatedly, along with new categories that promised exclusion from deportation. From the autumn of 1942 the Central Office for Jewish Emigration issued exemption stamps for 'foreign Jews' and for 'Portuguese Jews', whose status as Jews was hard to determine because of queries over their ancestry.[86] 'Jews by ancestry' (*Abstammungsjuden*) were spared for the time being because their 'racial' origin had yet to be clarified. Jews 'offered for exchange' (*Angebotsjuden*) too were temporarily spared, because they might be exchanged for Germans interned abroad. In addition, there were lists for the Jewish Council, for Protestants of Jewish descent, for 'armaments Jews' and 'diamond Jews', as well as for Jewish men and women with non-Jewish spouses, who were deemed to be part of mixed marriages (Doc. 112). Many Jews used all means available to them to get onto a list that seemed to offer them protection, with more than 30,000 persons thus listed by the end of December 1942. Coen Rood, a survivor of various camps, described in retrospect the attitude to life adopted by many Jews at that time: 'Every opportunity to stay is taken, and every transport that leaves without you on it is a step closer to liberation.'[87] At the same time, many assessed their situation very realistically, including the author and journalist Salomon de Vries: 'My wife and I had a few good chances [of being deported]. I had a couple of "exemptions", but these were on paper, and under very specific circumstances the Germans have traditionally shown a truly German disdain for everything that is written on paper and has had a seal put on it' (Doc. 76). Mirjam Bolle, an employee of the Jewish Council, described the situation in a letter written in February 1943: 'this Sperre [exemption] affair is a dark chapter indeed. The Germans tossed us a bone and watched with glee as the Jews fought for it.'[88] In practice, lists suddenly expired, depending on the needs and wishes of the Central Office for Jewish Emigration, while the number on the lists might be arbitrarily decreased or all those on the list deported as a group, as in the case of the 'privileged' Jews from Barneveld. For these reasons, an exemption stamp offered protection that was at most temporary.

To hide or 'go underground' was the only other way to avoid deportation. The family of Edith Samuel-Jakobs, for example, reacted immediately to their summons: 'When Rose and Martin, at the age of sixteen, were notified of their selection to report for "labour deployment", it was high time to disappear.'[89] There were various possibilities. One could try to lead a life as normal as possible in a new location with a false passport

86 A considerable number of Portuguese Jews applied to the German official in charge of 'racially ambiguous' cases, Hans Georg Calmeyer, seeking to be recognized as non-racially Jewish and thus to be exempted from anti-Jewish measures in general and deportation in particular. See Geraldien von Frijtag Drabbe Künzel, *Het geval Calmeyer* (Amsterdam: Mets & Schilt, 2008), and Jaap Cohen, *De onontkoombare afkomst van Eli d'Oliveira: Een Portugees-Joodse familiegeschiedenis* (Amsterdam and Antwerp: Querido, 2015), pp. 349–455.

87 Coen Rood, *Onze dagen: Herinneringen aan de jodenvervolging* (Amsterdam: Boom, 2011), p. 37.

88 Letter dated 2 February 1943, in Mirjam Bolle, *Letters Never Sent: Amsterdam, Westerbork, Bergen-Belsen* (Jerusalem: Yad Vashem, 2014), p. 57.

89 Rose Jakobs, *De roos die nooit bloeide: Dagboek van een onderduikster, 1942–1944* (Amsterdam: Arbeiderspers, 1999), p. 18.

that lacked the tell-tale 'J', for example helping with the harvest in the countryside. Many Jews sought shelter in the homes of friends and acquaintances as ostensibly distant relatives of their hosts. Parents tried to get their children to safety by lodging them under false names with the families of strangers; resistance groups provided many of them with food ration cards.[90] Anyone unable to obtain a false passport was left with no alternative to life in hiding. Not everyone managed to find relatively comfortable accommodation with the same success as the family of Anne Frank (Doc. 147), who lived in several rooms in a house that were accessible only through a secret entrance and who were provided for by employees of her father Otto Frank's former firm. In many cases, tiny rooms, cellars, or attic partitions served as hiding places which those who were being concealed sometimes could not leave for months on end. Approximately 25,000–28,000 Dutch Jews went into hiding.[91]

A considerable number of Dutch people were ready to help and took Jews who were in danger, even complete strangers, into their homes. In so doing they were taking a great risk. Some took payment for their help. Not infrequently people in hiding had to move to another hiding place because there was a threat of a roundup or because they had been betrayed. Every change of location brought fresh dangers and the challenges of adapting to a new environment. Albert Heymans, who went into hiding, recounted in his memoirs how difficult it had been to keep in touch with family members and to find new places to hide.[92] Conflicts between hosts and their illegal guests were common, the result of their living together in an extremely tight space and of the perilousness of the situation. 'I am aware of the fact that I am homeless, but that does not mean that I have to take insults from you,' said Toni Ringel, a Jewish woman in hiding, when she felt harassed by her 'landlady' (Doc. 106).

The attempt to escape to neutral Switzerland was no less risky. From the summer of 1942, members of the resistance movement in the occupied Netherlands were secretly in

90 Bert-Jan Flim, *Saving the Children: History of the Organized Effort to Rescue Jewish Children in the Netherlands, 1942–1945*, trans. Jeanette Ringold (Bethesda, MD: CDL Press, 2005 [Dutch edn, 1996]); Mark Klempner, *The Heart Has Reasons: Dutch Rescuers of Jewish Children During the Holocaust* (Amsterdam/New York: Night Stand Books, 2012).

91 Jozeph Michman and Bert-Jan Flim, *The Encyclopedia of the Righteous Among the Nations – Rescuers of Jews during the Holocaust: The Netherlands* (Jerusalem: Yad Vashem, 2004), p. xxxix. Scholars differ on the numbers of those who went into hiding. See de Jong, *Het Koninkrijk*, vols. 6/1, *Juli '42–mei '43*, pp. 356–360, and 7/1, *Mei '43–juni '44*, p. 441; and Marnix Croes and Peter Tammes, *'Gif laten wij niet voortbestaan': Een onderzoek naar de overlevingskansen van joden in Nederlandse gemeenten 1940–1945* (Amsterdam: Aksant, 2004), pp. 174–196. See also Marnix Croes, 'The Netherlands, 1942–1945: Survival in Hiding and the Hunt for Hidden Jews,' in Beate Kosmala and Feliks Tych (eds.), *Facing the Nazi Genocide: Non-Jews and Jews in Europe, 1941–1945* (Berlin: Metropol, 2004), pp. 41–72; Pinchas Bar-Efrat, *Denunciation and Rescue: Dutch Society and the Holocaust* (Jerusalem: Yad Vashem, 2017), pp. 25–27; and de Jong, *Jodenvervolging in Nederland 1940–1945*, pp. 1321–1322.

92 Albert Heymans, *Jood zonder ster* (Westervoort: Van Gruting, 1999), p. 81. On life in hiding, see Ad van Liempt, *Hitler's Bounty Hunters: The Betrayal of the Jews*, trans. S.J. Leinbach (Oxford: Berg, 2005 [Dutch edn, 2002]); Bob Moore, *Survivors: Jewish Self-Help and Rescue in Nazi-Occupied Western Europe* (Oxford: Oxford University Press, 2010); Marnix Croes and Beate Kosmala, 'Facing Deportation in Germany and the Netherlands: Survival in Hiding', in Beate Kosmala and Georgi Verbeeck (eds.), *Facing the Catastrophe: Jews and non-Jews in Europe during World War II* (Oxford: Berg, 2011), pp. 97–158.

contact with Switzerland. The so-called Swiss route was also used to convey information to the Dutch government in exile in London, and information about the persecution of the Jews made its way out of the Netherlands through this channel. Only a few hundred Jews, however, entered Switzerland via Belgium and France.[93] Another escape route, from the Netherlands via Belgium and France to Spain, was initiated by the Zionist Palestine Pioneers (Halutzim). They managed to rescue between 150 and 200 youngsters. Similarly, the 'Nanno' and 'Dutch-Paris' networks rescued hundreds of Jews by channelling them via the escape route to Spain.[94]

By the end of February 1943, a total of 46,455 persons – almost one third of all the Jews living in the Netherlands – had already been deported to Auschwitz, and the transports continued to depart from Westerbork regularly, at least once a week. Of the Jews deported by that date, usually no more than ten persons per transport survived the war. In a speech to the Germanic SS on 22 March 1943, Commissioner General Rauter affirmed the Germans' goal once again: 'We hope that in the foreseeable future there will no longer be a single Jew in the Netherlands walking around freely in the streets' (Doc. 113). Meanwhile, in January 1943 Het Apeldoornsche Bosch, a psychiatric institution for Jews, was emptied and all the patients deported, along with many of the nursing staff (Docs. 103 and 104). Not one of them survived. When making arrests, the German and Dutch police no longer spared the infirm, the elderly, or children. The destination of the deportation trains that left between March and the end of July 1943 was not Auschwitz, but rather Sobibor extermination camp. Of the 31,313 persons taken there on nineteen transports, only 18 survived the war. One of the survivors, Jules Schelvis, described the end of the train journey: 'Early Friday morning, after travelling for seventy hours, the last little grain of our endurance was used up. We could not bear any more. Extreme fatigue had rendered us so apathetic that we no longer took an interest in where we were going and what work we were to do.'[95] Almost all of the others who were deported to Sobibor were murdered in the gas chambers upon arrival. Selma Wijnberg-Engel was the only Dutch person to survive the uprising there in October 1943. She returned to the Netherlands after the war.

For the Jews who were still living legally in the Netherlands, the spring of 1943 brought a further restriction. In March, by order of Rauter, those living in the provinces of Friesland, Groningen, Drente, Overijssel, Gelderland, Limburg, North Brabant, and Seeland were forced to move to Vught camp. Only one month later the Jewish inhabitants of the remaining provinces – Utrecht, North Holland, and South Holland – suffered the same fate (Doc. 117). All the Jews still at liberty were thus concentrated in

93 Jenny Gans Premsela, *Vluchtweg: Aan de bezetter ontsnapt* (Baarn: Bosch en Keuning, 1990).

94 Moore, *Victims and Survivors*, pp. 168–170; Moore, *Survivors*, pp. 58–70; Igal Benjamin, *Faithful to Their Destiny and to Themselves: The Zionist Pioneers' Underground in the Netherlands in War and Holocaust* (Jerusalem: Yad Tabenkin and Ghetto Fighters' House, 1988) (in Hebrew).

95 Schelvis, *Er reed een trein*, p. 37. On the deportations to Sobibor, see also Elie Aron Cohen and Aad Nuis, *De negentien treinen naar Sobibor* (Amsterdam: Elsevier, 1979); Jules Schelvis, *Sobibor: A History of a Nazi Death Camp* (London: Bloomsbury, 2014); Saartje Wijnberg-Engel, *Dancing through Darkness: When Love and Dreams Survived a Nazi Death Camp* (Nashville: Dunham Books, 2012); Jules Schelvis, *Inside the Gates: An Authentic Story of Two Years in German Concentration Camps, 1943–1945*, trans. Senta Kushkulei-Engelstein and Gerda Baardman (Tricht: Elzenhorst, 1990 [Dutch edn, 1982]).

Amsterdam, which made it easier for the occupying forces to carry out roundups and arrests.[96]

In the spring of 1943 the mood shifted among the Dutch population, which had already increasingly turned against the occupiers over the course of 1942, as more and more Dutch men were required to perform forced labour in Germany. In late April 1943 more than 250,000 army personnel who had been quickly released from detention following Dutch capitulation in 1940 were required by the German occupiers to resume their status as prisoners of war, so that they could be deployed for forced labour in Germany. Strikes broke out in nearly every part of the country. Factory workers refused to work, as did employees of department stores and shops. Farmers stopped delivering grain. Only in Amsterdam, after the experiences of the strike of February 1941 did the situation remain calm. The German occupiers reacted with force and crushed the strikes within a week, with almost 200 persons losing their lives in the process.[97] Increasing numbers of Dutch non-Jews subsequently also went underground in order to avoid forced labour in Germany. The strikes in April and May 1943 marked a turning point in the occupation, with an increase in both organized resistance, which had previously remained slight, and support for those who were in hiding. Jews could now count on receiving greater help while living illicitly. For many, however, the shift in public opinion came too late – almost half of the 140,000 Jews living in the Netherlands had already been deported, and most of them murdered.

During this period, the Central Office for Jewish Emigration reduced the number of exemptions. In addition to the so-called armaments Jews and other groups, this cutback now affected the Jewish Council itself. On 21 May 1943 aus der Fünten notified the chairmen of the Jewish Council that half of its employees, around 7,000 persons, would be deported. The Jewish Council was to make the selection of employees. Despite grave reservations, both chairmen took on the task assigned to them. David Cohen justified that decision in his memoirs: 'It was no longer just the lives of those who had been selected and summoned that were at stake, but the lives of those whom the Jewish Council needed in order to obtain exemptions.' For this reason, the council tried to identify those who were essential to 'ensure the progress of the work'.[98] Harrowing scenes ensued in the days and nights that followed (Doc. 123). Although the Jewish Council had scraped together the prescribed number of employees for deportation, the number of people who turned up at the specified assembly point on 25 May was far too low to meet the Germans' requirement. As a result 3,000 people were arrested in a major roundup carried out by the German Order Police in Amsterdam's Jewish quarter. They were deported to Westerbork. Over the following weeks and months, several thousand additional Jews were arrested during several large-scale raids in Amsterdam and then deported. Ed van Thijn, who was later mayor of Amsterdam, described his impressions in retrospect:

96 Croes and Tammes, *'Gif laten wij niet voortbestaan'*.

97 B. A. Sijes, *De Arbeidsinzet: De gedwongen arbeid van Nederlanders in Duitsland 1940–1945* (The Hague: Nijhoff, 1966); Bart van der Boom, *Wij leven nog: De stemming in bezet Nederland* (Amsterdam: Boom, 2003); Barbara Beuys, *Leben mit dem Feind: Amsterdam unter deutscher Besatzung, Mai 1940 – Mai 1945* (Munich: DTV, 2012); de Jong, *Koninkrijk*, vol. 6/2: *Juli '42–mei '43*, pp. 799–862.

98 Cohen, *Voorzitter van de Joodse Raad*, p. 166.

'What still sticks in my memory is the tremendous noise that accompanied such a roundup. The stomp of boots as they marched along the street. The squeal of brakes bringing the trucks to a halt. The loud bellow of commands that left no doubt: "All Jews are to come with us!!!"'[99]

In addition, the German police intensified the search for Jews in hiding in the provinces. In the final large roundup, which took place on 29 September 1943, the last remaining employees of the Jewish Council, including both of its chairmen, were arrested and taken to Westerbork, as were all the other Jews still in Amsterdam. Cohen described his final moments in Amsterdam:

> So, during the night, I went to Amstel Station, where I met aus der Fünten, who told me that this was the total liquidation. [...] I was overcome by an enormous sense of relief because now, at last, I no longer had to keep saying goodbye to those who were leaving. Instead, I was myself part of a transport.[100]

Only a few individuals and Jews living in mixed marriages remained behind. The Jews from Barneveld camp and 300 Jews from Vught were also taken to Westerbork at this time. The Philips 'work squad', with more than 1,000 Jews, remained in Vught for the time being. Thus, at the end of September 1943, with the exception of the members of this work detail, those in hiding, and those in mixed marriages, all Jews remaining in the Netherlands, more than 30,000 in all, were imprisoned in Westerbork camp. From there, they were deported to either Sobibor or Auschwitz, to which transports had resumed in August 1943. There were between 1,000 and 3,000 persons on each transport. Although allowed to remain in the Netherlands for the time being, Jews living in mixed marriages were not left undisturbed, however. In May 1943 Wilhelm Harster, Senior Commander of the Security Police, stated that the Germans planned to allow Jewish women in mixed marriages over the age of 45, who could be assumed to be past childbearing age, to remove the yellow star from their clothing. He continued: 'For the rest of the Jewish men and women, voluntary sterilization is to be sought, and it is to be carried out in Amsterdam' (Doc. 118). The Christian churches lodged protests with Seyss-Inquart against these plans, arguing: 'Sterilization represents a desecration both of divine commandments and of human law' (Doc. 122). More than 8,910 Jews living in mixed marriages were affected by the plans for sterilization. Of the persons concerned, 2,562 either provided (often fake) proof of their inability to reproduce in light of their age or underwent sterilization. The remainder used various strategies to avoid sterilization and the deportation with which they were threatened if they refused, or they escaped the attention of the German authorities as time passed. The number of forced sterilizations performed cannot be accurately determined, but it seems likely that slightly fewer than 500 men and around 20 women were affected. The Netherlands was the only occupied country where sterilizations of Jews were carried out.

Those who refused to undergo sterilization initially remained with their families in the Netherlands. A directive from Berlin put paid to plans made by the Security Police's section for Jewish affairs to deport Jews in mixed marriages to the extermination camps

99 Ed van Thijn, *Achttien adressen* (Amsterdam: Augustus, 2004), p. 14.
100 Cohen, *Voorzitter van de Joodse Raad*, pp. 183–184.

in the near future.[101] For this reason, on 30 October 1943 Reich Commissioner Seyss-Inquart stated: 'The elimination of Jewish blood from the Dutch Volksgemeinschaft has, generally speaking, reached the level stipulated by the Reich' (Doc. 146). By this date, 87,351 Jews had been deported from the Netherlands.

The Reich Commissioner's statement did not mean that the deportations from the Netherlands were to be regarded as complete. The Jews in Westerbork were granted only a brief respite, with no deportation trains running between mid November 1943 and mid January 1944. Epidemics had broken out at Westerbork camp, which was placed under quarantine, and at the same time the trains were needed for military purposes (Doc. 152). On 11 January 1944, however, the transports were resumed, and 1,037 Jews were deported to Bergen-Belsen. Although the intervals were greater in the period that followed, nineteen more trains had left Westerbork by the end of September 1944. In addition to departing for Auschwitz, the trains now also ran to Theresienstadt and Bergen-Belsen.

The Theresienstadt ghetto in the Protectorate of Bohemia and Moravia, publicized by the National Socialists as a ghetto for the elderly and even presented to foreign visitors as a model Jewish settlement, had been established in November 1941. From 1942 onwards Jews who either were over the age of sixty-five or had acquired special merit in the view of the German authorities were deported to Theresienstadt.[102] From the Netherlands, the Security Police's section for Jewish affairs sent to Theresienstadt many Jews who until then had been regarded as privileged, that is, those who had been interned in Barneveld. It also sent the 'Portuguese Jews', whose applications to be classified as not being members of the 'Jewish race' had been rejected, as well as many Protestants of Jewish origin. In addition, numerous leading members of the Jewish Council and individuals who had 'made an outstanding contribution to the de-Jewification of the Netherlands and to the Westerbork camp' were deported to Theresienstadt.[103] In 1944 five transport trains carrying a total of 4,270 persons made the journey there.

As a result of German propaganda, the inmates of Westerbork considered Theresienstadt to be less dreadful than Auschwitz or Sobibor. Accordingly, being placed on the transport lists for Theresienstadt appeared to be the lesser evil. Gertrud Slottke, a German employee of the Security Police's section for Jewish affairs who was involved in organizing the deportations, recorded: 'While a fairly elevated mood prevailed among the Jews in the case of the first two transports to Bergen-Belsen and Theresienstadt, this mood plummeted again in the case of the transport to Auschwitz' (Doc. 152). But even Theresienstadt was no guarantee of survival. More than 3,000 Jews from the Netherlands were deported from there to Auschwitz, where most of them were murdered. David Cohen, the former co-chairman of the Jewish Council, was among the survivors of Theresienstadt; 433 other fortunate Dutch Jews were evacuated from Theresienstadt

101 Michman et al., *Pinkas*, pp. 191–192; Boterman, *Duitse daders*, p. 462, note 638; Coen Stuldreher, *De legale rest: Gemengd gehuwde Joden onder de Duitse bezetting* (Amsterdam: Boom, 2007), pp. 277–317 and pp. 328–337.

102 H. G. Adler, *Theresienstadt, 1941–1945: The Face of a Coerced Community*, trans. Belinda Cooper (New York: Cambridge University Press, 2017 [German edn, 1955]).

103 Letter from the Jewish Council to the commandant's office at Theresienstadt, dated 24 Jan. 1944: NIOD, 077/1290.

to Switzerland in February 1945, following negotiations between Himmler and Jean-Marie Musy, the former president of the Swiss Confederation.[104]

In April 1943 a 'holding camp' (*Aufenthaltslager*) was established within the Bergen-Belsen camp complex.[105] By July 1944 there were around 4,000 prisoners in the so-called Star Camp (*Sternlager*), which was designated for those Jews from Western Europe who were scheduled to be part of an exchange for German nationals interned in countries not under German control who were to be brought 'back to the Reich'. The largest group, some 3,500 in total, was made up of Jews from the Netherlands, who were deported to Bergen-Belsen from Westerbork.[106] The Central Office for Jewish Emigration, in co-operation with the Security Police's section for Jewish affairs, decided who was to be deported to Bergen-Belsen. Jews who held dual citizenship or citizenship of a Latin American country or who were in possession of a 'Palestine certificate', an entry permit for Palestine, or even an application for an entry permit, were eligible for exchange.[107] Diamond cutters, including Abraham Asscher, co-chairman of the Jewish Council, were also sent to Bergen-Belsen, as well as persons who had used their sizeable assets in an attempt to improve their chances of survival. Of the Jews with Palestine certificates, a total of 222 were selected in June 1944 for emigration to Palestine. In her diary, Mirjam Bolle described the horrendous scenes during the selection of those who were to make the journey and the unease of everyone when the departure was delayed. A few days later, she found out that she was one of the lucky ones: 'I'm on the train and I can't believe it,' she recorded.[108] A harsh fate awaited those who had to stay behind in Bergen-Belsen. From March 1944 prisoners from other camps, usually those located in Poland, had begun to be transferred to Bergen-Belsen, which became a site of horror, with devastating epidemics and completely inadequate food supplies. The so-called exchange Jews, until then among the privileged, had to fight for their survival along with everyone else in the camp.[109] The sisters Margot and Anne Frank were among those transported from Auschwitz to Bergen-Belsen. In the chaotic months of spring 1945, they perished at Bergen-Belsen, as did more than 17,000 others.

In October 1943 Reich Commissioner Seyss-Inquart had expressed satisfaction with the progress of the persecution of the Jews in the Netherlands. In July of the following year Otto Bene, representative of the Reich Foreign Office, went one step further:

104 See Adler, *Theresienstadt*, pp. 161–162.

105 Jo Reilly, David Cesarani, Tony Kushner, and Colin Richmond (eds.), *Belsen in History and Memory* (London: Frank Cass, 1997); Alexandra Wenck, *Zwischen Menschenhandel und 'Endlösung': Das Konzentrationslager Bergen-Belsen* (Paderborn: Schöningh, 2000); Eberhard Kolb, *Bergen-Belsen: Vom 'Aufenthaltslager' zum Konzentrationslager 1943–1945* (Göttingen: Vandenhoeck & Ruprecht, 2002).

106 Reilly et al. (eds.), *Belsen in History and Memory*, p. 46.

107 Chaya Brasz, 'Rescue Attempts by the Dutch Jewish Community in Palestine 1940–1945', in Jozeph Michman (ed.), *Dutch Jewish History: Proceedings of the Fifth Symposium on the History of the Jews in the Netherlands* (Jerusalem: Hebrew University of Jerusalem, Institute for Research on Dutch Jewry, 1993), pp. 339–352.

108 Letter dated 30 June 1943 in Bolle, *Letters Never Sent*, p. 270.

109 Abel Jacob Herzberg, *Amor Fati: Seven Essays on Bergen-Belsen*, trans. Jack Santcross (Göttingen: Wallstein Verlag, 2016 [Dutch edn, 1980]), pp. 23–24 and 63–64; Fré Melkman-de Paauw, *Hoe het verder gaat, weet niemand: Naoorlogse brieven uit Amsterdam naar Palestina* (Amsterdam: Contact, 2002), pp. 37–38.

> For the Netherlands, the Jewish question can be considered solved, now that the majority of the Jews have been removed from the country. The Jews still here are in camps or under constant supervision. Of the Jews who have gone to ground, several are picked up almost every day and taken to camps.[110]

By this date 99,216 persons had been deported from the Netherlands. By the time of the last transport, which left Westerbork on 13 September 1944, that number increased by 3,776 and included the last Jews from Vught camp, where the section designated for Jews had been permanently closed in early June 1944. The Jews in the Philips 'work squad' were deported from Vught directly to Auschwitz in November 1943.

Of the 28,000 Jews who had gone into hiding, close to 12,000 were tracked down in their hiding places by the police or by special 'Jew-hunters', mostly as a result of betrayal or denunciation.[111] One Dutchwoman described in a letter the arrest of a girl who had been hidden in her family's home (Doc. 163).

With the Allied invasion of Normandy, launched on 6 June 1944, and the advance of the Allied forces, the Dutch population hoped the occupation would soon end Resistance intensified and the Jews still living in the Netherlands, whether in hiding, in Westerbork or in limited freedom, mobilized all their strength in an effort to hold out until the anticipated liberation.

When it was rumoured on 5 September 1944 that the first Dutch town in the south-western part of the country had been liberated, panic arose among the Germans and their Dutch collaborators, many of whom hastily departed the western region of the country and sometimes even the Netherlands itself. The rest of the Dutch population, on the other hand, made ready for an end to occupation rule and prepared to welcome the Allied troops. But the rumour turned out to be false. In fact, Maastricht, in the far south-east of the country, was the first Dutch town to be liberated, and not until ten days later. The Allies continued their advance and liberated a wide swathe of land in the southern Netherlands, but the attempt to cross the Rhine at Arnhem failed and the capture of the regions north of the Rhine was delayed until the spring of 1945. Until then most of the Netherlands, including the large cities in the western part of the country, remained under German control.

The Allied advance once again brought many of the Jews living in hiding into great danger. Edith Samuel-Jakobs recalled this time with mixed feelings: 'We sat in the cellar for four days. Our hosts had been evacuated with all their neighbours, but we could not go with them because we had no fake identity documents.'[112]

The Jews in the northern and western regions of the country therefore still had to get through the winter of 1944/45. To support the advance of the Allies and thwart the German troops, in September 1944 the government in exile had called for Dutch railway workers to strike. The Reich Commissariat for the Occupied Dutch Territories responded by halting all food deliveries and fuel transports to the western part of the country for six weeks. Particularly in the densely populated region that included Utrecht,

110 Letter from Otto Bene to the Reich Foreign Office, dated 20 July 1944, PA AA, R 99 429.

111 Marnix Croes, 'The Holocaust in the Netherlands and the Rate of Jewish Survival', *Holocaust and Genocide Studies*, vol. 20, no. 3 (2006), pp. 474–499; van Liempt and Kompagnie, *Jodenjacht*, especially pp. 11–31 and 53–117; Pinchas Bar-Efrat, *Denunciation and Rescue*, pp. 90–95.

112 Jakobs, *De roos die nooit bloeide*, p. 127.

Amsterdam, and Rotterdam, this measure led to a catastrophic famine. The long, harsh winter exacerbated the situation, and more than 20,000 Dutch people died of hunger and cold.[113] The situation for the Jews in hiding was particularly dire. They were dependent on the help of their hosts, who themselves often did not have enough to eat. Foraging trips into the surrounding countryside were particularly dangerous because the German occupiers and their helpers were continuing to search for them. Even if the Jews who were in hiding still had any articles of value left after all the years that had passed, most of them had no opportunity to exchange them for food or fuel.

With the beginning of spring the Allies continued their offensive. After capturing the bridge across the Rhine at Remagen in Germany, some forces proceeded to the north-west and liberated the northern part of the Netherlands from German control. On 12 April 1945 Canadian troops reached Westerbork camp, which the German guards had abandoned shortly before, and 850 Jewish prisoners enthusiastically welcomed the soldiers (Doc. 171). On 5 May, after almost exactly five years of occupation, the German troops in the Netherlands capitulated. In Amsterdam, however, it was three more days before Allied forces entered the city. On 7 May 1945 German naval personnel shot into the celebrating crowds. Not until the day after this incident, which claimed 20 lives and injured more than 100, was the occupation also definitely over in Amsterdam.[114]

Of the 140,000 'full Jews' living in the Netherlands at the onset of the war, around 107,000 were deported during the years of the German occupation. Only just over 5,000 of them survived, most of whom returned to the Netherlands after the war. Approximately 500 Jews were killed in the Netherlands and around 750 took their own lives. The high mortality rate is explained in part by the success of the German occupiers in enforcing anti-Jewish measures in the Netherlands with exceptional speed and in carrying out an uninterrupted series of deportations in quick succession from July 1942 onwards. Additionally, for a long time the Jewish victims had considered themselves safe, because Dutch neutrality prior to occupation and the high level of Jewish integration into Dutch society had led the Jews to believe that they could count on the support of the Gentiles, the authorities, and their neighbours. Although many Dutch people did indeed help to hide and rescue Jews, the efficient state apparatus collaborated with the occupying forces in many ways and many ordinary Dutch people turned a blind eye. Moreover, the organized Dutch underground resistance did not take shape until 1943, a long time after the deportation of the Jews had begun. The Jewish Council established by the German occupiers in February 1941, which was under the direct control of and pressure from the Central Office for Jewish Emigration, an outpost of Eichmann's network, opted to cooperate with the Germans in the hope of thereby preventing something worse. Ultimately, the solidarity of the non-Jewish Dutch population came too late: 75 per cent of the Dutch Jews were murdered. This was the highest death rate in Western Europe and one of the highest in all the countries within the German sphere of control.[115]

113 Henri van der Zee, *De Hongerwinter: Van Dolle Dinsdag tot Bevrijding* (The Hague: BZZTôH, 1989).

114 Guus Meershoek, 'Onder nationaalsocialistisch bewind', in Doeko Bosscher, Augustinus J. J. Meershoek, and Piet de Rooy (eds.), *Geschiedenis van Amsterdam. Tweestrijd om de hoofdstad 1900–2000* (Amsterdam: Sun, 2007), pp. 235–335.

115 On this, see J. C. H. Blom, 'The Persecution of the Jews in the Netherlands in a Comparative International Perspective', in Michman (ed.), *Dutch Jewish History*, pp. 273–290; Bob Moore, 'Warum fielen dem Holocaust so viele niederländische Juden zum Opfer? Ein Erklärungsversuch', in Fasse et al. (eds.), *Nationalsozialistische Herrschaft und Besatzungszeit*, pp. 191–210.

Belgium

Belgium was under German military administration until shortly before its liberation in 1944. Two départements in northern France, Nord and Pas-de-Calais, were also put under the control of the military government in Brussels. General Alexander von Falkenhausen was the military commander in Belgium and northern France, with Eggert Reeder chief of the military administration. While the Belgian government in exile established itself in London, King Leopold III remained in Belgium as a prisoner of war held by the Germans. The secretaries general (the most senior ministry officials) cooperated with the occupiers in the attempt to preserve the provisions of the Belgian constitution and to pursue a policy of the 'lesser evil'.[116]

The Jewish population was registered by the Belgian administration in accordance with a German decree issued on 28 October 1940. The registration figures indicated that more than 50,000 Jews were living in Belgium at this time. In reality, however, that number may well have been greater than 70,000, because many Jews ignored the call to register; 93 per cent of the Jewish population were not Belgian citizens and most had only been in the country since emigrating from Central and Eastern Europe sometime between 1927 and 1932. The number of Jews who had fled to Belgium from Germany and Austria by May 1940 is estimated at 25,000. Less than half held either German or Austrian citizenship; more than 30 per cent were Polish.[117] Approximately 3,500 of them were deported to southern France by the Belgian authorities – in some cases voluntarily; many of them joined forces with the large numbers of Belgians fleeing to France, including Belgian Jews. The total number of Jews fleeing Belgium for France is estimated at 10,000–15,000.[118] Even among the 7 per cent of Jews in the country with Belgian citizenship, a considerable number originated elsewhere and had been naturalized before the mid 1920s.

In November 1941 the German military administration created the Association of Jews in Belgium (Association des Juifs en Belgique/Vereniging van Joden in België,

116 Werner Warmbrunn, *The German Occupation of Belgium, 1940–1944* (New York: Peter Lang, 1993); Mark van den Wijngaert, *Het beleid van het comité van de secretarissen-generaal in België tijdens de Duitse bezetting 1940–1944* (Brussels: K.A.W.L.S.K., 1975).

117 Insa Meinen and Ahlrich Meyer, *Verfolgt von Land zu Land: Jüdische Flüchtlinge in Westeuropa 1938–1944* (Paderborn: Schöningh, 2013), pp. 115–116.

118 Frank Caestecker, *Ongewenste gasten: Joodse vluchtelingen en migranten in de dertiger jaren in België* (Brussels: VUBPRESS, 1993), pp. 251–252; Rudi van Doorslaer, 'Les enfants du ghetto: L'immigration juive communiste en Belgique et la quête de la modernité (1925–1940)', in Rudi van Doorslaer (ed.), *Les Juifs de Belgique: De l'immigration au génocide, 1925–1945* (Brussels: Centre de recherches et d'études historiques de la Seconde Guerre mondiale, 1994), p. 61; Rudi van Doorslaer, 'Jewish Immigration and Communism in Belgium, 1925–1939', in Dan Michman (ed.), *Belgium and the Holocaust: Jews, Belgians, Germans* (Jerusalem: Yad Vashem, 1998), pp. 63–82, here p. 63; Maxime Steinberg, *La Persécution des Juifs de Belgique (1940–1945)* (Brussels: Vie ouvrière, 2004), p. 132; Lieven Saerens, 'De Jodenvervolging in België in cijfers', *Bijdragen tot de Eigentijdse Geschiedenis/ Cahiers d'histoire du temps présent*, 17 (2006), pp. 199–235; Meinen and Meyer, *Verfolgt von Land zu Land*, p. 89; Frank Seberechts, 'Les Juifs en Belgique durant l'entre-deux-guerres', in Rudi van Doorslaer et al. (eds.), *La Belgique docile: Les autorités belges et la persécution des Juifs en Belgique durant la Seconde Guerre mondiale* (Brussels: CEGES, 2007), pp. 45–53 (published in Dutch in *Gewillig België: Overheid en jodenvervolging tijdens de Tweede Wereldoorlog* [Brussels: SOMA, 2007], pp. 44–52). Subsequent references to this source will be from *La Belgique docile* with the page numbers from *Gewillig België* given in brackets.

AJB/VJB), with Chief Rabbi Salomon Ullmann as its chairman, to serve as the central representative body of the Jewish population.[119] The association was in constant contact with Kurt Asche, the official in charge of Jewish affairs at the Office of the Security Police and the SD in Brussels. A decree of 27 May 1942 made it compulsory for Jews to wear the yellow star from June 1942. This led to the first conflicts between the German occupiers and the Belgian authorities. In Brussels and Liège the relevant municipal administrations refused to distribute the badges.[120] In Antwerp, however, the Germans had already reshaped the municipal administration the previous year, strengthening the influence of the Flemish collaborationist party, Vlaams Nationaal Verbond (VNV). The new mayor, Leo Delwaide, was an advocate of unconditional collaboration, and he ordered the municipal officials to implement the decree without delay.[121]

Under German pressure, in September 1940 the Council of Secretaries General had already agreed in principle to the introduction of voluntary labour service in Belgium and in Germany.[122] On 6 March 1942 the military government issued a decree introducing labour conscription for adult Belgians for deployment within Belgium. This was followed on 11 March 1942 by a special decree on the compulsory labour deployment of adult Jews, which was subsequently amended on 8 May. Forced labour deployment for Jews was implemented predominantly in the labour camps of the Organization Todt along the Atlantic Wall in northern France, where manpower was urgently needed. This forced labour deployment was organized by the Belgian employment offices under the supervision of the National Employment Office, which the military administration had established the previous year. From mid June to mid September 1942, around 2,000 Jews were taken to the labour camps of the Organization Todt located between Calais and Abbeville.[123] The creation of this first forced labour detail aroused great anxiety among

119 Dan Michman, 'La fondation de l'AJB dans une perspective internationale', in Jean-Philippe Schreiber and Rudi van Doorslaer (eds.), *Les Curateurs du ghetto: L'Association des Juifs en Belgique sous l'occupation nazie* (Brussels: Labor, 2004), pp. 29–56, published in Dutch in Rudi van Doorslaer and Jean-Philippe Schreiber (eds.), *De curatoren van het ghetto: De vereniging van de joden in België tijdens de nazi-bezetting* (Tielt: Lannoo, 2004), pp. 25–45. Subsequent references to this source will be from *Les Curateurs du ghetto* with the page numbers from *De curatoren van het ghetto* given in brackets.

120 See PMJ 5/193. The mayor of Brussels, Jules Coelst, had already expressed his solidarity with the Jewish population in the spring of 1942 by making space in the city's schools available to the Association of Jews in Belgium for teaching Jewish children: see PMJ 5/195, and Rudi van Doorslaer, 'Conclusion finale', in van Doorslaer et al. (eds.), *La Belgique docile*, p. 1136 (*Gewillig België*, p. 1102).

121 Lieven Saerens, *Vreemdelingen in een wereldstad: Een geschiedenis van Antwerpen en zijn joodse bevolking (1880–1944)* (Tielt: Lannoo, 2000); Lieven Saerens, *Étrangers dans la cité: Anvers et ses Juifs (1880–1944)* (Brussels: Labor, 2005); Nico Wouters, 'La chasse aux Juifs, 1942–1944', in van Doorslaer et al. (eds.), *La Belgique docile*, pp. 547–662 (*Gewillig België*, pp. 555–557).

122 Referred to in *VOBl-BNF* (68), no. 2, 7 March 1942, pp. 844–845.

123 On labour deployment, see Sophie Vandepontseele, 'Le travail obligatoire des Juifs en Belgique et dans le nord de la France', in Schreiber and van Doorslaer (eds.) *Les Curateurs du ghetto*, pp. 189–231 (*De curatoren van het ghetto*, pp. 149–212); Frank Seberechts, 'Spoliation et travail obligatoire', in van Doorslaer et al. (eds.), *La Belgique docile*, p. 449 (*Gewillig België*, p. 439); Danielle Delmaire, 'The Fate of the Jewish Communities in the North of France during World War II,' in Michman (ed.), *Belgium and the Holocaust*, pp. 337–338.

the Jewish population in Belgium (Doc. 174). In October 1942 Jews from these camps were sent directly to Mechelen transit camp, and from there to the death camps.

The second call for the 'labour deployment' of Jews followed in July 1942. It was a product of the arrangements made at the Wannsee Conference in January 1942, and the concrete plans of the German officials in charge of Jewish affairs in Western Europe (Doc. 235). As a first step, 10,000 Jews were to be deported from Belgium to the East, ostensibly to be deployed as labour. An intervention by Reeder ensured that Jews who were Belgian citizens were not to be included initially because, as Werner von Bargen, representative of the Reich Foreign Office, noted in a report to Berlin, they were regarded as Belgians by the rest of the population (Doc. 175).

The German military administration was able to organize deportations on such a scale only with the support of the Belgian authorities. However, such support was not a foregone conclusion. Even when the first summons for labour deployment was issued, the individual municipal administrations reacted very differently. Two thirds of the Jews who had been taken to northern France to construct the Atlantic Wall came from the Greater Antwerp area. In Brussels, by contrast, in early July, Mayor Coelst had refused to have the city police arrest Jews who had not complied with the summons.[124] The German Oberfeldkommandantur turned to the governor of Brabant, who passed on the problem to Gerard Romsée, secretary general of the Ministry of the Interior. The latter, though a member of Vlaams Nationaal Verbond, supported the position of the mayor of Brussels in an official letter to von Falkenhausen. The arrest of Jews who refused to perform labour, he said, was 'undoubtedly one of the tasks' which must 'quite logically [elicit] psychological resistance on the part of the Belgian police.[125]

On 15 July 1942 Maurice Benedictus, the secretary of the Association of Jews in Belgium, received orders from Asche to make preparations for labour deployment in Germany. A register with the names of able-bodied Jews was to be created within ten days, and these Jews were ordered to appear at the Dossin Barracks in Mechelen when so ordered. The barracks at the town of Mechelen, located halfway between Brussels and Antwerp, became the assembly camp for transports to the East, similar to Westerbork in the Netherlands and Drancy in France.[126]

In the following weeks, 13,000 persons received notifications sent out by the newly established Labour Deployment Office of the Association of Jews in Belgium, but only slightly more than 4,000 of them reported as ordered. Marcel Liebman was thirteen years old when he was informed by letter that he and his brother were to report to the barracks at Mechelen within twelve hours:

124 Coelst, who had spoken out as late as 1939 in favour of restricting opportunities for immigration into Belgium, was dismissed from the municipal administration in September 1942 upon the creation of 'Greater Brussels'.

125 Letter from Coelst to the Oberfeldkommandantur in Brussels, 6 July 1942, and letter from Romsée to Falkenhausen, 29 August 1942, both cited in Wouters, 'La chasse aux Juifs', pp. 433, 532 (*Gewillig België*, pp. 436, 534). Only 86 of the 200 summoned for labour deployment had in fact left Brussels for forced labour in northern France on 26 June 1942: Vandepontseele, 'Le travail obligatoire des Juifs en Belgique et dans le nord de la France', p. 217.

126 Laurence Schram, 'La Caserne Dossin à Malines, 1942–1944', *Les Cahiers de la Mémoire Contemporaine / Bijdragen tot de Eigentijdse Herinnering*, no. 12 (2016), pp. 99–117.

> I remember those hectic hours well. We were in a state of excitement that was also bound up with a bit of fear and a kind of pride. […] When my brother and I visited a few friends that afternoon to bid them farewell, we behaved – without any coercion, without difficulty – in a resolute, unwavering manner, as if we were obeying a mobilization order that made us into soldiers of a noble cause.[127]

The first deportation train left Belgium on 4 August 1942, bound for Auschwitz. Of the 999 deportees – 426 women and 573 men, including 51 children under the age of 15 and 5 persons over the age of 61 – 254 were murdered immediately upon arrival. Of the 744 persons selected for forced labour, 7 survived the war.[128] The following transport left on 11 August with 999 deportees, of whom 3 survived the war. Salomon van den Berg, the chairman of the Brussels committee of the Association of Jews in Belgium, noted in his diary a few days later: 'Summer in Mechelen, where one only talks about the Jews who arrive by train or lorry and depart like livestock. When people talk about it, they have tears in their eyes, but it can't be helped; we are helpless in the face of this misfortune.'[129] Dreadful scenes unfolded over the course of these weeks in the offices of the association, which had to centralize the requests for exemption from forced labour. The father of Marcel Liebman observed 'mothers whose children had been summoned to report to Mechelen and who wanted to be reassured about their fate', as well as

> men and women who begged the heads of the AJB [Association of Jews in Belgium] to grant them an exemption because they would otherwise have to leave small children behind. An indescribable, confused mass of people was formed wherever these parents, all in tears, encountered the couriers going in and out of the AJB office, the bearers of the fateful calls.[130]

By 15 August three trains carrying 2,997 people in total had left Belgium for Auschwitz. This approach evidently would not enable the German Security Police to meet the quota that had been set: originally, 10,000 Jews were to be deported by the end of October, but in August the target had been increased to 20,000 persons by the end of the year.[131] As a result the German authorities turned to a method already tested in the Netherlands and in France: the mass arrest of Jews by means of roundups. They started with a large roundup in Antwerp during the night of 15/16 August 1942. With the support of the Belgian police, the German Security Police arrested between 998 and 1067 Jews and transported them to Mechelen.[132] Before the end of September, four more roundups

127 Marcel Liebman, *Né Juif: Une enfance juive pendant la guerre* (Paris: Duculot, 1977).

128 Wouters, 'La chasse aux Juifs', p. 537 (*Gewillig België*, p. 539); Ward Adriaens et al., *Mecheln – Auschwitz 1942–1944: De vernietiging van de Joden en zigeuners van België / La destruction des Juifs et des Tsiganes de Belgique / The Destruction of the Jews and Gypsies from Belgium*, vol. 1 (Brussels: VUBPRESS, 2009), pp. 281–282. This four-volume work provides a detailed overview of all the transports.

129 Diary of Salomon van den Berg, Wiener Library, PIII i/275, p. 67, entry for 18 August 1942.

130 Liebman, *Né Juif*, p. 54.

131 Adriaens et al., *Mecheln – Auschwitz*, vol. 1, p. 73.

132 Wouters, 'La chasse aux Juifs', p. 544 (*Gewillig België*, p. 546). Insa Meinen, *Die Shoah in Belgien* (Darmstadt: Wissenschaftliche Buchgesellschaft, 2009), gives the number of Jews arrested during the night of 15/16 August in Antwerp as 845 (p. 44).

followed at short intervals. They took place in Brussels, where the arrests were largely carried out by German forces (Security Police and SD, Feldgendarmerie (uniformed military police), Geheime Feldpolizei (secret military police), and members of the Wehrmacht); in the French regions that were part of the area controlled by the German military administration in Belgium and northern France (Doc. 270); and in Antwerp. During each of these roundups between 500 and 1,000 Jews were detained. The roundup in Brussels, carried out during the night of 3/4 September, concluded with 660 arrests and had to be chalked up as a failure by the German authorities, not least because the capital had the largest share of Belgium's Jewish population.

Salomon van den Berg described the arrests in the Belgian capital in his diary: 'The streets are blocked and the Germans haul the Jews out of their houses. Men, women, children of every age, in ill health or not, they have to leave everything behind and are carried off like livestock in trucks and sent who knows where, surely to Mechelen.' Because the raids always took place at night, van den Berg continued, foreign Jews tried not to stay overnight in their homes. Belgian Jews, by contrast, had not thus far been troubled, he noted. This immunity had been a concession to the king and the government, he wrote, 'so that they can say, after all, that they have done something for the Jews. I will admit that they can't change much and are doing everything possible, but it is insufficient.'[133]

What was the situation like for the refugees from Germany and Austria? On 6 June 1941 the Austrian writer Jean Améry, then still known as Hans Mayer, had successfully escaped to Belgium from the internment camp at Gurs in France. Almost forty years after the event, he gave an account of the situation for Jewish refugees in Antwerp:

> The inhabitants of Antwerp were truly mistrustful of the émigrés, who indeed brought about a foreign infiltration of certain parts of the city. Some of them were really well dressed and, because they were not allowed to pursue any work, sat around for hours in the cafés in the main street and engaged in animated discussions.

The refugees were, in turn, 'quite simply afraid of the locals: the ponderous, stocky, thoroughly Germanic type intimidated them, as did the language, which was related to the Low German dialect.' The relationship between 'native' Jews and foreign Jews, too, was perceived by Améry as problematic:

> The émigrés thus [lived] in a double ghetto: the local Jews did indeed provide for them, but had scarcely any personal contact with them, as their Yiddish culture, with its Flemish varnish, drew a clear line between them and the Germans and Austrians; the Belgians were altogether unwilling to get involved with the alien crowds of uprooted people that surged through the streets as an unfamiliar element.[134]

133 Diary of Salomon van den Berg, pp. 70–71, entry dated 3 Sept. 1942. On the experiences of Jews in Brussels during this period, see Lieven Saerens, *Onwillig Brussel: Een verhaal over Jodenvervolging en verzet* (Leuven: Davidsfonds, 2014).

134 Jean Améry, 'Verfemt und verbannt: Vor dreißig Jahren – Erinnerungen an die Emigration. Manuskript für den Deutschlandfunk 1968/69', in *Werke*, vol. 2 (Stuttgart: Klett-Cotta, 2002), pp. 804–805.

In Antwerp the roundups for the deportations to Poland took place concurrently with the call-up of workers for the Organization Todt in the départements of northern France governed by Brussels. The last transport to northern France left the city on 12 September 1942, one day after a large roundup in which 1,422 Jews had been taken into custody. To avoid mingling the two transports, the persons scheduled for the transport to Auschwitz were assembled at the railway station, while those recruited for forced labour in northern France were to gather in front of the employment office, although only 40 of the 500 who had been called up actually appeared, as word of the roundup the previous day had spread.[135]

For various reasons the number of Jews arrested in roundups in Antwerp was quite high, but the number for Brussels far lower. In Antwerp, Mayor Leo Delwaide had never prevented Belgian police from assisting with the arrests. The Belgian police were far more familiar with the local context than the German police forces. The roundup on 28/29 August was carried out predominantly by Belgian police, under significant German pressure (Doc. 180). After the war Delwaide declared that after this roundup he protested to the Germans and was promised that Belgian police would not be involved in any further arrests; however, they continued to participate in roundups. By contrast, in Brussels Mayor Jules Coelst, referring to the legal definition of the police's tasks, refused to permit his officials to cooperate and so the roundups were carried out exclusively by German forces, though including members of the Flemish SS.[136] In addition, the Jewish population in Brussels lived scattered throughout the city, whereas the relatively compact Jewish residential neighbourhoods in Antwerp made arrests easier.[137] In order to fill the planned transports to Auschwitz, from mid September 1942 the Security Police and the SD launched several manhunts, mainly in Brussels and Antwerp.

A total of 4,468 Jews were arrested in the various raids and deported to the East. During the last major roundup, which took place from 22 to 24 September 1942 in Antwerp, Jews with Belgian citizenship were also arrested and transported to Mechelen. That led the Belgian government to lodge fierce protests once more with Reeder, who in turn instructed Ernst Ehlers, representative of the Chief of the Security Police and the SD, to order that no more roundups of Belgian Jews were to take place.[138]

As a result, the German police switched to arresting individual Jews and entire families using the registration lists from 1941 as a basis. The number of Jews arrested in this way was remarkably high. Between August and October 1942 such arrests accounted for more than 40 per cent of the Jews deported to Auschwitz. Seeking to save their own lives, Jewish informants also assisted the Germans, with denunciations regularly leading to the arrest of Jews in hiding and creating a climate of general uncertainty (Doc. 209).[139]

135 Vandepontseele, 'Le travail obligatoire des Juifs en Belgique et dans le nord de la France', pp. 214–216.

136 Griffioen and Zeller, *Jodenvervolging in Nederland, Frankrijk en België*, pp. 529–530.

137 Saerens, *Vreemdelingen in een wereldstad*, pp. 592–649.

138 Meinen, *Die Shoah in Belgien*, p. 49.

139 Adriaens et al., *Mecheln – Auschwitz*, vol. 1, p. 104. A description of this manhunt is found in Maxime Steinberg, *L'Etoile et le fusil*, vol. 3: *La Traque des Juifs, 1942–1944* (Brussels: Vie Ouvrière, 1986), pp. 208–209; also see Insa Meinen, 'Facing Deportation: How Jews Were Arrested in Belgium,' *Yad Vashem Studies*, 36:1 (2008), p. 71. For detailed descriptions of several Jewish informants in Brussels, see Saerens, *Onwillig Brussel*, pp. 84–86.

The employees of the German Customs Service in Belgium also participated in the arrests. The Foreign Exchange Protection Commando (Devisenschutzkommando, DSK), which had operated in Western Europe since the beginning of the occupation in 1940, had a particular part to play. It took action on behalf of Göring's Office of the Four-Year Plan and cooperated closely with the military administration and the Security Police in order to pursue violations of the obligation to register foreign currency, gold, diamonds, securities and the like, a requirement which had been introduced by the military administration. Consequently, the DSK had quickly acquired an important role in the systematic expropriation of the Jewish population in Brussels and Antwerp. Its employees, who were not usually uniformed, were authorized to conduct house searches, make arrests, and carry out interrogations, and because they were not immediately recognized, they were able to apprehend many Jews who were keeping a low profile – such as the German refugee Rudolf Samson and his mother, who had risked escape from the Netherlands in August 1942 in the hope of reaching unoccupied France. They were captured in Brussels by the DSK and deported to Auschwitz eight days later (Doc. 179).[140]

To reach the targets established by the Nazi leadership in Berlin, 1,300 Jews who had been deployed in the summer as forced labourers along the Atlantic Wall were ordered back to Mechelen in October 1942 and included in the last two convoys of the year, which went to Auschwitz. Thus from July to the end of October 1942 a total of 16,624 persons were deported from Belgium on seventeen transports – almost two thirds of all the Jews deported by the Germans from Belgium during the entire occupation period.[141]

Immediately after Jews were arrested and transferred to Mechelen, the employees of the Western Office (Dienststelle Westen) of the Rosenberg Task Force, directed by its head of operations, Franz Mader, began confiscating household furnishings that had been left behind. By the time the occupation ended, under the supervision of the military administration's department for economic affairs more than 100,000 cubic metres of household effects had been taken to Germany or to German offices in Belgium.[142]

In mid September 1942 the military administration declared itself satisfied with the progress of the persecution thus far. The arrests, it stated, had taken place largely unnoticed by the Belgian public, and in any case the Belgian authorities were concerned solely about the Jews who held Belgian citizenship (Doc. 185). The illegal newspapers, however, insistently drew attention to the crimes and to the solidly united stance of the population (Doc. 181). And in his report 'on public opinion in Belgium' dated 1 December 1942, Paul Struye, a Brussels lawyer, also noted the outrage that the deportation of the Jews by the German occupiers had unleashed among local residents, despite the 'moderate antisemitism' prevailing most notably in Brussels and Antwerp. While the first coercive measures against Jews had met with indifference, Struye remarked, the

140 Meinen, 'Facing Deportation,' pp. 51–72.

141 In this connection, Belgian historian Maxime Steinberg refers to the 'hundred days' in which the majority of the deportations of Jews took place: Steinberg, *L'Etoile et le fusil*, vol. 2: *1942: Les cent jours de la déportation des Juifs de Belgique* (Brussels: Vie Ouvrière, 1984); see also Maxime Steinberg, 'The *Judenpolitik* in Belgium within the West European Context: Comparative Observations', in Michman (ed.), *Belgium and the Holocaust*, pp. 199–221, here p. 113; Thierry Rozenblum, *Une cité si ardente: Les Juifs de Liège sous l'Occupation (1940–1944)* (Brussels: Pire, 2010), pp. 158–159.

142 Johanna Pezechkian, 'La "Möbelaktion" en Belgique', *Bijdragen tot de Eigentijdse Geschiedenis / Cahiers d'histoire du temps présent*, 10 (2002), pp. 153–180.

forcible separation of parents and children in particular had engendered universal sympathy and a willingness to help.[143]

However, official protests, whether from the royal family, the Belgian administrative apparatus or the Catholic Church, failed to materialize. In contrast to the approach taken in France and in the Netherlands, in Belgium the Catholic Church confined itself to presenting exceptional cases to the occupiers in order to obtain a release. In the summer and autumn of 1942, the Belgian government in exile in London also displayed only limited interest in the fate of Jews in Belgium, although it was informed, at least to some extent, about what was happening in the extermination camps in the East. At an international protest meeting held in London on 29 October 1942, Prime Minister Hubert Pierlot, in a speech given at the Royal Albert Hall and broadcast one week later on Radio Belgique, continued to talk only very generally of 'persecutions' (Doc. 191). This reticence is all the more striking as the same radio station reported in detail on the crimes committed against the Jews in German-occupied Poland, about which the Allies had been informed by the Polish government in exile. Yet, right up until liberation in 1944, the transports of Jews from Belgium to the East were not clearly linked in the public pronouncements of the Belgian government in exile with the mass murder. The government in exile did participate financially in the aid provided to Jewish refugees who managed to escape from Belgium to neutral countries such as Switzerland, Spain or Portugal. In addition, at the request of the Jewish Defence Committee, it released substantial funds for the rescue of Jewish children in Belgium. However, the Belgian minister of colonies, Albert de Vleeschauwer, attempted from London to prevent Jewish refugees from settling in the Belgian Congo, although in September 1942 the minister of foreign affairs, Paul-Henri Spaak, had declared his willingness to supply the necessary visas (Doc. 185).[144]

In contrast to the Netherlands, in Belgium the participation of the Association of Jews in Belgium (AJB/VJB) in the preparations for the deportations met with criticism and resistance after just a few weeks. At the end of July, Maurice Benedictus was replaced as 'labour deployment' liaison between the military administration and the association by Robert Holzinger, a German refugee. On 29 August a group of Jewish communists made an attempt on the life of Holzinger, who died of his injuries a few hours later. The hope that the deportations might thus be stopped was not fulfilled. Nonetheless, during the period that followed, the Germans made less recourse to the services of the AJB/VJB. By the time of the large roundups, the association's assistance in organizing forced labour and in calming the Jewish population was no longer important. In September 1942 Kurt Asche had the chairman, Salomon Ullmann, along with Maurice Benedictus and other leading members of the organization, arrested and temporarily placed in the notorious Breendonk camp. From July to November 1943 Jean Améry was also at Breendonk, in detention cell thirteen, and he later wrote about the torture he experienced

143 The report is published in Paul Struye and Guillaume Jacquemyns, *La Belgique sous l'Occupation allemande (1940–1944)* (Brussels: Édition Complexe, 2002), pp. 157–194, here p. 167. On the relief efforts, see also Steinberg, *L'Etoile et le fusil*, vol. 3, pp. 27–28.

144 Mark Van Den Wijngaert, 'The Belgian Catholics and the Jews during the German Occupation, 1940–1944', in Michman (ed.) *Belgium and the Holocaust*, pp. 228–233; Emmanuel Debruyne, 'The Belgian Government-in-Exile facing the Persecution and Extermination of the Jews', in Jan Láníček and James Jordan (eds.), *Governments-in-Exile and the Jews during the Second World War* (London: Vallentine Mitchell, 2013), pp. 197–212.

there.[145] After his successful escape from Belgium in February 1943, Benedictus wrote a report for the Belgian government in exile about his experiences while in detention. Shortly after protests by various prominent Belgians, the leading members of the AJB/VJB were released: 'Upon our return home, each one of us received so many professions of sympathy and interest from the good Belgians, both known and unknown to us,' Benedictus wrote, 'that we were all proud to have paid this price' (Doc. 205). Rabbi Ullmann, who had been subjected to significant physical abuse during his imprisonment, announced his resignation as chairman of the AJB/VJB in early October 1942 (Doc. 188). He was succeeded by Marcel Blum.

On 25 September 1942 Reeder informed the Feldkommandanturen in Belgium and northern France that now 'the complete evacuation of the Jews from the area of command [would be] carried out', with Belgian Jews continuing to be exempted.[146] The chief of the military administration was evidently keen to avoid any disruption to German-Belgian collaboration: 'The office of the German Security Police is instructed to carry out the operation in such a way that it attracts as little public attention as possible and wins no sympathy for the Jews among the population' (Doc. 186). However, as elderly people, women, and children had also been arrested in the roundups, the pretence of 'labour deployment' could no longer be maintained.

In his message to the Feldkommandanturen, Reeder also pointed out that increasing numbers of Jews were attempting to leave the country to avoid arrest. Most of them, probably numbering several thousand, tried to make their way through France to Switzerland or to Spain and Portugal (Doc. 195) and got at least as far as France. In the attempt, they had to cross several borders and usually availed themselves of the expensive services of agents to help them escape. Many refugees were captured while still in France and were then deported via camps on French soil to the death camps in occupied Poland. Numerous records from the DSK and the offices of the German Customs Service prove that many attempts to escape failed even before the individual could leave Belgium, with those who were arrested sent to Mechelen camp (see Doc. 179).[147]

145 Markus Meckl, 'Unter zweifacher Hoheit: Das Auffanglager Breendonk zwischen Militärverwaltung und SD', in Wolfgang Benz and Barbara Distel (eds.), *Terror im Westen: Nationalsozialistische Lager in den Niederlanden, Belgien und Luxemburg 1940–1945* (Berlin: Metropol, 2004), pp. 25–38; Patrick Nefors, *Breendonk, 1940–1945: De geschiedenis* (Antwerp: Standaard, 2004) (French edition: *Breendonk, 1940–1945* [Brussels: Racine, 2006]); Jean Améry, 'Die Tortur', in *Merkur*, 208, no. 2 (July 1965), pp. 623–638; James M. Deen, *The Prisoners of Breendonk: Personal Histories from a World War II Concentration* Camp (New York: Houghton Mifflin Harcourt, 2015).

146 Jews with Belgian citizenship were to remain exempt in Belgium but not in northern France, while Jews with French citizenship were to be among those affected in Belgium, but not in northern France.

147 Meinen and Meyer, *Verfolgt von Land zu Land*, pp. 183–222; Ahlrich Meyer and Insa Meinen, 'Transitland Belgien: Jüdische Flüchtlinge in Westeuropa während der Zeit der Deportationen 1942', in *Theresienstädter Studien und Dokumente*, 14 (2007), pp. 378–431; Steinberg, *L'Etoile et le fusil*, vol. 3, pp. 30–32; Heini Bornstein, *Insel Schweiz: Hilfs- und Rettungsaktionen sozialistisch-zionistischer Jugendorganisationen 1939–1945* (Zurich: Chronos, 2000); Insa Meinen, 'Die Deportation der Juden aus Belgien und das Devisenschutzkommando', in Johannes Hürter and Jürgen Zarusky (eds.), *Besatzung, Kollaboration, Holocaust: Neue Studien zur Verfolgung und Ermordung der europäischen Juden* (Munich: Oldenbourg, 2008), pp. 45–79; Ruth Fivaz-Silbermann, 'Une migration urgente et transitoire: La fuite des Juifs de France en Suisse au temps de la "solution finale,"' *Diasporas*, 20 (2013), pp. 103–108.

Among them was Joseph Hakker who, in an account dated 1944, railed against the large number of fraudulent agents:

> Alleged patriots appeared, who, for a sum of 15,000 to 20,000 francs payable in advance, promised a safe escape to France. In addition, some – for greater safety – took the travellers' money and jewellery in trust. Then they quite simply handed their victims over to the Boche [Germans] at the French border or delivered the lorries in which they had locked their victims directly to the Gestapo. […] In their offices, the unfortunates were forced to write to their families to say that they had arrived safely. It goes without saying that the Jewish families who received such a letter in Belgium or Holland had full confidence in these journeys to Switzerland.[148]

Many Jews for whom an escape from Belgium was out of the question for financial or other reasons sought to keep a low profile when the roundups began in August 1942. They stopped spending the night at home or they changed their place of residence. But in the daytime too the risk of being caught up in an inspection of identity documents and then arrested was omnipresent, and people therefore wore the yellow star increasingly rarely.[149] On 6 October 1942, when Military Commander von Falkenhausen made forced labour in Germany compulsory for all Belgians – hence also for non-Jewish Belgians – outrage at the German occupiers escalated sharply (Docs. 191, 193) and there were increased expressions of solidarity with the Jews. The introduction of universal forced labour ultimately led to a rift between the occupiers and the population, and also between the occupiers and the Belgian authorities, which, up to that point, had been willing to collaborate, for now almost every Belgian family was affected. Resistance increased markedly, also encouraged by the weakening of the occupying forces after the Allied landings in North Africa and military setbacks in the East.[150] Within a few months thousands of Belgians had joined the underground movements, reinforcing the ranks of those who opposed German-Belgian collaboration. The relevant German local military authorities (Kommandanturen) tasked the German police with the arrest of thousands of fellow Belgians who had gone into hiding.[151] The Jews living in Belgium also profited from the increased willingness to resist, as they now encountered fewer difficulties in their search for hiding places, places to stay overnight, and food. The Independence Front (Front de l'Indépendance–Onafhankelijkheidsfront), a resistance movement established in March 1941 and closely allied with the Communist Party, mobilized non-Jewish locals: '*Now the Gestapo wants to deport the entire Jewish population of Belgium*. Tens of thousands of people are facing a horrible death. Time is running out. We must do everything to save them' (Doc. 193).[152]

148 Joseph Hakker, *La Mystérieuse Caserne Dossin à Malines: Le camp de déportation des Juifs* (Anvers: Editions 'Ontwikkeling', 1944), pp. 7–8.

149 Steinberg, *L'Etoile et le fusil*, vol. 3, pp. 28–29.

150 An overview can be found in José Gotovitch, 'Résistances et question juive', in van Doorslaer (ed.), *Les Juifs de Belgique*, pp. 129–136. The Military Commander's regulation is published in *VOBl-BNF*, 7 Oct. 1942, pp. 1050–1051.

151 Wouters, 'La chasse auf Juifs', p. 579 (*Gewillig België*, p. 582).

152 On the Independence Front, see José Gotovitch, *Du rouge au tricolore. Les communistes belges de 1939 à 1944: Un aspect de l'histoire de la Résistance* (Brussels: Labor, 1992).

As Belgium was a predominantly Catholic country, the attitude of the church authorities was of great importance. Several church leaders and church organizations, including seminaries and religious orders, were now more willing to help.[153] In September 1942 the Bishop of Liège, Monseigneur Louis-Joseph Kerkhofs, called on the priests in his diocese to help the persecuted Jews. Numerous children and adults found shelter in Banneux, a place of pilgrimage. They were supplied with food ration stamps and false identity documents that had been obtained by employees of the municipal administration in Liège.[154]

The Jewish resistance also began to establish itself. After the roundup in Brussels at the beginning of September 1942, engineer Hertz Jospa and others in the Independence Front had formed the Jewish Defence Committee (CDJ/JVC),[155] which became the most important Jewish resistance organization in Belgium. It supported Jews who had gone into hiding, looked after Jewish refugees from the Netherlands, and, via the Swiss route, made contact with international Jewish relief organizations such as the American Jewish Joint Distribution Committee (JDC), which provided money to support Jews in Belgium (Doc. 219). A report by the Jewish Defence Committee from the end of 1943 estimated the number of Jews receiving support at 6,500. The committee's main function, however, was to protect Jewish children from deportation. In this endeavour it could count on the support of the National Children's Welfare Society (Œuvre nationale de l'enfance) headed by Yvonne Nèvejean. Most of the children could be placed in various Catholic institutions or with non-Jewish foster families (Doc. 204). More than 3,000 Jewish children were saved this way.[156] Pinkus 'Pierre' Broder, a leading member of the communist resistance in Charleroi, emphasized in his memoirs how important it had been to separate parents in hiding from their children: 'The vast majority of these children spoke French or Flemish without any accent. They could thus easily pose as non-Jews, live freely, either in a family or in an institution, and go to school; in short, lead an almost normal life.'[157]

On 15 January 1943, after a pause of almost three months, the German occupiers resumed the deportation of Jews to occupied Poland, albeit on a more limited scale. By the summer of 1943 three trains, carrying 2,956 Jews in total, had left Mechelen for Auschwitz. During this period a relatively large number of Jews managed to escape from the trains.[158] More than 10 per cent of the deportees, 539 persons, succeeded in escaping

153 Dan Michman (ed.), *The Encyclopedia of the Righteous Among the Nations – Rescuers of Jews during the Holocaust: Belgium* (Jerusalem: Yad Vashem, 2005), pp. xix–xxvii.

154 Rozenblum, *Une cité si ardente*, p. 152.

155 Jean-Philippe Schreiber (ed.), *Hertz Jospa: Juif, résistant, communiste* (Brussels: Labor, 1997).

156 Steinberg, *L'Etoile et le fusil*, vol. 3, p. 32; Sylvain Brachfeld, *Ze hebben het overleefd* (Brussels: VUBPRESS, 1997), pp. 64–68 (French edition: *Ils ont survécu: Le sauvetage des Juifs en Belgique occupée* [Brussels: Racine, 2001], pp. 55–64); Lieven Saerens, 'Die Hilfe für Juden in Belgien', in Wolfgang Benz and Juliane Wetzel (eds.), *Solidarität und Hilfe für Juden während der NS-Zeit*, vol. 4: *Slowakei, Bulgarien, Serbien, Kroatien mit Bosnien und Herzegowina, Belgien, Italien* (Berlin: Metropol, 2004), pp. 193–280.

157 Pierre Broder, *Des Juifs debout contre le nazisme* (Brussels: EPO, 1994), p. 147. Pierre was the author's cover name in the resistance movement, and he kept it after the liberation of Belgium.

158 Tanja von Fransecky, *Flucht von Juden aus Deportationszügen in Frankreich, Belgien und den Niederlanden* (Berlin: Metropol, 2014); Rozenblum, *Une cité si ardente*, p. 159; Marion Schreiber, *Stille Rebellen: Der Überfall auf den 20. Deportationszug nach Auschwitz* (Berlin: Aufbau, 2001); Simon Gronowski, *L'Enfant du 20e convoi* (Brussels: Pire, 2005); Maxime Steinberg and Laurence Schram, *Transport XX Malines – Auschwitz* (Brussels: VUBPRESS, 2008).

from the five deportation trains that left between October 1942 and April 1943. Only seven persons had managed to escape from the fifteen previous transports, and only twenty-five persons managed to get away from the final seven trains that left Belgium between April 1943 and the end of July 1944. On two days the number of escapees was particularly high: on 30 October 1942, 240 people managed to escape from Transports XVI and XVII, and on 19 April 1943, more than 200 people escaped from Transport XX. Many of the escapees were later recaptured and deported again. The Jews had previously been taken to Auschwitz in third-class passenger coaches, which were more difficult to make escape-proof, but the transport of 19 April 1943 was the first to be made up of goods wagons and guarded more closely by members of the Order Police drafted in specially from Germany. This transport, which travelled at dusk, was particularly large, with 1,404 people on board. Members of the Jewish resistance had succeeded in staying together upon departure. Using tools they had smuggled in, they managed to set themselves free and jump from the moving train. In addition, three young resistance fighters, Youra (Georges) Livschitz, Robert Maistriau, and Jean Franklemon, launched an attack on the train from outside and freed more prisoners. This raid on a deportation train was the only occurrence of its kind during the entire period of the deportations of Jews in Europe. During this journey German guards shot and killed 26 people (Doc. 208) and 87 others were subsequently recaptured and sent to another transport, but 119 deportees managed to go into hiding until the end of the occupation and survived. Among them was Samuel Perl (Doc. 196), who had escaped for a second time, and 12-year-old Simon Gronowski, who later recalled:

> Suddenly my mother woke me up, I felt a fresh draught of air, the coldness of the night […]. The train was rolling, and the door was wide open. A cluster of people on the left side jumped from the moving train. […] My mother held my right hand in her right hand, and with her left she took hold of my left shoulder and led me to the door as if she were leading me into freedom and into life. […] My mother sat me down on the edge, so that my legs were dangling in the air.[159]

When the train slowed down, the 12-year-old jumped out. His mother had to stay behind in the train, which came to a stop after the discovery of the escapes. Simon Gronowski succeeded in escaping, and he was able to hide until the end of the occupation in the home of acquaintances in a Brussels suburb (Doc. 211); his mother was deported and did not return.

Early in 1943 the Reich Security Main Office planned to resume the deportations from Belgium and closely monitored the course of events. In early December 1942 the head of the Germany Department (Abteilung Deutschland, responsible for anti-Jewish policy), Martin Luther, had tried to put pressure on the German agencies in Belgium to include Jews with Belgian citizenship, particularly members of the Belgian resistance, in the next deportations. He asserted that 'Belgium will have to be thoroughly cleansed of Jews sooner or later, without fail' (Doc. 197). In response to the evasive answer given by Werner von Bargen, the representative in Brussels of the Reich Foreign Office, Luther

159 Gronowski, *L'Enfant du 20e convoi*, p. 97.

insisted that 'Belgian Jews also be gathered' in the assembly camps, and had the correspondence passed on to the Reich Security Main Office.[160] His petitions did not initially yield any concrete results. In 1942 Jews with Belgian citizenship had already been arrested on occasion and imprisoned in Mechelen camp for a lengthy period. After months of interventions by Rabbi Salomon Ullmann, the former chairman of the Association of Jews in Belgium, and other prominent advocates – as rumour had it, even the Dowager Queen Elisabeth of Belgium[161] – they were to be released in two phases. A first group was indeed allowed to leave the camp at the end of June 1943.

One of those concerned, Lucien Hirsch, reported in detail to the Belgian government in exile about the mistreatment and lack of provisioning in Mechelen, and about the preparations for the deportations (Doc. 217). The plans for releasing the other Belgian Jews from Mechelen were thwarted by Himmler's order that Jews with Belgian citizenship henceforth be included in the deportations.[162] Simon Gronowski's sister Ita had obtained Belgian citizenship when she was sixteen. Together with her mother and her younger brother, she had been arrested in March 1943 and that summer she was waiting for the release that had been announced. In mid August she wrote to her father

> Physically, I'm fine, but psychologically I'm quite ill, I think I'm suffering from neurasthenia. You will laugh, but it's true nonetheless. Not long ago I had a high temperature, I'm certain that it was a result of the transport. For things such as these, one needs to have a heart like a horse to endure the sight.[163]

Ita Gronowski was deported to Auschwitz on 20 September 1943. The German military administration had at first made an effort to delay the deportation of the Belgian Jews, concerned that 'once the intention to arrest Belgian Jews became known, the latter would go underground and the army of illegals and terrorist forces would thereby be reinforced' (Doc. 212). On 20 July 1943, however, General von Falkenhausen gave his consent. With that, the military administration's conciliatory approach towards the Belgian secretaries general was at an end. Yet cooperation had in reality already ceased: since autumn 1942 the policy of the secretaries general of pursuing the 'lesser evil' had given way in practice to perpetual crisis management.[164]

Jews with Belgian citizenship therefore became the target of the last large roundup in Belgium, which took place on 3 and 4 September 1943 (Doc. 214). The German Security Police and their auxiliaries arrested 750 Jews in Brussels and brought them to Mechelen. The majority of the 225 persons arrested in Antwerp had recently been released

160 Luther to Bargen, 25 Jan. 1943, published in Serge Klarsfeld and Maxime Steinberg (eds.), *Die Endlösung der Judenfrage in Belgien: Dokumente* (New York: Klarsfeld Foundation, 1980), pp. 61–62.

161 Adriaens et al., *Mecheln – Auschwitz*, vol. 1, pp. 84–85.

162 The original of Himmler's order has not come to light, but it is referred to in a telex from Department IV B of the Security Police in Brussels to all branch offices, dated 29 June 1943: see Ceges/Soma, AA 556, published in Klarsfeld and Steinberg (eds.), *Die Endlösung der Judenfrage in Belgien*, p. 70.

163 Letter from Ita Gronowski, dated 14 August 1943, in Gronowski, *L'Enfant du 20e convoi*, pp. 138–139.

164 Steinberg, 'The *Judenpolitik* in Belgium within the West European Context', p. 114; Wouters, 'La chasse aux Juifs', p. 586 *(Gewillig België*, p. 588).

from Mechelen, and they now returned to the camp under terrible conditions. During the journey nine persons suffocated in the completely overloaded and tightly sealed wagons. In Brussels, police officials also turned up at the residence of Salomon van den Berg, who had been warned a few hours before but believed that his prominent role as representative of the Belgian Jews would save him. He was able to avoid arrest by citing his position (Doc. 215). He informed Salomon Ullmann, who in turn notified the secretaries general. They asked the military administration – in vain – to release all those who had been arrested. For safety van den Berg and his family henceforth stayed in a different apartment each night. The people arrested in this raid, together with the Belgian citizens still detained in Mechelen, were deported to Auschwitz on 20 September 1943.[165]

The actions of the Germans aroused the indignation of the Belgian secretaries general, who now were able to bring themselves to write a letter of protest to von Falkenhausen in which, for the first and last time during the entire period of occupation, they condemned the persecution of the Jews unequivocally. Only now did they feel compelled to point out the violation of Article 43 of the Hague Convention on the Laws and Customs of War on Land, according to which an occupying power must observe the laws of the occupied country wherever possible. In the letter they also protested against the seizure of homes and the theft of Jewish possessions. These measures, they emphasized, ran counter to the Belgian constitution.[166] Their remonstrations went unheard and the arrest and deportation of Jewish citizens continued. The German police authorities acted alone or relied on assistance from the collaborationist parties and paramilitary militias. The Belgian police now received direct instructions only for minor and local arrest operations, which they generally carried out.

In Antwerp a legal existence for Jews was now impossible. In Brussels, by contrast, employees of the textile industry or members of the Association of Jews in Belgium could still be afforded protection through certificates of exemption issued by the military administration. In addition, Jews who were married to non-Jews, as well as children and elderly people who were housed in the homes of the association, were spared (Doc. 219). All others were in hiding somewhere in the country or had attempted to escape to another country. But in 1944, between January and July, 2,702 additional persons were deported to the East in five transport trains.

The Belgian population welcomed the Allied landings in Normandy in June 1944 with tremendous joy and optimism. Three weeks later Salomon van den Berg began a new diary, in which he expressed his happiness at the fall of Cherbourg: 'It's time to get ready for faster operations; everyone is full of hope.'[167] In July 1944, in a move that revived earlier German plans to convert the military administration into a civil administration affiliated to the Reich, the military commander was replaced by a Reich commissioner (the Gauleiter of Cologne-Aachen, Josef Grohé). However, in the new Reich Commissariat of Belgium, there was little opportunity to intensify the pursuit of the Jews who were in hiding. Plans to continue the roundups with a view to resuming the deportations could no longer be implemented because of the rapid advance of the Allies.

165 Meinen, *Die Shoah in Belgien*, pp. 56–57; diary of Salomon van den Berg, pp. 130 and 132, entries for 6 Sept. and 8 Sept. 1943.

166 Wouters, 'La chasse aux Juifs', p. 587 (*Gewillig België*, pp. 611–612).

167 Diary of Salomon van den Berg, p. 175, entry for 26 June 1944.

The only exception was in Liège, where the German police carried out another arrest operation in early July 1944, targeting Jews with Belgian citizenship.

On 3 September 1944 American troops liberated Brussels, followed by Antwerp one day later. On 31 July 1944 the last deportation train had left Mechelen camp. By that time 24,906 Jews, including 4,082 children, had been deported in twenty-seven transports from Belgium to the extermination camps in Poland.[168] Around 45 per cent of the country's Jewish population had been included in the deportations.[169] Only 1,207 of the deported Jews survived the end of the war.[170]

Luxembourg

On 15 October 1941 the last train carrying Jewish emigrants bound for Portugal departed from the railway station in Luxembourg City. One day later, the first deportation train left from the same station. It brought 331 Jews from Luxembourg to the Lodz ghetto in the Warthegau – the first Jews to be deported to Eastern Europe from a Western European country occupied by Germany.[171] Although 4,000 Jews had still been living in Luxembourg when the Germans invaded on 10 May 1940, only around 700 remained in 1942, most of whom were elderly and in poor health and unable or unwilling to emigrate. In the summer of 1941 the German civil administration had already made it compulsory for Jews to wear the yellow star. The measure had the desired effect: one Luxembourger later recalled that whenever one encountered a Jew with this star, one was 'unbelievably ashamed, but also no longer had the courage to approach him and do something'.[172]

In the summer of 1941 the former abbey at Cinqfontaines (Fünfbrünnen) in Troisvierges (Ulflingen) was repurposed as an assembly camp for approximately 300 inmates and officially named a 'Jewish home for the elderly'. Initially all sick and frail Jews housed in homes for the elderly run by Luxembourg City were required to relocate there. Later the occupiers forced all Jewish families to move to Troisvierges, with the result that the home soon became overcrowded. Only a few of those sent to the home, likely no more than ten, risked escape. The danger of being caught was too great.[173]

In the civil administration, which was under the authority of the Gauleiter of Koblenz-Trier, Gustav Simon, Department IV A was responsible for the registration and expropriation of Jewish property. By the autumn of 1943 it had concluded this bureaucratically organized theft. The value of the confiscated assets – bank accounts, real estate,

168 A total of twenty-eight trains were used for the transports: on 20 Sept. 1943 the same number was assigned to two trains (XXIIa and XXIIb).

169 Meinen, *Die Shoah in Belgien*, p. 184.

170 Ibid., p. 83.

171 Pascale Eberhard (ed.), *Der Überlebenskampf jüdischer Deportierter aus Luxemburg und der Trierer Region im Getto Litzmannstadt: Briefe Mai 1942* (Saarbrücken: Blattlausverlag, 2012).

172 Recollections of Ann Marie F., cited in Mathias Wallerang, *Luxemburg unter nationalsozialistischer Besatzung: Luxemburger berichten* (Mainz: Gesellschaft für Volkskunde in Rheinland-Pfalz, 1997), p. 189.

173 See Marc Schoentgen, 'Das "Jüdische Altersheim" in Fünfbrunnen', in Benz and Distel (eds.), *Terror im Westen*, pp. 49–70; and Paul Cerf, *Longtemps j'aurai mémoire: Documents et témoignages sur les Juifs du Grand-Duché de Luxembourg durant la Seconde Guerre mondiale* (Luxembourg: Editions du Letzeburger Land, 1974), pp. 87 and 92.

and household effects – is estimated at a minimum of 30 million Reichsmarks, of which a portion (exact data are not available) found its way into German hands. A report on the 'transfer of assets' of a Luxembourg firm in October 1941 recorded that Simon had 'initially proceeded on the assumption that, with regard to the "Aryanizations", Luxembourg would be first in line to be considered'. But, the report continued,

> various political considerations had led the Luxembourgers to exercise restraint in this respect, as the involvement in such dealings seemed too risky to them. For this reason, many plots of land, shops, and the few industrial companies had gone to Germans from the Old Reich, albeit with preference being shown to interested parties from the Gau of Koblenz.[174]

The Jews of Luxembourg were deported to the death camps in the East together with Jews from south-western Germany. The Einsatzkommando of the Luxembourg Security Police, under the command of SS-Obersturmbannführer Fritz Hartmann, prepared the transports. The Consistory of the Israelite Religious Community in Luxembourg, known after April 1942 as the Council of Elders of the Jews, was forced to notify those who had been selected for deportation, organize their transport to the railway station, and make arrangements for their provisioning.[175] At the end of April 1942, the second deportation train left Luxembourg, taking twenty-four Jews from Cinqfontaines via Stuttgart to either Lublin-Majdanek or Belzec.[176] In July 1942, when systematic deportations began in the rest of occupied Western Europe, trains ran in quick succession. 'Yet again the spectre of Poland hangs over us,' noted Alfred Oppenheimer, head of the Council of Elders in the Troisvierges home, on 7 July (Doc. 223). On 12 July 1942 a train took 24 Jews from Luxembourg to Chemnitz, where they were combined with a group of 300 Jews from the Reich and taken to Auschwitz. None of them survived.

On 26 July, 24 Luxembourg Jews were deported to Theresienstadt. Two days later another 157 were deported. A few days earlier, they had been required by the German Security Police to report to the railway station in Luxembourg City 'for the purpose of relocation to the Theresienstadt home for the elderly' (Doc. 227). Ester Galler, who had emigrated from Poland to Luxembourg in 1901, was seventy-four years old and living in Cinqfontaines when, in a letter to her cousin, she reported despairingly that all the residents of the home were now to be 'evacuated': 'I do not yet know when my turn will come; however, it will be within approximately 4–5 weeks. You can imagine how agitated I am. I am old, blind, and have problems with my legs' (Doc. 226).

The last sizeable transport, containing 99 persons, left Luxembourg for Theresienstadt on 6 April 1943. It was coupled to a freight train that travelled via Trier, Koblenz,

174 'Bericht vom 29.10.1941 bzgl. Interbank Luxemburg/Ideal-Lederfabrik Wiltz', copy in Mémorial de la Shoah, CLIV-78 (NI 2870).

175 Commission spéciale pour l'étude des spoliations des biens juifs au Luxembourg pendant les années de guerre, 1940–1945, *La Spoliation des biens juifs au Luxembourg 1940–1945: Rapport final* (Luxembourg: La Commission, 2009), pp. 39, 73, and 110.

176 Paul Dostert, 'La déportation des Juifs à partir du territoire luxembourgeois (1941–1943)', in Thorsten Fuchshuber and Renée Wagner (eds.), *Émancipation, éclosion, persécution: Le développement de la communauté juive luxembourgeoise de la Révolution française à la Seconde Guerre mondiale* (Brussels: EME, 2014), pp. 210–211.

Frankfurt, Eisenach, and Dresden, meaning that the journey took more than three days and four nights. 'Everybody is fine and everybody wishes this journey would never end, despite the cold and discomfort, for fear of what lies ahead,' wrote Selma Heumann, one of the deportees, in a letter to Alfred Oppenheimer (Doc. 232). Ester Galler was included in this transport. She died in Theresienstadt the following month.

Shortly afterwards the German police authorities closed Cinqfontaines camp. In May the Reich Security Main Office ordered the deportation of all Jews remaining in Luxembourg, including the members of the Council of Elders. As a result, on 17 June 1943 eight persons, including Alfred Oppenheimer and his family, were deported to Theresienstadt.[177]

For the first deportations the Jews had been taken by bus from their place of residence to the railway station in Luxembourg City, which explains why the non-Jewish population were largely unaware of these events. There were a few professions of solidarity, but overall the deportation of Luxembourg's Jews attracted little attention. They had scarcely any contact with the local population.[178] Moreover, Jews were only one of the groups that were persecuted. In the context of Germanization policy, in 1942 the German civil administration established a so-called ethnicity register (Volkstumskartei). This contained a precise breakdown of the 'ethnically alien' portion of the population, including Italians, French, Belgians, and Poles, and was intended to serve as a basis for resettlements or expulsions. These, however, were to be postponed for political and economic reasons until after the end of the war. At the end of August 1942, the announcement of general military conscription for male Luxembourgers born between 1920 and 1927 set off a wave of strikes, which was brutally quelled by the occupiers. Twenty-one strikers were shot, and many were put in concentration camps. Furthermore, from September 1942 to August 1944 more than 4,000 Luxembourgers were deported for 're-education' purposes, primarily to Silesia and the Sudetenland.[179] Around 40 per cent of those who were conscripted into the Wehrmacht went into hiding – around half of them in Luxembourg itself. Many of those who managed to reach England joined forces with the Allies and subsequently participated in the Normandy landings as members of a Luxembourg battalion within the Belgian Piron Brigade.[180]

In view of the rigid Germanization policy pursued by the civil administration and the measures taken against the strikers, the persecution of the Jews was of lesser interest to the general population. One woman from Luxembourg later summed up the situation by noting that while the Luxembourgers had indeed not been involved in the persecution, they had not helped the Jews a great deal either. While many hundreds of non-Jewish

177 Ibid., p. 215.

178 Marc Schoentgen, 'Luxemburger und Juden im Zweiten Weltkrieg: Zwischen Solidarität und Schweigen', in Marie-Paule Jungblut (ed.), *Et wor alles net esou einfach: Questions sur le Luxembourg et la Deuxième Guerre mondiale: Contributions historiques accompagnant l'exposition* (Luxembourg: Musée d'Histoire de la Ville, 2002), p. 159; Paul Dostert, *Luxemburg zwischen Selbstbehauptung und nationaler Selbstaufgabe: Die deutsche Besatzungspolitik und die Volksdeutsche Bewegung, 1940–1945* (Luxembourg: Imprimerie Saint-Paul, 1985), pp. 165–166.

179 Wallerang, *Luxemburg unter nationalsozialistischer Besatzung*, pp. 86–89.

180 Military units formed in 1940 and comprising Belgian and Luxembourg soldiers who had escaped to Britain. The units were named after their commanding officer, Jean-Baptiste Piron, and fought in Western Europe, for example at the battle of Normandy, in the Netherlands, and in the operation to liberate Belgium.

young men found people who helped them elude the clutches of the occupiers, she said, Jews had been given places to hide only on occasion. At first people had not really believed the Jews were in mortal danger, she maintained, 'then one saw how, little by little, some of them managed to get away; the rest were isolated, and everybody was preoccupied with themselves and ultimately concerned with the young men'.[181]

A number of antisemitic groups already existed in Luxembourg before the war, and even in some resistance circles it was said that Jewish influence must be curbed after the war. At the onset of the occupation, Luxembourgish collaborators, especially the members of the Ethnic German Movement (Volksdeutsche Bewegung, VdB) had been actively involved in anti-Jewish rallies and riots. Overall, however, they remained a small minority in Luxembourg.[182]

Until the summer of 1942 the prevailing impression among exiles was that the Jews who remained in Luxembourg were getting off relatively lightly. For example, in its August–September 1942 issue the English-language *Luxembourg Bulletin*, which was published in Montreal and New York by the government in exile, reported under the headline 'Religious Persecution':

> The Jews of Luxembourg suffered the same cruel fate as their co-religionists in other occupied countries. After the confiscation of their assets, they were expelled; most of them were forced to leave the country without any resources at all and faced a highly uncertain future. Nonetheless, they willingly concede that the situation for Roman Catholics is even worse.[183]

The authors were drawing on a report about the situation for the Jews in Luxembourg that Rabbi Serebrenik had prepared in March 1941 for the government in exile. Serebrenik had argued that the Catholic population had to suffer more, both mentally and physically, than the Jews. The latter, he said, were admittedly driven out of the country with terrible methods, but the Catholics were the objects of a 'mission' to turn them into Germans.[184]

During the second half of 1942, the fate of the remaining Jews in Luxembourg was brought into clearer focus. A leaflet produced in December 1942 by the Inter-Allied Information Committee, chaired by Georges Schommer, a Luxembourger, mentioned the deportation of Jews from Luxembourg to Poland and even assumed – prematurely – that all Jews remaining in Luxembourg had been deported to Theresienstadt (Doc. 230).

After July 1943 the only Jews still living in Luxembourg were either in mixed marriages or among the very few who were able to survive the period of occupation in

181 See Cerf, *Longtemps j'aurai mémoire*, p. 111; quote: recollections of Julie K., cited in Wallerang, *Luxemburg unter nationalsozialistischer Besatzung*, pp. 188–189.

182 Schoentgen, 'Luxemburger und Juden im Zweiten Weltkrieg', p. 160; Marc Schoentgen, 'Luxembourg', in Wolf Gruner and Jörg Osterloh (eds.), *The Greater German Reich and the Jews: Nazi Persecution Policies in the Annexed Territories, 1935–1945*, trans. Bernhard Heise (New York: Berghahn Books, 2015 [German edn, 2010]), pp. 290–315; on the Ethnic German Movement, see Dostert, *Luxemburg zwischen Selbstbehauptung und nationaler Selbstaufgabe*, pp. 217–241.

183 *Luxembourg Bulletin* (Montréal-New York), 2, August–September 1942.

184 Robert Serebrenik, 'Die Lage in Luxemburg, 6. März 1941, ANLux, Gvt exil 380', cited in Dostert, *Luxemburg zwischen Selbstbehauptung und nationaler Selbstaufgabe*, p. 166.

hiding. They lived in constant fear. As one Luxembourger later related: 'If somebody passed by somewhere in the street in the morning, then they thought they were about to be taken away.'[185]

Between 1941 and 1943 approximately 660 Jews were deported from Luxembourg, of whom around 50 were still alive at the end of the war. At least 565 persons managed to leave the country, mostly for France, but were later captured and sent to the extermination camps. In total around 1,400 Jews died as a result of the persecution in Luxembourg, a figure that represents one third of the Jews living in the country at the beginning of 1940.[186]

France

From the start of the occupation France was divided into zones. The Wehrmacht had occupied the northern part of the country as well as the coastal region all the way to the Spanish border, while southern France at first remained unoccupied and was administered by the collaborationist government of the French State (État Français), with its seat at Vichy, under Marshal Philippe Pétain. In the occupied zone, French administrative officials received their instructions from the Vichy government but additionally had to cooperate with the local representatives of the occupiers, these being the Feldkommandanturen and the commanders of the Security Police. In northern France, the two départements of Nord and Pas-de-Calais were assigned to the German military administration in Brussels. From 1940 Alsace and Lorraine, like Luxembourg, were under German civil administration and were de facto annexed. In addition, a narrow strip of territory extending from the Atlantic across the Ardennes to the Jura mountains was considered a restricted area. In the south-eastern part of the country, some communes in the départements of Savoie, Hautes-Alpes, Basses-Alpes, and Alpes-Maritimes were occupied by the Italian army; a strip 50 kilometres wide located west of that area was demilitarized. In November 1942 the Italian zone of occupation was extended to the Rhône and to cover the island of Corsica.[187]

Most Jews were located in the occupied northern zone and in the unoccupied southern zone. In the very first months of the war, the majority of the Jewish population in the annexed territories in eastern France, as well as a portion of the non-Jewish French population, had been evacuated or had fled. A noticeable change in the structure of the German occupation had begun in May 1942 with the appointment of Carl-Albrecht Oberg to the newly created function of Higher SS and Police Leader. The German police's position in relation to the military administration as well as to Military Commander Carl Heinrich von Stülpnagel, appointed in February 1942, had been enhanced as a

185 Recollections of Jean S., cited in Wallerang, *Luxemburg unter nationalsozialistischer Besatzung*, p. 188.

186 Commission spéciale, *La Spoliation des biens juifs au Luxembourg 1940–1945*, p. 10; Schoentgen, 'Luxemburg und Juden im Zweiten Weltkrieg', pp. 360–361; slightly different figures given in Ino Arndt, 'Luxemburg: Deutsche Besetzung und Ausgrenzung der Juden', in Benz (ed.), *Dimension des Völkermords*, pp. 103–104.

187 Eric Alary, *La Ligne de démarcation* (Paris: Perrin, 2003), pp. 25–32.

result.[188] In late 1941, at the urging of the Germans, the Vichy government had created the General Union of French Jews (Union générale des Israélites de France, UGIF), a representative body for all the Jews in the occupied zone and the unoccupied zone. The partition of France was reflected in the fact that the organization's two sections, 'North' and 'South', headed by André Baur and Raymond-Raoul Lambert respectively, worked largely independently of one another.

When the yellow star was introduced in the occupied zone on 7 June 1942, many of the French were outraged and declared their solidarity with the stigmatized Jews. Henri Plard was one of the non-Jews who sewed the star to their clothing: 'I was profoundly indignant at the humiliations that were imposed on our Jewish brothers.'[189] One month later, the occupation authorities denied Jews access to public events and amenities; they were allowed to enter non-Jewish shops and businesses only between 3 p.m. and 4 p.m. (Doc. 242). Such measures separated the Jews from the rest of the French population and prepared the general public for the deportations. The Vichy government refused to extend these measures to the unoccupied zone.

On 11 June 1942 the officials in charge of Jewish affairs from Brussels, The Hague, and Paris agreed that 100,000 Jews, drawn from both occupied and unoccupied France, were to be 'transferred to Auschwitz concentration camp to work' (Doc. 235).[190] Men and women between the ages of sixteen and forty were to be deported in three trains per week, provided they were required to wear the Jewish star and were not living in mixed marriages. It was stipulated that 10 per cent of the deportees could be 'Jews who are not fit for work'. However, in Paris it quickly became apparent over the following days and weeks that so many people could not be deported in such a short time. On 22 June, in an official letter both informing the Reich Foreign Office and ensuring 'that there are no objections to these measures on the part of the Reich Foreign Office either', Eichmann mentioned the deportation of only 40,000 persons.[191]

On the eve of the Second World War, some 300,000 to 330,000 Jews were living in France, approximately half of whom were French citizens. In June 1940, as the German

188 On the structure of the German occupation, see Hans Umbreit, *Der Militärbefehlshaber in Frankreich* (Boppard am Rhein: Harald Boldt, 1968); Herbert, *Best*, pp. 251–254; Barbara Lambauer, *Otto Abetz et les Français ou l'envers de la Collaboration* (Paris: Fayard, 2001), pp. 181–182; Gaël Eismann, *Hôtel Majestic: Ordre et sécurité en France occupée (1940–1944)* (Paris: Tallandier, 2010), pp. 97–109; and Gaël Eismann, 'The "Militärbefehlshaber in Frankreich" and Order and Security at the Local Level in Occupied France', in De Wever, Van Goethem, and Wouters (eds.), *Local Government in Occupied Europe (1939–1945)*, pp. 147–177.

189 Henri Plard, 'J'ai porté l'étoile en solidarité avec les Juifs', in Brigitte Leblanc and Christelle Chevallier (eds.), *Mémoires de la Shoah, 1933 à 1946: Photographies et témoignages* (Paris: Editions du Chêne, 2005), p. 66.

190 On the 11 June 1942 conference, see Serge Klarsfeld, *Vichy–Auschwitz: Die 'Endlösung der Judenfrage' in Frankreich*, trans. Ahlrich Meyer (Darmstadt: Wissenschaftliche Buchgesellschaft, 2007), pp. 78–81. The crucial document (RF 1517) was first published in 1947 in French translation in Henri Monneray, *La Persécution des Juifs en France et dans les autres pays de l'Ouest, présentée par la France à Nuremberg* (Paris: Éditions du centre, 1947), pp. 126–127.

191 Reich Security Main Office (Eichmann) to the Reich Foreign Office, 22 June 1942, published in *ADAP*, series E: *1941–1945*, vol. 3: *16. Juni bis 30. September 1942* (Göttingen: Vandenhoeck & Ruprecht, 1974), doc. 26; Klarsfeld, *Vichy–Auschwitz*, pp. 88–89; Ahlrich Meyer, *Täter im Verhör: Die 'Endlösung der Judenfrage' in Frankreich 1940–1944* (Darmstadt: Wissenschaftliche Buchgesellschaft, 2005), pp. 138–140.

troops advanced, many of them had fled to southern France. A French law of 4 October 1940 made it possible to intern foreign Jews, and by winter 1940/41 approximately 50,000 people were in the internment camps in Vichy France, mostly refugees or persons expelled by the National Socialist regime.[192] In 1941 this number decreased rapidly as a result of emigration, escape, and also release. In 1942 there were 10,000 to 12,000 persons in these camps.

In the occupied zone an estimated 7,000 to 8,000 Jews were held in internment camps. Most of them had been arrested during the three roundups in May, August, and December 1941. On 27 March 1942, in retaliation for assassinations carried out by the resistance movement, the Military Commander had ordered the deportation of 1,112 of these internees to Auschwitz. During talks in Paris in early May 1942, René Bousquet, the secretary general of the French police, informed Reinhard Heydrich of the Vichy government's desire to rid itself of the foreign Jews in the southern zone.[193]

After the meeting of the officials in charge of Jewish affairs held in Berlin on 11 June 1942, Eichmann had travelled to the French capital to assist Theodor Dannecker, who was in charge of Jewish affairs for the Security Police and the SD in Paris, in setting the deportations in motion. On 30 June 1942 Dannecker summoned all the Security Police's regional officials dealing with Jewish affairs in the occupied zone to come to Paris, where he gave them precise instructions for the arrest of the Jews in their areas of responsibility (Doc. 238). At the same time he demanded that Jean Leguay, Bousquet's deputy in Paris, instigate the proposed handover of 10,000 Jews from the occupied zone. In addition, he insisted upon the arrest of 22,000 Jews from the Paris metropolitan area, at least 40 per cent of whom were to be French citizens.[194]

In Vichy these demands caused a stir. The French government decided to make a clear distinction in the future between foreign and French Jews and to protect the latter from arrest. Dannecker's demands were then addressed on 2 July 1942 at a meeting between Higher SS and Police Leader Carl Oberg, Helmut Knochen, who was the Senior Commander of the Security Police and the SD, and Bousquet (Doc. 239). The priority of the French chief of police was to protect the local French police authorities from interference by German police and to preserve the independence of the French police as far as possible. Bousquet succeeded to a certain extent in this objective.[195] In return,

192 See PMJ 5/242 and 262, and Denis Peschanski, *La France des camps: L'internement 1938–1946* (Paris: Gallimard, 2002), p. 256.

193 There were four internment camps in the occupied zone: Compiègne, Drancy, Pithiviers, and Beaune-la-Rolande, of which the last three were under German administration. On the roundups in 1941, see PMJ 5, pp. 68–72. On the deportations on 27 March 1942, see PMJ 5/318; on the conversation between Heydrich and Bousquet, see Klarsfeld, *Vichy–Auschwitz*, p. 70.

194 Meyer, *Täter im Verhör*, pp. 146–147. Notes by Dannecker, dated 26 June 1942, Mémorial de la Shoah, Paris XXVI-33, published in Serge Klarsfeld, *Le Calendrier de la persécution des Juifs de France*, vol. 1: *Juillet 1940–août 1942* (Paris: Fayard, 2001), pp. 423–424. As Klarsfeld states, the goal of arresting 22,000 persons between the ages of sixteen and forty-five would not have been attainable in the Paris metropolitan area by detaining foreign Jews alone: Klarsfeld, *Vichy–Auschwitz*, p. 91.

195 Laurent Joly, *Vichy dans la 'solution finale': Histoire du Commissariat général aux questions juives, 1941–1944* (Paris: Grasset, 2006), pp. 340–341. A detailed description of the 'Oberg-Bousquet agreement' and its significance can be found in Bernd Kasten, *'Gute Franzosen': Die französische Polizei und die deutsche Besatzungsmacht im besetzten Frankreich, 1940–1944* (Sigmaringen: Thorbecke, 1993), pp. 71–73.

the German police authorities demanded that the French police undertake the arrest or handover of Jews. Jews with French citizenship could be excluded; the operation was to concentrate on stateless Jews. Bousquet agreed. Two days later Pierre Laval, the head of government, went one step further by suggesting that children who were under sixteen, and were therefore supposedly exempt from deportation, should be transported to the East along with their parents (Doc. 240). Most of these children had been born in France and held French citizenship. From this point on the Vichy regime played a central role in the deportation of Jews from France.

Two weeks later, on 16 and 17 July 1942, the French municipal police in Paris, under German instruction, carried out a large-scale roundup in which 12,884 stateless Jews were arrested. Dannecker had met representatives of the French police on 7 July 1942 to plan the mass arrest (Doc. 241). Evidently, a great many people received advance warning and managed to take shelter, for the number arrested was substantially smaller than the target of 22,000. Most of those arrested in the raid were women and children, who had believed themselves safe because they had been spared during the previous roundups (Doc. 245). Rachel Jedinak, a child at the time, recalled the divided reaction of the non-Jewish French:

> We went across the courtyard to get to the street and to the multitude of families, women and children, all likewise arrested. We were like a herd, and the inhabitants of the neighbourhood looked out from their windows or watched from the pavement as we passed. Some made the sign of the cross and wept; others, by contrast, laughed very openly and maliciously.[196]

Hélène Berr, a university student, noticed that the streets were blocked at Montmartre owing to the numerous arrests. In her diary she recorded:

> In Mlle Monsaingeon's neighbourhood, a whole family, the father, the mother, and five children, gassed themselves to escape the roundup. One woman threw herself out of a window […] Who is going to feed the internees at Drancy now that their wives have been arrested? The kids will never find their parents again.[197]

Families with children were initially housed in the Vélodrome d'Hiver, a sports stadium in Paris, and then transferred to the camps at Pithiviers and Beaune-la-Rolande. Rachel Polakiewicz reported on her first night in the stadium: 'We have hardly anything left to eat, we lack pretty much everything, how much longer are we to stay here like this? […] From time to time one hears the screams of women, it makes us shiver to hear them.'[198] Antonina Pechtner, a native of Lwów, appealed to friends on the second day of her captivity:

196 Recollections of Rachel Jedinak, in Leblanc and Chevallier, *Mémoires de la Shoah*, p. 72.

197 *The Journal of Hélène Berr*, trans. David Bellos (London: MacLehose Press, 2008), pp. 98–99, entry for 18 July 1942.

198 Letter from Rachel Polakiewicz, dated 17 July 1942, published in Karen Taieb (ed.), *Je vous écris du Vél' d'Hiv: Les lettres retrouvées* (Paris: Laffont, 2011), p. 98.

> I'm imprisoned, I think I'm going to be sent to Poland. I beg you, look after my child, ask the concierge for our things and take as many of them as you can. I don't want my child to die somewhere in Poland, I want to die without him. I trust you, take pity on my child, I entrust him to you, I am in the Vélodrome d'Hiver.[199]

Unmarried adults and families with children over the age of sixteen were taken to the camp at Drancy following the roundups on 16/17 July in Paris. A series of five deportation trains subsequently left Drancy for Auschwitz, the first of these departing three days after the roundups. Within 10 days, 5,000 people had been deported from Drancy to Auschwitz. In a 'special operation' (*Sonderaktion*) several days before the Paris roundups, stateless Jews in the rest of the occupied zone had also been arrested by German and French police; approximately 1,500 were detained in total and subsequently deported to Auschwitz.[200] Among them were the daughter and grandchildren of Ida Kahn from the Saarland. They had previously emigrated to Palestine but returned to France. They were arrested in Alençon on 13 July 1942 and detained in Pithiviers, from where they were deported to Auschwitz on 31 July and 3 August (Doc. 244).

During the week from 6 to 12 August 1942, the handover of 10,000 stateless Jews from the internment camps in the southern zone began (Doc. 248). In accordance with instructions from the French police headquarters at Vichy, those affected were not told of their actual destination. The prefect in charge of Gurs camp reported that there had been no problems with the first transport, but by the time of the second one, many Jews tried to avoid deportation, 'as if they had been tipped off by foreign radio broadcasts' (Doc. 256).

Karl Heinz Reinsberg wrote to his brother Ernst from Les Milles camp near Marseilles a few days before he himself was taken to Drancy: 'What has happened here is unprecedented in world history, but it must not go unpunished, the punishment will have to come one day. Children, women, and men locked up together, and a gendarme with a rifle every ten metres' (Doc. 254). Also gathered in the camp at Les Milles were all the refugees who already had French exit visas and were waiting to emigrate to a country overseas. They too were included in the lists.[201]

After mid August 1942, in accordance with Laval's suggestion, children under the age of sixteen who had been left behind by their parents were also taken to Auschwitz, where, in most cases, they were murdered upon arrival. Karl Heinz Reinsberg and his wife accompanied the first of these 'children's trains'. One eyewitness described the departure of the first group of children: 'The most terrifying moment was the morning of their deportation […]. As they left, a cry went up: Maman, Maman' (Doc. 259).

In mid August the Jewish labourers in 'Foreign Labourer Groups' (Groupements de travailleurs étrangers, GTE) made up the second large group transferred from the unoccupied zone into the occupied zone. These work squads had been formed by the Vichy government in the autumn of 1940 to employ foreign labourers, of whom there was a

199 Letter from Antonina Pechtner, dated 17 July 1942, ibid., p. 112.

200 Annette Wieviorka and Michel Laffitte, *À l'intérieur du camp de Drancy* (Paris: Perrin, 2012), p. 151; Meyer, *Täter im Verhör*, p. 162.

201 Doris Obschernitzki, *Letzte Hoffnung – Ausreise: die Ziegelei von Les Milles 1939–1942. Vom Lager für unerwünschte Ausländer zum Deportationszentrum* (Berlin: Hentrich & Hentrich, 1999).

'surplus' in the French economy. Even with the addition of this second group, the target figure of 10,000 had evidently not been reached. The French police therefore planned a mass arrest in the larger cities of the unoccupied zone for 26 August 1942, targeting all Jewish refugees aged between eighteen and sixty who had come to France since 1936. The only people to be spared in this roundup were those who were not fit for transport, 'visibly' pregnant women, the parents of children under the age of two, and spouses or parents of French citizens. The 6,584 people arrested, however, were still too few for the Germans, and consequently the operation was repeated in the following weeks.[202]

On 28 August 1942 the officials in charge of Jewish affairs from the countries of Western Europe, or their deputies, came together once again at the Reich Security Main Office for a meeting with Eichmann (Doc. 263). Eichmann insisted that the ongoing deportation programme targeting stateless Jews be concluded by the end of the year. The deportation of other foreign Jews would follow and was to be completed by June 1943; the details were still being negotiated with the Reich Foreign Office. The frequency of the transports was to be increased from mid September 1942 because the Reich Railways would probably not be able to provide transport between November 1942 and January 1943 (Doc. 263).

The French police arrested Jews and handed them over, with the exception of adults with French citizenship. Although the Vichy government had adopted its own discriminatory measures against all Jews in early 1940, it was not willing to participate in the deportation of French Jews.[203] The French police did, however, hand over to the German occupiers a large number of French citizens who had violated German regulations, for example Jews who had failed to wear the yellow star or had disregarded the curfew. This practice triggered a protest from the representative in Paris of the Vichy government's Interior Ministry to the chief of the French police (Doc. 316).

At the beginning of September 1942, the French authorities informed Heinz Röthke, the new head of the Security Police and the SD's section for Jewish affairs, that the number of handovers agreed upon could not be reached. In an attempt to meet the target set by Eichmann nonetheless, Röthke included in the deportations French Jews who were in German custody.[204] Among them was 22-year-old Anna Goldberg, who had been arrested in early August while attempting to enter the unoccupied zone illegally and detained in the camp at Poitiers and then at Drancy (Docs. 255 and 274). She was subsequently deported on Transport XXXIV to Auschwitz, where she perished.

The deportation of French Jews was a clear violation of the German-French agreements of July 1942. Nevertheless, René Bousquet instructed his local representatives not to interfere with the deportations, but rather to ensure that they took place without

202 Anne Grynberg, *Les Camps de la honte: Les internés juifs des camps français 1939–1944* (Paris: La Découverte, 1991), pp. 301 and 327; Klarsfeld, *Calendrier*, p. 950; Klarsfeld, *Vichy–Auschwitz*, pp. 183 and 193–195; Peter Gaida, *Camps de travail sous Vichy: Les 'groupes de travailleurs étrangers' (GTE) en France et en Afrique du Nord 1940–1944* (Morrisville, NC: Lulu Press, 2015).

203 During the arrest of French Jews by the German police, 'the French authorities were in the habit of expressing their disapproval mostly in protests that were as clear as they were ineffective'; Kasten, *'Gute Franzosen'*, p. 97. See also Klarsfeld, *Vichy–Auschwitz*, p. 110.

204 At this time, 4,000 French Jews were interned in the camps at Drancy, Beaune-la-Rolande, and Pithiviers: Klarsfeld, *Vichy–Auschwitz*, p. 201.

incident.[205] The French authorities subsequently intensified the roundups of foreign Jews in order to save French Jews from deportation. The circle of affected groups was gradually expanded, and the elderly, the sick, and others who had been exempted from the arrests were now included. From mid September 1942 the German authorities also arrested Jews who held citizenship of other European countries and had previously been spared. This course of action increasingly brought the German and French police authorities into conflict with the diplomatic representatives of Hungary, Romania, Italy, and Turkey, who initially prevailed in their insistence that their citizens be protected (Doc. 266). A few weeks later, however, the governments in Budapest and Bucharest abandoned their opposition.

Meanwhile, the number of handovers from the southern zone lagged far behind the Germans' expectations. At the beginning of September Röthke had notified the French authorities of an expansion of the programme of deportations from France, with 50,000 additional Jews to be deported to the East (Doc. 264). Instead, however, the pace of the deportations slowed down. Nonetheless, the original German targets set in July 1942 were ultimately achieved. Between 7 August and 22 October 1942, the Vichy authorities handed over more than 10,000 persons from the southern zone to the German occupiers. Between 27 March and 11 November, deportation trains took 41,951 Jews from France to Auschwitz. Upon arrival more than one third were assigned as forced labour; all the others were murdered immediately. Of these people deported to Auschwitz, only 785 of the men and 25 of the women survived the war.[206]

The mass arrests that began in July 1942 sparked panic in Paris and in the occupied zone in general. The number of attempted escapes to the unoccupied zone soared – as did the risk of being caught by German customs officials or the German police, who greatly intensified their surveillance (Doc. 250). The family of historian Jean-Jacques Becker were among those who left the place where they had been residing a few days after the Paris roundup: 'Theoretically, it was not a journey of no return, […] but even for optimists the German defeat lay so far in the future that it nevertheless resembled a journey of no return.'[207] The family crossed the demarcation line south of Nevers by wading across the Allier river, and then ensconced themselves in Grenoble.[208]

The intense persecution also led to a lasting change in the work of both Jewish and non-Jewish relief organizations. In addition to their legal and official work, which continued in the internment camps in cooperation with the Vichy authorities, they now also organized illegal rescue operations. Because the relief organizations were involved in the commissions that decided on exemptions, by arguing the case for exemptions they were able to prevent a few of those affected from being handed over to the occupiers. However, that only meant that others would take their place, an awareness that added to the sense of despair among the helpers (Doc. 257). It was nonetheless thanks to their tenacity that, for example, more than 1,400 of those arrested in the large roundup on 26 August

205 Ibid., p. 203; Klarsfeld, *Calendrier*, pp. 1141–1142.
206 Numbers based on Klarsfeld, *Calendrier*, pp. 1908 and 1916.
207 Jean-Jacques Becker, *Un soir de l'été 1942 … Souvenirs d'un historien* (Paris: Larousse, 2009), p. 80.
208 According to the report by the senior police official in Limoges for the month of July, in the département of Charente alone, 750 foreign Jews had crossed the demarcation line within a two-month period: Kasten, '*Gute Franzosen*', p. 95.

were not handed over. As of the end of August 1942 parents could no longer leave their children behind in the care of a relief organization. Both the relief organizations and the resistance organizations endeavoured to save the children and adolescents involved. In Lyons the Christian group Amitié chrétienne managed to smuggle around 100 children out of Vénissieux camp (Doc. 271) and place them with non-Jewish families or in children's homes, most of which were run by the Œuvre de secours aux enfants (Children's Aid Society, OSE).[209]

The Secours suisse aux enfants, a children's aid organization founded in 1937 during the Spanish Civil War and affiliated with the Swiss Red Cross since the end of 1941, looked after unaccompanied stateless children and adolescents. Depending on their age, adolescents entrusted to its care were also among those whom the French authorities planned to hand over. The residents of the children's home at Château de la Hille in the département of Ariège were saved at the last minute by the tenacity of the director and her immediate superior. Over the following months, the children were smuggled into Switzerland via secret escape routes. The relief organization Comité Amelot, which was established in June 1940 in rue Amelot in Paris and was later financed by the American Jewish Joint Distribution Committee (JDC), succeeded in bringing around 1,350 children and adolescents from France to safety in Switzerland in the autumn of 1943. Working for the Zionist youth movement, Sasha Racine Maidenberg brought children from the Italian zone across the Swiss border in October 1943:

> We had been walking for several hours when we saw the barbed wire that indicated the border. We came closer and suddenly panicked when we saw soldiers in uniform standing in front of us. It took a moment before we realized that they were Swiss, rather than Germans. It had instilled such fear and terror in the children that they ran away screaming. When things calmed down again, we gathered them back together and were able to cross the border without any problems.[210]

By contrast, Cécile Klein-Hechel, her husband and their four-year-old son, Claude, managed to cross the border only after an exhausting ordeal fleeing via Alsace, Vichy, and Grenoble (Doc. 324).[211]

With the beginning of the systematic deportations from Western Europe, the flow of refugees from the Netherlands, Belgium, and France into the countries bordering France that were not under German control, namely Spain and Switzerland, had increased substantially. At the same time, opportunities for escape declined abruptly. On 4 August 1942 the Swiss government issued a presidential decree in an effort to stem the 'influx of alien civilian refugees': this influx, it was stated, had been 'found to be increasingly

209 Sabine Zeitoun, *L'Œuvre de secours aux enfants (OSE) sous l'Occupation en France* (Paris: L'Harmattan, 2012); Grynberg, *Les Camps de la honte*, pp. 303–306; Renée Poznanski, *Jews in France during World War II*, trans. Nathan Bracher (Hanover: University Press of New England, 2001 [French edn, 1997]), pp. 282–283; Patrick Cabanel, *Histoire des Justes en France* (Paris: A. Colin, 2012), pp. 157–159.

210 Recollections of Sasha Racine Maidenberg, in Leblanc and Chevallier, *Mémoires de la Shoah*, p. 105.

211 Arno Lustiger, *Rettungswiderstand: Über die Judenretter in Europa während der NS-Zeit* (Göttingen: Wallstein, 2011), pp. 209–210.

organized' and facilitated 'by professional "passeurs" [smugglers]'. The cantons were now required to expel foreigners who had entered the country illegally, 'even if serious disadvantages (danger to life and limb) might arise from this for the foreigners affected'.[212] At that point the Swiss authorities already had information about the fate of Jews who had been deported to Poland, even though they were not yet aware of the Germans' policy of systematic murder. Not only Jews but also communist refugees now had little chance of being admitted to Switzerland. The elderly and the sick, adolescents travelling alone, families with children under sixteen, and pregnant women were considered hardship cases and exempted from deportation. Part of the Swiss population reacted with outrage to the expulsions, whereupon the Swiss authorities relaxed the measures temporarily. During the months that followed, several thousand refugees successfully crossed the border, which was only guarded fairly lightly, into Switzerland. However, the decree was not definitively rescinded until July 1944.

The escape routes from France mostly ran via Geneva, Lake Geneva, and the difficult terrain of the Jura Mountains. The focus was on the border at Geneva, where approximately 200 border crossings were recorded in August 1942, a further 2,000 in September 1942, and 1,300 in October 1942. Of the 9,860 Jewish refugees who by August 1944 had attempted to reach Switzerland, 9,000 did indeed find asylum there.[213] The number of border crossings increased again when the Germans occupied the southern zone in November 1942, and then the Italian zone in September 1943. Crossing the Pyrenees into Spain involved ever greater obstacles. Since November 1942, in addition to the French gendarmerie, German mountain troops had been guarding this border (Doc. 282). In February 1943 the area along the border was declared a restricted zone, with access to non-residents prohibited.[214]

Elli and Hans Friedländer were among those who sought to cross the border illegally in the late summer of 1942. In their despair they had entrusted their 9-year-old son to a Catholic boarding school in Montluçon, in the Auvergne, and agreed to his baptism. Elli Friedländer wrote at the end of August: 'If we must perish, we have one piece of great good fortune: the knowledge that our beloved child has been saved' (Doc. 261). A few weeks later, the couple's attempt to find safety in Switzerland failed (Doc. 278). The Swiss authorities handed over Elli and Hans Friedländer to the French gendarmerie, who transferred them to the assembly camp at Rivesaltes, from which Jews were taken to Drancy (Doc. 279). Just three days later, on 1 October 1942, refugees caught at the border ceased to be automatically handed over to the French authorities. Instead, they

212 Nationale Kommission für die Veröffentlichung Diplomatischer Dokumente der Schweiz, *Diplomatische Dokumente der Schweiz*, vol. 14 (Bern: Benteli, 1997), p. 720; see also Unabhängige Expertenkommission Schweiz – Zweiter Weltkrieg, *Die Schweiz und die Flüchtlinge zur Zeit des Nationalsozialismus* (Bern: Unabhängige Expertenkommission Schweiz – Zweiter Weltkrieg, 1999), pp. 93–94, 135, and 138; Unabhängige Expertenkommission Schweiz – Zweiter Weltkrieg, *Die Schweiz, der Nationalsozialismus und der Zweite Weltkrieg: Schlussbericht* (Zurich: Pendo, 2002), p. 116; and Georg Kreis (ed.), *Switzerland and the Second World War* (London: Routledge, 2014).

213 Fivaz-Silbermann, 'Une migration urgente', p. 109; Ruth Fivaz-Silbermann, 'Refoulement, accueil, filières: Les fugitifs juifs à la frontière franco-genevoise entre 1942 et 1944', in *Schweizerische Zeitschrift für Geschichte*, 51 (2001), pp. 296–317, here p. 298.

214 Robert Belot, *Aux frontières de la liberté: Vichy-Madrid-Alger-Londres. S'évader de France sous l'Occupation* (Paris: Fayard, 1998), pp. 76–80; Lustiger, *Rettungswiderstand*, p. 214.

were sent back – covertly – across the unmanned section of the land border. One month later the Friedländers were deported to Auschwitz, where they both perished. Their son survived, later took the name 'Saul' and became one of the most distinguished historians of the Holocaust.[215]

Police operations against Jews and the handover of Jews to the German occupiers frequently elicited outrage and sympathy among the French population. The press in both zones ignored the arrests for the most part, but the negative reactions filtered through in the reports on public sentiment compiled by the prefectures. The outrage intensified when leading representatives of the Catholic and Protestant churches repeatedly lodged protests with Pétain and also publicly protested against the deportation of the Jews (Doc. 246). On 23 August 1942, three days before the large roundup in the southern zone, the archbishop of Toulouse, Monseigneur Jules-Gérard Saliège, ordered that a letter be read aloud in the churches of his diocese. In this much-heeded text he publicly condemned the action being taken against the Jews. On 30 August the bishop of Montauban, Pierre-Marie Théas, followed suit with a similar initiative, and on 22 September Marc Boegner, head of the Protestant Association, also had a letter read out.[216]

During the night of 7/8 November 1942, Allied troops landed in Morocco and Algeria and opened the way for the Gaullist Free French Forces to enter these two regions. The strategic location of North Africa, which made an Allied landing on the coast of Western Europe substantially easier, meant Germany's supremacy in this part of Europe was directly threatened. In reaction, the Wehrmacht occupied the previously unoccupied southern zone of France.[217] Approximately 120,000 Jews were living in Algeria at the time of liberation in November 1942, but they had to wait until mid March 1943 for the repeal of the Vichy regime's antisemitic laws and regulations (Doc. 284). The Crémieux Decree that in 1870 had granted French citizenship to the Jews of Algeria and had been revoked by the Vichy government in the autumn of 1940 was reinstated in October 1943 following a declaration by the French National Liberation Committee.[218]

In Tunisia, by contrast, the situation for the estimated 66,000 Jews worsened dramatically in the same period. One third of the country, including Tunis, the capital, lay between two military fronts and was occupied by German and Italian troops in November 1942. During the six months of the German-Italian occupation, the Jewish popula-

215 See Saul Friedländer's own account in Saul Friedländer, *When Memory Comes* (New York: Avon Books, 1980), pp. 88–90. See also Ruth Fivaz-Silbermann, *Le Refoulement de réfugiés civils juifs à la frontière franco-genevoise durant la Seconde Guerre mondiale, suivi du mémorial de ceux parmi eux qui ont été déportés ou fusillés* (Paris: Klarsfeld Foundation, 2000), pp. 9–10.

216 Grynberg, *Les Camps de la honte*, pp. 323–326; Cabanel, *Histoire des Justes en France*, pp. 165–168; Klarsfeld, *Calendrier*, p. 632; Klarsfeld, *Vichy–Auschwitz*, pp. 176–179, 209; Poznanski, *Jews in France during World War II*, pp. 292–302.

217 What had hitherto been known as the *zone libre* or 'free zone' was now referred to as the southern zone.

218 Michel Abitbol, *The Jews of North Africa during the Second World War* (Detroit: Wayne State University Press, 1989), pp. 159–165; André Kaspi, *Les Juifs pendant l'Occupation* (Paris: Seuil, 1997), p. 206; Daniel J. Schroeter, 'Between Metropole and French North Africa: Vichy's Anti-Semitic Legislation and Colonialism's Racial Hierarchies', in Aomar Boum and Sarah Abrevaya Stein (eds.), *The Holocaust and North Africa* (Stanford: Stanford University Press, 2019), pp. 19–49. On the stance of the French churches, see Sylvie Bernay, *L'Église de France face à la persécution des Juifs, 1940–1944* (Paris: CNRS Éditions, 2012).

tion – with the exception of Italian citizens – was subject to persecution by the Tunis Einsatzkommando, which was led by Walther Rauff.[219] Indiscriminate and organized theft, forced labour and terror characterized the everyday life of the Jews (Doc. 303). Moïse Borgel, chairman of Tunisia's Jewish community, later recounted the arrest of the men, for the most part teachers, found in the school run by the Alliance israélite universelle in Tunis. German soldiers beat them with whips and forced them on a march of 65 kilometres. To put an end to the excesses committed against individuals during the first days of the occupation, senior figures in the Jewish community complied with German orders. They provided several thousand workers to develop the German-Italian line of defence, and they collected money and took out a bank loan to pay the 'fine' of 20 million francs that had been imposed on the community. This penalty had been levied as compensation for the damages inflicted by Allied bombing. Owing to the difficult transport situation, systematic deportations to Germany never took place, although Rauff had approximately twenty Tunisian Jews taken to German concentration camps, where most of them perished. Among them were Joseph Scemla, a textile dealer in Tunis, and his two sons, Gilbert and Jean, both students. In March 1943 they had tried to cross the border to Algeria and seek refuge with the Free French forces, but had been betrayed in the process. Following their arrest by German soldiers, they were taken to Germany by plane and placed in Dachau concentration camp, where, in May 1944, they were sentenced to death for espionage. They were executed two months later. During the six-month period of occupation, approximately 5,000 labourers were forcibly recruited. The number of Jewish victims during the German occupation in Tunisia is probably between 50 and 100.[220]

After the occupation of the southern zone of France by the Wehrmacht – whereupon the Italian army ordered its occupying troops to advance to the banks of the Rhône – the Office of the Higher SS and Police Leader was the only German authority in Paris that managed to extend its activities to include the newly occupied territory. Berlin declared this area an 'Operational Zone' and placed it under the control of the Commander-in-Chief West. The newly established Einsatzkommandos of the German police in the regional prefectures now had access to areas where Jews had thus far largely escaped persecution. According to German instructions, every assassination attempt by the French resistance movement was to be followed by arrests of Jews – they were to be tracked down in trains, at railway stations, and in other public spaces, and taken into custody. For this operation the German police were still able to count on the help of the French. On 9 November 1942

219 In dealing with the Reich Foreign Office, the Italian embassy in Berlin emphatically insisted that Jews who were Italian citizens be exempt from all anti-Jewish measures in Tunisia: Abitbol, *The Jews of North Africa during the Second World War*, pp. 120–121; Martin Cüppers, *Walther Rauff – in deutschen Diensten: Vom Naziverbrecher zum BND-Spion* (Darmstadt: Wissenschaftliche Buchgesellschaft, 2013).

220 Account by Moïse Borgel, 15 May 1943, published in Claude Nataf (ed.), *Les Juifs de Tunisie sous le joug nazi, 9 novembre 1942–8 mai 1943* (Paris: Manuscrit, 2012), pp. 25–38, quote: p. 30; Frédéric Gasquet, *La Lettre de mon père: Une famille de Tunis dans l'enfer nazi* (Paris: Le Félin, 2006); Abitbol, *The Jews of North Africa during the Second World War*, pp. 119–121 and 130; Kaspi, *Les Juifs pendant l'Occupation*, pp. 204–206; Cüppers, *Walther Rauff*, p. 176; Filippo Petrucci, *Gli ebrei in Algeria e in Tunisia 1940–1943* (Florence: Giuntina, 2011), pp. 150–214.

the French government issued a law prohibiting foreign Jews from moving freely from place to place or leaving their location of residence without explicit permission from the police. Although the Jews in the newly occupied zone remained exempt from the requirement to wear the yellow star, the law of 11 December 1942 made it obligatory for all identity documents and food ration cards to be stamped with the word 'Jew'. The Italian occupation authorities refused to implement such measures in their zone.[221]

In a meeting with Heinrich Himmler on 10 December 1942, Hitler – doubtless in anticipation of a future Allied landing – ordered the 'removal' (*Abschaffung*) of all Jews and 'other enemies' from France. This order led to the second major wave of deportations from France, in the course of which around 8,000 persons were transported to Auschwitz, Lublin-Majdanek, and Sobibor between 9 February and 25 March 1943.[222] To this end the German police authorities called for the remaining Jews in the internment camps of the southern zone to be handed over, while the commanders of the Security Police in the 'old' occupied zone received instructions to arrest and transfer to Drancy everyone who was eligible for deportation. The German authorities were determined no longer to permit any distinctions to be made between French and foreign Jews.[223]

In January 1943 roundups of Jews took place in Rouen and Marseilles, in both cases in the aftermath of assassination attempts by the French resistance movement. Following a German directive, on 12 January 1943 the French police arrested 222 Jews in Rouen, most of whom were French citizens.[224] For Marseilles, Reichsführer-SS Himmler had designed a 'radical and perfect solution [...] for clearing up the situation'. With the assistance of the French police and the Gardes mobiles, this involved carrying out mass arrests, which also affected Jews, and blowing up the port area which, with its large number of winding alleys and even subterranean passageways, offered an ideal hiding place (and not just for members of the resistance).[225] On 22 and 23 January 1943 French police arrested almost 6,000 people in Marseilles, 1,642 of whom were handed over to the occupation authorities and taken to Compiègne camp, north of Paris, the next day. Among them were many French Jews, who were transferred one month later to Drancy and shortly afterwards deported to Sobibor and Lublin-Majdanek (Docs. 287 and 298).

221 Michael R. Marrus and Robert O. Paxton, *Vichy France and the Jews* (Stanford: Stanford University Press, 1996), pp. 304–305. In the 'old' occupied zone such a stamp had been mandatory since the autumn of 1940.

222 Heinrich Himmler, *Der Dienstkalender Heinrich Himmlers 1941/42*, ed. Peter Witte, Michael Wildt, and Martina Voigt (Hamburg: Christians, 1999), p. 637. 'Other enemies' referred to Gaullists, the British, Americans (they were to be arrested), 'Red Spaniards' ('to be fed into the labour process' – presumably a reference to Organization Todt), and 'antifascist Italians', with 'truly dangerous figures' to be put in a German concentration camp. Deportation numbers from Klarsfeld, *Vichy-Auschwitz*, p. 370.

223 Knochen had raised this topic in discussion with the Reich Security Main Office on 21 Jan. 1943 and made reference to the 2,159 French Jews who were in Drancy camp in mid January. Eichmann's deputy, Günther, stated in his reply dated 25 Jan. 1943 that French Jews could also be deported: Klarsfeld, *Calendrier*, pp. 1318–1319 and 1331–1332.

224 Klarsfeld, *Vichy-Auschwitz*, pp. 230–231.

225 Himmler to the Higher SS and Police Leader in France, Oberg, 18 Jan. 1943, BArch, NS 19/2799 and NS 19/3402, published in Ahlrich Meyer (ed.), *Der Blick des Besatzers: Propagandaphotographie der Wehrmacht aus Marseille 1942–1944. Le regard de l'occupant* (Bremen: Edition Temmen, 1999), p. 171.

Simultaneously, SS Police Regiment Griese sealed off the northern part of the port neighbourhood and had its 20,000 inhabitants deported and temporarily interned in Fréjus, where German police selected persons for transport on to Compiègne (Doc. 306). In the first two weeks of February 1943, the Wehrmacht blew up the now-vacated port area.[226]

The roundups in Marseilles and Rouen, which were carried out primarily by French police, were 'special operations' insofar as they had been ordered by the German occupiers as reprisals for operations carried out by the resistance movement. With these exceptions, the French authorities continued to refuse to arrest French Jews. However, the French and German police cooperated effectively in tracking down foreign Jews, as was the case during the night of 10/11 February 1943, when 1,549 Jews were arrested in Paris. They included children who were living in the homes of the UGIF, as well as patients at the Rothschild Hospital, but it was primarily elderly people who were arrested; the average age of those detained was sixty-four.[227] Rachel Jedinak, who in July 1942 had managed to escape with her sister from internment in the Vélodrome d'Hiver, was now arrested for a second time, along with her grandmother. Jedinak recalled:

> They command us, my grandmother, my sister and me, to pack our things. Luckily, my uncle and aunt spent this night elsewhere. The concierge let them into one of the sealed apartments in the building. My grandfather can't be transported, so the police, without any qualms, decide to leave him behind, entirely alone. How could one ever forget the heart-wrenching parting of my grandparents?[228]

Rachel Jedinak, together with her sister and mother, succeeded in escaping her pursuers once again, but most of those detained were deported to Poland at the beginning of March.

After the French resistance movement assassinated two German officers in Paris, the order was issued to deport an additional 2,000 Jews. To prevent the inclusion of French citizens, the French police initiated an arrest operation in the southern zone on 20 February 1943 that targeted foreign male Jews between the ages of eighteen and sixty-five. The 1,778 men affected were deported on 4 and 6 March to Sobibor, where they were murdered.[229]

The second wave of deportations, which began early in 1943, again raised the question of French police collaboration. The deportations initially targeted many French Jews who had already been interned in Drancy camp for months or had been arrested in Rouen and Marseilles (Doc. 286). The continuation of the transports, however, depended on the renewed cooperation of the French police (Doc. 292). To expand the category of Jews who were 'able to be deported' (Jews without French citizenship), the German occupiers had already contemplated a collective denaturalization procedure as early as July 1942, and Prime Minister Laval had agreed to this in principle in August 1942 (Doc. 252). By

226 Ibid., pp. 26–29; Poznanski, *Jews in France during World War II*, pp. 371–373.

227 Wieviorka and Laffitte, *À l'intérieur du camp de Drancy*, p. 211; Klarsfeld, *Vichy–Auschwitz*, pp. 234–235.

228 Recollections of Rachel Jedinak, in Leblanc and Chevallier, *Mémoires de la Shoah*, p. 112.

229 Poznanski, *Jews in France during World War II*, p. 375; Klarsfeld, *Vichy–Auschwitz*, pp. 243–244.

December 1942 France's Commissariat General for Jewish Affairs had prepared a draft law on the deprivation of French citizenship for Jews naturalized after 1927. In addition, foreign Jews were as a rule to be denied naturalization in the future. The French government suggested moving the cut-off year from 1927 to 1932, which would still have meant around 20,000 people being deprived of French citizenship, but not the 50,000 envisaged in the draft by the Commissariat General, which was based on the German proposals. Röthke – the German official in charge of Jewish affairs – and Commissioner General for Jewish Affairs Darquier de Pellepoix forced through the original version.[230]

On this basis the German authorities prepared for the mass arrest of all Jews whose citizenship was to be revoked if granted later than 1927. At dawn on 24 June 1943, a few hours before the text of the regulation was made public, several thousand Jews were to be arrested by the French police, under German supervision. A special commando (Sonderkommando) led by SS-Hauptsturmführer Alois Brunner had been summoned to Paris especially for this purpose, the same unit that had previously set in motion the deportation of 43,000 Jews from Thessaloniki.[231] The date for the operation was postponed several times, and in the end the plan could not be carried out because Laval, with reference to the planned arrests that he had explicitly rejected, prevented the text of the regulation from being released. When Marshal Pétain officially confirmed this decision at the end of August 1943, it was clear that in this instance the French authorities would not cooperate. Röthke reacted by announcing that in future the German authorities would no longer distinguish between French Jews and foreign Jews. As early as July 1943, in a report on the 'present status of the Jewish question in France', he had made it known that if the denaturalization plan were to fall through, the German police and military forces would arrest every Jew they could get their hands on.[232]

During the first half of 1943, tensions also developed between the German and Italian occupying forces as a result of the German operations against the Jews. Immediately after the occupation of the southern zone in November 1942, German police authorities had ordered the resettlement of the Jews living in départements along the border and on the coast – including the area under Italian jurisdiction – to specific départements that were under German control. Jews who were potentially liable to deportation were to be taken straight to Drancy. The Italians put a stop to the plan for their area of influence, and open conflict broke out between the Italian and French authorities. The latter complained to the German Security Police. The Italian Armistice Commission in Turin forbade the French government to intern persons 'of the Jewish race' in the Italian zone.[233] Word

230 Joly, *Vichy dans la 'solution finale'*, pp. 716–723, text of the law reproduced on p. 717.

231 Hans Safrian, *Eichmann's Men*, trans. Ute Stargardt (Cambridge: Cambridge University Press, 2010 [German edn, 1993]), pp. 157–167. Klarsfeld, *Vichy–Auschwitz*, p. 274. Brunner's official position with respect to the Senior Commander of the Security Police (BdS) and his Dept. IV B4 seems unclear; presumably Brunner was directly subordinate to the Reich Security Main Office, as suggested in Meyer, *Täter im Verhör*, p. 192.

232 Report by Röthke, dated 21 July 1943, published in Klarsfeld, *Calendrier*, pp. 1583–1584.

233 Eberhard Jäckel, *Frankreich in Hitlers Europa: Die deutsche Frankreichpolitik im Zweiten Weltkrieg* (Stuttgart: Deutsche Verlags-Anstalt, 1966), p. 257; Marrus and Paxton, *Vichy France and the Jews*, pp. 315–321; Poznanski, *Jews in France during World War II*, pp. 386–390; Klarsfeld, *Vichy–Auschwitz*, p. 225.

spread very quickly, and tens of thousands of Jewish refugees sought shelter in the Italian zone of occupation.[234] In a report dated April 1943, Joseph Weill described the resultant onset of an 'out-and-out migration' (Doc. 299).

In mid February 1943 Helmut Knochen, Senior Commander of the Security Police, emphasized in a letter to the Reich Security Main Office that the inclusion of the Italian zone was a precondition for the planned deportations from 'France as a whole', noting that 'the migration of Jews into the Italian-occupied territory, which has already begun, would otherwise assume vast proportions' (Doc. 292). The Italian occupation authorities also vehemently opposed the French roundup on 20 February 1943, and anyone who had been arrested in the Italian zone had to be released. French protests at Italy's policy of obstruction were channelled from Paris to Berlin. The Reich Foreign Office already faced a similar situation in Croatia, which was partly occupied by the Italian army, alongside the German Wehrmacht. On 25 February 1943 Reich Foreign Minister Ribbentrop discussed this issue with Mussolini for the first time. One month later, on Ribbentrop's instructions, the German ambassador in Rome was supposed to increase the pressure on Mussolini (Doc. 296). But it became clear that Rome was continuing its placatory approach and delaying tactics, especially where Berlin was concerned.[235]

For the Jews the situation had deteriorated dramatically since the Wehrmacht had taken control of the southern zone. Many employees of the relief organizations that were part of the UGIF were arrested in 1943, and as a result the organizations had to discontinue their activities in the second half of the year.[236] In February 1943 a roundup spearheaded by Klaus Barbie, head of Department IV in the Office of the Commander of the Security Police and the SD in Lyons, heralded the end of the protection that the UGIF's employees had largely enjoyed (Doc. 291). At the end of November 1942 Darquier de Pellepoix had already ordered lists to be submitted of all UGIF employees in both zones. The lists were to record their address, citizenship, and date of naturalization, if any. Shortly afterwards Darquier de Pellepoix demanded the dismissal of non-French personnel by the end of February 1943, obviously again with the aim of enlarging the set of 'Jews able to be deported'. The heads of the two sections of the UGIF obtained an extension of the deadline to the end of March 1943 and a slight reduction in the number of dismissals. However, on 5 March the Commissariat General for Jewish Affairs provided the German Security Police with a list of the UGIF's foreign employees. It contained the names of 297 persons in total, 129 men and 168 women, listed by nationality. Although both the Commissariat General and the German authorities had been assured that those

234 See Meyer, *Täter im Verhör*, p. 187. Serge Klarsfeld estimates at 25,000 the number of (primarily foreign) Jews who were already present in the Italian zone on 1 Jan. 1943. The number increased rapidly after the roundups in Marseilles: Klarsfeld, *Vichy–Auschwitz*, p. 223. Renée Poznanski estimates at 30,000 the number of Jews who had been able to live fairly protected for several months owing to the attitude of the Italian authorities: Poznanski, *Jews in France during World War II*, p. 393. On the Italian zone of occupation, see Jean-Louis Panicacci, *L'Occupation italienne: Sud-Est de la France, juin 1940 – septembre 1943* (Rennes: Presses universitaires de Rennes, 2010).

235 Klarsfeld, *Vichy–Auschwitz*, pp. 246–247; Saul Friedländer, *The Years of Extermination: Nazi Germany and the Jews, 1933–1945* (London: HarperCollins, 2007), pp. 452–454; Daniel Carpi, *Between Mussolini and Hitler: The Jews and the Italian Authorities in France and Tunisia* (Hanover, NH: University Press of New England, 1994), pp. 102–135.

236 Poznanski, *Jews in France during World War II*, pp. 373–377.

affected would continue to be protected until the end of the month, Röthke ordered their arrest (Doc. 295), and approximately sixty of them were detained. Presumably some of the individuals involved had realized the danger or received advance warning. In addition, most of the addresses given to the Commissariat General were incorrect.[237]

The number of persons who opted to live in hiding increased rapidly in 1943. Not all of them were Jews; they included many non-Jewish Frenchmen, who since February 1943 could be called up for mandatory labour service (*service du travail obligatoire*, STO) in Germany.[238] The members of the Jewish-communist resistance movement already had experience of life underground, owing to the banning of the Communist Party in 1939, and therefore had the most efficient organization. Their output included numerous publications addressed to the Jewish population in French or Yiddish, as in the case of the newspaper *Unzer Wort*. Most of the material published illegally by the movement was, however, aimed at the French population as a whole and intended as a call for solidarity. From February 1943 the National Movement Against Racism (MNCR) encouraged solidarity through resistance newspapers such as *Notre voix*, *J'accuse* and *Fraternité* (Doc. 308). The papers provided detailed reports of roundups and the crimes against Jews in France or in the East, which the authorized press failed to mention at all.[239]

The armed Jewish resistance was largely communist-organized at first, particularly in the immigrant sections of the partisan organization Francs-tireurs et partisans – Main-d'œuvre immigrée (FTP-MOI). Its activities were directed against the German occupiers and their institutions and against French collaborators. Additionally, acts of sabotage targeted major infrastructure facilities such as railway lines and telephone lines. A group of young men in Toulouse founded the Zionist resistance group known as the Armée juive (Jewish Army), which was subsequently joined by the Jewish scouting movement in France (Éclaireurs israélites de France), which had gone underground in 1943, and the Zionist youth organization.[240] The Armée juive had branches in several large cities in the southern zone such as Lyons, Grenoble, and Nice. Jacques Lazarus wrote about the Armée juive in Nice, which had around fifteen members, both boys and girls. At its 'meetings [or] in the street, they exchanged the latest news and compared the lists of "those lost and those saved". The leaders handed out the money that was to be distributed, but also, in particular, envelopes that were full of false papers of all sorts'[241] (see also Doc. 319). In addition to helping people escape across the Swiss or Spanish border, the groups that made up the Armée juive sought to acquire information and to combat informers and collaborating French authorities. The cover of its Paris branch was blown in July 1944 by a double agent who claimed to be employed by the British intelligence

237 Michel Laffitte, *Juif dans la France allemande: Institutions, dirigeants et communautés au temps de la Shoah* (Paris: Tallandier, 2006), pp. 179–187.

238 On the history of the STO, see Patrice Arnaud, *Les STO: Histoire des Français requis en Allemagne nazie, 1942–1945* (Paris: CNRS Éditions, 2010); and Raphaël Spina, *Histoire du STO* (Paris: Perrin, 2017).

239 Poznanski, *Jews in France during World War II*, pp. 346–351; see also Adam Rayski, *Nos illusions perdues* (Paris: Balland, 1985).

240 Daniel Lee, *Pétain's Jewish Children: French Jewish Youth and the Vichy Regime, 1940–1942* (Oxford: Oxford University Press, 2014), pp. 181–184.

241 Jacques Lazarus, 'Juifs au combat', in Marek Halter (ed.), *Les Révoltés de la Shoah: Témoignages et récits* (Paris: Omnibus, 2010), pp. 40–41.

service and was simultaneously working for the Abwehr, the German military intelligence office. Also exposed through betrayal was the Westerweel Group, which had worked with the Armée juive to smuggle hundreds of young people out of the Netherlands to Spain, via Belgium and France (Doc. 335).

Allied forces landed in southern Italy in early July 1943. Consequently, that summer the Wehrmacht began to prepare to take over the Italian zones of occupation, including those in France. In early September Röthke and Brunner devised a plan for the arrest of the Jewish refugees in the Italian zone, who had been largely spared thus far (Doc. 310). After the proclamation of the armistice between Italy and the Allies on 8 September 1943, German troops promptly occupied this zone. A relentless manhunt was launched the same day. An anonymous account describes the arrests that began on 10 September in Nice, where there were more than 20,000 Jews: 'Without wasting any time, the Germans began persecuting the Jews 48 hours after their arrival [in the city].' Residential neighbourhoods were sealed off; 'physiognomists', who claimed to be able to recognize Jews by their facial characteristics, drove through the streets, and 'an army of informers got down to work'. Checks conducted at railway stations thwarted numerous escape attempts.[242] As the yellow star had never been introduced in the unoccupied zone, and as identity documents and food ration cards had thus far only rarely been stamped and were frequently counterfeit, Brunner resorted to his own methods. He ordered individuals who had been arrested as the result of (paid) reports, submitted openly or anonymously, to be taken to his headquarters in the Hotel Excelsior in Nice, where 'experts' were to examine them for physical similarities to Jews. For men circumcision was the decisive criterion. Under torture, those arrested were also interrogated about the whereabouts of relatives, and they were subsequently transferred to Drancy. From mid September to mid December 1943 Brunner's staff arrested more than 1,800 Jews in Nice and the surrounding area by this method alone.[243] Among those placed under arrest was the father of lawyer and Holocaust historian Serge Klarsfeld, who had taken the precaution of setting up a hiding place for his family behind a wardrobe:

> We heard the soldiers beating the Jewish neighbours and the children to make them disclose their brothers' hiding places. My mother, my sister and I went to the hiding place, and my father stayed. He opened the front door and claimed that we were out in the countryside. The Germans searched, they pushed the clothes in the wardrobe in all directions, but did not touch the interior wall.[244]

In the autumn of 1943 the Security Police and mobile Einsatzkommandos also intensified the persecution of Jews in other places in the southern zone, detaining Jews regardless of nationality, gender, or age, in line with Röthke's announcement. Jean-Jacques Becker observed the new methods in Grenoble:

242 Anonymous account, 'Nizza', dated 20 Dec. 1943, Mémorial de la Shoah, Paris, CCCLXVI-64.

243 Wieviorka and Laffitte, *À l'intérieur du camp de Drancy*, p. 261; Poznanski, *Jews in France during World War II*, pp. 390–391; Meyer, *Täter im Verhör*, pp. 194–198.

244 Reminiscences of Serge Klarsfeld, in Murielle Allouche and Jean-Yves Masson, *Ce qu'il reste de nous: Les déportés et leurs familles témoignent* (Paris: Michel Lafon, 2005), p. 194.

> German soldiers, who had arrived unobtrusively, suddenly blocked a square, a crossroads, frequented by many people. Everyone who was there was subsequently searched, interrogated and – if suspicious for one reason or another – placed under arrest.[245]

After Brunner's Sonderkommando took over Drancy camp, now called an 'emigration camp', or an 'assembly camp', the situation for the camp inmates deteriorated dramatically. The French officials from the prefecture of the Seine département were forced to leave the camp; only the French gendarmerie remained behind, as the outer guard. Inside the camp, Brunner had a separate security force established, made up of Jewish prisoners. The buildings were renovated and workshops set up. Brunner also introduced new punishments, such as beatings, torture, and detention in the cellars. His task was to arrange for the quick resumption of deportations to the extermination camps in the East, which had been suspended since the end of March 1943. Shortly before the first convoys left, Brunner personally interrogated the prisoners in order to assign them to groups, labelled 'A' to 'F', that were deemed either 'able to be deported' or 'not able to be deported'.[246] The internees who were earmarked for deportation were informed: 'We are sending you to labour camps, where you will live with your families and be paid for the work you do' (Doc. 334). Their heads were not shaved again before their departure. To increase the number of persons being deported, prisoners at the camp were forced to travel as so-called *missionnaires* (envoys) to Paris and the various regions of France to track down other Jews in hiding. Their family members stayed behind in the camp as hostages for the next deportation. By early September 1943 most of those found 'able to be deported' had left Drancy on four transport trains; one month later the deportations of those apprehended on the Côte d'Azur began. The leaders of the UGIF were now also affected. Raymond-Raoul Lambert and André Baur, together with their families, were deported to Auschwitz on 7 and 17 December 1943. Lambert was murdered upon arrival; Baur perished at Auschwitz in April 1944.

During this new phase, which was heavily influenced by Brunner and ran from the resumption of the deportations in June 1943 until their discontinuation in August 1944, Reich Railways trains transported almost 24,000 persons from France to the extermination camps in the East.[247]

Under the French chief of police, Bousquet, French Jews had been included in roundups only in exceptional cases. In late 1943, under German pressure, he had to vacate his position. He was replaced by Joseph Darnand, commander of the Milice française, the Vichy regime's paramilitary police force, who became secretary general for public order. Darnand was prepared to collaborate unconditionally with the Germans. As French police were proving less and less willing to take part in mass arrests, the Milice now played

245 Becker, *Un soir de l'été 1942 …*, p. 102.

246 Wieviorka and Laffitte, *À l'intérieur du camp de Drancy*, p. 219. From the end of June 1943, these interrogations were carried out by his assistants, Ernst Brückler and Josef Weiszl: ibid., pp. 222 and 226.

247 Meyer, *Täter im Verhör*, pp. 191–193; Wieviorka and Laffitte, *À l'intérieur du camp de Drancy*, pp. 249 and 255. The number of those additionally arrested in this way by September 1943 – mostly children and older relatives of Jews who were already interned – is estimated at 200 to 300.

an increasingly significant role in the persecution of Jews, members of the resistance movement, and those who were evading conscription for forced labour.[248] In addition, during the last months of the occupation many French Jews in the provinces were arrested and deported, for example in Bordeaux in late December 1943 and in Laon, Saint-Quentin, and Amiens in January 1944. Some prefects were troubled by these events. In Amiens, Charles Daupeyroux appealed to several higher-level French authorities, urgently requesting that they intervene (Doc. 320). Shortly thereafter he was relieved of his duties.

In Paris the municipal police focused on persecuting foreign Jews, while the Criminal Police continued to deliver to Drancy French Jews who had violated anti-Jewish regulations. The efforts by the German police to step up the deportations in the final months of the occupation are evident in the 'Information Leaflet on Increasing the Number of Jews Arrested', signed by Helmut Knochen, Senior Commander of the Security Police, and edited by Alois Brunner. Dated mid April 1944, the leaflet records, among other things, that nationality played no role in the arrests and that the 'entire network of relatives' was to be included (Doc. 329). Aline Vidal-Naquet almost fell victim to this new zeal. When the 11-year-old came out of school in Marseilles on 15 May 1944, a friend was waiting to warn her that she should not go home, because her parents had been arrested.[249] Soon afterwards the couple were deported via Drancy to Auschwitz, where they both perished. Their four children, one of whom, Pierre Vidal-Naquet, later became a historian of classical antiquity, managed to hide in the homes of acquaintances and thereby survived the war.

The Allied landings in Normandy on 6 June 1944 led to a sharp reduction in the number of detainees being transferred from the provinces to Drancy, so Brunner decided to concentrate on the Jews in Paris. In mid June Knochen briefed Military Commander Carl Heinrich von Stülpnagel, but von Stülpnagel opposed the plan because 'it [would] only bring turmoil to the thus far tranquil population of Paris'.[250] In any case Brunner was not in a position to execute his plan. Since the end of February 1944, the German police had been demanding the handover of the lists kept in the police prefecture that contained the names and addresses of the French Jews in Paris. The lists were not submitted to the Germans until early August, after several requests had been made to senior authorities, and the large-scale roundup sought by Brunner never took place. On 20 July 1944, however, he did manage to initiate the arrest of the children who had been taken in at the eleven homes of the UGIF in the Paris area following the deportation of their parents. Among them was Charlotte Schapira, who described in her memoirs the moment of terror when the police raided the home at 2 a.m. Between 21 and 25 July, 233 children were taken to Drancy, and most of them were deported to Auschwitz on 31 July.[251] The last transport, accompanied by Alois Brunner, left Drancy on 17 August 1944 with fifty-one deportees,

248 Kasten, *'Gute Franzosen'*, pp. 120–123 and 172.

249 Diary of Aline Vidal-Naquet, 15 May 1944, reproduced in facsimile in Pierre Vidal-Naquet, *Mémoires*, vol. 1: *La Brisure et l'attente, 1930–1955* (Paris: Seuil, 2007 [1995]), p. 135.

250 BA-MA, RH 19 IV, OB West, Ic, war journal (brief daily notes), fol. 134, records of the phone calls taken on 12 and 13 June 1944. We are grateful to Peter Lieb for bringing this document to our attention.

251 Charlotte Schapira, *Il faudra que je me souvienne: La déportation des enfants de l'Union générale des Israélites de France* (Paris: L'Harmattan, 1994), p. 48; Klarsfeld, *Vichy–Auschwitz*, pp. 343–344.

bound for Buchenwald. One week later, on 24 August, Allied and Gaullist armed forces under General Leclerc marched into Paris. At the end of November 1944 they liberated Strasbourg, and in February 1945 all of eastern France. A few harbour towns in western France that had been fortified held out until April 1945.

By Serge Klarsfeld's reckoning, between 1942 and 1944 a total of 73,853 Jews were deported from France to the extermination camps in the East, including 11,000 children – approximately 25 per cent of France's Jewish population prior to the occupation. Two thirds of them, or 56,500, did not hold French citizenship.[252] In addition, 3,000 Jews died in the French internment camps.

*

A comparison of the countries of Western Europe reveals a number of parallels in the persecution of the Jewish population, along with features specific to each country. In three of the countries – in France, Belgium, and the Netherlands – the timing of the introduction of discriminatory and exclusionary measures against Jews was virtually identical. And everywhere the German occupiers sought to take advantage of xenophobic and antisemitic tendencies already present before the war, and to reinforce them through targeted propaganda. The German officials in charge of Jewish affairs in these three countries also made joint decisions about mass deportation, and they coordinated the logistical preparations. Nonetheless, the percentage of deportees and murder victims among the Jews in each of these countries and in the other countries of Western and Northern Europe varied significantly. While more than 75 per cent of the Jews in the Netherlands lost their lives, the figures for the other countries were lower: approximately 50 per cent in Norway, 45 per cent in Belgium, 34 per cent in Luxembourg, 25 per cent in France, and 2 per cent in Denmark.

The reasons for this disparity are manifold. One variable that needs to be taken into account is the number of foreign or stateless Jews in the individual countries. That figure was small for the Netherlands, but relatively large for France and Belgium. In the latter two countries, foreigners and stateless persons were the first to be deported. This group had had little opportunity to integrate itself into Belgian or French society prior to the occupation. The German authorities declared foreign Jews to be enemies of the German Reich and invoked the laws governing warfare under which an occupying power was allowed to take action against such enemies or to adopt preventive security measures. The domestic authorities offered scant opposition to that line of action, but insisted that Jews who were citizens of the relevant country be exempt from deportation. For their part, the German Security Police made no secret of the fact that Jews who were local nationals would not be spared for long. In early 1943 the second phase of the deportations began, and both native and foreign Jews were targeted for persecution and deportation, without exception. For all Jews in the countries of Western Europe, it was now simply a question of trying to stay alive.

252 From March to November 1942 a total of 41,951 persons were taken to Auschwitz in 43 transports; 810 of these deportees survived the end of the war. Between 1943 and 1944, a total of 31,902 Jews were deported to Auschwitz, Lublin-Majdanek, Sobibor, and Buchenwald, with 1,759 of them surviving. In addition, there were several groups that were deported in separate procedures: Klarsfeld, *Vichy–Auschwitz*, pp. 368–371.

By contrast, most Jews in the Netherlands held Dutch citizenship. They were largely integrated into Dutch society and relied on the protection of the national authorities. Unlike in France and Belgium, in the Netherlands the Germans could not meet their deportation quotas by first rounding up mainly foreign Jews. From the outset, therefore, they were determined to target Jews with Dutch citizenship, and the government departments in The Hague were unable to resist this pressure. Unexpectedly and abruptly exposed to the violence of the German occupation regime, Dutch Jews were left entirely at the Germans' mercy. The vulnerability of the native Dutch Jews was increased by the fact that they had not experienced life as refugees or in hiding.[253] The result was paradoxical: Jews who were not citizens of the country in which they were living were persecuted early on and particularly severely in every country except the Netherlands, where no explicit distinction was made with respect to citizenship. But the number of victims was highest precisely in the Netherlands, where relatively few foreign Jews had lived. Participation in the raids by local police, who were familiar with the local geography, also appears to have played a significant role in the number of Jews seized, a conclusion suggested by the difference in the arrest figures for Brussels and Antwerp in summer 1942.

Another factor to consider is that in each country there was a correlation between the proportion of deportees and the extent to which state structures and institutions had been dismantled by the German occupiers. Prior to the collapse of Nazi rule in 1944–1945, the Danish and French governments had managed over the course of the war to exert some influence on the progress of the persecution of Jews; by contrast, the Netherlands had been placed under German civil administration at the onset of the occupation. The survival of at least 200,000 Jews in France until the retreat of the German occupation troops in the late summer or autumn of 1944 can be attributed not least to the differing circumstances in the various zones of occupation, and in particular to the opportunities for refuge, albeit only temporary, in the unoccupied southern zone. Moreover, it was easier to avoid persecution in a relatively large country like France than in smaller and more densely populated countries such as the Netherlands and Belgium.[254]

Finally, the structural differences between the various German occupation regimes were also of significance for the extent and pace of persecution. Only in the Netherlands was the local police force directly under the control of the German authorities. Here, the occupiers succeeded in enforcing anti-Jewish measures within a short time and, from July 1942, in carrying out deportations steadily and in quick succession. In Norway, command over the police formally resided with the Norwegian collaborationist government, which followed the instructions of the German occupiers without resistance. By contrast, the occupiers in Denmark were dependent on their own forces and could not count on the cooperation of the Danish police. Danish SS volunteers were the only potential auxiliaries who had local knowledge. In Belgium and France, political and economic

253 Griffioen and Zeller, 'Comparing the Persecution of the Jews in the Netherlands, France and Belgium', p. 78.

254 A systematic comparison of the conditions for survival in France is attempted by Jacques Semelin in *Persécution et entraides dans la France occupée: Comment 75% des Juifs en France ont échappé à la mort* (Paris: Les Arènes, 2013), pp. 799–855.

considerations also stood in the way of the relentless persecution of Jews. Here the Germans had to take care to avoid unsettling the local population unduly. They had also to ensure that the national authorities retained the inclination to collaborate, particularly in the case of the police, on whose cooperation they were dependent, not least because local officials had a far better record of success with roundups than the Germans did.

The attitude of the local population was also significant. In Denmark in October 1943 the deportations evidently came to a halt because they met with disapproval among the population. This was also the case for a temporary period in France and Belgium in late autumn 1942. Public opinion was also particularly influenced by the introduction of the conscription of non-Jews for forced labour in Germany – in the Netherlands in April 1942, in Belgium in October 1942, and in France in February 1943. From that point onwards, the Jews could increasingly count on support from segments of the non-Jewish population that had abandoned their previous wait-and-see attitude and turned against the occupiers. In France the conduct of the churches and relief organizations also played a part, as did the impressions left by the mass arrests in July and August 1942, and the deportation of Jewish children. As a result, in the autumn of 1942 the Vichy regime abandoned its policy of negotiation through collaboration and seemingly became more reluctant to be involved in open acts of persecution, though the precise extent of this reluctance remains subject to debate.[255]

When examining the persecution and murder of the Jews in Northern and Western Europe, an additional aspect of local collaboration with Nazi Germany should be considered, namely, volunteering for the Waffen SS and participation in the crimes committed by the Nazi regime in Eastern Europe. Nearly 50,000 so-called Germanic volunteers joined the Waffen SS. The largest group comprised between 23,000 and 25,000 Dutchmen, followed by some 10,000 Flemings, around 6,000 Danes, and approximately 5,000 Norwegians. Smaller numbers came from Wallonia and France and other countries outside Western Europe. There is no information on the involvement of SS volunteers from Wallonia and France who were sent to the Eastern Front from 1943 as part of anti-Jewish operations. However, more evidence is available about Dutch involvement in the practices of antisemitic persecution in Nazi-occupied Eastern Europe. Additionally, between 5,000 and 6,000 Dutch people – farmers, fishermen, construction workers, secretaries, artisans, and entrepreneurs – settled as colonists in the German-occupied Baltics, Belorussia, and Ukraine. They used Jews as forced labourers and were involved in atrocities. Some of these volunteers wrote about their actions and experiences in letters to their families that reveal their identification with German goals in general and towards the Jews.

It is clearly important to highlight the role played by local collaboration and cooperation in the persecution and the murder of the Jews of Western and Northern Europe. However, the overall picture of local responses remains complex. Obvious paradoxes remain: there is no direct correlation to be observed between the extent of antisemitism in individual countries during the decades preceding occupation and the subsequent proportion of Jews deported from each country. In the Netherlands antisemitism was

255 The exact reasons for the relatively high survival rate in France have been the subject of intense debate in recent years. See Jacques Semelin, *The Survival of the Jews in France, 1940–1944*, trans. Cynthia Schoch and Natasha Lehrer (Oxford: Oxford University Press, 2018).

far less pronounced than in France, where at the turn of the century the widespread condemnation of the Jews in the Dreyfus affair had caused a national crisis. And yet the proportion of victims among the Jews living in the Netherlands was three times that among the Jews living in France.

For all the importance of collaboration, complicity, passivity, and indifference on the part of the non-Jewish population – alongside the manifestations of solidarity, resistance, and help – ultimately the real driving force for persecution came from the German side. Reasons for the divergent death rates are to be sought primarily in the differing characters of the German occupation authorities, evident in their institutional structures and their personnel, and also in their access to suitable executive forces and the extent to which the specific circumstances within each occupied country were taken into account. The Germans' overarching objective, explicitly formulated at the Wannsee Conference and pursued with enormous energy, was to deport and kill all the Jews in the countries of Western Europe. The scale of their success, despite all resistance, is horrifying.

List of Documents

Denmark

Norway

Netherlands

173 On 10 May 1945, after her liberation from Auschwitz, Frieda Brommet writes a postcard to her friend Bep Steenbergen in Amsterdam

Belgium

174 On 2 July 1942 the Association of Jews in Belgium attempts to persuade Secretary General Romsée not to require Jews to perform forced labour outside Belgium

175 On 9 July 1942 the representative of the Reich Foreign Office, Werner von Bargen, informs his superiors of the plan to deport 10,000 Jews from Belgium

176 On 18 July 1942 Antoine Dubois asks the military administration to remove the names of his two illegitimate sons from the Jew registry

177 *Le Pays réel*, 23 July 1942: an article on the supposed privileges of the Jews calls for their removal from Belgium

178 On 15 August 1942 Theodor Pichier in the military administration's Department for Economic Affairs reports on the expropriation of the Belgian Jews over the past three months

179 On 19 August 1942 factory owner Rudolf Samson is arrested and interrogated about alleged foreign currency offences

180 In a report for the public prosecutor dated 31 August 1942, the Belgian policeman Jos Bouhon describes the course of action during a roundup in Antwerp

181 *Le Drapeau rouge*, August 1942: article calling for more active opposition to the deportation of Jews from Belgium

182 On 1 September 1942 Boris Averbuch writes to his girlfriend from the train to Upper Silesia

183 On 4 September 1942 Karl Holstein from the German military administration notes how Jews with diamonds or gold can buy their exemption from deportation

184 On 15 September 1942 the German military administration reports on the deportation of 10,000 Jews from Belgium

185 On 23 September 1942 Paul-Henri Spaak, the Belgian minister of foreign affairs, asks his British counterpart to relax the entry requirements for Jews from Belgium seeking admission to Britain

186 On 25 September 1942 the chief of the German military administration, Eggert Reeder, informs the Oberfeldkommandanturen and Feldkommandanturen that the deportation of the Jews can continue

187 On 7 October 1942 the Belgian underground organization Tégal reports to the government in exile in London about the start of deportations and raids against Jews

188 On 8 October 1942 Salomon Ullmann sends his letter of resignation as chairman of the Association of Jews in Belgium to the chief of the German military administration

189 On 8 October 1942 Frans de Groote asks the Queen of Belgium to protect his wife, who has been interned in Mechelen, from deportation

Luxembourg

France

DOCUMENTS

Denmark

Denmark
■ Camps
Skagerrak
North Sea
Skagen
Hirtshals
Gothenburg
Læsø
SWEDEN
Thisted
Aalborg
Kattegat
Nykøbing
Mors
Salling
Anholt
Viborg
Randers
Storå
Gudenå
Grenaa
Silkeborg
Aarhus
Ringkøbing
Jutland
Höganäs
Gilleleje
Helsingborg
Smidstrup
Horserød
Ramlösa
Snekkersten
Helsingør
Hillerød
Øresund
Horsens
Samsø
Copenhagen
Vejle
Varde Å
Esbjerg
Roskilde
Malmö
Kolding
Fanø
Zealand
Odense
Ribeå
Haderslev
Funen
Nyborg
Fakse
Stevns Klint
Næstved
Rømø
Aabenraa
Svendborg
Baltic Sea
Frøslev
Ærø
Langeland
Møn
Falster
Lolland
Nykøbing
Rødby
GERMAN REICH
0 20 40 60 km

DOC. 1

Kristeligt Dagblad, 20 June 1939: article on the arrival of Jewish refugees in Copenhagen[1]

Young Jewish refugees arrived in Copenhagen. Temporary residence in Denmark for half a year before children are moved on to Palestine[2]

One can hardly think of a worse tragedy than that which the Jewish emigrants are enduring at present. It does not matter where they turn, the borders are closed, and everywhere the miserable people are barred from going ashore from the refugee ships, which are at a loss as to where they should sail with their tragic cargo. But yesterday a small group of nineteen German Jewish children arrived in Copenhagen and will find temporary sanctuary in Denmark before they travel on before long to Palestine, where hopefully a brighter future awaits them than the one they could expect in their own country. The flock consisted of nine boys and ten girls between the ages of thirteen and fifteen.

From a refugee camp near Berlin

It was not too difficult to find Danish families that wanted to take in the children, but it was difficult getting the children into the country. However, the authorities have granted residence permits to twenty-five children for six months, and the six children still missing yesterday are expected later.

The children come from different regions in Germany and have spent a few months in a refugee camp[3] near Berlin.

Upon arrival, the young emigrants must have immediately felt they were in good hands. The National Council of Danish Women[4] has organized the stay, and friendly women met the children off the train.

They were brought from the main train station to the Women's Building,[5] where they sat around a plentifully laden table, while fair-haired young girls from Kathrinevej School sang both Danish and German songs for their comrades, who were each presented with a small welcome gift.

1 *Kristeligt Dagblad*, 20 June 1939, p. 1. This well-known daily newspaper was founded in 1896. It had a circulation of 11,000 copies in 1935, growing to 23,000 by 1948. This document has been translated from Danish.

2 Photograph with the caption 'Some of the Jewish guests photographed yesterday'.

3 Presumably a reference to one of the retraining (hachsharah) sites near Berlin that prepared people for emigration to Palestine.

4 The Danske Kvinders Nationalråd, the umbrella organization of Danish women's organizations, was founded as the Danish branch of the International Council of Women in 1899. In total, around 320 Jewish children from Germany, Austria, and Czechoslovakia were accepted into Denmark; later, during German occupation 43 of them were deported to Theresienstadt.

5 The Kvindernes Bygning was inaugurated in 1937; it contained exhibition space and lecture rooms, guest rooms for women from the provinces, and a restaurant.

We want to help you

'We warmly welcome you to Denmark', said Mrs Gloerfelt-Tarp[6] in a brief speech to the German children. 'There are many of us who wish to help you as much as we can. We cannot replace your mothers and fathers, but we wish you the very best for your stay in Denmark, so that later, when you arrive in Palestine, you will have pleasant memories of your time here. What we are doing for you is only what Denmark has done for other children in a difficult situation. I would like to remind you of the Viennese children who found a temporary home in Denmark after the World War.'[7]

Temporarily to Arresø[8]

The lawyer, Mrs Oppenheim,[9] said to the children: 'Even if your mother and father were sorry to be separated from you, I feel convinced that they are now happy to know you are in good hands. You have now taken the first steps to a new life and although I know that it is difficult to feel happy when one has seen such serious things as you have, I hope that after all you may find contentment during your stay here in our country. You are the first group of Jewish children who have been allowed to come into this country. Think about that and show your thanks with good behaviour.'

Then Supreme Court lawyer Henriques[10] spoke, and the small welcome ceremony ended with the Jewish children singing one of their own songs. Lawyer Max Rothenborg has already invited them to spend the first three weeks at his country house on Arresø, where they can get used to their new circumstances before they are placed in private homes.

6 Kirsten Gloerfelt-Tarp (1889–1977), administrator; chairwoman of the Danske Kvinders Nationalråd, 1931–1946; member of the Danish parliament, 1945–1960.

7 After the First World War, Danish families took in between 20,000 and 25,000 children from war-torn Vienna for several months. While they were in Denmark, the so-called Wienerbørn (Viennese children) were to recover from the effects of malnutrition.

8 A lake in the province of Zealand.

9 Correctly: Mélanie Oppenhejm (1897–1982), wife of the lawyer Moritz Oppenhejm (1886–1961); chairwoman of the Jewish Women's Association in Copenhagen from 1935; member of the steering committee of the Danish women's organization Dansk Kvindesamfund; co-founder of the Children and Youth Aliyah in Denmark. The couple were deported to Theresienstadt together with their children Ralph and Ellen in 1943; they all returned to Denmark in 1945. See also Doc. 25.

10 Probably a reference to Carl Bertel Henriques (1870–1957), lawyer; member of the representative body of the Jewish Community of Copenhagen; its chairman from 1930; imprisoned on 29 August 1943; released soon after; fled to Sweden in Oct. 1943.

DOC. 2

On 9 May 1940 the police in Lidingö provide information about Charlotte Friediger's and Hellmuth Jacoby's escape to Sweden[1]

Lidingö Police report concerning Charlotte Friediger,[2] signed Folke Johansson, Olaf Streijffert, dated 9 May 1940[3]

In connection with an application for a residence permit submitted to the Swedish National Board of Health and Welfare[4] by Danish subject Charlotte Friediger, whose application was forwarded here for comment, the undersigned can respectfully state the following. Police Officer Olof Streijffert was ordered to investigate the case and has informed us that on 13 April 1940 the following report was sent to the Swedish National Board of Health and Welfare:

Friday, 12 April 1940. Concerning *Jacoby*, Erich Hellmuth[5] (stateless).
On Friday, 12 April 1940, Mrs Karin Tarschys,[6] resident at 3 Hjortstigen in Lidingö I, came into the police station and reported that Erich Hellmuth *Jacoby*, who is stateless, and his fiancée, Danish citizen Charlotte *Friediger*, had arrived directly from Denmark at her above-named residence in Lidingö on 10 April 1940. Jacoby did not have a residence permit but had in his possession a Danish identity card for German refugees valid until 8 March 1941. Both of the above-named foreigners had fled from Denmark to Sweden in a fishing boat on 9 April, together with three other refugees. Mrs Tarschys stated that she has known Friediger for many years.

When questioned at this police station, Miss Charlotte Friediger informed Police Officer Olof Streijffert that she was born in Pohrlitz, in former Austria,[7] unmarried, the daughter of Danish subject, the Chief Rabbi in Copenhagen, Max Friediger,[8] and his wife, Danish subject Fanny Friediger, née Seegall. She also stated that she was engaged to be married to Erich Hellmuth Jacoby of Copenhagen, who is stateless, whom she intended to marry on 14 April. On the morning of 9 April at 6 a.m., she had awoken

1 Riksarkivet, Stockholm, Statens utlänningskommission, Kanslibyrån, F 1 ABA: 934. This document has been translated from Swedish.
2 Charlotte Friediger-Jacoby (1913–2006), chemist; fled from Denmark to Sweden in 1940; continued on to the Philippines in the same year; evacuated to the USA in 1945 after the end of the war.
3 The report was produced for the Immigration Office and the Swedish Foreign Ministry's passport department.
4 Swedish: Kungliga Socialstyrelsen; an agency within the Ministry for Social Affairs responsible for residence permits and social welfare.
5 Erich Hellmuth Jacoby (1903–1979), lawyer; legal counsel of the railway union in Germany; in 1933 fled to Denmark, where he worked as a trade union advisor and journalist; fled to Sweden in 1940; continued on to the Philippines in the same year; in 1945 evacuated to the USA, where he worked as a journalist; worked at the Food and Agriculture Organization (FAO) in Rome; became a Swedish citizen in 1956.
6 Karin Elisabeth Tarschys (1902–1988), teacher; held a doctorate in literature.
7 This refers to the former Habsburg Empire.
8 Dr Moses Samuel Friediger, also known as Max Moses (1884–1947), rabbi; chief rabbi in Copenhagen from 1920; arrested on 29 August 1943; deported to Theresienstadt on 2 Oct. 1943; returned to Denmark; reported on his internment in his book *Theresienstadt*, published in Copenhagen in 1946.

in her home at 21 Store Kongensgade in Copenhagen and had heard the sound of planes. She had quickly got dressed. After about an hour, her above-named fiancé and a Czech subject by the name of Friedrich Tejessy arrived at her home. A short time later Miss Friediger and the two other foreigners managed to get a lift by car to Helsingør, where they tried to get a ferry to Helsingborg. However, they found out that no ferry was due to depart from Helsingør. They therefore continued to Gilleleje, where together with two other German refugees – mechanics Hellmuth Bartberger and Mötsch from Copenhagen – they hired a fishing boat, with which they managed to cross over to Höganäs,[9] where they first went through customs and then immediately reported to the police station in Höganäs, where they were questioned. From Höganäs, all five journeyed to Helsingborg, where they took the evening train to Stockholm, arriving on the morning of the 10th. In Stockholm, all except Miss Friediger visited the refugee committee.[10] Miss Friediger was in touch with Professor Ehrenpreis, the chief rabbi.[11] The two above-named mechanics were given accommodation on Barnhusgatan. The Czech, Friedrich Tejessy, found accommodation with Särström, 68 Odengatan, 3rd floor, telephone 30 97 18.

Miss Friediger and her fiancé, Jacoby, lodged with Mrs Karin Tarschys at 3 Hjortstigen in Lidingö, where they planned to stay until they received word from the Swedish National Board of Health and Welfare. Jacoby stated that he was born on 5 July 1903 in Berlin, the son of Samuel Jacoby, deceased, a physician and German subject, and Käthe Jacoby, née Bernhard, his widow (resident at 3A Österportsgatan in Malmö). His further statements corroborated what Miss Friediger had said. In Copenhagen, he lived at 33 Vesterbrogade. Jacoby worked in Copenhagen as a journalist and was employed as a consultant by the Economic Council of the Labour Movement.[12] He had with him a Danish identity card valid until 8 March 1941. Miss Friediger had a Danish passport valid until 29 December 1944. Both passports were stamped by the police in Höganäs on 9 April.

Lidingö Public Prosecutor's Office, 13 April 1940.

When questioned on 9 May 1940, the applicant stated that the reason why she visited Sweden is that she wanted to live with her fiancé, Hellmuth Jacoby. There were no obstacles preventing her from returning to Denmark. Her parents were still living in Copenhagen, where her father was the chief rabbi. Grammar school teacher Bernhard Tarschys,[13] resident at 3 Hjortstigen in Lidingö, telephone 65 27 73, stated when questioned

9 Gilleleje, in the north of the Danish island of Zealand, and Höganäs, a Swedish coastal village, are only a few kilometres apart.

10 This refers either to the refugee committee of the Social Democratic Party (Arbetarrörelsens flyktingshjälp) or to the Stockholm umbrella organization for all refugee organizations (Stockholms centrala kommitté för flyktingshjälp).

11 Dr Marcus Ehrenpreis (1869–1951), rabbi; studied at the Higher Institute for Jewish Studies in Berlin; rabbi in Djakovar, 1896–1900; chief rabbi of Bulgaria, 1900–1914; then chief rabbi of Stockholm; helped Theodor Herzl in preparing for the First Zionist Congress.

12 The Arbejderbevægelsens Erhvervsråd, founded in 1936 by the Danish Confederation of Trade Unions and the Danish Employers' Confederation as an institute for academic research into labour conditions.

13 Bernhard Tarschys (1905–1978), grammar school teacher; member of the relief committee of the Jewish Community of Stockholm from May 1940; later elected chairman of the Jewish Community.

that Miss Friediger did not possess any assets to pay for her stay in Sweden. However, she was receiving support from acquaintances in Stockholm and additionally lived for free with the Tarschyses. He also stated that he would assume responsibility for ensuring that Miss Friediger did not become a financial burden on the state. Since the applicant moved to Sweden to be with her above-named fiancé and since according to her own information nothing prevents her from returning to her parents in Copenhagen, her application for a residence permit in Sweden is unfounded. For this reason the application can under no circumstances be approved. The applicant is not eligible to stay in the country at the present time.[14]

DOC. 3
On 15 January 1942 the Reich Foreign Office calls for the introduction of anti-Jewish measures in Denmark based on those in the Reich[1]

Speaking notes (marked 'secret'), signed Undersecretary Luther,[2] (D III 29g) for the Reich Foreign Minister,[3] Berlin, dated 15 January 1942[4]

Speaking notes on the topic of the Jewish question in Denmark

Thus far, the relevant section for Jewish affairs has directly approached neither the Danish legation nor the Danish government with regard to broaching the Jewish question in Denmark. Nor has the German legation in Copenhagen received any instructions to take up this question officially. The official in charge of Jewish affairs, Legation Counsellor Rademacher,[5] has, however, made repeated verbal requests to Envoy von

14 The Swedish authorities did not grant permanent residency to the couple, who were married in Sweden by a rabbi but not at a registry office. Both therefore left the country and travelled to the Philippines in Dec. 1940.

1 Copy in IfZ-Archives, NG-3931. This document has been translated from German.
2 Martin Luther (1895–1945), furniture haulier; joined the NSDAP and the SA in 1932; employed at the Bureau Ribbentrop, 1936–1938; employed at the Reich Foreign Office, 1938–1943; head of Department D (Germany), 1940–1943; representative of the Reich Foreign Office at the Wannsee Conference; imprisoned in Sachsenhausen concentration camp for attempting to overthrow Reich Foreign Minister Ribbentrop, 1943–1945; died in a Berlin hospital in May 1945.
3 Joachim von Ribbentrop (1893–1946), businessman; joined the NSDAP in 1932 and the SS in 1933; Hitler's foreign policy advisor (Bureau Ribbentrop) from 1934; ambassador to Britain, 1936–1938; Reich foreign minister, 1938–1945; sentenced to death at the International Military Tribunal in Nuremberg and executed.
4 The document contains handwritten notes and underlining.
5 Franz Rademacher (1906–1973), lawyer; member of the SA, 1932–34; joined the NSDAP in 1933; in the diplomatic service from 1937; in Uruguay between 1938 and 1940; legation counsellor, 1940; headed the section for Jewish affairs (D III) in the Reich Foreign Office, 1940–1943; became a naval officer in April 1943; went into hiding after the war; arrested in 1947 and sentenced to three and a half years in prison by Nuremberg Regional Court in March 1952; temporarily released in July 1952 and fled to Syria; returned to the Federal Republic of Germany in 1966; sentenced by Bamberg Regional Court in 1968 to five years in prison; released early on grounds of illness.

Renthe-Fink[6] that he might mention in conversation at a suitable opportunity that, in the words of the Führer, the Jewish question in Europe is being solved definitively, and it would thus be prudent for Denmark to adapt to this of its own accord in good time. The solution of the Jewish question would be made technically easier if Jew laws based on the German model were also introduced in Denmark. Envoy von Grundherr has spoken to Envoy von Renthe-Fink along the same lines on occasion.

Herewith presented to the Reich Foreign Minister through State Secretary Baron von Weizsäcker.[7]

DOC. 4

De frie Danske, December 1942: the illegal newspaper reports on protests in Sweden against the deportation of Norwegian Jews[1]

Fierce protests against persecution of Jews in Norway

On Sunday, 29 November, a service for the persecuted Jews was held in Gothenburg cathedral. The cathedral was filled to the last seat and the dean of the cathedral, Dean Nystedt,[2] gave a sermon. He stated, among other things:

> It was with disgust that we read about the slave raids of earlier times and about shiploads of slaves who were transported to America like cattle. Who would ever have dreamt of something so horrible – that such a ship should sail along our coast last week, laden with men, women, and children who could expect no fate other than that of slaves, not to mention that of cattle destined for slaughter, and not because they had been found guilty of some crime, but solely because they are of Jewish descent. The Church of Sweden cannot remain silent when something such as this happens on our borders. If we are silent, then the stones will cry out.[3] We are shaken to our core at the thought of those who suffer this misery, and we recoil in dread in

6 Dr Cécil von Renthe-Fink (1885–1964), lawyer; in the diplomatic service from 1913; joined the NSDAP in 1939; envoy in Copenhagen, 1936–1942; Reich plenipotentiary in occupied Denmark, April 1940–Nov. 1942; special representative to the French government in Vichy from Dec. 1943; interned in Denmark 1946–1948.

7 Baron Ernst Heinrich von Weizsäcker (1882–1951), diplomat; worked in the Reich Foreign Office from 1920; legation counsellor in Copenhagen, 1924–1927; envoy to Oslo in 1931 and to Bern in 1933; undersecretary in the political department of the Reich Foreign Office, 1936; state secretary, 1938; joined the NSDAP in 1938; ambassador to the Vatican, 1943–1945; sentenced to seven years in prison at the Nuremberg Military Tribunals in 1949; released in 1950.

1 *De frie Danske*, Dec. 1942, p. 9. This document has been translated from Danish. The illegal newspaper, set up by a middle-class conservative resistance group, was published from 1941. It contained photographs and was the work of professional journalists. At its peak, it had a circulation of 20,000 copies.

2 Bengt Olof Nystedt (1888–1974), theologian and pastor; dean of Gothenburg cathedral, 1938–1943; held various positions in Stockholm and other municipalities from 1943.

3 Luke 19:40: 'And he (…) said unto them, if these should hold their peace, the stones would immediately cry out' (King James Version, hereafter KJV).

> the face of the dragon's seed of hatred which is thoughtlessly sown.[4] What has happened to the Jews of France? What has happened and continues to happen in Poland? What awaits the Jews of Norway who are on their way there? What harvest will such deeds produce? We stand powerless. What will happen to the Jews who are still in Norway; can our government do something to help them? We implore the government to take up this matter with all seriousness and urgency.

Elsewhere in Gothenburg, a large demonstration was held against the persecution of the Jews in Norway. In the words of one of the speakers:

> A ship left Oslo's harbour with a cargo of suffering on board. I don't think that any of us can imagine what its passengers have suffered, are suffering, and will suffer. They leave behind an indictment which should shake the conscience of the North, if one exists. This is not a question of neutrality or politics, it is a question of humanity or inhumanity. Something such as this must never happen in Sweden. Indifference to crime *is* a crime.[5]

A resolution was adopted at this event, stating:

> In the name of Christianity and democracy, of humanity and justice, we protest against the mass deportation of Jewish compatriots from our nearest neighbouring country, deported not on account of crimes they have committed but because of their ancestry. We do so for the Nordic community, and we are equally incensed and troubled that Nordic men have been able to commit this shameful act. We do so for the sake of citizen rights, for without legal certainty, human order will perish, regardless of whether it is now called old or new.

4 This is probably a reference to an episode in classical mythology as told by Hyginus and Ovid: Cadmus, king of Thebes, sowed the teeth of a slain dragon in the ground, from which sprang a new legion of warriors.

5 The words quoted are those of Fredrik Natanael Beskow, an artist and lay preacher, who spoke at a gathering in Stockholm on 29 Nov. 1942. *De frie Danske* used a report from the newspaper *Dagens Nyheter* dated 30 Nov. 1942 as its source.

DOC. 5

On 24 April 1943 the Reich plenipotentiary in Denmark, Werner Best, warns the Reich Foreign Office that measures against the Jews would jeopardize cooperation with the Danish administration[1]

Letter from the Reich plenipotentiary in Denmark (II C 103/43), signed W. Best,[2] Copenhagen, to the Reich Foreign Office, dated 24 April 1943[3]

Re: the Jewish question in Denmark

I am reporting in reply to telegram no. 537, dated 19 April 1943,[4] with reference also to my written report of 13 January 1943 (II C 103/43).[5]

1) As I stated in my report of 13 January 1943, on the Danish side the Jewish question is viewed primarily as a legal and constitutional question. If the German side were to demand exceptional treatment of certain Danish citizens – specifically, the Jews with Danish citizenship – the Danes would view this first and foremost as an assault on their constitution, which guarantees the equality of all Danish citizens before the law. Once the first stone were pried from the edifice of prevailing constitutional law, they would fear a progression along these lines, leading to restrictions on the personal freedom of all citizens – for example, forced labour – and to a complete change in the legal and political status of the country.

Detailed examination of the Jewish question would thus encounter opposition from every constitutional component of the Danish state and – as Minister von Scavenius[6]

1 PA AA, R 100 864, fols. 75–78, published in *ADAP*, series E, vol. 5, no. 344. This document has been translated from German.

2 Dr Werner Best (1903–1989), lawyer; joined the NSDAP in 1930 and the SS in 1931; state police commissioner in Hesse, 1933; head of the SD's organizational department, 1933–1934; deputy chief of the Gestapo, 1935–1939; head of Department I at the Reich Security Main Office, 1939–1940; involved in the planning of the first Einsatzgruppen; head of the military commander in France's administrative staff, 1940–1942; Reich plenipotentiary in Denmark, Nov. 1942–1945; received death sentence in Copenhagen in 1948, subsequently commuted to five years' imprisonment; amnestied and released in 1951; thereafter worked as a lawyer and a management consultant; legal advisor to the Stinnes corporation in Mülheim an der Ruhr.

3 Two carbon copies were enclosed with the letter as attachments. The document contains handwritten notes and receipt stamps.

4 In the telegram the Reich Foreign Minister asked for an opinion as to whether the Danish government could be approached with demands in relation to the Jewish question without causing the government serious difficulties: original telegram no. 537, forwarded as no. 482, in PA AA, R 100 864, fol. 71.

5 In this report, referencing a meeting with Undersecretary Luther and Legation Counsellor Rademacher in Berlin on 7 Jan. 1943, Best had expressed his fear that the Danish government would resign if German demands for the introduction of Jewish laws were made. The text above accurately reflects the contents of the report: PA AA, R 100 864, fols. 79–81.

6 Erik Scavenius (1877–1962), diplomat; served in the Danish Foreign Office from 1901; legation secretary at the Danish embassy in Berlin, 1906–1908; president of the supervisory board of the newspaper *Politiken*, 1932–1940; foreign minister in the coalition government following the German invasion in 1940, and simultaneously prime minister from Nov. 1942 until the dissolution of the government in August 1943.

happened to tell me during a conversation – would result in the resignation of the government and make it impossible to form a new constitutional government.

2) The Jewish question plays such a minor role in Denmark quantitatively and objectively that no practical need for special measures is discernible at this time.

a) The total number of Jews in Denmark is approximately 6,000, and they are concentrated predominantly in Copenhagen.[7]

b) In public life, the Jews have over the last decades been ousted from all leading positions by the Danes.[8]

Not a single member of parliament or leading party politician is a Jew.

According to the information collected by my office thus far, in all of Denmark's public administration – including libraries, schools, and universities – 31 Jews are employed, and overwhelmingly in positions of little significance.

Among the lawyers in all of Denmark, 35 Jews have been identified.

In the entire Danish press, 14 Jews are employed as editors or the like (none as editor-in-chief).

In the fields of sculpture, painting, music, literature, theatre, and film, 21 Jews have been identified. In economic life, 345 self-employed Jews have thus far been counted, including 4 in banking, 6 in stock trading, 22 in manufacturing, and 313 wholesalers, whose significance has become quite minor as a result of the decline in business.

c) The Armaments Staff for Denmark,[9] which I have called upon to exclude Jews from the armaments orders transferred to Denmark, has ascertained that of the approximately 700 firms engaged, only six can be characterized as Jewish within the meaning of the German legislation pertaining to Jews. Of these, at the demand of the Armaments Staff one firm has induced the Jewish supervisory board to resign. Two firms are no longer of interest as the orders have been fulfilled and not renewed. In the case of three firms, efforts to eliminate Jewish partners, chairmen of the supervisory board and the like are still in progress.

d) In summary, it can be stated:

– that neither the political nor the economic behaviour of Denmark is noticeably influenced by Jews;

– that German interests do not presently necessitate any measures against the Jews in Denmark;

– that the small number and minor significance of the Jews in Denmark make immediate measures against these Jews appear unfounded and incomprehensible;

– that the small number of Jews in Denmark and the concentration of the majority of them in Copenhagen will facilitate an eventual comprehensive arrangement, in preparation for which my office is compiling data.[10]

7 In 1943 the number was probably approximately 8,000, including the Jewish refugees.

8 There is no evidence pointing to any such trend towards the exclusion of Jews from positions in Danish public life prior to the German occupation.

9 The Armaments Staff for Denmark (until Feb. 1943 the War Economy Staff) ensured that the material needs of the occupying troops were met, and organized the integration of the Danish economy into German armaments production.

10 No evidence has been found to suggest that the Reich plenipotentiary implemented a systematic census of all the Jews in Denmark before 29 August 1943.

3) At present, 1,351 stateless Jews who formerly held German citizenship (845 men, 458 women, 48 children) are living in Denmark.[11]

These Jews have thus far given no occasion for intervention.

In principle, all the considerations set out in 1) apply to them. That is, a German demand for general measures to be taken against these Jews would give rise to the response on the part of the Danes described above.

Not only the legal but also the psychological situation would be different if these Jews were to regain German citizenship, so that the Reich could deal with them without thereby touching upon questions of Danish sovereignty and Danish law.

I therefore request an investigation to ascertain whether it is possible to revoke or nullify the denaturalization of the Jews residing in Denmark, with the result that the now-stateless Jews would acquire German citizenship again.

If this question is answered in the affirmative, I will submit individual proposals regarding the timing of the revocation of denaturalization and further measures to be taken.[12]

DOC. 6

Jewish Chronicle, 3 September 1943: article on the initial measures taken against Jews in Denmark[1]

The Danish Crisis. Nazis Begin Anti-Jewish Drive.

Denmark has hitherto been the only country under Axis control where the Jews have enjoyed freedom from persecution. King Christian[2] and his government, loyally supported by the majority of the population, resolutely withstood strong Nazi pressure to introduce Jew-laws. Indeed, the king often bestowed marks of favour on his Jewish subjects, of whom there were about 6,000.

When, however, the Nazis assumed full control of Denmark and its administration at the beginning of the week, and proclaimed martial law, one of their first acts was to begin a drive against the Jews. The Chief Rabbi, Dr M. M. Friediger, and Mr C. B. Henriques, the 72-year-old head of the Copenhagen Jewish Community, were arrested, together with 400 other Jews.

According to messages reaching Stockholm, the communal leaders have closed the synagogue in Copenhagen until further notice because of the fear of provocative Nazi action during the services.

11 In Oct. 1940 SS-Brigadeführer Paul Kanstein, who was responsible for internal administration at the German embassy, launched a registration of Jewish refugees in Denmark. For some time, the Danish authorities refused to cooperate. In Feb. 1942 the occupation authorities were provided by the Danish National Police with information about foreign Jews drawn from the Danish index of foreigners.

12 This revocation of denaturalization did not occur.

1 *Jewish Chronicle*, 3 Sept. 1943, p. 1. The weekly newspaper, still published in London today, was founded in 1841.

2 King Christian X of Denmark (1870–1947); military officer; became king in 1912 after the death of his father, Frederik VIII; during the war he became a symbol of Denmark's striving for independence.

DOC. 7

On 8 September 1943 the Reich plenipotentiary in Denmark, Werner Best, proposes to the Reich Foreign Minister that the Danish Jews be deported[1]

Telex (no. 1032 – marked 'very urgent'),[2] signed Dr Best, Copenhagen, to the Reich Foreign Office (received on 8 September 1943, 2.25 p.m.), dated 8 September 1943

I request that the following report be forwarded immediately to the Reich Foreign Minister:

With reference to telegram no. 537 from your office, dated 19 April 1943,[3] and to my report of 24 April 1943 – II e 102/43,[4] I report the following concerning the Jewish question in Denmark in light of the new situation:

If the new course of action in Denmark is to be implemented consistently, a solution to the Jewish question and the Freemason question in Denmark [must] in my opinion now also be considered. The necessary measures would have to be taken during the present state of emergency,[5] because at a later stage they would provoke reactions in the country that would lead to the renewed imposition of the general state of emergency in circumstances likely more unfavourable than exist today. In particular, as I know from numerous sources of information, any existing constitutional government would resign, just as the king and the national legislature would cease to participate in the governing of the country. In addition, one would probably have to reckon on a general strike, because as a result of these measures, the unions would cease their activities and therefore halt their moderating influence on the workers. However, if the measures are taken during the present state of emergency, it is possible that a constitutional government can no longer be formed, with the result that an administrative committee under my leadership would have to be created and I would make law by decree.

For 6,000 Jews (including women and children) to be suddenly arrested and taken away, the police I requested in my telegram no. 1001 of 1 September 1943[6] would be required. The police would have to be deployed almost exclusively in Greater Copenhagen, where the vast majority of the Jews here live. Supplementary forces would have to

1 PA AA, R 100 864, fols. 93–94. This document has been translated from German.
2 By cryptograph ('G-Schreiber').
3 PA AA, R 100 864, fols. 93–94.
4 See Doc. 5.
5 On 29 August 1943 the German occupiers imposed a state of emergency after the Danish government allowed an ultimatum from the German government to elapse and resigned. In the face of a wave of strikes and acts of sabotage, the Germans had called for an aggressive response from the Danish police and the reintroduction of the death penalty. Following the formal resignation of the government, it was replaced by an emergency administration made up of the state secretaries of the ministries. Best's position was retained. See Introduction, p. 18.
6 In this telegram, Best had suggested to the Reich Foreign Minister that two additional Order Police battalions and 300 SD officials be dispatched to set up 25 police stations across the country and that German special courts be instituted. Without these measures, he said, lifting the state of emergency was out of the question: published in *ADAP*, series E, vol. 6, no. 271. The extent to which additional forces were dispatched to Denmark is not clear.

be provided by the commander of the German troops in Denmark. Ships would surely be the chief means of transport and would have to be summoned here in a timely manner. With regard to Freemasonry, one possibility would be the formal dissolution of all the lodges (to which all the key people in the country belong), the provisional arrest of the most important Freemasons, and the confiscation of lodge property. For this as well, strong executive powers would be required.

I request a decision on which measures I am to implement or to prepare for with regard to the Jewish question and the Freemason question.[7]

DOC. 8

On 17 September 1943 members of the Jewish Community describe for the Danish Ministry of Foreign Affairs how German police searched the Community's premises[1]

Letter from Max Rothenborg,[2] senior public prosecutor, 38 Skindergade, Copenhagen, with enclosed report, signed Ove Chr. Petersen and Josef Fischer,[3] to Director Svenningsen,[4] Ministry of Foreign Affairs (received on 28 September 1943), Christiansborg, Copenhagen, dated 17 September 1943

As agreed, I hereby send you enclosed a report about the incidents that took place on the property of the Mosaic Community at 6–12 Ny Kongensgade.

The report is, as you will see, signed by concierge Petersen and librarian Fischer and is, of course, in accordance with what happened.

You will appreciate that there is considerable tension within the Community – the information about what has happened has spread like wildfire throughout the city – and at any rate it would be of utmost importance if one could as soon as possible find out what is really going on, no matter whether the news is now good or bad.

I would be most obliged if you informed me about it, as soon as there is any news on this case – from 7 o'clock this evening, I will be in my private residence, telephone Ordrup 1111, where I probably will be tomorrow as well: if I go to the city centre, I will phone the foreign office.

7 On 17 Sept. 1943 Hitler ordered the deportation of the Danish Jews; Best was informed on 18 Sept. 1943. Office of the Reich Foreign Minister, PA AA, R 100 864, fol. 103.

1 Rigsarkivet, 120.D.43/1.a, Tysk aktion mod jøderne i Danmark. This document has been translated from Danish.

2 Max Rothenborg (1888–1956), lawyer; involved in aiding escapes; fled to Sweden, 1943; during his exile it was rumoured that he had betrayed his clients; he returned in 1944 and faced a trial in which he was given a prison sentence; released after the war.

3 Josef Fischer (1871–1949), librarian; emigrated from Hungary to Copenhagen, 1893; worked as religion teacher, librarian, and in poor relief for the Jewish Community of Copenhagen; after 1933 active in relief work for German refugees and for hachsharah (retraining in preparation for emigration); in 1943 lived in the Jewish Community premises; attempted to escape on 5 Oct. 1943; arrested and deported to Theresienstadt, where he was held until liberation in 1945.

4 Nils Svenningsen (1894–1985), diplomat; at the embassy in Berlin, 1924–1930; then head of the political-legal department. of the Ministry of Foreign Affairs; from 1941 state secretary, and worked with Minister of Foreign Affairs Erik Scavenius; after the war, served in various posts, including appointments as envoy in Stockholm and ambassador in London.

I also thank you very much for the urgency with which you are graciously attending to the matter.

Yours faithfully,

Max Rothenborg

Ove Chr. Petersen, the caretaker of the Jewish Religious Community building at 6–12 Ny Kongensgade, made the following statement:

This morning, Friday 17 September, at around 7 a.m., while he was opening the doors to the property, a German police vehicle 158 549 (Pol.)[5] rolled up in front of the building, and a German (but Danish-speaking) civilian[6] asked him if he was Mr Petersen, and when that was confirmed, he was told that he was under arrest. He was then guarded by two German soldiers with pistols, and he was told to open up the doors.

He was standing under guard while the aforementioned Danish-speaking civilian went up into the building. He came down again shortly after and asked Petersen to show him the way to the synagogue. Petersen was then brought to the car, still under watch, then driven to the synagogue. Petersen was then asked to walk in with the civilian, but instead Petersen made reference to Inspector Christensen and said that Christensen was more familiar with the surroundings. Christensen then went in, while Petersen remained outside, still under watch. Shortly after, the aforementioned civilian came back with the librarian, Fischer, and they drove back to 6 Kongensgade. Fischer and Petersen, while being watched from the stairway on the various floors, made their way up into the property, while the German police were still keeping watch on the street. The civilian together with another civilian and several uniformed persons then carried out a ransacking of the whole premises, including Petersen's private accommodation, which was carefully searched twice.

While Fischer was in the premises as it was being ransacked, Petersen was forced to remain under watch on the stairs. In the meantime Mrs Petersen received strict orders not to use the telephone. At around 10.30 a.m., the two civilians, as well as the soldiers, left the property in the police car with the various documents and other things that they had taken.

Josef Fischer, the librarian, reported as follows:

At 7.30 in the morning, Friday 17 September, some civilian Germans arrived at his place of residence, 6 Ny Kongensgade, and asked his wife where he was. Mrs Fischer explained that her husband was in the synagogue, and then a German, but Danish-speaking, civilian entered the synagogue and collected Fischer at the end of the service at 7.40.

This person showed Fischer a German police badge and let him know that if he behaved calmly, nothing would happen to him.

Mr Fischer was then forced to get into a large police car that stood in the synagogue courtyard; the driver was in uniform and alongside him sat a civilian. In the car sat Petersen, the caretaker, who had come from Ny Kongensgade, which is where the car

5 Part of the car registration number.

6 Fritz Renner (1912–1945), Oberscharführer at the Gestapo's section for Jewish affairs in Copenhagen; killed in the RAF bombings of the Gestapo headquarters in Copenhagen on 21 March 1945.

now headed, and where 6–8 soldiers were posted by the door and stairs, so that the private apartment was also under watch.

Mr Fischer now had to go in first to the reading room on the ground floor, where all the cupboards had to be opened; the German policemen took with them various German-Hebrew dictionaries, the *History of the Jews* in 12 volumes and Chief Rabbi Friediger's *History of the Jews*,[7] the commemoration volume for 1814,[8] and some other things.

At the same time, they examined the Torah Scrolls, which were rolled up and whose meaning Mr Fischer had to explain, after which they were put back.

They then went into the caretaker's room, which had previously been an office and where some old marriage contract forms were kept, among other things, while all the cupboards and drawers were thoroughly searched. They now moved up to the second floor in the library, where they went through everything as well. They took with them various biographical documents, ancestry records, all financial accounts from the Denmark Lodge (BB),[9] as well as the records of Lodge meetings and members list; and further records of all voting members of the religious community from 1935 and the provincial registers from the archive cupboard. In addition, they took the census records from 1911, 1916, 1921 relating to Jews. Finally, the card index for the historical archive and all books about Danish Jews; they also took a card index containing information on immigrants that had arrived since 1933, along with numbers, names, and dates of arrival.

They also went into the office where youth work is managed, and they took a card index with them. Miss Sussi Weigert, who works in this office, was made to stay in the office and her bag was meticulously searched; likewise, Hertz, the treasurer, who had since arrived, was forced to put his bag and lunch pack down so they could be searched.

On the first floor they went through the library[10] and museum, although nothing was taken. Nor was there anything taken from the meeting hall, the treasury, or accounting office.

The German civilian, who introduced himself as Mr Renner, next asked if there was any money stashed away, whereupon Mr Fischer answered that no money was held there, that the Community did not have any assets, and that the affiliation fees, which are administered by the representatives' committee of 7 members and which are held in a bank, were used to pay for the regular social and ritual expenses.

From the archive they took the last affiliation records from 1942–43. Finally, the private quarters were thoroughly searched – all drawers, linen cupboards, clothes cupboards and more, but they did not take anything.

At 10.40 everyone left the premises, civilians and those in uniform, without Fischer or anyone else being taken away.

Altogether, all those concerned came across as extremely polite.

7 Max Friediger, *Jødernes historie* (Copenhagen: P. Haase, 1934).

8 Probably the volume commemorating the 100th anniversary of the edict emancipating the Danish Jews in 1814: Julius Salomon and Josef Fischer, *Mindeskrift i Anledning af Hundredaarsdagen for Anordningen af 29. Marts 1814* (Copenhagen: Danmark Loge, 1914).

9 Branch established in 1912 of the international Jewish fraternal organization B'nai B'rith (Hebrew: sons/children of the covenant).

10 Presumably the library was located on both the first and second floors of the building.

DOC. 9

On 22 September 1943 the Wehrmacht High Command announces the impending deportation of the Jews from Denmark by the SS[1]

Telegram (marked 'top secret, top priority – to be handled by officers only') from the Wehrmacht High Command, OKW/WFST/Qu. 2 (N),[2] no. 66 23 33/43, top secret, top priority, p.p. Jodl,[3] to the Reich Foreign Office, for the attention of Ambassador Ritter[4] (received on 22 September 1943, 21:20), for information only to the Reichsführer SS and Chief of the German Police, SS Command Staff Hochwald,[5] for information only to the Chief of Military Armaments and Commander of the Army Reserve,[6] copy to the Commander of the German Forces in Denmark,[7] dated 22 September 1943

The Führer has ordered:
1) Reichsführer SS is authorized to recruit volunteers from among the former Danish members of the Wehrmacht who are to be released[8] and to send up to 4,000 men from the youngest age group to SS camps in the Reich.
2) Deportation of Jews to be carried out by Reichsführer SS, who is redeploying two police battalions[9] to Denmark for this purpose.
3) The military state of emergency will remain in effect at least until the end of the operations under 1) and 2). A special order will be issued for its termination.
4) The Reich Plenipotentiary[10] has been informed to the same effect via the Reich Foreign Office.

1 PA AA, R 100 864, fol. 107, published in *ADAP*, series E, vol. 6, no. 341. This document has been translated from German.
2 Wehrmacht High Command/Wehrmacht Operations Staff/Quartermaster 2. It is possible that 'N' is an abbreviation for Norden ('North').
3 Alfred Jodl (1890–1946), military officer; head of the Department for National Defence in the Reich Ministry of War, 1935; brigadier and head of the Military Operations Office of the Wehrmacht High Command, 1939; lieutenant general, 1940; colonel general, 1944; joined the NSDAP in 1944; signed the Wehrmacht's unconditional surrender at Rheims as the representative of Karl Dönitz in 1945; sentenced to death at the International Military Tribunal at Nuremberg in 1946 and executed.
4 Dr Karl Ritter (1883–1968), diplomat; in the Reich Foreign Office from 1922; ambassador by special appointment in 1939; in this function, liaised with the Wehrmacht High Command; sentenced at the Ministries Trial in 1949 to four years in prison.
5 Heinrich Himmler.
6 Friedrich Fromm (1888–1945), military officer; head of the General Army Office, 1934–1940; commander of the army reserve and chief of military armaments from 1939; after the attempted assassination of Adolf Hitler on 20 July 1944, established a court martial which sentenced the leaders of the plot to death; charged with having tolerated the attempted coup, he was convicted by the People's Court and executed in March 1945.
7 Hermann von Hanneken (1890–1981), career officer; representative for iron and steel procurement for the Four-Year Plan from 1937; commander of the German forces in Denmark, August 1942–Jan. 1945; convicted by a Danish court in 1948; acquitted on appeal in 1949.
8 The release of the Danish soldiers was intended to reassure the population. The soldiers had been interned by the Germans during the state of emergency.
9 It appears that only one police battalion was sent to Denmark. The exact date of its deployment could not be ascertained.
10 Werner Best.

DOC. 10

On 25 September 1943 State Secretary Nils Svenningsen advises representatives of the Jewish Community that Jews should not leave en masse[1]

Memorandum from the Foreign Ministry, signed Nils Svenningsen, dated 25 September 1943

Memorandum

The chairman of the representative body for the Jewish Community, Supreme Court lawyer Henriques, and vice chairman Mr Lachmann[2] met today at the premises of the undersigned because they were concerned that the Jewish question might be raised in this country.

I confirmed to the two gentlemen that Dr Best had personally informed me that the Jewish question had not arisen at all, and I added that in my conversation with Regierungsdirektor Stalmann[3] about the search carried out at the Community's office in Ny Kongensgade,[4] he had emphasized that this operation did not target the Jewish Community as such. Mr Stalmann said that the operation was carried out solely to secure evidence which could be compromising for individuals in terms of anti-German activities. It was not a racially motivated event.

Supreme Court lawyer Henriques asked who had been responsible for the aforementioned operation, as well as for the arrests that were carried out. I replied that General von Hanneken did not deal with these matters, and that responsibility must lie instead with the German authorities at the Dagmarhus,[5] that is, in the final instance with Dr Best.

The lawyer wished to know what position the 'government by the state secretaries'[6] would take if the Germans suddenly launched an operation against the Jews, for example, by arresting Jews for being Jews. He had understood that the Jewish question was something that the earlier Scavenius administration would have deemed an issue for the cabinet. Furthermore, he stated that this was known to the Germans, even though it was not officially recognized by the German authorities. How would the state secretaries react if the question became acute? I answered that it was entirely out of the question for the state secretaries to approve the implementation of measures against the Jews, and if the Germans implemented anti-Jewish measures of their own accord, that is, if they

1 Rigsarkivet, 120.D.43/1.a, Tysk action mod jøderne i Danmark. This document has been translated from Danish.

2 Karl Lachmann (1878–1956), engineer; director of the Thomas sugar factory; vice chairman of the Jewish Community; fled to Sweden in Oct. 1943.

3 Dr Friedrich Stalmann (b. 1902), administrative official; worked for the Gestapo from 1934; head of the Reich plenipotentiary's political department, April 1940; commissioner for domestic administration from summer 1943 with responsibility at the German embassy for the security of German troops in Denmark; from Feb. 1945 headed the Central Refugee Agency for German refugees in Denmark established by the Reich plenipotentiary; subsequently worked as an auditor.

4 Both the conversation and the search took place on 17 Sept. 1943: see Doc. 8.

5 The Dagmarhus in Copenhagen was the headquarters of the German occupation administration.

6 In the original: 'Departementschefregeringen'. The reference is to the leading ministerial civil servants who became responsible for day-to-day administration following the resignation of the Danish government.

presented us with a fait accompli, then I was in no doubt that the state secretaries would as one protest most vehemently to the German authorities.

Finally, the lawyer asked if it was conceivable that the existing situation with government by the state secretaries could persist. I replied by saying that such a possibility could not be completely ruled out. It is four weeks since the events of 29 August[7] and there was nothing that had happened in the meantime that could indicate that the Germans had definite plans. Mr Lachmann raised the question of the emigration of the remaining Jews. These comprise Danish Jews and German emigrants. To date, the Jewish Community's position has been to advise both Danish and foreign Jews against leaving the country. Should they continue to hold that position? I answered that it could only be a matter of illegal emigration and that in my opinion it would be questionable for the leadership of the Jewish Community to deviate from its position to date. Should there suddenly be a flood of Jewish refugees leaving the country, then in my opinion the risk of measures being taken against law-abiding Jews not attempting to flee would be greater.

DOC. 11
On 29 September 1943 the Bishop of Copenhagen protests on behalf of the Danish Church against the persecution of Jews[1]

Pastoral letter, signed H. Fuglsang-Damgaard,[2] dated 29 September 1943

On 29 September 1943 the country's bishops submitted to the highest German authorities via the state secretaries a letter stating the following:

The Church of Denmark's position on the Jewish question.
It is the duty of the Christian church to protest wherever the Jews are persecuted on account of their race or religion

1. because we could never forget that Our Lord Jesus Christ was born in Bethlehem of the Virgin Mary in fulfilment of the promise that God made to Israel, his chosen people. The story of the Jewish people up until the birth of Christ is preparation for the salvation revealed by God to all humankind in Christ. This is signified by the Old Testament being part of our Bible.

2. because persecution of Jews is contrary to the notion of charitable love that comes from Christ's message and that Christ's church is called to proclaim. Christ does not recognize personal standing and he taught us that everyone is precious in God's eyes. 'There is neither Jew nor Greek, there is neither bond nor free, there is neither male nor female: for ye are all one in Christ Jesus.'[3]

3. because it violates the Danish people's sense of justice, which has developed within our Danish-Christian culture over centuries. Accordingly, the constitution guarantees

7 See Doc. 7, fn. 5.

1 Frihedsmuseets Dokumentarkiv, 6E-2. This document has been translated from Danish.
2 Hans Fuglsang-Damgaard (1890–1979), Lutheran theologian; bishop of Copenhagen, 1934–1960; involved in the sending of food parcels to deportees in Theresienstadt.
3 Galatians 3:28 (KJV).

all Danish citizens equal rights and equal responsibility for the law and religious freedom. We understand religious freedom as everyone being able to worship God according to call or conscience. And thus race and religion can never be a reason for a person to be robbed of rights, freedom or property. Regardless of all religious differences, we will fight for our Jewish brothers and sisters to have the same freedom that we ourselves value higher than life.

As leaders of the Church of Denmark, we believe it our duty to abide by the law and not to oppose the authorities inopportunely, but at the same time we are responsible to our conscience, which calls us to defend the law and to protest against any violation of the law. In so far as is necessary, we therefore wish to make unmistakably clear that we will obey God more than human beings.

On behalf of the bishops
H. Fuglsang-Damgaard

This letter was read out in the churches on Sunday, 3 October 1943.

DOC. 12
On 29 September 1943 the Epstein family, in advance of their escape, grant Jørgen Holde power of attorney over their property during their absence[1]

Handwritten note, signed Abraham Gerson Epstein,[2] Leopold Epstein, Lise Epstein, and Dina Epstein, Copenhagen, dated 29 September 1943

Power of attorney
In the name of the Epstein family, Mr Jørgen Holde[3] is hereby granted power of attorney to make the necessary arrangements regarding the family's property, which consists of furniture, clothes, books, etc. in the residence at 35 III Willemoesgade.

It is expected that the arrangements which Mr Jørgen Holde makes are in the family's interests, insofar as conditions allow, in that the furniture is either retained for the family or, should it be appropriate to sell, the sums received should benefit the Epstein family as much as possible.

I issue this power of attorney to the undersigned on behalf of myself, my father Salomon, my mother Dina, my brother Leopold, and my sister Lise.

I have my family's full consent to issue this power of attorney, the contents of which are known to you.

1 DJM, 125X8. This document has been translated from Danish.
2 Abraham Gerson Epstein (1910–2002), teacher; fled to Sweden in Oct. 1943 with his mother, Dina Riba Epstein, née Berman (b. 1883), housewife; his father, Salomon (Salman) Movschov Epstein (1884–1957); and his siblings Leopold (b. 1913), physician, and Lise (also Lisa, Lea, b. 1911), journalist; taught refugee children at the Danish School in Gothenburg; worked as a language teacher in Aarhus after the war. See also Doc. 14.
3 In the original: Mr stud. theol. Jørgen Holde, the title denoting a student of theology.

This power of attorney is irrevocable and fully effective until at least two members of my family approach Mr Jørgen Holde and simultaneously provide a written declaration that they wish to take possession of the effects again and annul this power of attorney.

I agree with the above.
Jørgen Holde

DOC. 13
In late September 1943 State Secretary Nils Svenningsen attempts to prevent the deportation of the Jews from Denmark[1]

Notes, signed Nils Svenningsen, dated 30 September and 2 October 1943

As of late, there have been rumours circulating about action being taken against Jews in Denmark. These rumours have been persistent and have heightened dramatically in the last couple of days.

On Wednesday, 29 September, Jewish circles here were absolutely convinced that the deportation of Danish Jews would take place within the next few days. For this, a meeting of the state secretaries was called for 2 p.m., at which I explained the situation, stressing that the Ministry of Foreign Affairs had no certain knowledge whatsoever. From all that has been put forward, we had nevertheless to assume that there was a basis for the rumours. What position the heads of administration should adopt in this situation was discussed at length.

The result was that the undersigned, accompanied by State Secretary Eivind Larsen,[2] was to enquire with Dr Best. (For details of what occurred at the meeting of state secretaries, see the summary by Dahl as head of office.)

On Wednesday, 29 September, Mr Eivind Larsen and I were received by Dr Best at the Dagmarhus at 5.30 p.m. I began more or less as follows: the reason for our inquiry is that recently, and particularly in the last few days, persistent rumours have been circulating about an operation against the Jews. It is rumoured that such an operation is imminent. Normally, rumours should be left unheeded. Until now we have kept to that principle where the Jewish question is concerned, and – far from heeding the rumours – we have on the contrary worked hard to provide reassurance on the basis of statements received from the German side. The rumours have, however, taken on such forms, appeared with such tenacity, and are so detailed that we feel it necessary to enquire directly to Dr Best. If the Jewish question is actually raised and treated as has been reported, the consequences here in this country would be unimaginable. There is already a high state

1 Rigsarkivet, 120.D.43/1.a, Tysk aktion mod jøderne i Danmark. This document has been translated from Danish.

2 Eivind Larsen (1898–1971), lawyer; from 1940 public prosecutor for special affairs, in which role he was responsible for cooperation between the Danish police and the occupiers; state secretary in the Ministry of Justice from 1941; acting head of the Ministry of Justice after the government's resignation in August 1943; imprisoned in 1944; chief of police in Copenhagen, 1951–1968.

of anxiety, and it is difficult to say what the situation will be like if the operation is carried out. This issue is of enormous importance for the population in general, for the civil service, and for the heads of administration.

Dr Best answered evasively by asking various questions, such as: What are they saying? What are the rumours about? Where do they come from?

I explained to him plainly what the rumours are saying: deportation to Poland in the near future. Only full Jews. Ships are ready in the harbour. Furthermore, I referred to the fact that lists of Jews were seized during the two operations against the Jewish properties in Nybrogade and Ny Kongensgade. Everything pointed to there being a plan ready to be carried out.

Best again spoke in vague terms and claimed that the local German authorities do not have any plans. He was unaware of any ships being ready in the harbour. I asked him plainly if he could deny that he has instructions for carrying out an operation. It would be of utmost importance for order in this country if he could do so.

Dr Best remarked that it is always difficult to state that something will not take place and was of the opinion that an answer to my question would be tantamount to a political declaration. He was, however, willing to send a telegram to Berlin immediately asking if he is permitted to deny the aforementioned rumours to the [Danish] Ministry of Foreign Affairs. He would add a few comments to such a request to Berlin. He wanted nothing but peace and order in this country and for the situation to be normalized as soon as possible. He therefore regretted that the general had to give me the message the day before about the extension of the state of emergency until further notice and the soldiers' internment. A response from Berlin will probably not arrive until sometime on Thursday, 30 September.

30 September 1943

On Friday, 1 October, at 4.30 p.m. the government liaison officer arranged for me to meet Dr Best at the Dagmarhus at 6 p.m.

At 5.45 p.m. Dr Best's secretary rang to cancel the meeting. Dr Best had been called away suddenly. The secretary did not know where he had gone and also did not know when the Reich Plenipotentiary would return. It would probably not be possible for me to be received in the course of the evening.

At 6.20 p.m. I went to see Envoy Barandon[3] at the Dagmarhus, summed up my conversation with Dr Best on Wednesday, and said that I now wished to ask if an answer had been received from Berlin to the enquiry that Dr Best had promised me he would make. Envoy Barandon explained that he had nothing at all to do with this matter. He assumed that Dr Best had not achieved any result in Berlin. He did not think it would be possible for me to meet Dr Best in the course of the evening. I gave Envoy Barandon the letter from His Majesty the King, and Barandon promised to ensure that it was

3 Dr Paul Barandon (1888–1971), diplomat; in the German diplomatic service from 1909; member of the secretariat of the League of Nations in Geneva, 1927–1933; deputy head of the Reich Foreign Office's legal department from Feb. 1933; joined the NSDAP in 1937; envoy and permanent representative of the Reich plenipotentiary in Denmark from Jan. 1942; member of the commission and the arbitration tribunal for the London Debt Agreement, 1954–1960.

in Dr Best's hands as soon as possible. In addition, I passed on the Supreme Court's statement.

At 8.30 p.m. I got in touch with Mr Kanstein,[4] who promised that he would put me in contact with Dr Best.

At 8.40 p.m. Chief Administrator Herfelt[5] telephoned and reported that Public Prosecutor Hoff[6] from the Dagmarhus had received notice that the arrest of a series of elements 'hostile to the Reich' would be carried out during the night. The Dagmarhus had requested that police across the whole country be notified, in order to avoid clashes between the police and the German authorities who would be carrying out the operation. This notice was to be sent to the police via teleprinter.

Shortly thereafter the telephones were disconnected. For this reason, among others, it was not possible to meet Dr Best at the Dagmarhus until 11.15 p.m. State Secretary Eivind Larsen accompanied me. I referred to the conversation we had had on Wednesday and said that I had requested the opportunity to discuss the case with Dr Best earlier that day. In the meantime, this evening we had been notified that arrests of a number of elements hostile to the Reich would be carried out during this night. We understood that the reference was to the Jews, which Dr Best confirmed. Additionally, in response to our further enquiry, he confirmed that the plan was for those affected to be transferred to Germany immediately on Saturday morning. Those fit for work would be put to various forms of labour, and the elderly and those unable to work would be sent to Theresienstadt in Bohemia, a city in which the Jews have self-governance and live in decent conditions. From there, they would be able to communicate with the outside world, for example with their relatives in Denmark. After Dr Best confirmed that the talk was of immediate deportation, I made the suggestion of internment by Danish authorities here in Denmark by presenting a handwritten letter which read as follows:

> This evening I received word from Chief Public Prosecutor Hoff that the German authorities intend to arrest a series of elements hostile to the Reich. I understand that this message refers to the arrest of Jews.
>
> As I was not able to secure the opportunity to meet you today to discuss the matter in person, I wish to write these lines, albeit at the last minute, to ask you if there is any opportunity at least to prevent the deportation of those concerned. If it should really be the case that they are to be deported immediately, then Mr Eivind Larsen and I would be willing to do everything possible to make an arrangement for those sought by the German authorities to be assembled here in Denmark by our

4 Dr Paul Ernst Kanstein (1899–1980), lawyer; joined the NSDAP and the SS in 1933; head of the State Police head office in Berlin from 1937; from April 1940 at the German embassy, where he was in charge of the security of the German troops in Denmark; SS-Brigadeführer, 1942; transferred to Italy in summer 1943; briefly imprisoned after 20 July 1944 for having contacts within the resistance; interned after the end of the war.

5 Jens Herfelt (1894–1972), lawyer; in the Danish Ministry of Justice from 1921; in charge of police affairs, 1939; involved in drafting the legal basis for the arrest of the Danish communists, 1941; chief of police in Copenhagen and judge at the Supreme Court, 1948–1951.

6 Troels Hoff (1903–1961), lawyer; from 1933 in the Danish Ministry of Justice, with responsibility for German refugees; department head, 1938; from 1942 public prosecutor for special affairs, with responsibility for crimes against the German occupiers; head of the police intelligence department after the war.

own authorities. I therefore ask you to ensure that closer investigation of such a solution is not forestalled.[7]

I asked Dr Best if, in light of this Danish counterproposal, he could hold back the transport and request new instructions on how to proceed from Berlin. Best stated that it was impossible for him to hold back the transport as he has no ability to make decisions in this matter. He would, however, immediately forward my letter to Berlin and request instructions.

With regards to the scope of the operation, Dr Best said that it involves the arrest and deportation of 100% Jews, but that it does not cover a Jewish man or woman married to an Aryan. I asked if there are plans for further measures against the Jews, such as the confiscation of property, etc. Dr Best did not think that this would be the case. The king's letter had been immediately telegraphed to Berlin.[8]

Finally, Dr Best informed me that the question of releasing interned Danish soldiers is being resolved in connection with the matter of the operation against the Jews, as the order given last Tuesday that in the meantime the soldiers were to not be sent home has been lifted. He said the soldiers are now being released in accordance with the plan that had been made.

On Saturday, 2 October, Mr Kanstein telephoned at 9.20 a.m. on behalf of Dr Best to say that no response had yet been received to the telegram which Dr Best had sent to Berlin regarding the offer of internment here in the country. The individuals who had been arrested during the night had not been sent on to Germany, but their departure was presumed to be imminent. On enquiry, Kanstein explained that in his view one could completely rule out the possibility of another operation of the same character as the one that took place last night. The question now was what was to be done with the apartments that were left empty after the Jews had been arrested. It was not the plan for the arrested Jews' property and possessions to be confiscated, but arrangements must be made for the administration of the property and surveillance of the residences, safekeeping of keys, etc. Someone had to be assigned to this, and Kanstein raised the idea of whether it would not be right if we on the Danish side named a 'Treuhänder' or a 'Treuhänderkollegium'[9] to take care of such things.[10] If one were to consider placing this matter into Danish hands, it would solely be a protective measure. I remarked that it was impossible to take a position immediately on the question raised, but that it would be discussed at a meeting of the state secretaries. One would have to expect that the Danish side would be reluctant to be involved in anything to do with this matter, but there was also the issue of it being seen as a protective measure. This would have to be considered more closely.

At 9.40 a.m. Chamberlain Bülow rang and asked if there was any sense in the Danish Red Cross offering to intern Jews within the country. I informed him that an offer of

7 The text of the letter is in German in the original.

8 Best telegraphed the content of the letter cited above to the Reich Foreign Minister at 7.30 p.m. on 1 Oct. 1943. King Christian X pointed out that 'special measures with respect to a group of persons who have enjoyed full civil rights in Denmark for more than 100 years could have the gravest consequences': PA AA, R 100 864, fol. 145.

9 German in the original: 'trustee' and 'trustee council'.

10 The social services department within the Copenhagen city administration subsequently took over the task of securing the apartments and belongings left behind. As a result, the majority of the Danish Jews received their property back after liberation. See Doc. 24.

Danish internment was put to Best yesterday evening, but I thought I should in any case advise him to get in touch with Dr Best, as the latter would then be required to push Berlin for an answer.

2 October 1943

In the course of the morning, news came of a case in which a half-Jew was arrested and of the arrest of a Jewish lady who had been married to an Aryan man. The latter case concerns Mrs Schultz, the widow of a fleet commander. She was detained along with two daughters. These two cases were specifically brought to Mr Kanstein's attention, and at the same time I put forward a general request that the Ministry of Foreign Affairs and the Ministry of Justice be allowed to send representatives to where the Jews are being kept in order to check whether there were additional mistakes.[11]

Word was received that the communists from Horserød camp[12] had been detained and taken on board the steamer which was to take the Jews to Germany. An enquiry about this was also made to the Germans.

At 12.30 p.m. Mr Stalmann called to say that the steamer had already left early this morning as planned.[13] There was therefore no possibility of additional checks by representatives from the Ministry of Foreign Affairs or the Ministry of Justice. Follow-up inspection would be carried out on the ship, and in all instances of erroneous arrest those affected would be sent back. Mrs Schultz was on board the ship, but Stalmann was in no doubt that she and her daughters would come back. Mr Salomon was also on board, and it must be assumed that he also came back. With regard to the communists, he submitted that their removal had been necessary for reasons of security, and that they were also on board the ship and therefore on their way to Germany, where they would be placed in a camp and assigned to light labour. There was no reason to be concerned about their fate.

I remarked that the abduction of the communists was a serious matter as it concerned persons who were interned on the basis of Danish measures with a legal basis.[14]

Mr Stalmann was of the opinion that within the next few days the Ministry of Foreign Affairs would receive a complete list of the abductees, so that the Danish authorities would have the opportunity to examine each individual case.

11 This did not occur. In the case of the widow of a non-Jew, the Reich Security Main Office (RSHA) argued that as a result of the spouse's death, the widow came under the regulations for Jews. Additionally, no record of the follow-up checks mentioned below has survived. In all, probably no more than five of the deportees categorized as 'erroneously arrested' ever returned.

12 Horserød camp in North Zealand was originally established for the exchange of wounded prisoners of war from all the parties involved in the First World War. During the German occupation, it served as a Danish internment camp for stateless refugees and communists. After being taken over by the German occupiers on 29 August 1943, Jews and resistance fighters were also interned there.

13 On 2 October 1943 the ship *Wartheland* departed Copenhagen with 198 Jewish and 150 communist prisoners on board.

14 After the German invasion of the Soviet Union on 22 June 1941, officials from Danish communist organizations were arrested in several waves at the insistence of the Germans. The constitutional basis for these arrests and the law against communist activities that was passed in August 1941 remained controversial into the post-war period. The communists who were arrested were first held in Horserød camp under Danish guard, which protected them from German acts of violence and deportation to Germany until August 1943, when martial law was declared.

At 1 p.m. I had an opportunity to discuss the situation briefly with Legation Counsellor Scherpenberg[15] from the Auswärtiges Amt,[16] who is staying here for the trade negotiations. Mr Scherpenberg understood the difficulties regarding the abduction of the communists. He seemed to have no objections to this matter being raised on the Danish side by the legation in Berlin.[17]
2 October 1943

DOC. 14
Lise Epstein describes how she found out about the planned roundup of Jews in Denmark and was able to flee to Sweden with her family in early October 1943[1]

Typewritten report by Lise Epstein,[2] dated January 1944[3]

The escape
On Wednesday, 29 September 1943, a strange event occurred that suddenly tore us from our ordinary lives. It was Mother who conveyed the terrible news to us.

The first to come home was Lise. Leopold came a little later with his tennis bag, happy after being out playing tennis. We met Mother in the entrance, wailing, fully dressed in front of the house, with a face that was red and swollen from crying and despair. With a stifled voice she stammered that Mrs Storm (mother and mother-in-law to a pair of Leopold's old school friends) had learned from reliable sources that police raids against the Jews in Denmark were to be carried out that night. We were to get dressed as quickly as possible and to leave house and home, as we could no longer consider ourselves safe in our own place. Mother told me that she had rung Father, and we expected him at any minute. Abraham had not yet come home; he apparently knew nothing of the danger that hung over us. When Father came home he was astonished and said, 'You scared me to death on the telephone. What's happened? What's happened' – 'Mischugener, Mischugener, farsteist du nit, jetzt kumen die Nasisten. Tu aan deine kleider und leif avek.'[4] Father stood there confused and stammered, 'What should I do? What should I do?' In the kitchen there were pots full of food that Mother had calculated should see

15 Dr Albert-Hilger van Scherpenberg (1899–1969), diplomat; in the diplomatic service from 1926; legation counsellor and head of the Northern Europe section in the trade policy department of the Reich Foreign Office from 1937; sentenced by the People's Court in 1944 to two years in prison for resistance activities; worked in the Bavarian Ministry of Economics and the German Federal Ministry of Economics, 1945–1953; state secretary in the German Federal Foreign Office, 1958–1961.
16 German in the original: 'Reich Foreign Office'.
17 A review of the individual arrests did not take place. The Danish communists were imprisoned in Stutthof concentration camp, but from winter 1943 they received parcels on a regular basis via the Red Cross and saw an improvement in their treatment. Their mortality rate was low in comparison with other prisoner groups.

1 DJM, JDK207A1/24/125. This document has been translated from Danish.
2 Lise Epstein (b. 1903), journalist; see also Doc. 12.
3 The original contains handwritten annotations and additions. In the report, Lise Epstein writes about herself in the third person but uses the personal pronoun 'we' when referring to her family.
4 Yiddish in the original: 'You fool! You fool! Don't you understand? The Nazis are coming now. Get your clothes and let's run away.'

us through the coming two to three weeks. There was not enough time to sit down together to eat; everyone took what they could from the dishes. After a while Erna arrived, and when she realized our terrible situation, she was gripped by sympathy and tears poured down her cheeks. Within a short time we had gathered the most important things in small bags, and just as we were about to leave, Abraham turned up. He came, out of breath, from gymnastics. He was perplexed and baffled when he heard what possibly awaited us, but he did not want to miss out on eating, and after he had tucked away a solid meal, he headed out with us. He also stocked up with rye bread, a few cans of sardines and tomatoes, and honey, together with some money. We then left the house, each in a different direction, and over the coming days we constantly changed our quarters with friends and acquaintances. We were, however, still a little unsure that something really was about to happen, but nonetheless we were all suffering from anxiety and the uncertainty that we might be accosted or detained at any time. Only on Friday morning, on 1 October, was it clear to us what direction it was all heading in, and that the whole thing was deadly serious. On Thursday night, roundups had taken place all over Copenhagen, and the following day the Nazis announced in the newspaper that they had neutralized the Jews.

Each of us now worked on how we could leave the country by seeking to establish contact with illegal entrepreneurs[5] who could get us out of the country. We had different possibilities to choose from, but in the end we decided on a connection that Lise had made through G. M.[6] While these plans were being worked out, everyone tried to gather what could be saved from our home, and we granted power of attorney to Family H.[7] and to Erna and her family. It was touching to witness the kindness and zeal with which everyone contributed to helping us. Particular mention must be made of Erna, whose help to us was invaluable. Also Family H. from Tulipanvej, a family consisting of a pair of likeable young people and a sensitive mother in whom we had full confidence. Erna's sister also helped us as best as she could.

On Sunday evening, 3 October, Mother and Lise stayed with Family H. on Tulipanvej. While there they received word that the next day they would be able to travel to Sweden together with the rest of the family. The plan required them to go to the town of S.,[8] where they were to stay in a small summer guesthouse. At 6.30 p.m. Lise would meet a man on a specified street, who would give us more precise information about the opportunity to board a ship. Beforehand, we were all to meet the next day at 1.30 at H's. Mother and Lise were already there, then Father came, then Leopold and Abraham arrived by bicycle. Lastly, Erna arrived. She had been out to get Abraham's passport from Mogens, who had acquired it from the passport authorities under dramatic circumstances. An hour earlier Erna and Leopold had joined Abraham on G. road,[9] where he had rented a small room under the name 'Ekstein'. This name was the result of a series of misunderstandings on

5 The term alludes to the fact that many of those who helped the Jews escape accepted money in return for their services.
6 The identity of G. M. could not be established.
7 The Holde family; see Doc. 12.
8 Presumably a reference to Snekkersten, a village north of Copenhagen via which a large proportion of those fleeing travelled.
9 Presumably the street called Godthåbsvej.

the part of the hostess. When asked for his name, Abraham had said it indistinctly, and she had therefore misunderstood and said, 'Well, Mr Ekstein', and he had left her to believe what she believed. While still at the G. road Abraham and Leopold had decided to take time for a good meal. They opened a few tins of sardines and goose-liver pâté. The table was full of bread, tomatoes, and thick sandwiches. During this meal, we had several bright ideas. One of these ideas was that Abraham decided that it would be good if he could take his passport with him. Mogens was to get the visa for his passport in the Swedish travel agency at the main railway station. Abraham therefore asked Erna to go and meet Mogens to collect it. When Erna came back to Family H.'s, she gave a description of the upheaval that Mogens had gone through in order to retrieve the passport. Suddenly Frikorps men[10] had come in and arrested all the Jews present, whereupon they approached Mogens and asked what he was doing there. Mogens luckily had the quick thinking to turn around and push the passport back across the service desk, and when the Schalburg men[11] asked him what he was doing, he replied, 'I just wanted to know whether it's permitted to travel to Sweden on a little Christmas trip. Surely that's not forbidden.' In the meantime, the assistant winked at him to tell him he should follow him outside, and when they were standing in the arrivals halls at the main station, the assistant waved him on into the toilets, where he gave him back the passport. Mogens had earlier laughed at Abraham's vigilance and anxiety about this situation and had made a big joke about it, but now he realized that it was all deadly serious.

When it was nearly 2 o'clock, we left the H. house in small groups. Each of us took a briefcase or a small suitcase. Abraham did not want to take anything with him, though. He thought anything might happen. Among other things he reckoned that one could not exclude the possibility that one might have to swim at some point. Prior to the departure he had decided he was going to wear swimming trunks, but later he told me that in all the haste he had unfortunately forgotten to take this precaution. We obtained tickets from Godthåbsvej station[12] to the town of S. The first thing we asked ourselves was whether it would be very conspicuous for so many people to buy a ticket to S. station. Overall, we were incredibly suspicious and vigilant in every little thing we did, as we constantly assumed that these little things were of decisive importance for our safety. We immediately got on the train, but did not look at each other and did not speak to each other. The train was full of Jews. We were very afraid that someone might enter the train and attack us. We were already filled with a strange disquiet. On the train Abraham met Mr V., who lived out by Hørsholm and got off in Rungsted. Abraham spoke with him. He told Abraham about the protest by the bishops.[13] We finally came into town S. We had attentively observed who had got off at the stations before the town of S. How-

10 The reference is to the Frikorps Danmark, a volunteer unit created by the Danish National Socialist Workers' Party and the SS in 1941. The number of people involved in the Frikorps is unknown. In mid 1943 the remaining members were transferred to the SS-Division Nordland. In total, some 6,000 Danes fought on the German side as members of various organizations.

11 The Schalburg Corps was a Danish unit of the Waffen SS founded in Feb. 1943, named after the temporary commander of the Frikorps Danmark, SS-Sturmbannführer Christian Frederik von Schalburg (1906–1942). It was to be deployed against the growing Danish resistance. For many Danes the Frikorps and Schalburg Corps were synonymous.

12 Renamed Grøndal station in 1996.

13 On the bishops' letter of protest, see Doc. 11.

ever, it was only a few people. The big rush was for the town of S. We now split up into small separate groups to go down towards Strandvejen. We started out in the wrong direction, but when we realized our mistake, we quickly turned around to go in the opposite direction. Doubtless we attracted a lot of attention as we went along carrying our small bags and with expressions full of fear. We met only a few fishermen, who regarded us with curiosity and sympathy. There was a peculiar unease in the air that was particularly a product of the fact that on our way to Øl. Guest House[14] we met several fishermen who asked if we wanted to cross over with them. On the way, people in a guest house called out to Mother and said she should come inside quickly because it was dangerous to be out and about. The rest of us headed to Øl., and we were all gripped by a terrible feeling that something might have happened to Mother if she had gone into the wrong house, but a little later she turned up at Øl. We were quite hungry and so ate some of the food we had brought with us. We also drank a cup of coffee, which stood out as the most expensive coffee that we had ever, and would ever, drink. While we sat there and drank coffee, there was a knock at the door. A shiver ran through us all and in came a fisherman with one of those sailor caps on his head. He said, 'Is it you lot who are going over this evening?' We said that we had an appointment for 6.30 p.m. and we must first see what came of it before we could make other arrangements. He explained that getting to Sweden was a clear-cut matter. We could go straight down to the harbour, where the boat was, then be stowed away below in the cargo space, with the hatch closed over. The skipper would sail to the harbour master, get a stamp and then head out to sea. He said that this was happening in broad daylight, and that in fact the fishermen were doing nothing but ferrying people over to Sweden. There were intense discussions between us as to whether we should take up the fisherman's suggestion. Mother was particularly keen to get away. Lise adamantly took the opposite view, that not keeping to the original plan could possibly cause problems for other people, and therefore we stuck with waiting for the outcome of H.'s inquiries with the fisherman.

We were very grateful that we could be in a house before our escape and we thought we should express this gratitude to the landlady before we left. We reckoned that 10 kroner per person for coffee plus accommodation was a very reasonable price. The cost of the coffee thus came to 50 kroner, and she could not believe her eyes when she saw the money.

At 6.30 p.m. Leopold and Erna set off to find the street where we were supposed to meet the aforementioned man, but on the way we met young H. and Mr H. They could not say for sure whether we could cross over. They first had to go and discuss the matter with some fishermen. When they came back to Øl., they gave us the sad news that we certainly could not cross over that evening as the Gestapo had come to the harbour in S. We therefore decided to have supper at Øl. We had a delicious supper and the mood was cheerful. We ate, drank, and told jokes. In that moment we did not feel like refugees at all, but like ordinary happy people who were out celebrating. But we could not stay at the Ølgaard guest house. It was feared that there would be a roundup there later, so we were permitted to stay with a relative of the Holte family,[15] a very wealthy man whose house, so charmingly located down at the beach, was one of the prettiest you could

14 This refers to the Ølgaard guest house (see below).
15 Presumably another reference to the Holde family.

imagine. It was very tastefully decorated. Each of us was given a beautifully furnished room with an adjoining bathroom. We lived like lords. The next morning we were given breakfast and then we planned to leave. Now we were told that the Danish police had warned that there would be a roundup in Snekkersten, so we left for Humlebæk[16] station. On the way there we met many distraught Jews, while the locals looked on sympathetically. Several of the Jews we met did not think it was wise to head for Humlebæk, and instead suggested that it would be safer to go further inland, which later proved to be the wisest thing to do. At Humlebæk station lots of Jews were waiting for the train. There were many conflicting opinions as to whether we should get on the train or not. Some people approached us and told us that going to Humlebæk was the stupidest thing we could do as everyone was headed that way and in doing so increased the risk. We were advised to travel inland. In the meantime, one of my brothers, Abraham, ran over the railway tracks and into the forest to hide, while my younger brother, Leopold, with Erna, had quite calmly sat down on a bench, apparently entirely unaffected by the general commotion. My parents and I decided to go further inland and set off – with our small bags and several suitcases that we would later have to leave behind because one had as much as possible to avoid the impression that one was travelling. Just as we were about to leave the station, several young people approached us and asked if they could help us with anything. We didn't know them, but we were despondent and distraught and replied 'Yes, please' to the offer. They helped us carry our suitcases on their bicycles and, after we had walked for around twenty minutes, we asked the young man if he knew anyone who would put us up. He went into a farmhouse, whose owner he was acquainted with, to enquire whether it was possible, but the people did not want to take the risk since a farmhand there could not be completely trusted. We lay down on the field bordering the house, hidden behind some bushes, so that we could see who was coming down the road. It was a lovely autumn day and we spread out our coats, lay on them and sunbathed. In doing so for a brief moment we forgot our sad situation.

After some time, we saw Leopold and Erna walking down the road. We called over to them, and they lay down in the field beside us. Soon after, we saw a young man coming, and my mother, anxious about my brother's disappearance, asked him if he had by any chance seen my brother and gave a description of him. 'Yes,' he said, 'he is at our house.' What a remarkable twist of fate. It turned out that the young dark-haired man was the son of opera singer Skjær,[17] and we now all set off for his house.

There about ten people were gathered, all waiting for a chance to get on board a ship. A lawyer who was present and whose name I don't remember reckoned that we might be able to get away with the others. We were so happy that there was a possibility to depart. After we had paid several thousand kroner to the lawyer who was to organize it all for us, we were taken by car to Snekkersten harbour, where we were directed to a shoemaker, who received a certain sum of money from the lawyer to house us. The money was stuffed under the shoemaker's greasy shirt, and we were led into a tiny room, where we sat and waited from 2 o'clock in the afternoon until 7 o'clock in the evening. The room was small, and the air gradually became unbearable because of the tobacco

16 A small coastal village between Copenhagen and Helsingør to the north.

17 Eyvind Skjær (1923–1994), actor; son of opera singer Henry Skjær (1899–1991); active in the resistance and a member of the Danish underground army.

smoke and lack of ventilation, because we did not dare open the window. We sat as quiet as mice, and the mood was naturally very gloomy while we waited for the man who was to get us a place on a boat to come back and say that the coast was clear. It was around 4 o'clock in the afternoon when he first returned, but he said that getting away was hopeless because there were Gestapo men milling around the harbour. He left us and said that he would come back again at 7 o'clock regardless of whether or not we could depart. When the clock struck 7 he was back with news that the journey would have to be postponed. We got our money back, though minus a 'compensation' for his troubles: 200 kroner per family.[18]

We made our way back to the Skjærs, who now couldn't put us all up, so Father and Mother, my brothers and I were taken in by the Kramer family, the most kind-hearted, hospitable, and wonderful people I have ever met. What a wonderful reception he [Mr Kramer] gave us! The food was both exquisite and abundant. We stayed with this lovely man for a couple of days. We could have slept in the house itself, but my brothers, Erna, and I preferred to sleep in his hayloft, which was very high up and could only be reached by climbing a very tall ladder. My parents slept in the Kramers' house, while we 'kids' made our way to the hayloft, where we made ourselves comfortable dens in the soft, fragrant hay. We had a visit from the most delightful little cats, who purred and curled up with us gently, as if they wanted to comfort us and cheer us up, as if they were saying, 'Don't worry, everything will be all right.' I could feel their little paws on my chest and their velvety fur against my face.

So long as I live, I will never forget the kindness that was shown to us by the Kramer family. Of course we also received hospitality in other places, but with these people we found a rare kind-heartedness and goodness.

After some days Mr Kramer told us that he now had a good contact. He was in touch with a senior surgeon in Helsingør,[19] who had connections in turn with a fisherman who was sailing people over. It was decided that we should leave that same day in the evening. The doctor came to us in the afternoon and discussed with us where we should go. A car with a reliable driver was made available for us, and Mr Kramer very carefully explained to the driver in detail which route he should take in order to attract as little attention as possible. Mr K. knew the whole region like the back of his hand. At around 6.30 p.m. we took our leave of our hospitable host and of Erna, yes Erna, let's not forget her. She cried bitterly when we bid her farewell. She had followed us faithfully for the whole journey and had been of invaluable help. Now she stood with tears in her eyes and waved us goodbye.

Now, on 17 January, I have read in a newspaper that the Copenhagen police have been arrested.[20] Erna's father is a police commissioner on Årø[21] and her brother is a constable. What ordeals must her family and she herself have gone through! I thought about her all night. About the grief for her family. May the Nazi thugs get their

18 200 kroner was roughly half the monthly wage of a skilled worker. The average price for a crossing was 500 kroner.

19 See Doc. 19.

20 It is unclear what this refers to. The mass internment of Danish police by the German occupiers occurred only later, in Sept. 1944.

21 Island between the Danish mainland and the island of Funen.

well-deserved punishment for all their wrongdoing and for the sorrow and despair they have wrought on thousands of people.

The driver took us through winding forest roads and, as arranged, the doctor's wife was standing waiting for us on one of those forest roads, quite alone. We now went in small groups along the road in order to arouse as little attention as possible. As arranged, we entered the house where we were to meet. Once inside the house, we discussed the strange fact that a young man had been standing not far from the house and had keenly observed those who entered. We were a little nervous, but even if he had been an informant, he had arrived too late if he wanted to raise the alarm: it wasn't even five minutes before we were in the boat that was to take us to Sweden, after we had paid the money demanded.

The whole thing was marvellously arranged, and we cast off immediately. The elderly and the children were to be brought over first, and my parents went in the first boat. Then we others followed. There were around twelve people in our boat, my two brothers and I included. At the beginning we sat hunched and silent, but after we entered Swedish waters, the mood lightened, and we talked loudly and clearly with one another. The water sprayed in and over us as it was an open boat. My brother, who was sitting on the outside, got the worst of it, he caught one breaker after the other, but despite all that we thought it was glorious. The evening was actually mild and the water felt lukewarm. The polecat fur scarf I was wearing around my neck was completely drenched and so was my hat. But what did it matter …

The lights got closer and closer, we could see people on the quay, then the boat docked and friendly hands received us. A Swedish Lotte[22] took care of me. She didn't know what to say to me. She didn't know what she could say or do to make me feel better. She grabbed on to my arm so tightly that one would have almost thought I was unable to stand up on my own, but I felt completely fine. Suddenly I heard my mother calling my name. She was out here and was looking for me. Arm in arm we went to the assembly place, where a great number of people had already gathered. The delight at seeing each other again was of course great, and we saw a number of our acquaintances there.

Later, we heard of friends and acquaintances who had endured terrible tribulations; there were many who had found their graves beneath the cold waves, and many had been arrested by the Gestapo in their homes, along the coast, and on the beach. We heard of inhuman and bitter fates.[23] Mother cried every time someone told her of friends and acquaintances who had been taken or had perished, and in the big dormitory at Ramlösa we heard of many strange and harsh fates. I thank God that we all got to Sweden safe and sound. May the day come soon when Denmark and all other oppressed countries in the world will once again be free and independent. One night when Mother and I were staying with acquaintances, I was convinced that I heard someone trying to break down the door with great force. Never in my life have I been so terrified. I was shaking so much that the bed was almost shaking too. There was an alarm clock on the dressing table. I got up and brought it back with me to bed, where I put it under the covers. I was

22 Female military auxiliary.
23 At least 21 Jews perished in the attempt to flee to Sweden, and a further 20 took their own lives or died of shock or exhaustion.

afraid that it would ring at the wrong moment and betray us. The next morning it was evident that the whole thing had been in my imagination. Our acquaintances were insistent that there hadn't been anyone at the front door. I must have imagined it, my mind had been playing tricks on me, but my nerves were wrecked after this sleepless, troubled night.[24]

DOC. 15
On 2 October 1943 a Danish member of the Waffen SS records his experiences during the mass arrest of Jews[1]

Handwritten journal of Holger Gormsen,[2] entries for 30 September and 2 October 1943

30 September
Arrived in Copenhagen in the evening. We all had to go to 1 Jernbanegade, where we were told to report on Friday at 5 p.m. in uniform. So there is something on the agenda for tomorrow.

2 October
Met up at 5 p.m. at Jernbanegade.[3] Everyone divided up into two teams. One to the school in Algade, the other to the tennis centre in Pilealle; both places are barracks for the German police. I went to Algade.

We marched out along Vesterbrogade. When we got to the barracks, we stayed in the canteen until 8.30 p.m., where we were given time to drink beer and spirits. Then we were divided into teams, each with four Germans and one Dane, and all the teams were given a bunch of papers with the names and addresses of Jews who were to be arrested.

My workplace was Strandboulevarden – Bergens – Kristianiagade, it was a posh district. But in any case, they were all gone, they had sensed something was up and had disappeared just in time.

My team had no success. Out of four teams in the vehicle, only one of them made an arrest, two old Jewish ladies from Kastlevej, as well as an old tailor from Rugensgade with his wife and 11- or 12-year-old son. The tram depot at Strandvejen, just before Svanemøllen, was where the catch was handed over.

Then we drove back to the barracks, finishing our shift at 6 a.m.

24 The final paragraph was probably added later because it is on different paper and the page is not numbered.

1 Frihedsmuseets Dokumentarkiv, 23F-38. Excerpts published anonymously in Claus Bundgård Christensen, Niels Bo Poulsen, and Peter Scharff Smith, *Dagbok fra Østfronten: En dansker i Waffen-SS 1941–44* (Copenhagen: Aschehoug, 2005), pp. 128–130. This document has been translated from Danish.

2 Holger Gormsen, SS-Unterscharführer in the 3rd Panzergrenadierbataillon Danmark (as noted on the first page of the journal); member of the Waffen SS, June 1941–Jan. 1944, then served in the occupation regime's anti-sabotage guard; arrested by Danish resistance fighters on 5 May 1945; sentenced to three years in prison in Nov. 1946.

3 The headquarters of SS-Ersatzkommando Danmark (the recruitment office of the SS in Denmark) were at 7 Jernbanegade.

The Jews had to take with them two blankets, food for 3–4 days, and whatever valuables fitted in a small suitcase. Not exactly the kind of work that interested me, but orders must be obeyed as long as one is in uniform. The word is that the Jews were taken by boat to Danzig.[4]

DOC. 16

New York Times, 3 October 1943: article on the efforts in Sweden to save Jews from deportation[1]

Sweden offers aid to Denmark's Jews. Protests to Germans against mass arrests made during New Year festivities. Fate of 7,000 unreported. Stockholm fears prisoners may be sent to Poland – warns of repercussions.

By George Axelsson.[2] By wireless to the New York Times.
Stockholm, Oct. 2 – In a sweeping humanitarian gesture Sweden offered asylum today to some 7,000 Jews arrested by the Gestapo in Denmark on Sept. 30 during the New Year festivities.[3] The offer was made yesterday to German occupation officials through the Swedish Minister to Berlin,[4] but so far the Reich has not deigned to answer.

The Stockholm communiqué on the subject, released this evening, reads: 'In the last few days reports have reached Sweden that measures are being prepared against the Jews in Denmark similar to those already applied in Norway and other occupied countries. Acting on the Government instructions the Swedish Minister to Berlin[5] on Oct. 1 pointed out to the German authorities concerned the serious repercussions these measures might provoke in Sweden. At the same time the Minister conveyed the offer of the Swedish Government to receive in Sweden all Danish Jews.'[6]

German Reply Awaited
Stockholm political circles entertained tonight no illusion that the Swedish remarks in Berlin would receive a favourable answer if they received any at all. Stockholm was reportedly prepared for the first outburst of abuse of Sweden from the Wilhelmstrasse-inspired German press, similar to that levelled against this country following the Sweden protest at the end of August against the sinking with all hands of two Swedish fishermen by German destroyers. The Swedes rather expect soon to read in the German press a

4 Along with the Jews, 150 communists were deported from Denmark. The latter were taken to Stutthof concentration camp, near Danzig.

1 *New York Times*, 3 Oct. 1943, p. 29. This daily newspaper was founded in 1851.

2 George Axelsson (1899–1966), Swedish citizen; headed the Paris office of the *New York Times*, 1940–1941, the Berlin office in 1941, and the Stockholm office from 1942 to 1945; worked again as the Scandinavian correspondent for the *New York Times* based in Stockholm, 1948–1957.

3 The Swedish government offered to take in all Danish Jews. The actual number of Jews arrested in Denmark on 1 and 2 Oct. 1943 was 284.

4 Arvid Richert (1887–1981), diplomat; court clerk, 1914–1918; worked at the Swedish Foreign Ministry and in various diplomatic posts from 1918; ambassador to Berlin from 1937; governor of Älvsborg administrative district after 1945.

5 The author is referring to the Swedish ambassador.

6 This announcement was passed on to the Tidningarnas Telegrambyrå news agency on 2 Oct. 1943 and was read on Swedish radio at 6 p.m.

repetition of the hackneyed accusation of being Jew-ridden and infested with Anglo-Bolshevik plutocrats and Freemasons. The arrest of Jews in Denmark was heralded by the arrival in that country at the beginning of last week of some 1,800 German police and Gestapo agents. Definite news of the action reached Sweden in the early hours today. It was understood the measures applied were similar to those used against the Norwegian Jews a year ago when during the Rosh ha-Shanah observation the Gestapo forced its way into homes and synagogues, sending Jews into a concentration camp and subsequent deportation. The timing and procedure was the same with the 7,000 Jews in Denmark, 6,000 of whom are orthodox, including many Germans who had sought asylum in Denmark prior to its Nazi occupation.[7]

The United Press quoted the Swedish newspaper *Dagens Nyheter*[8] as saying tonight that the Germans had put 1,600 Danish Jews on a deportation ship, probably for transport to Germany,[9] but that many others had managed to escape the Nazis by slipping into Sweden.

Jews were reported fleeing Denmark by rowboat and every other means, running a gauntlet of German patrol boats to reach Sweden.

One of the refugees, it was reported, was Prof. Niels H. D. Bohr, famous atomic physicist and teacher who won the Nobel Prize in physics in 1922.

A cynical Berlin communiqué from DNB[10] tonight admits the round-up of Jews in Denmark, saying they have been 'removed from public life'. The official reason given is the usual one that 'Jews morally and materially supported terrorists, sabotage actions, and anti-German agitation and have materially contributed to the aggravation of the Danish situation.'[11]

Having been 'removed', the Nazi communiqué said, they would no longer be in a position to 'poison the atmosphere'.

As an integral part of the Nazi program now being carried out by stages in Denmark, it is believed here that the Danish Jews are facing the same fate as those in other countries under the German heel. In other words, they will be shipped to Poland, German-occupied Russia, and never will be heard from again. Information here today tends to show that preparations already have been made to deport the victims of the mass arrests to Poland.[12]

7 At the time of the German attack on Denmark there were around 1,680 Jewish refugees in Denmark.

8 '1600 judar på deportationsbåt' ('1,600 Jews aboard a deportation boat'), *Dagens Nyheter*, 3 Oct. 1943, p. 1.

9 Around 470 Jews were deported from Denmark on a total of four transports. The ship mentioned here is probably the *Wartheland*, which departed from Langelinie quay in Copenhagen with 198 Jews and 150 communists on board. The prisoners were separated at Swinemünde (Świnoujście): the Jews were transported to Theresienstadt and the communists to Stutthof.

10 Deutsches Nachrichtenbüro (German News Agency), founded in 1933; dissolved by the Allies in 1945.

11 The source could not be found, but the German authorities did indeed repeatedly justify the deportations with reference to alleged acts of sabotage committed by Jews.

12 With very few exceptions, the Danish Jews were imprisoned in Theresienstadt. Two of the Jews deported from Denmark perished in the camps in occupied Poland. Schmul Sender Jonisch (1899–1944) was included in Transport DX from Theresienstadt to Auschwitz-Birkenau on 20 March 1944; all of those on this transport were murdered in the gas chambers on arrival. Michael Rubin Singerowitz (1891–1944) was included in the fourth transport of Jews from Denmark, which did not go directly to Theresienstadt, but to Sachsenhausen (for men) and Ravensbrück (for women and children). He was transported on 6 Dec. 1943 from Sachsenhausen to Majdanek, where he perished on 21 Jan. 1944.

It is now believed that the Swedes also attempted to intercede at the time for the Norwegian Jews but with scant success because the Germans forbade the passage through Sweden of all the 'eliminated number', presumably except those able to pay a huge ransom in foreign exchange.

The Germans have a crying need for foreign exchange at present, and observers here think the action against the Danish Jews may be largely a financial operation, as evidence indicates the Nazis completely lost their heads over their reverses and once more were using the Jews as a whipping boy.

DOC. 17
On 3 October 1943 Danish students call a strike in protest at the imprisonment of Jews[1]

Pamphlet from the student organization De danske studenter, 3 October 1943

Sunday, 3 October 1943
On Friday night the Gestapo arrested around 1,000 Danish Jews. They were taken on board two ships, which have set sail for an unknown destination. This violation caused such great anger among the students that the Student Council adopted the following statement, which was conveyed verbally to the Senate[2] on Saturday afternoon.

> In view of the most recent events, the students expect the university to suspend all lectures at the university immediately. Should this not happen, the Student Council, as representative of the student body, believes it must counter the Senate's weak stance by calling a general student strike.

The Senate thereupon approved the following statement unanimously but for one vote:

> Due to the adversity experienced in recent days by Danish citizens, the Rector and Senate have decided to suspend all lectures at the University of Copenhagen for one week. Lectures are scheduled to resume on Monday, 11 October.

In addition, the Student Union cancelled a commemorative event for Henrik Pontoppidan[3] and adopted a resolution which Professor Niels Nielsen,[4] presiding senior professor, read out in the Dagmarhus:

> The fact that a group of our countrymen have been removed from the public eye is cause for the committee of the Student Union, as the leadership of a Danish cultural

1 Frihedsmuseets Dokumentarkiv, 6E-19, Forskellige protester mod jødeaktionen. This document has been translated from Danish.
2 The most senior body of the University of Copenhagen; at the time all its members were university professors.
3 Henrik Pontoppidan (1857–1943), Danish writer; winner of the Nobel Prize for Literature in 1917.
4 Dr Niels Nielsen (1893–1981), geographer; university professor in Copenhagen, 1939–1964; president of the university's student union.

institution, to condemn these abuses most strongly, for they are utterly irreconcilable with the Danish way of thinking.

We welcome the position of our student leaders and professors as the only right and dignified stance. It will be embraced by every student.

We assure our official leadership that they have the full support of the student body. This must be the fundamental basis for a courageous stance. This will enable professors, the Student Council, and similar leading individuals and assemblies to assume the moral responsibility that is always associated with a worthy and correct attitude.

DOC. 18

On 5 October 1943 the Reich plenipotentiary in Denmark, Werner Best, reports to the Reich Foreign Office on the arrests and the flight of many Jews to Sweden[1]

Telex (no. 1208 – marked 'very urgent'),[2] signed Dr Best, Copenhagen, to the Reich Foreign Office (received on 5 October 1943, 1.45 p.m.), dated 5 October 1943

In reply to telegram no. 1367, dated 4 October 1943,[3]

I report the following:

1) The direction of the Jewish operation in Denmark was entirely in the hands of Senior Commander of the Security Police SS-Standartenführer Dr Mildner,[4] who issued all directives for its implementation.
2) It is correct that the Senior Commander of the Security Police had issued instructions that locked apartments were not to be broken into. This was the case because it was already known that the vast majority of local Jews were no longer living in their own apartments, so the forced entry into vacant apartments would only have made an unfavourable impression that would then have been held against us.
3) It is correct that the Commander of the German forces in Denmark[5] declined to issue the regulation on the registration of Jews, the text of which had been conveyed in my telegram no. 1189 of 2 October 1943,[6] after he had agreed to do so in principle in a preliminary discussion. I did not insist that the regulation be issued, because the

1 PA AA, R 100 865, fol. 142. This document has been translated from German.

2 By cryptograph ('G-Schreiber').

3 In this telegram the Reich Foreign Office asked why only a small number of arrests had been made and whether it was true that the police had been forbidden to use force to enter residences. PA AA, R 100 865, fol. 139. This order had been given by Rudolf Mildner.

4 Dr Rudolf Mildner (b. 1902), lawyer; joined the NSDAP in 1931 and the SS in 1935; deputy chief of the Gestapo in Linz in 1938; from Dec. 1939 to March 1941 head of the Gestapo head office in Chemnitz, then in Kattowitz, where he was also head of the Gestapo in Auschwitz concentration camp; senior commander of the Security Police and the SD in Copenhagen from Sept. 1943; department head in the Reich Security Main Office (RSHA) from spring 1944; Gestapo chief in Vienna from Dec. 1944; interned and testified at the International Military Tribunal at Nuremberg; disappeared following his release in 1949.

5 Hermann von Hanneken (see Doc. 9).

6 PA AA, R 100 864, fol. 167. The regulation would have required all 'full Jews' still in Denmark, provided that they were not married to a non-Jew, to report to the nearest Wehrmacht office for labour deployment.

Senior Commander of the Security Police took the position that the regulation was no longer absolutely necessary and that he would use the resources of the Security Police to gradually record the Jews still remaining.

4) The number of 284 persons represents only the result of the arrests made during the night of 1 to 2 October 1943. Since then, additional Jews have continued to be detained, as in the case of the 60 Jews arrested during the night of 4 to 5 October as they attempted to leave Zealand island by boat.
5) The Senior Commander of the Security Police and I had foreseen that only very few Jews would be detained. I had also expressed this in earlier reports (telegrams no. 1162, dated 29 September, and no. 1187, dated 1 October 1943).[7] In interrogations by the German Security Police, the Jews who had been arrested stated that most Jews left their apartments immediately after the state of emergency was declared, because they had anticipated such an operation. Before the German police forces arrived here and the operation could be carried out, the Jews had an entire month, during which some went into hiding within Denmark and others left the country by crossing the Sound. These escapes across the Sound could hardly be prevented nor will they be easily prevented in future. Neither police nor military forces are available in sufficient numbers to ensure adequate control over that stretch of coast, which is more than 100 km long. Policing is hardly possible on the water either, because the German navy does not have sufficient vessels, or sufficient crews for the vessels taken over from the Danish navy.
6) Because the actual aim of the Jew operation in Denmark was to de-Jewify the country and not to carry out a headhunt that was as successful as possible, it must be noted that the Jew operation did achieve its aim. Denmark is de-Jewified, for no Jew affected by the relevant directives can legally reside or work here any more.

DOC. 19

On 6 October 1943 Sven Christiansen describes the efforts of Danish physicians to aid Jews in their escape to Sweden[1]

Handwritten report by Sven Christiansen,[2] Helsingborg, dated 6 October 1943

Summary of what I know about the Danish Medical Association's activities during the persecution of the Jews in Denmark, etc.

Upon the doctors' and hospitals' initiative, the hospitals in Denmark are open to the Jews; names are not given, upon the initiative and in consultation with the Medical Association.

7 In telegram no. 1162, dated 29 Sept. 1943, Werner Best reported on a discussion that day with Nils Svenningsen in which Best directly addressed the veracity of rumours of an impending round of arrests: PA AA, R 100 864, fol. 125; see also Doc. 13. In telegram no. 1187, dated 1 Oct. 1943, Best reported the king's protest, which Svenningsen had relayed to him that evening, as well as protests by various organizations even before the operation had begun. He warned that the rumours might cause the operation to fail: PA AA, R 100 864, fol. 145.

1 Frihedsmuseets Dokumentarkiv, 06E-10868–1. This document has been translated from Danish.

Right at the start of the persecution, numerous doctors and other individuals, acting on their own initiative, tried to take as many Jews across to Sweden as possible.

Those particularly active were:

Dr Gantzel and chief physician Sennels in Helsingør

Dr Gersfeldt in Snekkersten

Dr Borghild Andersen in Copenhagen

Chief physician Therp in Copenhagen

Dr Dich in Dragør

Insurance agent Abel in Copenhagen

Dr Algreen Petersen.[3]

In addition to the actions of these individuals, two secret organizations, one associated with the *Frie Danske*[4] newspaper and the other associated with the Communist Party,[5] were active in this area. Director Parkov and the brewer, Semler,[6] did the same as well as many fishermen in direct contact with the Jews.

Alongside these direct evacuation operations, attempts were also made to set up a central office, which collated addresses and then put those concerned in contact with the evacuation operations. One of these central offices was located at the Rockefeller Institute (Prof. Ege,[7] Dr phil. P. Brandt Rehberg[8] and laboratory supervisor Persson). Another central office exists, as before, in department O at Rigshospitalet[9] under the direction of Professor Helweg.[10]

All these individuals (except for Director Parkov) and organizations (except for 'Frie Danske' and presumably the communists) faced tremendous difficulties, as follows:

2 Sven Ivar Christiansen (1901–1987), physician; worked at Frederiksberg Hospital; active in relief efforts for refugees; fled to Sweden in Oct. 1943; from 1950 worked for the World Health Organization (WHO) in places including Afghanistan and Iran.

3 This is probably a reference to the following physicians: Dr Tage Urban Neergaard Gantzel (1911–1992); Dr Aage Sennels (b. 1890), chief physician at Øresund Hospital in Helsingør from 1926; Jørgen Gersfeldt (1912–1985) practised in Snekkersten; organized escape routes for Jewish refugees and later for the Danish resistance; fled to Sweden in May 1944; Borghild Andersen (b. 1903), active in the resistance, arrested in Jan. 1945 and interned in Frøslev camp until the end of the war; Holger Christian Storm Therp (b. 1891) joined the Danish exile police in Sweden and became medical director of the medical company Dich; and Dr Carsten Algreen Petersen (b. 1894).

4 On this resistance group, see Doc. 4.

5 This refers to the resistance group BOPA (Borgerlige partisaner, 'Civil partisans') founded by members of the Danish Communist Party; the group initially called itself KOPA (Kommunistiske partisaner, 'Communist partisans').

6 Knud Parkov (1884–1949), director of Wiibroe Brewery in Helsingør from 1932; provided money and shipping space for refugees. Arne Semler-Jørgensen, brewer; involved in organizing the mass flight. Both fled to Sweden in May 1944.

7 Richard Ege (1891–1974), biochemist; from 1928 professor in Copenhagen; as part of the resistance organization Ringen, co-organizer of the mass flight and of the shipment of aid parcels to deportees. The Ege family went into hiding in summer 1944.

8 Poul Brandt Rehberg (1895–1989), doctor of medicine; worked at the University of Copenhagen from 1921; helped with the shipping of aid parcels to Danish prisoners; imprisoned at the Gestapo headquarters in Copenhagen in Feb. 1945; escaped after the building was bombed by the RAF.

9 The National Hospital.

10 Hjalmar Helweg (1886–1960), doctor of medicine; head of the psychiatric department of the Rigshospitalet in Copenhagen from 1937.

1) The constantly rising prices, partly due to the growing alarm among the people and partly due to shrewd middlemen, who bribed the police and civil defence personnel and who were surrounded by a large number of people working for them.
2) The unreliability of some of the fishermen who would either increase prices (e.g. to double the amount) once the refugees were on board and refused to sail until the higher price had been paid, or would take the payment and then refuse to sail.
3) Finally, it also happened that in some cases it would be a trap, their money would be taken and the boats would set sail, only to take them directly to the German forces.[11]

Against the background of these financial and organizational difficulties, a group of doctors under the surgeon Professor E. Husfeldt's[12] leadership wrote to the Danish Medical Association's chairman, asking whether the General Danish Medical Association would be prepared to financially support Jewish doctors, and later all Jews, in leaving the country. The response from the chairman (chief surgeon Mogens Fenger[13]) was yes.

They also asked the chairman whether he, on behalf of the General Danish Medical Association, would contact the Catholic bishop and the bishop of Copenhagen and ask the former whether the Catholic Church in Denmark would open its religious houses and children's homes (which are private and therefore not subject to state supervision) to Jewish children.

The Protestant bishop was asked whether the national Church of Denmark[14] would be willing to organize collections to support the Jewish children under Catholic protection.

Already by Sunday afternoon, chief surgeon Fenger had contacted the two clerics, who agreed to the requests.

At the meeting with chief surgeon Fenger it was agreed that a committee would be put together and tasked with creating an organization which would gather Jewish children to take them to the convents and would also make contact with as many Jews as possible so as to get them out of the country in the safest way possible. All the decisions reached were of a strictly confidential nature and it was decided that the operation would be carried out as anonymously as possible.

The now founded committee comprises Dr Steffen Lund (inspector of Copenhagen municipality's hospitals) as chairman. Along with Prof. E. Husfeldt, Dr Ch. Højland Christensen, Dr Borghild Andersen, Dr Algreen Petersen, Dr Kirstine Ladefoged Jensen,[15] Dr Nellemann, Dr Sven Christiansen.

The work of the committee is such that it appoints a representative for each of Copenhagen's districts. The representatives contact trustworthy doctors in Copenhagen (i.e. all doctors apart from a few exceptions) and brief them about the case so that they know

11 This could not be confirmed.
12 Erik Husfeldt (1901–1984), surgeon; joined the resistance in 1941 (cover name: architect Jensen); professor in Copenhagen from 1943; member of the umbrella organization of the Danish resistance, the Freedom Council; chief surgeon at the Rigshospitalet from 1953.
13 Mogens Fenger (1889–1956), surgeon; worked at various hospitals in Copenhagen; chairman of the General Danish Medical Association, 1940–1945.
14 Danish: Folkekirke. Term for the Lutheran Church in Denmark.
15 Kirstine Ladefoged Jensen (1907–1964), doctor of medicine; practised medicine in Copenhagen from 1939; active in the women's movement.

what they need to do when Jews contact them to get their children out of the country or to leave the country themselves.

The committee has also appointed a subcommittee that is directly concerned with the shipment (Dr Borghild Andersen, Dr Algreen Petersen, Prof. E. Husfeldt and Dr Sven Christiansen). One part of this committee has made contact with the central office at the Rockefeller Institute and department O at the Rigshospitalet, another part has also tried to raise money by contacting private individuals, and for this last enterprise they also received an extraordinary amount of support from the haulier Tuxen (Tuxen and Hagemann, Amaliegade) and from Dir. Lipmann, Simonsen and Weel.

The committee decided that it was best to acquire sailing boats themselves and organize for them to be operated by reliable people whose associates would guarantee a certain amount of financial support in case the boat captain was arrested.

To look into the possibilities of buying the sailing boats, I went to Helsingør. Here I came into contact with Director Parkov and brewer Semler Jørgensen from Wiibroe's brewery. These two men have safely helped countless Danes get across to Sweden (both Jews and other refugees).

Here, Director Parkov came forward with another suggestion:

that one man be sent to Sweden, who would try and form an organization to transport Danish refugees to Sweden. This organization's vessels would sail as close to the Danish coast as possible and here pick up the Danes from small boats.

In Dir. Parkov's opinion, the risk for the Swedish boats would be less than for the Danish fishermen, since, in the worst case scenario, they would have to anticipate being detained in a Danish port for a few days, an event that would trigger political protest.

Yesterday, Director Parkov and I returned to Copenhagen and straight away went to find Prof. Husfeldt, who immediately approved of the plan and thought it was far preferable to the other projects.

After that, I was called to a meeting with Prof. Helweg and Prof. Engelbreth-Holm,[16] at which they wanted to put forward other plans. After I had introduced the two professors, they both declared that Dir. Parkov's plan was by far preferable to their own ideas, which were far from definite. Afterwards, it was finally decided that I would go to Helsingborg with a letter of introduction from Dir. Parkov to Mayor Laurin.

Dir. Parkov had previously spoken to Dir. Linden about the plan, which Linden approved. Dir. Linden thought, however, he couldn't give me a letter of introduction as this would greatly endanger the consulate.

I then headed to Helsingborg on a refugee boat dispatched by Dir. Parkov and then briefed the mayor on the matter.

During my stay in Helsingborg I came into contact with draughtsman Jorn Denize, 94 Vigerslev Allé, 2.v., whom I met on Monday afternoon when he arrived late for a refugee transportation which I had dispatched. He accompanied me to my accommodation from where I took him to a safe location. From that very point, he came across to me as a reliable person. At the refugee camp in Ramlösa,[17] Helsingborg, it emerged that

16 Julius Engelbreth-Holm (1904–1961), pathologist; professor in Copenhagen from 1941.
17 A central reception centre for the refugees was set up in the suburb of Helsingborg in Oct. 1943.

he had quite a number of acquaintances and friends among the Jewish refugees. He had come to Sweden on a boat whose owner was in contact with Mrs Adelson, who had done a lot of work helping refugees. She therefore had a lot of experience with Danish skippers and fishermen.

Mr Denize put me in contact with Mrs Adelson and he also gave me the address of the 'Frie Danske'[18] central shipping office.[19]

DOC. 20

In diary entries for 3 to 7 October 1943, Ivar Philipson from the Jewish Community of Stockholm describes the efforts to organize assistance for Jews fleeing Denmark[1]

Diary of Ivar Philipson,[2] entries for 3 to 7 October 1943 (copy)

3 October
6 a.m. instructions from Gunnar Josephson[3] to raise money and organize help to get refugees out of Denmark. 7.30 a.m. meeting with Massur and Arnheim.[4] The problem was discussed.

4 October
Phoned various people and collected 103,000 kroner in the morning.[5] Went to see Groschinsky. He first talked about a contribution of 5,000 kroner. I argued that I probably needed more money, and he said that the board of the Music Society would meet that afternoon and that the decision about the amount would be made then. In the meantime, however, I could expect 10,000 kroner from him and the society. At lunchtime I left for Malmö with Arnheim, Köpniwsky, and Bertil Gottfarb.[6] Discussion during the train journey. Arrived in Malmö around 10.30 p.m. Zadig[7] welcomed us at a Jewish Community meeting with around ten people, four of them Danish. After a few

18 This refers to the central refugee aid organization of the resistance group De frie Danske.

19 The plan was not carried out in this way, but various individuals and organizations in Sweden did try to hire vessels and come to meet the refugees. See Doc. 20.

1 YVA, 0.27/3, Copy in Frihedsmuseets Dokumentarkiv, 06E-10878-1. This document has been translated from Swedish.

2 Ivar Philipson (1901–1983), lawyer; had his own law firm from 1938; board member of the Jewish Community of Stockholm.

3 Gunnar August Josephson (1889–1972), bookseller; chairman of the Jewish Community of Stockholm, 1936–1962.

4 Correctly: Norbert Masur (1901–1971), businessman; representative of the Swedish section at the World Jewish Congress in the secret negotiations with Heinrich Himmler on the rescue of Scandinavian concentration camp prisoners. Franz Manfred Arnheim (1909–1971), lawyer; secretary of the relief committee of the Jewish Community of Stockholm.

5 By way of comparison: the annual salary of the rabbi of Malmö was 10,000 kroner.

6 Markus David Köpniwsky (1908–1992), lawyer; executive officer of the Jewish Community of Stockholm. Bertil Gottfarb (1909–1973), business studies graduate; involved in helping refugees in Sweden.

7 Albert Ferdinand Zadig (1879–1955), businessman; board member of the Jewish Community of Malmö.

minutes I asked to speak with Hollander[8] and [...][9] regarding my problem. Hollander reported that the Halutz boat[10] has twice been to Denmark in vain, but there are plans for additional boats. In the meantime, connections first need to be made with Denmark and these are being taken care of by Jensen,[11] who lived in Malmö but was very difficult to reach. It was decided that I should be introduced to Jensen tomorrow. Got home at 2 a.m.

5 October
Started with phone calls at 7 a.m. Failed to reach Jensen. Sought out Hansen: he reported on patrols involving twelve fishing boats. He has been in contact with the police authorities and the management of the naval district. Each boat cost 100 kroner per night, but the skipper provided the fuel. Now that the naval command is supplying the fuel for free, each boat would cost a bit less than 100 kroner, about 85 kroner per night. It was decided that I would bear this cost for the time being and would deposit 5,000 kroner in Allhem's account[12] for this purpose. Drove to the bank and made the transaction. Looked for Jensen again, unsuccessfully. Lunched with Hollander and Mrs Christensen. She came over two days ago with two friends in a dilapidated rowing boat, which they had bought for 2,500 kroner. She sat in the bottom of the boat with water up to her waist and bailed it with a man's hat. They arrived on land at Ven and were received in grand fashion by the Swedish military. She had been admitted to hospital for a few days but is fine now. It was agreed that Mrs Christensen, who is used to organizing, would be our link in Malmö and that we should rent her a room with a telephone.

In the afternoon I found Pfannenstill[13] and asked him to help me. He immediately asked the chairman of Limhamn's fishermen's association, Mr Fors, to come round. Mr Fors said that his brother and other fishermen might be willing to go across to Denmark. It was agreed that we would visit Fors that evening. Visit from Mrs Holm, head of the boatyard in Ystad. I asked her to look into the possibilities for getting fishing boats on the south coast. She said that some of the west coast fishermen are currently moored at Ystad and that they recently fished near Bornholm, but they would possibly be moving on, as they follow the fish. She promised to have her supervisor look into the possibilities and to call me in the morning. Hollander introduced me to a Danish skipper who normally travels between Denmark and Germany. On his latest trip from Denmark he had brought several refugees with him and they jumped ship along the Falsterbo Canal.[14] He didn't ask for any payment but didn't know when he

8 Dr Fritz Friedrich Salomon Hollander (1915–2004), businessman; emigrated from Germany to Sweden in 1933; board member of the Swedish section at the World Jewish Congress.

9 In the original, a blank space has been left here.

10 In spring 1943 Swedish Zionists had started preparations for the rescue of their Danish comrades (halutzim). For this purpose they purchased the *Julius*, a boat on which Danish Zionists had escaped. Although contact with the Danish Zionist youth organizations was not established around 280 additional Danish Jews were transported on the boat.

11 Robert Jensen (1900–1944), code name Tom, businessman; helped more than 1,000 people escape.

12 Probably a reference to the bank account of the Allhem publishing house. Its founder, Einar Hansen (1902–1994), was a patron, publisher, and shipowner and played a vital role in the assistance given to fleeing Jews.

13 Presumably Bo Pfannenstill (b. 1903), lawyer; employed in Philipson's law firm, 1931/1932.

14 Falsterbo Canal separates the Falsterbo peninsula from the Swedish mainland.

would return from Germany. Lunch with Hollander. Waited an hour for Jensen at his hotel, but to no avail. Several Danish refugees gathered there to listen to the radio. They had heard the rumour that Denmark has become a protectorate. Visited Fors, where we drank coffee with schnapps together with his brother and two Danish fishermen. The latter had come over the night before with a few refugees. They had earlier gone several times up to the border between Swedish and Danish territorial waters, but hadn't dared to cross over, as only in the last few days have the Swedish authorities permitted Danish boats to enter Swedish harbours. Previously passengers had to jump from one boat to the other and this was very difficult when the seas were rough – on one occasion the boats nearly crashed into each other. In other instances, the refugees had to jump into the sea from the Danish boats and swim to the Swedish coast. As a result, some of them arrived in Sweden with literally just the shirts on their backs. My informant had five people with him. One had been hidden in the small fore cabin. Three lay under the fishing nets and an elderly lady was in the cabin. The boat was searched by the German coastguard before leaving the Danish harbour, but when they wanted to look inside the cabin, the captain slipped them 500 kroner and they let the boat pass. The captain had talked to a pilot who had piloted a deportation ship as it left; 400 Jews and 200 communists had been on board.[15] The pilot knew one of the victims, but when this person gave a sign of recognition, he was taken away from the others and kept separate. The captain reported that many Danish fishermen have made a fortune in this period. One refugee paid 25,000 kroner for the crossing. The captain thinks that Møn[16] is the best place to leave from and he named several addresses, which I have passed on to Månsson. We then all went to Limhamn harbour. The scene would have looked good in a theatre. The wind was whistling through the mast tops and the rain was pelting down. A good 100 people were standing huddled together on the quay looking out across the sea. Every now and then a light appeared and people thought they were refugee boats, but they were only patrol boats. To shelter from the rain, we climbed down into the cabin of a small sailing boat, and I ended up sitting next to a man who was evidently a saboteur from Denmark. He had come over the day before, but the boat hadn't dared enter a Swedish harbour and instead had reached the coast directly south of Limhamn, where the passengers had to wade about 100 metres to shore. The man himself had carried a three-year-old child to shore. He told me that the Danish fishermen were earning up to 100,000 kroner in one night and that they were now on a permanent high. Just before his departure, the Germans opened fire on a group of people on a beach and around 25 people died.[17] In one village the Germans had decided that all boats should be pulled up into the square, where they were placed under German watch. Since no refugee boat had arrived by 11 p.m., I returned to Malmö. Conversation with Bermann, who reported that two young men have arrived from Gothenburg and have offered their help. It was agreed that they would meet me the following morning. In bed by 2 a.m.

15 These numbers are too high: ships for even the largest transports carried fewer than 200 Jewish deportees and around 150 communists.

16 A sparsely populated Danish island with long beaches off the southern coast of the island of Zealand.

17 This could not be verified.

6 October
Up at 5 a.m. Visit to the refugee camp at Ramlösa. Shown around by the head of the camp, an extraordinarily calm and decent man. The refugees have been housed in the infirmary, in a few small houses, and in the communal building. The beds were packed tightly together, in a few cases eighteen to a room. They have been provided with pretty bedcovers and linens. Food was served in a dining hall, with two meals a day. There was a large common room in the communal building with sofas, chairs and tables, and a radio. The camp commander was happy with the refugees, but complained that they were careless with lit cigarettes. Of course it was difficult to instil some discipline in them. This was also evident when meals were handed out, when the head of the camp would have liked to have everyone line up and almost had to hold onto each of them so they did not run away. It was unbelievably cramped in the administrative building, but the mood was good and relaxed. Two efficient ladies, one Swedish and one Danish, registered the refugees who had come in overnight. A distressed mother was sitting there with a child barely six months old. The child had been sleeping deeply for a long time because it had been given four shots of morphine to stop it from screaming during the trip. Almost all small children were treated that way. Just before the train was due to depart for Helsingborg, the two young men came to find me. They were Guy Welin-Berger and Sven Jonsson. One was newly qualified from Chalmers and the other was still studying there.[18] They had decided to help because they were interested in the cause. On arriving at Helsingborg, spoke to Köpniwsky. Then left for the factory, Leofabriken, to meet the manager, Karl Holtman.[19] His office was like an anthill. People were sitting waiting in every room. The phone rang constantly and Holtman was running around everywhere to talk to everyone. He was a nervous wreck and had recently suffered concussion. He was also working at least 22 hours a day. Next to him, on the table, was a revolver and he had another in his pocket. He claimed that the day before, three men had tried to get into his office to kidnap him. At the last minute he had managed to call the police, who detained the men. They turned out to be Gestapo dressed in green uniforms. Holtman kept a weapon on him at all times and had protection from a Danish policeman day and night. I asked Holtman what I could do, and it was agreed that I would try to buy one or more of the boats which they had had their eye on. I departed with my helpers for Påhlsson's boatyard in Råå, where we had to wait an hour for the boatyard owner. During this time we drew up a precise list of the equipment the boat should have. The *Kebnekaise* was inspected and was found to be an approximately 8 metre boat that could do 15 knots and should have space for 15 people. Back then to Holtman, who said we now needed to find fuel. When I said that in Malmö we had got fuel from the military authorities, Holtman rang a lieutenant in the defence staff and introduced me. I went there immediately and asked for 1,500 litres of fuel. The lieutenant replied that the matter should be presented to the colonel, who wouldn't arrive before 4 p.m. Inspected another boat and sent my helpers to look at a third boat. The lieutenant

18 Chalmers tekniska högskola, founded in Gothenburg in 1829 as a trade school for poor children, is a private technical university.

19 Correctly: Carl Ludvig Holtmann, born C. L. Cohn (1896–1986), pharmacist and entrepreneur; director of the pharmaceutical company Leo Läkemedel Aktiebolaget in Helsingborg from 1927; after the war received Swedish and Norwegian awards for his work in helping refugees.

now said that the defence staff couldn't provide the fuel but referred us to the adjutant at the naval command in Malmö. Spoke first with the adjutant and then with his superior, whom I knew earlier as a client. The latter first talked a while about old business and then asked whether the fuel would be used for patrols. When I replied that the idea was to go over to Denmark, the boss said he couldn't hand over fuel for this purpose. That had to be decided in Stockholm. I then drove to the fire chief, who said that at most he could advance 100 litres, but he suggested I call a district notary in Malmö, who could get hold of heating oil. During the phone call with the latter he sounded very sceptical and said it was a matter that would have to be forwarded to the Ministry of Foreign Affairs. After he had presented the matter to the county governor,[20] he rang me to say that the county governor shared his opinion and referred me to Stockholm. Then Mr P. M. appeared and claimed to have fuel in Landskrona. I was excited and suggested we go there immediately. At first P. M. was willing to do so, but then he remembered he could not travel until the following day, although he promised to get 200 litres in the meantime. Then visited Påhlsson and explained that I wanted to buy the boat if it could be ready the next day, which Påhlsson promised. It turned out that Påhlsson did not have enough fuel for a test run of the engine. I managed to get hold of the fire chief, who promised to get me 3 litres of fuel for 8 a.m. the next morning. Had dinner and a lively discussion with P. M., who was introduced to my helpers. In the evening we went down to the cordon at the harbour, and in the distance we could see several refugee boats coming in. They were very heavily laden and the people had to remain standing in the boat the whole time. In bed at 11 p.m.

7 October

Up at 7 a.m. Went to see the fire chief to fetch the test fuel. Visited the bank to withdraw 17,000 kroner. Brought 7,000 kroner to Welin-Berger and 10,000 kroner to Holtman. He had spent the whole night receiving refugees. He had seen a small rowing boat come in carrying 15 people with the rail just 2 cm above the water. He had also been called out by the police to identify 13 bodies which had floated ashore in the morning. Holtman mentioned that he had nearly been detained that morning by the Swedish secret police under suspicion of espionage. I told Holtman to calm down and made clear to him that he had to hand over a part of his work. Back in Malmö at midday. Just before I left, I was sought out by Mr Levitan, who had been sent down from Stockholm by Ehrenpreis and had looked for me in Malmö and then waited for me in Helsingborg. Levitan told me that after visiting the Prime Minister and the Minister of Foreign Affairs, he had succeeded in having the Swedish courier to Copenhagen permitted to carry news of where the refugees were staying, etc. Left for Malmö. Visited Hollander with Mrs Christensen. Also met Bertil Gottfarb and his sister,[21] who was upset about Levitan. On the train he had spoken freely about his involvement. One person had heard him and then

20 Presumably a reference to the governor of the county of Malmöhus, Arthur Natanael Thomson (1891–1977).

21 Inga Gottfarb (1912–2005), student, later social worker; involved in work for Jewish refugees in Sweden from 1938; helped her brother Ragnar Gottfarb with his work as representative of the American Jewish Joint Distribution Committee (JDC) in Stockholm; continued to work for the JDC after 1945.

said to the person sitting next to him, 'We've got one here', which suggested he was going to misuse what he had heard. Hollander said that some of the refugees had seen a column of Jews with their hands tied behind their backs being herded by the Gestapo along the main road near Helsingør. It was also reported that many refugees had been transported in coffins in order to get on board the boats. Some had been admitted to hospital under fictitious names, and neither the doctors nor the nurses had known who the patient was. To Stockholm by plane. In the evening Welin-Berger rang and said that they had still not got the boat going, but that they would work through the night on the engine.

DOC. 21
Benjamin Blüdnikow records in his diary how his refugee boat capsized on 7 October 1943[1]

Handwritten memoirs of Benjamin Blüdnikow,[2] entries for 7 and 8 October 1943[3]

A trip to Sweden

[…][4]

Chapter 4:

It was afternoon, and I was a good way through Kelvin Lindeman's *The House with the Green Tree*. In the morning, I had been surprised by a visit from our old doctor, through whom, via Knud Aage,[5] I had had some contact with my parents. He was able to tell me the good news: that my sister and brother-in-law, along with their children, had got to Sweden, and that my parents would be going over today.[6] He asked me how I was doing and asked things such as, 'Are you getting properly fed?' I looked at Helga, who stood over by the window. She had heard and looked furious. With a smile, I answered, 'I am starving to death.' But now I was in the middle of *The Green Tree*, when Leopold[7] rushed into the living room and shouted, 'Hurry, there is a car waiting. We're leaving now.' I scraped together a few things in my briefcase, and we crept out to the car. Before he came, he had gone and collected from the doctor the 1,000 kroner which Herman had

1 The original is privately owned. Copy in IfZ-Archives, F 601. Excerpts published in Bent Blüdnikow, *Min fars flugt: Jødiske skæbner i oktober 1943* (Copenhagen: Gyldendals Bogklubber, 2013), pp. 145–150 and 162–176. This document has been translated from Danish.

2 Benjamin Blüdnikow (1924–2016), student; continued his studies in Sweden after fleeing Denmark in Oct. 1943; subsequently joined the Danish armed forces in exile in Sweden; worked as an engineer for a telephone company after 1945.

3 According to Blüdnikow, these memoirs were written during his stay in a Swedish hospital between 18 August and 2 Oct. 1944.

4 In the previous sections, Blüdnikow describes how a friend advised him to hide and offered him shelter. It was there that he learned of the arrests taking place and of his parents' successful escape.

5 Knud Aage Madsen was a friend of Benjamin Blüdnikow's best friend from school, Leopold Recht. He hid several refugees in his apartment for a while.

6 Jacob and Gitel Blüdnikow fled to Sweden on 4 or 5 Oct. 1943.

7 Leopold Recht (1924–2001), student; Benjamin Blüdnikow's school friend; after 1945 gained a doctorate in medicine and settled in southern Sweden with his wife.

left me for this reason. We drove to an address in Ryparken, where we were accompanied by Leopold's sister, Dora,[8] and her 18-month-old child, Jette. The journey continued on to Klampenborg station, from where we went on to Snekkersten by train. I had been quite worried about this train journey, and with good reason, because there were raids on many trains. But it went well. When we disembarked, we could see that there had been a few refugees on the train. We were led to a house, where we remained, and at 11 o'clock at night we set off from there in the dark. Upon our departure, we were provided with a food parcel, which I hid under my jacket.

The destination turned out to be a barn, where we sat waiting for some time to find out when a ship would be ready. One of the men from the 'organization' told us, among other things, about how an officer, who had been on guard at the viaduct, had shown himself to be 'pro-German' the previous night, and it had become necessary to shoot him. – Suddenly, someone stuck their head through the door and shouted, 'Gestapo!' We tumbled out of the barn and were hastily led into a nearby forest; we groped our way forward along muddy paths for the next fifteen minutes in single file. Finally, we arrived at a new barn, where guards were posted outside. They were unnerving minutes, and they passed slowly in there. Jette had been given some sleeping pills but nonetheless lay crying, and an older lady was nearly hysterical because she was afraid that the crying could be heard. A long time went by before a message came that the Gestapo had gone, after which we went back to the old barn. Upon our return, we were told that there was space on a boat for four to five people. Those chosen were a German Jew, alongside Dora, Jette, Leopold, and me. A young man took the lead, and we began our walk through the darkened city. Once we saw a bicycle light and our guide immediately turned into a garden, in which we hid ourselves until the cyclist was gone. At another stage on our walk, we saw another bicycle light approaching, but we were on an empty street without any hiding places. The guide told us we should go to the side, while he would go ahead and, in the worst-case scenario, try to disarm the cyclist. But with an exchange of signals, it turned out to be one of the watchmen from the 'organization', who was patrolling the roads, and we continued, reassured.

After a long walk we reached our destination, which turned out to be a dentist's[9] home, which looked dark and closed up, but turned out to contain a crowd of guests. There were some from the 'organization', as well as six refugees. We were entertained with cigarettes, etc., and a doctor who was present gave Jette an injection to make her sleep. Throughout these nights, the doctors on the coast were busy giving these kinds of injections. The owner of the house led us up to a viewpoint. From there we could see the same sight that had made us stand still a couple of times on the way here. It was the coastline of Sweden, with shining pearls of unscreened light. An especially bright cluster of light indicated a city: Helsingborg. Upon catching sight of this, we had said to one another, 'Just over there. There is freedom. But will we make it over there?' The man pointed over to it and said, 'By that light there is the copper factory. You just steer south

8 Dora Thing, née Recht (1919–2002), student; active in the communist youth organization. The father of the daughter mentioned here was Børge Thing, one of the leading figures in the communist resistance.

9 Footnote in the original: '1979: According to Dr Gersfeldt, this was the now-deceased dentist Popp Madsen.' For more on Gersfeldt, see Doc. 19.

of that, and the current will take you right to Helsingborg.' I realised then that the idea was that we would be piloting a boat without the help of a 'professional', but I did not reflect further on this, because at that moment I had other things to think about.

It had been decided that there was only space for nine plus Jette in the boat. So one of us had to stay behind, but who? Since we were 'single', the choice was between the German Jew and me, and as I was in some way accompanying Leopold and Dora, the choice fell on the German. He would then have to wait until the next day. Lucky soul. There was a diagram assigning us our places in the rowing boat, and we were now to make our way down. We went two by two, with a couple of minutes' waiting time in between, each group led by someone from the 'organization'. My turn came, and we went down via some roads which led to the beach. Now and then a cyclist without lights went by, and a signal indicated that he was one of those who had the task of patrolling the roads. Suddenly a cyclist *with* a light came, and as we tried in vain to crawl into a hiding place, we saw, as he passed by, that he was a police officer. He did not even glance at us, and our guide explained that the police were quite loyal, which we later found out was true. A moment later, we scrambled down some steps and found ourselves on a foreshore. A short distance along was our rowing boat. Eventually we all arrived, and after a little squabbling, we found our places in the boat. Our helpers pushed the boat out, wished us safe passage, and our journey began. The time then must have been around 1 a.m.

Two of the boat's 'crew' had the task of rowing, and the rest of us sat and gave directions, criticized their rowing, and shushed one another. The rowing was indeed not exactly flawless, but nonetheless, over the next half an hour, we got ourselves some distance away from land, I would guess 2–3 kilometres. When we had completed half of this distance, the sirens began to wail from the dark land behind us, and we agreed that it could only be because of us. My feet got quite wet, as we took on a lot of bilge water. And then it happened. I heard someone behind me shout, 'Bail! Bail!', and I noticed that the bilge water had now risen considerably, and in the next fifteen seconds I saw – almost without knowing what was happening – how the water rose and rose, and just as it reached the gunwale, the boat capsized.

Chapter 5:
Who knows why it happened. The boat was old and fragile, but the 'organization' did not have many to choose from, and they probably did not have the time to inspect this old tub more closely. Furthermore, there were too many of us in it. But given the circumstances, it would not have been right to place the blame on anyone.

In any case, we were left swimming around.

I could not swim very well and instinctively tried to go back to the boat. Together with another young man, Harry, and his sister of the same age, Sonja, equally instinctively, we tried to right the boat, and we succeeded, with the result that the boat now lay at an angle and rocked, with its gunwale just under the surface. Luckily, there were no waves. Jette had fallen into the water when it tipped, but Leopold had immediately dived in after her, and we quickly found the best solution: letting Dora get into the water-filled boat holding Jette, while the rest of us lay in the water and held the gunwale and thereby prevented the boat from tipping again.

So, there we were now: Dora with Jette, Harry, Sonja, Leopold, and me. But what about the four others? We could hear someone shouting for help a little distance from us, but we were shouting ourselves and could not do anything. Of these four, three drowned, and I can tell their story now. One was a young man who had 'been visited by the postman';[10] he had made a previous attempt to flee with a couple of hundred others, [who] had gathered in a church in North Zealand, which got surrounded by the Gestapo. Apparently he was the only one who managed to escape, which he did by hiding behind the beams in the church tower.[11] And now he had drowned. The three others were the remaining members of a family: the mother and two children had been taken by the Germans. The father had saved himself by jumping from the third floor, but had broken bones in several places, so it was no wonder he could not keep himself afloat in the water, in spite of the fact that he was otherwise a good swimmer. Why the four of them did not keep close to the boat, I do not know. The two others in this family, a son and a daughter, Fanny, both 18–20 years old, tried to help their father, but only Fanny survived the struggle. She came to Sweden as the sole remaining member of the family. I do not think it is necessary to describe her emotional state.

Chapter 6:
And what was I thinking out there on the wreck? In about three weeks' time, it will have been one year since it happened, and of course I have forgotten things in the meantime, but I could barely remember it even the next day. Let me try to gather up the pieces of my state of mind. My first thought was, 'Could such a thing happen to me? It's unbelievable. This is my nightmare all over again. But we must be rescued.' And we screamed and shouted, and shouted and screamed. But no motorboats came our way. I had not noticed the cold water when I fell in, but the cold gradually took hold, and over the next couple of hours, my legs seized up several times. 'But how would a boat get out to us in the middle of the night? Will someone be able to hear us from the land? Have the others swum to get help?' And we shouted, and we froze. 'A boat will come soon. We might be in a warm cabin soon. I hope a boat comes, yes, even a German one!' Now and then the boat sank lower into the water, and each time I thought it would sink to the bottom. And then what? I was actually not afraid to die; I thought in passing of what my parents would say about me coming all the way out there and drowning, yes, and I also believe that I thought about what would become of my gramophone records. Between our cries for help, Leopold murmured something about how the others had surely not reached land, and therefore could not get help, and that he himself wanted to attempt to swim to shore. However, he was held back by his sister, Dora, who still stood in the boat with little Jette in her arms. She was inconsolable about how Jette had ended up in such a situation, and she stood there and cried, 'Jette, oh, Jette, whatever are we going to do?'

10 Note in the original: '[Han] havde "faat Paaringning af Postbudet"' (English: 'He "received a call from the postman"'). Presumably the author is playing on the title of the 1934 mystery novel *The Postman Always Rings Twice* by James M. Cain, in which an assassination attempt is foiled at the last second, only for the victim to be killed later.

11 This is a reference to the raid on the church in Gilleleje on the night of 7 Oct. 1943, during which 86 people who had been hiding in the church loft were captured. They were all deported to Theresienstadt. The name of the German refugee was Bruno Schmitz.

The cold water had partly reduced the effects of the injection, and as a result, Jette's crying merged with our cries for help. Eventually Leopold left and disappeared into the darkness. Incidentally, I lay in the water and noted that Harry, on the other side of the boat, despite all that had happened, still had his hat on. I myself still had a cap and glasses on, but the cap later disappeared. I began to feel tired and hoarse, and every once in a while, the water lapped over my mouth, nose, and eyes. Sonja said, 'Float on your front; it is much easier to hold yourself still.' I said, 'I can't because my legs float under the boat every time.' She said, 'Yes, you can. Just try.' I said, 'I have tried.' She said, 'Yes, and keep trying, you have to!' I said, 'Damn it, I just can't do it.'

The Danish side was dark, and no boat came. The Swedish side was starry with light, and I thought it was not very far away at all. I suggested that we could paddle the boat to Sweden, but the others said that this was an insane idea, and I have since come to agree with them. Now and then, someone shouted, 'Isn't that a boat light over there?', but no boat came. At first, I had thought that we should be able to cling to the boat until dawn in any case, at which point we would be seen, but gradually, as the cold, the cramps, and the tiredness came, I was less certain, and I gradually slipped into a state of unconsciousness. The others told me later that it was really unpleasant for them when I was in this state as I was making some horrible sounds because I instinctively shouted out even though my head was almost completely underwater.

Chapter 7:
From then on, I do not remember things clearly. Some episodes rush to mind, as if from a dream. Thus, suddenly I lay and looked up towards the stars in the sky, while my body was in a wet and convulsive state. I lay and moaned, I do not know why, and I tried in vain to stop the convulsions in my legs. I was not thinking at all, but nonetheless I noticed the smell of a wet tarpaulin which lay over me and a voice that said, 'There's no need to be afraid; you are on a Danish ship.' The next fragmentary image was of a car, which I deduced from the vibrations (I was already a little more lucid at that point). Dora sat and wailed; as far as I could understand, she presumed Jette was dead. I remember that I tried to console her, but I don't remember more. And the third glimpse began with the ambulance men carrying us into a hospital room. When one of them tried to get my clothes off by cutting my belt and pulling everything away, I suddenly realized that all of my dreams of lying next to a capsized boat, of looking up at the stars with the smell and the feeling of being in the sea, of driving in the ambulance with a crying woman and meanwhile trying to control my body's convulsions, *was not a dream*, but reality. I was relieved and proud, I think, because I, *yes me*, had been there to experience an event that seemed to be 'out of a novel'. Just then, the ambulance man pulled a wet, slimy bundle off my torso and threw it into the corner. It was the food parcel, which I had had under my jacket.

When I began to look around, I discovered both Leopold and Fanny. I did not reflect on it at the time, but they were both awake and conscious, having been taken to the hospital a couple of hours before us. Nonetheless, Leopold had been in such a state when he reached land that, when a policeman found him, he was incapable of informing him about us, and when he awoke later at the hospital, he thought we were probably long gone. So he was happy when we came in. And now he was strutting around between us with a blanket wrapped around him. He was the first one whom the policeman began lightly interrogating; he started by asking his name. 'Leif Olsen,' said Leopold confidently, looking boldly into the air. 'You have no need to be afraid. Just tell me your real name,' said the officer, smiling. 'We'll try to get you across,' at which point Leopold followed the recommendation. Then it was our turn, and after wrapping warm blankets around us, we slept.

I was nonetheless quite stiff the next morning, but the police came early to collect us, and we were driven to our old starting point, the dentist's, where they served us food. In the middle of the meal, we got a message that the Gestapo had arrived at the hospital and had begun to interrogate the doctors. This resulted in us moving as quickly as possible – carrying our meals – to a house that belonged to the dentist's family. After an uneasy afternoon spent waiting in my still damp clothes, we were interrupted in the middle of supper for the second time, as there were now some vehicles (led by a vehicle full of police officers) ready to pick us up for a new attempt at fleeing. We drove for half an hour, presumably northwards, then a short walk followed through the forest and we found ourselves at the beach. A motorboat distributed us – there were about fifty of us altogether, with some who had been in the cars and others who had been in the forest – into three fishing boats, which were chugging around just off shore. And then we were on our way to Sweden. Around half an hour later, the skipper told us that we were now in Swedish waters, and the mood on board lightened. Fifteen minutes after that, a Swedish customs boat came alongside, and a couple of minutes later, I stood with my torn-up coat twisted around the rest of my belongings, slightly chilly in my damp clothes, taking in the bright lights in Helsingborg, ready to shout a hurrah when we set foot on Swedish soil. The mood can be best described by noting that one of my fellow passengers chucked a bottle of poison out into the sea. He had no need for it any more. The time was 8.55 in the evening, as it said on Helsingborg's city hall when we went ashore, and it was Friday, 8 October 1943.

[…][12]

DOC. 22

On 8 October 1943 Johanna Salomon describes to her daughter in New York their family's escape from Denmark and reception in Sweden[1]

Handwritten letter from Johanna Salomon,[2] Jönköping, to Grete and Jack Poser,[3] New York, dated 8 October 1943

My dear, dear Grete and Jack,

At last I am able to write to you again. I assume that you have received the telegram I sent yesterday. Harald,[4] Elise, and Lilian sailed to Malmö in a fishing boat, but not all the way. For the last stretch to the coast they had to wade through the water. The German had warned us of this previously, and so I could not go with them. Harald had to leave

12 In the following chapters, Blüdnikow describes his experiences in Swedish exile up until his return to Denmark with the Danish Brigade on 5 May 1945.

1 The original is in the private collection of Norman Poser, author of *Escape: A Jewish Scandinavian Family in the Second World War* (New York: Sareve Press, 2006); copy in IfZ-Archives, F 601. This document has been translated from Norwegian.

that night, but it all turned out to be a very great physical ordeal for him. As he told us on the phone, he had to spend an entire hour in the water to get Else and the children ashore. They lost all their things and the clothes they were wearing, so when they got ashore all they had left was their underwear.[5]

We spent the last days before departure at the house of Harald's friends, who really put themselves out on our behalf. When Harald said that he did not dare leave me behind, they promised to make sure that I would join him in Sweden later.

Since I could neither go home nor stay any longer with Harald's friends, they hid me away in a hospital, where I spent two and a half days in bed before I was taken to a small motorboat with seven other women on board. We were safely brought to the coast, where Swedish soldiers helped us ashore and welcomed us. Then we were transported by bus to Ramlösa, close to Helsingborg, where we were given room and board. After that, I got in touch with Max,[6] and finally arrived here on the 7th of the month.

Nora and Max gave me a warm reception, and so did their two young girls. They were so sweet and affectionate that you would think they had known me their entire life. We also got a son and heir […],[7] who is now two months old. I feel comfortable here. In the meantime, we have received news from Harald: he has been offered a position with a large goldsmith's in Stockholm, which he will now visit, and he has another offer from a porcelain factory in Malmö. After all, he is well known in Stockholm, where the museum has an entire collection of his coins. Once more we have lost everything. I have nothing but the dress, the coat, and the shoes I am wearing. My last little suitcase containing the most essential items was left behind at the hospital, but we did save our lives!

Jews are arriving in droves in Ramlösa. Now I have told you everything, and please share this letter with Gerda.[8] Would you too, dear Gerda, please write to me and let me know how things are for you?

I have read the letters to Max that you sent here, and learned from your last one that you are not feeling well. Let me know everything – about Dodo, too! I will end this for now with my warmest greetings and kisses to all of my children and grandchildren.

Your loving Mother

2 Johanna Bella Salomon, née Eisenstein (1871–1957), housewife; arrested in Norway in Dec. 1942; on her release in Oct. 1943 left Norway for Denmark with the help of the Danish consul; fled to Sweden in Oct. 1943; returned to Denmark after 1945.

3 Margaret Poser, née Salomon (1901–1954), housewife; daughter of Johanna Salomon; emigrated from London to New York in 1939; took her own life. Jack Poser (1892–1976), fur trader; Margaret Poser's husband.

4 Harald Salomon (1900–1990), designer; son of Johanna Salomon; studied art in Copenhagen, 1922–1927; coin designer at the Royal Danish Mint from 1933; in Oct. 1943 fled to Sweden, where he worked in a porcelain factory; in 1945 returned to Denmark as member of the Danish Brigade, a military unit formed by Danish exiles in Sweden; worked again at the Royal Danish Mint.

5 Harald Salomon had to swim repeatedly back and forth from the boat to the beach to bring his family safely to shore.

6 Max Salomon, born Marcus Zola Salomon (1898–1971), fur trader; Johanna Salomon's son; on 15 April 1940 fled from Norway to Sweden, where he worked initially as a lumberjack and later for the Norwegian refugee aid; returned to Norway after 1945 and opened a leather-goods store; worked for the organization Redd Barna (Save the Children Norway) from 1960. See also Doc. 45.

7 One word is illegible.

8 Gerda Weill, née Salomon (1899–1992), Johanna Salomon's daughter; fled to Sweden in April 1940 and subsequently emigrated to the USA.

DOC. 23

On 16 October 1943 Max Lester writes to his ex-wife and children about his escape to Sweden[1]

Handwritten letter from Max Lester,[2] c/o Director Oscar Gyllenhammar,[3] 34 Avenuen, Gothenburg, telephone no. 166 872, to Rosa, his ex-wife,[4] dated 16 October 1943

Dear Rosa,
Dear children and little Inga,

You can only imagine how happy I was when on my arrival at Helsingborg I was told by Miss Michaelsen that she found out that you were in Sweden and therefore in safety. Having been picked up on Sunday at 1 o'clock, I only arrived in Sweden at 9.30 on Wednesday morning on the Swedish patrol boat that had taken us on board at the maritime border. It was a bad journey. There were thirty-two of us and we arrived at 4 o'clock in Humlebæk, where we were accommodated in two brick-workers' homes, consisting of two small rooms and a kitchen. The idea was that, on the same evening, we would board a fishing boat that lay ready and waiting. We had some sandwiches and waited in suspense for what would happen. One of those fleeing was a tailor, Lachmann, with his wife and an 8-day-old baby. At 11 p.m. we were told that we would not be able to get away before the early morning and that we should get some rest. There was a sofa, a chaise longue, and apart from that only chairs. The mother with the infant child and the other five children were settled down for sleep, having received something to calm them, while the rest of us sat on the chairs. At 1 o'clock we were all woken up … the Gestapo were approaching and we had to get out with our luggage, go over a muddy ploughed field, and hide behind a hedge. It was cold and we stood there for an hour. By then the danger had passed – the Gestapo had not found anything and had left again. We went back to our 'beds' and despite the fact that Mr Hirsch's snores were deafening, and once between snores he even delighted us with a mighty 'surprise', I managed to get another hour's sleep. The next morning we were given coffee and sandwiches again and at 12 o'clock a large removal lorry rolled up to the door. It's far from fun having to stand throughout a journey in such a vehicle – and we thought that we would drive to our final destination. But no, there was fear of an informant and we were being driven to two other workers' houses for the time being. They were small houses and basically very comfortable. We had a really good dinner: roast pork, sausages, and potatoes with parsley sauce, and it was very revitalizing – we were supposed to leave on Monday evening. We knew that it would have to be in the evening and when at nearly 10 o'clock the car came to collect us, our mood lifted. But, oh no, they explained to us that the Gestapo were still on our trail and that we would first have to get to Stevns Klint.[5] This dampened

1 Frihedsmuseets Dokumentarkiv, 6E-00-10894. This document has been translated from Danish.
2 Max Paul Lester (1866–1956); wholesaler.
3 Oscar Leopold Gyllenhammar (1886–1945), businessman; his company produced rolled oats.
4 Lester had been divorced from his wife Rosa (née Glückstadt) for at least twenty years when he wrote this letter. He had remarried in 1923, but his children were from his first marriage, and all adults (born between 1895 and 1900).
5 Coastal cliffs in the south-east of the Danish island of Zealand.

the good mood for most of us, but after only a short drive criss-crossing back and forth, we ended up at a large farm – we later found out it was in Smidstrup.[6] The mother and the young baby were given a place in the main building, while the rest of us were ordered up into the loft over the cowshed, where there lay a load of straw, which meant that we were to make ourselves at home up there as best we could. It prickled terribly everywhere, and by the time we were all frozen to the core, I ignored the ban, climbed down the loft ladder, and sat myself down on the only chair and waited for what might come. In the cowshed it was at least warm, but have you ever slept in a cowshed? The noise that the cows make is unbelievable. They were constantly pissing and doing their other business, and every time they got up and lay down again, they rattled their chains and they made so many other sounds. Simply put, I didn't get any shut-eye that night, and so that night felt as long as three nights and of course we weren't allowed to smoke – I confess that this night was my lowest, lowest point, and this was after, without wanting to flatter myself, I had previously kept up the spirits of the others. For there were a good few moaners among them.

But when the sun rose on Tuesday morning and at the same time a large pot of scalding hot coffee with bread arrived, my good mood also returned and the only unfortunate thing was that we had to stay in the cowshed; they did not dare have us in the house in case of a police raid. But I was able to nap for an hour, which helped.

We knew that we had to wait for dusk, and at 8 o'clock finally the hour of liberation struck and we left in teams of eight to slip down to Smidstrup Strand to wait for the boat. A woman who was frail was carried down in a yellow chair.[7] After half an hour, a boat came (a Danish policeman) so we all had to lie down flat, and at this point my heart was beating much faster.

We sensed something was happening around us, but after about twenty minutes the danger had passed and now we heard the fishing boat's motor and saw the rowing boat which was to take us out to it. Boarding took around an hour and then the boat set off. The children and the baby were in the little cabin, and the rest of us remained on deck. The sea was rough and there was a headwind, so one wave after the other splashed over the deck. I was drenched, even my trouser pockets were wet. The women and children vomited, but despite this when the captain announced that we had crossed over the Swedish sea border, we broke into song with 'Du gamla, du fria'.[8] Half an hour later we met the Swedish patrol boat and were taken on board. Then it was 1 o'clock and once again we adults had to spend the night, seated around the large table in the cabin. This third night was tough, but we were safe. We had to sail on with the patrol boat, and after the change of shift at 8.30 we docked at Helsingborg and were then taken by bus to the reception camp in Ramlösa park.

And now I am living with my dear old friend Oscar and feel as if I am in heaven. I am happy to have escaped. You can see that it is possible to be happy without money,

6 This refers to Smidstrup Strand, a seaside resort in northern Zealand. The reference could be deliberately incorrect, to mislead the Gestapo. From Copenhagen, Smidstrup is located in the opposite direction from Humlebæk and Stevns Klint.

7 Reference to a type of chair, usually yellow or orange, used to carry elderly or sick people.

8 Swedish: 'Du gamla, du fria, [du fjällhöga nord]' (Thou ancient, thou free, [thou mountainous north]): the first words of the Swedish national anthem.

because I have none as we had to leave so suddenly on Sunday. I hope you are all well, and that you are happy. How great the Swedes are in helping their Danish brothers. I have met many emigrants here in the town. It was strange how quickly my fellow emigrants and I became one big family. I haven't been able to find out in Helsingborg whether Anna and Grethe have also come over. Get in touch soon – I am worried for my two youngest children. Who knows what that rabble have planned!

My warmest greetings to you all,

Father

DOC. 24

On 23 October 1943 the Social Aid Department reports on how the property of Jews who have fled is safeguarded on behalf of the Ministry of Social Affairs[1]

Note, unsigned, dated 23 October 1943[2]

The Ministry of Social Affairs has called upon the Social Aid Department[3] to look after the interests of absent persons here in the country, including the care of property which they have left behind. The district managers of the Social Aid Department have been placed in charge of implementing this task. Since 2 October 1943 staff from the various offices of the Public Welfare Department, as part of the Social Aid Department, have taken on this task, with the support of selected social welfare employees, who have undertaken this work in the evenings. For this work, and for the work in general which is done outside office hours, in accordance with current regulations, salary supplements have been disbursed from public funds.

To date, the Social Aid Department has dealt with around 450 cases.

In summary, these cases are processed as follows:

Different sources inform the Social Aid Department about missing families. These reports come from private individuals who have made observations in this regard. The Social Aid Department also receives indications from friends and acquaintances of the absent persons, from landlords, caretakers, etc. as well as from the police, who have recently been investigating in the various districts to establish whether residents have abandoned their apartments. When such reports are received, the case is registered and an investigation is launched.

1 Københavns Stadsarkiv, Socialtjenesten, Administrationssag 1943–46, pk.1. This document has been translated from Danish.

2 The date was noted by hand in the original, which also contains handwritten corrections and additions.

3 In early 1943 the Social Aid Department (Socialtjenesten) was established within Copenhagen's municipal administration. Using resources from the Ministry of Social Affairs, the department was intended to assist those who had suffered losses as a result of war, particularly the victims of air raids. After 1 Oct. 1943 it primarily helped Danish Jews. In the period up to April 1945, the Social Aid Department investigated more than 1,900 apartments reported abandoned by neighbours and the police. It safeguarded around 350 apartments. In many cases this solution proved more favourable for those who fled than giving power of attorney to a private individual.

The investigation of individual cases proceeds as follows: the Social Aid Department's staff at the responsible social welfare office are instructed to investigate at the property concerned. This investigation consists of an inspection of the residence, for which access is obtained via the caretaker or another party who may be in possession of keys. If necessary, a tradesman (locksmith) may also be called in to help. Occasionally the official also contacts the relevant security firm. A summary inventory is then carried out at the residence. It is the responsibility of the authorized official to take notes on the state of the residence, and in particular, to determine whether any household effects or other items may have been removed. If there is any perishable or spoiled food in the residence, it will be removed, usually with the help of the Lotters,[4] who play a key role in these clearing operations. If any cash or valuables are found on the premises, the Social Aid Department arranges to store them in safes or security boxes, which are clearly labelled to indicate the origin of the contents.

When the Social Aid Department officials leave the residence, they must ensure that it is properly secured. In a number of cases, it has been necessary to arrange for the caretaker or a tradesman to replace glass panes, repair damaged doors, etc., and to install new locks.

Finally, it is the responsibility of the authorized Social Aid Department official to write up a report on the investigation. This report is then submitted to the appropriate head of section, along with any items which it may be necessary to store securely (as mentioned above). The head of section will then arrange further action as necessary.

This may involve, for example, the payment of any rent due, or in some cases, the termination of the lease and any resulting storage of furnishings, as well as the payment of any associated removal costs, etc. In cases where the residence is to be maintained, this is recorded in writing in view of any future rent payments.

It is not uncommon for third parties to contact the Social Aid Department claiming to be in possession of oral or written power of attorney on behalf of the absentee.[5] In such cases, the Social Aid Department must assess the credibility of the written or purported oral power of attorney. If the power of attorney and the accompanying circumstances appear to be genuine, then the authorized party is permitted to take all necessary steps on behalf of the absentee.

In those cases where the absentee is the owner of a business or real estate, or where it is otherwise determined that further measures need to be taken, the City Council's Main Department[6] is requested to appoint a guardian to look after the interests of the absentee. Such a guardian has also been appointed in cases where only one single action had to be arranged, such as the collection of garments, etc. which had been delivered to a relevant business for repair.

The Social Aid Department has reached an agreement with the security firms to the effect that, at the request of the Social Aid Department, surveillance [of the property] can be arranged on an individual basis.

4 A reference to the members of the Lottekorps, the Danish Women's Army Corps, which cared for and aided soldiers and the wounded, and carried out assignments with the Signal Corps.

5 For an example of a declaration of power of attorney, see Doc. 12.

6 This department was responsible for schools and cultural affairs as well as economic matters.

In addition, the Social Aid Department has contacted the insurance companies with the aim of ensuring that fire, theft, and water damage insurance policies taken out on behalf of the absentee's household effects remain in force.

The same applies to life insurance policies. It is hoped that an arrangement can be reached whereby the insurance policies remain in force even if the premiums are not paid.

The Social Aid Department has received from the German authorities a number of keys (ninety) for the residences of the families mentioned here.

DOC. 25

In his diary Ralph Oppenhejm describes his impressions as an inmate when a Danish delegation visited Theresienstadt on 23 June 1944[1]

Diary of Ralph Oppenhejm,[2] entry for 23 June 1944[3]

So the big day arrived. And it turned out well. I took time off again – also from the Swedish classes – because I had to experience this. I put on blue clothes for any eventuality – and shaved (why are we noble gentlemen after all?) and then we just waited.

Various people came to see the fuss, internal administration[4] and the Germans, and so we sat and waited.

Around 2 o'clock, we saw six splendid cars drive up and several people get out of them. A moment later Ebstein[5] came up and fetched Father[6] down to the common room, where the gentlemen were sitting. There were two Danes, exceedingly pleasant; one of

1 DJM, 207A35/18. This document has been translated from Danish.

2 Ralph Oppenhejm (1924–2008); deported to Theresienstadt in Oct. 1943 after a failed attempt to escape to Sweden; after 1945 journalist; author of *The Door of Death*, trans. Joyce Tufton (London: The Harvill Press, 1947 [Danish edn, 1945]).

3 Soon after the deportations of the Danish Jews, the Danish Ministry of Foreign Affairs and Ministry of Social Affairs sought to make contact with the prisoners and to visit them. Private organizations began sending parcels to the Danish deportees from Feb. 1944, though without the permission of the Reich Security Main Office (RSHA). Formal permission to receive parcels was only granted during the visit by the International Red Cross and the Danish civil administration to Theresienstadt on 23 June 1944. The ghetto was 'beautified' for this visit, in order to give the delegates a good impression of the living conditions.

4 This refers to 'Dept. I, Office for Internal Administration' of the Council of Elders appointed by the SS.

5 Correctly: Dr Paul Eppstein (1902–1944), sociologist; member of the board of the Federation of Jewish Youth Associations; Zionist; adjunct professor at the Mannheim Commercial College, 1926–1933; dismissed in 1933; taught sociology in the 1930s at the Higher Institute for Jewish Studies in Berlin; social welfare officer in the Reich Representation of Jews in Germany and their liaison to the Gestapo from 1935; deported on 26 Jan. 1943 to Theresienstadt, where he was the Jewish elder from Jan. 1943 to 27 Sept. 1944; murdered on 28 Sept. 1944.

6 Moritz Oppenhejm (1886–1961), lawyer; until 1933 legal advisor for the German legation in Copenhagen; representative of the Jewish Community. The Oppenhejm family attempted to flee to Sweden in early Oct. 1943. When their arrest was imminent, they all took poison. They were saved in Horserød camp by a physician who was a prisoner and deported to Theresienstadt in mid Oct. 1943. On his mother, Mélanie Oppenhejm, see also Doc. 1.

them was Frantz Hvass[7] from the Ministry of Foreign Affairs, the other Jual Henningsen[8] from the Health Authority. Father was seated next to the latter and on the other side was Mr Henner, whom he already knew from Horserød. Father preferred to speak German so there wouldn't be any misunderstandings later on. He had various greetings in his notebook from Thygesen and Esther Heiberg, Mrs Arntskov, and Ellinor, and Father asked him to send his regards to them and Jacobsen, whom he thanked for the 'large packages and the deliveries with eggs'. They discussed books and cigarettes, at which point J-H[9] remarked that he had noticed that people don't smoke here in town!! (I was at the post office this morning to collect a package from Allan and it was said that these days nothing's smuggled. Luckily there was a bit of coffee in it. The young Prtich girl was involved in the potato sorting yesterday and had to separate the bad ones from the good ones – by God, that is the first time that has ever happened. And today she had to sit in a newly prepared reading room and pretend to read, which she can probably do, despite everything.)[10]

Renner[11] remarked venomously: 'Ah, you are the Oppenhejms who wanted to flee on a Swedish ship? Why would you want to do that?' Father didn't answer (had he known that we would arrive in such a lovely place, of course he would never have done so). Second question (from the Germans): 'How long have you lived here?' – 'For a while and I lived in the same district before that.' Third question: 'There were some people called Hoffgaard[12] in Horserød, where are they?' – 'The wife and daughters live here.' 'And the husband?' 'That I don't know.' (The man tried to lead Father into a trap, but he didn't succeed.) Then the Danes asked about a Mrs Kielberg,[13] for whom they had a greeting. She had died of 'pneumonia'. Meyer[14] played up, of course, how splendid the town had become since the Verschönerungen.[15] Møss[16] said, 'Yes, listen to that, gentlemen! Don't forget to tell them back home. And when you speak about this town here,

7 Frants Hvass (1896–1982), diplomat; worked at the Danish Ministry of Foreign Affairs from 1922; head of the Department for Political and Legal Affairs; 1941–1945; state secretary, 1945–1948; Danish representative in West Germany, 1949–1966.

8 Eigil Juel Henningsen (1906–1992), physician; deputy head of the Danish Health Authority, 1940–1945.

9 This is a reference to Eigil Juel Henningsen.

10 Parentheses in the following as in the original.

11 Fritz Renner.

12 Sven Hoffgaard (1895–1965), bank employee; tried unsuccessfully to flee to Sweden with his family in 1943; deported to Sachsenhausen, where he was assigned to a currency counterfeiting unit established under Operation Bernhard. His wife, Karen (1896–1953), who was Jewish, and their children Lilian (b. 1920) and Kathe (b. 1928) were deported to Theresienstadt; the Danish authorities tried unsuccessfully to have Sven transferred to Theresienstadt to be reunited with his family. All four family members survived.

13 Rosa Kielberg (1877–1944); she died on 28 March 1944.

14 Ove Meyer (b. 1885), entrepreneur; married to a non-Jew, who died in 1942; deported in Oct. 1943 to Theresienstadt, where he was considered a 'high-profile' inmate as he held the title of Knight of the Royal Order of Dannebrog, an honour awarded for civil or military service to the Danish state.

15 German in the original: 'beautification'.

16 Correctly: Ernst Möhs, also Moes (1898–1945), bank employee; joined the NSDAP in 1940; SS-Hauptsturmführer, 1942; as a colleague of Adolf Eichmann at the RSHA, he had responsibility for Theresienstadt.

then you should really see Berlin.' (What's up with Berlin? Father really wanted to ask – we know nothing).

When they were about to go, Hvass hung back with Fridiger and whispered in his ear that he was to bring us heartfelt greetings from the king, whose thoughts are with us. Mr Renner turned around and asked Fridiger what the man had said. Ah, he was to bring greetings for me from Bishop Fuglsang-Damgaard.[17] Father thought you could see it had made a huge impression on them to see Danes with the Jewish star (we never notice it any more) and from the way they shook his hand long and hard, he could feel that they understood everything. And indeed, what there is in a handshake. (You just need to think of Fridiger, his is like a fish – dead, cold, and flaccid.)

Father said 'until next time' when they left – it is indeed very important that they really do come back and apparently that will be the case in September. It's Rahm's[18] next date for 'beautification' [of the ghetto]. So hopefully the Danes will not be carted off to another location, as we thought would happen, with the exception of the significant individuals.[19] They carried on to the orphanage, where they met Ellen.[20] She had been really nervous all day and said that she would definitely try to talk to them. She was wearing her hessian belt with everything possible on it, including a little Danish flag. They came and went out, at which point Ellen resolutely picked the little Fabian child[21] and carried her out to the toilet, talking loudly to the child in Danish, even though it didn't understand a word. J-H was taken aback and immediately asked: Sprechen Sie Dänisch?[22] Yes. What was her name. Ah, he had just spoken to her father. Meanwhile she sat the youngster on the potty and Renner stood alongside, with Moss right outside the door. 'Did you recognize her because of the flag?' Renner asked sharply. 'Ah, no, I know her from before.' 'Is there anyone I should send your greetings to?' 'Yes, Henning Schram, sincerely.'[23] He [J-H] took out his pocketbook to make a note. 'Well, surely you don't need to write it down, for you know him!' But he wrote it down anyway, at which point Ellen turned away and started to cry. He patted her comfortingly on her shoulder and said that he would do everything he could for her.

In the pavilion he asked how it was that everything was so new. Because of renovations, said Ebstein. What brains it took to achieve it, he added. Mother and I walked back and forth in front of the bank to snatch a look at the visitors and we were successful. The people crowded round them in their thousands, even though the older ones were

17 Rabbi Marcus Friediger corresponded from Theresienstadt with the Bishop of Copenhagen Hans Fuglsang-Damgaard.

18 Karl Rahm (1907–1947), machinist; joined the NSDAP and the SS in 1934; worked in the Central Offices for Jewish Emigration in Vienna and Prague from Feb. 1939; commandant of the Theresienstadt ghetto from Feb. 1944; sentenced to death by a Czechoslovakian court and executed in 1947.

19 The Danish prisoners were not aware of the agreement between Werner Best and Adolf Eichmann to leave the Danes in Theresienstadt.

20 Ellen Oppenhejm (1926–2020); worked for Denmark's National Office of Statistics after 1945.

21 Judis Fabian (b. 1941). Her father, Hans Erich Fabian, was an employee of the Reich Association of Jews in Germany. The Fabian and Oppenhejm families were 'prominent' inmates (*Prominente*) of the ghetto and lived in neighbouring accommodation.

22 German in the original: 'Do you speak Danish?'

23 Henning Schram (1914–1980), parodist.

not allowed to spend time outside. In the Sichenheim[24] the Danes said that it is certainly nicely fitted out here (during the previous week), but that the patients did not look so good (of course, those you could not beautify).

DOC. 26
Gilel Storch forwards the report from two Danish ministerial officials who had been shown around the Theresienstadt ghetto on 23 June 1944[1]

Report (#768-10/23/44-fh) forwarded by Hilel (Gilel) Storch,[2] to Dr Leon Kubowitzki,[3] World Jewish Congress, 1834 Broadway, New York, dated 10 September 1944[4]

Translation
At a meeting at the Danish Legation in Stockholm on July 19, 1944, the Head of the Department, Mr. Hvass of the Danish Foreign Ministry, reported on the visit he and Dr. Juel-Henningsen from the Department of Health had made to Theresienstadt on June 23rd as representatives of the Danish Red Cross. Present at this meeting in the Legation were the Secretary of the Legation, Hessellund-Jensen,[5] Professor Stephan Hurwitz,[6] and the undersigned, Director O. Levysohn and Lawyer Kai Simonsen[7] as representative of the Relief Committee for Refugees from Denmark. The Head of the Department, Mr. Hvass, stated:

We arrived in Prague on June 23, and went from there in cars to Theresienstadt, 33 miles from Prague. We were accompanied by different German authorities,[8] among

24 German in the original, correctly: 'Siechenheim' ('hospice').

1 AJA, The World Jewish Congress Collection, series H, H259, 8. The original document is in English.

2 Gilel (Hilel) Storch (1902–1983), retailer; in 1940 escaped from Latvia to Sweden, where he worked in the export sector; representative of the World Jewish Congress (WJC) and the Jewish Agency in Sweden.

3 Dr Leon Kubowitzki (1896–1966), lawyer; co-founder of the WJC, head of its Rescue Department and, from Jan. 1945, representative of the WJC in Europe; general secretary of the WJC, 1945–1948; in the Israeli diplomatic service from 1948; chairman of the Yad Vashem memorial from 1959 until his death.

4 In the cover letter of the report, Gilel Storch expressed his suspicions that the Nazis were using Theresienstadt to give the false impression that the Germans were treating the Jews in the occupied areas 'humanely', and that atrocities were being committed only by the local population.

5 Aage Hessellund-Jensen (1911–1974), diplomat; legation secretary in Stockholm, 1942–1946; diplomatic representative at the Danish embassy's refugee office, 1943–1945.

6 Stephan Hurwitz (1901–1981), doctor of law; professor in Copenhagen from 1935; leader of the Danish Refugee Office in Stockholm, 1943–1944; member of the Danish military commission in London, 1944–1944.

7 Otto Levyson (b. 1899), retailer, and Kai Simonsen (b. 1906), lawyer; both worked at the Danish embassy's refugee office after their escape to Sweden in 1943.

8 Apart from the Germans mentioned by name, the delegation also included, among others, the head of the Central Office for Jewish Emigration in Prague, Hans Günther, and his brother, Rolf Günther; Ernst Möhs, Fritz Renner, and Karl Rahm; the camp inspector, Karl Bergl; and Eberhard von Thadden from the Reich Foreign Office.

them a chief of the Gestapo in the Protectorate of Bohemia-Moravia;[9] further a Swiss physician, Dr. Rousell,[10] from the International Red Cross. We had with us about 25 kg. of valuable medicaments and serum from Denmark.

The visit in Theresienstadt took over eight hours, from 11 in the morning to 7 in the evening, on a nice summer day. We were free to see everything and to talk with everyone. Conversations were overheard 'in a discreet manner'. No one stopped us from asking questions, and answers were given freely. We also discussed relatives in Sweden.

Mr. Hvass went on to say that relatives of the deportees might be told that the conditions were much better than had been thought. The visit was most heartening for the Danish internees since it proved that the authorities at home still show great interest in them. Theresienstadt is far away from other cities. It is an old garrison whose former Czechoslovak inhabitants had been forcibly moved out. The Germans call the camp 'Jewish Home for the Sick and Aged', which gives it a special character. There are now about 37,000–40,000 Jewish deportees, divided as follows: from Germany about 94 per cent, from Holland about 5 per cent, from Denmark about 1 per cent (of which 296 are Danish citizens, and about 150 are stateless emigrants).[11] The city is not fenced in, but is guarded by a small group of Czech police. There are only 15 non-Jews in the city.[12]

Jewish self-government has been started. The Chairman of the Council of Elders is Dr. Eppstein, a famous personality and a former lecturer at a German university. He received the Danish representatives and those with them, in his office, which looked like a public office in Denmark. The Executive consists of a Council of 66 members, among whom is Dr. Friediger. There are about 1,200 officers.[13]

The average age in the city is 48 years. 59 per cent of the inhabitants are female. About 14,000 are over 60 years.[14] As can be seen, this is a camp mostly for old people, which accounts for the high death rate (about 10–15 per day). The average age of the dying is 72 years. Theresienstadt is not a transit camp, and nobody from Denmark has been deported from there.[15] Of three Danes who had been deported to Sachsenhausen by a

9 Dr Erwin Weinmann (b. 1909), physician; joined the NSDAP and the SA in 1931 and the SS in 1937; worked for the SD from 1936; head of Group IV D at the Reich Security Main Office (RSHA) from March 1941; head of Sonderkommando 4a, 1942; Senior Commander of the Security Police in Prague from 1942; declared dead in 1949.

10 Correctly: Maurice Rossel (1917–2008), physician; employee of the International Committee of the Red Cross (ICRC) from Feb. 1944; member of the Berlin delegation of the ICRC in April 1944; retired from the service after 1945; later took part in humanitarian missions in Vietnam (1966–1967) and Rwanda (1967).

11 These numbers are from a speech given for the visitors by Paul Eppstein, who, on the orders of the SS, stated this significantly higher number rather than the actual number of prisoners, which was 28,000. In total, 470 persons from Denmark were deported to Theresienstadt; around 70 per cent of them held Danish citizenship. Presumably, Eppstein's statements were designed to conceal the fact that thousands of prisoners had previously been deported.

12 Before the delegation's visit, fences and barbed wire were removed from the bastions.

13 These inflated numbers were also from Eppstein.

14 This number is likewise from Eppstein's speech and supported the deceptive presentation of Theresienstadt as the 'ghetto for the elderly'. In reality, the average age was lower.

15 Only the Danish prisoners and some of the so-called high-profile prisoners were protected from deportation. However, one Danish prisoner, Schmul Sender Jonisch (1899–1944), who had arrived in Theresienstadt on Transport XXV/3 from Denmark, was included on Transport DX to Auschwitz-Birkenau on 20 March 1944; he was murdered there on arrival.

later transport, one was transferred to Theresienstadt and the other two, if not already brought there, will be transferred in the near future.[16] Since the creation of the camp in 1942, there have been some marriages, and between 300 and 400 children were born. There are means for birth control, and abortion is allowed.[17]

Food is the same as in the whole Protectorate, but there is no butter, eggs, or cheese. Instead of butter there is margarine, although butter is shipped from Denmark. According to the information received, every person gets 2,400 calories daily, while at home, for a working person, one calculates 3,000 calories. The orthodox people are allowed to provide Kosher food.[18] Tobacco and alcohol are forbidden. About 24,000 of the city's inmates work a maximum of eight hours daily. All get first a physical examination. Thereafter, they are divided into four categories: 1 – those fully capable of work; 2 – formerly sick, now healthy; 3 – conditionally capable for work; 4 – incapable of working. In the beginning, people are divided into so-called 'Hundertschaften',[19] where they are put to all kinds of work, partly to train them in working cooperatively, and partly to see for what they are especially fitted. The young people do garden and field work, and some work in fields outside the city, guarded by gendarmes. They also work on silkworm farms. Women are occupied with special work and housecleaning. The intellectuals, such as engineers, physicians, lawyers and others, are put to work within their particular field. Room and board are gratis, and all get paid for their work. There is a special kind of basic money – Theresienstadt crowns – and the minimum salary per month is 100 T. cr., equivalent to about 10 marks, but with greater purchasing power than outside the camp. Through special work, one gets additional incomes, paid either in money or in extra meat. 50 per cent of the salary is withheld for taxes and other purposes. There are stores where, besides small items, one can buy clothing and shoes – mostly used or repaired. A suit costs about 350 T. crowns.

Dr. Eppstein said that he divided the people into two groups: the 'vegetating', who hold fast to the remembrance of the past, with no strength and willpower to get adjusted to the new conditions; and the strong and energetic, who look at the whole matter as temporary, something they have to come through. It so happened that the latter group was able to influence the weak, so that more and more got used to the new conditions. Thus, life has been functioning normally in the city, and the people in general have more courage to face life.

Visiting the city and the institutions, one got the impression that the city was clean; the inhabitants looked healthy and not undernourished.[20] All wear a Yellow Star. Order is kept by Jewish police, consisting of special people who enforce strong justice, knowing

16 One Danish prisoner remained in Sachsenhausen, and the other, Michael Rubin Singerowitz (1891–1944), was transported on 6 December 1943 from Sachsenhausen to Majdanek, where he perished on 21 Jan. 1944: see also Doc. 16, fn. 12.

17 This misinformation was meant to give the impression of normality. Probably no more than 230 children were born in Theresienstadt, and abortions were enforced. Two Danish children born in the camp died as a result of the poor living conditions.

18 In reality, nutrition in the ghetto was significantly worse, and the Danish prisoners suffered from hunger as well, despite the food parcels they received from their home country.

19 German in the original: 'groups of one hundred'.

20 The delegation was only allowed to see those Danish prisoners who by that point were no longer severely malnourished.

that this is necessary in order to maintain relatively good conditions in the city. There is a large open square in the city, a former parade-ground, with green trees and flowers, where an orchestra of 30 men plays daily.[21] Outside the city are vegetable gardens, and the vegetables grown there belong to the people who plant them. The houses are clean, but as the city originally had only about 10,000 inhabitants, and now shelters nearly four times as many, about 30 great barracks have been erected to make room for the over-population. There are some differences in accommodations; some people are in single rooms, while as a rule families live together, either in one room or in great dormitories with the double-decker system.[22] Some barracks accommodate only men, others only women; some rooms shelter several families who know each other and prefer to live together. The barracks are large, clean, and airy, with plenty of space between the rows of beds. The beds are of wood, equipped with woollen blankets, and with mattresses stuffed with hay. The dormitories have about 70 to 80 beds each.

Further, there are some youth and children's homes. There is electricity, water, toilets, and telephones, but no gas.[23] There is a special heating system. The food can be made either at home on the fireplace, or one can get it from a general kitchen, which we saw and found proper. There are also mess-halls which remind one somewhat of a Danish cafeteria. The food may also be taken home and heated in the barracks. At 10 p.m., everyone has to be indoors, unless one has a pass, which is given on special occasions. Newspapers do not exist, nor are there any radios. A Jewish Court, as well as a Court of Appeals, were established. The Chief of the Gestapo could change a decision made by the Court, but up to now this happened only once, and this one time it was changed to not guilty. The highest sentence given was six months.

Dr. Juel-Henningsen gave a detailed report on health conditions, and said they were good. There were no epidemics. A few cases of typhoid occurred, but there are none now.[24] Mental sicknesses are rare.[25] There are vaccinations against contagious diseases, especially against scarlet fever[26] and diphtheria, of which there have been some cases. There was only one old case of tuberculosis, and thanks to enough liver oil and vitamins, there were no cases of rickets. The camp has no lice or other insects, and the internees are forced to take a bath every tenth day.[27] There are showers and a swimming pool[28]

21 These facilities and the orchestra's public performance were part of the deception planned specifically for the visit. Previously, the square had been partitioned off by a wooden fence and was not open to the prisoners.

22 For the visit, some of the Danish prisoners had been allowed to move into better accommodation next to the living quarters of the high-profile prisoners. They also received new furnishings. With the exception of these privileged prisoners, inmates were usually housed in crowded dormitories, separated by gender.

23 Certain facilities of the Jewish self-administration temporarily had access to telephones. Private usage was strictly forbidden.

24 There were more than 1,000 cases of typhus in total. Larger typhus epidemics did not occur until spring 1945.

25 The SS had deported most of the mentally ill prisoners before the visit.

26 In reality, there were no vaccinations against scarlet fever. The frequent scarlet fever outbreaks in fact constituted a serious threat to the prisoners.

27 There was indeed a central bathing facility, but because of the overcrowding in the ghetto and the lack of water, lice and other pests were very common.

28 The swimming pool, built with the prisoners' forced labour in a fire water reservoir in the 'small fortress', the Gestapo prison, was reserved solely for the guards.

with chlorinated water which is changed twice a week. Everybody is entitled to 4 kg. of linen every three weeks, which seems to be adequate.[29] The camp has about 500 physicians, of whom 400 are practicing. Some of them are famous specialists. There is further a hospital with 2,150 beds, of which about 1,700 were occupied. The hospital rooms are very crowded, and contain about 40 or 50 people per room. But although the beds are closer together than in our hospitals, the place is clean and airy. Equipment for operations and taking x-rays is not fully modern, but it appears to be functioning well, and the hospital resembles somewhat the Danish province hospitals of the year 1935. Scientific research is being conducted in the many laboratories of the camp, which also has a 'Diät Küche'.[30] There is generally no free choice as to a doctor, but people may use the different medical stations in the city, where under certain conditions one may have a special physician. X-ray examinations are being made of the whole population. Up to now, about 50 per cent have been examined. There are good dental clinics; furthermore, there is a central pharmacy with four branches, which have plenty of medicaments (among others, insulin and sulfa drugs), a fact [noted] especially by Dr. Eppstein. While they have A and B vitamins, there is a shortage of C vitamins.

About 280 people are in homes for the aged. The oldest is 94 years, and most are bed-ridden. They are attended by fifteen physicians. The old people looked very downhearted and have generally not much hope. Much is being done for the children: there are schools (the visitors attended a singing lesson in Hebrew); playgrounds with swings, etc.; a special recreation hall, decorated with murals for children by a Dutch artist.

The post office, which is under Jewish care, appears to be good, and we had occasion to see the incoming mail and parcels from Denmark. The date of our visit was June 23rd, and there arrived parcels which had been sent from Denmark on June 14th. Parcels are also being shipped from the Protectorate, but the number is restricted by the authorities. The custom houses watch that no prohibited goods come in. One knows that every infraction of the law will hurt the whole population.

There are also banking institutions, which are under the supervision of a former Jewish bank manager. About 14 million Theresienstadt crowns are in circulation to cover the cost of labor and merchandise.[31]

We visited carpenter shops with mechanical saws which produce chairs, furniture and other things. There are also blacksmith shops. We further visited a larger bakery and tasted the bread, which was of the same quality as in the Protectorate.[32]

The fire-house was not modern. It had only one fire hose in bad condition.

The camp offered plenty of recreational facilities. In addition to the aforementioned orchestra, there was a theater which performed a children's opera[33] composed by one

29 The temporary water shortage and the overcrowding made such a laundry rotation impossible. Opportunities to do laundry more likely occurred every three to four months.

30 German in the original, reference to a kitchen producing a light diet.

31 The 'Bank of the Jewish Self-Administration in Theresienstadt' was put into operation by order of the SS in May 1943.

32 This concerns the former garrison bakery, which generally could not keep up with demand in the overcrowded ghetto. Bread was often a scarce commodity.

33 The opera *Brundibár* was composed by Hans Krása (1899–1944) in 1938 (libretto: Adolf Hoffmeister) and performed in the Jewish children's home in Prague in 1941. In Theresienstadt in 1942, Krása wrote down the musical score from memory and reworked it. This children's opera was probably performed fifty times in Theresienstadt. Krása and the majority of the performers were murdered in Auschwitz.

of the internees, as well as a choral composition by Verdi; the operas The *Bartered Bride*, *Carmen*, *The Magic Flute*, and others. Further entertainment was provided through classical music and lectures, and an outdoor stadium was being prepared for such occasion. The library is said to contain 166,000 books; reading halls were fully occupied. A restaurant sells soft drinks.

Mr. Hvass reported further that he and Dr. Juel-Henningsen had a long conversation with Dr. Friediger, Engineer Ove Meyer, and Lawyer Oppenheim regarding the deportees from Denmark. Mr. Meyer said that psychologically he was of course under pressure, but that physically and materially he had no complaints. Great developments had occurred in the past half year. He himself suffered of heart trouble, but the treatments he got were as complete as he could get in Denmark. – We talked to some 20 to 30 Danes, but there was no possibility to arrange for a meeting of all Danish internees: this would be making a distinction in relation to the other inhabitants, who had no visitors from the outside. Our conversations with them confirmed the impressions we had gathered before. One of the Danes, a Mr. Grun, asked us specifically to tell at home that 'things are much better than people believe'.[34]

Mr. Hvass stated further that permission has been granted to ship food from Denmark to Theresienstadt. Two parcels of 5–6 kg each per person and containing valuable food-stuffs and medicaments will be sent each month. In accordance with the wish of the German authorities, shipments will be made in collective consignments, but parcels are addressed to individuals. All deportees from Denmark will henceforth receive two parcels a month. A library of 1,000 books, containing scientific and other literature in Danish, as well as magazines of general contents, will also be sent from home in the near future. Further, permission has been obtained to send an amount of 10 marks per person to the internees. No assurance has been given that money may be sent more than once, but it is hoped that one may try again after a while.

Mr. Hvass said that the favourable overall impression which the Danish representatives got, concurs with that of the Swiss delegation.[35] He felt he should express his admiration for the Jews who head this self-government. For the whole population of Theresienstadt the idea prevails that all this is only temporary; hence they have remained hopeful. Mr. Hvass produced some photographs of Theresienstadt, which were taken by the Swiss delegates, showing, among others, children on playgrounds, in school, etc. Mr. Hvass, in reply to a question, said no possibility existed to have the Danish internees removed to Sweden or Denmark.

34 All these statements were made in the presence of the SS and were not freely articulated by the speakers.

35 The Swiss delegate of the ICRC in Berlin, Maurice Rossel, submitted a positive report on conditions in the camp to Geneva on 27 June 1944: Archives du Comité international de la Croix-Rouge, Geneva, B (Services généraux), B G 59/12–368. Rossel took the photos mentioned in the penultimate sentence.

DOC. 27

In April 1945 the Dane Kai Nagler experiences his liberation from Theresienstadt as part of the 'White Buses' operation[1]

Handwritten diary of Kai Holger Nagler,[2] entries for 9 to 20 April 1945

9 April 1945
The 5th anniversary of the occupation of Denmark. It's been spring for a month already, the fruit trees are in bloom, while the sun's rays are beating down hot from a cloudless sky. The air raid sirens are a daily occurrence, two to three times a day, and they say that the Russians are advancing in Slovakia and Austria, while the English are pushing forward everywhere in Germany from the west. We're now only looking at weeks or days. My March package arrived[3] (unexpectedly early) on Friday the 6th.

In a hurry on Friday the 13th at 8 p.m.[4]
The cars were expected on Saturday afternoon, but didn't arrive until the night and Sunday morning. Departure at 10 a.m.[5] Being parted from Margit was horrible and I understand her distress. A pleasant drive through Bohemia and the war zone. In Dresden by 3.30 p.m. Not a single house in the city was still intact and the devastation made for a gruesome sight.

During the night, the cars were driven to a forest road around 30–40 km from Potsdam, where we spent the night in the vehicles, while air raid sirens announced planes over Berlin. On Monday morning, the 17th,[6] we started off again at 6 a.m. After the air attacks during the night, Potsdam was now a terrible sight: 90 per cent of the area lay in ruins. From Potsdam, our route led via Berlin and Hamburg to Schwerin and Lübeck. From there at 8 a.m. via Neumünster, which was 80–90 per cent destroyed. On the way to Flensburg there were many delays owing to the air raid sirens and it wasn't until 6.30 on Tuesday morning that we crossed the border after another night in the vehicles. At several points we found ourselves very close to the front.

From 8 a.m. until noon, we stopped over in Padborg,[7] where we took a bath, relaxed and were able to eat as much porridge with cream as we wanted. At 2 p.m., we set off

1 DJM, JDK166A1. These documents have been translated from Danish.
2 Kai James Holger Nagler, born K. H. Cordosa (1895–1964); director of various companies.
3 From Feb. 1944 the Danish inmates received parcels, at first occasionally and then regularly. The shipments were arranged by a private network working in close cooperation with the Danish Ministry of Social Affairs and the friends and relatives of the deportees, as well as the Danish Red Cross, and Jewish relief organizations in Sweden, Switzerland, and the United States. The German authorities did not authorize these shipments until the visit by the delegation of the International Red Cross and the Danish civil administration on 23 June 1944.
4 The following entries give the impression of having been written on a single day rather than on separate days, especially as the dates given are wrong.
5 Since the start of the deportations the Danish authorities had sought permission for the return to Denmark of individual prisoners or entire groups. After negotiations by the vice president of the Red Cross, Folke Bernadotte, with Himmler, 15,000 Scandinavian prisoners were rescued in March/April 1945 and taken to neutral Sweden on white buses, in an operation undertaken by the Swedish and Danish Red Cross organizations.
6 The following Monday was 16 April 1945.
7 Danish border town.

and journeyed through South Jutland and an indescribable elation swept through us. It culminated in Apenrade and Hadersleben when masses of flowers, tobacco, chocolate, and much more, along with touching letters, were thrown into the vehicles. The hospital in Apenrade distributed milk and packages of delicious sandwiches to everyone. Lots of people lined the road to Odense, shouting 'Welcome'.

Arrived in Odense at 7 p.m., where we were sent to the municipal buildings. The Red Cross had prepared an excellent dinner (vegetable soup, Danish beef patties with onions and potatoes, coffee, and Danish pastries) and there was great joy and a wonderful celebration. It was 11 before we settled down and took a needed rest.

On the 18th, we set off at 4.30, everyone supplied with a package of tasty sandwiches. On the ferry they served ham with two fried eggs, bread and butter, coffee, and Danish pastries. At 9.30 we left Korsør. At noon, we arrived in Copenhagen via P. Bangsvej – Falkoner Allé – Østerbrogade to the airport, where Lilli, Anni, Kylle and Willy met me with tobacco, sandwiches etc. After a quick visit, the journey continued to Malmö, where I met Jytte and Sven.

At the free port in Malmö, we had to wait the whole day until we could be medically examined and were allowed to have a bath. It wasn't until midnight that we travelled through Halvdalen to Halmstad-Tylösand, where we were greeted with sausage, beer, and sandwiches. It was 5 o'clock the next day before I was given accommodation, although many had to wait another three hours before they were housed.

Norway

Norway
North Cape
Kirkenes
Hammerfest
FINNMARK
Veidal
Tromsø
TROMS
Narvik
Lofoten
Svolvær
Norwegian Sea
Bodø
NORDLAND
NORWAY
NORD-TRØNDELAG
Vaasa
FIN-LAND
Falstad
Östersund
SØR-TRØNDELAG
Trondheim
Kristiansund
Gulf of Bothnia
MØRE OG ROMSDAL
HEDMARK
Turku
OPPLAND
SOGN OG FJORDANE
SWEDEN
Uppsala
Stockholm
HORDALAND
BUSKERUD
Bredtveit
Grini
Oslo
Bergen
Baltic Sea
TELEMARK
Berg
Tønsberg
Fredrikstad
Hauge-sund
ROGA-LAND
Stavanger
AUST-AGDER
Gotland
Egersund
VEST-AGDER
Camps
Gothenburg
0 50 100 150 km
North Sea
OPPLAND
HED-MARK
BUSKERUD
OSLO
Bredtveit
Lillestrøm
Grini
Oslo
AKERSHUS
Töcksfors
Moss
VEST-FOLD
ØSTFOLD
Berg
Sarpsborg
Tønsberg
Fredrikstad
Halden
Stavern

DOC. 28

The Jewish Bulletin: in September 1942 the prime minister of the Norwegian government in exile in London condemns the persecution of Jews in his country[1]

A message from the Norwegian Prime Minister Professor Nygaardsvold[2]

In democratic Norway there was never any question of distinction between the class, race, or creed of Norwegian citizens. All men were equal and free to do what was right and proper.

The Jews in Norway – their numbers are not large – were never treated like their unfortunate kinsfolk in Germany. They were looked upon for what they were – fellow-men, peace-loving citizens, and hard workers; men and women who looked up to the Norwegian king and flag with the same love and ardour as the most loyal and patriotic citizen. This is their adopted land, and now that hard times have come for Norway the Jews strive with the same patriotic endeavour to build up the Home Front[3] as they strove to better the land in days of peace. Already some Jews have sacrificed their lives in the common fight against the enemy. They were not executed in a political purge against the Jews, but because they were men actively resisting the Germans.

There has never been a 'Jewish problem' in Norway. Jews have just been part of the community. But when the German hordes forced their way into our peace-loving country, they had to find a Jewish problem. Anti-Jewish demonstrations were staged by the Germans, windows were smashed, and insulting remarks were painted on the walls and windows of Jewish-occupied premises. They were deprived of their livelihood, their citizenship was removed; they were oppressed and starved. But they still fight on as staunchly as other patriotic Norwegians.

All these wrongs will be righted when Norway is once more a free land. The citizenship and equal rights of the Jews will be restored and, like other Norwegians, they will be helped to make good what they have suffered.

1 *The Jewish Bulletin*, no. 13, Sept. 1942, p. 1. The *Bulletin* appeared monthly between 1941 and 1945 and was published by the British Ministry of Information in cooperation with the chief rabbi of the British Empire. It was particularly widely circulated in the USA.

2 Johann Nygaardsvold (1879–1952), railway worker and politician; member of parliament for the Norwegian Labour Party, 1916–1949; president of the Norwegian parliament, 1934–1935; prime minister, March 1935–June 1945; in exile in London from June 1940. Here the term 'Professor' is to be understood as an honorary title.

3 'Home Front' is used in the sense of the Norwegian term *hjemmefronten*, which refers to resistance within the occupied nation. In contrast, the armed forces in exile were referred to as the 'forces abroad' (*utefronten*).

DOC. 29

On 7 October 1942 a Nasjonal Samling activist writes to Prime Minister Quisling with suggestions regarding the introduction of measures against Jews[1]

Letter from Halldis Neegård Østbye,[2] Lillevann V, Aker, to Prime Minister Quisling,[3] the Royal Palace, dated 7 October 1942[4]

Re: the Jewish question
With regard to our conversation a few days ago, allow me to make certain observations concerning the solution to the Jewish question.

In light of the rather tense mood, I do not think it advisable to take drastic measures at the present time. A country like Slovakia, for example, where there is no such internal division, can certainly introduce all of the necessary measures at the present time. Here, however, where the general mood is constantly at breaking point, it is somewhat different. All the more so because the vast majority of the Norwegian people do not yet have a full understanding of the Jewish problem, and there is great ignorance even among our own ranks. We can already sense the reactions to the measures that have been taken. For example, the bishop's pronouncements from the pulpit last Sunday.[5] London is still attempting a call to arms; the clergy are receiving new impulses for new disputes.[6]

I think it would be advantageous if the measures which must be taken were introduced as covertly as possible and *gradually.*

Above all, they must be accompanied by *systematic information about the Jewish problem,* and in particular information on why this or that measure must be introduced to protect the interests of our people.

I would also consider it wise to start by making *a clear and sharp distinction between specific types of Jews.* People are reacting so vehemently because Jews are all lumped together. For example, Mosaic Jews need to be set apart from 'Christian' Jews who entered the country before the last world war. Among the more recent immigrants, exceptions can be made for the so-called 'reputable' Jews, i.e. Jews who cannot be accused of any activities hostile to the state or of deceptive behaviour. Allow me also to suggest that

1 NRA, Landsvikarkivet, Bredtveit fengsel, L-sak 5/1949–50, no. 41. This document has been translated from Norwegian.
2 Halldis Neegård Østbye (1898–1983), alpinist and journalist; joined Nasjonal Samling as one of its first female members in 1933; soon part of Quisling's inner circle, head of propaganda in the party's women's organization in 1934, head of the party's Press and Propaganda Office, 1935–1940; editor of the party newspaper *Fritt Folk* from 1937; sentenced to seven years of hard labour by a Norwegian court in 1948, fled, and then returned to Norway and served part of the sentence; released in 1953.
3 Vidkun Quisling (1887–1945), career officer; minister of defence, 1931–1933; founded Nasjonal Samling in 1933, supported the German occupation of Norway, and then proclaimed himself head of government, although the German occupation authorities did not initially recognize him as such; prime minister of the Norwegian collaborationist government from Feb. 1942; sentenced to death after the war by a Norwegian court and executed on 24 Oct. 1945.
4 Receipt stamp for 28 Oct. 1942. The original contains handwritten corrections and additions.
5 This could not be found.
6 The reference is to the Norwegian government in exile in London and to the Norwegian clergy who resisted Nasjonal Samling's attempts to co-opt them in spring and summer 1942.

before there are any further regulations concerning Jews, a list of all those Jewish companies in the country specializing in bankruptcies be made public, along with an announcement that the assets of *these* companies have been seized in accordance with the current regulations on the confiscation of assets. As you may remember, we once had a list of all such companies in *Fritt Folk,*[7] taken from *Norsk Kjøbmannsblad,*[8] which campaigned against Jewish fraud. Within the business community and well beyond, there has been considerable bitterness about Jewish bankruptcy scammers for years.

The vast majority, and even the Jøssinger,[9] will certainly agree that *these* people should be apprehended. In this way we can nudge public opinion in our direction. And then we can go one step further.

Of great *urgency* is of course the *Aryan law,* so that all further mixing of races can be stopped. Furthermore, Jewish influence must be halted by barring Jews from anything to do with the education of children or the people, cultural life, etc. Jews with 'Aryanized' names must be required to re-adopt Jewish names immediately; the proprietor's name must appear in the shop windows and on letterheads, envelopes, etc. of the Jews who are allowed to continue trading for the time being.

Such measures are fairly uncontentious and will not provide much of a basis for agitation, certainly not from the pulpit. Everything else should happen on the quiet, like putting Jews in concentration camps, etc. – without official regulations. It is another matter when for example reports appear in the press that such and such a number of Jews have been put to practical work, such as road construction, tree felling, and the like. It will not be easy to say anything much against *that,* for many Norwegians have been drafted to do the same work.

The final settlement must of course be radical and unsentimental. But since we already have so many internal difficulties from before, a moderate line would certainly be best for us.

Some parties have proposed that Jews be identified by yellow stars. I would personally advise against this. It would simply produce a rush of sympathy and concern for the Jews among the Jøssinger, heighten hatred of the new order, and further worsen the mood among the people. Allow me to propose, rather – should anything of the like not yet have been discussed – that the upkeep of Jewish families be funded from confiscated Jewish assets and that a special *Liquidations Office* be set up for the management of Jewish assets and the allocation of the confiscated means, under satisfactory audit.[10]

7 *Fritt Folk* was the official newspaper of Nasjonal Samling.

8 Correctly: *Norges kjøbmannsblad.* This was the newspaper of the retailers' association.

9 Opponents of Nasjonal Samling. The name is taken from Jøssingfjord, which was where British troops captured a German ship in Feb. 1940; the Norwegian navy's failure to intervene was seen as a disgrace in nationalist circles.

10 Not every suggestion made here was implemented. The Law on the Compulsory Registration of Jews, which determined who was considered Jewish, was passed on 17 Nov. 1942, only shortly before the deportation of Norwegian Jews commenced: see Doc. 35. Jewish-owned shops were identified as such only on the initiative of regional German commanders. Jewish Norwegians were registered from spring 1942 onwards, and their identity documents were marked with a 'J': see PMJ 5/14, 20, 21. The yellow star was not introduced in Norway. There is no concrete evidence for a planned and comprehensive forced labour programme for Jews, but Jewish prisoners were used as forced labour. Quisling promulgated the Law on the Confiscation of Jewish Assets on 26 Oct. 1942. A Liquidations Office administered the possessions of those who were deported: see Doc. 44.

However, as long as we do not know *who* is Jewish, all provisions will be left more or less hanging in the air. Allow me therefore to propose that everything be done to expedite the comprehensive Jew registry that the NS Office for Statistics under Nylander[11] has been working on since last spring.

Concerning quarter-Jews, it was Dr Mjøen's proposal[12] that the decision should be made on an individual basis. Those who exhibited an Aryan mentality were to be declared Aryans, those who exhibited a Jewish mentality were to be declared Jews. Personally, I would add that cases where there is any doubt should probably be deemed Jewish.

It gets more complicated when it comes to marriage and progeny in connection with quarter-Jews, but that is surely a matter for racial biologists.

Could one not rather go about it in the following way: in all instances where there is any doubt, the person concerned could be allowed to choose between either sterilization or being declared a Jew. I mean cases where the person concerned does not yet have any Jewish children, or has children with such weak traces that they do not fall under the Aryan law. The problems would solve themselves over the course of one or two generations.

It does go without saying that the ultimate solution of the Jewish problem must be carried out without sentimentality when it comes to protecting our own people and Europe against a new Jewish onslaught. But a certain amount of humanity should be shown as long as it does not harm our own people. For example, there are two Jewish brothers here in Lillevann. One of them has always been, as far as I am aware, a model member of the community, clearly anti-communist, anti-English, and opposed to the old regime in all the time I have known him (10–12 years). He is married to a Swedish woman, one of the most excellent pure-blooded Aryans I have ever met. They cannot have children themselves and have adopted two Aryan children. One must admit that bringing about the downfall of this family would be inhumane and entirely superfluous. His brother on the other hand is a Jøssing, a common petty Jew, married to a Jewess with three or four insolent Jewish kids who have infected the other children up here with their hatred for NS[13] and the Germans.

I cite this example in order to show how necessary it is to be able to make decisions up to a point on an individual basis.

I also think it will profit us as a nation if we follow a *Norwegian* line. The treatment of Jews in Russia is in part such that I think the Nordic race is degrading itself by carrying it out. It is quite understandable that soldiers become enormously embittered at the sight of victims of Jewish sadism and that they feel an urge to torture Jews to death. But to actually *do* so is in my view un-Aryan. The old Vikings were certainly not angels; it was not unusual for them to gouge out the eyes of their defeated enemies, to torture and maim them. But I think it would be a great gain if the NS were to consider it one of the Germanic, or

11 Sigfried Nylander (b. 1891); emigrated from Sweden to Norway in 1917; joined Nasjonal Samling in 1934; head of the party's Office for Statistics; designed the questionnaire for Jews in Norway: see PMJ 5/21.

12 Jon Alfred Hansen Mjøen (1860–1939), pharmacist; married to a German; leading Norwegian eugenicist, involved in international eugenicist networks; published the periodical *Den nordiske Race* from 1920; published books on racial hygiene including *Det norske program for rasehygiene* ('The Norwegian Programme for Racial Hygiene'), 1932.

13 Here and below: Nasjonal Samling.

perhaps rather *Nordic*, virtues not to torture a defeated enemy but rather, when necessary, to shoot him quickly and mercilessly. It is the same as with animals. They should be killed quickly and painlessly, not horribly tormented. This should also apply to Jews.

Neither do I think that it is right that young SS men, men of Nordic blood, be used as *executioners* for shooting Jewish women, children, and old people. This should be left to Russians or Asiatic peoples, who are more than happy to take revenge on their tormentors. I find it appalling that *Norwegian* lads are also perhaps being given the role of executioner. They cannot possibly return to being normal human beings after that. War is brutal enough already without such horrors.

If I have permitted myself to convey these opinions, it is because – with the exception of the prime minister – there is no one within the movement who has looked as closely into the Jewish question as I have, and because I have worked more with propaganda than any other individual in the NS.[14]

Heil og Sæl[15]

DOC. 30

New York Times, 24 October 1942: article on the killing of a Norwegian border official and the impending annihilation of Jews[1]

Extirpation of Jews Expected in Norway. Two are Accused of Slaying Quisling Border Guard.

By telephone to the *New York Times*. *Stockholm*, Sweden, 23 October.
Extermination of Jews on the German model is widely expected in Norway after today's killing of a Quisling frontier guard by three young men, two of whom are officially stated to be Jews.

The men were Wille Scherman, from Oslo; Hermann Feldmann,[2] from Trondheim; and Harald Jensen,[3] from Lillestroem.[4] They were apparently on their way to the border, intending to escape into Sweden, when a frontier guard stepped into their compartment and asked to see their passports. The men pulled guns and shot the guard, then jumped out of the train. The shooting occurred near the Skjeberg station[5] and, surprisingly enough, the train was not halted until it reached the next station, Berg, some twenty miles farther.

14 In the original, the last part of the sentence has been placed in handwritten square brackets.
15 'Salvation and Bliss', the salutation of Nasjonal Samling.

1 *New York Times*, 24 Oct. 1942, p. 7.
2 Correctly: Willy Schermann (1918–1943), tailor, and Hermann Feldmann (1918–1943), salesman; both were arrested on 26 Oct. 1942; they were deported in Feb. 1943 to Auschwitz, where they were murdered in August 1943.
3 Harald Jensen was the alias given in the counterfeit identity documents of Karsten Løvestad (1916–1943), a firefighter, who helped people cross the border and who was to take the refugees to Sweden; it was he who shot the border guard. He was arrested on 27 Oct. 1942 and executed in Sept. 1943.
4 Lillestrøm is a small town around 20 km east of the capital, Oslo.
5 Skjeberg is located in the administrative district of Østfold, near the Swedish border. Since 1992 it has been part of the city of Sarpsborg.

When the murder was discovered all Jews on the train were arrested. An Oslo report says that these Jews were members of a 'sabotage gang'. But apparently they merely hoped to escape to Sweden.

According to late reports, Mr. Scherman and Mr. Feldmann have already been arrested and have told police that they killed the guard because of his brutal conduct against Norwegian Jews.

Anti-Jewish persecution, which until recently was on a rather mild scale, has lately greatly intensified. The chief rabbi of Oslo[6] and many other Jews have been arrested. During the state of emergency in Trondheim twenty-eight Norwegian Jews were taken as hostages. For some time the Quisling authorities have threatened Norwegian Jews with deportation to Eastern Europe, and it is generally thought that today's murder will become a signal for mass deportation and probable killing of Norwegian Jews.

DOC. 31
On 25 October 1942 the head of the Norwegian State Police orders the local police to arrest male Jews[1]

Telegram from the head of the State Police[2] to all police stations, unsigned, dated 25 October 1942, 10.30 a.m.

All male persons aged 15 and over whose identity documents are stamped with a 'J' are to be arrested and taken to 23 Kirkeveien, Oslo. Arrests are to be carried out on Monday, 26 October, at 6 a.m. Those detained must bring dishes and cutlery, ration cards, and all official identity documents with them. Assets are to be confiscated. Special attention is to be given to securities, jewellery, and cash, for which a search is to be conducted. Bank accounts are to be frozen and safety deposit boxes emptied. You are to retain confiscated items until advised otherwise. All registration documents are to be sent here as soon as possible. Administrators must be installed for businesses belonging to those arrested. Lists of those arrested with information about their citizenship status, especially regarding former German citizenship, must be sent here immediately. All adult female Jews must report daily to the criminal investigation department of the Order Police.[3]

6 Rabbi Isaak Julius Samuel (1903–1942) and some other Jewish men were imprisoned while on holiday in early Sept. 1942. Earlier, the Gestapo had repeatedly interrogated them over a period of days and had obliged them to report regularly to the police. Rabbi Samuel was deported in Nov. 1942 and murdered in Auschwitz.

1 NRA, S-1329 Statspolitiet, Hovedkontoret og Osloavdelingen, Ga, 15, 'Sachakten CII B2'. Published in 'Inndragning av jødisk eiendom i Norge under den 2. verdenskrig', *Norges offentlige utredninger* [NOU] 1997: 22 (Oslo: Statens forvaltningstjeneste statens trykning, 1997), p. 24. This document has been translated from Norwegian.

2 Karl Alfred Nicolai Marthinsen (1896–1945), career officer; joined Nasjonal Samling in 1933; head of the Norwegian State Police from summer 1941, head of the Security Police from Jan. 1944, and commander of the Hird, the paramilitary militia of Nasjonal Samling, from April 1944; shot dead by members of the Norwegian resistance movement on 8 Feb. 1945; in retribution for his assassination, Reich Commissioner Terboven ordered the execution of 34 Norwegians.

3 In total around 260 men were detained during this round of arrests.

DOC. 32

On 29 October 1942 Ruth Maier describes her dismay at the oppression of the Jews[1]

Handwritten diary of Ruth Maier,[2] Oslo, entry for 29 October 1942[3]

29 October 1942, Oslo
They are arresting Jews. All male Jews between the ages of 16 and 72. Jewish shops are closed. This does not come as a shock, it doesn't surprise me. It only makes me feel sick. I am no longer 'proud' of being Jewish. I can walk past a Jewish face without losing my nerve. But when I hear the words 'Jewish question', I get a bad taste in my mouth. I am tired of hearing that Jews are being arrested again. I think: that they can *bring themselves to do it*. Zionism, assimilation! Nationalism, Jewish capitalism. Oh! Just leave us in *peace*! It is so disgusting to hear about the yellow patches and the Jewish martyrs. It is so loathsome. It reminds me of nasty worms, of real, repulsive worms.

People are oppressed because of their opinions. People beat each other to death to defend their fatherland. But you do not punish or beat people because they *are* what they are, because they have Jewish grandparents. That is insane, idiotic. It's enough to drive one mad. It goes against all reason.

That the Jews endure it is something I do not understand. That they do not go mad. I no longer love them with the enthusiasm of a 17-year-old teenager. But I will stick by them. Regardless of how it turns out.

If you lock yourself in and see these persecutions and ordeals of the Jews only as a Jew, *then* you will surely succumb to some sort of psychological complex, slowly but surely. Salvation lies in seeing the Jewish question from a wider perspective. In the context of current world events. In the context of the oppressed Czechs and Norwegians, in the context of the labour question. Then Zionism becomes unimportant, no longer matters, becomes uninteresting. Only then will we be rich, once we understand that we are not the only nation of martyrs. That countless others also suffer, will suffer until the end of days, just as we do … unless … unless we fight for a better … Oh, no! I am too old, too weary, to have faith in that.

It creeps up on me, this Jewish martyrdom, like a disgusting worm. One that feeds on my thoughts. There is something nonsensical about it. I thought I was less sensitive. Why am I not equally agitated when they arrest Norwegians, shoot them by the dozen, as was recently the case in Trondheim?[4] Am I too selfish? Do I not see far enough? It is

1 HL-senteret, Oslo, Ruth Maiers arkiv 007. For a published English translation: *Ruth Maier's Diary: A Jewish Girl's Life in Nazi Europe*, ed. Jan Erik Vold, trans. Jamie Bulloch (London: Vintage Books, 2008 [German edn, 2008]), here pp. 406–407. This document has been newly translated from Norwegian and German.

2 Ruth Maier (1920–1942), student and writer; grew up in Vienna; came to Norway as a refugee in Jan. 1939; finished secondary school in 1940; in the voluntary Norwegian Women's Labour Service, 1940–1942, then earned her living through craftwork and by posing for artists; arrested and deported in Nov. 1942 to Auschwitz, where she was murdered. See also PMJ 2/104, 121, 138, and 202, and PMJ 5/3 and 24.

3 The first three paragraphs were originally in Norwegian; the remainder of the entry was originally in German.

4 During the state of emergency in Trondheim, which the Senior Commander of the Security Police and the SD Gerhard Flesch had declared in early Oct. 1942, ten Norwegians, including one Jew, were shot as 'hostages'.

the nonsensical aspect, I think, that causes me so much pain. Norwegians are fighting for their country. They are socialists, 'Jøssinger'.[5] We are being tortured because we are Jews. I would like to demolish this barrier that makes Jews Jews. I would like to see Jews without wounds. *Intact*. They should not weep any longer. They should walk tall.

Oh, my Muscherle.[6] It's been four years now since Vienna. And still the same pain. The same brokenness, this: Jewishness.

It nauseates me, this eternal striking out at defenceless people. It's like hitting something soft. It's unsavoury. Maybe they will take me away too. Qui sait?[7]

DOC. 33

On 4 November 1942 David Bermann writes to his wife from Veidal camp[1]

Handwritten letter from David Bermann,[2] Veidal prison camp,[3] Kvænangen, Oksfjordshamn, letter no. 4, to his wife and children,[4] dated 4 November 1942

Wednesday, 4 November 1942
My beloved sweetheart and our dear children!

Thank you so much for your lovely letter, as well as the snapshots, which I have looked at and studied with mixed emotions. Narvele, my heart's little treasure, he is like the glorious sun, oh how big and wonderful he is. And yes, our youngest, precious, dear Ingvar, he too looks so delightful. But you know, my sweetheart, I may not see much, but knowing that our beloved little darlings are thriving makes me so glad and happy, still it hurts me to know that I unfortunately have not yet been able to have the happiness and joy of seeing our little darling and holding him in my own arms, of feeling him close to me. But I hope by almighty God that I shall come home soon and take my place beside you again and that we can together feel the happiness and joy of being with our beloved, delightful little children. Oh, dear God, may this unforgettable, happy moment come soon – it is almost unbearable, the longing overwhelms me. Seven months have gone by, and I am into the eighth. Yes, it seems to me like eight years, given how long and oppressive this time has been for me. But I have never lost hope, just knowing that you are healthy and well has given me the strength to carry on. My dearest sweetheart, the 15 kro-

5 Opponents of Nasjonal Samling: see Doc. 29, fn 9.

6 Nickname for Ruth Maier's mother, Irma Maier (1895–1964), who had managed to flee to Britain in 1939.

7 French in the original: 'Who knows?'

1 The original is privately owned. Copy in IfZ-Archives, F 601. This document has been translated from Norwegian.

2 David Bermann (1898–1943), businessman; emigrated from Lithuania to Norway in 1903; arrested in March 1942; deported in Jan. 1943 to Auschwitz, where he was murdered. In this letter Bermann added the number 3298 to his name, presumably his prisoner number.

3 Veidal camp was a satellite camp of Grini police camp in northern Norway. From Aug. until Nov. 1942, prisoners from Grini and the Falstad prison camp had to undertake gruelling physical labour for Organization Todt.

4 Ida Bermann (1904–1975), housewife; fled to Sweden on 14 Dec. 1942; Narve Bermann (b. 1939) and Ingvar Bermann (b. 1942).

ner that you sent me in the letter have been returned by the censor, I hope that you have already received them. I suspect the money would have had to be sent by registered post, in that case I would have probably received it. You do not need to send me any money now, if I need any, I should be able to borrow it here. My dearest sweetheart, as for letters, we are allowed to write long letters, but no more than four pages, and you can also send me longer letters than you have been doing. My dearest sweetheart, thank you so much for the package I received 10–12 days ago, it was wonderful! The box with the jam in it was unfortunately torn open, so the underwear etc. was messy. Otherwise, everything was in order. The contents were: 1 large packet of crackers, 1 small packet of crackers, 1 can of Viking condensed milk, 1 can of beef, 4 rolls of malt drops, 1 sausage, apples, 1 box of tobacco, 2 packs of cigarettes, 1 can of spinach, 1 packet of cigarette papers, 1 set of underwear, 2 towels, etc. I do not remember absolutely everything, but I think that altogether the package was simply perfect, thank you very much for everything, and I hope that you are not lacking anything at home, and that you can feed yourself and the children well each day. Sufficient underwear and towels arrived too. Have you received the underwear from Skien?[5] Anyway, up here in the wasteland it is fully winter, extremely cold, but I will try to get through with the blanket you sent me. I would also need a good pair of winter trousers, but as it is difficult to get hold of ticking (that I had hoped you could buy at Blomberg's), I will just leave it be. But you could still send me my knickerbockers, although I do not know how much longer we will be up here before we move south, the work up here is almost finished. Everything takes time, it will take a long time for this to get to you and for you to answer and send a package, and by that time we might have left, but I do not know anything about our departure and therefore cannot say anything about it. I would also like you to send me my old grey winter coat, along with some handkerchiefs, but you may already have sent them, as I wrote about it in the last letter at the beginning of October (no. 3). Did you receive that letter??

My dearest sweetheart, you also write about having coughs and colds. Please, my sweetheart, look after yourself and the children. Wrap up warm; the change in the air, the cold etc. can be dangerous, so be careful and dress warmly. Did you get the cloth tailored in the summer? I hope that it is really beautiful and stylish. Or are you waiting for me to get home to have it tailored? How is it with the winter coat that you ordered for yourself before I left? I hope that it has been finished and that it looks beautiful, it was, after all, the same tailor who made your fur coat. I, your sweetheart, wish you good luck with everything. I hope I'll be home soon, and then we will enjoy all that is nice and beautiful together with our beloved, cherished little sons, and we will, God willing, get away for a bit to a guesthouse. Those who are now away will have hopefully returned and we can find out which beautiful places are good to visit in these times. I envy Mr Siew, who has the pleasure of our sweet, beloved little Narvele, I wish it had been mine. But I of course continue to hold on [to my faith in] almighty God and his righteousness, let us hope that I can return home soon. Otherwise, everything is more or less good here, but nothing can ease my boundless, oppressive homesickness, a longing for freedom, for home comforts and happiness together with our cherished, beloved little boys. Your letters console me and make me strong and steadfast. My deepest and most

5 Capital of the Telemark province in southern Norway.

heartfelt thanks for this strength and all the goodness that you provide me with in these dark times. May God's strength protect and keep you and our darling little ones. I await another letter with more pictures from you in the coming days, as well as a parcel from you and a parcel from the pharmacy which you wrote that you would get them to send to me directly. If I hear anything specific about our departure from our superiors here at the camp, I will ask for permission to telegraph. Otherwise, I can send greetings to you and the children from Hermann, Micke, and from others whom we know here.

Goodbye, and all the best, farewell, my deepest and most heartfelt thoughts and wishes and thousands of the sweetest kisses to you and our beloved, sweet little ones. I remain your longing and lonely David.

Kisses and hugs from Papa for our precious, beloved little ones

Write to the same address.

DOC. 34

On 10 November 1942 Norwegian church leaders protest against the arrest of Jews[1]

Letter, signed O. Hallesby, Ludvig Hope, J. Maroni, Henrik Hille, Andr. Fleischer, G. Skagestad, and Wollert Krohn-Hansen,[2] Oslo, to Prime Minister Quisling, dated 10 November 1942 (copy)

The prime minister's law on the seizure of Jewish property issued on 27 October this year[3] has caused our people great distress. And this distress increased when it became known that all Jewish men over 15 years of age are to be arrested.[4]

In turning to the prime minister, we are not attempting to defend the sins committed by Jews. If they have committed offences, they should be tried, convicted, and punished according to Norwegian law like any other citizen. But those who have committed no offence should enjoy the full protection of the law of this land.

For 91 years Jews have had the legal right to settle and make a living in our country.[5] But now their property is being taken from them without warning and the men are then

1 The original could not be found. Carbon copy in USHMM, Oskar Mendelsohn Collection, 1940–1991, RG-10.254.07, file 01. Published in Oskar Mendelsohn, *Jødenes Historie i Norge gjennom 300 å*, vol. 2: *1940–1985* (Oslo: Universitetsforlaget, 1987), pp. 102–103. This document has been translated from Norwegian.

2 The following signatories belonged to the secret provisional church leadership (Norwegian: Den midlertidige kirkeledelse): Ole Hallesby (1879–1961), theologian; professor in Oslo, 1909–1951; under the occupation, established the oppositional Kristen Samråd (Christian Community Council) with Eivind Berggrav and Ludvig Hope; imprisoned in Grini camp, May 1943–August 1944; Ludvig Hope (1871–1954), lay preacher; secretary general of the Norwegian Lutheran Mission, 1931–1936; imprisoned in Grini camp from May 1943 to Aug. 1944; James Maroni (1873–1957), theologian; bishop of the diocese of Agder, 1930–1947; and Henrik Hille (1881–1946), theologian; bishop of Hamar, 1934–1942. The other signatories were Andreas Fleischer (1878–1957), theologian; bishop of Bjørgvin, 1932–1949; Gabriel Skagestad (1879–1952), theologian; bishop of Stavanger, 1940–1949; Wollert Krohn-Hansen (1889–1973), theologian; bishop of Hålogaland, 1940–1952.

3 The law stipulated that assets of any kind that belonged to stateless or Norwegian Jews were to be confiscated and transferred to the state. By using the phrasing 'the prime minister's law' the bishops emphasized that it was a decree issued by Quisling and not a law based on the constitution.

4 See Doc. 31.

arrested and therefore unable to support their destitute wives and children. This is counter to not only the Christian commandment to love one's neighbour, but also all fundamental legal rights. These Jews have not been accused of violating the laws of the land in any way, let alone convicted in a court of law. And yet they are punished as harshly as are only a very few criminals. They are being punished for their ancestry, solely because they are Jews.

The authorities' failure to value the human worth of the Jews is absolutely contrary to the word of God. For this proclaims on page after page that all nations are of one blood, on which, see in particular the Acts of the Apostles 17:26. Yes, in few other places is God's word as clear as it is here: 'For there is no respect of persons with God', Romans 2:11. 'There is neither Jew nor Greek', Galatians 3:28. 'For there is no difference', Romans 3:22. And above all: when God became flesh, he chose a Jewish family and was born of a Jewish mother.

Thus, according to the word of God, all people have fundamentally the same human worth and thereby the same human rights. And our authorities are bound by our laws to respect this fundamental principle. Article 2 of the constitution states that Lutheranism is the state religion. And this means that the state cannot pass any law or statute which runs counter to the Christian faith and the teachings of the church.

We appeal now to the authorities on this matter because our conscience so earnestly demands it. By remaining silent on the legalized injustice against the Jews, we would become responsible for and complicit in this injustice. If instead we are to remain true to God's word and to the church's teaching, then we must speak out.

Our confession of faith states that the soul is not within the realm of the secular power, which 'using the sword and physical penalties, protects the body and goods against external violence': Augsburg Confession, Article 28.[6] And this chimes with the word of God, which states that rulers are of God, put there by him to be 'not a terror to good works, but to the evil', Romans 13:3.

If secular authorities become a terror to good works, so to those who have not violated the laws of the land, then it is the God-given duty of the Church as the conscience of the state to condemn this.

The Church is called upon and commissioned by God to proclaim God's law and God's gospel. Therefore it cannot remain silent when God's commandments are trampled underfoot. And now one of the fundamental values of Christianity is being violated: God's commandments, which are the basis of all human interaction, justice, and righteousness.

And here the Church cannot be dismissed with the suggestion that it is meddling in politics. The apostles spoke frankly to the authorities when they said: 'We ought to obey God rather than men', Acts 5:29. And Luther says: 'The Church is not interfering in

5 In 1851 the Norwegian parliament had revoked the 'Jew clause', § 2 of the Norwegian constitution of 1814, according to which Jews were not permitted to settle in the kingdom. The clause was reinstated by the government on 12 March 1942: see PMJ 5/23.

6 The Augsburg Confession, formulated by Philipp Melanchthon, was submitted to Emperor Charles V in Augsburg in 1530. It contains the central articles of faith of the Reformed and Lutheran churches and was adopted by the Norwegian Church. Article 28 of the original Confession dealt with the relationship between ecclesiastical and secular authority.

secular matters when it exhorts the authorities to obey the highest authority, who is God.'

By virtue of our calling, we thus exhort the secular authorities and declare in the name of Jesus Christ: stop the persecution of Jews and put an end to the racial hatred which is being spread by the press in our country.

And so in our proclamation we exhort our people to abstain from injustice, violence, and hatred. Those who live in hatred and incite evil bring down God's judgement upon themselves.

The prime minister has on many occasions maintained that the NS[7] will act in accordance with its programme and defend the fundamental values of Christianity. Now Christian values are in danger. If they are to be defended, they must be defended immediately.

We have mentioned it before, but are highlighting it again in closing: our appeal to you has nothing to do with politics. In all temporal matters we are obedient to the secular authorities as God's word demands.[8]

The Theological Faculty and Theological Seminary at the University:
Sigmund Mowinckel, Oluf Kolsrud, Einar Molland, Hans Ording, P. Marstrender
The Theological Lay-Christian Faculty and its Practical-Theological Seminary:
Olaf Moe, O. Hallesby, Karl Vold, Andr. Seiersatad, Johs. Smemo
The Norwegian Lutheran Mission Federation:
Joh. N. Wisløff, Henry Hansen
The Western Norwegian Home Mission Association:
Nils Larvi, G. Ballestad
The Norwegian Missionary Society:
K. O. Kornelius, E. Amdahl
Norwegian China Mission Association:
Olav Risan, Tormod Vaagen
The Norwegian Santal Mission:
H. Grosch, Ernst Hallen
The Nordic Christian Buddhist Mission:
Hans Ording, Jacob B. Natvig
The Norwegian Mission to Israel:
Chr. Ihlen, O. Duesund
Norway's Finn Mission Society:
Sigurd Berg, Sigurd Heiersvang
The Norwegian Seamen's Mission:
N. J. Hansen, V. Vilhelmsen
The Home Mission to Seamen:
Oscar Wilhelmsen, O. Dahl Geli
Norwegian Mission among the Homeless:
L. Koren, Oscar Lyngstad

7 Nasjonal Samling.
8 Here followed the signatures of the seven church leaders named at the start of this document, followed by a list of further signatories as below.

Norwegian Sunday School Union:
H. E. Riddervold, Sv. Seim
Norwegian Christian Youth Association:
Ragnvald Indrebø, Hans Sande
Norway's Christian Student and Junior College Student League:
Hans Høeg, Hans Hølvik
Norway's Christian Student Movement:
Alex Johnson, Einar Glöersen
Norway's National Church League:
Karl Vold, Th. Fagereng
The Blue Cross Norway:
Halvor Midtbø, John Theodor Hovda
The Christian Physicians' Association:
Einar Lundby, John Rø
Norwegian Deacons' Fraternal Association:
Thor Eriksen, Bredo Svendsen

The following free church societies and organizations in Norway have given the above declaration their full support:

The Norwegian Baptist Society:
O. J. Øie, Arnold T. Øhrn
The Methodist Church:
Alf Kristoffersen, Ths. Thomassen
The Norwegian Missionary Society:
L. K. Jegersberg, Chr. Svensen
The Norwegian Mission Alliance:
H. Hjelm-Larsen, I. Iversen
Norwegian Sunday School Union:
Arnold T. Øhrn, Chr. Svensen
Salvation Army:
J. Myklebust, O. Hovda

DOC. 35

The Law on the Compulsory Registration of Jews of 17 November 1942 stipulates who is to be considered a Jew[1]

Law on the Compulsory Registration of Jews

§ 1. Jews (full Jews, half-Jews, and quarter-Jews) who have their residence or abode in this country must register at the registration office in the municipality in which they live within two weeks of this law coming into force. In municipalities in which a registration

1 *Norsk Lovtidend* 1, no. 58, 20 Nov. 1942, pp. 761–762. This document has been translated from Norwegian.

office has not yet been set up, registration will take place at police headquarters in towns or at police stations in rural areas until further notice.

If the obligation to register transpires only after the law has come into force, then registration must happen within two weeks of the obligation to register transpiring.

The registration of minors is the responsibility of a parent or legal guardian.

§ 2. A full Jew is someone who has at least three grandparents who are fully Jewish by race. However, any person with Jewish blood who belongs to or has belonged to a Mosaic religious community is automatically a full Jew.[2]

Any half-Jew or quarter-Jew who is married to a full Jew at the time this law comes into force is also to be considered a full Jew, as is any other person of Jewish blood who is deemed by the Ministry of the Interior to be the equivalent of a full Jew.

§ 3. A half-Jew is someone who has two grandparents who are fully Jewish by race insofar as that person is not a full Jew according to § 2.

§ 4. All disputes over who is a full Jew, half-Jew or quarter-Jew according to §§ 2 and 3 will be decided by the Ministry of the Interior.

The prime minister can allow exemptions from the stipulations in §§ 2 and 3 on the recommendation of the Ministry of the Interior.

§ 5. The Ministry of the Interior can issue further regulations to supplement this law and for its implementation.

§ 6. Whosoever intentionally or negligently contravenes the terms of this law or stipulations issued on the basis of this law will be punished with a fine or imprisonment of up to one year.

§ 7. This law comes into force with immediate effect.

Oslo, 17 November 1942

Quisling

Prime Minister

Hagelin[3]

R. J. Fuglesang[4]

2 Here the Norwegian law goes further than the stipulations in Germany, as the Norwegian authorities could also classify persons who had only one Jewish grandparent and were members of a Jewish congregation as 'full Jews'.

3 Albert Viljam Hagelin (1881–1946), politician; lived in Germany, *c.*1900–*c.*1939; joined the NSDAP in 1933; joined Nasjonal Samling in 1935; Quisling's deputy from summer 1940; acting head of the Ministry of the Interior from Sept. 1940 and from February 1942 minister of the interior; condemned to death after the war by a Norwegian court and executed.

4 Rolf Jørgen Fuglesang (1909–1988), lawyer; from 1934 general secretary of Nasjonal Samling, and worked closely with Quisling; from 1942 minister for public enlightenment and culture; sentenced by a Norwegian court after the war to hard labour; released in 1956.

DOC. 36

On 25 November 1942 the Senior Commander of the Security Police and the SD in Oslo announces the transport of Jews to Auschwitz via Stettin[1]

Telex (no. 19 898 – marked 'confidential') from the Senior Commander of the Security Police and the SD in Oslo (B IV), signed SS-Sturmbannführer Reinhardt,[2] to the State Police head office in Stettin (received on 25 November 1942, 7.15 a.m.), dated 25 November 1942[3]

Re: deportation of Jews from Norway
Urgent, present immediately
Case file: none
For special reasons, I could not report until today that a transport by ship of approximately 700–900 male and female Jews of all ages from Oslo to Stettin will be carried out on 26 November 1942. The crossing will probably take around three days. Because the ship, provided by the German navy, will be needed again immediately after its arrival in Stettin, I request that preparations be made so that the Jews are immediately unloaded and transferred to accommodation after their arrival. The Jews are to be taken to Auschwitz. I have just informed the Reich Security Main Office, and I assume that further instruction will follow from there.[4]

1 Landeshauptarchiv Schwerin, ZB 7687 A. 02. Published in Tôviyyā Friedman, *Dokumentensammlung über 'Die Deportierung der Juden aus Norwegen nach Auschwitz'* (Ramat Gan: City Council, 1963), p. 1. This document has been translated from German.

2 Correctly: Hellmuth Reinhard, born Hermann Gustav Hellmuth Patzschke (1911–2002?), lawyer; joined the NSDAP and the SS in 1933; worked for the SD from 1935; head of Dept. II 225 in the SD Main Office in 1938; changed his name in 1939; head of the Central Office for Jewish Emigration in Amsterdam, August–Nov. 1941; head of the Gestapo in Norway, Jan. 1942–Feb. 1945; reversed his name change after 1945; convicted in 1967 by the Baden-Baden Regional Court; acquitted in 1970 by the Karlsruhe Regional Court.

3 The original contains receipt stamps from the State Police head office in Stettin, Office II B, dated 25 Nov. 1942, no. 1514g, as well as handwritten initials.

4 In fact, 532 persons were deported on this transport. They were taken from Stettin to Auschwitz and, with very few exceptions, murdered immediately upon arrival.

DOC. 37

On 25 November 1942 the Reich Security Main Office gives instructions for the deportation of Jews from Norway to Auschwitz[1]

Express telex (marked 'confidential') from the Reich Security Main Office, IV B 4 3771/42 g 1546, signed p.p. SS-Sturmbannführer Günther,[2] to the Senior Commander of the Security Police and the SD in Oslo, for information only to the State Police head office in Stettin (no. 18 069, received on 25 November 1942, 6 p.m.), dated 25 November 1942[3]

Re: removal of Jews from Norway
Subject: express telex no. 19 892 from your office, dated 25 November 1942[4]
Please ensure that you make full use of the opportunity suddenly afforded by the German navy to transport the Jews out of Norway. In determining which group of persons is to be evacuated, please observe the following guidelines precisely:

1) Only citizens of Norway, the German Reich, Slovakia, Croatia, and countries occupied by the Reich as well as stateless persons defined as Jews according to the current provisions in Norway are to be deported. (Reminder: according to the German decree of 28 July 1942 – IV B 4 a – 2644 / 42,[5] Jews who are citizens of the British Empire, the USA, Mexico, and the enemy nations of Central and South America as well as the neutral and allied states, such as Italy, Hungary, Bulgaria, Romania, etc., are not to be deported *under any circumstances*.)
2) To be initially exempted from evacuation are:
   a) Jews living in German-Jewish or Norwegian-Jewish mixed marriages and their family members.
   b) Jewish Mischlinge who are not considered Jews and their family members.

The separation of married couples and the separation from their parents of children under the age of fourteen are to be avoided.

Please ensure that the transports carry provisions in *sufficient* quantity for a period of at least fourteen days. In addition, every Jew is to come adequately equipped with good work clothing, footwear, underwear, bed linens, blankets, crockery and cups, etc. The following may not be taken along: securities, foreign currency, savings books and other valuables (gold, silver, platinum – with the exception of a wedding ring) – as well as livestock and pets. Prior to the departure of the transports, the Jews are to be searched for weapons, explosives, poisons, etc.

1 Landeshauptarchiv Schwerin, ZB 7687 A. 02. Published in Friedman, *Die Deportierung der Juden aus Norwegen nach Auschwitz*, pp. 2–4. This document has been translated from German.
2 Rolf Günther (1913–1945), commercial employee; SA member, 1929–1937; joined the NSDAP in 1931 and the SS in 1937; worked at the Central Office for Jewish Emigration in Vienna from 1938; Eichmann's deputy at the Reich Security Main Office in Section IV B 4, 1941 – March 1944; participant in the second follow-up meeting to the Wannsee Conference on 27 Oct. 1942; with the Central Office for the Settlement of the Jewish Question in Bohemia and Moravia in 1943/44; committed suicide while in custody in 1945.
3 Transmitted under messaging number 215 667 on 25 Nov. 1942 at 5.45 p.m. The original contains handwritten underlining and additions.
4 Probably a telex with the same wording as Doc. 36.
5 This document could not be found.

To safeguard the transports, an appropriately equipped escort led by an SS officer or police officer is to be deployed.

In addition, please ensure that the deported Jews lose their Norwegian citizenship once they leave Norwegian territory and that the Norwegian government asserts no further claims whatsoever with respect to individual Jews. The return of deported Jews to Norway is out of the question in absolutely all cases.

Please ensure that the Reich Security Main Office, IV B 4, and the State Police head office in Stettin are notified by telex of the departure of the transports, stating the number of people in the transport, the officer in charge, and the size of the escort, as well as the estimated arrival time in Stettin.

The State Police head office in Stettin will arrange for the Jews arriving in Stettin to be concentrated temporarily. Prompt onward transport to Auschwitz will be arranged from here.

In addition, I expect a final report.

Addendum for Stettin:
Please ensure, as requested by Oslo, that arrangements are made to concentrate the Jews temporarily who are expected to arrive in Stettin on 29 November 1942. The request for the special train needed for the onward transport of the Jews will be submitted to the Reich Ministry of Transport from here.

Further instructions will be issued.[6]

DOC. 38

On 27 November 1942 the head of the Norwegian State Police reports to Quisling on the arrest of Jews and their deportation from Norway to Auschwitz[1]

Report from the State Police, signed Karl A. Marthinsen, to Prime Minister Quisling, dated 27 November 1942

Evacuation of Jews
On Tuesday, 24 November 1942, 8 p.m., I received notification from the German Security Police, represented by Hauptsturmführer Wagner,[2] that all Jews whose documentation was stamped with a 'J'[3] are to be evacuated from Norway along with their families, and

6 Transport to Stettin was by ship, arriving at Stettin shortly after 11 a.m. on 30 Nov. 1942. In the afternoon, the deportees were taken in goods wagons to Auschwitz, where they arrived on the evening of 1 Dec. 1942. The majority of the deportees were murdered immediately after arrival.

1 NRA, Oslo, Politikammer, L-sak D3525 Ragnvald William Krantz. Published in 'Inndragning av jødisk eiendom i Norge under den 22. verdenskrig', *Norges Offentlige Utredninger* [NOU] 1997: 22, pp. 173–174. This document has been translated from Norwegian.

2 Wilhelm Wagner (b. 1909), teacher; joined the SS in 1935; responsible for 'Jewish questions' in the Greater Berlin sub-district of the SD; from Feb. 1941 head of Section IV B 4 at the Gestapo in Oslo with the rank of SS-Hauptsturmführer; sentenced to death by a Norwegian court after the war; sentence commuted in 1947 to 20 years' hard labour; pardoned in 1951.

3 For the wording of the decree, see PMJ 5/20.

that a ship has been made available for this purpose, to depart from Oslo on Thursday, 26 November 1942, at approx. 3 p.m.

After receiving this notification it was necessary for me to find a solution for the following tasks:

1) Transport the male Jews held in the internment camp at Berg[4] to Oslo.
2) Apprehend Jewish families residing in their former homes around the country and transport them to Oslo.
3) Detain Jewish males aged over 65 and transport them to Oslo.
4) Pick up all Jews in hospitals and other facilities and house them elsewhere until boarding could begin.
5) Procure temporary accommodation in Oslo.
6) Requisition and organize the necessary means of transport.
7) Procure provisions for the duration of the journey.

The same evening all officials within the State Police were summoned and the work was planned and tasks were allocated as follows:

1) Police Superintendent Kranz:[5]
   a) In the course of Wednesday, 25 November, detain and house Jews from hospitals etc.
   b) Locate and detain Jewish males aged over 65 in the Oslo and Aker police districts.
   c) Organize transport of the approx. 300 Jews interned at Berg.

To assist with this transport, the necessary units are to be requisitioned from the Emergency Services Department in Oslo.

2) Inspector Rød:[6]
   a) Detain Jewish families in the Oslo and Aker police districts and transport them to Pier 1.
   b) Set up the assembly point on Pier 1, including the necessary staff.
   c) Organize embarkation.

To assist with this, around 60 members of the Oslo Criminal Police and around 100 staff from the Oslo Emergency Services Department are to be provided as auxiliaries, and additionally 60 Hird men and 30 SS men from the Norwegian Germanic SS are to be made available to him.[7]

4 The camp was under the authority of the Norwegian State Police and was guarded by Norwegian personnel. It was used for the first time after the first roundup of Jews on 26 Oct. 1942. It was used to hold most of the male arrestees over the age of fifteen. Jews married to non-Jews and non-Jewish resistance fighters were also imprisoned there until the end of the war. After the end of the war, Berg served as a labour camp for Norwegians accused of collaboration: see Doc. 31.

5 Ragnvald Krantz, also spelled Kranz (b. 1904), policeman; member of the State Police from its creation in July 1941 until the end of the war; sentenced to hard labour for life in 1947.

6 Knut Rød (1900–1986), lawyer and policeman; member of Nasjonal Samling, 1941–Sept. 1943; police inspector in Oslo and Aker from 1942; member of the Norwegian State Police, July 1941–Sept. 1943; organized the detentions of Jews; arrested and charged with treason in 1945; acquitted in 1948 after several trials because he had been active in the Norwegian resistance; served again in the police, 1950–1967.

7 The Norwegian Germanic SS was a Norwegian SS unit created in July 1942 within the Germanic SS. It assumed police duties in Norway at the behest of the regime and in cooperation with the occupation authorities. At the end of 1944 it had 1,300 members.

3) Inspector Dürbeck:[8]
   a) Detain and transport Jewish families from Østland and Sørland[9] and also, if possible, from Trondheim and Bergen.
   b) House and feed them in Oslo until embarkation can commence.
   c) Transport them to Pier 1 when embarkation begins on Thursday morning.

To accomplish these tasks, the officials at head office, the local inspectors, and the rural departments of the State Police are to be made available to him.

4) Police Superintendent Lindvig:
   a) Procure the necessary means of transport for transports within Oslo – roughly 100 taxis along with a number of buses.
   b) Procure the necessary food supplies for the Jews during transportation.

At 11 p.m. on Tuesday, 24 November 1942,[10] the officers set to work and worked without a break until 4 p.m. on Thursday, 26 November 1942.

The most demanding and most difficult task by far was arresting the Jewish families (women and children) in the Oslo police district, above all because this operation had to be executed in a single strike and within a very short period because it proved impossible to procure suitable premises to house them in Oslo. The arrest therefore had to be postponed until 5 a.m. on Thursday, 26 November 1942.

Loading could not actually begin before 7 a.m. because the ship had not been unloaded earlier. The roughly 300 men who were available for this operation were therefore assembled to receive their instructions at 23 Kirkeveien[11] at 4.30 a.m. on 26 November 1942, and at the same time the 100 taxis were held ready on Kirkeveien.

The operation was carried out as follows.

The available forces were split up into roughly 100 patrols. Each patrol consisted of one policeman as patrol leader and two helpers (Hird, SS men or policemen).

Each patrol leader was provided with a taxi. The patrol leader was handed 4 dockets – 1 docket for each family to be detained, and was instructed to proceed as follows.

Helpers nos. 1 and 2 are each given a docket and are driven to the addresses on the dockets.

The patrol leader takes docket no. 3 and drives to the stated address, picks up the family, drives them to Pier 1, delivers the persons to the assembly point. He immediately drives back to where helper no. 1 is waiting, then drives that family in the car to Pier 1, giving docket no. 4 to helper no. 1 with orders to go to the address stated on the docket as quickly as possible to detain and prepare the family. After he has delivered family no. 2 to Pier 1, the remaining 2 families (helper no. 1 and helper no. 2) are collected and delivered to the assembly point as described above.

This arrangement proved very practical as all addresses were searched within a short time, which made it possible to initiate numerous additional searches for families who were not present at the stated addresses.

8 Sverre Johan Dürbeck (1912–1987), lawyer and policeman; joined Nasjonal Samling in 1940; member of the Norwegian State Police, 1941–July 1943; sentenced to six years of hard labour by a Norwegian court after the war.

9 Østland is the south-eastern part of Norway and includes the districts Østfold, Akershus, Oslo, Hedmark, Oppland, Buskerud, Vestfold, and Telemark. Sørland is the district to the west.

10 In the original (incorrectly): Wednesday.

11 Headquarters of the Norwegian State Police.

As for difficulties that arose during the operation, the following should be noted:

1) On Wednesday, 25 November, at about 8 p.m., I received notification from the German Security Police that the terms for the evacuation of Jewish families had been partially changed insofar as it had now been determined that families where one spouse was an Aryan were not to be evacuated at all. This caused us significant inconvenience in that we were already considerably advanced with the preparatory work on the basis of the original orders.[12]
2) On Wednesday morning I was to organize temporary accommodation to hold the Jewish families who were to come in from other parts of the country (by train, bus, and other means of transport) in the course of Wednesday and on Thursday morning, but that proved extraordinarily difficult because the Order Police refused to make available to us the only suitable venue in the town, namely the gymnasium at the Majorstuen police barracks.[13] The matter was resolved, however, after many hours of negotiation.
3) The time to prepare for such a comprehensive operation was far too short. I should have had as many weeks as I had days. This lack of time resulted in consequences, including:
   a) a good number of Jewish families arrived too late in Oslo from Trondheim, Bergen and other places, and I now have to intern them at Bredtveit[14] for an indefinite period.
   b) I did not manage to apprehend anywhere near all of the families because they had moved, gone away, were at work, etc.[15]

Attached is a list of the Jews who were evacuated from Norway in this operation – 524 persons in total.[16]

12 For the instructions given by the RSHA, see Doc. 37.

13 The barracks were located in requisitioned school buildings in the Oslo district of the same name.

14 Originally intended as a workhouse for juvenile delinquents, Bredtveit (also known as Bredvedt) was opened by Nasjonal Samling as a detention centre for political prisoners in 1941. Most of the Jews detained there were deported to Auschwitz on the *Gotenland* on 25 Feb. 1943.

15 The precise number is unknown. Most of those who had not been detained managed to escape to safety in Sweden.

16 The commandant of Auschwitz confirmed the arrival of 532 prisoners: Friedman, *Die Deportierung der Juden aus Norwegen nach Auschwitz*, p. 11.

DOC. 39

On 30 November 1942 the Swedish Ministry of Foreign Affairs endeavours to rescue several Jews who have been deported from Norway[1]

Letter (by courier) from the Swedish Ministry of Foreign Affairs [Hbg],[2] signed Engzell,[3] to envoy A. Richert,[4] Berlin, dated 30 November 1942[5]

Re: assistance for Jews with Swedish connections deported from Norway

Dear colleague,

I enclose herewith copies of both of today's telegrams[6] regarding assistance for certain Jews from Norway. The telegrams were sent at the order of His Excellency,[7] who, in light of the shocking deportations and the indignation it has aroused among the Swedish public, considers it is necessary to at least attempt to do something to aid those who have a connection to Sweden. In one of the telegrams we openly listed all such Jews whose relatives residing in Sweden have contacted the ministry with a request for assistance. Also, on 27 November, we communicated their names to the General Consulate in Oslo to ascertain whether they were still present or whether they had been deported on the 'Jew boat'.[8] Since one would hope that the best possible result of a démarche from the legation would be that those Jews who are mentioned and are now on board the boat would be separated off at the German port of disembarkation, His Excellency has recommended that the list be telegraphed without awaiting the consulate general's investigation. If these Jews, of whom two at most are Swedish citizens, have been transported farther into the Polish interior, we fear that nothing more can be done.[9]

1 Riksarkivet, Stockholm, UD, Hp 21 An 1070/II. Excerpts published in Paul A. Levine, *From Indifference to Activism: Swedish Diplomacy and the Holocaust, 1938–1944* (Uppsala: Uppsala University, 1996) p. 134. This document has been translated from Swedish.

2 The meaning of [Hbg] has not been established.

3 Gösta Engzell (1897–1997), diplomat; state secretary and director of the legal department of the Swedish Ministry of Foreign Affairs, 1938–1947; various ambassadorial posts, 1948–1963.

4 Arvid Richert (1887–1981), diplomat; court clerk, 1914–1918; at the Swedish Ministry of Foreign Affairs from 1918; ambassador in Berlin from 1937; governor of Älvsborg county after the war.

5 The original contains the receipt stamp for 30 Nov. 1942, as well as stamps and handwritten annotations.

6 The telegrams are in the file. They contain instructions to enquire with the German authorities about the whereabouts of 16 named individuals.

7 Christian Ernst Günther (1886–1966), lawyer; appointed foreign minister in the national unity government in Dec. 1939 after a career in the Swedish civil service.

8 This is a reference to the transport on the *Donau*, which departed on 26 Nov. 1942 from Oslo: see also Docs. 37, 38, 47, and 49.

9 The Germans rejected interventions on behalf of Jews who had already been deported. Most of those who had been deported had already been murdered. Subsequently, however, Jews who had connections to Sweden and were still in Norway were rescued with the aid of Swedish identity documents and granted refuge in the neighbouring country.

DOC. 40

On 1 and 2 December 1942 Norway's representative in Stockholm reports to the government in exile in London on efforts in Sweden to aid Jewish refugees[1]

Letter (no. 3241, marked 'confidential') from the Royal Norwegian Legation, Stockholm, signed Jens Bull,[2] to the Royal Ministry of Foreign Affairs, presently in London, dated 1 and 2 December 1942[3]

Guarantee for Jewish refugees
As already reported, Dr Natanael Beskow[4] has approached me confidentially on the matter of the deportation of Jews from Norway. Dr Beskow was the main speaker at a protest meeting which took place on Sunday, 29 November, here in Stockholm. (I draw your attention to the accompanying newspaper clipping from yesterday's *Dagens Nyheter.*[5]) The Baptist congregation and Stockholm Freethinkers' Association[6] also held protest meetings.

The deportation has caused a great stir here in Sweden and has provoked much outrage. Dr Beskow has spoken with prominent clerics, including Archbishop Eidem[7] and the newly appointed bishop of Stockholm, Manfred Bjørkquist,[8] regarding the possibility of some kind of action on behalf of the Norwegian Jews. I do not know who took the initiative for this. A number of free-church groups are also represented. The result, though, is that the archbishop and Bishop Bjørnquist are prepared to seek an audience with Foreign Minister Günther to try to persuade the government to inform the Germans that Sweden is willing to accept the Jews who are still in Norway.[9] A rough estimate suggests [that this concerns] a total of 300 Jews.[10] Dr Beskow phoned me to ask if one could reckon with the legation looking after these Jews should they come here. The archbishop had in fact said that he would not go to Günther with anything less than an assurance that the legation would do this. I told Dr Beskow that I could not answer this straight away and would first have to confer with the head of the refugee department,

1 NRA, S-2259, Utenriksdepartementet, Dyd (sakarkiv 1940–49), 10 392, 25.1/5. This document has been translated from Norwegian.
2 Jens Bull (1886–1956), diplomat; served in the Norwegian Ministry of Foreign Affairs from 1909; chargé d'affaires in Stockholm for the Norwegian government in exile from 1940; ambassador to the Netherlands and Denmark after the war.
3 The original contains a stamp and handwritten annotations.
4 Fredrik Natanael Beskow (1865–1953), theologian; headmaster in Djursholm, 1897–1909, and also preacher from 1896; president of the Swedish Association for Christian Social Life, 1918–1943; nominated for the Nobel Peace Prize as a radical pacifist in 1947.
5 Included in the file.
6 In 1934 the Freethinkers' Association (Frisinnade medborgerförening) had, together with the Liberal Union, founded the conservative People's Party.
7 Erling Eidem (1880–1972), Protestant theologian; archbishop of Uppsala from 1931; supported members of the German Confessing Church.
8 Manfred Björkquist (1884–1985), Protestant theologian; bishop of Stockholm from Nov. 1942.
9 In mid Dec. 1942 the Swedish government unofficially informed the Reich Foreign Office via the ambassador in Berlin that it was willing to take in all the Jews who were still in Norway; the German side delayed the process. A connection to the initiative documented here could not be established.
10 It is unclear how many Jews were still at liberty in Norway at this point. The total number of Jews who fled from Norway to Sweden is in fact probably about 900.

who was away when I spoke with Beskow. I also asked him whether anything had been done to ascertain whether wealthy Swedish Jews would do anything for their co-religionists. He answered that Mrs Löfgren[11] (presumably Mia Leche Löfgren, widow of the former foreign minister Eliel Löfgren) had contacted the Jews in Gothenburg and heard back that the issue of money should not cause any difficulties. However, Dr Beskow had not received any more details about this, and the whole thing therefore remained unresolved. I also asked Beskow whether contact had been made with the Mosaic Community here in Stockholm. This has not happened so far, but Beskow intends to do so.

Dr Beskow did not say anything about how long any potential guarantee from the legation might last. In my opinion it would be reasonable to expect wealthy Jews living here to take care of their Jewish co-religionists at a time like this, particularly as they are being persecuted because they are Jewish, and that the state would not step in to support them unless necessary. In other words, only if the matter cannot be resolved in any other way. On the other hand, I think the legation cannot simply refuse such a request, for the Jews are after all Norwegian citizens. We are talking here about Norwegian citizens whose life or freedom is in danger and who consequently fall into the category of Norwegian citizens who, according to the guidelines which the legation has followed until now, should leave the country and seek refuge in Sweden. But the difference between the two categories is that neither the government nor the legation has given any kind of guarantee at all for regular Norwegian citizens. If they arrive here, they are taken in. We ensure that they can obtain work and provide for them until they do. Jews would have to come with the assent of the German authorities and in accordance with a completely different arrangement than the one we have had until now. I therefore decided that I had to get the Foreign Ministry's decision on this matter. But I believe, as I have stated, that we must accept them. It is a question of defenceless people who could be threatened with deportation and exposed to mistreatment and who may perish in concentration camps in Poland. In my opinion, the whole thing should be seen for what it is, namely a question of helping people in need. But I have not told Dr Beskow that I have asked for a guarantee from the government because I wanted him to try as hard as possible to resolve the matter by organizing collections among Jews in Sweden. I told him that our expenditure on Norwegian refugees was now upwards of one million per month. We agreed that he would phone me tomorrow, Wednesday, and let me know the result of his conversation with the local Jews. I held out the possibility that by then I would be able to give an answer on the legation's position.

2 December

I did not get to talk with Lawyer Schjödt[12] yesterday because he was busy the entire morning with meetings with Social Affairs[13] and yesterday afternoon had a meeting

11 Ebba Maria Lovisa Leche Löfgren, known as Mia (1878–1966), writer; active in relief organizations for refugees.

12 Annæus Schjödt (1888–1972), lawyer; fled to Sweden, where in 1942 he was head of the refugee department at the legation of the Norwegian government in exile, for which he later worked in London; after the war chief prosecutor at the trial of Vidkun Quisling.

13 In the original 'socialstyrelse(n)' ('social services'). This was a reference to the Ministry of Social Affairs, which was responsible for all welfare matters. The Office for Foreigners was also under its authority.

with Martin Waldenström, director of the Grängesberg company.[14] It turned out that this last meeting was about the same matter as my telephone conversation with Dr Beskow. Lawyer Schjödt and I had a conversation about it this morning, and we agreed that the legation could not turn its back on this matter, but we were also in agreement that the Jews must first try to get help from their fellow Jews here in Sweden, where there is without doubt both an ability and a will to help. Lawyer Schjödt had said to Director Waldenström more or less the same as I did in the above-mentioned letter. He had not mentioned the formal concerns. It turns out that it was Director Waldenström who took the initiative in this matter. He is, if I am not mistaken, married to a Jewish woman.[15]

Shortly after my conversation with Lawyer Schjödt, Dr Beskow phoned again. He told me that at 12 o'clock today a deputation would have a meeting with the prime minister. The deputation would consist of President of the Court of Appeal Ekeberg[16] as spokesman, Dr Beskow, Director Waldenström, University Chancellor Unden,[17] and Bishops Aulén[18] and Björkquist. Undén wanted to try to get Archbishop Eidem to attend, but Dr Beskow was not certain that he would succeed. Dr Beskow was keen to hear now what position the legation was taking, and I answered that I could not say anything official or binding, but that I believed I could at least say off the record that he could assume that the matter would work out, that is to say, that Jews who come over here, whether as refugees or with a German exit permit, and cannot provide for themselves with either what they bring or with help from Jews in Sweden or through their own work would be looked after by the legation in the same way as it looks after other refugees. I told Dr Beskow that neither the legation nor the government guaranteed anything for our refugees because, among other things, we just cannot know how the matter is going to develop in the future. Until now we have been able to manage the outlay that the work with refugees has demanded, but it is impossible to know what we will have to reckon with in the future or what kind of difficulties there might be in continuing to transfer money to Sweden. We certainly believe that this matter must not be allowed to fail on account of money, but I also said to him that we could not really give a general guarantee because we would run the risk of it undermining efforts to get help from Jews in Sweden.[19] First and foremost, Jews must try to get what is needed through voluntary dona-

14 Martin Waldenström (1881–1962), lawyer; founder and partner in several law firms; director of the shipping, mining, and haulage company Grängesbergbolaget, 1930–1950.

15 Hedvig Waldenström, née Lion (1885–1973), housewife; active in refugee aid at the Jewish Community of Stockholm.

16 Birger Ekeberg (1880–1968), lawyer; professor in Stockholm until 1925; minister of justice, 1920–1921 and 1923–1924; judge at the Supreme Court from 1925; president of the Court of Appeal for the Regional and District Courts in the Stockholm area, 1931–1946.

17 Bo Östen Undén (1886–1974), lawyer; professor at Uppsala from 1917; member of parliament from 1934; foreign minister, 1924–1926 and 1945–1962.

18 Gustaf Emanuel Hildebrand Aulén (1879–1977), Protestant theologian; professor at Lund from 1913; bishop of Strängnäs from 1933; in 1946 awarded the St Olav's Medal for his efforts for Norway during the war.

19 In a further report for the British government dated 7 Dec. 1942, Bull recorded that he had informed Beskow as instructed that the legation was treating Jews on an equal basis to other refugees, but that they were expected to find means of support and to ask the Swedish Jews for aid: NRA, S-2259, Utenriksdepartementet, Dyd (sakarkiv 1940–49), 10 392, 25.1/5.

tions, but for those Jews who do not receive assistance in this way, we would do what we can. (Incidentally, this is roughly what Lawyer Schjödt had already told Director Waldenström yesterday afternoon.)

Dr Beskow asked me not to let the request to the prime minister become public.

DOC. 41
On 3 and 4 January 1943 Myrtle Wright and her friends make arrangements for the escape of several Jewish children to Sweden[1]

Diary of Myrtle Wright,[2] entries for 3 and 4 January 1943[3]

Sunday, 3 January. Was at home all day and wrote Christmas thank you letters. One of Bernti's[4] school friends dropped in to ask after him. Several of them do this for in some ways they envy him, and at least they feel he is taking the consequence of what they have done or would gladly do. His class at school have had a photograph made of themselves with their student caps on.[5] Bernti was already in prison when they became eligible to wear these, but they have asked that a former picture of him should be included so that he appears as the only one without a cap, recording for all time the history of this summer and the end of his school days …

In the evening Eva[6] came and was more anxious than I have seen her. Through her secret connections she has heard that Gerda has 'split' and told a great deal of what she knows.[7] This, if it is true, can put Eva and many others into direct danger. We debate the wisdom of her sleeping at home tonight and offer her a bed. She has not been at home for some time but just today has nowhere to go other than her own flat. This house is not much safer if this news is true, and she decided to take the chance and sleep in

1 NHM, Myrtle Radley Wright Private Archive, NHM 29. Excerpts published in Myrtle Wright, *Norwegian Diary, 1940–1945* (London: Friends Peace and International Relations Committee, 1974), pp. 128–130.

2 Myrtle Wright (1903–1991), British peace activist; active in the Quaker relief organization from Jan. 1940 in Denmark and from 6 April 1940 in Norway; worked for the Norwegian resistance; escaped to Sweden and returned to Britain in 1944.

3 The typewritten original contains handwritten notes and additions.

4 Bernt Henrik Lund (b. 1924), administrator and diplomat; arrested in May 1942 for distributing illegal newspapers and interned in Grini; imprisoned in Sachsenhausen concentration camp from 1944; liberated in the course of the White Buses campaign (see Introduction, p. 24); after the war, civil servant and diplomat; became president of the International Sachsenhausen Committee in 2018. His mother, Sigrid Helliesen Lund (1892–1987), was a key figure in the rescue operation described here: see also Doc. 46.

5 This is a reference to the mostly black-and-white uniform caps worn by high school graduates in Scandinavia.

6 Probably Eva von Munthe af Morgenstierne (1921–2017), student; active in the student resistance; escaped to Sweden in autumn 1943; her father, Georg Morgenstierne (1892–1978), was a board member of Nansen Relief.

7 'Split' is used here in the sense of 'betray confidence'. This was a rumour. Gerda Tanberg (1902?–1984), with the help of Sigrid Helliesen Lund, hid around 14 children in her apartment until all of them could be taken to Sweden. Tanberg was arrested and released again in Feb. 1943.

her own bed for once. She believes the children can be fetched tomorrow night at once.[8] She is a courageous and energetic soul.

We have decided that this house is too unhealthy for this diary and send it to a more secure place.[9]

Monday, January 4th. We rang up Eva early and found she had slept well and been troubled by no visitors in the night. So far so good but it is best to take all precautions. It seemed advisable to tell Gullimor[10] in case she has questions after Inge[11] and also to telegraph to Inge. In Stavanger she [will be] caught if she is searched for, for there is practically no way out except by train and it is impossibly far from the frontier. The telegram had to be sent anonymously from the station under an assumed name and read: 'Aunt very ill, advise come to Oslo'. With this she could get permission to travel to a sick relative if she decides to do more than go into hiding.

Tonight Ilse and Tommy are to be fetched.[12] Per[13] is to be at the house at 7. I went down to Nina[14] to make sure the plans were in order and to arrange what should be done if Eva and her transport people did not come. When I got there Nina had already collected little H[e]ini, and Ilse and Tommy had come. They had been sad when the strange 'policeman' had come to take them away. Tommy, aged 7, had asked if he was a kind policeman, and being told that he was, slipped his hand into Per's and trotted along trustfully. Ilse, who is 9, had been more thoughtful, and when she had suddenly seen a shooting star had said, 'Now I can have two wishes.' 'What are they?' asked Per. 'The first is that Father may come home soon, the other is a secret,' she replied. (This was her foster father, who had been sent more than year ago to Germany as a prisoner. Perhaps she had thought how lonely her foster mother was now that she had missed all three of them.) When they had arrived at Nina's Tommy had cast himself down on the floor with a book and was perfectly happy, but Ilse, feeling this was the beginning of a bigger and strange adventure, had said wistfully, 'I don't understand anything. It is so sad to leave

8 Following an initiative from Nansen Relief, 21 Jewish children from Vienna were taken to Norway in June 1938, and a further 39 Jewish children arrived from Prague in Oct. 1939. Some of them were put up in a children's home in Oslo. On 26 Nov. 1942, one day before the roundup of Jewish women and children, Sigrid Helliesen Lund and the child psychiatrist Caroline 'Nic' Waal, who treated the children, were warned. Together with Nina Hasvold, the director of the children's home, and other helpers, they managed to hide the children with Gerda Tanberg and others, and then take them to Sweden: see also Doc. 46.

9 The original contains the handwritten addition 'tell about this', probably as a reminder by the author to herself to mention the history of the diary. The manuscript pages were eventually hidden in the university library.

10 Pet name for Augusta Helliesen (1906–1953), Sigrid Helliesen Lund's sister.

11 Meaning unclear: possibly 'in case she has questions about Inge' or 'in case she is questioned about Inge'. Ingeborg Sletten Fostvedt (1917–1981), student; volunteered for Nansen Relief; warned Rabbi Samuel's family after his arrest and helped them escape.

12 Ilse Mautner (1933–2004) and Thomas Mautner (b. 1935) were two of the children from Czechoslovakia who were housed in Bergen, western Norway. Their foster mother took them to Oslo, from where they escaped to Sweden in Jan. 1943. Thomas Mautner emigrated to Australia in 1965 and was later professor of philosophy at the University of Canberra.

13 Per Lund was a relative of Sigrid Helliesen Lund.

14 Nina Augusta Prytz, née Eberhardt (1903–2000); hid some of the children in her apartment; interned in Grini from late Feb. until late May 1943.

those you are so fond of.' Nina was anxious about little Heini; his boots were too short for him and painful to walk in, and his chances of safety might depend on his ability to use his young legs. I had an address on a slip of paper with the address of a friend of her foster mother's which Ilse was to have with her and all three were to ask for Tove Filseth.[15] When she heard this last name Ilse was very much comforted, for then all must be well: she had learnt to trust and admire Tove. Just as I had given this paper to Nina the bell rang, and I waited breathlessly until she came back and whispered, 'They have come for the children.' I longed to take a hand in finding coats and hats and tying up boot laces and preparing packets of sandwiches, but the children knew me by sight and I dared not let them see me and so connect the whole story with Sigrid and with people they knew. So I only listened to the excited voices of the children and saw through a crack in the door the curly head of Tommy come and fetch his boots, and then while they were all for a moment out of sight of the front door slipped out myself and shut it quietly behind me. Coming out into the dark street I saw the dimmed lights of a big car, perhaps a tradesman's van, standing by the curb. A man walked up and down beside it, and I felt him watching me. I felt tempted to whisper 'Good luck,' but walked straight on. His passengers would come soon.

This was not the end of the day's events. Sigrid at home had had a telephone message from a Children's Home in Oslo where Vera[16] had been before she joined her brother, to say that the police had made enquiries about her address. We had no idea why they had suddenly taken an interest just in her, but it made it more difficult for Marie[17] to move her openly from the Pastor's Home, and it seemed best to warn her if we could. We decided to telegraph and ask her to telephone as soon as possible tomorrow. She might have already left for N.

The anxiety for Vera and for the three small onesmaking their way over the frontier nearly drove out of our heads the possibilities of any mid-night police visitations to us, though we made our nightly search to see that all dangerous papers were destroyed or hidden before we went to bed.

15 Tove Filseth (1905–1994), journalist; travelled to Czechoslovakia together with Odd Nansen in 1939 to help refugees; escaped in late 1942 to Sweden, where she was active in Nansen Relief and married the German-Jewish writer Max Tau.

16 Vera Taglicht (1929–1943) and Tibor Taglicht (1932–1943) fled from Czechoslovakia to Norway in 1939; lived in various hiding places, including with Pastor Aksel Mathias Kragseth (1903–1981) south of Trondheim; arrested after they were reported to the authorities in early 1943 and interned in Bredtveit; deported in March 1943 to Auschwitz, where they were murdered.

17 Marie Lous Mohr (1892–1973), teacher; head of the Norwegian department of the Women's International League for Peace and Freedom, 1934–1947 and again 1956–1961; active in Nansen Relief; involved in collecting the children from Prague.

DOC. 42

On 8 January 1943 exiled representatives of Norway's Jewish community urge the government in exile to do everything possible to save the deported Jews[1]

Letter, signed by Mendel Bernstein, former head of the Mosaic Religious Community, Oslo; Harry Koritzinsky, former secretary of the Mosaic Religious Community, Oslo; Marcus Levin, former chairman of the Jewish Relief Association, Oslo; Charles Koklin, former chairman of the Jewish Youth Association, Oslo,[2] Stockholm, to the Royal Norwegian Government, currently in London, dated 8 January 1943[3]

Norwegian Jews who currently live as refugees in Sweden think with steadily growing unease and anxiety about the fate that awaits our relatives who were deported from Norway to Poland. We know that powerful forces have been at work, and still are, to help these unfortunate people. In these efforts, however, no stone must be left unturned in seeking to help them in every way possible. We know that the chances of positive results are slim, but for our consciences' sake we cannot rest before we know that all conceivable options for saving them have been exhausted. In recent days certain people in Sweden have raised the idea of trying, if possible, to persuade the British government to exchange the deported Norwegian Jews (reportedly 532 in number) for an equal number of German prisoners of war who are unfit for duty, maybe with the help of Sweden. As far as we know, this solution has not yet been tried, and we therefore most urgently implore our honourable government to convey this proposal to the British government. As stated above, it is vital to us that everything is done to save the deported Norwegian Jews. And it is urgent. They face an imminent and appalling fate unless we secure swift and positive results. These deportees are channelling their calls for help through us. They are begging for their lives to be saved, if at all humanly possible.

1 The original could not be found. Copy in USHMM, Oskar Mendelsohn Collection, 1940–1991, RG-10.254.07 file 5. This document has been translated from Norwegian.

2 Mendel Bernstein (1890–1987); Harry Meier Koritzinsky (1900–1989); Marcus Levin (1899–1965), businessman; chairman of the relief association of the Jewish Community of Oslo, representative of the American Jewish Joint Distribution Committee (JDC) in Oslo; fled to Sweden in Nov. 1942; with the support of the Norwegian legation and the relief committee of the Jewish Community compiled a register of those who had been deported; worked for the Jewish Community of Stockholm's refugee committee until his return to Norway in 1946, and subsequently worked for the JDC; Charles Koklin (1914–1994), municipal auditor; former vice-chairman of the Tønsberg Left Party; forced out of his position in autumn 1941 by order of the Tønsberg NS mayor, despite local protests; fled to Sweden in Nov 1941, after being warned about pending roundups.

3 The date has been added by hand.

DOC. 43
On 26 January 1943 David Century turns to Vidkun Quisling out of concern for his relatives who have been deported to Poland[1]

Handwritten letter from David Century,[2] 16a Sturegatan, Uppsala, to Vidkun Quisling, Oslo, dated 26 January 1943

Mr Prime Minister Vidkun Quisling, Oslo,

As one of the Norwegian Jews who was lucky enough to avoid deportation to Poland, I take the liberty of appealing to you.

Some time ago a Swedish newspaper printed an interview you gave on this matter, and you are reported to have responded that the Norwegian Jews sent to Poland would start a new life there. I must assume that you meant what you said – that all these people have come to Poland to live, and not to be tormented to death. In newspapers and radio broadcasts outside Norway, the latter is so often asserted that it is difficult to suppress a feeling of profound fear that there might be some truth to these claims.

Most of us who escaped have one or more relatives who were deported to Poland. The fate that is befalling our loved ones is causing us growing anxiety – indeed despair. The only word we have received so far is your declaration, cited above, that they are to begin a new life. But you will surely agree, Prime Minister, that this is not sufficiently reassuring. You are the only person who can succeed in enabling the deportees to make contact with their loved ones. I appeal to you to take the necessary steps to make this possible for them, and at the same time to give those who want to the opportunity to send parcels with food and clothing to their loved ones in Poland. In taking such a step you would be acting in accordance with your own best traditions from the time when you and Nansen were personally involved in a great humanitarian operation in Eastern Europe – and you would, at a stroke, demonstrate to the world that the deported Norwegian Jews have not been carried off into the appalling conditions that have been written and talked about so much.

It may be that Germany needs these people for war work – but in any event let them live as human beings.

Yours truly,

1 NRA, Statspolitiet, Jødeaksjonene, mappe 29, Henvendelser til Quisling ang. jødeaksjonene. This document has been translated from Norwegian.

2 David Century (1897–1973), salesman; emigrated from England to Norway in 1917; fled to Sweden on 4 Nov. 1942; started a textile business following his return to Norway in 1945.

DOC. 44

In late January 1943 the Office for the Liquidation of Confiscated Jewish Assets informs returning SS volunteers about the sale of household items of deported Jewish families[1]

Circular from the Office for the Liquidation of Confiscated Jewish Assets,[2] unsigned, undated

Guidelines for purchases by frontline combatants[3] at collection centres
Two sales centres have been set up for the sale of inventory from Jewish estates:

A. The 'Furniture Centre' for the sale of second-hand furniture and other furnishings that fall into this category.
   The centre is located at the railway customs office, Schweigårdsgt., 4th floor.
B. The 'Kitchen and Bedding Centre' stocks tableware, curtains, linens, used items only.
   The centre is at 19 Storgata.

Frontline combatants may acquire a reasonable quantity of the available items at these centres for their own use.

Authorizations to make purchases are issued by the Liquidations Office, at 2c Gardevegen, 4th floor. Frontline combatants will be provided with a printed requisition form bearing the combatant's name, military unit, and current address, together with a note about quantity. Each person must present identification issued by the Frontline Combatants' Office confirming that he is a combatant. Authorizations are numbered and spread over several days, so that the centre's staff can process the requisition forms with due care.

Payment must be made in cash at the time of purchase. Exceptions can be approved only by the Liquidations Office.

Items from the 'Furniture Centre' will be delivered free of charge within city limits by the centre to the address provided by the buyer.

Items from the 'Kitchen and Bedding Centre' must be collected by the buyer at the time of purchase. The buyer must provide any necessary packaging.

Frontline combatants must have submitted a written request to the Liquidations Office in advance specifying the items they wish to acquire.

The sale will begin in early February 1943.[4]

1 NRA, S-1564 Justisdepartementet, Tilbakeføringskontoret for inndratte formuer, Dd, Likvidasjonsstyret, 69, 453, 'Salg av gjenstander fra jødiske bo'. This document has been translated from Norwegian.

2 The Office for the Liquidation of Confiscated Jewish Assets was established on 20 Nov. 1942 on the basis of the Law on the Confiscation of Jewish Assets of 26 Oct. 1942. During the period up to early 1943, the Ministry of the Interior established who was affected by the law. The Ministry of Finance was responsible for the administration of assets.

3 Frontkjemperes: literally translated as 'frontline combatants', the term refers to members of Norwegian volunteer divisions of the Waffen SS.

4 In total, more than 1,300 apartments and businesses belonging to Norwegian Jews were confiscated and either administered or sold by the Liquidations Office. Estimates for the total value of the confiscated assets vary.

DOC. 45

On 4 February 1943 Max Solomon gives his sister in the USA an account of the fate of Jews deported to Poland[1]

Letter from Max Salomon, Bjursås (Sweden), to Gerda Salomon,[2] New York, dated 4 February 1943

My dear Gerda,

At last a letter from you again, I got your letter of 1 December on 1 February. Thanks very much.

I sent a cable to Jack three weeks ago advising him of what happened to Mother, but as I have had no reply I do not know whether he received it or not. As perhaps you know she was at Vikersund Bad during the fall and early part of the winter, but suddenly she was arrested, apparently by Quislings state police, and taken to Bredtvedt at Grorud outside Oslo.[3] This happened on 14th December, and Gjörwad[4] got a chance to have a long talk to her at Oslo before she was taken away. She was very depressed of course, but she[5] has learned that she was in better spirits later on. Actually she was robbed of everything and they called up from Bredtvedt if Gjörwad could not send some underwear and stockings, so G. had to send some of her own. Well, these are the appalling facts, and I know nothing of what happened later or what is going to happen. I do not know if an old person can stand the shock and the treatment in the long run; I am afraid that all we can do is to be prepared for the worst and hope for the best. It is such a pity; she could easily have come across here, if she had only had the right advisers, but apparently she had a firm belief in Helliksen,[6] and I am inclined to believe that a very heavy blame rests upon him. He had phoned G. several times and said he would manage to get her out again before Christmas, but of course he cannot do a thing, even if he wanted to. The only consolation is that Bredtved is said to be the most humane of these places; they are not treated as brutally as in the places run by the Gestapo. In the meantime Harald is working on a slender chance to prove that she is a Danish subject[7] and to claim her release on these grounds. The Danish Consul has the case in hand, but I am afraid it will not work.

I went down to Stockholm on 13 January to have a conference with the Norwegian Legation in regard to another matter. While I was sitting in the ante-chamber a man in a white doctor's coat came out of a door. It was Dworsky.[8] He asked me to come to his office, and I learned that he had managed to come over just in time with his son. His wife and daughter-in-law came over three weeks later, and he himself got a job as the chief

1 The original is in the private collection of Norman Poser, author of *Escape: A Jewish Scandinavian Family in the Second World War* (New York: Sareve Press, 2006); copy in IfZ-Archives, F 601. The original document is in English.

2 On the Salomon family, see also Doc. 22.

3 Johanna Salomon probably escaped deportation because on 26 Nov. 1942 she was staying at the Vikersund spa resort. Because her husband, Simon Salomon, was a Danish citizen and her son, Harald, lived in Denmark, the Danish consulate in Oslo obtained her release and helped her emigrate to Denmark.

4 Correctly: Hellbjørg Gjørvad, the Salomons' maid.

5 Gjørvad.

6 Sverre Helliksen (1886–1974), lawyer; friend of the family; arrested as a collaborator after 1945.

7 Johanna Salomon had lived in Denmark for a number of years.

8 Presumably Isaac Dworsky (1886–1963), dentist; escaped to Sweden on 1 Nov. 1942.

dentist for refugees right away. So he was lucky, after all. He told me that the three Feinsilber girls are here, also the widows of Emil and Herman Feinsilber. Furthermore the Selikowitz boys, the Feins, Glotts, Koritzinsky and a number of others. Actually everything was wonderfully organized, and even people as old as 84 were carted to within half-an-hour's walk of the frontier. But the whole family Seligmann were deported on that steamer. Probably they were all taken to Poland, and so far nobody ever returned from there. The old people are actually done away with, and the younger ones are worked to death as slaves. The whole thing is so utterly unbelievable, and time and time again one has to ask oneself if it is not only a nightmare. – I know nothing about the fate of Hans and Elly.

But the Germans and even the Quislings are slowly realizing that they will lose. In Norway a number of people who have gone into the party are trying to get out now, but it is not so easy. Quisling doesn't let them, and no decent Norwegian will have anything to do with those people. They are the rats trying to leave the sinking ship. Many people here believe that the Germans will be done for this year; personally I believe it will happen sometime during 1944, but I would not mind if it were to happen earlier.

The food situation in Norway is a catastrophe; the child death rate has last year increased to 4 times the normal, and now they have stopped giving statistics; tuberculosis is spreading as well as other diseases. The people have lost 40 to 50 per cent in weight.[9]

Between 8 and 10 thousand are in Nazi prisons and concentration camps; 12 thousand are here in Sweden as refugees.[10] We have no contact with anybody except now and then Gjörwad and Bonnevies. I have no idea what happened to our other friends and acquaintances.

Thanks very much for sending us a gift parcel. But no boat has come from the U.S. since August last; if another boat comes there will be several parcels from Walter[11] also, and it would all be very welcome. We are all well, working hard, but also enjoying life as well as is possible under the circumstances. Fortunately the winter is not as severe as the previous ones, and it is quite tolerable to work in the woods.

With kindest regards to everybody,

DOC. 46

On 5 February 1943 Myrtle Wright describes the increasing difficulty of rescuing Jewish children[1]

Diary of Myrtle Wright, entry for 5 February 1943

Friday, 5 February. There have been arrests in Bergen, among them a woman teacher[2] who has been S.[3] link with the children there,[4] but the cause of her arrest is some other affair.

9 Despite severe rationing, hunger on this scale in Norway cannot be confirmed.
10 By the end of the war there were a total of 50,000 Norwegian refugees registered in Sweden.
11 Walter Herz (1904–1998), jeweller, Max Salomon's brother-in-law; owned the Gebrüder Friedländer jewellery shop on the Unter den Linden boulevard in Berlin; emigrated to the USA in 1938.

1 NHM, Myrtle Radley Wright Private Archive, NHM 29. Excerpts published in Wright, *Norwegian Diary, 1940–1945*, pp. 142–143.

I went to Nina to see what could be done about Vera and T.[5] She was anxious about them for they were difficult to keep quiet now. Eva, in spite of being in hiding, was working with a transport for them, but it is more and more difficult. A good many people have been taken and the routes are therefore reduced, and then the weather is bad too. While we sat and discussed, a message came that they could probably be fetched this evening. We rang to the person who knew where they were and asked her to bring the children 'to a party at 5.00 today'. She thought 'the children would be pleased to come and would bring some sandwiches with them', which means she understands they are to travel tonight. The bell again, this time a lady who is herself to go with the transport. She would like to meet the children before they start out and in any case must stay until they leave. They are to be at a meeting place in town at 6.00. Poor Nina, she has her sister-in-law coming to dinner at 3. The lady must be kept out of sight and she will try and ask her sister to be tactful and take an after-dinner nap about 5.00. May all at last go well with these two.

Nina told me about the three girls.[6] They had been fetched by a lady and gentleman who were to adopt them as their own daughters for the journey, they were to travel on false grensepasse.[7] She found it difficult to see how so fair a gentleman could have so dark daughters, but that would have to go as it could! The children had found it hard to have to leave everything of their own behind, especially a photo of their own mother, but this had a Czechoslovakian photographer's name on it. Nina would try and have it copied as an amateur snap and then get it taken to Sweden.

Sigrid got a letter from Signe F. which cheered and encouraged us. They had had a children's party with 37 there – only three had not been able to come, Robert Ris and Vera and T. Well, Vera and T. are on their way, and poor little Robert is at Bredvedt. But 37 are safe – all the effort and anxiety has been worthwhile. Signe speaks also about a skirt she is knitting – it has 685 stitches, 450 on the front and 235 on the back.[8]

The Russian are driving the Germans out of the Caucasus and threatening their retreat over Crimea.

2 Aslaug Blytt (1899–1966), teacher; worked in Bergen, 1935–1947; head of the Bergen-based Nansen Committee; assigned the children brought to Norway to host families and offered counselling; imprisoned in Grini, 1943–1944; worked as an art historian after 1947.

3 Sigrid Helliesen Lund (1892–1987), singer; member of the Women's International League for Peace and Freedom from 1935; employed at Nansen Relief from 1936; active in the resistance against German occupation; fled to Sweden in Feb. 1944; worked in development aid and with the Quakers after 1945.

4 For more on these children's origins, see Doc. 41, fn. 8.

5 Vera and Tibor Taglicht: see Doc. 41. The siblings' first attempt to flee with a group of refugees had failed, after which they were initially hidden near the town of Lillestrøm.

6 Presumably this is a reference to Vera, Edith, and Lia Kortner. The 15-, 14-, and 11-year-old girls came from Czechoslovakia and were rescued when they were brought to Sweden; their parents were murdered.

7 Norwegian in the original: 'border passes', special permission to reside in areas near the border.

8 According to Myrtle Wright, the number of Jews who were taken to Sweden totalled 450 men and 235 women: see Wright, *Norwegian Diary*, p. 143, fn. 1. In fact, approximately 900 Jews were able to make it to Sweden, and among them there were probably more women than men.

DOC. 47
Norsk Tidend (London), 7 April 1943: article detailing a police officer's account of the arrests of Jews in Norway[1]

When the Jews were deported

A Norwegian policeman, who was witness to the deportation of the Jews from Oslo on 26 November 1942, has given the following account of what happened:

On the afternoon of 25 November 1942, all the officers and constables of the Criminal Police Oslo received the order to meet at the State Police barracks at 24 Kirkeveien, with the exception of those who were assigned to other duties. Everyone had to sign a register confirming that they had received the order.

At that time, no one knew with any certainty what it was about. Most people thought it was the start of a new black-market raid.[2] Upon arrival, we saw that a Hird unit and a riot police unit were already in place. Police Inspector Rød of the State Police took a roll call of the members of the Civil and Criminal Police present. Thereafter he announced that all female members of Jewish families should be arrested along with those male family members who had not been arrested during the arrests of Jews about a month prior. All of them should be transported to the *Donau*, which was moored alongside the dockside shed of the *Norske Amerikalinje*.

Inspector Rød also informed us that a physician (he did not say which one) had seen to the required discharge of Jewish patients from all hospitals in town to which Jews were admitted. There was therefore no point in anyone claiming that they needed to go to a hospital. Nor was staying at home on grounds of illness a legitimate excuse. All of those concerned had to leave. Each person was allowed to take the following items: one set of daywear, warm underwear (how many sets was not stated), a knife, spoon, and fork, food for four days, toiletries. Taking anything more than this was strictly forbidden. We were specifically reminded that items of value such as gold, silver, jewellery, money, savings accounts, and so on were to be confiscated (if this had not already been done) and brought to the State Police, together with the keys to the apartments.

We were also instructed that half-Jews and Norwegian women married to Jews were not to be arrested, nor were any citizens of neutral countries. If in doubt, however, the person in question was to be arrested anyway and brought to the State Police. Most of the Hird men followed these instructions. They did everything possible to avoid exceptions to the main rule. Inspector Rød was asked how pregnant women were to be considered. To this he replied: 'Anyone up to and including six months must comply.' Furthermore, the inspector explained that if there was anyone who did not have food for four days, they were not to be given leave to procure any. They had two hours to arrange everything. No one was to be allowed to leave their apartment. The disabled and the elderly had also to comply, even if they were immobile.

1 *Norsk Tidend*, 7 April 1943, p. 11. This document has been translated from Norwegian. *Norsk Tidend* was the official newspaper of the Norwegian government in exile in London. It was published twice weekly between August 1940 and May 1945.

2 In original: *rasjonerings-razzia*, literally 'ration raid'.

We were split into groups of three: one from the Criminal Police, which was in charge; one from Hird; and one from the riot police. Each group was provided with a taxi and was to pick up between two and eight persons. Roughly 400 to 450 Jews were arrested that day. The State Police had set up their own office for the occasion in the dockside shed of the *Norske Amerikalinje*, led by Inspector Rød, with Lieutenant Holter as assistant.

I shall only recount one of the sad incidents which took place that day. A group was sent to a family in the city centre. After long and incessant ringing of the doorbell, a frightened woman opened the door. She was probably in her late twenties. When she found out what it was about, she turned white as a sheet and seemed on the verge of collapse. She managed to pull herself together sufficiently to do what was necessary to get ready. Then she went into the bedroom, where her two small children, aged two and four, lay asleep. With a great deal of effort and by summoning the last of her self-control, she dressed the two little ones. But when she came out onto the street and saw the vehicle waiting, she was completely beside herself with fear and screamed through sobs:

– You could save me and the children if you wanted to!

She repeated this constantly all the way to the quay, with her screams at times drowned out by the two terrified children, who were crying heartbreakingly and screaming 'Mummy!' At the quay they were received by the local hyenas,[3] German SS, and Gestapo, who revelled in this scene of the deepest human suffering. She was dragged out of the car, together with the children, heaved into a loading crate for animals, and with the help of a crane, lifted aboard and lowered onto the ship.

Here on the quay, the sick, the old, and the disabled were literally emptied out of the vehicles. No one was allowed to offer them a helping hand. These unfortunate people had to manage on their own, no matter how sick they were. They had to carry their own luggage. If they could not carry it, they had to leave it behind. There were enough greedy Germans around who knew what to do with it.

Quisling's top minions were in charge down there: State Police Chief Marthinsen, followed by the lackeys Holter, Myhrvold,[4] Homb,[5] Strange-Næs, and many others. All of them ready to carry out any order given by the German thugs, apparently without a moment's reflection on how many human beings they were driving into the darkest despair and the deepest misery.

3 This is a reference to the State Police, which was loyal to Nasjonal Samling.

4 This is probably a reference to Jørgen Wiermyhr (b. 1910), police officer; with the Norwegian police from 1940; chief inspector, 1942–1944; director of the Criminal Police, 1944–1945; sentenced to nine months in prison by a Norwegian court; worked in construction from 1946.

5 Ole Homb (1906–1989), police officer; with the Oslo police from 1930; joined Nasjonal Samling in 1940; member of the State Police from 1941; sentenced to two and a half years of hard labour by a Norwegian court in 1947.

DOC. 48

On 7 May 1943 a Norwegian textile manufacturer appeals to the Ministry of the Interior for the release of an employee who is in a so-called mixed marriage[1]

Letter from Gudbrandsdalens Uldvarefabrik,[2] Lillehammer, signed Ragnvald Svarstad,[3] to the Ministry of the Interior, Office of Constitutional Law,[4] Oslo, dated 7 May 1943

Engineer Aberle[5]
With reference to our earlier correspondence[6] concerning the question of the release of our engineer Ernst Aberle, allow us to report that Mrs Aberle[7] has now received the following information from her mother in Berlin: 'All Jews married to Aryans have been permitted to return to their families, with priority given to long-standing marriages and veterans of the previous world war.'[8]

We therefore graciously ask the honourable ministry to revisit the question of the release of our engineer Aberle, and refer you to our earlier account of the crucial importance of his assistance to the business. His absence is sorely felt, and we are now obliged to conduct an extremely onerous correspondence with him in Berg internment camp near Tønsberg, a correspondence which is far from satisfactory. In addition to the above, our assistant in the factory office, Arne Svarstad,[9] has now been ordered to northern Norway for work. We have attempted in vain to have him released. We trust that you can appreciate that this has caused us considerable difficulties in our office – at times like these when great demands are placed on us by the authorities and others.

We take the liberty of requesting that we might be permitted to obtain a report from the Norwegian Textile Authority[10] before the matter is addressed again, for we are in no doubt that the Textile Authority, with its extensive knowledge of our company's circumstances, will support our request. And if the situation for Jews who are married to Aryans is as described above in Germany, then surely the same must also be possible here in Norway.

1 NRA, S-1708 Sosialdepartementet, Våre Falne, Ee, 171, Aberle, Ernst. This document has been translated from Norwegian.
2 The textile manufacturer Gudbrandsdalens Uldvarefabrik in Lillehammer was founded in 1887 and has been owned by the Svarstad family since 1912.
3 Ragnvald Svarstad (1893–1965), businessman; held several managerial roles in the family business.
4 In the Office of Constitutional Law (Statsrettskontoret), which was part of the Ministry of the Interior, Nasjonal Samling wished to see the corporatist merger of employees and employers within individual branches of the economy. Civil disobedience thwarted the implementation of this plan.
5 Ernst Aberle (1898–1987), engineer; in 1929 emigrated from Germany to Brno, where he was employed by several factories; fled to Norway in Nov. 1939; arrested in Oct. 1942 and imprisoned in Bredtveit, Berg, and Grini; evacuated to Sweden in early May 1945; returned to Norway in June 1945, after the Norwegian authorities had initially denied him permission.
6 A letter dated 12 Jan. 1943 is enclosed in the file. It contains Svarstad's earlier appeal for Aberle's release: NRA, S-1708 Sosialdepartementet, Våre Falne, Ee, 171, Aberle, Ernst.
7 Gertrud Ella Aberle, née Grenzius (b. 1897), housewife.
8 This sentence is quoted in the original German in the letter.
9 Arne Svarstad (b. 1919), businessman.
10 Norges Tekstilstyre: national steering body for the Norwegian textile industry. In a report dated 18 May 1943 it supported Aberle's release.

We would also like to add that Ernst Aberle served as a volunteer – as described earlier – in the previous world war and was injured. He had a brother who was killed in the war.

We thank you very much in advance for the best possible treatment of our request.[11]

Yours truly,

DOC. 49
On 17 June 1943 Marcus Levin writes a summary of where the Jews deported from Norway have been taken[1]

Report by Marcus Levin (reg. no. 10 124), Stockholm, to the Norwegian government in exile, dated 17 June 1943[2]

After lists of Jews deported from Norway were sent in, new information gradually came in over time,[3] which made it possible to complete the lists. This mainly pertained to those cases which had been unclear up to then.

There was a great deal of confusion when the transport left Norway, which meant that several names were not on the lists. As a result, several Jews were left behind after they were called up and thus escaped these first deportations. They were transferred to Grini.[4] Other Jews who were accused of alleged misdemeanours, such as possession of illegal documents, hoarding, etc., were also transferred to Grini, where those who had been arrested while attempting to flee to Sweden were also assembled. These people have now been deported on various transports from Grini.

From information that has now come in it can be assumed that the overwhelming majority of Jewish men deported from Norway have been taken to various camps in Upper Silesia. In letters sent here by those who were deported, the designation 'labour camp' is used, while letters sent from here have been returned marked 'concentration camp refuses receipt'.[5]

It seems that the fate of the deported women and children remains unknown. We have had word from the Auschwitz labour camp from the group of women and elderly

11 Ernst Aberle remained in custody, as did the majority of Jewish men married to non-Jewish women. Shortly before the end of the war, thanks to the intervention of the Swedish government, he was evacuated to Sweden. His non-Jewish wife remained in Lillehammer and was supported by the Svarstad family.

1 NRA, S-2259 Utenriksdepartementet, Dyd, 10 393, 25.1/5 Jødespørsmålet II. This document has been translated from Norwegian.

2 The original document contains handwritten annotations and underlining.

3 Levin had already produced summaries of his enquiries for the government in exile in London and the embassy in Stockholm on 5 April 1943, working on the assumption that 747 persons had been deported. His reports do not always indicate the source of his information: NRA, S-2259 Utenriksdepartementet, Dyd, 10 393, 25.1/5 Jødespørsmålet II.

4 The former women's prison at Bærum near Oslo became Grini police detention camp in June 1941; around 20,000 people were detained there during the period up to 1945. After the end of the war, the camp was used to imprison Norwegian war criminals. Today the premises are part of Ila prison.

5 Most of the deportees had already been murdered.

men who were deported on 24 February this year. But there has been no sign of life from the group of women and children who were deported on the main transport, which left on 26 November 1942 on the *Donau*. Indirectly, we have received information in the meantime from which it can be concluded that after the men had been separated from the women, the transport is either still in, or at least passed through, the town of Ulm in Württemberg. At any rate, three different messages were posted from that town, and we know that an 82-year-old Jewish woman on the verge of death was taken to a hospital there.[6]

According to earlier reports, all the Jews, including those detained before the main operation took place, have, as far as we know, been subjected to the same treatment as the deportees and have been transferred to special camps for Jews, regardless of whether they were taken as hostages or accused of alleged offences. Exceptions may have been made for certain Jews who were convicted by German military courts or special courts or were prisoners of war. In this connection we can cite the Norwegian citizen Isidor Rubinstein,[7] born on 28 March 1909, who was sentenced in Oslo to four years in prison in November 1941 under German military law. He had been serving his sentence in Fuhlsbüttel prison in Hamburg and has now been transferred to Auschwitz concentration camp in Upper Silesia. Up until now, he has been able to receive letters and food parcels.

In Norway the Jews are mainly interned at Grini, both men and women, most of them Jews who are married to non-Jews. In one case where a Jewish woman married to a non-Jew was interned, her release was made conditional upon her husband being able to obtain an official attestation that she could no longer have children. The woman was childless and about 55 years old. The attestation was obtained, but the woman has not been released.

Most inmates in Berg are interned men who are married to non-Jews. Dr A. Ramson,[8] district physician in Sauda, Ryfylke, who was previously released, has apparently been rearrested, while Phillip Kröner has been released and has again taken up his position as departmental manager at Norwegian Music Publishing. The reason for the release is not known, but people who know him well think that Erpekum Sem[9] might have intervened on his behalf. In any event, it is known that Erpekum Sem has advocated strongly on behalf of his former pupil.

As of 1 April, all the Hungarian citizens who had been released earlier have been rearrested. Their subsequent fate is unknown.[10]

There are still a good number of Jews in hospitals in Norway who, as far as we know, have not yet been affected. There are still pensioners living under Nazi supervision in the Jewish old people's home on Holbersgata.

6 This could not be verified.

7 Isidor Rubinstein (1909–1945), sales representative; arrested in April 1941 and deported in Jan. 1942; murdered on 27 March 1945. He was Willy Rubinstein's brother: see PMJ 5/12.

8 Abraham Wulf Ramson (1904–1981?), district physician and physician for fisheries; married Barbara Nikoline Gulseth in 1932; converted to Christianity.

9 Arne van Erpekum Sem (1873–1951), Norwegian singer, singing teacher, and music critic.

10 A total of four Hungarian Jews were arrested with the permission of the Hungarian government. Three were interned until the end of the war because they were married to non-Jewish women. One Hungarian citizen was deported.

A few Jews who were not being sought by the authorities have recently come to Sweden, while a few are still at liberty in Norway.

Two more Jewish women who were detained in Norway, both Norwegian citizens, have come to Sweden on provisional Swedish passports. It seems, however, that this opportunity is not so far being made available to the interned men, even though they would have the same prospects as those released earlier on the basis of their birth and close ties to Sweden.

About 12 of 14 Norwegian Jews who were deported have been granted Swedish citizenship here in Sweden at the request of their families, and through the Swedish legation in Berlin an attempt is being made to obtain their release and permission to travel to Sweden. But because the German authorities will not recognize Swedish citizenship granted after 26 October 1942, the appointed day for the operation against male Jews, there currently seems to be little hope, although the case has not yet been definitively rejected.

DOC. 50

On 6 August 1943 Isaak Mendelsohn asks the representative of the Norwegian government in exile in Sweden to help save his deported relatives[1]

Letter from I. Mendelsohn,[2] 33 Brantingsgatan, to His Excellency Minister Bull, Stockholm (receipt stamp J.N 07 595/1943, dated 9 August 1943), dated 6 August 1943

With reference to our correspondence, please allow me to approach you with the following concern, in the hope that you might ask the Swedish Red Cross to obtain from the relevant German authorities the release of my relatives who were deported from Norway and whose present whereabouts are unknown.

The matter concerns:

My father, Aron Mendelsohn,[3] born on 17 November 1871, occupation: merchant.

My mother, Thora Mendelsohn, born on 19 March 1874, occupation: housewife.

My brother, Henrik Mendelsohn,[4] born on 4 November 1896, occupation: merchant.

Their last known address is Trondheim.

1 The original cannot be found. Copy in YIVO, Samuel Abrahamsen Coll., RG 1565–122. This document has been translated from Norwegian.

2 Isaak Mendelsohn (1900–1973), textile manufacturer; took over one of his father's textile factories in Trondheim in 1923; fled to Sweden in Nov. 1941; returned after the war and ran the company together with the widow of his brother Henrik.

3 Aaron Mendelsohn (1871–1943), businessman; born in Lithuania; emigrated to Norway in 1894; founding member of the Jewish Community of Trondheim, and saved the Torah scrolls before the requisitioning of the synagogue; arrested on 25 Nov. 1942; deported in Feb. 1943 to Auschwitz, where he was murdered.

4 Henrik Mendelsohn (1896–1944), textile manufacturer; the family business was forced to close on 7 Nov. 1941 and placed under provisional administration. Henrik Mendelsohn was arrested on the same day and again on 26 Oct. 1942; he was deported on 24 Feb. 1943 to Auschwitz, where he perished in spring 1944.

My brother, Henrik Mendelsohn, was arrested in autumn 1941, while my parents were arrested in November 1942. There are no obvious reasons for their arrest other than that they are Jews.[5]

After they had been interned in Bredvet[6] prison near Oslo, they were all deported from Norway on 24 February 1942.[7]

As my mother was born in Sweden and has Swedish family here, while my brother is married to a former Swedish citizen, upon application all three were granted Swedish citizenship on 19 March 1943 on grounds of the family's close ties to Sweden. I hope that this will lead to the immediate release of my family and the granting of permission to leave Germany. In connection with this matter I have, via the Swedish Ministry of Foreign Affairs, approached the Swedish legation in Berlin, which has now been dealing with the matter for months, but with negative results to date. As the prospects of getting my family released seem bleak, I appeal to you, Minister, to be so kind as to bring this case to the Swedish Red Cross, in the hope that in this way the German authorities can be moved to release my family and grant them permission to leave for Sweden.

Trusting in the understanding and goodwill that you, Minister, have previously displayed in similar questions, I allow myself to be so bold as to approach you in my hour of need, I hope you will forgive the inconvenience I have thereby caused you, and I hope for a favourable decision on my matter.

With best regards[8]

DOC. 51
Jewish Telegraphic Agency, 26 April 1945: report on five Norwegian Jews who survived Auschwitz[1]

Five Norwegian Jews at Buchenwald believed only survivors of over 1,200 deportees

London, 25 April (JTA)
A Swedish correspondent who has just returned from Buchenwald told the Jewish Telegraphic Agency today that he met there five Norwegians who believe that they are the only survivors of the more than 1,200[2] who were deported from Norway in November 1942.

5 On the arrest and expropriation of the Mendelsohn family, see PMJ 5/15 and 16.
6 As in original: more usually spelled Bredtveit or Bredvedt.
7 Error in original: should read 24 February 1943.
8 A handwritten note at the head of the letter states, 'Mendelsohn is informed that this matter must be handled via the Swedish Ministry of Foreign Affairs. For resubmission 18 August 1943, K.J.' Below the letter is a handwritten note stating, 'Swedish Red Cross declares that unfortunately the matter must be referred to the Ministry of Foreign Affairs. 18 August.'

1 Jewish Telegraphic Agency, 26 April 1945. Founded by Jacob Landau as the Jewish Correspondence Bureau in 1917, this news agency was called the Jewish Telegraphic Agency from 1919. It had offices in Berlin, Warsaw, and New York, among other locations, in the 1930s. The original document is in English.
2 At least 727 Jews were deported from Norway; 34 of them survived. Deportation ships left the port of Oslo in Nov. 1942 as follows: the *Monte Rosa* on 19 Nov., and the *Donau* and the *Monte Rosa* on 26 Nov. An additional 158 Jews were deported aboard the *Gotenland* on 24 Feb. 1943: see Introduction, p. 28.

The survivors – Samuel Steinman[3] of Oslo, Assor Hirsch, Asriel Hirsch and Julius Paltiel of Trondheim,[4] and Leo Ettinger of Moldo[5] – who range in age between 22 and 33, said that immediately after the deportations, the Jews were divided into two groups. Those unable to work were murdered, while the able-bodied ones were kept at Auschwitz until the approach of the Russians.

They were then loaded onto open trucks and sent to Buchenwald. Many died en route from exposure in the mid-winter cold. One of the five survivors told the correspondent that he was slated for extermination, but was saved by the arrival of the Allied troops. The Norwegian government is arranging to bring them to England pending liberation of Norway.[6]

It was reported today that Eliezer Gruenbaum,[7] a son of Isaac Gruenbaum[8] of the Agency executive, is among the survivors found at Buchenwald.

3 Samuel Steinman (1923–2015), student; deported to Auschwitz via Stettin on the *Donau* in Nov. 1942; later lived in Oslo.

4 Assor Hirsch (b. 1923), student; Asriel-Berl Hirsch (b. 1920), student; Julius Paltiel (1924–2008), student; all three were arrested in Trondheim in early Oct. 1942; they were imprisoned in Falstad prison camp and deported to Auschwitz via Stettin in Feb. 1943.

5 Correctly: Leo Eitinger (1912–1996), psychiatrist; fled to Norway from Czechoslovakia in 1939; worked in a hospital until the German invasion, then went into hiding as a manual labourer; arrested in March 1942; deported to Auschwitz in Feb. 1943; returned to Norway after liberation and worked at Oslo University Hospital; psychiatry consultant to the Norwegian army, 1952–1957; researched and published on post-traumatic stress disorder.

6 This did not happen. The five survivors managed to reach Copenhagen with the help of a British army chaplain and the Danish consul in Flensburg, and they returned to Norway with the help of the Norwegian refugee department in Stockholm.

7 Eliezer Gruenbaum (1908–1948), communist activist; fled to Paris after being arrested in Poland in 1931; fought in the Spanish Civil War and the French Resistance against the German occupation; arrested and deported to Auschwitz in 1942; died in the Arab-Israeli War in 1948.

8 Isaac Gruenbaum (1879–1970), lawyer and politician; emigrated from Poland to Palestine in 1933; worked for the Jewish Agency and was involved in its efforts to rescue Jews; one of the first 37 signatories of the Israeli Declaration of Independence; Israel's first minister of the interior.

Netherlands

Netherlands
Camps
North Sea
Afsluitdijk
GRONINGEN
Groningen
Leeuwarden
FRIESLAND
Assen
Beilen
Westerbork
DRENTHE
NETHERLANDS
NORD-HOLLAND
IJsselmeer
IJmuiden
Haarlem
Amsterdam
Zwolle
OVERIJSSEL
Leiden
Apeldoorn
Amersfoort
Barneveld
The Hague
('s-Gravenhage)
Utrecht
UTRECHT
GELDERLAND
Enschede
ZUID HOLLAND
Rotterdam
Arnhem
Dordrecht
Rhine
ZEELAND
Moerdijk
's-Hertogenbosch
Vught
Meuse
Middelburg
NORDBRABANT
GERMAN REICH
Eindhoven
Geldrop
Venlo
Antwerp
LIM-BURG
Breendonk
Mechelen
Düsseldorf
Scheldt
Meuse
Brussels
Hoensbroek
Waubach
Maastricht
Cologne
BELGIUM
0 20 40 60 80 100 km
Aachen
Rhine

DOC. 52
On 30 June 1942 the chairmen of the Jewish Council summarize the results of a discussion about labour deployment in Germany[1]

Minutes, unsigned, dated 30 June 1942 (carbon copy)[2]

Meeting of Hauptsturmführer aus der Fünten[3] and Hauptsturmführer Wörlein[4] with Mr A. Asscher[5] and Prof. D. Cohen[6] on Tuesday 30 June 1942 at 10 a.m.

We said that we had made every effort to put an end to the panic resulting from rumours that all Jews would be sent to Poland by announcing that this concerned an Arbeitseinsatz[7] of Jews to work camps in Germany, but that the passage in Mr Schmidt's[8] address stating that all Jews would be sent to Poland had countered our efforts.[9] We therefore asked for permission to issue another official statement saying this only concerned an Arbeitseinsatz, as we had been told on Friday evening.[10]

1 NIOD, 182/4. This document has been translated from Dutch.
2 The original contains handwritten notes and underlining.
3 Ferdinand aus der Fünten (1909–1989), businessman; joined the NSDAP and the SS in 1932; full-time member of the SS from 1936; worked in the section for Jewish affairs at the Reich Security Main Office (RSHA) under Adolf Eichmann; director of the Central Office for Jewish Emigration in Amsterdam from 1942; sentenced to death in the Netherlands in 1950; sentence commuted to life imprisonment in 1951. He was imprisoned in Breda until 1989; released on grounds of ill health and extradited to Germany; and died shortly after his release.
4 Karl Wörlein (1906–1978), bank employee; employed in retail, 1920–1934; joined the SA in 1921; took part in the Beer Hall Putsch in 1923; joined the NSDAP and the SS in 1931; with the SD from 1934; deputy head of the Central Office for Jewish Emigration in Amsterdam; head of the Household Effects Registration Office; thought to have returned to Bavaria in 1944; prisoner of war in Austria and Romania, May 1945–June 1949.
5 Abraham Asscher (1880–1950), diamond merchant; worked in the family business; liberal politician, chairman of the Ashkenazi Jewish Community, and from 1933 chairman of the Committee for Special Jewish Interests (CBJB), the activities of which included relief work for Jewish refugees; one of the two chairmen of the Jewish Council, 1941–1943; deported to Bergen-Belsen in 1943; freed when Bergen-Belsen was liberated in 1945. A Jewish 'court of honour' (*erenraad*), established by Jewish community activists after the war to try former Jewish Council members and collaborators, barred him from participating in Jewish organizations after 1945.
6 Dr David Cohen (1882–1967), historian and long-time Zionist activist; professor in Leiden and Amsterdam; from March 1933 headed the Committee for Jewish Refugees (CJV), a subdivision of the Committee for Special Jewish Interests (CBJB); one of the two chairmen of the Jewish Council from 1941; deported to Theresienstadt in 1943 and freed when Theresienstadt was liberated in 1945. A Jewish 'court of honour' barred him from participating in Jewish organizations after 1945.
7 German in the original: 'labour deployment'.
8 Fritz Schmidt (1903–1943), photographer; soldier, 1922–1926; freelance photographer, 1926–1934; joined the NSDAP in 1929; NSDAP Kreisleiter in Westphalia, 1932–1936; member of the Reichstag from 1936; in 1940, at Martin Bormann's suggestion, made commissioner general for special duties in the Netherlands; at the same time department head of the NSDAP's 'Netherlands Section' (Arbeitsbereich Niederlande); died in France in unexplained circumstances, 1943.
9 At an NSDAP and NSB training meeting on 28 June 1942, Schmidt had said that the Jews would be taken back to where they came from: *Deutsche Zeitung in den Niederlanden*, vol. 3, no. 25, 29 June 1942, pp. 1–2.
10 'Labour deployment' in Germany for Jews had been announced to the Jewish Council on 26 June 1942.

Mr aus der Fünten said this was indeed the sole intention, and that this was clear from the mere fact that postal traffic with the Lager[11] would be permitted. When we asked why the police rather than an Arbeitsamt[12] would be in charge – as is the case with non-Jewish labour service in Germany – he answered that the Polizei[13] would be better able to look after the Sicherheit der Judenschaft[14] in the camps. He told us the first departure would take place soon; he could not tell us anything about the number. Dutch and stateless Jews would be sent all together. The intention was to send the Jews in question from one town at a time. When we asked what the age range of those to be sent would be, the answer was that the upper limit would probably be 40. The intention was that families would travel together, so that if one family member was over 40, the family would not go. However, unmarried family members over an age still to be determined would be sent.

It was explicitly stated that the camps would be in Germany. Wherever possible, each person would be put to work in their own profession. It was also explicitly stated that the organization of the entire transport and the labour deployments are in the hands of the German police, whereas the calls for the Erfassung[15] would be issued by the Jewish Council.

When we asked whether any exceptions would be made, we were told that these would be decided place by place, and that we could put forward specific people from each place. There is no intention to exempt all people in a specific [occupational] category, as some of the physicians and other carers will have to travel along with the rest.

When we asked whether the capital owned by the people who are to be sent away will be kept for them so that they can continue to meet their obligations to support others as well as other obligations they have entered into, we were told that this matter had not yet been considered. We pointed out that this matter was of great importance to us, because major responsibilities would rest upon us if this was not permitted. We were assured that this would be further investigated, and that certainly the capital at Lippmann, Rosenthal & Co.[16] would remain in the names of those sent away.

When we asked whether those who had already been called up for labour deployment[17] in the Netherlands would undergo another examination,[18] we were told that everyone would be examined in the Durchgangslager.[19]

11 German in the original: 'camp'.

12 German in the original: 'employment office'.

13 German in the original: 'police'.

14 German in the original: 'security of Jewry'. *Judenschaft* is a derogatory term for the Jewish collective.

15 German in the original: 'registration'.

16 To facilitate the expropriation and theft of Jewish property, the German authorities established the 'bank' Lippmann, Rosenthal & Co. on Sarphatistraat in August 1941. The name was a front, identical to that of the renowned Jewish bank that already existed on Nieuwe Spiegelstraat, and used as a ploy to gain the trust of the Jewish population. Other than the shared name, the two financial institutions had nothing to do with each other. The German authorities later liquidated the Jewish bank and transferred its assets to the front institution. See Gerard Aalders, *Nazi Looting: The Plunder of Dutch Jewry during the Second World War* (London: Berg, 2004), pp. 127–145. See also PMJ 5/85 and 101.

17 The original uses the term *werkverruiming*. Prior to the German occupation, this term was used to describe work-creation schemes for the unemployed in the Netherlands, which were sometimes carried out in camps. In the context of the occupation, it referred to forced labour deployment.

When we requested permission for the provision of spiritual care, we were told they had never stopped any church from performing its role.

We were then told that the number of between 350 and 375 people which we had proposed was not acceptable. A total of 600 people will have to be processed daily. We commented that our technical advisors have deemed this impossible. The response was that the forms will be simplified even further than is the case already, and that this has been explicitly ordered. We requested permission for 350 people [to be processed] per day for an initial period. This was granted, with the comment that this period must not exceed eight days.

We were instructed to submit a list of diamond workers, as they will be exempted, at least if they have not been out of work for too long. All Jewish Council staff will also be exempted, as they perform Arbeitseinsatz in the Netherlands.

We then asked whether it might be possible to allow travel permits for visiting sick relatives. We were told that this might be the case, but that only the closest relatives would be allowed to go, and only in cases of very serious illness.

When we asked whether nurses and others who have a few days' leave each year and like to spend that time visiting their parents could be granted travel permits, the answer was that such special requests could be submitted on a case-by-case basis.

When we asked whether people had to carry the yellow registration card along with their identity card, the answer was negative. We drew attention to the fact that some police officers had demanded this and requested that they report this to Mr Damen von Buchholz,[20] which they said they would do.

When we asked about the suburbs,[21] we were told that this matter is being considered. It is likely that they will take the position that those municipalities which have their own post office, rationing office, and the like will not be regarded as suburbs. We pointed out that this would lead to major difficulties, as many municipalities overlap with one another, with the result that the boundaries are barely noticeable. It was promised that this would be given further consideration.

18 From Jan. 1942 Jews – at first the unemployed, and then others as well – were required to perform labour in the Netherlands. In total, approximately 5,000 Jews performed forced labour in around 50 different camps: see PMJ 5/110 and 111.

19 German in the original: 'transit camp'. Westerbork police transit camp was set up by the Dutch government in 1939 as a central refugee camp. With the occupation of the Netherlands in May 1940, it became a reception camp for detained German and Austrian Jews and by 1941 held 1,100 refugees. On 1 July 1942 the German authorities took over the camp, which now became the transit camp used to deport almost all Jews from the Netherlands. From mid July 1942 the deportation trains bound for the concentration and extermination camps – mainly Auschwitz and Sobibor – left from Westerbork.

20 Correctly: Rudolf Wilhelm Dahmen von Buchholz (1889–1967), military officer; joined first the NSNAP (National Socialist Dutch Workers' Party) and afterwards the NSB, both in 1940; police inspector in Amsterdam from March 1942; head of the Office for Jewish Affairs within the Amsterdam police from June 1942; sentenced to life imprisonment in 1945; released from prison in 1956.

21 This presumably relates to the question of which municipalities could be counted as part of Amsterdam. In the minutes of the Jewish Council meeting of 25 June 1942 (NIOD, 182/3), it was announced that all Jews outside Amsterdam would have to give up their bicycles; as a result, the question of the demarcation of the border between Amsterdam and the surrounding municipalities arose.

DOC. 53

Deutsche Zeitung in den Niederlanden: on 30 June 1942 Commissioner General Hanns Albin Rauter further restricts the freedom of movement of Jews in the Netherlands[1]

Second Directive of the Commissioner General for Security[2] *on the Presence of Jews in Public*[3]

Pursuant to § 45 of Regulation no. 138/1941[4] of the Reich Commissioner for the Occupied Dutch Territories[5] on the Protection of Order, I decree the following:

§ 1

Jews must be in their residences from 8 p.m. until 6 a.m.

§ 2

Jews are forbidden to be in living quarters, gardens, or other private facilities serving recreational or entertainment purposes and belonging to non-Jews, unless this is necessitated by an official request or by existing tenancy agreements or working circumstances. Jews who are married to non-Jews are exempt from this restriction.

§ 3

1) Jews may enter shops that are not marked as Jewish only during the period from 3 p.m. to 5 p.m. Pharmacies are exempt from this provision.
2) Jews are forbidden to have goods delivered to their homes.
3) This directive does not affect special regulations that have already been drawn up or will be drawn up for the City of Amsterdam by the Reich Commissioner's representative.[6]

§ 4

Jews are forbidden to enter barber shops and hairdressing salons and other paramedical[7] establishments or to use their services in any other manner, unless these businesses or establishments are marked as Jewish. Reference is made to § 2 of the Administrative

1 *Deutsche Zeitung in den Niederlanden*, vol. 3, no. 27, 1 July 1942, p. 1. This German-language daily was published in Amsterdam from June 1940 to May 1945 with a circulation of approximately 30,000–55,000 copies. It was the official newspaper of the German occupiers and replaced the *Reichsdeutsche Nachrichten in den Niederlanden*, which had been published by the NSDAP's Foreign Organization. This document has been translated from German.

2 Hanns Albin Rauter (1895–1949), military officer; in various Freikorps paramilitary groups in Austria and Upper Silesia, 1919–1923; active in antisemitic organizations in Austria, 1923–1933; fled to Germany in 1933; joined the SS in 1935; commissioner general for security and Higher SS and Police Leader in the occupied Netherlands from May 1940, where his responsibilities included organizing the deportation of the Jews; seriously wounded in an assassination attempt in March 1945; sentenced to death in the Netherlands in 1948 and executed in 1949.

3 The first Directive on the Presence of Jews in Public was issued on 15 Sep. 1941: see PMJ 5/93.

4 Under § 45 the Commissioner General for Security was permitted to issue directives and orders for the purpose of ensuring the security of public life. See *VOBl-NL*, no. 138/1941, 25 July 1941, pp. 583–584.

5 Arthur Seyss-Inquart.

6 Werner Schröder.

7 Customary term in the Netherlands for health professions which required no medical training.

Directive of the Commissioner General for Finance and Economic Affairs[8] of 30 June 1942 on the Regulation on the Exercise of Occupations by Jews.[9]

§ 5

1) Jews are forbidden to enter railway facilities and to use public and private transport of any kind.
2) Exempted from this remain:
   1. The use of ferries;
   2. Cycling within the municipal area of Amsterdam;
   3. Conveyance of goods by three-wheel cargo bikes (so-called bakfietsen) for business objectives within the scope of an occupation that is not off limits to Jews;
   4. Conveyance of the seriously ill by ambulance and of persons with severe physical handicaps by special vehicle;
   5. The use of local transport by persons holding the tickets submitted by the Netherlands Armaments Inspectorate and authorized by the Security Police;
   6. The use of railways with Security Police permission for travel;
   7. The use of transport by persons holding travel permits issued by the Central Office for Jewish Emigration.
3) Jews who are accordingly permitted to travel on public transport must use the lowest class of carriage (smoking compartments). They are allowed to board and occupy seats only if sufficient room is available for non-Jewish passengers.

§ 6

Jews are forbidden to use public telephone facilities.

§ 7

A Jew within the meaning of this directive is anyone who, under § 4 of Regulation no. 189/1940[10] on the Registration of Businesses, is a Jew or is considered a Jew.

§ 8

Implementing directives and additional exemptions from §§ 1–6 will be published in the *Jüdisches Wochenblatt.*[11]

§ 9

1) Anyone who violates or circumvents the provisions of §§ 1–6 will be punished – unless a harsher penalty is incurred in accordance with other regulations – with imprisonment for up to six months, or a fine of up to 1,000 guilders, or both. Anyone who causes, facilitates, or cooperates in a circumvention of these provisions is subject to the same punishment.
2) The right to impose Security Police measures is reserved.

§ 10

The directive comes into force on the day of its promulgation.

8 Hans Fischböck.

9 This directive was published immediately adjacent to the commissioner general for security's directive. § 2 stated which occupations were included in the 'paramedical' category.

10 See PMJ 5/42.

11 Dutch: *Het Joodsche Weekblad*, Jewish weekly newspaper published from April 1941 to Sept. 1943. Following the ban on other Jewish newspapers in Oct. 1941, it was the only Jewish newspaper in the Netherlands. The Jewish Council was responsible for ensuring the Jewish population was informed of German directives through the *Joodsche Weekblad.*

Den Haag,[12] 30 June 1942
The Commissioner General for Security and Higher SS and Police Leader
signed *Rauter*
SS-Gruppenführer and Lieutenant General of Police

DOC. 54

Writing in her diary on 3 July 1942, Etty Hillesum is convinced that the decision has been taken to annihilate the Jews and accepts the prospect of her own death[1]

Handwritten diary of Etty Hillesum,[2] entry for 3 July 1942

3 July 1942, Friday evening, 8.30 p.m.
Yes, I am still at the same desk, but I feel that I am going to have to draw a line under all that has gone before and continue in a different tone. We have to incorporate a new certainty into our lives and make a place for it: what is at stake is our demise and our annihilation, we should no longer have any illusions about that. They are out to destroy us completely, we have to accept that, and then we can go on from there. Today I was filled with terrible despondency at first, and now I shall have to come to terms with that as well. And perhaps, or rather certainly, that also comes from the four aspirin tablets yesterday. Even if we are consigned to hell, let us go there as gracefully as we can. But I did not really want to put it so bluntly. Why this mood at this particular moment? It is because I have a blister on my foot from the long walk through this hot city, because so many people have had sore feet since they were stopped from using the trams,[3] because of Renate's[4] pale little face; because she has to walk to school on her short little legs through the heat, an hour there and another hour back? Because Liesl[5] has to stand in a queue for hours and still doesn't get any vegetables? It is for such an awful lot of reasons, all of them just little things in themselves, but all of them part of the great campaign

12 Dutch spelling of The Hague as in the original.

1 JHM, Doc. 00 005 119, notebook 9, pp. 150–152, and notebook 10, pp. 1–7. Published in *Etty Hillesum: The Complete Works, 1941–1943*, ed. Klaas A. D. Smelik and Meins G. S. Coetsier, trans. from Dutch and German by Arnold J. Pomerans (Maastricht: Shaker, 2014), pp. 736–742. Reproduced by kind permission of the publisher. Etty Hillesum wrote her diary between March 1941 and Oct. 1943 in ten notebooks which she gave to friends; the last of these, written in Westerbork, she took with her on the transport to Auschwitz.

2 Ester (Etty) Hillesum (1914–1943); studied law and Slavic languages in Amsterdam from 1932; taught Russian courses; undertook welfare work in the Westerbork department of the Jewish Council from the end of 1942, returning periodically to Amsterdam; interned in Westerbork in the summer of 1943; deported from there to Auschwitz together with her parents and siblings in Sept. 1943; murdered in Auschwitz on 30 Nov. 1943. See also PMJ 5/68 and 143.

3 Use of the tram had been prohibited to Jews a few days previously: see Doc. 53.

4 Renate Hedwig Levie, later Hagar Rudnik (b. 1932), Liesl Levie-Wolfsky's daughter; deported to Westerbork in June 1943 and to Bergen-Belsen in Jan. 1944; returned to the Netherlands in June 1945; emigrated to Israel in 1951.

5 Alice (Liesl) Levie-Wolfsky (1910–1997); emigrated with her family from Berlin to Amsterdam in 1939; deported to Westerbork in June 1943 and to Bergen-Belsen in Jan. 1944; returned to the Netherlands in June 1945; emigrated to Israel in 1954.

to destroy us. And everything else is just grotesque for now and hard to grasp: that S.[6] is no longer permitted to visit this house, no longer has access to his grand piano and books, that I'm no longer allowed to visit Tide, and so on.[7]

I am attaching what Netty[8] wrote to S. It is still the case that I carry within myself the knowledge that my wish will be fulfilled, that I will go to Russia one day, that I will be one of the many small links between Russia and Europe. This certainty within me will not be upset by the new certainty: that what they are after is our annihilation. That too I accept. I know it now. I shall not burden others with my fears, I shall not be bitter if others fail to grasp what is happening to us Jews. The one certainty will not be corroded or weakened by the other. I continue to work and live with the same conviction and I find life meaningful – yes, meaningful – although I hardly dare say so in company these days. Living and dying, sorrow and joy, the blisters on my feet, sore from so much walking, and the jasmine behind my garden, the persecution, the countless meaningless cruelties, all of that is inside me as one mighty whole, and I accept everything as a whole, and begin increasingly to understand, just for myself, without yet being able to explain it to anyone how everything hangs together. I'd like to live for a long time so that I might be able to explain it one day after all, and if I am not granted that wish, well, then someone else will do it, and then someone else will go on living my life from the point at which mine was cut short, and that's why I have to live my life as well and as fully and as convincingly as possible until my dying breath, so that the one who comes after me doesn't have to start afresh and doesn't have such a hard time of it. Isn't that also doing something for future generations? After the last regulations, Bernard's[9] Jewish friend[10] had someone ask me whether I didn't now agree that all Germans should be done away with, preferably torn to shreds one by one.

And I thought: That would indeed best satisfy our personal resentment and our desire for revenge, but why take the cheapest and easiest course? Why only think of satisfying one's own ego? For that is what it really comes down to, isn't it? Then those who come after us are equally far away and have to start all over again, so why shouldn't we be able to try to take a little step forward ourselves? And then it's not a matter of theories, but rather of daily practices. For example, my sudden irritability and aggressiveness towards Käthe[11] because all at once I feel that she is defending her country inwardly, the goodness that exists in her country after all, because there are people living there who are just like us. And isn't that the case? You can spin as many theories as you like, they

6 This is a reference to Julius Spier (1887–1942), businessman and psychologist; ran a psychochirology practice in Berlin; emigrated to the Netherlands in 1939; worked there as a chirologist. Etty Hillesum became his secretary and lover in 1941; he died of lung cancer in Sept. 1942.

7 Henriette (Henny) Tideman (1907–1989), teacher; met Spier in 1939 and was in his circle of close friends, where she met Etty Hillesum.

8 Annette (Netty) van der Hof (1913–2000); orphaned at the age of 9; subsequently a frequent guest at the home of the Bongers family in Wageningen; met Julius Spier there and was in his circle of friends.

9 Bernadus (Bernard) Meylink (1911–1952), biochemist; until 1942 lived together with Etty Hillesum in a shared apartment in Gabriël Metsustraat; worked for the company Organon (insulin manufacturers) after 1945.

10 Samuel Parijs (1913–1943), chemist; deported on 26 May 1943 to Westerbork and from there on 1 June 1943 to Sobibor, where he was murdered on arrival.

11 Käthe Fransen, housekeeper; lived together with Etty Hillesum in Gabriël Metsustraat.

are people like us, and that is something we must cling to through thick and thin, and we must proclaim it against all the hatred.

Yes, we do indeed carry everything within us, God and heaven, hell and earth, life and death, and centuries, many centuries. The scenery and the plot of the external circumstances change. But we carry everything within us, and the circumstances are not the decisive thing, not ever, because there are always circumstances, good or bad, and we have to accept the fact that there are good and bad circumstances, which doesn't prevent us from devoting our lives to curing the bad. But we must know what motives inspire the struggle, and we must begin with ourselves, every day anew, with ourselves.

There was a time when I thought that I had to come up with a host of brilliant thoughts every day, and now I sometimes feel like a barren stretch of land on which nothing grows, but which is spanned by a low, silent sky. And it's better this way. Nowadays I mistrust the complexity of the thoughts welling up in me; sometimes I'd rather lie idle and wait. In the last few days an awful lot has been going on inside me, but now something has crystallized at last. I have looked our demise straight in the eye, our probably miserable demise, which has already begun in many small aspects of daily life, and I have incorporated this possibility into my attitude towards life, without that attitude having lost any strength as a result. I am not embittered or rebellious, I am also not despondent any more, and I am definitely not resigned. I continue to grow unimpeded from day to day, even with the possibility of destruction staring me in the face. I shall no longer toy with the words that merely evoke misunderstandings: I have come to terms with life, nothing else can happen to me; after all, it is not about me personally, and the point is not whether I perish or someone else; rather, it is about the demise that is setting in. Sometimes I say this to others, although there's not much point and it doesn't clearly express what I think, but that doesn't really matter either. When I say 'come to terms with life', what I mean is: the possibility of death has become a definite part of my life and as a result my life has, so to speak, been broadened by my looking death and destruction, any sort of destruction, straight in the eye and accepting it as a part of life. So not, as it were, sacrificing a part of life to death by fearing it and not accepting it – the failure to accept death and the fear of death leave most people with only a pitiful and mutilated scrap of life, which can barely be called life at all. It sounds almost paradoxical: When you shut death out of your life, you don't have a complete life, and by including death in your life, you broaden and enrich your life.

This is my first confrontation with death. I have never known what to make of death before. I have such a virginal attitude towards it. I have never yet seen a dead person. Just imagine, in a world strewn with millions of corpses, in my twenty-eighth year of life, I have never once seen a dead person. I have sometimes wondered: What do I really think about death? But I have never delved deeply into the question with regard to myself; there was no time for that then. And now death has suddenly come for the first time, as large as life, and nonetheless like an old acquaintance who is part of one's life and must be accepted. Everything is so simple. You don't have to have any profound thoughts on the subject. Death has suddenly entered my life, large, simple, unmistakeable, and almost silent. It has a place in my life now, and I know now that it is a part of life. So there you are, now I can go to sleep if I like, it is 10 p.m. I didn't do much today,

I took care of some odds and ends in the heat of the city, in the course of which the blisters on my feet gave me a good deal of trouble. Then I was overcome with despondency and uncertainty. And then I went over to see him.[12] He had a headache and was upset about it, as usually everything functions superbly in his strong body. I lay in his arms briefly, and he was so gentle and lovely, almost nostalgic.

I feel a new period is beginning in our lives. An even more serious and intensive time, in which one increasingly focuses only on what is absolutely essential. We are shedding a lot of the trivial things, more with every passing day. 'Es geht auf unsere Vernichtung das ist ja klar, darüber brauchen wir uns nicht zu täuschen.'[13] Tomorrow night I will sleep in Dicky's[14] bed, and he will sleep on the floor below, and in the morning he'll wake me. We've still got that. And the support we will be able to give each other through these times will grow. And the question of whether or not to marry, how that is to be, will also be resolved. Everything is growing, still, even if everything seems pointless. And now I'm going to bed.

Somewhat later:
And although this day didn't bring me anything, not yet that fine and final confrontation with death and destruction, I still mustn't forget the kosher German soldier who was standing at the kiosk with a bag of carrots and cauliflower. First he pressed a note into the girl's hand in the tram,[15] and later there came a letter, which I have to reread, saying that she reminded him so much of the deceased daughter of a rabbi, a girl whom he had nursed as she lay dying, for days and nights on end. And this evening he is coming to visit. –

When Liesl told me all this, I knew at once that I had to pray for this German soldier too this evening. Of all those uniforms one has been given a face now. There will be other such faces, too, from which we shall be able to read something we understand. And he is suffering too. There are no borders between suffering human beings, people are suffering on both sides of every border, and we must pray for them all.

Good night.

I have grown older again since yesterday, all at once I have become many years older and more serious. My despondency has melted away and been replaced by a greater strength than before.

And one more thing: By getting to know our own strengths and shortcomings and accepting them, we become stronger.

It is all so simple and is becoming clearer and clearer to me, and I'd like to live for a long time in order to make it clear for others as well. And now, really, good night. –

12 Julius Spier.

13 German in the original: 'Things are moving towards our destruction; that is quite clear, there is no need for us to deceive ourselves about it.'

14 Dirkje (Dicky) de Jonge (b. 1920), teacher; at an Oxford Group (an interdenominational Christian organization) met Henriette Tideman, who introduced her to Julius Spier's circle of friends. De Jonge and Spier lived in the same building in Courbetstraat in Amsterdam.

15 Liesl Levie.

DOC. 55

On 4 July 1942 a Rotterdam resident calls on the Archbishop of Utrecht and the Jewish Council to act[1]

Handwritten letter from De Rotterdammer,[2] Rotterdam, to His Excellency, the Most Reverend Archbishop of Utrecht, Monsignor Jansen,[3] Utrecht, dated 4 July 1942

Dear Reverend Monsignor,

A man from Rotterdam hereby very politely requests a few moments of your precious time to read the enclosed letter, which is a copy of the letter I am sending, at the same time as this one, to the two gentlemen of the Jewish Council of Amsterdam, Prof. D. Cohen and Mr Asscher.

The terrible conditions in which the Jewish people live here and elsewhere in Europe have now been driven to the extreme limit of what is possible, and it is unlikely that any authority still wishes to negotiate.

As things look at the moment, with their livelihoods destroyed, robbed of any possessions, repudiated and outlawed through disenfranchisement, this is bound to lead to major calamities, which can perhaps be prevented through the intervention of very prominent individuals.

Therefore I fully trust that you will also be favourably disposed to taking some kind of action, in the interest of all, for which I hereby express my sincere thanks in advance.

Yours faithfully,
De Rotterdammer
One enclosure

Copy of the letter to Prof. Cohen and Mr Asscher
Rotterdam, 4 July 1942

Dear Prof. Cohen and Mr Asscher,

As a non-Jewish man from Rotterdam, I would like to take this opportunity to politely draw your urgent attention to the following.

Due to all the regulations now weighing so heavily upon the Jewish people, a great tension has arisen among them, which will probably lead to major calamities very soon.

Based on different pieces of information, I believe it is highly likely that one or more overstressed individuals will very soon commit acts of desperation, the consequences of which – in the form of action that might be taken by the authorities as a result– are impossible to predict.

1 Het Utrechts Archief, 449/76. This document has been translated from Dutch.

2 The pseudonym 'De Rotterdammer' (in Dutch) was used during the Second World War by Hendrik Johannes van den Broek (1901–1959), a Dutch journalist who managed Radio Oranje for the Dutch government in exile in London. The name of the Rotterdam resident who employed van den Broek's pseudonym for this letter could not be found.

3 Johannes Gerardus Jansen (1868–1936), priest and theologian; archbishop of Utrecht, 1930–1936. He was the wrong addressee. In 1942, Johannes (Jan) de Jong was the archbishop of Utrecht.

This must be and possibly still can be prevented by talking to the authorities that issue all of these regulations.

If the current circumstances mean that you are both unable to do so, then have the courage to resign from your posts, as currently you and the weekly magazine[4] are the sole instruments they [the Germans] have commissioned to help them destroy the Jewish people in the Netherlands as quickly as possible.

If, however, you are still able to make an attempt to save the situation, do so immediately, as the circumstances are much worse and much more precarious than you realize.

Should the authorities no longer wish to speak to Jews, then in God's name non-Jews will have to try to achieve something, and the only possible way forward will be to direct your request in this respect to some prominent non-Jewish clergymen.

They can go and speak with a clear conscience and as representatives on behalf of humanity to the authorities mentioned, as these are still human beings after all, even though the laws they issue are harsh and cause distress.

This is the only possible route that can still be taken before it is too late.

Fully trusting you will do all you possibly can, I remain most sincerely yours, and am much obliged to you.[5]

DOC. 56
On 12 July 1942 Annie Bierman-Trijbetz bids farewell to a friend before being deported, ostensibly for labour deployment in Germany[1]

Handwritten postcard from Annie Bierman-Trijbetz,[2] Amsterdam, not addressed,[3] dated 12 July 1942

Dear Riek,

Although we have not been in touch for nearly a year, I decided to write to you to say goodbye. After everything we have already been through this year, which has been a lot more and a lot worse than you have been able to read in the paper, now we all have to go to Germany on the night of this Wednesday to Thursday.[4] There is a small chance that we will be able to leave the children behind with their grandparents, where they will

4 Presumably a reference to *Het Joodsche Weekblad*.
5 No reply to this letter could be found.

1 Herinneringscentrum Kamp Westerbork, 2143. Excerpts published in facsimile in Guido Abuys, *Het eerste transport 15 juli 1942 vanuit kamp Westerbork* (Hooghalen: Herinneringscentrum Kamp Westerbork, 2012), p. 5. This document has been translated from Dutch.
2 Marianne (Annie) Bierman-Trijbetz (1909–1942), housewife; married Herman Eduard Bierman in 1935; on 15 July 1942 deported together with her family from Westerbork to Auschwitz; murdered there on arrival, along with her children Francisca (b. 1935) and Robert (b. 1938); her husband perished a few days later.
3 The postcard was donated to the archives by the recipient's daughter: from this it was clear who the recipient was, namely Henderika (Riek) Zeijlemaker-Bosma (1907–1987), housekeeper; she was employed by the Bierman family until her marriage and afterwards remained on friendly terms with them.
4 On the night of 15 July 1942, the first transport to Auschwitz departed from Westerbork camp. The family had previously received a summons instructing them to prepare for deportation for the purpose of labour deployment in Germany.

be better off than over there with us. Three large transports will leave three nights in a row,[5] and we are not allowed to take anything other than some food and some clothes. We have lost everything else … I now often think of you and your husband[6] – you have been apart for so long. I find some consolation in the thought that at least we were together in our own house for all those years. Riek, in spite of everything, we keep our spirits up. Say hello to Trijn[7] from me, and I wish you and Lotteke[8] all the best.

Yours,

DOC. 57

On 13 July 1942 Pastor Willem ten Boom suggests to the secretary of the General Synod that people pray for a better relationship between Christians and Jews[1]

Letter from Dr W. ten Boom,[2] pastor, Hilversum, 15 Surinamlaan, to H. J. Dijckmeester,[3] secretary of the Synod, The Hague, 100 Javastraat, dated 13 July 1942 (typescript)[4]

Dear Colleague,

My opinion with respect to the protest regarding the persecution of the Jews in this country is as follows:

The time for protests in the ordinary sense is over. While initially the protests may have aroused some surprise and a certain degree of consternation in the occupying power, such an impact can no longer be expected. These protests are viewed as a constant, natural reaction by the Jewish victims, who will scream while they are beaten and will have others screaming on their behalf when they are no longer allowed to do so themselves. Our cry of indignation simply shows them [the Germans] how deeply Jewish influence has pervaded our people, and merely strengthens them in their desire to free the world from this Jewish plague permanently.

5 The second transport from Westerbork left on 16 July 1942, and the third just a few days later, on 21 July 1942.
6 Cornelis Zeijlemaker (1904–1983) was aboard a cargo vessel sunk by the Germans in 1939; he survived and was sent to a prisoner-of-war camp in Germany; upon the intercession of the Red Cross, he returned to the Netherlands in 1941 and lived there in hiding until the end of the occupation period.
7 Trijn Bosma (1905–1989), Riek Zeijlemaker-Bosma's sister.
8 Lolkje (Lottie) Anna Reurekas-Zeijlemaker (b. 1938), Riek Zeijlemaker-Bosma's daughter.

1 Het Utrechts Archief, 1423/2154. Published in German in Martin Bachmann, *Geliebtes Volk Israel – fremde Juden: Die Nederlandse Hervormde Kerk und die 'Judenfrage', 1933–1945* (Münster: Lit, 1997), pp. 359–360. This document has been translated from the original Dutch.
2 Dr Willem ten Boom (1886–1946), pastor; served as a pastor in the Dutch Reformed Church from 1913; mission pastor of the Dutch Association for Israel (NVVI), 1925–1942; awarded a doctorate in Leipzig, 1928; secretary of the Council for Church and Israel, 1942–1946; in 1944 arrested at his parents' home during a Bible study meeting for persons in hiding and imprisoned for two months.
3 Herman Jacob Dijckmeester (1895–1958), pastor; served as a pastor in the Dutch Reformed Church, 1921–1955; secretary of the General Synod, May–July 1942; responsible for negotiating with the German occupiers.
4 The original contains handwritten insertions and annotations.

And that is not all. All the protests held thus far were based on humanitarian resistance. I do not mean anything bad by this, but rather, together with countless other members of the Church, I am very grateful that the Synod has given such forceful and timely witness.[5] After all, the intention of large-scale extermination, which has been an underlying factor in modern racial antisemitism from the very start and has also been candidly expressed since the inception of this Movement, awakens all kinds of fundamental human emotions among friend and foe, which can only be pleasing to God the Creator, and which were already communicated, strengthened, and awakened in the earliest revelation to Israel (think, for example, of the book of Deuteronomy).[6] This is and remains the virtue of humanism, which appeals to the deepest feelings of the Church. But the same humanism has proved to be totally powerless against the fundamental outburst of demonic influences that occurred during the World War with which the twentieth century began,[7] and which I consider God's judgement upon the present generation, including our own Church. This judgement, which undermines all the humanitarian considerations of previous generations, and like all of God's judgements points directly to Christ, intends to show Jews what they are lacking and Christians their most important and most profound possession. If, therefore, our humanitarian resistance fails, as in my opinion is already the case, and by divine providence the Germans draw our attention to the weakness of nineteenth-century humanism, then resorting to renewed protests will yield no results. However, it will initiate a confrontation with the issue, in a way that will bring us all to our knees. Even though there is a clear degree of guilt (an element which humanism has grievously neglected), which consists in the fact that we have increasingly deviated from God and His Word: the deepest truth imposed on us by the current situation is that 'all have sinned, and come short of the glory of God'.[8] That is why I can so completely concur with the desire emerging within the circles of our Church, namely that the Synod should call upon us to join in prayer. But not only for the poor persecuted people, but also for the enemies who have put themselves forward as defenders of the destructive powers, and for us who are doomed to witness God's judgements with our hands tied. Prayer is our last and most important weapon, which counters all hostile powers, including those in our own heart, but also offers a way out to all who have a part to play on the sombre stage of the present time, including our worst enemies. The call for prayer, which many currently expect from the Synod, should therefore be considered from a collective point of view, encompassing Jews as well as Christians, and Dutch as well as German people. I envisage this as follows:

The terrible distress affecting our Jewish compatriots because of the latest measures taken by the occupying power, which could not be averted by our protests and have instead appeared to worsen as a result, oblige us to call the community to a special day

5 For example, the Protestant churches protested as early as Oct. 1940 against the dismissal of Jewish civil servants: see PMJ 5/43.

6 The Fifth Book of Moses, also known as Deuteronomy, in which Moses addresses the Israelites three times and strengthens them in their worship of God.

7 The First World War, 1914–1918.

8 Romans 3:23 (KJV).

of penance and prayer on Sunday …,[9] while requesting the pastors to make a good relationship between Jews and Christians in the current environment a special topic of intercession, so that Christian peoples bear witness to Christ through their deeds, and the Jews are converted to the living Christ, and God achieves his goal for both groups, 'that they all may be one'.[10]

You will know best, dear Colleague Rev. Dijkmeester, whether and to what extent you deem my letter, which I am sending to you entirely on my own responsibility, suitable for further circulation. I will leave that to your discretion. I think that it concurs with the few words you said at the latest meeting of the Church Forum,[11] which I listened to and completely agreed with.

Fraternally yours,

Your colleague,

DOC. 58

Het Joodsche Weekblad, 14 July 1942: supplementary edition on the arrest of 700 Jews as hostages[1]

Supplementary edition

Amsterdam, 14 July 1942
The Sicherheitspolizei[2] has informed us of the following:

Approximately 700 Jews have been arrested today in Amsterdam.[3] If the 4,000 allocated Jews do not depart for the work camps in Germany this week, then the 700 detainees will be taken to a concentration camp in Germany.

The chairmen of the Jewish Council of Amsterdam,
A. Asscher
Prof. D. Cohen

9 The General Synod did indeed ask all pastors to pray for the Jews in their services on 26 July 1942: see Doc. 65. However, this does not appear to have been a direct reaction to ten Boom's letter.

10 John 17:21 (KJV).

11 Correctly: Forum for Inter-Church Dialogue (Interkerkelijk Overleg, IKO). In June 1940, seven Protestant churches in the Netherlands founded the Convention of Churches (Convent van Kerken) to coordinate joint action. In 1941, when the Catholic Church wanted to join this body, the name was changed to Forum for Inter-Church Dialogue. The Council of Churches in the Netherlands, established in 1968, emerged from that organization.

1 *Het Joodsche Weekblad*, 10 July 1942 (incorrect date in the original). Published in facsimile in Jacques Presser, *Ondergang: De vervolging en verdelging van het Nederlandse jodendom 1940–1945* ('s-Gravenhage: Nijhoff, 1965), vol. 1, after p. 256. This document has been translated from Dutch.

2 German in the original: 'Security Police'.

3 In fact, approximately 540 persons were arrested and held at the SD headquarters in Euterpestraat. Most of them were released two days later.

DOC. 59

On 15 July 1942 Betsy de Paauw-Bachrach describes the departure of her brother, who has been called up for labour deployment in Germany[1]

Handwritten diary of Betsy de Paauw-Bachrach,[2] entry for 15 July 1942[3]

15 July 1942

The calls for 'voluntary' Auswanderung[4] are arriving in their hundreds; no, in their thousands. Our Demy[5] got one too, half an hour after he had been turned down *for the camps*[6] for the second time. He was *such a happy* fellow, and we were all so *relieved*. And then, immediately after the joy, *the* registered document … And it's all so much like Erlkönig: 'Und bist du nicht willig, so brauch' ich Gewalt.'[7] Violence – that doesn't suit the incredibly *dear soul* that is Demy. The poor, poor fellow! Thursday night last week: turned down for the camps. Friday night: off to Germany (Poland …?), off, within a few days … And those few days he had to spend largely with the German authorities or the Jewish Council. Walking, trudging along from one end of the city to the other, for Jews are no longer allowed to use the trams. Jews can no longer have a bicycle and may no longer use any means of transport.[8] Jews have to make sure that, one way or another, they get themselves to the central station by half past one in the morning, from whichever corner of the city, with a suitcase with *work* clothes, *work* shoes, medication, and provisions for *three* days. They also have to carry their two woollen blankets and two sets of bedclothes around their necks. And now he's gone. Forever?? Last night we said goodbye to him. And there he was: his bread bag hanging from his shoulder, his flask dangling beside it … A big, sturdy fellow, with the nature of an unspoilt child: the boys'[9] and Let's[10] good old uncle Demy, now with *the face of a dying man*. And then suddenly that question to us all: 'I will, won't I? I will come back! Otherwise you would surely have told me *that I shouldn't go*??'[11]

A little later, after we have all embraced him again and again, Louis brings his heavy suitcase down. In the dark landing he searches for our hands again, one by one, and then (oh, how will I ever forget that call), like a dying scream, we heard his last

1 JHM, Doc. 00 003 241. This document has been translated from Dutch.

2 Betsy de Paauw-Bachrach (1897–1943); married to the diamond cutter Philip de Paauw from 1920; deported to Westerbork on 20 June 1943, and then to Sobibor with her husband one month later; murdered there on arrival.

3 The original contains handwritten marking.

4 German in the original: 'emigration'.

5 David (Demy) Bachrach (1908–1942), office worker; deported to Westerbork on 12 July 1942, and from there three days later to Auschwitz, where he perished in August or Sept. 1942.

6 The labour camps for Jews in the Netherlands.

7 Quotation in German in the original: 'If you won't come willingly, I shall use force.' 'Erlkönig' (1782) is a poem by Johann Wolfgang von Goethe.

8 On the ban on the use of public transport, see Doc. 53. In accordance with a directive issued by Commissioner General for Security Hanns Albin Rauter on 20 June 1942, all Jews had to hand in their bicycles: see *Deutsche Zeitung in den Niederlanden*, 23 June 1942.

9 His nephews Israel de Paauw (b. 1924) and Robert Walter Pinto (1926–1943).

10 Alette Irene Pinto (1929–1943), arrested with her family in May 1943; deported on 1 June 1943 to Sobibor, where she was murdered.

11 From this point the original document changes to the present tense.

'byeeee'[12] from across the silent square. We shout 'bye' back to him, but he probably won't have heard that, the deaf man. Now we can't see each other any more either. It's a really dark night … We know 'our Demy' is over there … We don't know where he's going. Nor do we know if he'll ever come back …

When we are back upstairs, Grandpa[13] suddenly starts sobbing uncontrollably and laments: 'What are they going to do with him? Will I ever see him again?'

Grandpa is 72 years old. His heart is weak, and his only son has to go to Germany (Poland?). It's called: 'voluntary' Auswanderung.

It's a good thing that Grandma[14] is no longer alive!

DOC. 60

On 17 July 1942 the representative of the Reich Foreign Office in The Hague reports to his office in Berlin on the smooth progress of the first deportations of Jews[1]

Letter from the Reich Commissioner for the Occupied Dutch Territories, representative of the Reich Foreign Office (D Pol 3 No. 8/No. 998), signed Bene,[2] The Hague, to the Reich Foreign Office, Berlin (received on 29 July 1942), dated 17 July 1942[3]

With reference to the decree of 30 June 1942[4] – D III 516 g, and in connection with the report of 3 July 1942[5] – D Pol 3 Nr. 8/928
2 copies
Subject: deportation of foreign Jews
In connection with telex no. 250, dispatched today, regarding the revocation of the citizenship of all Dutch Jews,[6] it should be added that the first two trains have set off without difficulties of any kind, and accordingly the Higher SS and Police Leader[7] intends to

12 In the original: 'dââág'; correctly: 'dag'.
13 Simon Bacharach (1870–1943), mohel and teacher; worked in Oude Pekela and Nijkerk from 1899; deported to Westerbork on 6 May 1943, and then on 11 May 1943 to Sobibor, where he was murdered three days later. All of Simon Bacharach's children had changed their surnames to Bachrach before the war; this explains the different spellings.
14 Jetjen Bacharach-Frank (1868–1940); married to Simon Bacharach from 1894; mother of Betsy de Paauw-Bachrach.

1 PA AA, R 100 869. This document has been translated from German.
2 Otto Bene (1884–1973), businessman and diplomat; worked in the cloth trade; soldier and officer in the First World War; in the import/export trade in the interwar period; joined the NSDAP in 1931; held various positions within the NSDAP from 1932, including head of the regional NSDAP branch for Great Britain and Ireland, 1934–1937; in the German diplomatic service from 1936; posted in Italy from 1937; representative of the Reich Foreign Office to the Reich Commissariat of the Netherlands, 1940–1945; imprisoned in the Netherlands, 1945–1948, then worked for the Asbach Uralt brandy company in Germany.
3 The original contains handwritten notes and underlining.
4 See Doc. 53.
5 In this report, Bene indicated to the Reich Foreign Office how many foreign Jews were still in the Netherlands: NIOD, 207/702.
6 In this telex, Bene explained the Reich Security Main Office's proposal to revoke the Dutch citizenship of all Jews in order to prevent intervention by Sweden, as a protecting power, on behalf of the deportees: see *ADAP*, series E, vol. 3, pp. 185–186.

optimize arrangements so that as many as 4,000 Jews are transported each week. In the meantime, the able-bodied stateless and Dutch Jews are being conscripted for labour and transported to Westerborg[8] camp, so that 3,000 Jews are available there at all times. Jews living in mixed marriages and so-called Christian Jews are, for now, exempt from deportation. The number of so-called Christian Jews, as of 1 January 1941, probably represents around 1 per cent (approximately 1,500) of the total number of Jews in the Netherlands.[9] The representatives of the churches have approached the Reich Commissioner regarding these Jews.[10] The Reich Commissioner has intimated that, for now, no action against these Jews will be taken, provided the Church raises no difficulties of any sort in opposition to the deportation of the rest of the Jews. A binding promise has not been made, of course, and at some time the Christian Jews too will be deported, perhaps at some point by ship, to some country that wants to have the Jews. But this question is, as I said, not pressing at present. Rather, the attitude of the Reich Commissioner is to be taken as a tactical gambit.

DOC. 61

On 17 July 1942 the property management company De Administratie asks the Household Effects Registration Office when the release of an apartment belonging to deported Jews is to be expected[1]

Letter from De Administratie N.V., a property management company, signature illegible, Amsterdam, 393 Kerkstraat, to the Household Effects Registration Office of the Central Office for Jewish Emigration,[2] Amsterdam, 187 Apollolaan, dated 17 July 1942

We hereby inform you that, last Monday, the tenants of our apartments at 107 Nieuwe Achtergracht, 3e, and 105 Nieuwe Achtergracht, 1e, the Barzilay family[3] and the Bril family,[4] respectively, were instructed to go to Germany. The apartments have been sealed by the police, and they [the police] have taken the keys with them.

7 Hanns Albin Rauter.
8 Correctly: Westerbork.
9 In the Regulation on the Compulsory Registration of Persons who are Fully or Partially of Jewish Blood, all Jews were ordered to register: see PMJ 5/54.
10 On 11 July 1942, the Dutch churches sent a telegram to Reich Commissioner Seyss-Inquart protesting against the beginning of the deportations and advocating the protection of baptized Jews in particular. For the text of the telegram, see Doc. 65.

1 NIOD, 077/1490. This document has been translated from German.
2 The Central Office for Jewish Emigration, established in the early summer of 1941, was managed by Willy Lages and his deputy, Ferdinand aus der Fünten. In Feb. 1942 aus der Fünten took over the management. Until the autumn of 1943 the office was responsible for making preparations for the deportations and for supervising Jewish life in the Netherlands. The Household Effects Registration Office was responsible for making inventories of the residences of Jews who had been deported.
3 Correctly: Maurits Barzilaij (1904–1942), diamond cutter and rag picker, and his wife, Elisabeth, née de Rooij (1906–1942); on 15 July 1942 deported together with their brother/brother-in-law Samuel Barzilaij to Auschwitz, where they perished in Aug./Sept. 1942.
4 Jacob Bril (1903–1942), fruiterer, his wife Margaretha, née van Kleef (1914–1942), and their son Abraham (1940–1942) were deported on 21 July 1942 to Auschwitz, where they were murdered.

Because this is a special Jewish quarter, you will understand that it is not easy for us to find new tenants for the apartments, and we therefore wish to learn from you, at your earliest convenience, when we can expect to have the keys.

In addition, we would be pleased to learn how the rent will be paid in the meantime.

We await your reply with interest,[5] and we remain

Respectfully

DOC. 62

Storm SS, 17 July 1942: an inflammatory article demands further anti-Jewish measures and criticizes the Church's stance[1]

Volksgenoot[2] and Jew

A series of further measures to push back the Jews have been taken recently, partially driving them out of public life. We have since received many letters and complaints from comrades drawing our attention to the fact that all of these measures are only a stopgap and are therefore abused and evaded in all sorts of ways. And that is just how it is.

No one can be under the illusion that we can eliminate the Jews from our lives by means of a complex, laborious system of statutory rules, with all the corresponding, unavoidable exceptional clauses, transition periods, etc. And even if those stipulations were as simple as the 2 times table and as clear as crystal, our volksgenooten would still not benefit from them as long as we continue to have all kinds of institutions and civil servants that help evade these stipulations and protect the offenders.

The solution to the Jewish question is thus essentially still very much in a preparatory phase. Even the yellow star,[3] seemingly worn by many, is not being worn by many Jews, even when they fully and undoubtedly fall under the provisions.

As a result, Jews continue to travel around to their 'heart's content'.

And now that the Jews are no longer admitted to boarding houses,[4] their Aryan servants move from their own homes to boarding houses, while the Jews go and spend their holidays in the houses that have been vacated in this way. It would be well worth initiating a thorough investigation into the residents of a number of properties in Velp[5] and the surrounding area, where this system is being successfully put into practice. This

5 Handwritten note in Dutch at the bottom of the page: 'informed on 21 July by telephone, empty out in around three weeks'.

1 *Storm SS: Blad der Nederlandsche SS*, vol. 2, no. 5, 17 July 1942, p. 1. This document has been translated from Dutch. *Storm SS* was published weekly from April 1941 to May 1945. It was the newspaper of the Dutch SS and was published by the Amsterdam publishing house Storm, which was headed by Reinier van Houten (1908–1983). In summer 1942 it had a circulation of approximately 13,000 copies.

2 Dutch form of the Nazi term *Volksgenosse.*

3 See PMJ 5/130.

4 From the end of June 1942, Jews had to spend the night at the address where they were registered: see Doc. 53.

5 City near Arnhem (province of Gelderland).

would probably bring many things to light there – and also in many other nice, peaceful locations in our country – that smack of the Talmud and the Torah!

It also turns out that all sorts of men of Palestinian blood are still walking around freely, those who were already behaving particularly conspicuously during the system era.[6] And these gentlemen apparently still have so many obscure connections with mysterious protectors that the ordinary National Socialist with no special connections remains powerless against these criminals, who move among our people freely and unashamedly, and without a star. It is clear that all that has been achieved so far in terms of anti-Jewish legislation is still highly insufficient. And this is even more the case in broad strata of society in which our people's pride and self-respect are still so diseased and weak that thousands allow themselves to be willingly used by the shameless Jewish rabble for all kinds of slave jobs. The Jewish black marketeers have acquired Aryan servants, who now go to the countryside to sell their wares for them and come politely to settle up at the end of the day. Dutch gentlemen and ladies believe it is not beneath them – now that Jews are no longer allowed to go shopping at all hours[7] – to act as servants and maids to the Jews. They do so to the great amusement of the Jewish rabble, who, as soon as their obedient helpers are out of sight, grin with malicious delight over so much blind stupidity.

All this would be questionable enough in itself, but what is even more significant is that these volksvreemde[8] are represented day after day by all sorts of equally volksfreemde political-religious analyses as the oppressed innocent, while blood or race is dismissed as an incidental circumstance.

Thus the wicked Jew is praised again and again as a brother, an equal, and a full volksgenoot by all kinds of people who not only should have known better, but indeed in the past took no interest in him at all.

This particularly applies to political Christianity, which should therefore also be rendered harmless as soon as possible. Obviously, this would not destroy any of the Germanic religious values in the slightest; the opposite would be the case.

But the Church has become a political hotbed, emitting lies and sabotage. Crucifix-huggers and sermonizers[9] compete in making veiled insinuations, demonstrating opposition, and making trouble at the edge of the concentration camp. The fact that one of them occasionally crosses the line and disappears is only the logical consequence of these subversive activities.

It seems likely that it will take quite some effort to teach these gentlemen that they have no business here on earth with their cunning theories, and that they should only focus on the 'hereafter', about which they claim to know all the details.

6 'Systeemtijd', the Dutch translation of the German 'Systemzeit', a term used by the National Socialists to refer disparagingly to the period of the Weimar Republic; here apparently applied to the pre-war Netherlands.

7 Jews were permitted to make purchases only in Jewish shops, and only from 3 p.m. to 5 p.m.: see Doc. 53.

8 Dutch form of the Nazi term *volksfremd*: 'racially alien'.

9 The original Dutch uses the words 'kruismol' (lit. 'cross mole') and 'preektiiger' (lit. 'preach tiger'), both derogatory terms used by the Dutch National Socialists to describe clergymen.

We are happy to acknowledge that we have no theory or doctrine about this untrodden ground, but that even without this we are able to believe in the primeval forces that are beyond our understanding and that, as superhuman powers, decide our fate.

But there is another area, which is our area, which is where crucifix-huggers and sermonizers have no place – that is the earth, with everything that grows on it and has evolved from it.

Our people are among the organisms that have evolved from it – and Jewry does not belong to our people.

Crucifix-huggers and sermonizers apparently cannot understand these simple truths. Earlier this week, when we were having a rest on a bench in the public garden in the shadow of the famous St John's Cathedral in 's-Hertogenbosch, we noticed that the 'No Jews Allowed' signs prescribed for public parks and gardens are absent in this cathedral city.[10] Consequently there were Jews everywhere, and they had taken up all the best places.

However, the situation became comical when a somewhat larger-than-life-sized priest came solemnly striding along, walking past the benches taken up by Jews with much bowing and scraping and ostentatious nodding, thus personifying the highest level of affection for the Jews. Well, the result was certainly spectacular, for as soon as the tall friar was out of sight, the Jewish crowd came up with a volley of ghetto jokes, which would have been enough to keep twelve upright penitents in the confessional box for a long time.

Even political Christianity is a waste of time here – as it always has been – and the Roman Catholic Church would do best to return to its original point of view and to regard the Jews as its mortal enemies.

'But whomever the Lord wishes to destroy, He strikes with blindness' is a charming Jewish piece of wisdom,[11] and it looks like it will apply here too. And thus we see today's Christianity busying itself with setting up a brotherhood between the Jews and the Dutch, making the Jews – quite rightly – smile scornfully.

In practice, this means that the Church is welcoming back the alien blood that we have been trying to expel. This means that racial defilement is being facilitated under the guise of religion. This means propaganda about racial pollution, tolerance of the crime against the people that is mixed marriage, the begetting of bastards, and collaboration with the mortal enemies of the Germanic world.

This means that our people's physical and mental strength is harmed – at its very root, at the source of its blood.

In political terms, such politicized, alien Christianity is the main poisoner of our time, and the Church is a poison kitchen that is frequently abused by crucifix-huggers and sermonizers.

Considered against this background, it is clear that all laws and stipulations – even if their legal formulation and effectiveness were perfect – are and remain only a stopgap. Curtailing the Jews' freedom and banning them from public life is amateurish, shoddy work compared with the ever-present threat of the continuing existence of the Jews, who

10 From 15 Sept. 1941 Jews were no longer allowed to enter public parks: see PMJ 5/93.

11 A vague allusion to a quotation from *Antigone* by the Greek dramatist Sophocles (497/496–406 BCE).

are protected in a thousand ways. Here we are not even referring to the blatant madness of all kinds of regulations, which still avoid racial questions, and which still dredge up all kinds of matters of faith in order to determine who is a Jew and who is not.

No matter how often a Jew has joined or left some church or other – or whether he bathes in baptismal water on a daily basis – he will remain who he is: a born and bred Jew. Not even all the water in the River Jordan can wash that away.

When we look at the new anti-Jewish regulations in France, it seems that even there people are finally beginning to understand this.[12] But all of this is and remains shoddy work, as there is only one real solution: the complete and radical expulsion of all Jews from the Germanic world, to a place where they are still under Germanic control. An example of such a place is the East. It is located far enough away to keep the Jews out of European life. There is enough space to hold them, and there is plenty of work that needs to be done and is within their limited capabilities. It is also a place that meets all the practical requirements – and that is what is most important of all!

Therefore the situation is such that, from now on, regular transports of Jews to the East will take place, and at such a rate that by 1 June 1943 not a single Jew will be left in the Netherlands.

Jewry will then come to understand that the National Socialist vanguard cannot be conned. No rushed or bogus weddings, no hasty baptism ceremonies or church notices will avail, and Jewish servants and slaves will find out that their betrayal of our people and racial defilement is an evil that punishes itself!

DOC. 63

On 23 July 1942 a Dutch policeman tells the mayor of Beilen what took place when a train carrying Amsterdam Jews arrived in Westerbork[1]

Report, unsigned (Kornelis Jan Meijer),[2] to the mayor of Beilen,[3] dated 23 July 1942

Re: supervision of the deportation of Amsterdam Jews
The undersigned, Kornelis Jan Meijer, rural police officer in the district of Beilen, also unsalaried officer with the national police, stationed in Beilen, has the privilege to report to you, Your Worship, the following:

12 On the basis of the Ninth Regulation on Measures Against Jews (8 July 1942), Jews were largely excluded from public life: see Doc. 242.

1 Bestuursarchief Gemeente Beilen, 1146. Published in G. J. Dijkstra (ed.), *Gemeente Beilen 1940 bis 1945*, vol. 3 (Beilen: publisher unspecified, 2001), pp. 49–51. This document has been translated from Dutch.

2 Kornelis Jan Meijer (1904–1990), policeman; worked for the police from 1932; rural police officer in Beilen, 1940–1945; in Muntendam and Scheemda after 1945.

3 Hendrik Jacob Wytema (1906–1974), lawyer; mayor of Beilen, 1936–1942 and 1945–1948; in Oct. 1942 refused to continue participating in the deportation of Jews and was imprisoned for eight weeks; mayor of Alkmaar, 1948–1970. The small town of Beilen was very close to Westerbork transit camp.

On the morning of Thursday, 16 July 1942, at approximately 6 o'clock, I was in Hooghalen in this district, on duty and in uniform, to supervise the unloading of approximately 800 Amsterdam Jews and approximately 260 detained Jews from Amersfoort concentration camp,[4] who had arrived there at that time by train.

After these people had been unloaded, all of them apart from the 260 detainees had to go to the camp (Lager) in Oosthalen, Westerbork district, for registration.

The 800 Amsterdam Jews consisted of men, women, and children, including some very small babies who still had to be carried. The detainees were all male.

While the unloading was taking place, I was at one of the front carriages of this train. The persons in this carriage reported that during the transport one man had died from injuries suffered during loading,[5] and that another man was severely injured, so much so that he was unable to get off the train without help. One of the German officers present then gave the order to carry this man from the carriage and to put him on the grass beside the railway line. This was done by a number of the Jews from the train. A third injured person got out of the same carriage unassisted. Altogether there were six injured and sick people on this transport, in addition to the deceased man. On the orders of the same German officer, the corpse was transported to Assen to be handed over to the Dutch police. The injured and the sick were then transported by car from the camp[6] to the camp, and I have not seen them again. I therefore suspect that these people have not been transported onward by train from the camp. After these people were registered, all of them, including the detainees, were loaded onto another train consisting of two passenger carriages and freight wagons, approximately fifteen wagons in total.[7]

During the loading process, these people had to form a queue beside the wagons. As this was not done quickly enough, the officers shouted that they should hurry. I do not know the extent to which this had any effect, but several people were kicked to their places and loaded onto the train. An average of about seventy people had to sit in [each of] these wagons, none of which had a toilet. The accompanying guards from the German Wehrmacht took seats in the passenger carriages. I heard from several people in the wagons that they had been told they were on their way to Upper Silesia, on the Polish border, which meant they would be on the train for approximately three days.

I do not know whether there is anything to drink on the train for these people, but I do know that 1,000 loaves of bread were loaded at the yard, as well as various kinds of vegetables.

Several of the persons on board told me that the injuries had not been caused by the German Wehrmacht men, but by men from the Dutch SS who had kicked and hit them when they were loaded onto the train.

This report was prepared, concluded, and signed in Beilen on 23 July 1942.

4 Amersfoort camp was used as a police transit camp from 1941 to 1945. In addition to persons who refused to perform forced labour, Dutch communists and Jews were held there, usually for a short time, before they were sent to Westerbork transit camp (if Jewish) or to Germany for forced labour (if non-Jewish).

5 Thought to be Simon Mozes (1877–1942).

6 Presumably this should have been 'train station'.

7 This was the second deportation train to leave Westerbork. It carried 895 Jews to Auschwitz.

DOC. 64

On 25 July 1942 Dutch Prime Minister Pieter Sjoerds Gerbrandy, speaking from exile in London, condemns the start of the deportations in a radio address[1]

Text of the address by Prime Minister Gerbrandy[2] on Radio Oranje,[3] dated 25 July 1942

Fellow countrymen,

We have received notice of new measures the enemy has devised against Dutch Jews.

The implementation of these measures, which will have far-reaching consequences, has apparently already begun. They amount to nothing less than the removal of tens of thousands of full Dutch citizens to Germany, and probably further to the East from there. This marks the end of a centuries-old Dutch tradition.

This is also in breach of the Dutch constitution, according to which all citizens are equal before the law. Since time immemorial the Jews, as well as other persecuted people, have found a home in the country of our forefathers, where they lived on an equal footing with other Dutch people and, fully part of the nation and fully participating in society, were able to contribute to the greatness of our country in every respect.

At this hour, so tragic for our people, several names occur to me, such as that of our famous legal scholar Asser, the artist Jozef Israëls, men of letters like Querido and Heyermans, and in particular the poet da Costa,[4] whose prose and poetry are, in my personal opinion, the noblest expression of both the Jewish mind and that of the Dutch people.

No matter how appalling these reports are, they did not come as a complete surprise, either to you or to us. When we consider the various regulations that the enemy has issued against Dutch Jews over the past few months, they all point in the same direction. Forcing Dutch Jews to move to Amsterdam, visibly identifying the persecuted by means of the un-Dutch Jewish star, the ban on entering the houses of non-Jewish fellow citizens, the obligation to be at home at certain hours, the prohibition on travel, the prohibition on owning a bicycle,[5] … all of these measures are clearly intended to separate off a group of 180,000 Dutch citizens[6] in order to carry out in one stroke the act of violence against defenceless people which was clearly announced a number of weeks ago.

1 NIOD, Radio Oranje, 25 July 1942. Published in Pieter Sjoerds Gerbrandy, *Landgenoten! De radiotoespraken van Minister-president Prof. Mr. P. S. Gerbrandy in de jaren 1940–1945 gehouden voor Radio Oranje en De Brandaris* (Franeker: Wever, 1985), pp. 69–70. This document has been translated from Dutch.

2 Pieter Sjoerds Gerbrandy (1885–1961), lawyer; practised law in Leiden and Sneek from 1911; embarked on a political career from 1919; member of the Anti-Revolutionary Party (ARP); professor in Amsterdam, 1930–1939; minister of justice, 1939; prime minister of the Dutch government in exile, 1940 to June 1945; thereafter served as a member of the Dutch parliament and practised law until 1959.

3 During the German occupation, Radio Oranje was the radio station of the Dutch government in exile in London. Fifteen-minute (later thirty-minute) broadcasts in Dutch were transmitted via British Broadcasting Corporation (BBC) radio frequencies. The first broadcast was on 28 July 1940. Queen Wilhelmina also used Radio Oranje to address her subjects.

4 These figures, who were well known in the Netherlands, were Tobias Michel Karel Asser (1838–1913), who was awarded the Nobel Peace Prize in 1911; Jozef Israëls (1824–1911); Israël Querido (1872–1932); (correctly) Herman Heijermans (1864–1924); and Isaäc da Costa (1798–1860).

5 All of these directives were issued between 27 April (introduction of the yellow star) and 30 June 1942 (curtailment of the freedom of movement of Dutch Jews).

6 The registration of the Jews by order of the German occupiers revealed that there were 160,000 Jews in the Netherlands in 1941: see PMJ 5/90.

We know that it is not only us, but you too, fellow countrymen in the occupied territory, who have clearly recognized the correlation between all of these measures. Since we know you are still the same as you used to be, we trust that you have tried to think of means of assisting these innocent people as much as possible at this time of their deepest need. The enemy is listening in. Therefore I won't refer to such means in any more detail. All I say to you is this: follow your conscience, and act in Christian mercy. Your government is not yet able to alleviate the sorrow which has been inflicted upon thousands of Dutch people, non-Jews and Jews alike, and is threatening thousands of others.

We know that the enemy and its worthless servants are planning to inflict a similarly horrible fate on three million Dutch people.[7] Those currently affected may derive some strength in their distress from what one Dutch Jew said to me this afternoon: 'The Dutch Jews are suffering for a country that is absolutely worth suffering for.'

Fellow countrymen – at this time it befits us to pray to Our Father in heaven for all those who suffer violence. We know that these horrors provoke infinite sadness among you all. They will further strengthen the resolve of those who are left behind. Have faith and persevere. The weapons of tyranny will not subdue those of the mind forever.

Farewell, my poor sheep,
who are in deep despair.
Your shepherd will not sleep.[8]

DOC. 65

On 26 July 1942, in a statement to be read from the pulpit, the General Synod of the Dutch Reformed Church protests against the deportation of the Jews[1]

Statement by the General Synod of the Dutch Reformed Church, The Hague, sent out to all pastors in the Dutch Reformed Church, dated 26 July 1942[2]

(A)

We are living in a period of great need, both spiritually and physically. Two different needs in particular have recently come to the fore: the need of the Jews and the need of those who are put to work abroad.[3]

7 The Dutch government in exile suspected that the Dutch East Company (NOC), a Nazi organization responsible for settling Dutch citizens and coordinating business enterprises in German-occupied Eastern Europe, wanted to settle three million Dutch people as colonists in these territories: *The Times*, 17 July 1942, p. 5.

8 Beginning of the fourteenth verse of the Dutch national anthem, the 'Wilhelmus'.

1 Het Utrechts Archief, 1423/2129. This document has been translated from Dutch.

2 The accompanying letter, which is included in the file, requested pastors to read out Part A of the statement in their churches on 20 July 1942. Each pastor was to use his own discretion in rephrasing Part B, the prayer.

3 From April 1942 onwards Dutch men were subjected to compulsory labour deployment in Germany and were sent to work predominantly in munitions production. By 1943 approximately 200,000 Dutch people were performing forced labour in Germany.

We should all become deeply aware of these needs; that is why we are all reminded of them here. These needs also have to be brought to the attention of those who have authority in this respect. That is why the Synod, in association with virtually all the churches in the Netherlands, has turned to the occupying authorities by means including the following telegram:[4]

> The Dutch churches mentioned below, already deeply shocked by the measures against the Jews in the Netherlands, which exclude them from participating in the normal life of the nation, have been appalled at the news of the new measures, as a result of which men, women, children, and whole families will be taken away to Germany's territory and dependencies. The suffering this causes to tens of thousands of people, the knowledge that these measures contradict the deepest moral sense of the Dutch people, and above all the knowledge that they are in breach of what God requires of us in terms of justice and mercy impel the churches to appeal to you urgently not to put these measures into effect. For the Christians among the Jews, this urgent appeal to you is also inspired by the consideration that these measures make it impossible for them to take part in the life of the Church.
> The Dutch Reformed Church,[5]
> The archbishop and bishops of the Roman Catholic Church in the Netherlands,
> The Reformed Churches in the Netherlands,[6]
> The Christian Reformed Church in the Netherlands,[7]
> The General Mennonite Society,[8]
> The Remonstrant Brotherhood,[9]
> The Reformed Churches in the Netherlands in Restored Union,[10]
> The Reformed Congregations in the Netherlands,[11]
> The Evangelical Lutheran Church in the Kingdom of the Netherlands,[12]
> The Restored Evangelical Lutheran Church in the Kingdom of the Netherlands.[13]

4 This telegram was sent to Reich Commissioner Seyss-Inquart on 11 July 1942.

5 The Nederlands Hervormde Kerk, which adhered to moderate Calvinism, was the largest Protestant Church in the Netherlands until 2004, when it merged with the Reformed Churches to form the Protestant Church in the Netherlands.

6 The Gereformeerde Kerken were strictly Calvinist, but likewise merged to form the Protestant Church in the Netherlands in 2004.

7 The Christelijk Gereformeerde Kerk of the Netherlands emerged in the second half of the nineteenth century and also adhered closely to Calvinist traditions.

8 The Algemene Doopsgezinde Sociëteit was founded in 1811 as an association of several Mennonite churches in the Netherlands which adhered to Menno Simons's pacifist theology.

9 The Remonstrantsche Broederschap split from the Dutch Reformed Church in the seventeenth century due to a dispute concerning Calvin's teachings on predestination, which the Remonstrants rejected.

10 In 1926 the Gereformeerde Kerken in Nederland in Hersteld Verband broke away from the Old Reformed Church after a theological dispute. They aligned themselves with the Dutch Reformed Church in 1946.

11 The Gereformeerde Gemeenten arose as a nationwide faith community in 1907 as a result of splits within the Reformed Church Under the Cross and the Ledeboerian Congregations. They still exist today and represent a traditional form of Calvinism.

12 Evangelical-Lutheran Church congregations came into being as early as the sixteenth century, but a nationwide organization existed only from 1818. In 2004 they merged with other churches to form the Protestant Church in the Netherlands.

13 The Hersteld Luthersche Kerk split off from the Evangelical-Lutheran Church in 1791. It existed until 1952.

This has at least resulted in one of the commissioners general[14] promising, on behalf of the Reichskommissar,[15] that converted Jews will not be deported, provided they belonged to one of the Christian churches prior to January 1941.

Above anything else, these needs must be brought before God. That is why the Synod has set aside this service as an hour of humility and prayer.[16]

(B)

Almighty and holy God, God of Abraham, Isaac, and Jacob, Father of Our Lord Jesus Christ, whose judgements are all over the earth, we throw ourselves down before You in our great need. We do not merely want to lament so much suffering which is wounding Your people. Neither do we merely want to pity those whose suffering weighs heavily upon them. We beseech You to safeguard us, so that we do not solely accuse others, but first of all ourselves. Move us with Your Holy Spirit in such a way that we lament our sins above everything and in everything.

It is our sins, those of our country and our people, of our Church and congregation, of our families and our own, which have brought Your rightful judgements upon us. We have lived in self-satisfaction and confidence, in recklessness and conceit, with a worldly disposition and worldly pleasures, a life of duplicity and ambiguity, with a pretence of godliness and uprightness, while forgetting and trampling underfoot the authority You have over us and the call our neighbours can make on us in Your name. We have not taken Your authority or Your law seriously, or Your holiness and love, or the precious blood of Christ and the anointing of Your Holy Spirit.

And now Your judgements have arrived. We pray they may crush us and lead us to repentance, individually and as a congregation. For this, tear from our hearts all roots of bitterness, extinguish any flame of unholy hatred, and teach us how to bow before You in the community of sin and guilt with all people, including those to whom You give permission to humiliate and punish us. We also pray for their repentance.

Teach us to accept and to bear what You impose on us, as long as it pleases You to punish us, because we have deserved it.

Teach us to believe that You will forgive those who truly confess their sins to You.

Teach us to believe that through Your judgements, You want to draw us towards You and want us to find true safety and peace in Your presence, in spite of all that oppresses and threatens us. Teach us to believe that You are a God who performs miracles, who can make mercy prevail and make justice triumph, You who have conquered death.

We specifically bring to You the people of Israel, who are so bitterly tested in the present time. You will not renounce them forever, as You have made enduring promises

14 The commissioner general for special duties, Fritz Schmidt, promised this to the churches on 14 July 1942.

15 German in the original: 'Reich Commissioner' (Arthur Seyss-Inquart).

16 The Dutch Reformed Church had also signed the telegram, but its Synod decided on 24 July 1942 not to have it read aloud. The telegram was read aloud in the Catholic and the other Protestant churches. As a result, Reich Commissioner Seyss-Inquart decided to deport Catholics of Jewish origin. In an attempt to split the churches in the Netherlands, 'non-Aryan' Protestants were not subject to deportation at first: see Johan Martinus Snoek, *De Nederlandse kerken en de joden 1940–1945: De protesten bij Seyss-Inquart, hulp aan joodse onderduikers, de motieven voor hulpverlening* (Kampen: Kok, 1990), pp. 88–100.

for their future. Help them to hold out. We pray they will turn to You in repentance, in order that they may obtain the true redemption You have given to us through Christ, Your Son. In particular, we pray to You for the children of Israel, who are connected to us by the same faith. Give them the strength to bear their cross and to follow Him in whom they have found their Redemption.

We also fervently bring to You those whose fate it has been to live and labour in foreign lands, separated from their own families. Strengthen them in body and soul. Save them from bitterness and resentment, from despondency and despair, from estrangement and degradation. May they hold on to You and Your Word in their loneliness. Look after the families they have left behind, and may they remain united in the community of faith.

Oh merciful God, deliver all those who are tried and oppressed, prisoners and hostages, all those who are overshadowed by the black clouds of threat and mortal danger. Reveal Your power, show Your judgement, and may Your love move in its mysterious ways. Cast Your judgements in such a way that they become blessings, so that many who live without You turn to You, that the dividing wall of hostility between Israel and the peoples may prove to have been destroyed, that all those who believe in Your holy Name may also seek and find each other as brothers in You, forming one flock and one Shepherd.

Awaken in our congregations and throughout Your Church a genuine hunger and thirst for Your Word and Spirit. Teach us to set our minds on things above, not on earthly things. Give us all we need, including our daily bread. Give us endurance and patience. Also fill us with courage and boundless resilience, and a hope that will not be dashed. Make us weak in ourselves, so that we may be strong in Him who carried the cross for us and scorns disgrace, who is seated at Your right hand, He who is the King forever, to whom the future belongs, for whom the Church is yearning, hallowed be Thy Name, Thy Kingdom come, Thy will be done, on earth as it is in Heaven. Hear us, oh Lord, for Jesus' sake. Amen.

DOC. 66

The Times, 28 July 1942: article on the beginning of deportations in the Netherlands[1]

Depopulation of the Netherlands – Nazi Scheme Started
From a Dutch Correspondent

The Germans have begun to carry out their scheme of depopulating the Netherlands. As was to be expected, the Dutch Jews are the first victims. Every day 600 Dutch Jews, aged between 18 and 40, are transported eastwards.[2] Their property is confiscated by the

1 *The Times*, 28 July 1942, p. 3. *The Times*, founded in 1785 as the *Daily Universal Register*, has appeared under its current name as a daily newspaper in London since 1788. In the 1930s it had a circulation of 190,000 copies.

2 The number of Jews called up for labour deployment amounted to several hundred persons every day: see Doc. 52. The deportation trains departed from Westerbork approximately every four days until mid December 1942.

Germans. There are altogether about 200,000 Jewish citizens in Holland,[3] of whom 60,000 will be deported.

There can be no doubt that as soon as the Dutch Jews have been deported the Germans will start on the forced transportation of Dutch 'Aryans'. In a recent article in *The Times* it was stated that the Germans propose to move 3,000,000 Dutchmen to West Russia and the Baltic States.[4]

DOC. 67

Deutsche Zeitung in den Niederlanden, 3 August 1942: article on a speech given by Commissioner General Fritz Schmidt concerning the attitude of the German occupiers towards the Jews[1]

The German attitude is clear

Section Leader Head Schmidt[2] *spoke about current problems of the day at a ceremony on the occasion of the tenth anniversary of the local NSDAP branch in Waubach*[3]

DZ.[4] Waubach, 3 August

The oldest German National Socialist local branch in the Netherlands, Waubach in the province of Limburg, marked its tenth anniversary on Sunday. The main item on the programme at the celebration of its founding – which was attended by the district head of the NSB,[5] the Reich Commissioner's representative,[6] the district inspector[7] and his department heads and others – was an *address delivered by the head of the department, Commissioner General Schmidt,* who clarified several issues of particular interest in the Netherlands. At the beginning of his speech, the section leader presented a bust of the Führer created by the sculptor Ferdinand Liebermann[8] which the Reich Commission-

3 According to the census, there were 160,000 Jews in the Netherlands in 1941: see Doc. 64, fn. 6. Around 16,000 refugees who did not have Dutch citizenship were also among the 160,000 registered Jews.

4 *The Times*, 17 July 1942, p. 5; see Doc. 64, fn. 7.

1 *Deutsche Zeitung in den Niederlanden*, vol. 3, no. 60, 3 August 1942, pp. 2–3. This document has been translated from German. The *Deutsche Zeitung in den Niederlanden* was a German-language daily published in Amsterdam from 1940 to 1945, with a circulation of approximately 30,000–55,000 copies. It was the mouthpiece of the German occupiers and replaced the earlier publication *Reichsdeutsche Nachrichten in den Niederlanden*, which had been published by the NSDAP's Foreign Organization.

2 Fritz Schmidt.

3 Now a district in the municipality of Landgraaf (province of Limburg).

4 *DZ* is the abbreviation for the *Deutsche Zeitung in den Niederlanden*; it was not possible to ascertain which editor wrote this article.

5 Martinus Hendrikus Keller (1909–1944), district head of the NSB for Limburg, 1940–1941, and for North Brabant from 1941.

6 Wilhelm Schmidt (1898–1945), brother of the commissioner general for special duties, Fritz Schmidt; the Reich Commissioner's representative for the province of Limburg, 1940–1944.

7 Hans Quandt (1894–1967), Kreisleiter of the NSDAP in Limburg from 1940; died in June 1945 in a British internment camp.

8 Ferdinand Liebermann (1883–1941), sculptor; freelancer at Rosenthal Porcelain, 1909–1926; professor in Munich from 1926; worked on numerous state commissions after 1933, including as city councillor in Munich.

er[9] has donated to the local branch in Waubach as a token of his special recognition and his gratitude.

Starting with the first founding ceremony of the Party on 24 February 1920, the Commissioner General went on to speak about the ten-year history of the local branch in Waubach. He acknowledged the accomplishments of the Party comrades who, surrounded by hatred and scorn, resolved in those days to raise the swastika banner in Waubach.

The Jewish problem

After briefly describing the current state of the war, the Commissioner General dealt in detail with the *Jewish problem* in general, and for the Netherlands in particular. The Jews, he said, are the most dangerous and the most cunning enemies of National Socialist Germany. Poets and thinkers have always warned the German people against these parasites. Giving numerous examples, the Commissioner General described the sinister activities of the Jews. Names such as Karl Marx, who imposed himself as the alleged workers' leader of the disenfranchised masses of the working class in order to firmly entrench the power of the Jews, and names such as Rosa Luxemburg and Karl Liebknecht, who celebrated bestial orgies during the civil war and orchestrated bloodbaths, were key to this development. With the murder of the ailing regional NSDAP head Gustloff,[10] who was seeking recuperation, by the Jew David Frankfurter and, two years later, the murder of legation secretary Ernst vom Rath by the Polish national Herschel Grünspan,[11] international Jewry unmistakably conveyed its intention to destroy not only the National Socialists, but all Germans.

Citing further convincing examples, Commissioner General Schmidt showed how the Jews, especially in France, but also in England and America, incited war against Germany and systematically pressured the nations into war, and above all how they were to blame for the killing of 60,000 ethnic Germans in Poland.[12]

'Therefore, who will hold it against us Germans', Commissioner General Schmidt continued, 'if, in the fierce, decisive struggle that will define the next centuries, we eliminate this dangerous opponent? Whether it concerns a German, French, Belgian, Swiss, or Dutch Jew, he is always the representative of his race.' For this reason, the worst and most invidious enemy here also must disappear from the West. The western coast is heavily safeguarded, and the Siegfried Line[13] of 1939 has been pushed forward all the way to the ocean. This means we are strong and, as Dr Goebbels writes in his latest great article, will crush every attempt with our German military thoroughness, which is well known by now.[14] But to accomplish that, it is also essential for us to take all precautionary

9 Arthur Seyss-Inquart.

10 Wilhelm Gustloff (1895–1936), head of the regional NSDAP group in Switzerland, was shot by the Jewish student David Frankfurter (1909–1982) in Davos on 4 Feb. 1936.

11 Herschel Grynszpan (1921–1942), also known as Grünspan, attempted to assassinate the German diplomat Ernst vom Rath (1909–1938) in Paris on 7 Nov. 1938. Vom Rath succumbed to his injuries two days later. The Nazis used his assassination as the justification for the Kristallnacht pogroms against German Jews on 9/10 Nov. 1938.

12 Around 3,000–4,000 persons lost their lives in August and Sept. 1939 in the course of rioting against 'ethnic Germans' in Poland.

13 Known in German as the 'Westwall'.

14 Joseph Goebbels, 'Auch der Versuch ist strafbar', *Deutsche Zeitung in den Niederlanden*, vol. 3, no. 56, 30 July 1942, p. 1.

measures that must be taken. For every Dutchman, it is self-evident that we will not allow a single Englishman or American to be at large in this territory. That this applies all the more to our worst enemy ought to be clear to every level-headed Dutchman. This is why the Jew must leave the West.

We need manpower and have therefore placed these Jews in labour camps, some here in the Netherlands,[15] but the majority must work in the East and compensate for what they have brought about in this war through their warmongering. We are not barbarians; we also want to have the Jews be accompanied by their families, but they are expected to start doing clearance work out there in the devastated East, in the empty cities. Their lot will be hard; let us also not forget that in former times, destitute and lice-ridden, they came to our countries.

This historical mission that National Socialism has taken on will be carried out, and everyone who cuts across this path, which has been identified as simply the correct and necessary one, or prevents us from performing our task, regardless of his nationality, must expect to share the lot of the Jews. For this reason, the Dutch are expected to exercise restraint and to avoid interfering in matters that are decided between combatants.

Representatives of the churches have now approached the Reich Commissioner and Air Marshal Christiansen[16] with regard to this matter and have stood up for their Jewish co-religionists.[17] I have spoken with a representative of the churches and explained to him that nothing about our fundamental attitude can be changed, but that, in the process, a distinction can be permitted where smaller groups are concerned. A letter was read out last Sunday, particularly in the Catholic churches, in which the clergy criticize the measures that were taken against the Jews to safeguard our struggle against the arch-enemy of the Western world.[18] The clergy believe that they must champion the cause of the Jews, whose racial comrades in the East, in the Soviet Union, are indeed the true masterminds of Bolshevism, and the destroyers of the religions, and the murderers of the priests.

In some Protestant churches as well, announcements have been made in which a basic position was defined. Nonetheless, the representatives of the Protestant Church have informed us that the reading aloud of the complete declaration was not their intention, and that, due to technical difficulties, it could not be prevented everywhere.

However, when the Catholic clergy disregard negotiations to such an extent, we are compelled on our part to view the Catholic Jews as our worst opponents and to ensure that they are taken away to the East as quickly as possible.[19] That has occurred. Some day, the question of Jewry, too, will be solved in the Netherlands. On 12 February 1936,

15 See PMJ 5/110 and 111.

16 Friedrich Christiansen (1879–1972), soldier; initially captain of a merchant ship; soldier and pilot in the German navy, 1913–1922; worked for the Dornier aircraft manufacturer, 1922–1933; worked at the Reich Ministry of Aviation, 1933–1937; appointed air marshal (General der Flieger) in 1938; Wehrmacht commander in the Netherlands, 1940–1945; sentenced to twelve years in prison in the Netherlands after 1945; pardoned in 1951

17 On the churches' appeal to Seyss-Inquart, see Doc. 65.

18 On the different roles of the Catholic and Protestant churches, see Doc. 65, fn. 16.

19 On the differing treatment of Protestants and Catholics of Jewish descent with respect to their deportation, see Doc. 116, fns. 5 and 6.

by the grave of Gustloff in Schwerin, Adolf Hitler said: 'This act will rebound upon its perpetrator. It is not Germany that will be weakened by this, but rather the power that committed this crime, Jewry!'

[…][20]

DOC. 68
De Waarheid, 3 August 1942: appeal for a protest against the deportation and wholesale murder of the Jews[1]

Manifesto on the Reintroduction of Slavery[2]

Fellow countrymen,

In recent days we have heard the catastrophic news that the Jewish Council, acting on the instructions of the German occupying power, is organizing the deportation of almost all able-bodied Dutch Jews to Germany, Poland, and Silesia.[3] Men and women aged between 18 and 55 will be deported within the foreseeable future. About 90,000 Jewish citizens are affected by this measure.

This mass murder, planned in calm consultation and with staggering cold-bloodedness, can count on the full cooperation of a small political group, which in the past would open the doors of its movement to Jews, but whose black supporters[4] currently, with abhorrent statements of approval, act as lowly servants contributing to the performance of all that is mean, degrading, and spineless, and whose only excuse can be that they are rewarded for this.

As a result, we are on the eve of the greatest national disaster ever to hit our country. The Nazi terror will wipe out a large portion of the Dutch people. The introductory measures have already been taken. The streets of the neighbourhoods where the Jews are forced to live are completely deserted after eight o'clock.[5] The residents are in their homes. The ghettos can be closed off. Any time the 'Herren'[6] choose, the masses can be

20 The rest of the article addresses the confiscation of bicycles, the problem of the black market, the arrest of hostages, and the necessity of the second front.

1 *De Waarheid*, no. 51, 3 August 1942, pp. 1–2. This document has been translated from Dutch. *De Waarheid* was published from Nov. 1940 as the newspaper of the illegal Communist Party of the Netherlands (CPN), at first every two weeks and then weekly, and was one of the best-known illegal newspapers. The initial print run of 6,000 copies increased during the occupation period to 100,000. The newspaper continued to be published until April 1990.

2 The manifesto was published in various illegal newspapers. The author was Gerrit Jan van der Veen (1902–1944), sculptor; first worked for the Dutch railway and in Curaçao; freelance sculptor from 1930; active in the resistance movement from 1940, with roles including editor of the illegal newspaper *De Vrije Kunstenaar*; took part in armed resistance, including the arson attack on the Amsterdam population register in March 1943; arrested in May 1944; convicted and executed shortly thereafter.

3 See Doc. 52.

4 A reference to members of the NSB, who wore black uniforms. Until 1938 Jews were also allowed to become members.

5 See Doc. 53.

6 German in the original: 'masters'.

driven into the livestock wagons. And already transport after transport is being taken to the disgusting slaughterhouse called Germany.

But we, the true voice of the Dutch people, symbolized by all the newspapers and bulletins appearing illegally here in this country, we ask you: *What will you do?* Will you again confine yourself to shedding tears? Will your response to this mass murder be sufficient to merit the term compassion? Or will we soon speak of a furious outburst by the people, which will be able to bring the machinery of daily life to a halt? But if you still fail to act, even though you are aware of the tragic details that the Nazis have murdered 700,000 Polish Jews, and even though you are aware that the beast of 'fascism' will never be satisfied by any amount of blood, we ask you what needs to happen before you raise your voice, before you say to the 'Herren', the NSB: you cannot come after our blood without punishment.

Fellow countrymen, enough is enough!!!!
You have tolerated everything others decided to do to you. You have suffered hunger, cold, and hardship for the sake of an alien people, and you have allowed the lives of many of your sons to be taken without any serious protest. The slave-hunters insult you daily, and you allow yourself to be insulted.

But this is too much!!!! Come to your senses!!!! Organize the resistance!!!! Defend yourself, and defend your compatriots!!!!
Therefore, protect the Jews wherever you can. Hide them, give them shelter and food, however hard it may be for you!

Dutch police officers of the old school, think of your human and your true professional duty: do not arrest any Jews, or else merely pretend to carry out the orders given. Allow them to escape and hide. Be aware that you are the murderer of each man, each woman, and each child you inform on.

Railway workers, train drivers, be aware that each train, loaded with slaves, which you transport, is led to the slaughter!!!
Citizens from all classes of society, call on everyone to show resistance and opposition. Everyone can act in their own way, in their own circle, by speaking out, by writing, and – above all – through deeds!!! Save your persecuted compatriots from death. Be aware that we have no higher human obligation!!!

The blood of 90,000 Dutch people will stain the road, along which innocent men and women will go again and again, sacrificing the best they have to offer. Be aware that if you give in now, there will be a time when you too cannot do anything other than succumb to the tyrant and his henchmen.

Consider this manifesto a cry of disgust, rising up from the Netherlands like a scream, not for mercy, but as the daunting beginning of a new period in this horrible episode, a period when our people become aware of their empowerment, when we refuse to throw away our honour, and when we fight to defend life.

Long live our national solidarity!!! Long live our country!!!
The above is a manifesto jointly published by all the illegal newspapers in the Netherlands and distributed on a large scale. The fact that all the different branches of the

underground movement against the occupiers have come together in this protest is really encouraging. This can only contribute to an increased willingness among our people to fight.

This must be followed by action!!

The mass deportations have begun and are continuing systematically. They can only be stopped by means of mass protests and strike action. The extermination of our Jewish compatriots, which has now reached its peak, is not an isolated measure. It is related to the threat which the second front[7] posed to the Krauts.[8]

Therefore the Krauts not only bring troops and trains full of war equipment *into* the country, but they also want to send everything that poses a danger to them *out of* it.

The Dutch Jews have the honour of being regarded by the Krauts as their irreconcilable opponents. That is why they have to go! But it is not just them! All Dutch people who are enemies of Hitler's Germany are threatened with the same fate.

First it was the military officers, who were once again made prisoners of war.[9] Then it was the young skilled workers, who were deported.[10] Then it was the hostages.[11] Now it is the Jews, who are killed. Soon it will be the turn of the May 1940 soldiers, who will be made prisoners of war again.[12]

Will our people continue to stand by and watch this happen? That would be the equivalent of suicide. The time has come to take major action and to call a halt to the gang of criminals which calls itself the German Wehrmacht.

The strongest part of the Krauts' army is being held in the Soviet Union and systematically slaughtered. The battle will soon flare up in the West as well. But until that happens, we do not simply have to accept everything. On the contrary.

A massive protest campaign now – against starvation, the mass murder of Jews, the deportation of workers, and other Nazi terror – will weaken the enemy's strength and pave the way for freedom for our country.

No more hesitation or procrastination!!! The country demands action!!!

7 After the United States entered the war in Dec. 1941, a second front in Europe seemed increasingly probable.

8 The original uses the term *Moffen*, a long-standing satirical or pejorative Dutch term for Germans, used predominantly during and after the Second World War.

9 On 15 May 1942 all Dutch military officers had to report to their barracks to become prisoners of war again. This requirement affected 2,027 officers (only a few had gone into hiding beforehand), who were taken to Germany and held captive until the end of the war.

10 In April 1942, 30,000 Dutch workers were for the first time compulsorily drafted for labour deployment in the German metalworking industry.

11 On 4 May 1942 a total of 460 well-known Dutch citizens were arrested as hostages, followed by 600 more in mid July 1942. They were confined in separate camps in Sint-Michielgestel and Haren (province of North Brabant). In response to various attacks, 20 hostages were murdered in August and Oct. 1942.

12 See Introduction, p. 41.

DOC. 69
On 4 August 1942, after his wife's arrest, Kurt Vogel asks Bishop Mutsaerts to negotiate with the Germans[1]

Letter from Dr Vogel,[2] Eindhoven, 22 St Odastraat, temporary address: 17 Elzentlaan, to His Most Reverend Excellency Monsignor W. Mutsaerts,[3] Bishop Coadjutor, 's-Hertogenbosch, dated 4 August 1942 (copy)

Your Excellency,

The undersigned would like to take the liberty of presenting the following urgent matter to you:

I am a Catholic of Jewish descent, and I am currently in hospital. My wife,[4] who is also a Catholic of Jewish descent, was arrested on Sunday morning, shortly after 5 o'clock, and as reported by the 'Deutsche Sicherheitspolizei',[5] she was taken to Amersfoort[6] to be transported to Westerbork camp in Drenthe at a later stage, which has now happened.

At the same time, our house was sealed off by the police, and as reported by the 'Sicherheitspolizei', no one may enter it from now on. We are also unable to remove any items from the house.

The 'Sicherheitspolizei' states as the reason for the arrest and transfer to a camp that this was done in reprisal for the pastoral letter which was read out in all Catholic churches on Sunday, 26 July.[7] Such arrests reportedly took place among all Catholics of Jewish descent, who the Reichskommissar[8] promised would be exempt from deportation.[9]

For us, this consequence of the pastoral letter means the total disruption of our family life. It also means that, having already suffered severely under the special measures due to our Jewish origins, we are now also exposed to special persecution due to our Catholic faith.

Clearly the undersigned wishes to abstain from any criticism of the Episcopate's actions, but he nevertheless cannot refrain from respectfully but earnestly requesting the Episcopate to consider taking immediate steps to put a halt to these terrible consequences of the pastoral letter. The German authorities apparently take the view that their concession should not have been 'as it were' punished by means of this pastoral letter.[10]

1 Het Utrechts Archief, 449/76. This document has been translated from Dutch.
2 Dr Kurt Vogel (1899–1943), lawyer; emigrated to the Netherlands in 1937; deported to Westerbork on 13 April 1943, and from there on 20 April 1943 to Sobibor, where he was murdered on arrival.
3 Wilhelmus Petrus Adrianus Maria Mutsaerts (1889–1964), priest and theologian; ordained in 1914; appointed coadjutor in 1942; bishop of 's-Hertogenbosch from 29 June 1942 to 1960.
4 Gertrud Vogel, née Löwenstein (1904–1942), housewife; emigrated to the Netherlands in 1937; deported to Westerbork on 4 August 1942 and from there to Auschwitz on 7 August 1942; perished in Auschwitz on 30 Sept. 1942.
5 German in the original: 'German Security Police'.
6 Amersfoort police transit camp.
7 See Doc. 65.
8 German in the original: 'Reich Commissioner' (Arthur Seyss-Inquart).
9 On 14 July 1942 the churches had received the assurance that all Jews who had been baptized before 1941 would not be subject to deportation.
10 See Doc. 65, fn. 16.

As far as the undersigned has learned from a specific source, further measures against the Catholic Church are to be expected as a consequence of the pastoral letter.

The undersigned is of the opinion that an immediate attempt should be made, by means of direct negotiation with the German authorities, to arrive at an agreement, and so to overturn the arrests.

I fear the worst if this cannot be achieved, and that is without taking into consideration the risk of deportation mentioned in the newspapers.

As I stated above, I am ill; I would otherwise have liked to ask you for permission to explain this letter in person. Because this is not possible, I would politely recommend that you contact the lawyer F. Teulings,[11] who knows me, for any information. His Honour Mr K. L. H. van der Putt,[12] mayor of Geldrop, is also prepared to give you further information on this matter.

I trust that the Episcopate will wish to take note of this urgent appeal and will consider taking measures as soon as possible, and so put a halt to the terrible consequences of the pastoral letter of 26 July, in direct consultation with the German authorities. I assume Your Excellency will understand that there is absolutely no time to be lost.

The undersigned would very much appreciate your response.[13]

DOC. 70

On 13 August 1942 the lawyer Jaap Burger describes going to the Central Office for Jewish Emigration in an attempt to protect Jews from deportation[1]

Handwritten diary of Jaap Burger,[2] entry for 13 August 1942[3]

Let me continue where I left off in my previous letter.[4] My plans to have my hands free did not go as I had expected, and I am still in the same position of a lawyer. There is a small possibility that my plans will still go ahead, but there is considerably less chance this will happen than there was a month ago.[5] It is in fact not very pleasant to perform one's usual work just now, as this is a terrible time. When you are forced to witness the truly appalling suffering inflicted upon the Jews, everything else seems like nothing, and

11 Franciscus Gerardus Cornelis Josephus Maria Teulings (1891–1966), lawyer; member of the Dutch parliament, 1929–1948; minister of the interior, 1949–1951.

12 Hendrik (Harry) van der Putt (1887–1945), owner of a cigar factory; mayor of Geldrop, 1939–1944; refused to participate in the deportations in July 1944; thought to have perished in Bergen-Belsen.

13 The file does not contain a reply.

1 National Archief, Collectie 431 J. A. W. Burger, 2.21.254/262. Published in Jaap Burger, *Oorlogsdagboek*, ed. Chris van Esterik (Amsterdam: Bert Bakker, 1996), pp. 200–206. This document has been translated from Dutch.

2 Jacob (Jaap) Burger (1904–1989), lawyer; practised law in Dordrecht from 1929; escaped to Britain by boat as a so-called *Engelandvaarder* ('England sailor') in 1943; member of the Dutch government in exile there; minister without portfolio in 1943; minister of the interior, 1944–1945; member of the Dutch parliament, 1945–1962; member of the Senate from 1963; in the Council of State, 1970–1979.

3 The original contains handwritten notes.

4 Jaap Burger wrote his diary in the form of a letter to his cousin Bram Burger, who was employed aboard an oil tanker in Curaçao during the occupation period.

5 Presumably a reference to his plans to flee to Britain, which had already been made at this time.

you ask yourself in bewilderment if this can continue any longer. Prof. Bonger's chilling logic[6] has always frightened me somewhat, but I am now constantly reminded of how he refused to live in a non-democratic state and immediately after the occupation took his own life. In doing so, he spared himself insurmountable suffering. This past week it was the Dordrecht Jews' turn to be called up for departure tomorrow evening. In addition to Suus,[7] a total of 120 out of the 149 are within the age limit. I had to look after the interests of a family that I was trying very hard to release formally from their Jewish ancestors, for which purpose you devise the most ridiculous legal artifices, and the court pretends it does not understand or see through anything, accepts your assertions, and swallows everything whole. Indeed, our solidarity is still alleviating much suffering. Those with a dogmatic frame of mind keep harping on about the fact that proper Dutch office holders should relinquish their posts in protest, and many have done so; but if you stand up for individual people, it is always the ones who have not stood down who are still able to help you through the loopholes and also do so. A defiant attitude may be more appealing, but what is most useful only becomes apparent afterwards.

Yesterday I was at the Zentralstelle für jüdische Auswanderung in A'dam,[8] the fortress from which the scandal is conducted. I was successful there, but I have never before returned home feeling so downhearted. It makes your stomach turn and drives you insane in no time. As a matter of fact, my emotions have given me a lot of trouble again lately. Long queues of Jews are standing waiting at the – note my words – entrance for Jews; I, as an Aryan, may of course use the official entrance.

If you ever get to read this, you will think I would also have used the Jewish entrance in solidarity. We are all very familiar here with such and many other instinctive reactions, but a person who does not experience this will never come to know the sophistication and perversity of the National Socialist regime. These days I feel I have had enough of idiots like Gandhi,[9] who apparently do not understand what is going on at all, no matter how much I used to respect him.

Dr Heeroma[10] had his portrait in his room for many years, but when I visited him this week it was gone. So I take the entrance for Aryans – if you are not careful, you will first see Jews rather than Dutch people in that helpless crowd on the other side – and get serial number three hundred and something to get my case dealt with. Meanwhile, I find out – it is afternoon when I arrive – that there are people who have been waiting since 9 o'clock in the morning. It is therefore not the case that you are seen when it is your turn, but – and this is once again a case in point – on Friday all people who have not been seen have to go to Poland; their cases will definitely be dealt with there, as the

6 Willem Adriaan Bonger (1876–1940), lawyer; professor of criminology and sociology in Amsterdam; after the Netherlands capitulated, he and his wife took their own lives.

7 Suze (Suus) Benedictus (b. 1923); neighbour of the Burgers; in hiding with her family in the home of Jan Burger (Jaap Burger's uncle) in Dordrecht from 8 Oct. 1942 until the end of the war; emigrated to Israel after the war; co-founder of a settlement in the Mediterranean; worked as a secretary.

8 German in original: 'Central Office for Jewish Emigration' in Amsterdam.

9 Mahatma Gandhi (1869–1948), lawyer; political and spiritual leader of the Indian independence movement; advocated non-violent resistance and civil disobedience with respect to British colonial rule.

10 Presumably Dr Klaas Hansen Heeroma (b. 1879), physician; member of the Social Democratic Workers' Party (SDAP); briefly under arrest, 1944–1945.

German organization and administration never fails. You can imagine 'how' these people are waiting. I will be brief. When I left with the desired result at 5 o'clock, those from 9 o'clock were still waiting.

When I then got in fairly quickly, abusing my Aryan origin, my position as a lawyer, and the fact that I had left Dordt[11] at 7 o'clock to get here – the trains are running incomprehensibly smoothly, but now and again the network goes haywire – there was, believe it or not, one man in the room, a sort of bookkeeper, and that was all. This man had to process everything and claimed that he had not slept in three nights. He did indeed look confused and did not make any progress with his work; he mostly just kept pacing up and down. Dozens of men at the entrance of the building, the 'guards', were sitting there doing nothing, but apparently no assistance was available for this problem. I advised that it had been weeks since my clients had been put on the list of those whose descent is uncertain,[12] and how they had now nevertheless been called up for deportation. Where was my proof? But sir, surely you know as well as I do that German authorities never issue any proof. According to him, they are put on the list automatically. Errors never occur, and no proof is issued. Unfortunately I do not have that list!!! And that is the decision-making authority!!

To cut a long story short: one of my colleagues, the lawyer Miss Mazirel,[13] travelled to The Hague of her own accord to get – in what capacity? – a copy of the list and return to A'dam with it. That document was immediately accepted as authentic, and the machine kept moving. I asked her if she thought that the husband and child of my client, who was now safe, could be rescued. Reply: today, yes, so make use of the opportunity. And that is what happened. Clearly no one at the relevant authority takes any interest in how it fits together or whether it is correct. Justice does not come into it; this thought is completely alien. They simply carry out orders, and at most it occurs to them to think: if I set this man free, I have to call in someone else to arrive at the required number. That is awkward, or at least bothersome. You get a hopeless impression from this whole mess, and you ask yourself in vain who or what is the driving force here. For the fact remains that thousands of Jews are put on transports every week.

When my case had finally been dealt with, I ended up at the allerhöchste Stelle[14] for registration; this was a kind of corporal who had a secretary and, with a bored expression on his face, was writing out cards for the card index system with a pencil. When he briefly left the room, I tried to get a document from the lady confirming my people's exemption, which I had not managed to get anywhere else. She confided to me that this was not possible, as they had no 'Dienststempel'.[15]

11 Abbreviation for Dordrecht (province of South Holland), Jaap Burger's place of residence.

12 Many of the approximately 4,300 Sephardic Jews in the Netherlands, whose ancestors had emigrated there from Spain and Portugal since the sixteenth century, attempted to avoid deportation. They argued that, in accordance with the criteria laid out in German racial policy, they were not Jews at all. Four hundred of them were placed on an exemption list that promised them protection at first; the vast majority were nonetheless deported to Theresienstadt in Feb. 1944.

13 Laura (Lau) Carola Mazirel (1907–1974), lawyer; practised law, 1937–1955; championed the rights of minorities; active in the resistance from 1940; took part in organizing the attack on the Amsterdam population register in 1943; imprisoned briefly in 1944; emigrated to France in 1956.

14 German in the original: 'supreme authority'.

15 German in the original: 'official stamp'.

She also told me – the corporal had returned by then – that all of those Solomons and Moseses were beginning to give her nightmares. The corporal said: Madam, we are not interested in your private emotions. To me he said: I will not trouble you again, but I cannot guarantee that your clients will not be picked up during some roundup – that is not our department. If that happens, however, nothing can be done about it, and you will not be able to rely on the exemption.

I showed him a recommendation for a certain Jew which, according to the letterhead, originated from: der Reichskommissar für die Besetzten Niederländischen Gebiete, Generalkommissar für Finanzen und Wirtschaft, Wirtschaftsprüfstelle.[16] I had been able to obtain that recommendation in The Hague that morning, and I felt as safe with it as a Muslim with the Qur'an, but I was utterly astounded to hear the following from the corporal: anyone could write a note like that. Wer ist denn der Herr So und So[17] (making reference to the letter's signatory)? I answered his question, in response to which he said that his Kommandant, Obersturmführer auf der Fünten,[18] had just told him that enough exemptions had been granted, and Befehl ist Befehl,[19] according to the representative of the 'Supreme Court' for Jewish matters, Mr Liszt. I then decided to pay a visit to Mr auf der Fünten. Miss Mazirel told me in passing that the place was not in the least a mess – as had been my impression – and was apparently even better than other places, and then witnessed a scene in which the bookkeeper mentioned above, Mr de Haan, felt it would be humiliating to type a letter himself, and told the first Jew who came in to sit down at his typewriter to type the letter. Anyway, off I went to Mr auf der Fünten. Again a long queue of people waiting at his secretary's door. With the boldness of a Kraut[20] I went in and sat down with a German to wait. While I was sitting there waiting, a Jew came in whose parents had been picked up in the latest roundup, and he thought he could get them out because he was 'tätig'[21] for Nieuwe Doelenstraat[22] – I suspected he was a Jewish spy working for the Germans. The lady said that the Obersturmgruppenführer[23] had just left. I asked her why then she had asked me to wait. This was because the boss would return at 7 o'clock (it was 5 o'clock). Anyway, if I had to describe all my impressions, my notepad would be completely full; it was a disgusting matter, and when I left the place, I felt sick. And the strange thing is this: that this evening we are happy, as Suus has somehow miraculously been granted a deferment, and even though we know that tomorrow hundreds of people will be locked up in Depot 24 near the railway in Rotter-

16 German in the original: 'Reich Commissioner for the Occupied Dutch Territories, Commissioner General for Finance and Economic Affairs, Office for Economic Investigation'. The Office for Economic Investigation, established in 1940, was under the direction of Hans Fischböck, commissioner general for finance and economic affairs. All Jewish enterprises had to register there, beginning in Oct. 1940.

17 German in the original, 'Who is Mr So and So, then?'

18 Correctly: (Ferdinand) aus der Fünten.

19 German in the original: 'orders are orders'.

20 The original uses the term *Moffen*, a long-standing satirical or pejorative Dutch term for Germans, used predominantly during and after the Second World War.

21 German in the original: 'working for'.

22 After the February Strike in 1941, the German Security Police ordered Police Commissioner Douwe Bakker to establish a department for investigating political opponents and Jews as a branch of the Amsterdam police. The department offices were located at 13 Nieuwe Doelenstraat.

23 German in the original. Aus der Fünten held the rank of Hauptsturmführer.

dam[24] again, and that people are presently killing themselves with gas poisoning and other means, we feel immensely relieved. People are strange. And it saves all of us the – enormous – effort of hiding her and secretly providing her with food, as she would not have gone. But this should also be the case for the parents and Jules, as her parents would otherwise obviously be blamed for her disappearance.[25] Should you ever see and hear the secrets, about which I would not even dare to give any clues here, you would be amazed – not least by our unflinching resourcefulness.

And if there were no NSB members, we would let the Krauts beat their heads against the wall with all their regulations, as they would not be able to keep up the slightest pretence of order without direct and brutal violence.

We are worried again about the hostages as a consequence of several attacks that allegedly took place in Rotterdam;[26] the press is patient. But understandably, families will do everything they can to rescue their affected family members, even if this means involving NSB members, though the hostages themselves are usually emphatically against this happening. This is understandable, and the NSB plays the part of Absalom[27] and agrees with everyone, even when their interests are completely incompatible. However, all they achieve is that they are allowed to prepare the lists of hostages. When arriving at the hostage camp, those who qualify for release because of their old age are requested to stand separately; these expressions of sympathy are important. This is followed by those who desire release on the grounds of diseases or physical defects; even more sympathy. Finally, the same applies to those who hold high positions in the NSB or similar institutions.

The only result is that they are greeted with jeers. 'Nicht lachen',[28] the guards thunder. Buziau[29] was released due to 'Schwermütigkeit'.[30] We plod on and ask, 'How much longer?' How many persecuted people might have been able to escape if there had been another invasion of just one day, even if it was just because of messed-up records and a lack of means of transport? The latter is gradually becoming increasingly likely. Even in the Balkans,[31] all lorries – the few that are still there – are seized. They seized our bicycles to get their labourers to the factories.[32]

24 Warehouse 24 in Rotterdam served as a collection point for Jews who were deported from Rotterdam. It was situated in an isolated area of the port bordering Entrepotstraat.

25 The entire Benedictus family went into hiding on 8 Oct. 1942, in the building in which they had previously lived, and survived the occupation period.

26 See Doc. 68, fn. 11.

27 Biblical reference: in Absolom's quest to become king in place of his father, David, he sought to win over the people. He invited them to turn to him in case of disputes and took the side of every person who approached him: see 2 Samuel 15:1–6.

28 German in the original: 'No laughing'.

29 Johannes Franciscus Buziau (1877–1956), internationally renowned comic and cabaret artist; briefly imprisoned as a hostage in 1942.

30 German in the original: 'depression'.

31 One word is illegible.

32 A directive from Commissioner General Rauter on 20 June 1942 had already required all Jews to surrender their bicycles; this was also demanded of parts of the remaining Dutch population on 21 July 1942.

Recently, when a train was extremely overcrowded, Miss Stavens was pushed into a Wehrmachtsabteil,[33] which exists on every train. The conductor came to remove any civilians from that section, which he managed to do under protest. One civilian remained in his seat; the conductor urged him to leave, upon which the civilian hit the conductor in the face. It turned out the civilian was a German, upon which the most senior officer in the compartment snapped at the conductor, saying that if he dared to make a fuss about the case, he [the officer] would know where to find him.

In the crammed aisles of the carriage, people commented on this – I was recently in a first-class carriage with twenty other people – and among those who were listening were two German soldiers with their bicycles. One of them said they would make sure we would soon learn to speak German. One of the passengers said that they, being German, would probably soon have to learn English. But such jokes aside, the British are keeping us waiting for a long time.

DOC. 71

On 13 August 1942 the representative of the Reich Foreign Office in the Netherlands informs his superiors that it is increasingly difficult to fill the deportation trains bound for the East[1]

Letter from the Reich Commissioner for the Occupied Dutch Territories, the representative of the Reich Foreign Office (D Pol 3 no. 8; marked 'in connection with my report of 31 July 1942'[2] – D Pol 3 no. 8 – 2 duplicates), signed Bene, The Hague, to the Reich Foreign Office, Berlin (received on 17 August 1942), dated 13 August 1942[3]

Re: transport of the Jews
The situation has changed significantly since my above-mentioned report. Now that the Jewish community has figured it out and knows what is implied by transport or labour deployment to the East, they no longer line up for the weekly transports. Of the 2,000 summoned for this week, only around 400 turned up. Those who were summoned are no longer to be found in their apartments. There are therefore difficulties in filling the two trains, and it is not yet known how the trains are to be filled in the next few weeks. – Migration over the border to Belgium is in full swing. In exchange for money and fine words, the Jews always find accomplices to help them cross the border. There is talk of a daily migration of 1,000 Jews, but that is probably exaggerated.

So far,	8,500 Jews have been transported,
	1,500 [Jews] will be leaving this week,
in total, therefore,	*10,000 Jews have been deported.*

33 German in the original: 'Wehrmacht compartment'.

1 PA AA, R 100 876. Reproduced in *ADAP*, series E, vol. 3, pp. 315–316. This document has been translated from German.

2 The report is included in the same file; in it, Bene reports on the smooth progress of the previous deportations and the protests from the churches.

3 The original contains handwritten notes.

In addition, approximately 2,000 Jews have been deported to Mauthausen and other places.[4] The total therefore amounts to around 12,000 Jews, or 8 per cent. In any event, from now on it will be necessary to resort to strict measures in order to carry out the deportations. Moreover, the Jews are counting heavily on the second front, which they hope will result in the opportunity for them to resettle in England.

Exempt from transport are	around	22,000 Jews living in mixed marriages,
	[around]	3,500 armaments workers,
	[around]	1,200 diamond workers,
	altogether	*26,700 Jews.*

DOC. 72

On 14 August 1942 the police in Amsterdam accuse Abraham Abram of accepting money in return for hiding a Jewish woman[1]

Report from Amsterdam police headquarters, Jewish Affairs,[2] signed F. Veenis,[3] signed Dahmen von Buchholz (police inspector), dated 14 August 1942

Report

Accused is the Jew Abraham Abram,[4] born in Amsterdam on 25 May 1900, residing at 14 M.J. Kosterstraat, ground floor, in Amsterdam.

Re: He accepted 350 guilders from the Jewess Bertha Elisabeth Sonnenberg,[5] born in The Hague on 24 November 1897, seamstress, residing at 92 Van Baerlestraat, ground floor, in Amsterdam, who received a summons for labour service in Germany, in exchange for taking this Jewess to a safe place and hiding her.

Later she regretted it and voluntarily came forward to make a statement.

The sum of 25 guilders was found in *Abram's* apartment; according to *Abram's* statement, the remainder of the 350 guilders has already been spent.

Sonnenberg was released, as she must report this evening to the Hollandsche Schouwburg.[6]

4 On the situation of the prisoners, see PMJ 5/107.

1 NIOD, Coll. Bureau Joodsche Zaken. This document has been translated from Dutch.

2 At the suggestion of Hanns Albin Rauter, in late 1941 the Amsterdam chief of police, Sybren Tulp, established the Office for Jewish Affairs (Bureau Joodsche Zaken) as a separate department within the Amsterdam police. Working in close cooperation with the German authorities, this office was in charge of all police operations against Jews in Amsterdam. It was headed by an NSB functionary, Rudolf Wilhelm Dahmen von Buchholz (1889–1967).

3 Frans Hendricus Cornelis Veenis (1904–1989), soldier; radio operator for the Royal Netherlands Navy, 1922–1931; employed by the Amsterdam police from 1931; worked in the Amsterdam criminal investigation department, 1937–1943; worked in the Dutch criminal investigation department, 1943–1945; policeman in Amsterdam after 1945.

4 Presumably a false name, as no information on this individual could be found, either in Westerbork camp or in the population register in Amsterdam.

5 Bertha Elisabeth Sonnenberg (1897–1942), housekeeper; deported to Westerbork on 16 August 1942 and the following day to Auschwitz, where she perished in Sept. 1942.

6 The Hollandsche Schouwburg theatre was founded in 1892. From 1941 only Jewish artists were allowed to perform there, and the theatre was renamed Joodsche Schouwburg. From July 1942 the building served as the assembly point in Amsterdam for Jews before their deportation to Westerbork camp.

Witness: Police Detective F. Veenis, on duty, Section 5, Department 1

Abram was placed at the disposal of the Senior Commander of the Security Police and the SD, Amsterdam Field Office, on 14 August 1942.[7]

DOC. 73

On 19 August 1942 the farmer Jan Everhardus Blikman writes a letter to Westerbork camp requesting the temporary release of a Jewish harvest worker[1]

Letter from J. E. Blikman,[2] Vlagtwedde, to Westerbork camp,[3] dated 19 August 1942 (typescript)

Dear Sirs,

This summer a Jewish boy, W. Kosses,[4] has been working for me, and I have been happy with his work. On Tuesday he was taken away to the camp. Would it be possible for you to give him time off during harvest time, until about 11 November?

I have already been to the regional employment office in Winschoten, but they can't take a decision either. I am not sure whether they have also sent you a letter.

We have a large business and need many workers. Last autumn some of our potatoes were frozen because of a lack of workers, and surely that should be prevented if possible.

Yours faithfully,
your obedient servant,[5]

DOC. 74

On 25 August 1942 Emma Margulies asks the Central Office for Jewish Emigration to allocate an apartment to her and her Jewish husband[1]

Letter from Emma Lina Margulies, née Fiedler,[2] Amsterdam-Zuid, 23a Noorder-Amstellaan, to the Central Office for Jewish Emigration, Amsterdam (received on 4 September 1942), dated 25 August 1942 (typescript)[3]

Re:

Petition for provision of a small apartment for an impoverished family supported by the NSV[4] which has suffered war losses and is loyally German in its attitude, consisting of a married couple with a small child (a 22-month-old boy).

7 The head of the Amsterdam Field Office was Willi Lages.

1 NIOD, 2501/40. This document has been translated from Dutch.

2 Jan Everhardus Blikman (1889–1982), farmer; owned a farm in Vlagtwedde, a village in the south-eastern part of the province of Groningen.

3 The name of the addressee has not been recorded; the letter was found in the Westerbork transit camp files.

4 Wiardus Gompel Kosses (1924–1942); deported to Westerbork on 4 August 1942, and from there to Auschwitz on 24 August 1942; perished in Auschwitz in Sept. 1942.

5 The original contains a handwritten note in Dutch: 'gaat niet' (not possible).

1 NIOD, 077/1490. This document has been translated from German.

At the instigation of the NSV office, Amsterdam, 24 Sarphatystr.,[5] after a discussion with Mr Mielitzer[6] concerning this matter, I most respectfully venture to give reasons for my petition as follows:

I am a Reich citizen, an Aryan, and have been in the Netherlands with my husband[7] since November 1938 as a result of a series of special circumstances, which have been recorded in detail and made available to the senior commander for security,[8] SS-Gruppenführer Rauter, The Hague.

Regarding my husband, I can say that he has a well-deserved reputation with the relevant authorities, having acquitted himself well on account of his military discipline and due to his ideological awareness, which culminates in unquestioning obedience to the will of the Führer. It is precisely for this reason that he considers it his honourable duty to continue to prove himself worthy of the exception granted him so far within the scope of political possibility, in keeping with his silent pledge of loyalty. This extraordinary character trait sets him apart from typical Jews, who lack this propensity and are therefore thoroughly hostile to his attitude. Therein lies the primary reason for separating him from the Jewish Volkskörper.

He is a combat veteran, a former volunteer in the Great War of 1914–1918, injured in combat, awarded the Iron Cross Second Class, the Silver War Injury Badge, the Honour Cross for Combat Veterans, the Hungarian War Commemorative Medal, and the Austrian War Commemorative Medal.[9] His former active service for Germany is all the more commendable since he relinquished his Romanian citizenship, which he held at that time, solely because he felt German and, as a native Berliner, considered Germany his homeland, and drew the obvious conclusion: to offer up his life for 'Germany', which was and always has been his ideal.

His war experiences led him to become non-denominational after the war, and he later became Protestant as a result of our marriage.

In the course of the political transformation in Germany, my husband, with his characteristically insightful clarity about politically necessary requirements, always made it known through his actions that he was loyal to the Führer, in true comradely spirit. In a personal letter to the Führer in 1935, he openly pledged his commitment to him. Suppressing his own ego, he takes an active part in the development of current events with the same will to win, which cannot be surpassed by the most well-disposed Aryan.

2 Emma Lina Margulies, née Fiedler (1906–1993); married Wilhelm Margulies in 1934; returned to Germany before the war ended and was granted a divorce from her husband in Dec. 1944; lived in Erfurt after the war.

3 The original contains handwritten notes.

4 Nationalsozialistische Volkswohlfahrt (National Socialist People's Welfare Organization).

5 Correctly: Sarphatistraat.

6 Presumably correctly: Hans Johann Militzer (b. 1896), clerk; lived in the Netherlands from 1928 to 1946.

7 Wilhelm Margulies (1894–1982), businessman; emigrated to the Netherlands from Germany in 1938; detained in Westerbork from Feb. to July 1942; released from the camp because of his marriage to a non-Jew; returned to Germany in Oct. 1948; thereafter worked as a photojournalist.

8 Correctly: commissioner general for security (Hanns Albin Rauter).

9 The Iron Cross Second Class (EK 2) was a war decoration originally instituted by King Friedrich Wilhelm III of Prussia in 1813. In 1939 it was reinstituted by Adolf Hitler in a slightly altered version. The other awards listed are decorations from the First World War or in commemoration of it.

His fighting spirit reveals itself in the unshakeable belief in the Führer's greatness of heart, which will find its expression in some way in due time. He accepts all the phenomena of the times, with their logical, sometimes very unpleasant consequences, as litmus tests of fate, which he is able to face with dignity, and in this way he seeks to furnish proof of his worth.

When the Netherlands was occupied in May 1940 and there was a lack of good, trustworthy drivers at that time, he immediately made himself available to the Wehrmacht in June 1940. He was then deployed in several places including Bergen, N.H.,[10] at the airfield, where he was part of the permanent motor pool and in charge of an oxygen tank vehicle until January 1941. By then, a sufficient number of soldiers with a Wehrmacht driver's licence had been assigned to the L 14 401 station, and after eight months of loyally performing his duty he had to be dismissed, albeit with the best references.

As proof that it is not in fact a matter of mere lip service in my husband's case, one must also consider that he initially volunteered for Wehrmacht service even before leaving Germany, specifically while in Düsseldorf, on 30 September 1938, when the top-level meetings between Mussolini, Daladier, and Chamberlain were taking place in Munich.[11] In particular, however, he most recently distinguished himself when war broke out with the Soviet Union, by immediately volunteering on 30 June 1941 to join the ranks of the Waffen SS at the Northwest Recruiting Office in Groningen for frontline service against Bolshevism. At that time he was in Westerbork camp, when it was still under Dutch command,[12] and all the wishful thinkers and German-baiters there counted on the war ending soon and regarded the utter destruction of Germany as now being within reach. Without any support and completely surrounded by people with opposing ideological views, including not only Jews, but also Dutch Aryans who were sympathetic to the enemy side, he boldly attempted to get out of the camp [to join the Waffen SS] and thus, owing to his steadfast loyalty to the Führer and the Reich, incurred the hostility of all for the duration of his time there. They ensured that life was made as difficult as possible for us in every respect by spinning the basest webs of intrigue about us. My husband's efforts were of no avail here; his words fell on deaf ears. Finally, of his own accord, he provided information about his impressions and experiences in a confidential report to the SD office in Assen.

In connection with our German sympathies and the resulting world view, Dutch military personnel, seeking to shield their retreat to Calais back in May 1940, mistreated us by evacuating us from Sluis to France on a segregated transport with around 80 NSB members,[13] including Mr Rost van Tonningen.[14] At Béthune[15] we were literally left stranded on a road in the middle of the countryside, completely destitute. Prior to that, our German passports had been stolen, we were allowed to take only a small amount of

10 A small town in the province of North Holland (N.H.).

11 This refers to the discussions that led to the Munich Agreement of 30 Sept. 1938, which provided for the incorporation of the Sudetenland into the German Reich.

12 From Feb. 1941 Wilhelm Margulies lived in Westerbork refugee camp with his family. Why he had to report there at that time could not be ascertained. Until 30 June 1942 the camp was under the control of the Rijksvreemdelingendienst, the Dutch police for foreigners. After that the German occupation authorities assumed command.

13 Shortly before the German invasion, many Germans and Dutch National Socialists were interned by the Dutch police on 3 May 1940 and taken to France in an effort to prevent acts of treason.

luggage that we had to carry ourselves, we were given no rations, we received neither shelter nor money, and the luggage we had left behind, which contained our last remaining possessions, was stolen. The Dutch left us in the lurch, and in the combat zone near Ourton along the Béthune–St. Pol line we ended up being held under guard by French and English troops. I was five months pregnant and, along with my husband, had to endure heavy bombardments by our German dive-bombers back then, not to mention artillery fire and the other distressing occurrences. Until one day, the English, distracted by reports of a breakthrough from Valencienne,[16] left us unattended. For my husband, that meant an opportunity for us to find our way through a stretch of the front, which he happened to be familiar with from the Great War of 1914/18, and reach the German combat positions. A description of the boundless comradely assistance that we received from then on would not fit the pages of this report.

Owing to my husband's petitions and appeals to Commissioner General for Security Rauter in The Hague, we were finally released from Westerbork camp around five weeks ago. I am receiving support from the NSV, and my husband, as soon as his special case has been settled, will also be called on for labour deployment.

We have now been robbed by the Dutch for the second time. Our luggage from the transport was broken into and looted, so that we literally have nothing appropriate to wear any more.

In addition, my husband, my child, just 22 months old, and I have been poorly housed in *one small furnished room*. For lack of space, no beds can be set up. We have to improvise sleeping arrangements.

In view of the turbulent events that lie behind us and our general attitude, I request the provision of suitable accommodation, with cooking and washing facilities, for a family of three, provided the available resources permit this.

With a request for sympathetic handling of the present case as urgently as possible, signed

with German greetings,
Heil Hitler[17]

14 Meinoud Marinus Rost van Tonningen (1894–1945), lawyer; worked at the League of Nations, 1923–1928 and 1931–1936; joined the NSB in 1936; important party ideologue in his role as editor-in-chief of the NSB's daily newspaper, *Het Nationale Dagblad*; appointed president of Nederlandsche Bank and secretary general of the Ministry of Finance in 1941; arrested in 1945; died shortly thereafter, after falling from a prison building; the exact circumstances of his death are unclear.

15 A French municipality in the Pas-de-Calais département, near the Belgian border.

16 Correctly: Valenciennes. The Wehrmacht reached this town on 27 May 1940 and from there advanced towards the south and west in subsequent days.

17 The file does not contain a response to this letter. However, a resident's registration card for Wilhelm Margulies indicates that from 29 September 1942 onwards the family was living in a different apartment.

DOC. 75
From 8 to 10 September 1942 the writer Sam Goudsmit describes the anxiety caused by the evening arrests[1]

Handwritten diary of Sam Goudsmit,[2] entries for the period 8 to 10 September 1942[3]

Tuesday, *8 September 1942*
Continuation of: Expulsion etc.[4]
I have found it even more difficult than before to concur with the optimism around me. *I do not see a way out for the Jews of Holland.* The plan is to expel *all* Jews from this country, and so far all plans *of that nature* have been carried out in full. Rescue can only come from a British[5] occupation, if that happens very swiftly. Who among us believes in that? I will only believe it when I *see* it.

When a small squadron of twenty-one British planes flew over the River Amstel yesterday afternoon, the people of Amsterdam cheered and believed 'liberation' had arrived! They don't know our fears, otherwise they would make more demands for such a solution. Yesterday evening it remained 'quiet'. How long will it last?

(Meanwhile: the sun is moving towards the Hercules constellation at a speed of *60 million miles per year.* And: Arcturus (a planet) is moving through space at a speed of *22,000 miles per second,* says Jules Verne.)[6]

Wednesday, *9 September 1942*
Continuation of: Expulsion of Jews in Holland
Pause and new hunt
So yesterday and the day before, it was said – even in official quarters – that the removal from homes would cease again, while the call-ups would resume.[7]

Strange though this may sound, this gave us a bit of *breathing space.* Yes, to us *personally* this was a great relief, and a promise of freedom for the time being. For half a day we felt better; the pressure was reduced a little. But then! It was not to be.

Yesterday evening the Amsterdam police were 'on duty' again among the Jews, and over the whole evening another 400 were removed from their homes (around 100 of whom were released again; the rest have been 'sent on'). A very large percentage of them were older people, aged between 50 and 80; most of them were over 60.

1 Bibliotheca Rosenthaliana, HC-ROS-006. This document has been translated from Dutch.
2 Samuël (Sam) Goudsmit (1884–1954), writer; well-known author in the Netherlands in the 1920s and 1930s; survived the occupation period in hiding; kept a diary from 1909 to 1954.
3 The original contains handwritten notes and markings.
4 Goudsmit titled almost every page of his diary. From 17 July 1942 the title was *Expulsion of Jews in Holland.*
5 Here and below, the author uses 'English' rather than 'British' in the original.
6 Jules Verne, *Hector Servadac*, trans. Ellen E. Frewer (New York: C. Scribner's Sons, 1905 [French edn, 1877]), p. 50. This states that Arcturus (which is in fact a star) travels at a speed of eleven miles per second, that is, three times as fast as Earth.
7 Once the destination of the deportations became known, only very few Jews complied with the call to report for labour deployment. The Germans proceeded to come to their apartments and take them away.

And it continues this evening. The letters B and C have been completed; when will they get to our letter G? Those on the Jewish Council who are exempt are not to be picked up, in administrative terms. Two department heads said to me today: what of the 100 who have been sent back? *Yes, at least they can go back.* And that is why this evening and the following evenings will bring only blackness and fear. Every sound outside the house … and if the bell were to ring …

No, it is very bad in the evening. From 8 p.m. precisely it can start. At that time, the vehicles are parked at the police stations. Here and there it seems the non-Jewish population gathers in the street in large numbers, but it is accepted, albeit under protest.

A reliable source told me that on the day after the occupation in May 1940, the senior public servants assured the Jewish employees that the German authorities had given the guarantee that *'no one, including the Jews, has anything to fear'.*[8]

It seems that, apart from in Poland, i.e. in the West, the Jews are not treated as ruthlessly anywhere as in Holland.

Thank God, the clock strikes ten; just one more hour to go, and then it should be over again for one evening. One more hour of waiting! *But who says they might not 'work' a bit longer this evening??* Outside, rugs are being beaten. The entire Christian population can still be seen going about the city every day, on foot and *on the tram*,[9] generally quite cheerfully, especially of course the lower middle classes in these neighbourhoods: no, they do not give the impression that our dreadful life has affected them very much. *I believe they do not have the imagination to see what is going on.*

Thursday, 10 September 1942
Continuation etc.
Half past nine in the evening. This is how we spend the time night after night, scared of the bell. Exemptions, as far as they apply on a weekly basis – and it does happen that they *do not* apply! – in any case, as we are generally told, cannot protect against the Visit and being taken to the assembly point, where our fate and life will be decided. Half past ten seemingly no longer applies, as yesterday evening Jews were apparently taken away as late as midnight. This evening again four or five hundred victims, and we do not know yet if we will be among them.

So this evening again, thousands of Jews in Amsterdam, sitting together with narrowed eyes and the blood drained from their faces, waiting to find out if they will be allowed to sleep at home tonight or will be pounced upon at any moment, when the sound of the bell will cut straight through their heart, and they will have to leave their home behind forever. This is all unbelievable and baffling; I have not yet spoken to anyone who still has the peace of mind to understand and explain this. We know it, but that is not the same as understanding: understanding means being able to put yourself in the perpetrators' shoes, and we are unable to do so; we cannot put ourselves in the shoes of the perpetrators or the enforcers, or even in the shoes of those enforcers who object.

8 This also emerges from the statement made by representatives of the German occupiers to Amsterdam City Council: see PMJ 5/36.
9 Jews had been forbidden to use the tram since 30 June 1942: see Doc. 53.

Did I ever believe I would face the same fate as the Mainzer Anonymous from 1096, who obstinately maintained the chronicle of the slaughtering of the Jews in the Rhineland until he was killed himself?[10]

When I read this during my preliminary studies for *Simcha*,[11] I was struck by the dreadful, merciless and devastating nature of that task, under the ruthless pogrom machine of the Middle Ages. But doesn't everyone who reads this, including the person who has the capacity to identify more than others with this suffering, doesn't the law of nature continue to operate in each of us, which makes us believe – out of a sense of self-preservation – that the exact same fate could never befall us?

And look how far we have come since 1934, when I was occupied with this; will I, like that synagogue servant, have to write this chronicle[12] (also, probably like him, in order to *vent* my feelings of fear and at least keep myself occupied), while we are completely engulfed by fear and expect that we can be raided and taken away at any time? No more fear now for the near future; no concern about how the situation develops, but the full certainty and knowledge of the terrible facts: they are dragging away all the Jews from Holland, evening after evening, from 8 p.m. onwards, the hour from which we (for that very purpose!) have to remain at home, and each morning, if it has not yet been our turn, we get to hear a small part of what happened the night before, and the approximate number of people who have been taken away. First from the beginning of the alphabet, last week, and now last night apparently also from the end, and the letters in between. So there is no longer any respite for any of us, which could calm our fears for at least a few days or weeks and *make it possible* to prepare for the disaster in the end. Each of us can expect our destruction any evening, and it looks like all of this is deliberately done very systematically to unnerve all Jews and to make it as difficult as possible to escape.

And then, apparently, it is increasingly the anti-Jewish elements from the available police who are appointed to do the job, as the reports about more lenient police operations are diminishing, while those about hostile treatment and officers relishing the acquired power are increasing. 'Stop or I'll shoot', to a 14-year-old Jewish girl who briefly walked outside the police cordon in the street towards a friend. And an ambulance for a person suffering a nervous collapse … only to take him away. It is nearly 11 p.m., and I am still writing …

How will it be possible to settle the cost of all this in the future? Who knows? That is what is so perplexing, that there *no longer seems to be any sense of justice.*

10 A reference to the *Narrative of the Old Persecutions*, also known as the Mainz Anonymous, a Hebrew-language chronicle on the pogroms against Jews, dated 1096. During the First Crusade, more than 600 Jews fell victim to these massacres, which destroyed the city's entire Jewish community.

11 Novel by Goudsmit, *Simcha, de knaap uit Worms* (Simcha, the Boy from Worms) (Amsterdam: Querido., 1936), which deals with the persecution of Jews in the Rhineland during the First Crusade, 1096–1099.

12 At an earlier point in his diary, Goudsmit set himself the task of chronicling the persecution of Jews in the Netherlands.

2 a.m.
A sigh of relief
They did not come, I am still awake, and I am still writing. At five minutes past midnight, Judy[13] kissed me and said: *'they won't be coming any more today'*.

Was I sure about this? No. They can also come after midnight, why not?

But I also felt relieved at the thought that, in this campaign, they have so far always come before midnight.

And so we could breathe more freely, and I went upstairs and had the courage to take a coffee with me, because the fear and tension had been so extreme.

Coffee and a cigar because they did not come, and we will probably be free until 8 p.m. tomorrow; that is *20 hours* from now.

Until 8 p.m. tomorrow, then the game starts all over again, for the hundreds of thousands of Jews remaining in Amsterdam, and for the four of us[14] here.

Apart from the fact that our hearts will sink again tomorrow morning, when we hear about tonight's harvest.

DOC. 76
On 11 September 1942 Salomon de Vries describes the beginning of his life in hiding[1]

Diary of Salomon de Vries,[2] entry for 11 September 1942 (typescript)

11 September 1942
The last couple of nights we have not spent at home, as our home no longer felt like home. The story is now so familiar that it no longer needs to be repeated. Around all the houses where Jews were living, in among their obviously stolen household goods, German Dutchmen were loitering, those that are usually called Schalkhaar officers.[3] These are young men with a predestined inner void, which is replenished and filled with what is called the German soul. These people got the Jews out of their far too luxurious houses, loaded them into a German police van, and also accomplished many other small tasks, which tend to be part of the trade. They stole what could be carried away without being seen and filled their fit bodies with any ready-to-eat food they found in the dirty Jewish cupboards.

My wife[4] and I had a few good chances. I had a couple of 'exemptions', but these were on paper, and under very specific circumstances the Germans have traditionally

13 Judith Goudsmit-van der Bokke (1885–1949); married to Sam Goudsmit from 1917.
14 In addition to Samuël and Judith Goudsmit, their son Herman (1921–1943) and probably Paul Bernard Goudsmit (b. 1910), Sam Goudsmit's son from his first marriage, lived in the apartment.

1 NIOD, 244/174 III. This document has been translated from Dutch.
2 Salomon de Vries (1894–1974), journalist; worked for the newspaper *Groninger Dagblad*, the socialist daily *Voorwaarts*, and *Het Volk* from 1917; also worked as a radio play director and a radio editor from 1930; dismissed in 1941; lived in hiding, 1942–1945; continued his career as a radio editor after 1945; also worked in television from 1962.
3 The police training battalion was set up in Schalkhaar (province of Overijssel) in May 1941 to centralize police training and organize it according to National Socialist principles.
4 Sara de Vries-de Jonge (1901–1992); married to Salomon de Vries from 1923.

shown a truly German disdain for everything that is written on paper and has had a seal put on it. Choosing the safer option over the lack of safety offered by paper, my wife and I had left our house so we could feel at least a little bit at home. And where we were, that is where we saw it happen.[5] We saw those Dutch officers gather together in front of the skyscraper on Willinkplein,[6] we saw those traitors[7] give each other the German salute and then wait for the arrival of the German police van while casually chatting away. And when the clock struck eight, the raid started. A quarter of an hour later, the first rounded-up people appeared. With quickly packed rucksacks and bundles hastily tied together with a piece of string. Anxious and unsure, they walked beside men from […],[8] who were striding with broad German paces. Sometimes they came one at a time, sometimes whole families appeared. There were very young and very old people. A little old woman was taken from a home for the elderly located immediately adjacent to our hiding place, and the German Dutchman wanted to show his humanity without neglecting his German duty. 'Put your arms around my neck,' he said to the old woman, which is what she did. And then he carried this eighty-three-year-old to the police van and put her inside. I swear this is the truth. We saw this happen, right before our eyes. Evening after evening. The police vans came and went many times until after midnight. Each time with a new load of workers for Germany. As Herr Schmidt, the Oberdienstleiter,[9] clearly put it: 'The Jews were naked when they arrived from Poland, and naked they will return there.'[10] I have always thought – and I am quite sure about this – that I am from the old city centre of Groningen,[11] and – honestly – I do not feel anything for the Germans' Poland. I will stay as long as I can. And so will my wife and son.[12] And I absolutely do not fancy a game of poker with the Herren[13] of the Race, as long as they pinch the trump card and play it against my exemption aces. That is why we have withdrawn every evening. To watch and hear, to listen and learn. We have learned a lot, including on the evening of 10 September 1942. And at half past midnight, when the last police van for that night had gone to Adema van Scheltemaplein[14] with its load of Jews, we went to bed. Exhausted and our nerves in tatters.

'We have until eight o'clock tomorrow evening to recover,' my wife said, and I nodded, but this was not to be. When we arrived at our house the next morning, we saw that 'they' had been. A windowpane in the front door had been smashed with a hammer.

5 The de Vries family actually lived in Zuider Amstellaan (now Rooseveltlaan); it was not possible to ascertain where they hid overnight.
6 Daniël Willinkplein (now Victorieplein) served as an assembly point for Jews during the roundups and arrests.
7 The original here is 'sevenstuiversmannen' (lit. 'seven stuivers men'), a reference to the Dutch War of Independence against Spain (1568–1648), in which traitors betrayed their fellow countrymen to the Spaniards in exchange for seven stuivers.
8 One word in the original is illegible.
9 German in the original: 'senior manager'.
10 Fritz Schmidt, the commissioner general for special duties.
11 Salomon de Vries was born in Winschoten (province of Groningen).
12 Adolf Eduard de Vries (b. 1924); survived the occupation period.
13 German in the original: 'masters'.
14 Correctly: Adama van Scheltemaplein. The Central Office for Jewish Emigration was situated there from the end of June 1942. The inner courtyard of the former school served as an assembly point for Jews before they were deported to Westerbork.

And that had enabled them to put their claws inside and open the lock; that is how they had entered, and that is how they had made it impossible for us to return.

Looking pale, my wife, who had led the way, turned back and motioned to me: don't go any further. 'They' have been! And that is how we, on the morning of 11 September 1942, started our new, unknown life. We had lost our home, our household goods, and many other things. 'It's a shame about the blankets, which we only got back yesterday,' I said.

'There is more that is a shame,' my wife replied.

She did not say that it would have been better if I had taken away these famous blankets immediately yesterday, and that was kind of her. Not a single reproach, not even a reproachful look. And that in such a situation and after nearly twenty years of marriage. It was more than just kind, it was noble, don't you agree …?

We spent one more night in our nocturnal hiding place. Then we set off for our future home for both day and night. And even that journey was strange, for it is odd to go through your own town, through the familiar streets, past the familiar houses, in fear of being spotted. We went along the silent canals and through the back streets. In the early hours of the morning, like thieves in the night. With hidden badges and nervously beating hearts. We had been invited, spontaneously and honestly, when it was not yet necessary to go; what would it be like to arrive in this situation of extreme need? We acted normally, we were shy. And once we were inside, I sat down and talked. I talked like Lex. But I will talk about Lex later, as I have already said. I talked and talked, and then Els – you do not know her yet, but you will get to know her – put me in her room to calm down. And there was a little plate on the wall in that room with the words:

A wise old owl
Lived in an oak!
The more he saw,
The less he spoke,
The less he spoke,
The more he heard …
Why can't we be
like that bird?[15]

Since then I have been speaking less, and I think this at least has been appreciated. It can't be very nice to be stuck with a number of Jews, who can't help it, but who are nevertheless always there. Both day and night.

And now I often sit here and think: What is it like out there, in Real Life? For we are outside and beside real life, because we are inside. Remember that wise old owl, dear sir … And yet … In Holland there is a house.[16] And sometimes my thoughts wander to that house, and especially its surroundings, and the images begin to flood my mind. Imagine: you go for a short walk one afternoon. Just a simple stroll. And you come back and a representative of a different, new, and powerful race is standing at your door, […]

15 English in the original. This was a popular rhyme, originally from the United States, in circulation from the nineteenth century onwards.

16 Probably a reference to the nineteenth century Dutch children's song 'In Holland staat een huis' (In Holland Stands a House). It tells of a man, woman, and child who are thrown out of their house, which is set on fire and then rebuilt.

in hand,[17] and he says to you: Get out. What is inside is mine, and you can go and play a game of lotto.[18] At least, if you can borrow the game somewhere. It is quite possible that you still have a game of lotto in a cupboard in your house, but you are not even allowed to collect that. Do you think this is crazy? Whether you believe me or not, this is not even about a game of chance. There is more at stake, if I may put it that way, than a mere game of chance. Very well, it doesn't matter, wise old owl.[19] But my thoughts are wandering. Around the house in Holland. And among the people who have lived in it, and spent a lot of time there. In that house, there lives a gentleman. Well, a gentleman, that is perhaps taking it a bit far. A rather odd gentleman, perhaps …

DOC. 77

On 11 September 1942 Gerrit Vinke and his wife decide to hide Jews in their home and go to Amsterdam to fetch them[1]

Diary of Gerrit Vinke,[2] entry for 10 to 11 September 1942 (typescript and manuscript)

10 September 1942
Mien has just arrived and is telling us about the persecution of Jews in Amsterdam. Our attention is drawn in particular by a young man and woman with a child,[3] especially when Mien asks us if we could imagine taking these people into our home. The poor souls are terrified, as they may be taken away any time.

After talking this over for a long time, we agree that we want to sleep on it first, as this involves a great deal of risk, of which we are all too aware. We have asked Celi's mother,[4] who is staying with us, for advice, but she says, 'Listen, Celi[5] and Gerrit, it is up to you, I cannot give you any advice on this.'

In short, we went to bed with our heads full of worries. What is our Christian duty? Well, we know what it is, but there is the fear that something will go wrong. We offer our worries to the Lord before we go to bed and ask Him to come to our aid in this matter, which is so difficult for us.

We both sleep restlessly, but when the morning comes and we are awake, we have made our decision. We must help these people, and the Lord will watch over us. We are both fully convinced of this.

17 One word in the original is illegible.
18 In the original 'kienspel'. In Dutch, this refers to a 'game of chance', here presumably the parlour game lotto (similar to bingo), which was popular in the Netherlands at the time.
19 'Wise old owl' in English in the original.

1 NIOD, 244/95. This document has been translated from Dutch.
2 Gerrit Vinke (1904–1985), military officer; worked in the Veenendaal local administration during the occupation period; active in the resistance; hid eight Jews and other persons in his home from Sept. 1942, all of whom survived the war.
3 Siegfried Asch (1912–1983), his wife Selma, and their daughter Irma (b. 1941).
4 Rika Petronella van Langen-van Eden (1877–1952); lived in Utrecht.
5 Celia Elisa Vinke-van Langen (1903–1985), active in the resistance; supported Jews who were living in hiding.

11 September 1942
It is decided that Celi and Mien will take the 13.45 train to Amsterdam. When I get home in the afternoon, I realize they have taken the 11.45 train to Amsterdam.

By the time Celi and Mien are due to return home, Mother and I are waiting and dinner is ready. The women do not show up. I am beginning to feel a bit worried, as I fear something may have happened to them in Amsterdam. At about 10 p.m. I get on my bike and cycle to the station to see if they are perhaps travelling via Amersfoort. The train arrives, but no Celi and Mien. I am at my wits' end, and my heart is racing. I go back home and, thank God, I recognize their voices before I enter the house.

Here then is the story of Celi and Mien: what happened to them in Amsterdam and why they got back so late.

We took the 11.45 train from Veenendaal to Amsterdam and went to Vechtstraat. When we arrived there, we found a young woman with a nine-month-old child and two old ladies: one was the young woman's mother-in-law,[6] and the other was her brother-in-law's mother.

Mien said to the young woman, 'We've come to take you to Veenendaal to go into hiding at the home of this lady', pointing to Celi, 'and her husband.' Well, you should have seen her reaction; the woman did not know where to look. Nothing was said, no questions were asked about what kind of people they were, nothing like that, she just packed quickly.

As she had already prepared for departure so often, this did not take very long. She only packed the most essential things.

As soon[7] as we had finished this, we walked to Amstel station, during which time the woman took off her star. The pram was handed in as luggage with Veenendaal as the destination. Before we got on the train, Mien phoned the woman's husband to make sure he would be at the Utrecht station at 5 o'clock. Meanwhile it got later and later, and we arrived in Utrecht well after 6 o'clock. Naturally, the husband was not at the station. While Mien looked for the woman's husband, the woman, her child, and I sat down on the terrace of the Hotel Centraal. Then Mien returned and said the husband told her we had better get a taxi. However, we learned we would not be able to obtain a taxi. We then went to Lagerweij's house, where we ate and Cor sorted out some coffee; we did not have much appetite because of all the bad luck we had been having. We then rang the station to ask whether we would be able to catch a train, which was only possible after 9.15 p.m. to Ede. I was worried about mother and Gerrit, because they were waiting for us, of course. We then rode the bicycles to the station and left for Ede. In Ede we [...][8] at 22.05 and [took] Mien's bicycle [...][9] to Veenendaal, were we arrived at 22.30.

We were totally exhausted, but happy. And then, of course, we [went] to see mother and Gerrit to tell them what we had encountered. Naturally, I was surprised that our future guests stayed the night at Lagerweij's.[10]

6 Klaartje Asch-Keijser (1880–1960); emigrated from Germany with her husband to the Netherlands in 1933; survived the occupation.
7 From here on the original is handwritten.
8 One word illegible.
9 Several words illegible.
10 In the diary entry that follows, Gerrit Vinke reports that his guests arrived in Veenendaal the following day.

DOC. 78

On 16 September 1942 an employee in the Office of the Senior Commander of the Security Police and the SD in Arnhem summarizes instructions for a roundup of Jews[1]

Instruction sheet issued by the Senior Commander of the Security Police and the SD for the Occupied Dutch Territories – Arnhem Field Office – p.p. signed Bühe,[2] Arnhem, dated 16 September 1942[3]

Instruction sheet
for the operation against the Jews on 16 September 1942, 8 p.m.
At the direction of the Senior Commander of the Security Police and the SD,[4] the arrest of foreign Jews is to take place as a single swift action at 8 p.m. on 16 September 1942.

Enclosed are:

1) summonses,
2) address slips.

Lists of both groups[5] are to be prepared in six copies, one of which is to be provided to the officer in charge of transport for use as a transport list.

Five carbon copies are to be immediately forwarded to the Arnhem Field Office.

If the summons applies to the head of the household, the other family members – if they are of the same nationality – are also to be taken into custody. If the nationality of the family members is different from that of the head of the household, only the person named is to be taken into custody. With regard to health status, the only factor to be taken into consideration is fitness for transport; the age limit is not a criterion. Any exemptions, regardless of their nature, are not applicable. The residences of those arrested are to be sealed by the Dutch police. The keys of the buildings are to be left behind, with instructions to deliver them to Westerbork.

Both groups are to be transferred to Westerbork camp under guard. In the case of those provided with summonses, care must be taken to ensure that the objects listed on pages 1–2[6] are taken along.

An implementation report on whether arrests have been made based on each summons or address listed must be submitted by noon on 17 September 1942. These reports must include the reasons why the person in question was not arrested.

1 NIOD, 250i/40. This document has been translated from German.

2 Willy Paul Franz Johann Bühe (1902–1970), police detective; worked for the Urban Police and the Criminal Police, 1923–1939; joined the NSDAP in 1935; employed by the Security Police and the SD in Arnhem from 1940, from 1941 as official dealing with Jewish affairs; interned in the Netherlands from April 1945 to Jan. 1949 and then deported to Germany.

3 The original includes a handwritten list in Dutch at the end of the document with keywords indicating the information to be obtained on arrest – for example regarding bank accounts, valuables, and real estate.

4 Wilhelm Harster.

5 The two groups most likely referred to here are 1) Jews who had been summoned for 'labour service' or were due to receive a summons, and 2) persons who were registered in the address lists as Jews but, for various reasons, had not received a summons.

6 Not included in the file.

DOC. 79
On 18 September 1942 the Central Committee of the Jewish Council discusses its own role with respect to the deportations[1]

Meeting minutes, unsigned, dated 18 September 1942 (carbon copy)

Minutes of the 62nd meeting of the Central Committee,[2] held on Friday, 18 September, at 10.30 a.m. at 58 Nieuwe Keizersgracht.

Present: Prof. Cohen, chair; Mrs van Tijn, Messrs Bolle, Cahen, A. Cohen, Eitje, Frenkel, de Hoop, Hendrix, Krouwer, van der Laan, van Oss, Spijer, Meyer de Vries, van der Velde, Veffer, and Mr Brandon, secretary.
Absent: Messrs Edersheim, Slotemaker de Bruine, and Spier.

The chair opened the meeting and presented the minutes. They were approved.

The speaker then reported on the events of the previous week. The process of calling up people for labour deployment in Germany continues at an accelerated rate. Apart from the immense personal stress this causes, this week was also a very sad one for the Jewish community because certain people were deported.[3]

It is now virtually impossible to get anyone back from Westerbork.

Various organizations and offices have complained about the fact that their employees have been taken away.[4] However, these discussions have not yielded any result. As regards baptized people: in addition to the baptismal certificate, a declaration must be presented, stating that the person in question is still a member of the relevant church. That declaration alone is also no longer adequate.

As regards the Dutch labour deployment: this continues at the usual rate.[5] There are still problems in securing the release of our representatives.

Over the past week, a number of Jews of foreign nationality have been deported.[6] It is not yet known what their ultimate destination will be. Various identity documents for Jews are currently being stamped at the Zentralstelle,[7] by means of which a provisional exemption from employment in Germany is attained. This concerns baptized people, Portuguese people, diamond traders, etc.[8]

1 NIOD, 182/38. This document has been translated from Dutch.
2 The Central Committee of the Jewish Council consisted of its most important department heads. It met once a week to exchange information and discuss the way forward.
3 These included Josef Hersch Dinner, also known as Josef Hirsch Dünner (1907–1942), rabbi; chairman of the Central Cultural Committee of the Jewish Council; deported to Westerbork with his family on 11 Sept. 1942, and from there on 18 Sept. 1942 to Auschwitz, where he was murdered on arrival.
4 The German police had taken Jewish Council employees from their homes and deported them to Westerbork, often despite there being exemptions for the Jewish Council.
5 Dutch Jews began to be sent to labour camps in the Netherlands in Jan. 1942: see PMJ 5/11c.
6 See Doc. 78.
7 German in the original: 'Central Office [for Jewish Emigration]'.
8 On the system of exemptions, see Introduction, pp. 34–35 and 37–38.

The chair then informed the meeting that the Jewish Council's liquid assets are in a dreadful state. The departments were therefore explicitly warned not to start any new projects without consulting the chairmen first.

At Mr Eitje's[9] request, a discussion was then held on the Jewish Council's general course of action, and that of the chairmen in particular. This mainly concerns the fact that the heads of department deal not only with a large number of personnel, but also with a very important part of the Jewish community, and in the course of this contact, a frequently recurring question concerns the Jewish Council's reasons for participating in so many measures against the Jewish community. In response to this, several speakers argued for the need to cooperate. Ultimately, experience has shown that people ask us for both moral and material support, and they appreciate that the Jewish Council supports them until the end.

The chair added that it was his opinion that as leaders of a community, one has to do all of these things, and it would be criminal to let the community down when it is most in danger. Another consideration is that we should try at least to retain the most important people for as long as possible.

It was then expressly requested that no one visit the Expositur[10] in the evening for purposes other than official business. This agency is under extreme pressure due to the presence of employees who have no business there, which is disastrous for its good work.

It was then asked whether the circular[11] regarding the prohibition on going to the Expositur in the evening also applies to the heads of department. Following several comments, it was established that this is indeed the case. Heads of department can report arrests of their staff not only to the Expositur, but also to Dr van der Laan, Mrs van Tijn, the office at 80 Euterpestraat, and Mr Blüth.

It was agreed in principle that the Jewish Council cannot assist with the financial transactions of those planning to emigrate.

The offices of the Jewish Council will be closed on Saturdays and Sundays if possible, work permitting.

There being no further business to discuss, the chair closed the meeting.

9 Raphaël Henri Eitje (1889–1944), administrative official; worked in Jewish refugee relief organizations before the German occupation; worked for the Jewish Council, 1941–1943; deported to Westerbork on 29 Sept. 1943, and on 5 April 1944 from there to Bergen-Belsen, where he perished in Dec. 1944.

10 The Expositur, located at the Jan van Eyckstraat in Amsterdam, acted as a liaison with the Central Office for Jewish Emigration.

11 This is not included in the file.

DOC. 80

On 23 September 1942 the representative of the Reich Foreign Office confirms that Jews of foreign nationality are exempt from wearing the yellow star[1]

Letter from the Reich Commissioner for the Occupied Dutch Territories, representative of the Reich Foreign Office (D Pol 3 no. 8), signature illegible,[2] The Hague, to the Secretary General of the Ministry of the Interior,[3] The Hague, dated 23 September 1942 (copy)[4]

In reply to your enquiry of 23 September 1942 – no. 20 894, Afd. B.B.Bur.St.&A.R.[5]
Re: Foreign Jews
Jews who can prove possession of foreign citizenship by presenting a fully valid passport are exempt from wearing the yellow star, unless the yellow star has also been introduced in their home countries. However, they must *register* their assets with Lipman, Rosenthal & Co.[6] They are not exempt from the registration requirement.

Jews with Polish, Czechoslovak, Croatian, Romanian, or Hungarian citizenship, as well as Jews from the territories occupied by Germany, are to be treated as Dutch Jews.

At present, all citizens of the hostile powers are being transferred to internment camps in Germany, including the Jews from these countries.

DOC. 81

On 24 September 1942 Higher SS and Police Leader Rauter informs Himmler about the progress of deportations from the Netherlands[1]

Letter (registered, marked 'secret') from the Higher SS and Police Leader assigned to the Reich Commissioner for the Occupied Dutch Territories (logbook no. 837/42 g.), signed Rauter (SS-Gruppenführer), The Hague, to the Reichsführer SS and Chief of the German Police, Heinrich Himmler, Berlin, dated 24 September 1942[2]

Re: deportation of Jews
Reichsführer,

Allow me to submit to you an interim report on the deportation of the Jews.

1 NIOD, 020/1507. This document has been translated from German.
2 Otto Bene was the representative of the Reich Foreign Office in the Netherlands.
3 Dr Karel Johannes Frederiks (1881–1961), lawyer and political scientist; employed at the Ministry for Agriculture, Trade, and Industry, 1907–1919; employed at the Ministry of the Interior from 1919; secretary general of the Ministry of the Interior, 1931–1944; author of the apologia *Op de bres* (Into the Breach), published in 1945; placed on the retired list after liberation; dismissed in 1946.
4 Annotation in Dutch at the end of the page: 'to Dr Calmeyer'.
5 Afd. Binnenlands Bestuur Bureau Staats- en Administratief Recht (Ministry of the Interior, Office for Constitutional and Administrative Law). The letter of enquiry could not be found.
6 Correctly: Lippmann, Rosenthal & Co., Sarphatistraat.

1 BArch, NS 19/3364. Published in facsimile in Presser, *Ondergang*, vol. 1, after p. 272, and published in N. K. C. A. in 't Veld, *De SS en Nederland: Documenten uit SS-archieven, 1935–1945* (Amsterdam: Nijhoff, 1987), pp. 824–826. This document has been translated from German.
2 The original contains handwritten notes, such as 'Very good', with Himmler's initials and illegible stamps.

Up to now we have taken a total of 20,000 Jews off to Auschwitz, including the Jews who were deported to Mauthausen as a punitive measure.[3] Approximately 120,000 Jews are up for deportation in all of Holland. However, this number includes the Mischjuden,[4] who will remain here for the time being. There are approximately 20,000 mixed marriages in Holland. In consultation with the Reich Commissioner,[5] however, I am also deporting all the Jewish spouses in mixed marriages, provided no children have resulted from these mixed marriages. There will be around 6,000 of these cases, and so around 14,000 Jews from mixed marriages will remain here for the time being.

In the Netherlands, there is a so-called 'Werkveruiming',[6] a labour programme subordinate to the Dutch Ministry for Social Affairs, which forces Jews to perform various jobs in closed-off enterprises and camps. So far, we have not touched these Werkveruiming camps, in an effort to induce the Jews to seek refuge there. There are around 7,000 Jews in these Werkveruiming camps. We hope to reach a total of 8,000 Jews by 1 October. These 8,000 Jews have around 22,000 relatives throughout Holland. On 1 October the Werkveruiming camps will be occupied by me at a stroke, and on the same day the relatives outside the camps will be arrested and placed in the two large, newly built camps for Jews in Westerbork near Assen and Vught[7] near Hertogenbosch.[8] I will try to obtain three trains instead of two each week. These 30,000 Jews will be deported, beginning on 1 October.[9] I hope that by Christmas we will be rid of these 30,000 Jews too, so that 50,000 Jews in total – that is, one half – will then have been removed from Holland.[10]

For weeks now, preparations have been under way with the population registers[11] in the Netherlands to identify the mixed marriages, that is, to furnish proof that the Aryan spouses in these mixed marriages are indeed Aryan. These 13,000 Mischjuden have a note put in their Jew identity cards stating that they are entitled to stay in Holland. In addition, the armaments workers will be treated in the same way. The Wehrmacht still absolutely needs them here, around 6,000 + relatives = 21,000 in all. Included in this

3 On the situation of the prisoners, see PMJ 5/107.

4 'Mixed Jews', a reference to intermarried Jews.

5 Arthur Seyss-Inquart.

6 Correctly: 'werkverruiming', Dutch for 'work creation'. The National Work Creation Service (Werkverschaffings-Rijkedienst) was established in 1937 to counter the problem of mass unemployment in the Netherlands. The unemployed were required to perform work at specific locations and were sometimes placed in work camps. In 1939 the service was renamed the National Agency for Work Creation (Rijksdienst voor de Werkverruiming). During the German occupation it was also in charge of supervising Jews sent to labour camps between Jan. and Oct. 1942.

7 Vught concentration camp did not open until 5 Jan. 1943. By Sept. 1944 a total of approximately 31,000 prisoners, including around 12,000 Jews, were held there.

8 Correctly: ''s Hertogenbosch'.

9 The evacuation of the Jewish labour camps actually took place on 2 and 3 Oct. 1942. Around 12,000 Jews were deported to Westerbork.

10 By 12 Dec. 1942, a total of 38,578 Jews had been deported from Westerbork.

11 This refers to the State Inspectorate of the Population Register, which was established in 1936 and was subordinate to the Ministry of the Interior. It was headed by J. L. Lentz (1894–1964). The existence of a centralized and up-to-date population register made it difficult for many people to escape the reach of the German occupiers.

number are the diamond workers from Amsterdam, as well as certain paintings Jews and NSB Jews (20).[12]

On 15 October the Jews will be declared fair game, that is, a large-scale police operation will begin, involving not only German and Dutch police units, but also the local NSDAP organizations and its affiliated formations, together with the NSB, the Wehrmacht, etc. Every Jew who is found anywhere in Holland will be sent to the large camps for Jews.[13] Therefore, no Jew who is not among the privileged will be able to show his face in Holland any more.

Simultaneously, I am beginning to issue announcements to the effect that Aryans who have hidden Jews or helped them cross the border illegally or produced counterfeit identity documents will have their assets confiscated, and the culprits will be sent to a concentration camp. All this will be done to prevent the flight of the Jews, which has begun on a large scale.

With regard to the Christian Jews, the Catholic Jews have been deported in the meantime because the five bishops, headed by Archbishop de Jonge[14] in Utrecht, did not adhere to the original agreements. The Protestant Jews are still here, and we have actually succeeded in prying the Catholic Church away from the Protestant one and from this united front. Archbishop de Jonge has stated at a bishops' conference that he will never again participate in a united front with the Protestants and Calvinists. The attack launched by the churches, which started back at the start of the evacuation,[15] was thus dealt a severe blow and has abated.

The new hundred-strong units of Dutch police are carrying out excellent work with regard to the Jewish question and are arresting Jews by the hundreds, day and night. The only danger that arises in the process is that here and there one of the policemen makes a blunder and enriches himself by taking Jewish possessions. I have ordered trials of the SS and Police Court to be conducted before the assembled unit.

The Jew camp at Westerbork is now complete, and the Jew camp at Vught will be completed on 10–15 October.[16]

Heil Hitler!

Your most obediently devoted

12 'Paintings Jews' (*Bilderjuden*) referred to Jews who were supposed to acquire works of art in the Netherlands for Hitler's museum in Linz, or for Göring. 'NSB Jews' were Jews who had joined the NSB by 1938. The combined number of people in both groups amounted to just over 20 persons. They were deported to Theresienstadt in 1943.

13 This did not happen all at once. Rather, over the following months, there were continual deportations of small groups of Jews from many different towns to Westerbork, and from there to Auschwitz.

14 Correctly: Johannes de Jong.

15 See Doc. 65, in particular fn. 16.

16 See fn. 7.

DOC. 82

On 25 September 1942 Christiaan Broer Hansen itemizes the costs of the damage he sustained during the arrest of a Jew[1]

Report by C. B. Hansen,[2] Household Effects Registration Office,[3] Amsterdam West, 20 Joos Banckersweg, Parterre, dated 25 September 1942[4]

Report
While providing assistance during the arrest of a Jew on 24 September 1942, I sustained physical injury and damage to my clothes.

A wound above my left eye, probably inflicted by means of brass knuckles, was stitched by Dr A. J. van Reeuwijk.[5] A tooth was knocked out of my upper jaw.

My hat was lost. My raincoat, shirt, and tie were stained with blood, to such an extent that they can no longer be worn. My blood-stained trousers can be cleaned or turned inside out.[6]

I politely request permission, at the expense of the Hausraterfassung:[7]

1.	To make an appointment with a dentist for a tooth replacement, estimated at	fl. 25.00
2.	To purchase another hat, estimated at	fl. 7.50
3.	To get my raincoat turned inside out or choose a different one from the Jewish goods, estimated at	fl. 20.00
4.	To choose a shirt and tie from the Jewish goods, estimated at	fl. 5.00
5.	To get my trousers cleaned or turned inside out, estimated at	fl. 7.50
	Total	fl. 65.00

The physician's invoice will be covered by the health insurance fund.
Yours faithfully

1 JHM, Doc. 00 000 085. Published in facsimile in Joods Historisch Museum Amsterdam, *Documents of the Persecution of the Dutch Jewry* (Amsterdam: Athenaeum Polak & Van Gennep, 1969), p. 143. This document has been translated from Dutch.

2 Christiaan Broer Hansen (1904–1979), machinist; worked in shipping, 1922–1928; in the Dutch East Indies, 1929–1933; owner of a hotel in Amsterdam, 1934–1940; member of the NSB, 1940–1943; employed by Lippmann, Rosenthal & Co., June 1942 to 1944; went into hiding in Sept. 1944; arrested in Oct. 1944; in Amersfoort camp until Feb. 1945; interned from 1945; sentenced to six years in prison in 1948; released in 1952.

3 The Household Effects Registration Office of the Central Office for Jewish Emigration.

4 The original contains handwritten notes, some of which are in Dutch. 1: 'rejected, first Führer's order, 3 Oct. 1942', signature illegible; 2. 'notification to C. C. Hansen, 4 Oct. 1942', signature illegible; 3. 'was present here', Fr[au] E. Gerlinck, police employee.

5 Presumably Dr Adrianus Johannes van Reeuwijk (1904–1965), physician.

6 Because of the textile shortage during the occupation period, damaged or soiled garments were unstitched, the fabric was turned inside out, and then the articles of clothing were sewn back together again.

7 German in the original: 'Household Effects Registration Office'.

DOC. 83
Minutes of the Jewish Council meeting on exemptions from deportation for its own employees and on additional measures anticipated, 1 October 1942[1]

Minutes, unsigned, dated 1 October 1942 (carbon copy)[2]

Meeting of the Jewish Council on Thursday, 1 October 1942, at 11 a.m., at 58 Nieuwe Keizersgracht
Present: all members apart from Messrs de Beneditty, de Hoop, Soep, and Vos. Also present Messrs O. R. Frank and Wolff from the National Organization,[3] and Messrs v. d. Laan, Bolle,[4] and Brandon[5] from the office.

The chair, Mr Asscher, welcomed Mr Voet after the latter's lengthy absence due to indisposition.

He then said that the chairmen had had a meeting with Mr aus der Fünten about the *exemption (Sperr)*[6] *stamps for people working at the Jewish Council.* The lists submitted by the Jewish Council consist of approximately 35,000 names, including the women and children. Mr aus der Fünten was prepared to issue exemption stamps to approximately 17,500 of them. This meeting had been preceded by a meeting with the most important people on the Jewish Council, who, together with many members of their staff, after hearing the decision, worked from four o'clock on Sunday afternoon until approximately eight o'clock on Monday evening, for which we are very grateful. (Agreement.)

The current rate is 800 people with proof of identity (including the wives of members of staff, etc.) per day. Mr aus der Fünten announced that around 800 of the Jewish Council people from the provinces do not qualify for a stamp, as the provinces will be evacuated anyway. We were very sad to hear this. The stamps (according to a statement by Prof. Cohen) also provide exemption from working in Dutch labour deployment.[7] The relationship between the 'Sperr' system and the labour camps is currently still interpreted slightly differently by the Sozialreferenten[8] in various places, but the Zentralstelle[9] takes the final decision in this respect. Anyone who receives or has received a summons from the Regional Employment Office and now has a stamp would be wise to deregister

1 NIOD, 182/3. This document has been translated from Dutch.
2 The original contains handwritten notes.
3 The provincial branches of the Jewish Council.
4 Meijer Henri Max Bolle (1910–1945), auditor; head of the Keren Kayemeth LeIsraël (Jewish National Fund) in the Netherlands prior to 1940; chief executive of the Jewish Council, 1941–1942; deported to Westerbork and then to Auschwitz in 1942; perished in a camp near Dachau.
5 Jacob Brandon (1905–1944), administrative official; worked for the City of Amsterdam; secretary of the Jewish Council from late 1942; deported to Westerbork on 19 May 1944, then to Theresienstadt on 4 Sept. 1944, and finally on 16 Oct. 1944 to Auschwitz, where he was murdered on arrival.
6 German in the original, here and below. *Sperr* here is short for *Sperrstempel*, 'exemption stamp'.
7 From Jan. 1942, Jews – at first the unemployed and then others as well – were required to take part in labour service in the Netherlands. In total, approximately 5,000 Jews performed forced labour in around 50 different camps: see PMJ 5/110 and 111.
8 German in the original: 'social welfare officials'.
9 German in the original: 'Central Office [for Jewish Emigration]'.

themselves from that office. Those who have a stamp and are currently working in a Dutch camp will be allowed to return.

Transfers abroad etc. (statements by Mr Asscher)
It is thought that no further arrests will take place after tomorrow evening.[10] Yesterday evening the number was also relatively small. These people will generally stay in Amsterdam for the time being. This means the workload of all those involved in the Jewish Council will be slightly reduced, which is very necessary after the excessive working hours recently.

The chairmen made an appeal on behalf of very old people. What has happened to them is, of course, a major disaster.[11] The total number of people who have been sent on to Germany so far is more than 20,000.[12] This includes people from the provinces (yesterday 48 people from Alphen aan den Rijn arrested, families from Gorinchem, etc.). The efforts the chairmen have made to secure the release of rabbis Dünner[13] and Francès[14] and their families have been in vain, although they were told they could fulfil their roles as rabbis among the Dutch Jews in Germany. The efforts on behalf of Dr M. Pinkhof[15] and his family have been successful; they returned here yesterday.

The letters received from Germany are generally not too bad. Members of the Jewish Council can consult a summary report on this matter at Mr Brandon's office.

Further measures to be expected: Mr aus der Fünten has announced to the chairmen that Jews from everywhere outside Amsterdam (apart from the mental institution Het Apeldoornsche Bosch[16]), including Rotterdam and The Hague, will be evacuated in the months to come. They will go to the Westerbork and Vught camps, and if there is not enough room there, to Amsterdam. The intention is to send sick and elderly people to the camp in Vught.[17]

10 This hope was not realized. The families whose heads of household were in the Dutch labour camps were arrested on 2 and 3 Oct. 1942.

11 At the end of Sept. 1942, half of the Jewish homes for the elderly in Amsterdam were removed from the list of such homes that were under the Jewish Council's protection, and soon afterwards their residents were arrested and deported.

12 By this time, 18,918 persons had been deported from Westerbork.

13 Correctly: Josef Hersch Dinner.

14 Liaho Francès (1878–1942), rabbi; emigrated from Greece to the Netherlands in 1928; rabbi of the Portuguese Israelite Religious Community; worked for the Jewish Council from 1941; deported to Westerbork on 17 Sept. 1942, and then on 28 Sept. 1942 to Auschwitz, where he was murdered on arrival.

15 Dr Meijer Pinkhof (1892–1943), biologist; eldest brother of the writer Clara Asscher-Pinkhof; curator at Amsterdam Botanical Garden; arrested with his wife, Marianne Jeannette Pinkhof-Oppenheim (1896–1943) and their three youngest children on 13 Sept. 1942 and deported to Westerbork; the family members were released on 20. Sept. 1942 but then deported to Westerbork again in May 1943, and from there on 20 July 1943 to Sobibor, where they were all murdered a few days later. On their time in Westerbork camp, see Doc. 88.

16 The Jewish mental institution, established in 1909, was completely emptied on 21 Jan. 1943 and the residents and nursing staff were deported: see Docs. 103 and 104.

17 On 30 March 1943 all Jews still living in the provinces of Friesland, Groningen, Drenthe, Overijssel, Gelderland, Limburg, North Brabant, and Zeeland were told to report to Vught camp by 10 April 1943. On 13 April 1943 Jews were also forbidden to reside in the provinces of Utrecht, North Holland, and South Holland; only the City of Amsterdam was not included in the ban: see Doc. 117.

Although we have no idea how quickly this will happen, of course, this measure constitutes the worst-ever disaster to happen to Jewish people in the Netherlands. This was argued both by the chairmen, through Prof. Cohen, and by those who attended the meeting. Under the circumstances, the Jewish Council will do whatever it can to try to have as much of a say as possible in the camp's affairs in Westerbork and Vught, and it will also do everything possible to continue religious and cultural life there. If Vught remains at the same level as Westerbork, life will be bearable there – this was also confirmed by Prof. Cohen, who used to visit Westerbork frequently – and people will live and work there, with no intention to transfer them to Germany for the time being.

However, all of this will involve a major effort and a lot of work on the part of the Jewish Council, and all of its staff, with no exceptions, must be willing to be seconded to Westerbork or Vught for this purpose, if necessary. (Agreement.) During the transition months, committed cooperation between Jewish workers in Amsterdam and in the provinces will also be essential.

In accordance with a proposal by Prof. Cohen, the following notice will be included in the daily report to the members of the Jewish Council: 'Sending Jews to Germany for labour deployment will cease for the time being. The intention is to continue evacuating Jews from places outside Amsterdam. These evacuated people will go to camps in Westerbork and Vught; some will go to Amsterdam.'

Finances: (statement by Mr Asscher)
Following Prof. Cohen and Mr Asscher's meeting with the Beauftragte[18] and Messrs Rombach[19] and Korink,[20] a second meeting took place between Prof. Cohen, Mr Bolle, and Mr Krouwer[21] on the one hand and Lippmann, Rosenthal & Co. on the other. The results were not unsatisfactory. Although the provisions made for the deportees have required a large amount of money, we have now at least acquired a credit of fl. 300,000 based on the fl. 1,100,000 from the first instalment still to be collected from Lippros,[22] which will keep us going for the time being. After this the Jewish Council's second instalment will be collected; this will be done, insofar as the liable parties are account holders, by Lippmann, Rosenthal & Co. on behalf of the Jewish Council.

The next meeting will be called as and when required.

18 German in the original: 'representative'. The reference is to Werner Schröder, the Reich Commissioner's representative for Amsterdam.

19 Albert Rombach (1897–1968), lawyer; worked for the Prussian Ministry of the Interior in Münster, Arnsberg, Ratibor and Frankfurt an der Oder from 1929; joined the NSDAP in 1937; worked at the Reich Commissariat for the Occupied Dutch Territories, first as the representative for the City of Amsterdam, subsequently in the administration of the province of North Holland, and then again in Amsterdam, 1940–1945; chief clerk at Detmold welfare tribunal, 1954–1962.

20 Correctly: Paul Friedrich Gustav Ubbo Kohring (1902–1992), sales representative; aide to the representative for the City of Amsterdam.

21 Abraham Krouwer (1883–1965), retailer; member of the Jewish Council's finance committee; survived the war, presumably in hiding; barred by a Jewish 'court of honour' from participating in Jewish organizations after 1945.

22 Lippros is a seldom-used abbreviation for Lippmann, Rosenthal & Co. The reference is presumably to the amounts received by the Jewish Council from the so-called Liro funds – that is, from stolen Jewish assets – to cover its running costs.

DOC. 84

On 4 and 5 October 1942 Sam Goudsmit expresses indignation at British actions in the war and describes the progress of the deportations in Amsterdam[1]

Handwritten diary of Sam Goudsmit, entries for 4 and 5 October 1942

Sunday, 4 October 1942
Continuation of: Expulsion, etc.:
I will start by repeating what I wrote yesterday: *If you survive this, never again shake hands with an Englishman. This is not a code-word: I most certainly mean an Englishman, a member of the British nation. Never again shake hands with this hypocritical, selfish, and self-centred people.*

Meanwhile, I think that the chance of survival is steadily declining. No end to the war in sight for more than a year. And that is definitely too long for us.[2]

Half past three in the middle of the night –

This evening a Small Operation (I mean a small-scale hunt) probably took place, aimed only at women and their children, wives of those put to work, who were also paid a visit yesterday evening but were not yet taken away then.[3]

But, as usual, they will probably also have secretly taken away some other Jews. A special National Socialist police force has been engaged, brought here from other parts of the country, supplemented with the WA[4] of the NSB.[5]

Rumour has it that a *black week* has been announced. That would be this coming week.

A week *'such as the Jews have not yet experienced'*. It seems that this will be a terrible week for the Jews. No one knows yet what awaits us. But it looks like this coincides with more powers being granted to the Dutch NSB.[6] Perhaps it will now get the *power* here. And that power will certainly be used as a licence for a Jew hunt. A specific, small part of the Dutch people wants this to happen. And the other part, 95 per cent, allows this to happen – and so the fear and pressure will become even more intense.

Monday, 5 October 1942
Continuation of: Expulsion, etc.:
I am not obliged to update these chronicles about this onslaught against the Jews in Holland every day by virtue of my office. I cannot explain in more detail here why it is

1 Bibliotheca Rosenthaliana, HC-ROS-006. This document has been translated from Dutch.
2 Presumably Goudsmit is here referring to the failed Allied invasion of Dieppe on 19 August 1942.
3 On 2 and 3 Oct. 1942 the male Jews held in the labour camps in the Netherlands were deported to Westerbork. Simultaneously, their family members in Amsterdam were arrested and also deported. In total, approximately 13,000 Jews were affected by this operation.
4 Weerbaarheidsafdeling, Dutch for 'Defence Section'; the paramilitary arm of the NSB.
5 In the course of this operation, various German and Dutch units were deployed, including the German Order Police, the Dutch police, and members of the Dutch SS. The allegation that WA members participated in these arrests could not be proved.
6 Rumours repeatedly circulated alleging that Mussert, the leader of the NSB, was to be granted greater responsibilities, even extending to forming a government. However, this never came to pass.

taking place, as I have already done that. One can only repeat that, every day, the manner in which this extermination campaign is conducted against them again and again provokes the question: *But why is this happening?* Why, for example, should the Jews be the so-called enemy in this war, rather than each citizen of the occupied territory? And, if this slogan puts the conqueror in a negative light for the population of the conquered territories, why then constantly step up this persecution as if it were an operation against dangerous vermin? Why are women with many children, old men and women, the ill and the disabled dragged from their sleep at 5 or 6 o'clock in the morning, to be loaded onto trucks and taken to an assembly point, and then transported to the train, which takes three hours to get to a camp,[7] whence they will be subjected to a journey of about three days to arrive in Poland or Silesia, without knowing anything about what awaits them? And why is all of this done by police units who have completed a special course to develop their hatred of the Jews? Why does the leadership demand all this?

It seems as though they deliberately want to leave us in the dark about the development of the measures.

No one seems to know:
- whether or not deportation abroad will go ahead;
- whether those 'exempted' from camps will *remain* exempted;
- whether or not exemption from deportation is permanent;
- whether those who are exempted may stay at home or will be detained in a small ghetto, and if so, which measures would then apply …

It seems certain to me that this war will *not* end in 1942, but will last at least until the spring of 1943. This means that the chance that we will survive has become very small. For there is no doubt that this onslaught is directed against our lives, as has been openly stated, as everyone is aware. Is this a revenge campaign against the rich Jews who allegedly provoked the war? And who have nothing to fear from this campaign themselves? I am talking now of motives that are *stated*, rather than any deeper underlying causes that are more complex and more convoluted. Perhaps the police units that empty the Jews' homes and *seal* them the next day are aware of the underlying reasons for doing so in detail? They have been educated in economics, sociology, and politics. (?)[8]

7 Westerbork transit camp, from where almost all the deportation trains departed.
8 Question mark in the original.

DOC. 85

On 5 October 1942 Gerard Aleid van der Hal asks General Christiansen to exempt him from deportation because he is a severely disabled war veteran[1]

Handwritten letter from G. A. van der Hal,[2] Utrecht, 73 Petrarcalaan, to His Excellency the Wehrmacht Commander for the Occupied Dutch Territories Air Marshal Christiansen, 's Gravenhage (received on 8 October 1942), dated 5 October 1942[3]

The undersigned, while serving as a Dutch Jewish infantryman, was so badly injured in the fighting (May 1940) at the Grebbeberg[4] that he will be severely disabled for the rest of his life (see enclosed medical reports).[5]

Under these circumstances, I most respectfully request Your Excellency, if possible, to kindly instruct the 'Central Office for Jewish Emigration' that my name (and [those] of my wife and child[6]) is to be deleted from [the records of] this authority, and that I thus am ineligible for emigration.[7]

With most sincere gratitude to Your Excellency in advance, signed
most respectfully

1 NIOD, 077/1849. Published in facsimile in Presser, *Ondergang*, vol. 2, after p. 184. This document has been translated from German.

2 Gerard Aleid van der Hal (1909–1943), retailer; deported from a military hospital to Vught camp in the spring of 1943; on 8 June 1943 deported via Westerbork to Sobibor, where he was murdered upon arrival.

3 The original contains handwritten notes, underlining, and stamps.

4 In the battle at the Grebbeberg (11–13 May 1940), the Dutch army attempted to prevent the Wehrmacht from breaking through the Dutch defence line (the Grebbe Line). The Dutch army lost 382 soldiers and was unable to hold the line.

5 These are not included in the file. Van der Hal's right leg had been amputated and his left leg was badly damaged.

6 Klaartje van der Hal-Walg (1912–1943) and Benjamin Andries van der Hal (1935–1943) were also imprisoned in Vught camp and were deported along with van der Hal to Sobibor, where they were murdered.

7 There are two handwritten notes. The first, presumably by F. Christiansen, reads: 'A Jew is a Jew, whether he has legs or not, and if we do not defeat and eliminate the Jew, then he will eliminate us.' The second note reads: '8 June [19]43 East.'

DOC. 86

On 11 October 1942 Amsterdam resident Kurt Schroeter reflects on the uncertainty facing the Jews and the system of exemptions[1]

Handwritten diary of Kurt Schroeter,[2] entry for 11 October 1942[3]

Sunday evening, 11 October

Gloomy, anxious days full of uncertainty. And in spite of all the human goodness and kindness that one experiences in particular instances, there is so much, so very much, that is abominable, repugnant, and dreadful, both on a small and a large scale.

At the moment, it looks as if I am to be one of those left without even temporary protection from the clutches of the Nazis. In the face of the danger of deportation to eastern Germany, Poland, etc., it was (and is) possible here to 'exempt' certain categories of Jews.[4] To start with, those who work in some sort of enterprise that serves the Wehrmacht. Next, everybody who is part of the 'Joodsche Raad',[5] which is one of the worst, most dismal signs of the times. Originally a small organization intended to serve as an intermediary between the Jewish community and the German government, it has turned into a gigantic administrative apparatus, which, in practice, must implement, under the direct orders and command of the Nazis, all measures directed against the Jews – and, in addition, it offers advice and help to alleviate distress and lends support to individuals. This 'council' has of course made it possible for its members and employees, and then for their relatives, to secure the 'exemption stamp' (which reads 'pending further notice') and that has developed into an enormous opportunity for fraud, which is sickening. – Another piece of grotesqueness in itself is the fact that the 'baptized' Jews were privileged here,[6] whereby the Nazis' core principle, the racial doctrine, is simply obliterated, of course, but thousands are thus temporarily protected. The only category that, in compliance with German law, had to be officially exempted of course is spouses in a mixed marriage with children who are regarded as 'Aryan'. Nobody even doubted that these people would be in the same position here as in Germany. To register for this, I sent for your passports,[7] which were then duly submitted two weeks ago. And now comes the

1 The original is privately owned. Copy in IfZ-Archives, F 601. Published in Kurt Schroeter, *Tage, die so quälend sind: Aufzeichnungen eines jüdischen Bürgers aus Gröbenzell im besetzten Amsterdam, September 1942–Januar 1943*, ed. Kurt Lehnstaedt (Munich: R. Kovar, 1993), pp. 40–42. This document has been translated from German.

2 Kurt Schroeter (1882–1944), engineer and violin teacher; in 1937 emigrated from Germany to the Netherlands, where he worked as a violin teacher; arrested in August 1943 during a roundup in Amsterdam and sent to Vught concentration camp; on 15 Nov. 1943 deported to Auschwitz, where he was murdered on 2 Jan. 1944.

3 The original contains handwritten underlining.

4 See Doc. 79.

5 Dutch in the original: 'Jewish Council'.

6 On 14 July 1942 Fritz Schmidt, commissioner general for special duties, informed the churches that Christian Jews would not be deported as long as they had belonged to the Christian faith prior to January 1941: see Doc. 65.

7 Kurt Schroeter is evidently addressing his two daughters here: Marianne Schroeter (1913–1971), translator; emigrated to Sweden in 1936 and returned to Germany in 1952; Sigrid Schroeter (1920–1999), lived in Switzerland from 1935 onwards.

outrageous thing: some SS zealot here is attempting to establish that protection can be granted only to those whose children are under the age of 21 (others say even 18 or 16)![8] – There is as yet no certainty about this; one rushes to a different authority every day, trying to find out. If this limitation really goes through – and it seems likely! – then I am immediately at risk and, if I don't want to *immediately* go the way chosen by Dele and so many thousands of others, I must 'disappear' here, with the assistance of friends and other helpful people. That is also very dangerous, of course, and, if it has to continue for a long time, it is bound up with an almost unbearable degree of deprivation and want. – It is indeed the case that a decent individual, who has no idea how to 'scam' and how to find and take all the crooked paths, faces certain doom unless an unanticipated, quick turnaround in the war improves the situation, which at any rate is only to be *wished* for, can scarcely be *hoped* for, and is certainly not *expected*. – All of this is outlined here in just a few matter-of-fact words. But what one experiences in the midst of such events and hundreds of thousands of half-mad people; how one sees people in their naked helplessness and primitive self-centredness – on the other hand, in their readiness to help and their extreme dedication; how one strives inwardly for one's own continued existence; and how difficult it all is when one is alone, as I am, in the midst of all the others, who after all are almost all here as 'families'.[9] One would have to write a book to describe that, and be able to do so with the skill of a poet.

I don't want to speak in a personal way about all that one suffers inwardly in the process. The one person[10] who would fully understand it comprehends and knows it from her own experience without my needing to say it. – For you, my children, I want to say now that I intend to struggle along, trying as hard as I can, for as long as my strength holds out. Which of us knows exactly what drives and sustains us? Indeed, the drive for self-preservation clothes itself in desire and will. And, even if life does not have much more to promise me, I feel above all the wish and the desire to be united with you and Mother again after all, and to give as much love and goodness as might still be possible, indeed as must be possible precisely for someone who has suffered so long and so much, and yet has not been diminished and defeated in the process, as I may indeed say of myself. – Nonetheless: it *may* be the case that every day one is faced with the decision of whether it is wiser and more dignified to voluntarily end one's existence rather than to allow oneself to be martyred slowly by merciless brutes – at an age when one's strength will no longer suffice for years of misery. –

8 In Germany, so-called mixed marriages were regarded as 'privileged' if the marriages had been contracted before the 1935 Nuremberg Laws and the Jewish spouse as well as the legitimate children no longer belonged to the Jewish religious community: see PMJ 2/215. This was the case for Kurt Schroeter and his daughters, as he sought to prove by means of the passports sent to him. No evidence could be found for the tightening of the provisions for the Netherlands as mentioned here.

9 Kurt Schroeter had emigrated to the Netherlands alone; his wife remained in Germany.

10 Ilse Schroeter, née von Voigts-Rhetz (1887–1968), teacher; married Kurt Schroeter in 1920.

DOC. 87

In a Radio Oranje address on 17 October 1942, Queen Wilhelmina expresses sympathy for the plight of the Jews in the Netherlands and appeals to the population for solidarity[1]

Text version of the address given by Queen Wilhelmina[2] on Radio Oranje, dated 17 October 1942

Fellow countrymen,

Impeded by a slight indisposition, after which I had to rest, I have been unable to address you sooner. It is therefore an even greater pleasure to address you now.

I once again feel impelled to reflect with you for a few moments, with respect and consideration, on the memory of those who have fallen as victims of the senseless bloodthirst of the Moffen,[3] both those among them whose names and execution we are aware of, and all those who have been slaughtered in secret by the despicable fiend who has deemed it right to conceal this from us. Our heartfelt thoughts are with all those who mourn these martyrs.

The memory of these men will live on in your heart and mine.

May we find strength in this memory for the pure preservation of that for which they sacrificed their lives: the freedom and honour of the Netherlands.

May God give us the strength to do so.

The Wilhelmus[4]

With much attention and with great concern I follow your increasing difficulties and growing need in every area, and with equal interest I follow the increasingly unbearable uncertainty in your lives, which you are faced with day after day, and I follow the bitter suffering of the thousands of people in prison or in concentration camps; in brief, the mental and physical abuse inflicted upon you by the hated enemy.

I wholeheartedly share your indignation and sorrow over the fate of our Jewish compatriots, and together with all my people, I feel as a personal injustice the inhumane treatment, the systematic extermination of these compatriots, who lived with us in our blessed country for centuries.

Where you are not allowed to express your feelings, I now do so on your behalf.

We will endeavour to alleviate at least some of this pain as soon as possible.

1 NIOD, Radio Oranje, 17 Oct. 1942. Published in *De koningin sprak: Proclamaties en radio-toespraken van H. M. Koningin Wilhelmina 1940–1945*, ed. M. G. Schenk and J. B. Th. Spaan (Driebergen: Christelijk Lektuurkontakt, 1985), pp. 87–89. This document has been translated from Dutch.

2 Queen Wilhelmina of the Netherlands (1880–1962); became queen of the Netherlands on the death of her father, William III (1817–1890), though her mother Emma (1858–1934) was regent during her daughter's minority; married Heinrich von Mecklenburg-Schwerin (1876–1934), a German, in 1901; fled on 13 May 1940 to Britain, where she led the Dutch government in exile; in 1948 abdicated in favour of her daughter, Juliana (1909–2004).

3 A long-standing satirical or pejorative Dutch term for Germans, used predominantly during and after the Second World War.

4 The Dutch national anthem, the 'Wilhelmus', was played at this juncture.

Anyone who, in whatever manner, continues to collaborate with this terror regime will have to accept the consequences of this after our liberation, and will have to fully account for their deeds.

Fellow countrymen working in factories or workshops, I know how difficult it has been made for you to decide and act as you wish, to be and remain yourselves in the true interests of our people.

I know that you always have those interests at heart and, faced with difficult decisions, will take decisions like bold young Dutch men without hesitating, with a view to the future, and without reflecting on the possible drawbacks in the present.

Farmers and market gardeners, you who provide food for the people and see yourselves faced with an even heavier responsibility than ever before, you who feel rooted in your community and your land, which you would not want to relinquish at any price, I know that our people can count on you, on your tough nature, and that you are always prepared to make sustained efforts to help.

Your battle is now the battle for the survival of our entire people.

One day, your robust attitude and resilience will yield the most wonderful results, which will be worthy of all our appreciation and admiration.

These are the secret of the strength of our people, now and in the future.

And when we speak here of the strength of our people in its deepest essence, now and in the future, we mention in one breath its spirit of mutual willingness to help and its awareness that it constitutes one big family.

Speaking about that unity of our people, our thoughts automatically turn to our suppressed and suffering fellow citizens in the Dutch overseas territories in the tropics, whose fate is the same as yours, and who, in close mutual support and solidarity with you, stand firm in the mental battle against the common enemy.[5]

Under the fresh impression of the latest atrocities, carried out in all occupied European countries, the image familiar to all of us of a cat being driven into a corner and then leaping out springs to mind involuntarily amidst all my sorrow.[6]

And this is certainly not a discouraging image for us.

Fellow countrymen, we shall win the war, and we want to and we shall win the peace, which, from the present misery we are bearing together, will bring us renewal in every respect.

For whoever says liberation, also says renewal.

Forged and shaped in the sacred fire that inspires you; strengthened by a deep sense of responsibility for the enormous task you have taken upon yourselves; willing to give the best that your heart, your head, and your hands are able to give; that peace will guarantee a better future for our offspring.

We want to be ourselves, on our own free soil, we want to be able to live in good faith, with ourselves, with God, and with all our people in true community.

May God grant to us that this will come to pass in the not too distant future.

5 The Dutch army in the Dutch East Indies – today Indonesia – was forced to capitulate to Japanese troops on 8 March 1942. The Japanese occupied the entire territory until 1945.

6 The Dutch proverb 'Een kat in het nauw maakt rare sprongen' (lit: 'A cat in a corner makes crazy leaps') means that desperate people will do whatever it takes.

DOC. 88

Between 13 September and 19 October 1942 Detje Pinkhof writes a fairy tale for her sister Claartje about her time in Westerbork camp[1]

Handwritten fairy tale about Claartje Pink,[2] as told by Aunt Det,[3] with drawings by the author, created in the camp between 13 September and 19 October 1942[4]

Chapter 1
How Claartje Pink and her family arrived at the heathland camp[5]
Claartje Pink and her family lived in a large wood called 'Park Wood'.

They were city dwarfs and had lived in the city's Park Wood all their life.[6]

Claartje was from a large family; she had as many as four sisters.[7]

And she was the youngest dwarf sister.

Apart from the four sisters, there were also a father and a mother.[8]

Father Pink was a wise dwarf who received all kinds of little dwarfs in a large rabbit hole, where he taught them a lot about plants and animals.

Nearly all the dwarfs Claartje knew wore a marigold[9] on their chests …, and something terrible happened to them.

One night a thundering noise made the paths shake.

The little front doors of the unlucky dwarfs were torn open.

They were pulled out of their little holes and houses, and dragged away by huge giants.

Oh, how awful!

Oh, how dreadful!

1 The original is privately owned. Copy in YVA, P. 45/1, pp. 123–130 and 150–153. Published in Detje Pinkhof, *Een dagboek met sprookjes uit Kamp Westerbork* (Haarlem: Tuindorp, 1998), pp. 65–77. This document has been translated from Dutch.
2 Correctly: Clara (Claartje) Pinkhof (1928–1943); in May 1943 deported together with her parents and two of her sisters to Westerbork, and from there on 20 July 1943 to Sobibor, where they all were murdered several days later.
3 Correctly: Adèle (Detje) Pinkhof (1924–1943), nursery school teacher; Clara's sister; worked in the Jewish Council's nursery school; deported and murdered along with her parents and two of her sisters.
4 The fairy tale is part of Detje Pinkhof's diary. Part 1 was presumably written in the camp; the loose sheets were later pasted into the diary as part of the entry for 5 Oct., which is interrupted by the fairy tale. Part 2 was written directly in the diary, preceding the entry for 15 Oct. The Pinkhofs and three of their daughters were arrested for the first time on 13 Sept. 1942 and deported to Westerbork. On 30 Sept. 1942, they were allowed to return to Amsterdam, as the management of the botanical garden and the Jewish Council had interceded on Meijer Pinkhof's behalf: see Doc. 83.
5 Westerbork camp was situated in the heathlands in the north-east of the Netherlands (province of Drenthe).
6 The family lived in Amsterdam in the 'Plantagebuurt' neighbourhood, which is situated near the zoo and is characterized by the presence of many trees and other greenery.
7 Correctly: three. In total, including Clara, there were four sisters. Her sisters were Esther Roza (1922–1998), Adèle, and Sophie (1925–1943). Esther, who was married and did not live with the family, was deported to Bergen-Belsen but survived.
8 Meijer Pinkhof and his wife, Marianne Jeannette Pinkhof-Oppenheim (1896–1943).
9 The yellow star that Jews were required to wear as of 1 May 1942: see PMJ 5/130 and 132.

All the captured dwarfs were loaded onto small carts drawn by skunks.

Off they went, travelling all through the night.

Away from the wood.

'Farewell, wood! Will we ever see you again?' the dwarfs shouted.

At dawn the next day, they arrived at a large heath.

They heard a whistle.

And immediately hundreds and hundreds of dwarfs came running towards them. The giants unharnessed the skunks and left.

The city dwarfs were taken away by the heath dwarfs.[10]

Oh, how tired they were!

And how hungry they were!

But perhaps now they would be able to get some rest.

Chapter 2
Adventures in the camp

The heath dwarfs took the poor creatures to their houses among the heather roots. It was not nearly as pleasant there as it had been in their wood holes.

But still, things were not bad. Everywhere they saw city dwarfs who had been changed into heath dwarfs walking around. They said the skunks would occasionally come back and drag away some of the heath dwarfs.

Where to?

Why?

They could not say.

Claartje Pink and her family were taken to a small dwarf house. All the houses on the heath were already so full that not all the members of the large Pink family could be fitted in together.

So Father Pink and a few other dwarfs slept elsewhere.

Many dwarfs were already living in Claartje's house: Jo Sugar Bowl, Claartje Apple Cheek with her little calf Ali, and tiny Bennie Potato with his mother.

The house was a very noisy place.

In the afternoon they all went for a walk together.

First they were taken to the hamsters, who lived on the edge of the heath. The hamsters sniffed all their sacks and gathered together all their belongings, as hamsters do.[11]

How empty their sacks were!

Nothing was left!

Then they were taken to the Grand Heath Council.

There they had to promise to behave like good little dwarfs, and if they were found to be nice, then they would be allowed to stay.

They could only hope this was true.

10 A reference to the deportations; the trains to Auschwitz left from Westerbork almost every Tuesday morning.

11 Presumably an allusion to the Westerbork department of the bank Lippmann, Rosenthal & Co., where all valuables and money had to be handed in.

Chapter 3
What happened next in their little house
What a commotion there was in their little house at night.

The whole night, Jo Sugar Bowl prattled about her glow-worm, which she did not have with her, and Ali Calf's 'Moo, moo' could be heard throughout the house.

Bennie sang, for he was a cheerful little fellow, and all the Pinks shouted at the same time.

However, the cold and the noise made poor Claartje ill, and she had to go to the Field Hospital.

The clever Hare brought her there, as he was the physician.

There she went, poor Claartje.

She was taken there in a hollowed-out tree branch.

The hospital was in a mole tunnel. It was really well equipped.[12]

The nursing staff – burying beetles – scurried to and fro.

They drank from acorn shells and ate from flower petal halves.

Conclusion
The birthday
In spite of the good treatment, the comfortable bed made of moss, and the good food, Claartje cried the whole day.

She even left her little mug of dewdrops untouched.

At last the physician said that she had been cured. The Pinks were so happy!

An ant wearing an OD[13] band took her home.

And the next day was her birthday.

Not her ordinary birthday, but her flower birthday, as all dwarfs who wear a marigold have an extra birthday.[14]

They may not have been at home, but the family nevertheless hoped it would be a real flower day!

And you, children, who have read this little book, do you hope so too?

[...][15]

Part 2
Chapter 1
Claartje Pink's return
How the heath dwarfs changed into wood dwarfs
Many days passed. Claartje Pink was still living in the house on the heath. One night a wicked dwarf entered their house. He had a red nose with a drip on the end of it.

12 The hospital in Westerbork was indeed relatively well equipped. At one time there were 120 physicians and more than 1,000 nurses and orderlies taking care of the more than 1,700 patients.

13 The Order Service (Ordedienst – OD), which was made up of Jews, was responsible for guarding the punishment barracks and maintaining order in Westerbork camp.

14 Clara Pinkhof was born on 26 Sept. 1928. In the Jewish calendar, this date corresponds to 12 Tishri 5689. In 1942, 12 Tishri fell on 23 Sept.

15 Here follow 19 pages with diary entries for 7–15 Oct. 1942.

'Does Jo Sugar Bowl live here?' he thundered. But he had not come for Jo Sugar Bowl alone: he also came for all the other dwarfs in the little house, apart from the Pinks.

And the next day, they had all gone.

'Oh, how empty was the house!'

'Oh, how lonely they were!'

But do you think that the Pinks were allowed to stay in their little house?

You are wrong!

They had to move again.

They each tied an empty acorn on their back with a blade of grass and put their belongings into it. And so they went to their new home.

They did not live there very long, though.

One day Father Pink was summoned to appear before the Heath Council.

Oh dear! That gave the dwarfs a fright.

The Heath Council, which was aware how well-behaved Father Pink had been, had decided to change the family back into city dwarfs and send them back to Park Wood.

'Will you always behave well?' they asked Father Pink. 'Always!' he promised earnestly. Imagine how happy the Pinks were!

And the whole camp was happy for them too.

'We hope we will see you back in our wood again soon!' the Pinks said.

When they had said farewell to everyone, they had to appear before a bumblebee, who took his sting and waved it around in the air. At the same time he called out: 'Le Roli, Le Roli, Happesoupechai!'

And suddenly the Pinks were city dwarfs again.

Chapter 2
What happened while they were on their way
A field mouse, travelling to a neighbouring dwarf village with a cart full of grain, took them along for some distance. Farewell! Farewell! Goodbye! the Pinks shouted, and they waved with their handkerchiefs to the disappearing camp.

They had grown very fond of the camp. So much had happened there.

But now they were going back home, which was splendid.

After the Pinks had said goodbye to the field mouse, it was still a long walk to the beginning of a mole tunnel. How tired they were, those poor Pinks. Fortunately a few ladybirds appeared, who helped them carry their things.

A friendly fly asked Father Pink if he would get a worker ant when they reached the other end of the mole tunnel. (The mole tunnel led from the heath camp to Park Wood.)

The fly flew off quickly.

Then they all got on a long earthworm, and slowly they continued.

How impatient they became, and how desperate they were to get home. They stopped at every sideway. At last, the worm went back up, and they saw the clear blue sky again.

'Hurrah!' shouted all the wood dwarfs who had come to collect them. 'Here they are back again, who would have thought it?' They cheerfully returned to their hole in the willow. And oh, how well they slept that first night!

The End

DOC. 89

On 19 October 1942 two members of the Jewish Council describe the Jewish community's problems to the head of the Central Office for Jewish Emigration[1]

Record of meeting attended by Prof. D. Cohen and Dr E. Sluzker,[2] unsigned, dated 19 October 1942 (carbon copy)

Meeting of Prof. D. Cohen and Dr E. Sluzker with Mr Hauptsturmführer aus der Fünten on Monday, 19 October 1942

[1.] We pointed out to Mr aus der Fünten that the fact that the chief rabbi[3] and his family have been removed from their apartment and taken to the theatre[4] with the intention of deporting them to Germany has been a severe blow to the Jewish community. The Jewish Council was dealt an equally severe blow when the same happened to Mr Bolle[5] on Thursday, 15 October. We argued that his place in the Jewish Council cannot be taken by anyone else, which will lead to difficulties in following up on instructions.

1 NIOD, 182/4. This document has been translated from Dutch.

2 Dr Edwin Sluzker (1907–1965), lawyer; practised law in Vienna; fled to the Netherlands in 1938; worked in the field of refugee aid from 1939; head of the Expositur, 1941–1943; lived in hiding from 1944; practised law in Amsterdam after 1945.

3 Lodewijk Hartog Sarlouis (1884–1942), rabbi; chief rabbi of Amsterdam from 1936; member of the Jewish Council from Feb. 1942; deported to Westerbork in Oct. 1942, and then to Auschwitz, where he was murdered upon arrival.

4 The Joodsche Schouwburg.

5 Meijer Henri Max Bolle.

Mr aus der Fünten said that he was fully aware of all this, but the order had come from The Hague, and he had tried to have the order withdrawn, but had failed to achieve this. Any step on our part would therefore be fruitless. Both the chief rabbi and Mr Bolle would be sent to Germany with their families.

We asked him to conduct a hearing with them so that they could defend themselves against the charge. This was rejected as being impossible. We could not be informed of the reason [for the charge] either; it could only be indicated that it was apparently to do with letters, which had possibly been composed without any bad intentions.[6] (Perhaps it should be added here that both had been taken on 21 October to Westerbork, whence they were sent to Germany on 23 October, the chief rabbi as the spiritual leader of the transport, and Mr Bolle as the leader. Both have accepted their fate with the courage that matches their dignity.[7])

2. We then asked whether it would be possible to forward letters from Germany and offered to send someone to collect them. However, this was rejected because obtaining a travel permit would involve too much trouble. However, our proposal that we would take responsibility for censoring the outgoing letters was accepted; it was agreed that we would submit the opened letters in parcels, which would then be dispatched. In the course of the meeting, we pointed out that the link with Auschwitz is apparently so poor that we have not even received any notifications of any deaths, which surely must have occurred over time among such a large population.

3. We then pointed out that, according to the plans, Jews are to be concentrated in three locations, in Amsterdam, Westerbork, and Vught. We requested and were granted permission to submit memoranda regarding the Jewish Council's task in the two camps; Mr aus der Fünten declared that he was in principle willing to involve the Jewish Council in the work. We were told that workplaces will be created in Vught. We requested and were granted permission to provide assistance in this respect as well.

4. We stated that, in addition to the physicians already working in Westerbork, the Sicherheitspolizei[8] in 's-Hertogenbosch had invited Dr Diamant[9] to act as the leader of the medical staff in Westerbork, and later in Vught. We said that we would have liked to have been informed of the choice as, with all due respect to Dr Diamant, we would have preferred the appointment of a younger doctor as the head of medical care. It was promised that this would be considered.

5. We pointed out that moving to Transvaalbuurt is difficult, as in many cases the keys for the houses are not issued when permission is granted.[10] It was agreed that, if neces-

6 The grounds for the two men's arrest could not be ascertained.

7 The minutes were usually typed up a few days after the meeting; this explains how the fate of the two deportees was already known.

8 German in the original: 'Security Police'.

9 Dr Salomon (Sal) Diamant (1881–1958), physician; active in the Dutch Israelite Religious Community; briefly interned in Westerbork in 1942; interned in Barneveld in 1943; deported from there to Theresienstadt in April 1943; returned to 's-Hertogenbosch in 1945; thought to have returned to practising medicine.

10 Presumably this was about handing over the keys to apartments whose occupants had been deported to Westerbork; Jews who were forced to move to the Transvaalbuurt neighbourhood from the provinces or from other parts of Amsterdam had to move into these apartments.

sary, the Zentralstelle für jüdische Auswanderung[11] will issue a declaration, stating that the houses must be made available.

The other items to be discussed were postponed due to lack of time.

DOC. 90
On 19 October 1942 Leny Jakobs-Melkman reflects on whether she should put her children into hiding[1]

Handwritten letter from Leny Jakobs-Melkman,[2] Amsterdam, 49 Den Texstraat, to Theo Westerhoff,[3] Amsterdam, 115 Postjeskade, dated 19 October 1942

Dear Mr Westerhoff,

What I wanted to tell you, and what I could not say very easily over the phone, is that if we are going to be travelling,[4] it is highly likely we will take our children[5] with us. I had an address[6] where I could have put up Poortje, but that would mean we would have to hand her over now, and we would have to go into hiding as well. We cannot possibly go into hiding now, with a baby[7] due. Going into hiding is difficult enough in itself, but with a black child[8] it becomes really awkward. When you find an address where you can go, and the people there get to a point where it all becomes too much for them, you have nowhere else to turn. I have already come across this around here.

Perhaps we could approach Miss G. for an address where we could take the children, but it is always the case in such a situation that people prefer to get the children at once, and I cannot do that. I cannot send the children away from home now, while I can perhaps stay here for another couple of months. In any case, the neighbours would be aware of this. Poortje makes such a striking appearance in our street that everyone would notice her absence. And as not everyone is to be trusted, things would

11 German in the original: 'Central Office for Jewish Emigration'.

1 The original is privately owned. Copy in IfZ-Archives, F 601. Excerpts published in Hans Ziekenoppasser, 'Stem uit het verleden', *Nieuw Israëlietisch Weekblad*, 147, no. 27 (2012), pp. 68–71. This document has been translated from Dutch.

2 Dr Lena (Leny) Jakobs (also Jacobs)-Melkman (1910–1944), physician and educator; married the physician Jonas Jakobs (1908–1945) in 1936; went into hiding with her children at various locations; arrested without her children in June 1943; deported to Westerbork; deported in Oct. 1943 to Auschwitz, where she was murdered.

3 Correctly: Theodor (Theo) Westerhof (1906–2010), administrative official; secretary to the Dutch philosopher Philip Kohnstamm (1875–1951) from the late 1920s; moved with Kohnstamm to the Nut Institute (see fn. 15); lived in hiding from 1943; worked as a stenographer in the Dutch parliament after 1945.

4 The imminent deportation of the family.

5 The children Abraham (b. 1937) and Tzipora (Poortje) Jacobs (b. 1939) survived the occupation period in hiding; after 1945, they lived with their mother's brother's family and emigrated to Israel with them in 1957.

6 Presumably the address of Theo and Inge (Rob) Tangelder, with whom Tzipora was living.

7 Ada Jacobs (b. 1943) survived the occupation period in hiding; after 1945, she lived with her father's sister's family and emigrated to Israel with them in 1955.

8 A black-haired child, to whom a Jewish origin could quickly be imputed.

go wrong. I know parents who have been sent to Germany because their children were no longer at home.

Now we still have a chance that, if we are taken away, we can secretly leave the children at home and then place them in the good care of acquaintances, who should then drop them off at a good address. In the first place, the chances that this will work are very small, as lately houses have been sealed off immediately[9] after the occupants depart, and secondly, we have already experienced that scenario ourselves. We have already been taken to Adema van Scheltemaplein[10] in the evening once before, but fortunately we were allowed to leave. We were back home at half past six in the morning. It was a horrible experience, although the fact that we have lived to tell the tale here in Amsterdam is good. First of all, we had to walk back and forth in the street, in front of our door, from 10 o'clock till 11 o'clock, while waiting for a police van, and after that we were driven around until half past midnight to collect people everywhere. Initially we were hopeful that we would be released, but when we were still in Utrechtsche Straat after midnight, we thought it was getting too late for the Zentralstelle[11] and that we would go straight to the station. I was so terribly frightened thinking about what might happen to the children. We had managed to inform the neighbours, but it was still awful having to think that I would never see them again and would not know if they had ended up in good hands. And therefore, unless I am absolutely certain that they will end up in a good place, I cannot leave them behind. It is easy to think about what is best or would offer the best chances in theory, and perhaps even that is not as easy as it looks, but things are even more complicated in practice. I know a few children who have been left behind by their parents, and who are moving from one family to the next. You have to feel that once yourself, what it means to abandon your children like that, before you are able to judge what it means to sever this natural bond forever. The children are too little for this, and I cannot do it. Unless I am certain that this is what is best for them.

Meanwhile, we have our 'stamp'.[12] We had already unpacked our rucksacks, but I am going to pack them again, as the famous Bolle and the chief rabbi[13] have been arrested, and their stamp has been covered over by a 2nd stamp: 'ungültig'.[14] That is the true worth of all this stamping business everyone is getting so wound up about. The Jews are to be exterminated, and it would be foolish to think that you happen to be the one or among the few who will not be exterminated.

And yet you do have to be foolish enough to think this, as that is the only way to keep up your courage. For the other option, i.e. holding out until the end of the war, seems to be fading away.

9 Once the occupants were deported, the police would seal their apartments so that the furnishings could be inventoried by Rosenberg Task Force staff and passed on to other organizations or bombed-out families in Germany.

10 Correctly: Adama van Scheltemaplein. This was the location of the Central Office for Jewish Emigration, where Jewish detainees were assembled in the summer and autumn of 1942 before their deportation to Westerbork.

11 German in the original: 'Central Office [for Jewish Emigration]'.

12 Exemption stamps could provide a temporary respite from deportation; on the exemption system, see Introduction, pp. 34–35 and 37–38.

13 Meijer Henri Max Bolle and Lodewijk Hartog Sarlouis: see Doc. 89.

14 German in the original: 'null and void'.

It continues to surprise me that the Nutsseminarium[15] still exists. And that it does while there is an 'Educators' Guild'[16] and so many institutions have been discontinued. It seems to me that people are working hard behind the scenes for this purpose. In any case, it is certain that the leadership of the Nutsseminarium is in good hands.

I would like to speak to Prof. Langeveld[17] once again, but I cannot possibly visit him. I owe him so much. At a time when others, who imagined they had the right to show other people how to live their lives, had disappointed me exceedingly, Prof. L. was a true breath of fresh air to me because of his independent thinking. It was thanks to him that I learned to recognize again what I should and should not do, as before that I had completely lost my way. And that is why I am extremely fond of him. Please pass on my warm regards to him.

With very best wishes,

DOC. 91

On 28 October 1942 the German representative for the City of Amsterdam empowers his counterparts in the provinces to have the homes of Jewish deportees emptied[1]

Telex (no. 57, 28 October 1942, 10.18 p.m. – marked 'confidential') from the representative for the City of Amsterdam, signed Schröder,[2] to the Reich Commissioner's representatives in the provinces (received on 29 October 1942), dated 28 October 1942[3]

Re: Jewish residences in the provinces (excluding The Hague and Rotterdam)
In consultation with the Commissioner General for Security[4] and with the Rosenberg Task Force, I hereby inform you that the Reich Commissioner's representatives in the provinces are empowered to clear the residences of Jewish families that have become vacant as a result of evacuation, in cases where these residences are required for the accommodation of Dutch nationals returning from the coastal areas[5] or for other reasons.

15 As early as the eighteenth century, certain schools in the Netherlands advocated a tolerant, multifaceted, liberal education. In 1918 the Nut Institute (Nutsseminarium) was created at the University of Amsterdam to study and promote this pedagogical approach. It had a lasting impact on primary and secondary schools, and continued to exist until the 1960s. It was headed by Philip Kohnstamm from 1919 to 1943.

16 The Opvoedersgilde, founded in 1940, was an organization associated with the NSB. It promoted education along National Socialist lines. However, with 4,000 members at most in 1943, it was never influential.

17 Dr Martinus (Martien) Langeveld (1905–1989), teacher and educator; at the University of Utrecht from 1939; succeeded Philip Kohnstamm as head of the Nut Institute, 1943–1945.

1 NIOD, 086/397. This document has been translated from German.

2 Dr Werner Schröder (b. 1898); joined the NSDAP in 1933; the Reich Commissioner's representative for the province of Overijssel, 1940–1943; representative for the City of Amsterdam from 1942, and also for the province of North Holland from 1943; thought to have returned to Germany in 1946.

3 The original contains handwritten underlining and an illegible note, as well as receipt stamps from the representative for the province of Limburg.

4 Hanns Albin Rauter.

5 In May 1942 the German occupying forces declared the Dutch coast a prohibited zone. For fear of a possible Allied invasion, the Atlantic Wall was to be reinforced. Unless they were required for the war economy, the residents of the coastal regions had to move gradually to the interior of the country.

A short report is to be drawn up on the clearing of each individual residence, listing the individual items in the home. The local mayors are to arrange for a proper holding area for the items and for their safekeeping. The inventory lists are to be prepared in duplicate. One copy is to be sent to the office of the Rosenberg Task Force, Amsterdam, 264 Keizersgracht. The representatives are in each case to request the keys from the Central Office for Jewish Emigration, Amsterdam, 1 Adema van Scheltemaplein.[6] Commissioner General Schmidt[7] has instructed that an NSDAP political leader must be brought in and placed in charge of the clearing of the residences by Dutch authorities.

The properties owned by Jews are at the disposal of the Dutch Real Estate Administration,[8] The Hague, 10 Juliana v. Stolberglaan, to which the properties are to be surrendered individually.

A separate regulation will be issued for the cities of The Hague and Rotterdam.

DOC. 92
On 1 November 1942 Bob Cahen tells his family about life in Westerbork camp[1]

Handwritten letter from Bob Cahen,[2] somewhere in the Netherlands, dated 1 November [1942][3]

Dear all,

See, I'm starting a long letter again, and of course I'll tell you about my birthday first. First and foremost, many thanks to you all for the letters and parcels.

At midnight I was woken up by the night watchmen, who wanted to be the first to wish me many happy returns. Then I went back to sleep, and when I woke up in the morning, I found flowers that the patients and nursing staff had tied to my bed. Most inventively, they had put them in some urinals, which they tied to the posts of my apartment.[4] It was a truly lovely sight and gave me a sort of Amsterdam-allotment-garden feeling. On the ward, I was spoiled some more with cigars and cigarettes from the patients. I was even treated to a Viterna crispbake[5] with sugared aniseed[6] on it, along with small dabs and half a meatball.

6 Correctly: Adama van Scheltemaplein.

7 Fritz Schmidt.

8 This organization was established in August 1941 by the commissioner general for finance and economic affairs in order to manage Jewish properties which had to be declared pursuant to the Regulation on Jewish Real Estate (*VOBl-NL*, no. 154/1941, 11 August 1941, pp. 655–663).

1 Herinneringscentrum Kamp Westerbork, Doc. 408. Published in facsimile in J. Cahen, *Ergens in Nederland: Brief uit kamp Westerbork, 1 november 1942*, ed. Dirk Mulder (Hooghalen: Herinneringscentrum Kamp Westerbork, 1988). This document has been translated from Dutch.

2 Jonas (Bob) Cahen (1918–2000), electrical engineer; arrested in a police raid in August 1942 and sent via Amersfoort camp to Westerbork, where he worked as a nurse; deported on 18 Jan. 1944 to Theresienstadt, and from there on 16 May 1944 to Auschwitz; survived the death marches and was liberated in Lübeck; emigrated to Israel in 1958; returned to the Netherlands around 1978.

3 The original letter contains several drawings by Leo Kok (1923–1945), a fellow prisoner in Westerbork.

4 Here a reference to a bunk bed.

5 A protein-based food supplement.

6 *Muisjes* (literally: 'little mice'), a traditional Dutch bread topping made of little balls of sugar-coated aniseed, usually eaten on a round crispbake.

We had an enjoyable evening. We seized the opportunity to celebrate, and this opportunity was my birthday. All I can say is: I was greatly honoured.

There were around thirty of us in total, physicians, male and female nurses, and a few other guests. I got a huge number of gifts. The female nursing staff gave me a bowl of fruit. In addition, I was given tins of fish paste, tomato puree, condensed milk, cigarettes wrapped in flowers, and even a thermometer. Of course, I must not forget the main gift, and that's why I'm mentioning it last, as 'save the best for last!' As you all know, I have found a girlfriend at the camp. Very appropriately, her name is Eva. She was at the party too, of course, and from her I got a silver tiepin with my initials. She had it specially made for me. For me that was the best present of all, of course. All the more so as one can rarely get hold of silver these days, and in the camp at that! For this reason, too, you can see why I really treasure it.

So, as you see, I have been tremendously spoiled. The evening itself was really convivial. The birthday boy himself gave a recitation, and other artists presented songs or poems. You just can't imagine how much we enjoy an evening like that. How badly we need to let our hair down sometimes for an evening. And so that's what we did. An evening like that is so enjoyable precisely because it has an international flavour. When we all sit so cosily around the table, which is neatly covered with bedsheets,[7] topped with a few flowers and some syrup tins as ashtrays. In the background triple bunk beds, and other than that jackets, trousers, and rucksacks on all the walls; that gives you an idea of how picturesque our surroundings are. Naturally we couldn't make too much noise, because our room is right next to the patients' ward, and therefore we had to be quiet. But because the physicians were also there, we had a good excuse for singing, and to be honest, they sang along the loudest. At 10 p.m. the party was over and, just as in former times, we escorted our ladies back home, or rather to their barracks. That is always associated with a few difficulties – not what you're thinking, though. My goodness no, but first there is no lighting, second there are no paths, and third the rain has transformed the terrain into one big muddy puddle. So you'll understand how we have to walk.

7 In the original, the author uses the made-up term *dienstlakens*, a compound word made up of the Dutch for 'service' or 'work' (*dienst*) and 'sheets' (*laken*). The author is referring to hospital bedsheets.

This week I did a good deal. I traded my leather slippers for a pair of high rubber boots belonging to a patient. And in fact, on the condition that this deal is valid for the duration of his stay with us in the hospital. So I'll see to it that he stays with us a bit longer. So, dear folks, now I've told you that, and now we can get a bit more serious. The situation in the camp has been constantly changing of late. As you all know, around 17,000 Jews from all across the Netherlands arrived here in early October.[8] What we experienced at that time beggars all description. People arrived here herded like livestock. Some were buried beneath their luggage, others without any possessions at all, not even properly dressed. Women in poor health who had been hauled out of bed wearing just thin nightgowns, barefoot children in their sleepsuits, the elderly, the ill, the infirm – more and more new people came to the camp. The barracks were full, crammed full. There was room for 10,000 people at most, yet more kept coming. The blacksmiths worked flat out and produced beds non-stop. Straw sacks and mattresses had been unavailable for quite some time. People had to lie directly on the iron bed frames. The barracks became even fuller. People lay down or sat outside. They slept on or under handcarts out in the open.

There was not enough to eat. Sometimes hot food was provided only once every three days, and then there was too little of it. The infants got no milk; there was none. The pumps for the water supply were operating at full capacity and no longer working properly and they were no longer able to purify the water properly, with the result that people had to drink impure water – with the corresponding consequences. Barracks that, under normal conditions, held 400 persons were now full to bursting with as many as 1,000 people, who lay around all over the floor and everywhere else. The toilets were inadequate and were clogged up. Men and women lay in the same rooms; it was chaos. We had to work in between them, fetch the patients, and care for them. Our hospital filled up and was expanded by adding a new barracks with five additional wards. New personnel were hired: hurry up![9] One day later, everything was already full again. A large barracks was fitted out as an emergency ward. The people were put in triple bunk beds. Physicians worked day and night, supported by a staff of orderlies and nurses.

8 On 2 and 3 Oct. 1942, Jews were deported from the labour camps in the Netherlands to Westerbork, and at the same time, throughout the country, their family members were arrested in their homes and also taken to Westerbork – in all, around 13,000 persons.

9 In English in the original.

More and more patients arrived. Once again, 300 found shelter, and then this barracks too was full. The rest had to stay where they were. On the care itself: no equipment, no chamber pots or urinals available, no plates to eat from. There was no hot water, there were no towels or blankets. And then the first death occurred, and others followed regularly. Every day the suffering of two to three people came to an end.

The age of civilization – 'Germany is winning on all fronts', 'brings culture and civilization!' Civilization, when they let people lie on handcarts, on rucksacks, or simply on the ground? Culture, when one sees a mother in despair because she can't feed her child … no milk. No one can imagine what it means for us to be unable to help people adequately and to see their lives slowly slipping away. Can you imagine what it meant for me when a man whom I had been conscientiously nursing died in my arms, and his wife, out of gratitude, gave me his 'tefillin'? Those were his phylacteries, for he was a very devout Jew. Can you understand how a wife must feel when she gives away something of such value? You have never before taken part in a race with Death, when he stretches out his greedy fingers to seize new prey. There was one man who sought out death rather than enter into hell, 'The hell in Poland.' We found him lying on a table with his throat cut. He was still alive and said, 'Let me lie here quietly like this, friends, this way death is not so bad.' We entered the race, brought him to the hospital, everything was already prepared there. We won the race. He's still alive! He's doing better, and then he has to go anyway.

There are so many more cases that ought to be mentioned. And what I'm relating concerns the cases in which I was personally involved, but so many more things are happening. One of the transports brought us people from a home for the elderly in Amsterdam, old, lame, and blind! Workers for Poland. We put them all in a separate room where we could at least provide them with some care. One of them was an old man, 89 years old, who was completely paralyzed down one side. I looked after him for two days and when he left, he pulled a genuine old silver coin out of his jacket lining and said, 'This is for you, brother, because you have taken such good care of me.' Can you imagine what it means to be blind and then to come here and then to be completely dependent on others? Have you ever seen somebody go insane from fear, a fear that we can't imagine even here? And every week two [deportation] transports leave here, each of them carrying 1,000 to 1,500 people, sometimes more, sometimes less.

Here too, we come to help. By loading the 'livestock'! A long train, approximately twenty-five carriages more or less, luggage wagons, and the locomotive. The carriages, luckily, are still passenger carriages, made of very old, poor material. Carriages from all over the world, from Holland, Germany, Belgium, France – sometimes there is even an Italian carriage among them. They have broken windows, wooden seats. They are crammed full of people and their luggage, inadequate supplies of food and drink, no water, no WC, no medical care, that's how they embark on the journey, three days and three nights. A special carriage is designated for the sick, a second-class carriage, but there is no space to lie down.

People have to go on the transport even if they are ill and we put them on the train, one next to the other, until the train is full, and then it departs. Then it's time to get everything ready for the next transport, which you might be on yourself, for no one is safe here.

With every transport, one sees friends and acquaintances leave. 'Chin up, friends, we'll be back. Goodbye until we meet again!' And then we wave as the train pulls away and think, 'How much longer till it's our turn?' How much longer will the war last? How long must we continue to go through all of this, this tension, these rumours? It's going well, they say, but where? Not here, not at all!

And yet, we grow accustomed to it, to everything, but one does not want to become accustomed. We grow accustomed to the transports and to assisting with them. We even snap at the people when, in their nervousness, they fail to comply fast enough, or they do the wrong thing. We snap at them and castigate them while they are being sent away to Poland, because we have grown accustomed to being cruel, because we have to be cruel. Because this is what it's about: it's them or us. But don't think we didn't feel it. How we scream inside, and how it hurts when one sees a mother with a three-month-old baby leaving, the child wrapped in a blanket, no pram and no cradle for a bed, no milk for the journey. Can you understand that there are many people here who prefer to take their own lives rather than be deported? Do you understand that suicide is far more common here? That there are people who prefer to flee rather than to leave [on a transport], even at the risk of being shot in the process? Shot by the SS. The Dutch SS. Dutch against Dutch.

Civilization and culture … We Jews, in the Bible 'the chosen people' – and now 'the cancer of society'. Can you also understand a little how we live, hope, and dream here? Is our dream ever to become reality? Rumours, conversations, hope, progress, depression, and we're still alive. 1942 in Westerborg[10] – Jews.

We thought that the era of Emperor Nero with his persecution of Christians was over,[11] that the St Bartholomew's Day Massacre[12] was behind us. But what we are experiencing now is far worse! Husbands are separated from their wives, children from their mothers. 'We'll wipe the smile off the Jews' faces!' Hitler declared in a speech some time ago.[13] And indeed we aren't laughing any more; he is right about that, but still …

We are still alive; we still have hope. If we are sent to Poland anyway, then we'll go. But we will go as Dutchmen, as tough Dutchmen, as pioneers. We won't give up. We'll depart singing the songs of our country, our dear fatherland. That's how we'll go. You all know me, lads. You know who I am, and what I am like. We're still here now; tomorrow that may no longer be the case.

Be on the lookout; you'll see me before you, as if among the shadows. You'll see me laughing, laughing heartily; I'm waving, chin up, lads, I'll be back. Bon voyage. Until we meet again. That's how I will go, if I too get the order.

We don't know when that will be. No one day is like another here; the person sitting next to you at the table today may have to join the transport tomorrow. Now I'm coming to the end of my letter. Now you are more in the know again. You also know that we

10 Correctly: Westerbork.

11 The Roman emperor Nero (37–68 CE) blamed the Christians for a large fire in Rome in 64 CE and had many of them executed.

12 Synonym for a massacre. The reference is to the night of 23 August 1572, when the wars of religion in France escalated: Catherine de' Medici (1519–1589) ordered the killing of thousands of Huguenots who had gathered in Paris for the wedding of Henry of Navarre, the later Henry IV (1553–1610), and Margaret of Valois (1553–1615).

13 In a speech at Berlin's Sportpalast on 30 Sept. 1942, Hitler said: 'The Jews have once laughed at my prophecies, also in Germany. I don't know whether they are still laughing today, or if they have stopped laughing. But I can assure you now as well: Everywhere they will stop laughing.' See Saul Friedländer, *Nazi Germany and the Jews*, vol. 2: *The Years of Extermination, 1939–1945* (New York: Harper Collins, 2007), p. 402.

long for post. Write back when you've read this letter; be careful with it. Everybody should feel free to read it, because what I wrote is the truth. The drawings were done by a friend of mine. Keep this letter for me to have later, when I come back. Because that will definitely happen. You see: 'Bob is still Bob.'

I'm going to finish now. I wish all of you the very best. Write to me sometime; you know my address. 'Keep going. Stay strong.' See you again soon,

Your friend,

DOC. 93
On 2 November 1942 Salomon and Hanna Gotlib throw a postcard out of the deportation train to say farewell to their daughter and son-in-law[1]

Handwritten postcard, unsigned,[2] to O. Eberlé,[3] Rotterdam, 122 Gordelweg, dated 2 November [1942]

Dear children,

We are on our way to Birkenau, we think. In any case, we are heading somewhere. Keep your chin up. We do the same. Dad and I are together, and together we will return. Keep your spirits up.

Your mother and father,

DOC. 94
On 11 November 1942, after the deportation of Jewish colleagues, the staff of the Hollandia Works are called upon to strike[1]

Flyer, unsigned, undated (typescript)[2]

Jewish Hollandia[3] *workers taken away*

On Wednesday, 11 November, at about half past ten, a number of Krauts[4] from the Sicherheitspolizei[5] appeared at the Hollandia factories in Amsterdam North. The girls had to put their identity cards in front of them and sit down with their hands behind

1 JHM, Doc. 00 000 147. This document has been translated from Dutch.
2 The postcard is from the addressee's parents-in-law: Salomon Gotlib (1881–1942), musician; deported to Westerbork on 14 Oct. 1942 with his wife, Hanna Gotlib-van der Sluijs (1885–1942), and then on 2 Nov. 1942 to Auschwitz, where both were murdered three days later.
3 Oscar Paul Eugène Eberlé (1909–1993), sales representative; married Marjorie Winifred Eberlé-Gotlib (1914–2009) in 1939. After the war, his wife was the chairwoman of Hadderech ('The Way'), an association of Jewish Christians in the Netherlands, for more than fifty years.

1 JHM, Doc. 00 000 816. This document has been translated from Dutch.
2 Handwritten note on the document: 'Nov. 1942'. The name of the group that wrote the flyer could not be found.
3 Hollandia Confectiefabrieken Kattenburg N.V. was founded by the Kattenburg family in 1911 and was known for its waterproof raincoats. A non-Jewish administrator took over the operation in 1940. The Jewish employees, classified as 'armaments Jews', were exempted from deportation because Hollandia produced raincoats for the Wehrmacht. The factory was closed in the 1960s.
4 The original uses the term *Moffen*, a long-standing satirical or pejorative Dutch term for Germans, used predominantly during and after the Second World War.
5 German in the original: 'Security Police'.

their heads. Identity cards with a J were confiscated and the Jewish girls were taken away in cars and buses, with no opportunity to go home and sort out their affairs.

The male Jewish workers were also taken away. The family members of the married Jewish workers were also dragged away from their homes that same day.[6]

There were harrowing scenes at the factory. One of the Jewish supervisors was hit until he bled, and when he fell to the ground, he was kicked in the face. Another member of staff, who had been looking on with a grim face, could no longer control himself, made a comment, and was also hit. One of the Jewish girls slit her wrist. During the transport, which continued until late in the evening, a boy was standing outside watching. His face must have expressed disgust, as one of the Krauts hit him in the face.

The non-Jewish workers were very angry. On the ferry the next morning, the girls were still crying when they talked about this disgraceful event.[7]

But what difference does anger and crying make? Forceful action must be taken against this disgrace. The Hollandia factories, which employ more than 1,000 people, have worked continuously for the German Wehrmacht, including the Jewish workers. *And there are still many thousands of Jewish and non-Jewish workers, both male and female, who work for the Wehrmacht so that it can take action against us and our allies.*

Stop working! Sabotage is what we need!

An increasing number of companies are forced to stop operating or are disrupted in order to send the workers to Germany and steal our raw materials. A new attack on the staff of the municipal council is being plotted. *This time it is the cleaning staff's turn.*

Workers! Women! Mothers! Join the resistance! Fight against the Jewish persecution! Fight against the transportation! Fight against hardship! Fight for your life! *Follow the example of the French and Belgian workers!*[8]

DOC. 95

On 21 November 1942 Salomon de Vries weathers a suspected roundup from his hiding place[1]

Diary of Salomon de Vries, entry for 21 November 1942 (typescript)[2]

21 November

The anxiety! Indeed, sir, as you say, the anxiety! An unbelievable degree of anxiety! Oh well, you know what I mean, of course! A wealth of experience. Most certainly, sir! Of course, sir! The anxiety! It's in stock! It's amazing what you go through.

6 The Security Police and the SD used a tip about sabotage activities at the Hollandia Works as a pretext for carrying out a roundup there on 11 Nov. 1942. As a result, 367 employees and their family members were arrested and deported: more than 820 persons in total, of whom only 8 survived the various camps.

7 The Hollandia Works was in Amsterdam North, north of the IJ, which employees from the southern parts of the city had to cross by ferry every morning.

8 Assistance for Jews was indeed greater in Belgium than in the Netherlands; however, no evidence of targeted strikes on behalf of the Jews could be found. Evidence of corresponding strike action in France could not be found either. Whether this flyer's call for a strike was actually heeded could not be established.

1 NIOD, 244/174 III. This document has been translated from Dutch.

We all have days like that: you get up and you already know! Superstition! Of course, sir, you are quite right! There are also people who blame digestion, but that argument doesn't carry all that much weight any more, as the food the Dutch people are given to digest no longer has much weight! But what causes it is of little consequence: it exists! And yesterday was such a day! The anxiety! Yes, through and through!

'It' was there, the whole day! To-ing and fro-ing, and mostly for nothing! Out of the room in a frenzy and into the other half of the suite. Come back, it's Aunt Do. Or nothing. Or something else, which is also nothing. And so you skip through the hours. At least, if you can call something like that skipping. It doesn't matter what it is, because something rotten,[3] if not awful, remains.

And so the evening arrived and we thought calm was descending, but one should not praise the evening before night has fallen. We were sitting in the room. Saartje and Lex had been back for an hour or so. It was nearly half past eight. At that hour we were not expecting anything any more. Then the bell rang, and it was real. But as we were all in a state of incomprehensibly stable equilibrium, we did not heed the danger. Saartje even went out to open the door!!! My wife[4] was the first to recognize the danger, and she cried out in alarm! To-ing and fro-ing! Trouble! We acted, but of course did the wrong thing! We ran out of the room, leaving behind a table with three steaming hot cups of tea … Lex's bag was beside Saartje's chair. A pair of ladies' overshoes remained[5] next to the heater and 'pleasantly' attracted attention, and there was more. Anyone who entered did not have to be a detective to be able to draw his conclusions. Bags, shoes, and cups of tea were staring you in the face …

The four of us were standing in the pitch-black room next to the large living room. We did not dare to light a lamp, as that would give us away. Lex, in his nervousness – which he always says he has under control – was rustling a newspaper, which he had taken with him for a reason none of us understood, so loudly that I ripped the rag from his hand. Then he started to light his pipe!!!! According to the motto: more light![6]

The visitors were inside, and we slipped out to try to get to the stairs using an evasive manoeuvre, and then to reach our hiding place. We walked on tiptoes through the corridor in single file. There was laughter in the room. Good. A bit of loud laughter is distracting. We reached the door. The four of us went through it. Door shut, up the stairs! I take the lead. Just when I reach the highest step, I see light.[7] Light in the attic. I look back. The others also look pale. *There is someone in the attic!* And we have to pass through there, as there is no way back for us! Those are my thoughts in a split second, and I sprinted. Up into the attic. A gentleman with a portable lamp is standing there. Good evening, I say. Good evening, sir, is his friendly reply. I suddenly discover that I am on my own. The others have remained behind! I have to keep going … continue. But I don't have a key for the hiding place. I do have one for the attic though, our comfy room. So I

2 The original contains handwritten insertions and marking.
3 The words 'something rotten' are in English in the original, presumably an allusion to Shakespeare's Hamlet ('Something is rotten in the state of Denmark').
4 Sara de Vries-de Jonge.
5 One word inserted by hand is illegible.
6 An allusion to Goethe's alleged last words on his deathbed.
7 The change in tense here and below is in the original.

head straight for the door, put the key into the lock, turn the key and disappear. It is pitch-black. I don't dare to put on the light, as it would be visible through the keyhole. I let myself drop onto the bed. My heart is pounding, my temples are throbbing. I wait, and every second seems to last forever. In the attic, the gentleman continues to work quietly by the light of the portable lamp. Where are the others? I hear voices on the stairs, greetings, laughter. So there are people there too! Strangers! Where are the three Jews hiding? I don't know what to do, so I do nothing … I just sit there and wait …

After what seems like an eternity, the gentleman hangs up the portable lamp. I hear a key turn in the lock, and then footsteps … In the attic. On the stairs … I wait. And finally: a key is put into the door of the hiding place.[8] I hear a heavy footstep, an attempt to make it lighter, but this doesn't work. Lex, of course. I go towards him. He looks at me. Where is my wife? I ask in a whisper. Where is Saartje? asks Lex. We are standing in front of each other in the hiding place[9] and look at each other. The door opens again. My wife comes in. She looks pale and very nervous, and says in all honesty that that is how she feels. She drops herself into a chair and catches her breath.

– My God, I was so nervous, she says softly. Suddenly we hear a whistle. A signal.

– Saartje, says Lex, and he runs to the stairs. We are waiting.

– It was really awful, says my wife. Wherever we showed ourselves there were people, and everywhere we went we had to leave again!

Saartje came in, followed by Lex. She dropped into a chair and tears were running down her cheeks. She suddenly had to laugh. She had had a terrible laughing fit when she had finally reached the street, she said. She had been roaring with laughter, and suddenly she had thought: I hope the people can't hear me! And she laughed and laughed …

With hindsight, the course of events can be reconstructed as follows. When I had gone up to the attic, they had not followed me but had turned back. As soon as they were back on the stairs, though, they heard the bell ring at the neighbours' flat on the third floor. As quickly and as quietly as they possibly could, they went back up the stairs, but then they heard the gentleman, who had been upstairs, come down. My wife quickly went to the door of 'our' floor, and Lex followed her. As they went inside, they saw a gentleman and a lady come up the stairs: visitors for the third floor, apparently. Saartje had gone downstairs, but when she was on the first floor, she heard someone else who was also going down the stairs, and so the only way to prevent meeting that person was to go onto the street … And so she went out there in her blouse, skirt, and slippers … It was so funny it made her roar with laughter, she said afterwards …

Lex and my wife had ended up in the kitchen on 'our' floor, but once they were there, they did not feel safe, and so they went through the kitchen door to the veranda. It was very cold there and also very light, and therefore unsafe, so they decided to return to the kitchen. They peered up the stairs. People. Door shut again. They waited. And tried again. A chance. Up the stairs. Again, someone is coming down. It seems everyone is on the go tonight! At last: a chance. Up the stairs. Upstairs.

And so we were finally back together again. The four of us. And each was acting even more 'light-hearted', as if nothing had happened, you might almost say, more 'normal', than the other.

8 In the original, incorrectly: cellar-shelter door (*schuilkelderdeur*).
9 In the original, incorrectly: cellar shelter (*schuilkelder*).

Of course: this evening will later – God willing, and if we are still alive – be a source of priceless, roaring laughter. A bit like: Do you remember, that evening? In a horror film it would be an adventure that would make the cinema roar with laughter. For wherever the three Jews showed themselves on the stairs, or wherever they thought they might escape, there were people, or people were on their way. Wherever they went and stood still, doors opened and visitors or residents appeared. And the fourth person was in the attic in the pitch-dark, all by himself, peeking through the keyhole from time to time at the gentleman with the portable lamp, who just stayed there and never went away … Extremely funny … Later: but I say and say again: the anxiety!

DOC. 96

A concealed letter that successfully reached Westerbork describes the train journey to Auschwitz from 30 November to 1 December 1942[1]

Handwritten letter, signed S., dated 30 November and 1 December 1942[2]

30 November 1942
1. It is 11.50. We depart from Hooghalen.[3]
2. About 12.30. We are recoupled in Beilen. The heating comes on.
3. About 14.15. We pass Winschoten. All along the route, people greet us and catch our letters.[4]
4. About 14.30. Nieuweschans. Five minutes later we leave Nieuweschans; the Green Police post our letters.[5]
5. 14.40. We pass the first German station, *Bunen*.[6]
6. 16.50. We arrive in Oldenburg. After five minutes we depart again. Nothing special to report.
7. 18.00. We arrive in Bremer.[7] The compartments are closed on both sides. We have not had anything to eat or drink yet. It is nice and warm in the compartments. The police officers behave correctly.
About 18.30. We depart from Bremen.

1 Herinneringscentrum Kamp Westerbork, 2809. Published in Bob Cahen, *Brieven uit de trein Westerbork–Auschwitz (enkele reis)* (Haarlem: Tuindorp, 1996), pp. 11–13. This document has been translated from Dutch.

2 The letter, the author of which is unknown, was written on the journey to Auschwitz and was transported back to Westerbork on the same train, concealed in a secret letter box behind a ventilation grille. At the camp, it was removed from this hiding place by Bob Cahen, who, in his capacity as a medical orderly, was helping people onto the train for the next transport. In total, three letters reached Westerbork in this way.

3 Westerbork camp had its own rail connection from Nov. 1942. The actual train station, however, was in Hooghalen (province of Drenthe), 5 km away.

4 For an example of such a letter thrown from the train, see Doc. 93.

5 It appears that, in some cases, the German Order Police (known in the Netherlands as the 'Green Police') undertook the task of putting deportees' cards and letters into a postbox. In other cases, pieces of mail were simply tossed from the train in the hope that they would nonetheless be delivered.

6 Correctly: Bunde.

7 Correctly: Bremen.

8. About 20.15. We arrive in Soltau. The compartments are not lit. It's pitch-dark. We used our torch; had to hand it in initially but were allowed to keep it because it was for a baby. It still feels hot. The train has started moving again.
9. About 22.00. Kiel.
About 24.00. Lenstahl.[8]

1 December 1942
About 1.15. Probably Hamburg. Barrage balloons.[9] A lot of aeroplane noise. It is dark in the compartments and not very warm. We are still being treated correctly. We have not yet had any food.
10. 3 o'clock in the morning; it's dark. The train is speeding along through the night. Occasionally we stop at a station. There are four of us in the compartment and we find it easy to get some sleep. There are thirteen people in other compartments. They find it harder to sleep.
11. 8 o'clock in the morning. We stop in Kohlfurt.[10] The carriage guards and Sanitäter[11] get off the train and get bread and jam. ¾ of a loaf per person. One person has died so far. A 69-year-old woman, died from angina.
12. About 9.00. We enter Silesian territory.
About 9.15. We pass the small town of Bunzlau.[12] This is a beautiful region. A landscape of hills and valleys. Tiny pretty houses with sloping roofs and small windows. They look like the houses of little dwarfs.
9.50. We pass Kaiserwaldau.[13] The train is not going very fast.
13. About 10 o'clock. We pass Haynau.[14] A beautiful area. It looks incredibly peaceful. We can see a small village in the distance. Tiny white houses with red roofs. It has snowed a little. The temperature is the same as in the Netherlands. Twenty minutes later we pass an airfield to our right.
14. About 13.00. We are stationary in Köningszeld.[15] We were able to get some water on the platform just now. We have been told that we will arrive at our destination at 16.00?
14.30 We pass Schwiednitz.[16]
15. 14.40 We pass Reichenbach.[17] We are still in a beautiful mountain area. On some of the hills, houses have been built.
14.45 We pass Frankenstein (Silesia).[18] There is a thin layer of snow everywhere.

8 Correctly, presumably: Lensahn. A reason for the detour through Kiel and Lensahn could not be found.
9 Barrage balloons: large balloons tethered to the ground to serve as obstacles for approaching bombers.
10 Correctly, presumably: Kohlfurt (now Węgliniec, Poland).
11 German in the original: 'medical orderlies'.
12 Now: Bolesławiec (Poland).
13 Now: Piastów (Poland). The place name given is probably incorrect, as passing through it would have required a major detour.
14 Now: Chojnów (Poland).
15 Correctly: Königszelt (now Jaworzyna Śląska, Poland).
16 Now: Świdnica (Poland).
17 Now: Dzierżoniów (Poland).
18 Now: Ząbkowice Śląskie (Poland).

15.15 We are in Amenz,[19] where we have a half-hour delay. Meanwhile, we are writing a postcard home, which the police will post for us. (Hopefully.) We are passing through an area where lots of sugar beets are grown.

1 December 1942
My experiences!
All those rumours that: 1. your new clothes, your good food, and your cigarettes are taken away *is a lie!* The badges remain on the clothes. Until you get to the border, the compartment's windows remain *closed.* In German territory the windows may be *opened.* So far *nothing* has been taken off us. And here is a piece of advice: It is best to cut and butter the bread you take with you. It is easiest to transport babies in a travel basket. The Green Police are not bad, but do as they say and do it quickly. Everything has to be done quickly.[20]

DOC. 97

Krakauer Zeitung, 2 December 1942: article on the allegedly dominant position of Jews in the Netherlands before the war and the protecting hand of the royal house[1]

The Jewish protégés of the House of Orange. The Jewification of the Netherlands – commerce, art, theatre, and the press in racially alien hands

'Joodsche Wijk'[2] is written in huge letters on the big yellow sign standing at the entrance to a street in Amsterdam that, purely on the surface, at first glance, is no different from other streets in the Dutch capital. However, the people who walk along the pavement, gesticulating wildly, and who populate the streets here immediately evoke memories of Warsaw or other cities of the General Government. There would not even be any need for the yellow Star of David on the left-hand side of their chests. Even from a distance, one recognizes the Jews and notes that one is in the old Jewish quarter of Amsterdam, as the yellow sign also points out. Then, all of a sudden, one is standing in front of the big junk market,[3] and once again one feels transported to the East. This is no longer clean and tidy Holland, this is dirt and rubbish. Row after row of stalls, one filthier than

19 Correctly, presumably: Kamenz (now Kamieniec Ząbkowicki, Poland).
20 In Kosel (Koźle, now part of Kędzierzyn-Koźle, Poland), which is located between Groß-Rosen and Auschwitz, 170 of the total number of 826 deportees were removed from the transport and distributed among the surrounding forced labour camps run by the Organization Schmelt. The 655 deportees who reached Auschwitz on this transport were not given prisoner numbers, but were instead presumably murdered immediately after their arrival. On selections in late 1942 at Kosel for forced labour out of transports from Western Europe to Auschwitz, see also Doc. 308

1 *Krakauer Zeitung* – Reich edition, vol. 2, no. 285, 2 Dec. 1942, p. 3. The *Krakauer Zeitung* was published from 1939 to 1945, and the Reich edition, published from 1941 to 1945, was largely identical to it. As the only German-language newspaper in the General Government, it represented the opinion of the occupiers and reached a circulation of more than 100,000 copies at times. This document has been translated from German.
2 Dutch: 'Jewish quarter'.
3 This presumably refers to the daily antique and flea market on Waterlooplein, which continues to take place today.

the next, laden with everything that can be bartered or sold. There is simply nothing that might not be found here. From a rusty horseshoe nail to a brand-new telephone, from a used horse brush missing half of its bristles to a toilet lid, the most improbable things are on offer, but they find buyers. Even the idyllic canals are spoilt by the displays of the 'Jewish hawkers'. This is the El Dorado of the Polish Jews, who in Holland too have set the tone in the second-hand trade.

Their racial comrades from Portugal and the Jews who emigrated to the Netherlands after 1933 and after the assumption of power in Austria, however, found themselves a different domain. In our last article, we pointed out[4] that the Jew in Holland occupied a dominant position in trade as a whole, and the commissioner for Jews in the Netherlands, the Reich Commissioner's representative for the City of Amsterdam, *Dr Schröder,*[5] acquainted us with the Jewish invasion of the other spheres of Dutch life. Certainly, with the arrival of the German Wehrmacht, the Jews were eliminated from cultural life and the economy, as well as the civil service. Eating and drinking establishments, public grounds and parks, theatres and cinemas are off-limits to them. They are restricted to their own cultural establishments, and next to the old, extant Jewish residential quarter, three additional Jewish districts were created. Similar steps were taken in the country's other cities, wherever Jews reside. Since 29 April 1942, the Dutch Jews, like the German ones, have also worn the Star of David[6] and they are gradually being resettled, moved out of Holland, in connection with the Central Office for Jewish Emigration. The Jewish threat is thus averted here as well. Nonetheless, it is worth recalling the position of power that the Jew once held everywhere here.

In Holland, as in the Reich, the Jew set the tone in cultural life. He went about this with great skill. The conservative, markedly Christian attitude of the Dutchman would have put up the fiercest opposition to the anarchistic drives of the Jewish cultural Bolshevists if the Hebrew community had revealed itself here as it had done in Germany. A Christ with a gas mask[7] would have been unanimously rejected in Holland. Nigger sculptures, of the sort served up during the Systemzeit[8] in Germany as the ideal image of mankind, would have profoundly offended the Dutchman's religious notion of the act of creation. The Jew therefore dispensed with this sort of ethnic subversion, and slowly but surely crept in as a patron, donating hard cash wherever possible to unobtrusively exercise a destructive influence upon art and, beyond this, upon cultural life.

The art trade, for instance, was completely Jewified.[9] In 1940, 80 per cent of the art trade was in Jewish hands. Things were no different in the music world. With the lack

4 On 25 Nov. 1942 an article by Rudolf Steimer appeared in the *Krakauer Zeitung* (no. 279, p. 3), titled 'Die Juden in den Niederlanden. Völlige Herrschaft über den Diamanthandel. Amsterdam als jüdischer Kristallisationspunkt' ('The Jews in the Netherlands. Complete control of the diamond trade. Amsterdam as a Jewish focal point').

5 Werner Schröder.

6 On the measures taken by the end of 1941, see PMJ 5/104.

7 This refers to a drawing by George Grosz (1893–1959), 'Maul halten und weiter dienen' ('Shut up and continue to serve'), 1927.

8 German for 'system era'; a term used by the Nazis to refer disparagingly to the period of the Weimar Republic.

9 The data from the official censuses in fact show that the only sector of the economy where Jews could be said to predominate was the diamond industry: see PMJ 5/51.

of state and municipal theatres in Holland, the cultivation of the dramatic arts was often left to the initiative of private stage ensembles. In Holland, there were twenty-four professional theatre associations, two revue companies, and one operetta company, of which more than half had Jewish directors. Among the total number of 619 performers at 11 theatres in Amsterdam, there were 373 Jewish men and women. The city also had a drama school, at which eight Jews 'held office' as leaders. Of the almost 1,100 cinemas in Holland, 943 were associated with the 'Nederlandsch Bioscoopbon'.[10] Its manager, A. de *Hopp*,[11] and all thirteen supervisory board members were sons of the chosen people. Of thirty-six existing film distribution companies, thirty were headed by Jews. The Jew *David* held a senior position in the office for the postal distribution of films. It is not surprising that anti-German smear films were promoted in Holland with particular intensity. A total of 85 million guilders has been invested in Holland's cinemas and film companies. Of that amount, 66 million was Jewish capital. Native literature and poetry are to be found in Holland only to a modest extent. Émigré literature was to be found in the Netherlands all the more before the arrival of the Germans.[12] The leading press in Holland did willing stooge-work. No wonder. At 'De Telegraf'[13] and 'De Courant', with a combined circulation of 350,000, there were ninety Jews employed. The Jewish diamond producer Asscher had a large share in the 'Handelsblad',[14] likewise the Jewish textile manufacturer *Menco*[15] from Enschede, the Jewish art dealer *Goudstikker*,[16] and the Jewish paper manufacturer *van Gelder*[17] from Harlem.[18] They manufactured public opinion. In addition, more than half of Holland's book publishers were in Jewish hands. Jews represented 30 per cent, rather than 1.4 per cent, of the total population at the six national universities.[19] The particular prominence of Jews as judges in the justice system and in the liberal professions as physicians and lawyers is a phenomenon that was evident in every country in Europe. In terms of party politics, the Jew was in evidence mainly among the Social Democrats and the Communists. But he was pulling the strings of all the parties, even though he knew how to disguise himself skilfully and not to intervene directly anywhere in the field of politics. The administration alone remained

10 Correctly: Nederlandsche Bioscoopbond ('Dutch Cinema Federation').

11 Correctly: Abraham de Hoop (1895–1943), journalist; worked for the Vaz Diaz press agency, 1914–1929; chairman of the Dutch Cinema Federation, 1933–1940; employed at the Jewish Council from 1942 to 1943; deported to Westerbork on 6 Feb. 1943 and three days later to Auschwitz, where he was murdered upon arrival.

12 There were two major publishing houses, Querido and Allert de Lange, which brought out many books by German immigrants.

13 Correctly: *De Telegraaf.*

14 Correctly: *Algemeen Handelsblad.*

15 Correctly: Sigmond Nathan Menko (1877–1962), textile manufacturer; chairman of the Jewish Community of Enschede from 1930; Jewish Council representative in the province of Overijssel, 1941–1943; went into hiding in 1943; betrayed in 1944 and deported via Westerbork to Theresienstadt; returned to the Netherlands in 1945.

16 Jacques Goudstikker (1897–1940), art dealer; died in May 1940 while fleeing to Britain; his art collection was seized, and portions of it were returned to the Netherlands after 1945.

17 The Smidt van Gelder (Van Gelder en Zonen) family owned several paper factories. It was not possible to determine which member of the family was meant here.

18 Correctly: Haarlem, in the province of North Holland.

19 According to statistics for 1940, only 3.3 per cent of Dutch students were Jews and only 26 Jews worked at the various universities: see PMJ 5/51.

more or less closed to the children of Israel. This was surely not the fault of the Dutch government or even the Queen. On the contrary, the House of *Orange* was always favourable to the Jews, in line with the attitude of the Dutch business world. The Jew was regarded as a factor in the expansion of trade relations and the financing of monetary transactions, and thus he was automatically legitimized. Accordingly, the Jews always behaved like loyal, pro-monarchist citizens, and thus the feeble opposition of the Social Democrats is also understandable, for the Royal House was, so to speak, the guarantor for the safety of the Jews.

In fact, the Dutchman was not roused from his trance until, with the Jews who emigrated from Germany and the Ostmark, elements entered the country seeking to force their way to the top everywhere, with unprecedented ruthlessness. These émigrés lacked any tact or sensitivity. New businesses were daily occurrences in Dutch life, and in the process, the Jews energetically invoked the good relationships that they had all over the world. When one's own purse is being gnawed by these international rats, one must naturally put up a fight, and the measures ultimately taken by the Dutch government at that time against Jewish immigration are to be understood only in this way.[20] Unperturbed by the growing numbers of unemployed people, Jewish competition undercut high-quality indigenous workmanship and unhesitatingly squandered Holland's national wealth wherever an opportunity arose. The brazenness and power of Jewish émigrés in Holland are demonstrated in a complaint filed by a member of the Kamer van Koophandel en Fabrieken[21] in Amsterdam, the Jew Kahn.[22] He vigorously opposed all legal regulations that restricted foreign Jews in their business dealings in Holland in those days and stated that only the German émigrés, with the help of trained Jewish workers, were able to rebuild in Holland the ready-to-wear clothing businesses that had been forfeited in Germany. The Jew Kahn's cries of woe went largely unheard because worsening conditions in the labour market simply forced the government to control the Jews' activities, lest the masses be driven into the hands of the NSB, the mass movement. The instinct for self-preservation was the only driving force behind the resistance to Jewish domination.

Rudolf Steimer[23]

20 On 7 May 1938 the Dutch Ministry of Justice had refused to take in additional refugees: see PMJ 5/25.

21 Dutch: 'Chamber of Industry and Commerce'.

22 The Amsterdam representative of the Chamber of Industry and Commerce was Mr Bernard Arnold Kahn (1886–1941), lawyer; worked in the ready-to-wear shop Maison Hirsch; deported to Buchenwald as a hostage, probably in Oct. 1940; perished there in May 1941. The actual content of the complaint could not be determined.

23 Rudolf Steimer (1904–1972), journalist; joined the NSDAP in 1931; from 1932 editor of the National Socialist daily newspaper *Der Alemanne*; served in the Wehrmacht, Sept.–Oct. 1940; after the war worked as a freelance journalist for local newspapers and in commerce.

DOC. 98

On 11 December 1942 Adolf Eichmann refuses to allow Eduard Maurits Meijers to leave for Switzerland in exchange for a large sum of money[1]

Express letter (marked 'secret') from the Chief of the Security Police and the SD (IV B 4 1597/42g), p.p. signed Eichmann,[2] Berlin, to the Reich Foreign Office, for the attention of Legation Counsellor Dr Klingenfuß,[3] Berlin (received on 13 December 1942), dated 11 December 1942[4]

Re: emigration of the Jew E. M. Meyer[5] with his wife and daughter to Switzerland
Reference: express letter from your office, dated 2 December 1942 – no. D III 1059g – and letter from here, dated 1 December 1942 – IV B 4 a-1597/42g –[6]

As is well known to you there, in October 1941 the Reichsführer SS and Chief of the German Police[7] prohibited the emigration of Jews from the Reich and the occupied territories. Only in very special individual cases, for example, when it is in the interests of the Reich, does our office envisage granting permission for the emigration of individual Jews, after examining the case.

During the subsequent period, applications from Jews have been received by various agencies, including in particular the Reich Ministry of Economics and the Reichsbank, as well as lawyers, especially Swiss lawyers, in which a permit for emigration is requested in exchange for the payment of large sums of foreign currency. Despite the gravest political objections, which were and are being continuously raised from here, and despite explicit

1 Foreign Office – State Department Document Center. Copy in NIOD, 207/5547. This document has been translated from German.
2 Adolf Eichmann (1906–1962), sales representative; joined the NSDAP and the SS in 1932; worked at the SD Main Office in Berlin between 1934 and 1938; from March 1938 had a leading role at the SD in Vienna for matters pertaining to the Jews; de facto head of Vienna's Central Office for Jewish Emigration from its establishment in 1938 and in a similar role at the Central Office for Jewish Emigration in Prague after the establishment of the Protectorate of Bohemia and Moravia in March 1939; organized the deportation of Jews from the territory of the Reich at the Reich Security Main Office (RSHA) from 1939; head of section IV D 4 (evacuation affairs and Reich Central Agency for Jewish Emigration) from the start of 1940; head of the RSHA section IV B 4 (Jewish affairs and evacuation affairs) by March 1941; attended the Wannsee Conference in 1942; imprisoned, unrecognized, in an American detention camp, 1945–1946; escaped in 1946; in hiding, first in Germany, 1946–1950, then in Argentina, 1950–1960; kidnapped by the Israeli secret service in 1960 and tried in Jerusalem, 1961–1962; sentenced to death and executed in Israel.
3 Dr Karl Otto Klingenfuß (1901–1990), diplomat; employed by the German Foreign Institute, 1929–1937; joined the NSDAP in 1933; worked in the Reich Foreign Office from 1937; in Dept. D III (Jewish affairs) from June to Dec. 1942, then in Bern and Paris; interned in 1945; fled to Argentina in 1949; director of the German-Argentine Chamber of Commerce, 1951–1967; proceedings against him in Germany were dropped in 1960.
4 The original contains handwritten annotations, underlining, and official stamps of the Reich Foreign Office.
5 Correctly: Dr Eduard Maurits Meijers (1880–1954), lawyer; professor in Leiden from 1910; dismissed in Nov. 1940 due to his Jewish origins; deported to Barneveld camp in August 1942 and from there to Westerbork in Sept. 1943, and finally to Theresienstadt in Sept. 1944; reassumed his professorship in 1945; responsible for drafting the new Dutch Civil Code from 1947.
6 Both letters are included in the file. They state that Jews are not to be permitted to leave the country in exchange for foreign currency.
7 Heinrich Himmler.

reference to the dangerous repercussions that the issuing of such permits would have abroad, the Reich Ministry of Economics and the Reichsbank, taking into account the Reich's strained foreign exchange situation, attach great importance to the approval of emigration applications on a case-by-case basis when large foreign currency sums will accrue.

Temporarily putting aside the political objections that now exist in relation to the emigration of Jews per se in all cases, in view of the compelling economic reasons put forward it was agreed that an emigration permit will be issued by way of exception if certain prerequisites are met. These applications will be given further consideration only if the Jewish applicant and his relatives are of an advanced age, if no objections to emigration are raised by the Security Police, and if foreign currency in the amount of at least 100,000 Swiss francs per person is made available and receipt of the equivalent value is waived.

Permission for the emigration of the Jewish intellectual *Meyers* (formerly a professor in The Hague), for which the Swedish Legation is proposing the payment of 150,000 Swiss francs in exchange for a permit to emigrate, was denied – as reported earlier in my letter of 1 December 1942 – IV B 4a-1597/42g –[8] in view of his professional status, regardless of the amount of foreign currency offered.

DOC. 99

On 29 December 1942 Dutch nationals living in Palestine advocate the evacuation of Jewish children from the Netherlands[1]

Letter from the Advisory Committee for Immigrants from the Netherlands,[2] signed Metz Elias (secretary), Jerusalem, P.O. Box 46, to P. Rijkens,[3] London, Unilever House, Blackfriars, dated 29 December 1942

Dear Mr Rijkens,

The Advisory Committee for Immigrants from the Netherlands in Jerusalem has taken the initiative to set up a campaign to bring children from the Netherlands to Palestine.[4] We hope that the Dutch government will be willing to support this campaign. A petition was drawn up for this purpose, which has been signed by 268 Dutch residents of Palestine, a copy of which you will find below.[5] This petition was forwarded to London by the consul general of the Netherlands here.[6]

8 In this letter, the reason given for refusing the application was that E. M. Meijers was an intellectual.

1 Nationaal Archief; the original could not be found. Published in *Enquêtecommissie Regeringsbeleid 1940–1945: Verslag houdende de uitkomsten van het onderzoek*, vol. 6ab ('s-Gravenhage: Staatsdrukkerij- en Uitgeverijbedrijf, 1952), p. 197. This document has been translated from Dutch.

2 The Advies-Bureau voor Immigranten uit Nederland was established in May 1940. The organization Irgun Olei Holland (IOH) developed out of it in April 1943. The IOH represented all Dutch immigrants in Palestine. It is still in existence today.

3 Paul Carl Rijkens (1888–1965), entrepreneur; director of the Van den Bergh margarine factory from 1919; chairman of Unilever from 1937; in London, 1940–1954; subsequently returned to the Netherlands.

4 At the end of Nov. 1942, the Jewish Agency for Palestine had made public the systematic mass murder of Jews in Europe. In late 1942 it also received the British government's consent for 30,000 Jewish children to enter Palestine. For these reasons, the Dutch immigration organization became active.

5 The original petition is found in the Central Zionist Archives, J 24/43–2.

We trust that you will sympathize with this campaign, and therefore take the liberty to call for your support; by using your influence with the Dutch government, you will no doubt be able to bring this campaign closer to its fulfilment.

We hope that you will not refuse to cooperate in this matter and would like to thank you in advance for your efforts to rescue children from the Netherlands.

Through friends, we have submitted a similar request to Mr Van den Tempel,[7] Minister of Social Affairs.

Yours sincerely,
(sgd) Metz Elias, Secretary

Petition
Jerusalem, P.O. Box 46,
4 December 1942
To the Consul General of the Netherlands,
Jerusalem

Dear Sir,

The Dutch nationals in Palestine, almost all of whom are Jews, are deeply shocked by the many disasters which the foreign oppressors are inflicting on the Dutch, and latterly on the Dutch Jews in particular.

Any description of the current situation of this population group is superfluous, and we must not close our eyes to the sad fact that the outrages that have been committed and continue to be committed are aimed at the complete extermination of the Dutch Jews.

There is no doubt that this purpose can only be thwarted by the victory of the Allied Powers. However, this must not dissuade anyone from doing all they possibly can to bring this disaster to a halt, no matter how large-scale it has sadly become. In this context, we would like to point out that attempts have been made – not without success – in other countries in similar circumstances to save at least a number of children from doom. Such an attempt is currently being made with regard to Jewish children in the Netherlands. The mandate government[8] has already committed to the admission of 250 children from the Netherlands, within the immigration quota of 1,500 children. To cover the costs of transport, education, and maintenance, Jewish organizations and individuals from a number of countries have been approached. Although these circles have promised to cooperate, the sums needed for these purposes are such that only part of the costs can be borne by private organizations and individuals.

The Dutch nationals in Palestine therefore express their sincere hope and expectation that the Dutch government will play an active role in this campaign and will be willing to provide financial support.

6 Baron Herbert Paulus Josephus Bosch van Drakestein (1903–1965), diplomat; consul general of the Netherlands in Jerusalem from April 1942 until the end of 1943; consul general of the Netherlands in Munich, 1956–1957.

7 Dr Jan van den Tempel (1877–1955), house painter, trade unionist, and politician; general manager of the Netherlands Trade Union Federation (NVV) from 1906; member of Amsterdam City Council, 1910–1919; member of the Dutch parliament, 1915–1940; minister of social affairs, 1939–1945; fled into exile in London with the Dutch government.

8 From 1920 Palestine was under British supervision as a mandate. In addition to its role as the legislative power, the mandate government was responsible for issuing immigration permits.

This campaign is small – far too small – in terms of the scale of the emergency. Many thousands of children would qualify. We cannot ignore the fact that, unfortunately, the admission of such a large number would lead to objections, even if a step-by-step process were to be adopted. However, at least 500 children, in addition to the 250 already mentioned, should be taken into consideration. The Dutch nationals in Palestine therefore trust that the Dutch government will be willing to plead with the British authorities for an increase in the existing child immigration quota of 1,500, so that at least 750 Dutch children can be included.

The Dutch nationals in Palestine hope that Your Honour will communicate their request to the Dutch government promptly and would be grateful if you would also advise the government likewise on your own behalf.[9]

DOC. 100

On 11 January 1943 the SS Business and Administration Main Office states its requirement for fur and garment workers and diamond cutters for concentration camps in the East[1]

Telex (no. 146, 11 January 1943, 2.27 p.m.)[2] from the SS Business and Administration Main Office[3] Departmental Group D II, signed Maurer[4] (SS-Obersturmbannführer), Oranienburg, to the Senior Commander of the Security Police and the SD, for the attention of SS-Untersturmführer Werner,[5] IV B 4, The Hague[6] (received on 11 January 1943), dated 11 January 1943[7]

Re: transfer of Jews
With reference to the telephone call that took place on 9 January, I am notifying you that fur and garment workers as well as diamond cutters are needed. The diamond cutters are to be transferred to Auschwitz. However, until the numbers have been made known, I cannot inform you of the concentration camp to which the fur and garment Jews are

9 Over the following months, the question was discussed in the government in exile's Council of Ministers, and contact was made with the British mandate government. Neither an increase in the quota nor an actual exchange took place, however, because the German government demanded the handover of 500 German citizens who were in Britain as a quid pro quo. As this was unacceptable to the British government, further plans came to nought.

1 NIOD, 077/1317. This document has been translated from German.
2 Sent by the Message Transmission Service (no. 00 992).
3 The SS Business and Administration Main Office (Wirtschafts-Verwaltungshauptamt, WVHA) was created on 1 Feb. 1942. It grew out of the SS Administration and Business Main Office and the Main Office for Budget and Buildings, and it was headed by Oswald Pohl (1892–1951). Departmental Group D was responsible for the concentration camps.
4 Gerhard Maurer (1907–1953), retailer; joined the NSDAP in 1930 and the SS in 1931; from 1934 worked full-time for the SS; worked in the SS Administration and Business Main Office, 1939–1942; head of Dept. D II in the WVHA from May 1942; deputy inspector of concentration camps from Nov. 1943; went underground in 1945; arrested in 1947; sentenced to death in Warsaw in 1952; executed in Cracow in 1953.
5 Alfons Werner. No further details could be established.
6 Section IV B, under the Senior Commander of the Security Police and the SD, was in charge of combating ideological opponents of the Nazi regime; within this section, subgroup IV B 4 was responsible for all matters pertaining to Jews.
7 The original contains handwritten annotations and underlining.

to be transferred. Please let me know these numbers by telex. – Only male and female Jews who are fit for work can be used for the tasks envisaged. Please also inform me by telex of the number of diamond cutters, so that arrangements can be made for setting up the workshop in Auschwitz.[8]

DOC. 101
On 16 January 1943 Reich Commissioner Seyss-Inquart explains to the German commissioners general how to deal with confiscated Jewish assets[1]

Letter from the Reich Commissioner for the Occupied Dutch Territories (S-P),[2] signed Seyss-Inquart,[3] The Hague, to the Commissioners General Dr Fischböck,[4] Dr Wimmer,[5] Rauter, and Schmidt, Envoy Bene, and Regierungspräsident Dr Piesbergen,[6] dated 16 January 1943[7]

Directive
After consultation with Reich Minister of Finance Count Schwerin von Krosigk, I order that enemy assets, with the exception of Jewish assets, are to be forfeited to the Reich, while, in accordance with the agreement with the Reich Finance Minister, the management, liquidation, and reinvestment of these assets are to be performed by the Reich Commissioner. With regard to Jewish assets, it is anticipated that those assets that are owned by Jews who were formerly Reich citizens will be placed at the disposal of the Reich, but assets owned by Jews with Dutch citizenship are to be used specifically for Dutch purposes. With regard to Jewish assets, therefore, the present way of dealing with them will be

8 The plans of the SS Business and Administration Main Office to deport diamond cutters to Auschwitz and set up diamond-cutting machines there conflicted with Himmler's plans to transfer diamond-cutting machines to Vught concentration camp. The plans for diamond-cutting workshops in Auschwitz never materialized, but diamond-cutting machines were installed at Vught.

1 NIOD, 020/1517. This document has been translated from German.
2 The abbreviation stands for Hertha Santo Passo, Seyss-Inquart's secretary.
3 Dr Arthur Seyss-Inquart (1892–1946), lawyer; joined the NSDAP in 1931; member of the German-Austrian People's League (*Volksbund*) and the Styrian Home Guard; appointed Austrian minister of the interior in Feb. 1938 and chancellor and Reichsstatthalter of Austria in March 1938; deputy to the Governor General of occupied Poland, Hans Frank, 1939–1940; Reich commissioner of the Netherlands from 25 April 1940; sentenced to death at the International Military Tribunal in Nuremberg in 1946 and executed.
4 Dr Hans Fischböck (1895–1967), lawyer; director of the insurance company Österreichische Versicherungs-AG; in 1938, following the Anschluss, appointed Austrian minister for trade and transport; joined the NSDAP and the SS in 1940; commissioner general for finance and economic affairs in the Netherlands from 1940; also Reich commissioner for price setting in Germany from 1942; after 1945 fled to Argentina under a false name; returned to the Federal Republic of Germany in 1958
5 Dr Friedrich Wimmer (1897–1965), archaeologist and lawyer; archaeologist at the Lower Austrian State Museum from 1924; joined the NSDAP in Austria in 1934 and the SS in 1938; state secretary in Seyss-Inquart's cabinet in Austria from 1938; commissioner general for administration and justice in the Netherlands, 1940–1945; testified against Seyss-Inquart at the International Military Tribunal in Nuremberg; amnestied under the Austrian amnesty law in 1957; thereafter lived in Salzburg and Regensburg.
6 Dr Hans Heinrich Piesbergen (1891–1970), lawyer; Landrat in Fallingbostel, 1930–1939; joined the NSDAP in 1933; worked in the administration of the Protectorate of Bohemia and Moravia in 1939; head of the Reich commissioner's office in the Reich Commissariat of the Netherlands from 1940; arrested in 1945 and thought to have been in British captivity until 1949.
7 The original contains handwritten notes and underlining.

maintained for the time being; however, a lump sum is to be calculated, equivalent to the assets owned by the Jews who were formerly Reich citizens. A reasoned proposal in this regard is to be submitted to me.

DOC. 102

On 19 January 1943 Reich Commissioner Seyss-Inquart allows the secretaries general Frederiks and van Dam to name around 500 Jews who are not to be deported[1]

Note by the Senior Commander of the Security Police and the SD (IV B 4), unsigned, The Hague, dated 19 January 1943

From the notes of the meeting with the RC[2] on 19 January 1943:
Protected Jews:
The Reich Commissioner intends to allow Ministers *Frederiks* and van *Dam*[3] to name a certain number of Jews (around 500) who can continue to live in the country.

The Security Police will check the list for negative attributes. The grounds for intercession will not be assessed.

Together with the Representative,[4] the Security Police will determine the place of residence, scope of freedom of movement, and supervision.

After the clearing of Westerbork camp, these Jews are to be resettled in the main camp there.[5]

DOC. 103

On 21 January 1943 Claartje van Aals writes to her friend that she is being deported from Apeldoorn with all of her patients and colleagues[1]

Handwritten letter from Claartje van Aals,[2] Apeldoorn, to Aagje Kaagmans,[3] dated 21 January 1943

Dear Aag,

Please don't panic, my dear, but today we are off.[4] We don't know yet where we are going or what will happen to the people. Everything is complete chaos. I'm sitting in the

1 NIOD, 077/1319. This document has been translated from German.
2 Reich Commissioner Seyss-Inquart.
3 Dr Jan van Dam (1896–1979), Germanist; initially worked as a teacher; professor in Amsterdam from 1930; secretary general of the Ministry of Education, Science, and Cultural Protection from late 1940 to 1945; sentenced to seven years in prison after 1945; worked as a lecturer and teacher after his release in 1949.
4 Presumably a reference to Werner Schröder, the Reich Commissioner's representative for the City of Amsterdam.
5 As early as Dec. 1942 these Jews had been forced to move into two small castles in Barneveld (province of Gelderland). They were deported to Westerbork on 29 Sept. 1943, and from there to Theresienstadt on 4 Sept. 1944.

1 JHM, Doc. 00 012 189. Published in *Als ik wil kan ik duiken ... Brieven van Claartje van Aals, verpleegster in de joods psychiatrische inrichting Het Apeldoornsche Bosch*, ed. Suzette Wyers (Amsterdam: Thomas Rap, 1995), pp. 105–106. This document has been translated from Dutch.

corridor writing to you, and I'm ridiculously calm. I have bought a baby outfit for you only this week,[5] and I hope I will still get an opportunity to send it to you with your clothing card.[6] It would of course be awful if I can no longer return the clothing card to you, but I will do whatever I can. Just imagine, Aag: 1,500 people, patients and staff, are just taken away, and we have no idea what is going to happen to us. About half the staff have gone into hiding, and there are now only five nurses on the whole of [ward] G.[7] Last night I slept for two hours. From 3 to 5. A lot of men are sleeping upstairs, and it is a pigsty everywhere, as you can imagine. Agie, I have to leave everything behind. I can only take what is most essential, and what will become of us? It is just as if I am drunk. I can go into hiding if I want to, but I feel obliged to accompany the people, because my heart goes out to them. And if I no longer have Arno,[8] I no longer care about anything else. Agie, I am stopping here.

DOC. 104

An anonymous report dated 23 January 1943 on the complete evacuation of the mental institution Het Apeldoornsche Bosch and the deportation of the patients and nursing staff[1]

Report, unsigned, dated 23 January 1943 (typescript, carbon copy)

The deportation of the patients and staff of 'Het Apeldoornsche Bosch'
On Wednesday, 20 January 1943 at 4.30 p.m., one hundred Jewish people from the Ordnungsdienst[2] at Westerbork camp unexpectedly arrived at Het Apeldoornsche Bosch.

2 Klara (Claartje) van Aals (1922–1943), nurse; worked for the Dutch railway, 1938–1940; from 1940 trained as a nurse at Het Apeldoornsche Bosch, a Jewish mental institution founded in 1940; deported to Westerbork in Jan. 1943, and from there on 2 Feb. 1943 to Auschwitz, where she was murdered in March 1943.

3 Aagje Kaagmans (1921–2008); worked for the Dutch railway until 1942; worked in school administration in Edam after 1945.

4 During the night of 21 Jan. 1943, all the patients – 1,200 persons in total – together with 50 nursing staff at Het Apeldoornsche Bosch were deported to Auschwitz. The remaining members of the nursing staff were deported from Apeldoorn to Westerbork with the rest of the Jews: see Doc. 104.

5 Aagje Kaagmans had given birth to a son in Nov. 1942.

6 Like other necessities, clothing could be obtained only in exchange for coupons.

7 During preparations for deportation, the patients and the nursing staff had to remain in their wards.

8 Presumably Arno Walter Schwarz (1920–1991), precision mechanic; friend of Claartje van Aals; also worked at Het Apeldoornsche Bosch; deported to Westerbork on 21 Jan. 1943, from there to Auschwitz on 2 Feb. 1943, and subsequently to additional camps; returned to the Netherlands in Nov. 1945; moved to Hamburg in 1951.

1 Nationaal Archief, Medisch Contact 1941–1945, 2.19.53.02/19. This document has been translated from Dutch.

2 German in the original: 'Order Service'. This unit, made up of Jews, was responsible for guarding the punishment barracks and maintaining peace and order in Westerbork camp.

Shortly afterwards Obersturmführer Gemmincke,[3] the camp commandant of Westerbork, arrived, accompanied by Dr Spaniër,[4] the camp Chefarzt.[5]

Gemmincke asked whether those 100 people had arrived and gave the order that they should be provided with accommodation and a hot meal. At about 6 o'clock, aus der Fünten, Hauptsturmführer von der Zentralstelle für jüdische Auswanderung in Amsterdam,[6] also arrived. These three Germans left at about 7.30 p.m., without saying why they had come.

There were all kinds of speculations. Aus der Fünten had come to Het Apeldoornsche Bosch on 11 January to have a look around the asylum. He said nothing about the purpose of his visit, but his questions about whether there was a railway line to the asylum's premises and whether one had to get a train from Apeldoorn station if one wanted to travel by train from the asylum, as well as his request for a floor plan of the asylum, had raised major concerns. It was deemed unlikely that the asylum would be completely vacated, as ten new mentally ill patients from Westerbork had been admitted for care on Sunday, 17 January 1943.

On Wednesday evening the state supervisory inspector, Dr Audier,[7] received notification; he arrived from The Hague at about 10 o'clock on Thursday morning.

That same morning, the lawyer Leo de Wolf[8] from the Expositur division of the Jewish Council in The Hague also arrived to provide assistance.

Nothing happened that whole day; a list of non-transportable people was compiled, and patients' personal luggage was put out. In addition, food was prepared in case a transport would take place. Many of the nursing staff and[9] a small number of patients (fewer than 100) made their escape.

At 6.05 p.m. on Thursday, 21 January, a line of cars with armed SS men (they had carbines and guns) drove onto the asylum's premises.

The military personnel, including aus der Fünten and Gemmenincke, went into Dr Lobstein's[10] room. Aus der Fünten took over the management of the institution. He said that all patients would be taken to a military hospital in Germany, and that the staff would remain in the Netherlands.

3 Also called Gemmenincke below; correctly: Albert Konrad Gemmeker (1907–1982), policeman; served with the police from 1927; with the Düsseldorf Gestapo, 1935–1940; joined the NSDAP in 1937 and the SS in 1940; worked for the Senior Commander of the Security Police and the SD in the Netherlands, 1940–1942; commandant of Westerbork transit camp from Oct. 1942; arrested in 1945; sentenced in the Netherlands to ten years in prison in 1949; released in 1951; returned to the Federal Republic of Germany, and thereafter ran a tobacco shop.

4 Correctly: Dr Fritz Marcus Spanier (1902–1967), physician; admitted to the Netherlands after a failed attempt to emigrate aboard the refugee ship *St. Louis* in May 1939; in Westerbork, March 1940 to 1945; headed the camp hospital there; in Israel in 1949; returned to Germany in 1951.

5 German in the original: 'chief physician'.

6 German in the original: 'Hauptsturmführer of the Central Office for Jewish Emigration in Amsterdam'.

7 The reference is to the State Supervisory Authority for the Mentally Ill and Mental Institutions. Dr Arie Gijsbertus Audier (1903–1973), physician; joined the NSB in 1940; head of the State Supervisory Authority, 1941–1945; interned for a short time in 1945; subsequently head of cancer research at the University of Leiden.

8 Correctly: Leo de Wolff (1912–1945), lawyer and bookkeeper; employee of the Expositur department of the Jewish Council in Amsterdam from 1941; deported to Westerbork on 29 Sept. 1943, and from there to Bergen-Belsen on 11 Jan. 1944; died in Tröbitz in May 1945.

9 In the Dutch original, the word 'oom' ('uncle') appears here. The typo has been corrected in the translation.

When Lobstein said that there were non-transportable patients, aus der Fünten replied: 'Für uns sind alle Patienten transportabel.'[11]

Six (Aryan) staff members were called in and sent away. Dr Lobstein was put in the Committee Room with the administrative staff, so that he could no longer perform his work.

Dr Audier, who had met the Germans in the corridor, was greeted with the words: 'Ach, Audier, lieb, dass Sie hier sind, schön.'[12]

When Audier asked why aus der Fünten had come, referring to the Reichskommissar,[13] aus der Fünten replied that he did not normally give information about the purpose of his presence. Aus der Fünten pushed Audier aside, and the latter disappeared within ten seconds. The other physicians were given special orders.

Mr Mayer,[14] Hauptsturmführer[15] and physician, clearly coveted the instruments, the microscopes, and suchlike, and behaved particularly rudely by using insulting expressions. He took Dr Mendels[16] to the X-ray room, where the latter had to give information about how to operate the instruments, after which he had to hand over the keys.

Dr Speijer[17] had to accompany an SS officer and show him around the whole asylum, while the officer posted guards at the appropriate doors.

Dr Querido[18] had to do the rounds with a non-commissioned officer to retrieve torches and to lock doors.

As a result of these measures, the buildings were completely occupied; the telephone was disconnected.

The staff were separated from the patients and immediately locked up in a separate room in each pavilion. Following this – it was about 7 p.m. by then – the deportation of patients started. They were moved out of the main building and the pavilions between a double cordon of OD[19] people and loaded onto trucks without seats. Some were lying on stretchers.

10 Dr Jacques Lobstein (1883–1945), physician; at Het Apeldoornsche Bosch from 1908, and director there from 1936; forced to remain behind after his institution was evacuated; deported from there to Westerbork in Feb. 1943, and from there to Bergen-Belsen; died in Tröbitz on 7 May 1945.

11 German in the original: 'As far as we are concerned, all patients are transportable.'

12 German in the original: 'Oh, Audier, lovely that you're here, how nice.'

13 German in the original: 'Reich Commissioner' (Arthur Seyss-Inquart).

14 Correctly, presumably: Dr Eduard Wilhelm Paul Meyer (1898–1970), physician; joined the NSDAP and the SS in 1933; called up for the Wehrmacht in 1939; chief physician for the Waffen SS in the Netherlands from Sept. 1941; chief physician for the Higher SS and Police Leader from May 1943; returned to Germany in July 1944; prisoner of war in Germany, 1945–1946; interned in the Netherlands in 1948; subsequently returned to the Federal Republic of Germany.

15 German in the original.

16 Dr Jonas Mendels (1909–1944), physician; specialist in internal medicine and radiologist at Het Apeldoornsche Bosch; deported in Nov. 1943 from Westerbork to Auschwitz, where he perished on 31 Jan. 1944.

17 Dr Nico Speijer (1905–1983), psychiatrist; physician at Het Apeldoornsche Bosch, 1935–1943; deported to Westerbork on 23 Jan. 1943; freed when the camp was liberated in April 1945; head of the department of 'public mental health' in the Municipal Health Service (GGD), 1950–1965; professor in Leiden, 1965–1973.

18 Dr Arie Querido (1901–1983), psychiatrist; head of the department for nervous and mental illnesses at the Amsterdam GGD from 1933; physician at Het Apeldoornsche Bosch, 1942–1943; married to a non-Jew and therefore not deported; director of the public health service in Amsterdam 1949; professor in Amsterdam from 1952.

19 Order Service: see fn. 2.

These trucks drove to and from the station throughout the night. They returned with the empty stretchers.

Once a pavilion had been emptied completely, the staff who had been locked up in one of its rooms were transferred to the nurses' refectory, where all the lower-level staff were gradually being assembled.

Armed SS men were guarding over the staff in that refectory. One of them, SS Mann[20] Grüneberg, acted like a beast. He was swearing and cursing.

When Dr Lobstein appeared in that refectory during the night, Grüneberg beat him with a belt. When Dr Lobstein said he was the medical director, the SS Mann replied to him: 'Ach was, Direktor, ich bin der Direktor.'[21] This Grüneberg also forced Sister Heymans[22] to play songs on the piano in the refectory for an hour.

Once the physicians had carried out the orders mentioned above, they were also locked up in the committee room. They remained there until around midnight, were given bread and cheese, and were granted permission to sleep on beds prepared for them, under armed surveillance.

At 2 a.m. Dr Querido was woken up and ordered to guide aus der Fünten around the premises. The latter inspected a number of pavilions that had already been evacuated.

In these pavilions, Dr Querido saw all the luggage of the patients who had already left, both their personal belongings and all that had been hurriedly put together for them by the asylum.

It turned out that the food that had been prepared had not been distributed in several pavilions either.

When aus der Fünten went to the children's department, the Paedagogium Achisomog,[23] to inspect the evacuation process, Dr Querido tried to make it clear to him that severely maladjusted children rather than insane people were being cared for in this department. Aus der Fünten replied to that: 'Sie sind asozial, das ist die Hauptsache.'[24]

One of the public servants working at the Paedagogium explained to aus der Fünten on his arrival that his wife was eight months pregnant and asked permission for her to stay behind, following which aus der Fünten said: 'Sie kann auch draußen ihr Kind bekommen, Ausnahmen machen wir nicht.'[25]

He then went to the staff hospital.

Dr Querido pointed out to him that sick staff members were staying here, some of whom were seriously ill.

The dentist had sepsis, and there was also a patient with severe pulmonary tuberculosis.

Aus der Fünten said that he could not spare any staff to nurse these people. Anyone who was not able-bodied had to go with the patients.

20 German in the original: 'SS man'.
21 German in the original, 'Director indeed, I'm the director.'
22 Correctly, presumably: Henriette Heijmans-Bloemendaal (1887–1943), nurse.
23 The institution, founded in Apeldoorn in 1925 for mentally handicapped and disturbed children and adolescents, had moved to the site at Het Apeldoornsche Bosch in 1934. It reopened in 1945, taking in Jewish orphans at first. In 1966 it was officially taken over by the Christian mental institution Groot Schuylenburg, which had been located on the grounds of Het Apeldoornsche Bosch since 1952.
24 German in the original: 'They are asocial, that's the main thing.'
25 German in the original: 'She can also have her baby out there; we do not make exceptions.'

Dr Querido then asked him if he could give the dentist, who was dying, an injection to ease the discomfort during transport. He was allowed to do so. Aus der Fünten then left the small hospital, leaving Dr Querido behind.

That night the patients were locked up in wagons waiting at the station, so-called CH wagons.[26]

The patients, some of whom who were poorly clad or not wearing any clothes at all, including a young girl, were left in those wagons, which had no seats and in which some mattresses had been put on the floor, without any care being provided and without any supervision. Forty people were locked up in each wagon.

The sick staff members were locked up with these patients, and likely also staff members who were among the patients and had been locked up by mistake.

At about 7 o'clock on Friday morning, aus der Fünten ordered that fifty volunteers should be supplied from the nursing staff to travel with the patients. Twenty came forward, including some technical staff who, however, were rejected. A group of thirty who happened to be standing together were then selected, and the card index was used to verify whether they were nurses and unmarried.

It is thought that those fifty people did not travel in the same wagons as the patients but, if they were on the train, travelled in a separate wagon at the back. It is certain that more than 1,100 patients were deported without care being provided, without food, without a place to lie down or any cover, without heating, and without supervision, in a train consisting of goods wagons, which departed at about 7 o'clock via Bentheim for an unknown destination.[27]

At 8.30 on Friday morning, the order was given to the remaining staff that they and their families had to get ready for transport, and they were told they would be taken to Westerbork. The train, in which the physicians Speyer,[28] Mendels, de Vries,[29] and Spanjaard[30] were also travelling, departed for Westerbork at 11.30. Some patients who had been forgotten were also put on this train.

After the trains departed, Dr Lobstein, who had to remain in the asylum with part of the administrative staff, found an elderly female patient left behind in one of the pavilions, and a deceased person in another.

After the trains departed, all furniture and equipment were taken away, and SS soldiers searched the patients' remaining luggage. Aus der Fünten confiscated the money.

At 5.30 on Friday evening Dr Audier, the state supervisory inspector, returned to ask how everything had gone and to report to the secretary general.[31]

At 12 on Thursday, the secretary general had been informed of the situation as it was at that point.

26 Covered goods wagons; the abbreviation 'CH' is derived from the French 'charette' ('little cart').

27 In total, 1,200 patients and 50 members of the nursing staff were taken away. The train went directly to Auschwitz. The patients were murdered on arrival; the nursing staff were admitted to the camp. Not one of them survived until the end of the war.

28 Correctly: Nico Speijer.

29 Dr David Gerard de Vries (1918–1943), assistant physician; at Het Apeldoornsche Bosch from July 1942; deported on 9 Feb. 1943 from Westerbork to Auschwitz, where he perished in March 1943.

30 Jacob Spanjaard (1913–1985), psychiatrist; deported from Het Apeldoornsche Bosch to Westerbork; released from the camp on 15 April 1943; developed therapies for people returning from the concentration camps after 1945.

31 Mental hospitals were under the control of the Ministry of the Interior. Its secretary general was Karel Johannes Frederiks.

Summary

1. In the night from Thursday, 21 January, to Friday, 22 January 1943, more than 1,100 people from the psychiatric institution 'Het Apeldoornsche Bosch', of whom the vast majority were mentally ill, but a small proportion were sick and bedridden members of staff, were packed closely together in enclosed wagons without supervision, without care being provided, without covers or a place to lie down, and without food. They were in that train for hours while it was stationary at Apeldoorn station, after which they departed for an unknown destination via Bentheim at 7 o'clock.
2. The staff of this institution and their families have been transported to Westerbork.
3. The institution 'Het Apeldoornsche Bosch' has been closed down. The instruments and other items of furniture and equipment have been confiscated or removed.
4. The Germans who carried out these measures included:
   1. Hauptsturmführer aus der Fünten, von der Zentralstelle für jüdische Auswanderung in Amsterdam;[32]
   2. Obersturmführer Gemmincke, Camp Commandant of Westerbork;
   3. Chefarzt Dr Spaniër, Camp Physician at Westerbork;
   4. Hauptsturmführer Dr Mayer, Arzt,[33] and
   5. SS Mann Grüneberg.

Prepared truthfully according to information obtained on 23 January 1943.

DOC. 105

On 13 February 1943 the German soldier Charles Krause asks the camp commandant of Westerbork to permit his Jewish foster mother to attend his wedding[1]

Letter from Private First Class (Oberschütze) Charles Krause,[2] currently Amsterdam South, 7 III Geulstrasse,[3] to the German camp commandant of the Westerborg[4] camp, Hooghalen (Oost), Drenthe, dated 13 February 1943[5]

In view of my wartime wedding[6] and my leave of absence at short notice from the field to join my relatives in Amsterdam, I most politely request, Camp Commandant, that you grant a leave of absence allowing Mrs Adelheid Littwitz,[7] along with her husband and children, to travel to Amsterdam as of 18 February.

32 German in the original: 'from the Central Office for Jewish Emigration'.
33 German in the original: 'physician'.

1 NIOD, 250i/40. This document has been translated from German.
2 Charles Leonard Eugène Krause (b. 1919); soldier in the Wehrmacht from 1941; among other roles, worked in the Wehrmacht Rations Supply Office in Utrecht from June to Dec. 1943; thereafter in the Grenadier Replacement Battalion in Cologne.
3 Correctly: Geulstraat. Charles Krause's mother lived here from 1941 until the end of 1943.
4 Correctly: Westerbork. The camp commandant was Albert Konrad Gemmeker.
5 The original contains handwritten marking.
6 Charles Krause married Giuseppina Franca (b. 1922) on 13 Feb. 1943.
7 Adelheid Pauline Helene Littwitz, née Loewenheim (1899–1944), actress; lived in Berlin from 1915; emigrated to the Netherlands in 1936; deported from Westerbork to Theresienstadt on 5 April 1944 and on 4 Oct. 1944 to Auschwitz, where she was murdered.

Mrs Adelheid Littwitz was my foster mother in Germany for a considerable time, and the Littwitz family thus has a certain interest in this family event, despite the present-day circumstances.

Even though there is a certain contradiction between me as a soldier and the measures also affecting the Littwitz family, I request that you make an exception this once.

In anticipation of a favourable decision,[8] signed

Heil – Hitler!

DOC. 106

On 15 February 1943 Toni Ringel describes a conflict with the family who is hiding her[1]

Diary of Toni Ringel:[2] To our beloved children,[3] entry for 15 February 1943 (typescript)

15 February 1945

A small incident. The younger son[4] of the 'landlady',[5] probably upon her order, follows me around everywhere. During the first week I did not notice it, as I had too much on my mind. But gradually it dawned upon me, and I was deeply insulted. When the landlady came home, I went to see her in the kitchen and told her: 'Tomorrow I shall go into town and look for another shelter, and I hope to find one. If not, we shall give ourselves up. With the money we have got left, the chances are that we shall find something suitable. I am aware of the fact that I am homeless, but that does not mean that I have to take insults from you. I spit on your riches, whatever they are. I do not need any of your belongings and would not soil my hands by ever touching them.' I felt so embittered and insulted that I screamed to her face: 'You have not got enough to pay for my old shoes.'

Of course, I could not tell her that she judges others by one's[6] own actions. For instance, when she needs towels, she takes an expensive, initialled bath towel from Hedwig's trunk, cuts it up and hey presto, she has got six hand towels. When she needs sheets, she takes them from the belongings of Totje's[7] parents; and like that she pilfers many other items. – The woman did not know what to answer. Under no circumstances did she want us to go. She had never expected to hear such language from me but my dear children, she surely was impressed, and I was not bothered again.

8 Handwritten note: 'No', initialled by Gemmeker.

1 LBIJMB, MM II/14. The original is missing. The diary was presumably originally handwritten in German, but was translated into English and typed out by Robert Ringel, Toni Ringel's youngest son.

2 Taube (Toni) Ringel, née Hammersfeld (1888–1980); emigrated to Spain from Frankfurt am Main in 1933, and from there to the Netherlands in 1936; lived in hiding from Sept. 1942 until 1945; emigrated to the USA in 1947.

3 Toni Ringel's children were Amalia (b. 1907), Betty (b. 1909), Adolf (1910–2008), and Robert (1913–2004). Her sons had already fled before or during the war and had found refuge in Spain and Britain.

4 Bernard Veitz (b. 1923); emigrated from the Netherlands after the occupation.

5 Barendina Veitz-Hooijberg (1895–1981), laundrywoman; Toni Ringel and her husband lived in her family's apartment on Van Speijkstraat from Sept. 1942 until 1945.

6 As in the original; the meaning is presumably 'by her actions'.

7 Totje, correctly: Cato Rosetta Parfumeur (1920–2009), the fiancée of Adolf Ringel, Toni Ringel's eldest son. Both escaped to Spain in the autumn of 1942; they emigrated to Britain before the end of the war and later lived in the USA.

DOC. 107
In a pastoral letter dated 17 February 1943, the Dutch Catholic bishops oppose the persecution of the Jews and call for civil disobedience[1]

Pastoral letter from the Catholic bishops of the Netherlands, signed Dr J. de Jong[2] (archbishop of Utrecht), P. A. W. Hopmans[3] (bishop of Breda), Dr J. H. G. Lemmens[4] (bishop of Roermond), J. P. Huibers[5] (bishop of Haarlem), and W. P. A. M. Mutsaerts (bishop coadjutor of 's-Hertogenbosch), Utrecht, dated 17 February 1943 (typescript, copy)

From the Archbishop and Bishops of the Netherlands to the clergy and faithful under their care
Glory be to the Lord

Dearly Beloved,

The bitter suffering and great anxiety that weigh down so many, particularly as a consequence of the severe measures taken by the occupying power in recent times,[6] oblige us to write to express our sincerest sympathy. We are filled with the deepest compassion for all those who have to endure such great and bitter afflictions. But we would be failing in our task if we did not publicly speak out against the injustice done to so many of our people.

In this respect we follow the example of our Holy Father the Pope,[7] who said in his latest Christmas message,[8] among other things: … the Church would renounce itself and cease to be our mother if it remained deaf to its children's cry of fear and anxiety, which reaches its ears from all classes of society. It does not intend to choose sides for one or the other of the specific, concrete forms by means of which the different peoples and states seek to resolve the enormous problems of internal organization and interna-

1 Het Utrechts Archief, 449/152. Published in Siegfried Stokman, *Het verzet van de Nederlandsche bisschoppen tegen nationaal-socialisme en Duitsche tyrannie* (Utrecht: Het Spectrum, 1945), pp. 265–268. This document has been translated from Dutch.

2 Dr Johannes (Jan) de Jong (1885–1955), priest and theologian; professor at Rijsenburg Seminary from 1914; archbishop of the Archbishopric of Utrecht from 1936; active in the church's resistance during the occupation period; cardinal from 1946.

3 Adrianus Petrus Willem Hopmans (1865–1951), priest and theologian; worked for the Bishopric of Breda from 1897; bishop of Breda from 1914; represented by a coadjutor from 1945 until his death.

4 Joseph Hubert Guillaume Lemmens (1884–1960), priest and theologian; professor at Roermond Catholic Seminary, 1918–1932; bishop of Roermond, 1932–1958.

5 Johannes Petrus Huibers (1875–1969), priest and theologian; priest in Hoorn, 1928–1935; bishop of Haarlem from 1935; represented by a coadjutor from 1960 until his death.

6 Hundreds of students were held in Vught concentration camp in early Feb. 1943, following the fatal attack on the commander of the Netherlands Legion of the Waffen SS, General Seyffardt (1872–1943). In addition, more than 1,000 young men were arrested and taken to Germany for forced labour.

7 Pope Pius XII, born Eugenio Pacelli (1876–1958), theologian and lawyer; entered the Holy See Secretariat of State, 1901; professor at the Vatican's diplomatic academy, 1909–1914; appointed titular bishop and papal nuncio in Bavaria in 1917; nuncio for the German Reich, 1920–1929; appointed cardinal in 1929 and cardinal secretary of state in 1930; raised to the papacy in March 1939.

8 The complete text of the Christmas address delivered by Pius XII on 24 Dec. 1942 is published in Pope Pius XII, *Discorsi e radiomessaggi di Sua Santità Pio XII*, vol. 4, *Quarto anno di pontificato 2 marzo 1942–1 marzo 1943* (Vatican City: Tipografia Poliglotta Vaticana, 1955), pp. 327–346.

tional cooperation when they honour God's law. However, the Church, the 'pillar and ground of the truth' (1 Timothy 3:15),[9] and guardian of the natural and supernatural order through the will of God and the commission of Christ, should not fail to proclaim to its children and the whole world the sacrosanct fundamental principles, safeguarding them against being overturned, blurred, mingled, falsely interpreted, or deviated from in any manner.

Together with the main other religious communities, we have therefore now directed a letter to the Reich Commissioner with the following content:

> Reich Commissioner, the Protestant Churches and the Roman Catholic Church in the Netherlands feel obliged to write to you once more with great seriousness. They have turned to you on a number of occasions with serious complaints about the increasing level of injustice against the Dutch people,[10] which has also deeply affected the churches. As they have explained to you, they have made their voices heard by virtue of their mission received from Christ, also when the principles embedded in the gospel have been undermined in public life. They refer in particular to those principles that form the foundation of our Christian life: justice, charity, and the freedom of personal beliefs. They must profess that those in power are also subject to God's law and must refrain from deeds that are denounced by that law. The churches would stand condemned if they were to fail to point out to those in power the sins they have committed while exercising their power and to warn them of God's judgement.
>
> The churches have already pointed out the following:
>
> - the increasing lawlessness;
> - the deadly persecution of Jewish fellow citizens;
> - the imposition of an ideology and world view that are the direct opposite of the gospel of Jesus Christ;
> - the mandatory labour service as a National Socialist instructional institution;
> - the infringement of the freedom of Christian education;
> - the forced employment of Dutch labourers in Germany;
> - putting hostages to death;
> - imprisoning and keeping in prison many people, including religious office holders, in circumstances that are such that an alarming number have already had to sacrifice their lives in the concentration camps.
>
> The hunting down of thousands of young people like slaves and their capture and deportation have now been added to this list. All of these actions increasingly violate God's law.
>
> The churches preach against hatred and vindictiveness in the hearts of our people and raise their voices against expressions of this. According to God's Word, no one may act as their own judge. But at the same time, they are also called on to preach the following words of God: 'We ought to obey God rather than men'.[11]
>
> These words are a guideline for any moral conflicts, including those that are the result of the measures taken.
>
> Under God's law, a person may not assist in any acts of injustice, as this makes him also guilty of that injustice.

9 1 Timothy 3:15 (KJV).

10 See Doc. 65. The religious communities of the Netherlands had repeatedly approached Reich Commissioner Seyss-Inquart on other matters as well.

11 Acts 5:29 (KJV).

Reich Commissioner, it is in obedience to its Lord that the churches must address these words to you; they pray to God that He will guide you in His way towards the recovery of the law that has been so seriously violated in the exercise of power.

Here ends the joint letter to the Reich Commissioner.

Dearly Beloved,

With regard to all the injustice committed and the suffering taking place, our sympathy goes in particular to the young people who have been violently taken from their parental homes, and to the Jews and our fellow Catholic believers originating from the Jewish people who have been exposed to such great suffering.

However, we also feel deeply aggrieved by the fact that the implementation of the measures taken against these two groups of people requires the *cooperation* of our own fellow countrymen, such as [public] authorities, civil servants, and the governors of institutions.

Consequently, we are aware of the enormous moral dilemma in which the individuals concerned find themselves. Well then, to remove any doubt and uncertainty regarding this point, we emphatically declare that cooperation in this is morally impermissible. And, should the refusal to cooperate lead to sacrifices, be strong and firm in the knowledge that you are doing your duty towards God and the people.[12]

Dearly Beloved, we do not have any instruments of power. We therefore encourage you all the more to turn to the ultimate, never-failing resource of a humble prayer, in which you ask God to have pity on us and the world soon.

And this, our joint pastoral letter, will be read out on Septuagesima Sunday, 21 February, in all the churches belonging to our archdiocese and in all chapels where a rector has been appointed, in the usual way, during all planned celebrations of Mass.

Issued in Utrecht on 17 February in the year of our Lord 1943,

Dr J. de Jong, Archbishop of Utrecht
P. A. W. Hopmans, Bishop of Breda
Dr J. H. G. Lemmens, Bishop of Roermond
J. P. Huibers, Bishop of Haarlem
W. P. A. M. Mutsaerts, Coadjutor Bishop of 's-Hertogenbosch

PS. As regards reading out bishops' letters, follow the instructions of your own bishop exclusively.

12 This was the first time the Catholic Church had appealed for civil disobedience during the occupation period. Some of the civil servants and employees who were addressed reacted by refusing to cooperate in further operations initiated by the occupiers; as a result, they were arrested or forced to go into hiding.

DOC. 108

An anonymous report dated 22 February 1943 on conditions in the newly constructed Vught concentration camp[1]

Report, unsigned,[2] dated 22 February 1943 (typescript)

Report on the prison camp in Vught[3]
Approximately six weeks ago, the camp in Vught[4] was populated with prisoners. From a reliable source, we have learned the following about the conditions there in the first four weeks:

The camp is well constructed and the buildings are of a good standard. However, the camp had not yet been entirely completed. The hospital, for example, was not yet ready for use.

The camp has different divisions for: 1) Jews, 2) students etc., and 3) political prisoners and black marketeers, including some Jews. The treatment of the third group is the worst, and the black marketeers and Jews from group 3 are having a particularly hard time.

The camp is guarded by the SS, including a large group from the Wachbataillon[5] as well. A Hauptsturmführer[6] is in charge of the camp overall. However, German convicts act as 'overseers',[7] and it is their conduct in particular that gives rise to complaints.

The food is completely inadequate. On a repeated number of occasions, no food has been provided for 24 hours as a general punishment for minor negligence, a mistake during roll call, or due to an error on the part of the camp leadership. The food is prepared with unfiltered water. There is no proper drinking water.

The prisoners' clothing consists of old Dutch uniforms, which are usually completely threadbare and torn. No underwear is worn. The prisoners have to work outside in all weathers in these clothes, and they often stand in the cold wind for hours at roll call. (Striped prisoners' uniforms were allegedly issued a few days ago.)

1 Nationaal Archief, Ministerie van Justitie/Hooykaas, 2.09.56/47. This document has been translated from Dutch.

2 This document was found in the files of the acting secretary general of the Ministry of Justice, J. P. Hooykaas (1900–1971). The name of the author could not be found.

3 The Germans referred to the camp as Herzogenbusch concentration camp; in the Netherlands, it was called Kamp Vught. Geographically, the camp was located in the north-western part of the town of Vught, which is not far from 's-Hertogenbosch.

4 The first prisoners came to Vught from Amersfoort camp on 5 Jan. 1943. At this point, the camp had not been completed. It was simultaneously a state-run concentration camp and a transit camp for Jews.

5 German in the original: 'guard battalion'. The SS Guard Battalion North-West, established in early 1942, was responsible for guarding various camps. It was converted into the SS Brigade Landstorm Nederland in Nov. 1944.

6 Karl Chmielewski (1903–1991), woodcarver; joined the NSDAP and the SS in 1932; worked full-time for the SS from 1932, at Sachsenhausen and Gusen concentration camps and elsewhere; commandant of Vught concentration camp, Jan.–Oct. 1943; sentenced to 15 years in prison for embezzlement and interned in Dachau; fled to Austria in 1945; returned to Germany under a false name; sentenced to life imprisonment in 1961; released in 1979.

7 In the Dutch original: 'meesterknechten'; presumably a reference to prisoners who had been transferred to Vught from other concentration camps for deployment as Kapos (prisoner functionaries).

The treatment is often worse than barbaric. Apparently corporal punishment is officially prohibited, but it nevertheless often happens that prisoners are bludgeoned so badly that they are left for dead. The commandant takes pleasure in walking through the camp with a dog, which seems to have been trained to attack the prisoners. This dog then tears the prisoners' clothes and bits of skin from their bodies. If the prisoner shows any resistance to the attack, he is subjected to bludgeoning. Prisoners are given instructions they cannot fulfil because they are too weak, and they are flogged. The roll calls often last for hours. Those who are barely alive still have to appear. They are carried by their colleagues or transported on a wheelbarrow. One troop, which was recently suddenly detained, was made to believe throughout the night that they would be shot dead in the morning. One half-dead man, who had been carried away by his mates and put on a wooden bed, was kicked out by a Feldwebel amidst cursing and swearing. Of course the man was unconscious by then.

Some time ago, a fairly large number were released.[8] Most of them were so weak that they collapsed as soon as they left the camp. Some of them were collected on handcarts by the local people. Some time ago, there was a 'Propagandamarsch'[9] to Den Bosch,[10] where the prisoners had to work at the harbour. The local population, who saw this completely exhausted, starved troop go past in rags, will no longer be so easily impressed by the scenes from the film *Ohm Krüger.*[11]

An example of a sophisticated method of torture is getting the starved prisoners to unload bread. Anyone who dares to take a bite of bread or even just take the crumbs is flogged mercilessly.

A few incidents:

A prisoner was shot in the leg by mistake. This man had to wait for 12 hours with a splintered femur before receiving medical treatment.

During the transport to the camp, one student stooped down to pick up his rolled-up blanket. He was immediately stabbed three times with a bayonet. It was only through illicit means that he could be provided with medication and medical treatment.

Some of the labourers working at the camps have already had a nervous breakdown because they could no longer bear to see what was going on. These free labourers are also under great pressure. Minor offences such as providing food to prisoners are punished very severely.

There is virtually no medical treatment. The hospital is not yet finished.[12] There is no medication available. There does appear to be a German physician for the camp, and patients can report themselves sick, but they all seem to be extremely frightened to do so. The reason for this is not known. Even an engineer with diphtheria did not want to be treated, as he too was convinced that anyone reporting sick was doomed to die.

8 This could not be verified.

9 German in the original, lit.: 'propaganda march'.

10 Colloquial Dutch name for 's-Hertogenbosch.

11 German propaganda film (1941) depicting the struggle of the Boers against the British. Key scenes are set in a British concentration camp.

12 The camp infirmary did not open until July 1943. Until then, part of a barracks served as an infirmary. Owing to the poor hygiene conditions, an epidemic of dysentery broke out shortly after the camp opened.

In the first four weeks, 143 prisoners died. The dead are treated like dogs' corpses. They are completely undressed and thrown onto a pile in a shed. Their number is painted on their body. They were put into a pit that had been dug with so little effort that the corpses were exposed during heavy rain. This has changed over the past few weeks. There is now an incinerator in which the corpses are cremated.[13]

These prisoners also include men who secretly slaughtered a pig or a sheep once or twice and have been caught. When you then see the commandant, who carries out this punishment, eat ten-ounce chunks of 'black' meat[14] in the afternoon, you cannot help having murderous thoughts now and again.

The treatment of the prisoners has seen a change and an improvement over the past few days. There is a rumour that Rauter has intervened.[15] I cannot yet say how far-reaching these improvements are. In any case, a thorough investigation is highly desirable. Moreover, measures should be taken to prevent a situation in which prisoners are handed over to the will of sadists for a shorter or longer period of time in the future. It would be worthwhile to inspect the other camps as well. It is extremely difficult, however, to obtain reliable information, as most of the prisoners are too scared to talk.

People are increasingly aware of these conditions. Of course the stories will be exaggerated. But what has been said above must be more or less the truth.

DOC. 109
On 24 February 1943 Betty Jeannette Denekamp asks Georg Calmeyer to protect her from deportation, as she was formerly an NSB member[1]

Letter from B. J. Denekamp,[2] The Hague, 24 Ruychrocklaan, to Dr Calmeyer,[3] c/o Commissariat General for Justice and Administration, The Hague, 7 Binnenhof (received on 26 February 1943), dated 24 February 1943 (typescript)[4]

Dear Dr Calmeyer,

I would hereby like to ask you most respectfully to put me on a list (for example, Frederiks's list),[5] if possible, so that, as a Jewish woman, I am kept safe to some extent.

13 It was not until Dec. 1943 that a crematorium was officially brought into use inside the camp.
14 Meat from cattle slaughtered illegally.
15 Rauter planned to make Vught a model camp in the Netherlands, but his efforts repeatedly brought him into conflict with the SS Business and Administration Main Office (WVHA). In 1943 and 1944 he had two camp commandants replaced, but the prisoners were not treated substantially better as a result.

1 NIOD, 020/1544. This document has been translated from German.
2 Betty Jeannette Denekamp (1896–1943), shorthand typist; on 2 March 1943 deported to Westerbork, and on 20 April 1943 from there to Sobibor, where she was murdered upon arrival.
3 Dr Hans Georg Calmeyer (1903–1972), lawyer; practised law from 1931; took part in the campaign in Western Europe in 1940; head of the Decision-Making Body for Unresolved Questions of Ancestry (Entscheidungsstelle für Zweifelsfragen der Abstammung) in the Commissariat General for Administration and Justice, 1941–1945; interned in the Netherlands, 1945–1946; thereafter returned to Germany and worked as a lawyer.
4 The original contains handwritten notes and underlining.
5 In Jan. 1943 Dutch secretaries general Karel Johannes Frederiks and Jan van Dam were permitted to name around 500 Jews who were to be protected from deportation: see Doc. 102.

For approximately three and a half years, I was a member of the NSB and worked as a 'blokleidster' (inster),[6] among other things. I left the movement at the end of 1938 because I was afraid I would lose my job as an office worker.

Dr Fred. Stähle,[7] who advised me to contact you, is happy to provide you with all the requested information about me and my work for the NSB.

Looking forward to favourable news from you and thanking you most sincerely in advance for your efforts, I remain respectfully yours,[8]

Betty Jeannette Denekamp,
born in The Hague, 29 June 1896;
presently housekeeper for Prof. Dr E. Moresco,[9]
24 Ruychrocklaan, The Hague

DOC. 110

On 26 February 1943 the Dutch secret service gives the government in exile in London an overview of the measures against the Jews[1]

Report (JvH/HL.), unsigned, dated 26 February 1943[2]

Measures against the Jews in the Netherlands

The tightened measures of the German occupation government in the Netherlands against the Jews started with the deployment of Jews in Dutch work camps.[3] Initially, Jews aged between 18 and 40 who were found to be suitable for the work concerned after a proper medical examination by Dutch doctors were selected for this. The age limit was

6 Dutch in the original: 'block leader (collector [of donations])'. Until 1938 Jews were allowed to join the NSB.

7 Correctly: Mr Friedrich Conrad Stähle (1906–1991), lawyer; joined the NSB in 1933; administrator of liquidated companies and organizations from 1941; joined the Dutch SS in March 1943; interned, 1945–1948.

8 Handwritten notes: '1) Reply: I have recommended to the secretary general of the Ministry of the Interior that he put your name forward for protection, if at all possible. 2) Original to Dr Kloosterman, with a recommendation for approval of the request. Dr Stähle is a truly conscientious and reliable advocate. Perhaps the protection of Prof. Moresco can be combined with the protection of B. J. Denekamp. 26 Feb. 1942, p.p. signed Calmeyer.'

9 Emanuel Ephraim Moresco (1869–1945), civil servant; secretary general of the Ministry of Colonies, 1917–1922; professor in Rotterdam, 1924–1929; in 1943 deported to Barneveld, and from there to Westerbork in Sept. of the same year; one year later, deported to Theresienstadt; returned to the Netherlands in 1945.

1 NIOD, 226b/I-B. This document has been translated from Dutch.

2 The report is presumably the work of members of the Dutch secret service, as the context of the file suggests; the names of the authors could not be established. The original contains handwritten notes.

3 The National Work Creation Service (Werkverschaffings-Rijkedienst) was established in 1937 to counter the problem of mass unemployment in the Netherlands. The unemployed were required to perform work at specific locations and were sometimes placed in work camps. In 1939 the service was renamed the National Agency for Work Creation (Rijksdienst voor de Werkverruiming). During the German occupation it was also in charge of supervising Dutch Jews sent to labour camps in the Netherlands between Jan. and Oct. 1942. See PMJ 5/110.

gradually raised, first to 50, then to 60, and finally to 65. When the Germans decided that too many people were being declared unfit for work, the examination as well as the re-examination of those who had been declared unfit for work became the task of NSB doctors, in some cases assisted by German doctors. From then on, open tuberculosis was more or less the only reason why a person could still be declared unfit for work. The average duration of the examination is half a minute per person. Out of 850 persons aged between 18 and 65 called up in a specific town, 17 were declared unfit for work. Medical certificates from Dutch physicians were ignored. Heart patients, people suffering from angina pectoris, etc., and even people with one arm and one leg were passed without further ado.

The normal Dutch rations (without extra rations for heavy work) now apply in the work camps, as a result of which – due to the heavy work – malnutrition and its associated risks are becoming more and more apparent.

While the transfer to these work camps was taking place, the German authorities suddenly took measures to deport men and women with children to Germany, allegedly for the purpose of 'Polizeilichen Arbeitseinsatz'.[4] Initially, the age limit was between 16 and 40; for people who were married, the children were included. They were promised decent living conditions in every respect and that families would be kept together. Those who had been called up were given around three days to sort out their affairs before they had to report [for labour service]. Nevertheless, only around 400 out of 1,000 people who had been called up actually turned up. The previous experiences of Jews sent to concentration camps such as Mauthausen, virtually all of whom are now reported to have died,[5] raised the worst possible expectations for this new deportation. This was made even worse by a speech, given approximately one week after the announcement of this deportation, by General-Kommissar[6] Schmidt, who expressed himself in the most outspoken terms possible about the treatment to which the Jews would be subjected.[7] The number of people called up who actually turned up therefore remained well below German expectations. In one large city, only about 1,200 of the 5,600 people called up actually reported. From then on, instead of calling up the Jews, they were picked up. When those who were sought were not found, others were taken. Age limits or medical considerations were now barely taken into account. The only criterion for examination has since been 'Transportfähigkeit'.[8] Men and women of over 80, a six-year-old child from a Jewish orphanage, and a child aged two and a half whose parents had fled were deported without further thought. In the transit camp in Westerbork (Drenthe), there are already seven people who are completely blind. Many Jewish men and women aged 80, and even one aged 96, have already lost their lives.

Particularly in the beginning, the way in which the transports took place was inhuman. Sixty people were loaded onto a livestock wagon with a surface area of 21 m^2. People were told to gather with their luggage in places at a great distance from the railway, whence they had to walk to the station, dragging their luggage with them. This was

4 German in the original: 'police labour deployment'. See Doc. 52.
5 On the prisoners' situation, see PMJ 5/107.
6 German in the original: 'commissioner general [for special duties]' (Fritz Schmidt).
7 Presumably Schmidt's speech on 2 August 1942: see Doc. 67.
8 German in the original: 'being fit for transport'.

improved later. At least on the Dutch section of the route, the transport now takes place in passenger carriages. The management of Westerbork transit camp, which was originally in Dutch hands, was later transferred to German hands, with all the obvious consequences.[9]

From the Netherlands, victims are transported to southern Silesia, where an area of about 5,000 hectares near Gleiwitz seems to have been allocated as a Jewish reserve, with Auscewitz[10] as the distribution centre for all able-bodied Jews deported from Western Europe. It appears that Theresastadt[11] (on the Dresden to Prague line) has been allocated for the disabled, but some disabled people have been used to supplement transports to southern Silesia when there were insufficient able-bodied people to put together a full transport, while others have remained in Westerbork.[12] For many weeks at least two transports of a minimum of 1,000 people departed from Westerbork every week.

Since 15 September things have changed again in the deportation system. So-called 'Sperr'[13] lists of people who will remain exempt for the time being have been drawn up, for example under the Rüstungsinspektion, the 4-Jahresplan,[14] special categories such as residents and employees of homes for elderly men and women, recognized rest homes, etc., a number of so-called Christian Jews, and in specific cases spouses in a mixed marriage with children. All other Jews who fall into the hands of the Germans will gradually be deported. If Jews who have been in hiding are captured, the males aged over 16 among them will be sent to Mauthausen, from where one large town received 20 death notices in just one week. The females among them go to a concentration camp. Moreover, non-Jews who have provided shelter are severely punished.[15]

The Dutch churches are constantly protesting vehemently against the treatment of the Jews.[16]

The evident intention is to systematically make the Netherlands Jew-free. Jews from the provinces are placed in work camps or deported. All Jews from Utrecht and the surrounding area, with the exception of a small number who are exempted, have either been sent directly to work camps or to Germany, or forced to move to Amsterdam, whence many are sent to Westerbork as a transit camp before being sent onward to Germany. Their houses including the contents etc. are confiscated by the Germans. In The Hague and the surrounding area, the houses of very many Jews have also been confiscated, and in most cases the residents of these houses have been sent to Westerbork. An exception is made only for foreign Jews in cases where they are citizens of countries that are still neutral.

9 Westerbork was originally established by the Dutch government as a refugee camp and was under the authority of the Dutch Ministry of Justice. From 1 July 1942 the German Commissariat General for Security took over command of Westerbork, which became a police transit camp.

10 Correctly: Auschwitz.

11 Correctly: Theresienstadt.

12 More than 1,000 people had been deported by mid Feb. 1943 in just 15 of a total of 50 transports. The average number of deportees was between 700 and 850 per transport.

13 German in the original: lit. 'blocked', a reference to temporary exemption from deportation.

14 German in the original: 'armaments inspectorate', the 'Four-Year Plan'.

15 Helpers who provided Jews with false papers, food ration cards, and other things had to expect to be sent to a concentration camp if they were caught. People who sheltered Jews usually received little or no punishment if they claimed to have been unaware that their guests were Jews.

16 See Docs. 65 and 107.

DOC. 111

On 15 March 1943 IJnto de Boer criticizes policemen under his command who refuse to take part in the deportation of Jews[1]

Letter from the commander of the Marechaussee district of Groningen (no. 1221), signed Y. de Boer[2] (major, district commander of the Marechaussee district, simultaneously acting chief of police and acting district police chief in Groningen), Groningen, to the battalion commander, the Westerbork troop commander, the commander of the transport groups, district offices, senior clerks, and persons in charge of supplies, dated 15 March 1943[3]

Re: transport of Jews by the Dutch police

I hereby request that you instruct the group commanders under your authority to discuss the following with their staff.

Over the past few days, all Jews in the region had to be transferred to Lager[4] Westerbork on the order of the occupying power.[5] Sick Jews had to be transported by car, or by ambulance if necessary, to a separate camp for the sick.

This measure is a consequence of the Führer's decision to put an end to the situation in Europe whereby civilization is under threat from Jewry, which attempts, in accordance with the Jewish religion, to achieve world dominion by means of capital, Bolshevism, and other underground political forces, the reason being that once world dominion has been achieved, the Messiah of the Jews will appear on Earth. This aim poses a serious threat to Christianity.

The Jews consider Christ to be an impostor, and his followers may be freely deceived and cheated by the chosen people.

To break their power, all Jews are being removed from European society, and unless they are sick, they are transferred to Poland, where a large area of land has been set aside for them. The sick Jews are brought together in Lager Westerbork, where Jewish physicians are on hand to treat them.

It is everyone's duty, in the interest of their own culture, to cooperate in eliminating this danger.

1 Herinneringscentrum Kamp Westerbork, 8753–02. This document has been translated from Dutch.

2 Correctly: IJnto de Boer (1904–1988), career officer; teacher at various military academies from 1927; transferred to the Koninklijke Marechaussee (Dutch gendarmerie force) in 1940; joined the NSB in 1941; district commander in Maastricht, 1940–1942, and in Groningen, 1942–1943; chief of staff at police general headquarters in Nijmegen, 1944–1945; arrested in 1945; sentenced to eight years in prison in 1948; thought to have been released in 1951.

3 The letter also was sent for information – and for retention – to the police chiefs in the municipalities with their own police corps, with the request that their staff also be informed. It is not possible to tell which municipality applied the receipt stamp dated 16 March 1943. The original contains handwritten notes.

4 German in the original: 'camp'.

5 The last Jews were deported from the Groningen and Friesland provinces on 9 March 1943. Only a small number of persons who were not fit for transport and persons in 'mixed marriages' remained behind.

For the police, there is additionally the requirement that these forces organized along military lines immediately carry out the orders issued by the occupying power in this respect as commands.

Assembling the Jews is indeed a tough measure for these people, but compared to other acts of war, such as the bombing of cities, which involves killing women and children, its harshness should not be exaggerated, and it should not give rise to sentimentality.

Some believed that the Führer's words – that Jewry must be destroyed – should be interpreted in such a way that the Jews themselves would be destroyed. Of course, that is complete nonsense: if that were the case, we would not have to make such an effort to make the already scarce means of transport available for transporting Jews, and neither would we then need to transfer the sick Jews to a separate camp for the sick by ambulance.

In reality, therefore, not a single Jew who shows no resistance will be hurt in any way whatsoever. Any unnecessary harshness is avoided by leaving family units intact during transport.

In spite of the fact that all police officers should be aware of this, a number of Marechaussee personnel, all belonging to the Grootegast division, have refused to follow the orders they have been given.[6]

Following an attempt by the C. Division to make them fulfil their duty, in the evening I myself pointed out to them that their behaviour was entirely incorrect. The relevant personnel were then given one night to change their mind. The next morning, they were once again one by one given the choice, in the presence of German police officers, to either immediately follow the order that had been given, or to be taken to a concentration camp. Unfortunately, it turned out that the group commander, Sub-lieutenant De Witt,[7] and ten of his men, including three rural constables, had been fired up to such an extent by communist pamphlets, sermons from the pulpit, or ideas disseminated by British radio that they continued to refuse.

On orders from the Generalkommissar für das Sicherheitswesen,[8] the relevant personnel were immediately discharged from service, without entitlement to any pension or other income, and transferred to the concentration camp in Vught, whence they will be transported to Germany to work in machine factories.

Through this regrettable, stubborn attitude, as a result of which a number of families have been plunged into sorrow, those involved have also done a disservice to their divisions and to their people.

By acting in such a way, they render the Dutch police totally unreliable in the eyes of the occupying power. The only consequence of this will be that the occupier will be forced to put the Dutch police on non-active status and send the officers to Germany as labourers. The police forces could then be transferred to the German police; I have heard

6 On 12 March 1943 the Marechaussee group stationed in the municipality of Grootegast had refused to deport a Jewish family to Westerbork. All eleven members of the group were taken to Vught concentration camp, where they worked for the Philips electrical company until the summer of 1944. Some of the group were subsequently sent to camps in Germany, while others were released.

7 Jacob Derk de Witt (b. 1895), police officer; arrested on 13 March 1943 and imprisoned in Vught camp; deported in May 1944 to Dachau, where he was imprisoned until the camp's liberation in 1945; subsequently returned to the Netherlands.

8 German in the original: 'commissioner general for security' (Hanns Albin Rauter).

that one battalion has already been stationed in Assen. I do not need to spell out what this means for our people.

I therefore urgently appeal to the common sense of the Marechaussee personnel under my authority not to be dissuaded under any circumstance, by whatever influences, from fulfilling their duties in an absolutely reliable and loyal manner.

DOC. 112
Overview of Jews who have thus far been exempt from deportation, dated 16 March 1943[1]

Report, unsigned,[2] The Hague, dated 16 March 1943[3]

Re: Jews with deferment stamps
1) *Foreigners*:
a) *Neutral foreigners*
The number of neutral foreigners deferred by the Central Office in Amsterdam[4] amounted to *sixty-four persons*.

After the individual legations of the neutral countries had been asked by the Reich Foreign Office in Berlin to remove their Jewish citizens from the occupied western territories by 31 March 1943, the first country to remove its Jews was Switzerland. On 9, 11, and 13 February 1943, a total of sixteen Jews with Swiss citizenship left the Netherlands. The embassies of the other neutral countries have not yet provided the names of their Jews, but the following persons have, in anticipation, applied to leave the country and go to their homelands:

to Spain	3 persons
to Liberia	10 persons
to Denmark	7 persons
to Sweden	9 persons
to Turkey	5 persons
to Italy	thus far, none,
to Argentina	thus far, none.

The Liberian citizens are already in possession of Spanish entry visas but must delay their departure until the decision of the RSHA has arrived.

With regard to the Hungarian nationals, a group of thirteen persons is leaving the Netherlands on 18 March 1943, and a second group is currently being put together. The Hungarian ministry in charge has raised no objections to the return of these Jews. (Jews who are Hungarian citizens have not received any deferment stamps.)

1 NIOD, 077/1317. This document has been translated from German.
2 The document is in the files of the Commissariat General for Security. It was presumably written by employees of the section for Jewish affairs (W. Zoepf or G. Slottke), as suggested by the other documents in the files, which come from the same source.
3 The original contains handwritten notes and underlining.
4 This refers to the Central Office for Jewish Emigration.

b) *Citizens of enemy nations*

Thus far, eighty-one Jews who are citizens of enemy nations or of states that have broken diplomatic ties with Germany have been interned and have gone to the internment camps for the British in Germany. The list is as follows:

	Women	*Men*
San Domingo	1	–
Haiti	6	2
South Africa	1	1
Uruguay	3	1
England	34	11
America	19	2
	64	17

To date, no decision has yet been received from the Reich Foreign Office with respect to the evacuation or exchange of the Jews in Westerbork who are citizens of Central and South American countries.

c) *Exchange of English citizens for German ones*

The representative of the Reich Foreign Office in The Hague[5] submitted a list of the names of 289 Jews who are scheduled for a German–British exchange. These are persons who hold both Dutch and British citizenship. These 289 Jews are accounted for as follows:

still at liberty in this country	145 persons,
in Westerbork	41 persons,
in Vught	7 persons,
sent to the East	96 persons,
	289 persons.

In addition, the Reich Foreign Office has arranged for an exchange of a total of 30,000 Jews with Dutch, Belgian, French, Norwegian, and Soviet Russian citizenship,[6] but we are presently awaiting the decree to be issued by the Chief of the Security Police and the SD.[7]

d) *Foreigners with no deferment stamp*

With respect to foreign Jews with no deferment stamp (citizens of the Balkan states), around 400 were deported. There are still 136 citizens of the Balkan states in Westerbork camp at present.

Neutral foreigners (addendum)

Because the embassies of the neutral countries are taking a great deal of time to name the Jews who are to return to their homelands, the deadline of 31 March 1943 will probably not be met. It must be taken into consideration that those Jews who have already submitted their emigration applications to the Central Office will be exempted from the impending Jewish measures beyond 31 March 1943, until they leave the country.

5 Otto Bene.
6 This could not be established.
7 Ernst Kaltenbrunner (1903–1946).

2) *Protected Jews*[8]

a) *Exempt from the star requirement*

Forty-five Jews, forty-two of whom are still in the Netherlands, were exempted from wearing the yellow star. Three Jews have emigrated (Prof. Plesch and wife, and Benjamin Katz[9]), and three applications are now being processed.

Eighty-nine applications for exemption from wearing the star were rejected.

b) *Van Dam and Frederiks Jews (Barneveld)*

Prof. van Dam proposed	309 Jews
Sec. Gen. Frederiks proposed	276 Jews
	585 Jews

(including staff). Of these, presently located:

in de Biezen camp are	152 Jews
in Schaffelaar castle are	237 Jews
	389 Jews

c) *Doetinchem*

In Doetinchem there were *7 NSB Jews* on 15 March 1943.[10]

This stay in Doetinchem is a temporary one since the NSB members are supposed to be merely assembled there before being sent on to Theresienstadt

d) *Black Operation*[11] *(Four-Year Plan)*

At present, there are still twenty-six Jews (originally, thirty-nine Jews were deferred) working for the Black Operation.

3) *Clarifications of ancestry*[12]

The investigations of ancestry concerned a group of *2,197 persons*. According to information from Dr Wander[13] of the Decision-Making Body of the Commissioner General for Administration and Justice, decisions have been made regarding the ancestry of *1,362 persons* thus far, meaning that only *835 persons* still remain to be decided on. The decisions revealed the following:

8 The Dutch secretaries general Karel Johannes Frederiks and Jan van Dam were permitted to name around 500 Jews who were to be protected from deportation: see Doc. 102 and also b) below. These so-called protected Jews were interned in Barneveld at the places mentioned under b); on 29 Sept. 1943 they were deported to Westerbork, and from there to Theresienstadt on 4 Sept. 1944.

9 Benjamin Katz (1891–1962), art dealer; together with his brother, ran a world-renowned gallery with works by Dutch masters of the sixteenth and seventeenth centuries; traded paintings in order to obtain his freedom; after the war, there were a great many conflicts with the Dutch state over the restitution of his paintings.

10 From Jan. 1943, Jews on the 'protection list' of NSB chairman A. A. Mussert because they had been NSB members (until Jews were excluded from membership in 1938) were interned in Villa Bouchina in the town of Doetinchem (province of Gelderland). Of the original sixty-four residents, only nine remained in the villa until April 1943, when they all were deported via Westerbork to Theresienstadt.

11 'Schwarzaktion': a reference to the Jewish diamond workers who were made available for labour deployment as part of the Four-Year Plan.

12 The Decision-Making Body for Unresolved Questions of Ancestry (Entscheidungsstelle für Zweifelsfragen der Abstammung) in the Commissariat General for Administration and Justice was responsible for clarifying ancestry. It was headed by Hans Georg Calmeyer.

13 Dr Gerhard Wander (1903–1945), lawyer; joined the NSDAP in 1931; conscripted by the Wehrmacht in 1940; employed by Calmeyer from Oct. 1942 to Sept. 1943; assisted Jews and was transferred to the front as a result; deserted in 1944 and worked underground for the resistance movement in the Netherlands; found out and shot in Jan. 1945.

25 per cent remained full Jews,
50 per cent were classified as G I and not required to register,
25 per cent were classified as G II and Aryan.[14]
In Westerbork camp, the ancestry of *196 persons* is currently being investigated.

4) *Baptized Jews*
1,572 Jews who have been baptized Protestant were registered in the Bevolkingsregister[15] by 15 March 1943.[16] It is not possible to provide the exact number resulting from a decrease due to death, classification as Mischlinge, and the deportation of Jews arrested for criminal offences, since no statistics whatsoever were collected regarding these events.

The Commissioner General for Special Duties[17] is presently working on a proposed list that will be used as a basis for transferring the Jews named therein to a camp, which is yet to be designated. This list also extends not only to the group of Jews who are baptized Protestants, but also to Jews who, without baptism, have been associated with the Protestant Church, whether through instruction or only through church attendance. The total number of these Jews is estimated at around 1,600 to 1,700. The lists will be presented soon, but the deportation of these Jews cannot take place until around three to four weeks from now.[18] With regard to baptized Jews, there are now:

in Westerbork camp	133 Jews
together with family members	26 Jews
	159 Jews

The vast majority of these Jews are located in the cities of Amsterdam, Rotterdam, and The Hague. Only a small percentage of these Jews live in the provinces.

5) *Armaments Jews*
a) *Garment industry Jews*
The Central Contracts Office [ZAST][19] employed 2,300 Jewish garment workers. Of these, the following are to be made available:[20]

for November 1942	800
for December 1942	300
for January 1943	300
for February 1943	300
	1,700

14 In the table of racial classification used by the National Socialists, G I ('first generation') indicated 'half-Jews' – people with one Jewish parent or two Jewish grandparents – and G II ('second generation') referred to 'quarter-Jews', people with one Jewish grandparent. See PMJ 5/90.
15 Dutch in the original: 'population register'.
16 The State Inspectorate of the Population Register: see Doc. 81, fn. 11.
17 Fritz Schmidt.
18 In the spring of 1943 Protestants of Jewish origin were concentrated in Westerbork camp, where they occupied a barracks of their own. On 4 Sept. 1944, a group of 500 were deported from there to Theresienstadt.
19 The Central Office for Public Contracts (Central Contracts Office for short, or ZAST – Zentralauftragsstelle) was established in August 1940 by a directive issued by the Plenipotentiary for the Four-Year Plan, Hermann Göring. Its objective was to integrate Dutch industry into the German war economy.
20 'Made available' means here that these Jews could now be deported and were no longer protected on the basis of the importance of their work for the war effort.

with the result that, by mid March 1943, only 600 garment industry Jews will still be working for the ZAST. All of these Jews live in Amsterdam.

b) *Diamond workers*

The Four-Year Plan permitted *820 diamond workers and dealers* to obtain deferment from labour deployment. According to information from the representative of the Reich Diamond Office[21] in Amsterdam, the following are still working for the diamond industry:

c. 300	diamond workers and
c. 150	businessmen.
c. 450	Jews who live in Amsterdam.

c) *Armaments Inspectorate (Major Krummbein)*[22]

The following are still working here at present:

Army: engineers, mechanics, etc.	32 Jews
Navy: engineers, mechanics, etc.	44 Jews
Luftwaffe: engineers, mechanics, etc.	42 Jews
Administration:[23] furriers	291 Jews
Second-hand and waste materials	103 Jews
Metal dealers	137 Jews
Textiles	21 Jews
Chemists	25 Jews
Scrap-metal industry	56 Jews
Mining	17 Jews
Tobacco	2 Jews
Stones and earth	3 Jews
Leather industry	7 Jews
Petroleum	7 Jews
	792 Jews[24]

The Jews made available by the Armaments Inspectorate for late February/early March 1943 could thus far not [be] listed for the Central Office, owing to a shortage of workers; [the lists] are now under consideration and will come out in the next few days. The Central Contracts Office as well as the Reich Representative for the Diamond Industry and Major Krummbein mentioned that not all the Jews already named by the Central Office as having been assigned have been collected.

According to information from Major Krummbein, of this group of armaments Jews, only a very few from the scrap metal, metals, second-hand, and rags group are working in the provinces; similarly, the mining group is working in the province of Limburg; all the other Jews in these groups, however, are working in Amsterdam, Rotterdam, and The Hague.

21 The Central Office for Diamonds was established as a part of the Dutch administration on 18 Oct. 1940, by German order. Its task was to control the Dutch diamond industry and later to exploit it for the German war economy. The German representative for the Central Office was Dr Karl Hanemann (b. 1903), lawyer.

22 This presumably refers to Walther Krumrein (1890–1972), engineer; served in the Wehrmacht at the War Economy Office in Ulm and elsewhere from 1939.

23 In the German original: 'Verwaltung'. This was a category used by the Armaments Inspectorate for a range of suppliers producing indirectly for the war economy.

24 Added up correctly, the figures give a total number of 787 Jews.

Therefore, 1,842 Jews are still needed at present for armaments; with family members, this amounts to around 5,500 persons.

In Westerbork are:

87	armaments Jews and
72	family members
156[25]	persons

as well as

100	skilled workers (furriers, tailors, and diamond workers) and
115	family members
371	persons.

6) *Jewish Council*

According to information from the Central Office for Jewish Emigration, dated 16 March 1943, the number of Jews still deferred for the Jewish Council totals around *13,000 persons.*

In Westerbork there are presently around 180 Jews who have an exemption stamp from the Jewish Council. Jewish Councils continue to exist in the provinces in all the places where Jews are still present.

The Jewish Council in Westerbork camp comprises around *130 persons*.

7) *Mixed marriages*

The Rijksinspectie van den Bevolkingsregisters[26] reported on 16 March 1943 that the following have registered there thus far:

6,056 mixed marriages that have produced offspring,
252 mixed marriages in which children will be born in the coming months, and
1,065 childless mixed marriages in which the Jewish spouse is the wife.

However, as mentioned in the report dated 19 February 1943,[27] the number of Jews has decreased due to arrests made following criminal offences. Statistics on the departure of these Jews have not been collected by any agency.

Currently in Westerbork camp are:

180 Jews who are in a mixed marriage, and
10 prisoners who are in a mixed marriage.

8) *Theresienstadt*

Proposal list no. 1 was submitted to the Reich Commissioner[28] for approval. The following services worthy of merit were put forward:

a) *Peacetime services rendered*

for the völkisch movement	2 Jews
work in the civil service	7 Jews
academics	6 Jews
artists	2 Jews
consideration for friendly foreign nations	1 Jew

25 Correctly: 159 (incorrect tally in the original).
26 Dutch in the original: 'State Inspectorate of the Population Register'.
27 This is included in the file.
28 Arthur Seyss-Inquart. The list is not part of the file.

Red Cross awards		2 Jews
other services		4 Jews
		24 Jews
also:		14 family members
		38 persons

b) *Wartime services rendered*

Iron Cross First Class and Gold Medal for Bravery and War Injury Badge		21 Jews
Iron Cross Second Class and War Injury Badge		91 Jews
War Injury Badge		44 Jews
plus family members:	16 wives	
	3 children (for the Iron Cross First Class group)	19 Jews
plus family members for Group II (Iron Cross Second Class and War Injury Badge)		
	wives: 62	
	children: 9	73 Jews[29]
plus family members for Group III (War Injury Badge)		
	wives: 29	
	children: 3	32 Jews
Work in military service and the war economy		6 Jews
plus family members		3 Jews
		289 Jews
In total:		38 and
		289 persons
		327 persons

Of these, 174 persons are presently in Westerbork camp.

Additional applications from combat veterans are still being belatedly received, meaning that a supplementary list must be prepared.

29 Correctly: 71 (incorrect tally in the original).

DOC. 113

In a speech to the Germanic SS on 22 March 1943, Commissioner General Hanns Albin Rauter outlines arguments to justify the extermination of the Jews[1]

Shorthand transcript of Hanns Albin Rauter's speech released by the ANP,[2] unsigned,[3] Amsterdam, dated 22 March 1943 (copy)[4]

Report on the speech given by SS-Obergruppenführer Rauter[5]
[…][6]
In addition, a few words about the Jewish question in Holland. Everyone is aware that we have around 140,000 full Jews here in Holland, including the foreigners, although unfortunately certain foreigners remain beyond our grasp for international reasons.

All Jews are eligible for deportation to the East. I can say in front of this group – and I ask that you not report this to the outside world – that, as of now, we have deported 55,000 Jews from here to the East,[7] and that 12,000 Jews are still in the camp. That is therefore approximately 67,000 Jews who have already been removed from national life in the Netherlands. We hope to quicken the pace of the evacuation of the Jews from 1 April, to the effect that we will then have a train depart twice rather than once a week, so that we can then transport 12,000 every month.[8] We hope that in the foreseeable future there will no longer be a single Jew in the Netherlands walking around freely in the streets, with the exception of those mixed marriages with children, with whom we still have to talk. From 1 April we intend to impose a ban in the four northern provinces of Overijssel, Drenthe, Friesland, and Groningen, prohibiting all Jews from residing there. After that, it will be the southern provinces – Limburg, Brabant, and Zeeland. Then, starting on 1 May, we want to add Utrecht as well and, finally, North Holland and South Holland, and the City of Amsterdam.[9]

I would be very happy to see the Jewish question resolved at some point, because – and at the SD, they'll agree with me – always and everywhere, in every act of espionage

1 NIOD, 286/6. Excerpt published in A. E. Cohen, *Het proces Rauter* ('s Gravenhage: Nijhoff, 1952), pp. 41–43. This document has been translated from German.
2 The Netherlands News Agency (Algemeen Nederlands Persbureau, ANP) began operation on 1 Jan. 1935. During the occupation it was monitored by the Germans. It remains the largest news agency in the Netherlands today.
3 The transcript was prepared by Wilhelm Johannes Hubertus Winkelman (1915–1960), journalist and ANP correspondent.
4 The original contains handwritten notes and underlining.
5 The head of the Germanic SS, Johannes Hendrik Feldmeijer (1910–1945), had returned to the Netherlands in March 1943 after a ten-month deployment in the war against the Soviet Union. Rauter gave this speech at the ceremony in honour of Feldmeijer resuming command in Amsterdam.
6 In the first parts of the speech, Rauter welcomed Feldmeijer back to the Netherlands and addressed the following topics: Himmler's plans for organizing new SS divisions, the recruitment of volunteers from the labour deployment groups in Germany for frontline duty, the organization of the Landwacht (auxiliary police corps founded by the NSB), recruitment for military training camps within the youth organizations, and measures to combat the black market.
7 In reality, 49,629 persons had been deported by this time.
8 This goal was not met; there continued to be approximately one transport per week.
9 On 30 March 1943 all the remaining Jews in the provinces of Friesland, Groningen, Drenthe, Overijssel, Gelderland, Limburg, North Brabant, and Zeeland were asked to report to Vught camp by 10 April 1943. On 13 April 1943 Jews were also banned from being resident in the provinces of Utrecht, North Holland, and South Holland; only the City of Amsterdam was not included in the ban.

and terror that takes place here over time, there is a Jew involved, whether in organizing the bomb attacks, or in the financing, or as the person who hires a contract killer to kill a National Socialist. We will never get any peace until the Jews have been removed.

My aim is to remove the Jews as quickly as possible. This is not a pretty task; it is dirty work. But it is a measure that will be of great significance from a historical point of view. It is impossible to gauge what it will mean to have eradicated 120,000 Jews – who, 100 years later, might have been a million strong – from a Volkskörper. And in all of these measures of the Germanic SS[10] there is no personal compassion, for the Germanic peoples stand behind us. The actions for the benefit of the Volkskörper are carried out relentlessly, and there is no softness or weakness. Anyone who does not understand that or is full of compassion or humanist sentimentality is not fit to lead in these times. An SS man in particular must persevere mercilessly and without compassion. We only want to recover from this agony, and the Jewish question is to be resolved, definitively and totally.

The Führer, in his declarations over the past few months, indeed over the past few years, has repeatedly referred to the problem and has made it clear to the American Jews and the Freemasons that, if the American plutocrats were to unleash war and attack Europe, it would mean the end of European Jewry. And that is what will happen. Not one Jew is to be left in Europe. Hence the intended measure to make the first parts of the Netherlands free of Jews, beginning on 1 April.

If a policeman fails to participate, this policeman has to disappear. I no longer have any use for police in Holland who refuse to obey.[11] This is a regrettable manifestation, which is almost always attributable to the attitude of the church. Priests should stay in the church and leave the authorities in peace, and not issue church letters on these matters.[12] Anyone who does so should be rapped on the knuckles. They fight the battle on the backs of those who heed their appeals. I am determined to weed out the policemen who fail to do their duty, even if it might be 60 per cent of the whole police force.

I am glad that only a minuscule number of policemen obeyed the call of the priests. I do not understand why these people do not push the responsibility onto us when they say that they can't accept it before God. For what I have perpetrated against the Jews here, I will gladly pay with my soul in heaven!

Anyone who has realized the significance of Jewry as a people and as a race can act no differently than we do.

It is deeply regrettable that the bishops have also failed to realize the danger of communism in these times, and that they arrange for things and do things that are simply unbelievable at a time when Europe is engaged in a life-or-death struggle.

[...][13]

10 A reference to the Germanic SS in the Netherlands.

11 In early March 1943 various groups of Dutch policemen refused to continue arresting Jews. Among these groups were the Enschede Police Corps on 4 March 1943 and the Grootegast division of the Marechaussee on 12 March 1943: see Doc. 111, fn. 6. After Rauter threatened them with arrest, the majority of policemen resumed their duties, though a few went underground. The entire Grootegast division was sent to Vught concentration camp for continuing to refuse to carry out the arrests.

12 See Doc. 107.

13 In the rest of the speech, Rauter addressed the following topics: defence against Bolshevism, Dutch stubbornness, international acknowledgement of the ruthless attitude of the SS, and the world view of the SS. In conclusion, Rauter placed the leadership of the Germanic SS back in the hands of Johannes Hendrik Feldmeijer.

DOC. 114

On 25 March 1943 the Jewish Council addresses the progress of the deportations and its own powerlessness to prevent this[1]

Minutes of meeting, unsigned, dated 25 March 1943 (carbon copy)[2]

Meeting of the Jewish Council on Thursday, 25 March 1943, at 11 a.m., at 58 Nieuwe Keizersgracht

Present: all members apart from Dr Arons and Mr Mendes da Costa. Also present: Prof. Brahn from the Beirat,[3] the lawyers Mr de Haas and Mr Wolff from the National Organization,[4] Messrs Meijer de Vries and Brandon from the office.

The chairman, Mr A. Asscher, reported on the following items:

1) The *removal of Jews* has assumed appalling proportions; operations occur both during the day and at night; those without a Sperr stamp[5] are taken first. The sick and the elderly, in some cases very old people, also continue to be taken away. The chairmen have protested against this and urged moderation etc. in various discussions with the German authorities, but so far there has not been any noticeable result.

In addition, many arrests (so-called individual cases) have occurred, concerning which the chairmen have not been able to achieve very much, due to a lack of contact with the Sicherheitspolizei.[6] This also relates to several cases already known at the previous meeting, for example Dr Arons.[7]

Prof. Cohen said in relation to the above that those taken away who – still without a Sperr stamp – were working in the finance division at Vening Meineszkade[8] are still in the Joodsche Schouwburg, and it is hoped they will be released.[9]

Time and again it has been clear that stopping and looking around at the Joodsche Schouwburg is very dangerous; this can lead to one being apprehended and transported away. The warning, which has already been published in the *Joodsche Weekblad*,[10] is therefore reiterated emphatically.

The incident that took place yesterday, during which several persons were arrested in the vestibule of the Grote Synagoge,[11] has turned out not to be any kind of operation against visitors to the synagogue, but an expansion of the search for escapees from a

1 NIOD, 182/3. This document has been translated from Dutch.

2 The original contains handwritten marking.

3 German in the original: 'advisory council' (for non-Dutch Jews).

4 The provincial branches of the Jewish Council.

5 From the German 'Sperre', lit. 'block': a reference to the stamp granting temporary exemption from deportation.

6 German in the original: 'Security Police'.

7 Dr Jacob Arons (1882–1943), physician; chairman of the Joodsche Invalide, a Jewish home for the elderly in Amsterdam, from 1922; member of the Jewish Council from 1941; deported in 1943 to Westerbork, and from there on 31 August 1943 to Auschwitz, where he was murdered on arrival.

8 Sarphatikade, a street named after the Jewish physician Samuel Sarphati (1813–1866), was renamed Vening Meineszkade (after a Dutch geophysicist) during the occupation period.

9 It was not possible to establish whether this hope was realized.

10 *Het Joodsche Weekblad*, vol. 2, no. 51, 26 March 1943, p. 1. The later date is explained by the fact that the minutes were typed up a few days after the meetings.

11 Dutch in the original: 'Great Synagogue', Amsterdam synagogue dating from 1671.

transport of evacuees and sick people who had been held at the premises at 10 Houtmarkt. Those arrested in the synagogue were released soon afterwards, with the exception of one person without a Sperr stamp.

There was discussion of the issue of the Expo[situr] and the chairmen being overburdened with notifications of people being taken away. The Expositur has urgently requested that such instances be reported only once, and to the Expositur rather than to one of its staff in person. Notifications to the chairmen have also increased to such an extent that they are being deprived of essential hours of sleep at night. It should be borne in mind that between 1 and 6 a.m., in so far as reporting at that time is useful, the telephone at Dr van der Laan's[12] house should always be used, and on evenings when a transport to Vught takes place, the same applies to 58 Nieuwe Keizersgracht.[13] Transports to Westerbork normally take place on Mondays, Wednesdays, and Fridays at 7.30 p.m.; transports to Vught take place at less regular times, but the departure times are normally announced.

Mr Asscher also mentioned that an – albeit limited – number of diamond workers who have recently been taken away (although this was not part of a special operation against diamond workers) will now no longer be released on the basis of their Sperr, but instead are destined for Vught, because the original quota of approximately 290 people from the diamond sector has not yet been met.

2) *The whereabouts of deported Jews.* Mr aus der Fünten has told the chairmen that – in accordance with a recent Verfügung[14] – Dutch Jews who on account of their age are no longer able to work are taken to Theresienstadt, where conditions are thought to be favourable. Letters from there are still from German Jews only.

During their negotiations, the chairmen always urge that as many of the deported Jews as possible should be sent to *Vught* rather than to Westerbork.[15] As regards setting up Vught for industrial activities, there is cooperation on a practical basis with the Germans mentioned at the previous meeting.[16]

At *Westerbork* a crematorium has been in use since 15 March, in spite of attempts by the Jewish Council to prevent this. Burials can no longer take place there.

No decision has yet been taken regarding people who have requested the postponement of their departure to Barneveld through the Jewish Council. This means that they remain where they are for the time being.

3) *Admission of Jews to hospitals.* Decisions in this respect are taken by a committee of three, consisting of the alderman[17] and two others. Only patients in a serious condition

12 Dr Abraham van der Laan (1890–1945), veterinarian; member of the Jewish Council from 1941; deported to Westerbork in Sept. 1943, and from there to Bergen-Belsen on 15 March 1944; perished in Tröbitz in May 1945.

13 The Jewish Council's main building was located here.

14 German in the original: 'order'.

15 Because Vught camp was oriented towards industrial production (including for the Philips electrical company), the inmates seemed to be protected from deportation to Auschwitz for the time being. This hope was deceptive, however. The last Jewish inmates of Vught camp were deported to Auschwitz on 3 June 1944.

16 The minutes dated 11 March 1943 also make only a general mention of several German and Dutch persons responsible for this task: see NIOD, 182/3.

17 Presumably the City of Amsterdam's alderman for social affairs. From 1941 to 1944 this was Mr Frans Pieter Guépin (1904–1973), lawyer and NSB member.

who urgently need hospital care are being admitted, with the promise that they will be free to return home afterwards. In the provinces, admission to general hospitals can take place in acute cases.

The in-house staff of the three Jewish hospitals must remain fully prepared. The in-house staff of the Joodsche Invalide [home for the elderly] must also be prepared and present.

In this regard, the issue of *nursing at home* is also important. It is clear that – apart from a few, specially approved exceptions – it is considered prohibited to have a non-Jewish nurse at home to provide care. However, almost all Jewish nurses are obliged to stay in their hospitals. The Jewish Council is therefore currently organizing a nursing service – through its medical division – in order to provide the most urgent nursing care at home. It is hoped that further details in this regard will be available soon.

The so-called *district nursing* provided by the 'White Cross'[18] – permitted thus far, but now in doubt – is being further investigated by the mayor.[19]

4) Prof. Cohen said that the rumour that new *Sperren*[20] were being issued was based on a misunderstanding. All that has happened is that the Zentralstelle[21] has issued a few new Sperren, without any influence from the Jewish Council, to a number of owners of Jewish premises, and to some people who were taken away and later released again.

5) Within the next few days, Mr aus der Fünten will go through the list regarding the use of *bicycles.*

Chief Rabbi Dasberg[22] drew attention to:

a) *the ban on ritual baking,*[23] which has just been announced by the relevant trade association. Prof. Cohen said that this was being dealt with by Dr van der Laan's[24] division;

b) the urgent request for peace and quiet on the *Seder evenings.*[25] The chairmen will see what they can achieve in this respect.

The next meeting will take place on Thursday, 8 April 1943, at 11 a.m.

18 A welfare organization which was mainly involved in home nursing care.

19 Edward John Voûte (1887–1950), career soldier; officer in the Dutch navy, 1907–1915; held various administrative posts in the Netherlands, 1915–1941; mayor of Amsterdam from March 1941; member of the Germanic SS; sentenced to three years and six months in prison after 1945.

20 German in the original: a reference to the 'Sperr' stamps (see fn. 5).

21 The Central Office for Jewish Emigration.

22 Simon Dasberg (1902–1945), rabbi; chief rabbi of Friesland, 1929–1932, of Groningen, 1932–1943, and of Amsterdam, 1942–1943; deported to Westerbork in Sept. 1943, and from there in Jan. 1944 to Bergen-Belsen, where he perished.

23 This could not be found.

24 Abraham van der Laan was the head of the Jewish Council's General Affairs Department.

25 The Seder evening is the beginning of the Jewish holiday of Pesach (Passover); it involves a retelling of the story of the Jews' exodus from Egypt.

DOC. 115

Aufbau, 2 April 1943: article on the solidarity of the Dutch with their Jewish compatriots[1]

Hell in Holland. Nazi rage over solidarity between Christians and Jews

For four years I lived in Holland; for four years I saw with gratitude how this country, with a helpfulness which knew no bounds, was the very first of all countries to give new hope to uprooted refugees. All of those who provided me with shelter and support in those days are now refugees themselves, prisoners, or – dead. As reported in the last issue of *Aufbau*, Holland's great friend of the people, seeker of beauty, patron of art, and protector of nature Dr *Henri Polak* has died a miserable death.[2] A statesman, a patriot, a Jew.

But what moves the informed individual most of all is not the fact that this seventy-five-year-old man was among the many who succumbed to the ordeals suffered during imprisonment. Rather, what is most moving is a detail that is characteristic of that diabolical Nazi sadism: this man, who was hard of hearing, for whom listening to life meant life itself, had his hearing aid confiscated a long time ago by scoundrels with official authority. A Jew, a leader of socialists, has no need to hear. The Nazi fiends pushed him, still alive, out of life.

Before me are reports of this kind from Holland, often brought by refugees, often published by the Nazis themselves with perverse pride. When a free Holland sits in judgement on the perpetrators, these documents will give evidence of a Dutch people not shaken by any inhumanity.

The number of wandering, parentless children and abandoned infants has grown tremendously in Holland. As a result, the Nazis issued a regulation stating that such children would in future be regarded as Jewish by the authorities and treated 'accordingly'.[3] Any comment is superfluous.

But the Dutch steadfastly provide help. On a farm close to Windschoten,[4] near Groningen, five Jews who had been sheltered by the farmer were found in a raid.[5]

In Groningen itself, the town elders staunchly refuse to obey a Nazi decree requiring them to rename Oppenheimstraße and other streets named after Jews.[6]

1 *Aufbau*, vol. 9, no. 14, 2 April 1943, pp. 1–2. This German-language newspaper, published by the German-Jewish Club in New York, began publication in Dec. 1934 as a monthly, before shifting to weekly publication in 1939. It became one of the most important émigré newspapers and had a circulation of 26,000 copies in 1943. It has been published in Zurich as a monthly since 2005. This document has been translated from German.

2 Dr Henri Polak (1868–1943), trade unionist; founder and chairman of the General Dutch Diamond Workers' Union, 1894–1940; co-founder of the Social Democratic Workers' Party (SDAP), 1894; co-founder of the Netherlands Trade Union Federation (NVV), 1906; in custody from the summer of 1940 to July 1942; died of pneumonia in Jan. 1943.

3 On 15 Jan. 1943, by order of the German authorities, the Jewish Council announced that all foundlings would henceforth be treated as Jewish children: *Het Joodsche Weekblad*, vol. 2 no. 41 (15 Jan. 1943), p. 1.

4 Correctly: Winschoten.

5 This could not be confirmed.

6 Correctly: Oppenheimstraat. This street was in fact known as Hendrik Westerstraat from 1943 to 1945.

When the Jews of the small town of Weesp were deported, the other inhabitants carried their bags for them, and untraceable hands painted 'Tot Weerziens – See you again' on the walls, thereby enraging the Nazis.[7]

Out of all their belongings, Jews are allowed to take along only a small suitcase containing the bare necessities. When one of them managed to visit his house in Hilversum one more time, he found it had been completely looted. The Nazis had even taken away the washbasins.

The deportation of the Jews of Holland takes place broadly as follows: in one town after another, they are ordered to report, always equipped with the small suitcase, to the ghetto in Amsterdam.[8] Any delay in carrying out the order costs six months in prison and a thousand guilders as a fine.

The ghetto in Amsterdam is as crowded as a livestock wagon. Barbed wire encloses it. The historic drawbridge is pulled up.[9]

The next step is mass transport to the 'Hollandsche Schouwburg' at Leidsche Plein,[10] once a site for dramatic performances, today a house of horror. There are many who must cower there in the dark theatre building and are taken from their rooms without any family member ever learning their whereabouts.

Around midnight, they all are transported to the main railway station under guard. The final stop on their journey in Holland is the concentration camp in Westerbroek[11] in the province of Drenthe. Then comes Poland and – the next phase. No one knows precisely what the destination is. Even the chief rabbi of Amsterdam, Lodewijk B. Sarlouis,[12] has been lost without trace since his deportation.

Nine thousand Jews have thus far been deported to the East.[13] One thousand two hundred of them suffered under the burden of disruption to such an extent that they were officially termed 'mentally disturbed'. What lies ahead in Poland for such persons is known well enough.

The number of executions in Holland itself also continues to grow. Twenty-seven Dutchmen were recently executed. The rabbi of Haarlem is said to have been one of them.[14] Their crime? They were hostages …

7 This story of Weesp was circulated abroad. The teacher Daan Bouhuys did indeed put up such a sign at the railway station; however, the departure of the Jews of Weesp, who travelled to Amsterdam on a normal train on 29 April 1942, did not attract much attention among residents of the town. See Dick van Zomeren, *Geschiedenis van de joodse gemeenschap in Weesp: Ze waren gewoon ineens weg* (Weesp: Ark/Heureka, 1983), pp. 73–77.

8 The clearing of the provinces took place in two large operations, on 30 March and 10 April 1943, and the Jewish inhabitants had to report to Vught and Westerbork camps.

9 Some districts of Amsterdam had a majority-Jewish population, but an enclosed ghetto as such did not exist.

10 The Stadsschouwburg is located at Leidseplein, but the author was referring to the Hollandsche Schouwburg (from 1942 Joodsche Schouwburg) in Plantage Middenlaan.

11 Correctly: Westerbork.

12 Correctly: Lodewijk Hartog Sarlouis; see Doc. 89.

13 By April 1943, a total of 52,134 Jews had been deported from the Netherlands.

14 Philip Frank (1910–1943), rabbi; chief rabbi of North Holland from 1934; member of the Jewish Council's Culture Committee from 1942; in Feb. 1943 he was shot, along with nine other hostages, in retribution for an attack on a German soldier in Haarlem.

The Dutch Nazi paper *De Swarte Soldaat*[15] has vowed that all Jews will shortly vanish from the scene in Holland. For the time being, many still languish in labour camps as slaves. Accepted age: 18 to 65. The food rations are being systematically reduced. A leave of absence exists only in theory but not in reality, because it keeps being cancelled as a 'punishment' for anti-Nazi actions committed by other people, outside of the camp, somewhere in the country. The end is Poland – or the end.

None of the Jews has any resources remaining. After they were forced to deposit their assets with Lippmann, Rosenthal & Co., an Amsterdam bank taken over by the Nazis,[16] which was initially still allowed to release 250 guilders per month, a new order has now been issued. No Jewish individual is permitted to withdraw money. Any contributions go to the Jewish Council.[17]

But all the Nazis' attempts to galvanize the population into assisting with the policy towards the Jews have failed. Even when the Nazis take over a Jewish firm, they have no alternative but to retain at least its Jewish name, if the business is to continue. For example, one such firm, perforce, placed an ad in the Nazi paper *De Waag*: 'Buy your cakes from Cohen's!' – They have deported the owner, but not his reputation.

Even the Dutch Nazi leader Anton Mussert[18] had to concede that only 1 per cent of the population offers allegiance to him. His wife, together with other Quisling women,[19] was invited to Berlin by Magda Goebbels not long ago. The Dutch took note of it in their own way.

When a Nazi in a fully occupied train ordered a Jew, identifiable by his Star of David, to give up his seat for him, the train conductor claimed to know nothing of a rule to that effect, and a senior railway official in The Hague confirmed: 'Jews are our customers and will continue to be treated as such.' And, full of outrage, a Nazi newspaper from The Hague tells of a music teacher who taught her pupils Mendelssohn's lieder and Negro spirituals.

In front of the assembled class, she declared: 'Mijnheer[20] Mendelssohn was a Jewish aristocrat. His works are no longer allowed to be performed in public. So let us at least sing his lieder!'

Kurt Lubinski.[21]

15 Correctly: *De Zwarte Soldaat* ('The Black Soldier'), the newspaper of the WA (Weerbaarheidsafdeling), the paramilitary arm of the NSB.

16 See Doc. 52, fn. 16.

17 On 18 Dec. 1942 *Het Joodsche Weekblad* published the information that, as of 1 Jan. 1943, disbursements to Jews would have to be made through the Jewish Council, no longer through the Lippmann, Rosenthal & Co. bank.

18 Anton Adriaan Mussert (1894–1946), engineer; worked for the Provincial Water Management Authority in Utrecht; founded the NSB with Cees van Geelkerken in 1931 and became its leader; during the occupation, attempted to put himself forward as head of state for the Netherlands within a Germanic Reich, but never obtained Hitler's consent; declared 'Leader of the Dutch people' in Dec. 1942; interned in 1945; sentenced to death and executed in May 1946.

19 A reference to the collaborationist regime in Norway headed by Vidkun Quisling.

20 Dutch in the original: 'Mr'.

21 Kurt Lubinski (1899–1969), photographer; worked for the Ullstein publishing house in Berlin; emigrated to the Netherlands in 1933; fled to Britain in 1940; emigrated to the USA in 1943.

DOC. 116

On 4 April 1943 the mayor of Geldrop informs the archbishop of Utrecht about his failed attempt to intercede on behalf of Catholics of Jewish ancestry at the Reich Commissariat[1]

Letter from K. L. H. van der Putt (mayor of Geldrop), Geldrop, to His Most Reverend Excellence, Monsignor A. J. M. de Jong,[2] archbishop of Utrecht, Utrecht, dated 4 April 1943 (typescript)

Your Excellency,

Yesterday, 3 April, I was at the Reichskommissariat[3] to enquire about the plans for Catholic Jews. As usual I spoke to Mr Bühner,[4] adjutant to Generalkommissar Schmidt.[5] Our meeting had a very disappointing outcome. In view of the unpleasant consequences this may have for a number of co-religionists, I consider it my duty to report on this to you without delay.

1. The [exemption] stamp that has been obtained for the remaining Catholics after so much effort will cease to be valid on 10 April.[6] After that, a distinction will no longer be made between Catholic, baptized, and unbaptized Jews, and therefore the Catholics will be deported in the same way as the unbaptized in due course.
2. The camp that is being set up for Protestant Jews in Vught and will operate under the leadership of the Protestant churches will only be open to Protestant Jews. It is to be expected that these Jews can stay there until after the end of the war.[7]
3. No exception will be made for members of religious orders. This means they will be banned from residing in the provinces of Friesland, Drenthe, Groningen, Overijssel, Gelderland, Limburg, North Brabant, and Zeeland from 10 April onwards. I am sure I do not need to explain to you how vigorously I have pleaded in favour of allowing members of religious orders to stay in their monasteries and convents.

When I asked why the Reichskommissariat had tightened its position with regard to the Catholic Jews so suddenly, Mr B. told me the Reichskommissariat had been very displeased with the Catholic Church's lack of willingness to make concessions in comparison with the Protestant churches,[8] with which fruitful negotiations have taken place

1 Het Utrechts Archief, 449/76. This document has been translated from Dutch.
2 Johannes de Jong.
3 German in the original: 'Reich Commissariat'.
4 Friedrich (Fritz) Bühner (1911–1996); Unterbannführer, and later Bannführer with the Hitler Youth from 1934; joined the NSDAP in 1935; worked full-time for the NSDAP from 1936; soldier in the Wehrmacht from August 1939; adjutant of Commissioner General Fritz Schmidt in the Netherlands from Sept. 1940; recalled to the Wehrmacht in Jan. 1943; released from British captivity in August 1945.
5 Fritz Schmidt, commissioner general for special duties.
6 Many Catholics of Jewish origin had already been deported in the autumn of 1942, after the first dispute between the Roman Catholic Church in the Netherlands and the Reich Commissioner: see Doc. 65. In addition, 'non-Aryans' of the Catholic faith were later denied the stamp granting a temporary reprieve from deportation.
7 The Protestants of Jewish origin were in fact imprisoned in Westerbork camp. On 4 Sept. 1944 a total of 500 were deported from there to Theresienstadt.
8 Protestant and Catholic church leaders had sent a joint telegram of protest to Reich Commissioner Seyss-Inquart, but only the Catholic bishops took the further step of calling on members of their congregations to engage in civil disobedience: see Doc. 107.

in recent days about setting up a Christian camp, which will be put under the leadership of those churches. The Generalkommissar was very unpleasantly surprised by the refusal of a church funeral for the murdered mayor of Baexem.[9]

I am convinced that the latter event has been the decisive factor. The gentlemen were extremely angry about it. 'Warum diese Härte?'[10] asked Mr B., and he referred to the difference between the views of the Church here and across the border. 'Why would we render a service to the Church if it does not miss a single opportunity to thwart us? By withdrawing the ban in this case or tacitly agreeing to the funeral, the Church could at least have demonstrated its disapproval of the murder.' This is more of less what Mr B said.

In spite of all my efforts, I could not achieve anything. Until I insisted in the end on a short delay with regard to the requirement to report all baptized people; this to win time. I will receive further notification about this, but I do not hold out much hope for a favourable result.

The remainder of our meeting concerned the treatment of the Catholics in Auschwitz. As this issue is currently less important, I will leave this for the time being.

It is difficult to decide whether any action could still have a positive effect, but I would nevertheless like to urge you, Your Excellency, to make a final attempt to prevent the unfortunate victims from being deported. In my opinion, this could be done by means of a written request to the Reichskommissar, or even better by organizing a meeting between a representative of the Diocese and the Reichskommissariat,[11] during which a proposal could be put forward for setting up a Catholic camp for laypeople and leaving members of religious orders in the monasteries and convents and the sick in the hospitals.

In my discussions with the Reichskommissariat, I have been told repeatedly that there is absolutely no contact with the Catholic Church while there is, on the other hand, contact with the Protestant churches. Perhaps this would be an opportunity to restore this contact.

It is undeniable that the fact that there is no contact often gives rise to misunderstandings. Even if it were only to explain and clarify measures, and in doing so to prevent a situation in which certain statements and actions were misinterpreted, it would still appear to me that contact could be useful.

Finally, I would like to take this opportunity to point out to Your Excellency that if the Diocese is able to decide to do something, it should do so swiftly, as time is running out.

I am sending a copy of this letter to the Most Reverend Bishops of Breda, Haarlem, Roermond, and 's-Hertogenbosch.[12]

Sincere regards,

Your humble and devoted servant,

9 Willebrordus Albertus Hetterscheid (1895–1943), policeman; joined the NSB in 1940; mayor of Baexem from April 1942; shot by members of the Dutch resistance in April 1943.

10 German in the original: 'Why such harshness?'

11 Fresh discussions between the Catholic Church and the Reich Commissariat did not take place.

12 Adrianus Petrus Willem Hopmans (bishop of Breda), Johannes Petrus Huibers (bishop of Haarlem), Joseph Hubert Guillaume Lemmens (bishop of Roermond), and Wilhelmus Petrus Adrianus Maria Mutsaerts (bishop of 's-Hertogenbosch).

DOC. 117

Deutsche Zeitung in den Niederlanden, 13 April 1943: Commissioner General Hanns Albin Rauter orders the Jews to move from the provinces to Vught camp[1]

Directive of the Commissioner General for Security Concerning the Residence of Jews in the Provinces, The Hague, 13 April

Pursuant to §§ 47 and 52 of Regulation 1/43 of the Reich Commissioner for the Occupied Dutch Territories on Civil Protection,[2] I decree the following:
§ 1
With effect from 23 April 1943, residence in the provinces of Utrecht, South Holland, and North Holland is prohibited to Jews.[3] The City of Amsterdam is excluded from this provision.
§ 2
Jews presently residing in the provinces listed must relocate to Vught camp.
§ 3
For the purpose of relocation to Vught camp, it is permitted to take luggage and valuables. Before leaving their place of residence, the Jews must report to the local Dutch police authority in order to ensure that their home is properly locked and to obtain a travel permit for Vught camp.
§ 4
1) Jews in mixed marriages are exempt from the provisions of §§ 1–3.
2) For other cases where exceptions are made, the Central Office for Jewish Emigration in Amsterdam can grant permission for residence or for travel in the provinces listed.

§ 5
Within the meaning of this directive, a Jew is defined as someone who, under § 4 of Regulation 189/40 on the Registration of Businesses, is a Jew or is considered a Jew.[4]
§ 6
1) Anyone who contravenes or circumvents the provisions of §§ 1–3 is subject to punishment by imprisonment for up to six months or a fine of up to 2,000 guilders, or either of these punishments – except where the offence carries a more severe punishment under a different regulation. Anyone who causes, facilitates, or takes part in a circumvention of these provisions is subject to the same punishment.
2) The right to impose Security Police measures is reserved.

The Hague, 13 April 1943

1 *Deutsche Zeitung in den Niederlanden*, vol. 3, no. 309, 13 April 1943, p. 1. This document has been translated from German.
2 Under § 47 of this regulation, persons could be forbidden to reside in certain areas of the Netherlands, or a specific place of residence could be assigned to them; § 52 empowered the commissioner general for security to issue directives to ensure public safety: Regulation on the Protection of Order (1943), *VOBl-NL*, no. 1/1943, 5 Jan. 1943, pp. 1–39.
3 Residence in the other provinces had been forbidden to Jews since 30 March 1943.
4 According to § 4 of Regulation 189/40, a Jew was defined as someone with three grandparents who were considered full Jews, or someone who had two Jewish grandparents and belonged to the Jewish religious community or had a Jewish spouse: see PMJ 5/42.

The Commissioner General for Security
signed Rauter
SS-Gruppenführer and Major General of the Police

DOC. 118
On 5 May 1943 Senior Commander of the Security Police and the SD Wilhelm Harster summarizes further plans relating to the deportation of the Jews from the Netherlands[1]

Letter (marked 'secret') from the Senior Commander of the Security Police and the SD for the Occupied Dutch Territories (IV B 4), signed Dr Harster[2] (SS-Brigadeführer and Major General of the Police), The Hague, to the Central Office for Jewish Emigration, Amsterdam (two copies), Westerbork camp, Vught concentration camp, and all field offices, dated 5 May 1943[3]

Re: The final solution to the Jewish question in the Netherlands
Based on the latest instructions from SS-Gruppenführer Rauter and the discussions held with the representative of the RSHA, the following actions are to be carried out with respect to the handling of Jews over the next few months:
1) *General policy line*
The RFSS[4] wants as many Jews as is humanly possible to be transported to the East in the course of this year.
2) *Next trains bound for the East*
Because a new Buna plant is scheduled for construction in Auschwitz following the destruction of the plant in the West in an air raid,[5] the maximum number of Jews is required from the West, particularly in the months of May and June. It was agreed that, at first, the Jews made available for deportation will be transported, if possible in the first half of the month, by combining several trains. Therefore, the emptying of Westerbork camp will be accelerated. The target figure for the month of May is 8,000.[6] The Senior

1 NIOD, 077/1315. Published in facsimile in Joods Historisch Museum Amsterdam, *Documents of the Persecution of the Dutch Jewry*, pp. 95–97, and Loe de Jong, *Het Koninkrijk der Nederlanden in de Tweede Wereldoorlog*, vol. 6, 1 ('s Gravenhage: Nijhoff, 1975), after p. 366. This document has been translated from German.
2 Dr Wilhelm Harster (1904–1991), lawyer; official at Stuttgart police headquarters from 1929; joined the NSDAP and the SS in 1933; began working with the SD in 1935; head of the Gestapo in Innsbruck, 1938–1940; Senior Commander of the Security Police and the SD (BdS) in the Netherlands, July 1940–August 1943, and in Italy, 1943–1945; in British captivity from 1945; extradited to the Netherlands, where he was sentenced to twelve years in prison in 1949; pardoned in 1955; Regierungsrat in the Bavarian Ministry of the Interior, 1956–1963; sentenced in Munich to fifteen years in prison in 1967; pardoned in 1969.
3 The original contains handwritten notes and underlining.
4 Reichsführer SS (Heinrich Himmler).
5 Beginning in 1942, a subsidiary of the Buna plants, which belonged to the German chemical conglomerate IG Farben and produced synthetic rubber, was built in Monowitz, near Auschwitz. Auschwitz-Monowitz concentration camp was established in the grounds to house the Jewish forced labourers who worked there.
6 A total of 8,006 Jews were deported from Westerbork to Sobibor on the four transports in May 1943.

Commander of the Security Police and the SD in The Hague is arranging rail transport with the RSHA.

3) *Vught camp*

As the RSHA requires an additional 15,000 Jews in June, the point at which the inmates of Vught camp can also be drawn upon must be reached as quickly as possible.[7]

4) *Amsterdam*

This goal corresponds to the Gruppenführer's[8] intention to issue a directive to clear Jews out of Amsterdam once the current political resistance has been suppressed.[9] Clearance is to proceed in two stages. The Jews are to be induced to relocate voluntarily to Vught. The Central Office[10] must consider whether it is advisable for the clearance to proceed according to district (first the south and west, later the city centre and the ghetto)[11] or on the basis of other criteria, for example, in alphabetical order. In the course of the clearance operation, the majority of the Jewish Council would above all have to be included in the relocation.[12] No allowances are to be made for the Jew economy (the distribution of Jewish shops in the city's districts).[13]

5) *Armaments Jews*

As an absolute necessity, the Armaments Inspectorate etc. must abide by its pledge to discontinue the use of the armaments Jews before the end of May. Unless armaments industries are relocated to Vught, the armaments Jews, along with their families, can be transferred directly to Westerbork.[14]

6) *Portuguese Jews*

All Portuguese Jews (unless other grounds for exemption are present) are to be placed together in a special barracks at the camp (Westerbork), so that SS-Gruppenführer Rauter and the head of the Race and Settlement Main Office[15] can verify their ancestry there.[16]

7 On 6 June 1943 a total of 1,666 children were transported from Vught via Westerbork to Sobibor, where they were murdered: see Doc. 130. In the following weeks too, Jews were brought from Vught to Westerbork on several occasions, to be deported from there to other destinations.

8 This refers to the commissioner general for security, Hanns Albin Rauter.

9 On 29 April 1943 the occupying authorities instructed all members of the Dutch army to resume prisoner of war status and thus proceed to 'labour deployment'; as a result, strikes broke out all across the country, beginning at Hengelo (province of Overijssel). Within a week, the German occupiers brought the strikes to a bloody end (with more than 200 dead). The April–May strikes marked a turning point in the period of occupation; resistance, which had previously been slight, now intensified, and increasing numbers of people went underground.

10 This refers to the Central Office for Jewish Emigration.

11 See Doc. 115, fn. 8.

12 On 21 May 1943 the Jewish Council was asked to name 7,000 employees for deportation to Westerbork. When only a few turned up, a large roundup took place in Amsterdam's Jewish quarter on 26 May 1943: see Doc. 131.

13 Handwritten note in the margin: 'Who will be left in Amsterdam after the clearance? (mixed marriages, exemptions?)'; remainder illegible.

14 Many of the Jews held in Vught camp worked for the Philips electronics and engineering works. This strategically important work in the armaments industry initially protected them from deportation, but they were ultimately deported on 3 June 1944: see also Doc. 144.

15 The head of the Race and Settlement Main Office (RuSHA) was Richard Hildebrandt (1897–1951).

16 Various attempts were made to have these approximately 400 Jews with Portuguese roots, the descendants of the Marranos of early modern times, declared non-Jews within the meaning of Nazi racial doctrine. In Feb. 1944 most of them were deported to Westerbork, from where they were transported onward to Theresienstadt on 25 Feb. 1944.

7) *Barneveld*
First, the final lists are to be checked for negative attributes, and there is to be a visit to the camp. A prompt relocation of all inmates to Theresienstadt is to take place.[17]
8) *AB list*[18]
The Reichsführer SS intends to set up a camp in Germany for around 10,000 Jews with French, Belgian, and Dutch citizenship who are to be kept back for use as leverage, owing to their connections with foreign countries. Should the occasion arise, they are to be subsequently allowed to emigrate in exchange for German repatriates.
9) *Mixed marriages*

a) Jewish women over the age of 45 are to be summoned in turn to Amsterdam and exempted from the requirement to wear the Jewish star, so that it becomes known in this way that Jewish spouses in mixed marriages can stay, if it can be expected that they will produce no more offspring.
b) Jewish men in childless mixed marriages are to be transferred to the camp.
c) For the rest of the Jewish men and women, voluntary sterilization is to be sought, and it is to be carried out in Amsterdam. In the event of refusal, forced sterilization is to take place in Vught camp.[19]
d) Rapid enquiries are to be made into the economic activity and occupational status of the male Jews. A report is to be submitted to the Reich Commissioner.[20]
e) At the very least, people in mixed marriages in which the husband is a Jew are to be concentrated in one place, regardless of sterilization. For this purpose, the Gruppenführer has in mind some small town in the east or south-east of the country, as he wants Greater Amsterdam to be completely Jew-free for reasons of political control.[21]

10) *Bounties*
One must consider whether exemption from return to confinement as a prisoner of war should also be granted as a reward for procuring a sizeable number of Jews. If necessary, the WBN[22] will be approached in this regard.

17 The more than 500 so-called protected Jews in the municipality of Barneveld (province of Gelderland) were deported on 29 Sept. 1943 to Westerbork, and from there to Theresienstadt on 4 Sept. 1944: see Doc. 102.

18 The so-called AB list (*Austausch- und Beziehungs-Liste*, 'exchange and connections list') included Jews who could provide valuables in exchange for their exemption from deportation. For these individuals, exemption stamps, which were normally numbered in groups of tens of thousands, were provided with the number 120,000 and above: see also Doc. 135. In April 1943 the SS established a 'holding camp' (*Aufenthaltslager*) at Bergen-Belsen concentration camp for Jews who were to be exchanged for German nationals interned abroad. The holding camp existed until April 1945. A number of exchanges took place (with Palestine, Spain, Turkey, and Britain), involving several hundred prisoners in total.

19 The sterilization of Jews living in so-called mixed marriages aroused great outrage in the Netherlands: see Docs. 122 and 124. In a report titled 'On the De-Jewification of the Netherlands', dated 15 June 1944, the German authorities stated that of 8,610 mixed marriages, 2,562 men and 1,416 women had either allowed themselves to be surgically sterilized or were deemed infertile on the basis of their age: NIOD, 077/1317.

20 Arthur Seyss-Inquart.

21 This plan was never carried out.

22 Wehrmachtbefehlshaber der Niederlande (Commander of the Wehrmacht in the Netherlands), Friedrich Christiansen.

11) *Foundlings*
Arrangements must be made for all cases to be reported to the Security Police. Provision must be made for admission of the foundlings to a specific institution, where they will be genetically examined on the basis of the reports.

Please do not neglect the necessary preparations for these actions as part of your local responsibilities, despite the current political situation. Individual directions will be issued from here at the appropriate time.

DOC. 119
On 10 May 1943 Wilhelm Zoepf considers ways to meet the demand for an additional 8,000 Jews to be deported[1]

Letter from the Senior Commander of the Security Police (IV B 4), p.p. signed Zoepf[2] (SS-Sturmbannführer), The Hague, (1) to Westerbork transit camp for Jews (telex),[3] and (2) back to IV B 4 – Zoepf, dated 10 May 1943[4]

Re: filling the trains bound for the East
The Reich Security Main Office has demanded that 8,000 Jews must be shipped off at all costs in the month of May.

On 4 May 1943, a total of 1,200 Jews were deported on the first train of the month. There are 1,450 Jews lined up for 11 May 1943 (sick and elderly Jews from Vught). An additional 1,630 Jews are available in Westerbork for a third train this month.[5] As a result of the delivery of prisoners and the bounty-payment campaign, a maximum of 1,500 more Jews ought to reach Westerbork by the end of the month. That adds up to a total of 5,780 Jews for deportation for the month of May.

Therefore, at least 2,220 more Jews are needed to meet the monthly quota.

This latter number of Jews must, however, definitely be rounded up by the last week of May, on the basis of some sort of operation, and taken to Westerbork for onward transport. For this purpose, the following would be possible:

1) Immediate use of the Jews collected in *Vught* camp, most of whom are superfluous there (technically the easiest method, but psychologically the least advisable).
2) New *roundup operation in Amsterdam* (currently unenforceable because the Order Police are no longer available).
3) Results of a general clearance order for Amsterdam (difficult in technical and psychological terms because, firstly, rerouting through Vught means that transfer to

1 NIOD, 077/1317. This document has been translated from German.
2 Wilhelm Zoepf (1908–1980), lawyer; joined the NSDAP in 1933 and the SS in 1937; worked for the RSHA from 1940; head of the Central Office for Jewish Emigration in Amsterdam in 1941; SS-Sturmbannführer in 1942; official in charge of Jewish affairs for the Senior Commander of the Security Police and the SD, 1942–1944; fled to Germany in 1945; sentenced in Munich to nine years in prison in 1967.
3 Crossed through in the original, and replaced with the handwritten note: 'Miss Slottke'.
4 The original contains handwritten underlining.
5 On these three transports, the following numbers of people were deported to Sobibor: on 4 May, 1,187 persons; on 11 May, 1,446 persons; and on 18 May, 2,511 persons.

Westerbork would no longer occur in time, and, secondly, the immediate onward transport would scare the remaining Jews in Amsterdam).

4) Use of the *armaments* Jews who are scheduled to be phased out before the end of this month (for this purpose, the Armaments Inspectorate would have to be induced to provide, at least one week before the deadline, at least 800 of the Jewish workers who are in principle exempt until 31 May 1943, along with their families, but ideally all the armaments Jews and their families; then, with a police squad made available for two days, these Jews would have to be seized abruptly, taken to Westerbork, and transported onwards before the end of the month. On the other hand, this solution seems less reasonable in psychological terms, because it is precisely the Jews working for Germany who were originally to be kept longer at Vught and who are also counting most heavily on this).[6]

DOC. 120
On 12 May 1943 Gertrud Slottke from the Security Police's section for Jewish affairs visits Barneveld camp[1]

Report by the Senior Commander of the Security Police (IV B 4), signed Slottke[2] (police employee) and unsigned (SS-Sturmscharführer), The Hague, dated 12 May 1943

Re: Barneveld camp for Jews
On 11 May 1943, by order of SS-Sturmbannführer Zoepf, SS-Sturmscharführer Fischer[3] and Police Employee Slottke of IV B 4 made a visit to Barneveld camp for Jews by prior arrangement with the representative for the City of Amsterdam.[4] The protected Dutch Jews whose names were put forward by the secretaries general Frederiks and Prof. van Dam are in Barneveld camp. In only a very few cases did these Jews themselves submit requests for transfer to Barneveld. Rather, the secretaries general produced a list of names which was submitted without further documentation to Commissioner General for Special Duties Schmidt,[5] the representative for the City of Amsterdam, and the Central Office for Jewish Emigration in Amsterdam. After approval by Commissioner General for Special Duties Schmidt, summonses for relocation to Barneveld were sent out by the Departement van Binnenlandsche Zaken.[6]

6 In total, 8,006 persons were deported to Sobibor from Westerbork in May 1943. On the deportations to Sobibor from March to the end of July, see Introduction, p. 40.

1 NIOD, 077/1319. This document has been translated from German.
2 Gertrud Slottke (1902–1971), administrator; joined the NSDAP in 1933; worked for the Security Police's section for Jewish affairs in The Hague, and handled exemption requests from Jews, 1941–1945; briefly interned in 1945; sentenced to five years in prison by Munich Regional Court in 1967; released in 1970.
3 Franz Fischer (1901–1989), police officer; worked for various Criminal Police offices, 1925–1937; joined the NSDAP in 1933; worked for the Düsseldorf Gestapo, 1937–1940; with the section for Jewish affairs of the Security Police and the SD in The Hague, 1940–1945; interned from 1945; sentenced to life in prison and imprisoned in Breda in 1949; released for health reasons in 1989.
4 Werner Schröder.
5 Fritz Schmidt.
6 Dutch in the original: 'Ministry of the Interior'. Karel Johannes Frederiks was its secretary general.

The Jews in Barneveld are housed in two camps, specifically:

in Schaffelaar Castle	363 Jews
of these, male:	147
female:	216
of whom, children under the age of 18:	77
in De Biezem camp[7]	175 Jews
of these, male:	74
female:	101
of whom, children under the age of 18:	36

Among these Jews are three who are in mixed marriages and also one stateless Jewish woman. One Jewish man has died so far. – Scarlet fever has currently spread through Barneveld camp and sixteen affected children and adults have been transferred to a Jewish hospital in Amsterdam.

Dutch director *Wolthuis*,[8] a former Dutch officer, is in charge of administration for both camps and has a staff of six Aryan supervisors at his disposal. The Jews are deployed for housework and gardening, in accordance with a fixed daily agenda. No service personnel have been provided for them. The Jews are housed in the camps in separate women's and men's quarters. Only a few families live together as family units. They are drawn from certain categories: lawyers, physicians, officers, and civil servants. The process of selecting these groups was handled generously, as far as could be determined so far, as relatives such as children and children-in-law, who have no merits themselves, have also come with them to Barneveld. Some Jews invoked their personal acquaintance or connection with one of the two secretaries general.

Because no documents have so far been submitted to the Security Police to indicate what services were rendered that justify the Jews' placement in B[arneveld], such documents have been requested from the Departement van Binnenlandsche Zaken for review. A great many of the Jews in Barneveld are unlikely to stand up to this scrutiny, from the standpoint of the Security Police.

Upon arrival in Barneveld, the Jews must hand over all their cash. Until 1 March 1943 the individual Jews received a monthly sum, not to exceed fl. 200, from the monies deposited with the Lippmann, Rosenthal & Co. Bank.[9] These allowances have been discontinued as of 1 March 1943. Therefore, maintenance costs are now paid from the fund totalling fl. 58,000 that was created with the money taken [from the Jews upon arrival]. In addition, the Jews receive a monthly allowance ranging from fl. 5 to 10, paid out by the director in Schaffelaar. The salaries for the director and the Aryan supervisors are also paid from the fund of fl. 58,000. As this money has now nearly been used up, the Departement van Binnenlandsche Zaken has requested that the Representative of the City of Amsterdam make new allocations of funds from Lippmann, Rosenthal & Co. for payment.

7 Correctly: De Biezen, one of the two small castles used to house the Jews in Barneveld.

8 Eduard Wolthuis (1888–1973), career soldier; director of Barneveld camp from the end of 1942 to 1945.

9 From 8 August 1941 Jews had to deposit all their cash and assets with Lippmann, Rosenthal & Co., a bank that was used expressly to strip Jews of their assets; see PMJ 5/85. Up to May 1941 families were allowed fl. 1,000 per month to live on, which was paid out from their deposits; thereafter this was reduced to fl. 250 per month.

When relocating to Barneveld, the Jews can take their furniture and luggage with them. When instructed to relocate by the Departement, they will initially leave their furniture behind in their apartments. The furniture will then be fetched at the behest of the Departement and taken to Barneveld. There are five warehouses full of Jewish furniture in Barneveld camp. These Jewish furnishings were also used to equip Schaffelaar Castle. It was possible to establish that these apartments have been inventoried only in part by the Rosenberg Task Force. However, it is unlikely that the Jews sold or put aside furniture before deportation, because they could not expect that they would be able to stay in Barneveld.

In the event of a possible deportation of the Jews from Barneveld, the Rosenberg Task Force should be expressly notified of the existence of these furniture warehouses.

In conclusion, I also wish to mention that Schaffelaar Castle alone is not sufficient for housing the Jews. Three additional barracks – two for women and one infirmary barracks – have been put up, specifically because the arrival of sixty more Jews is anticipated.

DOC. 121

On 13 May 1943 David Koker describes his everyday life in Vught camp[1]

Handwritten diary of David Koker,[2] entry for 13 May 1943

Thursday

I did see Lehmann[3] the day after.[4] Made an appointment for yesterday evening. More about that and other things later. First the transport to Westerbork.[5] All day long my head was so heavy and so tired. In the afternoon they lined up. Old people, supported between young ones, who often went only for […],[6] all of them bowed down under

1 NIOD, 244/1657. The original document is in Dutch. The diary entry published here, with a few slight amendments, is from the English translation: David Koker, *At the Edge of the Abyss: A Concentration Camp Diary, 1943–1944*, ed. Robert Jan van Pelt, trans. Michiel Horn (Evanston, IL: Northwestern University Press, 2012), pp. 191–194, by kind permission of the publisher. Copyright © 2012 by Northwestern University Press. Published 2012. All rights reserved. Originally published in Dutch by G. A. van Oorschot as *Dagboek geschreven in Vught*, 1977.

2 David Koker (1921–1945), student; arrested with his family, Feb. 1943; deported to Vught, where he was assigned to the Philips electronics factory as a forced labourer; deported to Auschwitz, June 1944, and from there to Groß-Rosen; perished on the transport to Dachau in Feb. 1945.

3 Arthur Lehmann (b. 1892), lawyer; born in Berlin; emigrated to Amsterdam from Paris in 1936; deported to Vught on 15 Jan. 1943; head of the Jewish camp administration in Vught from Oct. 1943; deported on 20 March 1943 to Westerbork, from there on 23 March 1944 to Auschwitz, and subsequently to Mauthausen and Bergen-Belsen; returned to the Netherlands in August 1945; emigrated to the USA in 1947.

4 On 10 May 1943 Koker wrote in his diary about his hunch that the Jews from Vught would soon be taken to Westerbork. He intended to stay in Vught as long as possible, he wrote, and would therefore try to get an 'important job' in the camp. For this reason, he decided to approach Lehmann.

5 The transport of 8–9 May 1943, on which 1,280 persons were deported from Vught to Westerbork, consisted mainly of large families, the elderly, and the sick.

6 One word in the original is illegible.

luggage, loaded on their backs and shoulders, but also blankets in their arms, as if they were moving from one barrack to another and not to Poland. Parents with their children around them, and solicitous for their children and their luggage, which is also for the children, after all. The parents and children don't know it, but the others do. They are so timid in their distress. Grim, but not forcefully grim. They don't say anything, not because they can't spare the energy to speak but because they can't give voice any longer. The parents have been a curse to their children. They've dragged them here. And now the children become a curse to the parents: they're dragging them along to Poland. And this is so wretched that there's nothing more to be said. They stood there on the drill ground, 1,500 of them, but it seemed like a smaller group. The sky was very dark, and huge, ragged clouds sailed past. Those unable to walk were pushed along in wheelbarrows, their legs hanging down. The light was treacherous and changeable. The white patches on their luggage and bedding had a ghostly hue. Later that afternoon a shower of rain fell that was as sharp as hail, and there was a raw wind. They stood there for two hours and then were taken away.

Early to bed that evening. And at nine thirty: everybody out of bed! General roll call. The sick had to come too, except for the very seriously ill. They're allowed to stay in the dining hall, *fully dressed.* My blanket was like a hard board.[7] The smallest movement would have cracked it. I felt icy cold. My heart was beating as I had never felt it beat before. Transport to Poland I think, and we all think. And once outside: we stand and stand. At the outset the Germans stick around, but after a while they go to the women's camp, and then two people are carried out with a whole crew of children surrounding them. At first people wait in frozen anticipation, later they relax a bit, begin to talk nervously and volubly. And still later, when the rumour does the rounds that they are looking for 78 people who have made themselves scarce, the talking turns into exuberant joking. I myself utter one absurdity after another. I say: 'You mustn't think I am drunk. Nor that I'm talking so much because I'm nervous.'

When we got back to the barrack, people made themselves comfortable, sat at the tables, started eating and drinking, like the end of Yom Kippur.[8]

And since then the fear of being transported hasn't left us. And when I look at the camp now I think, just as I did at the outset: it's not for us they made it this nice. And this gives a voice to all of these dark thoughts. It even stirs them up further. Each time I hear that word 'Durchgangslager'[9] I go cold. In the morning, when I'm at roll call, standing there at the edge of the grounds, I'm glad not to hear that dreaded word. Anyway, the fear of Poland is just one thing. There is also fear of Moerdijk,[10] for which people are constantly drafted whenever a transport of sick people and so on returns. On days like that we warn each other to avoid doing things in particular: don't walk slowly with your hands in your pockets, don't talk too much while walking, don't walk through

7 This sentence is barely legible in the original.
8 Yom Kippur (the Day of Atonement) is the most important Jewish religious holiday of the year.
9 German in the original: 'transit camp'.
10 The largest subcamp of Vught concentration camp was located in Moerdijk from March 1943 to Feb. 1944. Prisoners in the external work details were forced to undertake heavy labour and were subject to mistreatment by the SS guards. In Oct. 1943 all of the Jewish prisoners at Moerdijk were brought back to Vught, from where they were deported to Auschwitz.

the sand outside the door when you go round the corner ('because people have already been nabbed for that'), and above all don't go to the women's camp. I don't keep to that last warning. Mother[11] was ill for a few days and my days were very empty. Something drives me towards her; is it a habit that I go there every afternoon, with all the attendant risks? In all fixed habits there is, after all, something that's alive, even if you aren't aware of it. And this isn't even a fixed habit, it's something I experience an urge to do every afternoon. But not an urge arising out of tenderness, rather out of a need the nature of which I'm unable to determine. Partly of a moral nature, but also to give everyday life a focus. I always get something nice to eat when I'm with her, and we talk very pleasantly, but on those days of panic I'm rigid and feel quite hunted. Now that I've started the ball rolling with Lehmann, Mother makes a big deal of my merits.[12] I have to recite my verses to admiring women, and am increasingly becoming the ladies' favourite. The pet poet! Mother yesterday: 'Mrs Jacubowski,[13] may I introduce my son?' Mrs Jakubowski is a lady who has lived in China, swarthy, but with a thick layer of matte makeup, with bleached hair, and chirping like a cheerful bird. 'My son writes poems even here,' Mother says in a tone of proud satisfaction. 'Do recite them for this lady.' I think of *Woutertje Pieterse.*[14] 'Oh I do so appreciate poetry; you must know that I'm an artist myself I have always associated with artists.' And I recite a poem for her, and she closes her eyes, shakes her head like a horse and says: 'I didn't know Dutch could sound like this.' And when she's heard everything: 'Oh, you must suffer terribly. Oh, how well I understand it' (everything in an immigrant's Dutch). 'I've experienced everything that same way. Just so, my dear (to Mother), we are kindred souls.' And then a paean of praise: 'When you leave this place, you will have grown and then your talent will open the way for you. You know, my dear, he's not strong, I mean in spirit.' Mother protests. 'But people who are so delicate, so subtle, etc., etc.' And yet she's not stupid. Suddenly: 'But I've seen you before. At Fritz H.'s. You know, my dear, I never forget anything. Everything that's in this head stays here. When I was taken away Fritz H. said: "One of my disciples[15] has been carried off." A highly talented young man who followed me (!!!), and now I care for nothing any more.'

This morning I was standing there watching a new (though not very interesting) transport from Amsterdam, and she appeared before me with a mug of the tasty bean soup that's being served up here today. And why is Mother doing this? I've wanted to write about this for some time. You have to make friends with everyone here. And to keep them as friends. And Mother is particularly good at it. She knows that people here are generally

11 Judith Koker-Presser (1892–1979), housewife; arrested with her family and taken to Vught in Feb. 1943; deported from there to Auschwitz in June 1944; survived and returned to the Netherlands in 1945.

12 David Koker was considered a gifted poet; he wrote poetry and also translated modern Hebrew poetry.

13 Hertha Jakubowski, née Gotthilf (b. 1895), housewife; emigrated with her husband from Shanghai to the Netherlands in 1937; imprisoned in Vught in 1943; survived the war and emigrated to the USA in 1947.

14 *Woutertje Pieterse* is a well-known novel by the Dutch author Eduard Douwes Dekker (1820–1887), who used the pen name Multatuli. In the novel, the young Woutertje, a talented poet, is asked by the devout spinster Miss Laps to write a religious poem for her uncle's birthday.

15 In German in the original: 'Jünger'.

not particularly refined and therefore doesn't recoil from any device, no matter how crude it may seem in my eyes. Does small favours for people, stays on good terms with the people in catering, with the women in the administration, deals with them all in a rather ostentatiously polite way. If she introduces her children, she praises them to the skies, so that people become embarrassed, but she gets what she wants. Father[16] has a rather clumsy style of flattery which gives me heart palpitations. It also costs cigarettes. I can't do it. Not because I object to it morally, although it does irritate me, but because I can't find the right way to do it. As I see it, every act of flattery is simply too obvious. That's because I overestimate the refinement of others, although from Mother's results it's clear that I'm mistaken. But it still gets in the way of acting effectively.

DOC. 122

On 19 May 1943 the Dutch churches criticize Reich Commissioner Seyss-Inquart's plan to sterilize Jews living in 'mixed marriages'[1]

Letter from the General Synod of the Netherlands Churches, unsigned,[2] The Hague, to the Reich Commissioner for the Occupied Dutch Territories,[3] The Hague, dated 19 May 1943

Letter to the Reich Commissioner concerning the sterilization of the spouses in 'mixed marriages'

After all the complaints which the Christian churches in the Netherlands have already felt compelled to raise with Your Excellency during the years of the occupation, particularly concerning our country's Jewish citizens, something so appalling is happening at this moment that we have no choice but to address Your Excellency in the name of Our Lord.

We have already protested about various actions of the occupying power that conflict with the spiritual foundations of our nation, which throughout its existence has at least endeavoured to live with its government in accordance with the Word of God.

And now, in recent weeks, the process of sterilizing persons in so-called mixed marriages has been initiated. But God, who created heaven and earth, whose commandment applies to all men, and to whom Your Excellency also must render account some day, said to mankind: Be fruitful, and multiply (Genesis 1:28). Sterilization involves a physical and psychological mutilation in direct contravention of the divine commandment that we should not 'dishonour, hate, injure, or kill'. Sterilization represents a desecration both of divine commandments and of human law. It is the ultimate consequence of a racial

16 Jesaja Koker (1886–1945), jeweller and diamond merchant; arrested with his family in Feb. 1943 and taken to Vught; deported from there to Auschwitz in June 1944; perished in a subcamp of Groß-Rosen concentration camp.

1 Het Utrechts Archief, 1423/2156. This document has been translated from a contemporary German translation of the Dutch original.

2 A different version of the same document lists the following institutions as signatories: the Dutch Reformed Church, the Roman Catholic Church, the Old Reformed Churches, the Reformed Churches in the Netherlands in Restored Union, the Christian Reformed Church, the Lutheran Church, the Old Lutheran Church, the Remonstrant Brotherhood, and the Mennonite Church: JHM, Doc. 00 000 628.

3 Arthur Seyss-Inquart.

theory which is anti-Christian and will ravage our people, a hubris beyond measure, a world view and an approach to life that undermine a truly Christian and humane life and ultimately render this impossible.

You, Your Excellency, are effectively the highest political authority in the Netherlands at the moment. As things now stand, you are entrusted with maintaining law and order in this country – entrusted not only by the Führer of the German Reich, but through an unfathomable preordination from the God whom the Christian church proclaims on earth. You, just like all other human beings – and especially so because you now occupy this high position – are subject to the commandments of this Lord and Judge of all the world.

Therefore, the Christian churches in the Netherlands tell you on behalf of God and on the strength of his Word: it is Your Excellency's duty to prevent the disgraceful procedure of sterilization.

We are under no illusions. We are well aware that we can hardly expect Your Excellency to heed the voice of the Church, that is, the voice of the gospel, meaning the voice of God. But what we cannot expect humanly, we may hope for in Christian faith. The living God has the power to incline even the heart of Your Excellency towards conversion and obedience. This, then, is what we ask of God and of Your Excellency, and for the good of our suffering nation.

DOC. 123

In a letter from Westerbork camp, secretary Mirjam Levie describes her distress when many Jewish Council employees had to be selected for deportation from 21 to 25 May 1943[1]

Handwritten letter from Mirjam Levie,[2] dated 4 July 1943[3]

Sunday, 4 July 1943, 4.30 p.m., Barrack 65, Westerbork

Dear Kobold,[4]

Although I can't muster the peace of mind to write and it's also rather difficult to write on the second tier of a bunk bed, with your head down so as not to knock it against

1 NIOD, 244/1480. Published in a slightly abridged version in Mirjam Bolle, *Letters Never Sent: Amsterdam, Westerbork, Bergen-Belsen*, trans. Laura Vroom (Jerusalem: Yad Vashem, 2014 [Dutch edn, 2003]), pp. 135–143. The English-language translation has been reproduced here with a few minor amendments; supplementary content from the original source has been newly translated from Dutch.

2 Mirjam Bolle, née Levie (b. 1917), secretary; employed by the Committee for Jewish Refugees (CJV), 1938–1941; subsequently worked at the Jewish Council; Raphaël Henri Eitje's secretary in May 1943; deported to Westerbork in June 1943, then to Bergen-Belsen in Jan. 1944; obtained a place on the 'exchange list' for Palestine and in July 1944 was among a group of Jews from the Netherlands exchanged for German nationals in Palestine; married Leo Bolle in 1944; worked at the Dutch embassy in Tel Aviv, 1948–1981.

3 This letter was written at Westerbork on 4 July 1943, but mainly describes events that occurred between 21 and 25 May 1943.

4 Leonard (Leo) Bolle (1912–1992), teacher; emigrated to Palestine in 1938; fiancé, and later husband, of Mirjam Levie, who wrote him numerous diary-style letters, which were hidden by a friend in Amsterdam. Mirjam Levie was able to take the diary she later kept in Westerbork and Bergen-Belsen with her when she was transferred to Palestine as part of the exchange of Jews from the Netherlands for German nationals. Leo Bolle's nickname 'Kobold' means 'mischievous sprite'.

the third tier, I want to find some comfort from you and tell you 'briefly' how we ended up here in Westerbork. The blow has come at last, and in some respects it's worse, in others less so, but certainly very, very different from what we ever imagined. In actual fact, we could never really form a picture of any of this. Such an awful lot happened during the month of May that I can't for the life of me mention it all. I saved some newspaper cuttings and notes, but it remains to be seen whether I'll ever lay hands on them again. I do remember a few things. For example, all the men in active service during the fighting in May 1940 have been made prisoners of war.[5] The paper keeps publishing call-ups for certain regiments. And all men aged 20–35 are being recruited for the Arbeitseinsatz.[6] Those students who didn't sign the declaration of loyalty have been deported to Germany.[7] Even all the Christians have to hand in their radio sets.[8] Unbelievable!!! What it comes down to is that, practically speaking, nobody will be left.

During May we received another nocturnal visit, and the blighters took down Father's[9] name and his Sperre number.[10] The following morning, when I made enquiries, I was told that we were bound to receive an Anweisung[11] to move to [Amsterdam-] Oost. Besides, that week we had just sent Mother[12] to the doctor's because she was so awfully thin, and he had found a small lump in her breast and referred her to Dr Kropveld.[13] I went with her, and he said she needed surgery. A dreadful thing in these precarious times of deportations and possible invasion, etc. Just what we needed. Then there was the added problem of housekeeping, but quite by chance I bumped into Selma Gazan[14] and she was prepared to come and help us. Except that this turned out to be impossible, because the JC [Jewish Council] needed qualified nurses very badly and they wouldn't allow her to do domestic work. By the grace of God, the JC's medical commis-

5 See Doc. 118, fn. 9.

6 From 1 April 1942 all Dutch men between the ages of 18 and 35 were called up by age cohort for labour deployment in Germany, unless they were needed for essential work in the Netherlands. On 7 May 1943 this was extended to include Dutch prisoners of war who had been released.

7 On 13 March 1943 the German occupying authorities demanded that students sign a 'declaration of loyalty' to the Third Reich. In response, the University of Nijmegen closed at the beginning of April. All the other universities forwarded the demand to their students. Most students refused to sign the declaration and were subsequently sent to Germany for labour deployment. Some of the students who refused to sign went into hiding in the Netherlands.

8 On 13 May 1943 all Dutch citizens were ordered to hand in their radios to the German authorities; approximately 75 per cent of the radios in the country were handed in.

9 Moritz Jacob Levie (1889–1965), businessman; company manager and member of the board of directors of the Dutch-Asian Trading Company; deported in May 1943 to Westerbork, and from there to Bergen-Belsen in Jan. 1944; transferred to Palestine in July 1944 as part of the exchange of Jews from the Netherlands for German nationals.

10 German in the original, lit. 'block'; here and below, a reference to the issuing of stamps providing temporary exemption from deportation. The exemption number would be stamped in an individual's identity documents.

11 German in the original: 'order'.

12 Sara Levie-Oesterman (1882–1975), housewife; deported to Westerbork in Sept. 1943, then to Bergen-Belsen in Jan. 1944; transferred to Palestine in July 1944 as part of the exchange of Jews from the Netherlands for German nationals.

13 Dr Aron Kropveld (1895–1972), physician; worked as a radiologist from 1923; deported to Westerbork on 28 Jan. 1944 as he was a spouse in a so-called mixed marriage; deported from Westerbork to Auschwitz on 3 March 1944; returned in August 1945; emigrated to the Dutch Antilles in 1970.

14 Selma Gazan (b. 1916), nurse; survived the war.

sion granted that if, after her release from the hospital, Mother was still too weak to do her own housekeeping, Selma could come and stay with us.

But it would all take a very different course. I headed to Oost on my bicycle to find a house. Houses are allocated, but if you say: 'I would like such-and-such a house,' and the woman in charge of allocating the houses (Mussert's niece!) is in a good mood, you usually get it. But I found nothing. Many of the houses were unoccupied, but they hadn't yet been 'pulsed'.[15] Besides, the Anweisung hadn't arrived yet, and Sluzker advised me against applying for one myself. I was in a hurry because of Mother's hospital admission and the fact that some kind of new Sperre process was hanging over our heads, which meant I'd be insanely busy again.

On Friday, 21 May 1943, the bombshell dropped. The JC was convened, and late in the afternoon it was announced that 'part of the JC will be called up for the Arbeitseinsatz[16] and everybody must be prepared.' (I forgot to tell you the trifling fact that those without exemptions had had to report to Polderweg,[17] but that only a very small percentage had showed up.) So now the JC's turn had come. I received word to go to Nieuwe Keizersgracht,[18] where Eitje was and I ran off there armed with staff lists. Everybody there looked glum, but what exactly was going on, the actual percentage [of Jewish Council employees affected], nobody knew. I was told to come back at eight in the evening. It was Friday evening and Mother was to go to the NIZ[19] that Sunday. But it couldn't be helped.

That evening the four of us (the flies here are driving me mad at the moment), Ro Leuvenberg, Meyer de Vries's[20] secretary, Lies Agtsteribbe (Brandon), Frouk de Lange (Prof Cohen), and I summoned all the departments that had to draw up staff lists, which were then to be presented to the Commission[21] for approval. In addition to the above-mentioned four, Henri Edersheim[22] from The Hague was also a member of this Sperre Commission. We went home at eleven o'clock and that was the last night I got any sleep

15 The homes of deported Jews were cleared by the Amsterdam-based removals firm owned by Abraham Puls (1902–1975) on behalf of the Rosenberg Task Force and the Household Effects Registration Office. This led to the coining of the colloquial verb *pulsen* ('to Puls').

16 German in the original: 'labour deployment'.

17 See Doc. 129, fn. 2.

18 The abbreviation 'N K.gr.' is used in the original. The main building occupied by the Jewish Council was located on Nieuwe Keizersgracht.

19 Nederlands Israëlietisch Ziekenhuis (Dutch Israelite Hospital). The hospital was founded at the beginning of the nineteenth century and was located on Nieuwe Keizersgracht. Patients and staff from the NIZ were deported to Westerbork on 13 August 1943.

20 Meijer (also known as Meyer) de Vries (1891–1980), civil servant; worked at the Ministry of Social Affairs until 1941; general advisor in the Jewish Council's secretariat and member of other Jewish Council commissions, 1942–1943; thought to have gone into hiding, 1943–1945; worked again as a civil servant in Utrecht, 1948–1956.

21 The Jewish Council's 'exemption commission' decided which Jewish Council employees would be put forward for exemption from deportation. It also had the task of drawing up lists of employees whose services the Council could most easily do without. The four secretaries were Rosine (Ro) Leuvenberg (1909–1987), Elizabet (Lies) Agtsteribbe (1912–1945), Froukje Debora de Lange (1916–2005), and Mirjam Levie.

22 Henri Edersheim (1885–1943), lawyer; secretary of the Jewish Coordination Committee in The Hague, 1941; representative of the Jewish Council in the Hague, 1942; imprisoned in Westerbork on 17 July 1943, deported a week later to Sobibor, where he was murdered on arrival.

for some time. I'm not in the mood now to give you all the details. It's a shame I didn't write it down sooner, for I can't possibly convey the tension and anxiety of those days now. Seven thousand people would have to be called up by Tuesday 25 May, and the Huns had immediately warned that 'terrible things' would happen if not enough people came forward.[23] The Professor took this to mean firing squads, but whether this was said in so many words, I don't know. It meant 60 percent (I believe) of the JC, so all people we know well. Not to mention … the parents! The four of us, the secretaries, could talk of nothing else.

Although I had seen that Bluth[24] had not let Father go, which very much amazed me, having seen the departmental lists, I realized they would never fill the quota. You see, every department had included on its list of those to be struck off[25] those people who were certain to be indispensable for another department. The seminary,[26] for example, had let Leo Seeligmann[27] go, knowing that the Jewish High School would keep him. All the departments were doing this, with the following result (Meanwhile, I've done the laundry, eaten some mash[28] and now I'll resume. A beautiful view: Some of the laundry is fluttering between two beds):

1. Mistakes were made, because the seminary, for example, said: The Jewish High School will put Leo Seeligmann on its list of indispensable people, so we can remove him. Meanwhile, the Jewish High School said: The seminary will certainly list him as indispensable, so we can strike him off the list.

2. The list was far too short, owing to the fact that too few were actually struck off the list of exemptions, because naturally people such as Seeligmann were not struck off and therefore not included in the required 7,000.

I hope this makes sense and, more than that, I hope to explain it to you in person. It's not easy to gather your thoughts in a barracks with 1,000 people, and so much happened afterwards that this has already faded from memory.

Saturday, 22 May
Worked with Eitje all day and into the night on the card index. I went home at eleven, where I said goodbye to Mother, who was going into hospital. As soon as she and Father had gone and I was by myself in the house, I cried my eyes out because I knew the game was up, and because I was so upset that the JC had once again lent itself to this barbarity instead of saying: Enough is enough, go hang. It reminds me of the following sick but very telling 'joke': Asscher and Cohen are sent for by the Huns and are told that the Jews

23 The chairman reported on this threat at the meeting of the Jewish Council on 21 May 1943: NIOD, 182/3.
24 Correctly: Curth Blüth (b. 1891), retailer; emigrated from Germany to the Netherlands in 1919; naturalized in 1935; head of the Jewish Council's Emigration Assistance Department; deported to Westerbork in Dec. 1943; returned to Amsterdam in 1945.
25 'Schraplijst', meaning a list of people to be deleted from the list of those exempted from deportation.
26 Netherlands Israelite Seminary (Nederlands Israëlietisch Seminarium).
27 Isaac Leo Seeligmann (1907–1982), lecturer; deputy chairman of the Jewish Council's Central Culture Committee, 1940–1943; deported to Westerbork in Nov. 1943, then to Theresienstadt in Sept. 1944; professor in Jerusalem from 1949.
28 *Stamppot:* a traditional Dutch dish made of mashed potatoes and vegetables.

are to be gassed, whereupon the Professor's[29] first question is: 'Will you supply the gas or should we?' Such was our predicament.

I slept until two, then went back to the office. There I had to strike all the bigwigs' friends and family off the (interim) call-up list. Nice, eh? In a word, I was given a list of their cronies and had to check whether they would be called up and, if so, I had to strike them off the list. I almost wept with fury and indignation, but there was nothing I could do. Home at half-past six, back at eight.

Sunday night, 23–24 May

I'll never forget that night. I was working on the call-up list, collating it with cards from the card index. Really nice people were sitting in my department, all heads of department, but now a really good bunch. A group of accountants had been called in to do the counting, Ab Vreedenburg and Karel Hartog among them.[30] You remember what I wrote to you about him, so I just couldn't understand why he now let himself get roped in to do this awful work (which we simply could not believe was real). I also forgot to tell you that Freddy[31] had refused to draw up the lists, as had Elie Dasberg.[32] But they knew they wouldn't be let go. And as for the parents: Elie's brother, Simon Dasberg (who has since become Amsterdam's acting chief rabbi), would take care of his mother, while your father,[33] as funeral director, was safe, so they could afford to refuse. But I did find it dreadful of Karel, and I had to think of it constantly because he really looked alarmingly ill. Apart from that, he was very nervous and got everyone riled by his uncivil behaviour. This team of accountants (I was helping Jo Pinkhof) did nothing but count and count, but the figures just didn't add up. They remained well below 7,000, which was quite understandable (see above) and had in fact been anticipated by us, but not by their lordships themselves. This resulted in a 'raid,' i.e. the entire card index was reviewed (so no longer just the departmental lists) and call-ups written for the cards that were pulled out. Utterly indiscriminate. Our team, who received the call-up lists – every now and then we were summoned to the Professor's office, the scene of the massacre, to fetch the lists – was beside itself with rage. Of course we kept coming across the names of good friends, colleagues, sometimes even relatives, brothers and sisters and even parents and children! The mood became more and more charged, until one of the men (a former

29 Presumably a reference to David Cohen, who was a professor of history.

30 Abraham (Ab) Vreedenburg (1909–1984), accountant; survived the war and emigrated to Israel in 1950. Karel David Hartog (1909–1995), auditor; from 1936 chairman of the Jewish Youth Federation; employee of the Jewish Council; interned in Westerbork, June 1942–July 1943, then released; chief executive of the Dutch Zionist League, 1945–1946; emigrated to Palestine in 1946.

31 Godfried (Freddy) Bolle (1914–1983), broker; active in Zionist organizations; head of the Jewish Council's Central Culture Committee, 1941; deported to Westerbork on 26 May 1943, then to Bergen-Belsen on 11 Jan. 1944; returned to the Netherlands in 1945; active in the re-establishment of Jewish organizations.

32 Eliazar (Elie) Dasberg (1904–1989), insurance broker; active in different Zionist organizations; head of the Jewish Council's vocational training centre, 1941–1943; deported to Westerbork on 29 Sept. 1943, then to Bergen-Belsen on 15 March 1944; emigrated in 1950 to Israel, where he worked as an insurance broker.

33 Mozes Bolle Jr (1879–1945), undertaker; deported to Westerbork on 29 Sept. 1943 and then on 11 Jan. 1944 to Bergen-Belsen, where he perished.

theatre director and impresario)[34] burst into tears and shouted that he refused to go on. At that point, we all chucked it in and one of us went to tell the Professor that we couldn't possibly do this insane and barbarous work.

Then the entire commission convened in our office and the Professor spoke to us as follows: 'If we fail to do this, terrible things will happen.' When he was told that there wouldn't be enough people in any case, he replied, 'Then that's the will of the people. But I can't shoulder the responsibility for refusing the order.' It all sounds very matter-of-fact, but everybody was crying and barely capable of voicing their objections. The Professor, too, was almost in tears.

Then I said, on the verge of tears: 'But Professor, surely the people would have wanted you to refuse this order. And if the terrible things you keep speaking of will happen anyway (you see, the Professor had told us the Huns had said that if insufficient numbers of people came forward the 'repercussions would be unimaginable'. He had also said that he was convinced the turnout would be poor), then why do this nauseating work instead of lying in the sun and gathering our strength for Poland?' Everybody agreed with me and nodded their approval, while I could hardly stop myself from weeping. The Professor replied: 'Miss Levie, that's not for you to judge.' I was incapable of replying that it's all very easy to fob somebody off like that.

The Professor looked round at all the sobbing men – I was the only woman – and said: 'Please don't make things difficult for us, the call-ups have to be dispatched.' (Remember, they had been given the order on Friday and the people were expected to report on Tuesday!) Anyway, we went back to work.

To cut a long story short, at six in the morning (i.e. Monday 24 May), Lies Agtsteribbe (who'd had a terrible crying fit, and out of fear for her parents. If it hadn't been for Father and Mother, I would have chucked it all in a long time ago and told them: Go hang, I quit), Ab Vreedenburg, Dorus Hijmans,[35] Karel Hartog and I were summoned to the commission and asked whether we were physically and emotionally fit enough to continue the raid through the card index, which had remained unfinished. We refused en bloc, whereupon the gentlemen looked at one another and said: 'In that case, we shall carry on ourselves.' Then Dorus H. and some others did do it after all, but the others left. Then we left. I got home at two, slept until four, and then went back to the office.

Meanwhile, many people had learnt that they were to be called up, e.g. from typists. The typists had suffered panic attacks that night, e.g., when they had to type out call-ups for their own parents. The first such call-up could usually be cancelled, but not the second. It was all so arbitrary, down to mood and chance. It was my task to receive these people and collect their details. At approximately six o'clock, we received news that staff at the NIZ, as well as any relatives living with them, would be interned at the JI[36] building

34 Walter Levy (b. 1883); emigrated from Germany in 1936; deported to Westerbork in May 1943, then to Bergen-Belsen in Jan. 1944; transferred to Palestine in July 1944 as part of the exchange of Jews from the Netherlands for German nationals.

35 Isidor (Dorus) Hijmans (1908–1943), businessman; worked in the Jewish Council's housing department, then on its finance committee; imprisoned in Westerbork on 29 Sept. 1943; deported on 16 Nov. 1943 to Auschwitz, where he was murdered on arrival.

36 The Joodsche Invalide, a Jewish home for the elderly, opened in 1938 in a large building at 100 Nieuwe Achtergracht and was run by an association established for this purpose. Its residents were taken to Westerbork in March 1943.

for five days. Panic and conjecture were rife. An hour later, the Professor issued a statement: The announcement is incorrect. Only hospital personnel *with* call-ups will be interned, without family. In the meantime, however, entire families had set off for the JI. But our minds had been put at rest, because we had thought that these people were to receive special treatment, whereas the revised version implied that the hospital staff would be safeguarded from the measures aimed at the rest of the population.

Home at approximately half-past six. Then to Freddy, because I wanted to talk to somebody. Everybody looked like they had done during the first few days of the war: nervous, pale and gaunt. I chatted to Freddy for a couple of hours, then (i.e. Monday night) returned home, slept (after two nights) and at nine o'clock on Tuesday 25 May went to Waterlooplein[37] to find out who had received call-ups and whether there had been any mistakes. By then I had already heard that dozens of friends and relatives had received call-ups, including Grewels,[38] other aunts and uncles, etc. At ten o'clock, to Keizersgracht. There I was summoned to the commission (the other secretaries hadn't arrived yet) and the game began all over again. Cancelling call-ups at the rate at which they had been issued. And it shows that we had been right in saying that it was an impossible task, because in a great many cases the committee said: Oh no, that's absolutely out of the question! And then the game of chance began all over again. Call-ups were cancelled until five in the afternoon, while the people were expected to report to Polderweg that very same day. One thousand call-ups were returned undeliverable, so things weren't looking good for the 7,000 quota.[39]

At half past six, Ro Leuvenberg and I asked our bosses whether we should come back again during the night, because the final list of call-ups had to be typed out. But they didn't feel that would be necessary, so we went home, completely exhausted.

Bye-bye, my dearest.

Maybe more tomorrow.

37 The Jewish Council's Department for Social Welfare was located on Waterlooplein at this time.

38 This refers to Israël (Isidoor) Grewel (1885–1943) and Channa Anna Grewel-Bolle (1894–1943), an aunt of Mirjam Levie's fiancé, Leo Bolle.

39 On the consequences, see Doc. 125.

DOC. 124

On 25 May 1943 the Dutch secretaries general draft a letter of protest against the planned sterilization of Jews[1]

Letter from the Dutch secretaries general,[2] unsigned, to the commissioner general for administration and justice, Dr E. Wimmer,[3] The Hague, undated (draft)[4]

Commissioner General,

It has come to our attention that the occupying authorities are planning to subject specific categories of Jews in the Netherlands to a sterilization procedure, or that this step may have already been taken. According to reports, the Jews in question face the choice of either being deported to Poland or voluntarily undergoing this sterilization procedure.

It appears to us, however, that as a result of the great uncertainty regarding people's fate in Poland and the severing of individuals' family ties in this country, this choice cannot be characterized as voluntary.

Irrespective of how much various regulations have placed the Dutch Jews in a situation that diverges sharply from that of other citizens, they have remained Dutch citizens under Dutch statutory law and, in accordance with the constitution, they continue to hold the same rights to the protection of their physical integrity and property as all persons who find themselves on Dutch territory. Apart from valid statutory law, this status and this right – as will not be unknown to you – are also based on the firm convictions regarding matters of legal principle held by nearly the entire Dutch population. We may add here that these convictions are not founded on a more or less friendly attitude towards Jews, but exclusively on a deeply rooted awareness of the principles of justice. They would apply to any other population group that found itself in a special situation under particular circumstances, as the Jews do at present.

As the heads of various principal constituent parts of the Dutch state administration, we therefore feel we have a duty to advise you of the feelings which the application of the aforementioned sterilization procedure will arouse in nearly the entire Dutch population.

The Dutch people regard the body and the individual's physical status as the most essential of a human being's possessions. Depending on whether one is of a more contemplative or pragmatic nature, they are felt by the Dutch people to be possessions protected by divine, statutory, or natural law.

1 NIOD, 101a/3d. This document has been translated from Dutch.

2 This letter was intended to be signed by the following secretaries general: Derk Gerard Willem Spitzen (Ministry for Water Management), Karel Johannes Frederiks (Ministry of the Interior), Jan van Dam (Ministry of Education, Science, and Cultural Protection), Hans Max Hirschfeld (Ministry of Trade, Industry, and Shipping), Otto Eduard Willem Six (Ministry of Colonies), and Robert Anthony Verwey (Ministry of Social Affairs). In a letter dated 2 June 1943, Jan van Dam refused to sign it. In the end, the letter was never sent to the German authorities.

3 Correctly: Friedrich Wimmer.

4 This document was enclosed with a letter from Secretary General Spitzen to Secretary General Frederiks, dated 25 May 1943.

Accordingly, Dutch people feel that any encroachment upon the integrity of these possessions is an encroachment on this divine, statutory, or natural law.

The confidence in these various types of law and the desire for them to be upheld are so great that, irrespective of the scale on which such measures are applied, and irrespective of the group to which they are applied, measures such as that referred to above will not cease to call forth the deepest consternation and outrage in all sections of the population. These sentiments will be of such an intense nature and so generally widespread among the population that we do not believe we have the right to maintain silence on this topic, even if the subject of this letter lies to some extent beyond the bounds of each of our departments' practical jurisdiction.

In our opinion, the above matter is of such profound seriousness that we would like to ask you to inform the Reich Commissioner[5] of the content of this letter, for which purpose we enclose a copy.

Yours faithfully

DOC. 125

On 28 May 1943 the Central Committee of the Jewish Council discusses how it can continue its work after many Jewish Council employees have been deported[1]

Minutes of meeting, unsigned, dated 2 June 1943 (carbon copy)[2]

Minutes of the 95th meeting of the Central Committee, held on Friday, 26 May 1943 at 10.30 a.m. at 58 Nieuwe Keizersgracht.
Present: Prof. Cohen, chair; Mrs Van Tijn, and Messrs Asscher, Aal, Blazer, Blüth, Cahen, A. Cohen, Diamand, Edersheim, Eitje, Hendrix, Kauffmann, Jacobs, Jacobson, Krouwer, Van der Laan, Moser, Van Oss, Sluzker, De Vries, and Mr Brandon, secretary.

The chair opened the meeting and reported on the events of the past week.[3] This has been one of the most terrible weeks in the history of Amsterdam's Jews. Our best and brightest people have fallen victim to these events, which will never be forgotten. Amsterdam has in Israel been described as a mother, and the history of the Jews is embedded here as it is in few other places. A history that dates back 300 years has been destroyed in a single day. We saw the people in Houtmarkt[4] and recognized many of our good friends among them; people who themselves and people whose ancestors have done much for Israel. They bore their fate with a pride in which the nobility of the Jews was evident.

5 Arthur Seyss-Inquart.

1 NIOD, 182/38. This document has been translated from Dutch.
2 The original contains handwritten marking.
3 See Doc. 123 and Introduction, p. 41.
4 Jonas Daniël Meijerplein (named after the first Jewish lawyer in the Netherlands) was called Houtmarkt from 1942 to 1945. It served as an assembly point for Jews who were arrested or summoned for deportation.

All we can do now is think about how we should proceed. Before doing so, we must offer a word of thanks for everything those who are leaving have done, wishing them the strength to bear their awful fate. All we can do is believe in better times and expect to be rescued and to be reunited with those without whom we cannot live.

The speaker then reported on his meeting with Mr Lages,[5] Mr aus der Fünten, and Mr Blumenthal,[6] which took place last Thursday. During this meeting it was reported that our organization has been destroyed, and we linked this with our request to bring back a number of our personnel from Westerbork. However, this was rejected. We have to try to rebuild the organization with the Jews who are present. An exception was made only for Chief Rabbi Dasberg and Mrs Eitje.[7] We may also submit a list of the deported wives and children of those who were working at the office at the time [of the roundup] and who have not been transferred to Westerbork. It is clear that the German authorities want the work of the Jewish Council to continue.

This was followed by an exchange of ideas about how a record of the remaining staff will be compiled and how the divisions will be reorganized. The decision was made to send out a circular in which the heads of the divisions will be urgently instructed to produce a list of employees.

With regard to the question of the extent to which information can be given about those whom the Jewish Council has called up for deployment in Germany, the reply was that nothing can be said about this, but it is likely that the operation has brought the transport issue to an end.[8] The possible transfer of employees from divisions with a surplus of workers to divisions with a shortage will also be considered.

Then the development of the card index system was discussed. A circular about this issue will be sent out in the course of the next week. In this regard, the speaker believes that the heads of the divisions should start thinking about the future reduction of their divisions. After some debate, the chair said he would return to this issue in the near future, at which time a decision will be made about how to handle this issue.

The speaker then appealed to the heads of the divisions to encourage people not to pay attention to the many rumours circulating in the Jewish community. According to the speaker, the underlying reason for such rumours is a lack of discipline, which is entirely inappropriate.

5 Willi (also Willy) Lages (1901–1971), police officer; joined the NSDAP in 1933 and the SS in 1935; member of the Braunschweig Gestapo, 1936–1940; headed the Amsterdam branch of the Security Police and the SD, 1941–1945; simultaneously headed the Central Office for Jewish Emigration in Amsterdam from March 1941; sentenced to death in the Netherlands in 1949; sentence reduced to life imprisonment in 1952; released and extradited to West Germany in 1966 on grounds of ill health.

6 Hans Carl Christian Blumenthal (1909–1987), tobacconist; joined the NSDAP in 1930 and the SS in 1932; with the SD from 1930; deputy head of the SD in Groningen in 1940; played a leading role in the Amsterdam field office of the Security Police and the SD from 1941; interned in 1945; sentenced to nine years in prison in the Netherlands in 1949; released in 1952.

7 Elisabeth Eitje-Kulker (1887–1945); married to Raphaël Henri Eitje, an important Jewish Council employee; deported to Westerbork on 29 Sept. 1943, and then on 5 April 1944 to Bergen-Belsen, where she perished.

8 This presumably means that those who had received a summons prior to the last roundup were no longer required to report for the time being.

Finally, a question was answered with the statement that there is no intention to issue declarations to indicate that an individual is not on the transport list. Someone then asked for the names of the women who were put on the transport who were the wives of employees working at one of the offices on the day of the operation, and this request was granted.

With no other business to be discussed, the chair closed the meeting.

DOC. 126

In early June 1943 the chairman of the choral society Kunst en Strijd circulates a farewell letter from its former choirmaster, Samuel Henri Englander[1]

Letter, unsigned,[2] Amsterdam, to the former members and sponsors of the choral society K. and S.,[3] dated June 1943[4] (typescript)

Dear Friends,

Following our last practice on 26 October 1941, the main purpose of which was to say farewell to our choirmaster (an afternoon never to be forgotten), our choir was dissolved by the government over the course of 1942. We nursed the secret hope that we would reassemble again soon, but so far this has not happened.

On the contrary, the terrible war continues, and the risk of our best friend and talented choirmaster Englander[5] also being deported was increasing by the day.

On Wednesday, 26 May 1943 we received the devastating news that Englander had been removed from his home with his family[6] and transported[7] to Westenborg,[8] where they remain as we prepare this circular.

Englander has shown himself to be a remarkably strong and above all deeply religious man, with faith in the future. When the police came to take him away, he and his son covered their heads, he gathered his family around the piano, and together they sang a few Jewish prayers, in the presence of the police. In his final letters, he wrote to us: We left singing, in good spirits. We are strong, please be strong too.

1 JHM, Doc. 00 007 649. This document has been translated from Dutch.

2 Based on the document, it appears the letter was composed by Antonie Kuil (1896–1977), book printer; worked at an employment office after the war.

3 The choral society Kunst en Strijd ('Art and Struggle') was established within the League of Workers' Choral Societies in Amsterdam North; various choirs and musical societies still exist under this name in the Netherlands today.

4 The original gives June 1943 as the date. The letter must have been written early in the month, as Englander was deported from Westerbork to Sobibor in the early part of June, and he informed Kuil of that fact in an undated postcard: JHM, Doc. 00 007 654.

5 Samuel Henri Englander (1896–1943), conductor; choirmaster at the Great Synagogue in Amsterdam from 1916; led various choirs in Amsterdam, including Kunst en Strijd from 1921; forced to give up his leadership role in all non-Jewish choirs in 1941; deported to Westerbork on 26 May 1943, and from there to Sobibor, where he was murdered on 11 June 1943.

6 The Englander family included Samuel's wife Judith Englander-Biet (1899–1943) and their children Cato (1922–1943), Lea (1925–1943), and Nathan Samuel (1932–1943).

7 Shortly before 26 May 1943 Englander wrote to Kuil that his deportation was imminent and asked him to forward a previously prepared farewell letter: JHM, Doc. 00 007 648.

8 Correctly: Westerbork.

A farewell letter, which he had written in advance, follows below, with no changes, as he requested.

With regard to the beginning of this letter, please note that he is referring to the gramophone records of the work *Avodath Hakodesh*,[9] performed by the choir.

We have kept this letter for nine months, and now fate compels us to reveal it to you.

Amsterdam City Centre, 4 September 1942

My dear friend Mr Kuil,

As promised, I hereby send you the needles which remained in my pocket last Thursday afternoon due to the dismal mood. You can definitely play two sides with one needle. They are the only ones I still possess. I hope that in doing so I have been of service to you. Should we depart from here, you will at least have the most beautiful and dearest of both of our memories, and the performance of the most important Kunst en Strijd event. Although there is certainly some scope for criticism here and there, anyone who listens to this performance will have to acknowledge that *our never-to-be-forgotten choir* has delivered a performance which is almost beyond all praise. I would like to thank you, Mr Kuil, as the chairman; the full committee; and all the ladies and gentlemen for this from the bottom of my heart.

I would also like to express my sincere thanks, also on behalf of my wife and children, for all of your great friendship and sacrifices during our most difficult years. You will understand what is on our minds. I would rather write this letter too early than too late, as it was announced yesterday afternoon at the Jewish Council that from now on, no proof of identity will be valid any longer. Any person who is taken away must be ready to leave their home and their belongings within ten minutes. We have started packing, and you will understand that this is not easy. There have been many tears and sighs, but they do not help us make any progress. We may be here for another two to three months, but we could also be arrested tonight or tomorrow night. We do not know anything! In any case, I wanted to write this to you in the hope that all of our people will receive this, for which I am grateful to you.

Of course, we all fervently hope that we will be able to greet each other soon, when peace for the whole of Humanity will have arrived.

I pray to the Almighty, Only Judge of the World that we may experience this soon. Amen! I would particularly like to thank you and your wife,[10] on behalf of us all, for the exceptional friendship you have offered us, and I can only add that I hope and wish to be able to repay you in full, but in better times.

I hope you will continue to live a happy life together for many years to come. Do not forget us; we will never forget you either, no matter what might happen.

Best regards to the Poort family and to everyone – too many to mention here.

Hope to see you again soon!

Yours,

S. H. Englander

9 A work by the composer Ernest Bloch (1880–1959) for baritone, mixed choir, and orchestra; first performed in 1934.

10 Anna Maria Kuil-van der Meer (1899–1967).

Friends, let us indeed remain strong, in spite of the devastating setbacks we have suffered and which are still to come. Let us take Englander as an example and have faith in the future. We hope to reconvene after the war and discuss together how we will proceed. It is our sincere hope, of course, that we will continue our beautiful labour of love *with* our much-loved, talented choirmaster.

Keep your spirits up!

DOC. 127

On 2 June 1943 Oskar Witscher sends the 1942 annual report to the trustee of Lippmann, Rosenthal & Co. bank, with information on the handling of Jews' assets[1]

Letter (marked 'confidential') from Lippmann, Rosenthal & Co., Sarphatistraat (Department Secretariat Sch.), signed Witscher[2] (representative of the trustee), Amsterdam, 47–55 Sarphatistraat, to President A. Flesche,[3] trustee of Lippmann, Rosenthal & Co., Central Amsterdam, 170 Herengracht, dated 2 June 1943[4]

Annual report 1942

Please find enclosed the *balance sheet* dated 31 December 1942,[5] signed by Dr von Karger,[6] with the relevant explanatory notes and appendices.

As instructed, the items listed in the profit and loss account were merged into the collective account when they were carried over into the new year.

Pursuant to the guidelines for trustees dated 31 July 1942, I wish to make the following comments about the most important events that occurred in 1942:

The most significant change in the course of 1942 was the issue of *Regulation 58/42 at the end of May.*[7] This regulation removed the previous exemption thresholds of fl. 10,000 for assets and fl. 3,000 for income, and reduced the exemption threshold for personal consumption from fl. 1,000 monthly to fl. 250 per month.

While so far only wealthy Jews and Jews with higher incomes had been obliged to concentrate their capital assets at Lippmann, Rosenthal & Co., Sarphatistraat, *all Jews,*

1 NIOD, 097/B IV. This document has been translated from German.

2 Oskar Witscher (1882–1952), German businessman; lived in the Dutch East Indies from approximately 1909 to 1924; resident in the Netherlands from 1924; joined the NSDAP in 1938; treasurer of the German Chamber of Commerce for the Netherlands from 1939; returned to Germany in 1946.

3 Alfred Flesche (1892–1986), banker; director of Rhodius-Koenigs Bank, 1924–1940; joined the NSDAP in 1933; president of the German Chamber of Commerce for the Netherlands, 1936–1945; fled to Germany in 1944; arrested and released again several times during 1945 and 1946 in Germany and the Netherlands; thought to have returned to Germany permanently in 1950.

4 The original contains the handwritten note: 'File', signature illegible.

5 Not in the file.

6 Dr Walter von Karger (1889–1975), lawyer; director at Deutsche Rentenbank, 1925–1935; partner at Wilhelm Ahlmann Bank in Kiel, 1937–1940; naval officer, 1940–1941; managing director of the Lippmann, Rosenthal & Co. Sarphatistraat bank, 1941–1943; imprisoned in Amersfoort camp, 1943–1944; interned in the Netherlands from 1947 to August 1948; board member of the credit institution Landmaschinen Finanzierungs-AG from 1950.

7 See PMJ 5/136.

including those with modest and extremely modest assets and incomes now have a duty to deposit such assets. As a consequence, the number of accounts and custody accounts we administered grew to 31,000 accounts and 9,300 custody accounts by the end of 1942.

In July and August, and even after that time, such a flood of large, small, and extremely small deliveries of securities poured into our premises, mostly in the form of packages, that prompt processing became impossible with our limited staff, and there was no other alternative than to keep the deposited assets initially without inspecting them, bundled or packed just as they had come. Our vaults soon became too small for this, and additional premises had to be rented. Furthermore, this development coincided with the transfer of the bulk of the securities deposited with Lippmann, Rosenthal & Co., Sarphatistraat, to Berlin.[8] Given the urgency with which this measure obviously had to be carried out, the bundles of securities deposited by our clients were transported to Berlin unsorted. They had been cursorily inspected, but apart from this, they were sent just as they were. As a result, the administration inevitably ran into difficulties, and the consequences of this measure have still not been conclusively overcome even today (June 1943).

Furthermore, Regulation 58/42 obliged Jews to declare *accounts receivable and rights.* In order to process this material, a new *department* has had to be set up,[9] which makes contact with debtors and collects the sums due. Given the massive scale of this task and the lack of trained personnel, this department initially had to limit itself to administratively recording the material that had accrued, to the best of its ability. It was only possible to reinforce the department with expert staff in 1943, when the *inspection* department was closed (on which more below), so that it was able to devote its energies to debt collection.

For more on the progress of this work, please refer to the most recent monthly reports.

The accounts receivable and rights to be declared also include the *benefits due* to Jews *from insurance companies* under current life assurance and pension policies. To deal with this sector, with its particular circumstances, it proved necessary to establish a special department that has since operated under the name *'policies department'*. At present (June 1943) this department has completed the inspection and registration of the policies deposited and is awaiting the issue of a prospective regulation that is to terminate Jews' insurance policies, making it possible for debts to be collected in the short term.[10] For the time being, it is processing each case individually.

Moreover, Regulation 58/42 ordered *gold, silver, jewels, and pieces of art* under Jewish ownership *to be deposited* with Lippmann, Rosenthal & Co., Sarphatistraat, and in this case as well, given the current shortage of expert staff, the inspection and registration of the more or less valuable material that accrued could only progress gradually. To begin with, the assets deposited had to be stored, and the premises required for this had to be

8 In June 1942, due to fears of a possible Allied invasion, all securities and bonds that had been received up until that point were sent to two banks in Berlin. Most of them were returned to Amsterdam at the end of 1943.

9 Presumably the accounts receivable department, a subdivision of the third department, which dealt with the sums owed to Jews by non-Jews, as well as Jews' insurance policies.

10 Regulation on the Termination of Jews' Insurance Policies, *VOBl-NL*, no. 54/1943, pp. 204–206, 11 June 1943.

obtained. As a consequence, a special *Commodities Department* had to be set up and organized. That it had to begin work with a considerable administrative backlog requires no further explanation. Only in the spring of 1943 was it to some extent up to date with its inspection, classification, and registration work. Its organization had to be modified and expanded on an ongoing basis, depending on the nature and volume of the materials that accrued; it was not possible for them to be accommodated entirely in the Muiderschans[11] building alone, in view of the amounts of items that were accruing.

The deportation of Jews from Holland began towards the middle of the year. In parallel, *the voluntary emigration operation* (processing through multiple official agencies) *came to an end*; the staff this freed up moved over to the Commodities Department.

Another significant change took place towards the end of the year. Whereas up until then the Jews had been reliant for their living expenses and the payment of their taxes etc. on Lippmann, Rosenthal & Co., Sarphatistraat, the Inspection Department of which examined their applications and approved or rejected them wholly or in part, towards the end of the year a senior authority transferred this task to the Jewish Council in Amsterdam, to which a fixed sum was made available for this purpose by Lippmann, Rosenthal & Co., Sarphatistraat, every month as of 1 January 1943, at the request of the representative for the City of Amsterdam.[12] The payment of taxes was stopped as well, and overdue tax payments were settled with a flat-rate sum. (The flat-rate sum was paid in 1943.) In connection with this, the *Inspection Department was closed*, some of its staff were made redundant, and some were moved to other departments with staff shortages (bank, custody accounts, accounts receivable, policies).

The list below provides information about the sums irretrievably disbursed in 1942:

Sums released for Jews by the Inspection Department:	
Living expenses	fl. 5,743,014.78
Taxes	fl. 10,601,108.38
Jewish Council	fl. 1,610,523.26
Mortgage interest and repayments	fl. 322,105.00
Various purposes	fl. 1,225,609.63
Subtotal: for Jews	fl. 19,502,361.05
Own expenses	fl. 1,665,121.32
Costs of requisitioning household effects (special household effects account I)	fl. 806,202.94
Total	fl. 21,973,685.31

With regard to the sums released by the Inspection Department and the bank's own expenses, I refer to the appendices to the balance sheet. In brief, the item 'requisitioning household effects' covers the following activities: on the basis of one of the Führer's decrees, the household effects and cultural goods that become available in the course of the resettlement and emigration of Jews are at the disposal of the Ministry for the Occupied Eastern Territories and are requisitioned here in the Netherlands by a special task

11 Sarphatistraat, on which the bank's building was located, bore the name of the Jewish doctor Samuel Sarphati (1813–1866); from August 1942 to 1945 it was called Muiderschans.

12 Werner Schröder.

force,[13] provided they are suitable for this purpose. The rest is transferred to Lippmann, Rosenthal & Co., Sarphatistraat, and processed according to the guidelines issued by senior authorities, which cannot be commented upon in detail here. The resettlement and emigration of Jews is a political operation, the implementation of which here lies in the hands of the SD, which has set up an organization for this purpose (the Central Office for Jewish Emigration) and has a workforce of employees and casual staff in its service. The costs incurred by the SD for this work are paid by Lippmann, Rosenthal & Co., Sarphatistraat, provided the invoices, declarations, etc. presented for settlement are marked: 'checked' or 'materially correct'. Further to this, reference is made here to the appendices to the balance sheet. In the course of this operation, a large quantity of household effects, furniture, pictures, carpets, fixtures and fittings, etc., which are not suitable for the task force of the Ministry for the Occupied Eastern Territories, have been arriving at Lippmann, Rosenthal & Co. for safekeeping and utilization, and are processed here with other materials and utilized by the Commodities Department.

In October detailed *guidelines* were issued concerning the utilization of securities, policies, accounts receivable, jewels, gold and silver, pictures, carpets, stamps, coins, and household effects. These have been amended or supplemented many times in the intervening period.

With regard to the *progress made in the handling* of the Jewish capital assets deposited with Lippmann, Rosenthal & Co., I refer to my monthly reporting. I enclose a list dated 30 April 1943 once again, for the sake of completeness.[14]

During the year under review, a stake was acquired in Phöbus N.V.[15] A balance sheet dated 31 December 1942 is enclosed.[16] This subsidiary was intended to collect Jewish accounts receivable abroad, insofar as this was possible. The accounts receivable were ceded to it by the Jews, who simultaneously issued mandates addressed to their foreign debtors and gave their account details, with which the Jews instructed the foreign debtors to pay the assets in question to Phöbus N.V. or place them at its disposal. Only time will tell the extent to which these documents fulfil their purpose; from a formal point of view, both the cessions and the mandates issued on the basis of Article 7 of Regulation 58/42 are null and void. At the same time, it has not been possible to find a more legally effective means of transferring assets that does better justice to the formal requirements and would stand up to any objections from foreign debtors. The total sum of the accounts receivable requisitioned in this way currently amounts to fl. 15,771,561.51 and is shown in the balance sheet on both sides. As indicated above, however, this is just a statistic, no more than a projection.

The number of *members of staff* at the bank was 482 at the end of 1942, compared to 265 at the end of 1941.

13 The Führer's decree of 1 March 1942 gave the Reich Ministry for the Occupied Eastern Territories a mandate to have cultural goods owned by Jews and opponents of National Socialism confiscated by the Rosenberg Task Force: BArch, B 323/257.

14 Not included in the file.

15 N.V. Phöbus, Association for Administration, Management, and Financial Affairs, was founded in Oct. 1942 but was unable to function because foreign states refused to settle German financial demands.

16 Not included in the file.

The changes that have occurred since then, which I would like to refer to under the rubrics of collective account,[17] handling of enemy Jews,[18] mixed marriages, and transfer to the VVRA,[19] have fallen within the 1943 financial year.

Heil Hitler!

DOC. 128

On 3 June 1943 Philip Mechanicus gives an account of the conflicts between German and Dutch Jews at Westerbork camp[1]

Handwritten diary of Philip Mechanicus,[2] entry for 3 June 1943

Thursday, 3 June

The other day a Dutch Jew and a German Jew had a disagreement about a seat on a bench. The Dutchman, who had been sitting there, stood up when a friend approached in order to say a word to him, and the German took this opportunity to sit down on the seat. After his conversation the Dutchman turned to the German and said: 'Excuse me, but this seat is occupied.' Whereupon the German snorted: 'Occupied, occupied, who are occupied – die Deutscher or die Holländer?'[3] The Dutch Jews took great umbrage at this tactless remark, which quickly did the rounds, not because the joke was in bad taste, but because it expressed exactly what the German Jews *really* feel about the Dutch Jews in the camp. This is one of the most sensitive issues you can raise, and you do so very tentatively and with the utmost caution.

There is something smouldering under the surface between these brothers of the same race – the fact that they cannot stand each other. The Germans despise their Dutch fellow inmates and the Dutch hate the German Jews, not as fiercely as they hate the German National Socialists, it is true, but they do hate them because they are *Germans–Prussians*. It is a complicated relationship. The German Jews act as if they are in charge here, just as the German Aryans are accustomed to acting as if they are in charge wherever they are.

17 On 24 Nov. 1942 a collective account was set up by order of Commissioner General Hans Fischböck, to which all credit balances held by Jews were to be transferred from 1943 onwards. Their individual credit balances were therefore de facto cancelled.

18 'Enemy Jews' in this context refers to Jews with the nationality of one of the Allied countries.

19 The Asset Management and Pensions Institute (Vermögensverwaltungs- und Rentenanstalt, VVRA, also VVR) had been established in May 1941 by order of Reich Commissioner Seyss-Inquart. Its task was to administer assets stolen in the Netherlands. After the war it was liquidated by the Netherlands Management Institute.

1 NIOD, 244/391. The original document is in Dutch. Published in Philip Mechanicus, *In Dépôt: Dagboek uit Westerbork* (Amsterdam: Van Gennep, 1964), pp. 25–29. The diary entry published here is a slightly edited version of the English translation in Philip Mechanicus, *Waiting for Death*, trans. Irene R. Gibbons (London: Calder and Boyars, 1968), pp. 29–35, by kind permission of Marion Boyars Publishing.

2 Philip Mechanicus (1889–1944), journalist; employed at various newspapers in the Netherlands and the Dutch East Indies; worked as a foreign correspondent for the *Algemeen Handelsblad* from 1920; detained in Sept. 1942 and deported to Westerbork via Amersfoort camp; deported to Bergen-Belsen in March 1944 and in Oct. 1944 to Auschwitz, where he was shot shortly afterwards.

3 'Die Deutscher' (correctly: 'die Deutschen'; 'the Germans') and 'die Holländer' ('the Dutch') are in German in the original.

They think they have a right to do so. Many ask their Dutch fellow Jews: 'What care and consideration have you ever given to us? What did you do to make our lot easier when we were flung in here by fate before you were ever subjected to the blight of the National Socialist regime? They reproach them, saying: 'You have fallen short in your duty as human beings.' To what extent is not very clear.

This camp was set up in 1939 for Jews who were roaming about in Holland illegally or as stateless persons. Some of the Jews who had made fruitless attempts to get into the United States on the *St. Louis*, which went on sailing demonstratively to and fro off the American coast, also found themselves in the camp.[4] Likewise the Jews who had been accommodated in different labour camps in Holland. By means of fixed voluntary donations Jews made it possible for many other Jews to stay in Amsterdam and elsewhere. The so-called Committee for Special Emergencies[5] defrayed the cost of admitting the Jews to Westerbork and maintaining them there. That was no small matter.

There are Germans who play this down and say the Dutch Jews ought to have done more, much more. That is one grievance. A second grievance is that the Dutch Jews did nothing to arrange for or encourage an outlet to America to be opened up for their German protégés who had come in perfectly legally. Either the money was not made available or they did not bring enough pressure to bear upon the Dutch government along these lines. Prime Minister Colijn[6] had held out a prospect of this being done, so, when they were put behind barbed wire in Holland, it came as a great disappointment to them. That is the second point. It is a matter of how you judge things. When someone feels embittered, and many Germans *do* feel embittered as a result of four years of camp life, he will demand the last drop from the barrel.

To explain and justify their dictatorial attitude the Germans say: 'We were in the camp long before the Dutch came. We have stood up to the miseries of the National Socialist regime since 1933 and have been chased perhaps two or three times from the places where we lived, but you only began to suffer these miseries in 1940.' That is no longer a question of *judgement*, but of character and comradeship. If anyone wanted to argue the point, he could say: 'Yes indeed, you *were* struck down by fate before the Dutch Jews, and you *have* endured all these miseries over a longer period than they have, but when you arrived in Holland they came to your assistance at the very first call for help, although not exactly in the way a number of you would have wished. At any rate, you *enjoyed* the hospitality of the Dutch Jews. And you could have shown a similar spirit of camaraderie and brotherly love when they were finally put in [the camp] beside you, overtaken by the same fate, and you could have divided everything up equally, even if only for the very reason that they were on home ground.'

4 In May 1939 the *St. Louis* left the port of Hamburg with 900 Jewish refugees on board, bound for Cuba. Its passengers were refused entry to Cuba because they had been sold invalid visas, and they were not taken in by other North American states either. Britain, France, Belgium, and the Netherlands all declared their willingness to take in some of the refugees after they had returned to Europe; only about half the refugees survived the war. See PMJ 2/290, 292, and 297.

5 This presumably refers to the Committee for Special Jewish Interests (CBJB), which was founded in March 1933 to support refugees from Germany.

6 Hendrikus Colijn (1869–1944), career soldier; member of the Dutch parliament from 1909; held various ministerial posts; prime minister of the Netherlands several times, 1925–1926 and 1933–1939; arrested in 1941 for supporting the resistance; placed under house arrest in Thuringia, where he died of a heart attack.

The first Dutch Jews did not come to Westerbork until the summer of 1942, accompanied by part of the Jewish Council from Amsterdam. The German Registration Department remained in the hands of the German Jews under the direction of Schlesinger.[7] When the Jewish Council had to plead for rights or obtain privileges for the Dutch Jews, it first had to approach the all-powerful head of the German Jews with the appropriate obsequiousness. It is generally known that Schlesinger does not pay any heed to the Jewish Council and treats it as a *quantité négligeable*[8] and it has very little authority. If a Dutch Jew wants to obtain anything, an exemption or a job [in the camp], then it is preferable for him to apply direct to the German Jews in authority if he knows them or else through German friends.

This does not mean to say that the German Jews have left the Dutch Jews out of things – oh no! Up to a certain level they have brought them into the administration of the camp. Dutch Jews are in charge of hospital barracks or assist in them, Jews, male and female, have become orderlies, nurses, barrack leaders, and are employed in a fairly large number of lower-level jobs, as stokers, as window cleaners, barrack cleaners, porters, or keep order in the camp or serve as members of the Flying Column.[9] In view of the large number of Dutch Jews coming in regularly and in view also of the large number of Dutch invalids and elderly folk admitted to the hospital barracks, the German Jews could not refuse to let the Dutch play a part in this way – indeed it was convenient for them to hand over certain jobs to the Dutch. But they held on resolutely to the key posts and more or less every one of the important jobs so that they could be in control of the whole organization and could give priority to the interests of German Jews.

The succession of German SS Commandants in the camp undoubtedly fostered the supremacy of the German Jews. Blood is, in short, thicker than water. When the transportation of Jews to Poland to join the 'polizeilicher Arbeitseinsatz'[10] began in the summer of 1942, the German Commandant at that time, Deppner,[11] promoted the two thousand or so German Jews still remaining out of the original three thousand to the status of Long-Term Residents who were not liable for deportation. One can only guess whose influence was responsible for this preferential treatment. It is said that the Commandant thought that the German Jews had suffered enough, and that it was the turn of the Dutch Jews now. But sentimentality of this kind or rather such sensitivity with regard to the just apportioning of all the violence and injustice inflicted on the Jews, is *not* as a rule in keeping with the National Socialist regime.

7 Kurt Schlesinger (1902–1963), mechanic; emigrated from Germany to the Netherlands in 1939; held at Westerbork from 1940; became camp elder in Feb. 1942; responsible for compiling deportation lists from August 1943; liberated at Westerbork; testified for the defence at the trial of camp commandant Gemmeker; subsequently emigrated to the USA.

8 French in the original: 'as if it didn't exist'.

9 At Westerbork the *Fliegende Kolonne* was responsible for transporting baggage and for other auxiliary duties when deportations were under way.

10 German in the original: 'police labour deployment'.

11 Erich Deppner (1910–2005), lawyer; joined the NSDAP in 1932 and the SS in 1933; first German commandant of Westerbork camp, July–August 1942; participated in shootings in Dutch camps; prisoner of war in the Soviet Union, 1945–1950; subsequently worked for the German Federal Intelligence Service (BND) and as an industrial and business consultant; later charged with involvement in the shootings, and acquitted in 1964.

One might venture to suppose that in settling Jewish affairs the Germans preferred to carry on discussions or negotiations or other business with German Jews than with Dutch. The example provided by Amsterdam gives rise to this assumption, namely the *Expositur*, which is directed by a German (Austrian), Edwin Sluzker, originally from Bukovina. They are closer to each other and understand one another better, both psychologically and as far as language and ways of behaviour are concerned. Deppner's successor, Dischner,[12] and Dischner's successor, Gemmeker, consistently maintained the position of pre-eminence of the German Jews. The last-mentioned even has a Jewish adjutant in the person of Mr Todtmann,[13] who forms the link between the Commandant and the Registration Department. The adjutant wears a uniform. He [Gemmeker] has awarded the now famous red stamps to German Jews. These safeguard their position and, moreover, give them certain concessions like freedom of movement within the camp and other privileges. So the Germans have bound the German Jews to themselves to a certain degree and play them off against the Dutch Jews. Not all German Jews will accept this ugly role, but some – and these are not the morally strongest among them – do. They feel invulnerable.

The German Jews have undeniably abused their position of supremacy and continue to do so. They form, as it were, an almost exclusive association for the protection of the interests of German Jews. As individuals and acting together, they do their best to save all Germans brought here from being deported and endeavour to keep them here. They have done this from the time that Dutch Jews began arriving at Westerbork. In this way they have, in point of fact, handed over the Dutch Jews to the Germans to suit their own convenience. Wherever possible, they have got the Germans into jobs and have kept the Germans here. The Registration Department with Schlesinger at its head has been able to do this. For example, during the seven months that I have been in the hospital,[14] it has *nearly* always been Dutch Jews who have been deported. On one single occasion German Jews were sent too. The same complaint can be heard from the residential barracks. In the last few months the nursing staff has been considerably thinned out, and it is the best nurses who have in some preordained way disappeared – *Dutch* Jews. The same thing happens in the other barracks – German Jews are seldom to be found among the deportees.

During the past five or six weeks, Dutch Jews who had up till then been doing certain jobs have been systematically replaced by Germans – as barrack leaders, porters, and foremen. Preference is given to the baptized. Among the Germans who have jobs to give out, the baptized Jews get priority. They are a clan, the members of which keep passing the ball to one another. The male nurse Gottschalk takes the lead. I have heard of the case of a leading Dutch Jew who was recommended by an honest German because of

12 Josef Hugo Dischner (1902–1989), commercial employee and window dresser; joined the NSDAP and the SS in 1932; worked full-time for the SS from 1933; on Himmler's personal staff, 1934–1936; worked in the civil administration of the General Government, 1940–1943; briefly camp commandant at Westerbork, Sept.–Oct. 1942; called up to the Waffen SS in March 1944.

13 Heinz Todtmann (b. 1908), journalist; emigrated from Germany to the Netherlands in 1939; a baptized Jew, he lived from Nov. 1939 in refugee camps; wrote the screenplay for the film about Westerbork made on Gemmeker's orders in spring 1944; liberated at Westerbork in 1945; is thought to have either returned to Germany or emigrated to Brazil.

14 After his detention in Sept. 1942, Mechanicus had been severely mistreated at Amersfoort camp; as a result, he was hospitalized at Westerbork from Nov. 1942 to mid 1943.

his abilities for a position in the Information Service, but he was very politely, but quite improperly, sent packing and palmed off by the powers that be. The most annoying case recently has been the appointment of Mr Grünfeld[15] as head of the Jewish Council instead of the notary Spier[16] who had moved to the 'Jan van Schaffelaar' camp at Barneveld.[17] It was said that the Commandant had more faith in a German Jew, but the German Jews accepted this as a matter of course. The Jewish Council has thus become a mere tool in their hands.

The German Jews do not only act as leaders by virtue of their official positions in the camp. They have evolved a certain measure of control in another respect, which creates permanent tension as far as the relationship between German and Dutch Jews is concerned. They dictate and bawl and snarl and bark and shriek and intimidate the others, often just like the National Socialists or Prussian soldiers. It is in their blood and without this they do not appear to thrive, they are not happy. This flaw is to be found mainly in the lower-ranking staff, in barrack leaders, porters, kitchen bosses, foremen, people who, for the most part, have been given authority and a say in things for the first time in their lives. They have been given some power and they abuse it completely. The Dutch Jews, who are hard put to it in any case, do not 'like' this tone of command, this throwing one's weight around, this self-importance – they hate it and the German Jews as well. Of course, the Dutch Jews are not all nice, and there is a good deal of riff-raff amongst them too, but they are used to different things. The German Jew, accustomed to *Tüchtigkeit*[18] and *Gründlichkeit*,[19] the German Jews cannot endure the lack of discipline or the touch of anarchy and individualism to be found in the Dutch Jews. That is why they do not like them. Also because of their matter-of-fact nature and their lack of enthusiasm for carrying out the measures laid down by the authorities. They despise them and show this openly. Leaving out of account the personal feelings of liking and friendship existing between German and Dutch Jews, and these are fairly common, there is a sharp emotional rift between the two communities. The Dutch say: 'Back to "Bocheland"[20] with them, bags and baggage; they don't belong here with us.' The great question is how many even of the Dutch Jews will ever see their native land and their homes again. The future is certainly not rosy as far as the German Jews are concerned. A large proportion of them do not want to return to Germany, which has given them such bitter experiences and such grim memories. But they cannot yet see where they, as stateless persons, will be accommodated after the war. This paralysing feeling makes them morally very vulnerable and, perhaps, over-sensitive.

15 Correctly: Fritz Grünberg (b. 1911); emigrated from Germany to the Netherlands; Jewish Council representative at Westerbork in 1943; returned to Amsterdam after liberation and emigrated to the USA in 1946.

16 Eduard Spier (1902–1980), notary; led the Jewish Council's Information Service from 1941; Jewish Council representative at Westerbork from August 1942; held in Barneveld camp, April–Sept. 1943; deported to Theresienstadt on 4 Sept. 1944; active in rebuilding the Jewish community in the Netherlands after the war.

17 Schaffelaar Castle was one of the two buildings at Barneveld where approximately 500 'protected Jews' were held between Dec. 1942 and Sept. 1943: see Doc. 102.

18 German in the original: 'efficiency'.

19 German in the original: 'thoroughness'.

20 The original uses the term 'Moffrika', a portmanteau of 'Mof' and 'Africa'. 'Mof' is a long-standing satirical or pejorative Dutch term for Germans, used predominantly during and after the Second World War.

DOC. 129
Storm SS, 4 June 1943: a malicious article on the deportation of the Jews[1]

Farewell

We have had to say farewell to our guests, guests who have 'shared' our bread with us for centuries and have been able to claim the best pieces for themselves. We have seen them off and have shouted our last farewell to them, at a site in Polderweg in Amsterdam East.[2] They were wearing large insignias – six-pointed stars – which behind the fence there served as proof that they belonged to the group travelling to Poland.

And so the Jews have officially disappeared from the Netherlands.[3] There are still some wandering around, but they only make up the plucky rearguard.

The Jews have bid farewell to the Netherlands, and we – the Dutch – have bid farewell to them. There were floods of tears on both sides, and we National Socialists were present and witnessed this leave-taking with a sense of bafflement. We saw the Dutch people taking their leave after this heartbreaking farewell. But we also decided to have a look behind the 'bars', behind the 'barbed wire', and to subject the Jewish travellers to a further investigation. What a difference! How alien this Jewish people has remained to us in every respect, in spite of the fact that they have lived here for many centuries. Off went the Dutch people, let us not call them good Dutch people here, extremely stiffly, as if they were opposed to the violence allegedly done to the Jews. Off they went with tears in their eyes, without any luggage, although they came here as the porters for the Jewish rabble. They were in a dismal mood, and we are convinced they continued to think of their Jewish friends for at least that whole evening, that they imagined where they might be at that time, which inhumane treatment they would be receiving at that hour and that minute, and many other such things.

And the Jews? While the Aryans withdrew, the Jews disappeared through the gate and were at the point of departure for faraway Poland. They were disappearing just as they had arrived in the past. While taking their final steps, they had to carry their own luggage, as their white friends were no longer allowed to accompany them. That was hard going. Even the mothers had to take their own children in their arms, and that too was a superhuman effort. But all this had also been done once upon a time by those who came to this country for a short or a longer period in the hope of finding a provisional land of milk and honey here, firmly resolved to find another land once the milk had been drunk and the honey had been digested, which they would then call their homeland.

And so they had gone through the gate to embark on their journey to the new promised land. We had expected a terrible outcry there behind the 'bars'. We had an image of the Wailing Wall in our minds, but the reality was different. The Wailing Wall was

1 *Storm SS: Blad der Nederlandsche SS*, vol. 3, no. 9, 4 June 1943, p. 4. This article has been translated from Dutch.

2 An assembly point was located on Polderweg, a street near Muiderpoort railway station. On 26 May 1943 Jews detained during a large roundup in Amsterdam were gathered here for transportation to Westerbork. The newspaper commissioned photo documentation of the area on this day, parts of which are published in Presser, *Ondergang*, vol. 1, p. 368.

3 It was not until Oct. 1943 that Reich Commissioner Seyss-Inquart deemed the deportation of Jews from the Netherlands to be virtually complete: see Doc. 146.

there, but it was outside the fence, where the non-Jews were bewailing their lost friends. Inside, however, things looked different. Once the formalities were over, completed by members of the Jewish Council, so that everything happened within a small aggenebbes[4] clique, the 'gentlemen' and 'ladies' found a place to sit in the sunshine. It had been many years since they had enjoyed as much sunshine as they did on this, the day of their relocation. It may have reminded some of them of the old days in Zandvoort,[5] in the same way as this comparison with that Jewish seaside resort came to our minds.

There they were, sitting on long benches, content and quiet at first, as they still had to become accustomed to this situation. But once they had done so and had adapted a little to feeling the sun's rays, their tongues started wagging. Small groups formed everywhere. Laughter and cheerfulness abounded. They seemed to reconcile themselves easily to the new situation.

There was absolutely no trace of any resistance or even any pent-up anger amidst this mass of Jewish bodies. Neither was there any sense of resignation to the circumstances, at least as we would understand this – if it were us, there would always be a degree of pride involved. There they were, sitting on the ground and eating their pancakes or chewing a sausage contentedly. There they were, shouting for water or milk, which the Jewish Council gave to them with sandwiches. And the Jewish Council had to ask around for mugs for this liquid, as there were no more mugs to be seen anywhere. Some of the borrowed drinking cups then reappeared from the bags and bundles. The Jews appeared to have interpreted these objects as farewell gifts.

This, however, was a sight that did not surprise us at all. What did surprise us was the fact that the two of us could walk among a couple of thousand 'enemies' without being disturbed, as we heard no comments from anywhere. Not a single hostile look, no one condescendingly turning their back on us, no sneer, nothing. Now don't think now: 'That is all well and good, but with machine guns aimed at you and bayonets pricking your belly, you would think twice before doing any of that.' There were no machine guns or bayonets to be seen here, and later in the day there was hardly even a uniform to be seen.

People always talk about the cowardice of the Jews. The reason for this has never been clearer to us than it was on this sunny afternoon. Would it ever occur to us to invite those who are about to deport us to eat a pancake with us? Would it ever occur to us, if it was us sitting there and the Jews were about to see us off, to ask them: 'Will you also take a picture of us?'

But that is just Jewish humour, you might say. However, this humour is also an expression of a specific attitude to life. Let us never forget that.

The Jews themselves, however, inspire little interest in us. That has always been the case and will not change now that we have bid farewell to them. What we think is important is what the Jews have achieved here among our people.

And the attitude of the non-Jews gave us a definite answer to this. Back then we managed to make sure that the Jewish mentality – which was on display when the Jews were riding their bicycle taxis[6] – was kept under control. Slave labour was thus prohibited. But

4 Correctly: *achenebissj*, Dutch Yiddish term meaning 'miserable' or 'shabby looking'.

5 A popular seaside resort in the province of North Holland.

6 The reference is to a *traptaxi*, a kind of bicycle rickshaw operating as a taxi. They appeared during the war when there was a shortage of other taxis and fuel.

here we saw all this reappear. A carrier tricycle carrying a fat Jewess, blissfully reclining on a pile of rags which had to go with her all the way to Poland, propelled by one youngster cycling and one pushing, both without a star. An edifying spectacle, and a clear indication that this measure was taken for good reason at the time.

And this was not the only vehicle the Jews used. They arrived in trucks, pony taxis, carriages, and even cars. Once again, they had to make use of the luxury items that they used to think had been created for them.

The true extent to which the veneration of Jews had penetrated our people became clear to us when we witnessed this farewell. How much blood has already been contaminated by the Jews, and how many bastards are walking our streets? We only got a true sense of the answer when we saw these scenes. Dull statistics were brought to life here. Reality confirmed our expectations.

But there is something even worse. We were well on our way to creating a respectable, blonde type of Jew with an almost Aryan face. They were walking around here, these Jews and Jewesses, a well-known floozy among them. Platinum blonde hair, so that no one was aware of her Jewish blood. There were dozens who could easily have become the bride of a good young Aryan man, without the man thinking for one instant that he was choosing a Jewess to be his wife. This posed a risk, and it was a great risk. It is good that measures have been taken.

And so the Jews have disappeared. We have bid our farewells. We saw them disappear into the trains. We did not feel sorry for them. And no one who had seen them would have felt sorry for them. Thousands of friends of the Jews, had they been present at such a departure, would have asked themselves whether they should have such 'humane' thoughts for those people and in that situation.

For us, it was not hard to bid farewell.

DOC. 130

On 5 June 1943 Richard Süsskind has to inform his fellow prisoners in Vught that all the children are to be taken to a special children's camp[1]

Public notice, signed Süsskind[2] (The Camp Management),[3] to all camp residents, Vught, dated 5 June 1943

It is with great regret that we have to inform you of a terrible calamity that has befallen us.

On orders from higher up, all children aged between 0 and around 16 must leave the camp in order to be housed – as we have been informed – at a special Children's Camp.[4]

1 JHM, Doc. 00 000 785. Published in facsimile in Joods Historisch Museum Amsterdam, *Documents of the Persecution of the Dutch Jewry*, p. 111. This document has been translated from Dutch.

2 Richard Süsskind (1910–1944), fashion designer; emigrated from Berlin to the Netherlands in 1933; deported to Westerbork in Jan. 1943, and from there to Vught, where he was camp elder until Oct. 1943; on 15 Nov. 1943 deported from Vught to Auschwitz, where he perished.

3 Vught camp was under German management. The Germans appointed Richard Süsskind to head the Jewish self-administration in the camp.

The rules for implementation have been defined as follows:

1. Up to 4 years old (children aged 0 to 3), the mothers must accompany their children.
2. Children aged 4 to 16 must be accompanied by one of their parents. Those who have been put to work in industry must remain here, but the father can accompany the child if he has not been put to work. If both parents are working, one of the parents will accompany the child.
3. Those fathers and mothers who have not been put to work, i.e. have not been assigned to camp work either, may both accompany their children.

   Only the following can be exempted:
   a. Half-Jews;
   b. Those whose 'Abstammungsverfahren' (proof of ancestry) has been requested or is pending.

As we are fully aware of the scope of this terrible blow which has befallen us, and the suffering affecting us all is hard to overcome, the Kommandantur[5] will maintain peace and order in the camp. We therefore kindly request you to observe peace and order as much as possible, in order that we be spared an even greater catastrophe due to stricter conduct on the part of the SS.

We will use all of our human strength to try to save anything that can still be saved, up to the last moment. We do not wish to leave you in any doubt, as this concerns approximately 3,000 people who will leave the camp on two transports on Sunday and Monday. Each person must wait to be summoned.

Finally, we would like to inform you that there is hope that the children will be housed here in the country, and that the parents will be able to return if they wish.

In view of this terrible situation, we declare an eight-day period of mourning for the entire Jewish camp and forbid any forms of entertainment until Saturday, 12 June, at 5 p.m.

Greetings to you all.

4 On 6 June 1943 children up to 3 years of age were deported with one parent to Westerbork; children between 4 and 16 years of age followed on 7 June 1943. The next day 3,017 persons in total (including 1,269 children from Vught) were deported from Westerbork to Sobibor, where they were murdered shortly after their arrival.

5 German in the original: 'camp headquarters'.

DOC. 131

On 6 June 1943 Otto Bene informs the Foreign Office in Berlin about the outcome of a major raid in Amsterdam[1]

Letter from the representative of the Reich Foreign Office (D Pol 3 no. 8/no. 987–2 copies), signed Bene, The Hague, to the Foreign Office, Berlin (received 10 June 1943), dated 6 June 1943[2]

Subject: confidential report from the Senior Commander of the Security Police[3] re: the Jews.

In his confidential report to the Reich Commissioner,[4] the Senior Commander of the Security Police gives the following interesting account of the deportation of Jews from Amsterdam Central Station:

After only a small proportion of the Amsterdam Jews had complied with their obligation to report to the authorities in response to the directive issued by the Commissioner General for Security[5] concerning the residence of Jews in the city of Amsterdam in contrast to those in the provinces,[6] the German Security Police made it incumbent upon the Jewish Council to provide 7,000 Jewish functionaries[7] for labour deployment. Yet again, only a small proportion of the individuals summoned turned up on the appointed date.[8] Our previous practice of rounding up Jews using individual summonses or an order imposing a general obligation to report (eviction order) therefore appeared to have failed, while the Jewish Council evidently wanted to let things come to a head in a trial of strength. Consequently, following meticulous preparation, *the historic Amsterdam ghetto (Jewish quarter I) was surrounded, sealed off, and cleared of Jews residence by residence,* with the involvement of the German Order Police, in the early morning of 26 May. Almost 3,000 Jews were picked up, made ready to travel, and transported to Westerbork, from where some of them have already been transferred on to the East. During this operation, it was notable that many Jews appeared just a short while after the call to the assembly points was issued by loudspeaker, and that they brought already tied-up, properly labelled pieces of luggage with them, so people had evidently been expecting to be taken away at any moment. By contrast, while the ghetto was being scoured, Jews were also picked up who had kept themselves hidden there with forged identity cards, and likewise a number of suspicious Aryans. Thanks to the simultaneous surveillance of the railway stations, several dozen Jews were prevented from emigrating illegally. Despite the streets being closed, disruptions of order and economic life were largely avoided during this day-long operation. The population, which is said to be Jew-friendly overall, did not display any strong reactions.

1 PA AA, R 99 428. This document has been translated from German.

2 The original contains handwritten notes in the margin: '1) Initially to group leaders for information, 2) Pol [Political Affairs] II for information, 3) file', signed with illegible initials.

3 Wilhelm Harster.

4 Arthur Seyss-Inquart.

5 Hanns Albin Rauter.

6 See Doc. 117.

7 This refers to Jewish Council employees.

8 See Doc. 123.

During the clearance of the ghetto, Jewish functionaries and businesspeople were also deported along with the others, irrespective of previous exemption stamps. Yet the proportion of Jewish Council members captured in this way was relatively small, so evidently the Jewish Council was largely able to evade this roundup as well. The resentment among the poorer Jews has grown even greater as a result, because they mostly blame the Jewish Council for the fact that better-off Jews have allegedly been spared again and again. People say they would welcome the rapid closing-down of this Jewish Council, which merely engages in its own machinations under the cloak of charity.[9] After this major operation, the head of the Jewish Council himself declared that the Jewish Council had gone through a triple Dunkirk on 26 May,[10] while attempts were made to have a number of captured Jewish Council members released again, attempts which the Security Police categorically rejected, however.[11]

Apart from the increased hopes of an invasion in the near future, the reason for the failure to comply with the orders concerning mandatory registration is also likely to be the fact that the *Jews no longer have any confidence in the Vught and Westerbork camps.* They are convinced they will not stay there long, even at Vught, particularly as Jews have already had to be deported from there via Westerbork to the East in the meantime.[12] These considerations now appear to have robbed the Jews of any willingness to report voluntarily, so the rest are waiting to be picked up individually, if they do not actually prefer to go underground.

The number of fugitives is also likely to have once again risen considerably recently, but because the willingness of the Dutch to hide Jews has simultaneously been declining, it is becoming *ever more difficult to find places to live illegally.* The Dutch have come to have a clear idea of the punishments for aiding and abetting Jews and are even less inclined to shield idle Jews because they themselves are being taken to Germany for labour deployment more and more often. As a result, in the overwhelming majority of cases, it is only possible for Jews to be taken in by Aryans if they deceive their hosts about the race to which they belong (forged identity cards). Where the fact that they are fugitive Jews is known, the Jew-friendliness mostly only lasts until the Jews' (sometimes not insignificant) stock of assets is exhausted, whereupon they are then sent out of the house under some pretext. In a few cases, Jews fleeced of their assets have consequently reported for labour deployment in the East themselves, due to their lack of funds. Housing difficulties have also led Jews to seek shelter in barns as well as in hunting lodges in more heavily wooded areas. On many occasions, cellars under buildings and in gardens have been discovered, into which Jews retreat when they are in danger.

In turn, there has been an increase in denunciations of fugitive Jews. Some of these are anonymous denunciations, while some denunciations have come from the circles of

9 The Jewish Council was dissolved by the German authorities on 29 Sept. 1943.

10 The meaning here is unclear. It may have been a reference to a disaster or defeat coinciding with a partial rescue: most Jewish Council employees evaded the arrests, and a large number of Allied troops evaded capture through the evacuation from Dunkirk in June 1940.

11 On 27 May 1943 the chairmen of the Jewish Council held a meeting to discuss the raid and potential candidates for release with the German officials responsible for these matters: see NIOD, 182/4.

12 See Doc. 130.

known middlemen. Thanks to the rewards[13] offered, several thousand Jews who are not exempt from deportation have been brought in since March, among them 1,500 criminal and fugitive Jews.

Unless they are in mixed marriages, *Protestant* Jews have moved into a special barracks at Westerbork camp (345 persons in total). Some baptized Jews who find themselves in Vught camp have refused to make use of this opportunity, because they are not confident that the Protestant Church has the power to prevent them from being transported onwards from Westerbork at a later date.

With regard to Jews in mixed marriages who have voluntarily reported for sterilization,[14] this procedure has begun at a Jewish hospital run by the City of Amsterdam under the supervision of the Security Police and German physicians. The yellow star has been taken from the sterilized Jews, and they have been granted exemptions from the restrictions on Jews enforced by the police. Dutch physicians initially refused to participate in this procedure, but now that Jews want to be sterilized of their own accord, it is becoming apparent that individual Dutch physicians wish to conduct private operations in order to qualify Jews for exemption from the star and, in exchange, to receive an appropriate fee.[15]

DOC. 132

On 16 June 1943 Michael Sommer asks Commissioner General Hanns Albin Rauter to permit the emigration of several Jewish metal wholesalers working for the Germans[1]

Letter (forwarded by the Department for Economic Affairs, Office of the Four-Year Plan) from Michael Sommer[2] (sworn expert for the Hamburg Chamber of Industry and Commerce), 84 Rokin, Central Amsterdam, to Higher SS and Police Leader, SS-Gruppenführer, and Major General of the Police W. Rauter,[3] The Hague, dated 16 June 1943[4]

Re: emigration of Jews

Dear Gruppenführer,

After consulting Mr Hans Plümer[5] from the Four-Year Plan, I venture to submit to you the following:

13 From March 1943 the Central Office for Jewish Emigration paid 7.50 guilders for anyone who reported on a Jew living in hiding.

14 From May 1943 the German authorities planned to make sterilization compulsory for Jewish partners in so-called mixed marriages who were to remain in the Netherlands: see Doc. 118.

15 Many Dutch physicians continued to refuse to carry out operations to sterilize Jews: see Doc. 140.

1 BArch, R 58/9279. This document has been translated from German.

2 Michael Sommer (1894–1970), captain; served in the German navy, 1910–1919; joined the NSDAP in 1932; worked as a ship calibration supervisor at the Port of Hamburg in the 1930s; purchaser for the Four-Year Plan, 1941–1943; served in the German navy in the Netherlands, 1943–1945; returned to Germany in 1946; extradited to the Netherlands in 1948 and interned in Vught camp until 1949.

3 Correctly: Hanns Albin Rauter.

4 The original contains handwritten notes and underlining.

5 Hans Plümer (1898–1961), businessman; initially worked as a businessman in Hamburg; during the occupation worked as head of section under the Plenipotentiary for the Four-Year Plan in the Netherlands.

Approximately two and a half years ago, the Office of the Four-Year Plan (Colonel Veltgens[6] and Mr Plümer) commissioned me to procure high-value metals, military engineering equipment, and the like for the German economy and the Wehrmacht in the East. At that time, I was required to expedite these purchases by any means necessary. In order to do so, I above all required specialized staff from the sector concerned. When I subsequently sought to make the purchases using Aryan staff, attempts to procure the goods came to nothing in virtually all cases, and as a result I was forced to have recourse to Jews.

The Office of the Four-Year Plan agreed to my appointment of Jews and had the Senior Commander of the Security Police secure them for this purpose.[7] Throughout this period, the Jewish staff have carried out excellent work, and I have received repeated recognition of my achievements via Berlin from the Reich Ministry of Economics (Ministerialrat Joseph Drex'l).[8]

When the question of the stars for Jews then arose, I discussed the matter with Ministerialrat Joseph Drex'l, and he stated that something definitely had to be done for the most important Jews in this regard, so as to ensure that my purchases, of metals in particular, did not grind to a halt. In addition, I spoke with the Office of the Four-Year Plan, and a tacit agreement was also reached with that party that something would have to be done for the above-mentioned Jews following the conclusion of our operation.

Since the Jewish question is very acute at the moment, I have conducted a survey of the Jews I employ in order to ascertain whether they would be in a position to raise a certain amount of money, through whatever channels, to facilitate their departure from the country.

The Jewish staff have given me assurances that they would be able to make available $5,000 in credit notes to each family.

In addition to this, there is also the individual service that the Jews have performed for the Reich, for if this work had not been done, I would not have been in a position to obtain approximately 7,000 tonnes of high-grade metals worth approximately fl. 10,000,000. In this respect, it also must be mentioned that these Jews have procured thousands of tonnes of iron and steel under the most difficult circumstances for the construction of fortifications and anti-tank ditches on behalf of the senior commander of the Waffen SS[9] and Organization Todt. This is not to mention the many other items procured, with a total value of millions of guilders.

I therefore maintain with a clear conscience that the Jews employed by me were the most valuable of all the Jews in Holland, and still are even now. I am convinced that my opinion will be shared by Mr Richard Fiebig, the representative of the Reich Minister

6 Correctly: Josef Veltjens (1894–1943), career officer; fighter pilot, 1914–1918; subsequently founded a shipping company and was involved in the arms trade; member of the NSDAP, 1929–1931; Plenipotentiary for the Four-Year Plan in the Netherlands from 1940; died in a plane crash.

7 Wilhelm Harster.

8 Correctly: Dr Josef Drexl (1895–1975); joined the NSDAP in 1937; Oberregierungsrat in the Reich Ministry of Economics.

9 Karl-Maria Demelhuber (1896–1988), business manager; joined the NSDAP in 1922, the SA in 1934, and the SS in 1935; from 1935 commander of various Waffen SS units; senior commander of the Waffen SS in the Netherlands, June 1942–Nov. 1944; interned in Germany, 1945–1948.

for Armaments and Munitions,[10] for whom I have made almost all the purchases in the last nine months, and also by the Office of the Four-Year Plan (Mr Hans Plümer).

The Jews earmarked for emigration are:

1.	Richard Messow,[11]	b. 6 February 1888 in Berlin, resident at 20 II Watteaustraat, Amsterdam, ID no. A 35/10969, exemption stamp no. 40 062.
	Martha Messow, née Ernst,	b. 16 January 1901 in Witten am Rhein, resident at 20 II Watteaustraat, Amsterdam, ID no. A 35/00348, exemption stamp no. 40 068.
	Jacques Goldwasser,	b. 6 March 1938 in Amsterdam, resident at 20 II Watteaustraat, Amsterdam, foster child and ward of Richard Messow. The whereabouts of the child's parents are unknown.
2.	Paul Friedrich Jonas,[12]	b. 30 April 1889 in Kiel, resident at 90 I Deurloostraat, Amsterdam, ID no. O 54/0026, exemption stamp no. 40 057.
	Rosa Jonas, née Isaak,	b. 9 July 1891 in Cologne, resident at 90 I Deurloostraat, Amsterdam, ID no. O 54/00023, exemption stamp no. 40 059.
3.	Erich Malachowski,[13]	b. 18 December 1899 in Hindenburg, Upper Silesia, resident at 284 I Uiterwaardenstraat, Amsterdam, ID no. A 35/10661, exemption stamp no. 40 055.

10 Albert Speer. The Reich Ministry for Armaments and Munitions (Reichsministerium für Bewaffnung und Munition) was renamed Reich Ministry for Armaments and War Production (Reichsministerium für Rüstung und Kriegsproduktion) in September 1943.

11 Richard Messow (1888–1944), businessman; emigrated to the Netherlands from Hamburg in 1914; married Martha Ernst (1901–1944) in 1942; the couple were deported to Westerbork with their foster child Jacques Goldwasser (1938–1944) in 1943/44, then to Theresienstadt on 25 Feb. 1944, and to Auschwitz in Oct. 1944. Jacques Goldwasser's biological parents survived the war, having been able to flee to Switzerland.

12 Paul Friedrich Jonas (b. 1889), retailer; thought to have emigrated to the Netherlands from Germany in 1936; deported to Westerbork on 27 Jan. 1944, then to Theresienstadt on 25 Feb. 1944, and to Auschwitz on 9 Oct. 1944; returned to Amsterdam in 1946. Handwritten note under his name: 'exempted from star'. His wife Rosa, (correctly) née Isack (1891–1944), did not survive Auschwitz.

13 Erich Malachowski (1899–1945), clerical worker; emigrated to the Netherlands from Stuttgart in 1933; married Milli Grünebaum in Amsterdam in Oct. 1933; deported to Westerbork on 28 Jan. 1944, then a month later to Theresienstadt, and on 28 Sept. 1944 to Auschwitz; perished in Dachau. His wife, Milli (b. 1907), who had also emigrated from Germany, probably went into hiding in 1943 together with their daughter, Yvonne Vera (b. 1938); both emigrated to Britain in 1952. David Malachowski (1864–1944), Erich Malachowski's father; emigrated to the Netherlands from Breslau in 1939; deported to Westerbork on 29 Sept. 1943, then on 25 Feb. 1944 to Theresienstadt, where he perished.

	Milli Malachowski, née Grünebaum,	b. 5 January 1907 in Holzheim, resident at 284 I Uiterwaardenstraat, Amsterdam, ID no. A 35/07939, exemption stamp no. 40 064.
	Yvonne Vera Malachowski,	b. 3 June 1938 in Amsterdam, resident at 284 I Uiterwaardenstraat, Amsterdam.
	David Malachowski,	b. 3 January 1864 in Borek, resident at 284 I Uiterwaardenstraat, Amsterdam, ID no. A 35/10660, exemption stamp no. 41 142.
4.	Hermann Wallheimer,[14]	b. 2 December 1909 in Oldenburg, resident at 121 III Olympiaplein, Amsterdam, ID no. A 35/14204, exemption stamp no. 41 133.
	Hildegard Wallheimer, née Freund,	b. 8 October 1913 in Berlin, resident at 121 III Olympiaplein, Amsterdam, ID no. A 35/07108, exemption stamp no. 41 134.
	Hedwig Wallheimer, née David,	b. 27 June 1889 in Krefeld, resident at 121 III Olympiaplein, Amsterdam, ID no. A 35/06202, exemption stamp no. 41 127.
5.	Gustav Scheiberg,[15]	b. 13 October 1893 in Münster/Westphalia, resident at 29 Jan Willem Brouwersplein, Amsterdam, ID no. A 35/604876, exemption stamp no. 40 291.
	Vera Scheiberg, née van Esso,	b. 13 August 1906 in Meppel, resident at 29 Jan Willem Brouwersplein, Amsterdam, ID no. A 35/526993, exemption stamp no. 40 292.
	Dorothea Scheiberg,	b. 27 December 1930 in Rotterdam, resident at 29 Jan Willem Brouwersplein, Amsterdam.

14 Hermann Wallheimer (1909–1979), businessman; emigrated from Bremen to the Netherlands in 1938; opened a metal-trading business at the end of 1938; worked as a buyer for the Sommer company, August 1942–March 1943; deported to Westerbork on 27 Jan. 1944, then to Theresienstadt a month later, and finally to Auschwitz; returned to the Netherlands in 1945 and reopened his business. His wife, Hildegard (b. 1913), survived the war, as did his mother, Hedwig (1889–1945), who later died in Amsterdam.

15 Correctly: Sally Gustav Scheiberg (1893–1945), businessman; moved from Germany to the Netherlands as a child; married Vera van Esso (1906–1944) in 1929; the couple were deported to Westerbork in 1943 with their daughter Dorothea (1930–1944), then to Theresienstadt on 25 Feb. 1944, and to Auschwitz at the beginning of Sept. 1944. Sally Gustav Scheiberg perished in Dachau.

6.	Alfred Gossels,[16]	b. 17 July 1907 in Osnabrück, resident at 28 Courbetstraat, Amsterdam, ID no. A 35/07720, exemption stamp no. 40 077.
	Emma Gossels, née Heilbrunn,	b. 3 March 1874 in Mühlhausen, Thuringia, resident at 28 Courbetstraat, Amsterdam, ID no. A 35/08352, exemption stamp no. 41 128.
7.	Justus Nussbaum,[17]	b. 1 March 1901 in Osnabrück, resident at 168 II Noorder Amstellaan, Amsterdam, ID no. A 35/11518, exemption stamp no. 40 050.
	Hertha Nussbaum, née Bein,	b. 7 January 1910 in Oberhausen, resident at 168 II Noorder Amstellaan, Amsterdam, ID no. A 35/04487, exemption stamp no. 40 051.
	Marianne Nussbaum,	b. 6 April 1935 in Osnabrück, resident at 168 II Noorder Amstellaan, Amsterdam.
8.	Erich Jonas,[18]	b. 14 March 1915 in Cologne-Deutz, resident at 90 I Deurloostraat, Amsterdam, ID no. O 54/00025, exemption stamp no. 40 067.
	Martha Jonas, née Simons,	b. 7 December 1920 in Cologne-Deutz, resident at 90 I Deurloostraat, Amsterdam, ID no. A 35/13334, exemption stamp no. 40 076.
9.	Ludwig Cahn,[19]	b. 24 March 1914 in Cologne, resident at 90 I Deurloostraat, Amsterdam, ID no. O 54/00015, exemption stamp no. 40 054.

16 Alfred Gossels (1907–1944), businessman; emigrated from Osnabrück in 1938; deported to Westerbork on 27 Jan. 1944 and to Auschwitz on 3 Sept. 1944; died at Burggraben, a subcamp of Stutthof concentration camp. Emma Gossels (1874–1944), Alfred Gossels's mother; emigrated from Cologne in 1939; deported to Westerbork on 29 Sept. 1943, and then on 25 Feb. 1944 to Theresienstadt, where she perished.

17 Justus Nussbaum (1901–1944), factory owner, and his wife (correctly) Sofie Herta (1910–1944) emigrated to the Netherlands from Osnabrück in 1937; the couple were deported with their daughter Marianne (1935–1944) to Westerbork in 1943, and then on 3 Sept. 1944 to Auschwitz, where Nussbaum's wife and daughter were murdered upon arrival; Justus Nussbaum perished at Stutthof concentration camp in Dec. 1944.

18 Erich Jonas (b. 1915), manager, and his wife Martha (b. 1920), employee of the Jewish Council from 1942 to 1943, were deported to Westerbork in Sept. 1943; they were released when the camp was liberated.

19 Ludwig Cahn (b. 1914), sales representative, and his wife Edith (b. 1913) were deported to Westerbork in 1943, and then to Auschwitz in Sept. 1944; Ludwig Cahn survived the Groß-Rosen and Buchenwald camps, and was liberated on 23 April 1945 at Wittenberg; the couple both returned to the Netherlands.

Edith Cahn, née Jonas,	b. 27 August 1913 in Cologne, resident at 90 I Deurloostraat, Amsterdam, ID no. O 54/00024, exemption stamp no. 40 070.
10. Erich Katz,[20]	b. 11 March 1903 in Duisburg, resident at 190 Noorder Amstellaan, Amsterdam, ID no. A 35/09676, exemption stamp no. 40 065.
Margarete Katz, née Meyer,	b. 4 January 1915 in Königshütte, resident at 198 I Noorder Amstellaan, Amsterdam, ID no. A 35/11070, exemption stamp no. 40 066.
Mirjam Lisette Katz,	b. 30 April 1937 in Essen, resident at 198 I Noorder Amstellaan, Amsterdam.
11. Philipp Nussbaum,[21]	b. 22 August 1872 in Emden, resident at 60 hs Legmeerstraat, Amsterdam, ID no. A 35/11524, exemption stamp no. 41 115.
Rachel Nussbaum, née van Dijk,	b. 14 March 1873 in Bunde, East Friesland, resident at 60 hs Legmeerstraat, Amsterdam, ID no. A 35/06516, exemption stamp no. 41 116.

Heil Hitler![22]

20 Erich Katz (1903–1945), metal trader, and his wife Margarete, née Meyer or Meijer (1915–1944) emigrated to the Netherlands from Essen at the end of the 1930s; the couple were deported to Westerbork with their daughter Mirjam in 1943, and then on 3 Sept. 1944 to Auschwitz, where Margarete and Mirjam Katz were murdered upon arrival; Erich Katz perished in March 1945.

21 Philipp Nussbaum (1872–1944), ironmonger, and his wife Rachel (1873–1944) emigrated to the Netherlands from Cologne in 1939; the couple were deported to Westerbork in Nov. 1943, and then on 8 Feb. 1944 to Auschwitz, where they were murdered upon arrival. Rachel and Philipp Nussbaum were the painter Felix Nussbaum's parents: see Doc. 206.

22 There is no reply to this letter from Commissioner General Rauter in the file.

DOC. 133
On 22 June 1943 Wilhelm Zoepf specifies how diamonds owned by Jews are to be dealt with[1]

Memorandum from the Senior Commander of the Security Police, IV B 4, signed Zoepf, The Hague, dated 22 June 1943[2]

Re: utilization of diamonds owned by Jewish diamond traders
Reference: meeting with Mr Plümer[3] and Oberregierungsrat Schüssler
According to the presentation given by Dr Schüssler, the Reich Marshal[4] places the greatest emphasis on bringing in foreign currency from abroad for the German war effort by selling the diamonds that are still to be obtained in the occupied territories. For this purpose, the diamonds registered to the various diamond traders in the Netherlands and the diamonds located in Arnhem are to be acquired in an inconspicuous fashion by a company using contracts of sale. These German intermediary companies are then to attempt to sell the diamonds abroad in exchange for foreign currency.[5]

So as not to alert hostile powers to this undertaking prematurely, the diamonds are not to be confiscated by an authority, but acquired expressly on the basis of contracts of sale and, as the sellers, the Jewish diamond traders will therefore be left at liberty for the time being. Some of the people included on this diamond traders list already hold the AB stamp.[6] This stamp is to be issued to the rest of these individuals in accordance with instructions that are yet to be issued by the Office of the Four-Year Plan. The remainder of these diamond traders are still to be left at liberty for the time being, but can then be deported once the diamonds have been delivered. The Security Police held out the prospect that no further operations to round up Jews would be carried out in Amsterdam for the time being, and so these Jews will remain undisturbed until the matter has been dealt with, even if they do not have stamps. Should some of these diamond traders have been captured and transported to Westerbork during the last major operation in Amsterdam, their immediate release will be arranged.[7]

The release of the diamond traders is in line with the RSHA's plans, as at a recent meeting in Berlin, SS-Obersturmbannführer Eichmann[8] said that he would agree with it. In general, there is no desire for the diamond traders to emigrate because, as experts in their field, they should not be put into a position to establish a diamond industry abroad at a later date. Accordingly, their further treatment on the basis of any AB stamps that may have been issued would only be appropriate subject to certain provisos.

1 NIOD, 077/1317. This document has been translated from German.
2 The original contains handwritten notes and the footnote: 'II. Mrs Slottke (e)'.
3 Hans Plümer.
4 Hermann Göring.
5 These transactions were executed via the Hamburg-based Bozenhardt brothers' diamond-trading business, for which the Jewish diamond traders were paid a total of fl. 9.4 million.
6 On the AB list, see Doc. 118, fn. 18.
7 The representative for the Central Office for Diamonds, Karl Hanemann, arranged the return of the diamond traders from Westerbork, but demanded more of the diamonds as his 'reward'. In total, he received approximately fl. 600,000 worth of diamonds, which he passed on to the Office of the Four-Year Plan. However, the 'Hanemann gift', as it was known, only gave the Jewish diamond traders a brief reprieve; most of them were detained again in Sept. 1943 and deported.
8 Adolf Eichmann.

DOC. 134
New York Times, 23 June 1943: article on the deportation of the last Jews from Amsterdam[1]

Netherlands Jews ousted by Nazis. Removal of Last Group From Amsterdam Completes Country-Wide Deportations. Terrible Journey Told. Asylum Patients Put in a Freight Car – Slovak Bishops Protest Persecution.

London, June 22 (U.P.)[2] – All Jews in Amsterdam have been deported by the Germans to Poland, thus completing the removal of the entire Jewish population of the Netherlands,[3] the Aneta[4] news agency said today.

The Netherlands had about 180,000 persons classified as Jews by Nazi standards at the time of the German invasion of 1940.[5] Some Jews, however, are thought to have escaped and to be still hiding in the provinces, aided by non-Jewish compatriots. The Germans have arrested scores of persons for harboring Jews.

The deportations, Aneta said, were carried out in three stages. April 10 was set for the beginning of the evacuation of Jews from eight of the eleven provinces. The remaining three were ordered evacuated beginning April 23, except for Amsterdam,[6] where a large concentration of Jews was held behind ghetto barriers.

The final stage began with a decree issued May 14 for the deportation of those in Amsterdam.[7]

Aneta reported that many of those deported died before reaching Poland. In one case, reported by underground newspapers, a Jewish asylum at Apeldoorn was evacuated and patients and nurses were packed into cattle cars,[8] eighty to a car, with the result that many died of suffocation before reaching the Polish border. Aneta said it was reported some of the survivors were executed by poison gas.

The Vatican radio has broadcast to Germany the text of a recent protest by the German Catholic Bishops[9] of Slovakia against the persecution of Jews, according to a British broadcast recorded in New York by the Columbia Broadcasting System. The broadcast on Monday quoted the Bishops as saying:

'No one has the right to harm Jews merely because they are Jews.'[10]

1 *New York Times*, 23 June 1943, p. 8.
2 United Press; news agency founded in 1907.
3 This presumably alludes to the deportation of 7,000 Jewish Council employees at the end of May 1943; see Doc. 123. However, the last comprehensive roundup, after which no Jews lived openly in the Netherlands, occurred on 29 September 1943, the eve of the Jewish New Year.
4 Algemene Nieuws en Telegraaf Agentschap (Aneta) was founded as the first press agency in the Dutch East Indies; in 1963 it merged with the Indonesian press agency Antara, which still exists today.
5 According to National Socialist criteria used in the 1941 imposed census of Jews, 140,000 Jews were living in the Netherlands at the time of the census. In addition, 20,000 were classified as *Mischlinge*: see PMJ 5/90.
6 See Doc. 117.
7 Such a decree did not exist, although the deportation of the majority of the remaining Jews living in Amsterdam did occur at the end of May: see fn. 3.
8 See Doc. 104.
9 The reference is to the Catholic bishops of Slovakia.
10 Presumably an excerpt from the Slovakian bishops' pastoral letter dated 21 March 1943, in which the bishops protested against further deportations: PA AA, R 100 887.

DOC. 135
On 25 June 1943 Wilhelm Zoepf issues a memorandum on the future handling of exemption stamps for Jews[1]

Memorandum from the Senior Commander of the Security Police, IV B 4 (L) (marked 'secret'), signed Zoepf, The Hague, dated 25 June 1943[2]

Re: AB list[3]
Reference: meeting on 25 June 1943 attended by
SS-Sturmbannführer Zoepf
SS-Sturmbannführer Meyer
SS-Hauptsturmführer Wörlein
SS-Untersturmführer Schmidt
SS-Sturmscharführer Fischer
SS-Unterscharführer Ohlendorf
Police employee Slottke
Police employee Werner.
I) *Memorandum:*
As a result of recent developments, the 120,000 stamp[4] now appeals so much to Jewry that it will be the main means of gaining the Jews' trust in the immediate future. In this respect, it is to be emphasized expressly that the Security Police has never disclosed to Jews what final treatment this stamp is intended to guarantee. Only in a few cases has the Central Office for Jewish Emigration indicated to Jews that they would at most be under consideration for inclusion on an emigration list if they have this stamp. In any event, these Jews should not go to the East for labour deployment.

Consequently, the question of the treatment of the Jews who have been issued with this stamp number has still in no way been settled per se. Instead of being deported for labour deployment in the East, these Jews have stayed in the country for the time being. However, nothing stands in the way of their transfer to Bergen-Belsen camp, as labour deployment in the East does not take place there, but it is rather a holding camp along the lines of Theresienstadt. They could potentially emigrate at a later date, but this would only be possible by means of collective exchange, because the procedure covered by stamp no. 40,000 still applies for preferential individual emigration.[5] Furthermore, the latter type of emigration has to all intents and purposes been brought to an end. At the same time, whether one or another Jew included on the 120,000 stamp list (the so-called 'AB list') actually ends up emigrating by means of exchange or not depends:

1 NIOD, 077/1317. This document has been translated from German.
2 The original contains handwritten notes.
3 The so-called AB list (*Austausch- und Beziehungs-Liste*, 'exchange and connections list') included Jews who could provide valuables in exchange for their exemption from deportation. For these individuals, exemption stamps, which were normally numbered in groups of tens of thousands, were provided with the number 120,000 and above.
4 Exemption stamp for the 'AB list'.
5 The stamps with numbers ranging from 40,000 to 50,000 were issued to 'protected Jews' and 'Jews offered for exchange' (*Protektions- und Angebotsjuden*) who were either under the protection of a particular individual or were to be offered in exchange for German citizens abroad.

a) on the particular character of the Jew,
b) on the consent of the foreign state in question, which is not yet to be assumed at present.

In order to gain the trust of the Jews, the AB list stamp (120,000 and above) is initially to be retained for all cases not to be earmarked for the East, but instead for Transvaal,[6] Westerbork, and finally *Bergen-Belsen*, without these subdivisions being made apparent. However, so that the reason for an individual's inclusion on the list is known at a later date, it is recommended that the following subdivisions now be recorded in the bottom part of the AB list:

1) Jews who have demonstrable *relationships* with hostile countries,
2) Jews who do not have such *relationships*, but have delivered *assets* that would otherwise not have come to light,
3) Jews whose deportation is to be deferred only *temporarily*, but who definitely want to emigrate abroad (diamond experts),
4) *distinguished Jews*[7] who were previously sent to Theresienstadt and are now to remain in Bergen-Belsen,
5) Jewish applicants about whose final fate nothing has yet been agreed.

II) To the Central Office for Jewish Emigration, Amsterdam
III) To Westerbork camp
IV) IV B 4 SS-Untersturmführer Schmidt
SS-Sturmscharführer Fischer
Police employee Slottke
Police employee Straszidlo

6 During roundups Transvaalplein was used as an assembly point for Jews from the Transvaalbuurt neighbourhood of Amsterdam. Jews who had to leave other parts of the city were concentrated in this neighbourhood; they were assigned the apartments of co-religionists who had already been deported.

7 *Verdienstjuden*: Jews who had been designated for preferential treatment by the Dutch secretaries general Karel Frederiks and Jan van Dam on account of their distinguished service to the Netherlands; they were imprisoned in Barneveld and later deported to Theresienstadt: see Doc. 102.

DOC. 136

On 20 July 1943 an unknown author writes a poem about the transports from Westerbork camp[1]

Handwritten poem, signature illegible, dated 20 July 1943[2]

Tuesday[3]

Three whistles fill the air all round,
It's like the shofar's[4] piercing sound;
Our hearts are by a hammer hit,
We dare not move the slightest bit.

And everyone, be he free and Jew,
Knows this sign, knows what it will do.
Away from here our brothers are taken;
The Jewish heart in us all awakens.

The train is gone, our breath comes back.
Life returns to its usual track.

DOC. 137

Vrij Nederland (London), 31 July 1943: article disputing the existence of a 'Jewish question' in the Netherlands[1]

The 'Jewish question'

There has never been a Jewish question in our good country.

Over the centuries, the Netherlands has opened its gates to all those who were oppressed. The Netherlands, cradle of freedom!

A historical refuge for thousands who were driven from their own countries of birth due to intolerance and who sought protection and safety, friendship, and decent living conditions.

And our readers will not hold it against me when I say that God has generously rewarded our country for this.

We had a blessed country, where truth and freedom, a sense of civic responsibility, and tolerance abounded.

1 NIOD, 250i/861. This document has been translated from Dutch.
2 The original contains handwritten corrections.
3 For much of the period 1942–1943, deportations left Westerbork for Auschwitz or Sobibor on Tuesday mornings.
4 Ritual musical instrument, generally made from a ram's horn, and used on important Jewish religious occasions, primarily on the High Holidays and sometimes in ceremonies.

1 *Vrij Nederland – je maintiendrai: Onafhankelijk weekblad voor alle Nederlanders*, London, vol. 4, no. 3, 31 July 1943, p. 25. This document has been translated from Dutch. In addition to the illegal *Vrij Nederland* newspaper that was published in the Netherlands, a newspaper of the same name existed in London, supported by the government in exile. The first edition appeared on 3 August 1940.

Among the thousands who settled in our country over the past centuries were many Jews.

The fact that there is a separate synagogue in Amsterdam for the Portuguese Israelite Religious Community is proof of the cosmopolitan nature of the Jewish community in the Netherlands.

The number of Jews was never more than about one and a half per cent of our population, and although their influence in certain trade circles was not insignificant – take the diamond trade, for example – Dutch Jews had their own, but not a separate, place in the community.

There are good Jews and there are bad Jews, just as there are good Christians and bad Christians. A distinction was never really made in our country.

This situation continued until the beginning of the 'thirties', by which I mean the period 1930 to 1940.

National Socialism in Germany, which had embraced antisemitism as one of its principles, compelled many German Jews to seek a safe haven in other countries.

In the Netherlands, too, there was a considerable increase in the Jewish population.[2]

Of course, these German Jews not only brought their virtues and skills, but also their vices, and one does not need to be a psychologist to discern that the lengthy period spent in Germany, the hard struggle to survive – especially in the years after Versailles – had left a certain mark on these people.

Just as you can't turn a foreigner into a true Dutchman within a week, you can't turn a German Jew into a Dutch Jew within such a short period of time.

It is therefore not surprising that these people stood out and provoked annoyance among others, including Dutch Jews.[3]

But something else happened …

As soon as Hitler came to power, antisemitism erupted in Germany. But this did not happen in Germany alone. Day by day, a sophisticated propaganda machine filled the atmosphere with a poison so intoxicating that it could not fail to have an effect.

All the misery Germany had brought upon itself as a result of losing the Great War was attributed to the Jews.

The animal instincts of fear and cowardice were systematically exploited to poison people's minds.

This propaganda had very little impact in the Netherlands due to the fact that the churches raised their voices against these wicked activities, and also because of the sense of tolerance characteristic of the Dutch psyche.

It is therefore not surprising that our people unanimously sided with the Jews when Hitler's gangs laid their dishonourable hands on their own people.

I am fully convinced that the Nazi gang has not succeeded in creating a 'Jewish question' in the Netherlands, and that it won't have to come to this after the war either.

However, this requires a few things. First of all, the Netherlands will only be able to accommodate 'Dutch' Jews: Jews who, in addition to the rights inherent in Dutch citizenship, will also understand their obligations and comply with them unreservedly.

2 Approximately 20,000 Jewish refugees from Germany found refuge in the Netherlands in the 1930s.

3 On the conflicts between Dutch and German Jews, see PMJ 5, p. 18 and Doc. 128 in this volume.

They have always been part of the Dutch community, and as such they belong here.

Secondly, those wishing to return to the Netherlands will have to do exactly the same as any other Dutch person would have to do: they will have to prove themselves worthy to return.

Someone once said that a man who wants to govern has to learn to 'serve discreetly'.[4] That applies to us all, whether we are Christians or Jews, but our high-spirited Jewish compatriots in particular must bear this in mind.

We really won't have time to think about Jewish questions after returning to the Netherlands. All Dutch citizens, irrespective of their origin, may be required to make all their energy and talents, ingenuity and money available for the recovery of our poor afflicted country.

I am convinced that the purpose of Nazi propaganda is to distract us from its main goal of world domination by blowing the Jewish question out of proportion.

Once again: there will never need to be a Jewish question in the Netherlands, and there should not be a Jewish question, as this would deprive us of the Almighty's blessing. According to the Bible, Shem will dwell in the tents of Japheth,[5] or translated into modern language: it is God's will that the Jews live among Christians, in order that both can serve each other in freedom and tolerance.

De Wit

DOC. 138

On 19 August 1943 the Dutch police officers Willem Henneicke and Willem Briedé deliver several Jews under arrest to the Joodsche Schouwburg[1]

Report, signed W. C. H. Henneicke[2] and W. Briede,[3] Amsterdam, dated 19 August 1943 (copy)[4]

Re: *the Jewish Rubens family*

The following individuals were found in the course of the one-off operation against Jews who were not exempt from deportation:

1. Jacob Rubens,[5] b. 20 February 1890 in Elburg

4 This could not be found.

5 Genesis 9:27 actually states this the other way round: 'God shall enlarge Japheth, and he shall dwell in the tents of Shem' (KJV).

1 NIOD, 249/317. This document has been translated from German.

2 Willem Christiaan Heinrich Henneicke (1909–1944), commercial employee; jobs included working as a taxi driver and a sales representative; served with the SD from 1941; joined the NSB in 1942; from 1942 worked for the Household Effects Registration Office, which was responsible for making inventories of the residences of Jews who had been deported; killed by resistance groups in Dec. 1944.

3 Willem Hendrik Benjamin Briedé (1903–1962), bookkeeper; joined the NSB in 1934; worked for the Household Effects Registration Office from June 1942; thought to have fled to Germany in 1945; sentenced to death in absentia in 1946.

4 The original contains handwritten notes and underlining.

5 Jacob Rubens (1894–1963), retailer. When they were deported from the Joodsche Schouwburg, he, his wife Eva (1906–1974), and their children succeeded in escaping by bribing officials; the family survived the war.

2. his wife Eva Rubens, née Themans, b. 14 August 1906 in Enschede
3. their child Rozetta Rubens, b. 29 June 1928 in Enschede
4. their child Salomon Rubens, b. 16 November 1933 in Enschede

Last resident at 47 Apollolaan, Amsterdam.

Reason:

We, the undersigned W. C. H. Henneicke and W. Briede, officers of the Henneicke Group,[6] Central Office for Jewish Emigration, Amsterdam, arrested the Jews detailed above at 10 p.m. on 16 August 1943.

The Jews had gone into hiding in the home of the Aryan Mrs Eusman,[7] 23(2) Westeinde, Amsterdam, who did not know they were Jews, which is why she was not arrested.

The Jew Jacob Rubens and his wife were in possession of fake personal identity cards, and they were not wearing stars.

The Jew Rubens was in possession of a sum of money to the value of fl. 4,014 and, in addition, the following items of value:

1 package containing financial papers (securities)
127 silver rings (with gemstones)
1 gold watch
1 gold chain with medallion.

The Jews detailed above have been delivered to the Joodsche Schouwburg, and the money and items of value have been handed in to the Security Police, Amsterdam office.

DOC. 139

On 28 August 1943 Adolf Eichmann informs the Senior Commander of the Security Police for the occupied Dutch territories that the Jews from Vught camp are to be deported to Auschwitz[1]

Letter (marked 'secret') from the Reich Security Main Office (RSHA) (IV B 4 KL. A 3233/41 – KL. C [1085]), pp. signed Eichmann (SS-Obersturmbannführer), Berlin (Nue[2] no. 153 257, 14.55 – Hab.), to the Senior Commander of the Security Police for the Occupied Dutch Territories, for the attention of SS Brigadeführer and Major General of the Police Harster (or his deputy), The Hague, dated 28 August 1943 (copy)[3]

Re: deportation of Jews from the occupied Dutch territories
Reference: meeting in The Hague
During my meeting on 27 August 1943 at the Business and Administration Main Office,[4] the issue of the approximately 2,400 Jews still present in Vught camp was raised.

6 The Henneicke Group consisted of 54 men who hunted down Jews in hiding on behalf of the Security Police and the SD. From March to Sept. 1943, they arrested approximately 8,500 Jews, receiving a bounty of fl. 7.50 per person.
7 Maria Cornelia Eusman (1885–1965), seamstress; lived at 23 Westeinde from 1938 to 1957.

1 NIOD, 077/1319. This document has been translated from German.
2 Abbreviation for *Nachrichtenübermittlung* ('communication'), here presumably a telegram.
3 The original contains handwritten underlining.
4 Wirtschaft-Verwaltungshauptamt.

It was agreed that these Jews would gradually be evacuated to the East (Auschwitz concentration camp) within the next few weeks, avoiding any significant disruption to production, unless the consultation between the head of Vught concentration camp[5] and SS-Obergruppenführer *Rauter*, planned for the next few days, reaches a different conclusion.

The diamond Jews and the eighty Jews deployed to perform important manufacturing work for the Luftwaffe are to remain exempt from evacuation for the time being.

Please make this position clear in The Hague as well, and report on the outcome of the meeting between the head of Vught concentration camp and SS-Obergruppenführer Rauter.[6]

Please register the 700 so-called protected Jews held at Barneveld for Bergen-Belsen detention camp.

The date for the deportation will be communicated following the creation of further reception facilities at Bergen-Belsen.[7]

DOC. 140

In August 1943 an illegal flyer appeals to Dutch physicians to refuse to sterilize Jews[1]

Leaflet, no signature, undated[2] (typescript)

A number of Israelites living in mixed marriages are currently urgently requesting Dutch physicians to sterilize them. Anyone agreeing to do so will be carrying out a severely damaging operation without a medical reason. The real reason is the persecution of the Jews, and the surgery can be performed by the Germans themselves under what would then be their unequivocally clear responsibility.

The fact that the person concerned prefers sterilization to 'wearing a star' and would rather be operated on by a Dutch than by a German physician does not fundamentally alter the essence of the matter: this is an operation for the purpose of escaping persecution. This is by no means a voluntary decision.

A physician who is willing to do this becomes the executor of a sentence he disagrees with, passed by a judge whose authority he does not acknowledge.

Furthermore, he would be acting in blatant contradiction of the standpoint consistently upheld.[3] If Dutch physicians were to deviate from this standpoint, the Germans could rightly say: the physicians who at first upheld their exacting standards are now collaborating with us.[4]

5 Karl Chmielewski.
6 There is no report of this kind in the file.
7 Barneveld camp was closed on 29 Sept. 1943, and its inmates were deported to Westerbork.

1 Nationaal Archief, Medisch Contact, 2.19.53.02/22. This document has been translated from Dutch.
2 Handwritten date: 'Aug. '43'.
3 This could not be verified.
4 In March 1942 the German authorities tried to exert control over Dutch physicians by establishing a medical association. Most of the physicians who opposed this measure banded together in an illegal group called Medisch Contact, the activities of which included organizing physicians' efforts to resist both performing medical examinations for 'labour deployment' and sterilizing Jews.

DOC. 141

On 11 September 1943 the district commander of the Groningen Marechaussee issues a wanted notice for two women who have escaped from Westerbork camp[1]

Telex (no. 1910) from the 1st Police Regiment, Groningen Marechaussee, unsigned, from the district commander of the Groningen Marechaussee[2] to all affiliates, dated 11 September 1943

The detachment commander of the Marechaussee in Westerbork camp requests that the following Jewish women be tracked down, arrested, and brought before the public prosecutor:

1. *Mathilde Bosman,*[3]
born in Rotterdam on 11 March 1923, office clerk, most recent address 8 Bersijnstraat, Rotterdam.

Description: height approximately 1.65 metres; of slim, strong build; attractive; not typically Jewish-looking; fair, frizzy hair; dressed in a dark skirt and a pink jumper, and probably wearing a light beige raincoat.

2. *Sophie Simons,*[4]
born 23 August 1922, most recent address 141 Van Diepenbroeckstraat, The Hague.

Description: height approximately 1.60 metres; not typically Jewish-looking; dark blonde hair styled in a roll; dressed in a dark blue skirt suit.

They are in possession of their identity documents but do not have their ration documents.[5] Both Jewish women belong to a group employed at a laundry in Meppel. They were last seen on 10 September 1943 at about 18:00 at the train station in Meppel. There is a well-founded suspicion that they departed in the direction of Zwolle. Publication in NAP is requested.[6]

1 Herinneringscentrum Kamp Westerbork, 2448/Doc. 3. This document has been translated from Dutch.

2 Presumably Willem Henri Wijnkamp (1897–1959), career officer; pilot in the Dutch air force before 1940; prisoner of war, 1940–1942; with the Marechaussee from July 1942; joined the SS in Dec. 1942; commander of the Groningen Marechaussee; thought to have held the post from April to Oct. 1943.

3 Mathilde ('Tilly') Bosman (b. 1923), office clerk; after her escape from Westerbork thought to have gone into hiding until 1945.

4 Sophie Marianne Simons (b. 1922), housekeeper; Jewish Council employee from August 1942; deported from Vught to Westerbork on 2 July 1943; after her escape from Westerbork, went into hiding in Leiden; nothing is known about her subsequent fate.

5 The ration coupons or cards for daily necessities such as food and clothing.

6 The *Nederlands Algemeen Politieblad* was published once a week from 1852. It published changes in the law and directives from the Ministry of Justice, as well as wanted notices and lists of missing persons.

DOC. 142
Report dated 29 September 1943 on the situation in Vught camp following the deportation of numerous Jews[1]

Report, unsigned, no author specified, 's Hertogenbosch, dated 29 September 1943

Report

In July of the present year, the size of the Jewish camp was cut from approximately 4,300 Jews to approximately 2,500 by means of two deportations to Westerbork.[2]

These transports transferred the remainder of the not entirely healthy adults and children as well as all the individuals whose ancestry is being verified, baptized Jews, etc. who were left.

The Jewish camp, which had been thrown into turmoil by the transports, soon calmed down after the composition of the transports appeared to prove that this had merely been a final purge, that is to say, the last deportations. The improvement in the inmates' health was also quite remarkable. Two deaths were recorded in July, none in August. The number of cases of sickness also decreased steadily.

The industrial plants were developed at an accelerated pace; the plants themselves rapidly chose the workers they needed to boost productivity in all areas, with the result that high production figures could very soon be achieved. In this regard, reference is made to the fact that, for example, the furrier's workshop managed a daily output of approximately 400 fur waistcoats, a very significant achievement bearing in mind that the largest privately owned fur business in Holland had a weekly production of 250 items. This was achieved notwithstanding the production of fur caps amounting to 250 items per day. One of the most important prerequisites for building up production to this level, while simultaneously establishing new plants, such as the Philips facility,[3] was the calm in the camp, and nothing could disturb this more than the prospect of the threat of new deportations.

The deportations represent the greatest source of terror for the Jews because, despite the transports being assembled with great care, family units are broken up, while the people who are left behind remain completely ignorant of the fate of those who depart, because there is no postal service to the camps in the East.

The Jews at the camp were therefore extraordinarily distressed when the deportations had to be recommenced in September, as a result of which the camp's workforce de-

1 NIOD, 250g/790. This document has been translated from German.

2 Two transports left Vught on 2 and 16 July 1943; they brought 1,687 persons to Westerbork.

3 Approximately half of the Jewish workers employed by Philips (the so-called Philips-Kommando) survived the occupation at this Philips plant. Royal Philips Electronics (Koninklijke Philips Electronics N.V.) was founded in 1891 at Eindhoven and developed from a light bulb manufacturer into a global electronics group that still exists today. Immediately prior to the occupation of the Netherlands, the management moved the legal seat of the company to Curaçao in the Dutch Antilles, arranged for its British and American activities to run under separate trusts, and established foreign subsidiaries, and the board of directors managed to flee the country. However, in the occupied Netherlands Philips was placed under German administration.

creased further, from approximately 2,400 to approximately 1,800.[4] These transports had to be assembled with the greatest care so that the impact on the industrial plants would not be too detrimental. A fall in production could not be avoided, due to the severe anxiety that took hold of the Jews.

At present, it is the case that every Jew in the camp is in fact deployed as labour, with the exception of nineteen children who arrived only recently and have stayed here on account of special circumstances.

In order to emphasize the significance of the industrial plants, a list of the numbers employed in the different departments is given below:

The following numbers were deployed on:	*17 July*	*29 Sept.*
Camp requirements	660	114
Camp operations	84	15
Diamond factory[5]	0	22
Philips factory	49	209
Military enterprises (tailors and furriers)	1,042	1,058
Unfit for deployment	322	120

Based on these figures, it is clearly evident that no one can be spared for further deportations. Everyone who can be deployed is being deployed. By contrast, the planned output for the plants envisages even greater volumes of work, since at present there are plans to extend the facilities at Philips further to manufacture light bulbs.

The Jews in the camp are naturally following the development of the labour statistics very attentively. It is clear to them that the population that remains here can hardly be reduced without harming production. This has in turn resulted in workers feeling reassured, which has again compensated for the decline in the production curve during the first half of September. Certainty that they would be able to stay here would undoubtedly lead to a further increase in output.[6]

4 Although not a single transport left in August 1943, transports left Vught on 11, 16, and 20 Sept. 1943, each carrying just over 300 persons, and travelled to Westerbork.

5 In mid 1943 diamond cutting machines were installed at Vught on Himmler's orders, following wrangling with the Business and Administration Main Office over an ultimately abandoned plan to install diamond cutting machines in Auschwitz and deport Jewish diamond cutters from Amsterdam to work them. In Vught, Jewish prisoners worked on the diamond cutting machines until May 1944; they and their families were then deported via Westerbork to Bergen-Belsen.

6 Two transports carrying a total of 309 persons were sent to Westerbork in Oct. 1943, too, before a large transport with more than 1,100 people left Vught on 15 Nov. 1943, headed for Auschwitz.

DOC. 143

On 14 October 1943 eight Protestant churches again urge Reich Commissioner Seyss-Inquart to protect Jewish partners in 'mixed marriages'[1]

Letter from the Dutch Reformed Church, signed H. M. J. Wagenaar;[2] the Old Reformed Churches in the Netherlands, signed Rutgers;[3] the Reformed Churches in Restored Union, signed J. G. Geelkerken;[4] the Christian Reformed Church, signed H. Janssen;[5] the Evangelical Lutheran Church, signed J. P. van Heest;[6] the Old Lutheran Church, signed Bik;[7] the Remonstrant Brotherhood, signed G. de Graeff;[8] the Mennonite Church in the Netherlands, signed van der Vlugt,[9] The Hague; to the Reich Commissioner for the Occupied Dutch Territories,[10] The Hague, dated 14 October 1943 (copy)

The Christian churches in the Netherlands have contacted Your Excellency more than once with regard to matters concerning our country's Jewish citizens, who have been settled in the Netherlands since time immemorial and accepted into the life of our people.[11]

Your Excellency felt he did not have to listen to the churches' urgent warnings. Most of our Jewish fellow citizens, who have until now still been living with a certain freedom, have recently been deported.

On their behalf, as well as on behalf of the very small group that still remains, we appeal most urgently to Your Excellency not to have any of them deported from the Netherlands, and instead to grant them privileged treatment in the Netherlands.

1 Het Utrechts Archief, 1423/2129. Published in Th. Dellemann, *Opdat wij niet vergeten: De bijdrage van de Gereformeerde Kerken, van haar voorgangers en leden, in het verzet tegen het nationaalsocialisme en de Duitse tyrannie* (Kampen: Drukkerij J.H. Kok, 1950), p. 627. This document has been translated from German.

2 Harmen Martinus Johan Wagenaar (1901–1999), lawyer; employed in the administration of the Dutch Reformed Church from 1926; director of the Council for Pastors' Stipends and Pensions, 1930–1967.

3 Dr Abraham Arnold Lodewijk Rutgers (1884–1966), biologist; lived in the Dutch East Indies, 1910–1928; governor of Surinam, 1928–1933; returned to the Netherlands in 1933; member of the Council of State, 1936–1959; active in the resistance and in church organizations, 1940–1945; held hostage from Jan. 1941 to Dec. 1942.

4 Dr Johannes Gerardus Geelkerken (1879–1960), pastor; in 1926 co-founded the Reformed Churches in Restored Union, for which he worked as a pastor until 1946.

5 Hector Janssen (1872–1944), pastor; lecturer, 1909–1919; military chaplain in the Dutch army and navy, 1919–1939.

6 Dr Johannes Petrus van Heest (1889–1969), pastor; secretary of the Evangelical Lutheran Synod of the Netherlands, 1943–1946; president of the Synod, 1946–1959.

7 Bertus Eliza Johannes Bik (1904–1969), pastor; founded his own church in 1948.

8 Baron Géorg de Graeff (1873–1954), engineer; employment included a post at the National Water Management Authority (Rijkswaterstaat); member of the Administrative Council of the Remonstrant Brotherhood, 1930–1937; chairman of the Administrative Council of the Remonstrant Brotherhood, 1933–1937; acting chairman while the official chairman was held hostage, 1942–1943.

9 Abraham Jan Theodor van der Vlugt (1894–1954), businessman; employed in the Dutch diplomatic service from 1912; from 1920 vice consul for Finland in the Netherlands, then consul, and finally consul general, 1940–1946; Dutch envoy to Finland, 1946–1954. The Mennonite Church in the Netherlands was known as the Algemene Doopsgezinde Sociëteit.

10 Arthur Seyss-Inquart.

11 See Docs. 65 and 122.

Furthermore, the churches are gravely troubled in view of the indications suggesting that on the German side renewed attention is now being paid to the problem of so-called mixed marriages, and that the intention is for the authorities to instigate divorce in at least a number of these marriages; just as in the case of sterilization, the severity of this planned measure may be mitigated by its supposedly voluntary nature. In this instance, too, the churches appeal to Your Excellency most emphatically: the path of the dissolution of marriage must not be taken. Our Lord Jesus Christ says – and He says it not just to His Church, but to the whole world, and also to Your Excellency – 'What therefore God hath joined together, let not man put asunder' (Matthew 19:6).

The churches therefore most urgently appeal to Your Excellency to allow these small groups, which have hitherto also come under consideration for exceptional provisions, to benefit also now from the opportunities for exemption from certain restrictions applicable to Jews that have recently been opened up for some of these groups.

It will not be possible to diminish the anxiety and indignation that are mounting for a wide variety of reasons if there is a continuation of measures that offend the deepest religious and moral feelings of the Dutch people.

DOC. 144

On 16 October 1943 the lawyer Albertus Swane approaches the German occupiers on behalf of Jews in 'mixed marriages' who are employed by the Philips Group[1]

Note by Mr A. A. Swane,[2] 1 Vughterdijk, 's-Hertogenbosch, unsigned, undated[3]

Note on individuals in mixed marriages on the Philips list
Introduction
The purpose of this note is to provide guidance to the relevant authorities concerning the Jews in mixed marriages brought together in the Eindhoven Sobü[4] Department at N.V. Philips Gloeilampenfabrieken.[5] This is to ensure that the group is dealt with as befits their previous history and their commendable service when any measures are taken by the authorities against individuals in mixed marriages – about which various rumours are circulating.
Previous history of the Sobü Department
There were only 82 Jews out of a workforce of approximately 25,000 at N.V. Philips Gloeilampenfabrieken in Holland. They were brought together at the end of 1941 in a separate Sobü Department. Since the beginning of the occupation, Philips's Jewish employees have worked exclusively for the Wehrmacht and under the control of a Wehrmacht agency. Since December 1941 they have carried out tasks that are important for the Wehrmacht in a self-contained unit known as the Sobü Department.

1 NIOD, 020/1493. This document has been translated from German.
2 Albertus Antonius Swane (1910–1997), lawyer; detained in various prisons and camps in 1944 for providing financial assistance to fugitives.
3 This note was found in the files of the Commissariat General for Administration and Justice. It has been dated based on another letter on the same topic that is included in the file.
4 Short for Sonderbüro (Special Bureau).
5 Philips Lightbulb Factories.

The work done by the Sobü Department has also been acknowledged by the German administration of the Philips Works and by various German military authorities that have inspected the department on many occasions. In view of this commendable service, and for other reasons, all Sobü individuals have received the 120,000 stamp for emigration and/or exchange.[6]

Apart from a few exceptions, the individuals in the department who were not in mixed marriages were transferred in August 1943 to Vught camp, where they are working for Philips in a self-contained unit.

The individuals in mixed marriages have remained at Eindhoven in the Sobü Department, undertaking development and production orders that are important for the Wehrmacht, and doing so in cooperation with the physics laboratory of N.V. Philips Gloeilampenfabrieken. Prior to the war, the employees in the Eindhoven Sobü Department were almost exclusively technicians. The minority who were not have been retrained as technicians since 1941. See the appendix for information on the size and structure of the group.[7]

Proposal

In view of the valuable work that the Philips Jews in mixed marriages have performed and are still performing for the Wehrmacht, and in view of the discipline of these individuals, which is assured by the Philips unit, it can be required that the laws applicable to German Jews in mixed marriages be applied analogously to the Philips Group.

In particular, in accordance with the spirit of the law, the day on which the legislation pertaining to Jews in the Netherlands was introduced is to be regarded as the cut-off date for marriages concluded between Dutch citizens, equivalent to the date on which the Nuremberg Laws were promulgated.[8]

Groups A.1 and B.1 in the appendix clearly fall within the definition of privileged mixed marriage b.[9]

However, again in view of the particular distinguished service provided by the Sobü Department for Wehrmacht production, I also wish to request that Groups A.2 and B.2 be placed on an equal footing with Jews in German privileged mixed marriages, and consequently that all Jews in mixed marriages in the Sobü Department be given the same preferential treatment.

Aryans married to Jewish women at the Philips Works

A small number of Aryans married to Jewish women are employed at the Philips Works. For reasons of fairness, equal treatment with corresponding German cases is also requested for these Aryans, who do not, of course, work in the Sobü Department.[10]

6 On the significance of this stamp, see Doc. 118, fn. 18, and Doc. 135.

7 A list of names of 'individuals in mixed marriages on the Philips list' is included in the file.

8 The original contains the handwritten note: 'For prohibited marriages? 1 Jan. 1941 at the earliest (see list of religions)'. The Nuremberg Laws were applied analogously in the Netherlands as of 1 April 1942: see PMJ 5/126. By analogy with the provisions in force in Germany, marriages between Jews and non-Jews concluded prior to this date were regarded as protected if they had produced children who were not being brought up in the Jewish faith. On the treatment of mixed marriages, see also Doc. 155, fn. 8, and Doc. 150.

9 This index is not included in the file. It was not possible to establish how the groups referred to here were defined.

10 There is no surviving response to this letter. Of the seventeen members of the Sobü Department in Eindhoven, one was murdered. All the others are thought to have survived the occupation.

DOC. 145
Vrij Nederland, 21 October 1943: article on the end of the Jewish Council and growing antisemitism[1]

The Jewish tragedy. The end is nigh. Deportation of part of the Jewish Council.

In the night from 28 to 29 September of this year, one of the final acts of the Jewish tragedy was unfolding in Amsterdam. That night, about 5,000 of the remaining Jews were taken from their homes, rounded up, and transported to Westerbork in the early hours of the morning.[2] Among those deported were also Prof. Cohen and Mr Asscher – the heads of the Jewish Council – and most of the officials from this organization were also taken away. Meanwhile the Jews from Barneveld, who had until then been under the protection of the Dutch authorities,[3] have also been taken to Westerbork. 'Genehmigungen',[4] [exemption] stamps, etc., often acquired at a very high price, no longer afford the least guarantee.

What remains of this hard-working, gifted segment of the Dutch population is a tiny number of isolated people, awaiting their turn. Tonight? Tomorrow night?

What are we to we say about these things? We cannot find the words to express our feelings. Hitler, in his megalomania, has made many promises which he has never kept. *However, it looks as though his wicked plans targeting the Jews will be fulfilled in every possible respect.* No matter how close our liberation may be, it is certain that it will come too late for thousands of our Jewish compatriots! And 'too late!'[5] is a terrible thing …

We also want to say a word of praise for the Jewish Council here. In our opinion, it is an established fact that at least the leaders acted with pure motives. They knew from the start that they could not achieve very much through direct action. Delaying, slowing down, procrastinating, postponing, at least holding on to a remainder until the British[6] arrived – that is what they considered to be their only chance, and that is what their 'collaboration' with their enemies was based on. But the British have not arrived. Not yet … And the work of the Jewish Council has been largely in vain. And we would also venture to doubt whether it was the right thing to do, but one cannot deny the leaders a certain degree of bravery. (We will not mention the various dishonourable, selfish motives of other members of staff.) Their bravery consisted in voluntarily taking on this unpleasant role, stigmatized by history … The best among them certainly did this for the benefit of others!

1 *Vrij Nederland*, vol. 4, no. 5, 21 October 1943, pp. 3–4. This document has been translated from Dutch. The first issue of the illegal Protestant newspaper *Vrij Nederland* appeared on 31 August 1940; Henk van Randwijk was its editor-in-chief from 1941 to 1950. The newspaper still exists today as an online publication and monthly magazine.

2 In this operation the majority of the Jews still living legally in the Netherlands were deported to Westerbork. The only Jews who now remained in Amsterdam were those living in so-called mixed marriages and those whose Jewish ancestry was still under investigation.

3 See Doc. 102.

4 German in the original: 'permits'.

5 Presumably an allusion to the illegal pamphlet by Jan Koopmans titled 'Bijna te laat!' ('Almost too late!'), in which the author appealed to readers to take a stand for the Jews before it was too late: see PMJ 5/52.

6 Here and below, the original refers to 'the English'.

This tragedy began with the 'harmless', 'purely administrative' signing of the Aryan Paragraph.[7] We are currently experiencing its conclusion. And may our people learn from this that with the Nazis there are never any harmless measures! Everything they do serves the dark, satanic intentions of Hitler and his heathen gang of pure-bred Teutons.

Indeed, we have learned this the hard way!

What is happening to mixed marriages?

Mixed marriages are left in peace for the time being. For how long? They are nonetheless being dealt with in a different, much more underhand, ten times more shameful manner. These approximately 10,000 people in mixed marriages are also subject to all the humiliating, restrictive measures. They too have been stripped of their freedom of movement, and they have been pushed out of their businesses and employment. However, they have so far been spared the final blow: deportation to Westerbork, and from there to Poland. To them, the executioners are 'big-hearted'. These 'privileged people' have the opportunity to remain in their country of birth, the country to which they feel a sense of attachment on account of their civil rights, their work, their language, and their religious institutions. They can acquire the privilege of being allowed to go out after 8 o'clock in the evening, ride a bicycle or go on a tram like any ordinary person, etc. Provided that …

This *provided that* demonstrates the deeply criminal nature of those who currently rule over us. In order to acquire the most basic freedoms, taken for granted by every citizen of a civilized nation, these Jews in mixed marriages must subject themselves to an unnatural procedure, which fills any right-minded person with horror when they first hear about it. *They can get themselves sterilized!*[8]

Just try to imagine this. Among these people in mixed marriages are young, healthy, strong individuals. Many of them have children, among whom there are many whose physical and mental health disproves everything that is preached by the insane pseudo-science which the Nazis call racial doctrine.[9]

In Westerbork, the victims had to choose between sterilization and Poland within an hour. Is it not understandable that many succumbed, especially older people?

As for the rest, the work is slowly but surely progressing, in silence. First it was done by German army physicians. They stopped doing it.[10] Then Dutch physicians were sounded out. They were all horrified when asked. Those who refused included a large number of Jewish physicians, who were promised significant benefits and security for themselves and their families.[11]

7 In Oct. 1940 all public officials had to sign an 'Aryan declaration' and Jewish employees and civil servants were dismissed: see PMJ 5/39. The Dutch secretaries general accepted this as a temporary measure: see PMJ 5/46.

8 See Docs. 118 and 124.

9 In the original, the word 'gevrijwaard' ('protected') follows here, between the sentences. Presumably it does not belong in the text.

10 This could not be verified.

11 In the absence of sources, it is impossible to ascertain who was performing sterilization operations. However, physicians made attempts to declare Jews in mixed marriages sterile before the surgery could be carried out. By June 1944 a total of 2,562 Jews had either been medically certified as sterile or surgically sterilized: Coen Stuldreher, *De legale rest: Gemengd gehuwde Joden onder de Duitse bezetting* (Amsterdam: no publisher specified, 2007), pp. 289–303.

Having escaped from one hunter – albeit permanently maimed – they fall into the hands of another …

Antisemites nevertheless?

In spite of all this injustice and suffering, which makes our hearts sink, there are symptoms of growing antisemitic sentiments among our people. The causes are well known: a few cases of negligence, immodesty, ingratitude, cowardice, and betrayal by Jews in hiding, in which those who have helped them have become the victims. We do not wish to deny these facts (we have experienced them first hand!) and most certainly do not wish to condone them. Nevertheless, we warn against rumours, which cannot be verified and are very much exaggerated, and often ten different stories are doing the rounds about one case. Moreover, it is always the wrongdoings of the Jews that are passed on. *Of course nothing is said about the thousands of Jews who are in hiding without any problems occurring at all.*

But there are also other reasons that prompt us to employ caution and self-criticism. Of course there are bad elements among the Jews, as there are among non-Jews. One might ask, however: why do so many of the cases identified above concern Jews?

The answer is simple. *All Jews, good and bad, brave and cowardly, nervous and calm, have to go into hiding. Each Jew must save his own skin. As far as non-Jewish Dutch people are concerned, it is usually the best, the strongest, and the bravest who find themselves on the wrong side of the Gestapo.* The cowards do nothing, the weak are obedient; the worst elements seek out the NSB and the WA, etc. Given the large number of those who conspire with the enemy, given the appallingly large number of Dutch people who do not become involved and wait to see how matters will pan out, etc., there is no reason whatsoever to put ourselves above the Jews.

But there is more, and worse: we are aware of several cases, which have been verified, in which Jews in hiding have been blackmailed: cases of scandalous financial exploitation, and betrayal, and fearfulness (withdrawing a promise to help, sending them away when controls are tightened, etc.).

Many Jews' efforts to obtain so-called Sperrstempel[12] are no different from the race for 'Ausweise',[13] exemptions, etc. on the part of labourers, prisoners of war, and suchlike.

We do not need to explain this side of the case in further detail; the criticism of many Dutch people and groups expressed in this newspaper and its sister publications makes it sufficiently clear that there is most certainly no reason why we should put ourselves above the Jews.

Let us instead be brave and self-critical, and increase our willingness to support those who suffer most, whether they are Jews or non-Jews.

This applies not only now, but also after the war. The poison of propaganda has affected us imperceptibly, and it will have long after-effects, especially on our children, who have become used to it and know no better than that a Jew always occupies a singular position. It is not without reason that the Nazis have declared antisemitism to be one of the decisive criteria for the National Socialist ethos.

12 German in the original: 'exemption stamps'.
13 German in the original: 'identity cards'.

The reverse is also true. *Wherever the hatred of the Jews is on the rise, democracy is losing ground, and people's minds are being surreptitiously nazified.* Let us be cautious! And let us be just!

DOC. 146
On 30 October 1943 Reich Commissioner Seyss-Inquart determines which Jews may temporarily remain in the Netherlands[1]

Letter from the Reich Commissioner for the Occupied Dutch Territories (S-P),[2] signed Seyss-Inquart, to SS-Obergruppenführer Rauter, Commissioner General Dr F. Wimmer, Commissioner General Dr Fischböck, Commissioner General Ritterbusch,[3] and Representative Dr Schröder, The Hague, dated 30 October 1943 (copy)[4]

The elimination of Jewish blood from the Dutch Volksgemeinschaft has, generally speaking, reached the level stipulated by the Reich. The situation must now be stabilized in order to prevent further concern arising from this issue. Therefore, it must be conclusively determined which persons of Jewish blood [are still living in the Netherlands], under which conditions they will be allowed to remain within the community, which of them are to be concentrated in Westerbork special camp, as well as which come into consideration for labour deployment in the East. Pending the final decision, which must be made in consultation with the central Reich authorities in charge, I hereby order the following provisional arrangement:

A

To remain outside the camps in the Netherlands are

1. Jews exempted from wearing the star
   a) who are among the approximately 60 persons included in a special list for a variety of specific reasons. In the majority of cases, the inclusion in the list is permanent. A small number have been temporarily exempted from wearing the star until a specific task has been accomplished, and will then join Group B 2[5] in Westerbork.
   b) Jews in mixed marriages who are unable to father children (due to age or voluntary sterilization).

   The members of this group, Group 1, have their identity cards stamped with the open (not filled-in) letter J, and their legal rights, or rather limitations, are defined in the Security Police leaflet regarding the obligations of Jews who are exempt from wearing

1 NIOD, 020/1561. This document has been translated from German.
2 The abbreviation stands for 'Hertha Santo Passo', Seyss-Inquart's secretary.
3 Wilhelm Friedrich Adolf Ritterbusch (1892–1981), teacher; joined the NSDAP in 1923; mayor of Piesteritz, 1933–1937; NSDAP Kreisleiter in Merseburg, 1937–1940; representative for the province of North Brabant, 1940–1941; worked in the NSDAP Party Chancellery, 1941–1943; commissioner general for special duties in the Netherlands, 1943–1945; arrested in the Netherlands in 1945; interned until Nov. 1947, then returned to Germany.
4 The original contains handwritten underlining.
5 This could not be found.

the star.[6] This also specifically applies to the labour deployment of these Jews, which must be arranged through the labour deployment offices, with the police merely checking to determine whether the requirements or restrictions have in fact been complied with. At any rate, this labour deployment will not be carried out within the established framework for Jews wearing a star who are not held in camps.

2. Jews who wear the star, that is, Jews in mixed marriages who are able to father children. Their identity cards are stamped with the filled-in J, and have a number between 100,000 and 120,000.[7] They are subject to all legal restrictions based on the regulations pertaining to Jews. As they are mostly unemployed and live off black-market trade, they must be put to work. However, this labour deployment must also be organized through the labour deployment offices, with the police ensuring that the relevant regulations are complied with. The labour deployment therefore takes place separately and in groups, but not in a closed facility. Furthermore, this deployment is supervised but not under guard as in the closed-off camps. Depending on the place of work, these Jews can live at home or visit their families on weekends, provided they are allowed to use public transport.

The activities outside of the camps of other Jews wearing the star, such as Jewish diamond workers, members of the Jewish Council, etc., must be phased out as quickly as possible. The Jewish diamond workers are to be put to work in a closed-off camp, the Jewish Council in Westerbork camp.[8]

The official responsibilities with regard to Group A will continue to be discharged by the Central Office[9] in Amsterdam (Schröder, Lages). Divorce will be made possible in the context of a reform of Dutch matrimonial law. The divorced Jewish spouse will, however, not be deported to the East, but rather placed in or kept in labour deployment, under guard, in the Netherlands.

B

Held in Westerbork are

1. the Protestant Jews whose names are included in a list. They are to be housed separately and will be visited weekly by a Protestant clergyman.
2. the privileged Jews (on the Frederiks and van Dam lists),[10] also listed by name, as well as those referred by the SD on a case-by-case basis. These are also to be housed separately and can receive weekly visits from representatives.

   Both groups are to be given suitable work in the camp.
3. Jews designated for exchange, including members of the Jewish Council, who will at most be taken to the exchange camp at Bergen-Belsen at some later date.[11] These are to be put to work in the camp for now.

The directives relating to assets remain unchanged.

6 These instructions were issued in Sept. 1943 and regulated the participation in public life of Jews who were 'exempted from wearing the star': NIOD 250i/961.
7 On the numbering of the exemption stamps, see Doc. 118, fn. 18.
8 The Jewish Council had in fact already been dissolved on 29 Sept. 1943, with the deportation of the two chairmen and the remaining members.
9 Central Office for Jewish Emigration.
10 See Doc. 102.
11 On the so-called holding camp at Bergen-Belsen, see Doc. 118, fn. 18.

C
All persons of Jewish blood who are not covered by the general regulations mentioned above, or to whom another specific regulation applies, such as former members of the NSB, etc., have been taken to the East for work or will be taken there for this purpose if they are still in the country in camps or have been apprehended after going underground.

DOC. 147
On 8 November 1943 Anne Frank writes about her changing moods in hiding in the Annexe[1]

Handwritten diary[2] of Anne Frank,[3] entry for 8 November 1943

Monday evening, 8 November 1943

Dearest Kitty,

If you were to read all my letters in one sitting, you'd be struck by the fact that they were written in a variety of moods. It annoys me to be so dependent on the moods here in the Annexe, but I'm not the only one: we're all subject to them. If I'm engrossed in a book, I have to rearrange my thoughts before I can mingle with other people, because otherwise they might think I was strange. As you can see, I'm currently in the middle of a depression. I couldn't really tell you what set it off, but I think it stems from my cowardice, which confronts me at every turn. This evening when Bep[4] was still here, the doorbell rang long and loud, I instantly turned white, my stomach churned, and my heart beat wildly – and all because I was afraid.

At night in bed I see myself alone in a dungeon, without Father[5] and Mother.[6] Or I'm roaming the streets, or the Annexe is on fire, or they come in the middle of the night to take us away and I crawl under my bed in desperation. I see everything as if it were actually taking place. And to think it might all happen soon!

1 NIOD, 212C/1a. Excerpt from Anne Frank, *The Diary of a Young Girl: The Definitive Edition*, ed. Otto H. Frank and Mirjam Pressler, trans. Susan Massotty (London: Penguin, 2007), pp. 144–145. This document has been translated from Dutch.

2 Two handwritten versions of Anne Frank's diary exist (version a and version b) because she revised the original in the spring of 1944. She did so in response to a call made over Radio Oranje on 28 March 1944 to save such documents for posterity; she hoped to write a novel based on her experiences in hiding. The *Definitive Edition* draws on both versions and does not include all the text from version b.

3 Anneliese (Anne) Frank (1929–1945); born in Frankfurt am Main; moved with her family to the Netherlands in 1934, after her father had relocated there; began her diary in June 1942; the family went into hiding in July 1942, but were betrayed and arrested on 4 August 1944. Anne Frank was deported to Auschwitz in Sept. 1944 along with the seven other people with whom she was in hiding. In Oct. 1944 she was deported with her sister Margot to Bergen-Belsen, where they both perished in February or March 1945, probably of typhus.

4 Elisabeth (Bep) Voskuijl (1919–1983), office worker; employed in Otto Frank's business, 1937–1947; helped with the daily provisioning of the group in hiding; remained in contact with Otto Frank for the rest of her life.

Miep[7] often says she envies us because we have such peace and quiet here. That may be true, but she's obviously not thinking about our fear.

I simply can't imagine the world will ever be normal again for us. I do talk about 'after the war', but it's as if I were talking about a castle in the air, something that can never come true.

I see the eight of us in the Annexe[8] as if we were a patch of blue sky surrounded by menacing black clouds. The perfectly round spot on which we're standing is still safe, but the clouds are moving in on us, and the ring between us and the approaching danger is being pulled tighter and tighter. We're surrounded by darkness and danger, and in our desperate search for a way out we keep bumping into each other. We look at the fighting down below, and the peace and beauty up above. In the meantime, we've been cut off by the dark mass of clouds, so that we can go neither up nor down. It looms before us like an impenetrable wall, trying to crush us, but not yet able to. I can only cry out and implore, 'Oh, ring, ring, open wide, and let us out!'

Yours, Anne

DOC. 148
On 11 November 1943 the Commissariat General for Administration and Justice rejects a draft regulation on the removal of Jewish cultural products from the public sphere[1]

Letter from the Interior Administration Department (C/W.), p.p. signed Calmeyer, The Hague, to the Legislation Department, Prof. Spanner,[2] The Hague, 8 L[ange] Vijverberg, dated 11 November 1943

Re: preventing the dissemination of Jewish cultural goods
Reference: your letter of 10 November 1943, file ref. Ve 1–II 19–20/42[3]
The draft directive on banning Jewish products from cultural life would not have met with any objections had it been submitted at the time that Regulation 189/40[4] was issued, or by approximately mid 1942. However, at the present time such a directive must, in my

5 Otto Frank (1889–1980), businessman; emigrated to the Netherlands, 1933; prepared the hiding place for his family in the rear building ('the Annexe') of his business premises; as the sole survivor of the family, dedicated himself after the war to the publication of his daughter's diary.
6 Edith Frank, née Holländer (1900–1945), housewife; born in Aachen; married Otto Frank in 1925; deported in 1944 to Auschwitz, where she perished.
7 Miep Gies, born Hermine Santrouschitz (1909–2010), secretary; emigrated from Vienna to the Netherlands in 1920; worked for Otto Frank from 1933; helped with the daily provisioning of the group in hiding; following the arrest of those in hiding, retrieved Anne's diary and personal effects from the Annexe.
8 Along with Anna and her parents, the following persons lived in in the Annexe: her sister Margot (1926–1945), Fritz Pfeffer (1889–1944), and the family Hermann van Pels (1898–1944), Auguste van Pels, née Röttgen (1900–1945), and Peter van Pels (1926–1945).

1 NIOD, 020/1491. This document has been translated from German.
2 Dr Hans Spanner (1908–1991), lawyer; worked in the state government of Styria, 1932–1936; held lecturer's posts at the universities of Vienna and Graz, 1934–1936; professor in Graz from 1937; head of the Legislation Department in the Commissariat General for Administration and Justice in the Netherlands, 1942–1944; professor in Graz and Munich after 1945.
3 Not included in the file.
4 Regulation on the Registration of Businesses: see PMJ 5/42.

opinion, cause consternation, first, because it raises a subject that is inconsequential in comparison with other problems, and second, because it inevitably creates the impression that Jewish products are inundating cultural life in the Netherlands. To the best of my knowledge, that is not the case. The German occupation does not need to expose itself to ridicule by searching this or that bookshop for a work which a Jew may have been 'discernibly involved' in producing.

Incidentally, the expansion of the term 'Jew' in § 4 is problematic.

I believe I must advise against issuing the drafted directive. To date, no special measures for the detection and removal of Jewish cultural goods have been necessary within the jurisdiction of the Internal Administration Department.

p.p. Calmeyer

Draft

Directive issued by the Commissioner General for Security[5] *on Banning Jewish Products from Cultural Life*

On the basis of § 14 and § 52 of Regulation no. 1/43 of the Reich Commissioner for the Occupied Dutch Territories on the Protection of Order,[6] I decree:

§ 1

It is forbidden to circulate Jewish products in the cultural sphere or to keep them in stock for this purpose.

§ 2

Within the meaning of this directive, products in the cultural sphere are:

1) literature;
2) sheet music and gramophone records;
3) paintings and sculptures.

§ 3

Jewish products within the meaning of this directive are those authored or created by a Jew or those which a Jew has played a defining role in making or in which a Jew is otherwise discernibly involved.

§ 4

A Jew within the meaning of this directive is

1) anyone who, under § 4 of Regulation no. 189/1940 on the Registration of Businesses,[7] is a Jew or is considered a Jew,
2) anyone who is descended from two Jewish grandparents.

§ 5

Within the meaning of this directive, circulation is defined as any type of artistic, scientific, journalistic, educational, and commercial distribution to the public, i.e. in particular the activities of displaying, performing, offering for sale, selling, and otherwise placing on the market, including artistic processing, mechanical reproduction, and reprinting.

5 Hanns Albin Rauter.

6 § 14 stated that the circulation of printed matter of all kinds could be prohibited by police directive, and § 52 empowered the Commissioner General for Security to issue directives to ensure the security of public life: see Regulation on the Protection of Order (1943), *VOBl-NL*, no. 1/1943, pp. 1–39, 5 Jan. 1943.

7 On the text of the regulation, see PMJ 5/42.

§ 6
The Commissioner General for Security is responsible for monitoring the implementation of this directive and for the granting of exemptions.
§ 7
1) Anyone who violates or circumvents the provision of § 1 will be sentenced to imprisonment for up to 6 months and a fine of up to fl. 5,000 or with one of these penalties, unless a more severe penalty under other regulations is applicable. The same punishment will be imposed on anyone who induces, facilitates, or contributes to a circumvention of these provisions.
2) The items to which the illegal act applies can be confiscated.
3) The right to impose Security Police measures is reserved.
§ 8
This directive comes into force on the day of its promulgation.[8]
The Hague
SS-Obergruppenführer and Police General[9]

DOC. 149
In November 1943 the American Jewish Joint Distribution Committee in Lisbon reports on its attempts to transfer Dutch Jews to Palestine in exchange for German nationals[1]

Letter (General Letter Nr. 581; HK/ML) from the American Joint Distribution Committee, signed Herbert Katzki[2] (secretary), Lisbon, 242 Rua Aurea, to the American Joint Distribution Committee, New York (received on 23 December 1943), dated 13 November 1943[3]

Re: exchange of Dutch Jews against Germans now in Palestine[4]
We refer to your cable in which you inquire regarding the possibility for exchanging Dutch Jewish nationals for German nationals in Palestine.[5] The situation is as follows:

Some time ago, when deportations of Dutch Jews from Holland were in full swing, an arrangement was made by the office of the Jewish Agency[6] in Geneva and in Jerusalem

8 This regulation was never issued.
9 Hanns Albin Rauter.

1 NIOD, 217a/1e. The original document is in English.
2 Herbert Katzki (1907–1997), American-born banker; worked for the American Jewish Joint Distribution Committee (JDC), 1939–1979; secretary of the European Executive Council in Paris from 1940; fled to Lisbon with his co-workers; worked for the War Refugee Board, 1944–1945; continued working in Europe for the JDC as its deputy director general after 1945; returned to the USA in 1967.
3 The original contains a receipt stamp with handwritten initials.
4 In German: *Palästina-Deutsche.* These were Germans living in various Templer settlements and colonies. The German Templer Society was established in the mid nineteenth century by Christoph Hoffmann. Its first colony in Palestine was established in 1868. In the 1930s and 1940s a considerable number joined the NSDAP Auslandsorganisation (the organization of Nazi cells outside Germany).
5 Not included in the file.
6 The Jewish Agency was founded at the Nineteenth Zionist Congress in 1929 and represented the Jews in relation to the British Mandate for Palestine.

for the preparation of lists of Dutch Jewish nationals[7] in Holland who might be available for exchange against German nationals in Palestine. Upon the entering of names on these lists the interested persons in Holland were advised that so-called 'exchange certificates' had been made available to them.

With these notes in hand, they had some measure of protection against deportation inasmuch as the Germans naturally had an interest in having available a group of persons subject to exchange for German nationals in Palestine.[8] While this procedure might have been regarded as a 'device', the interesting thing is that it worked for a while. Subsequently the procedure changed and the German administrators in Holland requested that the Dutch Jewish people included in the exchange list actually were in possession of immigration certificates or at least of immigration certificate numbers. These, too, were provided.

We now understand that the device has lost its efficacy or, at best, is working out only to a limited degree. People who had these so-called 'Exchange Certificates' have actually been sent to Westerbork for deportation or, in fact, have already been deported.

In terms of procedure, relatives or interested persons residing outside Holland who desired to have their relatives in Holland included in the exchange list requested the office of the Jewish Agency in Geneva to inscribe the names on the exchange list and at the same time the Jewish Agency in Jerusalem was notified so that it in turn could advise Geneva that the necessary steps had been taken in Jerusalem.

In our opinion the scheme was useful as long as it worked to prevent deportations. So far as we know, no one really thought that the exchange would take place. What the ultimate fate of these exchange certificates will be one cannot tell, nor can one forecast definitely how long, if at all, the exchange certificates will provide protection.[9] We do know that people with exchange certificates have been sent away.

As a side-[note] it is interesting to know that Dr Schwartz[10] advised us after his trip to Palestine that the German people in Palestine prefer to remain there and do not want to be repatriated to Germany.

7 Handwritten addition: 'and other Jews'.

8 Release stamps with the numbers 40,000–50,000 were scheduled for 'exchange Jews'.

9 At the end of 1943 around 1,300 people in the Netherlands (Dutch nationals and stateless Jews) possessed exchange certificates for Palestine. They were deported from Westerbork to Bergen-Belsen camp between Jan. and April 1944. In late June 1944 a total of 222 of these Jews were transferred from the so-called Star Camp (*Sternlager*) at Bergen-Belsen to Palestine as part of an exchange for German nationals, arriving in July. Of those remaining in Bergen-Belsen, few survived.

10 Dr Joseph Joshua Schwartz (1899–1975), rabbi and orientalist; rabbi in New York, 1921–1925; university lecturer, 1930–1933; welfare worker, 1933–1939; director of the JDC's European Executive Council, 1940–1950; board member of other Jewish relief organizations, 1950–1970.

DOC. 150
On 11 December 1943 Ministerialrat Friedrich from the Reich Court of Auditors summarizes the decisions regarding the administration of stolen Jewish assets and describes how they are implemented[1]

Report (X 51611–616/43) by Regierungspräsident (retd) Ministerialrat Friedrich,[2] Potsdam, dated 11 December 1943 (copy)[3]

Report
by Regierungspräsident (retd) Ministerialrat Friedrich on inquiries made locally [at offices and local administrative agencies of] the Reich Commissioner for the Occupied Dutch Territories in Apeldoorn, Arnhem, and The Hague in the period from 18 to 24 November 1943 (assignment from the director of the Court of Auditors of the German Reich, dated 20 October 1943 – Pr X 51600-530/43 –) regarding the *administration of Jewish assets.*
21 enclosures[4]

The proceedings were conducted:

In Apeldoorn on 18, 20, and 25 November at the governor's office with Regierungspräsident Dr Piesbergen and Treasurer Bartling.

In Arnhem on 19 November at the Office for Economic Investigation[5] with Diplomvolkswirt[6] Kolbmüller, deputy head of the Office for Economic Investigation Diplomkaufmann[7] Zumbrägel, and the lawyer Burghardt; and at the NAGU (Netherlands Public Limited Company for the Liquidation of Businesses) with board members Dr Veltjens and Kolbe.

In The Hague on 22 November at the premises of the Reich Commissariat (23 Plein) with Kammergerichtsrat[8] Dr Schröder, head of the Office for Economic Investigation; Dr Merkens, head of the Arnhem branch of the German Audit and Trust Company; Amtsgerichtsrat Zander, head of section at the Office for Economic Investigation; and Dr Iglseder, head of the Reich Commissioner's audit office; on 23 November at the Department for Settlement and Buildings and at the Netherlands Property Administration (NG) with the engineer Münster, head of the Department for Settlement and Buildings and

1 BArch, R 2/11443b. This document has been translated from German.
2 Werner Friedrich (1886–1966), lawyer; administrator in East Prussia from 1915; from 1938 Ministerialdirigent at the Reich Court of Auditors; chairman of the board of the Königsberger Diakonissen-Mutterhaus, a Lutheran training hospital, 1948–1965; awarded the Grand Cross of the Order of Merit of the Federal Republic of Germany (*Großes Bundesverdienstkreuz*) in 1951.
3 The report was sent by the Reich Court of Auditors to the Reich Minister of Finance on 23 Dec. 1943. It comprises 24 pages in total.
4 These are not part of the file.
5 Established in 1940, the Wirtschaftsprüfstelle reported to the commissioner general for finance and economic affairs, Hans Fischböck. All Jewish businesses were required to register with the authority, which worked closely with the German Audit and Trust Company (Deutsche Revisions- und Treuhand AG).
6 Professional title for the holder of a degree in economics.
7 Professional title for the holder of a degree in commerce.
8 Kammergerichtsrat and Amtsgerichtsrat below denote professional titles for a judge.

simultaneously manager of the NG; and Schneider-Arnoldi, his deputy; on 24 November with Reich Commissioner Reich Minister Dr Seyss-Inquart in person.

The results of the discussions are summarized in the report below.

Part One. Overview.

A. Legal basis, function, and structure of the assets administration procedure

1. As in other occupied territories, in the jurisdiction of the Reich Commissioner (RC) for the Occupied Dutch Territories, Jewish assets have been confiscated and placed under the administration of German agencies. The legal basis for this official intervention consists in a number of regulations (9) that the RC has issued on the basis of his legislative authority. The Jewish assets have not been seized in a single operation, but rather as part of a gradual process. In the autumn of 1940, mandatory registration for commercial enterprises was introduced,[9] and this was followed only six months later by the provisions regarding the de-Jewification of industry and commerce.[10] The next step was the de-Jewification of agriculture,[11] which was initially developed on the basis of voluntary Aryanization, but as of the spring of 1943 is being realized through forced Aryanization on the basis of supplementary provisions. The provisions on the de-Jewification of agriculture were followed in the summer of 1941 by the regulation on the de-Jewification of Jewish real estate,[12] which was executed from the outset by both methods: voluntary Aryanization and forced Aryanization. Simultaneously with this regulation, Jewish financial assets were also made subject to administration and sale.[13] Central to this was a regulation issued by the RC in the spring of 1942, which also made the remainder of Jews' movable assets subject to liquidation.[14] The only exceptions were furniture and other household effects, because other agencies (the Ministry for the East[15] and its task forces, previously the Rosenberg Task Force) are responsible for dealing with these assets.
2. The aim of the seizure is not only – as in the case of Reich assets – to secure the confiscated assets, but also to liquidate them, that is, to convert them into cash or other liquid assets (securities). Undecided as yet is the question which entity will subsequently have legal control over the proceeds. For now, announcing the forfeiture of the Jewish assets – for example, according to the model applied to Serbia[16] – has been avoided. However, it is probable that the proceeds from the Jewish assets will be confiscated to the benefit of the Reich, but will become assets designated specific-

9 See PMJ 5/42.
10 See PMJ 5/67.
11 Regulation on the Registration and Handling of Agricultural Land in Jewish Hands, 27 May 1941, *VOBl-NL*, no. 102/1941, pp. 388–395.
12 Regulation on Jewish Real Estate, 11 August 1941, *VOBl-NL*, no. 154/1941, pp. 655–663.
13 See PMJ 5/85.
14 See PMJ 5/136.
15 The Reich Ministry for the Occupied Eastern Territories.
16 Following the German occupation of Serbia in April 1941, the occupiers ordered the confiscation of Jewish assets. These assets were ostensibly to be used for the benefit of Serbia rather than the Reich, and the forfeiture of Jewish assets 'to the benefit of Serbia' was officially codified in an August 1942 regulation. In practice, the Reich authorities appropriated the assets on the pretext that they were required as compensation for war damage to Reich German and ethnic German property.

ally for expenditure in the Netherlands. The status of the assets as 'Reich assets-to-be' is already expressed in certain technical details of the procedure for administering assets, for example, the discontinuation of the process for maintaining separate accounts. For the time being, the proceeds from the Jewish assets remain blocked pending subsequent use.

3. The total value of the Jewish assets is estimated at fl. 6[00] to 700 million.[17] Standardized registration documents and their appraisal based on statistical principles are lacking. A reduction of the assets will result from the fact that approximately 10 per cent is to be set aside and made available to the Reich Minister of Finance as the share of the total proceeds from former German Jews. A further reduction of the proceeds will result from the fact that, owing to an easing of the provisions pertaining to Jewish assets – carried out solely via administrative channels – a substantial share of the Jewish assets reverts to the owners or their children. Jews living in mixed marriages who undergo sterilization are exempted from wearing the Jewish star and, as 'star-exempt' Jews, are given their assets back. Jews who do not undergo sterilization but live in a mixed marriage with children can gift their assets to their children, who then get them back from the administration.
4. The system for administering assets has an extremely diverse structure, perhaps as a result of the gradual implementation of the procedure for seizing assets. There is not even a uniform leadership, with the exception of the role of the RC. While the individual branches of the assets administration agency are all linked to the Commissariat General for Finance and Economic Affairs, within the Commissariat General itself they are subordinate to various departments. For example, a separate department known as the 'Office for Economic Investigation' has been created to deal with commercial assets, while a section of the Department for Enemy Assets[18] handles Jewish financial assets. The de-Jewification of real estate is the responsibility of the Department for Settlement and Buildings, and the de-Jewification of agriculture is administered by the Department for Food and Agriculture. In addition to the proliferation of responsibilities, the auditing process is also impeded by the fact that the individual offices of the assets administration agency are located in different places: in Arnhem, The Hague, and Amsterdam. In addition, a considerable number of very diverse private assets administration agencies have been entrusted with the actual implementation of the de-Jewification procedure. Apart from the individual trustees, there are collective trustees, sometimes in the form of associations under civil law, sometimes in the form of foundations with legal capacity.
5. Despite the highly diversified structure of the administrative apparatus, in this case – as in other areas – it has been impossible to prevent outside agencies from likewise concerning themselves with the registration and utilization of portions of the Jewish assets. In this regard, the offices of the assets administration agency point out in particular the role played by the Senior Commander of the Security Police and the

17 In summer 1945 the Jewish-owned monetary assets that were confiscated by Lippmann, Rosenthal & Co. bank were estimated at more than fl. 415 million. In total, it is likely that Jewish-owned monetary assets and tangible assets (such as real estate and plots of land) valued at fl. 770 to 900 million were stolen.

18 *Feindvermögen*: assets belonging to nationals of countries at war with Germany.

SD (BdS),[19] whose activities, not only in the form of individual confiscations in the context of criminal proceedings but also through general measures (the Fur Operation[20]), are said to have encroached on the responsibilities of the RC's assets administration agency.

5a. Alongside the administration apparatus, the RC has put in place a monitoring apparatus that covers all branches of the assets administration agency. It is operated partly by the German Audit and Trust Company[21] (Treuarbeit) subsidiary in The Hague (at present Arnhem), and partly by an 'Audit Office' created especially for this purpose.

6. As one must assume that the liquidation of Jewish assets will be completed in the not too distant future, apart from certain exceptions for war veterans – the offices of the Reich Commissariat speak of six months in their reports – proposals for a fundamental restructuring or sweeping reorganization of the administration apparatus are probably not appropriate. However, it will be important to ensure that the administration apparatus is dismantled as liquidation progresses.

7. The costs of administration, to the extent that they are not deducted from the assets, are covered by fees. The RC – either through his finance directorate or directly – has arranged for the resulting surpluses for the period up until 31 March 1943 to be collected for the Reich Foundation for the Netherlands (cf. report on this foundation).[22] He thus does not propose disbursing the administration cost surpluses to the private assets administration agencies as special funds; nonetheless, the RC's view has apparently not yet gained unanimous acceptance. One administration office – a foundation with a legal capacity – claims the administration fees it collects as its 'revenue' and the surplus as its 'profits'. In addition, with respect to the interest on the assets, which in the RC's personal view accrues to the total amount of the assets, ambiguities still seem to exist, and these must be resolved.

8. All of the proceeds are channelled into the 'Asset Management and Pensions Institute' (VVR),[23] a foundation under Dutch law that was established by the RC. This foundation has been assigned the task of managing the Jewish assets that are consolidated in it until a decision is taken regarding their confiscation and utilization.

[…][24]

19 Erich Naumann (1905–1951), commercial employee; joined the NSDAP in 1929, the SA in 1930, and the SS in 1935; worked full-time for the SD from 1935; commander of Einsatzgruppe B in the occupied Soviet Union, Nov. 1941–Sept. 1943; Senior Commander of the Security Police and the SD in the Netherlands, Sept. 1943–May 1944; returned to Germany; arrested in 1947; sentenced to death by a military tribunal in 1948; executed in 1951.

20 *Pelzaktion*: operation in which the fur and leather coats of murdered Jews in the occupied Eastern territories were distributed among bombed-out inhabitants of German cities.

21 The Dutch branch of the German Audit and Trust Company was established in summer 1940 and was responsible for administering 'enemy assets'.

22 This is not included in the file. The Reich Foundation for the Netherlands was a section within the Reich Commissariat's executive office.

23 Vermögensverwaltungs- und Rentenanstalt.

24 Under Item B in what follows, the regulations pertaining to Jewish assets are again cited in greater detail. The second part of the report deals with the individual branches of the agency for the administration of Jewish assets; the third concerns the Asset Management and Pensions Institute.

DOC. 151

On 11 January 1944 Sam Goudsmit wonders at the Jewish Council's submissiveness and the attitude of other Jewish groups towards the German occupiers[1]

Handwritten diary of Sam Goudsmit, entry for 11 January 1944

Tuesday, 11 January 1944
Concerns about the future. A spanner in the works.
Although I may not be around – I have now read for the second time an official statement from the Allied side about Germany after this war,[2] which leaves one in despair, yes, no less than despair. The second one appears in the paper this evening, in a 'Declaration from Moscow with regard to Poland.'[3] The Polish people can seek to cooperate with the Soviet Union, and 'also, if the Polish people so wish, on the basis of an alliance *for mutual assistance against Germany.*[4] Poland's entry into the recently concluded *Soviet-Czech* treaty[5] could serve this purpose.'

Will Germany therefore be given the opportunity to prepare a new war of aggression? There will be others, if they are alive, who, like me, will want to tear up the ground and bury the Bystanders,[6] the Bystanders. I am a Jew. 'I am the man who has witnessed the misery.'[7]

Faced with such prospects, with such plans made by the 'friends' and 'Allies' who have made such an effort to bring German power to a standstill and to divide Germany, etc., in short, to disable the German potential for aggression once and for all, even the most hopeful Wehrmacht news reports and other accounts become worthless and turn sour. What good would it be if this Germany were to collapse in a month, if new treaties have to be concluded against it anyway? Once again, a beautiful hill with bread and fresh water becomes the only ideal.

Evening
The Jews and their attitude towards the Occupier in Holland. This is a difficult issue. These are the crucial points:

1. *How would they have been able, without help from the non-Jewish population, to defend themselves against their downfall?*
2. *Why did they register as Jews in the beginning, when the Germans demanded that they do so?*

1 Bibliotheca Rosenthaliana, HC-ROS-006. This document has been translated from Dutch.
2 Presumably a European Advisory Commission statement in which the Allies stated plans for post-war policy.
3 It was not possible to ascertain the name of the newspaper in which this article appeared. The reference is to the Soviet government's statement concerning Poland's eastern border.
4 Note by the author in the original: 'Or do people say "Germany" but mean "America"? With its alliance partners?'
5 The Czechoslovak–Soviet Treaty of Friendship, Mutual Alliance, and Post-war Collaboration had been concluded on 12 Dec. 1943.
6 The original is barely legible at this point, but it appears to be 'Dulders', which could be a noun that the author has created from the verb 'dulden', meaning 'tolerate'.
7 Presumably an allusion to Lamentations 3:1: 'I am the man that hath seen affliction by the rod of his wrath' (KJV).

3. *Should and could they have refused to do so?*
4. *What would have been the consequences of a more or less complete refusal?*
5. Is the 'Jewish Council' to blame for that first surrender?
6. Is the Jewish religious community to blame?
7. Is the non-Jewish Dutch portion of the population to blame?
8. Is the Jewish Council to blame for the continued expulsion of Jews? The 'Allies'?
9. Is the non-Jewish population to blame?[8]
10. What would have been the consequences of further resistance by the Jewish Council, or by the non-Jewish population?

1. By refusing the first step: registering as Jews. And further, possibly also thereafter: by material resistance.
2. Largely out of ignorance of the Occupier's power and the duration of the war. Partly out of nationalist self-exaltation (due to that ignorance), partly also out of weakness towards the leaders'[9] suggestion to submit.
3. They could have refused. It would have been impossible to officially record people as Jews, at least in the case of many who were living outside the Jewish religious community.[10] Whether they should have refused will become clear in the future.
4. The consequences of a more or less complete refusal on the part of the Jews to state their ancestry would probably have been: major problems for the Germans in establishing the Jewish status of *all* Jews under German law. As a result, a much more violent approach immediately (which they wanted to avoid through 'voluntary' registration of the Jews). Bigger problems with the non-Jewish population as a result of violence employed too suddenly. And so many victims of that violence, especially among the Jews, of course. The violence would also have continued for a long time, as this Occupier does not want to refrain from this course of action, but it is very possible that the number of victims would have been smaller than it turned out to be, as many Jews who were not registered with the religious community would have escaped persecution, although one has to bear in mind *all the efforts* the Germans made to use any possible means of intimidation and *deception* until they had achieved their goal to the greatest extent possible. It is certain that, as things have turned out, they have completely achieved their aim: to bring all the Jews under their control without using any violence.
5. The Jewish Council is to blame for that first fatal step towards the Jews surrendering themselves. From the outset, it recommended submission in *Joodsche Weekblad*. Its own submission to the German demand that it set itself up in order to organize the persecution must be regarded as the first and the decisive fatal error.[11] That led to

8 Note in the original: 'The "alliance partners"? I have already dealt with these points in my earlier notebooks. My conclusion was: Yes, guilty. But it ought to be stated again here, briefly.'

9 Presumably a reference to the Jewish Council.

10 This statement is not correct. Religious affiliation was also recorded with the State Inspectorate of Population Registers, which would have made a census of the Jews possible.

11 In his 14 Feb. 1941 speech to mark the creation of the Jewish Council, Abraham Asscher, one of its two chairmen, had appealed to the Jewish community members' sense of responsibility and urged them to cooperate: see PMJ 5/56.

the situation described in point 4 above. The Jewish Council baulked at 'chaos', at resistance.

6. The Jewish religious community must be to blame to the extent that it
   1) demonstrated complete solidarity with the Jewish Council;
   2) according to information that needs to be verified, allegedly refused to destroy the records of the Jewish religious community (presumably because they believed they could use these records after the war, and that therefore their loss would be extremely detrimental to the power of the Jewish religious community and that of the rabbis).[12]
7. It is difficult to apportion blame to the non-Jewish population for that initial step on a superficial level. Where the Jews acted out of ignorance in terms of the duration of the war, the question of whether the non-Jewish population bears any blame is irrelevant. Where the Jews acted out of fear, it must be concluded that there was insufficient trust in the full (actual) solidarity of non-Jewish compatriots. And of course, the general culpability of the non-Jewish population is an established fact.
8. The Jewish Council is to blame for the continued expulsion of the Jews, since once it was under the Occupier's power, it tolerated and helped to implement each tightening of the rules, under the delusion that each time would be the last time as far as the Germans were concerned, and therefore the rest of the Jews would be spared; in the belief that the war would soon end with a German defeat; or, in the worst possible case, with the aim of rescuing a small portion of the Dutch Jews and, for that purpose, letting the others suffer the fate which the Jewish Council thought was unavoidable anyway. Personally, I believe that *all three* considerations, whether intentional or not, whether put into words or not, have played a part in this. It is hardly necessary to mention 'the Allies' here. They have promised everything and done *nothing* to rescue even one of the 100,000 Dutch Jews. Not half a litre of petrol. Not a teacup of oil.
9. The culpability of the non-Jewish population in terms of the continuation of the major process of expulsion and the deprivation of rights can also be briefly mentioned (and repeated) here. The non-Jewish population has allowed the Occupier to exclude the Jewish part of the population from it as a separate part of the Dutch nation. Although Dutch people have behaved extremely well individually or as members of small illegal organizations (and some of them have even sacrificed their lives), the Dutch people *on the whole* are to blame. They have not been anti-Jewish, but they have been weak and selfish.[13]
10. What the consequences would have been if the Jewish Council and the non-Jewish population had resisted has already been discussed under point 4. But as such resistance failed to materialize in the early stages, it became virtually impossible later. The more or less high number of Dutch people, officials working in public administration and enterprises (civil servants, tram and railway staff, etc.), who might have been inclined to offer resistance would certainly have received little or no support later and therefore had to anticipate their own downfall in the event of wilful disobedience.

12 Immediately after the Netherlands capitulated, the Jewish Community of Amsterdam had considered hiding the card index of community members. The community's council refused to do so.

13 Note in the original: 'The February strike had to be dropped because this small nucleus (of communists??) received no support. The enthusiasm of the masses proved to be a flash in the pan.'

I think that the registrars of the *Population Register*[14] in particular bear much blame. Without resistance and entirely at random, they entered *everyone* who could be considered a Jew in Amsterdam (indeed including those who were *not* registered with the Dutch Israelite Religious Community) in a separate register, thus handing them over to the Occupier. It is a testament to the spirit of the Dutch population that a large part of this Population Register was set on fire once this dirty work for the Germans had been completed, and it was the non-Jews' turn to be put to work in Germany.[15]

The question mark

What all this does not explain is how all of these Jews – particularly the well-educated ones, the 'intelligentsia', the smart ones, the lawyers, the astute traders – decided to hand themselves over into the power of their mortal enemy through that first registration as a Jew (with four Jewish grandparents). The only explanation I can come up with is the complete absence of any defiant *organization*. If the need for this was felt among individual people or small groups, it was absorbed by the Jewish Council. This is the case as far as the middle classes are concerned. The others, the lower middle classes, followed their ideology. And what about the 'proletarian' elements? Ninety-nine per cent were in the Social Democratic Labour Party or had an ideological affinity with it. And they were therefore far from demonstrating any defiance. The Occupier had an easy job with all of them. And it has won a complete victory, probably to its own amazement.

DOC. 152
On 27 January 1944 Gertrud Slottke notes the resumption of the deportations from Westerbork[1]

Note by the Senior Commander of the Security Police (IV B 4 e), signed Slottke (police employee), The Hague, dated 27 January 1944

Transports of Jews

After the lifting of the ban on the use of railway wagons and of the quarantine imposed on Westerbork,[2] the first transports set off on 11 January 1944. The first transport ran on 11 January 1944, carrying 1,037 Jews bound for Bergen-Belsen holding camp. Among

14 The State Inspectorate of Population Registers.

15 On 27 Feb. 1943 the State Inspectorate of Population Registers was set on fire by a group of resistance fighters, but only approximately 15 per cent of the registration cards were burned. In June 1943 twelve members of the group were put on trial and sentenced to death. At this point in time, the registration of Jews in the Netherlands had long been complete, and their deportation was well under way. In addition, in late March 1943 more than 200,000 non-Jewish Dutch nationals had already been taken to Germany to perform forced labour.

1 NIOD, 077/1317. Published in facsimile in Joods Historisch Museum Amsterdam, *Documents of the Persecution of the Dutch Jewry*, p. 106. This document has been translated from German.

2 On 19 Oct. 1943 a quarantine was imposed on Westerbork camp because of the outbreak of epidemics there. The train that carried 995 persons to Auschwitz on 16 Nov. 1943 was the only transport until Jan. 1944. Another train with 1,149 passengers left Vught camp on 15 Nov. 1943 and travelled directly to Auschwitz.

these Jews were 385 persons for the German-British exchange and 436 persons for the Palestine exchange,[3] along with Jews who had connections to enemy countries.

The second transport departed on 18 January 1944, carrying 870 persons to Theresienstadt. This transport consisted of Jews who had distinguished themselves through wartime and civilian service, Jewish children whose parents are already in Theresienstadt, parents of Jews who are on the Stammliste,[4] women whose husbands are prisoners of war, etc.

The third transport left for Auschwitz on 25 January 1944, with 948 persons aboard.

While a fairly elevated mood prevailed among the Jews in the case of the first two transports to Bergen-Belsen and Theresienstadt, this mood plummeted again in the case of the transport to Auschwitz.

Since the deportation of the Jews resumed, there has been a veritable flood of interventions. There were even petitions asking for Jews who are now being transported to be released once the war ends and sent back to the Netherlands.

DOC. 153

On 4 February 1944 the Westerbork camp commandant asks Wilhelm Zoepf to consent to the deportation of all sick Jews from Westerbork to Auschwitz[1]

Telegram (no. 101, 4 February 1944, 10.00 – BAEU,[2] marked 'Urgent. Present immediately') from Westerbork camp, signed Camp Commandant Gemmeker, SS-Obersturmführer, to the Senior Commander of the Security Police and the SD for the Occupied Dutch Territories, for the attention of SS-Sturmbannführer Zoepf, The Hague, dated 4 February 1944[3]

Re: deportation of sick Jews

Because the number of Jews in the camp has dropped to 6,500 but there are still approximately 900 sick Jews in the [camp] hospital, I consider it an urgent necessity to carry out the deportation of sick Jews, irrespective of whether they have infectious diseases and fevers. As a result of the large number of sick, a correspondingly large number of hospital staff are also needed, which impedes the transports to Auschwitz. –

In the case of the transports to Theresienstadt and Bergen-Belsen, it has also become apparent that the number of those unfit for transport was substantial and has caused a sharp decrease in the transport figures. My view is that if a radical deportation of the sick is carried out, the Jews will very quickly get better and no longer seek refuge in the hospital. I therefore propose that, with the exception of persons exempted from transport, all sick

3 Jews scheduled to be part of an exchange for German nationals interned in countries not under German control: see Doc. 149.

4 The *Stammliste* ('master list') comprised the 'original camp inmates' interned there since the creation of the camp; they held a privileged status. See Introduction, p. 36.

1 Herinneringscentrum Kamp Westerbork, 2725–3. This document has been translated from German.

2 The meaning of the abbreviation could not be ascertained.

3 Via news transmission service. The original contains handwritten notes and stamps.

Jews be placed on a transport bound for Auschwitz, unless they belong to the Barneveld group,[4] the Protestant group or are on the Stammliste.[5]

In this way, the number of sick Jews in the hospital would certainly be reduced by 400–500. –

For the transport on Tuesday, 8 February 1944, I have arranged for the deportation of all the Jews who are fit for transport,[6] including those with infectious diseases (scarlet fever, diphtheria, infectious jaundice, TB), and have ordered a correspondingly larger number of wagons.[7] I have told the camp physician[8] that no one will be considered unfit to travel on Tuesday's transport unless the sick Jew scheduled for transport would certainly die in the next 3–8 hours. –

I ask that a speedy decision be made, as this is essential for assembling the transport on Tuesday, 8 February 1944, and for equipping the train.[9]

DOC. 154

On 25 February 1944 a neighbour denounces Jacoba Albers-Metz to the German police for allegedly hiding Jews and providing them with food[1]

Handwritten letter, signed 'a neighbour from across the way', NSB, Amsterdam, to the German police, Colonial Museum,[2] Amsterdam, Mauritskade, dated 25 February 1944[3]

I would like to draw the gentlemen's attention to Mrs Alberts[4] at 22 I Preangerstraat. Two Jews in hiding have recently been removed from there. She does nothing but provide food to Jews in hiding. Could the gentlemen perhaps keep an eye on this lady? They are communists.[5] Also has a radio.

4 The 'privileged Jews' held at Barneveld camp had been deported to Westerbork after Barneveld was closed on 29 Sept. 1943.
5 See Doc. 152, fn. 4.
6 Jews who, for various reasons, were exempted from deportation.
7 A total of 1,015 Jews were deported from Westerbork to Auschwitz on this transport, including probably around 268 who were ill.
8 Fritz Marcus Spanier.
9 Handwritten note: 'yes; e) Sl.', Zoepf's signature stamp, 4 Feb. The abbreviation 'e) Sl.' presumably refers to Gertrud Slottke, who worked for subdivision E and was frequently entrusted with organizing and handling the transports from Westerbork.

1 JHM, Doc. 00 001 255. This document has been translated from Dutch.
2 The Colonial Museum, also home to the Tropenmuseum (Museum of the Tropics), was used as the German Order Police headquarters from 1940 to 1945.
3 The date is based on the postmark.
4 Correctly: Jacoba Albers-Metz (1901–1984), housewife; lived with her husband, the plasterer Johannes Baptist Albers (1897–1964), in Preangerstraat. No information could be found on her assistance to Jews in hiding.
5 Presumably the family of Isidore Vaz Dias, who lived on the second floor of the building. Isidore Vaz Dias (1900–1942), a hairdresser, was a communist and had already been arrested in 1941 and deported to Neuengamme, but his non-Jewish wife and their children were still living at the same address.

DOC. 155
On 28 February 1944 Reich Commissioner Seyss-Inquart informs Reichsleiter Bormann of his further plans for Jews living in 'mixed marriages'[1]

Letter from the Reich Commissioner for the Occupied Dutch Territories (S-P),[2] signed Seyss-Inquart, The Hague, to Reichsleiter Bormann (carbon copy for information only to the commissioners general and to Representative Dr Schröder), dated 28 February 1944 (carbon copy)[3]

Dear Party Comrade Bormann,

We have resolved the Jewish question in the Netherlands to the extent that is it now only a matter of carrying out the orders that have been issued. The Jews have been eliminated from the Dutch Volkskörper, and those not deported to the East for labour deployment have been grouped together in a camp. This primarily concerns the approximately 1,500 people who for particular reasons, such as intervention by the churches or by notable associates of ours, have not been transported to the East. It is common knowledge that I have staved off the churches' meddling in the entire Jewish question largely by keeping the baptized Jews in a closed camp in the Netherlands, where they are also visited weekly by a cleric.[4] Around 8,000–9,000 Jews have avoided deportation by going into hiding;[5] they are gradually being apprehended and sent to the East. At present, the number of Jews apprehended each week is around 500–600. Jewish assets have been confiscated and are being liquidated.[6] With the exception of a few businesses that have not yet been Aryanized but are being administered by trustees, this liquidation has been carried out and the wealth deposited in Reich investment securities. I am expecting proceeds of around 500 million guilders. The decision as to the future utilization of this money is to be made in due course in consultation with the Reich Minister of Finance,[7] but the Reich Minister of Finance agrees in principle that this money should be directed to purposes in the Netherlands.

Still open is the question of the Jews in mixed marriages. Here, we have gone further than the Reich and have required that these Jews must wear the star as well. I had also ordered that the Jewish spouses in childless mixed marriages should likewise be taken to the East for labour deployment. Our Security Police has taken action in several hundred such cases, but thereafter received instructions from Berlin to halt these deportations,[8] meaning that a few thousand of these Jews have remained in the country. Now

1 NIOD, 020/286. This document has been translated from German.
2 The abbreviation stands for 'Hertha Santo Passo', Seyss-Inquart's secretary.
3 The original contains handwritten notes and underlining.
4 This concerned Protestants of Jewish descent, who were housed in a separate barracks in Westerbork camp. The majority of the 'non-Aryan' Catholics had already been deported: see Doc. 69.
5 There were in fact more than 25,000 Jews living in hiding in the Netherlands in 1943.
6 See Doc. 127.
7 Count Johann Ludwig Schwerin von Krosigk.
8 In the Netherlands, Jews living in 'mixed marriages' were exempt from wearing the star if they could show proof of their infertility. Jews who were married to a non-Jewish partner and were still able to have children received an exemption stamp, but were otherwise subject to all the rules applicable to 'full Jews'. On 4 Dec. 1943 the Reich Security Main Office (RSHA) in Berlin ordered that Jews living in 'mixed marriages' were to be interned in Westerbork camp: see Stuldreher, *De legale rest*, pp. 328–332.

I have received word from Berlin of the wish to concentrate the Jewish spouses in mixed marriages in the Jew camp at Westerbork, in order to deploy these Jews as labour here for the time being. This raises the problem of the mixed marriages. It is a fundamental issue, and for this reason I am turning to you. The following must be considered with respect to marriages that produce offspring: if one parent is put in a concentration camp and presumably goes to the East sooner or later for labour deployment, the children born of these marriages will forever have the impression that we have deprived them of one parent. The Mischlinge actually cause more difficulties than the full Jews. For example, in political trials we can establish that it is the Mischlinge, first and foremost, who are involved as instigators and also as principal actors in most assassinations and acts of sabotage. If there is now to be an additional measure, which in my view will surely unleash hatred among these people, we will have in our community a group of people for whom segregation is our only viable course of action. Therefore, if a measure is planned that will result in Jewish spouses in mixed marriages with children being removed from the family unit, sooner or later we will have to apply the same measure to the children in this unit. I am therefore of the view that, for reasons of expediency, this should not be the course of action taken. Instead, depending on the decision made, either the whole family should be removed from the community or an attempt should be made to keep the Jewish spouse in the family unit, while observing certain Security Police precautions. In the former case, it would be a matter of placing the spouses in the mixed marriage along with their children in an isolated location, in much the same way as the Jews in Theresienstadt. Nonetheless, one must consider that in this case the Mischlinge will produce children among themselves, and so in practice it will not be possible to bring about a resolution to the Jewish problem unless, at some point, the entire group is removed from our Reich's sphere of interest. We are endeavouring to apply the latter course of action by exempting the Jew or Jewish partner in a mixed marriage from wearing the star if the individual is no longer capable of reproducing or submits to sterilization, and retaining him or her in the family unit. These star-exempt Jews – there are probably around 4,000–5,000 in the Netherlands at present – are subject to a certain level of Security Police control with respect to their residence and subject to certain restrictions on their gainful employment. For example, they are not allowed to run a business with staff or to hold a managerial position in such a business.[9] Volunteering to undergo sterilization is fairly widespread among the Jews. I also think that nothing more is to be feared from these people, because the decision indicates that they have reconciled themselves to the given situation. In the case of Jewish women, the issue is not straightforward because, as is common knowledge, a complicated surgical procedure is involved. Even so, I think this way of approaching the problem will lead to a certain degree of success over time, if the decision is made not to take the radical path I have described, i.e. to remove the whole family. For the Netherlands, I would consider the following course of action to be appropriate. I am of the opinion that we can bring an end to the Jewish problem here with the following measures:

1. The male Jewish spouse in mixed marriages, if not meanwhile exempted from wearing the star for the reasons given above, goes to Westerbork for segregated labour

9 The legal status of Jews in 'mixed marriages' and the restrictions applicable to them were determined at a meeting at the Central Office for Jewish Emigration on 18 May 1943: NIOD, 077/1317.

deployment, but this is not a measure that signifies permanent removal. Rather, it is enacted on Security Police grounds for the duration of the exceptional circumstances. These Jews are duly employed and also receive appropriate remuneration, with which they can maintain the family that has stayed behind. Approximately once per quarter, they are also given a few days of continuous leave. The childless female spouse in a mixed marriage can be dealt with in the same way. Here in the Netherlands, we have 834 male Jews in childless mixed marriages, 2,775 Jews in mixed marriages with children, and 574 female Jews in childless mixed marriages. Under certain conditions, these Jews can return to their families, for example, if they undergo sterilization, or if the reasons for the separation become less important, or if precautions are taken or circumstances arise that make the separation seem no longer necessary.

2. I would like to exempt the Jewish women in mixed marriages with children – numbering 1,448 here – from the requirement to wear the star. The following consideration is crucial in this respect: as the Reich Security Main Office agrees, one cannot take these Jewish women away from a family where there are still underage children, that is, children under the age of 14. Jewish women with children over 14, however, will mostly be at an age that entitles them to exemption from wearing the star, as they are hardly likely to still be of child-bearing age.
3. I now intend to have the Blood Protection Laws[10] implemented in the Netherlands and
4. to make divorce possible in the case of mixed marriages on the grounds of racial difference.[11]

These four measures, taken together, would resolve the Jewish question in the Netherlands once and for all. As this arrangement, in a certain sense, can have prejudicial significance for the Reich or, as the case may be, the regulations regarding mixed marriages in the Reich will also be applied to the Netherlands in the long run, I am informing you, Reichsleiter, of my plan in this regard and I request your comments.[12] I have written to the Reichsführer-SS along the same lines.[13]

Best regards and
Heil Hitler!
Yours

10 The so-called Blood Protection Law, adopted in Nuremberg on 15 Sept. 1935, prohibited marriage as well as extramarital relations between Jews and non-Jews: see PMJ 1/199.

11 In the spring and summer of 1944, several drafts of an amendment to the Dutch laws on marriage and divorce were indeed discussed in the Reich Commissariat, but a regulation was never published: Stuldreher, *De legale rest*, pp. 361–379.

12 No such comments were found.

13 This is included in the file. A few days later, on 2 March 1944, Commissioner General for Security Rauter wrote a similar letter to Reichsführer-SS Heinrich Himmler: NIOD, 077/1315.

DOC. 156
On 5 March 1944 the brothers Salomon and Chanine Silber move to a different hiding place with the help of a member of the resistance[1]

Diary of Salomon Silber,[2] entry for 5 March 1944 (copy of typescript)

5 March 1944
A few days later, we left this place[3] and moved in again with a miner's family,[4] where a small room was made available for us. This room was so small it could only hold one bed. Our freedom of movement was very restricted there. We would stay in this room, which was three metres long and two metres wide, the whole day. We had to talk calmly and softly. Due to the lack of exercise and fresh air, we both got an upset stomach. Chanine[5] complained almost every day about being insatiably hungry, while I was suffering from stomach cramps due to heartburn every day. We would spend almost the entire day studying the Bible, learning and reading Hebrew. Without this to fill our time, we would not have lasted out there.

The family consisted of a man, a woman, and three girls. They were pleasant, straightforward people. They were honest and sincere by nature. They made no distinction when dividing the food. When the man received something extra from the mine, such as sardines, they would give us our fair share. Fortunately, we did not have any problems with them. In early May, after two months, the secret was out, and we were forced to leave that cramped space.

At about nine o'clock in the evening, Ben,[6] one of the underground helpers, came to pick us up. We had already packed our humble belongings. He impressed on us the following: 'The route we are taking is dangerous. It is about a two-hour walk. We will also have to cross main roads before we arrive at your destination. In that place you will have more space, and the people are decent and nice.' These last words gave us the courage to undertake this dangerous journey. As always when we had to flee, we had our spiritual possessions, the Bible, tefillin, Hebrew books, and my diary, in a little suitcase. We would not go without these treasures. They were precious and dear to us. They were

1 The original is privately owned; copy in NIOD, 471/9e. Published in Salomon Silber, *Een joods gezin in onderduik: Dagboek* (Kampen: Kok, 1997), pp. 153–154. This document has been translated from Dutch.
2 Salomon Silber (b. 1922), retailer; emigrated from Poland with his family in 1933; lived with his brother in various hiding places from 1942; emigrated to Israel in 1953; worked in the film industry there until 1987.
3 From Dec. 1943 to March 1944, Salomon and Chanine Silber, along with up to 15 other Jewish young people and children, were sheltered by the family of Jo Broers, who was in charge of the pumping station for the Hendrik and Wilhelmina state coal mines and lived in the grounds.
4 Christian and Maria Deckers lived in Brunssum; the brothers stayed with the family for two months.
5 Chanine Silber (1926–1997); lived with his brother in various hiding places from 1942; emigrated to Israel in 1945; served as a soldier there, then worked for the post office after being wounded.
6 Presumably Bernardus (Ben) Fritz (1922–1987), commercial employee; went into hiding after being called up for labour deployment in Germany; joined the resistance group Naamloze Vennootschap, in which he was responsible for housing and provisioning Jewish children in Brunssum (province of Limburg).

our spiritual sustenance, which was often worth more than the food we ate. They filled us with belief, trust, and hope in God, who would protect us. We walked past woods and along quiet roads. As we approached the Emma mine in Hoensbroek,[7] Ben said to us: 'Now we have to cross a main road. About one hundred metres further along, there is a guard at the Emma mine. The guards are NSB members who respond to the smallest suspicious movement. If one of them stops us, we will grab him and kill him.' We were prepared for anything. We lay down behind the bushes and waited with pounding hearts to see which direction the guard would go. We lay there waiting for about half an hour. It was getting late: it was nearly 11 o'clock. There was hardly anybody out on the street. 'Now be brave, lads,' said Ben. Then the guard moved further along. We crossed the road quietly, and half an hour later we arrived at our destination.[8] The woman gave us a cup of tea, after which we went to sleep straight away in a decent bed in a wonderful, fresh, large room.

DOC. 157
On 9 March 1944 an unidentified author writes a poem for a woman who is living in hiding on the Beekhul country estate[1]

Poem, unsigned, dated 9 March 1944 (typescript)

We have here in our house a woman banished by the Krauts,
The longer lasts her banishment, the more her grief's drawn out;
No news about her husband has she heard,
As for a joyful reunion – so far not a word.

It's just as well we can't predict all things ahead
And sometimes, in time's rush, we forget suffering once it's fled.
She has been here now for six months straight,
Perhaps a good moment to pause and contemplate.

Her future's something she still works to build,
A thing she does with good faith, and brave-willed.
But what does she have here? How's her time occupied?
Would her life make others envious-eyed?

She has a piano, some books to flip through
And sometimes a friend comes to visit her, too.
But other than that, she has nothing here but air and trees
And of her future, all she can have is reveries.

7 The Emma mine was one of the largest coal mines in the Netherlands from 1911 to 1973.
8 The new hiding place was in the family home of Tjeerd and Trijntje de Boer in Hoensbroek (province of Limburg). The brothers stayed there for the remainder of the occupation period: see Doc. 166.

1 JHM, Doc. 00 004 462. This document has been translated from Dutch.

But … all this is not quite *everything*.
In her and us there's also one more resonant string.
She came here as a completely unknown guest:
Was it a gain for us, or a burden that oppressed?

The burden soon proved not to be too great,
It soon, in fact, became a thing to celebrate.
Not even mentioning the services she supplies,
We've received a greater and better prize!

It was …
Her bravely walking the paths of life,
Not worried about what fate might spring;
Her fresh and lucid mind
And calm perception of everything:
Her good humour and cheerful nature,
Not dwelling on her suffering;
Her sunny smile and pleasant manners,
Yes, we've welcomed all that these things bring.
…
…

Between us grew a mutual link,
A link that genuinely binds,
A friendship and affection
Such as a person rarely finds.

And finally, a paradox:

The longer she continues here,
The better it would be for us;
And yet we hope her banishment soon abates
And then she can depart for the better future that awaits!

'Beekhul,'[2] 9 March 1944

2 No information could be found on the place or the Jews in hiding there; there are several villages and one foundation with the name 'Beekhul'.

DOC. 158

On 21 April 1944 the Dutch Advisory Committee on Jewish Affairs in London makes recommendations to the Dutch Council of Ministers on measures to save the Jews[1]

Letter from the Advisory Committee on Jewish Affairs, signed Dr J. L. Polak,[2] S. van Zwanenberg,[3] M. Sluyser[4] (secretary), Berkeley House, London, to the Council of Ministers (received by the chairman of the Council of Ministers, 3 May 1944), London, dated 21 April 1944 (typescript)[5]

To the Cabinet in London

1. In a letter from His Excellency the Minister of General Warfare for the Kingdom, dated 22 February 1943 (AU 50/40),[6] the undersigned were informed that the government had decided, in view of the appalling treatment the enemy has inflicted upon members of the Jewish race and the urgency of the issues arising from this, to form an Advisory Committee on Jewish Affairs. The last of the undersigned was appointed secretary.

2. The committee initially maintained contact with His Excellency the Minister of General Warfare for the Kingdom, but after a few weeks he deemed it desirable to transfer that contact to His Excellency the Minister of the Interior.[7]

3. In the time that has passed since that transfer, the committee has found an opportunity to advise the minister concerned on looking after compatriots who were outside the enemy's reach but had not yet arrived in Britain. The committee would like to express its agreement with the Minister of the Interior's policy in this respect, which, partly because of his personal intervention, has helped to bring an end to much unnecessary suffering.

1 Nationaal Archief, Kabinet Minister-President, 2.03.01/384. Published in *Enquêtecommissie Regeringsbeleid 1940–1945: Verslag houdende de uitkomsten van het onderzoek*, vol. 6ab, pp. 198–199. This document has been translated from Dutch.

2 Jacques L. Polak (1883–1948), lawyer; director of Unilever in London; member of the Committee for the Regulation of Legal Relations in Wartime and the Advisory Committee on Jewish Affairs from 1940.

3 Salomon van Zwanenberg (1889–1974), entrepreneur; manager of a meat factory, 1912–1953; co-founder of Organon (a pharmaceutical company producing insulin) in 1923; took on various tasks for the government in exile, 1940–1945.

4 Meijer Sluijser, also Meyer Sluyser (1901–1973), journalist; worked for the socialist broadcasting company VARA from 1926 and for the newspaper *Het Volk* from 1929; fled to London in 1940 and headed the radio monitoring service there; returned to the liberated southern part of the Netherlands in 1944; founded the newspaper *Het Vrije Volk*; worked for the Dutch Labour Party (PvDA), 1951–1969.

5 This letter, along with an accompanying letter dated 25 April 1944, was sent to the chairman of the Council of Ministers, Prime Minister Gerbrandy. There is a receipt stamp on this letter.

6 This is included in the file. At the time, the minister of war was Baron Otto Cornelis Adriaan van Lidth de Jeude (1881–1952).

7 Hendrik van Boeijen (1889–1947), administrative official; worked in communications, 1915–1925; member of the Dutch parliament from 1923; member of the government from 1937; minister of the interior in the government in exile from 1940 to May 1944.

The committee has also advised the minister and his colleague, the Minister of Foreign Affairs,[8] on the planned attempt to exchange Dutch Jews for civilian prisoners of German nationality, regarding which the committee has received considerable assistance from the Advisory Committee for Immigrants from the Netherlands in Jerusalem and the Jewish Agency.[9] That neither this planned exchange nor the plan to evacuate Jewish children from the Netherlands has yielded any results is attributable to the attitude of the enemy.[10] The committee received promises of very generous financial support for the evacuation from private individuals, following the government's announcement that as a matter of principle the welfare of Dutch Jews is a government matter.

Furthermore, the committee would like to commend the successful action taken by His Excellency the Minister of Foreign Affairs, which means that passports and visas that had been irregularly issued to Dutch refugees by South American state consuls will nevertheless be temporarily recognized as bona fide by the relevant governments.

With regret, however, the committee has had to conclude that urgent requests to create an organization that would make it possible to move Dutch citizens residing in France to Spain, Portugal, or Switzerland – illegally if necessary – should all other means fail, have not achieved any results. The committee cannot escape the impression that when such operations were easy, advantage was not taken of good opportunities, and that later, when the circumstances had become more complicated, factors related to the competencies of different government organizations posed an obstacle to achieving positive results.

4. In the course of its activities, the committee has repeatedly asked itself whether and how it might achieve more satisfactory results in the interests of the victims concerned, albeit within the narrow limits imposed by the enemy's inhumane actions. After taking related measures, it soon arrived at the conclusion that the limited success of its interventions and those of the government in this respect are attributable in large part to the lack of a permanent government organization in which the handling of Jewish affairs, as set out in the letter from His Excellency the Minister of General Warfare, referred to above, is centralized.

The reason the committee did not previously push for such an organization to be set up is the fact that creating such an organization could, to some extent, imply recognition of the existence of a specific Jewish-Dutch question, which did not exist in the Netherlands before 10 May 1940.

5. However, the committee has gradually arrived at the conviction that, by persevering in this cautious approach, it is failing in its responsibility to both its Jewish compatriots and the government. It is strengthened in this conviction not only by the reports that are reaching it about the horrific fate of Dutch Jews, but also through its examination of what is being done with a certain degree of success by other, non-Dutch organizations in order to relieve the distress of the victims of the German extermination policy.

8 Eelco Nicolaas van Kleffens (1894–1983), lawyer; worked in the Ministry of Foreign Affairs, 1922–1958; minister of foreign affairs, 1939–1946; ambassador to the USA and to Portugal from 1947; played a major role in founding NATO; worked for the European Coal and Steel Community (ECSC), 1958–1967.

9 The names of both organizations are in English in the original.

10 See Doc. 99.

6. The committee has read various reports, including some of recent date, which describe the suffering of our Jewish compatriots, especially in Poland. Both the documentation in the possession[11] of the Government Commissioner for Repatriation[12] and other details create an impression that should fill any civilized person with horror.

The rations issued remain far below the required minimums in all cases. A calorie content which is only 21 per cent of the required minimum is probably one statistic that should be considered positive in comparison to most cases. According to details from the Institute of Jewish Affairs[13] in New York, 85,000 Dutch Jews were deported to Poland in September 1943 and 45,000 of them have already perished, i.e. 40,000 of them either perished during transport or died a violent death, and 5,000 died of starvation or as a result of epidemics. According to information – of Dutch origin – gathered on behalf of the Government Commissioner for Repatriation, the number of deported Dutch Jews has now reached or surpassed 100,000.

As a result of the policy pursued by the enemy, the aim of which is the complete extermination of the Jews in its territory, the mortality rate among the Jewish population in Poland since the German occupation is said to be about 90 [per cent], due to executions on a massive scale. While executions of our compatriots on a massive scale are also reported, there is reason to suppose that the mortality rate among Dutch deportees is not as bad as it is among Jews of Polish nationality.

According to the least pessimistic reports, it can be assumed that only about half of the Dutch citizens who were deported are still alive.

7. The committee would like to inform the cabinet that in its well-considered opinion, the circumstances do not pose an insurmountable obstacle to offering these compatriots some form of assistance, albeit inadequate, at this stage. The committee believes it cannot be ruled out that there may well have been opportunities to offer assistance to our compatriots without any Dutch government organization having been aware of this.

With regard to the Dutch people interned in Theresienstadt in Czechoslovakia, the committee has reason to believe that it would be possible to obtain details about their number and identity, in the same way as it has proven possible to get such information about Germans interned there. The committee also understands that fairly considerable consignments of food are regularly sent to the people interned in Theresienstadt by Czechoslovak Relief Action[14] and the American Jewish Joint Distribution Committee, and that these consignments do indeed reach their destination. The committee is painfully aware of the fact that, as far as it knows, until very recently neither any government

11 This could not be found.

12 G. F. Ferwerda was the government commissioner for repatriation from Oct. 1943 to 1945.

13 In English in the original. The Institute of Jewish Affairs was founded in New York in Feb. 1941 by the American Jewish Congress and the World Jewish Congress. Its purpose was to investigate the living conditions of the Jews and to secure legal rights for them after the end of the war. After the war ended and the institute moved to London in 1965, it continued to pursue its main objective of researching and documenting Jewish life worldwide.

14 Československá pomocná akce, an organization of the Czechoslovak government in exile, established in 1943. Relief supplies for the inmates of the camps in the East were financed by donations from expatriates. More than 65,000 parcels were sent from Spain and Portugal to Theresienstadt, and more than 12,000 went to Auschwitz and other places.

organization nor the Netherlands Red Cross had any knowledge of this, which therefore means that opportunities to do something for our compatriots have been missed.

8. In informal discussions arranged by or on behalf of the Government Commissioner for Repatriation with the relevant Polish government organizations, it has allegedly been confirmed that the Polish government, according to its own announcements, has been able to

a) gather details etc. about the fate of people interned in Poland via illegal means;
b) offer actual support to such people via the same means by providing them with false documents and/or the necessary funds to purchase food, which is allegedly obtainable in adequate quantities on the black market, provided enough money is available.

9. The committee believes it can by no means be ruled out that other opportunities to help our compatriots have arisen without any Dutch government organization being aware of this. It may be considered highly likely that, given the changing military situation, such opportunities may again arise. The committee believes it would be utterly irresponsible not to take measures which would make it possible to detect, promote, and utilize opportunities to provide assistance.

10. The committee is aware that concerns about Dutch Jews are also increasing within the circles of the World Jewish Congress,[15] both in America and in England. There has clearly been a growing tendency in these circles for organizations to put themselves forward as the candidate best placed to look after the interests of Dutch Jews. Although the committee greatly appreciates the work of the World Jewish Congress, it does not fail to recognise that if our compatriots are considered on a par with citizens from countries where Jews constitute a substantial minority or are equated with stateless persons of Jewish origin, this could create undesirable complications for the future position of our Jewish compatriots. This could indeed happen, as the World Jewish Congress is a political organization which could then put itself forward as a representative of Dutch citizens to the Dutch government and other governments.

11. The committee would like to take this opportunity to make the government aware that a number of Dutch citizens, apparently failing to comprehend the consequences of these issues, have set themselves up as the 'Netherland Representative Committee affiliated with the World Jewish Congress'.[16] The Advisory Committee on Jewish Affairs believes it has to conclude, based on notifications from the compatriots concerned, that the aforementioned organization is regarded by Her Majesty's Ambassador in Washington[17] (allegedly 'in consultation with London') as the organization promoting the interests of Dutch Jews. The Advisory Committee would like to point out in this respect that Dutch Jews were not affiliated with the World Jewish Congress before the war, and it is of the opinion that no such representative function can be ascribed to any organization currently based outside the Netherlands thereby enabling it to initiate such an affiliation 'on behalf of' Dutch Jews.

15 Here and below the name of the organization is in English in the original.
16 In English in the original.
17 Alexander Loudon (1892–1953), lawyer; in Dutch diplomatic service from 1916; envoy in Washington from 1938 and ambassador from 1942; returned to the Netherlands in 1947; member of the Council of State, 1947–1952; secretary general of the Permanent Court of Arbitration in The Hague, 1952–1953.

12. While we have touched upon several very urgent points above, the committee would also like to draw the cabinet's attention to a number of other issues.

In this regard, the committee is aware that, in addition to matters requiring urgent assistance, there are other issues, such as those mentioned above, that have become specifically Jewish issues, not as a consequence of discrimination on the part of the Netherlands, but as a result of the enemy's actions. In this respect, the committee is thinking in particular of problems that will arise immediately after the return to the Netherlands. As such large numbers of our Jewish compatriots have been deported, however, and as it is to be feared that those who are in hiding are in a severe state of shock, both psychologically and physically, it has to be accepted as a fact that, after liberation, far too few of our Jewish compatriots will be available to address specifically Jewish interests, or to help the government address them. The committee is not primarily thinking here of problems related to legal rehabilitation, although these should certainly not be neglected; it believes that, in the vast majority of cases, the general regulations will resolve these problems. Rather, the committee is thinking of the reconstruction of religious institutions and of Jewish orphanages, hospitals, sanatoriums, etc. It is thinking of the importance of restoring the once thriving Jewish charitable sector. It should not be considered to be in the general interest, and most certainly not in any Jewish interest, that the people in hiding and the Dutch Jews who are to be repatriated are the government's responsibility for even one day longer than is strictly necessary.

13. Our committee is of the opinion that it should therefore be deemed imperative that instructions are issued now to explore, draft, and prepare measures in London which will enable our compatriots to regain their social position as quickly as possible. It is of the opinion that for this purpose, compatriots should be appointed in London who, in our liberated country, in the absence of others, will assist the government in implementing these measures, as well as others still to be taken.

14. In light of all of the above considerations, the committee has decided to abandon its objections to the creation of a central government organization responsible for managing Jewish affairs. The committee hereby urges your cabinet in the strongest possible terms to decide to form such an organization, with broad powers, a generous budget, and adequate facilities. If such is decided, it should be made clear that the enemy's actions have temporarily changed the interests of Dutch citizens with equal rights into specifically Jewish interests. Furthermore, the committee considers it extremely desirable that this organization, accountable to the government for its actions, should have a board that comprises more people than our committee and powers defined in more detail; such an organization could then also contribute to putting our relationships in the United States back on an even keel.[18]

15. The committee feels that the responsibility for the task assigned to it in the abovementioned letter from His Excellency the Minister of General Warfare for the Kingdom has obliged it to submit these proposals to your cabinet. The committee strongly urges the cabinet to consider these proposals favourably.

18 No new committee was established. In the summer of 1944, the government tasked the Advisory Committee on Jewish Affairs with organizing aid for Dutch Jews.

DOC. 159

Trouw, late April 1944: article reflecting on Dutch society's attitudes to Jews since the occupation and its Christian duty to support Jews after the war[1]

The Jewish question

Until the moment when the steamroller of German Nazism entered our country, there was no Jewish problem within our borders. The Jews here were peaceful citizens, each of them earning a living in their own way. In some sectors they competed heavily with Christians, but this was generally not too much of an issue. Most of them had largely assimilated, while a smaller number were faithful to the Jewish tradition and thus isolated themselves to a certain extent. However, this did not lead to bitter clashes or any unpleasant friction.

The Jews' political affinities were distributed among the left-wing parties. The legend that Jews allegedly always have a hand in revolutionary disturbances was certainly not borne out in our country. We had Jewish communists, but also Jewish old liberals; there were even anti-revolutionary Jews. In any case, the Jews did not set the political tone in our country. Both Jewish ministers and Jewish mayors were an exception here. The Jews generally enjoyed popularity among the people, especially among the lower classes. The famous Amsterdam strike of 27 February 1941[2] is one notable example of this.

Antisemitism, as it occurs in other countries, barely existed here, although it was systematically encouraged in the final years before the war. All of this has changed since May 1940. The Nazis have succeeded in forcing their Jewish problem upon us, and we were insufficiently prepared for this. At first, we were still too naive: we thought we did not have to worry about the first measures affecting the Jews, which aimed to segregate the Jewish part of our population from the rest. Many, almost all of whom were civil servants, signed the notorious Aryan Declaration.[3] The Jews themselves registered as Jews en masse,[4] which resulted in them being led like lambs to the slaughter. We all helped with the comprehensive registration and meekly collected our proof of identity![5] We only realized the dangerous course we had taken once it was too late. We then tried to salvage what we could and reached out to those people whose rights we should have defended much sooner.

Now that the fact is that officially there are hardly any Jews left in our country, we are shocked that we have simply allowed this to happen. We lived according to Cain's

1 *Trouw*, vol. 2, no. 4, late April 1944, p. 5. This document has been translated from Dutch. The illegal Protestant-leaning newspaper *Trouw* was first published on 18 Feb. 1943. More than 100 of those involved with the publication were killed during the occupation. Since the end of the war, *Trouw* has been published daily.

2 Correctly: 25 and 26 February 1941. The first roundups of Jews in Amsterdam on 22 and 23 February provoked a general strike (the 'February Strike'), which brought public life to a standstill in Amsterdam and several other cities. The German occupiers took action to suppress the strike, which ended on the evening of 26 February. See PMJ 5/60–65.

3 See PMJ 5/39.

4 Under the Regulation on the Compulsory Registration of Persons who are Fully or Partially of Jewish Blood (10 Jan. 1941), all Jews were forced to register with the authorities: see PMJ 5/54.

5 The State Inspectorate of Population Registers introduced an ostensibly forgery-proof identity card for all Dutch people.

principle of 'Am I my brother's keeper?'[6] We forgot that an injustice inflicted upon others also concerns us. We did not realize that pity for others is a poor surrogate for upholding justice. We were willing to help, but only like the man who reaches out to a drowning person once he is safely on dry land.

The consequence of our weak, misguided attitude is that a Jewish problem based on a flawed, twisted perspective has evolved in our country. On the one hand, there is clearly an increasing closeness between Jews and non-Jews, but on the other, a deep divide has emerged which can hardly be bridged by our one-sided help. Unless we are extremely careful, we will continue to have a Jewish problem after the war, the practical side of which will be less of a cause for concern than the psychological one. In spite of all our good intentions and all the help which, fortunately, has been and will continue to be extended to the Jews, many nevertheless currently regard the Jew as a separate being, different from other Dutch citizens, to whom we should kindly offer our protection. If it then turns out that there are many among our charges who prove to be unworthy of our goodwill or, even worse, betray us if they are backed into a corner, then we will soon slip into rampant antisemitism and be completely in line with National Socialism.

It is therefore right that we seriously ask ourselves what our attitude to this Ancient People should be. First of all, let us consider the disappointments many of us have experienced in our dealings with Jews. This is completely natural. It has been said before that every Jew is in the same kind of danger, and that those who have been in hiding certainly include a large percentage of weak, nervous, selfish, dishonest, and inferior people. One may assume that the non-Jews who went into hiding for one reason or another generally belong to the best elements, the most courageous and the strongest, who were prepared to make sacrifices. Among the non-Jews, the dregs of society have separated themselves out – think of the behaviour of the Dutch SS and the WA during the arrests and in concentration camps – and the remainder constitute the best part of our population. But no such sifting has occurred among the Jews. Moreover, each instance of disappointing behaviour on the part of a Jew or Jewess can be immediately counterbalanced either by another example of a pleasant, positive experience, or by the disgraceful exploitation and robbery by so-called Christians who grossly abused the Jews' position of dependence. Indeed, as non-Jews we most certainly have no reason to boast and to exalt ourselves, as if on the whole we had been much better and more virtuous than our Jewish fellow citizens.

But none of this touches upon the core of the issue. We will be better able to accept all the disappointments, in both Jews and non-Jews, if we consider all that we do a necessary consequence of our Christian duty. We should not help the Jews because we feel so sorry for them due to their persecution, but because this persecution is a violation of God's law. Any persecution of people is contrary to God's command to love thy neighbour.

We should particularly take the oppression of the Jews to heart, as it is fundamentally based on heathen hatred for all that reminds us of the Almighty God. The fact that God once chose ancient Israel as the people of His covenant, from which the Saviour of the world was born, currently provides the basis for this fanatical madness, which aims to exterminate this people. And to us this same fact is the underlying reason for the tireless efforts to support and prop up today's people of Israel as much as we can, in spite of all the disappointments.

6 Genesis 4:9 (KJV).

What we perceive once again in our times is the harsh reality that no individual and no people can call down God's curse upon themselves without punishment. At the cross on Golgotha, the reckless 'His blood be on us, and on our children'[7] sounded like a scornful challenge, in which the rejection of the Messiah was expressed in most vehement terms.

But the bitter consequences of Israel's deepest fall must not serve as a guideline for our actions. Let us be wary of interfering with God's judgements, so that the same judgement will not fall upon us. All that applies to us is that we should recognize the Jew as part of God's creation, who has fallen into sin with us, but for whose salvation Christ died on the cross.

If that is our approach to the Jewish people, there will be no trace of antisemitism in us. We will then not only consider the Jews citizens with equal rights in the future, but also do everything we can to wipe out the vilification of the Jews, which must already have caused them unspeakable psychological damage.

DOC. 160

On 30 May 1944 the Dutch military attaché in Switzerland refuses to send two Jewish refugees as resistance fighters into a hostile foreign country[1]

Letter (1902) from the military attaché, unsigned,[2] to M. Elion,[3] Geneva, 9 rue John Rehfous, dated 30 May 1944 (carbon copy)

Mr Nieuwkerk,[4] Mr Keyzer,[5] and Mr Stibbe[6] have visited me in the course of this week.[7]

I would first of all like to express my great appreciation for the willingness with which these gentlemen have put themselves forward for such a dangerous task,[8] especially as their Jewish ancestry increases the risks considerably.

It is with regret that I must raise serious objections to the departure of Mr Keyzer and Mr Stibbe, for the reason that their Jewish appearance is unmistakable. I fear that the organization in B. would not be best served by their arrival.[9] They need people there

7 Matthew 27:25 (KJV).

1 Nationaal Archief Den Haag, 2.13.71/1308. This document has been translated from Dutch.

2 Aleid Gerard van Tricht (1886–1969), career officer; worked in the Dutch East Indies until 1938; Dutch military attaché in Switzerland, 1940–1944; military attaché and Dutch representative to the Combined Chiefs of Staff in Washington, 1945–1948; retired in 1948.

3 Max Elion (1895–1988), engineer; designed the Netherlands pavilion for the Paris International Exposition in 1937; lived in Switzerland, 1942–1945; returned to the Netherlands in 1945 and resumed work as an engineer.

4 Adolf Maurits Nieuwkerk (b. 1910).

5 Correctly: Joseph Keijzer (1916–1998); returned to the Netherlands in 1945.

6 David Eduard Stibbe (b. 1922), manufacturer; fled to Switzerland from the Netherlands; returned to the Netherlands with the Dutch army in 1945; founded a shoe factory after the war.

7 According to statements made by David Stibbe in 2010, he never met the military attaché A. G. van Tricht in person.

8 Precisely what task was involved could not be ascertained. According to David Stibbe, the three men offered to work for the Allies in Germany or in German-occupied countries.

9 It was not possible to establish which resistance organization in the Netherlands is referred to here.

who can move freely, not people who alone because of their appearance run the risk of drawing the attention of some Gestapo man or other, and therefore have very little freedom of movement. I am afraid they would – to avoid a much worse fate – quickly join the ranks of those whom the organization is supposed to protect and look after. They would needlessly expose themselves to the greatest possible dangers.

I discussed this objection in great detail with the two gentlemen and promised them that I would ask the Rev. Visser ’t Hooft[10] for his opinion first. He completely agreed with me, which means that I must now, *very much to my regret,* write to tell them that we have had to decide against their departure.[11]

Should Mr Nieuwkerk wish to go, which at our interview was not yet entirely certain, I do not have any objections.[12] I am currently unable to name another person who could go with Mr Nieuwkerk, but I will continue my search.

I look forward to hearing any further news about future plans.

DOC. 161

On 13 June 1944 the Jewish Coordination Committee in Geneva reports to the government in exile about its relief efforts on behalf of Dutch Jews[1]

Report by the Jewish Coordination Committee,[2] signed M. H. Gans,[3] dated 13 June 1944 (carbon copy)[4]

Report for the Dutch Government

Further to the memorandum we sent last February, with a letter from Her Majesty’s Envoy in Bern,[5] and the English report which Dr G. G. Kullmann took with him on our

10 Dr Willem Adolph Visser ’t Hooft (1900–1985), theologian; executive director of the Ecumenical Council of Churches in Geneva from 1938; organized the so-called Swiss route used by resistance organizations in the occupied Netherlands to convey information via Geneva to the government in exile in London.

11 The rejection letter is included in the file.

12 Whether Adolf Maurits Nieuwkerk actually went to a hostile country could not be verified.

1 NIOD, 249/1281. This document has been translated from Dutch.

2 The Jewish Coordination Committee (Joodsche Coördinatie Commissie, JCC) in Geneva was established by M. H. Gans, S. Isaac, and S. I. Troostwijk in the autumn of 1943. Its tasks included compiling an index of Jews deported from the Netherlands, sending parcels of food and medicine to Jewish deportees from the Netherlands in the camps and obtaining South American passports and ‘Palestine certificates’ to facilitate their emigration, and offering financial assistance to Dutch Jews in hiding in France and the Netherlands. After the liberation of the camps, the committee made lists of Dutch Jewish survivors and helped search for relatives. Isaac had been a member of the committee of the same name set up in the Netherlands in late 1940 to represent the interests of Dutch Jews, and dissolved by the German authorities in Nov. 1941.

3 Mozes Heiman Gans (1917–1978), antiques dealer specializing in jewellery; fled with his wife from the Netherlands to Switzerland in summer 1942; member of the JCC in Geneva, 1943–1945; active in the Dutch Israelite Religious Community from 1946; editor-in-chief of the *Nieuw Israëlitisch Weekblad*, 1950–1967; professor of Jewish history in Leiden, 1976–1977.

4 The original contains illegible handwritten notes.

5 This could not be found. The Dutch envoy in Bern was Johan Jeronimus Balthazar Bosch Ridder van Rosenthal (1889–1955).

behalf,[6] we are now pleased to be able to communicate that the expansion and coordination of all the support work for our Jewish compatriots set out in those documents is yielding such positive results that we believe it is appropriate to inform Her Majesty's Government of the most important details in brief.

1. Thanks to close contacts with the Netherlands,[7] we are able to make very considerable amounts available, mainly to pay the living expenses of people in hiding. More than fl. 200,000 has been made available so far.

2. Where possible, we send food to these people and their supporters via their Christian friends.

3. For those who are still in Holland, we produce, at their request, statements from South American countries.[8] This has been made possible partly through the intervention of Her Majesty's Envoy. In many cases, these documents have proven to be of great value.

4. We also send money, food, documents, etc. to our compatriots who are in hiding in France.

5. We send food to approximately 2,000 deportees, whose names and current whereabouts are known to us. From reports we have heard from witnesses, we know that most deportees are near starvation. Providing this food causes major difficulties, which we try to resolve in consultation with the Netherlands Red Cross representative in Geneva.[9] Our aim is to send as much as possible, as soon as we can.

6. In order to be able to carry out this work as effectively as possible, to expand it, and to be ready to provide all kinds of support, a number of people are working continually on developing a card index system, which already includes thousands of names. In March we sent out forms to all Dutch people in Switzerland, with a request to list as many Dutch Jews as possible: name, age, occupation, previous address, etc., and also details of deportation, if known. We have also tried to obtain details outside Switzerland by illegal means. Dr Visser 't Hooft has already sent you several very important lists.

The camps known to us where there are currently – or were until very recently – Jews from the Netherlands are: Theresienstadt, Bergen-Belsen (near Hanover), Vittel (France), Birkenau (Neubeuern), Monowitz, Sosnowitz, Auschwitz, Mechelen, Kattowitz,[10] Jawichowitz,[11] Dorohucza,[12] Wlodawa,[13] AF Lublin,[14] Kossow,[15] Majdanek, Maydan,[16]

6 This could not be found. Dr Gustave Gérard Kullmann (1894–1961), lawyer; active in refugee relief from 1933; commissioner for refugees at the League of Nations, 1938–1946; leading official of the United Nations refugee agency in Geneva and London, 1946–1954.

7 The so-called Swiss route was one of the most strategically important lines of communication for the Dutch resistance, by which information from resistance organizations in the Netherlands made its way via Geneva to the Dutch government in exile in London, and conversely, aid and money were conveyed from Switzerland to the Netherlands.

8 Presumably papers attesting to the South American countries' receptiveness to take in the people concerned, or to confirm that the document holders were citizens of a South American country.

9 Baron Jan Willem Jacobus de Vos van Steenwijk (1882–1970).

10 Sonderkommando Kattowitz was a subcamp of Auschwitz where a small number of prisoners were forced to build air-raid shelters from Jan. 1944 to Jan. 1945.

11 Correctly: Jawischowitz, a subcamp (at a coal mine) of Auschwitz.

12 Subcamp of Majdanek from March to Nov. 1943. Around half of the Jews imprisoned there were Dutch citizens who had been sent from Sobibor to Dorohucza. On 3 Nov. 1943 all the Jews in the camp, including 144 from the Netherlands, were shot as part of Operation Harvest Festival.

13 A Jewish ghetto existed in the city of Włodawa until 30 April 1943, when all of the inhabitants were deported to Sobibor. Whether Dutch Jews were among them could not be ascertained.

Trawniki,[17] Tarnowitz,[18] Warsaw, Riga, Drancy (France), Risa (?)[19] and/or Bergau,[20] Buchenwalde concentration camp,[21] Frauenlager[22] Ravensbrück, and Männergefängnis[23] Anrath (Rhineland).[24] We have just received the news, which has not yet been confirmed, that there are no longer any Jews in Vught[25] and that Lublin has been 'liquidated'. On the basis of information we have received, we are very concerned about the continued existence of Westerbork and Mechelen.

The telegram of 24 April 1944[26] from His Excellency the Minister of Foreign Affairs[27] regarding these details was presented to us by the delegate of the Netherlands Red Cross in Switzerland, London Committee. We were pleased to be able to conclude from this telegram that Her Majesty's Government does indeed support the development of a card index system.

7. Particularly in the aspect of our work involving the issue of providing initial support after the war, our committee is represented by Dr A. Polak Daniels[28] and his wife,[29] who are also members of 'Red Cross Committee P,'[30] which aims to train a team.

The Coordination Committee would also like to take in hand the training of social workers for the Netherlands and is in a position to finance all the preparatory measures for this initial support.

To ensure that all of this is properly organized, it would be very pertinent for Her Majesty's Government to send the aforementioned instructions for Dr Polak Daniels as

14 'Alter Flughafen' (Old Airfield) forced labour camp in Lublin, where Jewish men had to work between Feb. 1942 and Oct. 1943. The few survivors of this camp who were from the Netherlands later stated that they had been brought to the camp from Majdanek.

15 Presumably Kosów Lacki labour camp in Kreis Sokolow, where Jews were deployed to construct roads.

16 Presumably Majdan Tatarski ghetto, situated near the Lublin airfield; however, this ghetto had already been cleared in Nov. 1942.

17 Subcamp of Majdanek. The approximately 6,000 Jewish prisoners held there were shot in the neighbouring training camp Trawniki in Nov. 1943.

18 Presumably Lasowice forced labour camp near Tarnowskie Góry (Upper Silesia), in which Jews from Poland, Germany, and Western Europe were confined from 1940 to 1943.

19 Presumably Gröditz forced labour camp, near Riesa.

20 In October 1943 a group of 'exchange Jews' held in Bergen-Belsen were deceived into thinking they were to be sent to a camp called 'Bergau', near Dresden, pending their emigration from Germany. The camp 'Bergau' was a fiction: the group of 1,700–1,800 Jews were deported in late October to Auschwitz-Birkenau and murdered on arrival.

21 Correctly: Buchenwald.

22 German in the original: 'women's camp'.

23 German in the original: 'men's prison'.

24 Anrath men's and women's prisons between Krefeld and Viersen; prisoners were deployed as forced labour in a number of factories and businesses in the vicinity.

25 On 3 June 1944 the last Jewish prisoners, almost 500 persons, were deported from Vught to Auschwitz.

26 This could not be found.

27 Eelco Nicolaas van Kleffens.

28 Dr Anselm Polak Daniels (1901–1986), physician; fled to Switzerland in 1943; headed a committee to repatriate Dutch citizens from the Soviet-occupied territories, 1944–1945; thereafter returned to the Netherlands.

29 Ariane Margaretha Polak Daniels-Boon Hartsinck (1911–1980), psychologist; fled to Switzerland, probably in 1943; married Anselm Polak Daniels there in 1944; returned to the Netherlands in 1945.

30 Further information on the committee could not be found.

soon as possible, along with detailed tasks in this respect, also for the Jewish Coordination Committee.

8. The experience of the Jewish population's social and economic life which a number of us gained in the Netherlands before and during the war, the details gathered and the knowledge obtained about the condition of those who have been deported or are in hiding (including the hundreds of children in hiding without their parents) in the course of our work in Switzerland, and the contacts with the representatives of international organizations in Switzerland have motivated us to examine all aspects of the difficult problem of social and moral recovery in increasing depth, including the reintegration of the Jewish population in Dutch society, the restoration or replacement of many social institutions, and the incorporation of the group of Jews who were not born in the Netherlands and of whom a relatively large number have been rescued, and all this in the spirit of and according to the traditions of the long-established Dutch-Jewish community.

Given the above, our committee believes we may request Her Majesty's Government to provide us with information about the legal and concrete measures that have already been taken or are planned, and to involve us in their implementation. We have a number of people who would like nothing better than to get down to work (see also point 7). Prompt instructions from the government would therefore be very much appreciated.

9. Our committee currently consists of the following gentlemen:[31]

S. van Dantzig	formerly Hollandsche Bank Unie and Church Council, Rotterdam
M. H. Gans	formerly Premsela en Hamburger and Joodsche Invalide[32]
S. Isaac, LLM[33]	formerly Bijenkorf and a member of the Jewish Coordination Committee chaired by Dr L. E. Visser (founded independently of the Jewish Council, later dissolved by the Germans)
S. I. Troostwijk[34]	formerly a machine expert in Arnhem
Dr A. Polak Daniels	formerly acting director of the Red Cross Hospital in The Hague
Mrs A. M. Polak-Daniels-Boon	Hartsinck, psychologist

In financial terms, we are able to do all of this work mainly thanks to special cooperation with and support from Mr Saly Mayer,[35] a representative of the American Joint Distribution Committee.

31 The report refers to gentlemen (*heren*), although one of the committee members listed is female.

32 Premsela & Hamburger was a business in Amsterdam selling antiques, silver and jewellery; the Joodsche Invalide was a home for the elderly established in Amsterdam in 1938.

33 Siegfried Isaac (1900–1948), businessman; worked for the De Bijenkorf department store from 1925; editor of the journal *Joodsche Wachter*, 1927–1939; member of the Jewish Coordination Committee in the Netherlands, 1940–1942; fled to Switzerland in 1943; returned to Amsterdam in 1945.

34 Salomon Isaac Troostwijk (1903–1967), machinery dealer; lived in Switzerland, 1940–1945; returned to Amsterdam in 1945.

35 Saly Mayer (1882–1950); worked in the textile industry; secretary (1929–1936) and later chairman (1936–1943) of the Swiss Federation of Jewish Communities; representative of the American Jewish Joint Distribution Committee (JDC) in Switzerland from 1940.

Mr Roswell McClelland,[36] a representative of the War Refugee Board[37] and Special Assistant to the American Minister, also provides support and advice.

With much gratitude and appreciation, we would also like to mention the recognition of our work by Her Majesty's Envoy.

Particularly in view of the special situation in Switzerland, we value this highly. However, we would hardly be able to achieve anything in practical terms if we were not able to rely on the enormous daily contribution by Dr W. A. Visser 't Hooft, who also makes his extensive experience and important connections available to support the work on behalf of our Jewish compatriots.

In spite of all this highly appreciated support, it would nevertheless make a great difference if Her Majesty's Government were to decide to grant us financial assistance, possibly via the American War Refugee Board, particularly for office expenses and food dispatches.[38]

In the interest of our work for our Jewish compatriots, we would very much appreciate your prompt reply and instructions, by telegram if possible.

On behalf of the committee,

M. H. Gans

Due to the special circumstances, this report has been drawn up in haste. We would politely request that you also pass on the details provided to the army rabbi, Dr Rodrigues Pereira.

P.S. Mr McClelland is of the opinion that the War Refugee Board may well be prepared to pass on number telegrams[39] at the request of the Dutch government.

36 Roswell Dunlop McClelland (1914–1995); head of the Quaker relief agency American Friends Committee in Geneva, 1940–1944; representative of the War Refugee Board in Switzerland from 1944; US ambassador to Niger, 1970–1973.

37 The War Refugee Board, created by US President Franklin D. Roosevelt in Jan. 1944, provided financial and political support to victims of the National Socialist regime.

38 The Dutch government's provision of financial support to the committee can be documented only from Sept. 1944.

39 Presumably coded telegrams containing numbers, intended to keep the information transmitted secret.

DOC. 162

On 25 July 1944 Friedrich Moritz Levisohn informs the Catholic Archbishop of Utrecht about the Jews in Amersfoort camp and seeks help for baptized Jews in Amsterdam[1]

Letter from Dr F. M. Levisohn,[2] Doorwerth (Gelderland), Huize Eikenhof, to His Excellency, the Archbishop of Utrecht,[3] dated 25 July 1944

Monseigneur,

Many years ago, I made so bold as to write to Your Eminence to make a request and also to point out something.

At that time, I was filled *with burning concern*[4] for the immediate future of the Catholic brethren who were declared to be Jews through the application of the so-called Nuremberg Laws.[5]

The assurance Your Eminence gave me back then that everything was being done did not for a moment conceal from me the certainty that in problematic cases there was probably little the Church could do against the measures of the occupying authorities.

My fears have unfortunately proved well founded, and therefore only a very few Catholics 'of non-Aryan descent' are still at liberty in the Netherlands.

Back then, when I turned to Monseigneur to draw attention to the plight of these children of our Holy Mother Church, I did so under the fresh impression of my experiences in Amersfoort transit (concentration) camp.

At that time I, as a physician, was permitted to give assistance to some of the unfortunates. These were Catholics who had been arrested on 2 August 1942, one week after the well-known pastoral letter,[6] and for the most part sent to the East.

It was not only the many nuns (with the Jewish star) and monks (with the Jewish star) who continually proved what *true* children of the Holy Church they were. The laymen, too, movingly bore witness to their faith. I saw whole families there, even several generations. These included siblings, some of whom were monks, others nuns.

I will never forget how, on the day before they finally had to set forth, headed for a destination certain yet unknown, they all sang the *Confiteor*[7] in loud voices, while surrounded by the SS guards.

1 Het Utrechts Archief, 449/76. This document has been translated from German.

2 Dr Friedrich Moritz Levisohn (1905–1955), physician; managing director of Seppelfricke, a company producing cast metal; fled to the Netherlands from Germany in 1939; active in the resistance under an assumed name, 1940–1945; briefly imprisoned in Amersfoort in 1942; returned to Germany and to his old position in 1945; changed his name to Friedrich Maria Lenig in 1946; chairman of FC Schalke 04, 1946–1947.

3 Johannes de Jong.

4 This is a reference to the title of the encyclical 'Mit brennender Sorge', which was written in German rather than Latin and issued by Pope Pius XI on 21 March 1937. The encyclical was critical of those who had breached the 1933 concordat signed between the Holy See and the German Reich. It also condemned 'pantheistic confusion', 'neopaganism', 'the so-called myth of race and blood', and idolatry of the state, and it defended the Old Testament.

5 The Reich Citizenship Law of 15 Sept. 1935 made German Jews into second-class citizens and the regulations based on it defined who was to count as a Jew or a *Mischling*: see PMJ 1/198. The Blood Protection Law of 15 Sept. 1935 prohibited marriage and extramarital relations between Jews and 'Aryans': see PMJ 1/199.

6 See Doc. 65.

I myself readily acknowledge that they were no more saintly in life than their fellow believers in Christ, but the attitude they adopted in the camp made the deepest impression – and not only on me!!

It is not the aim of this letter to describe all the details of that time. I only want to add that, in those days, I made efforts on behalf of the deportees through the German Church's investigations office in Düsseldorf,[8] but that office is now no longer in existence.

Today I am turning to the Bishop of the Ecclesiastical Province of the Netherlands on a matter that fills me not just *with burning concern,* but also with *deep shame!*

It concerns the few Catholics with the Jewish star left in Amsterdam, who are either too old to undertake very heavy physical labour, or remain at liberty for similar reasons.

In some cases, the financial situation of these pitiable people is bleak. They must therefore rely on charitable payments.

Up until now, this has paid them a small subsidy. The appeal that reached me today speaks, in this individual's own case, of eight guilders (that's right: a whole eight guilders!) per week.

However, even this negligible support will cease in future.

Moreover, on receiving these subsidies, the recipients frequently got comments from the parish poor relief such as 'They are going to be keeping a close eye on the Jews now, especially in the Church.'

Comments in which mistrust and disdain are clearly evident.

Apart from the fact that I consider it objectionable to have such misgivings voiced by the parish Poor Relief Board, misgivings that are largely tantamount to malicious falsehood, only the clergy are entitled to make such admonitions, and propagating a 'Jewish question' within the Church is unquestionably inconsistent with the reasoning of the encyclical 'With Burning Concern'. Moreover, it seems unwise to me to create 'Marannos'[9] – heartless and un-Christian as well!

Then, as additional bonuses, these – truly – poorest of the poor get to hear: 'What we are doing is voluntary and is now coming to an end at last.' The word 'voluntary' looks strange alongside the axiom: 'What you do unto the poorest of my brethren – you do unto me.'[10]

Further, they are recommended to register with the [municipal] social welfare,[11] although one is aware, one says, how unwelcome Catholics wearing the star are there – but, one adds, the Jews did the very same thing after the dissolution of the Committee,[12]

7 The Confiteor (I Confess) is a prayer said during the Penitential Act of Holy Mass in the Catholic Church.

8 No information on this could be found.

9 Correctly: Marranos. The term was used in early modern times to denote the Spanish and Portuguese Jews who, under the pressure of the Inquisition, underwent baptism but often continued to practise their original faith in secret.

10 The wording from Matthew 25:40 (KJV) is: 'Verily I say unto you, Inasmuch as ye have done it unto one of the least of these my brethren, ye have done it unto me.'

11 This refers to the City of Amsterdam's Department for Social Welfare.

12 Presumably this refers to the Committee for Special Jewish Interests (CBJB) and its subcommittee for Jewish Refugees, which were dissolved by the German occupation administration in March 1941. Its functions were assumed by the Jewish Council.

and the Roman Catholic Poor Relief Board is no – Committee. To a man who has assuredly never been an idler in his life, it must sound like an insult when he is asked why he is not working. He can look for a job, he is told. Of course, he is too old for excavation work, he is told, but clerical work, that would still be a option, and in Germany all men under 65 work – the argument that nobody would hire him with his star and he is also not permitted to apply for jobs, but that he is asking [the] poor relief to place him, is rejected with the statement that it is not the task of the Poor Relief Board to place people in jobs. No one who notes such remarks with outrage can help wondering whether it is actually the business of the poor relief of a Roman Catholic parish in Amsterdam to respond in such a way to people highly unaccustomed to begging.

Even the shameful advice to go begging to wealthier friends or acquaintances and let them provide is given without hesitation. It will remain a mystery to me who is meant by 'wealthier friends or acquaintances'.

I have presented to Your Eminence only a selection from the most recent period, for the accuracy of which I can vouch. If requested, I would give the names of the individuals and parishes concerned, though only reluctantly – to avoid bringing even more ordeals and insults, rather than relief, to those affected.

Because I consider that the solving of the problem extends beyond the sphere of the Diocese of Haarlem,[13] I am appealing directly to you, Monseigneur, first, because of the dire need of Catholics who are déclassé for political and racial reasons, second, on account of the undeniable danger that threatens to ensue from this antisemitic attitude, which is not exactly a Catholic one!

As I am convinced that the spiritual leader of the Catholic Netherlands can provide a thoroughgoing remedy in this instance, which was certainly not possible in the case I set forth above, I most respectfully request protective measures for devout Catholics whose measure of earthly suffering is already more than ample, even without the humiliating lack of understanding on the part of the less disadvantaged members of our Holy Mother Church.

I ask that you receive this letter, my second one, in this way and only in this way:

Si linguis hominum loquar et Angelorum, caritatem autem non habeam,[14] – –.

Most respectfully seeking the blessing of Your Eminence, I remain, with an obedient kiss on the hand,

the most faithful son of Your Eminence[15]

13 Amsterdam was part of the diocese of Haarlem, now Haarlem-Amsterdam.

14 1 Corinthians 13:1 (KJV): 'Though I speak with the tongues of men and of angels, and have not charity …'

15 Handwritten note in Dutch: 'Do not reply, 2 August 1944'.

DOC. 163

On 3 August 1944 Elisabeth van Leest-van Oorschot writes a letter describing the arrest of Rebecca Aldewereld, whom she had been hiding in her home[1]

Handwritten letter, unsigned,[2] Tienray, dated 3 August 1944

Dear Sir and Madam,[3]

I very much regret having to write this letter to you, but it is my duty to do so, and I promised Truus[4] I would do this.

In the night from Monday to Tuesday *they* took Truus away from us; they also took my husband, and I will try to explain what happened.

It was 3.45 a.m. on Tuesday when there was a knock on the front door and another knock – or rather a bang – on our bedroom door at the same time. They shouted 'police', so we got up and opened the door, and there were six men with revolvers in their hands in our house, and they asked where that … was. I said we did not have one, but after a lot of lies and discussion, they just got on with it, and I had to precede them upstairs, first to the beds of my own children, whom they were not interested in, and then to the door of Truus's room. Oh madam, I had never before been as shaky as I was when I had to open that door, but once in the room, those men searched the place with their torches and the bed was empty. Truus had heard them of course and had hidden in the loft, but that could not save her, as they began to search everywhere, and they found Truus behind a few crates; it was as if part of my heart was torn out, but nothing else could be done. She had to go downstairs with them in her nightgown, and she was allowed to get dressed in our bedroom. Two men stayed with her at all times, and then a few more arrived; they kicked everything, which is how they found our radio,[5] and they made an awful racket. It was 4.30 a.m. by then, and they were ready to go.

Truus [stood] between two men, and the rest were there to watch over my husband, but then they reached the police van (it was parked a bit further away from our house), and they were going to use their torches to provide light to get Truus in the van, and then my husband saw his opportunity and fled. They went after him, but they ran into everything, but my husband knew the area inside out and soon had quite a head start. All the children, or rather all the … that were here in the village were taken away that night;[6] it

1 JHM, Doc. 00 007 692. This document has been translated from Dutch.

2 The married couple Martinus van Leest (1905–1965), railway worker, and Elisabeth (Lies) van Leest-van Oorschot (1914–2005), housewife, were honoured as Righteous Among the Nations by Yad Vashem in 1989 for having sheltered Rebecca van Aldewereld.

3 The unnamed addressees cannot be identified with certainty.

4 Alias of Rebecca Aldewereld (1924–2002) while in hiding; lived in various hiding places, 1942–1943; with the van Leest family from Dec. 1943; deported via Westerbork to Bergen-Belsen after her arrest; returned to the Netherlands in 1945.

5 On 13 May 1943 all Dutch citizens had been ordered to hand in their radios to the German authorities.

6 The midwife Hanna van der Voort (1904–1956), along with a few associates, had created an organization in Tienray that found hiding places for more than 100 Jewish children in the vicinity. On 30 July 1944 she was betrayed and arrested together with five hidden children and the male heads of the households which had taken them in; the children were deported, and the men returned home the next day. Hanna van der Voort returned home after nine days.

was pure betrayal [what happened] with the fathers of the family, but those people are all back again, those fathers I mean.

Truus put on a brave face, but when she gave me a farewell kiss, she fell apart. We had become so fond of each other, and for me it was a terrible blow to have to hand her over like that, but I hope we will see each other again soon, as they believe it will now soon be over. I have now told you some of the details but certainly not everything, as that is impossible in a letter, as you will understand. Those men came back at 10 a.m. that Tuesday, but they left again as they had come; I did not give them any information.

I have enclosed a note that Truus was able to give to someone else. It is torn, as it was hidden in a stocking, under the sole.[7]

I have now done my duty; please pass on my best wishes to *Marg*,[8] and tell her that I also loved her child very much; she was with us for seven months. I hope that I will soon be able to meet you all.

I wish you all the best, and please do get in touch. I still have Truus's grey jacket here, and a black blouse – that piece of fabric she got from Marg for her birthday – two pairs of shoes, and a beige dress she had only just received; she has taken the rest of her clothes with her. What should I do with them? That blue top Marg knitted really suited her.

When the photos of Truus and my twins are ready, I will send them to you; I have enclosed a small one,[9] but it is not very good. I hope the other ones will be better.

DOC. 164
In early September 1944 Willy Rosen bids farewell to Westerbork camp with a poem[1]

Poem by Willy Rosen,[2] written in early September 1944[3] (typescript)

Valediction of a veteran camp inmate[4]
My dearest Westerbork, I must part from you now,
It seems I can't avoid a little tear somehow.
You often proved a tough, unpleasant place to be,
Yet in the end, you did no harm to me.
My Westerbork, you plagued me quite a deal –
And nonetheless you had a certain sex appeal.

7 This could not be found.

8 Presumably the alias of Naatje Aldewereld-Wurms (1900–1970), housewife, mother of Rebecca Aldewereld, thought to have lived in hiding from 1942 to 1943. Rebecca's father was Simon Aldewereld (1898–1943), baker; deported via Westerbork in Nov. 1942; perished in Fürstengrube subcamp in June 1943.

9 This could not be found.

1 NIOD, 250i/338. Published in Volker Kühn (ed.), *Deutschlands Erwachen: Kabarett unterm Hakenkreuz 1933–1945* (Weinheim: Quadriga, 1989), pp. 295–296. This document has been translated from German.

2 Willy Rosen, born Wilhelm Julius Rosenbaum (1894–1944), composer and cabaret artist; in 1937 emigrated from Germany to the Netherlands, where he founded the Theater der Prominenten; in 1943 deported to Westerbork, where he ran the camp's cabaret; on 4 Sept. 1944 deported to Theresienstadt and from there to Auschwitz, where he perished.

'Servus', dear boiler house, I say in gentle tone;
One flute sound more, and then you're left alone.
Farewell, my back room where the little carpet lay,
I whisper nebekh[5] softly to myself today.
Farewell, you tiny kitchen, farewell WC.
The hot plate must be left behind, that sorrows me.
You often had short-circuits, oh, that wasn't great,
That always meant that one could watch good Tuerkel[6] get irate.
Adieu, my cupboard, and adieu, bookshelf,
It was a pleasure, I enjoyed myself.
Adieu, dear stamppot[7] and my vuilnisbak,[8]
I'm going on a hike now with my bag and pack.
EHBU,[9] for just one final time I squeeze your hands.
One more driepoeder[10] – after that, the curtain lands.
Farewell, you Service Sections, all so dear.
I've no more duties set for me, I yield, my space is clear.
Transports aplenty leaving did I see,
And now – now what is being ditched as scrap is me.
I board the train myself now, with my pack of stuff.
And just between ourselves: I think it's bad enough.
But sympathy and good advice I would decline.
Old combat veteran that I am, I'll cope just fine.
Of Westerbork affairs I've had my lot.
I'll get my tsores[11] in another spot.
Feed me my supplements, although they be the last.
I part with butter, and with much learned from the past.
I'm packing all my things and leaving nothing here,
I'll even take my wife,[12] whom I do hold so dear.

3 The dating is based on the fact that the last train from Westerbork to Theresienstadt left on 4 Sept. 1944, and Willy Rosen was among those on this transport.

4 'Alte Kampinsassen' was the term used for the German Jews who had lived in Westerbork refugee camp even before the occupation of the Netherlands. They were at the top of the Jewish prisoner hierarchy and held key positions within the internal organization of the camp, meaning that they were initially better protected from deportation than other prisoners.

5 Yiddish: 'what a pity', 'alas'.

6 Richard Türkel (1901–1984), electrical engineer; emigrated to the Netherlands from Vienna in June 1939; on 17 July 1940 deported to Westerbork, where he ran the technical service; lived in Hilversum after the war.

7 Traditional Dutch dish made from mashed potatoes and vegetables.

8 Dutch: 'waste bucket'.

9 Abbreviation for 'Erste Hilfe bei Unglücken' (First Aid). An EHBU ward was attached to the large, relatively well-equipped hospital in Westerbork.

10 Medicinal powder. Presumably a placebo prescribed by the physicians in Westerbork for all possible illnesses, but which had only a psychological effect.

11 Yiddish: 'troubles', 'problems'.

12 Olga Maria Rosen, née Krauskopf (1905–1945), seamstress; emigrated to the Netherlands from Merano in 1937; married Willy Rosen in 1942; in Nov. 1943 deported to Westerbork, where she worked for the Jewish Council; deported to Theresienstadt on 4 Sept. 1944 and, one month later, to Auschwitz.

Adieu, 'F.K.'[13] and 'V.',[14] adieu, the laundry too –
My laundry number's free to be assigned anew.
Farewell, dear Ipa[15] too, I have to move along,
So tell your shmontses[16] to the other throng!
You old camp inmates, all my brothers dear, farewell,
Perhaps we'll meet again in life – well, who can tell?
A picture postcard's something I can't send.
But here's how you'll perhaps remember your old friend:
I'm on the train, the whistle soon will sound,
Once more I sweep my gaze across the landscape all around –
I know it now – I'm grief-befallen.
Adieu, my Westerbork, Post Hooghalen.[17]

DOC. 165

In a diary entry for 4 September 1944, Aad van As, the administrative secretary for the municipality of Westerbork, records concern about the impending clearance of the camp[1]

Diary of Aad van As,[2] entry for 4 September 1944 (typescript)

I had intended to write every day again when the invasion[3] started, but I have not managed to do so. I do not have enough time. They are now advancing fast, and we may be free soon. They have already reached Belgium, and yet? A large transport has departed, one to Auschwitz and one to Theresienstadt.[4] My old neighbours, the Cohen family,[5] have also gone. The camp is empty; there are 588 people, 3,000 are gone. It's terrible. The mood was therefore very downhearted. The liberation so close, and then being

13 Flying Column (*Fliegende Kolonne*); unit responsible for transporting baggage and other auxiliary duties during deportations.
14 This presumably refers to Workplace V (Clothing).
15 Abbreviation employed in Westerbork for 'Israelite Press Agency', an ironic synonym for 'rumours'.
16 Yiddish: 'silly stuff', 'trifles'.
17 Hooghalen is the village next to Westerbork.

1 NIOD, 244/715. This document has been translated from Dutch.
2 Adrianus (Aad) van As (b. 1919), naval officer; head of the central rationing office in Westerbork camp from Sept. 1942, and thus one of the few non-Jewish civilians in the camp; involved in illegal operations against the German occupiers; appointed camp commandant in April 1945; emigrated to Australia after the war.
3 The invasion had begun on 6 June 1944, when Allied forces landed in Normandy.
4 On 3 Sept. 1944 a transport with 1,019 persons left Westerbork for Auschwitz; one day later, 2,087 persons were deported to Theresienstadt. The last transport left Westerbork on 13 Sept. 1944, taking 279 persons to Bergen-Belsen.
5 The Cohen family consisted of Levij (Lou) Cohen (1899–1968), ironmonger; his wife, Sophia Cohen-Joëls (b. 1903); and his mother, Elizabeth Cohen-van Emden. The family was deported to Theresienstadt on 4 Sept. 1944 and sent from there to Switzerland in Feb. 1945 as part of an exchange. All three returned to the Netherlands in 1945.

moved out of the country. It's unimaginable. I now have only three workers left from my original staff at the office: Mrs de Bree-v. d. Berg, Minni,[6] and Hanna.[7] The others have all gone now. The camp seems dead. The day before the transport, Gemmeker summoned everyone to the large hall and informed them that they would be evacuated and that the camp would be closed down. The people who were left would liquidate the camp and then also be sent away. If you work as hard in Theresienstadt as you have worked here, you will not be treated any worse, were his words. But what difference does that make? You are forced to leave the place where you were born, that's bad, and to go to a place from which no positive, uncensored news has ever been received, i.e. news from people allowed to write their honest opinion. Liberation in sight, but deported nonetheless. This is awful. This is not going to cheer people up. The camp is empty, deserted. What will the future hold? What happens now? We don't know. We have to wait and see.

DOC. 166
On 18 September 1944 Salomon Silber experiences the liberation of Hoensbroek by Allied troops[1]

Diary of Salomon Silber, entry for 18 September 1944 (copy of the typescript)[2]

As dawn broke, the deep-blue sky was covered by a dark cloak, while the Earth was filled with a thick grey mist that gradually began to dissipate. By 11 a.m. the sky was becoming clearer and clearer. The dark cloak was being torn apart. The sun occasionally peeked through the broken clouds, and by midday the glowing ball dispersed the clouds and now appeared as an invigorating, warming light.

German military vehicles are tearing up and down the road.[3] They are hurrying along at high speed to escape the approaching enemy. All morning and afternoon, defeated soldiers, fleeing and running, pass by the houses in the direction of Sittard.[4] Their faces and uniforms were covered in mud. They looked tired and dazed. They kept running as long as they could, carrying all of their gear, moving along at a fast pace. You could see boys of 16 and 17 going past. A commander shouted from afar, 'Soldaten, halt Mut.'[5]

6 Marieke (Minni) Gudema-Cohen (1916–2002); deported on 31 Dec. 1942 to Westerbork, where she was held until the liberation of the camp.

7 Johanna (Hanna) Gudema-Meijer (1918–2003), administrative secretary; worked for the municipality of Vlagtwedde, 1936–1941; deported on 3 Oct. 1942 to Westerbork, where she was held until the liberation of the camp.

1 The original is privately owned. Copy in NIOD 471/9e. Published in Silber, *Een joods gezin in onderduik*, pp. 165–168. This document has been translated from Dutch.

2 The original contains handwritten marking and corrections.

3 The change between present and past tense here and below is in the original.

4 At this time, Salomon Silber and his brother, along with their parents, were living in hiding in the home of Tjeerd and Trijntje de Boer in Hoensbroek (province of Limburg). The town of Sittard is almost 10 km north of Hoensbroek.

5 German in the original: 'Soldiers, don't lose courage.'

These encouraging words were silenced by approaching machine guns, probably American.

On the street you can hear voices shouting enthusiastically: 'The Americans are here.' I couldn't believe my ears. To me this was like a nocturnal dream full of beauty and splendour.

We first rush upstairs and look out of the window – but still through a narrow chink [in the curtains or shutters] – with longing and eagerness to catch sight of our liberators, but to our disappointment there is still nothing to be seen. We have to muster all of our self-control to make sure we put our heads out of the window as little as possible. Restlessly we go from one window to the other and back again.

When Auntie[6] happened to look out of the window, a German soldier asked her if she can get him a drink of water. She did not forsake her Christian duty of course, as she is obedient to God. If thine enemy be hungry, give him bread to eat; and if he be thirsty, give him water to drink: for thou shalt heap coals of fire upon his head.[7] The soldier put Auntie at ease with the words, 'Seien Sie ruhig, binnen drei Wochen kommen wir wieder zurück.'[8]

The American tanks can already be spotted in the distance. They shoot at the German troops with a great deal of noise and pandemonium.

Suddenly we hear cheerful, happy shouts: 'There's a flag over there, two flags, as many as ten.' I quickly run back upstairs, and now I dare to put my head out of the window. My eyes scan the open sky in all directions, I look to the left and the right and – after four years of sighing under the yoke of the Nazi regime – I once again see the Dutch people's proud flag of freedom. Its red, white, and blue, high and proud, is singing its song of freedom. It appears to be in its element. Determined and brave, it stood its ground while exiled from house and home, but now it proudly sings the song of freedom together with its oppressed people.

Our street is instantly transformed into a party with flags and decorations. Photos of the royal family are displayed in front of the windows. Impatiently and anxiously, the souls hankering for freedom stare into the distance. But suddenly their faces are beaming with happiness, expressing freedom and more freedom. Cheering and dancing, they shout: 'Look, the American tanks are coming.' I feel sheer joy when I see these happy faces.

My soul leapt in an extraordinary, wonderful way when my eyes beheld our liberators'[9] approach. At last, after watching and waiting for such a long time, the day of freedom had arrived. Not a single person remained inside: young and old, poor and rich went out onto the street, carrying flags of the House of Orange, of the Netherlands, America, and Britain. The whole street turned into a vibrant sea of people. From every corner and every street people appeared in front of us, dancing and cheering exuberantly. Among them you could see several people of our own race, filled with happiness twice over.

6 Presumably Trijntje de Boer-Germeraad (1893–1982).
7 Proverbs 25:21–22 (KJV).
8 German in the original: 'Don't worry, we'll be back within three weeks.'
9 'Liberators' in English in the original.

To me this experience was exactly like that of a bird that has been locked up in a cage, and then the door is opened wide, and the bird gets the chance to fly towards freedom. The bird first looks around timidly and distrustfully, and then it swiftly launches into the free world, spreading its clipped and subjugated wings with all its might, celebrating its freedom with song. Standing in the hallway all by myself, I looked around and asked Auntie warily: 'Can I also go outside?' 'Of course, come out here, the gates of freedom are wide open for you.' On hearing these delightful words, I leapt out of the hallway and found myself in the middle of the street with two small orange flags in my hands, which I got from our friendly neighbour. I cheered and danced with joy like a little child. My joy knew no bounds. Our neighbours rushed towards us from all directions and congratulated us on our glorious freedom.

God our Father has now surrounded many of His children with joy and happiness, and has taken away the sorrow from our heavy hearts. The people in hiding now resurfaced in large numbers and grabbed their priceless freedom with both hands.

DOC. 167
Jewish Echo, 13 October 1944: article on the situation of the Jews in Maastricht after liberation[1]

Hundred Thousand Jews Deported From Holland

Maastricht. – According to Dutch estimates, about three-quarters of the Jewish population of Holland, which before the war numbered 140,000, have been deported by the Germans. The old established Jewish community of about 80,000 souls was even [more] strong[ly] hit than the refugees who, owing to previous experience, were in a better position than their Dutch co-religionists to recognise the approach[ing] danger and to escape in time.

In Maastricht only half a dozen families who went into hiding when the mass deportations started remained of the 500 Jewish inhabitants of the town. Among those saved is the Shochet[2] of the local community, M. Isaac,[3] and his son-in-law.[4] While in hiding they were supplied with food cards by the underground movement. Mme. Isaac even gave birth to a child and had good medical attention.[5] The hundred-year-old synagogue of Maastricht was used by the Nazis as a warehouse. There are still piles of rejected debris of furniture in the building, broken chairs, tables, beds, lamps and pictures, while any furniture that could be used was shipped to Germany.

1 *Jewish Echo*, 13 Oct. 1944, p. 8. The *Jewish Echo* was published in Glasgow as a weekly newspaper from 1928 until 1992.
2 Hebrew, literally: 'slaughterer' or 'butcher'; a person officially certified as competent to kill cattle and poultry in the manner prescribed by Halacha (Jewish law).
3 Correctly, presumably: Isaac Mozes de Liver (1880–1948), kosher butcher; worked as a kosher butcher and precentor for the Jewish Community of Maastricht before the occupation.
4 Isaak Tugendhaft (1909–1976), businessman; leading member of the Jewish Community of Maastricht in the 1930s; chairman of the Dutch Zionist League in Rotterdam from 1947.
5 This probably refers to Isaak Tugendhaft's wife, Frida Tugendhaft-de Liver (1915–2000), who gave birth to a son in Nov. 1943 while living in hiding.

Since the end of 1942, the J. T. A.[6] correspondent was told, the Nazis used to round up 400 Jews every day. Certain categories such as diamond workers, rag collectors, and Jews living in mixed marriage[s] were exempt from deportation, but the others were brought to clearance camps and then sent to Eastern Europe. From the Westerbork camp, which has been cleared save for a few hundred prisoners, two transports of 1,300 deportees left every week for Poland.[7] Before sending the Jews to the camps, the Nazis secured all their property, including jewels listed in insurance policies. Latterly they ordered even Jews who are married to non-Jews to the labour camps, offering exemption to those who accepted sterilisation.[8]

They Bought 'Aryan' Grandparents

The story of how Jews, disregarding the enormous risk, participated in the hiding of Allied airmen in Holland was told to the J. T. A. correspondent here by one of the airmen, who reported to the Allied military authorities after the liberation of the town. Several airmen were hidden by Jews in secret chambers until the day of the Allied attack. Others were provided with false papers and smuggled into Belgium, whence they escaped home. The enormous risk the Jews were running will be realised when one considers that in Holland the Jews got a much rougher deal than in Belgium or France. Conditions were so terrible that many of them took refuge in Belgium. In Holland even people living in mixed marriage[s] were forced to wear the Yellow Star, whereas in Germany such Jews were exempted from this obligation.[9]

Nevertheless, the Nazis accepted much bribery. Border guards, if paid adequately, were even winking while Allied airmen crossed the Maas. In the same way some Jews 'bought' Aryan grandparents. They had to undergo a medical examination by a specialist who measured their noses, ears and eyes and for 30,000 guilders testified that their features revealed 'Aryan' descent.

DOC. 168

On 17 November 1944 the chairman of the Jewish Coordination Committee in Geneva again urges for the maximum possible assistance to be provided to Jews in the Netherlands[1]

Report, signed M. H. Gans on behalf of the committee,[2] dated 17 November 1944 (carbon copy)[3]

Report

Sadly, most of the Jews deported from the Netherlands have to be considered lost. In any case, we do not currently see any way in which we can do anything for them at all.

6 Jewish Telegraph Agency. The name of the correspondent could not be determined.

7 On average, one train left Westerbork per week.

8 See Doc. 155.

9 In general, all Jews in the Netherlands had to wear the yellow star; unlike in Germany, there were no 'privileged mixed marriages' in which the Jewish spouse was exempt from wearing the star. In the Netherlands, only Jews in so-called mixed marriages who underwent sterilization or were certified as infertile could be exempted from wearing the star.

1 NIOD, 249/1281. This document has been translated from Dutch.

The situation regarding those interned in Bergen-Belsen and Theresienstadt is slightly different, but we nonetheless ask ourselves with dread whether the poorly fed and poorly clothed people in Bergen-Belsen will survive another winter. It goes without saying that everything possible needs to be done if there is even the slightest chance of success.

We have recently received offers[4] to release at least 500 people for CHF 1,000 per person. We have studied these offers scrupulously. Our trust has been strengthened by the fact that nothing has to be paid until the persons concerned are in Switzerland. The War Refugee Board representative, Mr Roswell D. McLelland, is faithfully assisting us as always, but for financing we have had to approach the Joint [Distribution Committee] representative, Mr S. Mayer. The latter now takes the view that this is a task for the Dutch government.[5] In our opinion, the idea that the government can actually take such action has to be ruled out. We have not yet managed to persuade Mr Mayer – who is very critical of our government – to abandon his principle. He thinks it is about time the Dutch government substantiated its honourable reputation. The result is that for the Dutch people – as opposed to the other groups – nothing is being done. It would be a disgrace if, at some point, it were to be established that these people could indeed have been rescued if we had been able to spend CHF 1,000 per person.

We therefore *urgently appeal to you all* to ensure we have the required funds available as soon as possible. Whether you wish to raise that sum yourself or wish to intervene at the Joint is something you are best able to judge for yourself. The main thing is that this is done, and that it is done fast. Once again, nothing is given à fonds perdu.[6] Particularly with regard to this matter, it is a great shame that we, as opposed to the members of all the other non-Dutch committees, cannot leave Switzerland and hold talks in Paris and Brussels, for example, due to a ban imposed by the government.

Let us work together as closely as possible. If we do not address the aid work ourselves, absolutely nothing will happen. *People's lives are at stake!*[7]

2 The Jewish Coordination Committee in Switzerland, of which Mozes Heiman Gans was a member. See also Doc. 161.
3 The name of the addressee is unknown.
4 This is presumably a reference to the established contacts that led to a German–American exchange of civilians, in the course of which 301 prisoners with Central and South American papers were allowed to leave Bergen-Belsen in Jan. 1945 (136 went to Switzerland; the rest were interned in southern Germany); these contacts also led to the evacuation of 1,200 prisoners from Theresienstadt to Switzerland in early Feb. 1945. It was not possible to establish how many Dutch citizens were included in the two evacuations.
5 Part of the correspondence with Saly Mayer is included in the file.
6 French in the original: 'without a chance of getting it back'.
7 Nothing is known about the outcome of the enquiry.

DOC. 169

In February 1945 a flyer gives information about the founding of a Jewish Coordination Committee for the liberated Dutch territory[1]

Flyer from the Jewish Coordination Committee for the liberated Dutch territory,[2] Eindhoven, 23 Jan Luikenstraat, to the Jews in the liberated Dutch territory, undated[3]

First of all, we would like to congratulate you on your liberation.

We would like to inform you of what has already been achieved in the southern part of the Netherlands by and for the Jews. Your cooperation would obviously be appreciated. If you turn to us for support, we will do whatever we can to help you.

This January the 'Jewish Coordination Committee for the liberated Dutch territory' was established with the following aims:

1. To establish a centre to provide information and advice about specific Jewish matters to official and non-official organizations and persons in the Netherlands and elsewhere;
2. To act in a trusted capacity on behalf of foreign Jewish welfare organizations;
3. To cooperate with existing committees for Dutch Jews abroad, and those yet to be formed;
4. To initiate an investigation into the current whereabouts of Jews who were resident in the Netherlands on 10 May 1940 in order to, for example, reunite families as soon as possible. For this purpose, the Central Registration Bureau for Jews, which was established in November 1944 and is managed by Mr S. Roet,[4] has been included in the committee's remit;
5. To deal with the shortage of devotional items, partly caused by German destruction;
6. To take measures to provide support in the northern part of the Netherlands,[5] specifically where Jewish interests are concerned.

The Jewish Coordination Committee is made up of the following members: A. de Jong,[6] chairman; Captain I. Spangenthal,[7] vice-chairman; S. Eisenmann,[8] acting secretary; J. v. Amerongen,[9] treasurer; S. Roet, manager of the Registration Bureau; K. J.

1 JHM, Doc. 00 001 007. This document has been translated from Dutch.

2 The Jewish Coordination Committee for the liberated Dutch territory was established in 1945. It served as an umbrella organization for all Jewish organizations in the Netherlands. In the first years after the war, it was the most important point of contact for all Jews in the Netherlands.

3 The dating is based on the content of the document.

4 Salomon Roet (1892–1960), financial advisor; member of the Jewish Council's finance department; survived the occupation period, probably in hiding; lived in Israel, 1949–1956, and again from 1959.

5 The territory north of the Maas and the Rhine, which includes the largest cities in the Netherlands, remained occupied until May 1945. On the situation there, see Introduction, pp. 45–46.

6 Abraham de Jong, later Avraham Yinnon (1913–1995), teacher of religion; went into hiding in 1943; fled to the liberated southern part of the Netherlands in 1944; edited the first Jewish newspaper there; in 1947 emigrated to Palestine, where he again worked as a teacher of religion.

7 Dr Isidore Spangenthal, later Yitzhak Shatal (1900–1967), physician; went into hiding with his family in the summer of 1942; manager of the hospital in Eindhoven from 1945; emigrated to Israel in 1948.

8 Samuel Eisenmann (1904–1976), timber dealer; went into hiding with his wife and three small children in 1943; survived in various hiding places in Limburg; after the war, worked in Jewish organizations for the protection of children, 1945–1969.

Edersheim;[10] J. J. Hartogs;[11] S. S. Meyer;[12] Captain L. v. d. Rhoer; B. E. Spiero;[13] L. M. H. Sternfeld;[14] and Dr M. Spangethal-Pimkhof,[15] general advisor. All the members consider themselves interim post holders and will make their posts available when larger parts of Holland are liberated.

The Jewish Coordination Committee has set up the following research committees:
1. Religious and Cultural Affairs;
2. Organization of the Jewish Community;
3. Medical and Social Affairs and Repatriation;
4. Interests of Minors;
5. Legal Affairs;
6. Financial and Economic Affairs and Legal Rehabilitation;
7. Associations and Foundations.

Approximately 2,500 Jews who have emerged from hiding in the southern part of the Netherlands are registered with the 'Central Registration Bureau'. There are lists of:
Dutch Jews who have arrived in Switzerland from Theresienstadt and Bergen-Belsen;
Dutch Jews who have arrived in Palestine via Bergen-Belsen;
Dutch Jews in Belgium;
Dutch Jews in Bergen-Belsen (Celle);
Dutch Jews in Theresienstadt.
The last of these lists are incomplete.

Requests to search for specific persons can be submitted to the Registration Bureau.

The Dutch government has appointed Major S. Rodrigues Pereira as army rabbi of the 'Princess Irene'[16] brigade, and he has also been put in charge of looking after the interests of Dutch Jews. He has declared that he is prepared to take rabbinical decisions as long as no Dutch rabbi has emerged from hiding.

We hope to have as much contact with you as possible, as soon as possible. The address of the JCC is Jan Luikenstraat 23, Eindhoven, telephone number 2353.

With very best wishes,

9 Jacob (Jaap) van Amerongen, later Yakov Arnon (1913–1995), economist and auditor; deported to Westerbork on 20 June 1943, but soon released; went into hiding; chairman of the Dutch Zionist League, 1945–1948; emigrated to Israel in 1948; director general at Israel's Ministry of Finance until 1970.

10 Karel Josef Edersheim (1893–1976), lawyer; chairman of the Dutch Zionist League, 1927–1930; employed by the Jewish Council from 1941; Israel's envoy to the Netherlands, 1948–1950.

11 Jacques Josef Hartogs (1882–1963); member of the executive board of the Jewish Community of Eindhoven from 1931; survived the occupation period in hiding; chairman of the Jewish Community of Eindhoven from 1945.

12 Presumably Salomon Samson Meyer (1910–1986), antiquarian bookseller; deported to Westerbork on 14 Jan. 1943; escaped from the camp and went into hiding; again a bookseller in Amsterdam after 1945.

13 Barend Elias Spiero (1908–1988), dentist; chairman of the Jewish Community of 's-Hertogenbosch.

14 Leonard Maurits Herman Sternfeld (b. 1911), teacher; emigrated from Germany; survived the occupation period in hiding; involved in Jewish youth work from 1945.

15 Correctly: Dr Marianne Spangenthal-Pinkhof, later Miryam Shatal (b. 1903), musician and drawing teacher; married Isidore Spangenthal in 1930; emigrated to Israel in 1948.

16 The Prinses-Irene-Brigade existed from 1941 to 1945; it was made up of Dutch military personnel who had managed to get away from the German troops in May 1940, as well as refugees who had escaped from the Netherlands to England. The brigade was named after the second-eldest daughter of Crown Princess Juliana.

DOC. 170

On 14 and 15 March 1945 Toni Ringel records her hunger and the poor health situation in her diary[1]

Diary of Toni Ringel: To our beloved children, entries for 14 and 15 March 1945 (typescript)

Wednesday, 14 March 1945
My beloved children, I did not want to write any more about the famine. I had cheerfully welcomed the month of March, hoping that the food situation would improve. Unfortunately, it has become much worse than ever before.[2] I am suffering from diarrhoea and all my intestines hurt. Children dearest, one evening there was no food whatsoever left apart from one cold, raw, woody carrot. I ate it and during the night it almost tore me apart. From noon to night I had not eaten and then the carrot on an empty stomach. For Papa,[3] I had saved a few spoonful[s] of cabbage, and we did not get bread until the next morning at 8 a.m. For a whole week now, I am having trouble with my stomach. At a time [such] as the present one it is particularly aggravating, since there is nothing to cure oneself with, not a sip of tea nor milk, nor a spoonful of oatmeal to make a bit of hot cereal. The famine is simply [i]ndescribable. Believe me, children, despite diarrhoea and other discomforts, I am eating the black, sticky bread which makes one sick just from looking at it. But God is with us and He will make me well even with this bread.

15 March 1945
New days bring new worries. One cannot get any more cabbage. It is almost ridiculous to worry over cabbage. Unfortunately, for us this is of utmost importance. Since the beginning of October it has been our main dish. One cannot live on two kilos of potatoes, that is one kilo per person for a full week. Our 'landlords' do not know of such worries.[4] She brings home constantly potatoes and vegetables. The whole winter through they did not taste cabbage, that horrible stuff only good enough for Jews. When she has a lot of vegetables, she gives me some at a stiff price. In the begin[ning] they pitied us for the food we ate, such as tulip bulbs, sugar beet, etc. They had never seen anybody eating that kind of food. Soon, however, there was no more compassion. They hid all their foodstuff[s] and did not talk about their purchases. When she gets 30 kilos of potatoes, she says that she got 15 kilos. I don't ask her, and I don't want to know, and I can do without their pity.

1 LBIJMB, MM II/14. The original is missing. The diary was presumably originally handwritten in German, but was translated into English and typed out by Robert Ringel, Toni Ringel's youngest son.
2 The winter of 1944/45 was described as the 'Hunger Winter' in the Netherlands: see Introduction, p. 43.
3 Meilech Ringel (1877–1945), retailer; emigrated to Barcelona from Frankfurt am Main in 1933; emigrated from Spain to the Netherlands in 1936; lived in hiding from Sept. 1942; died of heart failure and malnutrition in hiding in April 1945.
4 From Sept. 1942 Toni and Meilech Ringel were in hiding at the home of the Veitz family on Van Speijkstraat in Amsterdam. The family consisted of Rudolph Veitz (1898–1964), bank employee; his wife, Barendina Veitz-Hooijberg (1895–1981), laundrywoman; and their two sons, Rudolf (b. 1923) and Bernard (b. 1929).

Papa causes me a lot of worry. He cannot stand on his feet anymore. The poor man is only skin and bones and is suffering from extreme malnutrition. He does not sleep nights. I ask him: 'Papa, why don't you sleep?' I know the answer only too well: 'I am so hungry that my heart aches, and that hurts so much.' I know the feeling, it is the same with me. I am not writing this down to arouse compassion, because only God can help us with a speedy liberation. I put this on paper, because it is my only refuge, where I can unburden my heartaches and worries. For almost 2.5 years I have not seen or talked to a person to ease my heavy heart. I [say] to the gentiles only what is necessary; they do not know what we are going through, and there is no need for them to know it. Would Jews behave better in times like these? I doubt it. I cannot discuss such things with Papa. The poor man is not aware of the situation we live in, and alas, he does not understand so many things. For several months already he has not smoked. A pack of 20 cigarettes cost[s] fl. 65. Can I pay that? From what funds? Maybe from the fl. 600 Ohm L.[5] lent me? For instance, Papa will ask me: 'Haven't you got some sugar for the coffee?' At present the price of sugar is fl. 65, but I don't want any. If I did, the price would then be fl. 75.

I just cannot talk to Papa about these hopeless problems. In the morning and late afternoon it is quite cold in our little room. We eat our supper by 4 p.m. and are in bed an hour later. Between 6 and 7 p.m. I smell the fragrance of freshly boiled potatoes and beans. The window pane of the upper part of the transom[6] on the door is broken and through the big hole enter all the odors, the good ones and others which are not so pleasant. Our 'landlords', parents as well as sons, have the habit of relieving themselves from the waste of potatoes and beans, etc. with the toilet door wide open. I am always well informed as to who is constipated or who suffers from diarrhoea.

Children dearest, please do not think of me as a gossip, because I am writing down all that is on my mind. Try to understand and not to condemn. It was all written down in moments of indescribable misery. Praised be the Lord that we are the victims and not you. Darlings, now that I have unburdened myself, I can weep with relief. When I put down my pen, I have the feeling of having talked to you. It calms me down immensely. Often I think how my children would console me and stroke my hair. My beloved sons did that so well. In such cold and strange surrounding[s] things are very much harder to take, and yet we have no reason to complain, because we are still alive. It will not take much longer anymore until the happy moment of liberation will come. We are on our way to freedom and happiness for all the persecuted and suppressed people.

5 Alexander Wellensiek (1887–1978), retailer; friend of the family who granted refuge to Adolf Ringel before his escape. Ohm stands for *oom* (Dutch for 'uncle').

6 Meaning a transom window above the doorframe.

DOC. 171
On 12 April 1945 Hans Bial welcomes the arrival of the Canadians and the liberation of Westerbork camp[1]

Handwritten diary of Hans Bial,[2] entry for 12 April 1945

The front is quite considerate. It allows us to sleep wonderfully, all night long, and does not open fire until around 7.15 a.m. Machine guns and presumably field artillery. That continues at intervals, sometimes scattered, sometimes more intense, throughout the morning. It comes from the south, from the canal or even between the canal and the farm, and from the west, probably the Beilen–Assen road.

It is 10.30 a.m. At 8 a.m. I heard the BBC reports for myself again, for the first time in my neighbour's room. He had already got hold of a radio. Around 9 a.m., radios are distributed; each large room gets one. At 10 a.m., a huge shout of joy. The Canadians are marching towards The Hague and Amsterdam. Caspar Israel[3] 'set out' at 8 a.m. with 3 others; I hope they manage to get through.

All the military really and truly pulled out by dawn, so that we are not threatened in this respect and are left to ourselves. At 11 a.m. everybody is running through the camp, holding a radio. I also get hold of what looks to be a good Philips 470A in the camp on the other side,[4] where the mob is already heavily engaged in looting, despite the NB blockade.[5] Pisk[6] and Meijer de Jong[7] stand there helplessly.

On the heath in the direction of Hooghalen, five tanks[8] were seen; the shooting actually seems to be WNW already.[9] Due to some heavy shelling, at 11.30 everyone is ordered to go inside the barracks. But it goes quiet again at once. As the mob is rampaging in the camp on the other side, I don't see why I shouldn't retrieve our curtains, which we recently had to surrender. People are hauling goods away by the cartload, things that for a long time must have been intended for commercial rather than personal use. After eating, I do the rounds of the offices and apartments at the customs office in order to gather information. A scene of devastation! Radios, telephones, old rifles, and gas masks were destroyed by the Germans themselves before they left, and then our people saw to

1 JHM, Doc. 00 005 318. The diary is titled 'Briefe an Hetty. Tagebuch aus dem Lager Westerbork 17. Sept. 1944–12. Mai 1945' [Letters to Hetty. Diary from Westerbork Camp, 17 Sept. 1944–12 May 1945]. This document has been translated from German.

2 Hans Walter Bial (1911–2000), retailer; fled to the Netherlands with his parents in 1938; worked for the Jewish Council from 1942; married to Karoline Oestreicher (1915–1975), known as Hetty, alias Maria Austria, from 1942 to 1945; deported on 17 August 1942 to Westerbork, where he managed the records office; held in the camp until it was liberated; subsequently returned to Amsterdam.

3 Casper Israël (1903–1976), retailer; in June 1944 deported to Westerbork, where he was held until the liberation of the camp.

4 Presumably a reference to the guards' living quarters.

5 The meaning here could not be established.

6 Arthur Pisk (b. 1891), retailer; fled to the Netherlands from Austria in 1939; from Feb. 1940 in Westerbork, where he was head of the camp's security force; held in Westerbork until it was liberated; thought to have returned to Austria after the war.

7 Meijer de Jong (1893–1976), post office worker; on 31 July 1942 deported to Westerbork, where he was held until the liberation of the camp; subsequently returned to Rotterdam.

8 'Tanks' in English in the original.

9 West-north-west.

the rest. Wherever they could not get in, windows were broken, walls kicked in, offices hacked to pieces, and the contents of the drawers lie on the ground. The only good thing: pictures of Hitler and other fallen greats trampled to pieces on the ground, some with red wine poured over them – fragments!

I find the draft of a letter, from which I gather that the camp was renamed on 31 March and designated an 'exchange and internment camp'.[10]

Only isolated shooting can be heard now, already rather far to the west. The surge seems to be over. However, from time to time one still hears a bang to the south. At 15.30, a full assembly of the camp in the large hall is called for 16.00. Van As asks for cooperation, the Tommies[11] may be here in a few hours, but it can also take another one or two days; meanwhile we are a no man's land and must try to feed ourselves. And just as he is about to conclude, Ottenstein[12] comes into the room and shouts: Mr van As is wanted on the telephone! The first Tommies are at the farm! And then the cheers break out, the rejoicing knows no bounds, and what happens now is indescribable in the truest sense of the word. The lads run out like mad things, heading towards the barrier in that direction, in front a horse-drawn cart that was standing there, now loaded with people, and the rest bringing up the rear on foot, all making for the farm. I went along with them; I didn't know that I could still run so fast. Around 50 m from the farm, we jump on to the first moving armoured vehicles, the soldiers get kisses, there are tears, laughter, rejoicing, and shouting. All the way to the camp, on both sides of the road, a solid row of cheering people, trying to catch hold of a hand from the vehicles and throwing flowers. Where have all the flowers suddenly come from? At the entrance, the vehicles stop, the soldiers are lifted on to inmates' shoulders, and the first English cigarettes are handed out.

In the middle of the convoy, its commander arrives. He is immediately escorted into the camp commandant's office, into the Ostuf[13] room, by van As, L. A. A. Cohen,[14] and Lambert Cohen[15] as interpreter. First, he asks: Is this Mr Gemmeker's camp? Is he still here, and are de Haan and de Jong still here? When I ask whether he has already heard of the camp while on the way here, he replies: Oh, about 4 years ago![16] He gives individual autographs (see enclosure)[17] and then wants to be left alone with van As. Then I chat

10 The renaming was officially announced by the camp elder, Kurt Schlesinger, only on 12 April 1945, the day of the camp's liberation. As a result, the camp was placed under the protection of the Red Cross: see JHM, Doc. 00 000 328.

11 Colloquial term used by the Germans to describe British soldiers, particularly associated with the First and Second World Wars.

12 Hans Simon Ottenstein (1902–1986), retailer; emigrated to the Netherlands from Germany in 1933; from Feb. 1942 in Westerbork, where he ran the applications office, which processed requests for exemption from deportation and presented them to the German authorities; returned to Amsterdam in 1945; emigrated to the USA in 1948.

13 This refers to the office of SS-Obersturmführer Albert Konrad Gemmeker.

14 Leon Albertus Alexander Cohen (1898–1980), police official; chief of the Jewish Council's Internal Service, 1942–1943; deported to Westerbork in Sept. 1943.

15 Lambert Gerrit Cohen (1901–1967), radio engineer; Jewish Council employee in 1942; deported to Westerbork on 30 Sept. 1943.

16 Reply in English in the original.

17 This could not be found.

with Zielke,[18] who had already been out along the canal since 12.30 and brought the Tommies here. If they had not learned from him that the way was clear, they would not have come until much later or even tomorrow, because they doubtless assumed that German troops were still here and wanted to encircle the camp first. Now a civilian limousine arrives, marked 'Nederlands Verbindings Officier'.[19] A pleasant chap in Canadian uniform gets out. Huge cheers! Jongens, een Nederlander![20] We don't need to tell him anything, he knows the SD, was imprisoned in the Oranje-Hotel[21] and then in Bochum, after which he took to his heels. 'I'm called Valk, but my real name's different, I won't tell it to you until Holland is completely free, because my family is still in the occupied territory.' The green uniforms of the OD[22] people who are trying to create a cordon create a misunderstanding; one said right away that he was an Austrian, and Valk says: 'Your guards who are foreign nationals are all prisoners of war,' and Lambert Cohen is too stupid to clear up the matter. It is then clarified, at my instigation, by Awerbach[23] and Meijer de Jong. Meanwhile, Todtmann is put in the commandant's office, under arrest. I take a very serious view of the matter, because if the combat troops, not the police, already have something against somebody, there must really be something serious involved. However, Capt. Morris[24] reassures Helga, saying 'not to worry about [it]',[25] and she is allowed to go to him.

Then Nathaniel[26] and some others come running up with the red, white, and blue flag, which is hoisted to the tune of Wilhelmus[27] and God Save the King.[28] Indescribable rejoicing, and meanwhile more and more armoured troops arrive. Also an officer in a paratrooper uniform, a Dutchman, whom we don't need to tell anything either, because he parachuted onto the heath here on Saturday night or early on Sunday.

Then everybody was assembled in the large hall: Capt. Morris addresses us: 'First: I am happy to be here with you and congratulate you on your liberation. Second: The war is not over!'[29] He advises us to maintain calm and order and asks us to stay here, because returning floods of people get in the way of the supply troops and thus make the war

18 Erich Joachim Zielke (1908–1976); fled to the Netherlands from Germany in Dec. 1938; from April 1940 in Westerbork, where he was head of the camp's External Service; held in Westerbork until it was liberated; emigrated to the USA in 1947.

19 Dutch in the original: 'Dutch liaison officer'.

20 Dutch in the original: 'Lads, a Dutchman!'

21 The so-called Oranjehotel in Scheveningen was a notorious German police prison during the German occupation.

22 Ordnungsdienst (Order Service).

23 Chaim Awerbach (1892–1967), timber dealer; deported on 19 Jan. 1943 to Westerbork, where he worked in the luggage section; liberated from Westerbork and returned to The Hague.

24 Douglas Francis Morris, later Monty Morriz (1905–1990), policeman; in the Canadian Scottish Regiment from April 1940; officer in the Security Service of the Second Canadian Division when Westerbork was liberated in 1945; head of the Security Service of the Canadian Occupation Army, 1945–1946; in the Secret Service of the British Control Commission in Germany, 1946–1948.

25 Quotation in English in the original.

26 Presumably Adolf Nathaniel (b. 1904), manager of the warehouses in Westerbork.

27 The Dutch national anthem.

28 The British national anthem.

29 Quotation in English in the original. On the notes made by D. F. Morris regarding this speech, see NIOD, 205i/976.

more difficult, and that's not what we want, is it? Is it? A roaring 'No'.[30] In addition, he points out that we would have to ask people for food along the way, people who have less than we do. He speaks of hardship in North Brabant and the big cities. We are to be patient for a few more days, not 2 or 3, but days nonetheless. He closes his speech, delivered with astonishing calm, composure, and level-headedness, by asking, OK? – Yes![31] The pressing crowd is asked to leave the area of the commandant's office; Morris wants to work. And people talk with every soldier they can about his battles, his route to this place, and ask whether one city or another is liberated. But the soldiers know no more than we do – no wonder, with the English radio available to us. In fact, they know even less, because they have had to fight hard in the last few days and therefore have had little time for reports. And then another long convoy comes along, tanks this time, from the farm and moves past the camp in seemingly endless numbers. Each one gets a cheer and flowers. Then, black from the dust raised by the monsters whizzing past, I go to eat my meal.

There really is no electric light from Groningen any longer. The generator is running, but only for water and for light for the commandant's office and the kitchen. So, candlelight! Naturally, I decline to play skat in Löw's room; I walk through the camp and hear music coming from the kitchen. I open the door and see a party there. On a high set of shelves there stands a jazz band made up of our people, and the Tommies and our girls are dancing to the music; it is just a joy to see. Around 22.00 it stops, the light is turned off, the national anthems are sung, and thus the truly spontaneous celebration comes to an end. Then I go to the barrier, find Prins and his wife[32] there in conversation with a Tommy, whom we then, as many others are doing, take home to Prins's place. I fetch coffee, we turn on the stove, and until 1.30 we have a very nice chat with Mr Smith from Vancouver. Then I am really tired.

Bobby Engel[33] meets his brother-in-law, now a Canadian and a soldier. He exchanged the first 10-guilder banknote of the new Dutch currency for me, and I am amazed that it has the same value as the old one. This is said to be due to technical difficulties.[34]

30 'No' in English in the original.
31 'Yes!' in English in the original.
32 Simon Prins (1910–1976), diamond cutter; deported from Scheveningen prison to Westerbork on 19 May 1944; in a so-called mixed marriage with Saapke Sonja Prins-van Rood (1908–1989) from 1940; the couple emigrated to New Zealand in 1951.
33 Robert (Bobby) Ernst Engel (b. 1923), precision engineer; emigrated to the Netherlands from Berlin in 1938; naturalized in the Netherlands in 1950.
34 The official currency reform did not start until 9 July 1945. On that day, all 100-guilder notes were declared invalid. The remaining banknotes were removed from circulation in Sept. 1945, and each household received 10 guilders of the new money.

DOC. 172
On 5 May 1945 Sam Goudsmit witnesses the liberation of Amsterdam[1]

Handwritten diary of Sam Goudsmit, entry for 5 May 1945

Saturday (night), 5 May 1945. Peculiar liberation day.
– Liberated Amsterdam, but under German surveillance![2]
– A national day of celebration, with no Dutch power.
– Thousands of celebratory flags and tens of thousands of people and children clad in orange, but with heavily armed SS and Greens[3] among them.

That was what the Dutch capital looked like today. It seems the 'Bündnispartner'[4] are unable to achieve anything for us. Even now, uncertainty, threats, arrests, and murder. Flags on public buildings and police stations. All shop windows, decorated carefully and with no holding back, display a national theme. Church bells chiming at the officially designated time.

And in the afternoon, an arrest by the SD! Following the morning, when the Dutch flag was raised over the Palace at Dam Square – three killed in a salvo fired by Dutch SS scoundrels.

Capitulation? But without disarmament! In my opinion an incredible phenomenon in war history. One paper writes: the situation will be completely resolved within a few hours, as the Allied Forces are about to arrive.

That was at 6 o'clock this morning; now, at 2 o'clock in the middle of the night, there is still not a single Allied soldier in the city.

Another paper claims: there are only a few technical measures that still need to be taken, but the capitulation as such is a fact: the whole of the Netherlands has been liberated! It says so in spite of the undisturbed actions of the German occupier.

A third paper declares: Eisenhower[5] ascribes the divided situation to a few groups of German occupiers, which imagine they do not have to accept the capitulation in full. That's *their* problem.

(But those 'few' groups can do what they like, and Eisenhower's voice alone cannot force them to obey, sometimes without protection,[6] as Eisenhower's troops have not entered Amsterdam, but leave the celebrations and the people permitted to take part in them to the superior strength of these 'groups'.)

1 Bibliotheca Rosenthaliana, HC-ROS-006. This document has been translated from Dutch.
2 On 5 May 1945 the German troops in the Netherlands capitulated, but no sizeable Allied units entered Amsterdam until 8 May 1945. The intervening days were characterized by a power vacuum; the German troops retained their weapons, and the Binnenlandse Strijdkrachten, the official umbrella organization of the Dutch resistance groups, could not yet exercise control over the city. On 7 May 1945 there was an armed conflict in which German navy personnel fired into a crowd of people who were celebrating, killing 20 and wounding more than 100.
3 A reference to the 'Green Police'.
4 German in the original: 'Allies'.
5 Dwight D. Eisenhower (1890–1969), military commander; led the Allied invasion of Europe; appointed supreme commander of the Allied troops in Dec. 1943; military governor of the American zone of occupation after 1945; president of the United States, 1953–1961.
6 This phrase is barely legible in the original.

Why then does Eisenhower not let his troops enter the city? And if that is not yet possible, well then, why does he proclaim that we are free and allow us to have *'moderate celebrations'*? The celebrations are moderate; the public was extremely quiet in the streets. A peculiar situation. A ridiculous situation. A shameful situation.

I walked around in the city for hours. In the busy streets, the quiet working-class neighbourhoods, the empty Jewish quarter, where the best houses, alongside piles of rubble, are inhabited by greedy Aryans, and many business premises are occupied by privileged businessmen. One half an Aryanized ghetto, the other half depopulated.

Fortunately, the warm-heartedness and the warm feelings and atmosphere did not throw me into confusion in terms of the vast crime. *And* I had walked around here like this before.

It is also wonderful that we no longer have to black out our windows. Our house is looking bright again.[7]

DOC. 173

On 10 May 1945, after her liberation from Auschwitz, Frieda Brommet writes a postcard to her friend Bep Steenbergen in Amsterdam[1]

Handwritten Polish Red Cross postcard from Frieda Brommet,[2] A 25 080, Auschwitz camp, hospital block 13, to Miss E. Steenbergen,[3] Amsterdam-Zuid, 2A Dintelstraat, dated 10 May 1945

Dear Bep,

Yes, a card from me. I hope with all my heart that you will receive this. Throughout this whole awful period, I have never forgotten how you were with me until the very last day, and what you sent to me in Westerbork. I'm very weak at the moment. I may be allowed to get up in a week's time. I've been lying in bed here for the last seven months. First I had scarlet fever, then I had typhoid, durchfall,[4] and now pleurisy on both sides. That's all (don't laugh). Mother is with me, fit and well. Father is on a transport to Germany.[5] My only desire is for the three of us to be united as soon as possible. May God grant us this. We got more kicks than we got food, but everything's fine now. At least bearing in mind the current war conditions.[6] Stone Bep[7] (do you remember?), hugs from Frieda

7 The last two sentences are written on a slip of paper pasted in the margin of the page.

1 JHM, Doc. 00 006 438. Published in facsimile in Ad van Liempt, *Frieda: Verslag van een gelijmd leven* (Hooghalen: Herinnerungscentrum Kamp Westerbork, 2007), p. 2. This document has been translated from Dutch.

2 Frieda Brommet, married name Menco (b. 1925); lived with her parents, Rebecca Brommet-Ritmeester (1897–1989) and Joël Brommer (1896–1945) in hiding from July 1942; they were betrayed in July 1944 and deported to Westerbork, and then to Auschwitz on 3 Sept. 1944; Frieda returned to the Netherlands with her mother in 1945; she subsequently became involved in the Jewish Reform community.

3 Elizabet (Bep) Steenbergen (b. 1924); non-Jewish friend of Frieda Brommet.

4 German in the original: 'diarrhoea'.

5 Joël Brommet is thought to have perished on a death march in 1945.

6 In the Dutch original, this sentence is grammatically incorrect, but presumably this is deliberate.

7 Because of her surname, Steenbergen (lit.: 'stone mountains'), Frieda's father always addressed her friend in this way.

Belgium

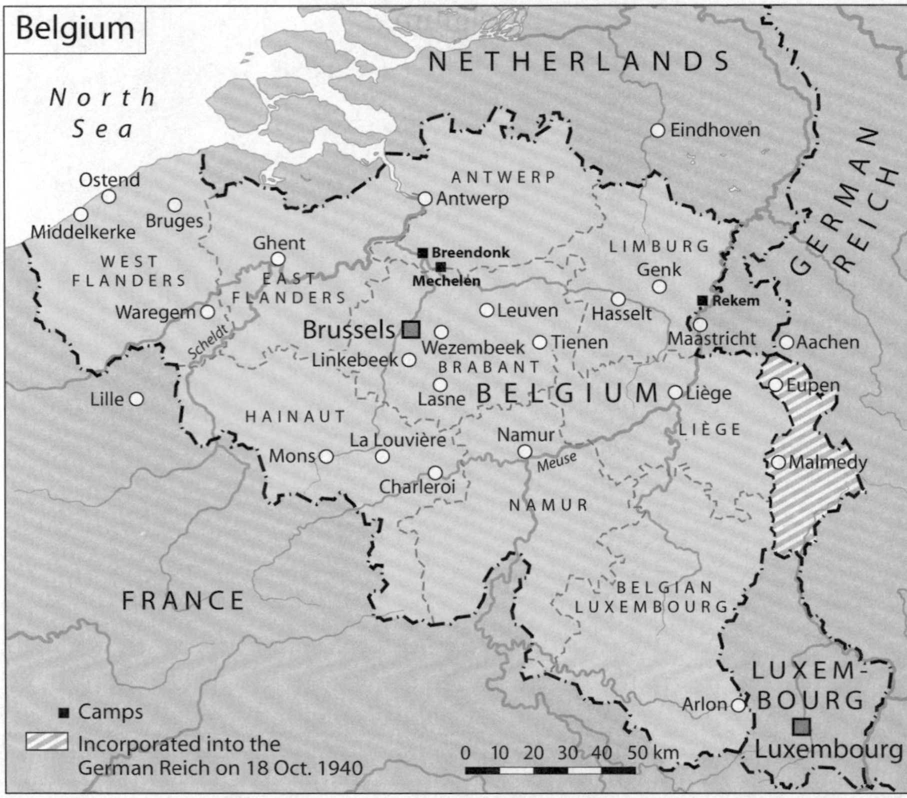

Belgium
North Sea
NETHERLANDS
GERMAN REICH
Eindhoven
ANTWERP
Antwerp
Ostend
Middelkerke
Bruges
Ghent
WEST FLANDERS
EAST FLANDERS
Breendonk
Mechelen
LIMBURG
Genk
Rekem
Hasselt
Leuven
Waregem
Scheldt
Brussels
Wezembeek
Tienen
Maastricht
Aachen
Linkebeek
BRABANT
Eupen
Lille
Lasne
BELGIUM
Liège
HAINAUT
LIÈGE
La Louvière
Namur
Mons
Malmedy
Meuse
Charleroi
NAMUR
FRANCE
BELGIAN LUXEMBOURG
LUXEMBOURG
Arlon
Luxembourg
Camps
Incorporated into the German Reich on 18 Oct. 1940
0 10 20 30 40 50 km

DOC. 174

On 2 July 1942 the Association of Jews in Belgium attempts to persuade Secretary General Romsée not to require Jews to perform forced labour outside Belgium[1]

Letter from the Association of Jews in Belgium (17.61.29, secretary's office, SU/EB D 345), signed (signature stamp) Chairman Dr S. Ullmann[2] and unsigned Administrator M. Benedictus,[3] to the Secretary General of the Ministry of the Interior, Romsée,[4] 7 Leuvenschestraat, Brussels, dated 2 July 1942 (carbon copy)

Dear Secretary General,

I have the honour of confirming today's meeting. As I explained to you, many Jews have had to leave the country over the past few weeks to work in the occupied territory of Northern France,[5] and it is likely that the same fate awaits many thousands. This compulsory relocation has led to an extraordinary degree of panic among the Jewish population and caused indescribable suffering among a large number of families. As far as I am aware, these people are not suited to heavy labour. I therefore politely request your kind intervention, in order that all those who are obliged to work are put to work in this country, preferably not too far from their current abode.

We can ensure that they will find suitable work in farming and factories. It is also desirable that war veterans be granted an exemption.[6]

Secretary General, please accept the assurance of our greatest respect.

On behalf of the Association of Jews

1 Kazerne Dossin – Mechelen, A008455. This document has been translated from Dutch.
2 Dr Salomon Ullmann, also Ullman (1882–1966), rabbi; from 1937 rabbi of the Belgian army; chief rabbi of Belgium, 1940–1957; chairman of the Association of Jews in Belgium (AJB/VJB), Oct. 1941 to Sept. 1942; interned in Breendonk camp for fifteen days in Sept. 1942; arrested again in 1944 and interned in Mechelen; emigrated to Israel in 1957.
3 Maurice Benedictus (b. 1907), cigar manufacturer; appointed vice president and administrator of the AJB/VJB by the German authorities; briefly under arrest in Sept. 1942; fled to Portugal in late 1942; volunteered to fight on the side of the Allies in the Belgian colonial army, the Force Publique, in Africa; returned to Belgium in Sept. 1945; emigrated from Belgium to South Africa, 1953.
4 Dr Gérard Romsée (1901–1975), lawyer; member of the Vlaams Nationaal Verbond (VNV) party leadership; governor of the province of Limburg, 1940; secretary general in the Ministry of the Interior and Public Health from 1941; fled to Austria, 1944; arrested after the end of the war and in 1948 sentenced in Brussels to twenty years in prison; pardoned and released, 1954.
5 On the introduction of forced labour for Jews in March 1942, see PMJ 5/197. The Belgian employment offices were subsequently assigned the task of sending Jews to Organization Todt labour camps in France, where 2,252 Jews in total had to work on fortifying the Atlantic Wall.
6 The Belgian authorities did nothing to prevent the transport of Jewish forced labourers to northern France or the concurrent deployment of so-called antisocial elements as forced labour.

DOC. 175

On 9 July 1942 the representative of the Reich Foreign Office, Werner von Bargen, informs his superiors of the plan to deport 10,000 Jews from Belgium[1]

Telegram from the Brussels division of the Reich Foreign Office (no. 602, dated 9 July 1942; in reply to no. 788 D III 516g., dated 29 June 1942), signed Bargen,[2] Brussels, to the head of Department D[3] (received on 9 July 1942),[4] dated 9 July 1942[5]

Military administration plans to carry out desired deportation of 10,000 Jews.
Chief of military administration[6] presently at headquarters to discuss matter with Reichsführer SS.[7]

Objections to measure could at some point result from the fact that there is no widespread understanding of the Jewish question here, and Jews with Belgian citizenship are regarded as Belgians by population. Measure might therefore be interpreted as the beginning of general forced deportations.[8] At the same time, Jews are largely integrated into the local economic process, so that problems in labour market might be feared. Military administration believes, however, that it can put misgivings on hold if deportation of Belgian Jews is avoided. At first, therefore, Polish, Czech, Russian, and other Jews will be selected, which could theoretically enable us to reach the target figure. Practical difficulties are to be expected, in that there is already some unrest among the local Jews because the deportations from France and Holland that are now beginning have become known, and Jews will therefore try to avoid being seized.[9] Police numbers are however not sufficient to enable the use of coercive measures.

Further report follows.

1 PA AA, R 99 406. Published in *ADAP*, series E: *1941–1945*, vol. 3, p. 125. This document has been translated from German.

2 Dr Werner von Bargen (1898–1975), lawyer; with the Prussian judicial service, 1923–1925; with the Reich Foreign Office from 1925; joined the NSDAP in 1933; worked for the Reich Foreign Office in Belgium, 1937–1943, then in Berlin and Paris; employed at various regional administrative courts in Lower Saxony, 1948–1951; in the Foreign Office of the Federal Republic of Germany, 1951–1963; from 1960, ambassador in Baghdad.

3 Martin Luther.

4 Copies of the telegram were sent to: (1) Task Force for Germany, (2) Reich Foreign Minister, (3) State Secretary, (4) Office of the Reich Foreign Minister, and (5) Head of the Political Department.

5 By cryptograph. The original contains handwritten notes and underlining.

6 Eggert Reeder (1894–1959), administrative official; joined the NSDAP in 1933 and the SS in 1938; Regierungspräsident in Aachen, Cologne, and Düsseldorf from 1933; chief of the German military administration in Belgium and northern France from 1940; again Regierungspräsident in Cologne and Düsseldorf, 1944–1945; interned and imprisoned from 1945 in Belgium; sentenced there to twelve years in prison in 1951; pardoned and released soon thereafter.

7 Heinrich Himmler.

8 During the German occupation of Belgium in the First World War, from Oct. 1916 almost 60,000 Belgians were sent to the Ruhr as forced labourers. The memory of these events was reawakened by the regulations on forced labour issued in March 1942 subjecting Belgians to labour conscription within Belgium and Jews in Belgium to forced labour, and in Oct. 1942 subjecting Belgians to deportation to Germany for labour deployment.

9 From late March 1942 to 9 July 1942 more than 5,000 persons were deported from France to Auschwitz on five trains. In the Netherlands, the first train left Westerbork camp on 15 July 1942. From late March 1942 to 9 July 1942 more than 5,000 persons were deported from France to Auschwitz on five trains. In the Netherlands, the first train left Westerbork camp on 15 July 1942.

DOC. 176

On 18 July 1942 Antoine Dubois asks the military administration to remove the names of his two illegitimate sons from the Jew registry[1]

Letter from Antoine Dubois,[2] Mons, 17 avenue des Canadiens, to the Military Commander in Belgium and Northern France,[3] Group XII, Department for Economic Affairs, Stones and Earth section, Brussels, dated 18 July 1942 (typescript)[4]

The undersigned, Antoine Dubois, born in Ghlin[5] on 13 November 1869, most respectfully ventures to submit the following confidential matter for your consideration:

From a liaison with a married woman, Hendrine Souweine,[6] I have two illegitimate sons, Edgar[7] and Leon,[8] the former born on 2 May 1901 and the latter on 16 March 1903, both in Brussels. Because the mother is a Jew and lives in a Jewish marriage, my sons, on paper, are Jews. However, they are married to Aryan women, have children, and are thus exempt from wearing the yellow star.

With advancing age, however, I am taking stock of the situation, and I have certain plans that concern my company. I see myself forced by circumstances to implement these plans in part possibly straight away. Because both of my illegitimate offspring are de facto non-Jews, but find themselves in a situation that is disadvantageous for them, I have decided after a long struggle to disclose the secret first to you. Decades ago, as a man of honour I made a vow to the woman to keep the fact a secret all my life, but I cannot reconcile with my conscience and my feelings the knowledge that my sons, by blood if not by law, are bearing the undeserved consequences.

Therefore, I am presenting you with the enclosed affidavit[9] as a legal basis for action and would be very grateful to you if you would help me unravel this now, in view of the delicacy of the matter, and restore to a concerned father his peace of mind.

I request the removal of the aforementioned Edgar and Leon Souweine from the Jew registry and their exemption from the legal restrictions pertaining to Jews.

1 MJB/JMB, Fonds Souweine-Cats. This document has been translated from German.

2 Antoine Dubois (1869–1949), businessman; co-owner of the stoneware factory in Saint-Ghislain, 1892–1909, then in Anderlecht, where the facility was destroyed in 1918; co-founder in 1920 of the 'Céramique Montoise' factory in Mons, which produced objects in the art deco style.

3 Baron Alexander von Falkenhausen (1878–1966), military officer; general staff officer on the Western and Eastern Fronts, 1914–1915; served with the German military mission in China, 1933–1938; military commander in Belgium and northern France, 1940–1944; imprisoned in Dachau concentration camp because of his association with the plot to assassinate Hitler on 20 July 1944; in 1948 extradited to Belgium, where he was sentenced to twelve years of forced labour in 1951; released and deported to Germany shortly thereafter.

4 The letter is written on the official stationery of Antoine Dubois's company.

5 Village north-west of Mons (province of Hennegau), which has been part of Mons since 1972.

6 Hendrine Souweine, née Cohen (1877–1967), housewife; wife of Félix Isidore Souweine (1873–1940), retailer and Antoine Dubois's business partner, co-founder of the first department store chain in Belgium (Sarma).

7 Correctly: Edgard-Isidore (known as Edgard) Souweine (1901–1988); initially technical director of a plate-glass factory; chief executive of the Sarma department store chain from 1945 until the 1970s.

8 Léon Souweine (b. 1905); member of Sarma's supervisory board in the 1970s.

9 This is included in the file.

I thank you most sincerely in advance for a sympathetic assessment of my situation and for your assistance, signed

with the highest esteem,

1 enclosure.

DOC. 177

Le Pays réel, 23 July 1942: an article on the supposed privileges of the Jews calls for their removal from Belgium[1]

What do they live on, these Jews?

The wearing of the yellow star, which has been imposed upon the Jews,[2] has the considerable advantage of making the public aware of the quantity of Jews infesting some of our cities, particularly Brussels and Antwerp. On some streets in Brussels, particularly the central boulevards, it is impossible to take a step without meeting not one, but several Jews in one's path. The streets are literally teeming with them.

And the question a great number of people are asking with increasing urgency is this: what are all these Jews living on?

Because the primary, striking, evident observation, even to the most blind or the most distracted, is this: among those Jews whom we meet walking at all times of the day, not even one wears work clothes; not even one has the outward appearance of a worker. Therefore, if the Jews were living from the labour of their hands, if they had any sort of normal job, we would not meet them wandering around all over town during working hours.

Previously a great number of these Jews had lucrative and not particularly tiring occupations in all sorts of areas from which they are now banned:[3] in the press, in cinema, in advertising in all of its forms, in various organizations in the entertainment industry, from music hall shows to dance marathons; they also worked in banks, in speculation, in foreign exchange, in trade and commerce, the sale of second-hand goods, etc. …

Today either these very specialized professions are banned, or the Jews have been excluded from them, at least officially.

These people no longer do anything, and they are living quite well. What a curious phenomenon. Doubtless this can be explained in some cases: during the time when they reigned supreme, they managed to amass piles of money, which today allow them to continue to live extremely well. Of course, there is also a certain solidarity among the Jews, and the neediest among them have a particular talent for living off the wealthy

1 'De quoi vivent-ils, ces Juifs?', *Le Pays réel*, vol. 7, no. 70, 23 July 1942, p. 1. This document has been translated from French. The daily newspaper of Léon Degrelle's Rexist Party was founded in 1936 and was published with minor interruptions until 1944. It was financially supported by the German military administration. The circulation before 1940 ranged between 40,000 and 80,000 copies; no reliable figures for the wartime circulation are available.

2 From 7 June 1942, Jews were forced to wear a yellow star in public: Regulation on the Visible Identification of Jews, 27 May 1942, *VOBl-BNF*, 79, no. 1, 1 June 1942, pp. 943–944; see also PMJ 5/193.

3 The regulations dated 28 Oct. 1940 and 31 May 1941 severely limited gainful employment for Jews: see PMJ 5/158, 159, and 168.

Jews when they need to. But we should not exaggerate in this respect either. Neither Jewish savings nor Jewish solidarity can explain why none of the restrictions which have affected the average Belgian have touched the wearers of the yellow star.

Almost every day, volunteer correspondents inform our editorial team that the Jews they know are literally overflowing with food supplies and all sorts of rationed goods. What is more, it is well known that in all areas of trade, the Jews are the most active elements in the black market.

They are not allowed to move around freely? An 8 p.m. curfew has been set for them?[4] They wouldn't let that hold them back. As much as they might be wandering around ostentatiously showing off their yellow star during the day in the areas in which they live, they also quickly rid themselves of the compromising star as soon as they start breaking the laws and regulations that apply to them.

One conclusion must be drawn from these few observations, which anyone could make, as well as from a few others, which it would be pointless to outline here: the myriad Jews who are still infesting our cities at the present time principally owe their subsistence to activities which in no way conform to our laws or our regulations and now more than ever, these activities are contrary to the social order.

The obligation imposed on the Jews to wear a distinctive sign is a prophylactic measure, and no one today would dream of contesting its necessity. But it is no more than a first step, and as important as it is, the protection it affords the indigenous population is only very limited.

It must be clear to anybody in their right mind that other measures must also be taken. We cannot hope to imprison the Jews with new regulations or to prevent their poisonous activities by passing even more rigorous decrees.

The only sane and fair solution, which is also a radical one, is simply to cleanse our cities and to rid our land of the Jews who infest it.

Deport them? The word is not quite accurate, since none of these people come from here; they are all foreigners.[5] What needs to be done is to 're-port' them. We need to re-port them to some territory in Europe or in the world where we can be sure they will not pose any threat to us. We have good reason to believe that such territories exist.

This 're-portation' of Jews will also be a very humane measure on their behalf. From the moment they are no longer allowed to live at our expense, they will be condemned to misery and hunger if they are kept within our borders. By sending them 'somewhere', as far away from us as possible, we will enable them to work to provide for their own subsistence.

We know that work is abhorrent to a Jew, a veritable form of torture. But we take a different attitude. And in this matter, it is our opinion that counts, not the opinion of the Jews.

4 The regulation dated 29 August 1941 imposed a curfew and a travel ban for Jews: see PMJ 5/173.

5 Around 90 per cent of the Jews living in Belgium did not have Belgian citizenship.

DOC. 178

On 15 August 1942 Theodor Pichier in the military administration's Department for Economic Affairs reports on the expropriation of the Belgian Jews over the past three months[1]

Report by the Chief of the Military Administration, Group XII (1/St. GA 3),[2] signed Pichier,[3] dated 15 August 1942[4]

Quarterly Report of Group XII
Mid May to mid August 1942

I) De-Jewification of the Belgian economy
The de-Jewification of the Belgian economy was at the forefront of the Group's work during the past quarter as well. All firms and enterprises under Jewish influence are now covered by the de-Jewification measures; for the most part, liquidation has already been completed. The utilization of the goods, factory equipment, machines, etc. from the total assets in liquidation is taking place in accordance with the guidelines given in the preliminary report[5] and predominantly with the involvement of the Registration Office.[6]

With respect to *Aryanization*, the findings already hinted at in the preliminary report have been confirmed in the quarter under review. Both German interest and Belgian interest in the acquisition of Jewish companies are decreasing from month to month, and the economic difficulties, especially the shortage of raw materials, are increasing in equal measure. Only for smaller companies originally scheduled for liquidation does Belgian interest continue to exist; the applicants are almost exclusively former employees etc. The initial cooperation of the Belgian Development Office for Commerce[7] and the Belgian professional organizations has declined, presumably for the same reasons that led Belgian and German applicants to back out.

All the profits accruing from Aryanization and liquidation are deposited in [a] collective account at the Société Française de Banque et de Dépôts.[8] The individual subaccounts of this omnibus account are in the names of the Jewish owners. Thus the first

1 NIOD, 039/35. This document has been translated from German.
2 Group XII was a division of the military administration's Department for Economic Affairs and was in charge of 'Enemy and Jewish Assets'.
3 Dr Theodor Pichier (1899–1977), lawyer; section head at the Nitrogen Syndicate in Berlin prior to 1940; head of Group XII in the Department for Economic Affairs of the Military Commander in Belgium and Northern France, 1940–1944; head of the legal department of a firm in Wuppertal, Herberts & Co., 1955–1970.
4 The report was sent on 18 August 1942 to the Reich Commissioner for the Occupied Dutch Territories for information only and was found in the files of the Commissariat General for Finance and Economic Affairs.
5 This is not part of the file.
6 The Registration Office for Jewish Assets (see PMJ 5/168) was set up on the basis of the Regulation on Economic Measures Against Jews (31 May 1941).
7 This presumably refers to the Liaison Office for Commerce (Verbindungsstelle des Handels), which provided 'Preliminary Reports on the Registration of Jewish/Enemy Assets' to Group XII, in which factors including the profitability of a Jewish enterprise were examined.
8 This subsidiary of the Société Générale de France was under the control of the Brussels Trust Company and served as a collection point for Jewish assets in Belgium.

step has been taken towards the planned centralization of all Jewish securities portfolios and cash assets, which until now have been scattered throughout the country and will be kept only at the aforementioned bank in future. The advantages of this measure (strict oversight; standardization and simplification of the exception-permit procedure; seizure at any time of the assets of former German Jews that are forfeited to the Reich) are obvious.

An administrative fee is charged for Aryanization and liquidation. It is to be paid to the Brussels Trust Company SPRL[9] and represents Reich revenue.

The present status of the de-Jewification of the Belgian economy is as follows:

Registered as under Jewish influence		7,419 firms
plus itinerant trade	+ 289	
minus duplicate registrations	– 87	202 firms
		7,621 firms
Eliminated due to self-Aryanization (negative certificate)[10]		391 firms
Included in de-Jewification		7,230 firms
Of these, currently still pending	1,444	
Aryanized or being Aryanized	173	
Liquidated	5,613	7,230 firms

II) Registration and evaluation of enemy and Jewish assets

In pursuance of the forfeiture of the assets of former German Jews in favour of the German Reich[11] and in the course of the ongoing E-action,[12] a comprehensive registration of Jewish private property is now taking place. Previously, only certain assets (enterprises, securities, real estate) were subject to mandatory registration. No information can be provided as yet on the outcome of the registrations.

During the quarter under review, the statistical recording of the enemy and Jewish assets under the control of Group XII was completed in its general configuration. Accordingly, the following have been registered thus far:

c.	74,000	private enemy and Jewish assets
c.	7,600	Jewish businesses
c.	1,700	enemy businesses
c.	3,100	Jewish real estate properties
c.	2,600	enemy real estate properties
c.	*89,000*	*Assets*

9 *Societé privée à responsabilité limitée*, Belgian legal entity for a company broadly equivalent to a private limited company.

10 Businesses previously under Jewish ownership which had carried out their 'Aryanization' on their own initiative received, upon request, a certificate (*attestation de négativité*) from the military administration stating that they no longer fell under the antisemitic provisions.

11 According to the regulation issued by the Military Commander in Belgium and Northern France on 22 April 1942, the German tax authority was officially permitted to seize the assets of German Jews living in Belgium: see PMJ 5/185.

12 This could not be identified. The abbreviation might stand for 'Entjudungsaktion' (de-Jewification operation) and thus refer to the prohibition issued in March 1942 that forbade Jews from engaging in business: see PMJ 5/183.

The assets above belong to around 34,300 owners, who can be broken down as follows into separate nationalities (X–XIII resident enemies):[13]

I	English	3,550
II	Palestinians[14]	37
III	French	14,700
IV	Egyptians	75
V	Sudanese	1
VI	Iraqis	14
VII	Monogasques[15]	8
VIII	Russians	125
IX	Americans	2,000
X	Belgians	5,650
XI	Neutrals and persons of unknown citizenship	7,500
XII	Germans	356
XIII	Poles	294
		34,310

In addition, there are around 4,000 formerly German Jews whose assets have been forfeited to the Reich but whose asset registration is still in progress at this time.

The configuration of the statistics is coordinated with the interested authorities in the Reich; the evaluation is likely to be assigned to a 'Central Office for Enemy Accounts and Enemy Portfolios',[16] which is to be set up with the assistance of the banking commissioners. This Central Office is a joint institution of various enemy banks, in which the enemy assets – pending further notice, the French assets remain an exception – will be centralized. The reasons for the consolidation of enemy assets are the same as for the centralization of Jewish assets.

III) Legislative measures

Through the Regulation on the *Forfeiture of the Assets of Jews in Favour of the German Reich* of 22 April 1942,[17] the prerequisite was created for the seizure of assets that are located in Belgium and forfeited to the Reich under the Eleventh Regulation on the Reich Citizenship Law.[18] The Brussels Trust Company SPRL has been assigned to manage and utilize the assets in question, specifically for the purpose of avoiding superfluous inquiries from Belgian notaries, banks, etc., by decree (Regulation of 1 August 1942).[19] The Brussels Trust Company will carry out the utilization in accordance with the guide-

13 This refers to Jewish citizens of enemy nations.
14 Jews from the British Mandate of Palestine.
15 Correctly: Monégasques.
16 This could not be verified.
17 See fn. 11.
18 As a result of the Eleventh Regulation on the Reich Citizenship Law (25 Nov. 1941), the German citizenship of all Jews living abroad was revoked and their assets were allocated to the German Reich: *Reichsgesetzblatt*, 1941, I, pp. 722–724.
19 The Supplementary Regulation to the Regulation on the Forfeiture of the Assets of Jews in Favour of the German Reich (1 August 1942) required everyone, on demand, to provide comprehensive information to the Brussels Trust Company and to allow the inspection of all documents: *VOBl-BNF*, 82, no. 1, 12 August 1942, p. 982.

lines coordinated with the Reich Ministry of Finance and will transfer the proceeds to the Reich in due course. Difficulties are likely to arise in the process of selling securities and real estate. In the case of securities, these difficulties arise from the need to prove ownership retroactively prior to 10 May 1940, while properties that are evidently owned by the Reich will probably find buyers at present only under exceptional circumstances, to all intents and purposes. By agreement with the Reich Ministry of Finance, therefore, the sale of these assets is not to be expedited for the time being. In principle, with respect to the forfeiture of assets, the following is also clarified, after consultation with the Reich Ministry of Justice:

In the case of *mixed marriages*, the forfeiture of assets is also extended to the assets of the Aryan spouse, on the basis of the Eleventh Regulation on the Reich Citizenship Law in connection with the Law on the Revocation of Naturalization and the Deprivation of German Nationality of 14 July 1933.[20] The decision on the revocation of naturalization and the forfeiture of assets rests in these cases with the regional tax director in Berlin-Brandenburg. In the case of dual citizenship held by a Jew whose assets are forfeited to the Reich under § 3 of the Eleventh Regulation on the Reich Citizenship Law, for the time being an exemption from the confiscation of assets is granted only if the Jew in question holds, in addition to German citizenship, citizenship in an enemy nation within the meaning of the legislation pertaining to enemy aliens.

The assets of Polish Jews – they do not come under the Eleventh Regulation on the Reich Citizenship Law – are likewise forfeited to the German Reich due to a Regulation of 17 September 1940 on the Treatment of Assets of Citizens of the Former Polish State.[21] Whether this regulation, like the Eleventh Regulation on the Reich Citizenship Law, should be extended by a corresponding regulation of the Military Commander[22] to include the Jewish-Polish assets in Belgium as well – an estimated total of 15,000 Polish Jews live here – is presently still being reviewed in consultation with the Main Trustee Office East.[23] As these Jews almost without exception will probably be selected for labour deployment in the near future,[24] in some circumstances the appointment of the Brussels Trust Company as administrator will be sufficient. Then the Brussels Trust Company, in its capacity as administrator, will move the assets being safeguarded at the Société Française de Banque et de Dépôts into the Reich. Once in the Reich, they are automatically subject to confiscation by the Main Trustee Office East.

IV) Administration of enemy and Jewish businesses

During the period under review, efforts to simplify the administrative apparatus and tighten its organization were continued. After some of the businesses placed under

20 According to this law, the citizenship of German citizens who resided abroad and 'harmed German interests through their behaviour' could be revoked and their assets seized. In its early years, the law was also used by the National Socialist authorities to dispossess Jews living abroad: *Reichsgesetzblatt*, 1933, I, p. 480.

21 The regulation dates from 17 Dec. 1940: *Reichsgesetzblatt*, 1940, I, pp. 1270–1273.

22 Alexander von Falkenhausen.

23 This office, established by Göring in Oct. 1939 as part of the Four-Year Plan, was responsible for the registration and management of Polish government-owned property and the assets of Polish citizens.

24 This refers to deportation to Auschwitz.

administration for the purpose of de-Jewification were Aryanized or liquidated in the course of the de-Jewification measures, the administrators who were appointed for these businesses were freed for other tasks. Further, 154 enterprises in total that were previously administered by single administrators were placed under the collective administration of the Brussels Trust Company. This measure, of course, does not take the pressure off Group XII with respect to its administrative duties (basic management and control of the enemy and Jewish assets, oversight of the businesses being administered and of the administrators themselves, decision-making as to continuation/sale/Aryanization/closure of the business/issuance of general guidelines for administrators, etc.), because these duties have remained the same whether the businesses are administered by single administrators or by the Brussels Trust Company. But the measures taken have the advantage that the management of the administered businesses can be made more uniform and thus more easily overseen and more tightly organized. In the course of these measures, 12 previous single administrators were removed and, as so-called administrative agents, transferred to employment with the Brussels Trust Company. The overall layout of the administrations that have been arranged is as follows:

In total, on the basis of the regulations concerning enemy assets,[25] Jews,[26] and management,[27] 1,124 firms, interests in other companies, and other major assets have thus far been placed under administration. Of these, it was possible to rescind 152 administrations after the purpose of the administrator's appointment (de-Jewification, liquidation, etc.) was achieved. The remaining 972 administrations can be broken down as follows:

Enemy assets regulation:	Administration of firm	337	
	Administration of interest	100	437
Jewish regulation:	Administration of firm	369	
	Administration of interest	20	389
Management regulation:	(predominantly trade unions)		146
			972

It is to be expected that, as liquidation progresses, the vast majority of the Jewish administrations can be rescinded in the foreseeable future. The figures above already include the administrations made necessary by the declaration of American assets as enemy assets; in each case, the individual selected as administrator was coordinated with the Reich Ministry of Economics.

V) Miscellaneous

The removal of the Jewish household goods stored in Antwerp (so-called lift vans)[28] can be regarded as completed. The goods in question are around 900 presumably complete sets of furniture, which can be made available to the bombing victims in Cologne as a contribution by the Military Commander to the emergency relief measures.[29]

25 Regulation Concerning Enemy Assets in the Occupied Territories of the Netherlands, Belgium, Luxembourg, and France (23 May 1940), *VOBl-BNF*, 2, no. 7, 17 June 1940, p. 39.

26 Regulation on Measures against Jews (28 Oct. 1940): see PMJ 5/158.

27 Regulation on Economic Measures against Jews (31 May 1941): see PMJ 5/168.

28 Large crates for the shipment of furniture and bulky items.

29 The Rosenberg Task Force confiscated the household goods and shipped them to Germany: see PMJ 5/190.

During the quarter under review, the officials dealing with these matters endeavoured to form a personal judgement on the administrators' proposals regarding the continuation or closure of the businesses in question. For this purpose, they visited the businesses under administration which they oversaw. However, owing to the severe depletion of the group's workforce, the visits could not always be made in the desired numbers, so that the question of the continued existence of the firm concerned had to be postponed in several cases.

DOC. 179
On 19 August 1942 factory owner Rudolf Samson is arrested and interrogated about alleged foreign currency offences[1]

Interrogation record, signed v.g.u.,[2] g.w.o.[3] R. Samson,[4] senior customs officer (F) Jaeschke[5] conducted the proceedings, administrative assistant Brendel took the minutes, Brussels, dated 19 August 1942

Rudolf *Samson* – personal data known – having been brought to the government office, appears and, upon being questioned, states in relation to the subject matter:

In January 1940, along with my mother, I set up a toy factory in Utrecht. Before the war, I had been trying to emigrate to the USA. My efforts to emigrate came to nothing once the war broke out.

On the 17th of this month my mother and I were called upon by the Central Office for Jewish Emigration in Amsterdam to appear at the Utrecht railway station on 18 August 1942 at 8 p.m. for transport to a labour camp in the eastern provinces. After receiving this summons, my mother and I decided to emigrate illegally via Belgium to unoccupied France. Some time ago a fellow Jew who has left Holland through illegal channels gave me the address of the person in Brussels who facilitates the transfer. We took all of our available cash with us and took the train from Utrecht to Tilburg. From there we took the bus to the border. We crossed the border on foot and travelled to Brussels by bus and then by tram. At around 8 p.m. we reached Brussels and went straight to the middleman, Jansen, I no longer remember the street, who gave us false identity cards and put us up in the hotel in the rue des Progrès. Today the middleman passed us on to another man,[6] who showed us the car that was to take us to France. We were motioned to a large car that was arriving, and then it brought us to the Foreign Exchange Protection Commando.

1 CegeSoma, AA 585/54/6. This document has been translated from German.
2 *Vorgelesen, genehmigt, unterschrieben*: read out, approved, and signed.
3 *Geschehen wie oben*: done as above.
4 Rudolf Hans Samson (1920–1944), factory owner; emigrated to the Netherlands from Germany with his mother, Rosa Samson, née Weiß (1890–1942); after the failed attempt to escape, both were imprisoned in St Gilles, handed over to the Security Police and the SD on 27 August 1942, and deported to Mechelen, then on 10 Oct. 1942 on to Auschwitz, where Rosa Samson was murdered upon arrival.
5 Hans Jaeschke (b. 1892), senior customs officer; joined the NSDAP in 1940; worked for the Foreign Exchange Protection Commando in Belgium from May 1942.
6 The middleman who betrayed the Samsons is listed in the Foreign Exchange Protection Commando files as 'undercover agent no. 193'. As a reward, he received 10 per cent of the assets confiscated from Samson.

In terms of cash, I was carrying 15,000 Dutch guilders in banknotes and four packets of unsorted stamps valued at approximately 5,000 guilders. I removed my Jew badge from my clothing before leaving Utrecht. I gave 7,000 Dutch guilders to the middleman. I got 1,500 Belgian francs back from the middleman. I do not know whether the middleman exchanged the Dutch guilders. He said he had exchanged them.

I am informed that the assets have been confiscated and I have been arrested for currency offences.

DOC. 180

In a report for the public prosecutor dated 31 August 1942, the Belgian policeman Jos Bouhon describes the course of action during a roundup in Antwerp[1]

Report by the police in the Deurne district (province of Antwerp) (No. 2130), signed Bouhon,[2] signed Hendrickx[3] (police commissioner), Antwerp, to the public prosecutor in Antwerp,[4] Antwerp, dated 31 August 1942 (copy)[5]

Official record of information regarding the arrest of […][6] Jews of foreign nationality by order of the German police *'Sicherheitspolizei'*[7]

Official Report
In the year nineteen hundred and forty-two, on the twenty-eighth of the month of August (28 August 1942)

We, Bouhon, Jos, deputy police commissioner in the municipality of Antwerp, duly authorized representative of the commissioner, report that we were invited by telephone at 17:45, as the police officer for the Deurne district on duty, to appear before the German police *'Sicherheitspolizei'*, 21 Della Faillelaan in Antwerp, at 19:00. On arrival, we and our colleagues from the 7th District of Antwerp and the districts of Borgerhout and Berchem were addressed by the duty officer, probably *Holm*.[8] We were told the following in German:[9]

1 Kazerne Dossin – Mechelen, A000846. This document has been translated from Dutch.
2 Jozef (Jos) Bouhon (b. 1905), policeman; worked for the Belgian police force, 1934–1947; accused of collaboration in 1945, but not convicted.
3 Robert Hendrickx (b. 1898), policeman; joined the Belgian police force in 1926; dismissed from the police after the war ended.
4 Edouard Baers, lawyer; closely affiliated with the Vlaams Nationaal Verbond (VNV); deputy public prosecutor in Mechelen prior to Feb. 1942; in Antwerp from Feb. 1942; remained a public prosecutor after 1945.
5 Parts of the original are underlined by hand.
6 Number illegible; presumably 250, as this number is mentioned later in the report.
7 German in the original: 'Security Police'.
8 Erich Holm (1912–1981), sailor and plumber; joined the SS in 1938; with the Hamburg Gestapo from 1939; official in charge of Jewish affairs in the Antwerp office of the Security Police and the SD, 1940–1944; initially reported missing after 1945; thought to have lived in Schwiederstorf, near Hamburg, from 1968. Whether Bouhon met Holm at this time is not certain; the person concerned could also have been Otto Desselman (1910–1943), head of the Security Police and the SD in Antwerp, or Alfred Thomas (1905–1943), head of department II (Churches, Jews and Freemasons) in the office of the Security Police and the SD for Belgium and northern France. The 'Jewish section' under Kurt Asche came under this department.
9 The text that follows is written in Dutch in the original.

> On 27 August 1942 I (*Holm*) organized a roundup of Jews with my force in Antwerp. For that purpose, I had summoned forty SS men and forty-five Feldgendarmen, and I had been given assurance of the cooperation of the Belgian police and gendarmerie. The Belgian police were given their orders at around 17:00, and the round-up with mass arrests was to start at 20:00. After I had been working with my men for half an hour, I discovered that the Jews had been warned in advance about what was going to happen by means of hastily written leaflets distributed by the members of the Belgian police. Many Jews had gone into hiding. As soon as I had discovered this and had solid evidence, I gave the order to withdraw and halted the planned arrests. The numbers and names of the accused police officers are known. Due to the betrayal by members of the Belgian police, I received the order from Brussels that, by way of punishment, the Belgian police must carry out the arrest and assembly of Jews on their own. That is the reason why I have summoned you. My lieutenant will give you the necessary instructions and orders, and each of you will arrest 250 Jews with your unit and deliver them to me by 8 a.m. tomorrow, 29 August. If this instruction is not carried out punctually and strictly with regard to the number, the relevant police authorities and you yourselves can expect to be sent to Breendonck concentration camp.[10] To be detained and assembled are all Jews aged over 12 months, without distinction on the basis of sex, and of the following nationalities: German, Estonian, French, Greek, Dutch, Lithuanian, Latvian, Norwegian, Austrian, Polish, Russian, Serbian, Czechoslovakian, and stateless. The Jews thus assembled will be put into a hall, whence we will collect them by motor vehicle. You can tell them they must have clothes, shoes, and food for at least two weeks with them. They may bring and keep their valuables, such as diamonds, jewellery, money, etc.; such items will not be taken off them. If you are unable to reach the number of 250 Jews in your area, for example in the Deurne district, then you must look for them in the Merksem district and the 6th District of Antwerp.

We also received the instruction that infants under twelve months should not be taken away and that only their respective mothers should be allowed to stay with them to look after them. Where a house or apartment was completely evacuated, it was to be locked up and sealed and later guarded, so that no Jewish movable goods would be misappropriated or embezzled by third parties. The arrest of the Jews had been proposed to relieve the burden on the Belgian treasury, as nearly all Jews had to be supported by the Belgian state. Severe measures based on martial law would be taken against any superior or any police officer attempting to sabotage the orders and their implementation.

We reported on this to our superior, the police commissioner, at about 21:30. Under his direction and with all personnel, the aforementioned Jews were arrested in the Deurne district. The roundup was extended to the Merksem district and the 6th District of Antwerp, as a result of which the number 250 was achieved at about 8 on 29 August. In Deurne, 134 Jews were assembled in the auditorium of the Plazza cinema, which had been appropriated specifically for that purpose. Most of those to be arrested were given

10 Fort Breendonk (also: Breendonck), built in 1906, used by the Security Police and the SD as a penal camp from Sept. 1940; until the establishment of Mechelen transit camp in July 1942, Jewish prisoners were also held there. Most of the inmates of Breendonk were gradually deported to concentration camps; only around half of the 3,500 prisoners survived the war: see PMJ 5/175.

time to pack and take everything they wanted and to make sure they had enough food. On 29 August 1942, at 16:30, the assembled Jews were collected by German police *'Sicherheitspolizei'* vehicles.[11] By order of the German government, Jews of Belgian, English, American, Italian, Swiss, Romanian, and Hungarian nationality as well as the nationalities not mentioned in the order were not apprehended. The Antwerp police authorities were notified of the orders received and were asked to cooperate. No incidents occurred.

Similar operations were carried out simultaneously by the respective police forces in the 6th and 7th Districts of Antwerp City and the districts of Borgerhout, Berchem, and Merksem.

In witness thereof,[12] concluded on 28 August 1942.

DOC. 181

Le Drapeau rouge, August 1942: article calling for more active opposition to the deportation of Jews from Belgium[1]

The disgraceful persecution of the Jews
Let us help the Israelites resist their executioners

The revolting measures taken by the occupier towards the Jews provoke general indignation.

For several weeks, massive deportations of young Jewish workers have been taking place, organized by the ONT.[2] The deported are sent to northern France to build fortifications[3] and are subjected to a very harsh regime in which they are maltreated and starved.

As the resistance movement is growing and an increasing number of Jews have realized that it is better not to heed official summonses, the Gestapo took matters into their own hands. They sent out the summonses themselves through the Association of Jews (which has been set up by the occupier), they took their victims from their own homes, carried out roundups on trains, and seized young men and young girls between the ages of twelve and eighteen in the streets. Entire families are now facing the threat of being

11 A total of 943 Jews were arrested during this roundup in Antwerp and deported from Mechelen to Auschwitz on Transports VII and VIII in early Sept. 1942.

12 In the original: 'Waarvan akte', meaning that this report constituted an official document that could serve as a piece of evidence.

1 'L'ignominieuse persécution des Juifs', *Le Drapeau rouge*, August 1942, new series, no. 33, p. 1. Published in facsimile in *Le Drapeau rouge clandestine: Pages glorieuses de l'histoire du Parti Communiste de Belgique* (Brussels: Jacquemotte Foundation, 1971), p. 177. This document has been translated from French. *Le Drapeau rouge*, the daily or weekly newspaper of the Communist Party of Belgium was published from 1921 until the early 1990s; it was also known as *La Voix du peuple* between 1936 and 1939. It continued to be published illegally after it was banned in 1939; it was again published under its original name from 1940. Seventy-three issues were published between Feb. 1941 and late August 1944.

2 Office national du travail: National Employment Office.

3 See Doc. 174.

sent off to Poland.[4] Hundreds of young Jewish girls are kept near Mechelen and risk a far more terrible fate.

There have been several instances in which people showed solidarity in the face of these vile practices. In Brussels, two hundred inhabitants of rue Haute accompanied a Jewish family all the way to the station. In Antwerp, hundreds of Flemish women created similar displays of fraternity, which brought the Feldgendarmerie to the scene.[5]

This is good, but we must resist even more actively. The bold move by some armed men who forcibly entered the offices of the Association of Jews, locked up the employees in a room, and burned the files compiled on the Gestapo's orders shows the way forward.[6]

It is with resolution and, where necessary, with violence that the victims must respond to their torturers. And they need to tell themselves that death itself is not worse than the fate that awaits them if they are deported. Everybody must stand with the threatened Israelites, help them escape, and tear them from the Gestapo's clutches.

Only by standing united will we be able to force our common enemy to retreat. We will only beat the Nazi oppressor and regain independence and freedom if all of us deal blows to the enemy, using all possible means.

DOC. 182

On 1 September 1942 Boris Averbuch writes to his girlfriend from the train to Upper Silesia[1]

Handwritten letter from Boris Averbuch[2] to Odette,[3] dated 1 September 1942

Tuesday, 1 September 1942
Dear Odette,

You presumably know what has happened to us: on Saturday at 4 o'clock in the morning the police[4] came to pull us out of our beds (my mother and me). We were taken to the police station; […][5] to a school where there were 200 people already. There, we were

4 The people deported in late June 1942 were taken to the Organization Todt labour camps in northern France; it was not until mid July that the German occupiers used call-ups for 'labour service' to deport people to the concentration and extermination camps in the East. The first roundup in Belgium took place on 22 July 1942 on a train between Antwerp and Brussels; in this raid, the Feldgendarmerie arrested approximately 60 to 100 persons, including a large number of women.

5 Neither of these events could be verified.

6 The index cards burned on 25 July 1942 were only copies; the originals had already been passed on to the Security Police and the SD. The operation was carried out by the communist resistance movement: Pierre Broder, *Des Juifs debout contre le nazisme* (Brussels: EPO, 1994), p. 124.

1 Kazerne Dossin – Mechelen, A000343. This document has been translated from French.

2 Boris Averbuch (b. 1917), teacher; emigrated to Belgium in 1919 and worked at a school run by the Association of Jews in Belgium (AJB/VJB); on 1 Sept. 1942 deported to Auschwitz, where he perished.

3 Odette Damoiseaux, Boris Averbuch's non-Jewish girlfriend.

4 The second large-scale roundup in Belgium took place in Antwerp during the night of 28 August 1942. It was carried out by the German police and Feldgendarmerie as well as the Belgian police: see Doc. 180.

5 One word is illegible.

loaded onto lorries for the Dossin Barracks at Mechelen.[6] So there we were. Today we left Mechelen for an unknown destination. I suppose to Upper Silesia via Germany (we've already gone through Leuven and Tienen). Our transport has 1,000 people, a passenger train, and it is the 7th transport.[7]

The first ten transports are all going to meet up in Upper Silesia they say.

For the trip we were given one loaf of bread, one meat ball, a bit of artificial honey, a package of fruit. An additional Red Cross carriage is attached to our train.

I am giving you these details so that you know exactly what is happening here.

Mechelen: in the morning a quarter of a loaf of bread with coffee, at midday soup, in the evening coffee and sometimes an extra, such as a little sugar, preserves, sausage, depending on what they managed to get.[8] In the morning, a bit of exercise. If you are on the staff or have contacts there, you can get everything: cigarettes, bread, as much butter as you want, fruit.

Dear Odette, I am very sad about what happened, I could have escaped several times, even from Mechelen, but I didn't want to, for fear they would take measures against my mother in retaliation.[9]

What troubles me is that I have neither clothes nor food because I did not have the time to take any with me.

They take everything *they see*, but not what they do not see because it is well hidden.

Dearest Odette, I am risking a lot by sending you this letter and I hope that you'll receive it. Let F. Van Herrewijen know, if you want, and Mr and Mrs […][10] in Antwerp.

With much love

DOC. 183

On 4 September 1942 Karl Holstein from the German military administration notes how Jews with diamonds or gold can buy their exemption from deportation[1]

File note by the Chief of the Military Administration, Department of Economic Affairs (Industry and Commerce, Section 2),[2] signed Holstein,[3] undisclosed location, dated 4 September 1942

1) File note

Re: registration of diamonds and gold owned by Jews.

On Monday, 31 August 1942, a discussion on the question of 'registration of diamonds and gold owned by Jews' took place in the office of the Feldkommandant in Antwerp.[4]

6 Mechelen camp in the former Dossin Barracks was initially under the command of Rudolf Steckmann; he was succeeded by Johannes Frank in March 1943. Jews who had been arrested were interned in the camp before being deported to Auschwitz. In total, 28 trains carrying around 25,000 persons left the camp between August 1942 and July 1944.

7 This transport took 555 female and 445 male prisoners – including 317 children under the age of 15 – to Auschwitz via Kosel in Upper Silesia. Of that number, 734 were murdered immediately after their arrival on 3 Sept. 1942.

8 Anything of value was removed from the prisoners when they arrived at the camp.

9 Luba Averbuch, née Lasowski (b. 1889), housewife; born in Polotsk (Belarus); on 1 Sept. 1942 deported to Auschwitz, where she perished.

10 Name is illegible.

1 AN, AJ 40/72. This document has been translated from German.

In addition to the representatives of the FK,[5] the participants included representatives of the SD, the Foreign Exchange Protection Commando, the Four-Year Plan (Mr Plümer), and Mr Frenssen[6] as an expert on the subject. Subject to the approval of the military administration, it was decided that Jews who hand in at least 100 ct.[7] of diamonds or gold or foreign currency (Sweden, Switzerland, and Portugal) to the value of approximately 50,000 Swiss francs from unreported holdings are to be exempted from the service obligation and evacuation, temporarily and informally, that is, without a written or binding declaration. The SD has explicit authorization from the Security Main Office in Berlin[8] to grant exemptions. This exemption is valid initially for approximately 6–8 weeks. A similar arrangement has been reached in Holland and has led to encouraging results there with respect to the handover of diamonds from non-authorized holdings.[9]

At my suggestion, it was decided not to accept the diamonds without compensation, but rather to pay as compensation the stop price[10] of 10 May, which must be put into a blocked account. The individual cases in question, which are confined to an estimated total of 50–100 persons, will be reviewed and processed by Mr Frenssen in consultation with the SD. He will also take delivery of the diamonds handed in on behalf of the Reich Office for Technical Products.[11] I have presented this planned arrangement to Kriegsverwaltungsrat Heym,[12] who has given his consent with the comment that the authorization of the Chief of the Military Administration[13] can thus be inferred as well. Thereupon I informed the FK in Antwerp that the outcome of the discussion on 31 August was approved by the military administration.

2 Department for Economic Affairs, Group I: Industry and Commerce, Section 2: Stones and Earth.
3 Karl Holstein (1908–1983), lawyer; joined the NSDAP in 1933; worked for the German Table Glass Factory GmbH from 1936; worked in the Department for Economic Affairs of the German military administration in Belgium, 1940–1944; worked in the glass industry again from 1946; chairman of the German-Belgian-Luxembourg Chamber of Commerce, 1967–1969.
4 Presumably Harry Botho Nadrowski (b. 1888); career soldier.
5 Feldkommandantur.
6 Correctly: William Frensel (1877–1944), retailer; employed at the Diamond Control Office of the Oberfeldkommandantur in Antwerp in 1940; worked in diamond control and, in addition, was the administrator of businesses formerly owned by Jews and the exclusive diamond seller to the Office for the Four-Year Plan from 1941.
7 Metric carat, a unit of weight for gemstones.
8 This refers to the Reich Security Main Office (RSHA).
9 In the Netherlands, the operation described also began in the late summer of 1942. The Jews who purchased a deferral of deportation in this way were given exemption stamps bearing numbers from 120,000 upwards.
10 This means a fixed price, which was pegged at the level of 10 May 1942.
11 In 1934 offices to oversee the movement of goods in industry and commerce were established within the Reich Ministry of Economics. Renamed the 'Reich Offices' in 1939, they dealt with the control and allocation of raw materials imports.
12 Dr Hans Günther Heym (1907–1979), lawyer; joined the NSDAP in 1930; worked in the administrations of various district and state governments, 1934–1940; personal aide to Eggert Reeder, the chief of the German military administration, 1940–1944; held the rank of Oberregierungsrat when he was dismissed in 1945; worked as a lawyer from 1961.
13 Eggert Reeder.

The entire operation covers only around two weeks, as the evacuation is to be completed within this time period.[14]
2) To Dr Jaeck,[15] Kriegsverwaltungs-Abteilungschef: please take note.[16]

DOC. 184
On 15 September 1942 the German military administration reports on the deportation of 10,000 Jews from Belgium[1]

Activity report no. 21 of the military administration for the period from 1 June to 1 September 1942 (no. 441/42 top secret), published by the Military Commander in Belgium and Northern France,[2] head of the military administration, signed Reeder, undisclosed location, dated 15 September 1942

[…][3]
6. Measures against the Jews
In accordance with a directive of the Reichsführer SS, the *transport of the Jews to the East* was begun on 1 August 1942.[4] The operation was begun initially as a labour-deployment measure and therefore pertained primarily to Jewish men and women who were fit for work. Only on the basis of subsequent directives from the Reich Security Main Office[5] did it take on the nature of a general evacuation of the Jews, so that Jews who are not completely fit for work have recently been transported as well. Citizens of the British Empire, the American and neutral states, and Italy, as well as the approximately 4,000 Belgian Jews and the approximately 500 French Jews in the area of the OFK[6] in Lille, are exempt from these measures. They are being made available to the OT[7] for construction work, mainly in northern France. *Thus far, 10,000 Jews in total have been transported to the East.* This operation naturally caused considerable panic among the Jews. Many tried to escape into unoccupied France, but for the most part were captured by the border guards and

14 The deportation of 10,000 Jews from Belgium was supposed to be completed by 15 Sept. 1942. According to a report by William Frensel dated 17 Oct. 1942, in the course of this operation 34 Jewish families handed in diamonds and gold with a total value of approximately 7–8 million Belgian francs in return for a temporary exemption: AN, AJ 40/72. Seven of these families were deported six weeks later, and four families managed to escape abroad. According to the report, the majority of the 23 remaining families were Dutch or Polish nationals.
15 Head of Group I (Industry and Commerce) in the German military administration's Department for Economic Affairs in Brussels.
16 Handwritten note: '3) for information. 200'.
1 BArch, RW 36/190. In the table of contents of the activity report, the portion quoted here can be found under the number A 6 on pages A 38–A 39. This excerpt published in Klarsfeld and Steinberg (eds.), *Die Endlösung der Judenfrage in Belgien*, pp. 44–45. This document has been translated from German.
2 Alexander von Falkenhausen.
3 The entire report contains 190 pages. Pages 1–71, the political section of the report, address the occupation administration's measures relating to general domestic policy.
4 See Doc. 235.
5 For the decisions taken by the Reich Security Main Office (RSHA), see PMJ 5, p. 29.
6 Oberfeldkommandantur.
7 Organization Todt.

French police authorities. Others attempted quickly to acquire Belgian citizenship, by marriage or by opting for citizenship.[8] These endeavours are futile, however, because such marriages are tacitly treated as invalid with regard to labour deployment. Furthermore, the possibility of opting for Belgian citizenship was quite some time ago made dependent upon the consent of the military administration. The operation did not cause too much disquiet among the Belgian public, because the Jews played only a minor role here and 9/10 of them were émigrés and other foreigners. Representatives of the Belgian Ministry of Justice and other Belgian authorities emphasized repeatedly that they want to lend their support solely to the Belgian Jews.
[…][9]

DOC. 185
On 23 September 1942 Paul-Henri Spaak, the Belgian minister of foreign affairs, asks his British counterpart to relax the entry requirements for Jews from Belgium seeking admission to Britain[1]

Letter from the Minister's Office[2] (no. 422/900), unsigned, to the Right Honourable Anthony Eden,[3] PC, MC, MP,[4] etc., dated 23 September 1942 (carbon copy)

From all sides I am being made aware of the increasingly tragic situation of Jews and political refugees in France.[5] I have been asked to intervene on their behalf.

For the Belgian government, this difficult question has two distinct aspects: the situation of the Belgian Jews on the one hand, and that of the foreigners on the other. As far as the Belgian Jews are concerned, I think I could help them, in fact most likely save their lives, if the English government were to modify somewhat its rules on Belgian refugees entering Britain.[6] If you could rule that Belgians can enter your country without the need for me to find them a post first, this would greatly ease matters. I could certainly get them visas for the Congo.[7] The journey to the Congo could then be made or not, depending on the respective cases. When it comes to money, I do not need to tell you

8 Once they reached the age of 16, the children of immigrants had the option of becoming Belgian citizens.
9 After this section, on pp. 74–190, the report addresses various administrative, fiscal, and economic policy questions dealt with by the military administration.

1 Fondation Paul-Henri Spaak, F 429/7149. This document has been translated from French.
2 Paul-Henri Spaak (1899–1971), lawyer; prime minister of Belgium, 1938–1940 and 1947–1949; minister of foreign affairs in the government in exile, 1940–1944; president of the first UN General Assembly, 1946; played a major role in founding the European Economic Community in 1957; secretary general of NATO, 1956–1961.
3 Sir Anthony Eden (1897–1977), British politician; foreign secretary, 1935–1938, 1940–1945, and 1951–1955; secretary of state for war from 1940; prime minister of the United Kingdom, 1955–1957.
4 Privy Counsellor, Military Cross, Member of Parliament.
5 This presumably refers to people who had fled from Belgium to France when the Germans invaded and who were still interned there in various camps.
6 In May 1940 the entry requirements for citizens of the Netherlands and Belgium seeking admission to Britain had been brought into line with the restrictive requirements in force for enemy aliens.
7 This refers to entry permits for the Belgian Congo colony.

that the Belgian government would be willing to cover all the living expenses for all the Belgian Jews.

I would also very much like to intervene on behalf of the foreigners, be they Jewish or not, but the situation is more complicated in their case. However, I think that, considering how tragic the situation is, it is imperative to examine it with the will to find a solution. Do you not think that the British government could take the initiative and set up a commission which would look into the practical steps necessary to save these people?[8]

DOC. 186

On 25 September 1942 the chief of the German military administration, Eggert Reeder, informs the Oberfeldkommandanturen and Feldkommandanturen that the deportation of the Jews can continue[1]

Letter (polit. group/political diary[2] no. 605/12 secret) from the Military Commander in Belgium and Northern France – chief of the military administration, Oberfeldkommandantur 672, administrative chief, diary no. 418/42s, signed Reeder, to the Feldkommandanturen and Oberfeldkommandanturen – administrative chiefs – in the command area, field office, dated 25 September 1942 (copy)

Re: evacuation of the Jews
After the previously implemented labour deployment of 10,000 Jews in the East, the complete evacuation of Jews from the command area is now being undertaken. For the time being, only Norwegian, Croatian, Slovak, formerly German, Polish, Czechoslovak, Austrian, Luxembourgian, Estonian, Latvian, Lithuanian, and stateless Jews will be evacuated as well as French Jews living in Belgium and Belgian Jews living in northern France. Jews who live in a mixed marriage or who are not required to wear the Jewish star are exempt from the measure. Other than that, care must be taken to keep families together when they are evacuated, and to proceed as unobtrusively as possible.

The implementation of the operation, which is initially expected to run until the end of October this year, is in the hands of the Security Police. Please make all reasonable efforts to make executive police forces available to the Security Police for registration in the case of larger operations. No attempt is to be made to call in the Belgian police. The Jews will first be assembled in Mechelen camp and then transported.

It must be ensured that the Jews currently in labour deployment also are transported along with their families. The Jews deployed in northern France with the Organization Todt will be released from that area in a few weeks, insofar as evacuation is now a possibility.[3] Further instructions will follow with regard to the Jews still deployed in armaments production.

8 Eden confirmed receipt of this letter the same day: Fondation Paul-Henri Spaak, F 429/7150. However, there is no evidence of any concrete steps taken by either the Belgian or the British government over the following weeks to rescue the Jews from Belgium who were at that time in France.

1 CegeSoma, AA 2143/2733 (copy). Published in Klarsfeld and Steinberg (eds.), *Die Endlösung der Judenfrage in Belgien*, pp. 46–48. This document has been translated from German.

2 'Gruppe polit.': see Doc. 188, fn. 2.

Finally, also in consultation with the Security Police, particular attention must be paid to the illegal emigration of Jews, which has recently been on the increase. Attempts by Jews to remove the Jewish star and illegally move out of the four big cities[4] and into the countryside or to smaller places must be prevented.

The office of the German Security Police is instructed to carry out the operation in such a way that it attracts as little public attention as possible and wins no sympathy for the Jews among the population.

DOC. 187

On 7 October 1942 the Belgian underground organization Tégal reports to the government in exile in London about the start of deportations and raids against Jews[1]

Report, unsigned,[2] dated 7 October 1942 (copy)[3]

Persecution of Jews

For the last three or four months, but above all over the course of these past weeks, the measures taken against the Jews have become so inhuman that the entire right-minded populace is revolted by them. The Gestapo is engaging in veritable raids upon these unfortunate people.[4] The Jews are being hunted down like dangerous animals. Cities such as Antwerp have been emptied of their Israelite populations entirely, and Brussels will soon follow suit. Initially, the Gestapo carried out the arrests on trains, or at random in the street, but now they have resorted to organizing roundups of Jews by sending out summonses, without any regard for age, sex, or social status. Thousands of people have been gathered in this manner and taken to Mechelen or Breendonck. From there, most are transferred to labour camps in France (coastal region) or to Silesia. Sometimes entire families are arrested, but most often families are torn apart. In Mechelen at the Dossin Barracks, the first assembly site, up to 5,000 Jews at a time are crammed together in the vilest possible way. For bedding they have only a bit of straw that is never changed. Men, women, and children are all muddled together in the dormitories and have to do everything in front of each other. It's a permanent seething cauldron in there. The detainees are allowed to go out into the courtyard for some fresh air for one hour in the morning and one hour in the afternoon. Body searches are performed at great speed: men on one side, women

3 1,300 Jews who had hitherto been used as labour to build the Atlantic Wall were transferred at the end of Oct. 1942 to Mechelen, from where they were deported to Auschwitz on 31 Oct. 1942.

4 This refers to the cities of Brussels, Antwerp, Liège, and Charleroi, where most Jews lived.

1 CegeSoma, AA 1105. This document has been translated from French.

2 The report was written by an unknown member of the Tégal underground intelligence service. This can be deduced from the document's context. Tégal was founded by Pierre Hauman immediately after Belgium surrendered. By 1943, the organization had spread across all of Belgium. Hundreds of agents, most of them French-speaking Belgians, collected military, political, and economic intelligence, which they passed on to the Allies. In late 1943, most of the organization's members were arrested. Those who remained at large joined Mill, another underground organization.

3 The original contains various stamps.

4 The first major roundup in Antwerp took place in the early hours of 16 August 1942.

on the other, in front of the children. Vermin crawling everywhere. The food is rotten and insufficient. All the provisions sent by the Secours d'Hiver[5] were sent back to the charity that had sent them. There had even been milk for the infants. People are beaten like dogs. A large number of them lack clothing. Money and items of value are confiscated from those who have any. For the past eight days, mass arrests have been carried out without any summons.[6] In the early hours, neighbourhoods spanning several streets are barricaded and blocked by soldiers. Then all the houses, without exception, must be opened up and searched from top to bottom. All the Jews are arrested and taken away on lorries. At the train station, they are locked up in livestock wagons in groups of 50. The raids usually last until 5 in the morning. Often one sees people taken by surprise, without having had time to get dressed: women in nightgowns, men in pyjamas. When the roundups are carried out during the day (which still occurs), it also happens that families are separated with skilful barbarity. Here are two facts from personal experience: in Anderlecht, 4 children who had been displaced from Mons were taken (the oldest aged 12), the parents remained at liberty (for the time being); on rue de Lenglentier in Brussels, the parents were taken, and a little girl of 11 was abandoned in the street. Neither age (in Antwerp, a 92-year-old woman; in Brussels, on the same list and one after the other, a 74-year-old woman and a 4-year-old child) nor one's state of health counts. At the moment, Belgians and foreigners are arrested, even the young men who fought in the 1940 campaign. The occupation authority no longer accepts interventions seeking the release of prisoners.[7] It is said that come October, not a single Jew will be free. Although initially the attitude of the population had been one of resigned passivity, now nearly everyone exhibits strident indignation. If a person is caught voicing their criticism too loudly, their identity card is confiscated and returned the following day to the Kommandantur[8] with the mark (stamp) 'Friend of the Jews' – an indication which is likely to get one into serious trouble later.[9] One particularly disturbing fact: it is no longer only the Gestapo who go around hunting Jews; individuals who belong to the Flemish or Wallonian guard (commonly known as 'the blacks' on account of their uniform) participate in arrests and appear to take to it with even greater zeal than the Germans. The population's hatred of them is also growing. This feeling was made manifest this month, on Sunday 6 September: a special film was screened for them at the Marivaux cinema (which, since the occupation, has been reserved for the exclusive use of the occupier). At around 10.30 a.m., a bomb exploded inside. We saw a lot of wounded people come out; a series of ambulances arrived on the scene. It is said (though we do not have definite confirmation) that there were seven deaths. The attitude of nearly everyone is: 'They had it coming. Shame the whole place didn't blow up.'

5 An umbrella charity organization in Belgium (Secours d'Hiver/Winterhulp), created by decree on 29 Oct. 1940, following the model of the Winter Relief which had been set up in Germany in 1933.

6 Because too few Jews had responded to the summonses, the German authorities launched a wave of arrests in order to reach the numbers set for deportation. The first wave of roundups began in mid August 1942 and lasted until the end of Sept.

7 Up to June 1943 it was possible in many cases for Jews with Belgian citizenship (approximately 6–7 per cent of the Jews living in Belgium) either to secure their release or at least to stay in the camp at Mechelen, since initially only foreign Jews were to be deported from Belgium. In July 1943 Military Commander von Falkenhausen gave the order to deport the Belgian Jews as well: see Doc. 212.

8 German in the original: local 'headquarters of the military administration'.

9 This could not be verified.

DOC. 188

On 8 October 1942 Salomon Ullmann sends his letter of resignation as chairman of the Association of Jews in Belgium to the chief of the German military administration[1]

Letter from the chief rabbi of Belgium,[2] signed Dr S. Ullmann, Brussels, to the Chief of the Military Administration,[3] 18 Wetstraat, Brussels, dated 8 September 1942 (copy)

Re: resignation request of the chairman of the Association of Jews in Belgium.
According to the certificate of appointment dated 22 December 1941, the undersigned was appointed chairman of the Association of Jews in Belgium.

However, as the events of the past weeks[4] have proved that he has been unable to function in this position to the satisfaction of the authorities, he most politely requests to be granted permission to resign from his office.[5]

With the highest esteem

DOC. 189

On 8 October 1942 Frans de Groote asks the Queen of Belgium to protect his wife, who has been interned in Mechelen, from deportation[1]

Letter (marked 'urgent, please') from Frans de Groote,[2] 85 rue Lamorinière, Antwerp, to Her Majesty Queen Elisabeth,[3] Laeken Castle, dated 8 October 1942

Your Majesty,

I take the liberty to address Your Royal Highness to ask for protection for my wife.[4]

Last August I married a Polish Israelite whom I love and who means everything to me.

1 CegeSoma, mic 41. This document has been translated from German.
2 The following addition is noted in the heading: 'Gruppe polit/Az. volk allgem 153'. This is likely to be a reference to the departments, known as 'groups', within the German military administration's executive office, including those for ethnopolitical questions ('volk') and political and Jewish affairs ('polit.').
3 Eggert Reeder.
4 The call-ups for 'labour deployment' in Germany, which the Association of Jews in Belgium (AJB/VJB) had to distribute and Ullmann had to sign, did not achieve the results that the German authorities had expected. Four large roundups subsequently took place in Antwerp and Brussels, in which 2,448 Jews were arrested and deported to Auschwitz via Mechelen.
5 After Ullmann's resignation, a turf war broke out over the naming of his successor. The military administration finally settled on the chairman of the Jewish Community of Brussels, Marcel Blum: see Doc. 205.

1 Archive of the Royal Palace, Archive of the Office of Queen Elisabeth/Sec RE 01/67. This document has been translated from French.
2 Frans de Groote (b. 1909), chemistry teacher; worked for several months as a liaison officer for the Belgian Ministry for War Victims in 1945.
3 Queen Elisabeth of Belgium (1876–1965); mother of King Leopold III of Belgium; after the death of Leopold's wife Astrid in 1935 she resumed the role of queen until the coronation of her grandson Baudouin and his wife, Fabiola, in 1951.
4 Probably Malvina Minczelez (b. 1924), born in Lwów (Poland); deported on 24 Oct. 1942 to Auschwitz, where she perished.

She was arrested last Friday[5] and is now detained in Mechelen.

I instructed my solicitor to take a written proposal to the Hauptmann[6] of the Dossin Barracks, in which I suggested I would go and work in Russia in exchange for my wife's release. Having studied chemistry and bacteriology, and having more than ten years' experience, I am better able to be of immediate service than my young wife.[7]

The Hauptmann rejected my proposal with contempt.

Given that my wife has become Belgian through marriage and that her deportation would be in breach of the Hague Conventions, and that our marriage was not entered into with the intention of avoiding the mandatory labour service the Israelites have to perform, I plead that You will kindly take my wife under Your protection so that she can remain in Belgium.

Especially considering I informed the Hauptmann that I have written to Reich Marshal Hermann Goering[8] to let him know of my grievances, and I do not want my wife to suffer the consequences of this.

I thank You in advance and assure Your Majesty of my deepest gratitude and devotion.

DOC. 190

L'Ami du peuple, 17 October 1942: a leaflet calls on people to report Jews living in hiding and those who help them[1]

The hour of the great departure is nigh!
No false pity, help us! It is in your interest, it is your duty as a good Belgian citizen!

We would like to draw our readers' attention to the contents of the anti-Jewish order of 1 June 1942,[2] which limits the free movement of Jews. This order stipulates that it is forbidden for Jews to leave their place of residence between 8 p.m. and 7 a.m.

The place of residence is the address listed in the Jew registry. Any other residence apart from the one mentioned above is forbidden for Jews.

The order includes details of prison sentences and fines for any person found to be in breach of this law. This applies not only to Jews, but also to all Aryans who illegally shelter them.

In addition, security measures can be taken against these people.

5 2 Oct. 1942.
6 German in original. Probably Rudolf Steckmann, who at that time was in charge of Mechelen camp as Philipp Schmitt's deputy.
7 Handwritten note: 'age 18.5'.
8 This has not been found.

1 'L'heure du grand départ a sonné' (leaflet), *L'Ami du peuple*, 17 Oct. 1942. This document has been translated from French. The newspaper, published by the Flemish nationalist organization headed by the lawyer René Lambricht (Volksverwering/Défense du Peuple), was targeted at francophone antisemitic readers.
2 Regulation on Residence Restrictions for Jews (1 June 1942), *VOBl-BNF* 79, no. 4, 1 June 1942, pp. 948–949.

It is patently obvious that many Jews attempt to avoid the work order and go into hiding to avoid the measures taken against them. They find shelter with obliging Belgians, who often provide them with room and board in exchange for money.

These antisocial elements must be hunted down without mercy.

We know that Jews have become masters of deceiving and betraying the peoples among whom they live like parasites. The Jews spread rumours, claiming they are mistreated. *This is absolutely untrue.* On the contrary, Jews are treated well, provided they do the work that has been imposed on them.

Let us save our mercy for our own compatriots, and let us not defend those who are responsible for this war and are the cause of all our ills.

Let us think of our prisoners in the Oflags and Stalags;[3] let us think of our dead who gave their young lives in those tragic days of May 1940;[4] let us think of all our comrades who are on the verge of malnutrition; let us think of the countless deaths that the current war causes; and let us never forget that the Jews alone are to blame for inciting this conflict. This is why we urgently appeal to all our readers to immediately notify us of any places where Jews are hiding. Write to the following address:

'La Défense du peuple'
Anti-Jewish League
52 rue Phillippe-de-Champagne
Brussels
Telephone: 12 59 07

All the information given to us will be passed on to the highest authorities, and we can guarantee that all information will be followed up promptly.

We have no doubt that our readers will understand where their duty lies, and we would also like to take this opportunity to appeal to those Belgians who, often for reasons that we understand perfectly, think they should still shun National Socialist Germany.

When presented with this unique opportunity to liberate the entire country from Jewish domination once and for all, everyone must swallow their resentment and disregard their personal preferences.

We know that there are also enemies of the Jews among the Anglophiles, because they suffered from Jewish competition before 10 May 1940. They must help us and understand their duty!

We must all work together to rid Belgium of the Jewish plague!

L'Ami du peuple

3 Prisoners of war held by the Wehrmacht were imprisoned in two different types of prisoner-of-war camps: camps for officers (Oflag, short for Offizierslager), and camps for NCOs and enlisted men (Stalag, short for Stammlager).

4 Around 12,000 persons died during the fighting in Belgium, approximately half of whom were civilians.

DOC. 191
On 23 October 1942 the prime minister of the Belgian government in exile protests against the persecution of the Jews in Belgium[1]

Address by the prime minister of Belgium (IV.LB.5196), signed Hubert Pierlot,[2] undated (transcription)[3]

Message from the Belgian Prime Minister to the meeting of protest against Nazi atrocities
Up to the moment of the invasion, Jews in Belgium received a most hospitable welcome. Protected by our Constitution which guarantees the freedom of opinion and creed, and by our laws which proclaim the equality of all Belgians, the Jews enjoyed the same status as other Belgians.

When a few years before the war, the Jews began to suffer from the first Nazi persecutions, Belgium was, once again, a land of refuge for the outcasts. The Belgian Government, supported by the unanimous opinion of the country did everything possible to relieve their sufferings.

When victory finally brings Nazi cruelties to an end, all citizens, without distinction of race or belief, will find in our country that regime of freedom which is traditional in Belgium.

Germany's conduct towards the Jews is one of the most atrocious dramas of history. To the honour of humanity, victory will put an end to it.[4]

DOC. 192
Representatives of the Belgian Jews report on their meeting on 27 October 1942 with Kurt Asche, official in charge of Jewish affairs for the Security Police and the SD[1]

Report, unsigned, attached to the minutes of the Association of Jews in Belgium (AJB/VJB) meeting on 27 October 1942, Brussels, dated 29 October 1942 (copy)[2]

Report on the meeting at the SD on 27 October 1942[3]
We asked in detail about the case of Mr Hellendall[4] and his family, and were told that Mr and Mrs Hell[endall][5] always went out without wearing a star. It seems they both

1 Algemeen Rijksarchief / Archives générales du Royaume, Archives des Cabinets du Premier ministre à Londres/313. The original document is in English.
2 Hubert Marie Eugène Pierlot (1883–1963), lawyer; worked in various government offices and held numerous ministerial positions from 1918; prime minister of Belgium, 1939–1945; fled in 1940 with other members of the government to London, where they established a government in exile; worked as a lawyer after 1945. Pierlot gave this address in London on 23 Oct. 1942 at an event protesting against the National Socialist terror against Jews; the event was organized by the Board of Deputies of British Jews.
3 This text was sent along with an accompanying message by the cabinet spokesman to the Belgian ambassador in London on 24 Oct. 1942: Archives des Cabinets du Premier ministre à Londres/313. On 31 Oct. 1942 it was broadcast on Radio Belgique/Radio België, the radio station of the Belgian government in exile.
4 Pierlot had already published an article with a similar message in the *Jewish Bulletin* in late April 1942: see PMJ 5/188.

1 Mémorial de la Shoah, Fonds Maxime Steinberg. This document has been translated from French.

denied it during their interrogation, but later confessed when confronted with somebody who had seen them in town without a star. Their release is out of the question, as they have arrived at their labour post by now.[6] We therefore asked whether an appeal for their release from Germany would be taken into consideration, in response to which we were told that people in higher places than us, and even Germans, had already begun such a procedure, and it had come to nothing.

We then submitted a request for the release of three of my employees, who were taken away today, and were informed that their release would only be considered if the officer who carried out their arrest were to confirm that they were not arrested for any special reason.

Mr A.[7] enquired about the current whereabouts of Mr J. Mehlwurm.[8] We replied that we had no knowledge of his address. We were then informed that Mr J. Mehlwurm, as well as Dr Spitz, is wanted by the police.

We raised the issue of schools and explained that they cannot continue when pupils and teachers are systematically taken away.[9] [We were told:] The pupils will be left alone if their parents have not been taken away for labour. As for the teachers, those who are indispensable will be selected and will receive a white card exempting them from labour service. The authorities[10] require a precise report on the schools, including the numbers of pupils and teaching staff; we were asked to provide precise and complete information on the latter.[11]

2 The original contains handwritten notes and underlining.

3 The conversation took place on 23 Oct. 1942 between Kurt Asche, Hans Berlin, and Noe Nozice.

4 Eugène Hellendall (1905–1945), retailer; member of the Brussels committee of the Association of Jews in Belgium (AJB/VJB); among the founding members of the Jewish Defence Committee (CDJ/JVC) in Sept. 1942; deported with his entire family from Mechelen to Auschwitz on 24 Oct. 1942; perished in Ellrich camp in March 1945.

5 Flora Rosalie Hellendall, née Cahn (b. 1907), housewife; thought to have been murdered immediately after her arrival in Auschwitz.

6 The couple had already been deported.

7 Kurt Asche (1908–1998), apothecary; joined the NSDAP in 1931 and the SS in 1935; worked for the SD from 1935; official in charge of the SD's section for Jewish affairs in Lublin, 1939–1940 and then in Brussels, where he was official in charge of Jewish affairs for the Security Police and the SD, 1941 to Nov. 1942, and continued to work in the section until Oct. 1943; forced to transfer in 1943; sentenced to 16 months in prison for embezzlement; lived after the war in West Germany, initially under a false name; indicted in 1975; sentenced to seven years in prison in 1981.

8 Jules Mehlwurm (b. 1899), retailer; born Juda Mehlwurm in Poland; settled in Charleroi in 1934; chairman of the local branch of the AJB/VJB in Charleroi; disappeared in Oct. 1942.

9 The AJB/VJB was finally established by the Regulation on the Establishment of an Association of Jews in Belgium (25 Nov. 1941): *VOBl-BNF*, 63, no. 3, 2 Dec. 1941, pp. 798–799. It ran the Jewish schools in accordance with the regulation issued by the Military Commander in late 1941. After the mass arrests in August and Sept. 1942, numerous schools were forced to close for lack of students. On 27 Oct. 1942 two women who taught at the Nos Petits school (see Doc. 219, fn. 16) in Uccle (Flemish: Ukkel) were arrested. One was released after the Belgian Ministry of Education intervened; the other, a Dutch citizen, was deported to Auschwitz four days later.

10 This presumably means the section for Jewish affairs of the Security Police and the SD.

11 By late Dec. 1942 all Jewish schools still operating in Brussels were closed. No new Jewish school had been established in Liège or in Brussels. The Jewish school in Antwerp, however, continued to operate until July 1943.

Furthermore, we learned that, contrary to information we received previously, a new transport will probably leave Mechelen for Germany next Saturday. In all probability, this will be the last transport.[12]

Following the acceptance of Dr S. Ullmann's[13] resignation, Mr A. requested that we make new proposals for the vacancy. Mr A. remarked that he cares little whether the new president is Belgian or foreign. What is of great importance to him is that it is somebody of high calibre. He would prefer one of the gentlemen from the former Rue de Ruyenbroeck Committee[14] to take up this role because these gentlemen have proved that they can find solutions to social problems on their own, without guidance from the authorities. Mr A. asked us for names, which we refused to give because we do not know whether these gentlemen, who are immigrants, feel up to taking on such a role.[15]

We informed Mr A. that the newspaper *Le Pays réel* published an article about the Association of Jews in Belgium, in which it offered interpretations of certain facts. Mr A. does not know of this article and requests that we send it to him.

Finally, we explained the Rossin case, a boy of fourteen[16] who made false statements and demanded that we obtain a permit (from the authorities) for him so he could follow his father,[17] who had left for his labour service posting via Mechelen. We did not conceal the fact that we tried everything to keep this young man here and provide him with everything. But his relatives feel we are responsible for this case and want to report us to the Belgian authorities for kidnapping. Mr A. asked that we provide a written report on the next steps taken in this case, because he finds it interesting to know how the Belgian authorities will act in relation to this situation. We promised to write a report if we are found liable.

12 The last two transports of 1942 left Belgium on 31 Oct. 1942. After a pause of two and a half months, the deportations resumed on 15 Jan. 1943.

13 See Doc. 188.

14 Correctly: Ruysbroeck. The reference is to the Hilfswerk der Arbeitsgemeinschaft von Juden aus Deutschland (Hidag), which was founded in autumn 1940 and based at rue de Ruysbroeck in Brussels. The agency, which provided support for Jews from the German Reich wishing to settle in Belgium, was incorporated into the AJB/VJB in March 1942.

15 Two days later, the AJB/VJB's board, suspecting former members of the Rue de Ruysbroeck Committee of secretly coming to an arrangement with the German occupiers, put forward a Polish-born member of the local AJB/VJB in Antwerp as the new head. Asche rejected this suggestion because he wanted to appoint the German refugee Felix Meyer. Asche's course of action was frowned upon by the German military administration, which continued to aim for the voluntary cooperation of the Belgians; as a result, Asche was replaced by Fritz Erdmann at the end of Nov. 1942, but he continued to work closely with Erdmann. Marcel Blum became the new president of the AJB/VJB.

16 Felix Rossin (b. 1928), originally from Vienna; deported on 24 Oct. 1942 to Auschwitz, where he perished.

17 Arthur Rossin (b. 1886) had been deported on 10 Oct. 1942.

DOC. 193

Bulletin du Front de l'Indépendance (Hainaut), October 1942: article giving the Belgian population practical advice on how to help persecuted Jews[1]

The Jewish question in Belgium

Fortunately, the FI's publications have always stressed the importance of the Jewish question in Belgium. From the very first anti-Jewish measures, it seemed clear that the deportations were only the prelude to other measures that would then affect the entire population. What we had foreseen is now happening. Today, the occupier's brutal fist slams down on all Belgians without distinction.[2] However, the fact that we are threatened with persecution should not prevent us from coming to the aid of our Jewish compatriots. On the contrary, more than ever we must stand in solidarity with them to resist the oppressor.

We know the reasons behind the hateful anti-Jewish measures. The occupier needed to compensate for the labour shortage which arose due to the massacres on the Eastern front. In spite of the enormous roundups carried out in Jewish neighbourhoods[3] and then the deportations of thousands of Israelites to the East and to France, Hitler still needs more and more workers.

Belgians will take to heart the call to provide effective help to persecuted Jews. After a thorough examination of this question, we can offer our committees the following list of practical measures to help the Jewish population.[4]

Practical measures to aid the Jewish population

1) *Make the crimes committed against the Jews known everywhere.* The enslaved press has been conspicuously silent about this. People in some of the large cities know what is going on. The occupier fears the people's indignation. We must spark this indignation by letting all Belgians know what is going on in Brussels, Antwerp, Charleroi, Ghent, etc.
2) *Help the Jews resist the roundups.* We must at least come out of our apartments during the roundups, reprimand the Gestapo agents, express our contempt to the soldiers who participate in these actions, and we need to get involved whenever fights break out to help the Jews resist and escape.
3) *Help the Jews go into hiding.* Here the help of the committees in the provinces is particularly valuable. We must distribute the Jews among the non-Jewish population to

1 *Bulletin du Front de l'Indépendance* (province of Hennegau), no. 4, Oct. 1942. This document has been translated from French. The news bulletin was published illegally by the Belgian resistance organization, the Independence Front (Front de l'Indépendance–Onafhankelijkheidsfront).

2 On 6 Oct. 1942 Military Commander Alexander von Falkenhausen issued a regulation enabling the conscription of Belgians for forced labour in the Reich: *VOBl-BNF*, 87, 7 Oct. 1942, pp. 1050–1051.

3 From August to Oct. 1942, large roundups took place in Brussels, Antwerp, Liège, and several towns in northern France, in the course of which 4,468 Jews were arrested and deported: see Docs. 180 and 217.

4 In Sept. and Oct. 1942 Ghert Jospa founded the Jewish Defence Committee (CDJ/JVC) within the Front de l'Indépendance. These recommendations probably came from people associated with this group.

ensure they will not be found by the Gestapo, which we know has only limited staff at its disposal.

Here are some suggestions which the local committees should examine carefully:

4) *Save the children.*

A) Are non-Jewish families willing to take in one or several Jewish children, for free or for a small sum of money? If the cost of their board is in excess of fifteen francs a day, it is advisable to put them in institutions where they can be educated.

B) Is there a home, a school, a crèche, a boarding school, or a convent in the local community which would be willing to take in Jewish children?

5) *Save the adults.*

A) Find families who are willing to take in a Jewish boarder.

B) Find people who would be willing to move into a bigger apartment, part of which could be made available to a Jewish family. Many Jewish families are quite wealthy and would be able to pay the removal costs, the extra rent, or even the entire rent, which would enable the family providing shelter to live there for free.

C) Find hotels in the community which would be willing to take between one and four lodgers without registering them.

D) Approach institutions in the community (convents, hospices, hospitals, etc.).

E) Find wealthy families who would be willing to take on a Jewish maid or a Jewish couple, where the husband could be a manservant or provide other services.

F) Find businesses, farms, etc. which would be willing to take on a Jewish worker or farmhand.

For all of these steps, it would be helpful to go through the Centre,[5] or at least to inform it immediately of what has been done.

The roundups are becoming ever more frequent.[6] We must therefore act quickly. It is advisable to draw up an exact list of tasks in each section and each member organization, and to carefully distribute these tasks.

Finally, it may be good for the local Committee[7] to publish and distribute an appeal. Local conditions will need to be taken into consideration when writing this. The following text could be used as inspiration:

Take up arms against the Gestapo.

The Gestapo's crimes against the Jewish people cause rightful indignation in everyone who has a heart. In the middle of the night, hundreds of men, women, and children are taken from their homes, beaten up, stripped of all their belongings, and taken to Mechelen to be sent to the East.

5 This presumably refers to the secretariat of the Communist Party in Brussels, which operated underground and coordinated the Front de l'Indépendance.

6 This report seems to have been written several weeks earlier, because the centrally organized mass roundups ceased for a time in Oct. 1942. From then on, large numbers of Jews were arrested individually or in small groups. In Sept. 1943 a new large-scale roundup took place: see Doc. 214. However, more than half of the Jews deported from Belgium were arrested in individual operations against Jews or in smaller roundups.

7 The Front de l'Indépendance had regional as well as municipal and local committees, which were supposed to gain the support of both the urban and the rural population for resistance efforts against the German occupiers.

Many secret letters have reached us from unfortunate people held in Mechelen. All can be summed up with this one cry: '*Risk everything, even death, to avoid this hell!*'

The fate that awaits them in the East is even worse. Sikorski,[8] the head of the Polish government, has given shocking accounts of the executions of Jews in Poland, saying that seven to eight hundred thousand people have been murdered in cold blood. Young girls are subjected to the sadistic lust of the revolting Wehrmacht characters. Able-bodied men are spared immediate death, but are condemned to a slow agony caused by exhausting labour beyond all human capabilities, scandalously little food, and mistreatment at the hands of their torturers.

Now the Gestapo wants to deport the entire Jewish population of Belgium.

Tens of thousands of people are facing a horrible death. Time is running out. We must do everything to save them.

Jews

Save your lives by hiding. If you cannot, forcefully resist the roundups. Barricade yourselves in your homes. Alert your neighbours. Take the guns from the Gestapo thugs and shoot them like dogs. If you resist, your fate will not be worse than if you let yourselves be led to the abattoirs in Poland.

Belgians

Show your solidarity with the Jewish victims of Hitlerite barbarity. Help the Jews go into hiding. Come out of your apartments during the roundups and show your contempt to the enemy's police. Come to the aid of your Jewish compatriots. Take in their children.

Let us prepare the second front by opposing the deportations of human beings.

Let us all together beat the Nazi beast, which is drained of all the blood it is losing on the Soviet steppes, and is frightened of the imminent attack of all free men.

Occupier, get out of our country

All united for the liberation of the fatherland

8 Władysław Sikorski (1881–1943), career officer; Polish prime minister and foreign minister, 1922–1923; prime minister of the Polish government in exile from Sept. 1939 to July 1943, and simultaneously military commander-in-chief of the army in exile; killed in a place crash: see PMJ 9/140.

DOC. 194

On 2 November 1942 an SD employee in Liège reports on the arrests of Zlata Weintraub and Izydor Bernstein for currency offences[1]

Report from the field office in Liège,[2] signed Stade[3] (Staffelhauptscharführer), Liège, dated 2 November 1942[4]

On 28 October 1942, the Jewess Slata *Weintraub*,[5] née Bergasi, born in Warsaw in 1890, previously living at 4 rue de l'Armistice in Liège, approached me and offered me 0.5 kg of gold if I would release her. I asked for time to consider, as I would have to think about the matter. When I returned to the office, I went immediately to the head of the office, SS-Obersturmführer *Graf*,[6] and made a report to him. By order of the office head, I accepted the offer. I escorted the Jewess out of the Citadel[7] and had her give me the gold. She presented me with 60 Dutch 10-guilder pieces and – as in her opinion, this did not amount to half a kilo – a gold wristwatch as well. After handing over the gold, she was released by me and, about 20 m away, arrested by SS-Oberscharführer Knauseder[8] and brought to the office. In order to ascertain where Weintraub resided, she was released again. The auxiliary police official Nossent was given the task of following the Jewess. She went to the building at 143 rue Feronstreè,[9] where she was arrested once again. On this occasion, her son Selig Weintraub,[10] born in Warsaw on 24 October 1920, residing in Liège with no fixed abode, was also arrested. He was in possession of a forged identity card. He claims not to know who made the card. Both were taken to the Wehrmacht military prison in Liège and transferred to Mecheln[11] on 30 October 1942.

Likewise, the Jew Izydor *Bernstein*,[12] born in Cracow on 5 September 1908, previously residing in Liège at 26 rue de la Madeleine, approached me and offered me the sum of

1 CegeSoma, AA 585–110 C. This document has been translated from German.
2 This refers to the field office (Außendienststelle) of the Security Police and the SD in Liège.
3 Presumably Willy Stade (1904–1950), wrought-iron maker; with the Urban Police from 1925 and the Criminal Police from 1937; official in charge of Jewish affairs with the SD in Liège, 1940–1944; declared dead in Germany.
4 The original contains handwritten notes and underlining.
5 Correctly: Zlata Weintraub, née Bergazyn (b. 1894), seamstress; emigrated to Belgium before 1940; after her arrest, she was deported to Auschwitz on 31 Oct. 1942 and is thought to have been murdered there upon arrival.
6 Georg Graf (b. 1890), carpenter; joined the NSDAP and the SS in 1932; with the Criminal Police in Berlin prior to 1940; headed the field office of the Security Police and the SD in Liège, 1940–1944.
7 Belgian resistance fighters and other prisoners were incarcerated in the Liège Citadel.
8 Rudolf Knauseder (b. 1913), sales assistant; joined the NSDAP in Austria in 1934; fled to Germany the same year; member of the SA, 1934–1939; returned to Austria after 1936; worked for the Criminal Police in Salzburg as a salaried employee; in Belgium from 1940; worked for the Security Police and the SD in Liège; acquitted in Belgium in 1951.
9 Correctly: Féronstrée.
10 Selig Weintraub (b. 1920), bookkeeper; emigrated to Belgium with his parents; deported on 31 Oct. 1942 with his mother to Auschwitz, where he perished.
11 This refers to Mechelen transit camp.
12 Izydor Bernstein (1908–1942), furrier; emigrated from Poland to Belgium before 1940; deported on 31 Oct. 1942 to Auschwitz, where he perished.

250,000 Belgian francs in gold if I would release him. Here too, I accepted this offer after reporting to the head of the office and being ordered to accept. I went to the Citadel of Liège and drove with Bernstein to Liège, rue Feronstree, where, in a fur shop. I was handed 5 – five – 20-dollar pieces, 44 – forty-four – 10-dollar pieces, and 130 – one hundred and thirty – English pounds in gold.[13] Since Bernstein still had luggage in the Citadel, I told him he should come with me in my car to fetch it. As the Feldgendarmerie had arrived there in the meantime to transport the Jews to Mecheln, Bernstein was immediately handed over to the transport commander for transfer to Mecheln. Bernstein was then transferred to Mecheln by train, departing at 11.14 on 30 October 1942.

The gold was counted and taken into safekeeping by the head of the office in the presence of the undersigned and the auxiliary police official Voss.[14]

DOC. 195

On 11 November 1942 Werner von Bargen informs the Reich Foreign Office in Berlin that fewer and fewer Jews are complying with the deportation order[1]

Letter (marked 'secret') from the Brussels division of the Reich Foreign Office (no. 2528/42g), signed Werner von Bargen, Brussels, to the Reich Foreign Office, Berlin (received on 17 November 1942), dated 11 November 1942[2]

Re: Jews in Belgium
On the basis of the obligation contained in the Military Commander's Jew Regulation of 28 October 1940,[3] around 42,000 men and women (over the age of 16) have registered. Of these, 38,000 were not Belgian citizens. In total, probably 52,000 to 55,000 Jews, including children not subject to the registration requirement, were living in Belgium.[4] Of that total, 15,000 men, women, and children have been deported to the East.[5] Additional transports will soon leave Belgium. Among the deportees are stateless persons, former Germans, Czechs, Poles, Dutch people, Romanians, Greeks, Slovaks, Russians, Norwegians, Luxembourgers, Croatians, and citizens of the three Baltic states. Likewise, a few Belgians are also included, who are being deported because they failed to wear the Jewish star when in public.

13 A file note dated 3 Nov. 1942 indicates that the 'English pounds' were actually Dutch guilders: CegeSoma, AA 585–110 C. According to a further file note dated 18 Nov. 1942, the undercover agent who had orchestrated the arrests received 10 per cent of the total amount confiscated – that is, 5,604 Belgian francs – as a reward: ibid.

14 Auguste Voss (b. 1907); worked as a translator from 1940, then as an SS-Unterscharführer and Stade's assistant; sentenced in Belgium to 20 years in prison after the war.

1 PA AA, R 100 862. Published in Klarsfeld and Steinberg (eds.), *Die Endlösung der Judenfrage in Belgien*, pp. 54–55. This document has been translated from German.

2 The original contains handwritten abbreviations and underlining.

3 According to this regulation, Belgian Jews were forced to enter their names in a so-called Jew registry: see PMJ 5/158.

4 The actual number was around 70,000, as not all Jews living in Belgium registered.

5 By this time, 16,624 Jews in total had been deported on 17 transports from Mechelen to Auschwitz.

Initially, a 'labour deployment order' was delivered through the 'Association of Jews'[6] to those affected by deportation. However, because compliance with the labour deployment order dwindled over time as a result of rumours about the slaughtering of the Jews etc., the Jews were seized in roundups and individual operations.

Recently it has been found that people are illegally emigrating to France, in particular into the unoccupied territory, and to Switzerland. According to a conservative estimate, it is likely that around 3,000 to 4,000 Jews have left the country and entered Switzerland. However, no precise information is available on this.

DOC. 196

On 3 December 1942 Samuel Perl is denounced to the Antwerp Security Police[1]

Handwritten letter from L. van Genechten to the Security Police (Feldkommandantur), Antwerp, Meir, dated 3 December 1942

Dear Sir,

Tomorrow, Friday, 4 December, at 12 noon, a Jew known for his foreign currency trade will be in Café Patria, 35 Gemeentestraat, Antwerp. He is around 21 years old and wears brown boots, a black overcoat, and a cap. His name is Perl, Samuel,[2] Romanian nationality. Has a Belgian passport.

Another five Jews are hiding in Namur[3] – 188 Chaussée de Waterloo. The house has two exits: one on the main road and one on the side street.

Always at your service in order to solve this problem.

Your obliging servant,

6 This refers to the Association of Jews in Belgium (AJB/VJB), which was required to send out the summonses for deportation.

1 CegeSoma, AA 585–466. This document has been translated from Dutch.

2 Samuel Perl (b. 1920), diamond cutter; born in Ruscova (Transylvania); after the arrest and deportation of his family in Antwerp in August 1942, fled to unoccupied France; thereafter, returned to Belgium; arrested in Dec. 1942 and interned in Mechelen; escaped from the transport that departed on 15 Jan. 1943, was arrested a few days later, but managed to escape again, from the transport that departed on 19 April 1943; went into hiding until the end of the war.

3 Namur (Dutch: Namen) is a town in the province of Wallonia.

DOC. 197
On 4 December 1942 Martin Luther of the Reich Foreign Office in Berlin advocates deporting Jews with Belgian citizenship as well[1]

Letter (secret – Ko to D III 1063g), signed Luther, Berlin, to the Brussels division of the Reich Foreign Office,[2] dated 4 December 1942

In reply to the report dated 27 November 42
No. 2855/42 g[3]
Undersecretary
In diplomatic cable no. 602 from your office on 9 July of this year,[4] agreement was expressed regarding the planned transport of a substantial number of Jews, but on the other hand it was requested that deportations of Jews with Belgian citizenship should not take place for the time being. After the interim completion of the deportation operation for this year, the summing-up report on the current situation now gives occasion to re-examine the position taken on the basis of the aforementioned diplomatic cable.

If the Jews remaining in Belgium are now flouting the orders of the Military Commander and are also trying in every possible way to hide their Jewish nature and crawl away into hiding places that are hard to clear out, and, furthermore, if efforts to involve these Jews in active resistance against the occupying power can already be detected, then the further spread of this source of danger needs to be prevented through vigorous intervention.

I therefore venture to request that, in consultation with the Military Commander,[5] options are considered to extend the measures to all Jews in Belgium and concentrate them in assembly camps until transports can be carried out. Individual questions regarding the exceptional treatment of certain Jews such as those in mixed marriages, those of the Christian faith or with children can be resolved in consultation with the Security Police.

Belgium will have to be thoroughly cleansed of Jews sooner or later, without fail. Given that previous transports have made the population sufficiently familiar with these matters and have prepared the Jews themselves for further measures, there is much to be said for carrying out the measures at the present time. The fact that all the Jews were evacuated in the neighbouring Netherlands should have left the Belgian Jews in no doubt in this regard. Moreover, in addition to the necessary elimination of the aforementioned dangers, it is advisable not to keep the population in a permanent state of unrest, but rather to carry out the unavoidable measures without interruption, one after the other. Postponing them to a later point in time might only have the undesired effect of making

1 PA AA, R 100 862. Published in Klarsfeld and Steinberg (eds.), *Die Endlösung der Judenfrage in Belgien*, pp. 55–57. This document has been translated from German.
2 The representative of the Reich Foreign Office in Belgium was Werner von Bargen.
3 In that report, von Bargen stated that almost 17,000 Jews had been deported from Belgium so far. Although black marketeering had been curbed, he reported, many Jews were now refusing to obey the orders of the military administration and were obtaining forged papers: PA AA, R 100 862.
4 See Doc. 175.
5 Alexander von Falkenhausen.

the oppositional propaganda campaign that is under way flare up again just when it has, for the most part, abated in this area.

A report on this matter is requested as soon as possible.[6]

DOC. 198

On 6 December 1942 the Association of Jews in Belgium complains to the Feldkommandantur in Antwerp about impostors in police uniforms stealing from Jews[1]

Letter (secretary's office JS/CE) from the Association of Jews in Belgium, Antwerp branch, signed Dr Marcel Laufer[2] and N. D. Workum, engineer,[3] to Feldkommandantur 520, Police Section, 24 Meir, Antwerp, dated 6 December 1942

As requested, we are sending you the statements we recorded, made by three victims of the activities of the uniformed men against whom we initiated legal proceedings during our visit on 1 December.

Three more victims have come forward, and we will send you the record of their statements at a later time.[4]

Dr Marcel Laufer

N. D. Workum, Engineer

Statement by Mrs Hanna *Lilienthal*, married to Dr Fritz *Basch*,[5] born in Wilmersdorf on 17 December 1904, German citizen, residing at 90 Pl. Moretuslei in Antwerp.

> On the night of 23/24 November at midnight, two men in uniform entered my apartment. They appeared to be 20 to 25 years old. One was tall, blond, with pale skin, and the other somewhat shorter with darker skin. Both wore caps with a death's

6 Von Bargen replied on 5 Jan. 1943 that the deportations could not be resumed until the spring of 1943 because of the shortage of means of transport. Until then, he said, the foreign Jews would be imprisoned in Mechelen camp. The deportations would affect foreign Jews first, he added, and only later Jews with Belgian citizenship, whose number the German authorities estimated at around 4,000 persons: PA AA, R 100 862. The deportation of Jews with Belgian citizenship did not actually begin until the summer of 1943: see Doc. 212.

1 Kazerne Dossin – Mechelen, A002930. This document has been translated from German.

2 Dr Marcel Laufer (b. 1907), lawyer; executive director of the Antwerp branch of the Association of Jews in Belgium (AJB/VJB); arrested in Sept. 1943; deported on 20 Sept. 1943 from Mechelen to Auschwitz, where he perished.

3 Nico David Workum (b. 1907), civil engineer; emigrated to Belgium from the Netherlands in 1929; Belgian citizen; architect at the Belgian Post Office; vice president of the AJB/VJB and chairman of its Antwerp branch; arrested in Sept. 1943; deported on 20 Sept. 1943 from Mechelen to Auschwitz, where he perished.

4 The accounts provided by these individuals are also in the file. On 9 Dec. 1942, the Antwerp branch of the AJB/VJB was informed by the administrative chief of Feldkommandantur 520 that the perpetrators had been found and arrested, and the records given to the Security Police and the SD.

5 Hanna Basch, née Lilienthal (b. 1904), housewife, and her husband Dr Fritz Basch (b. 1900), physician employed in Mechelen camp, had emigrated to Belgium from Germany; on 20 Sept. 1943 they were deported from Mechelen to Auschwitz, where they perished.

head and dark-brown leather coats with swastika armbands. They had pistols on their belts, but did not draw them. The first one had a briefcase, allegedly containing a warrant for my arrest. The first one said to me when he came in: 'Mrs Basch, your husband is in Mechelen; we have a complaint against you made by a Flemish man who claims that you possess firearms and foreign currency. We have been ordered to search the premises.' This so-called house search was simply laughable in its superficiality. While one stayed by my side, the other went quickly through the apartment and then said to the first one: 'Found nothing.' Then they asked me: 'Do you have any money?' I showed them my wallet, which was rejected, however. Then, in a drawer, I showed them 10,000 francs in banknotes, which were 'confiscated'. An ordinary camera, an old typewriter, and a good pair of opera glasses were rejected.

'Do you have anything else, gold, silver, jewellery?' they asked me. – 'Be careful, if you lie, you'll go where your husband is.' – 'What do you live on, anyway?' – I said that I received the salary of my husband, a physician in the Mechelen assembly camp.

At that point, a bogus telephone conversation took place:

– 'We are here in the … What's your name? … *Basch* residence; search concluded, nothing found except money, yes, yes.'

At that, the other one asked: 'Shouldn't we have the telephone tapped?'

Here came a second bogus telephone conversation: 'Please arrange for telephone number 288.39 to be tapped.'

The telephone conversation was definitely fictitious, because no voice could be heard at the other end, just the characteristic ringing.

Both spoke perfect German, and the short one, in my opinion, is definitely a German.

The caretaker told me afterwards that, when the two came in, they said the following: 'We're looking for a Jew, *Berkowitz*, who is hiding here.' – 'There's no *Berkowitz* here.'– 'Do other Jews live here, then?' –'The *Basch* and *Löwenthal* families.'

I have nothing else to add.

Antwerp, 1 December 1942.

Hanna Basch née Lilienthal.

Statement by Mrs Sara *Esquenazi*, married to Jacques *Menache*,[6] born on 20 January 1893, Belgian citizen, residing at 27 Ant. Van Dyckstraat in Antwerp.

Mrs *Menache* tells us:

On 30 November 1942 at 10 p.m., two men in uniform rang the bell and told me through the window that they had to examine my papers. Although I asked permission to postpone this until the next morning, I had to open the door. Before me stood two young men in dark-blue raincoats and death's head caps. The SS emblem was visible on their collars. The first one was tall, blond, and had pale skin. The other was somewhat shorter, with a round face and brownish hair. I had to show my papers, and then they asked about foreign currency. I showed them the certificate stating that my husband had regularly handed in his foreign currency in accordance with

6 Sara Menache, née Esquenazi (b. 1893), and Jacques Menache (b. 1878), diamond merchant; Jacques Menache had emigrated to Belgium from Constantinople in 1894. The Menaches were temporarily arrested and interned in Mechelen at the beginning of Sept. 1943; after their release, they lived in the Jewish home for the elderly in Anderlecht run by the AJB/VJB until early Oct. 1944. Both survived the war in Belgium.

the regulation and that his stock of diamonds had been registered with the Control Office. The men asked whether I had a telephone. I said no and referred them to the delicatessen at no. 3 on the same street. One of the men indicated that he would go there to place a telephone call to the office. Then they asked what we lived on, how much money we needed every month, and told me in a threatening tone: 'Give me everything you have, or else we will ransack the whole house, and if we find something, we'll send you to Mechelen.' At that, I gave them a platinum ring with a 6-carat blue sapphire and 12 to 14 brilliant-cut diamonds, valued at around 25,000 francs; I also gave them a gold ring with an oval turquoise bordered by small diamonds, valued at around 5,000 francs; a gold ladies' cigarette holder with the inscription 'From HPP. to H.P.'; 37.5 grams of 9-carat gold, valued at around 3,000 francs; also a gold tie-pin with a pearl and edged with small diamonds, valued at around 2,000 francs; finally, in addition I gave the men 9,800 francs in cash.

They said they would come back the next day between 6 and 8 p.m., after they had examined the validity of my statements.

The money and the pieces of jewellery were placed in special envelopes and sealed.

At that, my husband, who had until then taken virtually no part in these exchanges because he is hard of hearing, stated that he would not let them take the two envelopes but would take them to the Feldkommandantur himself. Upon hearing that, one of the two drew his gun. Then the two men left with their spoils.

The next day, I inquired in the shop at no. 3 in the same street whether a uniformed man had placed a telephone call there the previous night. I was told that no one had come in.

I lodged a complaint regarding the incident with the Security Service, 21 Della Faillelaan, Antwerp; after my statement was taken, I was given a slip of paper on which the following was written:

'The perpetrators are assumed to be Belgians, and the victims are also Belgians, so the Belgian police are in charge of the case.'

I went immediately to the police station for the 7th Wijk,[7] where a record of my statement was made.

Antwerp, 1 December 1942.
S. Esquenazi
Mrs J. Menache

Amendments to the statement by Mrs Sara Esquenazi, married name Menache.

When I gave the two men 9,800 francs in cash, I told them that this was all I had at home, but in addition I had an account at the Diamond Bank in Pelikaanstraat, in Antwerp, as well as 4,000 to 5,000 francs in a locker at the Diamond Club.[8]

After handing over everything, I had to sign a written confirmation, which also included this set expression: 'Requisitioned by the SS', in addition to an illegible signature and the date 30 November 1942.

A duplicate of this confirmation was handed to me. I provided it to the police station for the 7th District.

7 Dutch in the original: 'district', a reference to the headquarters of the 7th Police District in Antwerp.

8 In 1898 the Jewish diamond merchant Adolphe Adler founded the N.V. Diamantclub van Antwerpen as a trading centre. By 1930 four additional so-called diamond exchanges had been created.

When I was leaving, the people said that everything owned by my son, who is an English citizen, would definitely be given back the next day between 6 and 8 p.m. This amounted to 3,800 francs. The remainder, they said, would go into a blocked account.

The exact wording of the confirmation given to me by the S.D. is:

'As the victims are Belgians and the thieves are most likely also Belgians, the Belgian police are in charge of the case.'

Antwerp, 6 December 1942.

Statement by Mrs Seindel *Herskovics*,[9] married to Mozes *Löwenthal*, born on 13 May 1913, Belgian citizen, 90 Plantijn Moretuslei, Antwerp.

On the night of 23 November towards 11.30 p.m., two young men came to my apartment. My impression was that they were 19 to 20 years old. They wore an armband with a swastika and long raincoats. Both are of average height. They asked me: 'Who lives with you?' – My mother and a nurse. – 'Passports!' They made a note of the passports. Then one asked, 'Where is the nurse?' I pointed out the room where the nurse, Miss *Maitkes*, was sleeping. She was asked to establish her identity, and when she said she was authorized by Feldkommandantur 520, she received this reply: 'Oh well, you're OK', without any further searching for her papers.

After that, I was asked: 'Do you have a telephone in the apartment?' – I do not have one. – 'You've been betrayed; you have firearms, foreign currency, jewellery, diamonds.' I answered that they should go ahead and conduct a search, because I did not have any of those things; my husband was with the Organization Todt, I said and it had been a long time since I had heard anything from him.[10] 'You have money?' I showed them that I had 700 francs there with me. 'Then what do you live on and how do you pay rent, if that is all you have?' I explained that my husband had paid the rent for several months in advance before he was called up for the Organization Todt.

There followed a very brief search of the premises, which produced nothing. I was threatened: 'You know what to expect if you have lied to us. Is 5,000 francs really all you have?'

As they were leaving, they noticed the house telephone and said: 'Aha, so you have a telephone after all?' I explained that it was just the caretaker's telephone.

That is all I have to say; I was too upset to make a mental note of the precise details.

Antwerp, 2 December 1942.

S. Herskovics Löwenthal

9 Seindel Löwenthal, née Herskovics (b. 1913), housewife; born in Brusztura (Carpatho-Ukraine, now Ukraine); lived in Czechoslovakia and, from 1933, in Belgium; deported on 20 Sept. 1943 from Mechelen to Auschwitz, where she perished.

10 Mozes Löwenthal was presumably among the Jews who had been sent to the Organization Todt labour camps at the Atlantic Wall in the spring of 1942. Nothing could be ascertained about his fate.

DOC. 199
Brüsseler Zeitung, 12 December 1942: article alleging that Jews are hiding in vacant apartments in the city[1]

Corpus delicti

In certain buildings in Brussels, mysterious things have been happening over the last few months. In the evening hours, four, seven, or more persons gathered in an apartment – no resident of the building had ever seen them before – and set up camp there. The next morning, the little nameplate next to the main doorbell had strange names on it.

One day a woman encountered a young girl on the street, an acquaintance from earlier times, and wished her good day. She was doing tolerably well, she said; perhaps they might start to visit one another once in a while. 'Where are you living now?' In reply to this question, the girl did not give a satisfactory answer but displayed a certain wariness in her response that, because she was a Jew and wanted to live somewhat incognito, she lived in a different place every day. Now with these acquaintances, now with those. The other Jews, she said, were doing the same. The woman never learned where the Jewess was living …

In that same four-storey apartment building, on one level of which the unknowns assembled every evening – the reader has guessed by now that these persons, too, were Jews – a master tailor had also set up his workshop. A hardworking expert in his field, and therefore highly valued and in demand. Politics was of little interest to him; he had his work and was glad that he always earned enough to feed his family.

Things went well until, one day, the Jewish colony in the building where he lived on one floor was hunted out; the whole group were in possession of fake passports. The nameplate next to the doorbell contained false names, of course, and a huge gang of tricksters and dishonourable types was exposed. Because there are always people who pity even the greatest frauds and blackguards, there were some who wanted to see the master tailor as the betrayer of the Jewish gang that was brought to light. Evidence of that could not be found, of course – and, in fact, it had not been he who betrayed them – but, just a few weeks earlier, had he not *received an order for uniforms for three Rexists? Of course, one knew that he was not a Rexist, but this order … if that's not a real corpus delicti.*

There are in fact non-Jewish customers who have avoided the tailor ever since, just because a few Jews made trouble for him. Such demonstrative avoidance may one day be a very unpleasant piece of evidence against them; indeed, the final chapter has yet to be written.

ei.[2]

1 *Brüsseler Zeitung*, 12 Dec. 1942, p. 5. This daily newspaper was published by the German military administration from July 1940 to Sept. 1944, with a circulation averaging 100,000 copies on weekdays and 200,000 on weekends. This document has been translated from German.

2 The author of the article could not be identified.

DOC. 200

On 14 December 1942 Moshe Flinker describes going to see the film *Jud Süß*[1]

Handwritten journal of Moshe Flinker,[2] entry for 14 December 1942

14 December, midnight

Yesterday I went to the cinema with my sister.[3] When I was still in The Hague, before the occupation by the Germans, I did not go to the cinema much. After the Germans had been in Holland for some time, they forbade Jews to go to the cinema.[4] Then they began showing antisemitic films at the cinemas. I wanted very much to see these films, but I could not because my identity card was stamped 'J' for Jew. And if they had even the slightest doubt, they could have asked me to show that card, and for such an offence, I believe, people have been sentenced to six months' imprisonment. But now that I am in Belgium, and here I am not registered as a Jew, I can go to the cinema, and here they are not so strict about it. When I came here, there was nothing written yet on the windows [of these cinema buildings] to say that Jews could not enter, except for a few places whose owners were antisemites. Now, however, in front of every cinema is posted: 'By order of the German authorities, Jews are forbidden to enter cinemas.'

Nevertheless, I went to see the film *Jud Süß*.[5] What I saw there made my blood boil. I was red in the face when I came out. Now I knew what these villains were planning, I saw through their tricks, how they strive with all their might to inject the poison of antisemitism into the gentiles' blood. As I watched the film, I suddenly remembered something this scoundrel had said in one of his speeches: 'Whichever side wins the war, antisemitism will spread and spread until the Jews are no more.'[6] He said something like that. And here I observed the ruses he will use to attain his goal. And I realized that unless something changes, he will surely be able to get that toxin into their blood.

The way he stirs zealotry, hate, and enmity among the gentiles is simply impossible for me to describe. Similarly, I do not have words to describe how devious he is. One thing I know for sure: unless we are saved now by some miracle from heaven, our end is as certain as the fact that I am sitting here. For not only the body of Israel is being attacked, but also its spirit. Here he is giving the Jews such a bad name among the gentiles that even rivers of persimmons will not be able to banish it. When I left the cinema, I

1 The original is privately owned. Copy in IfZ-Archives, F 601. Published in *Young Moshe's Diary: The Spiritual Torment of a Jewish Boy in Nazi Europe* (Jerusalem: Yad Vashem, 1971), pp. 42–44. The original diary was written in Hebrew. This document is based on the published English translation, with additional content translated from the original Hebrew.

2 Moshe Ze'ev Flinker (1926–1944/1945); born in The Hague; fled with his family to Brussels in 1942; arrested in April 1944; deported from Mechelen to Auschwitz in May 1944; perished either in Auschwitz or in April 1945 in Vaihingen.

3 Moshe had five sisters, who were deported along with their entire family from Mechelen to Auschwitz in May 1944; they survived the war and emigrated to Israel.

4 From 9 Jan. 1941 Jews in the Netherlands were forbidden from visiting cinemas: *Het Parool*, 14 Jan. 1941, p. 4.

5 This antisemitic film by director Veit Harlan, personally commissioned by Reich Minister of Propaganda Joseph Goebbels, was released in 1940. It was intended to strengthen antisemitic stereotypes through the negative depiction of the Jewish banker Joseph Süß Oppenheimer (1698–1738).

6 This is probably a reference to a similar declaration in a speech given by Hitler on 30 Jan. 1939: see PMJ 2/248.

realized the nature of the fiend and all his little fiends. I studied him and I understand him and when I left, I knew what I had to do to achieve my objective, God willing.

In the film, Jew Süss says to a young girl: 'We too have a God, but this God is the Lord of Vengeance.' These words, placed in the mouth of an actor playing a Jew, are false and deceitful. Our Lord is the same Lord who said, 'Love thy neighbour as thyself.'[7] However, precisely because He is now a Lord of Vengeance, may He now appear in that form. Now I shall ask of him:

O Lord of Vengeance, please come forth
Avenge the blood of Your servants
And Your dignity and that of Your people
Whom the gentiles, the ugliest and most disgusting of them,
Have sullied.

Either way, the quarrels at home are multiplying every day. Despite the bitter fate of the man who fled to Switzerland and had to return to Brussels, thanking God a thousand times over for having achieved this at least, despite all this my mother[8] still wants to go to Switzerland. And whenever there is an opportunity, she says that this or that thing would not have happened to us had we gone to Switzerland, the land of gold, silver and precious stones. And my father[9] rarely takes this lying down; eventually he answers with biting comments to which my mother has no lack of retorts. Most of these fights end with my father insulting my mother's family and my mother insulting my father himself by accusing him of never listening to her. And each time my parents fight or quarrel, I become angry all over again and my heart fills with hatred for those people who are responsible for pitting my parents against each other.

There is no portion of my people whom I truly hate. I love them all. I even love the merchants, whose occupation I hate, just as I love the rest of my people. I do, however, loathe one group. They are responsible for at least half the disasters in the family of the past generation and for some of those in this generation. I mean the matchmakers. They, and they alone, are guilty of the quarrels that occur in my family. They trade in love, which many sages define as the most exalted thing in the world. They treat it like merchandise. And a family life that is built on such a rickety foundation obviously reflects this. On their heads be this sin. And I strongly doubt whether they can repent for it. A person can repent for his sins only when he sees the results of what he has done. What can I say about the repentance of these murderers? When these people see that a match they brokered has 'not gone well', they look at it merely as a business transaction that did not turn out satisfactorily. They will pay for all the pain that they have caused, if payment is even possible.

These past few days I have not done or learned much. I pass the time idly. But it does not matter. The time will come when I will take revenge and make up for lost time and I will finally get everything done at once. Either way, we have not received our permits yet, but my father still remains hopeful and keeps expecting them every day. Of course

7 This commandment is found in the Torah in Leviticus 19:18.

8 Mindla Flinker, née de Rochanini (1895–1944), housewife; born in Warsaw; emigrated to the Netherlands; arrested in April 1944 and deported from Mechelen to Auschwitz in May 1944.

9 Lajzer Noech Flinker (1898–1944), businessman; born in Yalta; emigrated to the Netherlands; deported along with his family from Mechelen to Auschwitz in May 1944.

this too is a source of quarrels. When we get the permission, perhaps there will be less fighting, or it might even stop altogether. While I was at the library today getting some books, I heard the librarian say that the Rexists have been trying for the past few nights to set the Great Synagogue on fire, but so far they have not been successful.

DOC. 201
On 5 January 1943 Fritz Mannheimer asks the Trappist monk Father Eustachius to find a hiding place for a Jewish child[1]

Handwritten letter from Frederic Meierle,[2] Brussels, to Father Eustachius,[3] St Sixtus Abbey,[4] Westvleteren, dated 5 January 1943

Most Reverend Father Eustachius,

I am pleased to take the opportunity today to send a few lines to you. I hope that you are enjoying the best of health, as I can say of myself as well. After taking my leave early on New Year's Day, I arrived back at my abode towards 4 o'clock, after changing trains several times. It is certainly no pleasure to undertake journeys in this day and age, but we are subject to the times in which we live. I am particularly happy to have made your acquaintance there, Most Reverend Father Eustachius, as a fellow believer and a compatriot, and I can also assure you today of my most sincere friendship. For all the courtesies you have shown me, I can only say to you today, with all my heart, God bless you; I will not fail to include you in my prayers. I also have a heartfelt wish to express my gratitude to the Reverend Father Bursar as well and to the Father who exchanged the food coupons for me so that they didn't expire, but I do not have their addresses for correspondence. I would be very grateful to you for this information. I will also write separate letters to the Reverend Father Abbot, Father Prior and Father Hotel-keeper.

Now, concerning the matter of finding a place for the little 6-year-old boy by the name of Henricus Rudolph *Meenen*,[5] about which I also sought your advice, I cordially request once again, Most Reverend Father Eustachius, that you lend your support to this case and discuss it in detail with Reverend Father Prior again, possibly also with the

1 Archief Sint-Sixtusabdij, 4.WO2/Oorlog 1 Mannheimer 1 1942–1945/letter no. 1. Published in Rosine De Dijn, *'Du darfst nie sagen, dass du Rachmil heißt': Die Geschichte von Laja Menen und ihrem Sohn Rudi* (Munich: Deutsche Verlagsanstalt, 2005), pp. 194–196. This document has been translated from German.

2 Siegfried (Fritz) Mannheimer, also known as Frederic Meierle (1888–1950), retailer; converted to Catholicism; imprisoned in Dachau in Nov./Dec. 1938; fled to Belgium in 1939; incarcerated in French camps, 1940–1942; fled back to Belgium in July 1942; returned to Germany in 1946.

3 Father Eustachius (1890–1967), priest; born Franz Mütsch in Württemberg; emigrated to Belgium in 1910; took holy orders there in St Sixtus Abbey; lived in a monastery in the Eifel, 1914–1921, then returned to St Sixtus Abbey.

4 St Sixtus Abbey was founded in 1831 by the Trappist order, a branch of the Cistercian order. The Abbey still exists today.

5 Correctly: Rudolf Rachmil Menen (1936–2003); born in Berlin; came to Belgium with his mother in 1939; baptized a Catholic in 1942; hidden in the home of the Verplaetse family from Jan. 1943 (see Doc. 204); joined the US Army in the 1950s to obtain US citizenship; emigrated in 1961 to the USA, where he worked as a retailer.

other Fathers. As I have already mentioned, this case is urgent, since the boy's mother[6] is extremely worried about her child. Reverend Father Prior knows the case in great detail, and he also thinks, as he told me, that he can place the boy with a family of his acquaintance or with a childless couple whom he knows.[7]

No more for today, please accept my warmest regards, Reverend Father Eustachius
Most respectfully

Please address letters to Mme Suzanne Bourgeois in Brussels, 2 pl. Surlet du Choqier[8]

DOC. 202

On 15 January 1943 the representative of the Chief of the Security Police and the SD reports that more and more Jews are fleeing to avoid deportation[1]

Excerpt from the reports from Belgium and northern France (no. 1/43, marked 'secret, present immediately') by the representative of the Chief of the Security Police and the SD for the area of the Military Commander in Belgium and Northern France,[2] unsigned, Brussels, dated 15 Jan. 1943

Jews

Over the course of the past month, the *transfers of Jews* to Mechelen, which have continued on a reduced scale, have resulted in most Jewish families no longer living together. Their hope is that this tactic will somehow enable them to avoid the deportations to the East after all. In contrast to earlier times, therefore, operations against Jews now only rarely result in the arrest of full family units. There are even cases where sizeable numbers of Jewish children, whose parents have either fled or been taken to Mechelen or are living illegally in Brussels or in the countryside, are found living with Aryan families. Sometimes these children are even registered by name with the Belgian Children's Welfare Society[3] as having been placed with the Aryan families. The extent to which the Jewish population has already gone underground is clearly indicated by a report from Antwerp, the city well known for having the largest number of Jews in all of Belgium. In the Jewish school that still exists there, only 100 Jewish pupils in total are now being taught.

6 Laja Menen (1915–1943), housekeeper; born in Warsaw; worked for a Jewish family in Torgelow, 1932–1937; fled from Berlin to Belgium in 1939; arrested in May 1943; deported to Auschwitz on 31 July 1943.

7 See Doc. 204.

8 Correctly: place Surlet de Chokier.

1 CegeSoma, AA 553. This document has been translated from German.

2 Ernst Ehlers (1909–1980), lawyer; joined the NSDAP in 1928 and the SS in 1932; worked at the Saxon Ministry of the Interior, 1935–1937; with the SD from 1938; from Dec. 1941 representative of the Chief of the Security Police and the SD in Belgium and Northern France, in charge of the deportation of the Jews from these territories; judge at the Schleswig Administrative Court after 1945; committed suicide while awaiting trial.

3 Founded in 1919, the Œuvre nationale de l'enfance, an association governed by public law, was responsible for all aspects of child welfare. During the occupation, the local sections in Antwerp and Brussels worked closely with the Association of Jews in Belgium (AJB/VJB) and tried to protect Jewish children from deportation: see Doc. 219.

The deadline for the completion of the total evacuation of Jews from the territories occupied by Germany is generally assumed to be 1 May 1943. It is therefore also expected in Jewish circles that Jews holding citizenship of enemy nations will shortly be included in the evacuation as well.

The improvement in morale that was observed in Jewish circles after the military and political events in North Africa has subsided again, now that the anticipated great successes of the English and American landing forces have failed to materialize.[4] Incidentally, the attempts to assassinate members of the Wehrmacht in Brussels[5] have aroused great consternation in Jewish circles. Given the well-known anti-Jewish attitude of the German authorities, it was seen as likely that the sharpest reprisals would also be directed against the Jews in particular. This was even more the case as it was rumoured in Jewish circles that Jews had been involved in the attempted assassinations of members of the Wehrmacht and citizens of the Reich.

The flight of Jews to foreign countries also continues. Switzerland and the Italian-occupied territories in the south of France are viewed as the preferred destinations for refugees.[6] The Italians are said to be still treating the Jews extremely well. It is said that the Jewish question in Italy and in the territories occupied by Italy can never be handled in the same way as in the territories under German control, because the influence of the Vatican would not permit this. The route to Spain and Portugal has begun to be avoided by Jews in many cases, as these countries are rumoured to be unofficially occupied by the Germans.

[…][7]

DOC. 203

On 22 January 1943 Moshe Flinker records his consternation at the deportation of a family[1]

Handwritten diary of Moshe Flinker, entry for 22 January 1943

16 Shvat[2]

Yesterday my mother told me to visit the sexton, whom I have already mentioned, to buy from him coupons for clothing and, if he had any, for bread. I went to him. I was mildly happy. It was warm. The sun was shining. I felt that spring had already arrived, even though we are only at the fifteenth of Shvat. I took the number 5 [tram] to see him. When I reached his house I rang once, twice, three times, but nobody opened the door. Until then, I had been ringing the bell that he had made for himself so that visitors who want

4 On the night of 7 Nov. 1942, Allied troops had landed on the coasts of Morocco and Algeria. The fighting in North Africa continued until May 1943.

5 In Dec. 1942, there were 52 attacks and acts of sabotage directed against the German occupiers in the Brussels metropolitan area alone. For the most part, these were carried out by the immigrant sections of the partisan organization Francs-tireurs et partisans – Main d'œuvre immigrée, FTP-MOI), which also included Jews.

6 See Introduction, p. 55 and Docs. 195 and 299.

7 The remaining sections of the report could not be found.

1 The original is privately owned. Copy in IfZ-Archives, F 601. Published in *Young Moshe's Diary*, pp. 69–71. This document is based on the published English translation, with additional content translated from the original Hebrew.

2 This corresponds to 22 Jan. 1943 (Shvat/Shevat is the fifth month in the Jewish calendar).

to visit him could ring without disturbing the tenants living on other floors. Then I rang the house bell for the whole building, and after I had rung twice, I heard someone coming to the door. The door opened and a woman appeared. I could see that she was trembling all over, I asked her whether the people I had rung for were not at home. She answered me in French that yesterday these people had been taken away, in a car. Hearing this news, I was entirely shaken. A tremor surged through my body. I felt as if I was face-to-face with the Angel of Death. To be absolutely sure, I asked her who it was who had come to take this family, [and] the woman told me: the Germans. After having said that, she showed me the doors to the apartment which had been sealed, with a swastika imprinted on the seal. I told the woman that I understood everything, because she told me in an apologetic tone of voice that she had not been home when they were taken. Then I left. As I stood in the street, I saw that the shutters were closed. I thought: this man took such pains to hide from the Germans and now, despite all his efforts, he has been snatched – he, his wife, and his two children. The younger was a four-year-old girl. As I walked to the tram, I was still trembling all over. I did not know what to think. This time it seemed to me that I had personally witnessed this abduction. On other occasions when acquaintances of mine had been abducted, I had heard about it before I had to go to them. In those cases, it was as if those people had disappeared from my world. They no longer existed for me. They had gone to another world that very much resembled the World of Truth.[3] But in this case everything was different. I had known nothing. Unsuspecting I went to visit them to buy something I needed and then leave. But it was as if the Germans did not want that to happen and so snatched him and his family away beforehand. Nothing remained of the little happiness I had had on the way there. Anguish and sadness took its place. On my way there, I had told myself that in the summer I would stroll in the woods near my home, but when I got home, I put aside all the strolls and everything else that I had thought to do that summer. I did not want to enjoy anything. I wanted to grieve and stay at home all summer long. I do not want to grant myself the slightest happiness. I only want to seek ways to torture myself. With all my body and soul, I wish to be with my people and share its bitter fate. When trouble befalls it, so should it befall me. I want to be at one with my people. I do not know how I can banish even the smallest joy from my heart, but I will find ways. I thought: in what state were those people when they got into the car? Weeping? Or perhaps they steeled themselves and climbed in with the spirit of 'Into thy hand, I commit my spirit'?[4] That man[5] had moved to a new place just two weeks ago. It had cost him much effort. Yet he had had to do it, otherwise he would have been caught. At home, Mother told me that she had visited the family only two days ago. And the woman had invited her to sit down. And after my mother had sat down, the woman told her that their previous house had been searched a few days earlier. And she added that she had left the place just in time and that the Holy One Blessed be He will define it as a lucky moment, a mazeldike minut as they say in Yiddish. As she spoke, her husband sat there deep in thought. And now they are no more. This man had been persecuted in Germany before

3 Meaning: 'the hereafter'. In the Jewish faith, the soul leaves the body after death and merges with a spiritual world of truth.

4 Based on the beginning of the liturgical poem 'Adon Olam' (Master of the World), which is recited daily at the beginning of the morning prayer and also commonly sung on Shabbat in synagogues.

5 The reference is to the synagogue sexton.

the war. This was the second time he and his family had fallen into the Germans' hands. The first time he had been able to flee from Germany with ten marks. This time he took nothing with him. I did not know what to think, what to say, what to do. I saw in the street that the goyim[6] were happy and rejoicing, none of it affecting them at all. It is like being in a great hall where many people are rejoicing and dancing and carousing but there are also a few people who are not happy, are not dancing. And every now and then a few people of the latter kind are led away to another room and strangled. The happy, dancing people in the hall do not care about it at all. It almost seems that they are happier as a result and their celebrating even more exuberant.

Yes, that is how it is, no other way. The goyim are literally animals. The day will come when they will pay for their behaviour.

As I said the afternoon prayers that day, I wanted to pour out my heart to God through the Shmone esre.[7] But I found this form much too small. I could not fit into it all that I had in my heart. I did not know whose zechut[8] could make it possible for me to pray. Our forefathers are too far from us. Our people? It seems to have no zechut at all; otherwise, so many troubles could not have befallen it. Maybe the most effective prayer would be to pray for the magnitude of the woes. Even if our sins cannot be counted, our woes are already great. A few more and we will be done for entirely.

DOC. 204
On 27 January 1943 Marie-José Verplaetse agrees to take in a Jewish boy to live with her family[1]

Handwritten letter from Marie-José Verplaetse,[2] Waregem, Nieuwenhove, to Rafael Verbeke,[3] dated 27 January 1943[4]

Wednesday evening, 9 o'clock

Dear cousin Rafaël,

You will see that this time I am much quicker to respond – as it was only this morning that we received your postcard.

6 Goyim (plural, from goy): term commonly used in Jewish discourse to refer to a Gentile.
7 The eighteen, also called Amidah, which comprises 19 (formerly 18) praises and requests, is central to Jewish liturgy. The prayer is recited three times a day.
8 Zechut (plural: zechuyot), literally: 'merit(s)'. In traditional Jewish thought zechut/zechuyot means the accumulated power of good deeds to protect someone (or a community) from danger or their own sins; this accumulated power is transferred from parents to children. The zechuyot of forefathers ('zechut avot'), especially those of the founding fathers of the Jewish people (Abraham, Isaac, and Jacob), are considered to be especially protecting; this is what Flinker is referring to here.

1 Published (partly in facsimile form) in De Dijn, *'Du darfst nie sagen, daß du Rachmil heißt'*, pp. 208–210. This document has been translated from Dutch.
2 Marie-José Verplaetse (b. 1917), teacher; taught in Nieuwenhove from the early 1930s; moved to Antwerp after her marriage in 1947.
3 Rafael Verbeke, religious name Father Idesbald (1898–1974), priest; from 1930 at St Sixtus Abbey, where he was novice master, master of ceremonies, and subprior; also cellarer at the abbey, 1940–1958.
4 The abbreviation 'J.M.J.' was added by hand on the top left; it is unclear what this refers to.

And I had no trouble at all working out what our dear cousin from Westvleteren wanted from us.[5]

Father, Mother, brothers, sisters, and I[6] all completely agreed that the boy can come and stay with us. 'Where there's enough food for nine mouths, there's enough to feed a tenth,' Father and Mother said. 'If another mouth to feed should put us in the direst need, we'll not despair nor fear our plight, the Lord will help us with his might!'[7] There was only one problem we had to solve: 'Where will the boy sleep?' When all nine of us are at home, all the bedrooms are full. But where there's a will, there's a way! And the three brothers have rearranged things as well as they can to make sure the 'new little brother' also has a good place to sleep. We will all do our best to make sure the boy will soon get used to staying with us and will feel *'at home'* among us.

We will also try to teach him the Dutch language, as well and as quickly as possible. The boy will certainly also have to do his best at school, as he will be taught by Master Albert![8]

As far as food is concerned, Mother will take care of that. The boy will not lack for anything. The only thing Mother wanted me to ask, dear Rafaël, is that he brings his ration card with him (if that is possible and if his parents allow him to do so). And, in addition to his clothes, also some underwear – as we currently do not have any garments for a small boy any more.

As you can see, dear cousin Rafaël, we are all very much looking forward to *your arrival with the boy from the city.* The sooner the better!

Could you please send us a card with details of when we can expect you both? Once again, just come as soon as you can!

Dear cousin, warmest greetings from us all; we will see you in a few days, God willing!!

Your cousin[9]

5 Fritz Mannheimer had approached St Sixtus Abbey to ask for help in finding a place for the Jewish boy Rudolf Rachmil Menen: see Doc. 201. As a result, Father Idesbald asked his cousin's family whether they could take him in.

6 The family consisted of the parents, Clement Verplaetse (1881–1949), teacher, and his wife, Augusta, née van den Broucke (1890–1956), and their children, Marie-José, Léon, Cécile, Jeanne, Julienne, Albert, and Julien.

7 Here the author of the letter quotes the last stanza of an old Flemish song.

8 This presumably refers to Albert Verplaetse, who, like his father, was a teacher at Waregem primary school.

9 Rudolf Rachmil Menen went to live with the Verplaetse family at the end of Jan. 1943 and remained with them until the end of the occupation period.

DOC. 205

On 18 February 1943 Maurice Benedictus reports on the arrest of the board members of the Association of Jews in Belgium and his own imprisonment in Breendonk in the autumn of 1942[1]

Report, signed M. Benedictus, Lisbon, dated 18 February 1943 (typescript)

Report[2]
on the arrests of Messrs S. Ullmann,[3] chief rabbi of Belgium, S. Van den Berg,[4] A. Blum,[5] E. Hellendael,[6] M. Benedictus, and their stay in Breendonck concentration camp from 24 September 1942 until 3 October 1942

On 22 September 1942 the management board of the A.J.B. (Association of Jews in Belgium) assigned Mr M. Benedictus and his deputy, Mr M. Nocyze,[7] to go and discuss the situation of the A.J.B. staff with Obersturmführer Asche.[8] The aim was to avoid further staff members being arbitrarily arrested in the roundups carried out for the purpose of deporting the Jews of Belgium. Asche received Mr Benedictus in a particularly hostile manner and accused him of being involved in the terrorist attack that took place at 36 boulevard du Midi,[9] involving the assassination of Mr Robert Holsinger,[10] and in the intervention by Her Majesty Queen Elisabeth.[11] He declared that these activities would not go unpunished, and that even though the perpetrators of Mr R. Holsinger's assassination and the attack on Bd du Midi had not yet been found, the Gestapo was well aware of who had instigated them, and heads were going to roll. Mr Benedictus answered that he had had nothing to do with any of those events, that R. Holsinger had always enjoyed the trust of all the members of the board, and that his murder had

1 CegeSoma, mic 41. This document has been translated from French.
2 The report, along with other notes on the treatment of Jews in Belgium, was compiled at the request of a representative of the Belgian secret service at the embassy in Lisbon and delivered to the Belgian government in exile in London.
3 Salomon Ullmann.
4 Salomon van den Berg (1890–1955), furniture dealer; emigrated from the Netherlands to Belgium with his parents in 1902; active in the Jewish Community of Brussels; chairman of the Brussels committee of the Association of Jews in Belgium (AJB/VJB) and member of the AJB/VJB board, 1941–1944; went into hiding after the voluntary dissolution of the AJB/VJB in August 1944.
5 Alfred (Freddy) Blum (1904–1989); son of Marcel Blum; born in Basel; in Belgium from 1921; secretary of the Brussels committee of the AJB/VJB; head of its children's department from 1943.
6 Correctly: Eugène Hellendall.
7 Correctly: Noé Nozice (1905–1965), fur dealer; born in Teschen (Austria-Hungary, now Cieszyn, Poland); head of the AJB/VJB in Liège; arrested with his family on 13 April 1943; deported from Mechelen to Auschwitz six days later, and from there to various other camps. He was the only member of his family to survive, and he returned to Belgium in 1945.
8 Kurt Asche.
9 This refers to the raid on the AJB/VJB premises at 56 boulevard du Midi/Zuidlaan on 25 July 1942, during which copies of the list of Jews were burned: see Doc. 181, fn. 6.
10 Correctly: Robert Holzinger (1898–1942); from July 1942 responsible within the AJB/VJB for 'labour deployment in the East'; shot by Jewish resistance fighters on 29 August 1942: see Introduction, p. 54.
11 On 1 August 1942 three members of the AJB/VJB had an audience with Queen Elisabeth, who reacted with great concern upon hearing their reports and promised to intervene. Maurice Benedictus was not part of this delegation.

profoundly dismayed them all. After this, Asche accused Mr Benedictus of having formally approached her Majesty Queen *Elisabeth*. Mr Benedictus declared that he had never had the honour of being received by the sovereign and that he did not know those who had had this honour. All he knew was that the Belgian Red Cross, through its president, His Highness the Prince A. de Ligne,[12] had made it known in a letter to Mr S. van den Berg that a certain degree of protection had been granted to Belgian Jews. Mr Benedictus then remarked that, as usual, Asche would have been notified of this by his informant, F. Meyer,[13] who had been furious ever since the Belgian Jews were afforded this protection. Asche then told Mr Benedictus to assemble the twenty most prominent Jewish figures from among those on the list entitled 'A.J.B. Central Administration' in order to choose a replacement for R. Holzinger. Asche added that he no longer wanted to deal with Benedictus, who was suspected of not being loyal in his dealings with the occupier. This meeting was convened for 24 September 1943 at 10 a.m. The most eminent figures who still played a role in Belgian Judaism reported to 510 avenue Louise in Brussels[14] and were received by Asche and his assistant, Franck (a second-rate individual).[15] The names and duties (as far as I remember) of the 20 people summoned can be found in the list attached to this document.[16] Important fact: Meyer was not summoned to the meeting. Asche took a roll call and announced that he had had enough of the A.J.B.'s passive resistance and of the acts of sabotage inspired by certain members, that it was no longer a matter of putting the Jews to work, but of their final removal from the country, that there would be no more summonses to meetings or opportunities for the A.J.B. to intervene in favour of its members, that he was sending Mr Ullmann, Mr van den Berg, Mr Blum, Mr Hellendael, and Mr Benedictus to Breendonck camp until the removal of the Jews from Belgium was completed, and that they would remain in the camp as hostages in order to serve as an example to the other members of the A.J.B. In addition, Mr Rothkehl[17] would be deported because he was a foreigner. Those six thus condemned had to step out of the ranks. The five destined for Breendonck were taken to the corridor which leads to Asche's office, where Franck took their identity cards off them. Rothkehl disappeared into the cellar, and we never saw him again.

A few minutes later, our colleagues left Asche's office, where he had threatened them once again, and to which he summoned Mr Nocyze the next day to discuss certain administrative questions.

12 Prince Albert Édouard Eugène Lamoral de Ligne (1874–1957), diplomat; ambassador in Washington, 1927–1931, and at the Vatican, 1931–1937; later vice president of the Belgian Red Cross.

13 Presumably Felix Meyer (1875–1950), engineer; head of the Rota Works in Aachen; developed the 'Rota arm' for amputees in 1915, together with the physician Pauwels; emigrated from Germany to Brussels in 1938; member of the relief agency known as the Rue de Ruysbroeck Committee in Brussels: see Doc. 192, fn. 14.

14 The location of the headquarters of the Security Police and the SD.

15 Correctly: Johannes (Hans) Frank (1905–1964), police officer; worked in the section for Jewish affairs of the Security Police and the SD in Brussels, 1940–1943; head of Mechelen transit camp from 1943; interned in Belgium after 1945; extradited to the Netherlands in 1948; sentenced to six years in prison; released in 1950 and returned to Germany.

16 This is not included in the file.

17 Correctly: Edouard Rotkel (1898–1945), office worker; born in Budapest; emigrated via Danzig to Belgium in 1938; secretary of the Jewish Community of Brussels from 1940; deported from Mechelen to Auschwitz on 26 Sept. 1942; perished in a satellite camp of Mauthausen.

We saw our colleagues file out ahead of us, with odd expressions on their faces. My fellow prisoners and myself, as curious as it might seem, finally felt a certain relief that this terrible fear of being arrested had become a reality. In a low voice, I told my colleagues: 'No one will ever be able to say that we were collaborators again!'

A few moments later, all five of us were taken to the infamous cellar. Fortunately, because I had seen it coming, I had put some chocolate and a few packs of cigarettes in my briefcase. Since the building at 510 avenue Louise was an apartment building, we were in a relatively spacious double cellar, with one chair between the five of us, a bucket of water, and a toilet bowl. Morale was excellent. Our first observation was that Asche, like a good Kraut, had made the worst mistake of his career, since by arresting us he would rally all the loyal public opinion in Belgium behind us and open the eyes of all those who had not understood our attitude up to this point.

We were left in the cellar until 10 a.m. the next morning, without food or drink. Dr Ullmann, with his usual calm and optimism, told us that we would not have to wait long, and that Asche had overstepped his authority. At around 4 in the morning someone came to empty the other cellars, which contained our friend Rothkehl and other Jews who had been rounded up over the course of the day. They were taken away in a lorry to the Dossin Barracks,[18] to be sent east.

At around 10 o'clock, a big brute from the SS came to fetch us and allowed us to go to the toilet. He told us that if someone tried to escape along the route, he would shoot. Mr van den Berg insisted that he wanted Asche to receive him one more time so that he could protest against our arrest. To no avail!

We were put into a beautiful Buick and driven to Breendonck, a former fortress which can be found on the new road between Antwerp and Brussels, 13 km from Boom and 4 km from the village of Villebroock.[19]

The drive passed without incident, and our SS man handed us over to the guard squad. We were then taken to the camp office, where, after a fairly long wait with our faces turned to the wall and watched over by a guard, we were led in one at a time. We were made to hand over any money, cigarettes, in short anything that we had in our pockets, except personal papers. Three staff members were there, all from the VNV, members of the SS. They spoke German to us. I personally was not welcomed with slaps, but Dr Ullmann and van den Berg, who probably did not empty their pockets quickly enough, were beaten.

After our pockets had been emptied and the registration completed, we were taken to a barrack to receive our prisoner uniforms. These are old uniforms from the Belgian army, in quite poor condition, particularly the shoes. Our civilian clothes and all that we still had in our pockets, with the exception of one pencil, were put into a blue bag. The tailor, a Jewish prisoner, sewed our patches onto our uniforms, both on the chest on the left-hand side and on the back. This patch was made up of a yellow bar for Jews with a red 'I' across it, which signified that we were 'disloyal', that is to say, not loyal to the occupying authorities. Then a scene of unbelievable brutality took place, the first in a whole series! An SS officer entered holding a 50-franc note on which the three letters

18 Mechelen transit camp was housed in the buildings of the former Dossin Barracks.

19 On Breendonk camp, see PMJ 5/175.

RAF and the word Ullmann[20] had been written. He asked what this signified, and Dr Ullmann was brutally beaten with a stick and with fists. He told us later that on the note there had been an 'umlaut' on the letter U in his name,[21] and that his name had been written in the same characters as the letters RAF.

We were then taken to our room by a Flemish SS man, who treated us to various 'caresses'. In the dormitory, our fellow detainees, all Jews, gave us a warm welcome. There we made the acquaintance of the two work detail leaders, Jewish prisoners named Kessler[22] and Obler,[23] about whom I will say more later.

In addition to the patches, we each had a number. In my case it was 11 and had been made from the old metal numbers of the Belgian army regiments.

Then the soup was handed out. The soup never changed during our entire stay: a liquid with some white cabbage swimming in it, without any salt. Each prisoner had the right to receive half a litre of it in a bowl. After this meal, we were made to go to the hairdresser, and as it turned out, this role was performed by the two individuals named Kessler and Obler, who were allowed to keep their hair. For Mr Ullmann, having his hair and beard cut was very distressing, because the beard is particularly significant to religious Jews, which I know nothing about. In order to make my report clearer, I will talk about the diet in the camp at the end, and will first talk about what we lived through and had to put up with. After the meal we were taken to work, and at 6 p.m. we were back in our dormitory. There we were able to get to know our fellow prisoners a little better and to learn more about what was in store for us in that hell. What frightened us was that our companions were so thin and were all suffering from terrible hunger. Some even had to be sent to the Brugmans hospital[24] in Brussels to be treated for hunger oedema. At 9 p.m. it was lights out. Each prisoner had a bed, which is to say three wooden crates stacked on top of one another, with wood planks as a base, a sack of straw, and two blankets. Among our companions there were two Belgian Jews, one imprisoned for supposedly coming back from France too late, and the other a composer imprisoned for having written a piece of music entitled 'Gestapo Blues'. The others, all Germans or Poles, were imprisoned for different reasons, ranging from black market activities to returning home after 8 p.m. There were two political prisoners among our comrades: a young Austrian writer and a Polish architect who had only just got out of two months in solitary confinement; he was still regularly taken to the torture chamber for questioning and was therefore in a piteous state.

20 Presumably this was meant to suggest a connection with Britain's Royal Air Force.

21 In Belgium the name Ullmann is pronounced with an initial close front rounded vowel (/y/). Presumably Ullmann's comment was to indicate that the words were written by a German.

22 Presumably Leo Kessler (1913–1973), retailer; emigrated from Germany to Belgium; released from Breendonk in Feb. 1943; rearrested in July 1944 and interned in Mechelen; returned to Germany after 1945; later went to live in Yugoslavia.

23 Walter Obler (1906–1947), factory worker; fled from Austria to Belgium in 1938; interned in France in May 1940; imprisoned in Breendonk camp from Oct. 1940; Kapo (prisoner functionary) there from 1942; deported to Auschwitz, then Sachsenhausen, and then Mauthausen in Sept. 1943; arrested in Vienna in 1945 and extradited to Belgium; sentenced to death in 1946 for complicity in at least ten murders; executed in April 1947.

24 The hospital, which opened in 1923 and was named after Georges Brugmanns (1829–1900), still exists today.

During our stay the rhythm of life remained the same infernal round. The only moments of peace occurred when the parcels were distributed and during the Saturday morning shower; otherwise the atmosphere was that of a labour camp, made worse by an air of torture and death. Can the reader imagine that when I passed through there, there were prisoners in this vile, horrible place who had been there since the start of the occupation!

The camp garrison: The camp garrison is made up of fifty or so Wehrmacht soldiers who solely perform different guard functions. I never saw them pay any attention to the prisoners. Two Wehrmacht NCOs lead the prisoner roll call several times a day: nothing special to report, apart from a few kicks and screams.

The jailers: The internal camp command is in the hands of SS men who take orders from Major Schmidt.[25] He is the perfect example of a sadistic Nazi brute. However, he does not condescend to beating the prisoners, as this is no doubt beneath the dignity of an 'Übermensch'.[26] He lives in a villa outside the camp, and his wife regularly enters the camp. They say that she concerns herself with the female prisoners in the camp and that she does everything possible to improve their lot. Next is an Obersturmführer:[27] he had not been there for very long, but from what I saw, I can be sure that his favourite pastime is to beat prisoners with a riding crop and a dog whip. He was the one who beat me the most. Unfortunately I do not know his name.

Then comes a Sturmführer who is the head of the camp administration.[28] A short, brutish scoundrel who shouts and indiscriminately uses his riding crop to lash out at people all day. His beatings are less serious than those meted out by his immediate superior. I do not know his name.

Apart from these three despicable individuals, there are a dozen SS men. I still blush with shame when I think that they are Flemish; they supervise the work and beat their poor victims for any little thing; they are the dregs of humankind who have nothing left of their humanity but the exterior form, the most abject toads formed by the most shameful of regimes. I do not have words to describe them further.

The inmates: At the time when I passed through this hell, around 450 (four hundred and fifty) male prisoners and two women were held there. One hundred or so were Jews, the rest non-Jews. The proportion of Walloons seems to be higher than that of Flemish prisoners. There are men of all ages, up to and including a prisoner who has only one leg. Aryans and Jews are separated; the Aryans do not have their heads shaved and do

25 Correctly: Philipp Schmitt (1902–1950), bank clerk; joined the NSDAP in 1930 and the SS in 1932; worked at the SD Main Office, 1936–1939; head of Breendonk camp, 1940–1943; simultaneously head of Mechelen transit camp, 1942–1943; dismissed for black marketeering; sentenced to death in Belgium in 1949; executed in 1950.

26 German in the original: 'superman', a reference to the term coined by the German philosopher Friedrich Nietzsche to refer to the ideal superior man of the future who could create and impose his own values.

27 Johann (Hans) Kantschuster (b. 1897), unskilled worker; joined the NSDAP in 1928 and the SS in 1932; guard and commandant of the detention block at Dachau concentration camp from 1933; later deployed to Ravensbrück, Mauthausen, and Sachsenhausen concentration camps; at Breendonk, Sept. 1942 – April 1943; his subsequent fate is unknown.

28 Presumably Arthur Prauss (1892–1945), butcher; joined the SS in 1933 and the NSDAP in 1937; chief guard at Breendonk, probably from 1941; returned to Germany in 1944; killed during the battle of Berlin in 1945.

not receive quite so many blows as the Jews. Since they offer more resistance to their jailers, they are often forced to work with a sack filled with 20 kg of stones on their backs. They have two work detail leaders who are much more decent than those of the Jews. The prisoners in charge of the Jews are the two bandits called Obler and Kessler, both German Jews who beat prisoners as hard as the SS men. It is true that they are privileged; they get more to eat and do not have their heads shaved. They have the right to a certain portion of the contents of food parcels.

The food: The prisoners have to hand in their ration cards and receive the bread ration for heavy labourers: 325 g per day. At noon a bowl of cabbage soup and the bread, with either a bit of sugar or artificial honey, or a knob of butter or margarine. Apparently the food has greatly improved lately. In addition, we were able to receive parcels. Unfortunately, 50 to 60 per cent of their contents were stolen by the guards. Parcels were banned after our release, and in spite of all the efforts on the part of the Belgian Red Cross and the A.J.B., this prohibition was still in place at the end of December 1942. Apparently this measure was taken as retaliation for an escape.

The premises: The premises are situated in a former fortress, which is scrupulously clean and has very nice shower facilities. In addition, there are cells where a man can barely stand upright and a torture chamber where the prisoners are interrogated. There is an infirmary, but you need to be all but dead (that's the only way you can put it) to be admitted.

The labour and treatment of prisoners: Prisoners work ten hours a day filling in the ditches around the fort with sand loaded on tipper wagons. The brutes described above supervise. Blows and injuries rain down on prisoners continually. When there is fog, there is no work because of the possibility of escape. The Jews have to sing when they march to and from work. On Sunday morning, prisoners do chores, cleaning the courtyard, etc. Brutality reigns, and on Saturday morning in the shower you see so many bruises, contusions, and wounds of all kinds on those poor, emaciated bodies that it makes you shudder with horror.

Our release: We were released one Saturday morning at 10 a.m. A few minutes before this astonishing piece of news was announced, the Sturmführer beat me up for not having properly handled the broom on courtyard duty.

The brutes particularly targeted Mr Ullmann, who is 62 years old, and he put up with all of the maltreatment they inflicted on him with admirable stoicism and courage.

We were released thanks to the intervention of Cardinal Van Roey[29] and the secretaries general. Upon our return home, each one of us received so many professions of sympathy and interest from the good Belgians, both known and unknown to us, that we were all proud to have paid this price.

29 Jozef-Ernest van Roey (1874–1961), priest and theologian; vicar general of the Mechelen archdiocese, 1907–1926; archbishop of Mechelen from 1926; cardinal from 1927.

DOC. 206

On 1 April 1943 the painters Felix Nussbaum and his wife, Felka, express their gratitude to their friends Margrit and Dolf Ledel for giving them a place to stay[1]

Handwritten letter from Felix[2] and Felka Nussbaum,[3] Brussels, 6 avenue Nouvelle, to Margrit and Dolf Ledel,[4] dated 1 April 1943

Dear Margrit and dear Dolf,

Because we became upset over what were essentially minor domestic issues and have become such a burden to you, and because of the resulting conflicts, I feel it is best to put some space between us so that we preserve our mutual esteem for each other, which is rooted far more deeply in our souls than the things I have just mentioned. – What is essential, and what counts, is the spontaneous gesture you made when you opened the doors of your home to us a few months ago. – Before we now, as I said, separate 'physically' from each other, I would like to put a few words down on paper instead of saying a 'thank you' that will get lost in the ether. At the same time, these words will be a document that is not uninteresting to Karin, still a little girl today; they tell her that it brought honour to her parents to have sheltered two homeless, wandering Jews in their home during the great war, thereby violating the laws of the occupation. You, dear little Karin, will no longer remember Uncle Felix and Aunt Felka when you read these lines. But maybe your first big bed, modern at one time, stands somewhere in your apartment. We gave it to you with genuine pleasure, and we have left on it all our good wishes for your future as we take leave of your parents to seek another hiding place, from which we hope soon to emerge, healthy and liberated.

1 Felix-Nussbaum-Haus, Osnabrück. Published in facsimile in *Felix Nussbaum, Fragezeichen an jeder Straßenecke: Zwölf Briefe*, ed. Peter Junk and Wendelin Zimmer (Bramsche: Rasch, 2003), p. l. This document has been translated from German.

2 Felix Nussbaum (1904–1944), painter; exhibited his works in Germany from 1928; lived in exile with Felka Platek from 1933, initially in Italy, then in 1935 in Paris, then Belgium; imprisoned in St Cyprien camp in France in 1940; lived in hiding, 1942–1944; in June 1944 arrested and deported to Auschwitz, where he was murdered on 2 August 1944.

3 Felka Nussbaum, née Platek (1899–1944), painter; emigrated to Berlin from Warsaw in 1923; lived in exile from 1933 with Felix Nussbaum, initially in Italy, then in 1935 in Paris, then Belgium; in 1937 married Felix Nussbaum, with whom she went into hiding; arrested and deported; perished in Auschwitz.

4 Adolphe (Dolf) Ledel (1893–1976), sculptor; offered the Nussbaums a hiding place in his home from August 1942; he himself went into hiding in the Ardennes with his family in spring 1943.

DOC. 207

On 17 April 1943 Felix Lipszyc writes from Mechelen to his wife, Anna, and hints at his plan to escape from the deportation train[1]

Handwritten letter from Felix Lipszyc[2] to his wife, Anna, via Mr Emile Delhaye,[3] 74.76 rue F. S. Navez, Schaerbeek, Brussels, dated 17 April 1943

Mechelen, Saturday

My dear little wife,

This is to let you know that I have received all the parcels as well as my bags and the good rucksack, which I am very happy with. Jakie told me that you wanted to come here, which would have been a terrible mistake, and that you are working to get me out of here. It would be better if you did nothing at all and did not spend a single penny on it because it would not serve any purpose, and besides I hope to come home one of these days. You are giving yourself so much worry and trouble and you do not look well, while I am very well and resolute and I would like you to be the same. Régine, Henri, and Madeleine are still here and in very good health. Mr Lachmann is here and in good health and will probably do the same thing as me.[4] We believe that we will leave from here on Monday or Tuesday evening.[5] I hope my mother still does not know anything.

My dear Anna, you will see that our separation will not last long and that I will soon be home. I hope that the whole family is in good health. You try to stay strong and to stay healthy. I will end my letter. I send you a thousand hugs and to the entire family. Regards to all acquaintances.[6]

1 Kazerne Dossin – Mechelen, A000974. This document has been translated from French.
2 Fiszel Abram (Felix) Lipszyc (b. 1923), tailor; born in Łódź; deported to Auschwitz on 19 April 1943; survived the war.
3 Non-Jewish neighbour of the Lipszyces.
4 Allusion to an attempt to escape during the impending transport from Mechelen.
5 The next transport left Mechelen for Auschwitz on Monday, 19 April.
6 Two days later Felix Lipszyc wrote a postcard from the deportation train saying that he had been unable to escape from the train because 'the head of the wagon was no good': Kazerne Dossin – Mechelen, A000974. Those designated 'head of the wagon' were selected from among the Jewish deportees before the trains departed. They were often fathers with family members on the train. They were held responsible for any escape attempts that occurred.

DOC. 208

On 20 April 1943 the Belgian policeman Albert Decoster reports to the public prosecutor in Leuven on prisoners who escaped from a deportation train[1]

Report, unsigned, to the public prosecutor in Leuven, dated 20 April 1943 (copy of the carbon copy)[2]

Regarding persons killed and injured by gunshot
We, *Decoster*, Albert,[3] were informed that a certain *Withof*, Louis Ferdinand, born in 1892 and residing at 415 Leuvenschelaan T/S, came to the police station to declare, on the instructions of the physician *Debuyst*, residing at T/S in Leuvenschelaan,[4] that a person had knocked on the door of *Withof*'s house, asking for help. As said person, who was accompanied by a woman, later identified as his wife, was seriously injured, *Withof* called the physician, Dr *Debuyst*, who lived nearby. When the latter arrived, the man had died as a result of a gunshot wound to his abdomen.

We hastened to the address, where we found Dr *Debuyst*, who was attending to another injured woman. We were told then and there that a bit further along, by the railway line, there was another injured woman, whom we found and also brought to the physician.

All the persons concerned had gunshot wounds and told us that they were of Israelite origin, as such had been imprisoned in Mechelen concentration camp, and that, while being transported by train to Germany, they had jumped off the train under fire from the guards.[5] According to their statements, such escapes took place all along the route the train was taking, starting from *Mechelen*.

As the injuries were severe, we had the injured taken to the town hospital, but we were stopped on the way by the Feldgendarmerie, who, having been alerted to the facts by the mayor of Zoutleeuw,[6] where there were also several dead and injured at the railway station, had immediately started to search the area.

The Feldgendarmerie took charge of transporting the injured and ordered us to take the corpses to the mortuary. The man who died in *Withof*'s house could be identified through the intervention of his wife as *Westermar*, Julius, born on 13 May 1901, place unknown, and residing in Brussels at 53 rue Souverain, bearer of cardboard tag no. 879, husband of *Westheimer*, Meta, born in Berlin on 9 November 1904 and residing at the same address. The woman in question, who was suffering a nervous collapse, was also taken to the hospital.

1 Directorate-General for War Victims / Directie-generaal Oorlogsslachtoffers / Direction générale Victimes de la Guerre, Brussels, 497 181–910. This document has been translated from Dutch.
2 The original contains handwritten notes.
3 Albert Decoster (1893–1960), policeman. Normally the policeman's place of employment is noted on the report form, but such information is not included in this carbon copy. It is clear from the file, however, that he was a member of the police force in Tienen (French: Tirlemont), which is located on the railway line between Mechelen and Aachen. The train stopped for thirty minutes at Tienen station to allow the locomotive to be replaced.
4 Correctly: Leuvenslaan. This is a very long road; the abbreviation presumably indicates the Tienen/Stad section of it.
5 This was Transport XX, which departed on 19 April 1943. On escape from the deportation trains, see Introduction, pp. 57–58.
6 Correctly: Zoutleeuw (French: Léau), city in the province of Flemish Brabant.

The two other women, also seriously injured, declared that their names were as follows:

Goldering, Marie, born in Leipzig on 13 August 1920, residing at 4 rue du Ham in Ukkel;

Aronsfrau, Lore, born in Dresden on 8 September 1920, residing at St Gillies, Brussels, 47 rue Jordan.[7]

None of the dead or injured was in possession of any proof of identity or any money, as all this had been taken from them during their time in the concentration camp.

At dawn, the body of another woman was discovered beside the railway line on the edge of town, killed by a gunshot and without any proof of identity.

A little later we heard from the railway station that the staff there had also found the body of a woman killed by a gunshot, lying on the track about a hundred metres before the station, in the direction of Kumtich.[8]

Finally, the body of a man who had been shot was found in the canal alongside the track at the Paardenbrug level crossing between the stations at Tienen and Grimde. He was wearing a cardboard tag with the number 1407 on it,[9] probably his prisoner number at the concentration camp.

All of these corpses were taken to the local mortuary, pending further instructions from the occupation authorities.

All of the items found on the bodies of the dead and injured as well as the items left behind by those persons were claimed by the Feldgendarmerie T/S.

In witness thereof,

We are continuing our investigations with the aim of obtaining further information on the identity of the deceased persons. A further official report with a description of these persons will follow.

In witness thereof,

7 The individuals in question were Julius Westheimer (1901–1943), butcher, born in Cannstatt; Meta Westheimer, née Boas (b. 1904), seamstress; correctly: Marie Goldring (b. 1919), film actress; and Leonore Aronsfrau (b. 1920). The women were deported on the next transport to Auschwitz, where they perished: see Doc. 219, fn. 64.

8 One of the two victims is thought to have been Helene Zylberszac (1927–1943); arrested in Jan. 1943 and interned in Mechelen.

9 This number was worn by Rudolf Kahan (1900/08–1943), sales representative; born in Łódź; emigrated to Belgium.

DOC. 209

On 23 May 1943 Salomon van den Berg describes in his diary the arrest of an acquaintance who had been in hiding and the flight of fifteen children from a convent[1]

Diary of Salomon van den Berg, entry for 23 May 1943 (copy)[2]

Last week was once again very chaotic. Last Tuesday as I was coming back from Mechelen in the evening, André[3] shouted to me from his balcony that another disaster had struck us and our friends. I didn't faint, as one expects anything and has got used to everything. But when I went up I was told that the Gottlobs, with whom we have been friends since I saved the young girl, had just been seized in the street by the infamous Jacques,[4] that horrible Jewish individual who arrests most of the people. I went to their place straight away. There I found Mrs Gottlob,[5] who luckily had been at the hairdresser's. She had just come back five minutes earlier, just after the Gestapo had left with her husband.[6] She had no idea of the terrible misfortune that had befallen her. I took her home with me and she and Hilda[7] spent the night there. I immediately alerted Beilin[8] and Rosenfeld,[9] who are in charge of intercessions. Mr Gottlob had been to see his parents-in-law, and when he left, he bumped into a Mrs Goldwein,[10] an acquaintance of his. They had been speaking for a few minutes in the street when the Pol car pulled up.[11] He was asked for his papers, which were forged, like those of all foreign Jews who do not

1 Copy in Wiener Library, P III i/275, pp. 112–115. This document has been translated from French.

2 Salomon van den Berg continued the diary begun by his daughter Nicole from 10 May 1940, the day of the German invasion of Belgium, and he wrote entries up until 1945. Nicole van den Berg (b. 1924); fled to the south of France with her family in May 1940, and they all returned in Sept. 1940; later worked for the Association of Jews in Belgium (AJB/VJB); survived the war. The handwritten original of the diary is owned by the family.

3 André van den Berg (b. 1920); son of Salomon van den Berg; drafted into the Belgian army in 1940; worked for the Association of Jews in Belgium (AJB/VJB) from June 1942; survived the war.

4 Icek Glogowski (b. 1899), night porter; also called 'fat Jacques'; emigrated to Belgium from Poland in the 1930s; his wife and children were deported to Auschwitz in Oct. 1942; subsequently worked for the Germans as a 'catcher' (*Greifer*); members of the resistance made several unsuccessful attempts to assassinate him; fled to Germany in June 1944; his subsequent fate is unknown.

5 Gertrude Caroline Gottlob, née Stern (b. 1898), housewife; was not deported.

6 Siegfried Gottlob (b. 1907) was released from Mechelen in Jan. 1944 after van den Berg filed numerous petitions; after his release, he worked in a home operated by the AJB/VJB.

7 Hilda Gottlob (b. 1925), the couple's daughter; later worked in the mail office of the AJB/VJB's Department for Special Assistance, which mostly dealt with sending provisions to internees at Mechelen camp.

8 Correctly: Hans Berlin (b. 1894), tailor; former Reichswehr officer; married to a non-Jew; fled to Belgium from Cologne in 1939; member of the Brussels-based relief agency known as the Rue de Ruysbroeck Committee; head of the AJB/VJB's Department for Interventions with the Occupying Power at the end of 1942.

9 Louis Rosenfeld (b. 1889), factory owner; member of the Rue de Ruysbroeck Committee; appointed to the AJB/VJB by Fritz Erdmann; headed the AJB/VJB's Department for Special Assistance and was in charge of contacts with the German occupiers from Dec. 1942.

10 Probably Marianne Goldwein (b. 1926); deported in late July 1943 to Auschwitz, where she perished.

11 German police cars, which regularly drove slowly through the streets of Brussels, could be recognized by the abbreviation 'Pol' stamped on their licence plates.

want to get arrested. But a few well-placed blows are often enough to bring out the truth about where one lives, even with people who live in hiding. This was the case with the Gottlobs. There are now three charges against him: possession of forged papers, living in hiding, being out in public without a star. I am writing all of this down for future reference, so that the humiliations inflicted upon the Jews are made public. Wednesday went by without me being able to do anything, because Mr Ertman,[12] who is in charge of these cases at the SD, was not there. Thursday something else happened. Fifteen Jewish children were hidden in a convent.[13] Some Germans came to take them away. The convent's Mother Superior, who wanted to save the children and gain some time, asked if they could leave the children there until she could come to some agreement with someone in a position of authority. They agreed, while insisting that they would return the next day. In the meantime, Mr Rosenfeld, having heard about it, interceded on the very same day with Mr Ertman and obtained from him the assurance that the children could stay there. He returned home, very happy with this result. The next day, on the Friday, he was to have another meeting with Ertman to plead for Mr Gottlob's release, something he had already been more or less promised during Mr Ertman's unannounced visit to the A.J.B. Midi and boulevard d'Anvers,[14] where he had found everything to be completely to his satisfaction. But as he arrived at Ertman's on the Friday, Mr Beilin learned, to his great astonishment, straight from Ertman's mouth, that the fifteen children had been kidnapped from the convent in the early hours of Friday by masked men with guns.[15] Beilin flew into a rage. He immediately summoned the board members of the A.J.B. In the meantime, I learned that Mr Heiber[16] and his wife,[17] who had taken on the task of finding places for children on behalf of the A.J.B. and others, had been arrested at their home that very morning at eight o'clock. The people who were doing the same in Antwerp and Liège were also arrested.

So it looks like the war against children has started. A few days earlier, Ertman had said to Rosenfeld that he knew that some eight hundred children were in hiding. I see a very clear link between his words and the facts. We, the current members of the A.J.B., Blum Sr,[18] Lagare,[19] myself, Rosenfeld, and Beilin, were seen at half past ten by Ertman, whom I had not met before, but who made a very good impression, so good, in fact, that

12 Correctly: Fritz Erdmann (1900–1955), police officer; joined the NSDAP and the SS in 1931; with the SD in Chemnitz from 1935; with the Reich Security Main Office (RSHA) from Sept. 1941; from Jan. 1942 with the Senior Commander of the Security Police in Brussels, where he headed Dept. IV B from Dec. 1942 to Oct. 1943; sentenced to four and a half years in prison for corruption in May 1944.

13 The convent of the Sisters of the Divine Redeemer at 70 avenue Clémenceau in Anderlecht.

14 The AJB/VJB headquarters were on boulevard d'Anvers/Antwerpselaan; the Department for Special Assistance was on boulevard du Midi/Zuidlaan.

15 The operation was in fact carried out by the Jewish resistance, the Partisans armés. Afterwards the children were taken either to their parents or to new hiding places. All of them survived the German occupation.

16 Maurice Heiber (1908–1981), perfume dealer; born in Stryj (now Ukraine); lived in Belgium from late 1925; fled to France in May 1940; after his return, worked for the AJB/VJB's social welfare department; head of the children's welfare department of the Jewish Defence Committee (CDJ/JVC) from Sept. 1942; arrested in May 1943; released from Mechelen in Jan. 1944; in a Swiss sanatorium, 1944–1947.

17 Estera Heiber, née Fajersztein (1903–1992); born in Warsaw; lived in Belgium from 1924; member of the CDJ/JVC's Committee for the Rescue of Children in 1942; arrested with her husband in 1943; interned in Mechelen; subsequently released.

one cannot fathom how such a mild-mannered man can be a member of a police force which commits so many crimes. He asked us whether we knew of Heiber's work outside the association and about the provenance of the funds (50 to 60 thousand francs a month) which Heiber had claimed were at his disposal for this. Ertman then said that if there were such a large sum at Heiber's disposal for this purpose, he could well have money to pay terrorists operating in the interests of the Jews. We pointed out to him that we had no idea about this and that the very fact that these children had been kidnapped was against our own interests. We were let go after being lectured for not knowing what was happening outside the A.J.B. But poor Gottlob still remained in the […][20] with the woman with whom he had been arrested. On Saturday morning, however, Rosenfeld received Ertman's guarantee that he would be released; unfortunately, he has not come back yet and has in the meantime been taken to Mechelen, from where we very much hope to get him back. This whole time, the Gottlobs' flat has been sealed off, and mother and daughter have nothing to wear. They were promised that the flat would be unsealed.

On Sunday, I attended the wedding of Workum, the vice president of the A.J.B. His bride is very nice and an accomplished pianist,[21] and she gave us a sample of her art by playing Liszt's 'La Campanella' for us.

Afterwards, I went to a bridge party at Mr Oestrich's. On the military and political front, nothing much has changed in this past week. We still await Italy's surrender.[22]

DOC. 210

On 9 and 14 June 1943 Liba Stern tells her mother, who has managed to escape arrest, about life in Mechelen camp[1]

Handwritten letter from Liba (Loulou) Stern,[2] Mechelen, to her mother, Idesa Stern,[3] dated 9 and 14 June 1943

Above all, do not show this letter to anyone.
Mechelen, Wednesday, 9 June 1943
This morning I will write this note without knowing if I will find a way to send it to you. But it doesn't really matter anyway. I hope mostly to pass the time, because I feel terribly down at the moment and am profoundly sick of everything. Also, I hope to make myself

18 Marcel Blum (b. 1883), factory owner; father of Alfred Blum; chairman of the Jewish Community of Brussels; president of the AJB/VJB from autumn 1942; survived the occupation; acquitted of all charges of collaboration in 1947.
19 Presumably David Lazer, vice president of the Orthodox community in Brussels; member of the AJB/VJB board from spring 1942.
20 Word missing in original: probably 'basement'.
21 Anna Rutzki (b. 1920); deported with her husband in Sept. 1943 to Auschwitz, where she perished.
22 The Allies landed in Sicily on 10 July 1943. However, the German occupation of northern Italy prevented an early end to the war in Italy.

1 MJB/JMB, Fonds Stern 084. This document has been translated from French.
2 Liba Stern (1921–1943), university student.
3 Idesa Stern, née Erlich (1896–1962), housewife; born in Radoszyce (Poland); lived in Belgium from 1920.

feel better by pouring my heart out a little in this letter. It has been three months already that I have not seen you, my dear sweet mum! Good Lord! This is the first time that I am able to say it: Mum, my sweet mum! Three months since that terrible Friday afternoon when, luckily for all of us, you were at the hairdresser's. How I would have liked to see you then! How pretty you must have been, with your lovely head of hair! When I think of what it must have been like for you to come back and find the doors shut and your husband and two children gone,[4] I swear I will no longer dare to complain about anything. That must have been awful for you, my dear. That was all I was thinking of when they took us to the Gestapo. And for you as well, my dear little Billy,[5] it must have been awful not to find your dear little Stern[...],[6] but I hope you rose to your duty and supported our dear mum as much as possible.

Today, all of that already seems very far away, but it is far from forgotten! Here in Mechelen with the parcels, life would be entirely bearable for me if we did not worry so much for those in Brussels, and if we weren't so frightened every time of seeing one of you arrive on the famous lorry. The days in Mechelen can be summed up like this: reveille at 6 o'clock, washing in the 'Wachraum'[7] or eating breakfast on one's bed. Roll call is at 8. Everyone goes down to the courtyard; 30 minutes of exercise, then a walk until 9 (still in the courtyard). Then they pick a group of men to clean the staircases. This is almost nothing, and yet you should see how little Sus[8] hides in order to try to get out of it! As for dad, he always manages to sneak off. He has a good network, you understand! Influential contacts! The foreman of the cobblers, for example! You should hear him boast about it. Meanwhile I go back up (we are quartered on the 3rd floor), and most of the time I mend my stockings, because you cannot imagine how quickly we wear them out here! At around 11 o'clock there is another roll call. This means you have to walk around in circles for an hour (you can walk with whomever you want and talk as much as you like).

For women, this programme alternates every other day with a session of peeling potatoes. Just after the transport, when all the people had gone,[9] there were of course very few women. These sessions went for as long as 6 to 8 hours per day. And all of it standing up! Currently, we have to peel for 2 to 3 hours every other day, because unfortunately the barracks is filling up at an incredible speed. Every day they bring in 20, 30, or 50 people on the infamous lorry. This week they brought in 50 people from a boarding house in Woluwé.[10] Among them were Mrs Gabinet and her two children.[11] Each time they bring a new arrival from Brussels, I am worried that I might recognize one of you, my dears, among those defeated faces!

4 On 20 March 1943 Jacob Eliezer Stern (1892–1943), a leather salesman born in Łódź who had emigrated from Germany to Belgium in 1919, and two of his children, Liba and Willy (1927–1943), were arrested and interned in Mechelen; on 20 Sept. 1943 they were deported to Auschwitz, where they perished.

5 Nathan Stern, known as Billy (b. 1923), brother of Liba; arrested in Uccle (Flemish: Ukkel) on 14 July 1944 and deported from Mechelen on 31 July 1944 to Auschwitz; returned to Belgium in the summer of 1945.

6 Part of name illegible: presumably the nickname of the siblings' youngest brother, Willy.

7 German in the original (correctly: 'Waschraum').

8 Presumably another nickname for Willy Stern.

9 Meaning a deportation.

Monday, 14 June 1943
It was impossible to get back to writing this letter until now. Ever since 'Postsperre'[12] was declared, writing has been seen as very suspect, and it is difficult to hide in a room with 50 people. (The Belgians are slightly privileged, because in the other rooms there are around 100 people! We have beds! Well, in a manner of speaking! Iron beds with straw mattresses on them. That wouldn't be so bad if there were not also fleas, the scourge of the camp!)

I don't know how I manage to write to you so calmly. It is true that I have the impression that it was all a dream: yesterday, I saw my adored mum! I saw Georgine! I really feel I must have had a vision, and my little Pegotty[13] feels the same by the way. This morning, as I was waking up, his words were: 'Can you believe it, Loulou, we saw Mum yesterday!' Why, dearest mum, did you do that! It is really too imprudent. I absolutely do not want that to happen again. In any case, how did all of that even help? I am certain that you must be much sadder after having seen us, a 10-minute visit is so very short. We barely had enough time to squeeze one another and then it was already time to be torn away from each other, for us to return to our place between those four big yellow walls, and for you to go back to the city of Brussels, which is full of dangers.

The whole week we had been living in anticipation of the visit Georgine was going to try to arrange. We did not have much hope that it would happen, because even the authorized visits only last five to ten minutes. And then the *Sturmscharfuehrer*[14] was in a bad mood. Mariette and Bann will be able to confirm that. They saw him. Luckily for us, he was not there, because Dad had found a way through one of his acquaintances to come to an arrangement with the sentry and the officer. Don't think for a minute that it could have happened in the way it did otherwise. We would have had to consider ourselves very lucky to have been able to speak with you for three minutes (and not ten) in the hallway! Several people weren't even allowed to come in. When I saw Georgine enter, pretty, elegant, in a word, exuding Brussels, I had to make a huge effort to contain myself, but when I saw my darling mum appear behind her, I thought that I'd go crazy! No, I assure you my beloved mum, you should not have done that. And in such attire! What an ugly hat, and what an ugly dress! And then I imagined your hair as it would have been after you had been to the hairdresser's, and I only saw grey hair badly combed – what is going on? I want you to remain the young and elegant mother that you have always been, and of whom we have always been so proud!

I have nothing to add about the visit itself. You know what happened.

We were extraordinarily lucky. The soldiers were particularly indulgent. I thank you again, my darling mum, for the beautiful bottle of cologne, and naturally also for the cigarettes and the strawberries. How unfortunate that we weren't able to eat the cherries from our garden together!

10 Correctly: Sint-Lambrechts-Woluwe (French: Woluwe-Saint-Lambert), a municipality in the Brussels metropolitan area.
11 Maria Gabinet, née Szczupak (1905–1943); deported from Mechelen to Auschwitz on 31 July 1943, along with her children Liza (1928–1943) and Leo (1935–1943); they all perished in Auschwitz.
12 German in the original: 'mail ban'.
13 Presumably another nickname for Willy Stern, possibly alluding to the Peggotty family in the novel *David Copperfield* by Charles Dickens (1850).
14 Presumably Johannes (Hans) Frank.

As for Georgine, I cannot find the words to express to her the effect that the bouquet of roses had on me.

Nothing could have given me more pleasure. Flowers, and especially roses! I had not seen any for three months, and people miss flowers when they can no longer breathe fresh air, I can assure you! In your next letter, I want you to include the postcard that our poor dear Bernard sent you. I saw a postcard from Upper Silesia where they say they are working in the fields and are very well.[15] And still nothing from Léa and Willy? And have Nathan and Anna still not sent you any news either? Don't forget to tell us about them in your next letter.

I can imagine how you must have felt, my dear big Billy, when you had to wait for Mum to come back with news from us. My beloved little brother! I hear that you have become very thin. Why? You miss your little Sus, don't you? And maybe even your annoying sister a little bit. As for your Dad, you must miss his daily remarks too. I certainly miss you terribly, my big brother. Maybe I just miss arguing with you, but I miss you a lot. In spite of everything I said to you, I know very well that deep down you are a decent fellow, especially now that I suppose you have become more serious. I hope that you are still just as handsome a boy as before? More handsome than ever, no doubt, now that your hair has grown back. What I wouldn't give to see you again, my dear old Billy.

What a catastrophe! I don't have any more space and I feel like I haven't said anything. What happened to Paul? Is he in hiding with Pacha? And where? And the two little children, where are they and how are they doing? I want you to tell me more about them. As for Dad's friends, I don't know what to say to them, except that the war will end one day and that then we will be able to express all of our appreciation to them, all of our gratitude for the kindness they displayed towards us in such times. They are what you call good folk. And that is so rare!

I really wonder how I will ever manage to hide such a long letter in a cardboard box. Don't forget to briefly let me know if you have received it. I assume you understood what I asked of you in the note I gave to Georgine. I hope I'll get a visit tomorrow. You should understand that I'm doing the impossible. It's the same with the postcards. I can only send a few because I am protected. Please send me some more – well camouflaged, obviously.

I must stop writing to you because I cannot add any more paper. That would make the parcel too thick. If Willy and Dad add nothing to this letter, it is because he[16] knows nothing about it. I will only tell them about it once it's been sent. The danger really is too great! One more time I beg you, be careful! The smallest thing is enough to get you here. I do not have any more space, alas. I embrace you all warmly, also for Dad and Willy.

Your Loulou

PS. Tell us also about our friends and acquaintances. I cannot believe that Simone has abandoned me after all she did for me. Something must have happened! All the best to

15 This is likely to have been one of the postcards which prisoners were forced to write to give the impression that they were safe and well, in this case presumably sent from Auschwitz.
16 Probably a reference to her father.

Mr and Mrs Polydore, to Mr van den Bosch, to Moederke and Vader, to Maurice and his wife, and finally to everyone. I won't continue to enumerate them for fear of forgetting some. This time I really am going to finish. Another thousand kisses.

Your Loulou

NB. Here is what we get each day: In the morning: coffee (hot water with bromide in it),[17] a quarter of a loaf of bread (around 200g). At noon: soup. In the evening: soup from the Secours d'hiver.[18] It is awful how quickly the barracks fill up. They are bringing new victims here every day.

What are they saying in Brussels about the Belgians? Are they still talking about their release? Here they are talking about releasing around 25 who have been here for eight, nine, ten months, the old and the sick.

What happened with the note Billy received from the Oberfeldkommandantur?[19] I cannot wait to hear more news. Again and always: be careful!!!

All the best to Myriam and her family.

DOC. 211

At the end of June 1943 Simon Gronowski writes to his father from his hiding place[1]

Handwritten letter from Simon Gronowski[2] to his father,[3] dated June 1943

My dear Papa,

I have received your two letters, as did Madame Delsort.[4] In your second letter you asked me how I am. I am very well. I hope the same is true for you. You can set your mind at rest and need not worry at all as far as I am concerned, as I only go out once a week for a very short time and in the evening, so that I am not seen. I don't go near the window, and I don't speak to anybody. I am very careful. Madame Delsort is happy with me, and I feel calm. Fortunately, I have quite a lot of books, and Raymond[5] comes by now and then to visit me. I help Madame peel the potatoes, the carrots, cut the

17 It was a widespread though apparently unfounded rumour among inmates of Nazi camps and prisons that they were being dosed with bromide.
18 The Belgian Winter Relief organization.
19 The note has not been found.

1 Kazerne Dossin – Mechelen, A000828. Published in facsimile in Simon Gronowski, *L'Enfant du 20e convoi* (Brussels: Luc Pire, 2005), pp. 133–134. This document has been translated from French.
2 Simon Gronowski (b. 1931); lived with his family in hiding from Sept. 1942; arrested with his mother and sister on 17 March 1943; interned in Mechelen and deported with his mother on 19 April 1943; escaped from the train and survived in various hiding places.
3 Léon (Leib) Gronowski (1898–1945), leather goods dealer; born in Radziejów (Congress Poland); prisoner of war in German captivity in Lithuania, 1916; moved to Belgium in 1920; lived with his family in hiding from Sept. 1942; escaped arrest in March 1943; died shortly after the end of the war. See also Doc. 222.
4 Madame Delsort was a friend of the family who had hidden Léon Gronowski in her home until Simon arrived. From then on Simon stayed with her, while Léon moved to a different hiding place in June 1943.
5 Raymond Rouffart, a friend of Simon's, whom he had met in the Scouts.

cauliflower and the salads. So you see I have become a housekeeper. And I play the piano. Papa, you cannot imagine how happy I was when Madame Rouffart,[6] returning from the Association,[7] told me that Mama[8] had written that she was in good health. She is in Upper Silesia, so we must write to her, and Mama will be able to write back to us.[9] You can be delighted about this as I am too. And what is more: Maggy and Eliane went to see Ida;[10] she is very well. Madame Rouffart has done a lot to secure Ida's release, and this is why I am expecting my sister to arrive on Saturday, Sunday, Monday, or Tuesday, 3, 4, 5, or 6 July.[11] You can imagine how glad I am about this. You can see that we have only good news. Papa, do you remember the letter you sent to that rural patrolman?[12] Well, the exact address is: Monsieur le Garde-Champêtre at Beeringen, near Hoepertingen, Limburg, Belgium. So please write to him and explain the misunderstanding, because the address was not correct.[13]

Papa, I have to leave you now, and I'm sending you a thousand kisses. Don't worry.

6 Madeleine Rouffart, Raymond's mother, helped the Gronowski family go into hiding in Sept. 1942. After their arrest in March 1943 on the basis of an anonymous tip-off, she sent parcels to Mechelen through the Association of Jews in Belgium (AJB/VJB) and made sure that letters between father and son were delivered.

7 This refers to the AJB/VJB.

8 Chana Gronowski, née Kaplan (1902–1944/1945), housewife; born in Jurbarkas (Lithuania); moved to Belgium in 1923 to marry Léon Gronowski; arrested with her children on 17 March 1943; deported on 19 April 1943 from Mechelen to Auschwitz, where she perished.

9 On two occasions, in May and June 1943, the family received post from the mother, who was imprisoned in Auschwitz-Birkenau extermination camp, through the AJB/VJB.

10 Ida Gronowski (1924–1944/1945), student; interned along with her mother and brother in Mechelen in March 1943; deported on 20 Sept. 1943 to Auschwitz, where she perished. Maggy Rouffart, Madeleine Rouffart's daughter, and Eliane Taburiaux were close friends of hers.

11 In the original, incorrectly: June. At the end of June 1943, Ida Gronowski, like all other Jews with Belgian citizenship, was supposed to be released from Mechelen, but she was never freed. She shared this fate with around 200 others.

12 The French term is 'garde-champêtre', which roughly translates as rural patrolman, a combination of forest ranger and police officer in rural areas; the role existed in Belgium until 1998 and was under the control of the municipal administration.

13 On 21 April 1943 the father had written a letter to the man from Borgloon who had helped Simon after his escape from the deportation train and put him on the train to Brussels. However, Simon did not know his name (Jean Aerts) and wrongly thought he was a rural patrolman, As a result, the letter was addressed, with no name specified, to the rural policeman who had handed Simon Gronowski over to Aerts at the Gendarmerie: Jules van Hoenshoven (1907–1987), tailor; rural patrolman in Berlingen (correct spelling of the place name) from 1939; thought to be a member of the VNV; attacked by members of the Belgian resistance in July 1944. After the war, van Hoenshoven was interned as a suspected collaborator but released due to lack of evidence. The aforementioned letter helped him avoid conviction for collaboration. See Gronowski, *L'Enfant du 20e convoi*, pp. 106–121.

DOC. 212

On 26 July 1943 the Security Police in Brussels records the agreement of Military Commander Alexander von Falkenhausen to the deportation of Jews with Belgian citizenship[1]

File note (L IV),[2] signature illegible, Brussels, dated 26 July 1943

1) *Note:*
On 20 July 1943 a meeting took place in the office of Military Commander General von Falkenhausen, during which the arrest also of the Jews with Belgian citizenship was discussed. General von Falkenhausen was of the opinion that the Jews living illegally in Belgium should be rounded up first, because once the intention to arrest Belgian Jews became known, the latter would go underground and the army of illegals and terrorist forces would thereby be reinforced. However, in the end General von Falkenhausen too had no objections to an immediate operation against the Belgian Jews, but he requested that this exclude Belgian Jews who are for any reason declared by the military administration to be unsuitable for evacuation. This assurance was given, with the request that the military administration provide a list of these Jews to the local office as soon as possible.[3] As General von Falkenhausen remarked, as a rule these would be very elderly Jews unfit for labour deployment.
2) To be forwarded to IV B 3 for further processing.[4]

1 CegeSoma, AA 556. Published (with a different date: 28 July 1943) in Klarsfeld and Steinberg (eds.), *Die Endlösung der Judenfrage in Belgien*, p. 74. This document has been translated from German.
2 The meaning of L IV could not be established.
3 No such list has been found.
4 Following von Falkenhausen's agreement, a large roundup, primarily targeting Jews with Belgian citizenship, was carried out in Antwerp and Brussels during the night of 3–4 Sept. 1943: see Doc. 214.

DOC. 213

On 25 August 1943 Ezryl Anielewicz writes a card from Jawischowitz camp to his wife in Belgium[1]

Handwritten postcard[2] from Ezryl Anielewicz,[3] Jawichowitz,[4] Labour Camp, Building no. 10, Upper Silesia, to Mr Mirel Delcroix,[5] 7 Terliststr., Antwerp, dated 25 August 1943[6]

My dear wife Lea,

I can report that I have received your lovely card with joy, and what you sent. It was very fine. I am well and work in construction. I hope you are well and strong. That gives me joy.

From your husband who loves you and thinks about you always.

Best wishes to all.

DOC. 214

On 1 September 1943 Fritz Erdmann, official in charge of Jewish affairs for the Security Police and the SD in Brussels, draws up a plan of action for the imminent roundup of Jews[1]

Letter (IV B 3, Erd/Pl), unsigned[2] (SS-Hauptsturmführer), Brussels, dated 1 September 1943[3]

Plan of action[4]

Operation against the Belgian Jews during the night of Friday, 3 September, and early morning of Saturday, 4 September 1943.

During the night of 3–4 September 1943, the arrest of Belgian Jews for deployment in the East,[5] as required by the Reich Security Main Office, will begin for the first time

1 USHMM, 199 211. This document has been translated from German.

2 In 'official' correspondence of this kind, which was censored, prisoners were forced to write in German. This letter contained mistakes and unusual wording in the original German.

3 Ezryl Anielewicz (1921–1945), tailor; thought to have emigrated to Belgium from Poland; deported on 31 Oct. 1942 from Mechelen to Auschwitz, where he was held in the Jawischowitz subcamp; thought to have died of typhus shortly after the end of the war.

4 Correctly: Jawischowitz, subcamp of Auschwitz; the prisoners held there worked in the nearby Brzeszcze coal mine.

5 This refers to his wife, Mireille (Lea) Anielewicz, née Delcroix (b. 1923); married Ezryl Anielewicz in 1942, shortly before his deportation; survived the war in hiding; after the war married the widower of her sister and in 1957 emigrated to the USA with her family.

6 On the reverse is a stamp of the Association of Jews in Belgium (AJB/VJB) and a handwritten annotation in Dutch: 'Unknown. Return to VJB'.

1 CegeSoma, AA 556. Published in Klarsfeld and Steinberg (eds.), *Die Endlösung der Judenfrage in Belgien*, p. 78. This document has been translated from German.

2 The authorship is inferred from the file reference; the head of Dept. IV B 3 at this time was Fritz Erdmann.

3 The original contains handwritten annotations as well as archival stamps that were added later.

4 Other documents in the same group of files indicate that these roundups were to be carried out under the codename Operation Polecat.

with a large-scale operation. The operation will be carried out [as in Brussels] simultaneously in Antwerp in accordance with exactly the same principles. The other field offices, which cover only a very small number of Jews, will be informed of the impending operation and also urged to begin arresting Jews of Belgian nationality as soon as possible.

In total, 14 motor cars will be needed for the operation, each of which is to be manned by a member of Section IV B or IV. For support, each of these officials will be assigned either two men from the Feldgendarmerie or alternatively, if possible, two members of the guard platoon.[6] The lead official will pick up the addresses of the Jews before departure, around 20 at most – and will begin independently with the detention and transfer of the Jews to 510.[7] If required, the garage at 510, which would be manned by an Unterführer[8] and 4 or 6 men, will be made available to receive the Jews. Transport to the Mecheln[9] camp will take place in the morning hours using official vehicles from this office.

In total, therefore, 14 members of Department IV, of whom 7 would be provided by Section IV B, would be needed. The remainder of the officials would have to be made available by Department IV. To support these officials, 28 additional members of the Flemish guard platoon and around 6 men must be available to guard the Jews who have been arrested. I deem it important to start this operation without the help of the Feldgendarmerie.[10]

In addition, the Foreign Exchange Protection Commando will participate at full strength in the operation. The Foreign Exchange Protection Commando has already made a note of a number of Jews of Belgian nationality who are in possession of sizeable amounts of foreign currency. The Foreign Exchange Protection Commando will immediately take control of the Jews' apartments, order the residents who are present to pack their bags, and also begin searching for and securing all tangible assets that are of importance to the Foreign Exchange Protection Commando. SS-Obersturmführer Asche, with 2 members of the guard platoon and 2 drivers from the Foreign Exchange Protection Commando, will be in charge of transporting the Jews detained in their apartments by the Foreign Exchange Protection Commando.

The entire operation is expected to be concluded around 6 a.m.

Remaining in the office will be:

1. SS-Hauptsturmführer Erdmann,
2. Fräulein Plum as typist.

In summary:

The operation will be carried out by the Security Police, with 7 men from Section IV B and the rest from the other administrative sections of Department IV.

5 On 29 June 1943 the Security Police and the SD in Brussels informed all field offices in a telex that Reichsführer SS Himmler had ordered Jews with Belgian citizenship to be included in the deportations from now on; this telex is included in the file.

6 Presumably this refers to members of the Germanic SS in Flanders who formed a guard troop for the headquarters of the Security Police and the SD in Brussels.

7 The headquarters of the Security Police and the SD in Brussels were located at 510 avenue Louise.

8 Rank equivalent to non-commissioned officer.

9 Correctly: Mechelen.

10 The roundup was actually carried out for the most part by members of the German police, in a few cases with the support of Belgian collaborators.

28 men from the guard platoon and
6 additional men from the guard platoon for special guarding of the Jews in the building at 510. In addition
14 official vehicles from the office.

It is requested that consent to the impending action be granted.[11] There is no intention to apprehend Jews in whom the military administration might have a special interest.[12] Should particular objections still be raised, it is possible to release Jews of this sort or perhaps transfer them to the home for the aged or to some other Jewish institution.

DOC. 215
On 6 September 1943 Salomon van den Berg records how he avoided arrest early on 4 September in Brussels[1]

Diary of Salomon van den Berg, two entries for 6 September 1943, pp. 128–130 (copy)

6 September:[2]
On Friday morning[3] I was told by a *reliable source* that they would come to take all the Belgian Jews during the night between Friday and Saturday. At first I gave little credence to these stories, since so many tall stories are being told, but as a precaution and in sworn secrecy I warned some friends. As for me, I was very tired. We had spent the evening as usual and had gone to bed around 11 p.m. I could certainly have gone to stay somewhere else, but Nicole had a temperature of 39 degrees and a bout of angina, and I decided to stay and to defend myself if anyone came.

Around 5 a.m. someone rang our neighbours' bell on the ground floor for about 20 minutes, or so I was told, but I didn't hear anything. After a short time the caretaker went to open the door, and there were three protecteurs[4] who burst into our place. I asked them who they were. Members of the German police. Was wünsche[n] Sie? Das werde i[ch] Ihne[n] gleich sagen.[5] Then come in, I said. So, I said, tell me, what can I do for you. They answered by just saying: Get yourself ready and come with us. I told them that this was not possible because Nicole was sick and could not get up, and, in any case, I had documents that I could use to protect myself. But they would not hear of it. As they were in a hurry, we were to get dressed. But I insisted and told them that they were making a mistake, that I was the president of the Brussels AJB, that I had been

11 This is not part of the file. The roundup was carried out as planned. In all, 750 Jews were arrested in Brussels and 225 Jews in Antwerp, and they were deported to Auschwitz on 20 Sept. 1943. Following protests by the Belgian authorities on 6 Sept. 1943, Eggert Reeder, the chief of the military administration, complained that the Security Police and the SD had not given the Oberfeldkommandanturen in Brussels and Antwerp sufficient notice of the operation: CegeSoma, AA 556.

12 See Doc. 212.

1 The original is privately owned. Copy in Wiener Library, P III i/276. This document has been translated from French.

2 In the diary, both this entry and the next are dated 6 Sept. 1943.

3 3 Sept. 1943.

4 French in the original: 'guards'.

5 Faulty German in the original: 'What do you want? You're about to find out.'

given the position by President Rocher[6] and that his signature should be respected. In the end – at my suggestion and after I had given him the telephone number – he called the head of the Gestapo[7] and informed him about all these documents I had shown him, and was told he had to let me stay at home. At which he said: Sie haben Schwein or, You're in luck, you can stay. But we are nevertheless going to do a little search to see if we can find any valuables or gold or money. They searched through everything but did not find anything, and after ten minutes they left very politely and we breathed a huge sigh of relief. We went back to bed, and as early as 7 a.m. I telephoned Mr Beilin[8] to tell him what had happened to me. He told me that his telephone had been [ringing] since 4.30 a.m., that almost all of the Belgian Jews had been arrested during this one single night, and that in Antwerp all of the Belgian Jews had also been arrested, including the members of the Association's management board.[9] On Saturday morning I immediately telephoned Mr Ullmann, even though he does not answer the telephone on Saturdays, and because I kept persevering he ended up answering, or actually his daughter did, and I brought him up to date on the situation. He then went straight to the Director General of Justice, Mr Platteau,[10] who promised to intervene right away and to get in touch with the other secretaries general so that they could draw up a joint démarche. He promised to be very firm and to threaten complete disruption if their requests to release all the Belgians[11] and not touch their possessions were not honoured. I doubt anything will come of it. I also saw Mr Grauls[12] […][13] Brussels, and Mr Frédericq, head of the king's office, and all promised their support, but I have the impression that we are heading towards the end of the war and that [the Germans] want to take revenge on the Jews for all of their misfortunes. I think that we have no choice but to disappear for some time, even though it is repugnant to me to abandon everything at the Association, but I have to look after the safety of those closest to me before all else.

6 September:
Today we will see again how the gentlemen from the Gestapo are disposed towards the attitude of the secretaries general. A first meeting between the latter and the military

6 Presumably a reference to Eggert Reeder.
7 The diary entry for 10 Oct. 1943 indicates that van den Berg was referring to Kurt Asche, who had been working for the section for Jewish affairs since the previous year: see Doc. 192. The head of the section was actually Fritz Erdmann, who had indeed stayed in the office with his typist during the roundup: see Doc. 214.
8 Correctly: Hans Berlin.
9 The reference is to the Association of Jews in Belgium (AJB/VJB). Management board member Nico David Workum and several employees of the Antwerp branch, together with the Belgian Jews released from Mechelen in June 1943, were summoned to the headquarters of the German police in Antwerp on the eve of the Brussels roundup and arrested there.
10 Léon Platteau (1905–1974), office manager for the secretary general of the Ministry of Justice; interceded with the German occupiers to obtain the release of Belgian Jews; minister of justice and Belgian ambassador in the Netherlands after the war.
11 i.e. all Jews with Belgian nationality.
12 Jan Jozef Grauls (1887–1960), linguist and administrative official; governor of the province of Antwerp, 1940–1942; mayor of Greater Brussels, 1942–1944; sentenced to five years in prison in 1945 but released in 1947; worked as a textbook editor.
13 The original has the word 'Bzatuche' here, which makes no discernible sense and has therefore been left out.

government has taken place,[14] [the military government] proposed releasing the elderly and the children, but [the secretaries general] rejected that; they want the liberty of all the Belgians.[15]

The military situation is very poor for the Germans.

Ciano[16] has been arrested.

DOC. 216

On 17 September 1943 the Antwerp Feldkommandantur forbids the confiscation of household effects belonging to Jews who have not yet been deported[1]

Letter (marked 'by courier!') from the chief of administration at Feldkommandantur 520 (III pol. no. 804 Dr L./M), unsigned (military administration department head), Antwerp, to the field office of the Ministry for the Occupied Eastern Territories,[2] 1 Gretrystr., Antwerp, dated 17 September 1943 (carbon copy)

In the large-scale operation against the Belgian Jews, approximately 800 Antwerp Jews were arrested.[3] As became known here, matters have progressed to the point where the furniture and entire household effects of these detained Jews are being removed. According to the notification from the Chief of the Military Administration,[4] the question of the deportation of these Jews has not yet been decided. It must be expected that in individual cases the release of Jews who have been arrested will be ordered, for example on grounds of their advanced age. Naturally, significant distress will arise if the Jews who are released find on their return that their former apartment has been emptied. During the previous operation against the Jews, in which furniture was removed before the transport of the Jews had actually taken place, substantial difficulties occurred when a

14 As the representative of the secretaries general, a senior official in the Belgian Ministry of Justice (presumably Léon Platteau) lodged a protest on 6 Sept. 1943 with the chief of the military administration's 'politics' group ('polit' for short, dealing with political and Jewish affairs), opposing the arrest of Belgian citizens and indicating that the secretaries general might not continue their work should these citizens be deported.

15 On 17 Sept. 1943 Reeder told the chairman of the Council of the Secretaries General that he could not promise that those who had been arrested would remain in Belgium, but that he had ordered further arrests of Belgian Jews to be suspended and had initiated an investigation into the events in Antwerp: see Doc. 218. Three days later, those who had been arrested were deported to Auschwitz. Finally, in early Oct. 1943 the secretaries general submitted a protest note, which had no further consequences.

16 Galeazzo Ciano (1903–1944), lawyer; Italy's minister of foreign affairs from 1936; broke with Mussolini in Feb. 1943; arrested in Sept. 1943 and sentenced to death; executed in Jan. 1944.

1 Wiener Library, P III i/279. This document has been translated from German.

2 This refers to the field office of the Rosenberg Task Force for the Occupied Eastern Territories. On the role of the Rosenberg Task Force in the confiscation of household effects from the apartments of arrested Jews, see PMJ 5, p. 64 and PMJ 5/141; on these confiscations, see also Docs. 217 and 218 in this volume.

3 This figure was inflated. The actual number of Jews arrested in Antwerp during the major raid on 3–4 September 1943 was 225: see Doc. 214, fn. 11.

4 Eggert Reeder.

good number of these Jews subsequently had to be released after attestation of a mixed marriage.[5]

For this reason, I consider it necessary that the removal of the furniture and household effects of the Jews arrested in the last operation against the Jews must wait until the deportation of these persons has actually been carried out.[6] The Chief of the Military Administration has been informed of my decision. Please use the enclosed acknowledgement of receipt to confirm receipt of this decision.

DOC. 217

After his release in late June 1943 from Mechelen camp, Lucien Hirsch describes the roundups and life in the camp in a report for the Belgian government in exile[1]

Report by Lucien Hirsch,[2] unsigned, undated[3] (typescript)

Notes on the life of Jewish internees in the Dossin Barracks in Mechelen (September 1942–June 1943)

These notes were written by one of the first Belgian prisoners, who was arrested in his house in September 1942 and released as a Belgian citizen in June 1943. These pages reflect only some aspects of life for prisoners of the Gestapo. The release of a few Belgians was merely a ruse on the part of the Germans, since the Sicherheitspolizei[4] arrested all the Belgian Jews two months later and deported them to the East in huge numbers.[5] Only a few were lucky enough to escape the Nazis' clutches.

The Roundups

Since the Germans invaded Belgium, the Israelites have been subject to the most senseless harassment. Vexatious orders have been issued at fairly regular intervals: registration in a special register, defacement of identity papers with a stamp, curfew from 8 p.m. to 7 a.m., no access to public funds or mortgage loans, confiscation of radios, liquidation of Jewish businesses, mandatory wearing of the yellow star, forced labour in the Organization Todt for men, etc.

But the most malicious acts, aimed first and foremost at foreigners living in Belgium, were perpetrated from July 1942.[6] Without any warning, roundups were organized by the

5 See Doc. 217, fn. 51.
6 On 20 Sept. 1943 a total of 794 persons were deported; all the others were placed in institutions (children's homes and homes for the elderly) of the Association of Jews in Belgium (AJB/VJB).

1 CegeSoma, AB 1324. This document has been translated from French.
2 Lucien Hirsch (b. 1911), estate agent; worked in his father's business; arrested on 23 Sept. 1942 and taken to Mechelen; as a Belgian citizen, he was released in late June 1943; after his release, he was active in the resistance movement.
3 According to post-war statements by the author, the report was written after his release from Mechelen and delivered to the government in exile in London through secret channels at the beginning of 1944.
4 German in the original: 'Security Police'.
5 This refers to the raid of 3/4 September 1943: see Doc. 214.
6 More than 90 per cent of the Jews living in Belgium did not hold Belgian citizenship.

Gestapo and their Flemish SS lackeys.[7] These took place on trains, at food supply points, in the streets, in shops, and in people's homes. At that time Belgian citizens[8] were not subject to harassment. People were brutally arrested and thrown into the cellars of the Gestapo building in Brussels, herded into a disused cinema or a public hall in Antwerp. The same evening or the next day, the victims were put on lorries which were then hermetically sealed, and transported, packed together like cattle, to the Dossin Barracks in Mechelen, which served as a transit camp. Needless to say, the people who were arrested while they were out in public did not have any luggage with them. Many of them were sent to Poland in a summer dress or in a suit with no overcoat. Arrests at home took place both during the day and at night, and all the Israelites were taken away regardless of their age, infirmities, or illnesses. Women whose children were at school, babies who were home alone without their parents, children in the streets, the sick in their beds, all were arrested.

At the time of these arrests, the following people in Antwerp stood out in particular because of their brutality and cynicism:

a) SS Sturmscharführer Holm[9] of the Gestapo;
b) Lauterborn[10] from Flanders in Deurne (Antwerp);
c) Janssens,[11] another Flemish man, manager of the Belgica Café on avenue Isabelle in Antwerp.

In Brussels:

a) SS Sturmscharführer Kaizer[12] and
b) Hascher,[13] both from the Gestapo on avenue Louise;
c) Sturmscharführer Rodenbusch,[14] secretary to Hascher.

Officials in charge at Mechelen

The leaders at Mechelen camp were:

a) SS Sturmbannführer Schmidt[15] from Berlin, in charge of camp administration. This officer was infamous at Breendonck camp, where he was in command. But the actual active leader of Mechelen camp until March 1943 was

7 Several large roundups, during which 4,468 Jews were arrested and deported, took place between 15 August and 23 Sept. 1942, primarily in Brussels and Antwerp. In addition, there were frequent arrests of smaller groups or individuals. By 26 Sept. 1942, 11,781 persons were deported to the East: see Docs. 180 and 188.

8 This refers to Jews who were Belgian citizens.

9 Erich Holm.

10 Felix Lauterborn (1895–1956), journalist; member of the antisemitic Flemish Volksverweering; worked as an informant for the Security Police and the SD in Brussels from mid 1942; sentenced to death in Belgium in 1948; sentence commuted to life imprisonment in 1950.

11 Karel Emiel Janssens (b. 1911); member of the Flemish SS from 1941; fled to Germany in 1944 and joined the SS; sentenced to death in Belgium in 1948; sentence commuted to life imprisonment in 1950; released in 1963.

12 Correctly: Karl Walter Kaiser (1907–1973), retailer; served with the police in Halle/Saale from Sept. 1933; worked in the section for Jewish affairs of the Security Police and the SD in Brussels; deployed to Mechelen from July to Sept. 1942, then returned to the Security Police and the SD in Brussels.

13 This presumably refers to Kurt Asche.

14 Correctly: Hans Rodenbüsch (b. 1908); transferred to Belgium from the Düsseldorf Criminal Police in 1940; served as Asche's deputy from August 1942; thought to have remained in post until Sept. 1944.

15 Correctly: Philipp Schmitt.

b) SS Hauptsturmführer Steckmann,[16] of an unbalanced mind, alcoholic, diabolically evil, deceitful, spying and prying everywhere. Sent inmates who could have stayed at Mechelen to Poland on any pretext. His immediate subordinate was

c) SS Untersturmführer Meinzhausen,[17] a butcher by trade, a real beast who terrorized the camp. This Nazi spread panic everywhere he went. Never seen without his truncheon, an alcoholic of a bestial character, he constantly slapped and beat inmates.

d) Another miserable character was Dr Krull[18] (rumour had it that he was in fact called Zetser and had been a lawyer in Chemnitz). He only dealt with administration and served as a middleman for the Treuhandgesellschaft.[19] He was the one who transferred the loot to this bank when the new inmates arrived. Although he had nothing to do with life inside the camp, he played sinister and sadistic pranks over which his sidekicks rejoiced. Woe betide the old man or woman who failed to greet him when he crossed the yard. He would bludgeon them in the face and kick them relentlessly. Only rarely did he target young men.

His subordinates were:

e) the German woman Graf (or Graffe);

f, g) the VNV [member] Albers[20] and his sister,[21] from Mechelen.

And then there were:

h) SS Sturmscharführer Kriminalsekretär Boden[22] from Leipzig. A shrewd, shifty Saxon, he would sometimes defend inmates and alleviate punishments. Despite this, he was vulgar and hypocritical, uttering obscenities and swearing with no regard for who was listening.

i) The SS man Probst[23] obeyed his superiors' orders, led the sessions of punitive 'sport', and inflicted corporal punishments on anyone who made a misstep.

16 Rudolf Steckmann (1912–1956), office worker; joined the NSDAP in 1931 and the SS in 1937; personnel manager for the SD in Berlin, 1936–1940; with the Security Police and the SD in Belgium, 1940–1944; spent 18 months of that time as camp commandant in Mechelen; returned to the SD in Berlin in Jan. 1944.

17 Correctly: Karl Meinshausen (1907–1962), joiner; with the Security Police and the SD in Brussels from 1940; worked in the section for Jewish affairs; in Mechelen, July 1942 – April 1943; dismissed for embezzlement; returned to Germany and served as a soldier from May 1944; in Allied captivity in Germany from April 1945; released in July 1946.

18 Correctly: Erich Crull (1901–1975), retailer; conscripted in Litzmannstadt (Łódź) from Oct. 1939 to 1940; with the Brussels Trust Company in Mechelen, Nov. 1942–Oct. 1943; dismissed for embezzlement and conscripted into the Wehrmacht; in captivity, April 1945–Oct. 1946.

19 German in the original: 'Trust Company', i.e. the Brussels Trust Company.

20 Correctly: Albert Jozef Aelbers (b. 1917), bookkeeper; joined the far right Vlaams Nationaal Verbond (VNV) before 1940; a regional leader (*gouwleider*) of the VNV's youth movement from 1940; worked for the Brussels Trust Company in Mechelen from July 1942; arrested in France in 1944 while attempting to flee with several suitcases full of jewels; sentenced to 15 years in prison in 1947; released in 1950; rehabilitated in 1968.

21 Hubertine Aelbers (b. 1912), retailer; member of the VNV's girls' organization; worked for the Brussels Trust Company in Mechelen from 1942; arrested with her brother in 1944; sentenced to four years in prison in 1947.

22 Max Boden (1891–1974), policeman; with the Leipzig Gestapo from 1935; joined the NSDAP in 1939; with the Security Police and the SD in Brussels, 1940–1944; posted at Mechelen camp from the summer of 1942; arrested in Rotterdam in 1945; extradited to Belgium in 1947; sentenced to eight years in prison in 1950; released and returned to Germany in 1951.

23 Heinz Probst, sailor; member of the SS; worked for the Brussels Trust Company in Mechelen from July 1942; headed the Flemish guard troop outside the camp, Jan.–May 1943.

j) The Flemish SS man Poppe,[24] from Bassevelde (East Flanders), must be considered a murderer just like his superiors. He is greedy, rude, and inherently evil, and is responsible for more than one death.
k) The kitchen was managed by the SS man Stark,[25] who, like all the leaders at Mechelen, enriched himself considerably. Secretarial work was done by
l) a young female VNV member, Miss Louise […],[26]
and health (?) services were under the supervision of
m) Oberstabsarzt Pohl,[27] a high-ranking medical officer in the Wehrmacht. He allowed people who were gravely ill in the infirmary or in hospital to be deported.

The guard troops were provided by the Wehrmacht until November; after that they were made up of Flemish SS men. They had nothing to do with life inside the camp.

In March 1943, all the staff in the camp were replaced, except for Dr Krull, Boden, and Stark. These changes were prompted by the atrocities against the prisoners, the thefts, and the misappropriations of funds committed by the gang mentioned above. Word of the numerous abuses got out and caused some commotion in Berlin. Then the replacements happened.[28]

Hauptsturmführer Erdmann[29] took over the leadership of the antisemitic section in Brussels.[30] Sturmbannführer Schmidt was relieved of his duties, and his job was eliminated. Steckmann was transferred to Breendonck and, after some prompting from Brussels, ceded his position to Sturmscharführer Hans Franck,[31] assisted by Rottenführer Noppeney[32] and four Flemish SS men: Journee from Brussels, Stubbe, Blietge, and van Kol[33]

24 Jean Poppe (1907–1947), ship steward; member of the Flemish SS; in Mechelen, August 1942–March 1943; dismissed for embezzlement; arrested in Brussels in August 1945; sentenced to death and executed in 1947.

25 SS-Unterscharführer Stark (b. *c.*1907), born in Austria; cook; in Mechelen from Jan. 1942.

26 Louisa van de Poele (b. 1922), secretary; worked for the Flemish extremist group De Vlag in Brussels and Antwerp; secretary at Mechelen camp; returned to De Vlag until August 1944; fled to Germany; sentenced to permanent loss of civil rights in 1946; sentence reduced to five years in 1948.

27 Presumably Dr Karl-Otto Pohl (1897–1998), physician; with the Wehrmacht from April 1941; head of health services at Mechelen camp in 1943; prisoner of war until Dec. 1945.

28 In March 1943 most members of the German administration at Mechelen camp were replaced because rumours had reached Berlin about them enriching themselves with possessions belonging to Jews. Charges were subsequently brought against several members of the administration (Asche, Schmitt, Erdmann, and Crull).

29 Fritz Erdmann.

30 This refers to the section for Jewish affairs of the Security Police and the SD.

31 Correctly: Johannes (Hans) Frank.

32 Ferdinand Noppeney (b. 1902), bank employee; joined the NSDAP in 1933; member of the SS; worked for the Security Police and the SD in Brussels; in charge of the warehouses in Mechelen, March 1943–Sept. 1944.

33 Jean-Baptiste Journée (b. 1907), toolmaker; served on the Eastern front, 1942–1943; with the Flemish guard troop, Feb. 1943; in Mechelen, April 1943–April 1944; interned in May 1945; released into the American sector, April 1946. Correctly: Robrecht Josef Antoon Strubbe (b. 1903), painter and pastry chef; sentenced to 20 years in prison in 1945; rehabilitated by the Brussels Court of Appeal in 1966. Correctly: Franciscus Cornelius Hubertus Blietgen (b. 1908), mechanic; sentenced to death in 1945; sentence commuted to 20 years in prison in 1947. Lodewijk van Kol (1913–1966), shipyard worker; joined the VNV in 1940; worked for the Security Police and the SD from Sept. 1942, first in Brussels; in the Netherlands from Nov. 1944; taken prisoner in May 1945; extradited to Belgium; released in Dec. 1958 and moved to Germany.

from Antwerp. The latter, a former butcher, had been a member of the SS since 1933 and wore Nazi insignia under his Belgian uniform. He too was brutal and beat up several inmates immediately after his arrival.

But under Franck's leadership there was a distinct improvement in the moral and material conditions in Mechelen camp. The inmates were no longer harassed, and the first releases took place. Occasionally, prisoners with particular talents were allowed to perform in the camp yard.

In Mechelen

The disused line regiment barracks served as a human warehouse for the unfortunate victims of Nazi persecution before they were deported to the East. The barracks, which in peacetime could house two infantry battalions, had to hold up to 2,300 people.

The inmates were divided into separate groups and had to carry a cardboard tag with their number. First there was the 'staff', made up of foreign men and women who had been seized right at the beginning of the roundups. The 'staff' worked in the office, the warehouses, and the infirmary, and carried out other specific tasks in the barracks. They enjoyed better treatment and a few privileges. However, this did not prevent three-quarters of them from being deported to Poland as soon as they were no longer required for organizing the camp.

Then there was the 'mixed' group, men and women in mixed marriages or half-Jews, arrested by mistake, who stayed in Mechelen for nearly nine months. Some were deported if Steckmann did not like their physical appearance, or if he considered their papers to be false. The Belgians formed another category altogether. Around 140 were also arrested 'by mistake' in September 1942, and we were promised that we would be released soon. As no other Belgians were arrested, there was no reason to keep 140 people imprisoned. Nevertheless, their imprisonment lasted nine months and cost several of them their lives. Apart from the members of this group, some of the Belgians arrested on the basis of German ordinances (wearing the star etc.) were deported, but from November 1943[34] it was official that the 'mixed', together with the Belgians arrested in September – who, from the German perspective, had done nothing wrong – and the Belgians arrested thereafter would not be sent to Poland. In many cases, people had had their stars torn off and were then considered in contravention of the ordinance. Their file was stamped 'ohne Stern' – without a star – and no amount of protest, nor the threads which showed that they had been wearing the star, could change the Nazis' minds. This is why there were 300 Belgians in Mechelen in June 1943, who had been promised that they would be released, following the interventions of highly placed people.[35] Two hundred of them were released, and the remaining one hundred were sent to Poland during the final roundups of all the Belgians. German promises …

The Belgians and the inmates in the mixed group were put up on the third floor, on beds with straw mattresses in the damp, rundown attic of the barracks. The skylights did not close properly, and water ran down the walls. The beds were wedged together side by side, and sixty people slept in spaces that were meant to hold only half that number. But, as they slept in bunks, their fate in this respect was a little better than that

34 This should presumably be 1942.

35 The Belgian secretaries general had called for the prisoners' release: see Doc. 215.

of the 'transport' groups made up of foreigners, who slept on straw, eighty to a hundred per standard soldiers' room. The straw was laid down when the camp was opened in 1942 and was not changed even once until January 1943.

How many people will have slept in this dirt! At the beginning of 1943, bunks were built with canvas on a wooden frame; these bunks were built one on top of the other, so that more than one hundred inmates could be squeezed into each room. Although there was less dust, it was teeming with vermin (the straw used to fill the bunks was still that which dated back to July 1942). The whole barracks was very quickly infested with insects.

While the 'mixed' group and the Belgians were able to get their hands on a little leftover coal, the dormitories for the transport groups were not heated at all. Men, women, and children slept in the same quarters, side by side, and all had to get undressed in public.

Arrival at the camp

When the lorries arrived, people assembled in the yard and were split into two groups: Belgians and foreigners. Then the inmates were taken to the office: this was the ghastly Aufnahme.[36] They had to go to each department and were stripped of one thing after another: their money, their keys, their jewellery, pencils, penknives, rings, watches, penholders, torches, all their valuables, and their official documents. Valuables were put into envelopes and taken to the Treuhandgesellschaft. Needless to say, when the object was too tempting, these gentlemen would take it for themselves. Similarly, only part of the money was put in the bank; the rest lined the pockets of the Nazis, who made considerable fortunes in this way. They first stole from the inmates, and then from their government.

The search was accompanied by humiliation, insults, slaps, truncheon blows, and cologne sprayed into women's eyes (a specialty of Dr Krull's). If somebody had managed to smuggle in a ring or some jewellery or silverware in the hem or fold of some garment, and if this 'theft' was discovered, the inmate was led away, stripped completely, and severely beaten. Their screams would ring out in the yard.

Women, particularly if they were young, were immediately stripped of their clothes and examined in a closet. They were turned round and round in a way that decency prevents me from describing. The sadistic drunkards had great fun.

Next was the inspection, or more precisely the theft, of the luggage. They took the suitcases, which the inmates had just managed to pack in time, and everything was removed: clothes that seemed too nice; leather handbags; the suitcases themselves, if they were made of leather; furs, soap, razors, scissors, alarm clocks and small clocks, and all food apart from bread. Everything was thrown into baskets, and at night the Germans and the Flemish guards would rummage through these things.

This search was carried out by young girls from the 'staff' under the supervision of two Germans. I have to pay special tribute to these young girls, who very often managed to alleviate the prisoners' terrible misery somewhat, at great risk to themselves.

Prayer books and religious items were also taken away and sometimes burned on a bonfire in the middle of the yard.

36 German in the original: 'registration'.

Then, stripped of all their possessions, with no other identification than the numbered cardboard tag around their neck, the inmates went to the communal rooms to wait for their departure to Poland.

Several suicides occurred at the Dossin Barracks.

Food

In total, the daily ration was made up of a quarter loaf of bread in the morning, with a black brew that was referred to as coffee; a ladle of watery soup, in which floated some potatoes and vegetables, at lunchtime; and a spoonful of sugar and a spoonful of jam with coffee in the evening. That was all. Very bad mouldy bread was delivered by a baker from Heyat-op-den-Berg,[37] a certain Brinkers, who is in cahoots with the Germans and whose business was booming from his revolting bread ingredients and his cheating on weight. Twice a week, we were given a second portion of soup in the evening, and the bread ration was reduced to one eighth of a loaf per person.

Poppe managed the kitchens while Stark was on leave, and for almost three weeks the soup, which was often completely without salt, was thinner than ever. He sometimes also forgot the evening sugar ration. Months later, this Belgian traitor would boast in the hall: 'When I was feeding you …'. This of course was said in German; he never spoke to us other than in German, with lots of mistakes. It was the official language.

The inmates were allowed to receive parcels from outside the camp. Of course, only people with rich relatives could get food parcels and clothes. These parcels were usually distributed the day after their arrival and were subjected to the same inspection as the luggage.

Tins of food, butter, chocolate, and sweets were mercilessly removed, 'für die Kinder',[38] they would say. Never during Steckmann's rule did the children get any sweets!

Every night, a collection for the poorest would be carried out in the dormitories among the lucky ones who had received parcels. But what good could two extra slices of bread a day really do in the face of this systematic starvation?

Very often our guards were drunk or in a foul mood. Then the distribution of parcels would be postponed until the next day, which meant that food cooked by friends on the outside had to be thrown away, as it had gone bad.

Sometimes the parcels were held back for several days as a punishment. This would then bring the whole camp close to starvation. The food items from the parcels would then be thrown into the soup whole, except for the butter and the sweets. We would find sandwiches, gingerbread, cooked dishes, sauerkraut, and even razor blades that had been smuggled in and not discovered.

Children and old people got a little milk, but when the barracks were full (before a transport), there was not enough milk for everyone.

The Belgian Red Cross was able to send some parcels, and the recipients sent a receipt back. These parcels were inspected like the others, and often the food was removed. When the parcels were not handed out in January 1943, Meinzhausen, with his truncheon in hand, forced the recipients to sign the receipt requested by the Red Cross. After these events, the sending of parcels was abolished.

37 Correctly: Heist-op-den-Berg (province of Antwerp).

38 German in the original: 'for the children'.

I must add here that the entire running costs of the barracks, including food, toiletries and cleaning products, the few medicines, etc., were paid for by the Association of Jews in Belgium, an organization created by the Germans.[39]

Life in the camp

Reveille was at 6 a.m. At 8 a.m., exercise for the men, for just under half an hour; this was 'excellent' for the empty stomachs of most of the inmates. Then the various cleaning chores, and then nothing after that. The inmates lived in a permanent state of waiting for something to happen. They were waiting for their departure to the East and speculating about the likelihood of certain events, which depended on the mood the guards were in and how drunk they were. Bedtime was irregular and depended on the whims of the officer in charge, ranging from 7.30 to 9.30 p.m.

For a few months, workshops were set up, and two to three hundred inmates carried out prison work: gluing envelopes and cardboard boxes, tailoring, and leatherwork. The workers engaged in this labour received some slight advantages in terms of food rations, but the programme was soon stopped.

Punishments

In addition to flogging and solitary confinement without any food except for the camp rations, and sometimes even less, inmates were beaten with fists, always in the eyes or on the nose, and kicked in the legs or the stomach. But these gentlemen also came up with other ideas: as the fancy took them, they would suddenly summon a young girl into the yard, make her go into the office, and force her to take off all of her clothes. Sometimes they would ridicule an old man by shaving one side of his head, his moustache, or his beard. Then they would cover his face in red ink and force him to walk around the yard in front of everybody.

But the most damage was done by the bullwhip in Meinzhausen's hands, Probst's truncheon, and Krull's and Poppe's fists on the days they were drunk.

After an evening of drinking, Boden would quite often wake the inmates up in the middle of the night and utter such vulgar obscenities in front of women, girls, and children that I dare not repeat them.

Foot inspections were another occurrence which took place fairly frequently at night. If a prisoner's feet were not judged clean enough according to the inspectors' liking, the unfortunate prisoner would be forced to run around the yard several times, barefoot, in nightclothes, in the middle of winter. The SS men would sometimes throw buckets of water on them and beat them. This is how Boden and Poppe caused the death of one of our compatriots in February 1943.

Delousing

Since our officers felt that the inmates were infested with too many vermin, they decided to have them deloused in a facility they had spontaneously set up in Antwerp. Flanked

39 The Department for Special Assistance of the Association of Jews in Belgium (AJB/VJB) organized the aid parcels for Mechelen camp in cooperation with the Belgian Red Cross and the Belgian Winter Relief. At the same time, the Antwerp branch of the AJB/VJB had set up its own department for supplying camp inmates who had been deported from the city.

by many guards, we were taken by tram to Antwerp and had to shower in groups of forty to fifty people at a time. While our clothes were being disinfected, we had to wait, completely naked, for over an hour.

Needless to say, these German and Flemish clowns were also parading around in their uniforms in the room reserved for women and young girls, who had also been forced to wait, completely naked, for their clothes to be disinfected.

Departure for Poland

Twice a week in the beginning, then each Saturday, then every fortnight, and later every two or three months, inmates were sent, wearing a transport number, to their deaths in Poland.[40]

They were gathered in the yard and were then, one after the other, brutally herded into the cattle wagons which would take them to Muyzen-Mechelen station.[41] Those who had had the time to have some warm clothes or food sent to them carried suitcases, which were often put in different wagons and got lost during the transfer to third-class carriages in Muyzen. The inmates who had arrived at the barracks a day or two before often had no more than one loaf of bread for four days and the one meatball which the Germans granted them. Many children left for the East without their parents, and many mothers without their children, only equipped with bread and the meatball, as per regulations.

Particularly in the beginning, boarding was unbelievably violent and brutal. If old people did not climb into the wagon quickly enough, thugs like Poppe, Probst, or Meinzhausen would beat them savagely. The other officers, drunk since the day before, could not even stand up and were swaying between their victims.

After a good number of escapes, the Germans decided to make the prisoners do the whole trip to the East in livestock wagons.[42] The wagons contained fifty people, their luggage, water to drink, and two buckets for toilets. The wagons were locked and sealed, and the windows barred. But in spite of all these precautions, which also included twenty-odd armed Schupos,[43] some inmates still managed to escape from the trains.[44] But how many did not make it to the destination alive! Everybody was sent off. I saw lame people, blind people, infirm old men over eighty, mental patients taken from their asylums and the mentally abnormal, this entire human cargo dumped off their stretchers together onto the straw in the wagons. It was a massacre! Pregnant women, babies only a few days old, all of them made up what they pompously called 'Arbeitseinsatz im Osten' (labour deployment in the East). And all dispatched without any papers, to be lost in the death camps in Poland.

40 In total, 27 transports of Jews left Mechelen for Auschwitz.

41 Correctly: Muizen, a village south-east of Mechelen. It was an autonomous municipality until being incorporated into Mechelen in 1975.

42 During the transports, individuals had frequently managed to escape from the third-class passenger coaches that were used initially. The freight wagons used from late April 1943 were easier to seal and supervise.

43 German in the original: this refers to members of the Schutzpolizei (Urban Police) assigned to guard the transports.

44 This is a reference to Transport XXII (19 April 1943), from which more than 200 prisoners managed to escape.

Many of them departed in good spirits, holding their thumbs up in the English fashion. Others were resigned and softly whispered prayers. Others held each other upright, their eyes full of panicked fear of the Nazi and Flemish truncheons, and quietly thanked members of the staff group for the small but heartfelt help they were able to provide.

Those who witnessed these scenes of terror reminiscent of the Middle Ages will never be able to erase them from their memories.

Some atrocities

On 1 January 1943 there was an escape from Mechelen camp.[45]

All the male inmates, young and old, were summoned to the yard. All the NCOs went round the rooms, truncheon in hand, to ensure nobody could hide. The inmates, hatless in the pouring rain, were chased from one side to the other, pushed against the walls by the savage Meinzhausen, who, mad with rage, stoked their panic by cracking his whip randomly. The guards threatened prisoners with their machine guns. Some people, pushed down by the crowd, were left lying stretched out; an inmate was breathing his last on the ground. Meinzhausen beat him up, and finally some SS men poured buckets of water over him to shut him up. Two inmates were forced to run around the yard until they collapsed from exhaustion.

After two hours of waiting and being threatened, we were finally allowed to go back to our quarters, frozen through.

Special exercise

Sometimes Probst would call up all the men, young and old, without any apparent reason, and order them to do punitive exercise. These are some of the exercises: prisoners had to bend their knees and remain half-crouched, or lie down on the ground in the mud and bend their arms. If this was not executed quickly enough for his liking, the men would be beaten with truncheons. Then they had to run several times around the yard with their arms up or their knees bent. This was called 'sport'. Sometimes Major Schmidt would participate in this entertainment and fire his revolver into the air to increase the panic among the inmates even more, and sometimes his dog would hurl itself at them and maul them savagely.

Torture

If an inmate managed to escape from a transport to Poland and was unfortunate enough to be recaptured in a roundup, the worst punishment awaited him: he would be beaten to a pulp and held in solitary confinement, his head would be shaved, and he would be kept in isolation until the next transport departed.

One day, Dr Krull found one and took him to the office. He first beat him up and then burned his genitals with his cigar.

Very often, the bullwhips would not strike the victims' backs or shoulders, but cut into their stomach or genitalia. German Kultur!

45 This could not be verified.

The incident on 6 January 1943

It was discovered that parcels addressed to the inmates were disappearing.[46] Eventually, two culprits were picked out, passing over the complicit Flemish SS, who had concealed the goods. False accusations were made, innocent people were arrested, and eleven men in total were beaten up and thrown into solitary confinement. Later, in the snow, they were whipped, forced to throw themselves face down on the ground, then stand back up, and run, chased by their torturer Probst. This went on for two hours and was followed by Meinzhausen beating them with his bullwhip and by an encounter with Major Schmidt's savage dog. Finally, all the inmates in the camp were gathered in the courtyard.

Before us we saw eleven spectres, covered in blood, shivering with cold and fever. Then all the assembled men were forced to lynch them, which of course they only pretended to do. Can one imagine these eleven men, many of them innocent, thrown like this into the crowd of inmates, who themselves were terrified by the officers yelling at them? Then the eleven men were thrown into two cells with no blankets or food.

These sessions in the yard, led by Probst, with the prisoners forced to run and then crawl in the mud and snow, continued for three or four days.

Finally, seven of the eleven men were deported under terrible conditions, several of them with frozen limbs. One was pardoned, two were sent to Breendonck, and the last one, a young man of nineteen, H. H.,[47] innocent, was admitted to hospital as an emergency case; there they amputated his leg above the knee (frozen foot and gangrene), as well as four toes on his remaining foot. A few months later, despite all efforts to secure this poor victim's release, he too was deported to Poland in the horrible livestock wagons.

All evidence of the events of 6 January 1943 had to disappear forever. But the murderers will have to atone for their crimes!

These dreadful days made other things pale into insignificance: the inmates' suffering and humiliation, the women and men hit in the face, the mothers crying for help for their children, the people dying on their straw pallets, stripped of their belongings and covered in vermin.

The whole gang – Schmidt, Steckmann, Meinzhausen, Krull, Probst, and the Fleming Poppe – will eventually get what they deserve, even though five of them left the barracks in March 1943.

The Belgians' release

After the people in mixed marriages were released, there was talk of releasing the 300 Belgian inmates, including the 140 people arrested 'by mistake' in September 1942. After long deliberations, the leadership in Brussels[48] decided to release us in groups of 100 at a time.

46 This incident came to light on 1 Jan. 1943. The punitive measures in Mechelen lasted for ten days. On 11 Jan. 1943, 37 people who had been accused of embezzlement were transferred from Mechelen to Breendonk camp. Many of them did not survive.

47 Herman-Israël Hirsch (1923–1943), electrician; left Germany to settle in Belgium; deported to Auschwitz on 31 July 1943; thought to have been murdered immediately upon arrival.

48 This refers to the German military administration in Brussels, which, for political reasons, decided not to deport the Belgian Jews for the time being and to release those who had already been imprisoned.

At last the day we had awaited and feared arrived. Would it be another trick? So many promises had been made to us since our internment![49]

We had to sign a declaration that we would never divulge anything that had happened at the barracks; we also had to sign that we had 'willingly' given up everything that was stolen from us; and finally, with 20 francs in our pockets, we were able to return to our homes, which had been totally stripped of all furniture and memories.[50] Nothing was left, unless it had been left behind by mistake!

We were assured that we were free. Holm in Antwerp even apologized for the imprisonment and assured us that some furniture would be made available to former inmates. Then he wished them good luck. Two hundred people were freed in this way and had to make a living somehow and find somewhere to live.[51] The remaining one hundred waited in vain for two more months.

On 3 September 1943, the Germans again went back on their promises. General roundups of Belgians in Antwerp and Brussels. The removal trucks in Antwerp were so full that nine people suffocated during the journey to Mechelen.[52]

Then there were the deportations, despite the formal assurances given to highly placed officials that no Belgian citizen would be sent to Poland.

A few managed to escape the clutches of these scoundrels. After the war, they will help the judiciary to unmask and punish them.

DOC. 218

In November 1943 the German military administration reports on the first deportation of Belgian Jews and the distribution of confiscated Jewish property[1]

Excerpts from activity report no. 25 of the military administration for the months July–September 1943 (no. 751/43, top secret), produced by the Military Commander in Belgium and Northern France, Chief of the Military Administration,[2] undisclosed location, dated 1 November 1943

[…][3]

10. *Jews*

After the military administration had initially refrained from deporting the approximately 3,000 Belgian Jews to avoid further aggravation of the general situation,[4] *on in-*

49 On 26 June 1943, 143 Jews were released; on 29 June, 160 more Jews were released. Further releases were blocked after Fritz Erdmann intervened, and the third group scheduled for release remained imprisoned in Mechelen.

50 These homes were emptied by employees of the Western Office (Dienststelle Westen), part of the Rosenberg Task Force. Most of the furniture was taken to Germany in freight wagons and distributed to the victims of air raids.

51 Most of the Belgian Jews who were released were housed in AJB/VJB facilities. Many of those who returned to Antwerp were arrested again on 3 Sept. 1943 while meeting with Erich Holm regarding the return of their furniture, and then deported.

52 The 225 Jews who were arrested were taken to Mechelen on two lorries. The second transport, carrying 145 Jews, was delayed by a breakdown and needed much longer to make the half-hour trip. As a result, 9 Jews suffocated and 14 others had to be taken to hospital upon arrival in Antwerp.

1 AN, AJ 40, vol. 5. Excerpt published in Klarsfeld and Steinberg (eds.), *Die Endlösung der Judenfrage in Belgien*, pp. 81–83. This document has been translated from German.

structions from the Reichsführer SS[5] *regarding the evacuation of the Belgian Jews, the deportation measures have now been implemented.* On 20 September 1943 the first transport train departed, carrying 793 Belgian Jews into Reich territory. In the course of the arrest operations on 3 and 4 September 1943, accidents occurred in Antwerp. Nine Belgian Jews died from suffocation while being transferred to the assembly camp in overcrowded lorries.[6] This incident provoked protests by the secretary general at the Ministry of Justice[7] and leading Belgian administrative officials. The matter is being investigated by the SS and police court at the behest of the Chief of the Military Administration.

[...][8]

2. *Jewish assets*

Recently *difficulties have arisen in the de-Jewification of the Belgian economy* in that the Belgian registration authorities have been refusing of late to recognize the acting administrators of Jewish companies as legitimate representatives of the mostly absent Jews. This attitude can undoubtedly be attributed to political and military developments.

Thus far it has not been possible for the sale of Jewish real estate properties to get under way, *owing to the refusal of Belgian notaries to provide the required certification.* During the period under review, efforts to reach an agreement with the relevant Belgian authorities have been unsuccessful. The intention is now – as in the Great War – to issue a decree to allow certification by German notaries.

The *registration and emptying out of Jewish apartments that have already been freed up or are becoming available* are continuing through the operational command in Belgium that was appointed for this purpose by the Reich Ministry for the Occupied Eastern Territories.[9] It is currently not feasible to confiscate furniture, household objects, etc. from the Belgian civilian population for the benefit of German bombing victims, however desirable this would be, because of the staff shortage and the danger of political repercussions. We must therefore draw on Jewish-owned furniture as much as possible. Between the onset of the registration operation (September 1942) and 30 August 1943, the Reich Ministry for the Occupied Eastern Territories sealed 4,015 apartments and cleared out 3,868 apartments. From this stock, 408 complete apartments, 418 complete sets of room furnishings, and 11,173 individual pieces of furniture have been made available to German offices in this command area to meet local billeting needs. The vast bulk of the furniture, comprising 54,057 cubic metres of furniture and household goods, was transported to the Reich and made available in complete sets to German cities. This is the equivalent of 1,800 railway wagons carrying 15 tons each or 45 trains, each with 40 railway wagons.

2 Eggert Reeder.
3 The full report is around 200 pages long and deals with political (Part A), administrative (Part B), financial (Part C) and economic issues (Part D) within the remit of the military administration. This excerpt is from Part A, pp. 50–51.
4 See Doc. 197.
5 Heinrich Himmler; see Doc. 214, fn. 5.
6 See Doc. 217, fn. 52.
7 Gaston Schuind; secretary general of the Ministry of Justice, April 1941 to Sept. 1943; forced by the military administration to resign with immediate effect on 17 Sept. 1943; sentenced after the war to five years in prison for collaboration.
8 The following excerpt from the report is from Part D (economic issues), pp. 27–28.
9 The reference here is to the Rosenberg Task Force for the Occupied Eastern Territories.

DOC. 219

At the end of January 1944, the Jewish Defence Committee reports on its work and the situation for Jewish children in Belgium since the beginning of the occupation[1]

Report, unsigned,[2] dated late January 1944 (typescript)[3]

Report on the situation of the Jewish children in Belgium from 10 May 1940 to 31 December 1943

When the storm swept across Belgium on 10 May 1940, almost the entire Jewish population left or sought to leave the country to seek refuge abroad.

In a number of cases where leading Committee members had left [their positions] at Jewish children's homes, these homes were placed in the care of subordinate staff, who acted on their own initiative to save the children. In some cases the children were returned to their parents, and in others they were transferred to non-Jewish institutions, while a few institutions set off for France en bloc. After the ceasefire was signed, all those who had failed to reach the free zone of France or a neutral country slowly began returning to Belgium. In taking stock with regard to Jewish children, we were to discover that the three large colonies – Villa *Johanna* in Middelkerke, by the sea, the Maison *de Cure* in Wesembegk,[4] near Brussels, and Villa *Altol* in Capellenbosch,[5] north of Antwerp – were occupied by the Germans.[6] We learned that a group of children who had emigrated from Germany had settled in unoccupied France,[7] while another group of young emigrants from Germany, led by their director, had returned to this country after a circuitous tour through France and were looking for a property in order to re-establish their home.[8]

In 1940 there was hardly any organized Jewish social work in Belgium worth mentioning. The year 1941 was not characterized by any especially noteworthy activity either. It should be emphasized that the Central Jewish Welfare Organization (OCIS)[9] organ-

1 Lavon Institute, III-37A-2-13A. The document is part of the collection of Nathan Schwalb (1908–2004), who ran the World Centre in Geneva of the Zionist youth organization Hehalutz, whose aim was to prepare halutzim (pioneers) for emigration to Palestine; together with the American Jewish Joint Distribution Committee (Joint, JDC), the World Jewish Congress, and the Swiss Red Cross, he helped organize relief operations for the Jews in the German sphere of influence. This document has been translated from German.

2 The report is thought to be the work of Yvonne Jospa, née Have Groisman (1910–2000), welfare worker; born in Popouti (Bessarabia); married Ghert (Hertz) Jospa in 1933; active in the Communist Party and the International League against Racism and Antisemitism in the 1930s; involved in children's relief in the Spanish Civil War; co-founder of the Jewish Defence Committee in 1942.

3 The original contains handwritten underlining.

4 Correctly: Wezembeek (now Wezembeek-Oppem), municipality in the province of Flemish Brabant.

5 Correctly: Kapellenbos, now part of the town of Kapellen, north of Antwerp.

6 All three institutions were founded in the 1920s as holiday homes for Jewish children, and Villa Altol has retained that function to this day. Before the occupation of Belgium, children of Jewish refugees were also housed in these homes.

7 This presumably refers to the ninety-two children who lived in Château de la Hille in the Pyrenees from 1941: see PMJ 5/152 and 153.

8 Presumably this is the group mentioned later in this report; see fn. 11.

9 Œuvre centrale israélite de secours, relief organization founded in 1926.

ized a service in Brussels to enable children in need to take their meals in the homes of middle-class families and in a few restaurants, as well as daily excursions into the countryside around Brussels during the summer, in cooperation with non-Jews. Some people organized a children's colony on a small scale for a limited number of children. The Jewish Community of Brussels established a number of Jewish supplementary schools, which were attended by a great many pupils.

At the same time, a horticultural and agricultural school for retraining young people was set up in Ramée,[10] though recruitment was slow at first. When in 1942 the institution was really starting to flourish, the German regulations made it impossible for its work to continue. Thanks to a private initiative, a private orphanage was established in Brussels. Its nucleus consisted of a group of emigrant children who were mentioned earlier in this report.[11]

When the Association of Jews in Belgium (A.J.B.) was established on 25 November[12] by order of the occupation authorities, the situation for the Jews changed fundamentally, as the only schools the children were allowed to attend were those especially established for Jewish children. This regulation came into force on 1 January 1942[13] for secondary schools and vocational schools, while the regulation was suspended for primary schools until the A.J.B., working with the Ministry of Education, established special primary schools. Shortly after the promulgation of this regulation, a teachers' training school and a Jewish 'athénée'[14] were opened as the result of a private initiative. With regard to the primary schools, however, both the ministry and the A.J.B. managed to prolong the discussion of the issue until the autumn of 1942, and by this time there was no longer any talk of special instruction, because of the deportations.[15]

For the year 1942 we highlight the founding of an association known as 'Nos Petits' (Our Little Ones).[16] This institution established a number of schools, which were particularly well run and had great success. Unfortunately, these schools were only very short-lived, as the events of the autumn[17] made their continued existence impossible.

At the beginning of September 1942, a resistance group was established in Brussels which later adopted the name *Jewish Defence Committee*.[18] The goal of the Committee was

10 The school for agriculture and horticulture at Chateau de Ramée near Jodoigne, in the province of Walloon Brabant, one of several institutions run by the Association of Jews in Belgium (AJB/VJB), provided young Jews with stable employment and thereby protected them from deportation. It was closed in June 1943. Some students were deported; others went into hiding.

11 This presumably refers to the Jewish orphanage in the rue des Patriotes/Patriottenstraat in Brussels, which had existed before the occupation and was reopened by Maurice Heiber in 1941 at the urging of Edouard Rotkel. Heiber became head of the AJB/VJB's social welfare department; in addition, he was involved in the Jewish Defence Committee.

12 See PMJ 5/176.

13 Regulation on the Jewish School System, 1 Dec. 1941, *VOBl-BNF*, 63, no. 4, 2 Dec. 1941, p. 801.

14 Secondary school.

15 See Doc. 192, fn. 11.

16 In April 1942 Dr Felice (Fela) Perelman, née Liwer (1909–1991), historian, founded schools for Jewish children on behalf of the AJB/VJB. From May 1942, first three and then four 'Nos Petits' schools operated in Brussels. Through her contacts with both the parents and the AJB/VJB, Perelman procured hiding places for many Jewish children.

17 This refers to the roundups in August/Sept. 1942, in which thousands were arrested and deported.

18 In French: Comité de défense des Juifs. Though the author does not use the full name in French, later in the report the abbreviation C.D.J. is used.

to wage war against the occupier, within the framework of the Belgian resistance movement, by taking part in resistance activities within the Belgian national plan,[19] organizing the resistance of the Jewish population to the occupier's regulations pertaining to them.

In practical terms, we first had to consider the problem of saving the children who had been left behind when their parents were deported, as well as the children threatened with the same fate. In the initial phase of the deportations, the Germans summoned people individually without any regard for family units. After the Belgians objected, the Germans agreed for 'humanitarian reasons' to stop separating the families and instead to send them to their workplaces together.[20] It is clear that once the Jewish population had grasped the true nature of these departures, many parents made an effort to save at least the children by trying to place them in the homes of non-Jews as boarders, with people whom they trusted. Some of the parents were able to find accommodation for themselves, but the number of children was too large for an operation dealing with individual cases to succeed, and the group that had just been established recognized that its first act had to be to systematically find lodgings for the children.[21]

Beginning on a small scale, in the very first weeks the Committee was inundated by this task. The small number of welfare workers who took the first steps to obtain possibilities for accommodation were well received everywhere and realized that the possibilities for accommodation were greater than one dared hope. It turned out that a large number of colonies for frail children, boarding schools, children's homes, and Catholic and secular orphanages declared themselves willing to work with us by taking in children without shrinking from the risks that might possibly result. Contact was also made with a great many private individuals who were willing to temporarily adopt Jewish children. The pressure from the parents who wanted places for their children was so great during the first months of work that the Committee was forced to avail itself of every opportunity for accommodation that was offered. Naturally, one would have preferred to place all the children in middle-class families, where the children were best off with regard to social position and material care and where there was often reluctance to accept money for room and board. However, to accommodate a large number of children, it was necessary also to draw on institutions and modest boarding houses that required payment.

The children who were to be housed came to us in various ways. The nature of the work of course made it necessary to proceed with a great deal of caution. In addition to the children who were nominated by relatives of the Committee members personally, enquiries were often also received from two left-wing Jewish political organizations[22] that continued their activities after 10 May 1940, and from persons who headed Jewish nursery schools in 1942, while a few welfare workers from the A.J.B were in contact with our Committee and sent cases to us indirectly.[23]

19 Presumably this refers to the plan by the Independence Front to bring as many of the smaller resistance groups as possible together in an umbrella organization and to plan for the liberation of Belgium.

20 This refers to so-called labour deployment in the East, i.e. deportation to Auschwitz.

21 The children's welfare department of the Jewish Defence Committee had five main members; its head was Maurice Heiber.

22 This probably refers to the Zionist-socialist workers' movement Poale Zion Left and the liberal General Zionists.

In addition, in a number of cases the Committee had to take back children whose parents had already placed them but were then no longer able to look after their children because of lack of funds or because they had been deported.

As regards the organization, the work took on such a scale that over the course of a few months the staff totalled around 20 welfare workers and officials. In addition to administration and bookkeeping, the work included a local service to scout out accommodation, selection and medical examination of the children, as well as accommodating them and accompanying the children when they had to travel, regularly sending them food parcels and transferring payments and contributions by parents who are able to cover part of the costs for board and lodging.

The administration consists of an index card system covering all the children who have been placed and specifying all the necessary information. Each child has a number, and care has been taken to record separately the assumed names and the correct ones, the addresses of the lodgings, the addresses of the parents and sponsors, and other references for the children, so that in the event that the German police uncover the administrative committee, they can never find the children.[24] On the other hand, all steps have been taken to keep the children from losing their real identity after the war and to ensure that they can be returned to their parents with no difficulty.

From a technical standpoint, the problem of food ration cards was especially thorny. In fact, since the children were accommodated under assumed names and the real parents were absent or unable to fetch the ration cards, the officials of the organization had to pick up the children's food ration cards every month under a pretext of some sort and with the tacit consent of the municipal officials. Then the cards were passed on to the institutions or private individuals. The contribution of money continually decreased because of the deportations and the impoverishment of the parents. Although the institutions and private persons generally made do with very modest disbursements for room and board and although the instances of accommodation being provided free of charge were not uncommon, the financial burden constantly increased and caused a great problem. It was extremely difficult if not impossible to scrape together the necessary funds by asking for charity, all the more so because the illegal nature of the work made all promotional efforts impossible. Only several months after the work had begun was contact made with the management of one of the most major welfare associations in the country, who took a lively interest in the work we had undertaken, and if it was possible to carry on with new placements without interruption, then it was thanks to the moral and financial support provided from this quarter.[25]

23 Parents or relatives who turned to the AJB/VJB were urged to place their children where they would be hidden or to entrust them to the Jewish Defence Committee.

24 The system developed by Estera Heiber for the children's welfare department consisted of individual file cards that could not be decoded without the numerous notebooks kept by 'Madame Pascal' (i.e. Estera Heiber). Each notebook contained different information, and links between the notebooks were created by numbers assigned to the children that always remained the same. The originals of the notebooks and the index card system are now in the archive of the Directorate-General War Victims, Brussels.

25 Through cooperation with Yvonne Nèvejean (1900–1987), the head of the National Children's Welfare Agency, about 4,000 Jewish children were saved.

In May 1942 the situation became especially critical after the arrest of the head of the children's welfare department, as well as his wife,[26] while at the same time the financial problem entered a particularly difficult stage as a result of the new placements made the previous month. The number of children reached approximately 1,300, and the financial needs amounted to 7[00,000]–800,000 Belgian francs, taking into account the replacement of clothing, as well as the children placed in Antwerp, Liège, and Charleroi. Luckily, very significant contributions were received at this time from this organization, while in June contact was made with the American Jewish Joint Distribution Committee [Joint], which from July on supported our work on a regular basis. After that it was possible to stabilize the situation and to undertake new placements.

It must be highlighted that the organization of which we spoke supplied us regularly with vitamins, flour-based products, condensed milk, cod-liver oil, fish pies, sardines, tuna, meat pies, chicken, chocolate, oranges, banana pastries, etc., while we were also helped to obtain clothing and shoes for the children. Generally speaking, the children's nutrition is satisfactory for the most part, but clothing and equipment for the children is a problem. The few things the children brought with them when they were entrusted to us were exhausted long ago, and must urgently be repaired or replaced. Thanks to a collection of clothes from various quarters, which continues to grow and is beginning to be well stocked, we hope to make improvements in this area. For the festivals, such as St Nicholas' Day,[27] the organization prepares little gifts and sweets for the children.

The children are in excellent health.[28] Cases of serious illness are extremely rare. It does happen, however, that children suffer from scabies because of the shortage of soap and the poor quality of the pharmaceutical products that substitute for it. Apart from the cases of two babies, there were no deaths. A project is about to be carried out with regard to the medical inspection service, which we want to enhance by securing the services of a female physician and several nurses and welfare workers. The vast majority of the children who have been placed attend school or receive regular instruction.

The number of children who were taken by the occupying forces is extremely small and is limited to ten cases. Often these concerned placements that the association had to take back and where placement elsewhere had not yet been able to occur. Mention must be made of the case of a convent in the centre of Brussels where there were around 16 girls and which received a visit from the Gestapo at which it was demanded that the children be handed over. The Mother Superior managed to persuade these gentlemen to postpone the abduction of the girls to the next day, on her responsibility. During the night, armed 'bandits' were able to creep into the convent and rescue the children.[29]

A rather large number of children were regularly arrested by the Germans in roundups and taken to Mechelen, which was an assembly camp for deportations to the East. The treatment of the children there was poor due to the poor hygienic conditions. Many children suffer from impetigo, scabies, and other infectious diseases. Naturally what be-

26 The date given in the text is incorrect: Maurice Heiber and his wife were not arrested and transported to Mechelen until May 1943. See Doc. 209.
27 This festival, known in Belgium and the Netherlands as Sinterklaas, is celebrated on 6 December.
28 This statement is at odds with the comment further on in the document that cases of illness among the children living in placements were above average.
29 See Doc. 209.

came of these children after their departure is not known, but the situation in Mechelen and the conditions of the transport lead one to assume the worst. In the summer of 1942, it was possible to secure the release of ten or so children, who were then placed in official homes of the A.J.B., and since then it has happened more often that children found by the Germans were not taken to Mechelen, but rather handed over to the A.J.B. directly.[30] To further increase security, a large number of children who had been accommodated were provided with false identity cards with proper registration in a municipality. Thanks to the help of the Belgian resistance movement, it was thus possible to obtain new, officially registered identities for many children, and we hope to be able to continue until all children for whom this matter is of interest can obtain such cover.

It has been ascertained that contact between the parents and their children must be avoided as far as possible, and a certain toughness in this regard is necessary. The moment the parents learn the address of the children, they find it hard to resist the temptation to visit them, which is of course highly imprudent. However, a correspondence service exists for a certain number of cases, and the parents are frequently shown photos of the children.

Although extreme caution is exercised in all the organization's services, unfortunately recently one of the young girls working for the organization was arrested in the street and sent to Mechelen.[31]

To raise the standard of the accommodation, an effort is being made to systematically eliminate the institutions and landlords that are less good, by removing the children who are there and finding better lodgings for them. There is no point in naming the organizations that took in our children, but it is interesting to note that recently a large number of children were accommodated at no charge by an organization that specializes in the housing of sickly, frail children in the cities and in the countryside.[32]

It is understandable that in some institutions and various private settings, the children are heavily under the influence of the Catholic Church. There are no more than several dozen cases of children who have now been baptized. The fact that Cardinal Van Roey has prohibited baptisms of children during the war without parental permission has surely contributed to this. Besides, only a minority of the children are housed in religious institutions.

The number of children who have been placed is around 2,000. This number includes the children accommodated in Antwerp, Charleroi and Liège. In Charleroi the local committee of the A.J.B started working as a clandestine organization at the beginning of the

30 The German occupiers did not keep their promise to transport only entire families for 'labour deployment'; as a result, a number of children under the age of 16 were left on their own in Mechelen. The AJB/VJB was able to place these and other orphaned children in Jewish orphanages, which, although under the control of the military administration, were organized by the AJB/VJB and maintained with the support of the National Children's Welfare Agency. In total, more than 500 Jewish children survived the occupation period in these orphanages.

31 Many girls and young women, most of them under the age of 20, made themselves available to the Jewish Defence Committee as messengers and to deliver money or false papers. Several of them were arrested, including Hénia Hass (b. 1913) from Antwerp, who might be the person referred to here. She was picked up in Schaerbeek in mid Nov. 1943.

32 Presumably a reference to the Young Christian Workers, founded in 1924, which from 1941 maintained various homes for sick and frail children and also offered Jewish children a hiding place.

deportations and took over housing the children,[33] while in Liège the church-related groups seized the initiative regarding placement of Jewish children and were very active in finding accommodation for them.[34] At the moment, all the work in Brussels is carried out by the National Committee for the Defence of the Jews, which was established as such in November 1941.[35] If we take into account that necessary purchases must also be made for maintaining the children's wardrobe, we must reckon that the average cost for a child comes to 600 francs per month. The expenditures from 15 September 1942 to 31 December 1943 were in

Brussels:	room and board	Frs.	6,513,413.45		
	miscellaneous	Frs.	272,881.85		
	stipends	Frs.	187,020.—		
	clothing	Frs.	104,612.35		
Charleroi:		Frs.	340,425.35	Frs.	7,418,353.—

The number of children living with parents who are more or less in need of support is estimated at 1,000. The Committee is also looking to find accommodation for these children, as it is an inescapable fact that, both for security reasons and in order to feed them properly, they will have to be separated from their families, particularly those from poor families. It is especially important to note that it is almost impossible to provide children who live with their parents with a good education.

The number of children recently placed with friends and acquaintances by their parents is also estimated at 1,000, although it cannot be ruled out that this number is lower in reality.

A certain number of Jewish children were sent privately to Switzerland in 1942. Apparently in many cases the children were simply put on the train with the necessary instructions about changing trains and border crossings. The organization has often tried to arrange a departure service for the children by arranging to have them accompanied. After some failures and some arrests along the route, this effort was discontinued.[36] One indeed does not dare risk exposing the children to these dangers, which are greater than those if they remain in this country. Nonetheless, we are still working on the question of evacuation, and as soon as an opportunity with some degree of secur-

33 In Sept. 1942, the Germans asked the local AJB/VJB committee for a list of the current addresses of the Jews living in Charleroi. As a result, the committee's members went into hiding and passed on the remaining funds to the Jewish Defence Committee.

34 The bishop of Liège, Louis-Joseph Kerkhofs (1878–1962), supported the accommodation of Jews in the convents, monasteries, and schools of his diocese. The Catholic lawyer Max-Albert van den Berg (1890–1945) was also very active in helping Jews until his arrest in April 1943. He died in Neuengamme concentration camp.

35 This refers to the Jewish Defence Committee, but this was not founded, as the current document also correctly states in an earlier passage above, until Sept. 1942. The date given here may have been mixed up with the publication date of the first issue of the Yiddish underground paper *Unzer Wort* (at the beginning of December 1941), which was considered to mark the beginning of Jewish resistance in Belgium. There were continuities, for instance Abusz Werber was involved in both *Unzer Wort* and the Jewish Defence Committee.

36 For example, in early Dec. 1943 Jacques Weingarten (b. 1922) and Bayla (Betty) Jacubowicz (1925–2000), Belgians who helped Jews escape and took refugees to Switzerland, were arrested in the French town of Belfort, not far from the Swiss border.

ity presents itself, the question will be taken up once more. However, efforts in support of the evacuation of one or more groups of young people to a neutral foreign country have been successful.[37]

If I am not mistaken, the *Association of Jews in Belgium* operates five homes for children, while a sixth is currently being prepared.[38] These are:

The orphanage in rue des Patriotes,[39] Brussels
The Maison de Cure de Wesembeeck, near Brussels
The home for infants, rue Victor Allard, Nesle[40]
The children's home in Linkebeek[41]
The children's home in Lasnes.[42]

The number of children housed in the 5 homes is around 300. So far, the occupying power has spared these homes. An incident in 1942 must be mentioned when several lorries from the Gestapo arrived in Wesembeeck to take away all the staff and children and take them to Mechelen. Thanks to interventions from different influential Belgian circles, all of them were brought back the same evening.[43]

Although the children understandably suffered dreadfully from the devastation in their families, both psychologically and morally, and although uncertainty about the future weighs heavily on the atmosphere in these homes, spirits are reasonably good. The food situation is very satisfactory, as they are generously provided for by Belgian organizations.[44]

Although one must also admit that the children are not safe and that an abrupt change in the Germans' position on the homes is not impossible, it must be stated that the homes of the A.J.B. perform an important role, even though it is one of disguising their role and even covering up the fact that a large number of children are hidden. In addition, they serve as an address for the children who are apprehended or found by the Germans and for those who are liberated from Mechelen.

37 With the help of Zionist socialist youth organizations in Switzerland, around 80 young people from Belgium illegally entered Switzerland in 1942 and 1943.

38 Absent from the following list are the home for infants in Etterbeek, east of Brussels, which was opened in Sept. 1943, and the home at Aische-en-Refail in the province of Namur, which was not established until early 1944.

39 This was a Jewish orphanage which had existed before the war (see fn. 11).

40 In fact the home in Uccle (Flemish: Ukkel) south of Brussels, which was opened in Jan. 1943.

41 This home at the city limits of Uccle was established in the summer of 1943. Most residents were children of parents who had been deported.

42 Correctly: Lasne, municipality in the province of Walloon Brabant. The home was originally the Antwerp orphanage, but its residents moved to Lasne in 1943.

43 On 30 Oct. 1942, the Security Police arrested all the children living in this home. At the request of Yvonne Nevejean, the director of the National Children's Welfare Agency, Queen Elisabeth of Belgium intervened with Military Commander Alexander von Falkenhausen, and brought about the release of the children.

44 The National Children's Welfare Agency, the Belgian Red Cross, and the Belgian Winter Relief supported the homes with money and foodstuffs. Because the AJB/VJB listed many more children than were actually living in the homes, these resources could also be used to support children who were living in hiding.

Report on the Jewish population in Belgium, from September 1942 to the end of December 1943.
[…][45]

Referring to our earlier report,[46] it suffices to note that since the appearance of the first anti-Jewish laws, which were published in the *Verordnungsblatt* on 23 and 28 October 1940,[47] a series of regulations have been issued with the aim of systematically destroying the legal and social position of the Jews in Belgium, in pursuit of the ultimate goal of cutting them off completely from economic life and bringing about their total deportation from the country.

One must dwell in particular on the regulations of 11 March 1942 and 15 May 1942,[48] which envisage a special status for Jews with regard to work, with the chief of the German administration in principle authorized to control the labour situation of the Jews. The death sentences were not long in coming, and in July the first orders to appear for forced labour in northern France were sent out.[49] After the failure of this 'labour deployment', the Jews began to be called up for compulsory labour. When the Jews were to comply with this summons, the Germans did not hesitate to organize roundups[50] on a large scale, emptying entire Jewish neighbourhoods in the most brutal manner.

At this tragic time in the existence of the Jewish people, left to their fate by the Jewish association in Belgium that was created on 25 November 1941 by the occupying authority, the resistance group began its activities.

To maintain morale and stay in touch with the Jewish population, the decision was made to publish two newspapers, one in French and one in Flemish, which simultaneously helped to enlighten the non-Jewish population about the German campaign of terror against the Jews.[51]

In practical terms, the first thing that had to be considered was the problem of saving the children who were left behind as a result of their parents' deportation, as well as the children awaiting the same fate. In fact, as soon as the Germans began to deport the Jews on a large scale, as soon as it was realized that it was not about forced labour but was really a deportation into the unknown under circumstances that led one to fear the worst, many parents tried at least to save their children, by placing them as boarders with non-Jews, with people they trusted. A certain proportion of the parents managed to find places for themselves, but the number of children was too large for individual initiatives planned individually to succeed. The group that had just been formed understood that the first activity had to be a systematic effort to find places for the children.

It must be emphasized that the situation for all those who saved themselves from deportation by going into hiding was also extremely critical. The financial circumstances

45 There follows a repetition of the seventh paragraph (establishment of the Jewish Defence Committee).
46 This was not found.
47 Regulation on the Prevention of Cruelty to Animals during Slaughter, 23 Oct. 1940, *VOBl-BNF*, 18, no. 1, 25 Oct. 1940, pp. 251–252; see also PMJ 5/158 and 159.
48 Regulation on the Employment of Jews in Belgium, 11 March 1942, *VOBl-BNF*, 70, no. 2, p. 857, 18 March 1942, and Implementing Regulation to the Employment of Jews in Belgium, 8 May 1942, *VOBl-BNF*, 76, no. 2, 15 May 1942, pp. 911–912.
49 See Doc. 174.
50 See Doc. 180.
51 This presumably refers to the newspapers published by the Independence Front, *Bulletin du Front de l'Indépendance* and *België Vrij*.

of many people who were no longer able to practise their profession and had already long been forced to live off their savings could no longer sustain them, especially as living underground meant a massive increase in the costs of living. A great many impoverished people no longer dared to leave their homes out of fear of being nabbed by the German police and had to forgo the assistance due to them from public bodies. Sometimes the day spent in the shadows came with the loss of the necessary ration stamps. Unfortunately, the financial resources were not sufficient to provide all these persons living illegally with financial assistance. We[52] created a service to locate apartments that were 'very safe'; likewise, we managed to provide false papers, which life 'underground' required, as well as food ration cards. We frequently took steps with the municipal authorities to support the people in hiding, so that their food ration cards would not be revoked. Although we encountered a great deal of sympathy and goodwill on the part of the municipal personnel, achieving our goal was not always possible. On the other hand, we regularly gave a stipend to the Jewish families whose head of household was shot during the political struggle or was in prison or a concentration camp, while the fighters likewise received support on a regular basis. The Committee effectively supported the young people and families who wanted to go to Switzerland or Spain. Several 'emissaries' were sent forth to create 'lines', that is, to identify safe stages on the route to be followed. Core groups of partisans eagerly collaborated in the activities of the Belgian patriots, and Jewish names were often found among those of the 'terrorists' and saboteurs who were shot by the Germans.[53] The few Jewish snitches and traitors who worked with or for the enemy could be brought down. Jewish partisans raided the office where the archives of the A.J.B. were located and set fire to the index cards where the names of the members are recorded.[54] The most daring Jewish fighters come from the ranks of the communists or left-wing Zionist workers. This latter group publishes a newspaper in Yiddish, which appears along with the newspapers of the Jewish Defence Committee in French and Dutch.[55]

After this compressed overview of the activities of the Committee, we must discuss the placement of the children in a little more detail.

[…][56]

Fortunately, contact with the Joint was successfully established during this period. Beginning in July, it sent money on a regular basis, and this not only gave a new impetus to practical activities but also had an extremely good influence on morale. We knew that we were no longer alone and that the Jews abroad acknowledged and supported the work

52 This refers to the Jewish Defence Committee.

53 Many Jews in Belgium took an active part in armed resistance, including as part of the military arm of the Independence Front, the Belgian Partisan Army. At the end of 1943 and beginning of 1944, following assassinations, 116 persons were shot as 'terrorist hostages' by the occupiers. The exact number of those killed cannot be ascertained, but the total is thought to have been more than 200.

54 Only copies of the file cards were damaged during the operation: see Doc. 181, fn. 6.

55 From Dec. 1941, the Poale Zion Left published the illegal newspaper *Unzer Wort*. From March 1943 the Dutch-language *De Vrije Gedachte* was edited by Leopold Flam (1912–1995), and the French-language *Le Flambeau* is thought to have been edited by Ghert Jospa until his arrest.

56 A repetition of the ninth paragraph (placement of the children and financing of the rescue operations) follows.

that was being done. Likewise, gratitude must also be expressed for the important gift that reached us from Palestine in July.[57]

The period from September to July was plagued with a great many roundups in the large centres where the Jews lived; assembly in Mechelen in the Dossin Barracks,[58] from where the unfortunate were deported to Upper Silesia, as well as to Poland, as soon as 1,800 to 2,000 people were gathered together. After a great many Jews had changed their residence to avoid the dangers of the roundups, the Gestapo employed informers, and thanks to them, a number of victims fell into the Gestapo's hands. One figure with particularly unfortunate notoriety was the infamous 'Jacques',[59] a Jewish informer who drove around Brussels with the Gestapo agents in their car and pointed out several thousand Jews. Regrettably, all efforts to bring this wretched fellow to justice have been unsuccessful so far. Another Jewish spy by the name of Wechselmann was shot dead by the partisans in late July. During the transports from Mechelen, a certain number of young people full of daring and audacity succeeded in saving themselves by jumping off the train carrying them to the West[60] when it was moving slowly. To prevent such escapes, for the 20th transport, which was to take place in April, the Germans made up a train consisting solely of baggage wagons, which were completely sealed.[61] They did not reckon with the indomitable will for freedom of those destined for deportation. Scarcely was the train under way when several young people, equipped with the necessary materials, began to saw the iron bars of the small opening in the roof of the wagon and managed to escape from the train in large numbers by lowering themselves onto the tracks with the help of ropes that were held fast inside the wagon.

The same train was the object of a bold undertaking on the part of the Jewish partisans, who formed an armed party to stop the train and thus allowed a large number of Jews to escape the fate awaiting them. Although around 100 people were wounded and approximately 60 were felled by the bullets of the police who were operating the train, an estimated total of 400–500 persons of the 1,700 who belonged to the transport managed to escape.[62] This heroic deed is a marvellous page in the book of the Jewish resistance movement. Eight Jews wounded in the fighting who were being kept in hospital in Tirlemont under the control of Gestapo agents[63] were abducted by partisan groups.

57 Through the mediation of Zionist groups in Switzerland (which included Nathan Schwalb), the Jewish Defence Committee succeeded in obtaining funds from the Belgian government in exile for the rescue of Jewish children. In July 1943 the government in exile made 4 million francs available. Through contacts with the JDC, additional funds could be utilized in Belgium on a regular basis until the war ended.

58 No large roundups took place between the autumn of 1942 and the summer of 1943; Jews were instead arrested singly or in small groups.

59 Icek Glogowski: see Doc. 209, fn. 4.

60 Correctly: East.

61 Up until the departure of this convoy on 19 April 1943, third-class passenger coaches had been used: see Doc. 217, fn. 42.

62 Using tools that had been smuggled in, more than 200 persons were able to escape, including Simon Gronowski, who subsequently survived the war in hiding: see Doc. 211. As a result of an armed attack by three resistance fighters – Youra (Georges) Livschitz (1917–1944), Robert Maistriau (1921–2009), and Jean Franklemon (1917–1977) – 17 additional persons could be freed; 26 were killed as they tried to escape: see Doc. 208. The idea for the attack originated within the ranks of the Jewish Defence Committee.

63 A ninth wounded man succumbed to his injuries in hospital.

Unfortunately, however, after a denunciation, they fell into German hands once again. During the abduction of the Jews from the hospital, there was fighting between the partisans and the Feldgendarmerie, which resulted in the loss of 8 people, while the Jews were able to withdraw without any losses.[64]

During the September–July period, the A.J.B. made special efforts to send food parcels and equipment parcels to Mechelen, to people who were awaiting deportation. The food parcels often arrived in good condition, but it seems that the equipment quite frequently was not received. The A.J.B. was also tasked with creating and running several orphanages, children's homes and homes for the elderly, and with organizing social welfare.[65] For this last function, it made use of the OCJS[66] (Œuvre centrale israélite de secours – Central Jewish Welfare Organization), a semi-official undertaking that was already in existence before the war. On the other hand, the A.J.B. frequently intervened with the Gestapo, sometimes with success, to obtain the release of certain persons under arrest, such as the sick, the elderly, children who had been left behind, officials of the A.J.B. etc.

It must be said that while the A.J.B. in Brussels and in Antwerp carried out the orders of the German authorities without the slightest resistance, the local committee in Charleroi successfully concealed all the Jews of this town when the first summons for deportation arrived.[67] The secretary of this community has subsequently played a major role in the resistance movement.[68]

The Jewish Defence Committee suffered a very serious loss when in May and July four of its leaders, the most important ones, were arrested and sent to Mechelen and Breendmark.[69] They conducted themselves very bravely and refused to give information about their activities and their comrades. Two of them were released in Mechelen in January 1944, while the other two are still in Breendmark, where they are treated extremely harshly.[70]

64 The prisoners in Tierlemont were freed by two units of the Belgian resistance movement under Emile Lovenvirth (b. 1920) and Albert Bailly (b. 1916) on 4 May 1943. No members of the resistance were lost during the operation; it is not known whether any Germans were injured. Of the eight persons who were freed, seven (and not, as noted here, all eight) were recaptured, including Meta Westheimer, Marie Goldring, and Léonore Aronsfrau: see Doc. 208. Only one injured man managed to elude his pursuers, travelling in a Red Cross vehicle.

65 From summer 1943 the AJB/VJB's social welfare programme was headed by Chaïm Perelman (1912–1984), lawyer; husband of Felice/Fela (see fn. 16); worked for the AJB/VJB from the autumn of 1942; founding member of the Jewish Defence Committee, where he also worked in social welfare; in hiding from June 1944.

66 Correctly: OCIS.

67 See fn. 33.

68 Pinkus (Pierre) Broder (1901–1994?), shopkeeper; before the war, member of the Communist Party; member of the Jewish Defence Committee in Charleroi during the war.

69 Correctly: Breendonk.

70 The arrests (made independently of each other) in the early summer of 1943 led to the formation of a new committee. Those arrested were Maurice Heiber; Ghert (Hertz) Jospa (1905–1966), engineer; communist, member of the Independence Front and founder of the Jewish Defence Committee, in June 1943 arrested and imprisoned in Breendonk, in May 1944 deported to Buchenwald, returned to Belgium in 1945; Emile Hambresin (b. 1907), engineer and journalist; member of the Independence Front; in Sept. 1942, as a non-Jew, founding member of the Jewish Defence Committee; arrested in mid 1943 and deported to Germany, where he perished; Maurits Bolle (b. 1890), sales representative; helped many Jewish refugees escape to southern France; arrested in July 1943; survived the war.

Six other colleagues, very loyal to the C.D.J. were arrested in October and November because of their work for this Committee and are still in prison. On 1 August, during the departure of the 21st transport, which included 200 children, some people tried to escape, but unfortunately they all were killed while attempting to flee.[71]

Until September [1943], the Germans abided 'grosso modo'[72] by their commitments not to touch Jews who were Belgian nationals unless these persons contravened the regulations. During the night of 3 to 4 September, a gigantic roundup was organized in Antwerp and Brussels, during which all the Jews in Antwerp and hundreds in Brussels were arrested.[73] The Jews from Antwerp were forced to climb 200 at a time into a lorry that had room for a maximum of 45 people, with the result that 14 persons had already suffocated by the time the vehicle reached Mechelen.[74] Despite protests by various influential circles in Belgium, the Belgian Jews were not released again and were deported within the month. The sole concession made by the Germans was to take all men over the age of 65 and the women over the age of 60 to a home for the elderly in Anderlecht, run by the City of Brussels.[75] Since then, all those arrested who have reached the given ages have been taken to the institution in question.

In the course of November 1943, the Jewish Defence Committee in Brussels met with the underground Jewish committees of Antwerp, Liège and Charleroi to create a national defence committee of the Jews for all of Belgium, so that activities could be integrated on a national basis.[76] Among the various Jewish communities in Belgium, clandestine Jewish work was organized best and most quickly in Brussels and Charleroi, while in Liège it was chiefly the church groups that were very active in organizing the rescue of children and adults as soon as the deportations began.[77] The clandestine reaction in Antwerp, by contrast, was rather feeble and was not undertaken seriously until the end of 1943. The decision was made to affiliate with the Freedom Front,[78] which offered a seat on its general council to a representative of the C.N.D.J.[79] During the creation of the National Committee for the Defence of the Jews, it was made clear that the Committee is primarily a combat and resistance organization and that the important welfare work that is arranged must always be clandestine and anti-German in nature, and must never degenerate into simple charitable relief. The Jewish Defence Committee in Brussels has expanded its base by asking two non-Jews to join the Committee.[80]

71 Transport XXI left Mechelen on 31 July 1943 with 174 children among the 1,562 deportees. Although the train was heavily guarded, ten persons attempted to escape during the journey: four were killed in the course of this attempt; two were recaptured; four managed to escape.

72 'Generally speaking.'

73 See Doc. 214.

74 Correctly: nine persons suffocated on the journey to Mechelen: see Doc. 217, fn. 52.

75 The home for the elderly and invalids admitted its first residents on 7 Sept. 1943. It was under the oversight of the Belgian welfare authority. By the time of the liberation, almost 500 Jews had found refuge in this home and thus survived the occupation period.

76 Independent groups of the Jewish Defence Committee had initially been formed in various cities, but over the course of 1943 they established links with each other.

77 This refers to Bishop Kerkhofs's network mentioned above.

78 This refers to the Independence Front.

79 The Comité national de défense des Juifs was founded in the autumn of 1943 to coordinate the distribution of the relief funds procured through Switzerland (see fn. 57). The first general assembly, held in Dec. 1943, was not followed by another meeting, and the Committee had little influence.

In December 1943, Zionists of every hue established a Palestine Office, which knew how to organize and gather the Zionist forces still present in the country.[81] They made contact with the Palestine Office so that it could assign them to distribute veterans' certificates and other certificates of exchange for Palestine.[82] According to the various pieces of information received, the German authorities in Belgium recognize the certificates for veterans and assure those who hold them that they are protected from all deportation measures. This raises the question of the limit for the number of certificates that can be requested without compromising those already given out.

At the end of 1943 the situation of the Jewish population in Belgium is that out of 105,000 persons before 10 May [1940], around 29,000 have been deported.[83] From this number, a large number of Dutch Jews who were arrested in this country while in transit to Spain must be subtracted. According to an estimate, 17,000 persons are still here, the majority of them living in hiding. In the census taken by the Association of Jews in Belgium at the end of 1941,[84] 42,000 people were recorded, so assuming that several thousand Jews did not register, 55[000]–60,000 persons left Belgium between 10 May 1940 and the end of 1941.

The present population, according to an approximate estimate, is made up of the following:

a) Jews not directly threatened by the deportation measures: around 900 persons associated with or related to people associated with the A.J.B. These are persons who are employed in the central office of the A.J.B, in the service that sends parcels to the camps at Mechelen and the children's homes, orphanages and homes for the elderly, and who are therefore under the special protection of the Gestapo, which exempts them from the deportation rules. At present there are six children's homes and orphanages and three homes for the elderly, while a fourth is being set up.

Around 1,000 persons, elderly people and children, who live in the official institutions of the A.J.B and are recognized by the Gestapo.

Around 1,000 persons who work for 'Lustza', along with their families. Lustza is a non-Jewish company that does furrier work for the occupier.[85] This company has

80 As a result of the arrests in the early summer of 1943, three new members joined the Jewish Defence Committee in Brussels at the meeting on 29 Dec. 1943: Yvonne Nèvejean; Emile Allard, a professor at the Free University of Brussels; and Jacques Pels, a banker from the Netherlands. Nevejean and Allard were not Jews.

81 The Office Palestinien de Bruxelles, established in Dec. 1943, compiled lists for the Palestine Office in Geneva with the names and addresses of Belgian Zionists who were to be rescued. The initiative strengthened the influence of the Zionist members of the Jewish Defence Committee. In addition, the Belgian Palestine Office negotiated through the AJB/VJB with the German authorities for the recognition of (ultimately four) lists of names and the issuing of exchange certificates.

82 The Palestine Office of the Jewish Agency in Switzerland attempted to secure the emigration of Jews from western Europe to Palestine by arranging to exchange these persons for interned German citizens.

83 It has been estimated that before the war there were around 90,000 Jews in Belgium, including illegal immigrants; by the end of 1943, those deported numbered 22,557.

84 The registration of the Jews by order of the German military administration took place as early as late 1940: see PMJ 5/158.

85 Correctly: Lustra. The firm made padded waistcoats for the Wehrmacht, and for this reason its Jewish employees were protected from deportation.

accepted a number of Jewish workers whose terms and conditions of work are outrageous but who do enjoy a certain protection.

Altogether around 2,900 persons.

b) Jews who are at risk of deportation and live illegally:

c. 1,500	persons	Antwerp and vicinity
c. 1,500	persons	Liège, Charleroi, and vicinity
c. 2,500	persons	in rural areas
c. 5,500	persons	in Brussels
c. 2,000	children	placed with non-Jews by the J.D.C.
c. 1,000	children	placed by their parents individually
c. 14,000	persons	

Examination of the social welfare work of the CNDJ at the end of 1943 reveals that while the problem of the children was largely solved, due to lack of funds the assistance for adults was sorely lacking. Around 2,000 children – mostly of Belgian nationality – have been placed and are supervised by the CNDJ, under very satisfactory conditions.[86]

Even though there are not enough qualified employees to make regular visits to these children possible, there have been enough appreciative signals for us to assume that in general the children are well placed where they are. The percentage of children taken by the Germans is extremely low. Cases of illness, meanwhile, are above average. Negotiations are in progress to appoint a female physician, as well as several welfare workers, to expand the inspection service. The children in most instances attend school and periodically receive supplementary foodstuffs as well as vitamins, sardines, tuna, cod-liver oil, oranges, chocolate, milk, etc. which are indirectly made available at no cost from official quarters. The children's clothes and equipment have been subjected to general scrutiny for some time now, and the Committee has already begun large-scale replacement of sorely needed items of clothing and footwear for the children. [...][87] It must be noted that in certain Jewish circles there is concern as to whether the raising of Jewish children in Catholic circles might not detach these children from the faith of their forefathers. Cardinal von Roeyayant[88] has prohibited the baptism of Jewish children during the war without the authorization of the parents; the known cases of religious conversion are relatively few in number.[89]

Projects for moving the children to neutral countries are being examined, but there is reluctance to subject them to the dangers of travel as the risks in Belgium are minimal. However, the Committee has played an active part in moving around fifty young people into a neutral country.[90] It should be emphasized that the operation on behalf of the children meets with sympathy among all sections of the non-Jewish population, while various official circles provide very significant financial aid, indirectly of course.

86 Yvonne Jospa kept an exact tally of the children provided with accommodation by the CDJ/JVC: in Dec. 1942, a few weeks after the founding of the Committee, she counted 424 children who had been hidden. One year later there were 1,678, and by the summer of 1944, the number had grown to 2,104.

87 The repetition of a passage follows (children who live in hiding in their parents' homes).

88 Correctly: Cardinal van Roey.

89 Nonetheless, research has shown that the number of baptisms of children was not insignificant, and after the war the question of the baptism of Jewish children and their being raised in Christian families led to heated debates between Jewish and Christian organizations.

As for the adults, the first payments made by the Joint have allowed us to provide summary assistance to a portion of those in need. To get this help to them, which is to keep them from starving to death and to enable them to keep fighting, to resist, the employees of the C.D.J go from house to house in the evenings, at the greatest risk.

It is impossible to describe typical cases of this sort. Each case is special and indescribable. But we can list the man with TB who sells his milk ration card so he can pay his rent; the family that likewise sells its butter and sugar rations; the man who sold his winter coat in the summer and is freezing now; the unfortunates who actually sell their shirt to buy potatoes; and the other man who sells his children's shoes and his little boy stays at home in slippers.

At the moment, the Committee counts 3,500 persons who are registered, a number that is constantly increasing, however, and soon will reach 4,000.[91] The minimum income sufficient for basic needs averages 1,000 Frs. per person, including heat, light, rent, etc., and taking into account that living underground increases the cost of living many times over. Last year the minimum was stated as 500 Frs., because at this time a certain number of persons were able to pay their living expenses in part. Even counting on a certain amount of regular support from the Joint, the Committee has available approximately 20 per cent of the necessary funds, so that only a proportion of those in need can be helped, and even then only inadequately. The service for adults has complete index cards for all those in need of support, so that help could be provided very effectively upon receipt of the requisite funds.

These past few months, the Committee has been receiving indirectly 2,000 to 3,000 parcels per month with foodstuffs from Belgian associations, containing tins of meat, gingerbread, sugar, meat pies, dried peas, jam, etc., which naturally make it possible to ease the situation for a large number of those in need.

The monthly budget follows below, while the status of income and expenditures from 15 September 1942 to 30 November 1943 and the status of expenditures for December 1943 and a transcript of the meeting of the C.D.J. of Brussels on 29 December 1943[92] are on a separate sheet that is enclosed here.

One may conclude that if the financial means exist and can be made available to the Committee, there is a good chance of saving the majority of the Jewish population remaining in Belgium. In fact, the Germans are finding it increasingly difficult to find the Jews who are still in the country, and the number of arrests for the past few months, 200 in total, indicates a further notable downward trend.

As to the future, there are very serious problems with regard to the return of the deported Jews, if they are still alive, and their readjustment and employment after their return home. We must also set up an organization for the purpose of rehabilitating and

90 Fifty-four persons were saved by the escape route into Switzerland arranged by Betty Perkal, née Jacubowicz; see fn. 36. In addition, from Nov. 1942 the Belgian children's aid organization tried, with the help of the JDC and the Jewish Agency, to enable Jewish children to emigrate from Belgium to the United States or Palestine through official channels. It is not known, however, whether and to what extent such emigration was actually able to take place.

91 In Nov. 1943, a few weeks after the increase in aid for adults, the Jewish Defence Committee was already supporting 1,750 persons in Brussels alone; by Feb. 1944 the number had increased to 3,600.

92 This is not included in the file.

reintegrating the Jews who managed to survive in this country, although they were driven from their homes and lost their belongings, while the problem of them returning to their previous occupations and jobs will also require special attention in order to allow for possible professional readjustment.

Likewise, we are already working on solving the problem of the thousands of children who will be unable to find their parents after the war, and who will have to be financially supported by the C.D.J. or its post-war successor organization. It would be extremely interesting if the C.D.J. could get in contact with the Belgian government in London and the international Jewish organizations that are interested in the post-war problems for Jews, in order to have an initial exchange of views about the problems outlined here.

Monthly Budget
Expenditures

around 3,500 to 4,000 adults at 1,000.– each	3,500,000–4,000,000	Fr.b.
around 2,000 children housed at 600.– each	1,200,000	Fr.b.
around 1,000 children to be housed at 600.– each*	600,000	Fr.b.
	5,800,000	Fr.b.

* These are children who are still living with their parents at the moment. As most of these children belong to families that have not received support so far, there is no reason to deduct this amount from the first item.

Income:

Contribution from official circles	600,000.–
Contribution from a bank	250,000.–
Contribution from the Joint	c. 1,000,000.–
Various donations	50,000.–
	1,900,000.– Fr.b.
A.J.B aid for a certain number of people in need from the OCSI[93]	150,000–200,000.–
	2,100,000.– Fr.b.

PN.[94] The Independence Front approved in principle a contribution of 100,000 for the month of December. As of 15 January, no payment has been received.

It thus follows that the sum of 3,700,000 that is required to ensure social welfare provision is lacking.

93 Presumably correctly: OCIS.
94 The abbreviation could not be identified, but presumably it has the same meaning as PS or NB.

Financial position of the Jewish Defence Committee in Brussels
from 15 September 1942 to 30 November 1943

Income[95]		Expenditure		
B.B.	Frs. 950,000.–	*Children*	Room and board	Frs. 5,810,217.35
Sse.	Frs. 1,989,648.–		Gen. expenses	Frs. 247,071.05
U.F.	Frs. 2,487,419.–		Wages	Frs. 155,570.–
Freddy	Frs. 272,000.–		Clothing	Frs. 78,963.–
Loan	Frs. 55,000.–	Adults	Assistance	Frs. 928,151.45
Advance from F. (to be repaid in December)	Frs. 175,000.–		Gen. charges	Frs. 44,521.45
Vign	Frs. 231,600.–		Wages	Frs. 46,892.–
Cards	Frs. 444,468.25		V. family	Frs. 141,500.–
Donations	Frs. 1,136,517.–		Lodging	Frs. 80,386.–
Solicitations	Frs. 445,875.–		Expenditure	Frs. 163,855.–
			Org.	Frs. 157,645.–
			id. Antwerp	Frs. 65,000.–
			id. Charleroi	Frs. 40,000.–
			Lost (A)	Frs. 62,312.–
			Special expenses	Frs. 63,750.–
			Special operation	Frs. 50,173.50
			Debt ref.	Frs. 25,000.–
			Sze Fund (to be repaid)	Frs. 3,000.–
			Balance	Frs. 23,615.90
	Frs. 8,187,528.25			*Frs. 8,187,528 25*

The balance is made up as follows:

Gen. funds	N.	64,272.–		
	F.	290,345.–	354,617.–	Credit
Relief fund			3,016.10	Credit
Gen. service fund	debit	8,345.50		
Children's fund	debit	372,903.50	23,615.90	balance 30 Nov. 43
	Frs.	381,249.–	Frs. *381,249.–*	

Committee for the Defence of the Jews in Charleroi
1 October 1942 to 30 November 1943

Income		*Expenditure*	
A.J.B. Charleroi	24,675.–	Aid for adults	315,694.–
A.J.B. Brussels	43,000.–	Aid for children	311,425.35

95 A number of abbreviations in the following could not be expanded, with the exception of U.F. (presumably: Unabhängigkeitsfront, 'Independence Front').

Solidarity J.	35,745.–	Rent	50,091.10
Donations	199,450.–	Medical aid	10,864.–
Ration cards	468,614.50	Aid for prisoners	14,582.75
Aid for children	50,366.–	Special expenses	112,970.30
Contribution for F.S. Charleroi	108,758.–	Expenses, travel	34,868.95
C.D.J. Brussels	20,000.–	Office expenses	3,700.–
Miscellaneous	2,872.–	Expenses for ration cards	79,384.90
		Officials	18,400.–
		Contribution for La Louvrièr[96]	25,920.–
		Miscellaneous	16,924.90
	953,480.50		994,826.25

Expenditure	994,826.25
Income	953,480.50
Deficit up to 1 December 1943	*41,345.75*

Expenditure, December 1943, C.D.J. Brussels

Adults		
Aid	Frs. 221,875.–	
Families of victims	Frs. 29,100.–	
Organizations	Frs. 40,000.–	
Charleroi	Frs. 10,000.–	
Liège	Frs. 25,000.–	
Food ration cards	Frs. 7,750.–	
General expenses	Frs. 7,982.–	
Special operation	Frs. 41,750.–	
Special expenses (interest)	Frs. 2,200.–	Frs. 385,657.–
Children		
Room and board, Brussels	Frs. 667,796.10	
Room and board, Liège	Frs. 15,000.–	
Room and board, Charleroi	Frs. 29,000.–	
Clothing	Frs. 25,644.35	
Food ration cards	Frs. 20,400.–	
General expenses	Frs. 22,728.85	
Wages	Frs. 31,450.–	
Expenses: doctor, pharmacy	Frs. 1,418.–	
Rent and expenses locally	Frs. 936.–	
Office expenses	Frs. 727.95	Frs. 815,101.25
		Frs. 1,200,758.25

96 Correctly: La Louvière, town in the province of Hennegau.

DOC. 220

Vrijheid, March 1944: article describing the scenes that unfolded in Mechelen before the departure of a deportation train[1]

A transport of Jews departs for Poland

On 15 January 1944 the 23rd transport of Jews departed for Poland. This time there were not only Jews, but also about 700 Gypsies.[2]

While we are calmly going to work, somewhere in a large yard of a former barracks,[3] people are standing in long lines, with numbers on their chests. Flemish SS men pass between the lines, sticks in hand, maintaining order among this desperate mass of defenceless people. Look at the faces of these victims of the Nazis. Pale, eyes full of sadness, eyes bidding a silent farewell. The children are crying. A mother is soothing her baby of just a few months old, while her four-year-old daughter with blonde curly hair starts crying. The woman is alone with her elderly mother. Her husband was deported a long time ago. Now it is her turn - and she will not even be in the same wagon as her mother, as she has a different number, having arrived in Mechelen at a later date. Another woman has a broken arm, but she has to come too, to join the German Arbeitseinsatz[4] in the East. Everyone has to go. A mother with two mentally handicapped children with a fever of 39 degrees. They are all good enough for the Arbeitseinsatz, because they are all going to the slaughtering block.

And they know it, these innocent victims of the Nazi terror. That is why there is such a nervous atmosphere among them, such despair; that is why they embrace so fervently the few lucky ones allowed to stay behind, as if it is for the last time. People bid farewell to each other as if they are going to the front, where a certain death awaits the soldiers, and the voice of the camp leader,[5] who is calling out the numbers of his sheep, is like an incessant undertone. During the 22nd transport, at least the young people were still singing and dancing,[6] so that at least the enemy did not see how their hearts were breaking. Now everything is quiet, now despair prevails. They thought they had escaped the dance of death, and that they were at the end of this whole tragedy, and yet they ended up between the teeth of this giant monster and were deported, just as liberation is around the corner.

People leave the yard in groups of fifty that are led into livestock wagons, which have some straw on the floor and buckets to relieve oneself. Those who escaped from previous transports have said that there is so little room that most people cannot find the buckets

1 'Een jodentransport vertrekt naar Polen', *Vrijheid, Orgaan van de V.B.J., Vrije Belgische Jeugd/ Jeunesse Belge Libre*, March 1944, pp. 2–3. This document has been translated from Dutch. Of this underground newspaper from the province of Antwerp, only this one issue dated March 1944 has survived. The names of the authors and publishers are unknown.

2 Transport XXIII carried 659 deportees; aboard Transport Z, which made the journey at the same time, there were 351 Sinti and Roma.

3 This refers to the Dossin Barracks in Mechelen.

4 German in the original: 'labour deployment'.

5 Johannes (Hans) Frank.

6 This could not be verified. Transport XXII consisted of two sections; 639 foreign Jews were transported to Auschwitz in Section A, while 794 Jews with Belgian citizenship were deported to the same destination in Section B on the same day, 20 Sept. 1943.

and eventually have to relieve themselves standing up, on the person standing next to them …

Wagon after wagon is filled. The doors are closed and sealed with lead. SS men stand guard. One would have thought that the people inside are the worst possible criminals. The sky, which was clear in the morning, has now turned grey. Darkness is falling over the country, bringing silence and sadness. The barracks is still […], calmly and […], with no appearance of cruelty.[7] The last wagons are brought. These are the wagons for the sick and the 'Flitsers'[8] (those who had escaped from the previous transports). Not that the wagons for the sick are any better than those for the others. The only difference: there is more straw and more room. During the 22nd transport, they put a young child with a broken leg and another one with diphtheria in there, as well as a woman who had been so badly beaten by a German that she had a nervous collapse and was taken to the 'Sanitätswagen'[9] on a stretcher, paralysed and a complete wreck.

Finally, the wagon for the 'Flitsers' arrives. They are wearing a red band around their left arm. The men's heads have been completely shaved. There is no straw in their wagon. They are not getting any blankets either. Their wagon has been specially selected and has been reinforced. Who knows how they will be treated during the transport … Just imagine, these people had the courage to jump out of a train travelling at a speed of 40 km per hour, while the Germans were firing dumdum bullets. These people knew what awaited them in Poland; that is what gave them the courage to jump out of the train. They escaped, but some were recaptured and are now put into a special wagon as 'Flitsers'. They are braver, and also calmer. They have stood the test. During the 22nd transport they were even singing, in order to provoke the Germans deliberately: 'We're not scared'. Their wagon fills up quickly too and disappears into the darkness.

The transport is now complete, and the ghost train will depart to Poland at the crack of dawn, guarded by SS men (who are giving their all to combat Bolshevism) and Schupos.[10] We have a small question for the Nazis' bootlickers, who made such a fuss about the ghost train that took them to Abbeville in 1940.[11] You at least had something to answer for, and your family was left in peace. But what do you have to say about this, you most honourable Borms or [H]ermans,[12] or whatever your names might be? Instead of protesting against it, you cannot get enough of grovelling to your bosses. But be aware that the heart of each and every patriot is with these innocent victims, and be aware that the time will come when you are brought to justice.

7 Parts of the sentence are illegible.

8 Dutch in the original; *flitsen* means to flash or dart. This transport included twenty-two persons who were classified in this special group.

9 German in the original: 'medical wagon'.

10 Members of the Schutzpolizei, the urban police. Because Jews frequently tried to escape from the deportation trains, Schupos who had travelled from Germany escorted the transports from Mechelen to the German border.

11 After the German invasion of Belgium, the Belgian government, fearing acts of treason, had some people – including members of nationalist parties – sent to internment camps in France, such as the one at Abbeville. After the onset of occupation, these people returned to Belgium.

12 August Borms (1878–1946), teacher, and presumably Ward Hermans (1897–1992), writer (the first letter of the name in the original is illegible); both Flemish nationalists who were well known in Belgium. After the war, Borms was sentenced to death for collaboration and executed in 1946; Hermans was in prison until 1956, and thereafter worked as a journalist and writer.

DOC. 221

On 15 June 1944 the representative of the Chief of the Security Police and the SD complains that Jews living in Belgium have not been deployed as labour[1]

Excerpt[2] from the reports from Belgium and northern France (no. 12/44, secret, present immediately) by the representative of the Chief of the Security Police and the SD for the area of the Military Commander in Belgium and Northern France,[3] unsigned, Brussels, dated 15 June 1944 (carbon copy)

Jewry

Despite considerable difficulties, on average 80 to 100 Jews continue to be taken into custody each week.

The difficulties lie particularly in that 80 per cent of all Jews are in possession of counterfeit identity cards. In addition, they find broad support from many Aryan Belgians. Apartments, food and other things are frequently made available to them. Recently it has often been noted that the Jews are disguising themselves by wearing work clothing such as the blue overalls of mechanics.

As was to be expected, the landing of the Anglo-Americans has caused great glee among the Jews.[4] They are convinced of an Anglo-American victory. Wall maps with the course of the front indicated, always as the line specified by the enemy, have been found in almost every home where Jews have been living illegally. From this it can be concluded that the Jews continue to have access to an excellent intelligence service.

To date a particular problem has been caused by the labour deployment of Jews living in mixed marriages. The vast majority of them are slackers and idlers. The Belgian employment office, which is subordinate to the labour recruitment office of OFK 672,[5] refuses to call these Jews for labour deployment. This state of affairs results in a peculiar situation: many men and women who are fit for work are not working at a time when almost everyone must put their efforts into war production. As is hardly to be otherwise expected, the Jew who is in a mixed marriage has made life as comfortable as possible for himself. He can be seen in the café, playing or conducting some sort of shady business.

The greatest contribution to living expenses, of course, must be made by the Aryan spouse. In conversations, one often hears a Jew living in a mixed marriage commenting scornfully:

'It's fine by him [says the Jew] but he cannot understand why the German occupiers literally force the Aryan spouse to work for the Jewish spouse, since the Jewish partner in a mixed marriage is off limits and can continue his life of idleness.'

This evil has now been eliminated. All Jews living in mixed marriages have been registered here with the local office of the labour deployment authority so that they can

1 CegeSoma, AA 553. Published in Klarsfeld and Steinberg (eds.), *Die Endlösung der Judenfrage in Belgien*, pp. 86–87. This document has been translated from German.
2 The file contains the present excerpt (pp. 18 and 19) but not the entire report.
3 Ernst Ehlers.
4 The Allied troops had landed in Normandy on 6 June 1944.
5 Oberfeldkommandantur 672 was headquartered in Brussels.

be called on for labour deployment with the Reich Ministry for the Occupied Eastern Territories.[6]

The offering of bounties[7] has proved worthwhile thus far. [...]

DOC. 222

After 3 September 1944 Leib Gronowski records in his diary the Belgians' joy at their liberation and his own despair[1]

Handwritten diary of Leib Gronowski, entry after 3 September 1944

Sunday, 3 September 1944
At 7.20 in the evening, the first English and Americans enter Brussels, the liberation has come.[2]

People wander around the streets. They are crazy with happiness. People cry, laugh, and sing. Everyone is kissing each other. It's a real Yom Tov.[3]

A mass happiness that expresses itself in holy, pure mass feelings and devotion.

The happiness is complete.

For me, the liberation has not yet come. I am even more sad and depressed than before ... Everyone is rejoicing, redeemed. I am not ... My [illegible] are still in the camp.[4]

... and so begin what are for me terrible days and nights.

Even worse than before ... I started to get used again to freedom ... I walk and wander around the streets. Aimless. With a terrible pain in my heart.

The redemption is not meant for me.

6 Jewish individuals who were married to non-Jews were initially protected from deportation. Nonetheless, there were isolated instances of deportation even before June 1944. Five persons from 'mixed marriages' were deported on the last transport to leave Mechelen, on 31 July 1944.

7 Rewards of 100 to 150 Belgian francs, paid by the German police: Maxime Steinberg, *L'Étoile et le fusil*, vol. 3: *La Traque des Juifs 1942–1944* (Brussels: Vie Ouvrière, 1986), p. 213. Labour deployment for Jews with the Reich Ministry for the Occupied Eastern Territories presumably meant that the Jews were used as forced labour in the transport of furniture and household goods confiscated from Jews by the Rosenberg Task Force.

1 Kazerne Dossin – Mechelen, A000821. This document has been translated from Yiddish.

2 Brussels and Antwerp were liberated at the beginning of Sept. 1944, and the Belgian government in exile returned from London on 8 Sept. But Belgium was definitively liberated only on 4 Feb. 1945 following the failure of the German offensive in the battle of the Bulge.

3 The Hebrew (two words) and Yiddish (expressed as one word) Yom Tov/Yomtef means '[Jewish] holiday', meant here as a celebration with special religious dimensions.

4 Leib's wife, Chana Gronowski, and daughter, Ida, were deported and murdered. The only members of the family to survive were Leib and his son, Simon, who had gone into hiding: see Doc. 211.

Luxembourg

Luxembourg
Ardennes
BELGIUM
Troisvierges
(Ulflingen)
Cinqfontaines
(Fünfbrunnen)
Clerve
Wiltz
Our
Sauer
Prüm
GERMAN REICH
Bitburg
Diekirch
Medernach
Sauer
Echternach
Moselle
LUXEMBOURG
Arlon
Alzette
Trier
Grevenmacher
Hinzert
Luxembourg
Moselle
Nennig
Bettembourg
Esch-sur-Alzette
FRANCE
Merzig
Thionville
Camps
0 10 20 30 km

DOC. 223
On 7 July 1942 the Jewish elder in Luxembourg, Alfred Oppenheimer, has to announce additional deportations[1]

Handwritten master copy of the speech given by Alfred Oppenheimer[2] to the residents of the Fünfbrunnen home,[3] dated 7 July 1942

Yet again the spectre of Poland hangs over us. Yesterday morning the Gestapo's Jewish Department informed me that a new transport to Poland is envisaged – I would receive details early this morning. When I went back again, I was given the following information:

The transport will contain, as was the case last time,[4] 24 persons and must be in Chemnitz by next Monday, 13 July, because the journey will continue at 24:00 the same day.[5]

Those affected will probably receive the registered letter to this effect tomorrow morning.[6] This time, all married couples up to the age of 60 will be affected, as well as some individuals whom the Gestapo refrained from including in the most recent transports for some reason.

I will only be informed of the names of the individuals as [...][7] tomorrow morning, so after the registered letters have been sent. However, I fear that all the couples who work here are included. –

I pointed out to the official in charge of Jewish affairs[8] that without sufficient support staff the home can no longer be sustained, for he could indeed see for himself on his last visit how high the rate of illness is amongst us. I repeated the same information to the chief of the Gestapo[9] a few minutes later. The reply was a shrug and the comment that the home would not exist on this scale much longer anyway. And meanwhile we would just have to struggle on as best we can.

I need not tell you how difficult it is for me to keep coming before you with such news. Unfortunately, this time there is again no opportunity at all for me to intervene in

1 ANLux, FD-083-25, C.I. 02. This document has been translated from German.

2 Alfred Oppenheimer (1901–1993), businessman; born in Metz; lived in Luxembourg from 1926; from 15 Oct. 1941 president of the Consistory; retitled 'Jewish elder' by the Gestapo in April 1942; in June 1943 deported to Theresienstadt; in Oct. 1944 deported to Auschwitz; in Jan. 1945 liberated from Blechhammer camp by Soviet troops; in May 1945 returned to Luxembourg; in 1961 testified at the Eichmann Trial.

3 In the summer of 1941, a Jewish home for the elderly was established in the former Abbey of Fünfbrunnen (municipality of Ulflingen). Jews who remained in Luxembourg were forced to relocate to this home, which simultaneously became the collection and transit camp for transports to the East.

4 This refers to the transport on 23 April 1942; see PMJ 5/223, 224, and 225.

5 The transport left Luxembourg on 12 July 1942 and presumably went next to Stuttgart, and then, via Chemnitz, to Auschwitz.

6 See, for example, Doc. 227.

7 A word is illegible.

8 Presumably Detective Sergeant Otto Schmalz.

9 Walter Runge (b. 1895), police official; head of the Gestapo in Luxembourg from Aug. 1940; sentenced to death in absentia by the Luxembourg Military Tribunal in 1950.

some way to mitigate the situation, because the order, as Dr Hartmann[10] informed me with a sneer, comes directly from Berlin. I was able to convince myself of the truth of his assertion. –

Words cannot express what I feel, what the Consistory feels. Consolation is cheap. Unfortunately, I can give you no other comfort than the hope and the assurance that we will indeed see each other again – that the sun must some day shine again for us Jews after this long period of suffering.

Let us be brave and grit our teeth. This is a hard lot; it is a Jewish lot. Today it is now visited upon younger and stronger people who will easily come through this period of suffering. Next time it will be the old and frail who must leave.

And nonetheless let us firmly believe, let us hope with trust in God, that we Jews too will see better times.

DOC. 224

On 9 July 1942 the Council of Elders appeals to the members of the Jewish Community to donate food rations for those threatened by deportation[1]

Letter from the Council of Elders of the Jews, Luxembourg, signed the Elder, Alfred Oppenheimer, to the members of the Community, dated 9 July 1942 (copy)

To our Community members,

On Sunday, 12 July, 24 of our brothers and sisters in faith are to leave our Community to be resettled in the East. The food parcel given to them by the Community to take with them to see them through the early days in their new place of residence contains among other things:

flour – oats – noodles – sugar – jam – *cold meats.*

To that end, we ask you to send us *immediately* the *stamps that can be spared* from every card.

We are certain that our request will not be in vain.

10 Dr Fritz Hartmann (1906–1974), lawyer; SS-Obersturmbannführer; head of the Gestapo office in Koblenz from 15 Jan. 1940; leader of the Einsatzkommando of the Security Police and the SD in Luxembourg and head of the Gestapo office in Trier from 8 March 1941 to 9 April 1943; subsequently transferred to the Waffen SS; arrested in 1946; sentenced to death in Feb. 1951 by a war crimes tribunal in Luxembourg, and later pardoned; on 19 Dec. 1957 expelled to the Federal Republic of Germany, where he worked as a lawyer in Düsseldorf.

1 ANLux, FD-083-25, C.I. 02. This document has been translated from German.

DOC. 225

On 15 July 1942 Jews who have been evicted from their homes ask the Council of Elders for support[1]

Memorandum by the Council of Elders of the Jews, signature illegible, Luxembourg, dated 15 July 1942 (copy)

Regarding: Salomon family, Marx Herz, and Mr and Mrs Ludwig Ermann.
Mrs Salomon Herz[2] calls at 8 a.m. and reports the following:

On 14 July 1942 at 6.50 p.m., the mayor[3] appeared at their home with a policeman[4] to inform them that they were to leave the building within half an hour. They were permitted to take with them only undergarments and clothing, no food at all; the mattresses, too, which were at first promised to them, had to be left behind. In the rush it was not possible for them to take the most necessary undergarments and clothing with them, so that they all are in great difficulties on this account. They are no longer permitted to enter the building. The homeless spent the night as follows.

The Salomon Herz family with Mrs Henriette Kahn[5]

Marx Herz[6] and Mr and Mrs Ermann[7] with Lippmann Herz.[8]

The above-named ask for our intervention and our assistance.

1 ANLux, FD-083-40, C.I. 06. This document has been translated from German.

2 Delphine Salomon Herz, née Meyer (b. 1897); deported from Medernach via Fünfbrunnen to Theresienstadt in the summer of 1942, and from there in late Jan. 1943 to Auschwitz, where she was murdered.

3 Jean-Baptiste Arend (1886–1960), farmer.

4 In the original: 'Gendarme'.

5 Henriette Kahn, née Hertz (b. 1892); deported from Fünfbrunnen to Theresienstadt at the end of July 1942 and from there in late Jan. 1943 to Auschwitz, where she was murdered.

6 Marx Herz (1858–1943), livestock dealer; deported in late July 1942 via Fünfbrunnen to Theresienstadt, where he perished.

7 Ludwig Ermann (b. 1864) and Clara Ermann, née Lurch (b. 1867); deported via Fünfbrunnen to Theresienstadt in late July 1942, and in late Sept. 1942 to Treblinka, where both were murdered.

8 Lippmann Herz (1865–1943), grocer; deported via Fünfbrunnen to Theresienstadt, where he perished in early Jan. 1943.

DOC. 226

On 19 July 1942 Ester Galler, aged seventy-four, writes to her cousin that she is to be taken to Theresienstadt within the next few weeks[1]

Handwritten letter from Ester Galler,[2] Fünfbrunnen, to a cousin, dated 19 July 1942 (copy)

Dear Cousin,

I am surprised that to date I have received no reply to my last letter.

Unfortunately, I must give you the sad news that all the residents of our home are to be evacuated. They will be deported in groups according to age to Theresienstadt (Bohemia). I do not yet know when my turn will come; however, it will be within approximately 4–5 weeks. You can imagine how agitated I am. I am old, blind, and have problems with my legs.

Everything must be left behind, because other than bedding and cookware, we can take with us only what we can carry.

My children have provided for me well, but whether they will ever see me again alive is a big question, as I am not in the condition to endure such hardship. Grumbach[3] is also leaving.

This may be the last letter I write to you. Warm regards and kisses to your whole family as well as to your siblings.

Ester Galler

My children should not have left me alone to have to go through all this.

I have received no more news from Albert.[4]

Whether Aunt Blima[5] will go with me is not certain.

1 The original could not be found; a copy is privately owned. Copy in IfZ-Archives, F 601. This document has been translated from German.

2 Ester, also Esther, Galler, née Schupak (1868–1943); born in Belchatów (Poland); thought to have emigrated to Luxembourg in 1901; widowed in 1933; from autumn 1941 in Fünfbrunnen (Cinqfontaines) camp; on 6 April 1943 deported to Theresienstadt, where she perished.

3 Ferdinand Grumbach (1871–1942); emigrated to Luxembourg from Baden in 1897; as of autumn 1941 in Fünfbrunnen camp; deported to Theresienstadt on 26 July 1942; deported in mid Sept. 1942 to Treblinka, where he was murdered.

4 Albert Galler (1904–1942); son of Ester and Henri Galler; prisoner in Breendonk camp in Belgium; from there deported in mid Sept. 1942 via Mechelen transit camp to Auschwitz, where he was murdered.

5 Blima Kalinsky, née Schupak (1874–1943); born in Poland; sister of Ester Galler; thought to have been deported on 28 July 1942 from Fünfbrunnen to Theresienstadt, where she perished.

DOC. 227

On 23 July 1942 the Einsatzkommando of the Security Police and the SD in Luxembourg gives Karl Stern precise instructions for his transfer to Theresienstadt[1]

State Police order of the Einsatzkommando of the Security Police and the SD (B. no. 1586/42 II B 3), Luxembourg, signed SS-Obersturmbannführer and Oberregierungsrat Hartmann, to the Jew Karl Stern,[2] Ulflingen, dated 23 July 1942

For the purpose of relocation to the Theresienstadt home for the elderly, you – and if any family members are present, they too – must report ready for departure to the main railway station in Luxembourg City – Customs Clearance – on Tuesday, 28 July 1942, at 6 a.m. Note the following:

1) Permitted luggage:
   a) one suitcase or knapsack per person
   b) 2 parts of a three-part mattress, 2 woollen blankets and 1 pillow and 1 dish plus a spoon,
   c) 50 Reichsmarks in cash per person,
   d) complete set of clothing, provided that it is worn on the person,
   e) provisions for eight days.
2) You must duly de-register by presenting this order to the police registration authorities and the appropriate food office.
3) The current residence must be cleaned, tidied, and locked when you leave. The key is to be provided with a tag on which your exact address must be visible and is to be turned over to the representative of the Council of Elders before your departure.

Failure to appear will result in your immediate arrest and detention in a concentration camp.

1 ANLux, FD-083-31, C.I. 03. This document has been translated from German.
2 Karl Stern (1880–1943), retailer; emigrated to Luxembourg from Frankfurt am Main; deported in late July 1942 via Dortmund to Theresienstadt, where he perished in Feb. 1943.

DOC. 228

On 29 July 1942 Curt Edelstein describes for Alfred Oppenheimer his deportation to Theresienstadt[1]

Handwritten letter from Curt Edelstein[2] to Alfred Oppenheimer, dated 29 July 1942[3]

My dear A. O.,

Up until Dortmund, the journey went well enough.[4] Mrs Altmann[5] suffered from travel sickness but soon recovered. *Lt Schmalz*[6] was very nice but did not talk to me about personal things. I had to check the number of my fellow travellers against a list of names, and it turned out that we actually had a passenger who was not on the list, namely Mrs Emma Kahn,[7] so we are *157 altogether.* The journey really does not agree with Inge,[8] she is surely much more unwell than we both thought. It was catastrophic in Dortmund. No organization at all. A change of trains. From the local community, a couple of helpers, who were busy with their own transport. No help getting off the train, train did not stop at the ramp, no help transferring the luggage to the other train. No one from the local leadership was at the railway station at 8.30 a.m., not even for the local community's own transport. Dreadful barking of orders. Incredible effort to haul the bags 300–400 metres. For the short distance remaining, finally get a small cart for 5 Reichsmarks, which helped. Some items seem to get lost. After repeatedly trying to speak to the local elder, I accidentally address an Aryan, get a slap in the face and three kicks, and am forbidden to leave the railway wagon again. Try harder to reach the gentleman, unfortunately in vain. Food: soup, not bad, but cold. Our milk cans are supposed to be filled up with water, but don't come back to us. I really felt like expressing my thanks for the hospitality. Scandalous. The train is too long, we are given wagons with fewer axles. One freight wagon is to be left behind, thus far impossible to learn whether all the luggage is

1 ANLux, FD-083–25, C.I. 02. Published in French translation in Paul Cerf, *Longtemps j'aurai mémoire: Documents et témoignages sur les Juifs du Grand-Duché de Luxembourg durant la Seconde Guerre mondiale* (Luxembourg: Editions du Letzeburger Land, 1974), pp. 129–130. This document has been translated from German.

2 Curt Edelstein (b. 1894); emigrated to Luxembourg from Mannheim in Feb. 1932; with his wife, Edith, and the Heumanns, a married couple, ran the internment camp in Fünfbrunnen Abbey from Aug. 1941 to July 1942; deported to Theresienstadt on 28 July 1942, and in Sept. 1944 to Auschwitz, where he perished. During the journey from Luxembourg to Theresienstadt, he was responsible for the transport.

3 Receipt stamp, presumably that of the Consistory, dated 31 July 1942. Pre-printed on each page of the original: 'i. C. Edelstein & Wife, Post Office / 2. 1'.

4 The train, consisting of freight wagons and one passenger coach for the police escort, had left Luxembourg on 28 July 1942. The deportees presumably also had to change trains in Düsseldorf. In Dortmund, they were attached to convoy Da 72, bound for Theresienstadt and transporting 968 persons.

5 Minna Altmann (b. 1867), housewife; thought to have survived.

6 Otto Schmalz (b. 1904), police official; with the Gestapo in Trier from 1936; joined the NSDAP in 1937; assigned to the section for Jewish affairs of the Security Police and the SD in Luxembourg from 1940.

7 Emma Kahn, née Seckler (1870–1952), housewife.

8 Inge Edelstein (1922–1944), daughter of Curt Edelstein; in May 1944 deported from Theresienstadt to Auschwitz, where she perished.

with us. Forwarding as express freight may be possible if the freight charge is paid in advance. Request that it be handled from there. Inspection of the luggage has not yet taken place, but the taking of 50 Reichsmarks per person has. Here too, addressed in an unbelievable tone of voice. After I delivered the money from my group, I had to jump through the window into the moving train. We are glad to be out of Dortmund. We have far less room in the wagons, had to take in other people in addition. Hardly any room to move around in the corridors. Terrible, nowhere to wash, no water! Care provided in Trier was kind, helpful. Hope you all are spared this strain and stress. If only we were already there. If only we knew what will become of us. I'm anticipating something bad. Nonetheless, mood here not bad, at most somewhat anxious.

Warm regards to all, your dear family, the Heumanns, the dear, dear young people, the rest of the community, the rest of the council.[9]

To you, a friendly handshake

Yours, CE.

Please let Denise read this letter too.

DOC. 229

On 21 October 1942 the Council of Elders of the Jews asks that Leo Salomon not be deported, to avoid jeopardizing the care of the occupants of Fünfbrunnen[1]

Letter from the Council of Elders of the Jews (O/J), signed Martin Israel Meyer,[2] official in charge, and Elder Alfred Israel Oppenheimer, Fünfbrunnen, to the Einsatzkommando of the Security Police and the SD (Department II B 3),[3] Luxembourg, dated 21 October 1942 (carbon copy)

Our community member Leo Israel Salomon,[4] along with his family, is to be placed under the authority of the Berlin Gestapo for the purpose of resettlement. We venture most respectfully to present the following for your consideration:

Salomon, along with his family, was exempt from the first resettlement to Litzmannstadt, on 16 October of last year,[5] on the basis of his military papers. We subsequently utilized Salomon for community tasks, while his wife helped look after those living here. The two daughters (16 and 20 years of age) volunteered the very next day after this first transport to help with housework and with care for the elderly and sick in Fünfbrunnen.

9 Otto Schmalz, who presumably escorted the convoy as far as Dortmund, gave the letter to Alfred Oppenheimer after returning to Luxembourg.

1 ANLux, FD-261-09, C.I. II. This document has been translated from German.

2 Martin Meyer (1890–1944), retailer; emigrated with his family to Luxembourg from Germany in 1939; deported from Fünfbrunnen to Theresienstadt in early April 1943, and from there in mid Oct. 1944 to Auschwitz, where he was murdered.

3 In 1942 the director was Fritz Hartmann.

4 Leo Salomon (b. 1881), retailer, his wife Erna, née Hertz (b. 1892), and his daughters Margot (b. 1922) and Sonja (b. 1926) emigrated to Luxembourg from Gießen in Sept. 1936 and relocated to Fünfbrunnen in the summer of 1941; the family were deported to Theresienstadt on 6 April 1943 and five months later from there to Auschwitz, where they were all murdered.

5 See PMJ 5/215.

We sought to have the Salomon family exempted from the last two transports to Theresienstadt[6] because Mr and Mrs Salomon, despite serious abdominal problems and rheumatoid arthritis respectively, volunteered for the heaviest work, the laundry, as we neither had nor have the workers who can do this work.

The occupancy of the home is presently 89 persons. Of these, 55 are permanently or almost permanently bedridden, while 16 persons are ill and unfit for work. The remaining 18 are divided among the following tasks:

director of the home[7]	1	must also attend to Community business and provide support for the mixed marriages.
bookkeeper[8]	1	
co-director[9]	1	
launderers	2	with so many who are bedridden and helpless, far more laundry
ironers	2	needed than previously
aides	2	for cleaning the ward and taking care of the 55 who are presently bedridden and helpless.
worker	1	for carrying coal, chopping wood, repairs in the building
gardener	1	fetching provisions in Ulflingen and garden work.
clerk	1	to date correspondence has been handled in part from Luxembourg.
kitchen	2	
female workers	4	for daily cleaning of 29 rooms, the dining room, hallways, water closets and staircase. Also, washing-up and bringing meals to the bedridden.

We have to have our staff work from 6 a.m. to 10 p.m. with almost no interruption just to be able to cope after a fashion. In addition, sometimes one or other of our workers becomes ill because of overexertion and then the others have to do the work of the person who is sick as well. For example, at the moment the wife[10] of the signatory on the right and a female worker are receiving medical treatment.

The resettlement of the Salomon family would mean for us a loss of four able-bodied workers. As a result we would no longer be able to maintain the home for the infirm in its present state of cleanliness, and the risk that epidemics and diseases might spread would be not insignificant.

For these reasons, the Council of Elders ventures to ask most respectfully that the decision to resettle this family is reversed.

We thank you most sincerely, Oberregierungsrat, in anticipation of your gracious approval of our request, and sign

with the highest esteem

6 See Doc. 228.
7 Martin Meyer, Curt Edelstein's successor.
8 Hugo Heumann.
9 Selma Heumann.
10 Aline Oppenheimer, née Cahen (1892–1943); deported on 17 June 1943 along with her husband, Alfred, and son René to Theresienstadt, where she perished five months later.

DOC. 230
In December 1942 the Inter-Allied Information Committee describes the situation for Jews in occupied Luxembourg[1]

[…][2]

Luxembourg

The oldest historical events concerning the Jews of Luxembourg date back to the thirteenth century. However, sustained Jewish emigration in modern times goes back to the French Revolution. At that time the Jews received complete equality with other citizens, a principle which was upheld by the Constitution of 1868. Judaism is officially recognized by the state in the same way as the Christian religion, and the Grand Duchy's Chief Rabbi is a civil servant.

In 1935 there were 3,144 Jews in Luxembourg. Around two thirds were of foreign origin, German refugees for the most part. They were concentrated particularly in Luxembourg City, the capital, and in two other cities.

The treatment inflicted upon this little community in Luxembourg is characteristic of the desperate misery which afflicted most of the Jews of Europe. At the start of the war, on 19 May 1940, the purely Luxembourgish Jewish population numbered around 2,300, and the German refugees who had been permitted to remain in the Grand Duchy numbered 600.[3] A short time after the German occupation and the armistice with France, a German civil administration was set up, and the antisemitic laws were comprehensively applied. Those refugees who had left Germany 'illegally' were thrown into concentration camps. Others, particularly Austrian refugees, were granted permission to leave Luxembourg if their emigration papers were in order.

A number of well-off Luxembourgish Jews had left Luxembourg before 10 May 1940 (the date of the invasion), and around 600 others were to leave the Grand Duchy on the day of the invasion itself.

'Aryanization' began with the registration of the Jews on 31 May 1940.[4] A decree on 5 September 1940 brought the totality of German antisemitic legislation into force.[5] (It should be recalled that Germany considered Luxembourg 'incorporated into the greater Reich'; therefore, the laws which applied to Germans also applied in their entirety to the Luxembourgers.) The decrees of 19 December 1940[6] and of 7 and

1 Comité d'information interallié, *La Persécution des Juifs: Les conditions de vie dans les territoires occupés* (His Majesty's Stationery Office: London, 1942), pp. 9–10. This document has been translated from French.

2 The brochure begins with a preface, dated 18 Dec. 1942, from the committee president Georges Schommer (1897–1961), judge; secretary general of the Ministry of Foreign Affairs of the Luxembourg government in exile. A general introduction into the persecution of the Jews in German-occupied Europe is followed by depictions of the situation in particular countries.

3 At the start of the German occupation about 3,900 Jews lived in Luxembourg, including approximately 1,000 citizens of Luxembourg.

4 This could not be verified.

5 See PMJ 5/199–201.

6 Presumably this refers to the announcement of the implementation of the Regulation on Jewish Assets, 18 Dec. 1940, and the Implementing Regulation to the Regulation on Jewish Assets in Luxembourg, 19 Dec. 1940: *VOBl-L*, 1940, no. 72, 24 Dec. 1940, pp. 433 f.

18 February 1941[7] covered the registration of the Jews and the confiscation of property belonging to them. On 18 December 1940,[8] Rabbi Robert Serebrenik,[9] who represented the Jewish community to the Nazi government, received the order that all Jews were to leave the territory within a fortnight.[10]

Thanks to the efforts of the Grand Duchess and Jewish aid organizations, particularly the American [Jewish] Joint Distribution Committee (JDC), more than 2,000 Jews were able to leave Luxembourg.[11] Of those who stayed, 338 were sent to Poland[12] and a hundred or so left the country illegally. The elderly and the infirm, 334 in total, had to be left behind; they were separated from the rest of the inhabitants, and most of them were placed in a former monastery. The Jewish Consistory administered their property and served as an intermediary between the Jews and the Gestapo. The local farmers showed their humanity by helping the Jews as much as they could; without the help they received in this way, few of these Jews would have survived their ordeal. Finally, the Jewish community was liquidated when the 300 remaining Jews were deported; on 28 July 1942 they were transferred to the Theresienstadt fort in Bohemia-Moravia.[13]

Mr Hugues le Gallais,[14] minister-plenipotentiary of Luxembourg, declared on 21 July 1942 at a gathering in New York held in protest against Hitler's atrocities:

> I would like to use the occasion of a protest demonstration against the Hitlerian atrocities to express the unreserved admiration and sympathy of the government of Luxembourg for the Jewish people who are being martyred and are resisting in occupied Europe, and the hope that after the victory their tormentors will not escape the just punishment which awaits all German war criminals.
>
> I am aware of the intolerable suffering that has been inflicted upon my Jewish compatriots who were cruelly driven out of their homes and their country by the pitiless oppressor of my homeland. In their suffering, they have all the help and the full sympathy of the government and the population of Luxembourg, which itself is a victim of Hitler's barbarism.

7 Regulation on Measures concerning the Assets of Jews and Emigrants, 7 Feb. 1941, *VOBl-L*, 1941, no. 12, 11 Feb. 1941, p. 90. A further decree dated 18 Feb. 1941 could not be found.

8 Correctly: 12 Sept. 1940.

9 Dr Robert Serebrenik (1902–1965), rabbi; chief rabbi of Luxembourg, 1929–1946; went into exile in May 1941; with other refugees from Luxembourg, he founded the Ramath Orah congregation and the Luxembourg Jewish Information Office in New York in 1942.

10 See PMJ 5/202 and PMJ 5, p. 56.

11 At least 890 Jews from Luxembourg were able to escape the German sphere of influence in Western Europe. At least 1,374 more were trapped in France and 217 in Belgium; only 599 and 78 respectively survived the occupation, with at least 475 in France and 90 in Belgium caught up in the deportations.

12 By the end of 1942, a total of 551 Jews in total had been deported from Luxembourg to the East.

13 In April and June 1943, 99 and 8 Jews respectively were deported on two further transports to Theresienstadt.

14 Hugues Le Gallais (1896–1964), merchant and diplomat; manager of a branch of a Luxembourg company in Tokyo, 1927–1938; chargé d'affaires of Luxembourg in Washington, April 1940–1958; simultaneously plenipotentiary of Luxembourg in Canada, 1949–1958; worked for the International Monetary Fund from 1956.

Martyrdom is never in vain. The systematic and concerted martyrdom of the Jewish population, which shows how German barbarism behaves towards defenceless men, women, and children, and shows how the Germans would behave if they were to win the war, has inspired millions throughout the world in their struggle against a common enemy.

The cause of the persecuted Jewish community is the cause of the civilized world.

[…][15]

DOC. 231

In late 1942 the Council of Elders reports on previous financial donations for deportees to Litzmannstadt (Lodz) and appeals to the remaining Community members to continue to donate[1]

Appeal, unsigned, undated (carbon copy)

Donations to our brothers and sisters in faith who have been resettled in the East.

The donations received did not pass through the coffers of the Community and the Fünfbrunnen home for the elderly. A few days before the first large Poland transport to Litzmannstadt on 16 October 1941,[2] the Administration of Jewish Assets[3] had indicated that resettled persons who were registered with this administrative office and had money on account or held secure accounts with restricted access were to receive 50 Reichsmarks per person each month.

Assured that in addition they could continue to count on food supplies from Luxembourg, our brothers and sisters in faith took their leave of us. It was not possible to supply food from here. The Administration of Jewish Assets did not permit shipments to Litzmannstadt in any form. Therefore the Community members who remained here had to use their limited means to provide the urgently needed support. As soon as we knew the addresses of even a part of those who were relocated to Litzmannstadt on 16 October 1941, as a test on 12 December 1941 we sent each one a postal order for 10 Reichsmarks, 3,250 Reichsmarks in total. The entirety of this sum was raised through voluntary donations.

After the vast majority of those who had been resettled from here confirmed they had received the money, we have been sending funds regularly to Litzmannstadt and have taken advantage of every opportunity to ask for donations.

15 There follows in the brochure a description of the situation of the Jews in Norway, the Netherlands, Poland, Bohemia and Moravia, Slovakia, and Yugoslavia.

1 ANLux, FD-083-69, C.I. 17. This document has been translated from German.

2 See PMJ 5/215.

3 Department IV A of the civil administration responsible for the 'administration of Jewish and emigrant assets'.

During the period from 10 December 1941 to 31 December 1942
receipts and disbursements were as follows

Receipts:		*Disbursements:*	
12 Dec. 1941–31 Dec. 1941	RM 3,250	12 Dec. 1941–31 Dec. 1941	3,250
1 Jan. 1942–31 July 1942	RM 14,203	1 Jan. 1942–31 July 1942	15,189
1 Aug. 1942–31 Dec. 1942	RM 8,108	1 Aug. 1942–31 Dec. 1942	6,795
	RM 25,561		RM 25,234
		Holdings on 31 Dec. 1942	RM 327
	RM 25,561		RM 25,561

The first remittance to Litzmannstadt, sent on 12 December 1941, should be understood as a test. Each member of the Community has contributed to the amount raised according to his ability. The total receipts of RM 22,311 for the period 1 January 1942–31 December 1942 have been divided into two time periods in order to show that after the large deportations in July 1942, the remainder of the Community – around 100 persons, in contrast to a total average of 300 strong in the first half of 1942 – contributed especially strongly to the funds raised. Every appeal, whether made in a circular letter to the Community members or later through solicitation among the residents of the Fünfbrunnen home, was successful. The donations raised would have been many times greater if our Community members had still had access to their assets.[4] They were dependent upon the monthly maintenance payment, from which the donations to us were made. In particular, it is worth emphasizing and paying tribute to the fact that the later donations, at a time when only pocket money was being made available, can be regarded as substantial.

In some cases, individuals placed the entirety of their pocket money at our disposal. Special occasions for remembering the unfortunate who had been deported, such as our main holidays, the festival of Hanukkah, always yielded good results.

The sum of RM 25,234, which is spread across 1,647 postal orders and giro transfers, is made up almost exclusively of sums for Litzmannstadt. It was not possible to send money to the transports of 23 April 1942, with 24 persons for Izbica in District Lublin,[5] and 12 July 1942, with 24 persons supposedly for Auschwitz in Upper Silesia,[6] and to the two transports of 26 and 28 July 1942 for Theresienstadt, because news of the deportees on the first two transports never reached us here and sending money to Theresienstadt was not allowed.

We know that with an initial head count of 325 and even with the 80 to 100 persons we estimated to be in Litzmannstadt at the end of 1942, the remittances should have been many times larger.[7] Unfortunately, the circumstances meant that the remaining Community members were not able to manage that. But we do also know that our

4 Bank accounts belonging to Jews in Luxembourg were converted into blocked accounts in autumn 1940. Jews were also required to deposit any cash they held in a blocked account. From the end of 1941, they were permitted to withdraw only 50 Reichsmarks per person per month for their maintenance, rather than the original 125 Reichsmarks.

5 See PMJ 5/224 and 225.

6 The transport of 12 June 1942 did go to Auschwitz.

brothers and sisters in faith in exile receive everything we send with great gratitude and with understanding. And as long as it is still necessary and we are still able, we shall also strive during 1943 to do our duty and to act according to the motto

'To give quickly is to give double.'

DOC. 232

From 6 to 9 April 1943 Selma Heumann reports to Alfred Oppenheimer from the train to Theresienstadt[1]

Handwritten letter from Selma Heumann[2] to Alfred Oppenheimer, dated 6 to 9 April 1943

Dear A. O., all you dear ones,

The first night is over. It is 9.30 a.m., and we are in Bettenburg.[3] Geographically we are so close to you, but in reality already far away. The night was very cold, but bearable. We were in Luxembourg on schedule and continued the journey an hour ago.[4] Our wagon is the best equipped.[5] Thanks to the energy and prudence of my husband, we all had a place to lie down and above all had all our things with us. Mr Fuchs,[6] who was still complaining loudly about the change of allocated place and saw the other wagons today, is now quite content to be here with us. The sick people are all calm; only Mr Winter[7] is in poor condition. He has vomited several times and Renée[8] and I were often in the wagon. The Kliatzkow group,[9] to which he belongs, is horrified, not helpful at all, selfish and heartless. We could have made good use of your authority there, Mr President. My thoughts are always with you. My wish for you is that you continue to be spared such a journey. However, we can't complain. Our escorts are decent to us. They will have their hands full. How glad I would be to help.

7 In Oct. 1941, 322 Jews had been deported from Luxembourg to Litzmannstadt (Lodz). Many of them had already been murdered in spring 1942, at Kulmhof (Chelmno); others were taken to labour camps. The basis on which the Council of Elders established its estimate could not be determined.

1 ANLux, FD-083-40, C.I. 06. This document has been translated from German.

2 Selma Heumann, née Dalberg (1893–1990); married Hugo Heumann in Germany in 1920; left for Luxembourg in April 1939; along with her husband ran the Jewish home for the elderly at Fünfbrunnen from 1941 to 1943; from April 1943 in Theresienstadt, where she was held until liberation in May 1945; returned to Luxembourg in Aug. 1945 and emigrated to the USA in 1948.

3 Correctly: Bettembourg, railway hub in southern Luxembourg.

4 The train had left Fünfbrunnen on 5 April 1943 and travelled via Luxembourg City to Germany.

5 The Consistory had requested third-class coaches for this transport, but the Reich Railways in Saarbrücken had provided five freight wagons. These were fitted out with straw and mattresses for the 99 passengers on the train.

6 Alexander Fuchs (1874–1947?), teacher of religion; cantor in Luxembourg.

7 Samuel Winter (1863–1943); emigrated to Luxembourg from Germany; perished a few days after the transport's arrival at Theresienstadt.

8 Presumably Renée Cerf (b. 1915); deported in early Sept. 1943 from Theresienstadt to Auschwitz, where she is thought to have been murdered.

9 Correctly: Kliatzko. May (b. 1900), Gertrud, née Hirsch (b. 1909), and Marianne Kliatzko (b. 1937) were deported at the end of Oct. 1944 from Theresienstadt to Auschwitz, where they are thought to have been murdered.

Thursday morning[10]
Yesterday went well, the mood is satisfactory. The night was less peaceful. We were in Koblenz for several hours and were often shunted from one track to another, which is not pleasant. Mrs Sara Levy[11] was very restless, in spite of taking drops. She disturbed all the occupants and […].[12] In the daytime it looks like a gypsy caravan in here, and at night it is like being in steerage. Renée is holding up marvellously; I haven't seen much of all the other girls yet. It is stormy and raining; the weather is a good match for our sad journey. Around 8 a.m. we were in snow-covered Frankfurt and anyone who wished was allowed to leave the railway wagon for 5 minutes. I used the time for my morning wash: there was hot water from the locomotive. The paraffin lamps for the escorts didn't come with us. We helped out with candles. Meanwhile I made my inspection visits. Everybody is fine and everybody wishes this journey would never end, despite the cold and discomfort, for fear of what lies ahead. The details you will probably hear from the girls, who all are writing, and I don't want to repeat myself. Sometimes I wish, Mr Oppenheimer, that I could pop into your office for a little chat, to share my observations with you and discuss our views on life. I hope Renée and I can continue to work together. She is a good comrade, prudent, kind to the old people and full of good humour. The other girls are nice too. They are happy when I come to see them, but it is different. With Edith and Denise[13] I feel as if they are looking forward cheerfully to what comes next.

Friday morning[14]
Last night was bitterly cold. We have been in Dresden for hours in the marshalling yard but cannot get off the train because it is too dirty here. Did it snow where you are too? The mood is good. Fr[…][15] had even […][16] her two neighbours last evening and Mr Rothschild,[17] who is very weak and takes only liquids, answered very nicely. I was so glad, because I had been worried that he would not survive the journey. A great deal of cooking is being done in the other wagons. We have no time for that and are glad if we can get the coffee hot for everybody. Meyerlein brought us soup yesterday, which greatly delighted us. Our people make sure that we do not get bored. We are now slowly starting to pack up. Now you know everything and it will also interest you that the problem of the smallest room was also solved successfully.

And now most likely my last regards for a long time, stay healthy and think of us sometimes.

10 8 April 1943.
11 Sara Levy, née Oppenheimer (1858–1943); emigrated to Luxembourg from Germany in 1889; perished a few days after arriving at Theresienstadt.
12 A word is illegible.
13 Edith Levy (b. 1917); employed at Fünfbrunnen from Nov. 1941; in Theresienstadt she married Gert Edelstein; in early Oct. 1944 deported first to Auschwitz and then to a subcamp of the Groß-Rosen concentration camp; returned to Luxembourg in June 1945; see also PMJ 5/206. Denise Levy (b. 1923) was deported on 9 Oct. 1944 to Auschwitz, where she is thought to have been murdered.
14 9 April 1943.
15 A word is illegible.
16 A word is illegible.
17 Louis Rothschild (1861–1943); perished shortly after arriving at Theresienstadt.

In constant friendship,
Yours,
Selma Heumann

Dear friends! My wife's report is so detailed that I have only to add my best regards to it. I know that you won't forget us, just as we will retain our friendship for you all our lives.

With a very warm handshake to you all,
Yours,
Hugo Heumann[18]

DOC. 233
In early 1944, while in Theresienstadt, Hugo Heumann writes a personal account of the persecution of the Jews in Luxembourg[1]

Handwritten account by Hugo Heumann,[2] Theresienstadt, undated[3]

[…][4]
The increasing pressure from the Gestapo and the many emigrations that resulted, both to unoccupied France and to countries overseas, caused [Helene][5] and her children to think seriously about emigrating to the USA. As they had sufficient capital there, the question of a visa was quickly resolved. The family thus also faced the prospect of a life as emigrants and hence gained a better understanding of the lot forced upon us, and from this time on, their manner towards us improved.[6]

18 The train reached Theresienstadt on 10 April 1943.

1 Simon Wiesenthal Center Library and Archives, Los Angeles, CA, 2000–057. Published in Hugo Heumann, *Erlebtes–Erlittenes: Von Mönchengladbach über Luxemburg nach Theresienstadt: Tagebuch eines deutsch-jüdischen Emigranten*, ed. Germaine Goetzinger and Marc Schoentgen (Mersch: Centre Nationale de Littérature, 2007), pp. 51–54, 57–59. This document has been translated from German.

2 Hugo Heumann (1876–1973), textile manufacturer; partner in his father's textile company in Gladbach from 1905; the firm was Aryanized and Heumann briefly detained in 1938; emigrated to Luxembourg in April 1939; with his wife, Selma, he managed the Jewish home for the elderly at Fünfbrunnen from 1941 to 1943; deported to Theresienstadt in April 1943; returned to Luxembourg in Aug. 1945 and emigrated to the USA in 1948.

3 Hugo Heumann wrote his diary for his son Walter (b. 1921, electrician), who had worked for Philips in the Netherlands, survived the war in hiding, and emigrated to the USA in 1947. This entry was written in Jan. or Feb. 1944.

4 Heumann first describes the flight of the family from Mönchengladbach and their life as refugees in Luxembourg, initially in relative freedom and then in the Fünfbrunnen home for the elderly.

5 After Hugo Heumann's death, his wife, Selma, made the names in the original unidentifiable. With the permission of the family, the names have been added here in square brackets. Helene Bonn, née Heumann (1881–1948); sister of Hugo Heumann; emigrated to the USA in May 1941.

6 Elsewhere in the diary, Heumann describes a dependence on his sister that he found uncomfortable.

Many things were sold, with which [Uncle Moritz][7] and I often helped, other things, particularly linens, rugs, and the like were given to friends and acquaintances for safekeeping. But carrying out their plans took a considerable time, and as a result […][8] in particular became so nervous that one sometimes had to doubt his sanity. [Uncle Moritz] also used all possible means to obtain a visa, which he managed to do on the basis of the paperwork sent to him by Karl.[9] It went on all winter long, and not until April [1941] could [Lex],[10] as a solo traveller, start on the long journey, followed in late May by all the rest of the family in a larger group.[11] I cannot express in words how we felt to see them leave, how we felt to stay behind.

Before leaving, [Lex] had made an agreement with the Community administration according to which his mother's large house passed into the Community's possession without payment, on condition that it would be turned into an old people's home for the elderly people who remained behind and that Mutti[12] would be made head of the home. The Gestapo had given its consent to this plan.[13]

On 1 May the home was opened, with 2 residents at first; by the end of May there were 5 persons, it was all going quite well, our only difficulties were with Mrs [Cohn],[14] who had arrived on 1 May and was very demanding, especially for Mutti, but she did not put up with anything from her and finally prevailed, so that this relationship too became bearable.

During this time an episode occurred that I don't want to leave unmentioned. One Friday evening towards the end of April,[15] the synagogue was attended as usual by older persons. The cantor was roughly midway through Lecho Dodi[16] when loud voices caused a noisy disturbance at the door, and a few moments later a man in black breeches and a white shirt (the uniform of the Ethnic German Movement[17] and equivalent to the brown uniform of the NSDAP) stood on the almemor,[18] struck the cantor's lectern with his hand and forbade the service to continue 'in the name of and by order of his party'. All attempts to negotiate produced no result. He threatened to order his people, who

7 Moritz Heumann (1874–1952), textile manufacturer; partner in his father's textile company in Gladbach from 1905; travelled to Luxembourg in April 1939, and two years later to the USA.

8 Name not known.

9 Karl Heumann (1913–1978); son of Moritz Heumann; lived in the USA.

10 Alex Bonn (1908–2008), lawyer; nephew of Hugo Heumann; supported and partially financed the emigration of the Heumanns to the USA; vice president and secretary of the Consistory in 1941.

11 The Bonn family left Luxembourg at the end of May 1941 along with 66 other Jews to travel to the USA via France and Portugal.

12 Selma Heumann.

13 The building at 42 rue Notre Dame in Luxembourg City was transferred to the Consistory on 30 March 1941. Several Jewish families in Luxembourg made their residences available as homes for Jews who were elderly and in need of care. With the transfer of most Jews to Fünfbrunnen Abbey in August 1941, these private homes for the elderly were gradually closed again.

14 Presumably Auguste Cohn-Grünbaum (1878–1942); died in Luxembourg.

15 Correctly: on 9 May 1941.

16 Hebrew: 'Come, my beloved', liturgical song recited to welcome Shabbat.

17 The Ethnic German Movement (Volksdeutsche Bewegung, VdB) was founded after the German occupation in May 1940. The chairman was the teacher Damian Kratzenberg (1878–1946). The VdB was aligned with the NSDAP in terms of its world view, organization, and appearance, and undertook intensive propaganda for the integration of Luxembourg into the German Reich.

18 Hebrew: bema, podium in the synagogue from which the Torah scrolls are read.

were manning the doors, to shoot unless the 'Jew church' was cleared immediately, and thus there was no choice but to leave. It was probably one of the most shameful events I have experienced in my life, and even today as I write these words I feel the awful dread that seized us all at that time.

The next day a complaint was lodged with the Gestapo. The Gestapo said that such things would not be repeated, but no religious service was held in the synagogue again, especially as the rabbi[19] emigrated to the USA a few weeks later, travelling in the same group as [Aunt Helene]. The synagogue building was vacated[20] in winter 1941–1942, the seforim[21] and other religious objects having been removed beforehand.[22]

It was envisaged that we should receive a number of additional residents at the home in July–August in order to make the operation viable; then one morning in early July, 2 P.G.[23] in uniform appeared and demanded that the house be vacated within 2 hours. Reference to the written permission issued by the Gestapo and the assurance given to [Lex] before his departure that the house would not be confiscated led to nothing. The only thing achieved was that we were given until noon the next day to get out. The Consistory immediately organized several removal vans and a sizeable number of helpers. First the furniture and belongings of the residents were transferred to other homes, and then our bedroom furnishings and possessions were put in a room in the home of [Felix Kahn][24] that had been cleared out, and everything else from [Helene's] large house, her furniture, her tableware, kitchen equipment, etc., went into storage with a haulier. There was an enormous amount of work to be done to get everything packed up, but it was accomplished. By noon the next day, the house was completely empty; incidentally, it continued to stand empty for weeks before it was utilized for its new purpose.

From early July until the end of July, we lived as, so to speak, pensioners.[25] The Consistory wanted to establish a new home for us and entered into negotiations about several properties with the Administration of Jewish Assets[26] and with several landlords. But before any decision could be made, the news came from the Gestapo around 25 July that the abbey of Fünfbrunnen near Ulflingen had been designated for the establishment of a home for the elderly and infirm and must be put into operation as soon as possible. The Consistory asked Mutti whether she wanted to take on the management of the home together with a Mr [Curt Edelstein]. Mutti's reply was worthy of her: 'If you trust me to take it on, I want to do it.' And with that, a complete change from our previous way of life began.

19 Robert Serebrenik.
20 The building had been erected in 1893/94. After an arson attack and the raid, it was closed, and it had been completely demolished by autumn 1943.
21 Hebrew: term for the Torah scrolls.
22 The objects were brought to safety at the State Museum of Luxembourg and returned to the Jewish community after the war.
23 Parteigenossen = Party members.
24 Felix Kahn (1894–1981); member of the Consistory in 1941, in charge of the Jewish homes for the elderly; left Luxembourg in mid Oct. 1941 on the last transport headed west and reached the USA via Portugal.
25 From this point on, the family was entirely dependent on financial support from the Consistory.
26 See Doc. 231, fn. 3.

[…][27]

Towards mid November 1941, the Consistory was informed that all the Jews in the country, around 350 in number, were to be concentrated in Fünfbrunnen, and barracks were to be built to house them. The construction of these barracks was assigned to a Cologne firm,[28] which sent up a foreman in early December, under whose direction the digging of trenches for the foundation walls began immediately. It was very hard work, as the terrain consisted entirely of rock. At first, an attempt was made to manage with 10–12 younger men who were sent to us as 'labourers'.[29] Then a contractor from Ulflingen was given the job, but the barracks were never finished, because later the plan was changed, and instead of being brought to Fünfbrunnen, our poor brethren and fellow sufferers were transported to Poland, Birkenau, and Theresienstadt.[30]

The accommodation of the approximately 100 persons present at the end of November had only been made possible by having the big dormitory room for the religious pupils divided under the direction of [Curt Edelstein] into around 25 single rooms, each with an area of roughly 9–10 square metres. However, they were separated from each other only by simple wooden partitions and therefore were anything but soundproof, which was often disturbing. These small spaces had room only for the beds and a few small pieces of furniture, while the cupboards had to be set up in the central corridor, where 12 to 15 stoves for the makeshift heating of the entire space were also placed. In addition to these small rooms, the large spaces on the ground floor were divided into several rooms by mesh and plaster walls.[31] Later, when occupancy became substantially higher, every little nook that could be used in some way was converted into accommodation. We wanted to avoid adapting the chapel or the attic to house the home's residents, a move the Gestapo had repeatedly proposed.

[…][32]

I took it easy for a few more weeks and then gradually resumed my customary life and my customary work, but also the customary agitation. It was primarily the Stapo[33] that made sure I had no lack of the latter. The first major transport to the East, specifically to Litzmannstadt, had departed as early as 20 October 1941[34] and included, among others, the [Obermeiers].[35] The whole transport comprised more than 100 persons,[36] around 25 of whom came from our home. It was sad to see these poor expellees setting

27 In what follows, the author describes Fünfbrunnen, the preparations for housing the Jewish residents, their relocation to the abbey, and their daily life together.

28 The work was taken on by the firm Franz Schlotmann Concrete Engineering. The construction of the barracks had to be financed by the Jewish community.

29 These were Jewish forced labourers.

30 The work was halted at the end of July 1942 because of the shortage of materials and the beginning of the deportations.

31 *Rabitzwände*: light dividing walls made of powdered gypsum and plaster of Paris or cement on wire mesh.

32 In the following section, the author describes falling seriously ill. He spent several weeks in a hospital in Luxembourg City.

33 Gestapo.

34 Correctly: 16 Oct. 1941.

35 Presumably Siegfried Obermeyer (1883–1942) and his wife, Amalia, née Scheiberg (1895–1944); before the war they lived in Bad Salzuflen; both perished in Litzmannstadt.

36 In all, 322 Jews were deported; 12 of them survived the war.

out with the meagre belongings they had prepared for this journey out of the remnants of their often very considerable possessions which they had brought with them when they came to us. Unfortunately, we often had to see this scene repeated on a smaller or larger scale, until we experienced the same fate when we were taken off to Theresienstadt. A second source of upset and continual alarm was the inspection visits made by the Stapo. In most cases, to be sure, we were notified about these visits beforehand, but now and then they were entirely unsuspected. One such unexpected visit took place on 17 January 1942, and by the Stapo chief himself[37] at that, accompanied by several SS men. A piece of toilet soap, still almost new, which he saw lying on the washstand in the first room, gave him occasion to confiscate all the toilet soap in the whole building and order that it be delivered immediately: for 'both he and the soldiers at the front had only war soap, so the Jews didn't need to wash with toilet soap'. Since the delivery did not proceed quickly enough for him, the following punishments were imposed: (1) house arrest for all inmates[38] with the exception of those working in the administration insofar as this was necessary to procure what was needed to meet daily needs; (2) strict ban on smoking, (3) ban on reading, both for newspapers and books.[39] One must imagine how the sick and elderly were affected by these three measures, which were only relaxed months later in that free movement in the immediate vicinity of the building was allowed during the hour between 11 a.m. and noon. The other two bans were never lifted, but they were frequently not observed by the residents, and we were generous! enough to look the other way.

[…][40]

The spring of 1942 was by and large not particularly eventful, other than that the letters from Oma[41] sounded increasingly frightened; she feared that she too would very soon be lined up for one of the transports, which had begun on a large scale and mostly went to Poland. Unfortunately, her suspicions were not wrong. In June 1942, with more than 1,000 fellow sufferers, she was forced to start the journey to Theresienstadt, while Siegm. Rosenstein[42] and his siblings followed only in September 1942. We never saw Oma or Siegm. again. They both died on the same day, 16 March 1943, around 3 weeks before we arrived in Th[eresienstadt]. Incorrect, misleading information from the Reich Association of Jews in Berlin[43] kept us from sending letters and parcels to her, which probably

37 Fritz Hartmann.

38 Fünfbrunnen had no walls or fences and was entirely unguarded. Nonetheless, escape was hardly possible for the residents, most of whom were weakened by age or illness.

39 The measures were ordered by the Gestapo, and the directors of the Jewish home for the elderly were required to announce them on 18 Jan. 1942.

40 There follows a description of religious ceremonies and traditions in Fünfbrunnen.

41 Presumably the mother of Selma Heumann, Friederike Dalberg, née Breyer (1870–1943); deported in mid June 1942 from Cologne to Theresienstadt, where she perished the following year.

42 Siegmund Rosenstein (1870–1943), retailer; friend of the family; lived in Cologne; in mid Sept. 1942 deported to Theresienstadt, where he perished.

43 The Reich Association of Jews in Germany originated in the Reich Representation of Jews in Germany, which was forced to change its name in 1939; the Reich Association was under the control of the Reich Security Main Office (RSHA) and tried at first to arrange for the emigration of Jews and to organize care for those who remained behind; finally, it was forced to take over auxiliary services for the deportations from Germany.

would have been possible and which she had waited for so eagerly.[44] We too were informed at various times that we were to get ourselves ready for deportation, and various small transports were also dispatched, each carrying 10 to 20 persons from our home, but as they were solely for labourers, they covered only the younger people who in their time had come to us as workers.[45] But around 20 July we received notice that a large transport from Dortmund to Theresienstadt would be dispatched at the end of the month, for which Luxembourg would have to deliver 220 persons.[46] Our home had to provide around 80 of these, so that of the approximately 145 residents whom our home had grown to include over time, only around 60 were left, of whom 6 to 8 were always in hospital in Luxembourg or Wiltz.[47] It had taken real skill to house all these people, and we brought it off only by utilizing every last little nook and cranny, and by putting as many people as possible in each individual room. Naturally, feeding so many people caused difficulties as well. The kitchen first had to adapt itself, and the dining room had space for 90 persons at most. But when needs must, anything is possible, and the more work and duties she had, the better Mutti liked it. When the aforementioned large transport left on 27 July 1942,[48] we had to see the [Edelstein] family, who had become real friends of ours as a result of our work together, leave with the others. Saying goodbye to them was especially hard for us. Mr E. and Mutti, who were around the same age, always got along well; they shared the worries of running the home, but we also spent many pleasant and enjoyable evening hours together, chatting away. Later, we met them again in Theresienstadt, but the old relationship could not be rekindled.

[…][49]

44 Delivery of parcels weighing up to 2 kg were permitted in Theresienstadt only from Dec. 1942 onwards; from Jan. 1943, parcels weighing up to 20 kg could also be sent at times.

45 This refers to the transport to Izbica on 23 April 1942, in which 14 of the 24 Jews deported are thought to have come from Fünfbrunnen; the transport to Auschwitz on 12 July 1942, when 7 of the 24 Jews deported from Luxembourg are thought to have been from Fünfbrunnen; and the transport to Theresienstadt on 26 July 1942.

46 This was the transport of 28 July 1942; see Doc. 228.

47 Town in north-western Luxembourg.

48 Correctly: 28 July 1942.

49 In what follows, the writer describes how after the deportations mentioned in the document the home became a 'home for the infirm', with almost half of the residents in need of nursing. At the same time, the threat of soon being deported oneself was ever present.

DOC. 234
New York Times, 21 July 1944: report on an appeal by the prime minister of Luxembourg[1]

Luxembourg Bid to Jews. Premier Invites Their Return. World Congress Reports.

Jews will be welcomed back to Luxembourg. Pierre Dupong,[2] Prime Minister of the Luxembourg Government in Exile, said in a letter addressed to the Luxembourg Committee of the World Jewish Congress, dated June 6, according to that body.

The Prime Minister's statement follows:

'I have submitted to my colleagues the question which you have put to me, in the name of the World Jewish Congress, concerning the return of the Jewish aliens who, before the invasion, had their residence in Luxembourg. My colleagues and I share the idea that there can exist no controversy on the subject.

The Jewish aliens who had their domicile in Luxembourg up to the moment when they had to flee from the Nazi menace, may, at the end of the war, return and establish themselves anew at Luxembourg.'[3]

1 *New York Times*, 21 July 1944, p. 21.

2 Pierre Dupong (1885–1953), politician; prime minister, 1937; head of the Luxembourg government in exile in Canada, 1940–1944; co-founder of the Christian Social People's Party in Luxembourg, 1944.

3 The Jewish community in Luxembourg was almost totally eradicated by the end of the war; in Sept. 1944, only 70 Jews lived in the country. At the end of August 1944, a few weeks after Dupong's announcement, the government in exile founded a repatriation committee for all the refugees who had left Luxembourg due to the war. Some of the survivors returned: in 1947, a total of 870 Jews were living in Luxembourg.

France

France
BRITAIN
London
Amsterdam
NETHERLANDS
GERMAN REICH
Cologne
Rhine
Calais
Brussels
BELGIUM
Dannes
Camiers
Lille
English Channel
Amiens
LUXEMBOURG
Luxembourg
Compiègne
Royallieu
Rheims
Metz
Strasbourg
Caen
Rouen
Paris
Drancy
Châlons-sur-Marne
Nancy
ALSACE AND LORRAINE
Seine
Rennes
Alençon
Pithiviers
Beaune-la-Rolande
Vittel
Mulhouse
Orléans
Tours
Occupied zone
occupied from June 1940
Dijon
Besançon
Basel
Baden
Nantes
Vierzon
Loire
SWITZER-LAND
Coastal military zone
(access prohibited)
Poitiers
Montluçon
Chalon-sur-Saône
Geneva
Saint-Gervais
La Rochelle
Vichy
Aix-les-Bains
Limoges
Clermont-Ferrand
Lyons
Izieu
Megève
ITALY
Nexon
Atlantic Ocean
Grenoble
Le Chambon-sur-Lignon
Italian-occupied zone
Nov. 1942–Sept. 1943
(then under German occupation)
Bordeaux
Garonne
Unoccupied Zone
Under German occupation
from Nov. 1942
Rhône
Sisteron
Septfonds
Montauban
Avignon
Brens
Nîmes
Nice
Menton
Hendaye
Toulouse
Montpellier
Les Milles
Aix-en-Provence
San Sebastián
Gurs
Pau
Noé
Le Vernet
Récébédou
Bram
Marseilles
Rivesaltes
Perpignan
Saint-Cyprien
SPAIN
ANDORRA
Mediterranean Sea
Barcelona
Camps
Zone with restricted access
Annexed to the German Reich
Zone attached to the German military administration in Brussels
Italian-occupied territories (1940–Nov. 1942)
Demilitarized zone (1940–Nov. 1942)
0 50 100 150 km

DOC. 235
On 15 June 1942 the official in charge of Jewish affairs for the Security Police and the SD in Paris, Theodor Dannecker, sets out further plans for deportations of Jews from Western Europe[1]

Note by Section IV J – SA 24, Office of the Senior Commander of the Security Police in France[2] (Dan./Ge.), signed Dannecker,[3] Paris, dated 15 June 1942 (carbon copy)[4]

Re: further transports of Jews from France[5]
1. Note:
On 11 June 1942, a meeting took place in the Reich Security Main Office – IV B 4. In addition to the undersigned (SS-Hauptsturmführer Dannecker), the participants also included the officials in charge of Jewish affairs from Brussels and The Hague.[6]
a) *Subject*
For military reasons, an evacuation of Jews from Germany to the Eastern area of operations can no longer take place during the summer. The Reichsführer SS[7] has therefore ordered that larger quantities of Jews either from the south-east (Romania) or from the occupied Western territories are to be transferred to Auschwitz concentration camp to work. The central requirement is that the Jews (of both sexes) must be between 16 and 40 years of age.[8] Up to 10 per cent of those sent may be Jews who are not fit for work.
b) *Agreement*
It was agreed that 15,000 Jews will be deported from the Netherlands, 10,000 from Belgium, and a total of 100,000 from France, including the unoccupied territory. In addition to setting the age limit, it was determined at the suggestion of the undersigned that

1 Mémorial de la Shoah, XXVI-29. Published in Klarsfeld, *Vichy–Auschwitz,* pp. 410–411. This document has been translated from German.
2 Dr Helmut Knochen (1910–2003), English teacher; joined the NSDAP in 1932; member of the SA, 1932–1936; joined the SS and the SD in 1936; head of the Paris office of the representative of the commander of the Security Police in Belgium and France, August 1940–May 1942; Senior Commander of the Security Police in France, May 1942–August 1944; arrested in 1945; sentenced to death in Paris in 1954; sentence commuted to lifelong hard labour in 1958; released in 1962; subsequently worked as an insurance broker in Offenbach.
3 Theodor Dannecker (1913–1945), retailer; joined the NSDAP and the SS in 1932; with the SD from 1935; in Berlin at the SD's section for Jewish affairs from 1937; official in charge of Jewish affairs for the Security Police and the SD in Paris, 1940–1942; worked in the section for Jewish affairs at the Reich Security Main Office (RSHA), 1942–1945; assistant to the German police attaché in Sofia, Jan.–Sept. 1943; head of an Einsatzkommando in Italy, Sept.–Dec. 1943; member of Eichmann's Sondereinsatzkommando in Budapest, March–Dec. 1944; committed suicide in a US Army internment camp in Bad Tölz.
4 The original contains handwritten notes and underlining. The document was submitted to Helmut Knochen and Herbert Hagen on 18 June 1942.
5 On 27 March and 5 June 1942 a total of 2,112 Jews were deported from Compiègne and Drancy to Auschwitz.
6 Kurt Asche and Wilhelm Zoepf.
7 Heinrich Himmler.
8 Five days later, the age limit was raised to 55 for the deportation of 2,000 Jews from the Pithiviers and Beaune-la-Rolande camps; thereafter, it was set at 45.

those to be deported will include only Jews who are required to wear the star and who are not living in mixed marriages.[9]

c) *Technical implementation*

I. At the instruction of the RSHA, the undersigned are to contact ETRA Paris (Lieutenant General Kohl) to enquire about the provision of means of transport.[10] The question of the ten transport trains required for Belgium must also be resolved then. The transports are to begin on 13 July 1942 – approximately three each week.

II. By means of direct or indirect negotiations, the French government must be made to issue a law similar to the Eleventh Regulation on the Reich Citizenship Law,[11] under which all Jews who live beyond French national borders or who subsequently emigrate will lose their citizenship and right of residence.

The costs of transport, as well as the per capita payment (around 700 Reichsmarks per Jew), must be borne by the French state. This also applies to providing food and supplies for the Jews for a period of two weeks, starting from the day of deportation.[12] Section IV B 4 of the RSHA – SS-Obersturmbannführer Eichmann – has ordered that the officials involved are to report to Berlin again on 2 July 1942 for a final discussion. (Telex request will follow.[13])

2. Submitted to Knochen for information
3. Submitted to Lischka[14] for information
4. Follow up with IV J

9 The Military Commander in France's regulation on the wearing of the yellow star came into force on 7 June 1942: see PMJ 5/323. It applied to Jews with French, Dutch, Slovak, Croatian, Belgian, Romanian, Yugoslav, and Soviet citizenship as well as stateless Jews, i.e. former German, Austrian, Czech, and Polish citizens.

10 Dannecker's enquiry to the Wehrmacht's Railway Transport Department (Eisenbahntransportabteilung, ETRA) revealed that the planned transports could not be carried out with the trains available in France. At Eichmann's request, the Reich Ministry of Transport subsequently procured most of the trains.

11 This regulation, enacted on 25 Nov. 1941, revoked the German citizenship of Jews who lived abroad permanently; their assets passed to the Reich: *Reichsgesetzblatt*, 1941, I, p. 722.

12 In contrast to Croatia or Slovakia, for example, where the respective governments actually paid for the deportation, this plan was not put into effect in France.

13 What was presumably the next meeting in Berlin of the officials in charge of Jewish affairs did not take place until 28 August 1942: see Doc. 263. In the meantime, Eichmann was in Paris on 1 July for a short visit. Knochen added a handwritten note to the document reproduced here: 'Speed things up, if the transport problem in particular is resolved by then. Please submit only a brief report to Higher SS and Police Leader Oberg.'

14 Dr Kurt Lischka (1909–1989), lawyer; joined the SS in 1933 and the NSDAP in 1937; worked for the Gestapo from 1935; worked for the representative of the Chief of the Security Police and the SD in Paris from Nov. 1940; commander of the Security Police and the SD in Paris from Jan. to Sept. 1943; at the Reich Security Main Office from Oct. 1943; company secretary in Cologne after 1945; sentenced in absentia to lifelong hard labour by the Permanent Military Tribunal in Paris in 1950; sentenced to ten years in prison by the Cologne Regional Court in 1980; released in 1985.

DOC. 236

On 23 June 1942 Paul Zuckermann writes to his fiancée from Drancy to tell her about his fellow prisoners' deportation and to urge her to be especially vigilant[1]

Letter from Paul Zuckermann,[2] Drancy,[3] to Berthe Rachline,[4] Paris, dated 23 June 1942

My darling, I have too many things to tell you, and too little time to write to you by hand. Just this once, as an exception, I'll type up everything I want you to know. The great drama is over. You've read all those letters that I could not get out to you and that I'm attaching, in order. And this means you'll have experienced all my fears. There must have been 180 of them. All of the veterans of the 39/40 war were taken away!![5] And to my great sorrow, K. P.[6] was among them, as well as Cordier,[7] who wrote the song about the lice. I narrowly escaped, very narrowly thanks to the gentleman who was with me that memorable Saturday. There was nothing to be done, absolutely nothing. We were terribly sad. K. P. was called up on Saturday evening at 6 p.m. The next morning, he went to another staircase, where nobody could contact him from noon until the departure, which took place between 5 a.m. and 8 a.m. yesterday morning. 934 prisoners left the camp! This has been an appalling, horrifying time for me. I haven't had much sleep over the last eight days, and I feel I have aged terribly. This is the worst, the most awful of all the departures because of who is on board. They are either sick and will not be able to survive this ordeal, or they are good friends of mine. The only thing that alleviates this slightly is that the search carried out by the Police for Jewish Affairs[8] was less

1 Mémorial de la Shoah, Fonds Sarquier, MDCXVIII, Doss. 8. Published in Paul Zuckermann, *Berthe chérie: Correspondance clandestine de Paul Zuckermann à sa fiancée. Drancy, août 1941–septembre 1942*, ed. Michel Laffitte (Paris: Éditions du Retour, 2014), pp. 445–454. This document has been translated from French.

2 Paul Zuckermann, later Paul Sarquier (1913–1996), office clerk; arrested during the roundups in August 1941 (see PMJ 5/276); worked in the hygiene department of Drancy camp; released in Sept. 1942; went on to work for the social welfare service of the General Union of French Jews (UGIF) and helped to hide Jewish children with non-Jewish families; went underground in August 1943.

3 Following the German occupation of France in 1940, the Wehrmacht requisitioned the buildings of an unfinished commercial and residential complex in the Parisian suburb of Drancy and used them as an internment camp for French and British prisoners of war. From late August 1941 foreign Jews were interned in the camp. From spring 1942 to 1944, it served as a transit camp for deportations from France to occupied Poland.

4 Berthe Rachline, later Berthe Zuckermann and Berthe Sarquier (b. 1916); worked for the UGIF, 1942–1943; went underground in August 1943 under the assumed name Sarquier, which she kept after the war.

5 A deportation transport with 934 men and 66 women on board had left France on 22 June 1942.

6 Most likely Paul Kohen (1911–1942), cabinetmaker; arrested in the course of the roundups in August 1941; imprisoned in Drancy; on 22 June 1942 deported to Auschwitz, where he perished two weeks later.

7 Roger Cordier; wrote the song 'Y'a des Poux' ('There are Lice') to the tune of 'Y'a d'la Joie' ('There's Joy') by Charles Trenet.

8 The Police aux questions juives (PQJ) was established in Oct. 1941 by the French Ministry of the Interior as one of three special political police units. It later also carried out investigations on behalf of the German Security Police. In the spring and summer of 1942, the PQJ carried out between 10 and 20 per cent of its investigations on behalf of the German occupiers, while the rest of its work was based on requests from the Commissariat General for Jewish Affairs, the prefectures, and the Vichy government's Ministry of the Interior. In Drancy camp, one of its tasks was to search the prisoners who had been earmarked for deportation.

rigorous than the last ones. I even managed after the search to hand K. P. all the things they would possibly have taken away. He left well provisioned. And he left in good spirits, convinced that this terrible nightmare would be over in a few months. I would be only too happy to believe him, and Laval's[9] speech, which I just read, convinced me: this SOS reminds me of the one Paul Reynaud sent out during the night of 13/14 June 1940.[10] Dear Berthe, will you please assure Mrs K. P. of my great affection, and ask her not to hold it against me that I stayed behind: who knows, I may be next. If that were to be the case, I would feel very alone, because all of my friends have left together: there were 16 from our dormitory. K. P. will have good company. Tonight, we expect 160 new arrivals from I don't know where,[11] but most importantly, it seems there will be 500 more arriving at the end of the week: supposedly those will be Jews whose papers need to be renewed every month. If you know any, my dear, be sure to warn them. Is my uncle from Champigny not in that situation? I think they will all be summoned to the prefecture, and from there they will be taken directly to Drancy. And all of this does not mean there won't be any other roundups. Laval's speech will inform you of the need for labour in Germany. Here, Danécker[12] declared: 'There are still too many Jews in Paris, and I am going to bring them to account.' But I have heard something even more horrible, a thousand times more horrible. There were also 68 women on the transport, taken from the rue des Tourelles camp!![13] One was the wife of the well-known lawyer Idskowski,[14] who is here. He doesn't know it yet. And the sister of two of the inmates who were also taken away themselves! At every departure they shave all the prisoners' heads, and I fear it was exactly the same at the rue des Tourelles camp. It is revolting to deport women this way and leave their children behind. It is hateful! And you know, my dear, if they are locking people up in the rue des Tourelles, as they are here in Drancy, simply because they did not wear the patch,[15] as is the case for quite a few, you can imagine the fate that awaits them! I beg you, be careful. As you asked me, with this message I am including two patches I was able to procure. Wear them everywhere. Don't start taking them off again before you enter the dry cleaners; I'd rather go without the parcel. Don't ever take them off, and do not take anything, anything, at all lightly. You people in Paris don't seem to fully realize what reign of terror the Jews are subject to. The inspectors who arrest the Jews have to ignore it themselves. They have not realized what kind of work they are lending themselves to. Yesterday, when they saw that veterans, many of whom had been decorated, were being deported, several were completely shocked: to be deported for

9 In a radio broadcast on 22 June 1942, Head of Government Pierre Laval had called for French people to volunteer for labour deployment in Germany. In exchange, the Germans were to release from prisoner-of-war camps French prisoners who were agricultural workers: *Le Figaro*, 23 June 1942, p. 1.

10 During the night of 13/14 June 1940, shortly before the French surrender, Paul Reynaud, then president of the Council of Ministers, had given a radio address: *La Croix*, 15 June 1940, front page.

11 On 24 June 1942 a total of 163 Jews were transferred to Drancy from Compiègne camp.

12 Here and below, correctly: Dannecker.

13 The barracks in the rue des Tourelles on the north-eastern edge of Paris were used as an internment camp by the German occupiers from 1940. In 1942 its prisoners included women who had been found to be in breach of anti-Jewish regulations.

14 Rosette Idzkowski, née Bardia (b. 1902), wife of René Idzkowski (b. 1896); both were deported on 22 June and 23 September 1942, and both perished in Auschwitz.

15 The yellow star.

having been five minutes late one evening, that's the fate that awaits a human being here. The German does not see us as human beings. He hates the Jews. Everything he does, all those young Germans dying on the battlefields, it's all done to hurt the Jews. The communists are Jews, the Freemasons are Jews, behind capitalism is the Jew, it's always Jew, Jew, Jew. And an entire people is suffering and dying just to satisfy the hatred harboured by some Nazis against the Jews. Remember this. Remember it well. And don't think I'm too influenced by what I have lived through here. Yes, I certainly am, but none of you understands anything, that is certain. Don't ever take your patch off, don't ever be late. And make sure neither Papa nor Albert[16] ever leaves the house without good reason. Don't ever get caught doing anything illegal. Take all possible precautions, more than they do in crime novels. Be careful when you're on the phone, or when you argue with people who might end up reporting you. You need to hold on for another few months. – Waldmann[17] was in tears when he departed. He had nothing left and I gave him 50 francs. He wanted Mrs Ruben to go and visit his wife regularly. – Among those who left were the two brothers Bornstein,[18] who made me suffer so much during the first few days of the great heroes,[19] my former business partner's brother, Salomon the orchestral conductor, Zaidmann,[20] our acquaintance's brother, Paul Dubouillon's friend, who'd only recently arrived, Sahna's nephew etc. etc. All of them, the whole neighbourhood must have been taken away. Don't tell people that I remained behind, I'm almost ashamed of it. My God, what a departure. We just learned that young Brout, who lives at no. 21, managed to escape at the station.[21] He wanted us to visit his wife. Don't go there, because now that he's escaped, his wife in particular will be under surveillance. The Germans ordered that Jews who are married to Aryans would not be taken away. And in the midst of this great drama, a tragicomic episode was played out: The Shammash[22] of the local synagogue didn't want to come forward for fear he'd lose his job. A Shammash married to an Aryan!! And this got him deported. The poor man. – In addition to those that you already know, my dearest Berthe, I have one more hope of escaping deportation left: it seems that Jewish Affairs[23] have permitted the camp administrator to draw up a very short list of people who are absolutely indispensable for life in the camp. If only it is true. I'll keep you informed, of course. But, as always, discretion is key! I didn't have any luck with the post this week, you must have been terribly worried!! Yesterday, there was a release. It was that famous headmaster who's supposed to organize the Jewish school system and who was set free by Danécker especially for that. I asked him to call you yesterday evening to reassure you. I hope he did. I also told him about

16 Both Paul Zuckermann's father Maurice (1881–1966) and his younger brother Albert (b. 1920) had also been arrested in August 1941. Albert Zuckermann was released on grounds of poor health in Oct. 1941, and Maurice due to advanced age a month later.
17 Isaac Waldmann (1891–1942) perished in Auschwitz one month after his arrival.
18 Godel (b. 1896) and Alexandre Bornstein (b. 1901).
19 Presumably an ironic reference to the early days of German occupation.
20 Most likely Moszek Zajderman (b. 1897).
21 No evidence of this escape could be found. Victor Brout (1912–1942), leather goods manufacturer; lived next door to Paul Zuckermann; on 22 June 1942 deported to Auschwitz, where he perished.
22 Hebrew: warden at a synagogue.
23 The Commissariat General for Jewish Affairs.

Suzanne[24] because he will certainly need staff. I'll give you his address. I expect that those who work with him will be a little better protected, like those who work for the UGIF. The UGIF employs 300 people, and they should have nothing to fear. It might be useful to look into this for Suzanne, maybe even for Albert. Papa or someone else should go and see him on my behalf and tell him that I was the young man who'd seen him in his office, Mr Kohn's[25] assistant. I asked him for his address. His name is Mr *Schentowski*,[26] École Lucien de Hirsch, 70 avenue Secrétan, Botzaris 84-14 – This would even be good for Papa, but, alas, he is not cultured and educated enough. He should go and see him anyway.[27] Because I know that Jews are summoned to the prefecture, particularly those who declared they were of modest means, and they are then asked how they manage to live. What is the administrator doing? And what about the money in the bank? I'm sure it would be advisable to sell the house and to pretend to live off the proceeds. If he gives it to us, that is. We need to be very careful in this respect, too. Once again: don't think I'm just pretending to be a bundle of nerves or in a panic. What I am saying here is extremely serious and extremely grave. – I received the letter you wrote on Sunday without any problems. I'm going to ask the man if he would be willing to visit you in the apartment. In any case, he should come at some point on Thursday evening, unless we hear otherwise, which is always possible. Make the necessary preparations concerning Ginette from Neuilly. Her husband is still in prison. He should be in for nine days more. He was lucky because he stated he was married to an Aryan. If anyone finds out, he might have to pay dearly. Ginette was wrong to have hidden the truth from him, although, on the other hand, it was what saved him this time around. It would be better to say nothing to Ginette. – I have not said anything to him. – I am now going to answer your letters. – Zola is not in the kitchens: he is now the official tailor at the storeroom, and he was to become the head of the planned tailoring workshop. – His son was terribly wrong to come back!! And he isn't really aware of it either!! Yes, C. D. was worried, she told me so, and she was right to be. Poor Mrs K. P., my heart goes cold when I think of her. You must tell her how much I share her sorrow. I could not stop crying, and now the camp is empty, very empty. How well you write, my dear, how one can feel the sincerity of your feelings, and how they are alive. I swear I've never read more beautiful love letters, and I'm devastated that I can't make you understand how much I adore you. I don't easily open up by nature, and I very much regret now not having told you better, in person with my own voice. My love … As you continue to have so many money worries, I'll write to Maman[28] straight away to get her to give you my money?[29] I want to be sure once and for all that you want for nothing, not even the smallest of whatever superfluous things can still be had in these times. I am not there to spoil you as I would

24 Suzanne Rachline (1925–1943), secretary and Berthe Rachline's sister; arrested with her sister Julia and their parents, Ita and Leiba Rachline, in mid July 1943; deported a few days later to Auschwitz, where all of them perished.

25 Georges Kohn (b. 1884), engineer; head of the Jewish camp administration from May 1942; escaped from Lévitan satellite camp in Paris in July 1944.

26 Nathan Schentowski (b. 1884); deported in early Sept. 1943 to Auschwitz, where he perished.

27 In Sept. 1942 Maurice Zuckermann found work in an orphanage run by the UGIF and was therefore able to achieve Paul Zuckermann's release.

28 Rachel Zuckermann, née Lipa (1888–1966).

29 Question mark as in the original.

love to do, but I want to at least be sure that you have the means yourself. So the question is settled: Maman will do it because I will ask her to. – As for the lottery tickets, it seems more rational not to cancel them now because they might win. You must either reimburse Ginette or buy two more for her, whichever she prefers. – You can eat at Ginette's and then leave later. At the moment you shouldn't care too much about conventions, we're at war, and in the thrall of persecution. The rest doesn't matter that much, and I'm sure she'll like that. If I know her, she wouldn't do it if it didn't please her. Please pass on my best wishes to her and tell her that I'm looking after her husband as well as I can. But make sure that her brother Loulou leaves quickly, otherwise I might have to look after him too. M. has been an immense comfort to me, and I can assure you that you have no reason to fear. Besides, I can see that you are joking. – 'Rêverie' is not by Cordier, but by Paul K. – Thank Mr. Nimbus 'from me'; I will never be able to be grateful enough for those friends who were prepared to 'selflessly' help those I love during my absence. I'm very serious … So, my dear Berthe, I think I've answered your last letter. Now I need to deal with the material questions. The parcels are always very good. Of course, I've completely recovered from my indisposition. I'm supposed to eat only very small amounts of charcuterie and eggs, and now I'm wondering what I can eat at all. – You'll need to send off my laundry parcel soon, the day after tomorrow I think. Please include the following: my brown shorts, well I think I have two pairs, and for the larger a belt (because of my belly …), my short-sleeved white tennis shirt, and one or two pairs of ankle socks. – Can I also ask you, in addition, to send a separate package with my fur-lined Canadian jacket, just in case I eventually do have to leave? I will mention it to you again. – From my end, I'll send my regimental boots back to you, for urgent repairs, and if possible, my overcoat.

Time flies, and it is almost one o'clock. I need to go and make myself something to eat with my little stove very quickly, because I have a huge amount of work, needless to say. – How empty and sad the camp is. But I prefer it this way, in fact I'm afraid of seeing the buses arrive to fill it up again, just like almost a year ago now. – There is some small news from the camp: a man has arrived who was Harry Baur's[30] cellmate at the Santé prison.[31] Harry Baur was given three months in prison by the Germans for not declaring that he is Jewish. After that, he'll be sent here. – That will teach him to receive Heinrich Georges[32] and to write for *La Gerbe*.[33] – Berthe, do you remember when we saw him in 'Jazz' at the Gymnase?[34] The people next to us said, 'He may be Jewish, but that doesn't prevent him from being talented.' It only prevented him from having any common decency. He doesn't deserve our pity! Berthe, I need envelopes and stamps. Could you please give some to you know who? And could you also give him a deck of 32 cards in good condition, if you have one in the house. My beloved Berthe, I am going to stop here and leave some space in case any other ideas come to me before the letter is sent

30 Harry Baur (1880–1943), actor from Alsace; acted in German films from 1940; arrested in May 1942 because of his Jewish-sounding name; released in Sept. 1942; died a few months later of a disease he had contracted during his imprisonment.

31 A prison built in the 1860s and located in the south of Paris.

32 Correctly: Heinrich George, born Georg A. F. H. Schulz (1893–1946), German actor.

33 The antisemitic and pro-collaboration weekly *La Gerbe* was published between July 1940 and August 1944 by Alphonse de Châteaubriand.

34 *Jazz* by Marcel Pagnol at the Théâtre du Gymnase in 1940.

off. I'm worn out, as you can imagine. Yesterday, I saw a photograph in the newspaper of an outdoor swimming pool with a whole crowd of people. That really made me feel sad. Do you remember last year around this time at the beach in Champigny? We're suffering here, and people continue to live well, without a thought for us. … My dear little Berthe, the storm is over for a little while, I hope. We now know that there will be a deportation about once every month: 'Drancy will be the station from which all the Jews will be deported,' announced Danécker. He said he'd even have a special train station built at Le Bourget. This isn't idle gossip, I heard it directly from those who heard it with their own ears (from the civil authorities). So it's a done deal, at least officially, that the camp will be evacuated … Such a lot of tall stories from Paris as well. My nerves are slowly relaxing. Laval's speech betrays such disorder that it is some consolation for the German victories in Africa. Once more: let us be calm and have courage, and do not wear out those pretty eyes of yours, my dear. It's true, you have wonderful eyes, I must be the only person who has never said that to you. It's true that I love you, and not for your eyes, but for your heart. You really are my wife, and now I understand what is meant when you read that people are tied together by physical and material bonds that are impossible to break. Give my love to your family for me, to Ginette and Albert and especially Maman and Papa, and I kiss your adored lips with all my love and all my tenderness.

DOC. 237

On 23 June 1942 Wigdor Radoszycki notifies his wife of his impending departure from Pithiviers for forced labour[1]

Handwritten letter from Wigdor Radoszycki,[2] Pithiviers camp,[3] to Sonia Radoszycki,[4] no place given, dated 23 June 1942

Pithiviers, 23 June 1942, 6 a.m.[5]

My precious little Sonia,

Only yesterday evening I learned that the letter I wrote to you on 18 June unfortunately did not reach you, as it was returned to me. Of course that annoyed me greatly, but woefully there is nothing to be done about it.

My one and only beloved little Sonia, the situation here has changed greatly since Sunday. Sunday afternoon there began to be talk of a départ[6] on Thursday, 500 persons, it was said, for work in France. On Monday there was a change; now they say 800 to

1 Mémorial de la Shoah, CMLXXXVI(3)-16. This document has been translated from German.

2 Wigdor Radoszycki (b. 1907), hairdresser; emigrated to France from Poland in 1933; arrested in the first large roundup in Paris in May 1941 and interned in Pithiviers camp; on 25 June 1942 deported to Auschwitz, where he perished.

3 The camp at Pithiviers (Loiret département) served as an internment camp for Jews who had been arrested in the occupied zone from May 1941 onwards.

4 Sonia Radoszycki, later Rzeznik, née Chwatiuk; Wigdor's wife.

5 These details are in French in the original letter.

6 French in the original: 'departure'.

1,000, destination unknown, probably not in France; they even say that the whole camp will be sent away. So, my precious little Sonia, this time we can expect a very large départ to leave. We don't know exactly where it will go to, but we can assume with some certainty that the destination will not be in France, and it is assumed that everybody in the camp will be sent away. My darling, I won't become discouraged; I'm keeping my head held high and I'm approaching it all with great courage, because there's a feeling in me that tells me I will survive this too, and that it will not last too long. And there's a will in me to see my one and only beloved little wife again, whom I hold deep in my heart, and wherever I may be and whatever the circumstances, my only thought, all my inner striving and thinking, will always be solely of you, my precious little Sonia, and of being reunited with you as quickly as possible. Don't cry, my darling, I beg you, don't cry; take courage and be patient a bit longer. I know you are young and have not enjoyed much of life. I can't ask you to lock yourself up like a grandmother. Therefore, if you can live your life, then go ahead and do so. So, once again, we must expect that I will also be sent away on Thursday, and the situation will be as follows: Papa[7] is already gone; if this is now also to happen to me, then you and Mama[8] are left alone. This has made me think that perhaps the right thing for the two of you to do would be to sell everything and cross over into the Zone non occupé.[9] Maybe you'll have more peace and quiet there. Of course that must be carefully thought over, and I rely completely on you two to handle it; at any rate, be careful and consider everything thoroughly with regard to what you should do. I hope I will still have the chance before the departure, my dearest little Sonia, to write a few words to you. At any rate, I will try my best to keep you informed, my dear little Sonia; please don't be sad, don't lose heart and hope. After all, millions of people are suffering. The main thing is that it does not last too long, and then we will be happily reunited, my dearest one in the world! I'll leave you in the hope that my letter will find you in the best of health. I'm sending love and kisses to you from the bottom of my heart. I remain your husband, who always thinks only of you, who hopes to be with you again as soon as possible, my dear little Sonia. Once again, chin up, my little Sonia; hope to see you again soon, Yours, Wigni

Warmest regards and kisses to dear Mama. She should not be sad. I feel I may perhaps say bonjour to dear Papa in person. See you again soon, Wigni

Give my best to all our acquaintances.[10]

7 Presumably Szmul Chwatiuk (b. 1895), tailor, Wigdor's father-in-law; arrested in the roundup in August 1941; in early June 1942 deported to Auschwitz, where he perished.
8 Wigdor's mother-in-law.
9 French: 'unoccupied zone'.
10 The next day, Wigdor Radoszycki informed his wife that his name was on the list of those being deported; Radoszycki assumed that he was to be sent to East Prussia for agricultural labour. The transport left on 25 June 1942: Mémorial de la Shoah, CMLXXXVI(3)-16.

DOC. 238
At a meeting in Paris on 30 June 1942 the officials dealing with Jewish affairs in the occupied zone are given instructions for the deportation of the Jewish population[1]

Note from Section IV J – SA 261 c, Office of the Senior Commander of the Security Police in France[2] (Rö/Ge), signed SS-Hauptsturmführer Dannecker, Paris, dated 1 July 1942

Re: meeting with the officials dealing with Jewish affairs in the Security Police (SD) commandos held at Section IV J on 30 June 1942
1. *Note:*
The officials dealing with Jewish affairs in the Security Police (SD) commandos were invited on 30 June 1942 for the purpose of coordinating the practical implementation of their tasks and receiving essential instructions.

Officials from 8 commandos took part in the meeting. The official from Poitiers was unable to attend before the afternoon of 30 June 1942. The Nancy commando, which was not represented, will be informed about the outcome of the discussion by the Châlons-sur-Marne commando.

During the meeting, the following points were discussed in detail:

1) General status of the Jewish problem in the occupied and unoccupied territories.
2) Wait-and-see attitude, often negative, of the French government representatives and authorities regarding the Jewish question; this makes uncompromising action on our own initiative necessary.
3) Long-term objective: completely cleansing the provinces of all Jews; then there will only be Jews in Paris, and the rest will be deported from there.
4) Overview of the essential laws pertaining to the Jews.
   Definition of a Jew according to the Seventh Regulation on Measures Against Jews of 24 March 1942 and the French Statute [on Jews] of 2 June 1941; discrepancies between the two definitions and conclusion:
   Because the French definition goes further, it is to be taken as a basis in case of doubt.[3]
5) Regulation on the yellow star: Uncompromising, drastic measures must be taken in cases of non-compliance.
6) Now in preparation, the Ninth Regulation on Measures Against Jews,[4] in addition to implementing provisions from the Higher SS and Police Leader.
7) Transport of Jews from the occupied territory to Auschwitz. Immediate implementation of the preparations for the transports (see special note on transports).[5]

1 Mémorial de la Shoah, XXVb-45. Klarsfeld, *Vichy–Auschwitz*, p. 420. This document has been translated from German.
2 Helmut Knochen.
3 The Military Commander in France's Seventh Regulation of 24 March 1942 established a new definition of who was to be considered a Jew: *VOBl-F*, no. 58, 15 April 1942, pp. 375–385. Conversions and marriages to non-Jews were henceforth recognized only if they had taken place before the cut-off date of 25 June 1940. The Vichy government's Second Statute on Jews of 2 June 1941 stipulated that the spouse's descent also had to be taken into account when classifying someone as a Jew: see PMJ 5/270.
4 See Doc. 242.
5 This is included in the file.

8) Report on implementation of the transport preparations due by 6 July 1942.
9) Discussions of individual questions and problems that have arisen.
At the meeting, the officials dealing with Jewish affairs in the SD commandos were handed information charts on the German and French laws and regulations concerning Jews currently in force in France, as well as instruction sheets on the transport of Jews to Auschwitz.
2. Submitted to SS-Standartenführer *Dr Knochen* for information.
3. Submitted to SS-Obersturmbannführer Lischka for information.
4. Follow up with IV J.

DOC. 239

On 2 July 1942 the heads of the German and the French police discuss how they will cooperate in arresting Jews in France[1]

File note (log no. 267/42) from the Higher SS and Police Leader[2] in the territory of the Military Commander in France,[3] signed Hagen,[4] Paris, dated 4 July 1942[5]

Re: discussion with Secrétaire général à la Police *Bousquet*[6] on 2 July 1942
On 2 July 1942 a meeting with Secrétaire général à la Police Bousquet took place in the office of the Higher SS and Police Leader.

The meeting was attended by the following:
SS-Brigadeführer *Oberg*,
SS-Standartenführer Dr *Knochen*,
SS-Obersturmbannführer *Lischka*,
Lieutenant Colonel von *Schweinichen*,

1 Mémorial de la Shoah, XXVI-40. Published in Klarsfeld, *Vichy–Auschwitz*, pp. 422–425. This document has been translated from German.
2 Carl-Albrecht Oberg (1897–1965), commercial employee; member of a Freikorps (paramilitary unit), 1919–1920; joined the NSDAP in 1931 and the SS in 1932; in the SD Main Office from 1933; chief of police in Zwickau, 1939; SS and Police Leader in Radom, 1941; Higher SS and Police Leader (HSSPF) in Paris from May 1942; arrested by US troops in 1945; sentenced to death in Paris in 1954; pardoned in 1965.
3 Carl Heinrich von Stülpnagel.
4 Herbert Hagen (1913–1999), businessman; joined the SS in 1933; in the SD Main Office from 1934; travelled with Eichmann to Palestine and Egypt in 1937; head of the branch office of the Security Police and the SD in Bordeaux, 1940–1942; aide to the HSSPF in France, 1942–1944; in charge of anti-partisan combat under the HSSPF Alpenland, 1944–1945; sentenced to lifelong hard labour in absentia in Paris in 1954; CEO of the West German company IND-APP (Industrieapparatebau GmbH); sentenced to 12 years in prison by the Cologne Regional Court in 1980; granted early release in 1984.
5 The original contains handwritten notes and underlining.
6 French in the original (correctly: secrétaire général de la police): 'secretary general of the police'. René Bousquet (1909–1993), lawyer; secretary general of the Châlons-sur-Marne prefecture, 1939–1940; prefect of the Marne département, 1940–1941; head of the Vichy government's police authority, April 1942–Dec. 1943; played a central role in roundups and deportations of Jews from France; arrested by the Gestapo on 9 June 1944 and placed under house arrest in Bavaria; charged with collaborationist crimes and 'compromising the interests of national defence' by the French Haute Cour de justice in 1949, acquitted of the latter charge in light of his involvement with the resistance, but sentenced to loss of civil rights for five years; worked in finance and in the French press; charged with crimes against humanity in 1989; murdered before the start of his trial.

Major *Runkowski*,
SS-Sturmbannführer *Hagen*,
SS-Obersturmführer Dr *Schmidt*
in one party,[7] and
Secretary General *Bousquet*, accompanied by the
interpreter *Wilhelms*
in the other party.

All the issues touched upon in the meeting were related to issues raised at a previous meeting on 16 June 1942.[8]

[…][9]

7) *Special police*

a) When asked how the establishment of special police forces was going, Bousquet stated that it was 'not going well'.[10] The laws against the Jews were generally being implemented, he said, but an inspection service with thoroughly vetted staff needed to be established.

To this end, Bousquet said, he was placing all available resources at *Pellepoix*'s disposal.[11] However, Pellepoix had told him that he wanted to carry out raids, which he could not allow, as he wanted a unified police force that is neither fragmented nor under several different commanders.

He is willing to set up a 'section spéciale' as part of the overall police force and under his command.[12]

SS-Standartenführer Dr Knochen emphasized that this solution was fully in keeping with our intentions. However, he said, this section had to be put together immediately, so that the previous record of success in fighting our enemies did not decline. Therefore, he added, it was necessary to begin with the fight against communism, the Jews, and the Freemasons.

The Senior Commander of the Security Police and the SD[13] emphasized that the Higher SS and Police Leader and he himself had the impression that the stagnation in

7 Bolko von Schweinichen (b. 1896), police officer; commander of the Order Police in France, 1944; Rudolf Runkowski (b. 1897), police officer; Dr Julius Schmidt (1913–1945), aide to the Senior Commander of the Security Police and the SD.

8 During this meeting with Oberg and Knochen, Bousquet had agreed to hand over 10,000 stateless Jews from the unoccupied zone to the German police: Klarsfeld, *Calendrier*, p. 406.

9 Notes on the following topics have been omitted here: agreements with the French police, police schools, mobile reserve units, railway protection, the Paris fire brigade, and the gendarmerie.

10 This refers to the special police agencies created by the French Ministry of the Interior in 1941: Police aux questions juives, Police anticommuniste, and Police antimaçonnique du service des sociétés secrètes (Anti-Freemasonry Police). Bousquet's objective was that his office should unify and centralize the management of all the police agencies.

11 Louis Darquier de Pellepoix (1897–1980), journalist; mainly unemployed, 1919–1935; participated in the February riots organized by far-right leagues in Paris in 1934; member of the Paris municipal council, 1935–1942; founded an antisemitic association in 1937; prisoner of war in 1940; French Commissioner General for Jewish Affairs, May 1942–Feb. 1944; fled to Spain in 1945; sentenced to death in absentia in 1947.

12 The Police aux questions juives was disbanded by a decree issued on 5 July 1942. It was replaced by the newly established Section d'enquête et de contrôle (SEC), which, against Bousquet's wishes, was placed under the authority of the Commissariat General for Jewish Affairs. It was intended to detect violations of antisemitic regulations.

13 Helmut Knochen.

this area was due to the French government not yet being in full agreement among themselves when it came to the fight against these enemies. This was the only explanation, he added, for why Pellepoix had not yet been assigned a budget.

Bousquet, on the other hand, emphasized that this was down to Pellepoix himself. But he said he was willing to intervene on Pellepoix's behalf with the Minister of Finance.[14]

Bousquet said he doubted that the Minister of Finance, as reported by the Senior Commander of the Security Police and the SD, based on information from P[ellepoix], had refused to pay out money to the Commissioner General for Jewish Affairs. Rather, he believed that Pellepoix had merely failed thus far to submit an organizational plan for the allocation of the funds he requested.[15]

Finally, when challenged by the Senior Commander of the Security Police and the SD, Bousquet conceded to Pellepoix the right to propose to carry out operations against Jews. For the implementation itself, Bousquet will put his police force and his knowledge at Pellepoix's disposal. To settle this question, a meeting between the Senior Commander of the Security Police and the SD, Pellepoix, and Bousquet was arranged.[16]

b) The enquiry about the status of the deportation of Jews from the unoccupied territory, as agreed on 16 June, revealed the following:

Bousquet discloses that SS-Hauptsturmführer Dannecker had sent for Bousquet's secretary in Paris, *Leguay*,[17] and demanded that Leguay immediately organize the arrest of 10,000 Jews in the unoccupied zone and 20,000 Jews in the occupied zone, on the basis of the agreement that had been reached between Laval and the Senior Commander of the Security Police and the SD on the one hand, and the Higher SS and Police Leader and Bousquet on the other.[18]

He had made the suggestion to Laval based on what Leguay had presented to him, and Laval in turn had said that he was not up to date on this question.

On the basis of an intervention by the Marshal,[19] Laval had suggested that the French police should not carry out the arrests in the occupied territory. Instead, he would like to see these arrests carried out by the occupying forces.[20]

14 Pierre Cathala (1888–1947), lawyer and politician; minister of finance and economics, 1942–1944.

15 Pierre Laval, head of the Vichy government, had promised Darquier de Pellepoix additional financial resources when the latter took office, but he still wanted to appoint a secretary to work alongside Darquier de Pellepoix so that he could control his activities. He also sought to strip Darquier de Pellepoix of certain responsibilities relating to the Aryanization of the French economy. When the latter opposed these efforts with German support, Laval refused to increase his budget.

16 This took place on 4 July 1942, and one result was the formation of a committee, presided over by the Commissioner General for Jewish Affairs, which planned the mass arrests which took place on 16 and 17 July 1942: see Docs. 241 and 245.

17 Jean Leguay (1909–1989), lawyer; worked in the French administration from 1935; Bousquet's permanent representative in Paris, April 1942–Dec. 1943, then prefect in Alençon; dismissed from the civil service in 1945 and emigrated to the USA; charged with crimes against humanity in 1979; died before the trial ended.

18 On 25 June 1942, Dannecker demanded that the French police arrest men and women between the ages of 16 and 45; at least 40 per cent of these had to be French citizens.

19 Philippe Pétain.

20 Dannecker's demands had been discussed by the French Council of Ministers in Vichy on 26 June 1942, and Laval had rejected them. Leguay notified Dannecker of this on 29 June 1942.

Following the Marshal's intervention, Laval had suggested that, for the time being, only Jews who are foreign nationals should be arrested and handed over in the unoccupied zone.

In response to this stated position, the Senior Commander of the Security Police and the SD declared that one could observe that on the part of the French the introduction of the yellow star in the occupied territory had indeed been accepted, but that the Jewish question had obviously not yet been fully understood to the extent that arrests of Jews would be implemented without further ado. The Senior Commander of the Security Police and the SD stressed that this suggested that the problem had not yet been understood in Vichy.

At that, Bousquet declared that, on the French side, there was no opposition to the arrests per se, it was simply that it was *génant*[21] in Paris to have the arrests carried out by the French police. This had been the particular wish of the Marshal, he said.

In response, the Senior Commander of the Security Police stated that the Führer, in all his recent speeches, had emphasized nothing more clearly than the absolute necessity of a definitive solution to the Jewish question. Therefore, it was only this attitude, and not that of the French government, that was going to influence our measures. He added that, were the French government to resist carrying out the arrests, the Führer would have little patience with this kind of attitude.

The following agreement was therefore made: as no Jews who hold French nationality are to be arrested in France for the time being, owing to the Marshal's intervention, Bousquet consents to have Jews who hold foreign nationality arrested in a coordinated operation throughout France in the numbers we requested. Bousquet emphasized that this would be a first-time course of action for the French government, and that they are aware of the difficulties that will arise from it.

In this context, Bousquet pointed out the problematic treatment of the Jewish question in Africa. Steps were indeed being taken against Jews who hold French nationality, he said, but taking action against Jews who hold Italian nationality was still prohibited.[22]

Asked once again about his relationship with Pellepoix, Bousquet agreed to impose all restrictions upon the Jews, although it would be necessary for Pellepoix to make the relevant proposals, he said. When asked, he said it was not possible that Pellepoix had been refused permission to give a radio address for no good reason. The reason was rather Laval's universal directive that no member of the government may give a radio address without his permission.[23]

For the purpose of implementing the agreement on the arrests of the Jews, a meeting with Laval was promised for Saturday, 4 June.[24] The Senior Commander of the Security

21 French in the original: 'embarrassing', 'awkward'.

22 In North Africa, Jews were dismissed from public service and forced out of economic life. Jewish children and teachers were largely excluded from the state school system: see Doc. 284. However, the Italian government insisted that these measures should not be taken against Italian citizens. Around 5,000 Italian Jews were living in Tunisia.

23 The Commissariat General for Jewish Affairs produced a weekly programme on 'the Jewish problem in France and in the world' on Radio nationale from late Sept. 1942. This was the first explicitly antisemitic series of programmes broadcast on French state radio. Following this first broadcast, Darquier de Pellepoix himself was on air once or twice per week.

24 Correctly: 4 July. The original contains the handwritten addition: 'Has now taken place.'

Police and the SD then explained that, for our part, the reason for refusing to carry out the arrests of the Jews was that we wanted to get to a point where we did not have to make use of our occupying *power*.

On the basis of this comment, Bousquet declared that the actual reason for the Marshal's objection had been the question of Jews who are citizens of Alsace. The Marshal, he said, had so many connections to Alsace that he was unwilling to take action against these Jews.

[...][25]

DOC. 240

On 6 July 1942 Theodor Dannecker urges the Reich Security Main Office to decide whether children under the age of 16 can also be deported from France[1]

Telegram from Section IV J SA 225a (marked 'urgent, to be presented immediately', dated 6 July 1942, 16:20), signed Dannecker, Paris, to the Reich Security Main Office, Section IV B 4,[2] Berlin, dated 6 July 1942

Re: deportation of Jews from France
Case file: discussion between SS-Obersturmbannführer Eichmann and SS-Hauptsturmführer Dannecker in Paris on 1 July 1942

The negotiations with the French government[3] have produced the following result:

All stateless Jews in the occupied and unoccupied zones have now been designated for deportation.

President *Laval* has suggested that children under the age of 16 be taken along as well when Jewish families from the unoccupied territory are deported. The question of Jewish children remaining behind in the occupied territory is of no interest to him.

Therefore, I urgently request a decision by telex as to whether children under 16 can also be deported, maybe beginning with the fifteenth transport of Jews from France.[4]

As a final point, let me also mention that, in order to get the operation going at all, we have for the time being only been able to discuss stateless or foreign Jews. Later, during the second phase, we can begin to deal with the Jews who were naturalized in France after 1919 or after 1927.[5]

25 The remaining passages deal with the Anti-Freemasonry Police and the Freemasonry question, the campaign against black market trade, and possibilities for recruitment to the police.

1 Mémorial de la Shoah, XLIX-35. Published in Klarsfeld, *Vichy–Auschwitz*, pp. 427–428. This document has been translated from German.

2 This section was headed by Adolf Eichmann.

3 Dannecker is referring to the talks held on 2 and 4 July 1942: see Doc. 239.

4 On the age limit, see Doc. 235, fn. 8.

5 On 7 August 1942 the Reich Security Main Office agreed to deport the children of stateless Jews. However, it was decided that a certain number of adults also had to be included in these transports: see also Doc. 259.

DOC. 241

On 7 July 1942 Theodor Dannecker and the French police authorities prepare for the planned arrest of 22,000 Jews in the Greater Paris area[1]

File note from the section for Jewish affairs (IV J SA24), Office of the Senior Commander of the Security Police and the SD,[2] signed Dannecker, Paris, dated 8 July 1942[3]

Re: further transports of Jews from France – first meeting of the operation committee[4]
1. File note:
Present during the meeting:
A) SS-Hauptsturmführer Dannecker,
SS-Unterscharführer Heinrichsohn
B) Darquier de Pellepoix
Mr Leguay, representative of the chief of police,
Director François, head of the internment camps,
Director Hennequin, chief of the street police,[5]
Director Tulard, in charge of the Paris prefecture's Jew registry,
Director Garnier, representative of the Seine département prefect,
Director Schweblin, anti-Jewish police,
Mr Gallien,[6] Darquier's chef de cabinet,
Mr Guidot, staff officer of the street police.[7]

In his introductory remarks, Darquier pointed out that the occupation authority had declared its willingness to relieve the French state of the Jews and that this meeting had been called to discuss the technicalities of the deportation. After that, the actual discussion began, and SS-Hauptsturmführer Dannecker ascertained:
1) *whether all the gentlemen present were authorized representatives of their agencies*, so that the decisions reached today would be binding and any further queries or changes would be out of the question. At that, all the gentlemen stated that they had the requisite authority.

1 Mémorial de la Shoah, XXVb-55. Published in Klarsfeld, *Vichy–Auschwitz*, p. 428. This document has been translated from German.
2 Helmut Knochen.
3 The original contains handwritten notes and underlining.
4 The meeting took place on 7 July 1942: see Doc. 239, fn. 16.
5 In the original 'Strassenpolizei', meaning the municipal police (*police municipale*).
6 Correctly: Pierre Galien (1898–1978), office supervisor for the commissioner general for Jewish affairs.
7 Jean François (1884–1972), deputy prefect of police in Paris, head of the department Police générale which oversaw the section for foreigners and Jewish affairs; simultaneously head of Drancy camp, August 1941–July 1943; Emile Hennequin (b. 1887), director general of the Paris municipal police, July 1942–Feb. 1944; André Tulard (1898–1967), head of the section for foreigners and Jewish affairs at the Paris Police Prefecture; Garnier, head of the supply department of the Prefecture of the Seine département, in charge of food supplies and facilities in Drancy camp; Jacques Schweblin (1907–1945), head of the Police for Jewish Affairs in the occupied zone and of its successor organization, the Section d'enquête et de contrôle (SEC); Georges Guidot (b. 1908), police inspector of the Paris municipal police.

In the course of the meeting,

2) *the number of Jews under consideration in the Paris metropolitan area was discussed.* According to the special guidelines, there are around 28,000 Jews (stateless etc.) in Paris who are to be arrested. In addition, there are Russian Jews (both White and Red),[8] so that, after subtracting those who are ill, unfit for transport, and too old, we can assume a total number of 22,000 Jews in Paris.

Subsequently,

3) *the actual arrest measures were discussed in detail.*
Inspectors from the prefecture and the anti-Jewish police, as well as female assistants, will select the file cards in question and sort them by arrondissement.[9]

These cards will then be given to Director Hennequin (police municipale), who will distribute them to the police inspectors of each arrondissement.[10] The latter must make the arrests on the basis of the cards and return the cards for Jews who have not been found. The sorting of the cards will be concluded by Friday, 10 July 1942, and on Monday morning (13 July 1942) the operation can take place in all arrondissements at the same time.[11] Then the Jews will be assembled in the respective municipal administration offices and, in conclusion, transported to the main assembly point (Vel d'hiver).[12] Transport to the individual camps will be organized by the French themselves. The age limit has been set at '16–50 years'.

Children who remain behind will also be assembled at a central site. The General Union of French Jews will then take charge of them and transfer them to children's homes.

All Jews within the age limit will be arrested, provided that they are fit for transport. (Not those living in mixed marriages!)

Following the operation in Paris,[13] the same operation will be carried out in the Seine-et-Oise and Seine-et-Marne départements, in collaboration with the Paris police.

In this context, there was

4) *discussion of the capacity of the individual internment camps.* Hauptsturmführer Dannecker set the following figures:

Drancy:	6,000 Jews	(men and women)
Compiègne:[14]	6,000	» » »
Pithiviers:	5,000	» » »
Beaune-la-Rolande:[15]	5,000	» » »

8 This is a reference to the Russian Civil War, where opponents of the Bolsheviks were identified as 'White' and its supporters as 'Red'.

9 Municipal administrative district within Paris.

10 From 1940 the Service juif, a special agency headed by André Tulard, kept the registration lists of the Jewish population, which were required by a regulation issued by the Military Commander in France (see PMJ 5/238). In 1942 this registry included the details of 27,361 foreign and stateless Jews.

11 The arrests were made on 16 and 17 July and were carried out by the municipal police and the national police force.

12 During the roundups in July 1942, the Vélodrome d'Hiver sports stadium in Paris was used as a temporary detention centre for Jews.

13 This refers to the Seine département.

14 Royallieu camp in Compiègne, around 60 km north-east of Paris, had been set up in June 1941 by the German occupation authorities to hold communists and other political prisoners. It was under German control.

15 The Beaune-la-Rolande (Loiret département) and Pithiviers camps served as internment camps for Jews in the occupied zone.

5) *Actual deportation of Jews to the East*
It was determined that one transport per week will depart from each camp. This course of action was decided upon because each transport requires thorough preparation (searching the Jews, rations, lists, etc.). This means that four trains, each carrying 1,000 Jews, will leave the occupied territory for the East each week.

The trains will be guarded by the French gendarmerie, overseen by a German Feldgendarmerie commando consisting of one lieutenant and eight men.

6) *Provisions and supplies for the Jews*
Each Jew is to be supplied as follows:

a) 1 pair of sturdy work boots, 2 pairs of socks, 2 shirts, 2 pairs of underpants, 1 set of work clothes, 2 woollen blankets, 2 sets of bedding (covers and sheets), 1 bowl for food, 1 mug, 1 field bottle, 1 spoon, and 1 sweater, in addition to the essential toiletries.
b) Each Jew must carry with him rations for three days.

Only one piece of luggage in total (1 suitcase or rucksack) may be taken along.

c) In addition, the transport is to be supplied with food for a total of two weeks (bread, flour, potatoes, beans, etc. in sacks) in a separate goods wagon.

The representative of the Seine prefecture saw no problems in providing this.

2. Submitted to the Senior Commander of the Security Police and the SD for information.
3. Submitted to *SS-Obersturmführer Lischka* for information.
4. Carbon copy for the Higher SS and Police Leader.[16]

DOC. 242
With the Ninth Regulation on Measures Against Jews of 8 July 1942, Jews are largely excluded from public life[1]

Ninth Regulation on Measures Against Jews
Dated 8 July 1942

By virtue of the authority vested in me[2] by the Führer and Supreme Commander of the Wehrmacht, I decree the following:

§ 1

Ban on visiting public events and facilities
Jews can be prohibited from attending public events and using facilities available to the public.

Detailed provisions will be issued by the Higher SS and Police Leader.[3]

16 Carl-Albrecht Oberg.

1 *VOBl-F*, no. 69, 15 July 1942, pp. 414–415. This document has been translated from German.
2 Carl-Heinrich von Stülpnagel (1886–1944), military officer; senior quartermaster in the general staff of the army, 1938–1940; chairman of the Franco-German Armistice Commission in Wiesbaden from June to Dec. 1940; commander-in-chief of the 17th Army, Dec. 1940–Oct. 1941; military commander in France, Feb. 1942–July 1944; sentenced to death and executed for participation in the attempted assassination of Hitler on 20 July 1944.
3 Carl-Albrecht Oberg.

§ 2
Restrictions on visiting businesses engaged in trade and commerce
Jews may visit department stores, retail firms, and commercial enterprises, or have others make purchases for them in such businesses, only between 3 p.m. and 4 p.m.
§ 3
Exceptions
Visits to purely Jewish businesses that have been specially identified as such are exempt from the prohibitions under §§ 1 and 2.
§ 4
Penalties
Contravention of the provisions of this regulation or the directives issued on the basis of this regulation will be punished with imprisonment or a fine or both.
§ 5
Police measures
In addition to or in place of sentencing, police measures can be ordered, in particular placement in a camp for Jews.
§ 6
Entry into force
This regulation comes into force upon its promulgation.

The Military Commander in France

DOC. 243

Je suis partout, 10 July 1942: Lucien Rebatet praises the antisemitic film *The Eternal Jew*[1]

On the screen: Israel's dirty mug. The Eternal Jew at the César.[2]

Often one finds oneself saying to the good but not very clever people whose understanding of the Jewish question is very limited: 'You need to see the Jews in the real ghettos in Romania or in Poland.' It is this journey that the film *The Eternal Jew*, several clips of which were shown at the exhibition at the Berlitz Palace, now makes available to all Parisians.

For the most part, the film was shot in the Polish ghettos by Wehrmacht cameramen during the 1939 campaign or shortly thereafter. For two years now, each week we have

1 *Je suis partout*, vol. 12, no. 571, 10 July 1942, p. 7. This article has been translated from French. The weekly newspaper, founded in 1930 by the publisher Fayard (Paris), was close to the right-wing nationalist, monarchist and antisemitic movement Action française, founded at the time of the Dreyfus affair. Publication was interrupted for several months during the occupation period but resumed in Feb. 1941. Thereafter the paper became one of the major publications of the French collaborationists. By 1944 its circulation had increased from 100,000 to 300,000 copies.
2 *The Eternal Jew* (in German: *Der ewige Jude*; in French: *Le Péril juif*), Germany, 1940; director: Fritz Hippler; scriptwriter: Eberhard Taubert. This antisemitic propaganda film was produced at the behest of Goebbels's Ministry of Public Enlightenment and Propaganda and made use of footage shot by Wehrmacht soldiers in Poland shortly after the German invasion.

been able to admire both the intrepid spirit and the talent of all these filmmakers from the propaganda units in their 'feldgrau' uniforms.[3] Among the Polish Yids, these courageous camera soldiers, familiar with shells and bullets, only had to brave the bedbugs, lice, and all the other manifestations of the Jewish pestilence. But they have given us a masterpiece of a report.

I know them well, the parts of the world where they have worked: the ghettos of Galicia, the one in Cracow, the Kazimierz neighbourhood, one of the largest and most hair-raising ghettos in Europe, as well as almost identical ones in nearby Bukovina, which are even more filthy, if that were even possible; Czernowitz, where the ghetto has practically absorbed the whole city, and cleaning it up will be no mean feat for our friends the Romanians.[4] In Cracow, that fairy-tale medieval city, it seems like one crosses an actual border when one arrives in Kazimierz and walks towards the Vistula river. One enters a different world in which Polish Christians practically never set foot. Wherever he looks, the traveller who strays into these alleyways will only see Jews in boots, with beards and sidelocks, wearing their fox-tail hats even in the hottest and brightest continental summer, their caftans flapping at their heels. As he brushes past these ridiculous or hideous figures, constantly the target of thousands of mean and sidelong glances, the Aryan feels as lonely and as alienated as if he were among an Amazonian tribe. The Jew, a person like any other? What a joke! Like everywhere else, there are Aryan scoundrels in Eastern Europe who trade with Jews. But there is not a single Christian who is not an antisemite in his heart of hearts.

Anyone who has spent some time in these cities of European Judea can bear witness to the extraordinary truthfulness of a film like *The Eternal Jew*. With a surprising sense of the 'things seen',[5] the reporters have captured these daily scenes of Judaism: the vile and filthy hovels where the Yid, not at all put out or uncomfortable, stacks up his brood of children and his banknotes; the interminable pilpul[6] in the street, conducted in the awful Yiddish jargon; all these furtive and clandestine negotiations smell of fraud, fencing stolen goods, usury, and credit fraud. It has something of the nonchalance of the raptor observing its prey out of the corner of its eye, or the restless and teeming activity of rats. The faces shown present all the varieties of deception, fraud and duplicity.

The commentary, which is remarkably well put together, underlines the parasitical existence of these short, fat crooks, stuck to the skin of a nation, getting fat off what others produced, never contributing anything of their own creation, with the exception of dreadful diseases.

The images of Israel at work, picks and spades in hand, standing on piles of rubble after a bombing, are priceless. But they do not fully satisfy our need for revenge, because

3 German in the original: 'field-grey', a reference to military uniform.

4 In the weeks following the German invasion of the Soviet Union, the Romanian army had reoccupied Bukovina; one year earlier, the Romanian government had been forced to cede the region to the Soviet Union. During the invasion of Bukovina, special Romanian units targeted the Jewish population, displaying exceptional savagery; they murdered between 12,000 and 20,000 Jews in only a few weeks. The survivors were expelled or deported to Transnistria, where thousands fell victim to additional massacres.

5 'Pour la "chose vue"': most likely an allusion to the book *Choses vues* (1887/1890) by Victor Hugo.

6 Hebrew: method of studying the Talmud through intense textual analysis; used polemically here to mean nitpicking and hair-splitting.

we need to remind ourselves that our workers and our farmers are still feeding almost one million of these unbelievably lazy scoundrels, even though they can no longer feed off our wealth and sell for their profit what we produced with our own hands.

We go further, into their atrocious kosher slaughterhouses, where we witness the savage and disgusting throat-slitting of cattle, which can only be explained as a centuries-old sadism that has survived in the rabbinical schools and the synagogues, which are not at all havens of spiritual life, but centres of hate where the little Jews learn to trick and rule over the Christians.

Simpletons might say: 'All of this is happening far away. We are dealing with different Jews here.' The screen itself will provide the answer. Look at the famous film industry trade fair in Amsterdam, where all the films in the world were bought and sold. In spite of the elegant full suits, the silk ties, the impeccably combed and parted hair of Parisian, London, or American Jews, they display exactly the same gestures, they cut exactly the same shady deals. In the Galician fleapit, on every street corner, before every hovel, we immediately run into the bearded and caftaned brothers and cousins of our big Yids from the rue de la Faisanderie, from the avenue Foch, the Maurois, the David-Weills, the Ephrussis, the Louis-Dreyfuses, the Sterns, the Wildensteins, the Veil-Picards, the Baders.[7] By Jehovah! There is the famous orchestra conductor Monteux, the midget Géo London, the illustrious Professor Hadamard, the Jewess Simone, Tristan Bernard, Armand Bernard, the filmmaker Chenal, the Jewess Marie Dubas, who still sang in Lyons last winter (they are not easily put off, our friends from Lyons).[8] The only difference between an elegant dress rehearsal in Paris in 1938, a party at Bagatelle,[9] or a Petits Lits Blancs[10] ball around the same time and the ghettos of Przytkyk, Skierniewice, Wlodzimierz Rzeszow, or Przeworsk[11] lies in the degree of hirsuteness and odour.

Without even speaking of race in a geographical sense, 'French' Jews are a tiny minority. There were barely three thousand Jews in Paris in 1800. Eighty years later, Drumont,[12] to his horror, counted forty thousand. In 1939, on the eve of the war, their number in our capital had reached half a million! Back then, we established in this newspaper that, at the very most, one tenth of the Jewish families in all of France were able to claim that they had lived on our soil for more than one hundred years, only one quarter had been here more than fifty years, and barely half more than twenty-five years. And these calculations were generous at that.

We can say that almost all the Jews living in France arrived from the ghettos of Eastern Europe one or two generations ago, and very rarely three. They brought with them squalor and dishonesty, festering hatred, and insolent and crazy messianic beliefs. Their names are Kirzbaum, Aziza, Aiache, Kislik, Youdkevitch, Grimblatt, Yacobichvili, Birtchansky, Zakroistchik, Zizine, all those barbaric and grotesque words that still fill up French phonebooks and directories by the tens of thousands in 1942. They have carefully

7 Well-known and wealthy French families from the community of Jewish big business.
8 All of these were prominent figures in French cultural life in the 1930s.
9 Park in the western part of Paris.
10 Charity gala that took place in Paris and at various glamorous French resorts between 1918 and 1935.
11 Towns in Poland. Correctly: Przytyk.
12 Édouard Drumont (1844–1917), journalist, writer, and politician; one of the most significant representatives of antisemitism in France around 1900.

reconstituted their exotic Jewish ways, which are anathema to our race, through hundreds of associations. Up to the start of the war these were called Adarsyercim (rue Cadet), Acoudath Atereth-Sion and Eth-Laasoth (67 rue de Bretagne), les Enfants de Cracovie, les Enfants lithuaniens, La Jeunesse de Nowo-Radomsk, le secours mutual de Rowno, les Amis solidaires de Brzeziny, les Amis de Szydlowiec, la Société Bickor Cholim (do not confuse this one with the Bicolor-Cholim!) of Montmartre, 100 rue Ordener, etc.[13] And by the way, many of the appalling shops we listed here in the spring of 1939 have reopened since then, on the banks of the Rhone or on the Mediterranean.

All French people have a duty to see films like *The Eternal Jew*. No matter how much they may already know about the matter, a film like this will prove instructive and enlightening for them. And this in turn will show that not all French people have become idiots.

François Vinneuil.[14]

DOC. 244

On 15 July 1942 Ida Kahn writes in her diary about the arrest of her daughter and two grandchildren[1]

Handwritten diary of Ida Kahn,[2] Alençon, entry for 15 July 1942 (copy)

The 13th, oh unhappy day. At 9 p.m., Feldgendarmen came to take Gustel, Berthold, and Edith.[3] Order to pack suitcases, with bed linen, one change of underwear, toiletries, a bowl, a spoon, and food for three days. Then they were taken away in a car without saying where. I almost forgot, it was specially mentioned that they were to take along work boots and work clothes, no money.

By chance or through good people, we heard that they would be leaving this morning at 11.30, so they were still here in a barracks for two nights. Lilli and Rudi[4] went to the railway station and managed to give them some food. There were a number of others with them going through the same thing, around twelve in total.

13 The names of these organizations are all either in Hebrew or refer to places in Eastern Europe.

14 Pseudonym of Lucien Rebatet (1903–1972), journalist and writer; worked for the extreme right-wing newspaper *L'Action française* from 1929; wrote for *Je suis partout*, 1932–1944; promoted collaboration with Nazi Germany and vehemently criticized the Vichy government; fled to Germany in 1944; arrested in Austria in 1945; sentenced to death by the Paris Court of Justice in 1946; sentence commuted to life imprisonment in April 1947; released in 1952; subsequently worked again as a journalist and writer.

1 YVA, O.33/6760. Copy in Mémorial de la Shoah, CMLXXXVI(13)-6. This document has been translated from German.

2 Ida Kahn, née Kaufmann (1878–1942), housewife; wife of Julius Kahn, in Merzig (Saarland) until 1935, then in Neufchâteau (Vosges) and Alençon (Orne département); arrested in early Oct. 1942; deported on 6 Nov. 1942 from Drancy to Auschwitz with her husband and a grandchild.

3 Gustel Bonnem (1903–1942), housewife; daughter of Ida Kahn; lived with her husband, Marcel Bonnem (1902–1942), and their three children in Palestine, 1935–1937, and subsequently in Alençon; her son Berthold (1925–1942), apprentice baker and confectioner; her daughter Edith (1927–1942). After their arrest, they were interned in Pithiviers camp; Gustel and Berthold Bonnem were deported from there to Auschwitz on 31 July 1942, and Edith was deported to Auschwitz three days later.

Now if only a bomb had killed everyone, all the misery would be over for us! And now the difficult task of informing Marcel and the siblings! Today there was post from them all. Alfred[5] is slowly making progress. Grandma Bonnem[6] turned 79 today, a sad birthday.

There was a disturbance on our street on Monday evening and it came close to a physical altercation. Outrage prevails all over the town and there is much sympathy. Regulations and restrictions are increasing for us Jews. The swimming baths, cinema, theatre, concerts, many public squares, and parks are off limits, even the markets. We are also barred from using the public phone boxes.

DOC. 245

Heinz Röthke, the official in charge of Jewish affairs for the Security Police and the SD in Paris, reports on the results of the large roundup on 16 and 17 July 1942[1]

Report by Section IV J of the Security Police (SA 225a, Rö/Ge), signed p.p. Röthke,[2] Paris, dated 18 July 1942

Re: deportation of stateless Jews
1. *Additional note:*
I. The arrest operation targeting stateless Jews on 16 and 17 July 1942 yielded the following final result:

Men	3,031
Women	5,802
Children	4,051
Total	12,884

The high percentage of women among those arrested is striking. The variance from the number of men arrested can be explained when we remember that it was mostly men who were arrested in the earlier roundups, and that it was probably easier for men than for women to get themselves to safety in good time before the arrests.

Those arrested come mainly from the lowest stratum of the Jewish race.

4 Germaine (known as Lilli) Meyer, née Kahn (b. 1913), piano teacher; daughter of Ida Kahn; became a French citizen in 1937 by marriage; arrested in mid Oct. 1942; deported in mid Feb. 1943 from Drancy to Auschwitz; and her nephew Rudolph Bonnem (1929–1942), son of Gustel Bonnem, arrested in early Oct. 1942; deported in Nov. 1942 from Drancy to Auschwitz; both perished there.

5 Alfred Kahn (1904–1990), retailer; eldest son of Ida Kahn; dealer in second-hand materials in Alençon, 1935–1940; interned from 1940; farmworker in Bellegard (Tarn département); went into hiding with his family from Nov. 1942; returned to Alençon in 1944.

6 Rebecca Bonnem, née Hanau (1893–1942), housewife; mother of Marcel Bonnem; arrested in early Oct. 1942 and deported one month later from Drancy to Auschwitz.

1 Mémorial de la Shoah, XLIX-67. This document has been translated from German.

2 Heinz Röthke (1912–1966), lawyer; worked for the regional administrative authority in Munich; Kriegsregierungsrat in Brest (France) in 1941; official in charge of Jewish affairs for the Security Police and the SD in Paris, 1942–1944; head of Drancy camp, 1942–1943; sentenced to death in France in absentia in 1945; after the war, lived in Wolfsburg, where he worked as a legal consultant.

Of the Jews arrested, 6,000 men and women in total (unmarried individuals or couples without children) were taken to Drancy camp for Jews while the operation was still in progress. The rest of those taken in were provisionally transferred to the Vélodrome d'Hiver.

Section IV J has been informed by many different sources that a substantial portion of the stateless Jews learned of the operation in advance and went into hiding.

In several instances, French police officers are said to have told the people they were to arrest, namely well-off stateless Jews, of the planned roundups and advised them not to be at home on 16 and 17 July 1942. Those who supplied this information have been asked to provide concrete examples, specifying the police officers concerned. So far, however, there has not been a single case where such particulars have been provided, even though the accuracy of this information cannot be doubted.

While around 9,800 persons were apprehended on the first day of the arrests, the French police arrested around 3,000 persons on 17 July 1942, only a fraction of the previous day's result, as was to be expected.

In several instances, the French population expressed sympathy for the arrested Jews and their disapproval, particularly concerning the arrest of children. The transport of the Jews who had been arrested was frequently not carried out discreetly, so that sections of the non-Jewish population had the opportunity to gather in small crowds and discuss the arrest of the Jews.

The French press repeatedly approached the propaganda department,[3] even as early as 16 July 1942, and expressed the wish to report on the arrests. The propaganda department was advised that for now – until further notice – there should be no press coverage of the arrests. As additional operations are planned for later, it will be expedient for the press to only report on the arrests in general terms. All reporting must be agreed in detail with the propaganda department in advance. The press coverage might point out that the Jews have continued to behave so arrogantly that drastic measures were necessary, and that for the most part the Jews arrested were active in the black market, dealing in forged passports and identity cards, and continuing to engage in bribery, large-scale scams, and all kinds of other crimes.[4] In addition, it should be pointed out that the security of the occupying power demands the strictest measures against the Jews, who verifiably circumvent the directives of the Military Commander and the Higher SS and Police Leader in hundreds of instances every day and are in violation of French laws.

II. On the morning of 17 July 1942, a discussion was held in the office of Section IV J on the question of where to house the Jewish children who were arrested. The meeting was attended by:

1. SS-Sturmbannführer Hagen,
2. the undersigned,
3. the police representative, Leguay,
4. the director of the police from the Police Prefecture, François,
5. Director Tulard,

3 Office within the military administration that was subordinate to the Reich Ministry of Public Enlightenment and Propaganda; its responsibilities included censorship and the allocation of paper for French publications.

4 See Doc. 258.

6. Darquier de Pellepoix, and
7. his secretary general Gallien.[5]

The Commissariat General for Jewish Affairs, which was tasked with directing the round of arrests, had initially proposed that the Jewish children be housed in buildings in Greater Paris and in suburbs of Paris. According to information provided by the Commissariat General, that would be possible. During the discussion, however, the following proposed solution was found to be preferable: the Jewish children are initially not to be separated from their parents, but rather transported along with them to the Pithiviers and Beaune-la-Rolande camps. The transport will be undertaken by the SNCF; the operation will be overseen by the French police.

There are, however, now already 6,000 Jewish men and women at Drancy camp who are either unmarried or married but without children. These Jews can now be taken away.[6] For the moment, one must wait and see what decision is made at a higher level (Reich Security Main Office) on the possibility of deporting the Jewish children.[7] The representatives of the French police repeatedly expressed the wish for the children to be included in the transports to the Reich. Should this not be possible for the moment, the adult Jews will be taken to Drancy from the Pithiviers and Beaune-la-Rolande camps on trains carrying 1,000 persons each according to the capacities here. If it is possible to take the Jewish children away, the parents should be deported along with them. The French police will be in charge of conveying the Jews from Pithiviers and Beaune-la-Rolande to Drancy. The French police, in consultation with the Commissariat for Jewish Affairs, have also assumed responsibility for provisioning the Jews.[8] As on previous occasions when Jews were assembled in camps, the Jews will hand in their food ration cards and receive meals through mass catering.

The Union will be in charge of medical care.[9] The transports from Drancy to the Reich border will be escorted by a French gendarmerie officer and thirty men. For supervision, a Feldgendarmerie commanding officer and eight Feldgendarmerie officers will be added to each detachment.

The distribution of the Jews currently still housed in the Vélodrome d'Hiver will take place from 19 July 1942 and is to be carried out as quickly as possible, i.e. within a few days.[10]

2. Submitted to SS-Obersturmbannführer Lischka for information.
3. Submitted to *SS-Standartenführer Dr Knochen* for information.
4. Carbon copy to SS-Brigadeführer Oberg.
5. Follow-up with IV J.

5 Correctly: Galien.

6 More than 5,800 persons were deported on six trains from Drancy to Auschwitz between 19 and 29 July 1942.

7 See Doc. 240.

8 Equipment and food for Drancy camp were made available by the Seine prefecture.

9 This refers to the General Union of French Jews (UGIF); medical care was also the responsibility of the Seine prefecture.

10 Beginning on 19 July 1942, for four days 2,000 persons per day were deported from Paris by the French National Railway Company (SNCF); 4,544 were taken to Pithiviers camp and 3,074 to Beaune-la-Rolande.

DOC. 246

In a letter to Marshal Pétain dated 22 July 1942, the Catholic cardinals and archbishops of France stress the sanctity of the rights of the individual[1]

Letter from the cardinals and archbishops of France, signed Cardinal Suhard,[2] Paris, to Marshal Pétain,[3] Vichy, dated 22 July 1942 (copy)[4]

Dear Marshal,

We are profoundly moved by what we are told of the mass arrests of Israelites carried out last week and of the harsh treatment that has been inflicted upon them, particularly in the Vélodrome d'Hiver, and we cannot stifle the voice of our consciences.[5]

It is in the name of humanity and of Christian principles that we raise our voices in protest and in favour of the inalienable rights of the individual human being. This is also an anguished cry for pity in the face of immense suffering, particularly that of so many mothers and children.

We ask you, Marshal, to consider this, so that the requirements of justice and the law of charity are adhered to.[6]

DOC. 247

On 26 July 1942 Pierre Lion notes how Paris has changed under the occupation[1]

Diary of Pierre Lion,[2] Barèges, entry for 26 July 1942 (copy)[3]

Saturday – Sunday 26 July 1942

So now I have completed this trip, which I prepared and thought through so carefully for months, and which my friends[4] (André D. most of all) advised against until the last minute. Now I am so glad that I made my plans a reality.

1 AHAP, 1 D 14, 8. Copy in Mémorial de la Shoah, XXVc-196. Published in Klarsfeld, *Calendrier*, p. 575. This document has been translated from French.

2 Emmanuel Suhard (1874–1949), priest and theologian; bishop of Bayeux and Lisieux, 1928–1930; archbishop of Rheims, 1930–1940; cardinal in 1935; archbishop of Paris, 1940–1949.

3 Philippe Pétain (1856–1951), military officer and politician; commander at the battle of Verdun, 1916/1917; commander-in-chief of the French army, 1917/1918; appointed marshal, 1918; inspector general of the army, 1922–1931; minister of war, Feb.–Nov. 1934; ambassador in Madrid, 1939–1940; prime minister of France, 16 June–10 July 1940; head of state of the Vichy regime, 11 July 1940–20 August 1944; in exile in Sigmaringen, August 1944–April 1945; sentenced to death by the Haute Cour de justice on 15 August 1945. President de Gaulle commuted the sentence to life imprisonment.

4 The annual conference of the French cardinals and archbishops had taken place in Paris on 21–22 July 1942.

5 In what became known as the Vél d'Hiv roundups, 13,000 Jews were arrested in Paris on 16–17 July 1942.

6 This letter was given to Marshal Pétain by Monseigneur Chappoulie, representative of the episcopate in Vichy, on 25 July 1942: Sylvie Bernay, *L'Église de France face à la persécution des Juifs, 1940–1944* (Paris: CNRS Éditions, 2012), pp. 325 f.

1 The original diary is privately owned. Copy in IfZ-Archives, F 601. This document has been translated from French.

The undeniable risk was reduced to a minimum thanks to G.,[5] but I still felt it quite strongly when crossing the line at V.,[6] both going and coming back, as well as during a few unpleasant chance meetings in Paris (Bunt, Mrs Liotier!).

I did accomplish my goal of seeing my friends again and reconnecting with my city. After seven and a half months of separation, I found it not much changed, but more tense, sadder than before, and with much more of an atmosphere of war to it.

More tense, sadder: Indeed, *terror* reigns there more and more, both for the villagers in general and especially for Martin.[7] This is because the *Gestapo's* hold on the place is becoming ever stronger. Wick told me last Tuesday that, faced with the failure of 'friendly collaboration' (!), the Reichswehr[8] has increasingly ceded the surveillance of Paris to the Gestapo.[9] And we know what that means: mass arrests, often without even the semblance of a motive; people disappearing and never being heard of again. Many executions. The only thing the Parisians are talking about is the word 'Shot'. (Harry Baur, the actor, a few days ago.[10])

The terrible poster about the 'cousins' covers the walls of the Metro, no longer bearing the name of the Militärbefehlshaber,[11] but that of the chief of the Gestapo.[12]

Naturally, Martin is first in line among the victims of this terror. Four days before my arrival, during the night between the 16th and the 17th, a horrible operation took place, which left Paris completely distraught when I arrived. 25,000[13] Martins (foreigners) were arrested, including women and children, and mothers were separated from their children if they were over four years old! It was a night-time operation that went on until the small hours of the morning. The operation was carried out by the French police on their own, which, for our government, is utterly despicable. In executing the operation, the police were as humane as possible; some policemen were dismissed and shot for refusing to obey orders. One member of the Garde Mobile committed suicide on the night of the operation. Every witness reported appalling details: women killing

2 Pierre Jules Lion (1896–1977), mining engineer; employed in the French civil service, 1919–1921; businessman from 1921; French representative at international conferences on energy; obtained an exemption from the French Council of State in 1941, which would have allowed him to re-enter the civil service despite the provisions of the Statute on Jews; served in the Free French Forces, 1942–1944; primarily employed by the Schneider electronic and armaments corporation from 1947.

3 The original contains handwritten additions.

4 Lion had been in Paris from 21 to 23 July 1942; since late 1941 he had been living in the unoccupied zone, after he narrowly escaped the roundup of Jews in Paris in Dec. 1941. On the Dec. 1941 roundup, see PMJ 5/299.

5 G. stands for Gauthier, the name on the false documents Pierre Lion had used to travel to the occupied zone.

6 Presumably Vierzon, an important crossing point on the demarcation line.

7 Lion used the term 'villagers' for the inhabitants of Paris and the name 'Martin' for Jews.

8 German in the original: reference to the Wehrmacht.

9 After a Higher SS and Police Leader (HSSPF) was appointed in France in May 1942, the military administration reduced its involvement in anti-resistance operations.

10 At this time, Baur was in fact in Gestapo custody; he was released in Sept. 1942: see Doc. 236, fn. 30.

11 German in the original: 'military commander'.

12 In early July 1942 HSSPF Oberg used publicly displayed posters to announce that family members of alleged would-be assassins would be held responsible for acts of resistance unless the perpetrators handed themselves in within ten days.

13 Crossed out in the original and changed to 10,000. Correctly: 12,884: see Doc. 245.

their children before throwing themselves from windows, children jumping out of the buses that were taking them away, etc. They were all taken to the Vél d'Hiv and to the Parc des Princes. There were invalids among them, births, operations. No place to go to the toilet. After six days of torture, they were crammed into livestock wagons and sent to Pithiviers. And then?

All of my friends fear that the same thing will happen to the French. Although the Parisians are all perfectly kind, the *yellow star* presents them with a terrible moral dilemma. I always travelled in the last carriage when I took the Metro, the only one permitted to Martins. I saw the star-wearers, some brave but with a tense expression, others ashamed, hiding it under a newspaper or behind a book.

In addition, the faces of all the travellers on the Metro are gloomy, crushed by this atmosphere of terror. There is only silence. I would say there is an atmosphere of war in the city. I could feel it before my train pulled into Austerlitz station, when I saw the hundreds of sausages[14] guarding the perimeter of Paris, especially near the Vitry North power station.

Then the preparations for *air-raid alarms* (I experienced one during the night of Wednesday to Thursday; the sirens went off all over the city, but there was no bombing): the officers with their helmets on their belts; anti-aircraft units are more or less everywhere in the city, on the rooftops of many buildings. (I saw companies of them positioned on the boulevard Lannes, across from number 55, on the St Cloud and Sèvres bridges, on the turf at Longchamp.) The night is more intense than ever in the streets of Paris in the evening. Judging by the number of troops around, there are about as many Germans in the streets, but they are older. On Tuesday I saw a motorized regiment go by on the Champs-Elysées.

I was in *Boulogne–Billancourt*, looking at the results of the bombing of the Renault factory,[15] and in general it was remarkably precise. All throughout the factory building, there are destroyed halls, collapsed walls, other walls riddled with shrapnel, particularly along the Seine. As for the ruined houses, they can be found almost exclusively in the area immediately surrounding the factory. On the two evenings when I cycled through Billancourt, I was moved to see crowds of people walking around normally, and children were playing right next to the ruins of the bombed-out houses.

From a personal point of view, this unforgettable trip finally re-established the contacts I had desired, with my city and with my friends. I travelled around a lot in the 16th arrondissement, the 8th, the 17th, and the centre, the first two days by bicycle (borrowed from Maîtrejean)[16] and the third by Metro, to see the Place de la Concorde, the Champs-Elysées, and the boulevards again (although I wasn't allowed to enter them).[17] Alas on

14 Colloquial term for the airships guarding the airspace over Paris.

15 The Royal Air Force had bombed the Renault, Rosengart, and Salmson plants in Boulogne–Billancourt near Paris which worked for the German armaments industry. The attack destroyed two thirds of the factory complex. No air-raid alarm had been sounded. A total of 623 persons lost their lives, and 1,500 were injured.

16 The person with whom Pierre Lion was staying, not otherwise identified; mentioned again below.

17 In connection with the regulation issued on 8 July 1942 (see Doc. 242), the Parisian press had announced on 10 July 1942 that Jews were forbidden from using the Champs-Elysées and other major boulevards in Paris: front pages of *Le Petit Parisien* and *Le Matin*, 10 July 1942. Such an order could not be verified.

Wednesday I came across German music coming down the Champs-Elysées, as in the past, at a quarter past 12.

On Tuesday morning, even before arriving, the first church of the Île de France[18] …

The kindness shown by all my friends is deeply touching. Saw Jacques W. again (dined with him on the first day in the rue Bonaparte, the second at Darde's, at Austerlitz on the third), Darde all three days (dined with him and went to rue Chauchat), Maîtrejean (stayed at his place, right from the first day, with Gérard at rue Marbeuf). The little crew from my office (Mrs Linotte, Meurisot, Paulin, Miss Launin), sad and courageous, […] (lunched on the third day at rue Chauchat), Alfred, Geneviève, Michou, Marcel, and finally Miquette, whom I tried to convince to come back here. I met Francin, Mény …[19]

But what a shock to have to put on a mask in one's own city, to move around like a hunted man, fearing some incident every second, which would no doubt have tragic consequences …

And then the return trip with D.,[20] who was so brave during this journey, and finding peace and quiet back here again …

Over the course of this week, things have been happening in *Russia*. With great speed, the Germans succeeded in occupying the whole territory within the Don river bend, all the way to the confluence of that river with the Donets. After taking *Voroshilovgrad*, they managed to encircle *Rostov* on three sides, and claim to have taken it on the 24th.

It even seems that they have crossed the Don in the direction of Stalingrad and have cut off the Stalingrad–Krasnograd railway line in the direction of the Caucasus.[21]

So the surge of the invasion is flowing both towards the Caspian Sea and the Caucasus. Stalingrad, a place of huge importance, is under threat. All of that is certainly disturbing, but it was to be expected. The Germans are pushing forward, but how long will they be able to continue such a colossal effort? The Russians have managed to avoid being encircled, and the numbers of prisoners do not compare to those of last year's campaigns.

In *Egypt*, Auchinleck started an offensive on the 22nd, which appeared to have the sole objective of taking a few positions before reaching El Alamein and apparently succeeded in doing so.[22] Apart from that, things are quiet, and Rommel remains blocked.

Bombings in the Ruhr, but not on the same scale as those at the start of June. Why? That's what everyone's wondering.

18 This refers to Notre Dame Cathedral.

19 Several names are illegible.

20 Lion's wife Daisy (Marguerite) Lion-Goldschmidt (1903–1998), museum curator and art historian; born in Brussels to a Jewish family originally from Frankfurt; settled with her family in France in 1912; studied art history at the Sorbonne; spent the war in the southern zone looking after her three young children and elderly parents; after the war, continued career as expert on Asian art, porcelain and sculpture.

21 Rostov fell to the Wehrmacht on 23 July 1942. On the same day, Hitler ordered his forces to proceed simultaneously towards Stalingrad and the Caucasus. On 25 July the Wehrmacht's 6th Army reached the River Don (85 km from Stalingrad).

22 As of mid July, British onslaughts under General Auchinleck led to breaches along the front lines, near to the El Alamein position that Field Marshal Rommel was defending.

In general, I don't hear anything really new in my conversations in Paris, compared to the information I get in the free zone. Everyone is convinced (the Germans at the Majestic[23] as much as our people) that the rope has been stretched to the point of breaking, and that this machine will collapse one day. Many, like myself, believe that this day may come soon. Others see it further off in the future.

It has been corroborated that discontent is growing in Germany (most of all among the Catholics). But how far are we from the explosion?

Domestically, Doriot's[24] propaganda is intensifying in the occupied zone, and we still fear seeing him in power sometime soon. Déat[25] is taking action too, but not exactly in the same direction. The press is even more dreadful and intellectually inferior than in my day. Disgusting pseudo-humoristic posters mocking the British or Martin deface the walls and make no impression.

The people in the occupied zone feel further and further away from those in the free zone. The Vichy government is increasingly discredited, and its attitude in this business of the 25,000 last week[26] shocked everyone, when it not only failed to protest, but even loaned its police for the operation. People deplore the mistakes made by the English, but all the hatred is still directed against Dupont,[27] and the bombings have done nothing to change that.

All of this is terrible, confusing, sad, and the strain put on millions of people's nerves is such that it is time for it all to stop. But the villagers are nevertheless determined to carry on for as long as necessary.

23 The German military administration was quartered in the Hotel Majestic.

24 Jacques Doriot (1898–1945), metalworker; member of the French Communist Party (PCF) and communist delegate in the French Chamber of Deputies, 1924–1934; excluded from the PCF in 1934; councillor for the Seine département, 1924–1936 and 1937–1940; co-founded the extreme right-wing Parti Populaire Français (PPF) in 1936 and the Legion of French Volunteers Against Bolshevism (LVF) in 1941; editor of the collaborationist newspaper *Le Cri du peuple*; deployed in the war against the Soviet Union several times up to 1944; fled to Germany in 1944; killed in an air raid.

25 Marcel Déat (1894–1955), politician; served in the First World War; joined the French Section of the Workers' International (SFIO) in 1920; deputy for the Marne, 1926–1928, and in Paris, 1932; expelled from the SFIO in 1933; minister of aviation, 1936; supported the Munich Agreement in 1938; advocated collaboration with Germany after the occupation of France; co-founder of the far-right collaborationist party National Popular Rally (RNP) in 1941; minister of labour and national solidarity in the Vichy government in 1944; fled to Germany after the Allied landing in Normandy; fled to Italy in 1945 and lived under an assumed name; lived undiscovered in a convent; sentenced to death in absentia by a French court in June 1945.

26 This is a reference to the mass roundup of Jews on 16 and 17 July in Paris: see Doc. 241.

27 Lion's synonym for the German occupiers.

DOC. 248
On 29 July 1942 the French Police Directorate asks the Ministry of Agriculture to provide food for the Jews in the unoccupied zone who are to be taken to Drancy[1]

Letter (marked 'top secret', no. 7937) from Section 9 of the French police, signed Cado, prefect and deputy director general of the police,[2] Vichy, to the state secretary for agriculture and food supplies,[3] department for distribution and consumption, dated 29 July 1942 (copy).[4]

Re: transfer of Israelites
I am writing to inform you that a number of Israelites of both French and German nationality – men, women, and children – who are currently in the camps in the unoccupied zone, will be sent into the occupied zone by order of the German authorities, starting on 6 August.

They will be divided up and put on four transports, the planned points of origin and composition of which are as follows:

1st transport: 6 August: 1,000 leaving from Gurs camp (B. P.).[5]
2nd transport: 8 August: 740 from Gurs camp (B. P.),
190 from Vernet camp (Ariège),[6]
100 to 150 from Récébédou camp (Haute-Garonne),[7]
trains will merge at Toulouse.
3rd transport: 10 August: 500 to 600 from Rivesaltes camp (P. O.),[8]
200 to 300 from Les Milles camp (B. D. R.),[9]
trains will merge at Avignon.
4th transport: 12 August: 800 from Les Milles camp.

1 AN, F7, vol. 15 088. This document has been translated from French.

2 Henri Cado (1903–1979), lawyer; served in various prefectures; prefect and chief of police in Marseilles in 1939; relieved of his post in 1940; prefect again from 1941; deputy director general of the French police from April 1942; suspended in 1944; sent into retirement in 1946.

3 Jacques Le Roy Ladurie (1902–1988), farmer and major landowner; leading figure in the agricultural cooperative movement, 1929–1945; mayor of Moutiers-en-Cinglais, 1929–1945; state secretary for agriculture and food supplies, April–Sept. 1942; fought in liberation battles on the side of the French Resistance in Orléans, 1944; again mayor of Moutiers-en-Cinglais, 1947–1983; delegate to the National Assembly, 1951–1955 and 1958–1962.

4 The original contains the handwritten note: 'Passed on to Mr Winck, who promises to give the necessary order.'

5 Gurs camp in the Basses-Pyrénées département was until Nov. 1942 the largest internment camp in the unoccupied southern zone. Between Oct. 1940 and Nov. 1943, a total of 20,000 prisoners were held there, some only briefly, others long term. A total of 17,000 of these prisoners were Jews.

6 Foreigners (mostly Jews) considered 'suspicious' or 'dangerous' were interned in the former military camp known as Le Vernet from autumn 1940. Around 40,000 prisoners were interned in the camp over the period up to 1944.

7 Récébédou camp, located south of Toulouse, was opened in 1941 as a 'model camp' in response to internal criticism of the poor hygiene in the camps in the unoccupied zone; it was closed in Oct. 1942.

8 Rivesaltes camp was a former military training camp located in Rivesaltes, in the Pyrénées Orientales département. From Dec. 1940 refugees from Germany and territories under German control were interned at the camp. In early Sept. 1940 Rivesaltes camp became a transit camp for Jews who were to be taken to Drancy. After the Wehrmacht occupied southern France, it became a German military camp.

9 Les Milles camp was set up in Sept. 1939 in a former tile factory near Aix-en-Provence in the Bouches du Rhône département. From late 1940, it initially served as a transit camp for German refugees who were leaving France for overseas destinations. Later it served as a transit camp for Jewish concentration camp prisoners.

The first part of the journey should take between 24 and 36 hours and, for reasons of public order, cannot be interrupted to distribute hot meals. It is therefore absolutely necessary that each person concerned should be provided with food to last for the entire duration of the journey, right up to the destination.

I would be grateful to you if you would authorize the Gurs, Le Vernet, Les Milles, Rivesaltes, and Récébédou camps to receive, on the day before the fixed departure date, sufficient food supplies and canned food to ensure that those concerned can be fed over 48 hours.

I insist that it is necessary to guarantee enough food for these detainees during the entire transport in order to avoid any possible incident. Furthermore, given that these departures will significantly ease your administration's workload, it seems to me that it must be possible to allow the individuals concerned to benefit from a relatively good diet for a few days.

I would be grateful if, given the urgent nature of the situation, you would be willing to give all the necessary orders to help implement all the measures described above as quickly as possible.

DOC. 249

On 29 July 1942 the French Police Directorate instructs the prefect of Pau on how to prepare for the impending transports of prisoners from Pau camp[1]

Telegram from Section 9 of the French police (dated 29 July 1942, 11.30 a.m., LQ/NK), signed Cado,[2] Vichy, to the prefect of Pau[3] (secretariat general) (copy)[4]

Confirm de Quirielle's[5] instructions given during visit on 21 July as well as my telephone communication of 27 July.

1) Cancel visits and reinforce camp guard squads from 1 August. You will have at your disposal the Pau Mobile Reserve Group and possibly gendarmerie. Further instructions to follow.

Confirm that from now on all permissions have been suspended. Take necessary precautions to avoid all incidents inside and outside the camp.

Will send definitive list of people who are certainly to be taken away, as well as list of guards.

2) On 2 August offer choices concerning: a) children under 18 of those who must leave, b) their spouses, older relatives, and children who are exempt from transport in prin-

1 AN, F7, vol. 15 088. Published in Klarsfeld, *Calendrier*, p. 606. This document has been translated from French.

2 Henri Cado.

3 Emile Ducommun (1887–1971), lawyer; worked at the French Ministry of Finance, 1914–1940; prefect of the Basses-Pyrénées département, 1940–1943; state secretary in the Vichy Ministry of Finance, 1943–1944; forced to retire in 1945.

4 The original contains handwritten annotations. The telegram was also sent to the regional prefect and the police commissioner in Toulouse for information.

5 Louis de Quirielle, a high-ranking official in the French police, had visited Rivesaltes, Noé and Récébédou, Le Vernet, and Les Milles camps on 21, 22, and 23 July 1942.

ciple. Telephone liaison officer Lieutenant Philippe (Cabin Drou, S&L,[6] military post) to send list before 4 August of those opting not to leave as well as of those who were struck from the list at the last minute for whatever reason. Do not reveal actual destination to those concerned, but tell them they will be taken to another camp currently under construction.

3) They will also be allowed to take their funds which they deposited at the camp or to leave them with the head of the camp. Remember verbal instructions given by my delegate to your secretary general. Send me receipts for sums and items belonging to those who choose second option.[7]

4) Departure of first transport, which comprises 1,000 persons plus guards, is scheduled for the morning of 6 August. Second transport with remaining passengers plus guards will follow, departing on the morning of 8 August. Guards will likely be provided by the gendarmerie. Make sure each person has rations for five days. Do not let them keep blankets or any materials belonging to the state. But supply them with plates and cups, cardboard or otherwise, as far as possible.

Transports with guards will be directed to Chalon-sur-Saône, where the German authorities will take charge of them. Second transport will be merged with that of prisoners from Vernet and Noé-Récébédou in Toulouse. Provide head guard with five copies of the list of passengers (send me one copy) and tell him to have the German authorities officially discharge him from his duties.

5) Set up transport medical service with doctors and nurses from among the passengers. Acknowledge receipt of these instructions and report any difficulties in their implementation.[8]

Reminder: you must transmit the list de Quirielle asked for by Friday morning at the latest.

6 Saône-et-Loire département.

7 The prisoners' funds were deposited with the Caisse des dépôts et consignations (CDC), a state financial institution responsible for the centralized administration of blocked accounts.

8 See Doc. 256.

DOC. 250
On 30 July 1942 the Security Police outpost in Vierzon reports that thousands of Jews are fleeing to the unoccupied zone[1]

Telex from the Vierzon outpost (no. 173, dated 30 July 1942, 9.10 a.m.), signed SS-Hauptscharführer Bauer,[2] to the Senior Commander of the Security Police and the SDMA[3] (no. 15 185, received on 30 July 1942), Paris, dated 30 July 1942[4]

Re: mass flight of Jews to the unoccupied territory of France
The Orléans Security Police post has received word that a mass flight of Jews to the unoccupied French territory from Holland, Belgium, and Paris has started over the last eight days. Almost without exception, the Jews are carrying newly issued identity cards which do not identify them as Jews.[5] For example, the local office detained about seventy Jews at Vierzon railway station over the course of three days. The other border railway stations cannot be monitored from here due to staff shortage. However, the Feldgendarmerie and customs offices here report that thousands of Jews are moving to the unoccupied territory illegally. All the roundups carried out so far in this context have been successful; numerous agencies in The Hague, Brussels, and Paris engage in people smuggling and the procurement of fake identity papers. Word of the operation to detain Jews at Vierzon railway station has spread, which is why the flight of Jews has already eased off here. Instead, the Jews are now using other railway stations along the border. It is therefore urgently requested that any persons arriving at border railway stations be checked by special Security Police units, particularly this coming Saturday and Sunday. Because of the staff shortage, the Vierzon outpost will not be able to monitor the 80 km border strip assigned to it.[6]

1 Mémorial de la Shoah, XXVI-51. This document has been translated from German.
2 Wilhelm (Willy) Bauer (b. 1912), brewer; head of the Security Police and SD outpost in Vierzon; subsequently worked at the section for Jewish affairs at the Office of the Commander of the Security Police and the SD in Marseilles; following the Allied landing in southern France, he took part in an operation to execute French resistance fighters at Cannes on 15 August 1944.
3 Senior Commander of the Security Police and the SD: Helmut Knochen. The reason for the abbreviation SDMA rather than SD is unknown.
4 The original contains handwritten annotations.
5 From mid Oct. 1940 Jews' identity papers were marked with a special stamp in the occupied zone.
6 The document contains a handwritten instruction from the official in charge of Jewish affairs for the Security Police and the SD in Paris, Röthke, asking for guards from the relevant Security Police and SD detachments to be posted to all the railway stations involved to carry out checks on travellers.

DOC. 251

On 2 August 1942, in an anonymous letter to Marshal Pétain, veterans protest against the antisemitic measures taken in recent weeks[1]

Anonymous letter, Grenoble, to head of state Marshal Pétain, Vichy (received on 6 August 1942), dated 2 August 1942

A news item about the measures taken against Israelites in the liberal professions,[2] which appeared in the press a few weeks ago, has obliged us, sir, to respectfully bring to your attention the grave consequences such a regulation might have.

This is based on the fact that art and science have no national homeland, that they both belong to all of humanity, and that all who practise them are honouring universal civilization.

We, veterans of the old war, the Great War, the one that gave you victory, we have not forgotten and cannot forget that men of all races, religions, and political persuasions died by our side.

They all sleep their last slumber side by side after giving their blood in defence of the nation.

Do not stain your glorious past by making common cause with the author of *Mein Kampf* and his despicable carnage. Cruelty degrades man.

We have heard from the occupied zone, and particularly from Paris, that the occupying authorities are subjecting our former brothers in arms to the most undignified harassment and are supported in their cowardly activities by shady individuals in their pay.

They believed they could get French people worthy of the name to side with them by forcing [the Jews] to wear a star with an inscription which, from our point of view, is in no way dishonourable. You are surely aware, Marshal, that they were seriously mistaken, and that this grotesque sanction has rebounded on them.

We veterans, whether members of the Légion d'honneur or not, but French above all else, are determined to put a stop to such a practice should it be extended to the free zone. Our protest will certainly make itself widely felt, and the goal of national reconciliation that you advocate would be far from being achieved.

We dare to hope that, as a powerful authority, you will not tolerate such an outrage to our country and that, inspired by the wise words 'Do unto others as you would have them do unto you', you will leave the responsibility for the cruelties that rest on its conscience to the monster and let it await the punishment it deserves, which will not be long in coming.[3]

Allow us to assure you, Marshal, of our deep devotion and profound respect for you.

A group of Frenchmen who want to remain Frenchmen.

1 AN, AJ 38, vol. 67. This document has been translated from French.

2 In the second Statute on Jews, issued on 2 June 1942, the French government prohibited Jews from practising the liberal professions and other occupations: see PMJ 5/270.

3 Throughout the entire German occupation, and despite the efforts on the part of Commissioner General Darquier de Pellepoix, the Vichy government avoided introducing mandatory visible identification of Jews in the southern zone.

DOC. 252

On 4 August 1942 the Senior Commander of the Security Police records that the Vichy regime's head of government, Pierre Laval, is insisting on a gradual approach to actions against the Jews[1]

Excerpt from a file note from Section VI, Office of the Senior Commander of the Security Police France,[2] signed SS-Sturmbannführer Hagen, to Section IV J, Paris, dated 4 August 1942[3]

Excerpt from the file note on the meeting with Laval[4] on 3 August 1942
Re: Jewish question
Asked once again by the Senior Commander of the Security Police about the deportation of stateless Jews from the unoccupied territory, Laval explained, with occasional assistance from Bousquet, that he was trying to deliver the stateless Jews to us by all means possible. In any event, he said, the first transport would be taken across the demarcation line on 8 August.[5] By 15 August all the Jews already in concentration camps would be transferred to us. He added that the remaining Jews of Polish, Czech, etc. and also Hungarian nationality who still live in the unoccupied territory would be swiftly detained after 15 August and transferred to concentration camps, and could be deported from 20 August. The information that Jews with Hungarian nationality could be detained along with the others was particularly well received by Laval and Bousquet. Laval merely wanted confirmation that the Hungarian government had agreed to this. This was confirmed to him.

Bousquet explained that on account of this extension, the specified number of 11,000 Jews would be exceeded by at least 3,500. He said for our part we would need to create the facilities to take up these additional Jews.

In addition, the Senior Commander of the Security Police brought up the denaturalization of the Jews who had been naturalized in France after 1933.[6] He pointed out that Berlin had expressly drawn his attention to the need for such a provision.

Based on the information he had received earlier from Bousquet, Laval agreed in principle to proceed in this way. However, he emphasized that, in his view, a gradual approach in the form specified was necessary for psychological reasons. From Berlin it would certainly look very nice if everything were to be speeded up in the desired manner, but the setbacks this would cause would be greater than the benefits achieved.

1 Mémorial de la Shoah, XXVI-54. Published in French translation in Klarsfeld, *Calendrier*, p. 651. This document has been translated from German.
2 Helmut Knochen.
3 The original contains handwritten annotations and underlining.
4 Pierre Laval (1883–1945), lawyer; held various ministerial posts from 1925; senator, 1927–1940; prime minister of France, 1931–1932 and 1935–1936; played a crucial part in the transfer of executive powers to Marshal Pétain in July 1940; deputy prime minister and prime minister, 23 June–13 Dec. 1940; head of the Vichy government, April 1942–August 1944; exiled in Sigmaringen, 1944–1945; fled to Spain in 1945; extradited to France; sentenced to death by the Haute Cour de justice on 9 Oct. 1945; executed.
5 See Doc. 249.
6 See Introduction, p. 78.

He said he had also talked to Cardinal Suhard about dealing with the Jewish question in its current form and had met with great understanding. The meeting, he said, had otherwise mainly addressed the widespread claim that children have been separated from their Jewish parents.[7]

DOC. 253

Gringoire, 7 August 1942: an article by Philippe Henriot warns against compassion for the persecuted Jews[1]

The Romance of the Star[2]

Are they going to start up a new Dreyfus affair for us now?[3] Not content with invading the hotels, the cities, and the countryside, are they going to invade our conversations as well? My word, we talk of nothing but them! One would think that they are the only preoccupation we have at the moment. Why? Because they provoked the war and the catastrophe we suffered?[4] Because they are the ones behind the black market everywhere? Because their resurgent arrogance exasperates the French-born French people, who feel at least as much at home here as those who came from the ghettos of Bukovina or Poland and have been naturalized? No, none of the above. The reason is that they have been forced to wear the yellow star in the occupied zone![5]

This very simple measure, which ought to flatter people so proud of their race, has provoked an explosion of compassion among the tender-hearted and resulted in sentimental whining about the fate of these unfortunate victims of terrible persecution. People who owe nothing to the Jews but what we ourselves suffer, people who have no personal sympathy for Israel either, are beginning to feel sorry for these victims of oppression in the name of Christian charity, of democratic pity, or of an incurable, foolish sentimentality which has already led us to make so many stupid mistakes.

Over the centuries, kings and popes have taken steps time and again to limit the eternally poisonous character of the Jews. They locked them up in ghettos; they passed special legislation for them; they rigorously kept watch over them and punished them. And because today these Jews are being asked to declare themselves Jews by wearing the yellow star, we should feel pity for such a cruel fate!

7 See Docs. 240 and 259.

1 *Gringoire*, 7 August 1942, front page. This document has been translated from French. The right-wing weekly *Gringoire* was published from 1928 to May 1944. During the occupation it received financial support from the Vichy government and was only published in the unoccupied zone, with a circulation of 300,000 (1936: 650,000).

2 The title is an allusion to a scene in act 3 of Wagner's opera *Tannhäuser* and the aria 'To the Evening Star'.

3 Alfred Dreyfus, a Jewish army captain, was accused – unjustly, as it later turned out – of espionage for the German Reich and convicted of treason in 1894 and again in 1899. His conviction sparked fierce protests and divided French society. The affair is considered as a culmination of French antisemitism. Dreyfus was exonerated and rehabilitated in 1906.

4 This refers to France's defeat in June 1940.

5 The yellow star was not introduced in the unoccupied zone.

Honestly, what are the French thinking? Have they forgotten the appalling misdeeds of international Jewry? You only need to think back a few years! Have they forgotten that the spectre of Bolshevism has hovered over humanity for the last 25 years, and that it is the Jews who keep it there? In Russia, the leaders of the first Soviet government were Jews, and they have not stopped multiplying. And when the revolution unleashed its force in Germany, it was led by two Jews: Karl Liebknecht and Rosa Luxemburg, who were supported by a third Jew in Bavaria: Kurt Eisner. In Hungary, the Jew Béla Kun was one of the most sinister executioners ever to horrify humanity, piling torture on top of assassinations and ruins. In Spain, the Jew Rosenfeld took over the leadership of the revolutionaries, and when it came to torturing, he brought in Latvian and Russian Jews to teach the reds of Barcelona how to do it. In France, while they were waiting to do the same, the Jews had to be content with stripping the French of their savings and occupying posts on government committees to prepare for the moment when they would seize power. From Stavisky[6] to Léon Blum,[7] the racial chain was unbroken; all were at their posts, ready to rob France. The bankers were Jews, the cocaine traffickers were Jews, the ministerial attachés were Jews, the cinema directors were Jews, the newspaper owners were Jews, the professors and doctors were Jews … They controlled everything: money, vice, power, propaganda, influence, and the youth. You had to be called Lévy at the very least if you wanted to get anywhere, and it was clear that Bloch was a step ahead of Durand when it came to being awarded the Légion d'honneur. They all thundered at political meetings and whispered in the salons. And Léon Blum, who played the aesthete among princesses, would go in shirtsleeves to show off at the Vel d'Hiv[8] just after leaving a dinner party where pretty women had swooned over his intelligence and education.

The Jews came up with the idea of the Front Popu[9] as a transition that would take the French on the road to Bolshevism. Everything, right down to this uncouth abbreviation,[10] bore the mark of the degradation to which we were being condemned. First it was: 'Put Blum in power!', then: 'Let Blum get down to business!', but what it meant was: 'Make way for the Jews!' With great discipline, the simple-minded electorate fell in line, and we were well served. We got Blum. We got Mendès-France.[11] We got Zay.[12] We

6 Alexandre Stavisky (1886–1934), banker; protagonist in a corruption scandal which caused turmoil in France's domestic politics in 1934.

7 Léon Blum (1872–1950), lawyer and politician; France's first socialist and first Jewish prime minister, 1936–1937 and March–April 1938; indicted by the Vichy government on charges of war guilt, 1940; tried in 1942; imprisoned in Buchenwald by the German occupation government; liberated by Allied troops, May 1945; headed the month-long interim French administration, Dec. 1946; retired from public life in 1947.

8 Vélodrome d'Hiver, sports stadium in Paris. It was used as a temporary detention centre for Jews arrested in the roundups of 16 and 17 July 1942: see Docs. 241, 246, 259, and 265.

9 This refers to the Front Populaire, the alliance between the socialists (SFIO), the communists (PCF), and the Parti Radical that won the French elections in 1936; the SFIO and the Parti Radical subsequently formed the first Popular Front government.

10 The abbreviation Front Popu was sometimes used by the French Right.

11 Pierre Mendès-France (1907–1982), politician; delegate of the Parti Radical, 1932–1940; French prime minister, 1954–1955.

12 Jean Zay (1904–1944), politician; delegate of the Parti Radical, 1932–1940; minister of education, 1936–1939; murdered by the Milice française, the Vichy regime's paramilitary force.

got Mandel.[13] This meant war, the obligatory prelude to defeat and revolution. We got war. We got defeat. Did anyone really think that these people would abdicate and give up after achieving such successes? Do the French really have nothing better to do than to pity those who are the cause of disasters everywhere?

Let them keep their pity for those who deserve it and who have been forgotten. Yes, indeed! We have our dead, our poor dead, who died needlessly in the war and during the exodus;[14] we have the countless victims piling up on our soil and that of our empire due to the cowardice and savagery of the British; we have the starvation victims of Djibouti, the prisoners of French Equatorial Africa and South Africa;[15] we have our prisoners; we have thousands of compatriots who are suffering from hunger and from being separated from their homes and families; we have a full share of distress and suffering, enough to use up all the tears and all the pity in the world. And the French, forgetful of these prisoners and of these dead, feel sorry for the Jews who have to wear the yellow star in Paris! Weighed down with victims, they feel sorry for the executioners. This is the height of confusion, stupidity, and thoughtlessness.

Unfortunate? The Jews? But even in the occupied zone, they strut about and flaunt themselves with that incurable pride, drawing on what others would take as humiliation to glorify themselves. In the unoccupied zone, they run around the countryside to secure food, first for themselves, and then for the black market. Unfortunate? Those people who fill the café terraces in Marseilles, in Toulouse, in Nice, in Montauban? I will stop there. Hundreds of readers will write to us tomorrow, saying: Do you think there are fewer of them where we are? And so?

So, let's talk about something else, if you will. There is, alas, enough real grief; there are enough urgent worries which require our pity and our care. We must not waste our time pitying people who do not need pity and who are the source of all our suffering. The French have to rebuild everything. This is not the time to lean out the window of a ruined house to listen tearfully to the organ grinder playing a new 'Romance of the Star' among the rubble and ruins in the courtyard. Do not waste your money. Because the organ grinder is not really blind, and he has not even been naturalized.

Philippe *Henriot*[16]

13 Georges Mandel (1885–1944), politician; long-term delegate of the moderate right; served as a minister several times; last minister of the interior under the Third Republic; murdered by the Milice française.

14 This refers to the mass flight of French civilians before the advancing German troops in 1940.

15 This refers to actions taken by the British against the French colony in French Somaliland, blockaded in summer 1941; French prisoners of war were held in the Congo following the surrender of Vichy troops in Gabon in November 1940.

16 Philippe Henriot (1889–1944), teacher and essayist; member of the Chamber of Deputies, 1932–1940; lived in the unoccupied zone of France from 1940; supported collaboration with Germany; Radio Vichy broadcaster from Feb. 1941; joined the Milice française in March 1943; served as a propagandist for the Vichy regime; appointed secretary of state for information and propaganda in Vichy in Jan. 1944; murdered by the French Resistance in 1944.

DOC. 254

On 8 August 1942 Karl Heinz Reinsberg writes a letter of farewell to his brother from Les Milles camp[1]

Handwritten letter from Karl Heinz Reinsberg,[2] Les Milles camp, to his brother Ernst,[3] dated 8 August 1942

Dear Erni,

Sent you a telegram yesterday that we are in the greatest danger, yet everything seems to be too late because everyone is expecting a deportation within the next forty-eight hours. What has happened here is unprecedented in world history, but it must not go unpunished, the punishment will have to come one day. Children, women, and men locked up together, and a gendarme with a rifle every ten metres. It is terrible what heartbreaking scenes have already taken place, but the worst is yet to come when the deportation starts. Ulla[4] is one of the few women who are being spared […],[5] but if it should start, I […][6] not do anything differently. I want to tell you now that I have put all our large luggage in storage at *Francceschi*, 89 boulevard Plombières, Marseilles, and you will be able to reclaim it there later, because in my opinion it is very doubtful whether we will see each other again. There is a one in a hundred chance. The most tragic thing about the whole business is the following: eight days ago I had news from Mother[7] that she wanted to visit us, and a suitcase that belongs to her has already arrived; she is coming […][8] to a fine place.

I will write to her today, and I hope it will be in time. Just imagine the poor woman was caught up in this business as well. She wants to come here precisely on account of just such an operation. You can well imagine the state the poor people here are in. It is the greatest disappointment of my life. I, who had always thought so highly of the French, their sense of honour, their concepts of liberty, etc., and it has all been dragged through the dirt like this. One ought to think it was just a dream, but unfortunately it is all bitter

1 Sammlung Mahn- und Gedenkstätte Düsseldorf, GED-31-552–300. This document has been translated from German.

2 Karl Heinz Reinsberg (b. 1914), retailer; emigrated from Düsseldorf to Belgium in 1936; trained as a furrier in Liège; imprisoned in Gurs camp from May 1940, later at Les Milles; transferred to Drancy on 13 August 1942, and deported four days later to Auschwitz, where he is thought to have perished.

3 Ernst Reinsberg (1917–2003), physician; from 1936 studied in Scotland, where he was interned as an 'enemy alien' in 1940; subsequently taken to Canada and held in internment camps until April 1941; later continued his studies in Britain and became an ear, nose, and throat specialist.

4 Ursula Reinsberg, née Devries (b. 1919); emigrated from Duisburg to Belgium in 1937; married Karl Heinz Reinsberg in 1938; fled to France in 1940; interned at Gurs, then Les Milles; transferred to Drancy in August 1942; on 17 August 1942 deported with her husband to Auschwitz, where she is thought to have perished.

5 Illegible, probably: 'from deportation'.

6 Three words are illegible.

7 Martha Reinsberg, née Hermanns (1890–1980), housewife; fled to Brussels in 1937 following the violent death of her husband, Albert, a fur trader; in 1940 fled to the south of France, where she survived the war in hiding; emigrated to Israel in 1945; returned to Düsseldorf in the late 1950s.

8 Illegible.

truth. Maybe we will see each other once again in this world after all. Tell Kurt,[9] Ilse,[10] etc. about our fate. If Kurt had honestly wanted it, we would already have been in safety long ago, but over there they never wanted to acknowledge the danger in which we have always been here. They bear a great deal of the blame for our misfortune. May God protect you, dear Erni, from all misfortune. In the hope that we will see each other once again in better circumstances after all, I embrace you most affectionately, your brother

Karl Heinz

DOC. 255

In a letter from Poitiers internment camp dated 9 August 1942, Anna Goldberg tries to comfort her mother and asks for supply parcels[1]

Letter from Anna Goldberg,[2] Poitiers internment camp,[3] to her mother,[4] 64 boulevard Ménilmontant, Paris 20, dated 9 August 1942 (copy).

Sunday – morning

Dear Maman,

I am no longer in Angoulême, but in Poitiers. This is a camp where we are doing well. The Red Cross looks after it. We eat well, and we live in barracks. Unfortunately we are not going to stay here for more than a few days.

Maman, what hurts me the most is not what is going to happen to me. I am young, I will find a way out, it is only a question of time and you will be able to help me with parcels. What tortures me is the sense that you are suffering even more than me. You must not think that it is your fault that I am here. Things happen as God wills them, and that is how it is. You must not have any regrets. This was my destiny, and that is all. You[5] went through it, and thousands of others did as well, and me too. I will get out one day. I am young and in good health, and if I suffer for a year or two, I will get over it afterwards and that is all. I have never once cried for myself since I was arrested. I cry when

9 Kurt's identity has not been established.

10 Ilse Guttmann, née Reinsberg (1911–1991); sister of Karl Heinz Reinsberg; born in Brussels; married Dr Ernst Guttmann, a dentist from Breslau, in 1932; emigrated to Palestine in 1933; returned to Germany in the late 1950s with Martha Reinsberg.

1 YVA, O. 9/255. This document has been translated from French.

2 Anna Helene Goldberg (b. 1920), student; arrested in Angoulême when trying to enter the unoccupied zone; interned in Poitiers camp; transferred to Drancy in early Sept. 1942; on 18 Sept. 1942 deported from Drancy to Auschwitz, where she perished.

3 Poitiers internment camp, also known as the Camp de la route de Limoges, had been set up to house republican refugees from Spain in 1939, but then mostly used to intern Roma people. From 1941 the camp was increasingly used to intern Jews who had been arrested in the Poitou-Charentes region.

4 Esther Goldberg, née Herzog (1892–1976), housewife; born in Łomża (Congress Poland); emigrated to France before 1914; mother of Rosalie and Anna; later emigrated to Israel; died in Jerusalem.

5 During the First World War, Anna Goldberg's parents had been interned in a French camp for enemy aliens in Vire (Normandy). Anna's father was from Mielec (Galicia).

I think that you are unhappy because you tell yourself that it is your fault, that I did not want to go, etc. … More than anything, you must not harbour any regrets. It is done, and that is that. It would be easier for me if you could assure me that you have no remorse,[6] that you regret nothing. It is when you tell me that you will be sad and unhappy that I begin to weep; if you do not, I am fine. So if you forget all of that and stop having regrets, I will not be unhappy any more. Now here is what you can do: I do not know how long I will be staying here. Here, I want for nothing. Even so, I would like you to send me parcels. One can send two per month. There are no coupons or weight limits. As I do not really need anything here, I would like to have things which will keep, to create a little reserve for later – for example: sugar, chocolate, biscuits, salted butter. Anything of this sort you can find and spare. I know that this will be difficult for you. Just do what you can.

I would also like you to send me my blue suitcase (if you do not have another even smaller one), my winter coat (the navy blue one), some underwear, a warm jacket, woollen socks, a scarf and gloves, if possible in a suitcase that can be closed (and locked, if possible). All that is for later, but I would like to have these things with me. Send what you have, do not buy anything, that would be too difficult, I will make do with whatever you send. I would also like a pencil, stationery, stamps, another pen, a knife or pocket knife, a spoon, a fork, a tin bowl or something made of aluminium that I can eat and drink out of. We have some here, but they belong to the camp. I need to be prepared for later. If you can do it, I would also like to have some money transferred to me (the maximum allowed is 300 francs). Please send all of this to me as soon as possible, before I leave here, because I do not know when and how I will be able to receive parcels afterwards. Send all of this in one or two parcels, whichever you prefer (there is no weight limit). As one can receive two parcels per month, I would like to get them as long as I am still here.

For now, I thankfully have some linen and soap. It was a good thing I brought all of that. I have a towel – do send me some shoes as well. We can correspond as much as we want. I will write to you again on Tuesday, because this letter will be sent out tomorrow. Write a lot to me, give me all the news of Rosette.[7] If there are any postcards from her to me, you can send them to me in an envelope, I think that that will get through. I also want you to send me a Bible, the one in two volumes in French. It is a bit heavy, but never mind.

For the time being, we are very happy here, and you do not need to worry about me. Write to me often, and don't be sad. Do not go to too much trouble with the parcels. All the more because you don't have any bread rationing cards, and me neither. We must have hope. Tell me all about how things are.

Big hug,

Nana

6 Anna Goldberg's mother had wanted to send her daughter to stay with relatives in Nice.

7 Anna's sister Rosalie (b. 1916) had recently left France with her husband, Aaron, and wanted to get to England via Senegal.

DOC. 256

On 11 August 1942 the prefecture in Pau reports to the French Police Directorate on the first transports of Jews interned in Gurs[1]

Report no. 1358 CAB S.G.) from the prefect of the Basses-Pyrénées département, unsigned (the prefect),[2] Pau, to the director general of the French Police (section 9),[3] Vichy, dated 11 August 1942 (copy).[4]

Re: transports of 6 and 8 August, departing from Gurs camp for Chalon-sur-Saône.
Reference: instructions from Mr de *Quirielle*, head of section 9, made both verbally and over the telephone, and your telegrams of 29 July 1942, 30 July, and 1 August 1942.[5]

I am writing to inform you that I ordered, in accordance with the conditions set out in your instructions quoted above, the formation and departure of two transports from *Gurs* camp, which comprised:

- 1,004 inmates on 6 August
- 600 inmates on 8 August.

The lists were drawn up with the utmost care. Only persons who did not belong to one of the groups who were exempt from being taken away were included.

The material organization of the transports and the necessary provisions only presented minor difficulties which were solved within the time required. The material that was sent from *Septfonds* camp[6] (jugs and sanitary pails) did not arrive, and so I requisitioned the necessary utensils from the stock for the refugees. I will of course try to get them back once the shipment from *Septfonds* camp arrives.

As for the provisions, I was able not only to provide each inmate with two days of rations (including fruit), but also to secure an additional reserve that should last for three days of travel for each transport.

I also need to mention the significant contribution from the aid organizations and particularly from the *Quakers*.[7]

The bus and lorry service for the 34 kilometre journey between *Gurs* and the train station in *Oloron* worked perfectly. The turnaround of the vehicles was organized so that all of the inmates could be transported in the most perfect order, each lorry corresponding to one railway car.

The two transports could thus leave *Oloron* on time at 8.55 a.m. as per your instructions.

1 AN, F7, ed. 15 088. This document has been translated from French.
2 Emile Ducommun.
3 Henri Cado.
4 The original contains handwritten underlining. This document was sent to the regional prefect and the police headquarters in Toulouse for information.
5 See Doc. 249. Both telegrams dated 30 July and 1 August 1942 were about the practical implementation of the transports.
6 Septfonds camp was established in 1939 for refugees from the Spanish Civil War. It was located in the Tarn-et-Garonne département.
7 A number of aid organizations worked in the internment camps of the southern zone with the permission of the French authorities. Apart from the Quakers (officially the American Friends Service Committee), organizations such as Cimade, Secours suisse, Service social d'aide aux émigrants, HICEM, OSE, ORT, and Amitié chrétienne were active in Gurs.

The organization of the first transport was relatively easy. The preliminary measures taken, such as drawing up the lists, as well as assembling the inmates and holding roll calls, made the loading much easier. I only have to note that the transport *leader* found it necessary to place much of the luggage inside the railway cars that held the inmates. This was because the SNCF had only made two luggage cars available to me instead of the three that had been promised.

No incident worth mentioning occurred during the first transport.

This was not the case when it came to preparing the second transport and getting it under way.

While the foreigners who left on 6 August were certain they would be transferred to another camp in the free zone, those who left on 8 August collectively behaved as if they had been tipped off by foreign radio broadcasts, which, as you know, had announced the date, time, and destination of the transports. It must also be noted that the Swiss newspaper *Israelitisches Wochenblatt*[8] also mentioned the departure of this transport in its 24 July issue. This paper had been confiscated by the camp's censors.

Despite all efforts, quite a few of the inmates were willing to try anything in order to escape from the transport. The roll call showed that 42 prisoners were missing. They had escaped in the following ways:

- 23 inmates had hidden in the outlying buildings of the camp and were found only after the transport had left. They were put in the penal section.
- 4 people had also hidden but were found in time to be put on the transport.
- 7 people escaped and have not yet been found.
- 6 people tried at the moment of departure to take their own lives; one of them could still be put on the transport.

The camp leadership was therefore forced to significantly modify the transport list, which had already been altered, namely by removing all of those who worked with the Quakers and the rabbis.[9] The blanks thus created were filled by putting back on the list several inmates whose names had been taken off the original list (in accordance with your telegram no. 11 604),[10] and by putting the volunteers on it whose requests[11] could not be fulfilled up to that moment.

In spite of these incidents, inmates were added to make up the required 600 people and the transport could leave Oloron train station at 8.55 a.m. precisely.

Please find attached the list of names of the foreigners who were on the 6 August transport. I will send you the same list for the second transport very soon, along with the reports from the commanders of the guard squads.

I believe I should also point out the efforts of Chief Superintendent *Kayser*, the commandant of *Gurs* camp, who performed admirably under the circumstances. Through-

8 German-language Jewish weekly which was published between 1901 and 2001 by Marx in Zurich. It served as the central publication of the Jewish community in Switzerland.

9 Jewish and non-Jewish aid organizations, which looked after the inmates, were involved in drawing up the lists: see Doc. 257 and Introduction, pp. 71–72.

10 In his telegram no. 11 604, dated 8 August 1942, Cado ordered that if the designated number of Jews to be handed over could not be achieved, the list was to be supplemented with the 'least important persons' from the original list, whose names had at that point been deleted (see footnote 5 above).

11 Some categories of prisoners were exempt from the transport but could opt to leave with parents or relatives: see Doc. 249, point 2.

out these important and delicate operations he showed all of the necessary firmness, but also a good deal of tact and understanding. His entire team assisted him with intelligence and dedication, most notably Superintendent *Ants*.[12]

All of the personnel performed their duty, whether they were civilian guards, management, members of the medical service, or nurses.

The gendarmerie and the Mobile Reserve Group from Navarre, whose first mission this was, were equally up to the task.

Nevertheless, I have to draw your attention to the special report I sent you today. This concerns Doctor *Guvigny*, assistant to the chief physician, on whom it would appear necessary to impose disciplinary sanctions for a serious matter which is unrelated to the operations of 6 and 8 August.[13]

The Prefect

DOC. 257
Pastor Henri Manen describes the situation of the inmates in Les Milles camp between 6 and 12 August 1942[1]

Report by Henri Manen,[2] typescript marked 'do not publish', Aix-en-Provence, undated[3]

In the depths of the abyss[4]

Thursday, 6 August: At the grocer's I hear that 'people from the camp are being handed over to the Boche'.[5] I do not attach much importance to what seems to me to be a fabrication, because if anything serious had occurred, would I not have been warned, either by the camp leadership, the General Chaplaincy, or the French Protestant Federation?[6] On Sunday my parishioners from the camp were at the service and did not say anything to me. Nevertheless, that afternoon one of my parishioners, whom I met in town, confirms to me that this is a sweeping measure aimed at all the internment camps. I leave immediately for the camp.

First police barriers at the level crossing. Very interesting conversation with a dozen police officers regarding the inmates and our views on human, national, and spiritual

12 Correctly: Albert Antz, police inspector.

13 In the file. The doctor had a relationship with a Jewish woman due to be included on a transport.

1 SHPF, DVP 119. Published in Henri Manen, *Au fond de l'abîme: Journal du Camp des Milles*, ed. Philippe Joutard (Maisons-Laffitte: Éditions Ampelos, 2013). This document has been translated from French.

2 Henri Manen (1900–1975), theologian and pastor; pastor in Mulhouse from 1937; Protestant chaplain in Aix-en-Provence and, on his own initiative, in Les Milles camp from 1940; assisted interned prisoners to escape to Saint-Privat-de-Vallongue (Cevennes) in August 1942; honoured together with his wife, Alice, as Righteous Among the Nations by Yad Vashem in 1986.

3 The report was written between 9 and 13 August 1942 and sent to pastors Boegner (Nîmes) and Freudenberg (Geneva) a few days later.

4 Initially the diary was titled 'Du fond de l'abîme' ('From the depths of the abyss'), an allusion to Psalm 130 ('Out of the depths have I cried unto thee, oh Lord!'). Manen later changed it to 'Au fond de l'abîme' ('In the depths of the abyss').

5 French pejorative term for the Germans that had been in use since around the time of the First World War.

6 The Fédération protestante de France (FPF) was founded in 1905 as the central organization for French Protestants. Pastor Marc Boegner was its president from 1929 to 1961.

questions. General agreement with this group of policemen, with whom I chat for quite a long time while waiting for a freight train to leave and open the way. I arrive at the camp. The commander of the police unit refuses to let me enter. I appeal to the camp director, who is busy and says he will see me shortly. While waiting, I manage to enter the courtyard discreetly. One of my parishioners, Mr F.,[7] runs over and throws himself into my arms in a touching show of joy. He briefly gives me some information: he arrived at the camp on Monday, brought in from a work detail who were not as lucky as those from X[8] (at X the officer informed them in time of the fate that awaited them, so that they could escape). But we are spotted, and a policeman comes over to remind me that I do not have permission to enter the camp. He accompanies me to a little waiting room, where he asks me to sit … I wait … Finally I am before the camp director.[9] He sadly and politely informs me that it is impossible for him to let me enter the camp. I insist. He refuses again. I stress that this is the first time in my ministry that I have not been allowed to provide spiritual support to people who are suffering. Under the 'ancien régime'[10] I had been a prison chaplain, a chaplain at asylums and for mental patients, and never once encountered the slightest hindrance. Today, I must follow my vocation as a minister of God and of the Church. The director hides himself behind orders from higher up.[11] I refuse to leave. I sympathize with the director's awkward situation. We agree to make a telephone call to police headquarters. The same prohibition, the same argument, the same refusal. He promises to refer it again, and to give me an answer the next day by telephone. To be fair, it was quite late. I was supposed to receive the answer at noon the next day, Friday, which would allow me to enter the camp from Saturday morning.

I leave the director's office – and enter the camp. I find Mr F. again; he quickly brings me up to date on several people, tells me about the heavy, oppressive atmosphere of the camp, about the agony of waiting that everybody at the camp has to endure, now that they are deprived of all contact with the outside world and guarded by a formidable police force. This anxiety really makes itself visible on all the faces I see.

Back home, I write to President B.[12] to inform him about what I know of the situation at the camp, and in particular about the ban on entering the camp under which I find myself at the moment.

Friday, 7 August: Early in the morning I write to Pastor T.,[13] informing him of the steps I am taking, and ask him for any information or suggestions. I telephone the YMCA. We arrange that in the afternoon my wife[14] will go to see Mr L.,[15] who will be back from Vichy. At 12.30 I receive a telephone call from the camp director, who informs me on

7 Hans Fraenkel (1888–1971), journalist; converted from Judaism to Lutheranism in 1897; Italy correspondent for the conservative German daily *Deutsche Allgemeine Zeitung*, 1924–1933; emigrated to Switzerland after the war.
8 Most likely Foreign Labourer Group (GTE) 104 at Salin de Giraud, a village west of Arles.
9 Robert Maulavé.
10 This term normally refers to the pre-revolutionary monarchy in France, but is used here to denote the Third Republic, i.e. France before the German invasion.
11 See Doc. 249.
12 Marc Boegner (1881–1970), theologian and pastor; pastor in Passy (Paris), 1918–1954; president of the FPF, 1929–1961; member of the Comité de Nîmes from Nov. 1940; member of the Vichy government's National Council from 1941.

behalf of the police superintendent[16] that I will be able to enter the camp freely as of the next morning. At 2 p.m., Mr B[oegner] telephones to bring me up to date on the steps he took at Vichy. He tells me there is nothing to be done. In addition, the entry ban for the camps, of which I was the object, has affected all the chaplains of all religious denominations.[17]

Upon her return, my wife gives me a decidedly pessimistic account of her meeting. Nothing can be done in Vichy; perhaps pastoral action might obtain some results locally. In three camps, Christians[18] were not put on the lists of those due to leave.

Saturday, 8 August: I am at the camp at 8 a.m. sharp. I gather my parishioners together. Right from the first contact I am struck by a strong impression, which is confirmed over and over again during these terrible days, not only in observing my parishioners, but also in the attitude of the inmates in general. First of all, there is the piercing terror of the spectre of deportation. Then, in spite of this, there is the courage with which each person looks their own fate in the face. Finally, there is the love they all continually show one another – each one trying to lessen the burden of his brother's cross and trying to help save whoever he can. I appeal to the camp director, who tells me that he himself cannot do anything for the Christian community – Protestants or Catholics. We decide to request a meeting with the police superintendent at …[19]

I call on the inmate who is the lay leader of the Catholic community in the camp.[20] I tell him of my wish to have a joint Christian initiative. He is very grateful and asks me to go and see the priest,[21] who has not yet been seen at the camp. I take myself to the rectory, and I am very well received by the priest, who is in a very awkward position on account of the absence of orders from his superiors and in principle approves of the steps to be taken, but does not think that he himself will be able to come to … during the day because of the obligations of his ministry. Back home, I request a meeting for the afternoon. I telephone the priest. He cannot accompany me, but asks me to speak on his behalf as well as my own.

In …, I wait in the police headquarters office. Finally … I am received. I explain the attitude of the Christian Church in detail: all who suffer and are persecuted have the right to our sympathy and our aid, but the 'baptized' are limbs of the body of Christ, and we cannot allow these to be torn off; we cannot accept the idea that they could be sent to the ghetto. I hand over the list of my parishioners. I demand all of them, without

13 Pierre-Charles Toureille (1900–1976), pastor; in charge of chaplaincy for Protestant foreigners in France at the FPF.

14 Alice Manen, née Bertrand (1903–2001).

15 Donald A. Lowrie (1889–1974); representative of the YMCA in France; chairman of the Comité de Nîmes from 1940; met with Pétain on 6 August 1942, when Pétain told him he regretted the deportations but there was nothing he could do about them.

16 Maurice Rodellec du Porzic (1894–1947), naval officer; police superintendent in Marseilles; responsible for rounding up Jews and handing them over to the German occupation authorities.

17 In marked contrast to the occupied zone, religious aid organizations from various denominations were allowed to visit the internment camps in the southern zone: see Doc. 256, fn. 7.

18 People who converted from Judaism to various Christian denominations.

19 Here and below: ellipsis and sentence break as in the original.

20 Hans Schwann, journalist and writer.

21 The camp's Catholic chaplain.

exception [be exempted from deportation]. I sense that in the other camps the Christians have not yet been sent away. In the name of the priest and in my own name, I demand all the Christians in the camp [be retained]. The answer I receive is: 1) that the measures taken in favour of Christians in some of the camps were possible because those camps had to hand over a smaller percentage than ours, and that no exceptions are to be made in principle, according to what they've been told; 2) that this is an ethnic regrouping measure, and however hard it may be, it is still in the interest of France … 3) that I can expect no promises whatsoever. I get home late from M…, dismayed by this meeting.

Sunday 9 August: I am at the camp at 8 a.m. Despair. The day before, I had announced on behalf of M. L. that children under the age of 18 whose parents would have to leave could be left in the care of the YMCA, which would endeavour to have them sent to America. I had asked the leader of the group to talk to the parents and insist that they all agree to the separation in the interests of their children. There was no need to insist. To the families, this was a great relief and a weight off of their minds. However, on Saturday evening an order was issued which annulled this arrangement. (This order would again be overturned.)[22]

We assemble for the service in the little office of the Quakers, where their admirable activity has continued uninterrupted day and night. The reality of the Church … The reality of prayer … The reality of God … 'How much then is a man better than a sheep?'[23] I repeat this to them as a message from God. To men, they are less than cattle, but to God, they are worth infinitely more than anything else. And because they are under the sign of the cross, they are God's treasure and the Church's treasure. In fragile earthly vessels, they carefully carry the precious treasure of the saints and the martyrs in order to obtain the crown of glory one day … Our communion is intense – I would even say it is almost peaceful. I meet with my parishioners individually. Their steadfastness is their faith. One of them says to me: 'Write to my wife and tell her that I left with confidence in God.' In pain, hearts will open up. In all of this distress, there is nothing base or vile at all. I have noticed this in all the inmates with whom I have passed this nightmarish week. Their dignity, their humanity, their nobility of spirit. Discussion with the camp director: we still don't know who will be on the list.

Monday 10 August: The anguish has reached its peak! The departure of the children under 18, who will be sent to America, is an unforgettable spectacle. Terrible scenes of separation. A tall, handsome boy of 17 or 18 stands between his father and his mother and embraces his mother, putting his arms around her neck. He does not cry. But he leans alternately to one and the other, rubbing his face against theirs, slowly and gently, with all the tenderness in the world. Not a word. The father and the mother cry incessantly, so full of anxiety. This goes on and on. No one speaks. Finally the buses set off. From the oldest to the youngest, everyone is in tears. Not a cry, not a gesture. Only tense faces wanting to behold something in an instant that will last an eternity. Around me the police officers' faces are

22 There were only 11 children among the 3,429 prisoners who were taken to Drancy between 9 and 14 August 1942 on four trains from the camps at Gurs, Récébédou, Noé, Le Vernet, Rivesaltes, and Les Milles.

23 Matthew 12:12a (KJV).

pale. One of them tells me the next day: 'I was in the colonial army. I was in China; I've seen massacres, war, and famine. I've never yet seen anything as horrible as that!' For the moment, no one can speak or move. The bus has disappeared. Finally, a mother falls down, writhing on the ground in a nervous collapse. All day, the rabbi, two French Jewish gentlemen, and myself are with the police superintendent, pleading the case of these unfortunate people, whose departure seems to us worse than a death sentence.

Here are among others some cases of Protestants whom I endeavoured to wrest from this atrocious fate.[24]

G.,[25] a captain in the merchant navy. Shipped his vessel along the coasts during the war on behalf of the Netherlands, Britain, and France. His father and his two brothers were shot by the Nazis as enemies of the Third Reich. He is therefore under no illusion. I demand he be pardoned and am refused. He is already with those scheduled for departure when I have to inform him that there is nothing anyone can do. He looks at me courageously and thanks me.

X.,[26] a former public prosecutor from one of the large German cities. Rigorously argued his cases in the first trials against the Nazis. Sentenced to death in Germany. Very distinguished man. His wife,[27] whose love and serenity never stop shining in this darkness, was free but chose to join her husband in the camp and volunteered to become a prisoner to share her husband's fate, however hard it may be. Their son is a French soldier in the Foreign Legion.[28] Initially I have to accept a refusal in their case, which I have to communicate to them. She takes the blow admirably, finding the strength to comfort her husband … and to smile at him. He picks himself up, withdraws into himself – and only asks me if I could give them Communion before their departure. I go back to the police superintendent's office and implore him again – stressing the fact that the couple's son is a French soldier. The superintendent demands proof. I go and ask the parents if they have a recent letter from their son. Alas, they burned everything because they did not want anything to be found among their papers that could be used to harass their child. She remembers that they might still have a certificate of their son's enrolment in the Legion, a certificate that they forgot to destroy. With their poor hands trembling feverishly, they rummage through their parcels and discover the life-saving document. I run off to show it to the police. After examining it, they explain to me that this certificate does not prove that the son is currently still in the Legion, as it is dated 7 March 1942. My protests are futile. We decide to send the Legion's commander in Saïda[29] an urgent telegram with a prepaid reply. The Xs do not leave until Wednesday, the day after tomorrow. We also telegraph Pastor T., the Legion's chaplain general, who met the young legionary last month, and we ask him to testify. A difficult wait all of

24 In the original: 'whom I wrested'.

25 Hans Goldschmidt (b. 1903); born in Breslau; on 14 August 1942 deported from Drancy to Auschwitz, where he perished.

26 Dr Franz Heinsheimer (b. 1879), lawyer; converted to Lutheranism in 1897; chief public prosecutor in Karlsruhe, 1927–1932; fled to France with his family in Oct. 1940; interned in Gurs, Récébédou, and Les Milles camps; escaped to Switzerland, most likely via Le Chambon-sur-Lignon.

27 Gertrud Heinsheimer, née West (b. 1885); came from a Lutheran family; married Franz Heinsheimer in 1905; mother of three sons.

28 Erich Heinsheimer (1910–1943), civil engineer; died in the battle for Tunisia.

29 City in north-western Algeria, where a regiment of the French Foreign Legion was stationed.

Tuesday and all of Wednesday. No answer. In spite of my efforts, the Xs are taken away on Wednesday at 4 p.m. and led to the train. As they pass me, he says heavily: 'It's over.' I answer: 'No!' He gets on the livestock wagon; there are 42 men and women per wagon, and only a small pail for them to relieve themselves. The doors are closed and locked with an iron bar. And still no answer to our telegram. One hour later I manage to get the police superintendent to agree that they will be released and will not have to leave. It takes almost another hour to get the wagon door open and take them back to the camp. They only have the strength to silently praise God. As I accompany them back to the camp, the head of the Catholic group, an inmate, Doctor Y.,[30] hugs me and weeps for joy. All of their friends surround Mr and Mrs X., comforting and congratulating them. An hour later, when everything has already ended happily for them, we receive the reply from Mr T[oureille], who had received our telegram very late.

Z., an Aryan, was not supposed to leave. As I'm walking through the ranks of a group of prisoners assembled for departure – I always carefully check the composition of each group in this way because I fear there might be some errors – I notice a face turned towards me with that expression of fear and pleading that I've had to see so many times during these days, because these unfortunates are no longer allowed to speak once they have been assigned to these ranks, not even to defend themselves if there has been a mistake. I walk up to him, quickly get some information, and run to the director's office, where I am immediately satisfied at the very last minute.

Y., a father, a mother, and a son who is 20 years old. Only the son is on the list of those who have to leave. I manage to make sure he can stay. The inmates are assembled in the courtyard from morning until evening, those leaving as well as those not leaving, while the police search the 'dormitories' for weapons or for people who have hidden. Indeed they discover a few inmates and some knives, saws, and axes, which are brought to the director's office while I am there. A little later, the chief rabbi[31] arrives. Important items were stolen from the inmates during the police searches. I cannot believe this and think that some of the inmates must have misplaced their things in the panic and confusion. But alas, it's later confirmed. The next day, the camp physician and trustworthy inmates tell me that 154 items, ranging from a gold watch to a pair of shoes, were stolen during the police search of the camp, while up until that point nothing had ever been stolen.

The transport is full. The Quakers go to the railway cars and hand out food. The train leaves on Tuesday at 8 a.m.

This brief account of the day would not be complete without mentioning that a man and a woman opened their veins and were taken to the hospital in a critical condition.

Tuesday, 11 August: Part of the morning is spent sending telegrams and making phone calls on behalf of various people. The rest of the day at the camp, licking our wounds, strengthening ourselves for tomorrow. Two attempted suicides.

30 Hans Schwann.

31 Israël Salzer (1904–1990), rabbi; chief rabbi of Marseilles, 1929–1975; chaplain at Les Milles camp; in hiding at the Miramas seminary from 1943; thereafter escaped to Switzerland. Chief Rabbi René Hirschler, who was in charge of chaplaincy in the internment camps, sent a rabbi to each of the camps threatened by the deportation operation. Their task was to put pressure on the prefectures and selection committees in order to keep the number of deported Jews as low as possible.

Wednesday, 12 August: Ten attempted suicides mark this horrifying day. From 10 a.m. the inmates are assembled in the courtyard under the scorching sun. In the afternoon, a policeman crosses the courtyard with a pitcher of water, which he takes to his comrades on guard duty. He walks up to a group of prisoners, and one of these unfortunates timidly holds out his metal cup with an imploring gesture and without saying a word. The policeman passes by on the other side[32] and insults him. Later the policemen in charge of the first group of those leaving on the train will not hesitate to maltreat them. The chief rabbi and I protest to the police superintendent, after which we do not witness anything similar again.

Some events I was involved in:

Mrs L., who was free, came to the camp to have herself imprisoned so she could leave with her son. However, he had managed to escape in the meantime. Mrs L., in spite of all my efforts, will have to leave on the train, a victim of her own motherly love.

Q.,[33] an important personality whose photograph appeared in the newspapers several times as a typical example of an enemy of the Third Reich. He must leave in spite of my entreaties. He takes this blow admirably and asks me to pass on his last wishes to his wife, without moving a muscle on his face. In the evening, I manage to have him taken off the list at the very last minute. He writes me a beautiful letter.

G.[34] On Monday I was promised that he would not leave. Driven by a premonition, his wife, who had just had an operation, presents herself at the camp to be interned and to leave with her husband. The camp director, who has always shown himself to be very humane, does not let her enter and sends her home with the assurance that her husband will not be leaving. But Wednesday at 4 p.m. a German general arrives. After his visit to the police superintendent, there is a veritable manhunt in the camp. A large group of men who were not supposed to be leaving is assembled to be 'screened', that is to say, to have their situation examined again. G. is among this number. He is 58 years old. Things go very badly for him. In the end, it took until 8 p.m. for him to learn that he will not be leaving. But the strain was too much for him, and he is completely shattered.

At 9.15 p.m. I save another prisoner, a young Lithuanian, by speaking up on his behalf. When he returns to the circle of his comrades, they pummel him with punches to express their joy. One of them runs over to me and shakes my hand, saying: 'Pastor, you are a very good man!' Another, as a sign of friendship, wants me to join the general fracas. I just barely manage to remind them of the sacred character of my presence and, with some confusion, to stop a fist a few millimetres from my ribs. Nevertheless, I do have some regrets about missing this friendly punch-up.

Night has come. It is terrifying! I timed it: a man's fate is now decided in the space of 30 seconds! Distress, humiliation, disgust, indignation, heartbreak, infinite sadness. Ruins, lives trampled upon, permanent stains, unforgiveable crimes.

32 This is an allusion to Luke 10:31: 'And by chance there came down a certain priest that way: and when he saw him, he passed by on the other side.'

33 Willi Wolfradt (1892–1988), art critic; wrote for Weimar Germany's cultural weekly *Die Weltbühne*; escaped to Switzerland in 1943.

34 Kurt Grelling (1886–1942), mathematician; member of the Berlin Society for Empirical Physics; deported from Drancy to Auschwitz with his wife in mid Sept. 1942.

The testimony of His Church beneath the cross in the camp of Les Milles: God has brought it forth in truth and it deserves to be set down in record.

The testimony of Israel: God made it great and moving. These people suffered with dignity, with verity, with humility and nobility.

Admirable example of women who voluntarily joined their husbands. A sense of fraternity and general mutual help. I felt an intimate, warm bond with the rabbi.

I must say that I saw these unfortunate brothers look after others as much as after themselves, rejoicing in the delivery of their friends and profoundly sympathizing with their misery, and I did not see them try to harm one another. However much of this was hideous and disgusting, it was not so with them.

One piece of statistical information: 36 Protestants were on the lists, seven departed.

DOC. 258

Le Petit Parisien, 15 August 1942: report on the arrests of Jews in the occupied and unoccupied zones of France[1]

4,000 stateless Jews have been arrested in the unoccupied zone

The first of the recent arrests carried out among the Jews of Paris and in the occupied zone only targeted stateless Jews. Several thousand individuals without clear nationality were taken to concentration camps and will soon be deported.

The same measures were applied in the unoccupied zone, where four thousand stateless Jews were apprehended by the French police. They joined those who had been arrested in Paris.

Those Jews who had hoped to escape the decrees that concern them by moving to the unoccupied zone will have to abandon such hopes. If they succeed in crossing the demarcation line, they will find themselves subject to the same regulations on the other side. They will be wanted by the police, and it will not take long for them to be reunited with others of their race in the occupied zone.

A number of French Jews, all significant traffickers in the black market, were arrested along with the stateless Jews. These kings of the black market were hoarding significant quantities of food supplies and all kinds of other products, like the infamous Korenbild, who hoarded 50,000 metres of fabric. It is worth noting that hundreds of fake identity cards were seized at one Jew's home, 3,100 kg of cotton at another's, and 1,500 kg of wool were found at a third's. All have been detained and will be put on trial before French courts.

These measures are only the first steps towards the elimination of all French or foreign Jews from the French community, because they are the organizers of the black market.[2]

1 *Le Petit Parisien*, 15 August 1942, front page. This document has been translated from French. The major French daily was published from 1876 to 1944. In 1942 it had a circulation of more than 500,000 copies (1940: 1,000,000).

2 The newspaper clipping is included in the Section IV J files of the Senior Commander of the Security Police and the SD: Mémorial de la Shoah, XXVb-129.

DOC. 259
A Jewish welfare worker describes the dramatic scenes at the deportation of children from Drancy in mid August 1942[1]

Handwritten account of events in the Pithiviers and Drancy camps between mid July and mid August 1942 by a Jewish welfare worker, unsigned, undated[2]

I was arrested on 16 July.[3] As I was without children, I was not taken to the Vélodrome d'Hiver, but directly to Drancy. Families with children under 16 were taken from the Vélodrome d'Hiver to Pithiviers and Beaune-la-Rolande.

When I arrived at Drancy, I found thousands of people on the stairwells and outdoors with their luggage and bedding in an indescribable mess. The screaming and crying were deafening.

Then they started assigning us to rooms. On the wall of one room I found the following inscription: 'Our dear friend Mojsze Bernstein was taken from here to be shot on 16 December 1941.' The gendarmes hadn't dared to erase this inscription.

Two days after the roundup, on 18 July, the deportations began. Because I was able to prove that I had worked as a social welfare assistant with the rue Amelot committee,[4] I was assigned a similar task in the camp, which saved me from being deported.

The children who were with us at Drancy were over 16 years old. The Germans considered them adults. The deportations were carried out with the well-known method: separating family members from each other. The men were separated from the women, the children from their parents.

These moments were terrifying, but above all I want to tell you about the deportation of children. To me, these moments are a spectre that haunts me every single moment of my life. I was released after two months of internment, and thus I did not have to endure the drawn-out misery that my compatriots had to go through, but what I saw severely affected my health and my mental state, and it is only due to my friends' devoted care that I have been feeling like myself again, though only for a few months now.

After they had deported everyone they could find at Drancy, they brought the adults from Pithiviers in, who told me about the separation from their very young children.

One morning the Pétainist police announced that all the women would have to leave and that they would have to leave their children behind. This order was met with resistance from the women. First, they cried and protested, and they offered active resistance by throwing bottles, rocks, and bricks at the policemen. They reacted so vigorously that the camp administration was forced to request police reinforcements and the German armed forces.

The German officer asked the women to go back to the barracks and to select a delegation. But the delegation was not received by the commander.

1 YVA, O.9/268. This document has been translated from French.
2 It can be deduced from the text that it was written in late 1942 or early 1943.
3 On the Paris roundups of 16/17 July 1942, see Docs. 241 and 245.
4 The Comité de la rue Amelot was founded in Paris in June 1940. It was a member organization of the General Union of French Jews (UGIF) and its purpose was to support immigrant and foreign Jews both secretly and through the UGIF.

The next day at 4 p.m., the Nazi murderers announced over the loudspeakers that the women would have to leave the camp two days later at 8 a.m., and that by 6 a.m. they would be separated from their children; each child was to have their bundle ready by that time.

All resistance proved futile. With bleeding hearts, the mothers were separated from their babies and began to meticulously prepare their paltry little bundles and mark them with the children's names.

The next day the babies were left all alone. In some families there were four or five children, aged between 3 and 8, and so the older children looked after the younger ones. The gendarmes attempted to calm the children, but they pushed them away indignantly.

In August, the children were taken to Drancy by train with 750 children per transport squeezed into sealed livestock wagons.[5] In the scorching heat, they travelled for 12 to 13 hours with only one bucket of water to quench their thirst and one sanitary pail per wagon. They arrived at Drancy sick and exhausted.

As you can imagine, the sanitary pails filled up quickly. A boy of 14 pulled up a floorboard in his wagon so that he could empty the bucket. When the train arrived, the Nazis noticed this deed, and the officer announced that if the criminal did not come forward of his own accord, four adult Jews would be shot. At this, the 14-year-old criminal stepped forward out of the ranks, head held high, looking the officer straight in the eye, and declared: 'It was me.' The officer could not bear the child's proud and dignified gaze; he turned away and did not punish the boy.

The children arrived at Drancy on one of those exceptionally hot August days. On that day, the heat was almost unbearable. The buses took them away at 2 p.m. and dropped them off at the infamous yard surrounded by barbed wire.

They were all exhausted, stricken with the heat and thirst, their faces were contorted with suffering. They let themselves fall to the ground and put their little heads against their bundles. Some had their belongings wrapped up in pillowcases, others in rucksacks. The sun was burning, the children had no strength left. And the children were kept there, exposed to the blazing sun, until the roll call at 6 p.m. Some of the little ones could not even remember their names any more, and as a result, 94 children were left nameless. They were given numbers, which were attached to their bodies.

The children's silent despair broke our hearts. The littlest ones held on to their older siblings as if to seek protection there.

Until the end of my days I will not be able to forget the scene where two little ones with blonde hair and bright blue eyes, three and four and a half years old, held on to each other, their little arms wrapped around one another as if for mutual protection. They were hunched over their little bundle that their mother's careful hand had prepared, her heart breaking. Their faces were blistered from the heat and their lips were dry from thirst. I sat down beside them, took them onto my lap, and attempted to comfort these two little broken hearts by pressing them to my chest. Their expressions, so full of gratitude, cut into me like a knife. Alas, in the evening I was separated from them, because the welfare assistants were not allowed to enter the stairwells of those being prepared for deportation.

5 The first train to Drancy left Pithiviers and Beaune-la-Rolande camps on 15 August 1942 with 1,054 children on board, accompanied by 5 men and 218 women.

The most terrifying moment was the morning of their deportation,[6] when they were woken up at 4.30 a.m. and gathered in the infamous yard surrounded by barbed wire, the yard where the searches took place. As they left, a cry went up: Maman, Maman. And seven hundred and fifty little children, even the babies, their legs unable to support them, cried and called out to their dearest, sweetest Maman!

All of Drancy was crying: Maman! Maman!

The babies were gathered together so that their luggage and clothing could be searched, and even their little bodies, to look for money. Hidden where?! On children between three and eight! They were pitilessly tortured in the yard until 8 a.m.; it was true torture. Ah, the criminals! The police inspectors, the Pétainist police,[7] not a hint of pity, no restraint at all!

And at 8 a.m. the buses took away 750 little ones accompanied by 250 women who were supposedly meant to look after them.[8]

Forever I will be haunted by one thought only: vengeance!

DOC. 260

On 24 August 1942 French resistance groups warn the Lyons police commissioner against carrying out the planned roundups of Jews[1]

Anonymous letter, signed The Resistance Movements, to Police Superintendent René Cussonac,[2] Lyons, dated 24 August 1942 (carbon copy)[3]

Police Superintendent,

Yesterday, mandated representatives of all the Resistance movements of the free zone met in your city.[4] They were informed of the measures put in place by your government

6 The first deportation train with 530 children under the age of 16 from Pithiviers camp left Le Bourget-Drancy station on 17 August 1942. Two days later, the transport reached Auschwitz, where the children were murdered upon arrival.

7 The searches before the deportation were carried out by the Police for Jewish Affairs (Police aux questions juives, PQJ) and, from summer 1942, its successor organization, the Section d'enquête et de contrôle (SEC).

8 Eichmann had approved Dannecker's and Röthke's requests for the deportation of the children from Pithiviers and Beaune-la-Rolande with the proviso that they had to be accompanied by a certain number of adults. Among the adults on board transport no. 20 on 17 August 1942 were 310 German Jews, including the Reinsbergs, who had been transferred to Drancy three days earlier from Les Milles camp. See Docs. 240 and 254.

1 AN, F60, vol. 1678. This document has been translated from French.

2 René Cussonac (1894–1944), police officer; senior official in the Lyons State Police, 1934–1938; worked for the military intelligence agency, 1939–1940; police commissioner in Lyons in 1942; regional police chief, 1943–1944; sentenced to death in Lyons in Nov. 1944 and executed.

3 Stamp: Commissariat national à l'information (National Commissariat for Information), Service L.T.E., Documentation, France Libre (Free France).

4 In 1942 the city of Lyons had become a major centre of the French resistance movements and the place where contacts with de Gaulle's Free France were made. At the beginning of the year, Jean Moulin had been sent to the region as de Gaulle's representative to bring the different movements together and put them under de Gaulle's control.

to deliver foreign Jews to the Germans and thus to repeat in Lyons, just as in Toulouse and in Marseilles, the abominable crime[5] which has dishonoured Paris.

We believe it is necessary to warn you that we have taken measures to make sure this operation does not go unnoticed, in spite of the instructions you received. You also need to know that, thanks to the powerful instruments we have at our disposal, we can now determine who is responsible for what in this terrible business. This will be useful once the time has come for scores to be settled. But in your case we need to explain matters further.

Your file is in no way ordinary, and we hold your decorations in the highest esteem.[6] The grounds for your five commendations, which were cited in 1918 when you were put forward for a Military Cross,[7] the magnificent circumstances under which you were wounded at the Somme and at Verdun, make it impossible to consider you a blind executor of the invader's orders. You know what is asked of you: to destroy families overnight, to forever deprive children of their parents, and even of their own identity; to collaborate in the extermination of those poor souls; and most unforgivably, to dishonour France.

Sir, some believe it is necessary to be sly and to make the worst compromises in order to save our unfortunate country. But when the ruse only helps the executioner, when it forces a French official, a French police force, to begin a process of persecution which will actually lead to the worst pogrom, this ruse only helps to sink the country further into moral bankruptcy. Your mentor, Professor Le *Chatelier*,[8] who so fittingly defined national integrity in terms of both spirit and morality, would not have spoken any differently to you. We have entered an era in Europe when the politics of the likes of Quisling, Hacha, and Antonescu have made hitherto morally untarnished countries into partners in crime.[9] This is worse than defeat.

We address this letter to the honest man that you are. A copy of this letter will be sent to the Commissariat of the Interior of the real government of this country, that of Fighting France.[10] Another copy of this letter will be handed to each of your colleagues who are likely to receive this shameful order. To them and to you we say: Beware! A written, explicit order will not protect you. All that Prefect Angeli[11] has is a vague tele-

5 This referred to the French police operation planned for 26 August 1942 against stateless Jews in the unoccupied zone.

6 Cussonac had been awarded six military decorations and the War Service Cross.

7 'Military Cross' in English in the original.

8 Presumably Alfred Le Chatelier (1855–1929), senior French colonial officer in Africa; professor at the Collège de France, 1902–1925. Le Chatelier was an important figure in propaganda efforts to mobilize the population in the First World War.

9 Vidkun Quisling (1887–1945), Norway's prime minister (1942–1945), stood for unconditional collaboration with the German occupiers. Emil Hácha (1872–1945), president of Czechoslovakia (1938–1939) and later president of the Protectorate of Bohemia and Moravia (1939–1945), agreed to let German troops enter Prague in March 1939. Ion Antonescu (1882–1946) was the prime minister and de facto leader of Romania (1940–1944) when the country was a vassal state of the German Reich.

10 The name 'Fighting France' (France Combattante) was first applied to the Comité national français, founded in London in 1941; from summer 1942 it was applied to the resistance movements that fought on the Allied side, under de Gaulle's leadership, against the German occupation. The committee viewed itself as the counterpart to the existing governments in exile established by other countries.

11 The prefect Alexandre Angeli was concurrently regional prefect of the Lyons region and thus in charge of the police stations in the region's ten départements: on Angeli, see also Doc. 271.

gram[12] signed by Cadot.[13] At every level of the hierarchy, officials are evading their responsibilities or hiding. But at the end of this chain of abasement is the agency which carries out the orders: the French police. The police will have to answer to their conscience first and foremost. They will forever lose the privilege of enforcing the law, the clear and generous French law, which they will violate in a night of crime.

We ask you not to consider this letter a threat. It does not make any requests. We were asked to turn to you and your staff, to speak to you as Frenchmen. That is what we have done. We will not do it again.

The French Resistance Movements

DOC. 261

On 28 August 1942 Elli Friedländer asks an acquaintance of the family to save her son[1]

Handwritten letter from Elli Friedländer,[2] Néris-les-Bains, to Mrs Macé de Lepinay,[3] Néris-les-Bains, dated 28 August 1942

Esteemed Madam, I am turning to you today in my great need and despair because I have learned through my husband[4] that you have sympathy for us and understand our sad fate.

By the grace of God, we managed to save our little lad,[5] at least for the moment. As Frau Frenkel[6] has already told you, dear Madam, he has somewhere to live for the moment. I would not like to leave him there because these days you can no longer place your trust in a Jewish institution.[7]

12 The upcoming round of arrests had been announced to the relevant regional prefects as early as 5 August 1942; the exact date was disclosed on 18 August with orders to maintain strict secrecy.
13 Correctly: Henri Cado.

1 The original is privately owned. Copy in IfZ-Archives, F 601. This document has been translated from German.
2 Elli Friedländer, née Glaser (b. 1905); daughter of a businessman in the textile trade from Rokytnice nad Jizerou (Bohemia); fled to Paris with her family in 1939, then in 1940 to Néris-les-Bains in the southern zone; after a failed escape attempt, she and her husband were handed over to the French gendarmerie in Sept. 1942 by the Swiss authorities; deported from Rivesaltes transit camp to Drancy, and from there a month later to Auschwitz, where she perished.
3 The de Lepinays were friends of the Friedländers, and Henri Friedländer taught Macé de Lepinay German. Macé de Lepinay saved Paul Friedländer's life by putting him into a Catholic school under an assumed name.
4 Hans Friedländer (1897–1942), lawyer; officer in the Austro-Hungarian army, 1914–1918; subsequently deputy manager of the Czechoslovak branch of a German insurance company; deported with his wife at the beginning of Nov. 1942 to Auschwitz, where he perished a month later.
5 Paul (later: Saul) Friedländer (b. 1932), historian; born in Prague; attended school in France; emigrated to Israel in 1948; studied in Paris and Geneva from 1955; appointed professor in 1969, taught at various universities in Jerusalem, Tel Aviv, Geneva, Los Angeles and elsewhere, 1969–2011. His publications include *Nazi Germany and the Jews* (2 vols., 1997 and 2007), and he won the Peace Prize of the German Book Trade in 2007 and the Pulitzer Prize in 2008.
6 Grete Frenkel, née Schindler (b. 1905), married to Walter Frenkel.
7 The Œuvre de secours aux enfants (OSE) ran several children's homes, including one at La Souterraine, where Paul Friedländer stayed only briefly because immediately after his arrival the French gendarmerie demanded that all children over the age of ten be handed over. See Doc. 279.

Now my great, heartfelt request to you, Madam, is for you to take in our child and bestow your patronage upon him until the end of this terrible war. I do not know how he can best be protected, but I have the utmost confidence in your wisdom and kindness.

My fate and that of my husband now lie in God's hands alone. If it is His will that we are to make it through, we will see the end of this terrible period. If we must perish, we have one piece of great good fortune: the knowledge that our beloved child has been saved.

The boy is very generously provided for with clothes, linen, and shoes, and there is enough money for him, too. I will leave everything with you should you have the indescribable kindness to say 'yes'.

Now another thing. I will need a place to live for my husband by the time he comes out, if they let him stay in hospital for a while,[8] and for me as well. We cannot live openly any more. I will only be able to stay a few more days where I am now. I think a *ferme*[9] in the vicinity of Néris would be the suitable thing. Ideally, they would have to be reliable people, but also possibly poor, so that we could offer them something materially for their services. It is important that it is in the vicinity of Néris because I have friends in Néris who would supply me with the necessary food.

Would it be possible for you, dear Madam, to make inquiries in this regard?

I do not know how I can thank all the people who have helped us in our great need. It is such an enormous consolation for us to find so much kindness and helpfulness among our friends.

Please forgive the appearance of this letter, my hands do not obey me any more.

I kiss your hands
and remain yours truly, E. F.

DOC. 262

On 30 August 1942 French Police Chief René Bousquet demands that the regional prefects in the unoccupied zone take harsher measures against foreign Jews[1]

Telegram from the secretary general of the French police (Section 9, no. 13 224/13.226. Me 30/8), signed Bousquet, to the French regional prefects in the unoccupied zone, dated 30 August 1942 (carbon copy)[2]

Drawing your attention to noticeable gap between number of foreign Israelites on registers and number arrested.[3] Continue and intensify ongoing police operations with all police and gendarmerie staff available. Resort to roundups, document checks, home visits, and searches in order to arrest individuals not exempted by provisions outlined in the

8 Hans Friedländer suffered from a serious stomach complaint.

9 French in the original: 'farm'.

1 AN, F7, vol. 15 088. Published in Klarsfeld, *Calendrier*, p. 957. This document has been translated from French.

2 The original contains handwritten notes. This document was sent to the prefects of the départements for information.

telegram of 18 August and more recent telephone communications[4] concerning combat veterans. Where applicable, inform your colleagues in the départements where those concerned were living of any arrests made.

After a transport has departed from your region, send individuals under arrest to Rivesaltes camp[5] in groups under guards. Further transports will be assembled after the prefect of the Montpellier region and the prefect of Perpignan have been informed that they are on their way.

Reminding you that only the Directorate General of the National Police can give orders concerning these operations. Keep me regularly updated on the results of operations and inform me of anything noteworthy.

DOC. 263

On 1 September 1942 Horst Ahnert from the section for Jewish affairs at the Office of the Senior Commander of the Security Police and the SD in Paris reports on a meeting at the Reich Security Main Office[1]

Note by Section IV J/SA 16 (Ah/Bir), Office of the Senior Commander of the Security Police in France,[2] signed pp. SS-Untersturmführer Ahnert,[3] Paris, dated 1 September 1942 (carbon copy)[4]

Re: meeting on Jewish questions at the Reich Security Main Office, 28 August 1942
1) Note:
On 28 August 1942 a meeting on Jewish questions was held at the offices of Section IV B 4 of the Reich Security Main Office Berlin, which the undersigned attended on behalf of SS-Obersturmführer *Röthke*.

The morning meeting consisted of hearing reports about the current situation with regard to the Jewish problem, in particular the evacuation of Jews in the occupied foreign states, by officials in charge of Jewish affairs for these states. In the course of the meeting, SS-Obersturmbannführer *Eichmann* announced that the current evacuation problem (deportation of stateless Jews) will have been solved by the end of this calendar year.

3 On 26 August 1942 a total of 6,584 persons were arrested in roundups in the unoccupied zone. In a conversation with Röthke on 28 July 1942, Leguay had announced the arrest of 12,000 stateless Jews in the unoccupied zone: Klarsfeld, *Calendrier*, p. 597.

4 According to a telegram from Bousquet dated 18 August 1942, the following categories of non-French Jews were to be exempt from these operations: those over the age of 60, those not fit for transport, 'visibly' pregnant women, parents of children under the age of two, and those with a French spouse or a French child: ibid., p. 759.

5 After the first wave of deportations from Gurs, Rivesaltes, Le Vernet, Récébédou, and Les Milles at the end of August 1942, Rivesaltes became the assembly camp for all further deportations of foreign Jews to the occupied zone.

1 Mémorial de la Shoah, XXVI-59. Published in French translation in Klarsfeld, *Calendrier*, pp. 929–930. This document has been translated from German.

2 Helmut Knochen.

3 Horst Ahnert (b. 1909); worked for Dannecker and Röthke in Section IV J of the Office of the Senior Commander of the Security Police in Paris; listed as missing after 1945.

4 The original contains handwritten annotations.

The end of June 1943 is envisaged as the date when the deportation of the other foreign Jews will be concluded. SS-Obersturmbannführer Eichmann pointed out that the scale of the deportations should be increased as much as possible over the next few months because the Reich Railways will probably not be able to make the required means of transport available in November, December, and January.

After the end of the meeting, the following questions were discussed with the relevant officials in the Reich Security Main Office:

a) *Increase of deportations in October*[5]
The Reich Security Main Office is prepared to have the Reich Railways make one transport train a day available during October, and if possible from as early as mid September.

The Reich Security Main Office must be informed immediately of the date when this will become possible.

b) *Loading difficulties due to the longer hours of darkness in October*
The undersigned asked for the departure times of the transport trains to be rescheduled to about two to three hours later because the preparatory work for the deportations will be more difficult as a consequence of the longer hours of darkness from October onwards.

The Reich Security Main Office proposed that the preparation and loading be carried out the day before and arrangements be made to have the trains guarded accordingly until their departure, because it is hardly possible for the departure times to be brought forward.

c) *Provision of blankets, shoes, and dishes for individuals on the transports*
The commandant of the Auschwitz internment camp demanded that the requisite blankets, work shoes, and dishes must be sent along with the transports. They are to be forwarded on to the camp immediately where this has not been done to date.

d) *The problem regarding nationalities*
The Reich Security Main Office was informed about the particular difficulties arising because of the foreign Jews who are exempted from wearing the star.[6] In particular, it was pointed out that various foreign consulates (Italian, Portuguese, Spanish, and Swiss consulates) were interceding very insistently on behalf of their Jews. Among other things, the question was raised as to whether foreign Jews could also be deported along with the others if they have infringed the current rules in any way or have a criminal record. The Reich Security Main Office explained that initially only stateless Jews can be deported. Negotiations are still under way with the Foreign Office concerning the other foreign Jews and have not yet been concluded. The repatriation of foreign Jews to their countries is certainly not desirable. The request from the Swiss consulate for a number of Jewish families holding Swiss nationality to be deported to Switzerland cannot be granted.

5 Handwritten annotation in the margin of the document, probably by Hagen: 'But Jews to be got from where?'

6 Jewish citizens of 'friendly' or 'hostile' states did not have to wear the yellow star and were largely exempt from antisemitic measures. By contrast, as of early Sept. 1942, the yellow star was introduced for Jews with French, Dutch, Slovak, Croatian, Belgian, Yugoslav, and Soviet citizenship as well as for stateless Jews, i.e. former German, Austrian, Czech, and Polish citizens.

Foreign Jews' assets cannot yet be confiscated because various foreign legations are interested in their Jews' assets. Negotiations on this question are also ongoing between the Foreign Office and the foreign legations.

The Reich Security Main Office pointed out that Bulgarian Jews are now also required to wear the star and can be deported with the others.

e) *Purchase of barracks*

SS-Obersturmführer Eichmann requested that the barracks ordered by the Senior Commander of the Security Police in The Hague be purchased immediately. The camp is to be established in Russia. The barracks can be taken there by conveying three to five barracks on each transport train.[7]

2. To *SS-Standartenführer Knochen* for information
3. To *SS-Obersturmbannführer Lischka* on his return, for information
4. Carbon copy for *SS-Sturmbannführer Hagen*

DOC. 264

Higher SS and Police Leader Carl-Albrecht Oberg notes President Laval's request of 2 September 1942 that the German authorities stop pressing for the extradition of Jews from the unoccupied zone for the time being[1]

File note (Hg./Lg) by the Higher SS and Police Leader[2] for the sector of the Military Commander in France, signed p.p. SS-Sturmbannführer Hagen, Paris, dated 3 September 1942 (carbon copy)

I. *File note:*

Re: discussion with President Laval on 2 September 1942

On 2 September 1942, on the occasion of a dinner hosted by Ambassador de Brinon[3] at which Ambassador Abetz and others were also present, a discussion took place between SS-Brigadeführer Oberg and President Laval. The following points from this discussion are noted:

1) *Jewish question:*

a) President Laval explained that the demands we have put to him concerning the Jewish question have run up against extraordinary resistance from the Church in the last few days. This opposition to the government is being led by Cardinal *Gerlier*.[4] Since

7 No further details of this operation could be found.

1 Mémorial de la Shoah, XLIX-42. Published in Klarsfeld, *Calendrier*, pp. 1035–1036. This document has been translated from German.

2 Carl-Albrecht Oberg.

3 Fernand de Brinon (1885–1947), journalist and politician; worked as a journalist from 1919; co-founder of the Franco-German Committee in 1935; delegate general of the French government in the occupied territories, with the official title of ambassador, Dec. 1940–August 1944; sentenced to death by the Haute Cour de justice and executed.

4 Pierre-Marie Gerlier (1880–1965), lawyer and cardinal; worked as a lawyer before being ordained in 1921; became bishop of Tarbes and Lourdes in 1929; appointed archbishop of Lyons in 1937, and cardinal the same year; delivered a public declaration of loyalty to Pétain in 1940; published a letter of protest against the mass detention of Jews in early Sept. 1942 and supported initiatives to save them; honoured as Righteous Among the Nations by Yad Vashem in 1981.

Laval did not wish to detain the Cardinal himself, he had his right-hand man, the head of the Jesuits in the Lyons area,[5] arrested on 1 September and committed to a 'résidence forcée'.[6] In this context, Laval remarked very ironically: 'And that's quite something in a state under the leadership of Marshal Pétain.'

In view of this opposition from the clergy, President Laval requested that, if possible, no new demands be made of him at the moment concerning the Jewish question. He said it is particularly important that he not be given any figures in advance for the Jews to be taken by Germany from the unoccupied territory. The demand had been made for 50,000 Jews to be supplied for the fifty available trains, for example.[7] He asked that he be trusted to be entirely scrupulous in fulfilling the pledges given to us concerning the Jewish question, but, he said, the transfer of Jews was not like going to 'a one-price bargain shop', where one could get as many items as one liked at the same price. Furthermore, he did not want – and he made this remark in an intentionally humorous manner – to raise the issue of what he could expect to get in return.

He again confirmed that, in accordance with the agreements reached after the transfer of the Jews who had previously held German, Austrian, Czech, Polish, and Hungarian nationality, those with Belgian and Dutch nationality would also be transferred. Then, as had been discussed, those Jews who had acquired French nationality since 1933 would be transferred.

President Laval's inquiry as to whether the Higher SS and Police Leader currently has further demands to make in this area was answered in the negative. In response, President Laval again requested that in view of the difficulties that have arisen, no particular pressure be exerted with regard to this matter.

b) In this context, he returned once more to the question of *Darquier de Pellepoix*, which, incidentally, is dealt with in a very ironic fashion at every meeting with him [Laval]. He emphasized that he has told Darquier de Pellepoix, who keeps coming to him with impossible requests, that he will not get the special police he would like to have.[8] He said he had again confirmed to Darquier de Pellepoix that he could for his Jewish affairs deploy trusted informants within the jurisdictions of the regional prefects, but that their information is to be passed on from him to Bousquet.

In this context, he pointed out that, as far as he is concerned, an arrangement like this set up by Darquier de Pellepoix would be very welcome, because, as he unfortunately has to admit, he cannot rely entirely on his police.

Apart from this, Laval commented, as he has done repeatedly, that although Darquier de Pellepoix may be a 'bon garçon',[9] he is incapable of undertaking orderly administration. (The repeated ironic allusions to Darquier de Pellepoix's incompetence created the impression that President Laval wished him to be removed from office. This is particu-

5 Pierre Chaillet.
6 French in the original: 'mandatory place of residence'. In fact, Chaillet was being detained in a psychiatric clinic. See Doc. 271.
7 At a meeting with Jean Leguay's head of office on 1 Sept. 1942, Röthke had announced the expansion of the German deportation programme, which was to affect more than 50,000 Jews by the end of Oct. 1942; Röthke's report, dated 1 Sept. 1942, was published in French translation in Klarsfeld, *Calendrier*, pp. 1015–1017. See also Doc. 263.
8 See Doc. 239.
9 French in the original: 'good lad'.

larly evident from the fact that during the meeting today he remarked that Darquier de Pellepoix raises hardly any objections in meetings with him, but after the discussions constantly sends him letters containing accusations against the various ministers.)

c) Further, President Laval asked whether we have already received the law he has drafted that would transfer the Aryanization of enterprises to the Land Office.[10] He was informed that as yet we know nothing of this law, but that inquiries will be made into the matter immediately.

d) In addition, when the Jewish question was discussed, President Laval indicated that he may request permission for the Jewish wife of the Jew *Citroen*[11] to travel to the unoccupied territory so she can visit her children. However, he said, this question is not urgent at present. He emphasized in this context that as of yet he has not submitted an application for exemption and will not be submitting one. However, he said, it is a fact that the Jew Citroen[12] has done a very great deal for the French automotive industry by creating his standardized automobile and that indeed the occupying army had also benefited from him in using this very good vehicle.[13]

In passing, he remarked, slightly ironically, that so far only Marshal Pétain has submitted applications for exemptions, which indeed have been approved by the Higher SS and Police Leader. Besides this, he asked the Higher SS and Police Leader to tell him whether there were protected Jews in Germany as well. This question was answered in the negative by the Higher SS and Police Leader, while Ambassador de Brinon remarked to Laval that exemptions of this kind would only be approved in the Reich if they are in the interest of the Reich.

[…][14]

II. Submitted to SS-Brigadeführer Oberg
III. Carbon copy to the Senior Commander of the Security Police
IV. » to VI B
V. » to IV K
VI. » to IV J

10 The Land Office (Administration des domaines) was in charge of implementing the Aryanization of intangible assets such as shares, securities, etc. on the basis of the law of 22 July 1942. The reference here is probably to related legislation that was intended to reallocate related responsibilities.

11 Correctly: Georgina Citroën, née Bingen (1892–1955).

12 Correctly: André Citroën (1878–1935), founder of the French automotive company of the same name.

13 Probably a reference to the Citroën 23, a small truck. Following the invasion of France, the Germans had these trucks manufactured for them in Citroën plants.

14 Other points under discussion concerned the restructuring of the fire brigade regiment (Régiment de sapeurs-pompiers), the independence of the gendarmerie and Paris Police Prefecture from Secretary General Bousquet, and Minister of Agriculture Jacques Le Roy Ladurie. Supplementing this file note, Hagen wrote on 4 Sept. 1942 that during this discussion Laval had also asked for 'an agreed line' on the destination to which the Jews extradited from the southern zone would be transported. It was agreed that the responses to enquiries from foreign diplomats should mention 'deportation to the General Government for labour deployment': Mémorial de la Shoah, XLIX-42.

DOC. 265
Manchester Guardian, 3 September 1942: a special correspondent reports on the arrests and Aryanizations in France[1]

How the Jews in France were rounded up. Terror still growing.

From our Special Correspondent
The roundup of Jews in occupied France was begun on July 14 and reached its height on the night of the 15th to 16th.[2]

Twenty-eight thousand people, including Jews of foreign origin, French Jews, and other French subjects regarded as suspects were wanted by the French and German authorities.[3] Many were warned in time of what was to come, in several instances by the French constabulary. In Paris thousands of them tried to hide in the Eighteenth District. Of those who were taken into custody after their money and valuables had been forcibly taken from them, the men were brought to the Velodrome d'Hiver and the women carted off to the Parc des Princes.[4]

Not a single soul whom the police could lay hands on was allowed to go free. Inmates of the Rothschild Hospital, which had been set apart for patients from the camp at Drancy, were placed under arrest regardless of their condition and no matter how recently they had been operated upon.[5] Children over three years old were separated from their mothers, about 5,000 of them being herded together in three school buildings, whither they were taken in lorries after their parents had been seized and their homes locked up by the police. Quite a number of the smaller children are unable to give their names and cannot be identified.

Efforts are now being made by the Quakers, the Salvation Army, and the Israelite Union of France[6] to improve conditions in the camps to which the adults were eventually transported. The prisoners are half-starved and deprived of the most elementary comforts. There is no proper sanitation, no medical supplies, and no kitchen equipment.
Children left in streets
In and around Paris foreign Jews formed the majority among the victims, but in the provinces, where German police carried out the arrests, French and foreign Jews alike

1 *Manchester Guardian*, 3 Sept. 1942, p. 6. The *Manchester Guardian* was established as a British daily newspaper in 1821 and has appeared under the name *The Guardian* since 1959.
2 The roundups actually occurred on 16 and 17 July 1942: see Doc. 245.
3 The number is an overestimate. A total of 22,000 people were supposedly arrested by French police in the Greater Paris area; figures for the rest of the occupied zone do not exist, though it should be assumed that this concerned fewer than 2,000 persons.
4 The Parc des Princes was a football stadium on the western outskirts of Paris. In fact, childless couples and unmarried persons were immediately brought to Drancy; families with children were first detained at the Vélodrome d'Hiver in Paris and then, from 19 July 1942, in the camps at Beaune-la-Rolande and Pithiviers.
5 The Parisian hospital of the Rothschild Foundation, founded in 1852, received sick inmates from Drancy camp from Dec. 1941. After several patients escaped in spring 1942, three remote buildings on the hospital premises were enclosed with barbed wire and placed under guard by French police.
6 This refers to the General Union of French Jews (UGIF).

were rounded up.[7] Thousands of them, men and women, were provisionally interned in a camp at Pithiviers. Children were simply left in the streets and the neighbours expressly forbidden to take them in. The police turned up even in out-of-the-way places for the purpose of arresting the solitary Jewish family known to be living there.

The plight of the French Jews was relieved to some extent by help and sympathy shown to them by their non-Jewish countrymen. Some were enabled to escape and numbers of children were given shelter and smuggled later into unoccupied territory, in spite of the danger involved. Others who evaded arrest are trying desperately to reach unoccupied France, and there is an almost uninterrupted stream of fugitives towards the demarcation line.

Persecution now fiercer

There is as yet no sign that the persecution is abating – on the contrary it is becoming more fierce. Parisian Jews are not allowed to use the telephone and are given one hour only, and that the hour before closing-time, in which to buy the barest necessities of life.[8] Open acts of terror are growing in number, and the Doriotistes lately plundered the famous Paris synagogue in the rue de la Victoire.[9]

On July 23 the *Pariser Zeitung*,[10] the German newspaper published in the capital, reported that to date 31,699 'non-Aryan' businesses in occupied France had been provisionally taken over by 'Aryan commissioners'. Of this total, 24,114 were located in Paris and the remaining 6,785 in the provinces.[11] The journal added that the process of Aryanization was being applied to 2,158 further enterprises and that 600 more cases were still under examination. The manner in which the anti-Jewish regulations are being applied in France is almost incomprehensible. Reliable estimates of what the Germans call non-Aryan businesses have never exceeded 12,000.

It is thus highly probable that the official figures now given conceal a more comprehensive system of robbery directed not only against Jews, French or otherwise, but against Frenchmen towards whom the Germans, for one reason or another, bear a grudge that they are now working off.[12]

7 In the rest of the occupied zone, the Security Police and SD command had prepared for the arrest of foreign and French Jews from the beginning of July, but because of the arrangement between German and French police, French Jews were not prosecuted in the end: see Doc. 239.

8 See Doc. 242.

9 On the night of 20/21 July, six supporters of the Parti Populaire Français (PPF), founded in 1936 by Jacques Doriot, who collaborated with the German occupiers, infiltrated the Grand Synagogue in Paris and damaged the interior.

10 The daily and later, from autumn 1943, weekly newspaper of the German occupiers, which was published in German and French in occupied France by Europa-Verlag between 1941 and 1944.

11 The calculation error is in the original.

12 According to estimates, an 'Aryanization procedure' had been introduced for close to 50,000 companies by 1944; of these, close to 30,000 were located in the Greater Paris area, approximately 12,000 in the occupied zone, and close to 8,000 in the southern zone. However, in the Greater Paris area, for example, only slightly more than half of these procedures had actually been completed by 1944. No reliable numbers exist for the southern zone, where there were multiple instances of Aryanization procedures having been introduced against persons mistakenly identified as Jews.

DOC. 266
On 7 September 1942 Otto Abetz, the German ambassador in Paris, calls for the revocation of the special status held by Jews of certain nationalities[1]

Telex from the German ambassador (no. 1738/42g, marked 'confidential'), signed Otto Abetz,[2] Paris, to the Reich Foreign Office, Berlin, dated 7 September 1942

Introduction of the star in France was initially welcomed very warmly by the French population, in particular by those with antisemitic views.

However this favourable mood soon transformed into its opposite, especially among the antisemites, when it became known that foreign Jews, who the French understandably like even less than their own Jews, were exempt from these measures.[3]

This change of mood has not only resulted in these exempted Jews behaving more arrogantly and shamelessly from day to day, but also in their consulates interceding on their behalf more than ever.

In individual cases this has already led to severe tensions between the Italian consulate and the SD.

What is more, the implementation of our regulations is being hampered by the lack of opportunities to carry out checks, because in each individual case the nationality of the Jews must first be determined, and over the last few weeks large numbers of Jews have been attempting to become nationals of states that are exempted from visible identification.

Furthermore, enemy propaganda immediately seized upon the differing treatment of the Jews depending on nationality and made the most of this, with slogans stating that, as can be seen, the Jewish problem is not a matter of race for the Germans after all, but a matter of nationality.

It is claimed that Germany does not even dare take action against Jews from allied or friendly states. That its situation is so weak it has to make allowances everywhere.

Since the visible identification of all Jews apparently cannot yet be pushed through at the moment, the embassy and the SD propose that it be suggested to those states whose Jews are currently still not visibly identified that they remove their Jewish citizens from France by 31 December 1942, and that the SD already be empowered to promulgate a regulation under which from 1 January 1943 all Jews without exception will be subject to visible identification and to all previously promulgated and forthcoming regulations.[4]

1 PA AA, R 100 867. This document has been translated from German.

2 Otto Abetz (1903–1958), art teacher; joined the SS in 1935 and the NSDAP in 1937; worked at the Bureau Ribbentrop, Oct. 1934 – April 1940; at the Reich Foreign Office, 1940–1945; Reich Foreign Office representative in Paris and Sigmaringen, June 1940 – Dec. 1944; appointed ambassador on 15 August 1940; sentenced to twenty years of hard labour by a French military tribunal on 22 July 1949; pardoned in 1954.

3 See Doc. 263, fn. 6.

4 In mid Sept. 1942 Abetz informed the Foreign Office exactly how many foreign Jews in Paris were exempt from wearing the yellow star and from being detained: 500 Italians, 3,790 Romanians, 1,570 Hungarians, 3,046 Turks, 1,416 Greeks, and 258 Spaniards and Bulgarians: note dated 15 Sept. 1942, PA AA, R 100 867. Soon afterwards the Romanian government withdrew its protection of its Jewish citizens. Ribbentrop gave instructions for all other governments to be called upon to repatriate their Jewish citizens before 1 Jan. 1943. However, the number of persons actually evacuated remained small.

DOC. 267
On 8 September 1942 Ida Kahn realizes that her daughter and grandchildren have been deported from Pithiviers camp[1]

Handwritten diary of Ida Kahn, Alençon, entry for 8 September 1942 (copy)

This morning a mandate we had sent to Pithiviers came back, a sign that our loved ones are no longer there. Max Kaufmann has not had any news from his family either, nor has Laura.[2]

In the afternoon a card arrived from Edgar[3] dated the 31st. He spent a whole day with Marcel[4] in Bram[5] before his departure. He met several acquaintances there, including Paul Weil Merzig. As Marcel hopes to see his wife and children again, he is in good spirits.

1 YVA, O.33/6760, copy in Mémorial de la Shoah, CMLXXXVI(13)-6. This document has been translated from German.
2 Max Kaufmann (1881–1965), costume jewellery salesman; emigrated from the Saarland to Paris; interned in Drancy at the beginning of August 1944. Laura: probably Laura Cahen, née Schwartz (1879–1944), a cousin of Ida Kahn's who lived at Château-Gontier (Mayenne département) murdered in Auschwitz.
3 Edgar Kahn (1907–1943), mason; Ida Kahn's son; lived with his family at Lavalanet (Ariège), 1940–1942; detained in late Feb. 1943 and transferred to Drancy, then deported a few days later to Sobibor, where he was murdered.
4 Marcel Bonnem.
5 Bram was one of the camps set up in the unoccupied zone in 1939 for refugees from Spain.

DOC. 268

On 10 September 1942 the Swiss envoy, Walter Stucki, reports on his intervention with Pierre Laval because Jewish children from Swiss children's homes in France have been detained[1]

Letter (A.4.1.42) from the Swiss envoy, Walter Stucki,[2] Vichy, to the head of the Federal Political Department, Federal Councillor Pilet-Golaz,[3] Bern, dated 14 September 1942[4]

French measures against the Jews

Dear Federal Councillor,

As I had agreed with Minister Bonna[5] on the 7th of this month, immediately after my return I asked for an audience with Head of Government Laval, who then asked me to meet him as early as Thursday, 10 September. He received me with the words: 'Est-ce que vous aussi, vous voulez venir me faire de la morale à cause de mes mesures contre les juifs?'[6] I replied very calmly that I certainly wished to talk to him about some of the effects the measures taken against the Jews in France were having on Swiss-French relations, but that I was entirely aware that it could not be Switzerland's role to lecture France in this respect. I explained that the fact that Jewish children had been removed from Swiss children's homes in France by armed members of the gardes mobiles[7] and taken away in the middle of the night had provoked a very considerable uproar in Switzerland.[8] Not only the sizeable groups that support and finance Swiss Children's Aid both in Switzerland and in France, but also the Federal Council itself has been unpleasantly surprised by this measure. Any repetitions of such brutal interference could certainly cause significant damage to the charitable work for French children undertaken

1 CH-BAR#E2001D#1968/74#358. Published in *Documents diplomatiques suisses / Diplomatische Dokumente der Schweiz 1848–1945*, vol. 14 (Bern: Chronos, 1997), pp. 763–766. This document has been translated from German.

2 Dr Walter Stucki (1888–1963), lawyer and diplomat; director of the Trade Division of the Federal Department of Economic Affairs, 1925–1935; member of the Swiss National Council, 1935–1937; Swiss envoy in Paris in 1938; in Vichy, 1940–1944; negotiated the peaceful liberation of Vichy in 1944; head of the Foreign Affairs Division of the Political Department from 1945.

3 Dr Marcel Pilet-Golaz (1889–1958), lawyer; member of the Swiss National Council, 1925–1928; elected to the Swiss Federal Council in 1928; head of the Department of Home Affairs in 1929; head of the Postal and Railway Department, 1930–1939; head of the Political Department in 1940; resigned in Dec. 1944.

4 The original contains handwritten underlining and annotations.

5 Pierre Bonna (1891–1945); minister and head of the Foreign Affairs Division of the Political Department from 1935.

6 French in the original: 'So do you too want to lecture me about my measures against the Jews?'

7 French in the original: 'mobile guard forces'.

8 During the Spanish Civil War private Swiss citizens had established a children's charity which became the Swiss Children's Aid (Secours suisse aux enfants) in Jan. 1940. In cooperation with the American Quakers, it took care of children interned in the southern zone. In late 1941 the agency was affiliated with the Swiss Red Cross. In the course of roundups on 26 August 1942, forty-five young people in a children's home run by the agency at Château La Hille near Toulouse were detained by French gendarmes and interned at Le Vernet camp. The group were able to return to the home a few hours before they were due to be handed over to the German authorities.

by Swiss circles, as a result of which the children would inevitably suffer. I therefore asked him if at all possible to give me very specific guarantees that in future the children's homes in France managed by the Swiss children's aid organization would no longer be the target of such interference under any circumstances.

Laval first insistently attempted to convince me that the measures he has taken in general against Jews of specific nationalities are entirely appropriate. He said the Jews are largely to blame for France's collapse. Even then, he said, his measures were much less about reprisals for what happened than about prophylactic measures. He claimed the Jews were, without exception, opposed to him and the regime, they were Anglophiles and above all Gaullists, they were agents of underground subversion, and if revolutionary activities were to break out, Jews would undoubtedly be in the vanguard. Finally, he added that they were also largely responsible for the black market and the difficulties it has caused. He said he therefore wanted to and had to free France as far as possible from this plague. For the moment, he said, his measures were very limited: they only affected citizens of the territories occupied by Germany, with the exception of Norway, Belgium, and Holland. Consequently, they applied to German, Polish, Austrian, Czech, Greek, and stateless Jews and, what was more, only to those who had sought asylum in France not in the normal course of events but prompted by the hostilities, i.e. those who had taken up residency in France since 1936. He was going to free himself of these Jews under all circumstances, he said, 'même si tous les jours 50 diplomates étrangers et les représentants de toutes les Églises du monde'[9] protested to him about it.

Specifically, when it came to the measures against the residents of Swiss children's homes in France to which we have objected, two things should be kept distinct, he said: first, where children over the age of 16 were involved, they would be equated with adults and treated as such. With regard to them, he said, he could state only that in future the homes concerned would be properly notified in advance, and the approach taken would be very gentle. Second, when it came to children under the age of 16, the measure had been applied purely so that the children would not be separated from their parents, but instead allowed to share their fate. Indeed, people had previously protested strongly to him about children being separated from their parents. However, in view of the great work done by Switzerland for French children, which he wholly appreciated, he wanted to give me a firm declaration that the French armed forces would no longer under any circumstances force their way into Swiss children's homes in France and take children away from them. If special circumstances arose, he would contact me in advance.

Besides, Laval said, the operation had largely been concluded. Approximately 12,000 Jews in the categories cited above had been repatriated to their countries of origin. However, he said, he now knew that numerous Jews who fell into these same categories were hiding throughout the country and in monasteries and convents. These people were to be sought out by all available means and would then also be deported.

With regard to the fate of the children of deported Jews who for some reason were not deported to the East with their parents, the Ministry of the Interior was dealing with them in collaboration with the Assistance publique[10] and specifically the Comité de

9 French in the original: 'even if every day fifty foreign diplomats and the representatives of all the world's churches'.

10 French in the original: 'State Welfare Authority'.

Coordination des Œuvres des Réfugiés en France[11] in Marseilles. Moreover, the Dominican Republic had kindly declared that it was willing to take in 3,500 of these children, almost all of them, and he said he would do everything he could to ensure this proposal was acted upon. It would be desirable, he said finally, for other countries to show the same willingness to help. I answered merely that Switzerland was already flooded with refugees of all kinds, proportionally more than other countries, and also had to be careful in view of the difficulties involved in provisioning them.

I therefore reiterate that with regard to Jewish children under the age of 16 who live in institutions run by the Swiss children's aid organization in France, certain guarantees have been given by the Head of Government personally, and that the whole operation's current stage appears to be largely concluded. However, I feel it is not impossible that new operations against Jewish citizens of France itself or other nations may be undertaken at a later date.

I will report on the domestic political implications of Laval's most recent measures on another occasion.

Respectfully yours,
The Swiss Envoy

DOC. 269
On 11 September 1942 the United States chargé in Vichy urges the State Department to admit Jewish children from France into the USA[1]

Telegram (no. 1346) from the chargé d'affaires in France, Tuck,[2] Vichy, to the US Secretary of State,[3] Washington, DC, dated 11 September 1942 (copy)[4]

I am greatly disturbed as to the fate of foreign Jewish children in the unoccupied zone who have been and are still being separated from their parents. I am convinced that it is useless to expect any moderation in the restrictive measures now being enforced against foreign Jews young or old.[5] I therefore strongly advocate that our Government should

11 French in the original: 'Committee for the Coordination of Refugee Charities in France'. Correctly: Central Commission of Jewish Aid and Charity Organizations (Commission centrale des œuvres juives d'assistance); see PMJ 5/287.

1 NARA, 851 4016/92. Published in *Foreign Relations of the United States: Diplomatic Papers, 1942*, vol. 2, *Europe* (Washington, DC: United States Department of State, 1962), pp. 712–713.

2 Somerville Pinckney Tuck (1891–1967), diplomat; vice consul and later consul in Alexandria, 1916–1917; in Samsun (Turkey), 1921; in Vladivostok, 1922–1923; in Geneva, 1924–1927; US chargé d'affaires in Vichy, 1942–1944; special envoy to Egypt, 1944–1948; ambassador from 1946.

3 Cordell Hull (1871–1955), politician; member of the House of Representatives, 1907–1921 and 1923–1931; member of the Senate, 1930–1933; US secretary of state, 1933–1944; awarded the Nobel Peace Prize in 1945 for his contribution to establishing the United Nations.

4 The letter was sent in two parts: part 1 was received on 11 Sept. 1942 at 3.19 p.m., and part 2 at 4.52 p.m. The original contains handwritten underlining and stamps as well as the note: 'The telegram must be reformulated before disclosure to third parties.'

5 On 25 August 1942 Tuck pointed out in a conversation with Laval that the American public would view the arrests of Jews in France very negatively. Laval thereupon rejected any kind of interference in French domestic matters.

if humanly possible give immediate consideration to the advisability of presenting through this Embassy a concrete proposal to Laval that as many of these children as we may be prepared to accept should be permitted to emigrate to the United States. I have reason to believe that Laval would accept such a proposal if only because it might in a measure calm the storm of criticism which his inhumane policy has aroused throughout the country.

In conversation he has twice sarcastically referred to the 'high moral tone' adopted by certain governments in connection with the treatment of foreign Jews in France, remarking that these governments at the same time consistently refused to admit Jewish refugees within their own border. He mentioned in this connection that the only concrete offer that he had so far received had been from the Dominican Republic, which had declared its willingness to admit 3,000 Jewish children.[6] (Laval, I believe, might even be induced to consent to the emigration of certain categories of adult foreign Jews.)

The situation of these separated children is desperate. Many of them from the occupied zone are now filtering into southern France, and this movement will probably continue. It is estimated that in the unoccupied zone alone between 5,000 and 8,000 of these children will soon be in the charge of welfare agencies. As it appears to be the intention of the Nazi authorities that their deported parents should not survive the treatment they are now undergoing, many of these children may already be considered as orphans. To leave them in France is to expose them to constant danger, to the threat of possible Nazi aggression (even against Jewish children) and to the serious difficulties of feeding, clothing and sheltering which face the whole population of France during the coming winter.

I am remaining in close contact with Dr. Donald Lowrie, who continues to give this tragic situation his earnest attention. He has been appointed Chairman of an Emergency Committee set up in Geneva which groups a number of organizations religious and nonsectarian, such as the National Migration Service and Save the Children Fund.[7] The primary purpose of this Committee is to bring all possible pressure to bear in order to secure the necessary immigration authorizations from our Government for foreign Jews in France.

I fully realize the difficulties which such a proposal entails, particularly insofar as transportation and funds are concerned. Nothing, however, can alter the fact that the fate of these little people hangs in the balance. Should the Germans decide to order them over the demarcation line into the occupied zone, they may be considered as lost.[8]

6 The specific details of this offer could not be determined. In any case, this proposal was not implemented.

7 The emergency committee led by Donald Lowrie existed from August 1942 until Oct. 1943. It estimated that 22,000 children were directly affected by the roundups in summer 1942.

8 In early Oct. 1942 Tuck was able to inform Laval that the US government would issue entry visas for 1,000 Jewish children and that it would be prepared to receive a total of 5,000 Jewish children. The Vichy government, however, insisted that this should not pertain to those children whose parents had been deported, but rather to children identified as orphans, and therefore protracted the operation. The Allied landing in North Africa at the beginning of Nov. 1942 and the resulting occupation of the southern zone by the Wehrmacht put a premature end to these efforts.

DOC. 270
On 12 September 1942 the sub-prefect of Valenciennes informs the prefect in Lille of the arrest of the Jews of Condé[1]

Report from the sub-prefect, signed Devroe,[2] Valenciennes, to the prefect of the Nord département,[3] Lille, dated 12 September 1942[4]

Arrests of foreign Israelites

Following on from my dispatch of today, I have pleasure in sending you (attached) a copy of a report by the police superintendent of Condé, in which he announces that six Israelites living in Condé have been arrested.

This brings the total of Jews (men, women, and children) who were arrested by the Feldgendarmerie[5] on 11 September in my district to 65. To make these arrests, the Feldgendarmerie requested the assistance of the French gendarmerie and of the local police in Condé.

These Israelites were taken to Valenciennes station, whence they left for Douai and Lille at 1.18 p.m.

The departure took place without incident, but the station platforms had been evacuated in advance.

I must add, however, that this operation has caused some upset among the general public.

1 AD du Nord, 1W1844. This document has been translated from French.
2 Joseph Devroe (1892–1964), civil servant; worked in the Périgueux municipal administration, 1916–1918; in the prefecture of the Nord département from 1920; in the Valencienne sub-prefecture, 1939–1953; thereafter retired.
3 Henry Darrouy (b. 1897), civil servant; worked in the département administration in Algeria, 1916–1918; in the prefecture administration from 1920; deputy to the prefect of Lille, 1941–1944; suspended and arrested in 1944; acquitted in 1945; pensioned off in 1946; named 'honorary prefect' in 1953.
4 The original contains handwritten notes and underlining.
5 German in the original: military police unit of the Wehrmacht.

DOC. 271

On 12 September 1942 the Free France intelligence service in London provides information on church-based relief organizations' opposition to handing over Jewish children to the police[1]

Memorandum from General de Gaulle's general staff (no. 39 d/BCRA/NM, LV/MCD – marked 'top secret'),[2] France Combattante,[3] unsigned, London, to National Commissioner of the Interior André Philip,[4] dated 12 September 1942[5]

Source: B.X. 09[6]
Telegram dated: 5 September 1942
Received on: 9 September 1942
After the Vichy government asked Prefect Angeli[7] to arrange the transport of 800 Jews from the Lyons area to the occupied zone, Angeli asked a relief organization, some of the members of which have knowledge of German, to help the police with its work.[8]

Some of the Jewish children who were meant to be deported had been taken away to safety, and the police demanded that they be handed over.[9] The prefect summoned (the Jesuit) Father *Chaillet*[10] and threatened to intern him at Fort *Barraux*[11] if he did not hand over the children. The priest declared that he was in full agreement with Cardinal

1 AN, F60, vol. 1678. This document has been translated from French.
2 General de Gaulle's general staff was established in Sept. 1941 under the command of Lieutenant Colonel Pierre Billotte (1906–1992). From Jan. 1942 the Free France intelligence service (BCRA) was part of de Gaulle's personal staff.
3 See Doc. 260, fn. 10.
4 André Philip (1902–1970), lawyer and politician; member of the Chamber of Deputies for the French Section of the Workers' International (SFIO), 1936–1940; worked for Free France in London from 1942, first as commissioner of the interior, then as commissioner in charge of relations between the Committee for National Liberation in Algiers and its consultative assembly; member of the Chamber of Deputies, 1946–1951; minister of economics and finance, 1946–1947.
5 The memorandum was also sent to the national commissioner for information; the National Commissariat of the Interior (CNI); Free France's weekly newspaper, *La Marseillaise*; and the archival service.
6 The abbreviation indicates the agent who conveyed the information to London.
7 Alexandre Angeli (1883–1962); held a doctorate in law; prefect in 1931; removed from the occupied zone by the occupation authorities in Dec. 1940; regional prefect in Lyons; sent into early retirement in Jan. 1944; convicted of high treason in Dec. 1944 and sentenced to four years in prison and permanent loss of civil rights.
8 On 26 August 1942 a total of 1,016 Jews had been arrested in the Lyons region and interned in Vénissieux camp. Members of various relief organizations, including two representatives of the Christian aid organization Amitié chrétienne, were present at the selection of the 800 persons to be deported to the occupied zone.
9 At the last minute, Amitié chrétienne smuggled the 108 children scheduled for deportation out of the camp and housed them first with the Jewish Scouts (EIF) in Lyons, and then in various convents and boarding schools, as well as with families.
10 Pierre Chaillet (1900–1972), priest; active in the resistance movement; co-founder of Amitié chrétienne; forcibly confined in a psychiatric hospital in Privas in autumn 1942; released following an intervention from Cardinal Gerlier; thereafter lived under a false name in Paris; recognized as Righteous Among the Nations by Yad Vashem in 1981.
11 The fortress, which dated from the sixteenth century, became an assembly camp for Jews from the region in summer 1942.

Gerlier. Cardinal *Gerlier* had also had a long meeting with the prefect and then with the chief of staff of the secretary general of the police *Bousquet*, and had said to him: 'There are limits which a Christian conscience cannot overstep. These children will stay in our custody, and you will know their place of residence only if the government gives us formal assurance that they will not be handed over to Germany.'

Father *Chaillet* has just been sent to an 'enforced place of residence' in *Privas* in the Ardèche département. The conflict between the Vichy government and Cardinal *Gerlier* is ongoing.

DOC. 272

On 12 September 1942 Otto Abetz complains to the Reich Foreign Office about the approach taken to Aryanization in Tunisia[1]

Telegram from the German ambassador, Abetz (no. 4021 – marked 'urgent, confidential'), Paris, to the Reich Foreign Office, Berlin (received on 12 September 1942, 6 a.m.), dated 12 September 1942[2]

Reply to wired ordinance no. 3909 of 7 September 1942[3]
No pressure has been put on the French government to accelerate the implementation of its legislation on Jews in Tunis by either the embassy or the Security Service. Pressure has generally only been put on the French government to pursue the solution to the Jewish question in the French motherland and the overseas French protectorates and colonies with the requisite vigour.

From discussions with Laval and the secretary of state in the Ministry of the Interior, Bousquet, it has emerged that the French have ordered Aryanization measures in Tunis, and Italian Jews have come forward as buyers. Occurrences of this kind are harmful in the highest degree to Italy's standing and to the implementation of National Socialist racial policy.

I request that it be ensured the Italian government does not raise any objections to the Aryanization of Italian enterprises in Tunis and that it takes the necessary measures to prevent Italian Jews from coming forward as buyers when French Aryanization measures are undertaken.

Conversely, the French government would have to be asked not to permit the involvement of French buyers when Italian firms are Aryanized, so that Italy does not suffer any economic harm as a result of the Aryanization measures taken in Tunis.

1 PA AA, R 100 867. This document has been translated from German.
2 Transmitted by secret code teleprinter.
3 In early Sept. 1942 the Italian government had complained about antisemitic measures being applied to Italian citizens in French North Africa. See also Doc. 259.

DOC. 273

On 14 September 1942, in a letter to the Commissioner General for Jewish Affairs, a delegate of the Parti Populaire Français reports a Jewish woman for failing to wear the yellow star[1]

Letter from Colonel Morel, delegate of the Paris regional group of the Parti Populaire Français, 1 rue Volney, Paris 2, to the High Commissioner[2] for Jewish Affairs, Paris, dated 14 September 1942

I have the honour to pass on to you the following for your information:
The matter concerns Miss Champan,[3] Jewish, living with her mother, a seamstress working from home, at rue Richer (Paris 9).

This person currently works as a shorthand typist for the Organizing Committee for the Chemical Industry (OCCI)[4] at 40 avenue d'Iéna, Paris 16.

About three weeks ago, Miss Champan told the head of personnel at OCCI, a certain Mr Macaire, that, as a Jew, she would probably have to wear the yellow star.

Since then, and in spite of a telephone warning to the organization employing her, Miss Champan has persisted in not wearing her star.

She has declared to colleagues that 'she would be forced to go to the free zone if she was made to wear the star'.

Given her origins, it is surprising enough that this Jew works for a publicly regulated organization and that the management treats her with some indulgence.

I think this calls for direct intervention from the High Commissioner for Jewish Affairs; in addition, this would also free up a job for an Aryan woman, maybe the wife of a prisoner of war or a war widow whose husband died in 1939/40?

I am eager that the necessary measures are taken to force Miss Champan to respect police orders.

Yours respectfully[5]

1 Mémorial de la Shoah, XXX-85, Dossier Champan. This document has been translated from French.
2 Correctly: Commissioner General (Darquier de Pellepoix).
3 Madeleine Champan (b. 1919), born in Paris; her parents had moved to France before the First World War and had subsequently been naturalized.
4 The Comité d'organisation des industries chimiques was formed in 1940 to centralize, control, and reorganize the chemicals sector; it was established by a law of 16 August 1940. The committee compiled a survey of all existing enterprises and issued binding guidelines for restructuring, reallocation, and production.
5 One week later, a deputy department head from the Commissariat General, René Ziegler de Loës, made a surprise visit to the Organizing Committee and ensured that Madeleine Champan was dismissed.

DOC. 274

On 16 September 1942 Anna Goldberg describes her life in Drancy camp in a letter to her mother[1]

Letter from Anna Goldberg, Drancy camp, to her mother, 64 boulevard Ménilmontant, Paris 20, dated 16 September 1942 (copy)

Wednesday, 16 September 1942

Dear Maman,

I received your parcel on Monday afternoon and your card on Monday evening. I cannot tell you how happy I was! I feel so lonely here, so deprived of news. The parcel is very useful, first of all, but it also makes me very happy to know that you are thinking of me, that somebody outside is looking after me.

The parcel was very, very good. Do thank Stern for the chocolate. I ate it all in one go – that's how good it was! What was really good was the sugar. I still have some, by the way. I eat it on its own because it's nourishing. I really needed a parcel badly; I had nothing left of the ones from Poitiers. Imagine, everything's gone after ten days! You don't forget anything any more; you even put in what I'd forgotten to write about. Maman, your parcels are such a pleasure. Everybody keeps saying to me, 'Your mother must be so nice!' The bread was wonderful, and the biscuits especially. In short, everything was wonderful.

Where did you house the hen that lays the eggs? That's so funny. Mrs W. is very kind. We'll cook it (the hen) when I come home. She'll have had time to have thirty-six chicks by then. As for my documents, I really need a citizenship certificate, which you will need to get from the police station in the 20th arrondissement. I'm counting on you to send it as soon as possible. There was no nationality specified on my transit papers, and they're not official documents anyway. Everything you tell me about Marina, Bienf.,[2] [and] Lussi gives me some hope. There is no chance of me being released, unless it comes from outside. Anyway, I know you are doing everything that can be done, and St. must help you; I'm sure he's informed.

There is no canteen here. We get 275g of bread a day, some coffee, and two portions of soup. We need the parcels. Charles D. is at Hermele's.[3] A makeshift shul[4] was set up for Rosh Hashanah.[5] I attended the service. It was very sad knowing that you, too, are on your own and sad, and I'm here. But we must keep our hopes up.

The news you sent me of Rosette made me very happy. How wonderful not to have to fear for them. It's lovely to know they are safe, in good spirits, and free. I got a card from Regine from Poitiers. They are frightened of running into Mendel's sisters, it's terrible. I'm awfully scared for them.

1 YVA, O.9/255. This document has been translated from French.
2 Rue de la Bienfaisance, address of the General Union of French Jews (UGIF).
3 Friend of Anna Goldberg's father.
4 Yiddish in the original: 'synagogue'.
5 In 1942 the Jewish New Year fell on 13 September.

I see that things are improving with the shop.[6] All of these things you have to worry about! I'm pleased that you saw Ida's parents,[7] and that all is well. From what I can tell from your card, you haven't seen Edith? I'm pleased that all is well for her and Mrs Wolmut. I'd like to hear more about her husband. It's really sad that I don't get to hear more from you. You can imagine how lovely it was in Poitiers to receive mail every morning and to be able to write to you! It's hard to be almost completely cut off from the outside world. Soon I'll send you my dirty laundry, but for now, as it isn't cold, I wash it myself.

Are you feeling less sad? Of course now it's the holidays, and I don't think that they've ever been as sad before.

The days here are sad, long, and boring. I sleep a lot. I sometimes see Alice's friend. My bed is next to Ida's; there are a few of us from Poitiers together in one big room. I am counting the days. I don't dare to hope for anything. What is more, you see so much suffering here that you constantly have a heavy heart. It is therefore very, very precious to feel that someone out there is thinking of me and is trying to make my time here easier. Take good care of yourself, follow the rules carefully.[8] I know that you are careful, but you just can't be too careful. It helps me to know that you are safe at home.

Leon B. is in Pithiviers. I am always scared to bump into people I know here. It's painful seeing people here, but thankfully it has not yet happened to me. I hope I won't see Reg. or Mend.

Some days I have lots of courage, like when I receive a parcel; that cheers me up. Send the parcels in the morning before eleven so I'll get them in the afternoon.

Say hello to Alice, Marina, Wolm., Edith, Stern, to everybody. I'd like him to write to me, but that's not possible. Give him my thanks.

Is it still possible to write to Rosette?

I'll soon send you a clothing coupon. A Happy New Year to you, dear Maman, and to all Jews. I hope that this year we will all be reunited. I thought of you throughout Rosh Hashanah. I did get a very small piece of apple with honey.[9] We need courage and lots of hope. Lots of love, dear Maman.

Your daughter,

Nana

Thank you for the fruit; it was beautiful and tasted really good.[10]

6 This is a reference to the business owned by Anna's father, the retailer Rubin Goldberg (b. 1890).

7 Ida was a friend of Anna's from Poitiers camp.

8 At the time, Jews who held French citizenship were not included in the ongoing roundups. However, they were arrested by the French police and taken to Drancy camp if they did not comply with antisemitic regulations.

9 Traditionally, Jews eat apples dipped in honey for Rosh Hashanah as a symbol of optimism and to ensure a 'sweet' new year.

10 Two days later, Anna Goldberg wrote her final letter to her mother, which she threw out of the deportation train to Auschwitz: YVA, 0.9/255.

DOC. 275

On 16 September 1942 Jean Leguay notes that the German authorities are planning to deport French Jews to Auschwitz as well[1]

Handwritten note, unsigned, and memorandum (carbon copy) signed Leguay, Paris, for the secretary general of the French police, René Bousquet, dated 16 September 1942

Telephone communications
16 September 1942
Call from Mr François P.P.[2] 5.40 p.m.
Message
Mr Heinrichsohn[3] telephoned Mr François to tell him to get the train ready for the 18th.[4] Mr François confirmed to him that he had only 558 Jews who fit the designated requirements. Mr Heinrichsohn told him to fill up the train with French Jews.

Mr François is asking for instructions. He will do nothing before he has received your orders.[5]

Paris, 16 September 1942
Note for Mr Bousquet[6]
Today the German authorities asked Mr *François*, the police prefect in charge of Drancy camp, to ensure the departure of the transport which is to leave Drancy for Germany on 18 September, according to the German transport programme.

The numbers in Drancy camp are currently as follows:

Deportable Jews	588
French Jews	876
Foreign, non-deportable Jews	193
Infirmary	124
Total	1,781

As the number of Jews who have to be on this transport is 1,000, the German authorities have made it clear to Mr *François* that it is necessary to fill up the train with French Jews[7]

1 AN, F7, vol. 14 887. Published in Klarsfeld, *Calendrier*, p. 1108. Both documents have been translated from French.
2 Préfet de police (prefect of police).
3 Ernst Heinrichsohn (1920–1994), lawyer; employed in the section for Jewish affairs at the Office of the Security Police and SD in Paris, 1940–1944; practised law in Miltenberg after 1945; sentenced to death in absentia in Paris in 1956; Christian Social Union (CSU) mayor of Bürgstadt, 1978–1980; sentenced to six years in prison by the Cologne Regional Court in 1980; released on probation in 1982.
4 The deportation of Jews from the unoccupied zone had resumed on 15 September 1942 after a ten-day pause.
5 According to the Franco-German agreements on the French police handing over Jews to the German authorities, Jews with French citizenship were exempt from deportation: see Doc. 239.
6 Handwritten note in the original: 'Forwarded to the directorate general via telex at 7 p.m.'
7 From here on, the text is a handwritten addition.

selected from among the inmates at Drancy. For the most part, these were arrested[8] by the French police at the request of the German authorities during the operations carried out in August 1941.[9]

DOC. 276

On 18 September 1942 Chief Rabbi René Hirschler asks the French minister of the interior to refrain from deportations to the occupied zone on Yom Kippur[1]

Telegram from Chief Rabbi René Hirschler[2] (no. 99 299, 3.37 p.m.), Marseilles, to the French minister of the interior,[3] Vichy (no. 18 429, received on 19 September 1942), dated 18 September 1942 (copy)[4]

Confirming my letter dated 7 September 1942 and entreating you in name of humanity and out of respect for religious conscience not to order departure of foreign Israelites to occupied zone next Monday, 21 September, Jewish holiday of atonement and fasting starting Sunday evening and finishing Monday evening.[5]

DOC. 277

On 25 September 1942 the Senior Commander of the Security Police, Helmut Knochen, warns the Reich Security Main Office about the consequences of an operation to arrest French Jews[1]

Telex from the Senior Commander of the Security Police (Dr Kno./Wo.), signed SS-Standartenführer Knochen, Paris, to the Reich Security Main Office, IV B 4, Berlin, dated 25 September 1942 (carbon copy)[2]

Re: deportation of Jews from France
After the arrests of foreign Jews in the occupied and unoccupied territories were completed, efforts were also made to bring about the arrest of Jews with French

8 See PMJ 5/276.
9 In fact, 350 French Jews were on the transport that departed on 18 Sept. 1942. The next train, on 21 Sept., also took 1,000 Jews with French citizenship from Pithiviers to Auschwitz. Two days previously, René Bousquet had instructed the prefect in charge not to oppose the deportation and to take precautions to ensure that the process would be orderly.

1 AN, F7, vol. 15 088. This document has been translated from French.
2 René Hirschler (1905–1944), rabbi; served as rabbi in Mulhouse, 1929–1939; chief rabbi of Strasbourg, 1939–1943; secretary general of the Commission centrale des œuvres juives d'assistance, an umbrella organization of Jewish charities, 1940–1943; rabbi for inmates in internment camps, 1942–1943; imprisoned on 23 Dec. 1943; in early Feb. 1944 deported to Auschwitz, where he was murdered.
3 Pierre Laval.
4 Distribution list: 1st and 2nd police sections as well as the head of the political bureau.
5 Yom Kippur is the holiest day of the year in Judaism. On 21 Sept. 1942 no train bound for Drancy left the unoccupied zone.

1 Mémorial de la Shoah, XXVc-177. Published in French translation in Klarsfeld, *Calendrier*, p. 1156. This document has been translated from German.
2 Communicated by the Message Transmission Service (Nachrichten-Übermittlungsdienst, NÜ), no. 22 230. The original contains handwritten corrections. The carbon copy, initialled by Heinz Röthke, was sent to Section IV J.

nationality.[3] The political situation and the position of President Laval do not permit them to be seized without consideration of the consequences.

I consulted with the French police chief, Bousquet. Based on the outcome of this discussion and the statement made by Laval, and in view of the current situation, the Higher SS and Police Leader[4] sent a telex to the Reichsführer SS[5] indicating that, given Pétain's attitude, an operation would have the most severe consequences.[6]

The Reichsführer SS agreed with the assessment given there and ordered that no Jews with French nationality would be arrested for the time being. The deportation of significant contingents of Jews is therefore not possible.

The arrest of all Romanian Jews is currently under way (notice that Romanian Jews could be arrested was given by the embassy here).[7] Efforts are to be made by all possible means and in cooperation with the Reich Foreign Office to obtain approval for [the arrest of] other foreign Jews. (According to information from the embassy, the negotiations for [the arrest of] Italians and Hungarians have been taken up energetically.)[8]

The deportation of Romanian Jews will go ahead immediately, but the number will not exceed 3,000.

DOC. 278

On 30 September 1942 Elli and Hans Friedländer tell a French acquaintance about their failed attempt to escape across the Swiss border[1]

Handwritten letter from Elli and Hans Friedländer, Saint-Gingolph, to Mrs Macé de Lepinay, Néris-les-Bains, dated 30 September 1942

Dear Madam,

We reached Switzerland after a very tiring journey and were turned away. We were not given the right information,[2] and we are now waiting for our transport to Rivesaltes camp, where our fate will be decided in the way you know very well. We cannot even begin to describe our sadness and despair. What is more, we do not have our luggage with us. Can you imagine our physical and mental state? If anybody can, it can only be you, with your deep kindness and sympathy. Perhaps an intervention on our behalf in Vichy could spare us the worst. We are not scared of the camp, as you know. If you have even the slightest chance of helping us, do not hesitate, we entreat you. Please act quickly.

3 Knochen is referring to a proposal for a large-scale roundup of 5,000–6,000 French Jews in Paris that had been drawn up by Röthke and rejected by Knochen himself: Klarsfeld, *Calendrier*, pp. 1135–1138.
4 Carl-Albrecht Oberg.
5 Heinrich Himmler.
6 This telex has not been located.
7 A total of 1,574 Romanian Jews had been detained by the Paris City Police since the previous day.
8 See Introduction, p. 71.

1 The original is privately owned. Copy in IfZ-Archives, F 601. This document has been translated from French.
2 From early August 1942 the Swiss government severely restricted entry to the country for Jewish refugees: see Introduction, pp. 72–73.

A solution can surely be found in Vichy which would be less catastrophic for us. Please do not forget our little boy! May God bless you and your whole family!

Elli and Jan[3] Friedländer

We hope that Mme de Vd.[4] will be kind enough to inform Mme Tud.[5] as well. Maybe she will be able to do something to help us. We really hope that she has better news. She also greatly deserves our gratitude, and we kindly request that you give her our regards.

DOC. 279
On 9 October 1942 Walter Frenkel writes to inform Cilli Glaser about the fate of her daughter Elli Friedländer and her family[1]

Letter from Walter Frenkel[2] to Cilli Glaser,[3] 35/I Sandelsgatan, Stockholm-Gärdet, dated 9 October 1942 (copy)[4]

Dear Madam,

I am very sorry to have to write you this letter. Sorry because I became a good friend of your poor children Elli and Hans. However, the latter asked me to inform you if something were to happen to him, which he had long feared.

In the course of the general measures ordered against Jewish foreign citizens, your children Elli and Hans were sent to an 'unknown place of residence' on the 5th of this month. This means either to Germany itself or otherwise to one of the Jewish reservations.

They have been through so very, very much. A warrant was first put out for them towards the end of August. Hans was able to save himself by going to a hospital, Elli by staying with friends, and somewhere was found for Paul to stay.[5] Elli's situation became untenable, but she too was able to be taken to the same hospital, where they both stayed until around 25 September. During this period they wrote to you several times through my offices or through the offices of my friend, who will post you this letter as well[6] and whom you or your son may contact if you wish to write to me. Around 26 September, driven to the brink of despair, when they were certain that they would not be able to return to the place where they had been staying because the police had been ordered to

3 'Jan' is the Czech form of the German name Hans.
4 Could not be identified.
5 Could not be identified.

1 The original is privately owned. Copy in IfZ-Archives, F 601. This document has been translated from German.
2 Walter Frenkel (b. 1904), industrialist; Protestant; lived in Milan in the 1930s; moved to Néris-les-Bains in Dec. 1938; later arrested, then deported in late 1944 from Drancy to Auschwitz, and from there to Natzweiler, Buchenwald, and finally Dachau, where he is thought to have died of typhus in March 1945.
3 Cäcilie Glaser, née Schütt (1869–1946); widowed; emigrated from Bohemia to Sweden with her son Hermann in Oct. 1939, with the intention of travelling on from there to join her sons in Palestine; died in Stockholm.
4 The original contains handwritten underlining and corrections.
5 On Paul (later Saul) Friedländer, see Doc. 261, fn. 5.
6 The letterhead records the following name and address: B. Lebovits, 24 Nüschelerstrasse, Zurich, beneath which is written: 'So you can reply to me, Lebovits. 9 Oct. 1942.'

detain them, they decided to flee to Switzerland. For this purpose, they scraped together all the money they could, indeed they were forced to borrow substantial sums as well. After much effort they succeeded in getting there, but an inhumane understanding or interpretation of the law or the two poor things' particular misfortune induced the Swiss authorities to hand them over to the border authorities here after a few hours. They transferred them both to the Centre d'hébergement de *Rivesaltes*, Ilot K (P.O.).[7]

When I received the terrible news a week ago, I set everything in motion, mobilized influential friends, but before all this could have any effect, the transport left on 5 October and I received a farewell card from them both yesterday. It ends with the request to look after the child and inform their relatives. Apart from you, I have also to write to Mr Paul Glaser[8] and Dr Alfred Fleischner[9] in New York, which I am doing right now. I have given the very last place where your children were staying so precisely above and also cited the date of their departure because it is possible that these facts may be of service to you in the searches you will set in motion through the Red Cross. I will also set in motion the same searches. I hope that the ignominy of this account and the greatness of this tragedy will move the censors who read this letter to forward it nonetheless.

What could not be done for the unfortunates (Elli and Hans), namely save them unequivocally (there is no saving Jews here), was achieved for little Paul. I have the task of also informing you about him in the greatest detail, all the more so because I have no way of knowing how long I will still be able to stay in this country unscathed.[10] For reasons that will be readily apparent, however, I will not be using names in this letter, but will replace these names with numbers. My friend will let you know the names with the numbers in the letter that follows on from this one.

So when the raids started, Paul was initially taken to a Jewish children's home, a branch of the same home in which he had been back before the war, not far from the capital here.[11] However, as it was not at all safe there, because children were sought out and taken away from there, too, he was brought back again (he was picked up at the time by the author's wife), and in all their despair and in all their helplessness, Hans and Elli decided to take him to a Catholic home.[12] This was instigated by that family and in particular Mrs One,[13] who proved to be a particular friend to your poor children overall during this period. To begin with, Hans and Elli paid this lady 10,000 francs, and in their farewell card to me they informed me that the Quakers' aid organization had accepted 6,000 francs, a gold bracelet, and a wedding ring from them, with the instruction that they were all to be sent to Mrs One as well. This sum is enough for more than a year. Paul now had to be baptized as well, which also happened with his parents' consent.

7 French in the original: 'Rivesaltes accommodation centre [internment camp], Block K, Pyrénées-Orientales département.'

8 Elli Friedländer's oldest brother, who lived in Palestine from 1939.

9 Alfred Fleischner emigrated to the United States shortly before the outbreak of the Second World War.

10 Two days previously Frenkel had received an order from the prefecture that he was to leave his place of residence; the notification was revoked shortly afterwards.

11 A reference to the OSE children's home at Montmorency: see Doc. 261, fn. 7, and PMJ 5/231.

12 Paul Friedländer lived under the name Paul-Henri Ferland at the Œuvre des Samuels home in Montluçon.

13 Probably Mrs Macé de Lepinay.

However, he had to take a different name so as not to stand out, that is to say Paul Two, and was put up quite a long way away from here, at Address Three.[14] To date he knows nothing of his parents' tragic fate, he only knows that they were in hospital and that they have now been arrested. Neither I nor Friends One have the courage and consider it appropriate to tell the child. If you want to write to the child, write to the address of the person who will pass on today's letter for the time being, and add that the letter is to be forwarded to me. Should I not be here, I will let you know in good time; should I have to go away abruptly, you will notice that there is no quick reply, and then you will send the letters for Paul with an accompanying letter to Family One. But I will also be glad to be at your disposal as far as anything else you might now be planning for Paul is concerned. One possibility is to leave him here for the duration of the war. He is safe and nothing will happen to him. The Ones are looking after him, they write to him every ten days, and I want to do the same. But how will the child grow up influenced by his surroundings, and how will he have changed at the end of the war and be estranged from the milieu into which he was born? Maybe you know that Hans and Elli have good friends here, and that this goes back to before the war. In particular the daughter Miss Jacqueline Propper, Address Four, has proved to be very nice, and when they both were in hospital, she came to take the child with her. However, it was not advisable to give him to her at that time, because it was still too unsafe for a Jewish child to travel. But this Miss Propper is now in contact with Mrs One and continues to be willing to take Paul in. This lady and those around her, whom Paul is already familiar with, moreover, would be better for him in my opinion. I will write cautiously to this lady now and ask her whether her offer still stands, and then I will ask her to overcome the resistance that might come from the Ones. For it must not be forgotten that these people, who are highly esteemed and prepared to help, regard it as an honour and a duty to bring the child up religiously in accordance with their own beliefs, and they are themselves doing everything they can to this end, and that ultimately they can argue in their favour that they received the instruction to care for Paul directly from the child's parents. Which is the truth.

There are other solutions too, e.g. to have the child taken in by the Secours Suisse[15] [and] taken to Switzerland. However, for this to happen, it would have to be requested by some Swiss family. I do not know anyone there, and maybe if you explained the matter to the (Swedish) Red Cross there, you could even get them to bring Paul to you.

There is also the possibility of abandoned children reaching America through the OSE. Without taking it upon myself to make any decisions about this, today I asked a mutual acquaintance to put the child on the list for a transport of this kind, just in case. I do not know whether she will do this, because it is a scheme for Jewish children and not for children who are being well looked after by Catholics, but this could certainly be sorted out.

In this case, however, i.e. should he be accepted, I would first await your consent and then attempt to overcome the resistance that might be put up by the Ones.[16]

You can count on me and tell me what to do in relation to all these questions.

14 A reference to the boarding house at Beaulieu-lès-Loches in the Indre département, a Catholic children's home attached to a farm.

15 French in the original: 'Swiss Children's Aid'.

16 Paul Friedländer stayed at Saint-Béranger until after the liberation of France.

I am particularly sorry that I, someone who had a particularly warm friendship with Elli and Hans, someone who instilled courage in this man through two sad years, who shared every worry with him, now have to inform you of this in such an unemotional and seemingly impassive fashion. Dear Madame, keep up your determination and your hopes of seeing your children in good health again soon. Of course, all that has been said also applies to your son who lives in Sweden, whose first name I do not know.

The rest of the couple's possessions are stored with friends here, and I believe they will be well looked after. I will report on this the next time if you wish me to.

The last two food parcels that were sent have unfortunately been returned to your address. I was no longer able to get them at the post office, otherwise I would have had them delivered to Paul. Should you want and be able to send Paul something to eat, such as sweets, chocolate, then send it to his name, Paul Two, Address Three.

I feel for you completely in this pain, I know how much the uncertainty hurts because my father is in Poland (deported from Vienna) and I have heard nothing of him for about a year.[17]

Please accept my sympathy, and my best wishes. I kiss your hand.

DOC. 280

On 13 October 1942 Joseph Fisher gives the Zionist Executive in Jerusalem an overview of the Zionist movement's activities in France[1]

Letter from J. Fischer,[2] Marseilles, to the Zionist Executive,[3] Jerusalem, dated 13 October 1942 (copy)

I will take this rare opportunity to send you some news about our lives. The events of last August (the imprisonments and mass deportations of Jews) greatly disrupted our work, which is hampered by staff reductions (especially among young members). However, we continue to carry out our duties in the hope of better times and are certain that all of our current efforts to keep our movement and organization going in these difficult times will be justified later, and that what we are now sowing will enable us to reap generous rewards after the war.

Most importantly, France's Zionist Organization is still operating under its *management committee*, made up of representatives of all the different strands (including Alsatians).[4] It holds meetings periodically, and in fact directs all Zionist activities.

17 Max Frenkel (1876–1942); born in Buczacz (Galicia); deported in early 1942 from Vienna to Riga, where he perished.

1 Central Zionist Archives, KKL 5/12/49. This document has been translated from French.

2 Correctly: Joseph Fisher, from 1952 Ariel Fisher (1893–1964), Zionist; expelled from Odessa as a Poale Zion activist in 1924; went to Berlin, then to Palestine, and then to Paris in 1925 as the representative of the Keren Kayemeth LeIsraël (KKL); managing editor of the Zionist newspaper *La Terre retrouvée* from 1928; became a French citizen in 1932; member of the Central Consistory and the directorate general of the General Union of French Jews (UGIF) in Marseilles in 1943; moved to the Italian zone in 1943; moved to Israel permanently in 1950; Israeli ambassador to the Benelux countries, 1952–1957; co-founder of Yad Vashem, the World Holocaust Remembrance Center.

3 The Zionist Executive, the governing body of the World Zionist Organization, was formed after Theodor Herzl's death in 1905 to define the overall policy guidelines of Zionism.

The *funds* are continuing their practical work very discreetly, on a very reduced scale.[5] They have been dissolved as independent organizations, and their activity has mostly been integrated into that of the General Union of French Jews (UGIF). Furthermore, M. F.[6] as the representative of the KKL in Jerusalem, authorized by the Ministry of Finance in consultation with the Commissioner [General] for Jewish Affairs, has been given the task of compensating Jews going to the USA who donate their wealth to charitable Jewish organizations and who will be paid back upon their arrival in the USA. The relationship with the UGIF is good and built on trust, and a good level of cooperation has been established where social and financial issues are concerned.

Vaad Aliyah[7] has not been dissolved yet (no doubt an oversight). Its director, Mrs Wolff, holds her meetings at HICEM. We are currently reorganizing the membership of Vaad Aliyah while we wait for the immigration certificates which we have been promised. Currently emigration to Palestine is very difficult, both for administrative reasons – the government is refusing to issue exit visas – and financially. But we hope we will be able to overcome all of these difficulties. Send us the certificates![8]

Political parties: Zionist parties are in a fairly precarious situation. The Jewish state is completely non-existent here, due to a lack of fighters. The General Zionists, whose leading figures have for the most part emigrated, do not officially exist, but are in the process of regrouping.[9] Poale Zion–Hitahdut and the left-wing Poale Zion both occasionally convene their old central committees for consultations, often the day before management committee meetings.[10] They are very active in the life of the Federation presided over and led by Marc.[11] The Mizrahi,[12] and young people in particular, display a lot of energy and devote themselves mainly to cultural activities in almost all the cities of the free zone, where there are local groups led by and made up of Zionists of all

4 The Organisation sioniste de France was founded in Lyons in early 1942; regional committees were formed in Limoges, Toulouse, Nice, Grenoble, and Roanne. Before the war, Jews from Alsace and Lorraine had been organized separately from the other French Zionists.

5 As the representative of the KKL, Fisher distributed funds – mostly provided by the American Jewish Joint Distribution Committee (JDC) – to the Jewish relief organizations in France.

6 Presumably the author is referring to himself here (M. F., 'Monsieur Fisher').

7 Organization that promoted emigration to Palestine.

8 In 1939 the British Mandate had restricted immigration into Palestine to a maximum of 75,000 persons over the subsequent five years. Anyone who wanted to emigrate to Palestine required one of the strictly limited certificates. Not a single certificate reached France after Nov. 1940. In addition, the number of certificates actually issued was far smaller than the guidelines specified; only 60 per cent of the quota was met. Of the 4,411 persons who managed to leave France between Jan. 1941 and April 1942, only one emigrated to Palestine legally.

9 The liberal wing of Zionism pursued the goal of establishing a Jewish state and rejected other ideological or political goals.

10 Poale Zion–Hitahdut and Poale Zion were Zionist-socialist workers' parties.

11 This refers to the Fédération des sociétés juives de France (FSJF), officially the umbrella organization of around 20 associations supporting destitute Jewish immigrants from Eastern Europe, established in 1928. Marc Jarblum (1887–1972), politician; representative of the World Jewish Congress in France; president of the Zionist Organization of France from 1936: president of the FSJF from 1937; one of the founders of the Federation of Young Zionists and Pro-Palestinians in 1938; fled to Switzerland in 1943; from there organized aid for the Armée juive resistance organization, the Zionist Youth Movement, and the FSJF; returned to Paris in Oct. 1944; head of the Palestine Bureau in Paris, 1948–1953; emigrated to Israel in 1953.

12 Middle Eastern Jews.

strands. We also have a strong Youth Movement, organized within the Zionist Youth Association, which also brings together people of all political stripes.[13] This association carries out very important cultural work. In August it organized a ten-day leaders' camp. Several leading members of our movement in France spent a few days with a team of thirty youth leaders to discuss in detail the basic difficulties of the lives of Jews and Zionists within the framework of a carefully planned programme of lectures and discussions. The *Zionist Youth Association* works very closely with the Jewish Scouts of France, where a growing Zionist trend can be observed.

Hachsharah:[14] Around mid August we were running two agricultural training centres: Frettersseps, near Toulouse, and Blémont, near Limoges. We also contributed to the development of agricultural training centres founded and run by the EIF.[15] Our farms developed normally. We were about to start a third centre. The farm had already been rented, and a new kibbutz was starting work there when the deportations hit us very hard. The new centre was dissolved. It was made up almost entirely of haverim[16] who had come to France after 1933 (and were therefore 'deportable'). Its members were forced to flee, some to Spain, some to Switzerland, and some are still in hiding now. Only six out of thirty members are left at the Frettersseps centre. By contrast, the Blémont centre was unaffected. We are currently working with the EIF to fill up Frettersseps with French people. We can now confirm that the farm will not be closed and that its operations will continue.

In spite of the setbacks that hit this farm, we must recognize that the efforts have not been entirely in vain, because all the people who worked there for one or two years will one day be able to use their knowledge and experience in their future work in Eretz.[17] Hehalutz is currently in the planning stages. The events of August have delayed its establishment.

Vaad HaChinuch:[18] The work is going well. The Vaad head offices are in Marseilles. Its president, Mr Israel Jeffroykin,[19] who has now emigrated, has been replaced by Mr N. Grinberg.[20] Also appointed are the lawyer Leopold Metzger[21] (from Strasbourg) as general secretary, and Mr J. Fisher as treasurer. Mr Metzger will be in charge of the whole

13 By 'Association de la jeunesse sioniste' (as in the original), Fisher presumably meant the Zionist Youth Movement (Mouvement de la jeunesse sioniste), which had been created by Simon Lévitte in May 1942 and was closely linked with the management committee through Fisher and Jules Jefroykin.

14 Hebrew for 'preparation': occupational and agricultural training of young Jews on Zionist collective farms in preparation for emigration to Palestine.

15 Éclaireurs israélites de France (Jewish Scouts of France).

16 Plural of *haver*, Hebrew for 'friend', in Zionist discourse also 'member', 'comrade'.

17 Eretz Israel, Hebrew for 'Land of Israel', a biblical term used by Zionists with reference to the desired re-establishment of a Jewish state.

18 Committee promoting the teaching of the Hebrew language and Jewish history.

19 Israel Jefroykin, correctly: Jules (known as Dika) Jefroykin (b. 1911); lawyer; born in St Petersburg; member of the FSJF from 1926; later its chairman; member of the Armée juive, 1942–1944; representative of the JDC in Marseilles, 1942–1944; president of the Zionist Youth Movement from 1942; member of the Comité de Nîmes; fled to Spain in spring 1944; owned a travel agency from 1945; head of the Zionist newspaper *La Terre retrouvée*, 1962–1971.

20 Possibly Reuven (Ruben) Grinberg, also a member of the FSJF and co-founder of the Comité de la rue Amelot: see Doc. 259, fn. 4.

organization. Local committees will be formed everywhere. The new courses (Hebrew, history, literature, and Palestine studies) are being set up. A textbook for learning Hebrew, entitled *Chaienu*,[22] has just been published. However, this work is also hampered by the mass deportations of children and young people.

We continue to disseminate news about Palestine in the form of private letters (written by the undersigned) and through the dissemination of the newsletter from Geneva (*News from Palestine*).[23] This work helps us keep in touch with our friends. Although we do not have a fully fledged organization with regular conferences and meetings, we still have Zionist *social circles* and a Zionist *atmosphere*. We have a *directorate*, and we are maintaining both the technical and the financial structure (we do not lack the necessary funds for our activities) as well as the practical activities of all involved. All of this together will enable us, at the opportune moment, not just to take up *all* of our activities again, but perhaps also to create a better organization (more united and with a large base of young people) than the one we had before the war.

Our relationship with the Consistory:[24] Over the last few months, there has been a rapprochement between the Consistory and foreign Jewish circles[25] as well as the Zionist Organization. Although neither side has taken the necessary steps to have candidates selected by the various communities (they insisted on co-opting them, which is contrary to our statutes), at least a permanent form of contact has been established.[26] From time to time the Consistory's leadership will organize consultations with representatives of all the aid organizations, including the Federation and the Zionist Organization. Such a meeting took place on 8 October, with the aim of informing each other of all of our activities and of the steps necessary to defend our interests, both legally and morally. These meetings will take place periodically. The Zionist Organization was represented by the lawyer Mr Léonce,[27] Dr R. L-D, and the undersigned. Incidentally, the latter joined the Consistory last month as the representative of the [Jewish] Community of Nice. The Federation was represented by Marc, N. Grinberg, and E. Lewin.

This should give you a brief summary of our activities.

A most heartfelt shalom

Yours

21 Leopold Metzger (b. 1897), lawyer; employee of the General Union of French Jews (UGIF) in Strasbourg, Marseilles, and Limoges; arrested by the German police in Oct. 1943 and taken to Drancy camp; deported on 20 Nov. 1943 to Auschwitz, where he perished.

22 Hebrew: 'Our Life'. The organization managed to distribute two thousand copies of the first edition of this textbook.

23 The newsletter of the Permanent Bureau of the Jewish Agency in Geneva was sent out twice a month.

24 Under its president Jacques Helbronner, the Consistory – established in 1808 as the central representative body of the Jewish population in France – had successfully resisted compulsory inclusion in the UGIF: Laurent Joly, *Vichy dans la 'solution finale': Histoire du Commissariat général aux questions juives* (Paris: Grasset, 2006), pp. 264–268.

25 This refers to the FSJF (see fn. 11).

26 Following the forcible integration of all the Jewish organizations into the UGIF, the Zionist Organization operated within the Consistory.

27 Presumably Léonce Bernheim (b. 1886), lawyer; represented France at the 15th Zionist Congress in Zurich in 1927; arrested in early Dec. 1943, when he was living in Grenoble; deported to Auschwitz via Drancy with his wife a few days later.

DOC. 281
On 19 October 1942 Robert Lévy-Risser suggests how parents can identify their children again in case of enforced separation[1]

Letter from the head of the Rouen delegation of the General Union of French Jews (UGIF), signed Robert Lévy-Risser,[2] 55 rue de Crosne, to Armand Katz,[3] UGIF Service 1,[4] 19 rue de Téhéran, Paris 8, dated 19 October 1942[5]

Dear Mr Katz,

I have the honour to confirm to you my letter of 11 October.[6] Since that date, I have had the pleasure of obtaining the liberation of the *Erdelyi* family. The Hungarian consulate confirmed that Mrs *Erdelyi*, of Romanian origin, had acquired Hungarian nationality through marriage; she was therefore released along with her three daughters.[7] The other people, who were joined by seventeen of our co-religionists from Eure and la Manche [départements], were taken to Drancy on the 16th of this month.

I hope that you were able to undertake all appropriate steps in order to bring about the rapid liberation of the French Israelites arrested by mistake.[8]

Ways for people arrested to find their children again in case of enforced separation

One of the greatest worries of our co-religionists is how they may verify the identity of their children if they are reunited with them after a long period of separation. Two methods, which can be used in combination, can be suggested to parents:

1) Take one or two copies of the fingerprints of the ten fingers of each of their children.
2) Have each of their children marked with a small, distinctive tattoo.

I have recommended these procedures to the Department Hygiene Service, and in several cases I have carried them out personally.

Respectfully yours

1 Mémorial de la Shoah, CDXXIII-9. This document has been translated from French.
2 Robert Lévy-Risser (b. 1890), engineer and industrialist; briefly under arrest in May 1942; interned in Drancy in mid Jan. 1943 with his family members and other employees of the General Union of French Jews (UGIF); on 20 Nov. 1943 deported to Auschwitz, where he perished.
3 Armand Katz (1895–1944); interned in Drancy in August 1941 and released in late Oct. 1941; from autumn 1942 to 1943 secretary general of the UGIF; interned in Drancy again in summer 1943; probably deported to Auschwitz on 7 Dec. 1943.
4 Service 1 of the UGIF was part of Group 1 (General Services); it included the administration and the secretary's office.
5 Portions of the original have been underlined by hand.
6 Not included in the file.
7 After repeated intercessions by the Hungarian consul in Paris, Hungarian Jews were exempted from antisemitic measures. Nesca Erdelyi née Cataf (1911–1943), born in Chişinău, and her husband, Georges (Gyorgy), an electrician born in Csengerbagos, Hungary, as well as their three daughters born in France, Berthe (b. 1938), Michèle (b. 1939), and Annie (b. 1941), were detained in a mass arrest in mid Jan. 1943 and deported on 11 Feb. 1943 to Auschwitz. Of the family, Georges Erdelyi was the only one to survive.
8 In all, 842 persons had been transferred to Drancy on 16 Oct. 1942, including 45 Jews from the Rouen metropolitan area. In addition to Romanians, Poles, Russians, and Balts, 19 French citizens were among those transferred.

DOC. 282

On 14 November 1942 Otto Abetz informs the German consul in Vichy that the German occupation authorities are demanding that the borders with Spain and Switzerland be completely closed[1]

Telegram from Administrative Office I (Schl/Schm) of the German embassy in Paris (no. 1511, marked 'very urgent'), signed Abetz, to Consul General von Krug,[2] Vichy, dated 14 November 1942 (copy)[3]

At the joint suggestion of the ambassador, the Commander-in-Chief in the West,[4] and the Military Commander,[5] a discussion about travel permit issues took place this morning in the office of the Chief of Staff of the Military Commander.[6] The Commander-in-Chief in the West called for an explicit ban on travel by civilian citizens of the Reich into the French territory that is to date unoccupied.[7] Permits will be issued only if there is a truly compelling reason for travel and if this reason is confirmed by one of the three authorities named above.

Travel arrangements for French citizens remain unchanged.

Wehrmacht travel is regulated separately.

As the French government has at present closed the Spanish and Swiss borders solely to citizens of enemy nations, and observations so far indicate that Jews and emigrants are fleeing across the border in large numbers,[8] it seems absolutely essential to demand that the French government provisionally close the borders completely until negotiations on the assumption of control of the external borders of France's unoccupied zone by German authorities are concluded.

The customs officers currently deployed in the unoccupied territory believe that, in the event of a total closing of the borders, they can use their advance units to monitor the borders to a degree, to ensure that the border closure is enforced. The complete closing of the borders could be rescinded, in consultation with the relevant German

1 Mémorial de la Shoah, CXXV-114. This document has been translated from German.

2 Dr Roland Krug von Nidda (1895–1968), diplomat; member of a Freikorps (paramilitary unit) in Leipzig, 1920; joined the SA and the NSDAP in 1933; Reich Foreign Office legation secretary, 1920–1925; foreign correspondent in Moscow, London, and Paris, 1928–1939; head of the press office and Gau office of the NSDAP Regional Group in Paris, 1934–1939; representative of the Reich Foreign Office to the Wehrmacht High Command (OKW) in 1940; head of the office of the German representative in Vichy, 1941–1943; freelance writer after 1945.

3 By secret code teleprinter. The document was used in the Nuremberg Trials (doc. no. NG-3192).

4 Gerd von Rundstedt (1875–1953), field marshal, commander-in-chief of the Western Front from March 1942.

5 Carl Heinrich von Stülpnagel.

6 Karl-Richard Koßmann (1899–1969), colonel, chief of the general staff for the Military Commander in France from April 1942.

7 On 11 Nov. 1942, following the Allied landings in North Africa, Wehrmacht troops had invaded the southern zone of France.

8 Approximately 22,000 persons – Jews and non-Jews – illegally crossed the French–Spanish border after the German occupation of southern France. By the end of 1943, the number had risen to 30,000. Crossing the border into Switzerland had been made considerably more difficult by the Swiss authorities in early August 1942 (see Introduction, pp. 72–73). Nonetheless, from Sept. to Dec. 1942 a total of 7,372 refugees were allowed to enter the country and 1,264 others were turned back. Between Jan. and August 1943 a total of 4,833 were admitted and 2,243 were turned back.

military offices, at the point when the control of the Swiss and Spanish borders has been taken over by German authorities.[9]

With these points in mind, please discuss the matter immediately with Secretary General Bousquet and if necessary with President Laval, and report by wire on the outcome for the purpose of informing the Military Commander and the Commander-in-Chief in the West.

DOC. 283
In late 1942 a leaflet calls on the French population to help the victims of antisemitic persecution[1]

Anonymous leaflet (initials M/R), place and date unspecified (late 1942)

We call for help!

As soon as the German army invaded France, the representatives of the Nazi regime quickly began to do their best to associate our country with the same disgrace into which Hitler's Germany has fallen in the eyes of the civilized world.

They have introduced the Nuremberg Laws in the country of the Declaration of the Rights of Man, in the country which represented justice and liberty to all human beings worthy of the name. They have sought to bring about a regime that through antisemitism discriminates against an entire swathe of the French population.

Those who signed the emergency decrees of October 1940 and June 1941[2] have brought dishonour upon our country, regardless of whether they were the actual authors of these decrees or whether they signed them voluntarily or under duress.

Honest workers who had dedicated their labour and their physical strength to France have been deprived of their livelihoods; thousands of people have been robbed for the benefit of a few; widely respected intellectuals have found themselves banned from practising their professions; scientists and men of letters have been forced into silence, and with them the voice of our country can no longer be heard.

And as if that were not enough, the internment camp, the prison, and the firing squad have become the fate of entire families, who are condemned to misery, despair, deportation, and death.

For the Jews, it was the concentration camps: Drancy, Compiègne, and Pithiviers in the occupied zone, Gurs, Rivesaltes, Ruffieux,[3] Le Vernet, Brens, and others in the unoccupied zone; these have become the sad replicas of the Nazis' Dachau.

There the same scenes are played out, the same misery prevails, the same methods are used. Brutal violence or slow death through hunger and abuse, firing squads, and

9 From mid Nov. 1942 the French–Spanish border was guarded by forces of the German customs authority, the German police, and the Feldgendarmerie. The French border officials had been completely ousted by summer 1943. The north-eastern part of the Swiss border (Jura Mountains) had been guarded by the German authorities since 1940. The southern portion of the border (Alps) remained under Italian control until Sept. 1943.

1 AN, AJ38, vol. 67. This document has been translated from French.

2 This refers to the Vichy government's Statute on Jews of 3 Oct. 1940 and the second Statute on Jews of 2 June 1941: see PMJ 5/241, 242, 244, 270, and 271.

deportations. And for those who cannot withstand it any longer, there is one way out: suicide. Men, women, and children, everyone is subject to the same fate.

And now they are hunting down those who still seem to enjoy a semblance of liberty. The foreign Jews in the unoccupied zone are assigned a place of compulsory residence; in some places, French and foreign Jews find themselves banned from practising their religion; French Jews are banished step by step from the cities; they can no longer move around without reporting to the police.[4] And finally, evoking scenes from the darkest periods of the Middle Ages, they have set out to visibly identify the entire Jewish population of our country with a defamatory sign. With the 'yellow star' they have sought to create a pogrom atmosphere in the occupied zone.

And what of the unanimous reaction of the French people? We know what nobility, what generosity they have shown to those who have been oppressed, humiliated, and persecuted in this way. We know that many among us who have expressed solidarity with the Jews have had to suffer the same fate as they did and have been taken to the same camps.

New crimes are being committed, others are being prepared.

We have received extremely serious news from Paris. The internment camps in the occupied zone have been emptied and the inmates, including the women, deported to unknown destinations. And those women who protested have suffered brutal violence. Thousands of arrests have just been made. Women, children, the sick and the elderly, all have been taken away. *Dozens of women and children have killed themselves so as not to fall into the hands of the Nazi functionaries.* The deportation of all Jewish families from the occupied zone is currently on the verge of being completed. And similar measures have not been ruled out for the unoccupied zone.

Are you going to allow the same crimes to be committed in France as in Croatia, in Yugoslavia, in Czechoslovakia? Will you allow the same crimes to be committed in France as in Poland, where 700,000 Jews have lost their lives since the German invasion, and where fathers have been forced to dig their children's graves before being shot in front of them?

We are determined no longer to passively wait for death. We are determined to defend ourselves!

With all our might, we will insist that we are human beings. Human beings for whom the only life worth living is one of work, freedom, and dignity.

But we cannot defend ourselves unless you help us in this struggle against our common enemy.

Because this really is our common enemy.

Antisemitism is the weapon of division.

Nazism, our common enemy, is lashing out and will lash out harder still tomorrow against Christians, intellectuals, veterans, workers, against all those who do not want to bow to the will of the slave-driving regime that the occupation and its minions have imposed on our country, and against all who dare or will dare to speak out for freedom and justice.

3 Non-French workers from the 974th Foreign Labourer Group (GTE) were held in Ruffieux camp in the Savoie département in the French Alps. In early 1942 the Jews on this work detail (approximately 200), referred to as the 'Palestinian group', were separated from the other inmates.

4 The law of 9 Nov. 1942, which was published in early Dec. 1942, banned foreign Jews, though not French Jews, from leaving their district of residence without a permit issued by the police.

Today, the Nazis are trying this out on the Jews, but Jew or non-Jew, if you let these crimes against a section of the population with limited means of defence be perpetrated today, you will be imprisoned, interned, deported, or shot tomorrow.

But now, nobility of spirit and generosity are no longer enough. You must help us by any means possible.

You must loudly proclaim solidarity with all who have given their lives and with all who are prepared to give their lives in the fight which will decide the fate of all French people.

Help us! Help us with all your power!

Workers, employees, shopkeepers, veterans, intellectuals, all of you non-Jews, remember that those who persecute us today are the same who devastated our country, who are holding two million of our people prisoner,[5] ruining their bodies and their spirits; they are the same people who organize upon our own soil the trafficking of our workers[6] and who have killed and are still killing thousands of the best people among us every day.

DOC. 284

In its report for December 1942 the French prefecture in Algiers outlines the situation of the Jewish population in Algeria[1]

Report by the French prefecture, Centre d'information et d'études,[2] Algiers, on the 'activity of the local population in the Algiers département'[3] in December 1942 (excerpt)

[…][4]
VI. The Israelites Question
a. Jewish demands
Last month we noted a rapid rise in Jewish demands[5] following the Anglo-American landings. A report on this subject by an Israelite from Algiers has probably been sent to the Allied authorities (see Appendix II).

5 In 1940 between 1.5 and 1.8 million French citizens were captured by the Germans. In late 1942 the Vichy government's state secretariat for war veterans recorded 1.1 million French prisoners of war still captive in the German Reich.

6 From spring 1942 the Nazi regime's drive to recruit French workers for deployment in the Reich, with the cooperation of the Vichy regime, became increasingly coercive. The measures introduced included the *relève*, through which French prisoners of war were brought back to France from June 1942 in (unequal) exchange for larger contingents of French workers dispatched to the Reich.

1 ANOM, GGA 40 647. This document has been translated from French.

2 The CIE was established in 1940 and secretly funded by the French Ministry of the Interior. It consisted of an intelligence service and an active police unit (*Groupe de protection*). It was deployed against opponents of the Vichy regime, especially communists, Jews, and Freemasons: see Jean-Marc Berlière, *Policiers français sous l'Occupation* (Paris: Tempus Perrin, 2009), pp. 29–31.

3 Between 1937 and 1951 the prefecture in Algiers prepared a monthly report on 'activité indigène' in the département; this report was intended to reflect the mood of the local population.

4 The topics covered at the beginning of the report include the general situation, representation of the locals and their former deputies, reformist Islamic legal scholars, the Algerian People's Party, and European parties' activities among the local population.

Several weeks went by without any modification being made to the legislation in force, and the American authorities have made it known that they only came to North Africa to wage war. At the end of the month, many Israelites seem to have resolved to be patient a while longer. The declarations made by Admiral *Darlan*[6] on this subject were nevertheless warmly welcomed in these circles.

'A new dawn' (it says in the December issue of the Jewish Societies' Bulletin[7]): 'Admiral *Darlan* declared to General *Eisenhower*:[8] French Africa[9] must make the maximum military effort. This will be accomplished through the unity of all of its citizens, regardless of their political or religious affiliations. The admiral indicated that all measures which were inspired by the Germans or which aim to persecute people on the grounds of race or religion will be suspended. Let us wait and hope …'

Among the locals, by contrast, this declaration caused some concern.

b. Approaches made to the Muslims

Several leading Jewish figures (above all the doctors *Aboulker* and *Loufrani*, and Mr Elie *Gozlan*) continued their persistent solicitation of the Muslim leaders of all parties to bring them to join a 'United Action Front'.[10] The Muslims, careful to preserve their independence, remain reserved, though they have condemned racism.

Thus one 'reformist', called upon to declare that 'the Muslims have no hostility towards the Jews', limited himself to declaring that they had 'no intention of attacking them'.[11]

'Islam does not allow for a chosen race' (this is the response of one of the deputies from Algiers). 'That the Judeo-Christian minority enjoys a privileged status and the Muslim majority is subject to special laws[12] is due to the actions of the political institutions. The repeal of the Crémieux Decree,[13] far from making the Muslims happy, on the contrary

5 During the night of 7 Nov. 1942, Allied troops landed in Morocco and Algeria. Admiral Darlan signed the ceasefire agreement. The antisemitic Vichy laws remained in force, and only individual points were made less stringent or overturned.

6 François Darlan (1881–1942), naval officer; deputy head and later head of the Ministry of Naval Affairs, 1926–1934; commander of the navy from 1937; appointed admiral, 1939; minister of the navy, 1940–1942; deputy prime minister, Feb. 1941–April 1942; ordered an armistice on 8 Nov. 1942 after the Allied landing in North Africa; high commissioner of France in Africa with US support after the Allied landing in North Africa; murdered in Algiers in Dec. 1942.

7 Correctly: *Bulletin de la fédération des sociétés juives d'Algérie*, a monthly journal founded by Elie Gozlan in May 1934 as the official publication of the Jewish community in Algeria.

8 Dwight David Eisenhower (1890–1969), military officer and politician; commander-in-chief of the Allied armed forces in North Africa; president of the United States, 1952–1960.

9 On 23 Nov. 1942 the governor general of French West Africa also pledged his support to Darlan, which meant that all of French North-West Africa came under the control of the new French authority in Algiers, which was on the side of the Allies.

10 In French: 'Front commun revendicatif.'

11 The readiness of parts of the Muslim population to employ violence against Jews had noticeably increased since the early 1930s, owing to increasing colonial political tensions. It reached a peak in Constantine in 1934, when clashes resulted in more than 25 dead and a large number of injured.

12 While Algerian-born Jews had enjoyed French civil rights since 1870, Muslims remained 'French subjects' (*sujets français*) who were subject to sharia law as well as special French laws and regulations. Under a law passed in 1881 which contravened general French law, Muslims who were found to have broken the law were liable to particularly harsh and even collective punishments.

13 In 1870 this decree granted Algerian Jews French civil rights and citizenship. The decree was rescinded in Oct. 1940 by the Vichy government: see PMJ 5/244.

gave them an increased sense of their own inferiority. They have suffered too much from racial injustice themselves not to condemn it wherever it may come from. They hope that, before long, Muslims and Jews will have the right to live in justice and harmony in a unified French Algeria.'

'Wherever they come from' (writes another), 'special measures always awaken painful memories in the hearts of Algerian Muslims …'

During an important meeting, important Muslim individuals from Algiers and the interior (reformists, elected officials, PPA,[14] and communists) were petitioned once again to commit to 'shared support for all demands from the Jewish and the Muslim communities that aim to establish their equality with the Europeans'. However, they avoided making any promises, but obtained for their part a commitment from the Israelites that they would 'not accept any advantages from which the Muslims are excluded'. The Israelites did not receive any commitment in return.

At the end of the month, the proposal for a 'United Front' remained a proposal, and it does not seem to be going anywhere. Three points seem to emerge from the many discussions that have taken place recently:

- There remains a deep mistrust of the Jews and their 'scheming character' among a large number of Muslim intellectuals.
- The local population would perceive a simple return to the situation before the war (by reinstating the repealed Crémieux Decree) as an injustice. 'The Jews, who have made far fewer sacrifices for France than the Muslims, should not in any way be favoured over them'.
- However, the intellectuals unanimously condemn the racial doctrines and measures, and they see anti-Judaism today as nothing more than a 'divisionary manoeuvre from which the Muslims have nothing to gain'.

[…][15]

Appendix II

Report on the racist measures implemented against the Jews of Algeria by the public authorities (extracts)

(drafted by a prominent Israelite from Algiers)

Opening remark

This report aims to present a concise picture of all of the transgressions committed in this country against the honour, the dignity, the person, the right to work, and the private property of French citizens of Jewish origin …[16]

Who are the Jews of Algeria?

The Jews of Algeria have lived in this country from time immemorial and today number around 130,000 people.[17] The Senatus Consulte[18] of 1865 made them French subjects of French nationality, along with the indigenous Muslim population.

14 The Algerian People's Party (PPA) campaigned for the autonomy and emancipation of the Algerian population, and after being banned in 1939 continued its activity underground until 1943.

15 The remaining items in the report address economic matters and miscellanea.

16 All the antisemitic regulations passed in France itself were applied in North Africa as well.

17 According to the 1941 census, 111,021 French Jews and 6,625 foreign Jews were living in Algeria at this time. Their number had increased rapidly over the preceding decades (1881: 35,663 Jews).

18 A French Senate resolution that had the force of law.

On 24 October 1870 the Government of National Defence, going back to a plan formed under the Second Empire,[19] collectively granted the Jews of Algeria French citizenship rights.

The Jews of Algeria have contributed extensively and broadly to the consolidation of French authority in Algeria; their role in the economic and intellectual development of this country has been significant.

They did not shirk their duty and answered the call of the Motherland loyally, both in 1914–18 and in 1939–40. They fought with valour to defend the country, and the great number of dead, wounded, citations, and decorations among them are testimony to this.

Revocation of citizenship

In spite of so much evidence of their attachment to France, the decree of 7 October 1940 took citizenship away from the Jews of Algeria, after 70 years of them exercising their rights and after two wars.

This loss of political rights, which according to the French Penal Code only affects those found guilty of infamy under common law, was applied to all the Algerian Jews, with the exception of those who fought in the 1914–18 or 1939–40 wars and were awarded the Legion of Honour in a military capacity, the Military Medal, or the Croix de Guerre.

This loss of rights also affected war widows, veterans of the two wars who did not receive one of the decorations listed above, war orphans who are wards of the nation, and the parents and grandparents of soldiers who died for France.

Nor did it spare the descendants of the Jews who had been allowed to keep their citizenship rights.

Even if the law of 18 February 1942 expanded the categories of Jews who could benefit from these rights,[20] it imposed upon veterans, wards of the nation, war widows, and the descendants of veterans the humiliating procedure of having to request as a favour what their sacrifice and valour should have secured them as an inviolable and sacred right.

And what is one to say about the prisoners of war, who learned in the Oflags and Stalags[21] from their conquerors that from now on they were nothing more than subjects of the French state …

Dispossessed of their political rights, the Algerian Jews were then declared unworthy of serving in the chantiers de la jeunesse (law of 15 July 1942)[22] or of serving as jury members in the assize courts (law of 25 November 1941).[23]

19 The Second Empire, established by Napoleon III in 1852, ended in 1870 with his arrest during the Franco-Prussian War and the proclamation of the Third Republic.

20 Under this law, the following groups were exempt from the revocation of citizenship: veterans; holders of the War Merit Cross of 1941, the Legion of Honour, or the Military Medal; war orphans cared for by the state (the so-called 'wards of the nation'); and the parents and children of soldiers killed in the line of duty: *Journal officiel*, 22 Feb. 1942, p. 762.

21 German prisoner-of-war camps during the Second World War (Oflag refers to the German 'Offizierslager', a camp for officers; Stalag refers to 'Stammlager', a camp for NCOs and enlisted men).

22 The Vichy government introduced the *chantiers de la jeunesse* (youth camps) in 1940 as a form of mandatory service for young people. According to the law of 15 July 1942, only young people who were non-Jewish French citizens were allowed to participate: *Journal officiel*, 19 July 1942, p. 2481.

23 The *cour d'assises* was a criminal court dealing with serious crimes against the person, such as murder, robbery, rape, etc. The law of 25 Nov. 1941 regulated the balance of power between the jury and the judge in these courts. In addition, Article 381 specified which groups, including Jews, were excluded from jury service: *Journal officiel*, 12 Dec. 1941, pp. 5354–5358.

Denial of the right to work
Public service: Jews have been driven out of all the posts they held in the army, the police, the judicial authorities, the higher civil service, and the teaching professions, with no regard for any military ranks they might have held (a complete list of these positions follows) …

In addition, the law of 3 October 1940, the Statute on Jews, stipulated that in all sectors of the administration other than those listed above, Jews could only be retained in any position if they were able to prove they held a military rank.[24]

The law of 3 October 1940, amended by that of 2 June 1941,[25] stipulated a two-month period for the removal of all Jewish public officials. This process was completed by 18 December 1940.

Public service licensed operators
A significant number of lower-paid Jewish employees, including salaried staff and skilled and unskilled workers, have been dismissed without any compensation from companies licensed to offer public services – public transport, gas and electricity, and other services.

Private sector employment
The racist legislation has aimed systematically to eliminate Jews from the Algerian economy.

The laws of 3 October 1940 and 2 June 1941 (Art. 5) banned Jews from accessing and practising the following professions, with no possible exceptions: directors, managers, editors of newspapers and magazines with the exception of scientific publications, theatre, radio broadcasting, banking, currency exchange, advertising, real estate agents, commercial real estate agents, commission brokers, forestry enterprises, gaming concessions.

By the decree of 30 October 1941, Jewish ownership of such companies had to end by 15 December 1941 …

The liberal professions
Quota of 2 per cent for lawyers, physicians, dentists, midwives, architects, ministry officials …

Denial of the right to education
Higher education: The decree of 23 August 1941 stipulated a quota of 3 per cent for universities and other higher education institutions.

Primary and secondary schools: On 30 September 1941, the GG[26] decided that a quota of 14 per cent would be applied in state schools, starting on 1 January 1942.

This arbitrary decision, with no legal basis and in complete disregard of the organic law which makes primary education compulsory for all, has driven thousands of Jewish children out of state schools.[27] With great difficulty, the Jewish communities of Algeria have managed to place these children in Jewish schools.

The quota was halved to 7 per cent at the start of the new school year in October 1942, again without any legal basis.

The quota was confirmed by the law of 19 October 1942.

24 See PMJ 5/241.
25 See PMJ 5/270.
26 Governor general. From Sept. 1940 to Nov. 1941, General Maxime Weygand (1867–1965) held this post.
27 In autumn 1941 a total of 11,962 Jewish children were expelled from state schools in Algeria.

Measures against property

To complete the elimination of Jews from the Algerian economy, the decree of 21 November 1941, amended by that of 13 April 1942, allowed for the appointment of temporary administrators for:

1) all industrial, commercial, real estate, or trade and craft businesses;
2) any properties, any property rights, or any leasehold rights;
3) any movable goods, securities, or movable property rights if the owners or managers are Jews, or if there are Jews among the owners or managers.

Hundreds of temporary administrators were appointed for thousands of Jewish-owned buildings.

The task of the temporary administrator is to issue receipts, to carry out the sale of movable goods, and to deposit the funds with the Caisse des dépôts et consignations,[28] after deducting his fees, of course, which are charged proportionally as determined by the decrees of 16 December 1942 and 25 March 1942. The person whose property is under administration has the right to request financial support under certain conditions.

In addition, special laws have been passed:

1) For commercial enterprises (businesses), the decree of 3 March 1942 and the regulation of 13 April 1942 ban Jews from acquiring, holding shares in, pledging as collateral, or leasing any commercial enterprise without the permission of the prefecture.
2) For real estate, the decree of 15 March 1942 bans Jews from owning more than one building, and this must serve as the family home.
3) For licensed public houses, the law of 2 July 1942 and the decree of 7 July 1942 forbid Jews from owning, operating, or managing such establishments.

The excesses of the Algerian administration

The Algerian administration has never failed to apply these laws much more widely than the legislators envisaged …

Jewish housekeeping staff in nursery schools are sacked under the pretext that they are part of the teaching staff.

Jewish newsagents are forbidden from working (based on the law against Jews working in the press).

Jewish students at fine arts schools have been thrown out without any legal basis.

This even happened to Jewish students at the Maison-Carré Agricultural Institute,[29] an establishment which has been erroneously classified as a higher education institution.

As soon as a law against the Jews is passed in France, the Algerian administration hastens to make sure it is also applied in Algeria.

Conclusion

Collectively, the Jewish population has been the target of unrelenting legal oppression. In spite of the legitimate, fierce indignation directed against the initiators of this persecution and those who willingly implement it, the community has been able to preserve its honour and its dignity. Nevertheless, unemployment and poverty have severely devastated Algerian Jewry, a community already placed outside the law and subjected to

28 The Caisse des dépôts et consignations (CDC), a state financial institution founded in 1816, was responsible for the centralized administration of blocked accounts. It managed Jews' assets which had been placed under administration or were already Aryanized.

29 The institute is east of Algiers.

tyranny. This has resulted in a profound sense of turmoil within the Jewish community. Today, the Jews of Algeria expect fair moral and material reparations. They see the emergence of the confident hope of a free and dignified life.[30]

DOC. 285

An anonymous report dated 8 January 1943 describes aid provided to refugees by Christians in France[1]

Report (marked 'confidential'), unsigned,[2] Geneva, dated 8 January 1943[3]

Excerpt from a letter about refugee work in France.

1. *General remarks.* Since the occupation of southern France, regular reporting by our French friends is no longer possible. Telephone and telegram exchange has ceased, and since 21 December the postal service has also been interrupted. Only in the past few days have a few unimportant letters made their way to us. Therefore, we are largely dependent on messages sent by word of mouth that are occasionally brought by refugees, as even legal travel has been completely halted.

As a result, we must give our French friends completely free rein in structuring the work and putting the funds to use. The magnificent spirit of the French teams, their caution, and their unshakeable courage justify our confidence that, despite constant danger, all that is humanly possible is being done to help refugees. All the refugees with whom we are able to speak here praise the helpfulness, the spirit of self-sacrifice, and also the organizational accomplishments of the French women and men who provide assistance. It is uplifting to learn how impartially Protestants, Catholics, and Jews work together to aid the beleaguered refugees. Moreover, these are not merely small groups of helpers, for the refugee service is backed by the sympathy of the broadest sections of the population, including official bodies. One can say without exaggeration that a spirit of brave humanity and a heartening commitment to the sacrosanct entitlement to hospitality have prevailed in deeply afflicted France. It is a marvellous sign of divine providence that it was the cause of the despised, mostly Jewish, refugees that led people to remember these high moral values. The churches, the brave pastors, their wives, and especially the tireless workers of the Cimade[4] form a vital part of this spiritual move-

30 The Vichy regime's antisemitic legislation was not repealed until March 1943, under Allied pressure; the limits placed on Jews' access to the educational system had been rescinded one month earlier. The Crémieux Decree did not come into force again until Oct. 1943.

1 La Contemporaine, Archives Cimade, Files of the General Secretariat, F delta 2149/5001. This document has been translated from German.

2 The text is thought to have been written by Pastor Adolf Freudenberg, secretary general of the Ecumenical Council of Churches, Geneva.

3 Handwritten note: 'file: Cedergreen' (probably Hugo Cedergren (1891–1971), secretary general of the World Alliance of YMCAs).

4 The Cimade refugee aid organization was founded in 1939 by Protestant youth movements to support people evacuated to southern France from Alsace and Lorraine when the war broke out. During the occupation, it extended its activities to include all refugees and became one of the most important non-Jewish aid organizations for Jews.

ment. Only against this backdrop can one appreciate the inherently inconspicuous refugee work in France and recognize what blessings our help can bestow.

2. *Homes:* the Cimade home Le Côteau Fleuri in Le Chambon currently provides living quarters for around 50 refugees, and approximately 25 are lodged in Les Roches student dormitory in the same town.[5] The refugees from both homes who were placed on the deportation list in August of this year and since then have been hidden and moved elsewhere – more than 40 persons in total – have, with few exceptions, reached Switzerland; an achievement of our French friends that was carried out amidst great danger.

The home that was opened by the Cimade in October in Mas du Diable, Bouches du Rhône, with 15 occupants, had to be evacuated in early December shortly before the official opening.[6] By all accounts it has been reopened, but we lack reliable information. Likewise, we do not know whether the long-planned third Cimade home in Le Vabre/Tarn has begun operation by now; it is possible, and we hope so; we await further information.[7]

Since the occupation, the situation of all foreign refugees, the non-Aryans and the political refugees, is under immediate threat. The exceptions previously made for a few categories (children, the elderly, etc.) are no longer in force. Nonetheless, one is safer in the homes than in the camps. In particular, whatever rescue operations are still possible can be most easily carried out from the homes.

We must reckon on maintaining the homes for some time to come.

3. *Camps:* the large assembly camp at Rivesaltes near Perpignan was closed down in early December. The majority of its inmates, namely 1,300 persons, were taken back to Gurs. In Gurs, a Cimade team is operating in the usual manner, as always with the strong support of the YMCA and YWCA. Not far from Gurs, around 500 refugees are living, under restrictions that forbid them to leave the immediate locality, in the health resort of Eaux-Bonnes, known for its good air quality …[8] They too are looked after by an Assistance Protestante[9] under the management of Miss Merle d'Aubigné,[10] a person of outstanding merit. In addition, Cimade teams are working in the smaller camps at Nexon near Limoges and Brens-Gaillac.

The Aumônerie Protestante[11] continues to look after the labour camps and work squads, of which there are still a great many, and it administers to the needs of refugees

5 In Le Chambon-sur-Lignon, a town in the Cévennes region, a first Cimade home, Le Coteau Fleuri, had been opened in March 1942. It had room for approximately 100 women and children. The student dormitory, operated by the European Aid Fund for Students (Geneva), was used to house young men from the internment camps in the unoccupied zone. After a raid at the end of June 1943, in which 18 students and the teacher Daniel Trocmé were arrested, the home was closed.

6 The prefect in charge had demanded that only non-Jews be housed in the home near Pomeyrol, south of Avignon, and therefore it had to be closed again.

7 Such a home, with space for 12 persons, was indeed opened and maintained by Pastor Robert Cook.

8 The German occupation authorities had housed Spanish Republicans, Jews, and other former Gurs internees in several hotels in this resort town in the Pyrenees. They were to be transferred to Drancy in mid Jan. 1943 but managed to escape during transport.

9 French in the original: Protestant welfare organization.

10 Jeanne Merle d'Aubigné (1889–1975), welfare worker and nurse; worked in Gurs camp until Oct. 1942, then at various Cimade care centres.

11 French in the original: 'Protestant chaplaincy'.

in other camps such as Le Vernet and Noé, and stays in close contact with many isolated refugees. The individual subsidies granted by the Aumônerie continue to be paid, and the visiting service is very active.

4. *Work of the Cimade outside the camps and homes:* the entire service's focus has shifted heavily in this direction. Since the beginning of the deportations, and especially since the German occupation, it has been imperative to save human lives by every means imaginable. In this respect, the Cimade and its associates unquestionably bear the heaviest responsibility today. Madeleine Barot[12] permits herself not a minute's rest, shuns no danger, but sets about her task with shrewd judgement.

Great caution is obviously called for when making this work public, and it must specifically be ensured that no names of organizations or individuals are given. However, we think that some of the examples mentioned below are highly suitable for publicity.

For months now, hundreds of refugees have been kept hidden. New, large groups continue to seek shelter with the Cimade, which does not differentiate between the religious faiths. One realizes what dangerous work is being done here, and what large financial resources are increasingly needed, when one considers that this entire service must be performed underground, in the presence of authorities and police organizations that view these refugees as Enemy No. 1.

During the warm season, many refugees were hidden in forests and barns. Now, in wintertime, many parsonages, Catholic convents, monasteries, and the homes of private individuals have become places of refuge that open their doors to those seeking a safe haven.

We will mention a French mother of 10 who gave food and shelter to 30 refugees in a single month. There are parsonages that take in 20 visitors some nights and house 4 to 5 refugees at all times. Refugees have come to us who had met with a warm reception in convents or monasteries for more than two months, in sizeable groups. After the poor harvest, the cutting off of North Africa and the German invasion, the shortage of food in France is even more extreme than before. The refugees who are living underground have no entitlement to food ration cards. This means that the hosts, who themselves are underfed, are making painful sacrifices to feed their guests. But these sacrifices are not enough. Our staff are constantly busy trying to procure food at exorbitant prices and bring it to the places of greatest need. Some refugees are hunted so fiercely and in such danger that they had to be hidden far away from any human abode. There was one artist who spent many weeks in a dark little well house. The woman helping him who brought food once a day, at night, reported that he was on the verge of insanity. We continue to help by receiving and passing on the costly Colis Suisses and the Portuguese sardines provided by the Unitarian Service.[13] But the contents of the Colis Suisses are increasingly meagre, and export from Portugal is presently at a standstill. The French helpers are therefore forced to make very expensive and complicated purchases.

12 Madeleine Barot (1909–1995), librarian; secretary general of the Cimade, 1940–1956.

13 Freudenberg organized food parcels from Switzerland (*colis suisses*) and Portugal through the Swiss Workers' Welfare Organization in Zurich and the American Unitarian Service in Lisbon. The parcels were distributed by Cimade to refugees in need in the southern zone: Uta Gerdes, *Ökumenische Solidarität mit christlichen und jüdischen Verfolgten: Die Cimade in Vichy-Frankreich 1940–1944* (Göttingen: Vandenhoeck & Ruprecht, 2005), pp. 124–127.

For understandable reasons, we must refrain from giving details about the challenges which the refugees had to overcome when trying to escape to Switzerland.

Often, the attempt to reach Switzerland fails the first and the second time. People from our circle then spent further weeks in lonely mountain huts and other remote shelters until, eventually, the final attempt to escape was successful. Only with the help of loyal, courageous friends can such odysseys reach their goal and be seen through in these times.

A great many refugees also fall into the hands of the police. If these police officers are French, a prison sentence for false papers and attempted illegal border crossing is imposed. Once the time has been served, a transfer to Gurs camp is ordered in the best of cases. At any rate, there is some hope in these cases, as there has been a sharp decline in the deportations carried out by the French.

5. *Refugees in Switzerland:* the majority of the refugees enter Switzerland through the canton of Geneva. Their luggage consists, at most, of a rucksack or a small bag, and most have no financial means. Often their shoes are soaked from wading through streams. Their only coat, jacket, or pair of trousers is torn from negotiating the barbed wire. They tell us the story of their odyssey. The anxiety they have suffered for months speaks from every glance and gesture. They have been forced to leave their closest relatives behind, doomed to perish or in the greatest peril. They can hardly believe in their own deliverance from danger. They tell us how they fled from Belgium to northern France with the locals and the military, under aerial bombardment and machine-gun fire, how the Gestapo was on their tracks in Paris, how wives were separated from their husbands and parents from their children, and then were interned in various camps after what were often long and harrowing transports. They tell us of the manhunts carried out in this time of deportations.

We met a man who, after receiving the summons for deportation, managed to get away from the camp and hid for a few days, only to learn that his wife had been arrested and deported in the meantime. Now, after a successful escape across Lake Geneva, he and his young daughter are in a Swiss camp.

A man barely 30 years old, who had to leave his wife and 7-year-old daughter behind in Brussels and was able to escape to Switzerland after a long stay in France, had to learn here that his wife had been deported and that insurmountable barriers separated him from his child.

We are particularly glad about the rescued children, now that the project for emigration to the USA, which had been quite advanced, has come to a stop because the war has spread. Many children come here, and they are gladly given help to escape. Recently we talked with an old lady, herself a refugee, who took four small children with her and brought them all through the barbed wire successfully.

On another occasion, we will report on the enormous growth in refugee work in Switzerland. Since the early summer of 1942, way over 8,000 persons have been admitted: Jews, Jewish Christians, Poles, Czechs, and recently many Alsatians. Many are wary and frightened, but the eyes of many shine with gratitude when they speak of the Christian charity they have encountered during the past weeks.

6. After what has been said, the great need for money to fund the work in France hardly needs to be justified. In November we still estimated the amount required by the Cimade and Aumônerie for the next six months at 40,000 Swiss francs. As a result of the growing

number of persons seeking shelter, the rising prices and the other circumstances, this estimate no longer applies. We must expect to require at least 30,000 francs more.

Of this total amount of 70,000 francs, we have so far been able to make around 30,000 francs available to our French friends, to a significant extent thanks to Swedish assistance.

DOC. 286

On 21 January 1943 the Senior Commander of the Security Police in Paris presses the Reich Security Main Office for a quick resumption of deportations from Drancy[1]

Telegram (no. 3440, marked 'secret') from Section IV J-SA 225a, Office of the Senior Commander of the Security Police in France (Rö/Ne), signed SS-Standartenführer Knochen, Paris, to the Reich Security Main Office, Section IV B 4, Berlin, dated 21 January 1943 (copy)[2]

Section head and author of report: SS-Obersturmführer Röthke
Re: transport of Jews to Auschwitz from Drancy camp for Jews near Paris
Drancy camp for Jews presently holds around 1,200 Jews who meet the requirements for deportation. As the head count for the camp now stands at 3,811, additional Jews are being admitted daily, and the feeding of the Jews and the heating of the camp are causing certain difficulties. For these reasons, I request instructions as to whether one to two transports of Jews to Auschwitz can soon be set in motion. The view here is that the current weather conditions in France permit the transports to be carried out. I would ask you to inform me whether, if necessary, the transports can take place using goods wagons even if there is a hard frost. Transport in passenger coaches cannot be arranged because there is a lack of sufficient guard personnel. In the event that an imminent deportation is desired, I also request that I be informed of the precise railway schedules and the provision of guard personnel from the Reich border onwards.

Also interned at present in the aforementioned camp for Jews are at least 2,159 Jews with French citizenship, most of whom are imprisoned for violation of German directives pertaining to Jews. I request guidance as to how I should proceed with respect to the following questions:

a) Can Jews with French citizenship who are guilty of offences be deported under the deportation directives currently in existence?
b) Are we to deport Jews who have violated directives pertaining to Jews and are living in a mixed marriage?
c) How are we to deal with Jews who were interned on the basis of roundups of Jews in late 1941 and in 1942 and are French citizens?[3]

1 Mémorial de la Shoah, XXVc-195. Published in French translation in Klarsfeld, *Calendrier*, pp. 1318–1319. This document has been translated from German.

2 Conveyed by message transmission service on 21 Jan. 1943 at 24:00. The original contains handwritten annotations and underlining.

3 On 25 Jan. 1943 the Reich Security Main Office (RSHA) replied that special trains could be provided. Jews under a) and c) could be deported, but Jews living in a so-called mixed marriage could not be deported for the time being. If they had violated directives, however, they could be deported along with political prisoners: Mémorial de la Shoah, XXVI-70.

DOC. 287
On 27 January 1943 the Central Consistory lodges a protest with Pierre Laval against the mass arrests in Marseilles[1]

Telegram from the Central Consistory,[2] Lyons, to the head of the French government,[3] Vichy, dated 27 January 1943 (copy)

We were astounded to learn of the arrests by French police of several thousand perfectly law-abiding French Israelites,[4] specifically veterans, people from Alsace and Lorraine, returned prisoners of war, young girls, and minors, who were all taken to unknown destinations. We urgently demand they are afforded the safety to which they are entitled and we protest most indignantly against such measures, which have shocked the conscience of the nation.

Respectfully

DOC. 288
On 2 February 1943 Ivan Hock asks Adolf Hitler for the release of his wife, who has been deported[1]

Letter from Ivan Hock,[2] 4 rue de la Cure, Paris 16, to the Office of the Reich Chancellor and Führer Adolf Hitler, Berlin W, Wilhelmstrasse (received on 8 February 1943), dated 2 February 1943[3]

The undersigned, Ivan Hock, a full Aryan (attachment no. 1: Aryan certificate),[4] residing in Paris at 4 rue de la Cure, Paris 16 (business address: Assistant Manager[5] of Hauts Fournaux de la Chiers, 20 rue de la Baume, Paris), ventures to submit the following matter with the request that you kindly send the wife of the undersigned back to her place of residence and thus return her to her family.

Statement of reasons

My wife, Anna Hock, née Goron,[6] of non-Aryan descent, born on 3/16 March[7] 1875 in Kovno (formerly Lithuania), married to me since 19 August 1902 (attachment no. 2), was

1 Mémorial de la Shoah, CCCLXVI-45. This document has been translated from French.
2 The president of the Central Consistory was Jacques Helbronner (1873–1943), lawyer; member of the French Council of State, 1899–1940; removed from office under the provisions of the Statute on Jews; president of the Central Consistory in France, 1940–1943; arrested on 23 Oct. 1943; deported in Nov. 1943 from Drancy to Auschwitz, where he was murdered.
3 Pierre Laval.
4 On the arrests in Marseilles, see Introduction, pp. 76–77.

1 PA AA, R 99 406. This document has been translated from German.
2 Ivan Hock (b. 1880).
3 The original contains handwritten underlining.
4 The attachments mentioned here and below are included in the file.
5 In the original: 'Unter-Direktor', presumably derived from the French 'sous-directeur', roughly equivalent to an assistant manager.
6 Anna Hock, née Goron (1875–1942); Belgian citizen, deported to Auschwitz on 30 Sept. 1942.
7 As in the original. The dual dating appears also on the couple's marriage certificate, reflecting the different dating systems of the older Julian calendar formerly used in the Russian Empire and the Gregorian calendar adopted in 1918.

arrested by the German police in Paris on 29 September 1942, taken to Drancy and from there deported on 30 September 1942, destination unknown.

Since my wife, according to the enclosed medical certificate (attachment no. 3), is ailing and already 67 years old, and the only son resulting from our marriage was killed in action as a Belgian soldier[8] during the present war, in Flanders (attachment no. 4), I request most respectfully and sincerely that my heartfelt plea be dealt with favourably.

Additionally may it also be noted that my wife had completely distanced herself from Judaism, which is indicated by the fact that, as according to the enclosed letter of confirmation (attachment no. 5), she has not been a member of the Jewish religious community. Our son, who, as noted above, was killed in action, was baptized a Roman Catholic (attachment no. 6), was married to an Aryan woman, and also had his son baptized a Catholic (attachment no. 7).

It also bears mentioning finally that my wife and I were forced to flee from the Bolsheviks and leave Russia in 1918 and lost everything in so doing. I had worked in Russia for fifteen years, most recently as director of the 'Russian Company for Pipe Manufacture' in Ekaterinoslav. To explain why my son fought in the Belgian army, I note that although resident in France, I am a Belgian citizen by birth and have never relinquished my Belgian citizenship.

Finally, may I take the liberty of noting that I had already submitted an application to the appropriate authority in Paris for the release of my wife; this application was processed and ultimately rejected by the Security Police and SD Section IV J (case handler Untersturmführer Ahnert). It was remarked, however, that my wife *would have been released if she had been in French territory at the time of the decision;* that this was no longer the case is the only reason that prevented the re[lease][9] of my wife.

In anticipation of your favourable decision, [I] sign, most honourable Reich Chancellor,

With the expression of the greatest esteem[10]

8 Boris Octave Oscar Hock (1906–1940), soldier; born in Russia; married; killed in Belgium during a bombing raid in May 1940.

9 Part of word illegible.

10 The Reich Foreign Office asked the Reich Security Main Office (RSHA) for information regarding the whereabouts of Mrs Hock and the possibility of her release in view of her advanced age and illness. In late June 1943 Section IV B 4 of the RSHA informed the Reich Foreign Office that Mrs Hock's location was not known: PA AA, R 99 406.

DOC. 289

On 9 February 1943 Madeleine Roy appeals to the prefect of her département to intervene with the German authorities on her behalf[1]

Letter from M. Roy,[2] La Tremblade, rue de la Jonction, presently Camp de la route de Limoges, Poitiers, to the prefect of Charente-Maritime,[3] La Rochelle, dated 9 February 1943 (translation)[4]

I am writing to present my case to you:
I am a Jew, a Frenchwoman, and was arrested in my apartment in La Tremblade on 1 February and interned in Poitiers camp for not wearing the yellow star. When I went to the mayor's office in La Tremblade to register, no one informed me that I was required to wear this star.[5] I am the only Jewish person in La Tremblade, am 64 years old and my husband is a Catholic. Until 1 February I did not know that I was meant to wear the star.

Therefore, Monsieur Préfet, I appeal to your benevolence, in the hope that you exert influence upon the German authorities with a view to my release.

Respectfully[6]

1 AD de la Charente Maritime, 15/W/11. This document has been translated from German.

2 Madeleine Roy, née Lévy (1878–1943), housewife; lived in Suresnes, near Paris, until the German occupation in 1940; fled to La Tremblade (Atlantic coast); interned by the French gendarmerie at the order of the German police on 1 Feb. 1943; taken to Drancy in late May 1943; deported to Auschwitz in mid July 1943.

3 Robert Martin (1895–1957), senior administrative official; prisoner of war in German captivity from Sept. 1914 to 1918; administrative career from 1919; temporarily taken hostage by German troops while sub-prefect in Montbéliard in 1940; prefect of the Charente-Maritime département in La Rochelle from Nov. 1942; regional prefect in Rennes in 1944; sentenced to life imprisonment with hard labour in 1945.

4 The German translation of the original letter was forwarded by the prefect Robert Martin to the field office of the Security Police and the SD in La Rochelle on 12 Feb. 1943.

5 After arrests of Jews in La Tremblade in Dec. 1942, Madeleine Roy had registered as a Jew with the local mayor's office in Jan. 1943. The registration was passed on by the mayor to the prefect in La Rochelle and by the latter to the Security Police and the SD, where a list of the Jews living in the département was kept.

6 In a letter dated 19 Feb. 1943, the German police refused to grant release: AD de la Charente Maritime, 15/W/11.

DOC. 290

On 10 February 1943 Heinz Röthke, official in charge of Jewish affairs for the Security Police and the SD, comments on the French attitude towards the deportation of Jews with French citizenship[1]

Notes by Section IV B, Office of the Senior Commander of the Security Police in France,[2] SA 225a (Rö/Ne), signed Röthke, Paris, dated 10 February 1943[3]

Re: deportation of Jews with French citizenship from Drancy camp for Jews to Auschwitz/Upper Silesia

1. *File note:*

At present, there are 837 Jews with French citizenship in Drancy camp for Jews, who were taken there in the course of roundups of Jews in December 1941 and in 1942. Also in Drancy are 661 Jews with French citizenship who have been transferred there by various offices of the Security Police and the SD, the Feldgendarmerie, etc., because of punishable offences.

In reply to an enquiry from this office, the Reich Security Main Office has decided that transports of Jews to Auschwitz can now begin.[4] All preparations have been made to dispatch trains on 9, 11, and 13 February, one train on each of these days, each carrying 1,000 Jews.

The first train left Le Bourget-Drancy railway station on 9 February 1943 with 1,000 stateless and otherwise deportable Jews.

Another 1,000 Jews who are stateless or whose citizenship makes them subject to deportation await departure on the second train.

Those prioritized for dispatch on the third train, due to depart on Saturday, 13 February 1943, are Jews who are French citizens and have been imprisoned in Drancy for various offences. In addition, the French police wanted to carry out a small roundup of their own by 11 February 1943 to arrest Jews subject to deportation. (The French police themselves made this offer to arrest these Jews through the police chiefs François and Tulard from the police prefecture, because they wanted to prevent Jews with French citizenship from being deported at all. In particular, they wanted to arrest the Jews who had been in hiding during earlier roundups but have now resurfaced due to the stamping of food ration cards.)

This afternoon, Prefect Leguay's aide Sauts, as well as the police chiefs François and Tulard, paid me a visit. Sauts told me that the question of deporting Jews with French citizenship had been brought to Bousquet's attention by Leguay. He said Bousquet had ordered him to inform me that the question of deporting Jews holding French citizenship has not yet been settled between the German and the French governments. Therefore, he said, Bousquet cannot permit the French police to assist with the deportation of these Jews as long as this issue remains unresolved.

1 Mémorial de la Shoah, XXVc-204. Published in French translation in Klarsfeld, *Calendrier*, pp. 1358–1359. This document has been translated from German.

2 Helmut Knochen.

3 The original contains handwritten annotations and underlining.

4 See Doc. 286, fn. 3.

In reply to my question as to whether this also applied to Jews holding French citizenship who are guilty of offences, Sauts answered in the affirmative.

I told the gentlemen that I had taken note of Bousquet's message, but that this attitude surprised me because we deported Jews with French citizenship who had violated the regulations in force pertaining to Jews as early as 1942.[5]

Sauts went on to state that the position taken by Bousquet meant that we could deport all Jews holding French citizenship who are in Drancy; the French police, however, could not assist with this process.[6]

The Senior Commander of the Security Police and the SD made an immediate decision on the phone, after which I informed Sauts that the transport on 13 February 1943 would depart without fail.

Sauts told me in conclusion that Bousquet was still in Paris today and that he would immediately inform Bousquet of our decision.

I will submit the deportation question straight away this evening to SS-Obersturmbannführer Eichmann of the Reich Security Main Office.

2. Submitted to SS-Standartenführer Dr Knochen for information.[7]

DOC. 291

On 11 February 1943 Klaus Barbie reports to the Senior Commander of the Security Police on arrests in the office of the General Union of French Jews in Lyons[1]

Letter from the Lyons Einsatzkommando of the Security Police (SD) (log no. 563/43), signed p.p. Barbie,[2] to the Senior Commander of the Security Police and the SD[3] for the sector of the Military Commander in France, Paris, dated 11 February 1943[4]

Re: roundup of the Jewish committee 'General Union of French Jews' (UGIF), Lyons
Case file: none.
Enclosed: 86 arrest and committal warrants, 80 envelopes with identity documents and valuables and a summary (in duplicate).[5]
The local office has learned that there is a Jewish committee in Lyons at 12 rue St Catherine, which supports emigrants and helps Jews wanting to flee from France to

5 See Introduction, p. 67.
6 Knochen underlined this last passage and put exclamation marks in the margin of the document.
7 Knochen requested submission of the document to Higher SS and Police Leader (HSSPF) Oberg, who made a note on the document the same day, intended for Knochen: 'Urgently consult embassy'.

1 Mémorial de la Shoah, XLVI-A. This document has been translated from German.
2 Klaus Barbie (1913–1991), policeman; joined the SS in 1935 and the NSDAP in 1937; worked for the SD in Berlin in 1935; in Düsseldorf in 1936; worked for the Security Police and the SD in The Hague and then Amsterdam, from 1941 for the Central Office for Jewish Emigration; head of Section IV in the Office of the Commander of the Security Police and the SD (KdS) in Lyons in Nov. 1942; sentenced to death in absentia in France in 1947; fled to Bolivia; extradited to France in 1983; sentenced to life imprisonment for crimes against humanity in 1987; died in Lyons.
3 Helmut Knochen.
4 The original contains handwritten annotations.
5 This is not included in the file.

Switzerland with their preparations for illegal border-crossing.[6] On 9 February 1943 an operation was carried out to arrest the committee. When the raid started, more than 30 Jews were already in the offices. All these individuals were detained. More Jews arrived over the course of the next hour, and a total of 86 persons were arrested.[7] All those detained were put in one room and, before they could be individually searched, most of the Jews destroyed their forged identity cards and identity documents. Most of these Jews were planning to escape from here to Switzerland in the near future. When the office premises were searched, a considerable amount of valuables, foreign currencies, etc. were found, the owners of which are known. Some of the owners have probably already fled to Switzerland. These valuables were confiscated and are enclosed in a separate envelope (see attached list). Further valuables and currencies were found when these individuals were searched; they are enclosed in the case file in separate envelopes, together with the identity documents, for further processing.

All 86 persons arrested will be taken to the Wehrmacht military prison[8] in Chalon s. S.[9] today to be processed there.

It was established that the committee was supported by financially well-situated Jews in France and above all by a Jewish committee in Geneva.

Since the Wehrmacht military prison in Chalon s. S. is overcrowded, the prisoners will be transported onwards to the appropriate camp, as per consultation with Chalon s. S.

DOC. 292

On 12 February 1943 the Senior Commander of the Security Police complains to the Reich Security Main Office that the French and the Italians are preventing the deportation of French Jews[1]

Letter (BdS/E) from the Senior Commander of the Security Police in France, signed Helmut Knochen, Paris, to SS-Gruppenführer Müller,[2] Office IV of the Reich Security Main Office, Berlin, dated 12 February 1943 (copy)[3]

Re: final solution to the Jewish question in France
Case file: consultation with SS-Obersturmführer Eichmann in Paris
The message from SS-Obersturmbannführer Eichmann about the evacuation of all Jews holding French citizenship[4] has prompted me to give my view briefly on this question and, in outlining the present situation, to indicate the items that are essential for implementation so that difficulties posed by the French government are kept to a minimum.

6 This refers to the Lyons office of the Committee for Assistance to Refugees (CAR) and the Federation of Jewish Societies in France (FSJF). Both aid organizations saved Jews from deportation by arranging for forged papers, places to hide in the homes of non-Jews, and opportunities to escape to Switzerland.
7 Correctly: eighty-four persons were arrested and taken to Drancy.
8 In the original: Kriegswehrmachtshaftanstalt.
9 Chalon-sur-Saône.

1 Mémorial de la Shoah, XXVI-71. Published in French translation in Klarsfeld, *Calendrier*, pp. 1368–1371. This document has been translated from German.

1) As announced in the various reports, the French government, responding to German pressure, has consented to have Jews without French citizenship, including stateless Jews, placed under arrest and also handed over by the French police to the German police for deportation to the Reich.
2) However, the French government, that is, primarily Marshal Pétain, is resisting every attempt to extend the anti-Jewish measures to Jews who are French citizens. The French government declined to decree the introduction of the star. In the formerly occupied territory, the star was introduced through German regulations.[5] It has not yet been introduced in the newly occupied territory because the French government persists in its refusal to adopt for this territory the same directives used by the German military administration in the formerly occupied territory. In the newly occupied territory, the French government is so far still sovereign.[6]
3) All attempts to change the stance of the French government have ended in failure. Even the efforts of Commissioner for Jewish Affairs Darquier de Pellepoix produced no result. Even if President Laval claims that he too would be personally willing to apply the measures to all Jews, this statement cannot be taken seriously because he always talks his way out of it at the decisive moment by saying that

a) the Italians do not even allow restrictions to be applied to Jews; on the contrary, in the Italian-occupied territory they take on the protection of Jews of all nationalities and do not allow the French government to issue measures even against Jews with French citizenship.[7]
b) Marshal Pétain would allegedly voice his opposition to the concentration or deportation of Jews who are French citizens in the strongest terms. Pétain, according to Laval, would even threaten to resign.

4) The attitude of Marshal Pétain becomes evident when one considers that the French police – Bousquet, the French chief of police, personally – do everything possible to prevent Jews with French citizenship from being deported. The following will serve as an example:

2 Heinrich Müller (1900–1945), aircraft mechanic; worked at the police headquarters in Munich from 1919; worked for the Political Police (anti-communist measures) from 1929; joined the SS and the SD in 1934, and the NSDAP in 1938; transferred to the Gestapo Central Office in Berlin in 1934; manager of the Reich Central Office for Jewish Emigration and head of Office IV at the Reich Security Main Office from 1939; attended the Wannsee Conference in 1942; died at the end of the war.
3 The original contains handwritten annotations.
4 Knochen is presumably referring to a conversation with Eichmann during the latter's brief visit to Paris on 11 Feb. 1943.
5 See PMJ 5/323.
6 After the occupation of the southern zone in Nov. 1942, the German authorities administered the two zones separately, using the terms 'altbesetzt' (formerly occupied) and 'neubesetzt' (newly occupied). The newly occupied territory was not put under the control of the military administration in charge in Paris; instead, it was directly subordinated, as a 'zone of operations', to the commander-in-chief in the West, General von Rundstedt. This was intended to preserve the illusion of ongoing French sovereignty.
7 In the Alpes-Maritimes département, the Italian occupiers prevented, for example, the application of a French decree which, in Dec. 1942, ordered the stamping of Jews' identity documents and the forced resettlement of all post-1938 Jewish immigrants to the German-controlled Ardèche département.

Jews with French citizenship were supposed to be deported from the camp for Jews if they had been arrested for failure to wear the star or for other transgressions. Bousquet made it known that these Jews could be deported, but that the French police would not be willing to carry this out. Upon receiving the reply from this office that the deportation would then be carried out by German forces, the French police responded by conducting a roundup and immediately arresting 1,300 Jews who were not French citizens.[8] These Jews were handed over to the German police with the suggestion that they be deported in place of the Jews who were French nationals. It is clear that both categories of Jews will be deported in this case.

5) If measures against all Jews with French citizenship are now issued on a large scale, one must expect political repercussions. And just as in other territories the overall military situation gives rise to the view that Germany will lose the war, such attitudes are especially evident in France, where there is an expectation that the American efforts will restore North Africa to France and also guarantee a strong France. In France, owing to this 'wait-and-see attitude', which is particularly pronounced at the moment, there will be an attempt to allow no further measures against Jews in order to demonstrate to the Americans a refusal to do the German government's bidding.

To support the arguments they put to the Germans against the measures, they cite the Italians. They point out that the Italians – and these are facts that are also reported and emphasized by every office of the Security Police as well as other German authorities – champion the Jews everywhere east of the Rhône. Not only do the Italian authorities send notes to the French government in which they forbid the visible identification of the Jews[9] and, by so doing, stand up for Jews of all nationalities, but in addition, excellent relations have come to prevail between the Italian occupation troops and the Jewish population. Italians live in the homes of Jews and allow Jews to invite them and pay for them, so that the impression is created down there that the German point of view and the Italian one are totally different. On the French side, it has already been suggested that, because of Jewish influence, pacifist and communist subversion has been successful among the Italian soldiers, and, as a result, a pro-American sentiment is on the rise. At the same time, these Jewish middlemen are creating a very good relationship between the Italian soldiers and the French population with the suggestion that the French and the Italians, as Latin races, understand each other far more readily than the Germans and the French or the Germans and the Italians. Everything possible is being attempted in the conscious effort to criticize the German–Italian relationship in harsh terms and, conversely, to advocate a French–Italian rapprochement and thereby at the same time to sow subversion among the entire population with the suggestion that, in the event of an invasion by the Americans, the Italians will not put up any resistance. Instead, it has been suggested, peace will ultimately be brought about by the Americans.

8 The roundup took place in the Paris metropolitan area during the night of 10 Feb. 1943; in the process, the French police arrested 1,549 Jews in total, including a great many elderly people. See Introduction, p. 77.

9 This refers to the stamping of identity documents; see fn. 7.

Because of the current military situation,[10] this state of affairs gives the French government a dual incentive: first, to speak out strongly against Italy, as they have seen themselves as superior to the Italians from time immemorial, but second, to resist the German demands concerning the Jewish question.

6) If the final solution to the Jewish question in France is now ordered, one must anticipate that

a) Pétain will oppose this, i.e. will not allow the French police to carry out the executive measures, or will threaten to resign. (Given the overall situation in Africa and the fact that French citizens keep trying to get to North Africa, without Pétain issuing any regulations or implementing any measures to stop this, it is open to question whether Pétain is still an asset to the German Reich as the French head of state, or whether Pétain is playing a role as the figurehead of Franco-German conciliation, while at the same time acting as a rallying point for all Frenchmen and keeping a close eye on events in North Africa in the hope of a favourable outcome for France.)

b) Laval himself will countenance the measures against the Jews if he receives in exchange some political pledge from Germany to the French people.[11] In a discussion on 12 February 1943, Laval stated that the Americans have already pledged to France that France will receive all the former Italian colonies and will get the French colonies back, and that France will obtain more than the Rhine border in Europe. The Germans, he said, have made no promise of any sort to him with respect to the post-war period. In my view, Laval will swallow the measures against the Jews if he receives a political assurance of some sort.

7) For the implementation of the measures against Jews in the newly occupied territory, the use of the French police is essential. This would be guaranteed by Laval personally under the preconditions enumerated under point 6.

8) To implement the measures for France as a whole, the prerequisite is that the measures must be carried out in the Italian-occupied territory as well. Otherwise, the migration of Jews into the Italian-occupied territory, which has already begun, would assume vast proportions, and implementation would stop at only half measures.[12]

10 Knochen was referring here to the German defeat at Stalingrad and the loss of Libya by the Axis powers.

11 German policy towards Vichy had become noticeably more hard line since spring 1942. Although the French government complied with the Germans' economic and military demands, the occupation regime did not ease its approach.

12 In early 1943 there were more than 25,000 Jews in the eight Italian-occupied départements. Most of these Jews were in Nice and the surrounding area. The influx did not subsequently abate, owing to the wave of arrests in Feb. 1943: see Introduction, pp. 78–79.

DOC. 293

On 3 March 1943 David Burkowsky writes a farewell letter to his daughter on the eve of his deportation from Drancy camp[1]

Letter from David Burkowsky,[2] Drancy, to his daughter, Pierrette Burkowsky,[3] 22 rue de la Chapelle, Paris, 18th arrondissement, dated 3 March 1943

My dearest Pierrette,

It is in continuing good spirits that I am writing to you.[4] Tomorrow morning we will be leaving for Germany. I think of you constantly, and I hope more and more that I will see you again. Grandfather[5] left the day before yesterday with great courage. I think I will meet him again. As for Grandmother,[6] it might be better to hide the truth about me from her and to tell her that I'm in the countryside. Don't worry, my dear little Pierrette, I'm still sure that I'll see you all again in good health. Please give my love to everyone and be sure to tell them that I've not forgotten anyone – I am taking your last postcard and your photos with me; they'll give me courage. I'm sending you lots of love, my dear Pierrette. Be a good girl now, because in spite of everything we have had to endure, you are still just a little girl. I embrace you and remain full of hope.

Your Papa

I just received the parcel. What joy!

1 The original is privately owned. Copy in Mémorial de la Shoah, CMLXXXVI(2)-11. This document has been translated from French.

2 David Burkowsky (b. 1902), warehouse manager; emigrated from Odessa to Paris in 1906; volunteered for the French army, 1939–1940; worked for a trading company in Paris; arrested by the French police on 21 Feb. 1943; imprisoned in Drancy camp and deported on 4 March 1943 to Majdanek or Sobibor, where he perished.

3 Pierrette Burkowsky (b. 1928), still in school at the time; went into hiding in Nantes until the end of the war; thereafter worked as a seamstress and shop assistant, and from 1977 as a commercial employee.

4 Two days earlier, David Burkowsky had written to his daughter to inform her of his own and her grandfather's imminent departure.

5 Ephraïm (François) Burkowsky (1870–1943), tailor; born near Kyiv; emigrated to France with his family in 1906; arrested by the French police on 11 Feb. 1943; on 2 March 1943 deported from Drancy to Auschwitz, where he perished.

6 Berthe Burkowsky, née Lev (b. 1878), housewife; born in Odessa; most likely not deported.

DOC. 294

On 12 March 1943 Raymond-Raoul Lambert writes to André Baur to explain his reservations about the planned restructuring of the General Union of French Jews[1]

Letter from the director general of the General Union of French Jews (UGIF) (unoccupied zone), signed Raymond-Raoul Lambert,[2] 101 rue Sylvabelle, Marseilles, to André Baur,[3] vice president of the UGIF (occupied zone), Paris, dated 12 March 1943

Re: your letter 1-AB/SBL, dated 4 March 1943
I have pleasure in confirming receipt of your letter of 4 March, which I was keen to discuss with several of my colleagues on the board after I returned from my trip before informing you of our opinion.[4]
Foreign staff:
The UGIF (unoccupied zone) foreign staff members were made redundant on 10 March, as per the instructions from the Commissariat General for Jewish Affairs,[5] which was kind enough to grant me 12 (twelve) exemptions for long-serving technical staff at the charities and for veterans who are indispensable to the continuation of our social welfare measures.
Reorganizing the UGIF:
We have taken note of your proposal of 3 March,[6] and I have to admit that it left us somewhat astonished. I will put it to the board meeting, which I have called for 29 March at *Grenoble*, and I will inform you of our decision on this matter.

1 YVA, O.9/28. This document has been translated from French.
2 Raymond-Raoul Lambert (1894–1943), Germanist and journalist; teacher in Germany, 1913–1914; worked for the Inter-Allied Rhineland High Commission in Bonn from 1918; on the council of the Zionist Association of France from 1927; editor-in-chief of the weekly newspaper *L'Univers israélite*, 1935–1937; secretary general of the Committee for Assistance to Refugees (CAR), 1936–1942; served in the war, 1939–1940; head of the General Union of French Jews (UGIF) in the southern zone from 1942; interim president of the UGIF from March 1943; co-founder of the Centre for Contemporary Jewish Documentation (CDJC) in Grenoble; arrested on 21 August 1943; deported on 7 Dec. 1943 with his family to Auschwitz, where he was murdered three days later.
3 André Baur (1940–1944), banker; president of the Zionist-leaning Union Libérale Juive in the 1920s; treasurer of the Keren Kayemeth LeIsraël de France (Jewish National Fund of France) until 1940; head of the Comité de coordination des œuvres de bienfaisance juives, the precursor organization to the UGIF, from June 1941; head of the UGIF North from 1942; resigned in Feb. 1943; interned in Drancy in late July 1943; deported to Auschwitz on 17 Dec. 1943.
4 In this letter, Baur had informed Lambert that Heinz Röthke had refused to allow the UGIF headquarters (in the unoccupied zone) to be moved from Marseilles to Lyons. In addition, Baur had announced that he would cease his efforts on behalf of UGIF foreign staff members because he feared that these efforts might lead to the persecution measures being expanded to include French Jews.
5 Lambert continued to refer to the northern and southern zones of France as the occupied and the unoccupied zones, although German troops had also occupied the southern part of the country in late 1942. Until spring 1943 employment with the UGIF shielded foreign Jews from arrest and deportation. However, in late 1942 the Commissariat General for Jewish Affairs had ordered all non-French Jews to be dismissed by 28 Feb. 1943: see Introduction, p. 79.
6 Baur had submitted far-reaching proposals for a reform of the UGIF, which included merging the sections in the two zones and giving predominance to representatives of the northern section. This reform, which also envisaged pooling the budgets of both sections, was intended to save the northern section from a looming bankruptcy.

First of all, to make sure there is absolutely no misunderstanding between us, I would like to point out the following: if you believed that you could deduce on my part any approval of a total and immediate synchronization on the basis of the private agreement in principle which I communicated to you during our brief conversation on the subject in Lyons, you mistook my intentions.

To be quite frank, the way I understood the idea of a regional reorganization of the UGIF (unoccupied zone) was that its goal was to concentrate the administrative and technical responsibilities in the hands of regional delegates – as per the wishes and due to the presence of the occupying authorities. But, based on what has been our doctrine for more than a year, I understood that the different head offices of the UGIF[7] (unoccupied zone) would continue to work as technical and social welfare agencies. Specifically, I thought to model our organization in the unoccupied zone on the military organization of an army corps, in which the regional director would take on the role of the commander, while the regional head offices would function as the high commands do in the military.

I am sure you are aware that the withdrawal to the unoccupied zone of the executive staff of institutions which have been active in Europe and in France for more than a hundred years in some cases represents a moral obligation to respect certain technical and social traditions. This should in no way elicit any disapproval from the French or the occupying authorities.

In addition, I believe I was given to understand in the very important talks that I had at Vichy, both in the General Commissariat for Jewish Affairs and in the circles around the head of state and the head of government, that both the French authorities and even the occupying authorities themselves admit that the two zones are to be governed differently, even after the relaxation of the demarcation line.

Under these conditions, I feel that an immediate and complete synchronization would not only hinder our social welfare work, but also discourage our donors, on whom we are counting to keep our budget in balance. As you know, the donors formally insist that their voluntary contributions are specifically allocated.

Under these circumstances, I doubt that my administrative board will consent to committing hara-kiri so quickly,[8] and for my part, I cannot see what role a general directorate would play, as according to your plan it would become a simple medium of transmission between Paris and the regional delegations.

I hope you will not hold it against me that – in order for myself and my colleagues from the unoccupied zone to disclaim responsibility from the outset – I feel obliged to advise the Commissioner General for Jewish Affairs that I cannot adopt a view regarding your proposal of 3 March without having first submitted it to my colleagues and informed them of my reservations.

7 Any charitable organization incorporated into the UGIF normally had its own 'head office', i.e. formed its own department. After the German invasion of the southern zone, all Jewish charitable organizations had to be incorporated into the UGIF.

8 Baur's suggestion was to keep the UGIF headquarters in Paris. The merged management board was to have twelve members, with only three from the southern zone. By contrast, the heads of the southern section of the UGIF wanted to maintain its existing structure, as the disparate operations of the two sections offered the charities more leeway in how they carried out their operations and thereby created more protection for Jews and better opportunities for them to escape.

I am sure you will agree that it is imperative that we get back in touch as soon as possible so that we and our colleagues in Paris can take a unified stance on the matter. I would therefore ask whether it might be possible for you to come to see us and attend the board meeting on 29 March, at which you as well as our friend Mr *Katz* or any other of your colleagues would be most welcome.[9] If for any unknown reason you should have any difficulties in obtaining another permit, I would suggest that you ask for three permits in Paris so that my secretary general, Mr *Brener*, and my two fellow board members, Mr *Gamzon* and Mr *Lazard*,[10] who are all perfectly up to date on the issues of organization and charity work, can come and make contact in Paris with our colleagues from the board in the occupied zone.[11]

I would have liked to ask you to do the same for myself, but the new powers conferred on me by the decree of 1 March[12] mean I must not be away for a longer period of time because I have to sign papers and liaise with the authorities.

UGIF (unoccupied zone) contribution to the UGIF (occupied zone) budget:
In your report of 3 March, you informed the Commissariat General for Jewish Affairs that a monthly sum of 3,500,000 francs would be placed at your disposal. I must remind you (as our minutes clearly confirm) that we only made a commitment for two months, which is to say for February and March 1943, for a total of 5,000,000 (five million) francs.

Information on social welfare services:
I thank you for the information you sent me on the way your social welfare services work. I am pleased to know that our services in the unoccupied zone are organized in the same way and that the application forms have more or less the same format.

Prisoners from Lyons and Marseilles:
It is with regret that I have read Mr Israelovicz's[13] letters of 1 March on the issue of Leiba, as well as the news of our officials currently in Compiègne and what you told me about a possible release.[14]

9 From Jan. 1943 Baur and his secretary general, Armand Katz, were issued passes that allowed them to travel to the southern zone.

10 Maurice Brener (1912–1978), Lambert's secretary; representative of the American Jewish Joint Distribution Committee (JDC) in France, 1943–1945; had ties to the French Resistance; arrested by the German police in Paris in May 1944, but managed to escape. Robert Gamzon (b. 1905), electrical engineer; founder of the Jewish Scouts of France (EIF); organized the Scouts' integration into the armed resistance from 1943. André Lazard (b. 1894), silk merchant; member of the administrative board of the UGIF South; arrested in mid November 1943 in Nice; a few days later deported to Auschwitz, where he perished.

11 In mid May 1943 Maurice Brener, Robert Gamzon, and Jules Jefroykin travelled to Paris and met with the directorate of the UGIF North.

12 On 1 March 1943 the Commissariat General for Jewish Affairs had appointed Lambert to the post of interim president of the (entire) UGIF.

13 Correctly: Leo Israelowicz (1912–1944?), opera singer; born in Vienna; in charge of liaison with the German authorities at the UGIF; on 17 Dec. 1943 deported to Auschwitz, where he perished.

14 This is a reference to UGIF staff from Marseilles and Lyons who had been arrested in the roundups. Baur thought there was little chance of their being released. David Leiba (1902–1944), prisoner of war in Germany in 1940; released for health reasons; head of the UGIF South's 5th directorate (refugee support); arrested in Jan. 1943 in Marseilles; deported via Compiègne and Drancy to Auschwitz, where he perished in early April 1944.

As for Compiègne, it was once again officially confirmed to me in Vichy that the French authorities are negotiating with the occupying authorities and that we should not lose hope.[15]

I therefore wonder – and I would be grateful if you could look into this – whether it would be useful for you to intervene to ensure that the prisoners from Marseilles who are currently in Stalag 122 in Compiègne receive either the same treatment as those in *Drancy* or as the prisoners of war, which is to say that they are at least given the chance to correspond.

The regional prefecture in Marseilles has informed me that the prisoners in Compiègne can now also receive parcels and money transfers, and has communicated their prisoner numbers to their families, either directly or through us. Both we and the regional prefecture would like to know the exact number and weight of the authorized parcels as well as the maximum amount of the money transfers.

New composition of the board:[16]

I have not yet obtained approval from Dr Joseph Weill, and I doubt that he will agree to work with us if the plan you have envisaged is realized. I hope I will be able to see him again next Tuesday and will strongly insist that he agrees in advance.

And finally, I would like to thank you most sincerely for letting the occupying authorities know that the charge against the UGIF (unoccupied zone), namely that it was getting involved in political issues, had no basis in reality.

I have always ensured, and will continue to do so in the strictest possible way, that our centres' activities and also the attitudes of my staff do not allow for any ambiguity in this respect.

It seems to me that this charge is based on a matter that I would like you to clarify when you have the opportunity. Until 11 November last year, the UGIF (unoccupied zone) was engaged in certain activities at some of its centres which differed completely from those of the UGIF (occupied zone). Specifically, it continued – with the permission and under the strict control of the French authorities – to organize emigration; to administer schools and charitable organizations in Morocco and Tunisia, both then still under French authority; and to maintain relations with international charitable organizations authorized to operate in the unoccupied zone, i.e. the Quakers, the American Red Cross, the YMCA, and our organizations in Portugal and Switzerland.

Of course, as I have made clear to the authorities, all of these activities have ceased as of 11 November 1942.[17]

Director General of the UGIF (unoccupied zone)

15 This is a reference to the people arrested in the roundups in Marseilles in Jan. 1943, which were carried out by the German and the French police: see Introduction, pp. 76–77.

16 See fn. 8.

17 Most of these activities and contacts continued clandestinely after German troops occupied the southern zone.

DOC. 295
On 15 March 1943 Heinz Röthke asks the Paris Police Prefecture to arrest 720 Jewish workers and the foreign employees of the General Union of French Jews[1]

Letter from Section IV B, Office of the Senior Commander of the Security Police in France,[2] SA 225a (Rö/Ne), signed p.p. SS-Obersturmführer Röthke, to the Paris Police Prefecture, dated 19 March 1943 (carbon copy)[3]

Re: arrest of Jews
Case file: none
I request that on one day this week, the following categories of Jews are arrested and immediately taken to Drancy:

1) The Jews specified in the 720 sets of identity cards for fur workers that were handed over to Director François today, provided they are citizens of any country subject to deportation in accordance with the current provisions.[4]

   To this end, I request that their citizenship is established first by reference to the card indexes held by yourselves.

2) All Jews who appear on the lists of foreign personnel employed by the General Union of Jews in France, which were handed over to Director François today,[5] provided the names of these Jews are not marked with a red or blue cross.

   The Jews from the Union whose names are not marked with a cross are also to be arrested along with their family members. For this category, however, an exact address must first be determined by reference to the indexes.

I request that the arrest operation be kept secret until the last moment. The arrests are to be made in the early hours, before the Jews are permitted to leave their apartments.[6]

1 Mémorial de la Shoah, XXVI-72. Published in facsimile in Joseph Billig, *Le Commissariat général aux questions juives (1941–1944)*, vol. 1 (Paris: Centre de documentation juive contemporaine, 1955), pp. 384–385. This document has been translated from German.
2 Helmut Knochen.
3 The original contains handwritten annotations and underlining.
4 The Jewish fur workers were employed by various Paris companies in connection with Wehrmacht commissions. They therefore had so-called 'company identity cards', which should have protected them and their relatives from being interned and deported.
5 The UGIF administration had passed on the list, together with the fur workers' identity documents, to the Commissariat General for Jewish Affairs in mid March 1943. Of the 920 employees, around 230 Jews who did not have French citizenship had been dismissed. The identity cards should have protected them from arrest until 31 March 1943.
6 In the operation during the night of 17/18 March 1943, a total of 350 fur workers were arrested along with their family members. A few days later most were released and sent back to their workplaces. They were arrested again four months later. Many of the non-French employees of the UGIF had evidently received advance warning, as only a minority were at their listed residences.

DOC. 296

On 20 March 1943 the German ambassador in Rome reports to the Reich Foreign Minister about Mussolini's willingness to take harsher action against Jews in France[1]

Telegram (Geh.Ch.V.)[2] from the German embassy in Rome (no. 1311, marked 'secret Reich business'), signed Mackensen,[3] Rome, to the Reich Foreign Office, Berlin (received on 20 March 1943, 22:20), dated 20 March 1943

With reference to telegram no. 1117 of 14 March[4] and in response to telegram no. 1246 of 17 March.[5]

Bastianini[6] asked me to come to his office this morning so that he could inform me of the following on behalf of the Duce[7] in connection with my conversation with the latter on 17 March:

With regard to taking action against Jews etc. (i.e. citizens of enemy powers) in parts of France occupied by the Italians, Bastianini said that the Duce has now opted for our *solution no. 2* and issued the corresponding order.[8] I replied to Bastianini that this surprised me somewhat, in that in his conversation with me, the Duce had clearly decided in favour of solution no. 1 and had used arguments that I found convincing to justify his opinion. Bastianini replied that my impression was indeed accurate, as he had gathered from a conversation with the Duce that took place immediately afterwards. Subsequently, he said, the Duce summoned Colonel General Ambrosio[9] to issue the necessary instructions. From the latter's presentation, the Duce gained the impression that the objective deemed crucial both by him and by us could definitely not – as matters stand –

1 PA AA, R 100 869, fols. 155–158. This document has been translated from German.
2 Short for Geheimes Chiffrier-Verfahren, secret coding method.
3 Hans-Georg von Mackensen (1883–1947), diplomat; personal aide-de-camp of Prince August Wilhelm of Prussia, 1905–1919; diplomat in Copenhagen, Rome, Brussels, Albania, and Budapest from 1920; state secretary in the Reich Foreign Office from 1937; German ambassador in Rome, 1938–1943; suspended from his post as ambassador in late Nov. 1944; prisoner of war in French captivity, 1945–1946.
4 In this telegram Ribbentrop instructed the German embassy in Rome to ask Mussolini to intervene in person because the Italian military command posts in France were refusing to carry out measures against Jews: PA AA, R 100 869, fols. 155–158; see also Doc. 292.
5 Report on Mackensen's conversation with Mussolini, which the former sent to Berlin the same day: PA AA, R 100 869, fols. 155–158.
6 Giuseppe Bastianini (1899–1961), politician; vice secretary of the Italian National Fascist Party, 1921–1923; diplomat from 1927; Italian ambassador in London, 1939–1940; governor in occupied Dalmatia, 1941–1943; voted against Mussolini in the Fascist Grand Council in July 1943, then fled Italy; sentenced to death in absentia in 1944; acquitted in 1947.
7 Benito Mussolini.
8 Ribbentrop had proposed three possible solutions to Mussolini: 1) order the Italian military authorities in France to stop obstructing the French police in the implementation of antisemitic measures, 2) assign the implementation of antisemitic measures to the Italian civilian police (a suggestion made by Heinrich Himmler), or 3) leave such measures to the German and French police.
9 Vittorio Ambrosio (1879–1958), military officer; commander of the Italian 2nd Army (Yugoslavia), 1939–1941; Italian chief of staff in Yugoslavia in 1942; chief of the Italian general staff in 1943; participated in the arrest of Mussolini and the negotiations with the Allies in July 1943; inspector general of the army in 1943; retired in 1944.

be achieved by the French police alone, for the reasons outlined by Colonel General Ambrosio. Ambrosio reportedly stated that according to all the reports he had to hand, in particular the one from General Vercelling,[10] the French police had indeed clamped down in some instances or at least given the impression of a clampdown, but in numerous other instances it had been clearly established that cooperation between the Jews and the French police had spread, and that Jewish money had played a role in this, as had the Jewish ladies and the fact that many Italian officers were even billeted in Jewish homes, with the result that a great many Jews had managed to evade arrest.

In response to my comment that – as I had also proved to the Duce by citing concrete cases – in our view the French police had failed primarily because the Italian military authorities had held them back and even countermanded arrests that had already been made, Bastianini replied that according to the account given by Ambrosio, who did not dispute these facts per se, these were merely a few exceptional cases which have no significance for the overall situation. As a rule, he said, in reality the French police simply do not get on with the job and do not even want to get on with the job because, in addition to the motives mentioned above, they are reluctant to lend themselves to the implementation of measures demanded by the Berlin–Rome axis. Therefore, he said, the Duce preferred the second solution, which we had also described to him as desirable, and to this end, following the audience with Ambrosio, he immediately summoned Senise,[11] the chief of the Italian police, to his office and in Bastianini's presence directed him to take over responsibility for the operation on his own, completely independent of the Italian military. For this purpose, he reported, he selected one of the vice inspectors of police from a list of four names submitted to him by Senise and had him leave for occupied France yesterday evening, with the appropriate instructions. From among the four names he selected Police Inspector Lospinoso, whom he, the Duce, personally knew to be especially dynamic.[12] The Duce, Bastianini said, simultaneously sent strongly worded written orders to both Lospinoso and General Vercelling, which have by now been delivered to the latter by a special officer. In reply to my question whether the Italian police really have the manpower to carry out the operation, Bastianini said that the forces are indeed sufficient for complete registration of the Jews, but that they would of course make use of the forces of the French police to implement the arrests, deportations and so forth ordered by the Italian police.

With regard to the execution of the operation, Bastianini said that an order had already been issued by which all Jews in Italian-occupied France are no longer permitted to leave their present place of residence, where they had previously still enjoyed some freedom of movement. Police Inspector Lospinoso, Bastianini said, had been assigned to launch the broader operation without delay. It consists in immediately transporting

10 Correctly: Mario Vercellino (1879–1961), commander of the 4th Army in Italian-occupied France, Nov. 1942–Sept. 1943.

11 Carmine Senise (1883–1958), police officer and prefect; at the Italian Ministry of the Interior from 1908; prefect and vice chief of police in 1932; chief of the Italian police, 1940–1943; arrested in Sept. 1943; interned at Dachau.

12 Guido Lospinoso (1885–1972), police official; Italian consul in Nice in 1928; worked at the Italian Ministry of the Interior in 1939; transferred to southern France as 'Inspector General for Racial Policy' in March 1943; provisionally retired in 1944; senior ranking police officer in Caserta in 1947 and in Udine in 1949; retired with official honours in 1953.

all Jews etc. to remote interior regions of France that are relatively easy to monitor closely and housing the Jews in all available homes and hotels there, which will be requisitioned for this purpose, as no concentration camps are available there and their construction would take months.[13] When I asked what was to become of them from there, in other words, whether deporting them was being considered, Bastianini replied that as of yet this was not the intention.

Police Inspector Lospinoso has been ordered to return to Rome after an appropriate period and to report in person on the measures he has taken and on their implementation.

When I asked in conclusion whether there was also sufficient guarantee that the Italian military authorities would not somehow obstruct the Italian police's operation, as had happened previously, Bastianini said that the order given by the Duce to General Vercelling in this regard was unambiguous and strict and even went so far as to stipulate that members of the Italian forces would be made accountable if they were to act as protectors of the Jews or other undesirable elements in any way.

DOC. 297
On 26 March 1943 the prefect of the Marne département reports on Jews trying to escape from a deportation train[1]

Letter from the prefect of the Marne département,[2] Châlons-sur-Marne,[3] to Council of State member and the secretary general of the police,[4] Paris (received on 29 March 1943), dated 26 March 1943[5]

I am writing to inform you that on 25 March, around 2.30 p.m., the alarm signal in a train carriage containing the military guards was sounded just as the train pulled into Epernay station. The goods train was transporting Jews from Drancy to an unknown destination.[6]

The train was stopped by the military guard on board when they noticed that a number of Jews had escaped by cutting open a side panel. The soldiers of the escort made use of their weapons and shot five of the fugitives, four of whom were picked up straight away and put back into the train, which immediately started again. One of the prisoners was wounded, but still managed to get away.[7]

13 Thousands of Jews from the Côte d'Azur, who according to the German military authorities represented a threat to military security, were to be interned at least 100 kilometres into the Italian zone of occupation.

1 AN, F7, vol. 15 088. This document has been translated from French.
2 Louis Péretti della Rocca (b. 1885), lawyer; practised law, 1907–1912; in the French administration from 1912; appointed prefect in 1930; worked in the colonial and the finance ministries, 1930–1931; regional prefect in Châlons-sur-Marne and prefect of the Marne département, 1942; relieved of his duties in Nov. 1944; retired in 1945.
3 Renamed Châlons-en-Champagne in 1995.
4 René Bousquet.
5 The original contains handwritten annotations and underlining.
6 The 53rd deportation transport had left Le Bourget-Drancy station that day, carrying 527 men and 472 women. With the exception of 15 men, all on board were murdered in Sobibor.
7 At least sixteen persons tried to escape from the train; only three of them survived.

So far, the search for him has been unsuccessful.

When the train arrived at Châlons station, two corpses were literally thrown onto the platform by the train guards and then left there for everyone to see until the notified French authorities – the mayor and the local police commissioner – arrived and had them put into coffins.

The two victims[8] were temporarily deposited at the morgue, where the police commissioner tried to determine their identity from the few papers that they had been carrying.

It must be noted that no French identity documents or foreigners' permits were found on them. I think we will only be able to establish their identity with some certainty through the correspondence cards they had on them.

The two individuals who were wounded were bandaged and then placed in the care of their co-religionists. They were put onto a different wagon, along with the people from the wagon where the side panel had been sawn through.

This incident has caused quite an outcry among those who witnessed it, particularly at Châlons train station.

I will send you any further information on the identity of the two victims gleaned by the Châlons police commissioner.

The prefect

DOC. 298

On 3 April 1943 Émilie Carpe asks the French minister of war to intervene and bring her husband back from Upper Silesia[1]

Letter from Mrs Carpe,[2] 25 boulevard Battala, Marseilles, to the French minister of war,[3] dated 3 April 1943 (copy).

Dear Minister,

I am writing to inform you of my husband's case, which will surely attract your particular attention.

I must inform you that he has been the victim of an error, as he should have been protected by the law which stipulates that all Frenchmen who have received the Military Medal must not be interfered with, regardless of their denomination.

I am attaching to this letter the relevant documents to support his case, and I would be most grateful if you were to give them all the attention they require.[4]

8 This word was crossed out by hand on the original document and changed to 'bodies'.

1 AN, 2 AG, vol. 82. This document has been translated from French.
2 Émilie Marguerite Thérèse Carpe, née Lacombe (b. 1885), housewife; Paul Carpe was her third husband.
3 Eugène Bridoux (1888–1955), military officer and politician; made a general in 1938; in German captivity, 1940–1941; state secretary in the Ministry of War, later Ministry of Defence, 1942–1944; fled to Sigmaringen in 1944; arrested by US troops in 1945; fled from France to Spain in 1947; sentenced to death in absentia in 1948.
4 These are included in the file.

My husband, Paul *Carpe*,[5] born in Toul in 1880, is a veteran who served as a volunteer for the entirety of the 1914–1918 war. During that war, he was awarded the *Military Medal* for an act of brilliant courage, as mentioned in his citation. He was also decorated with the Croix de Guerre with laurels and I have attached the authenticated copies.

My husband converted to Catholicism in October 1933. Since his parents were of Israelite origin, he complied with the law requiring that he acknowledge his Israelite origin through his parents and he thus fulfilled his legal obligations.

I would like you to note as well that he is married to a French Aryan, born Émilie Marguerite Thérèse *Lacombe*, now *Carpe*. In this envelope you will also find the corresponding birth and baptismal certificates.

Despite all this, he was arrested at his home during the roundup of 22 January 1943 at around 2 in the morning because his identity card bore the word *Jew*. He was sent to Compiègne and given the prisoner number 8394. He was then transferred to the Drancy camp, staircase 3, room I, and from there to Metz. Now I have just learned that he was sent to Upper Silesia. Before receiving this last piece of information, which I learned from a third party, I was without news. In his last postcard, he told me that he would have been able to avoid deportation if he had been given enough time, but the time was too short for us to obtain all the necessary birth and baptismal certificates, which I am sending you herewith.

Please confirm receipt of this letter.

Yours faithfully,

DOC. 299
In April 1943 Joseph Weill sums up the desperate situation of the Jews in southern France[1]

Report (marked 'strictly confidential') by Dr Joseph Weill,[2] no place given, dated April 1943

In all occupied countries, an anti-Jewish central authority is gradually implementing the programme of extermination of Jews in its sector according to the methods established in Berlin, which it adapts to the local economic conditions and mentalities.

In France, it is section J4 under the command of an Obersturmführer which is engaged in solving the Jewish question.[3] Sections J1, J2, and J3 respectively are in charge of controlling the communists, the Gaullists, and the Freemasons and theosophists.

5 Paul Carpe (1880–1943), antiques dealer; arrested in Marseilles in Jan. 1943; imprisoned in Compiègne and Drancy; deported on 23 March 1943 to Sobibor extermination camp.

1 OSE, Fonds Tschlenoff, box 2. This document has been translated from French.

2 Joseph Weill (1902–1988), physician; relocated from Strasbourg to the Dordogne region in 1939; from 1940 worked as a physician for the Jewish population and refugees, in Gurs and Rivesaltes camps and elsewhere, and within the OSE welfare organization; member of the Comité de Nîmes; relocated to Geneva in March 1943; returned to Strasbourg in 1947; president of the consistory of the Bas-Rhin département. Author of *Contribution à l'histoire des camps d'internement dans l'anti-France* (Paris: Éditions du centre, 1946).

3 This refers to Section IV J (also IV B or IV B 4), headed by Heinz Röthke, in the Office of the Senior Commander of the Security Police and the SD.

In the areas administrated by a prefecture, the J4 Kommandanturs,[4] each headed by a specialist Sturmführer, carry out the directives issued from Paris and occasionally directly from Berlin. These headquarters are located in Marseilles, Lyons, Toulouse, Vichy, etc.

The experience gained in the different zones of operation has shown that the German police take two to three months to completely organize a newly occupied region. This is also what happened in the unoccupied zone, which is now officially called the formerly unoccupied zone and which the occupying power calls the southern zone, as opposed to the northern zone (the formerly occupied zone).[5]

The first steps of the German police's anti-Jewish activities were the compulsory stamping of all of the identity cards and the food rationing cards, for both the French and the foreign Jews, and the establishment with the help of the prefectures of a list of names of all Israelites from countries under German control. This list also indicates the heads of families, spouses, children, and anybody who depends on the head of the family.

As soon as this measure became known, recalling the events of August[6] in France, a new wave of panic swept over the affected Israelite families, who tried to escape this cruel fate. We witnessed the terrible flight of people in all directions. Some went into hiding, others tried to cross the borders guarded by the German army. Hunger forced the first to return to their homes, while a considerable number of the second group were arrested as they crossed the border and were then deported.

This meant that a significant number were arrested when the roundups started in January.

The programme of persecution was established in advance by Franco-German negotiations; during these talks, all of the foreign Israelites were sacrificed and abandoned without further consideration. In exchange, the French Jews were to be excluded from these collective measures in the same way as the people from Alsace and Lorraine and the escaped [prisoners of war]. But we cannot understand the true extent of this agreement if we ignore that it ended with an addendum according to which the Deutsche Polizei[7] reserved the right to take any appropriate police measure to ensure the protection and security of the occupying army. In expert hands, these few words became a formidable weapon against the French Israelites. On 22 January 1943 the SNCF received the order to fire up eight locomotives and to prepare eight long trains with empty goods wagons.

Soon after the evacuation of the Old Port,[8] whose population contained several hundred Israelite families, 10,000 police officers set up roadblocks in the heart of the city, in one neighbourhood after the other, street after street, and proceeded to methodically search each building, from the attic to the basement, as well as check the identity documents of all passers-by.[9]

Men, women, and children were arrested with absolutely unheard-of brutality, at all hours of the night, as they were getting off trains, in the squares in front of the train

4 German in the original: correctly 'Kommandanturen', here 'main offices'.

5 In Nov. 1942 German troops had also occupied the previously unoccupied zone in the southern part of the country.

6 This refers to the large-scale roundups by the French police in the unoccupied zone on 25 August 1942: see Doc. 262.

7 German in the original: 'German police'.

8 Of Marseilles.

9 See Introduction, pp. 76–77.

stations, on the tram, in train carriages, in their apartments, many of them barely dressed. They were not allowed to take any warm clothing or food with them, and then they were locked up in Mazargue[10] prison, thousands of them, both French and foreign.

A certain number of non-Jews were also arrested for as little as not having their food rationing cards on them in addition to their identity card. Later in Drancy they had to prove that they did not belong to the Jewish race.

Thousands of these people remained locked up for 48 hours without any food or water and without being able to stretch out, as they were crammed together so tightly in the cells.

The number of suicides was relatively high. Several women were seen grabbing hold of electric cables; children covered in blood threw themselves on their mothers' dead bodies, crying, and these scenes made a much deeper impression on the population than the regrettable evacuation of the Old Port.

Nevertheless, the roundups became more and more extensive. The local police were eager to support the German police, which meant that these measures threatened to affect the entire Israelite population of Marseilles. There was a real atmosphere of St Bartholomew's Night[11] about the city. No less than the personal intervention of the minister and secretary of state for the police[12] was needed: he was hastily sent there and eventually threatened to shut down the entire centralized police administration and leave the whole responsibility for security in the Bouches du Rhône département to the German authorities if the persecutions did not stop.[13] At midnight on the third day, the order ending the roundups was finally secured.[14]

A few prisoners who managed to jump out of the moving trains gave details of the extremely harsh conditions under which the transport to Drancy took place. The National Aid[15] was able to provide 900 grams of bread for 12 people, as well as half a tin of sardines and a cup of coffee at the moment of departure for each individual passenger to last for the entire journey (30 hours).

There were many dramatic incidents and some deaths, cases of insanity, and suicide attempts among the unfortunate travellers.

After the urgent intervention from the French government, which was completely overwhelmed by the unforeseen seriousness of the events, the occupying authorities committed to let the French Israelites return home. Not one among them has come back up until now.[16] On the other hand, 48 non-Jewish people, whose family names begin

10 Municipal district of Marseilles.

11 Synonym for a massacre: see Doc. 92, fn. 12.

12 René Bousquet.

13 Such a course of action could not be verified. However, during negotiations beginning in Jan. 1943 on French police participation in the planned operations, Bousquet and Higher SS and Police Leader Oberg had agreed that German police officials were to be kept out of the picture, if at all possible, and that only convicted resistance fighters and German deserters were to be handed over to the northern zone.

14 The police operation began on 22 Jan. and ended on 27 Jan. 1943.

15 The Secours national was a state relief organization founded in 1914 to support soldiers, their families, and the population affected by the First World War. The organization was re-established in 1940 and mostly collected donations to help civilians suffering from the consequences of the war.

16 The Jews arrested, most of them French, were deported to Sobibor, Majdanek, and Auschwitz in March 1943.

with the letters A to C, were able to return to Marseilles two and a half months after these tragic nights. Those in charge of the police in Marseilles were dismissed.[17]

Ten days or so later, a raid by German police took place at the office of the Amitié chrétienne organization in Lyons, which was charged with collaborating with Israelite organizations, with intervening in favour of Jews, and with other subversive schemes. The management staff and the foreign Israelites who were found in the offices were arrested, with the exception of the French Israelites present.[18] After four weeks, the management was released, and the Israelites deported.

One month later, again in Lyons, the police force their way into headquarters of the UGIF, armed with machine guns and revolvers.[19] The staff of the charities are beaten up and arrested, and all those they have been helping, too, including the sick, who happen to be in the offices. All of the people who have come to attend the medical and social welfare consultations provided by the charities between 3 p.m. and 6.30 p.m. are arrested one after the other in this manner.[20] In the end, 100 people are arrested and – with the exception of two who remain in Drancy – they are deported, after being stripped of their coats, their handbags, their wallets, and all of their personal belongings.

At the end of the same month, all the foreign staff members of the UGIF are dismissed from their jobs,[21] with the exception of 54 in Paris and 12 in the formerly unoccupied zone. The next day, many of them are arrested and deported. The police break into several branch offices of charities in the southern zone during the night in order to arrest the non-French physicians, teachers, accountants, kitchen staff, and gardeners five days before the expiry of the administrative protection which guaranteed them the freedom to work. It was only due to a watch-keeping rota which some of those concerned had organized themselves and kept day and night on the roofs of houses that most of them were able to escape deportation.

The difficult problem of lodgings and the almost insoluble one of getting provisions, the obligation to move to other lodgings regularly, having to go out only in the dark of night for supplies; all this makes this existence of a hunted animal unbearable for many. Many youngsters live in hiding in forests without a tent or a sleeping bag, without even the possibility of preparing a hot meal because any smoke could give their location away.

Since early March, the roundups to seize foreign Israelites whose names were on the lists drawn up by the prefectures in November and December 1942 at the request of the German authorities have been taking place in all cities, in smaller towns, and even on remote farms. If the wanted individuals are absent, they take their fathers or grandfathers, their wives or their children, because every transport has to carry exactly the required number of people. When the inmates arrive at Gurs selection camp[22] after an interminable journey, they are transferred to a different livestock wagon on the same

17 On 18 Feb. 1943 Robert Andrieu replaced the senior police official (*intendant de police*) in Marseilles, Maurice Rodellec du Porzic.
18 On the association Amitié chrétienne, see Doc. 271.
19 Change of tense in the original.
20 See Doc. 291.
21 See Doc. 294.
22 After Rivesaltes was closed in late 1942, Gurs became the new assembly camp for the southern zone.

night with no straw, without benches, sealed and hermetically closed, to be sent off to destinations in Germany and beyond.

The roundups continue incessantly, and throughout March an uninterrupted succession of smaller transports has been pouring into the regulatory camp in the Seine département.[23] Since then this traffic seems to have been interrupted until new orders arrive.[24]

Children are not spared from the systematic and forced evacuation of the foreign Jews. As well as the 3,200 children from Paris who were torn from their parents last August and deported several weeks later, at a rate of 60 children aged between 2 and 14 per sealed carriage, without supervision, without food, without water, to an unknown destination, several hundred children have just been dealt the same fate. The German authorities had instructed the UGIF to place these children in accommodation in the countryside and then demanded that the organization bring them back in early January and hand over the children to them so they could be sent to an unknown destination. Beforehand, all of their identity documents were destroyed. To the nurses of the Red Cross who rose up against the conditions in which the transports were taking place, the doctor in charge replied that a 30 per cent rate of losses during a journey (Reiseausfall)[25] was considered normal.

The French police have just set up, still under the orders of the occupation authorities, a new list of all the foreign Israelite children between 2 and 16 years of age whose parents have been deported. Several thousand abandoned children in the two zones are thus targeted and at risk of sharing an alarming fate.[26]

Charities from all the religious denominations, unifying their means and their efforts, have courageously attempted to save a certain number of these youngsters. Time will tell how far these courageous, delicate, perilous operations, sometimes undertaken under heroic conditions, will succeed. In any case, they represent a magnificent example of solidarity and social dedication.

Until a few weeks ago, the foreign Israelites who still lived in the zone occupied by the Italian army found themselves in a better situation. The identity of Israelites residing in the Alpes-Maritimes département were not stamped.[27] The foreigners rounded up in the Isère, Savoie, and Haute-Savoie départements, who had been taken to barracks to be transferred to Gurs under guard from the French police, were protected against these measures by the Italian army, which was under orders to oppose the removal of these individuals with force. It seems that by taking this stance in the Savoie and Alpes-Maritimes départements, they sought to distance themselves from the German army. This meant that the British and the Americans arrested throughout the country by order of the German army and deported to the southern zone were protected from the French police by the Italian army in the same manner, and after two days, the individuals who had been arrested were sent back home. The difference between the heavy, tense, and

23 This refers to Drancy camp.

24 The deportations from France were briefly suspended between 25 March and 23 June 1943.

25 German in the original.

26 From the summer of 1942, the UGIF North had used seven homes in the Paris metropolitan area to accommodate children under the age of 15 whose parents had been deported. Numerous children were housed privately, mostly with 'Aryan' families. In early 1943 the German police began to take children from these homes to fill up transports that were not at capacity.

27 See Doc. 292, fn. 7.

menacing atmosphere in the German zone and the peaceful, properly regulated, and occasionally cordial one in the Italian zone is striking. This difference in atmosphere has understandably attracted a considerable crowd of foreign Israelite families to the départements situated on the coast and on the left bank of the Rhône. We have witnessed an out-and-out migration that eventually began to worry the Italian authorities themselves. Clusters of impoverished men and women carrying their last belongings and surrounded by children in rags literally besieged the Armistice Commission and, after being sent away from there, the offices of the charity organizations. The Italian authorities have been increasingly insisting on the exceptional and possibly temporary character of their attitude, particularly as it does not depend only on their own goodwill, and have been warning the Israelite public against the possibly negative consequences of a continued influx of refugees.

Over the last few weeks, the measures taken by the Italian authorities have become somewhat more rigorous: compulsorily assigned residence in deprived little villages in the Basses-Alpes département, which are poorly supplied with food and without any sanitary facilities, and where people suffer from hunger;[28] a curfew for foreign Israelites from midnight until 6 a.m.; and the expulsion of a certain number of foreigners from the Italian zone.[29]

However, the concentration of foreign Israelites in Megève as a place of assigned residence can still be considered a measure aimed at protecting a number of Israelite families who are under threat, even more so because the evacuation of Megève, which had been imposed on Vichy, has quite different goals. But in any case, the obligation to leave behind in their former homes their food reserves, the produce of their vegetable gardens, and their stocks of fuel all burdens families with financial obligations that are sometimes unbearable and makes the problem of feeding these people very difficult. In addition, the evacuation of the coast has delivered many families into the hands of the German authorities, families who had serious reasons for fleeing them.

The plan to transfer 20,000 foreign Israelites to Italy, which has been explored over the past few weeks by the authorities in charge and regarded favourably, has not so far been put into action.

Until new orders arrive, the French police are no longer exercising their authority over the foreign Israelites in the Italian zone.

The very large number of Israelites who make up part of the foreign labourers groups continue to be targeted for deportation by the German authorities. Particularly labourers assigned to private companies or farms have so far been affected by these measures. Deportation of whole groups has been relatively rare, and where this was the case the Jewish workers were deported along with their non-Jewish supervisors.

The release and the registration of numerous inmates from Gurs are currently under way, and the majority of them were directed to the Hautes-Alpes and the Basses-Alpes

28 The villages that were designated as locations of compulsorily assigned residence for Jews were Saint-Gervais and Megève (both in the Haute-Savoie département), Saint-Martin-de-Vésubie, Venanson, Vence (Alpes-Maritimes), and Barcelonnette (Alpes-de-Haute-Provence). Within a few weeks around 4,000 Jews had been taken to these places from the Côte d'Azur.

29 The Italian authorities decided to continue granting their protection only to those who resided in their zone from 26 March 1943.

départements to be placed under the authority of the Italian army, but lately these départements have no longer taken them in.

Altogether, it can be said that the authorities in charge of foreign workers have made a huge effort to keep both the non-Jews and the Jews under their protection from the Germans' grasp, with mostly satisfactory results overall.

While the plight of the foreign Israelites in France and particularly in the southern zone is growing bleaker by the day, plunging every family into mourning, the situation of French Israelites in turn is getting worse, along with that of their foreign co-religionists, and at the same speed as that of all their compatriots.

In all cities large and small, Israelites are being arrested and deported for the most diverse reasons, and they are never heard from again. This past winter, several thousand Jews were arrested as they were trying to cross the border.

We have no figures for the number of French Israelites who have been arrested, but there is now practically not a single family which has not had one or several of its members taken away, imprisoned, deported, or executed. One day it is the father, the next the mother, and the day after it is the children, the parents, the other relatives, who are successively rounded up. One day, it is the families from a particular neighbourhood or a specific street who are arrested, as was the case for example for the rue Paradis in Marseilles or the Villeurbanne neighbourhood in Lyons, and nobody knows why the roundups stop at a particular house. After several turbulent weeks, complete calm suddenly descends for several weeks, but the heavy silence does not stop the gnawing anxiety eating away at the Jews' nerves. Denunciation plays an important part in all these cases, and there are even Jews who do not hesitate to become informers. Chronologically, these measures seem to affect the very wealthy families first. French Israelites are arrested later, as well as their compatriots, technicians, former NCOs, and anybody suspected of harbouring any sympathies for the other side.

Unlike the attitude that the occupying authorities have shown towards the UGIF in Paris, the UGIF 'South' appears very politically suspect to the German police. Quite a number of the leading personnel are already wanted, and the police raid at the Lyons UGIF was based on precisely these concerns.

In addition, the scope for action of the charities united within the UGIF is continuously limited further and further. In certain regions, commitments had had to be made which practically put their entire activities under German control. And it is very difficult for the charities' staff to extricate themselves from these obligations without risking arrest, even if they resign. Four weeks ago, the UGIF was asked to provide a complete list of all people they were helping, including their addresses, the names of family members, the amount of benefits they received, and divided into two separate sections according to whether or not the individuals were French or foreign citizens. The organization has tried to avoid handing over this list up to now, but we must fear that it will eventually have to comply.

There is no doubt that the Italian attitude has been a blessing. Thus the ban on travel, already signed by the head of government and announced on the German radio, was not enforced because of Italian opposition.[30]

30 See Doc. 283, fn. 4.

But Radio Paris and the interviews in the militant anti-Jewish newspapers such as the *Pilori*, the *Gerbe*, the *Nouveau Temps*, as well as the *Pariser Zeitung*, constantly announce the introduction of new anti-Jewish measures. According to the Commissioner [General] for Jewish Affairs, these consist primarily of the requirement that all Israelites have a Hebrew first name; the compulsory assignation of a place of residence which one is forbidden to leave, which also applies to French Israelites; wearing the star; not being allowed to own telephones, radios, and bicycles.

There have also been threats of a mass denaturalization, which would extend all the way back to the files from 1919. As of now, several dozen Israelites are denaturalized every day without any regard for the individual's merits or what they did for the country. The daily denaturalization quota is met without looking at the files.

Handing over Jewish businesses to administrators has given rise to some sensational scandals which have reached even the most senior civil service circles and most notably the Commissariat itself, and all of them were hushed up. Their commodities are flooding the black market, and large companies are sold twice so the amounts that are officially deposited with the CDC[31] are only small sums. The profits are divided between the administrators and the civil servants.

Bankruptcies of old and sound businesses are now frequent, and people are finally noticing that this unscrupulous management has begun to affect the French national wealth. As for the owners, they end up swelling the ranks of the newly poor, in growing numbers.

Removal from the lists of Jews, deletion of files in the Commissariat [General] for Jewish Affairs, fiddling with census records; all such activities have become commodities that can be purchased.

While it may not actively participate in this hunt, the central administration in Vichy is a powerless witness to this wave of persecution and expropriation, and is often ignorant of the extent and the precise character of the measures. It learns from private sources of the creation and location of new camps.

The people, in their vast majority, often overtly express their sympathy for the victims of persecution. It would be fair to say that, overall, the aggressive antisemitic propaganda has completely failed. It should be noted that, since June 1940, the Jewish question is the only issue which has led to the people rising up en masse and taking to the streets. The echo was infinitely more resounding than what happened when the French workers were targeted.[32]

The Israelites themselves live in complete insecurity and are exposed to the demoralizing effects of all the false news. They have to look on as their livelihood and opportunities for life are reduced further every day, and they feel the net they are caught in closing around them more tightly and mercilessly every day. According to the leaders of French Judaism, there is no doubt that the Israelites will not be able to put up with the consequences of this regime for many months longer without their very existence being threatened.

April 1943.

31 On the Caisse des dépôts et consignations (CDC), see Doc. 284, fn. 28.
32 It is not clear here which action taken against French workers is being referred to.

DOC. 300

On 7 May 1943 the Security Police records an increasing number of Jews in Paris with forged documents[1]

Report by Section IV B, Office of the Senior Commander of the Security Police in France,[2] signed Horst Ahnert (initials), Paris, dated 7 May 1943 (excerpt)[3]

d) Jews

During the reporting period,[4] in cooperation with the French police, a total number of 137 Jews were arrested and interned in Drancy camp for Jews. The arrests were made largely on the basis of information provided by anti-Jewish circles and reports from police informants. The number of cases of Jews using forged documents to pass themselves off as Aryans is increasing day by day. It must be assumed that the number of Jews with forged identity documents in Paris is quite high and constantly growing. Numerous Jews are thus able to evade arrest. Only through reports from anti-Jewish circles is it possible to unmask 'Aryanized' Jews. It is worth noting that precisely these Jews are adept at cultivating close relations with German circles. During the reporting period, for example, a Jewish woman was arrested who frequented a bar to which only German officers are admitted. Another Jewish woman was found to have various letters from Wehrmacht soldiers with whom she had been socializing.

In general, it can be said that the broad mass of the population still fails to understand the Jewish problem. We observe time and again that the Jews are supported and pitied by the population.

DOC. 301

On 21 May 1943 the regional prefect in Poitiers informs the French Police Directorate in Paris of the German order to arrest children whose parents have been deported[1]

Telegram (in code, no. 1029, dated 21 May 1943, 18:40) from the regional prefect in Poitiers[2] (police headquarters) to the prefect and representative of the Ministry of the Interior – Directorate General of the French Police,[3] Paris (received on 22 May 1943)

German police Poitiers region order arrest on 24 May at 5 a.m. by the French police and military police of Jewish children whose parents are foreign nationals and have already been taken to Germany.

1 AN, F7, vol. 15 148. This document has been translated from German.
2 Helmut Knochen.
3 Excerpt from the general situation report of the Security Police and the SD; the remaining portions of the report are not in the file. The original contains handwritten annotations.
4 The 'Reports from occupied France' have survived in only a few cases or only in excerpted form, making it impossible to determine the exact reporting period. It was not possible to locate the report in its entirety.

1 AN, F7, vol. 14 887. Published in Klarsfeld, *Calendrier*, p. 1508. This document has been translated from French.

These children are to be transferred to Paris on 26 May to be entrusted to the General Union of French Jews.

Request that you notify us telegraphically of agreement to implementation of these measures.[4]

DOC. 302

On 8 June 1943 the German Feldgendarmerie in Paris arrests Marie-Antoinette Planeix for wearing the yellow star although she is not Jewish[1]

Arrest report from the Paris Feldgendarmerie Detachment, signed Sergeant Manfel, dated 8 June 1943 (copy)

Re: the French subject *Planeix*[2] wearing the Star of David although she is not a Jew.
Reference: none
Arrested: 8 June 1943, at approximately 11.45 a.m., on boulevard St Michel (5th arr.)
Imprisoned: 8 June 1943, at approximately 7.45 p.m., in La Santé prison
Evidence: confession
Arrest report
During a search operation for Jews on 8 June 1943, at approximately 11.45 a.m., Planeix, who is further identified in the attached personal information record,[3] was found wearing the Star of David although she is not a Jew. The star was made out of paper. She was arrested and taken to 'La Santé' prison. The Star of David made by the arrested woman is attached.
Record of Planeix's interrogation on this matter overleaf.[4]

2 Louis Bourgain (1881–1970), qualified lawyer and military officer; naval officer, 1902–1941; appointed prefect of the Vienne département and regional prefect of Poitiers in summer 1941; sentenced to eight years in prison as well as loss of civil rights and confiscation of his assets in 1945.
3 Jean Leguay.
4 Leguay gave his consent the same day: Klarsfeld, *Calendrier*, p. 1508. On 26 May Drancy camp recorded the arrival of 44 prisoners from Poitiers, including 13 children.

1 Mémorial de la Shoah, XLIXa-71. This document has been translated from German.
2 Marie-Antoinette Planeix (b. 1920), student; wore a yellow star that she had made out of paper and inscribed with 'INRI' (from the Latin 'Ieusus Nazarenus Rex Iudaerum', meaning 'Jesus of Nazareth, King of the Jews'; traditionally depicted in art as the inscription over Christ's head at the Crucifixion).
3 Included in the file.
4 The interrogation record includes this statement by Marie-Antoinette Planeix: 'I made the Star of David at home. I attached it to my dress before going out. I wanted to attest to the fact that Christ was the first King of the Jews. I have nothing else to add.'

DOC. 303
On 15 June 1943 the North African Economic Board outlines the situation of the Jews in Tunisia during the German occupation[1]

Airgram[2] (no. 60, marked 'secret') from the North African Economic Board,[3] Algiers, to the Combined Committee for French North and West African Civil Affairs[4] and to the Secretary of the Treasury, Morgenthau[5] (received on 19 June 1943), dated 15 June 1943 (copy)

Re: property changes under German rule – Tunisia
BOC A-60.

1. Tunis, as the first sizeable city recaptured from Nazi occupation,[6] offers a realistic indication of the problems which will arise in the return of property and the indemnification of discriminated groups who have suffered at Nazi hands. Our preliminary study of this matter, presented herewith, is based primarily on the treatment accorded to Jewish people in Tunis and was gleaned from conferences with the heads of Jewish groups and other persons in Tunis. Exact figures are not available at present.
2. There are about 90,000 Jews in Tunisia as a whole.[7] About 80,000 are descendants of people who have been in the country 2,000 years. They are not subjects of the French, but of the Bey. There are about 5,000–6,000 Italian Jews, sent to Tunisia as colonists about 150–200 years ago, who have remained subjects of Italy. Lastly, there are about 5,000 Jews who are French subjects.
3. Shortly after the arrival of the Germans in Tunisia on about 8 November 1942, the Nazis commenced to requisition buildings of the Jews for use as offices and dwelling houses. A typical case is the following: A middle-class Jewish family in Tunis was notified one evening in early December that they would have to evacuate their apartment the next morning, since it was to be taken over by Italian officers as a residence. The family, more fortunate than many, packed up most of its belongings during the night and moved out the next morning. After 8 May, with the departure of the Italians, the family returned. In many cases in which houses were requisitioned for use by the Germans or Italians, damage was done to fixtures and furniture. Rugs, hangings, furniture, etc. were taken. The Nazis also requisitioned the vehicles owned by Jewish people and obliged them to turn in their radios, refrigerators, firearms, etc. Many of these requisi-

1 NARA, 740 00113 European War 1939/938. Published in *Foreign Relations of the United States: Diplomatic Papers, 1943*, vol. 2, *Europe* (Washington, DC: United States Department of State, 1964), pp. 280–282.
2 Confidential letter transported by diplomatic courier.
3 The North African Economic Board (NAEB) was founded in early December 1942 by the US government to secure economic provision for North Africa and to represent the interests of the USA. Its notifications to the US government were marked with the abbreviation 'BOC'.
4 Representative body of the Allied High Command in Washington.
5 Henry Morgenthau (1891–1967), agriculturalist; US secretary of the Treasury and advisor to President Roosevelt, 1934–1945.
6 The war in North Africa ended with the surrender of the German Army Group Africa and the Italian First Army on 12 and 13 May 1943. Tunis had been liberated five days earlier.
7 According to estimates based on the results of the 1931 census, there were 66,000 Jews, of whom 7,000 were French citizens and 3,000 were Italian citizens; 195,000 Europeans; and 2.1 million Muslims living in Tunisia in 1936.

tioned vehicles were damaged and some were sent to Europe. Most of the radios, refrigerators, etc. were sent to Europe. The total cost of this phase of Nazi oppression was estimated at about 30,000,000 francs. While some of the requisitioned vehicles have been found and returned, there is, as yet, no program developed for compensation for losses incurred as the result of this type of activity.

4. On 6 December 1942, the Council of the Jewish Community in Tunis received an order from the German authorities to produce 2,000 workers, under an arrangement whereby food, clothing, wages, etc. were to be paid for by the Jews. At the cost of an additional 1,000 laborers a 24-hour extension was obtained. On 9 December 1942, the request not having been complied with, a reign of terror commenced, in which synagogues and schools were broken into, Jews beaten and threatened, and obliged to march long distances. At this point the Jewish Community organized itself and set up services for drafting laborers, feeding, clothing and paying them, as well as supplying them with transportation and medical aid. About 4,000 workers were obtained, and put to work at the airport and harbor in Tunis, at Bizerta, Mateur, Enfidaville, and Cheylus, all points of nearly constant Allied air attacks. The Jews also had to act as policemen, to ensure that the workers remained at their jobs despite heavy bombings and maltreatment.

5. The Jewish Community was obliged also to shoulder the financial burden of caring for Jewish refugees who came to Tunis from Bizerta and similarly destroyed cities as well as those who lost their homes by other means.

6. The funds to meet the expenses referred to above, including the costs of feeding and care for the labor gangs, were obtained by the Jewish Community by imposing a capital levy of 10–15 per cent upon the property of its members. Mortgages, sales, etc. were resorted to to raise these funds, which were estimated at 60,000,000 francs. At the present time, these mortgages are still outstanding, and in the hands of banks principally.

7. On 22 December 1942, the Germans imposed a levy of 20,000,000 francs on the Jewish Community to 'pay' for the Anglo-American bombings of non-Jewish property, for which the Jews were said to be responsible because they were friends of the Allies. The head of the Jewish Community[8] endeavored, without success, to raise these funds at the private banks in Tunis, and was obliged to appeal to the Government for aid.[9] The latter authorized the Caisse Fonciere,[10] a semi-public institution, to advance these funds in the form of a loan at 8 per cent interest, with commissions and carrying charges running it up to about 12 per cent. The loan was secured by mortgages on Jewish estates, those in the country being insisted upon because there was less danger from bombing. The Caisse Fonciere received the funds from the Bank of Algeria, Tunis Branch, and we have been advised that payment was made in Bank of France notes. It was said that these Bank of France notes were subsequently distributed among the Arab and Italian followers of the Nazis. The former head of the Jewish Community has recently approached the Government in Tunisia with a view toward adjusting or deferring the payment of this loan, which

8 Moïse Borgel (1872–1959), chairman of the Jewish Community of Tunis.

9 The representative of the Vichy government on the ground was Admiral Jean-Pierre Esteva (1880–1951), resident general in Tunisia.

10 The French authorities established the Caisse Foncière de Tunisie to provide the agricultural sector run by European settlers, which was heavily indebted following the economic crisis, with uncomplicated access to credit, thereby counteracting the numerous foreclosures.

the Jews are not in a position to meet at present. The Caisse Fonciere threatened foreclosure, and a six months interest payment of 1,500,000 francs is due. At first the Government was said to have advised the head of the Jewish Community to repay the loan, with interest, and to place a claim against the Germans after the war. The latest indications were that the French authorities had not yet reached a definite decision on the question but were thinking in terms of a moratorium.

8. On 15 February 1943, the Germans, because many of the forced Jewish laborers were leaving the work camps, imposed a fine of 3,000,000 francs on the Community. This fine was paid without resort to the banks, by the sale of jewels, etc. belonging to individual members of the Community.

9. On the basis of present estimates, the measures taken by the Germans and Italians against the Jews in the Tunis area, from 8 November 1942 to 8 May 1943, cost the latter about 100,000,000 francs. No indemnification or relief measures have yet been taken by the French, and, insofar as the bulk of the problem is concerned, none appears to be contemplated.

10. From the fact that this memorandum is confined largely to the Jews, it should not be inferred that this class stood alone in regard to discrimination. The case of the Jews is probably the most glaring, because the great majority of them could not be considered enemies of the Nazis or Italians in the technical sense. Furthermore, there appears to have been more physical hardships, and the imposition of fines seems to be an additional measure of oppression. However, vehicles, houses, factories, etc. were requisitioned from the French in Tunis. Machinery was taken away, and forced labour was at least threatened, if not in fact realized. We are canvassing this side of the picture more fully at the present.

11. Likewise, a counterpart of this story which we will canvass is the matter of increments to Italians and Arabs as the result of this discrimination. Rumors as to these matters have reached us, but it is, of course, more difficult to develop this side of the problem.

12. We are also studying the question of real property transfers made during the occupations and endeavouring to obtain as much information as possible on this score.

13. We should appreciate your view on the problems. In this connection, reference might be made to the United Nations Declaration on property transfers.[11]

Action: Treasury, State

Distribution 'A'[12]

11 At this point, the 16 governments allied with Britain and the USA, as well as Charles de Gaulle's French National Committee, constituted the United Nations. In the Inter-Allied Declaration against Acts of Dispossession Committed in Territories under Enemy Occupation or Control, dated 4 January 1943, the signatory governments reserved the right to invalidate any transactions implemented during the war in territories directly or indirectly controlled by the enemy.

12 US President Franklin D. Roosevelt responded to the report in a personal letter to Cordell Hull on 29 June 1943. In the letter, Roosevelt wrote that the authorities of the National Committee in North Africa were to be informed that Washington condemned every attempt at foreclosure or collection of capital interest on mortgage loans that arose from taxes imposed by the Axis Powers; see fn. 1.

DOC. 304

On 21 June 1943 Anna Dreksler asks acquaintances to hide her child[1]

Handwritten letters from Anna Dreksler,[2] Drancy, to Yvonne Larousse,[3] Paris, as well as Mrs Baglin and Miss Essayan,[4] Neuilly-sur Seine, and Mr Perret,[5] Saint-Maur-des-Fossés, dated 21 June 1943 (copy)

My dear friend,

I'm sure you'll find that I'm writing in disjointed sentences, but what I'm going to tell you is very urgent and very serious. It's possible, and it's even official, so to speak, that there will be a deportation this week, either on Wednesday or Thursday.[6] Because I told them that Maurice[7] was in Grenoble, I was told that I had to write to him so that he could leave with me, and they would bring him here. As for my husband,[8] I also said that he was in Grenoble, and I was told that they would be here with me within ten days and we would all leave together.[9] So the first thing you need to tell the concierge is that if ever anyone comes asking after Maurice, she must say that she doesn't know where he is. The little one must disappear, whatever it takes. So far, my only consolation has been that I didn't have the little one with me here, and now I'm very anxious about him and worried sick. I beg you, dear Mrs Larousse, please, you can place the little one anywhere, but he must not stay where he is. I know that up to now you've done everything in your power for my good and believe me, my very dear friend, that no matter what happens to me, I will *never* forget you and all of my other friends. But I beg you, put my little one in a safe place. This is the greatest worry in my life. Be sure to tell the concierge to say that she hasn't been in the building for very long and that she doesn't know where my husband or my child may be found. She mustn't let herself be intimidated. As my little one has been registered as residing in the free zone, she

1 The original is privately owned. Copy in Mémorial de la Shoah, CMLXXXVI (13)-12. This document has been translated from French.

2 Anna (Chinka) Dreksler, née Laks (b. 1905), secretary; born in Szydłowiec (Congress Poland); naturalized in France; arrested by the French police in late March 1943; deported three months later from Drancy to Auschwitz, where she perished.

3 Yvonne Larousse (1898–1947), concierge; lived in the same building as Anna Dreksler and her family with her husband, Fernand.

4 Both were colleagues of Anna Dreksler.

5 Georges Perret (1899–1949), businessman; head of a British coal import company; employed Anna Dreksler.

6 The deportation train left Le Bourget-Drancy station on Wednesday, 23 June 1943.

7 Maurice Dreksler (b. 1933); as a schoolboy, arrested with his mother in March 1943, released at her request and entrusted to Yvonne Larousse; survived the war in hiding in the home of Georges and Amélie Perret, his mother's former employers, in Saint-Maur-des-Fossés near Paris; worked in the administration of the French national railway company SNCF after the war.

8 Henri (Arja Yehuda) Dreksler (1902–1942), tailor; born in Będzin; married Anna Laks in 1932; arrested by the French police in mid May 1941; interned in Beaune-la-Rolande camp; deported in late June 1942 to Auschwitz, where he perished in mid August 1942.

9 In preparation for further deportations in June 1943, Alois Brunner ordered approximately 1,400 internees to step forward one by one in the yard of Drancy camp to be interrogated about their family members living in freedom. Anna Dreksler was one of the 1,002 persons selected in that process for the next transport.

won't be risking anything. Note that it's possible that no one will come asking about him, but it's better to be prepared. I know that you'll be careful about everything and I have great confidence in you and in all of my friends. Lots of love to you and Maurice. Hide the truth from him for as long as possible, poor little boy without a father and mother. I know very well that he will want for nothing if they don't get their hands on him, but please destroy this letter as soon as you receive it and don't mention it to anyone.

Your friend forever

Dear Mrs Baglin and Miss Essayan,

I believe that this will be the last time I'm writing to you. I have great courage and I'm ready for anything, but I beg you not to let my little one fall into their hands. Do whatever you want, but have pity on him. If you haven't bought my summer shoes yet, there is no point in doing so now. I'm sending both of you and your families lots of love. The little one absolutely mustn't be found where he is now. Perhaps Clara is staying but that is not yet certain.

Goodbye. Yours, Chinka

Dear Mr Perret,

Before leaving I wanted to thank you for all that you've done for me and for Maurice. Perhaps one day I'll have the chance to tell you in person. Forgive me for having caused you so much trouble. I would like to thank Mrs Perret from the bottom of my heart for all her kindness towards my son, and I hope with all my heart that you'll not have to go through what I'm going through at the moment.

Goodbye, dear Mr and Mrs Perret. Rest assured of my eternal gratitude.

When you receive this, dear Mrs Larousse, please get in touch with my friends immediately. Whatever happens, the little one will have to leave the house. Telephone Miss Essayan, please. A thousand thanks.[10]

10 Amélie and George Perret subsequently hid Maurice Dreksler in their home in Saint-Maur-des-Fossés until liberation. Amélie Perret (1906–1992) gave this document to Maurice Dreksler shortly before her death. Mr and Mrs Perret were recognized as Righteous Among the Nations by Yad Vashem in 1997.

DOC. 305
On 28 June 1943 Aimée Cattan writes from Marseilles to Marshal Pétain to find out whether her relatives are still alive[1]

Letter from Mrs Aimée Cattan,[2] 4 boulevard d'Accès, Marseilles, to head of state Marshal Pétain, Vichy, dated 28 June 1943[3]

Dear Marshal,

Please forgive me for disturbing you in this way, but it is not humanly possible to remain without any news of the three members of my family who were taken away on 22 January 1943.[4] It has now been five months that we have been living in a state of anxiety and unable to give the slightest help to our sisters and our aunt. Already in the first days of *January*, just after the *roundup* had taken place, I approached all the services which I thought might be in charge of these matters without achieving even the slightest result. I even took the liberty of writing to Dr Menestrel,[5] your private secretary, who responded in May[6] that my family had again been sent to an unknown destination.

For clarity's sake, it will probably be necessary for me to give you some fuller details about the case, which I will now submit to you:

On Friday, 22 January 1943, when the mass roundups were taking place in Marseilles, three members of my family were taken away for the sole crime of being *Jewish*. They are:

- My aunt Henriette *Cattan*,[7] widow of Moïse *Amaoua*, born in *Sousse*, Tunisia, in March 1890, a war widow from the 1914/1918 war on a full pension, who only had one preoccupation: to bring up her daughter well.
- My sister Suzanne *Cattan*,[8] wife of Marius *Saltalamacchia*,[9] born in *Sousse*, Tunisia, on 9 December 1909, mother of three children (two boys, one aged 6½ and the other 3½, and a little girl, who is 20 months old); her husband being a Catholic, the children were baptized in the Catholic faith. My sister is a Ward of the Nation.[10] The worst thing about her case is that in addition to her three young children, my sister was expecting another child in three months at most, and we had hoped that this situation would mean

1 AN, 2 AG, vol. 82. This document has been translated from French.
2 Aimée Aziza Cattan (b. 1912), secretary; born in Sousse, Tunisia; French citizen; arrested in Marseilles in early April 1944; sent to Drancy camp; deported to Auschwitz in mid April 1944; returned to France in May 1945.
3 The original contains handwritten additions.
4 On Franco-German police operations in Marseilles in Jan. 1943, see Introduction, pp. 76–77.
5 Correctly: Bernard Ménétrel (1906–1947), physician; hospital manager in Paris; personal physician and close advisor to Marshal Pétain from 1936; Pétain's private secretary, 1940–1943.
6 This is not included in the file.
7 Henriette Amaoua, née Cattan (1890–1943); deported to Sobibor extermination camp on 23 March 1943.
8 Suzanne Simonne Cattan (b. 1909), book printer; is thought not to have been deported.
9 Marius Sauveur Saltalamacchia (b. 1914), book printer.
10 Ward of the Nation (*pupille de la Nation*) is an official status the French state grants to children who have lost a parent in a war or in the performance of public duties. These children are granted a regular allowance.

that we would be able to see her again as soon as possible. Alas, this has not been the case.

– My sister Georgette *Cattan*,[11] born in *Sousse* (Tunisia) on 17 February 1918, also a Ward of the Nation; almost five years ago, my younger sister suffered a severe case of typhus; her health is therefore very delicate, and she needs a lot of care.

My family's only crime is to have been born *Jewish*. My relatives have scrupulously adhered to the racial laws that are currently in force. And if their identity cards had not been stamped with 'Jew' in red capital letters, I am sure that I would not need to tremble in fear of the fate in store for them.

As I have said and repeated to the various institutions I approached: we may have always been *Jewish*, but we have also been *French* for generations, and our relatives have done their duty every time that circumstance required them to (my great-grandparents in 1870, my Father, my uncles, etc., etc. in 1914 – which is when we became war orphans – my brothers, cousins, brothers-in-law, etc., etc. in 1939). We would never have thought that the fact that we were born *Jewish* would result in us being treated in this way having so generously spilled our blood for our *fatherland*.

After my relatives were no doubt taken to various concentration camps and then to *Royallieu* camp in *Compiègne*, they were sent to *Drancy* camp; I was almost happy to learn that they were finally in a fixed spot, where we would be able to alleviate their unjust situation as much as we could. Unfortunately, this happy time did not last very long, as not even two weeks after their arrival at Drancy, my sisters and aunt wrote me a letter, dated 22 March 1943, to tell me that they would be leaving again the next day, 23 March, for an '*unknown destination*'.

Do you fully understand what words such as '*unknown destination*' mean for us in times as troubled and as evil as those in which we are living?!!! Imagine your loved ones in these awful concentration camps, and on top of that God knows where?!! The unjust measures directed against us, the worry brought on by such a long silence, it all exacerbates our anguish; we imagine the situation to be even worse than it probably is. This is perfectly normal, and I am sure you will understand the mental state we are in.

Although the normal thing would be to release my sisters and my aunt, I do not even dare to ask as much, and for the moment, I only want to know if they are still alive and where they can be found, so that I can send them some items of clothing and alleviate their suffering as much as possible. It would pain me too much to see them having to bear another winter without me being able to send them some clean, warm clothing. It seems to me that this desire comes from the most basic degree of humanity.

I venture to hope that you will be able to reassure me regarding their situation, and I also hope, with all my heart, that they are still in *France*; if you could confirm this for me, you would lift an immense weight from my mind.

I thank you in advance for anything you can do, not only to give me certainty about their situation, but also to reduce the length of their imprisonment.

Rest assured of my deepest gratitude, Marshal.

Yours,

11 Georgette Cattan (1918–1943); deported to Sobibor extermination camp on 23 March 1943.

DOC. 306

On 29 July 1943 the Marseilles police chief reports to the Vichy government's Ministry of the Interior on the fate of deported Marseilles residents[1]

Letter no. 3390 L/POL from the Marseilles regional prefect,[2] signature (illegible),[3] the chief of police, to the head of government,[4] the minister and secretary of state for interior affairs,[5] dated 29 July 1943

Re: situation of people transferred to Compiègne after the evacuation of the Old Port neighbourhoods in Marseilles

The many enquiries with which I am currently being flooded show that the groups concerned are increasingly upset about the fate of some of the inhabitants of the old neighbourhoods who were transferred to *Compiègne* when the old port neighbourhoods in *Marseilles* were evacuated. There are indeed elderly people over 60 as well as young people and girls under 20 among them, who have never given occasion for any complaint.

In order to describe the problem more precisely, I think it would be useful to briefly remind ourselves of the conditions under which these people were transferred to *Compiègne*. The individual transports differed markedly from each other in their composition.

The first transport was made up of people who had been arrested in the different neighbourhoods that were searched on 22 and 23 January during preliminary police operations. The French authorities were planning a detailed examination of their situation. However, for unknown reasons, these people had to be loaded onto the train at dawn on 24 January. Only a few people, for whom being taken away would have been too obvious an injustice, were able to be released before the final composition of the transport was established. In the end, it was made up of almost 1,300 residents of the different neighbourhoods of *Marseilles*.

The second transport was put together at *Fréjus* by the German authorities and was made up of the part of the population of the old neighbourhoods which had been taken to Puget-sur-Argens camp following the selection procedure. This transport, the make-up of which is difficult to ascertain, primarily consisted of men of all ages, most of whom had been employed in Marseilles and had never attracted the attention of the police on grounds of political activities.

The French authorities were unable to obtain any information as to the intended destination of these evacuee transports. Later, the *delegate* sent by the secretary general

1 AD des Bouches-du-Rhône, 76 W, vol. 104. This document has been translated from French.

2 Antoine Lemoine (1888–1962), lawyer; prefect from 1940; prefect of the Haute Vienne département and regional prefect in Limoges, April 1942–Jan. 1943; subsequently prefect of the Bouches-du-Rhône département and regional prefect in Marseilles; appointed secretary of state for internal affairs in Dec. 1943; sentenced to the loss of civil rights for five years in 1948; the sentence was later annulled due to his involvement with the resistance.

3 Most likely Robert Andrieu (1908–1979), public official; secretary general of the Cher département prefecture from 1940; deputy chief of police in Lyons from Nov. 1942; chief of police in Marseilles from 1943; had contacts with the French Resistance; resigned in Jan. 1944; returned to public administration in August 1945; prefect again from 1951; decorated several times.

4 Pierre Laval.

5 René Bousquet.

of the police in the occupied territories[6] was able to confirm that 1,300 individuals from *Marseilles* had arrived at Royallieu camp in *Compiègne*.

When asked, the German authorities almost immediately agreed to collaborate with the French services in the selection procedure. The French authorities were also able to submit requests for the release of individuals in cases where they felt this was appropriate. But the selection committee had to interrupt its work having compiled almost one thousand individual records.

Over the following days, the cases of those for whom an individual record had been compiled were further examined, not only at the department of criminal records at police headquarters, but also at the archives of the Criminal Police and the police intelligence service.

After this preparatory work, the following proposals were submitted on 18 February by *Prefect Leguay* to the Senior Commander of the Security Police attached to the French Military High Command[7] (74 avenue Foch):

1. Wanted individuals who will be handed over to the responsible public prosecutor's office: 8.
2. Suspect individuals who are to be administratively interned[8] by the French authorities: 91, including 68 Israelites.
3. Individuals who have been detained for no reason: 1,019. This number includes foreign Israelites, with regard to whom the German authorities seemed to oppose any plans for release from the very beginning.

During this meeting on 18 February, the commander of the German police informed the French authorities that all of these proposals would be submitted to the higher German police authorities. At the same time, he stated that General *Oberg* was planning to have 49 people who were interned in Royallieu camp released, and that a list of their names would be provided later. On 25 February, the French authorities did indeed receive a list of 42 people who had been released on 18 February.

Since then, several individuals have been released without the French authorities being notified, except by these individuals themselves. Under these conditions, the French police services have no way of knowing with any certainty what fate is in store for those who have been put forward for release or for internment.

The police services were unable to carry out any kind of tally of the people on the second transport which left *Fréjus* after the German authorities' selection procedure.

Since these first interventions, which did not yield the desired results, several people have been brought to Prefect Leguay's attention individually. However, the results of these efforts have not been announced.

Therefore, it seems that the situation in which these people find themselves, as most of them are on the verge of being deported to Eastern Europe, ought to be the subject of renewed talks with the higher German police authorities.

6 Jean Leguay.

7 This refers to the Senior Commander of the Security Police and the SD, Helmut Knochen.

8 The 'mesure administrative d'internement' (literally: 'administrative internment measure') was introduced in Nov. 1939. It allowed the state to intern people suspected of acting in contravention of the nation's defence or public security interests, without a warrant and for an unlimited period of time. It was mostly used against foreigners. During the German occupation, this measure was also used to intern political opponents, primarily communists.

In addition, it must be stressed that any interventions with the local German authorities are completely futile, as even the chief of the German police[9] declared that he had no authority in this matter. However, in recent correspondence about a request he had sent to me for evaluation, he revealed that he would not be opposed to the return of those evacuees whom the French police do not consider undesirable.

DOC. 307
On 30 July 1943 Commissioner General Darquier de Pellepoix is informed of the arrest of the Jewish leaders and non-Jewish employees of the General Union of French Jews in Paris[1]

Report (Cab. D./J.L., no. 8[?]478), unsigned,[2] to the Commissioner General for Jewish Affairs, Paris, dated 30 July 1943, 4 p.m. (carbon copy)[3]

I have the honour to report on two events which, although they concern different categories of people, both relate to incidents which arose from the reorganization[4] of Drancy camp.

First, I have to describe and emphasize in particular the following case, which exclusively concerns Aryans working for the bookkeeping agency of the UGIF, of whom several are civil servants in the Ministry of Finance.[5]

Here are the facts without further commentary: on 30 July at noon, an Aryan employee of the bookkeeping agency, Miss Susanne Berniolle,[6] was in the offices of the UGIF at 29 rue de la Bienfaisance on official business, when a German police raid took place. Miss Susanne Berniolle did not have her identity documents with her, and therefore telephoned her sister, Miss Andrée Berniolle,[7] to ask her to bring them to her. In order to certify that the employee in question was an Aryan, Mr Boussard and Mr Lebon, both section heads in the bookkeeping agency, accompanied Miss Andrée Berniolle to 29 rue de la Bienfaisance and were arrested at the same time as their two employees. Mr Couturier, treasurer and auditor for the UGIF, protested vigorously and requested a personal intervention from the Commissioner General to ensure that these four individuals would be released and no longer mixed up with the Jewish prisoners.

9 From late 1942 the SS and police regiment in Marseilles was under the command of Bernhard Griese (1887–1964).

1 Mémorial de la Shoah, XXVIII-82. This document has been translated from French.
2 This document was probably written by Robert Duquesnel (b. 1884), who from 1942 at the General Commissariat for Jewish Affairs was in charge of overseeing the General Union of French Jews (UGIF). In spring 1943 Duquesnel wrote a report on the UGIF's secret efforts to rescue Jews; his superiors forwarded that report to the German Security Police.
3 The original contains handwritten underlining.
4 In July 1943 the Germans took over direct control of Drancy camp, with Alois Brunner as commandant. See Introduction, p. 82.
5 The UGIF's bookkeeping was supervised by Maurice Couturier of the French Ministry of Finance.
6 Suzanne Angèle Marie Berniolle (b. 1916), office worker; lived with her mother and sister in Paris; worked at the bookkeeping agency from early April 1942.
7 Andrée Berthe Berniolle (b. 1919), office worker; worked temporarily at the Caisse des dépôts et consignations, a state institution that administered blocked accounts, 1938–1943; worked at the bookkeeping agency from early July 1943.

The second series of arrests was aimed at the leaders and section heads of the UGIF. On 22 July, Mr André *Baur*, the Union's vice president, was arrested in the offices of the UGIF along with Mr *Israelowicz*, head of liaison with the occupying authorities, as guarantors for the return of two escapees from Drancy camp.[8]

Mr *Israelowicz* was released a few hours later and ordered to continue the search for the fugitives. In order to satisfy the German authorities, Mr *Stora* and Mr *Weil Halle*,[9] members of the board of the UGIF, went to Nice and Lyons in the hope of finding more information – which, incidentally, they were unable to obtain.

On the morning of 29 July, Mr Ernest Weill and Mr Brunner,[10] heads of the canteen service, were summoned to the camp for a meeting on the issue of supplies for Drancy camp.

For the same reason, Mr Marcel Lévy,[11] head of the food and provisions service, and Mr Israelowicz were also summoned to the camp at 11 a.m. Mr Armand Katz, the secretary general, who, the evening before, had attended a meeting with the prefecture of the Seine département and the food and provisions service, accompanied them voluntarily.

At 6 p.m. the same day, the UGIF was informed that none of them would be returning and was asked to send them their luggage.

On 30 July at around 11.50 a.m., the headquarters on the rue de la Bienfaisance were surrounded by the German police. All of the staff, including the Aryan employees of the bookkeeping agency who were mentioned in the first part of this report, were taken away on two buses, probably to Drancy.[12] The headquarters are now closed and under guard.

At around 2 p.m., Mr Stora and Mr Edinger, both members of the board, received phone calls asking them to come to Drancy camp to meet with Hauptsturmführer Brunner at 5 p.m.

The UGIF staff, as well as all the directors who continue to hold their posts, are extremely worried about what these various arrests could mean.

In accord with Mr Couturier and in conclusion to this account, I would like to ask the Commissioner General to take action with a view to getting the Aryans who were imprisoned released. Their arrest was without doubt a mistake, as there is no plausible motive for it.[13]

8 Correctly: after two internees escaped from Drancy – one of whom was André Baur's cousin, Raymond Ducas – Brunner summoned Baur to the camp on 21 July 1943; he was initially held in solitary confinement there.

9 Marcel Stora (1906–1945), translator; deputy managing director of the UGIF North from Dec. 1941; interned in Drancy in early Sept. 1943; deported to Auschwitz with his family in mid Dec. 1943; perished in Buchenwald. Correctly: Benjamin Weill-Hallé, paediatrician; uncle of André Baur; member of the French delegation of the Jewish Agency, 1937; board member of the UGIF in Paris from 1942.

10 Correctly: Ernest Weil (b. 1881), butcher; after his release, he went into hiding until the end of the war. Léon Brunner (1880–1944), restaurateur; arrested in late July 1943; deported from Drancy to Auschwitz in late June 1944; murdered in Auschwitz.

11 Marcel Lévy (b. 1888), retailer; manager of the Galeries Lafayette department store, 1940–1942; head of provisioning for the UGIF North from 1942; UGIF board member from 1944.

12 Approximately 50 persons had been arrested.

13 They were released the same day.

Secondly, it seems to me that so far there has been no legislative intervention to modify the French law of 29 November 1941, which established the UGIF as a public institution, and straightforward logic would dictate that the union should not be rendered unable to perform the task it was given. At the current moment, with Mr Edinger and Mr Stora under arrest, there is no longer anyone with the authority to sign off on payments.[14]

DOC. 308

Fraternité, 1 August 1943: article featuring an eyewitness account of a deportation train and selections for forced labour in Upper Silesia[1]

New mass arrests and deportations of Jews from France to the torture and death camps[2]

Let us express our wish to put an end to these massacres in hundreds of thousands of protest letters sent to the authorities.
Come to the aid of all victims of racism!
At a time when French Jews are once again being arrested in huge numbers (in Paris, Nîmes, Avignon, Montauban, Clermont-Ferrand, etc.) and are all then deported to the East, we would like to present to our readers two documents which depict inhuman suffering and the dreadful ends of thousands of innocent lives.

Told by two eyewitnesses, one a non-Jewish Pole, the other someone who miraculously managed to escape from an indescribable hell, the facts they describe show how far the Nazi brutes' savagery and sadism extend. Their leaders destroyed all spiritual and moral values in their home country before attempting to do the same across occupied Europe and here, in France.

With a barbarity unparalleled in modern history, they exterminate entire peoples, executing men, killing infants, murdering women and the elderly. And they dare to call themselves 'defenders of civilization and the rights of nations'.

And they find French people who will lend them a hand in this work of destruction and annihilation.

Civil servants, police officers, and all those who directly or indirectly collaborate in the arrests and deportations of Jews must know they have turned themselves into the Nazi killers' accomplices.

Let it be known that they will be held to account, just as the Nazis themselves will.

Let it be known that by helping the enemy deport and murder the Jews, they are helping the enemy prepare new terror tactics to be used against the entire population, as well as new deportations of young people.

14 Only Marcel Stora, Georges Edinger, and the 12 employees from the rue de la Bienfaisance office were subsequently released.

1 *Fraternité: Organe du Mouvement national contre le racisme (zone Sud)*, special issue, 1 August 1943, pp. 1–3. This document has been translated from French. The Mouvement national contre le racisme (National Movement Against Racism) was founded in autumn 1942, following an initiative by the communist resistance group Francs-Tireurs et Partisans Main-d'Œuvre-Immigrée (FTP-MOI). Its aim was to encourage the French population to offer solidarity and aid to persecuted Jews, especially Jewish children.

2 The preceding issue of *Fraternité* (July 1943) had centred on the situation in Drancy camp.

As for the people of France, they refuse to adopt these barbaric and bloody racist ideas, just as they refuse to follow the men in Vichy.

With great energy, faithful to the principles of equality and fraternity, they have placed themselves resolutely on the side of the victims of racism.

All those who have saved thousands of families through their actions to date, whether they are workers or intellectuals, believers or free thinkers, come together in solidarity with all victims of racism. In so doing, they will contribute to defending their own undernourished children and our young people living under the threat of deportation, just as they will contribute to the battle the French people are waging for their own liberation.

Torture and massacres of Jews deported from France, from Belgium, and from Holland to Poland:

Account of an escape[3]

Truthful account from a witness who was arrested along with hundreds of other families in the region of Nice by the Vichy police in August 1942.

> Crammed into livestock wagons, we leave Nice for an unknown destination. The train arrives in Marseilles. The cries of the women and children draw the attention of the locals, who gather around the train. Seeing that resentment is rising, the Vichy police solemnly declare that the detainees locked up in the wagons will not be handed over to the Germans, but that the men will be sent on work detail, and the women and children will be sent to a mandatory place of residence.
>
> But these families' hopes of not being handed over to the Nazis did not last very long. When the train arrived at the demarcation line, the Nazis directed it towards Drancy.
>
> When we arrived at the camp, they stripped us of all our possessions: money, linens, toiletries, etc.
>
> Once again crammed into livestock wagons (men, women, and children), 70 per wagon, we travelled for three days without anything to eat or even a drop of water to drink. The children's screams were terrifying. It was not until we reached Koziel[4] (Upper Silesia) that the wagons were opened and we were led to a camp. At the end of the journey, 68 dead were counted.
>
> At this camp, a selection is carried out: men between 16 and 50 years of age, as well as young women, are assigned to work. All have their heads shaved. Everybody receives six yellow stars, which they have to sew on by themselves, first cutting a hole in the clothing where the stars are supposed to be attached, one on each knee, two on the shoulders, two on the chest.
>
> The elderly, the women, and the children who cannot work are sent to Oschewitz[5] camp.

3 A similar version of this account was published in an issue of the underground periodical *Notre voix* on 1 August 1943.

4 Koźle (German: Kosel), today a district of the city of Kędzierzyn-Koźle on the Oder river in Poland. Deportation trains were stopped here on the orders of Albrecht Schmelt, head of the Organization Schmelt. Prisoners selected for slave labour were deployed in camps run by the Organization Schmelt. The camps were known from the end of 1942 onwards as forced labour camps for Jews (*Zwangsarbeitslager für Juden*). They included Sankt Annaberg (near Koźle) and Laurahütte.

5 Oświęcim/Auschwitz.

Oschewitz is the camp which makes every Jew tremble. As the Nazis cynically say: 'It's where you go to snuff it.'

What I saw with my own eyes at this departure for Oschewitz is tragic and indescribable: 10-year-old children declared they were 16; 70-year-old men tried to pass themselves off as being 50; all to avoid Oschewitz.

The beatings and torture meted out at the labour camp itself surpass all imagination. And then there is the hunger. Even during the meals, which are just soup made from dirty water, the blows keep raining down on the shaved heads.

Every day, teams of 600 people are formed and assigned to construct roads and railway lines at Koenigshütte, Bismarckhütte, and Varahütte.[6]

Every day, between 12 and 18 people per group die during work.

In order to humiliate the tortured prisoners even more, the Nazis offer the dead person's rations to those who carry the body from the worksite back to the camp. The hunger is so great that there are always more than enough volunteers to do this job.

One day, two Dutch Jews felt ill but did not dare to report this before work (to be ill is the most serious crime and is punishable by death). At the worksite, they collapsed from exhaustion. The Nazi thugs fell on them, beating them until they lost consciousness completely, and then finished them off with their boots.

Such scenes took place every day.

After work, everyone is stripped of their clothing and left only with their underwear. This is done under the pretext of preventing escapes.

There is a hospital in the village of Schapiniec,[7] where women about to give birth are taken. As soon as the babies are born, they are put into a bag and killed. The mothers are sent to Oschewitz camp, 'from where no one ever comes back'.

As the number of prisoners in the labour camp gradually dwindles due to the many deaths, and because all who appear too exhausted are immediately sent to Oschewitz, new victims are shipped in from Western Europe to replace them.

The person who witnessed all of these events was able to escape with the help of a non-Jewish Pole. He would like to add that, as a general rule, the Polish population will help the unfortunate deportees by any means necessary.

[…][8]

6 Correctly: Laurahütte.
7 Correctly: Szapiniec.
8 The article continues with another eyewitness account of the 'massacre of Jews in Poland'.

DOC. 309

On 31 August 1943, in an anonymous letter to the commandant of Drancy camp, employees of the Rothschild Hospital in Paris denounce their Jewish colleagues[1]

Anonymous letter (marked 'confidential'), from the 'Aryans of the Rothschild Hospital',[2] 15 rue Senterre, Paris, to the German commandant of Drancy camp,[3] dated 31 August 1943 (copy)

Dear Commandant,

Please excuse us for taking the liberty of writing to you again, but we, all the Aryans at the Rothschild Hospital, are extremely shocked following some of the Jewish inmates' escapes from the hospital. A few days ago a woman escaped, and this morning it was a Jewish inmate who was supposed to be on a transport to Drancy.[4]

We would like to repeat and to emphasize, Commandant, that we, *all the Aryans*, are in no way responsible for these escapes. We are doing our duty without fail, and we are carrying out the *very severe and very strict instructions* from the hospital's Aryan management, which is also not at fault at all. But how can we combat the scheming of Jews *when they are helped by the Jewish hospital staff? Because it is only the Jewish staff* who support and facilitate these escapes. We got further proof of that this morning.

If it is in your power, it would be useful and necessary to take the appropriate and well-deserved action against the Jewish staff, beginning with:

the finance officer, the Jewess Arjkuski;
the supervisor, the Jewess Chili;[5]
the switchboard operator and receptionist, the Jewess Fanny Jellikover; and
the foreign Jewish internees (a dozen) on the medical staff.

All of these Jews hold an *identity card* given to them by the infamous *General Union of French Jews*.[6]

They believe these cards will afford them protection from sanctions and will make them unassailable, and they take advantage of this and make a mockery of everything. We Aryans are wondering: to what kind of permit can these Yids[7] have a right?

1 Mémorial de la Shoah, CMLXXXVI(13)-9. This document has been translated from French.
2 On the Rothschild Hospital, see Doc. 265, fn. 5.
3 Alois Brunner (b. 1912), commercial clerk; born in Austria; joined the NSDAP and the SA in 1931; member of the Austrian Legion, 1933–1938; joined the SS in 1938; Eichmann's secretary in Vienna in 1938; coordinated the registration and deportation of the Austrian Jews in 1939 and 1941–1942, of the Jews from Berlin in winter 1942–1943, from Thessaloniki in spring 1943, from France between July 1943 and August 1944, and from Slovakia in Sept. 1944; commandant of Drancy camp from July 1943; went underground in Germany under an assumed name after the war; sentenced to death in Paris in absentia in 1954; thought to have fled to Syria in the 1950s and to have died in Damascus.
4 When Alois Brunner took over Drancy camp, the French police's supervision of the Rothschild Hospital also came to an end. The hospital management subsequently hired a private detective agency. The Jewish staff were held responsible whenever an interned patient escaped. However, successful escapes continued to occur, for instance on 26 August 1943, when Riva Chisner managed to get away after eleven months in the hospital.
5 Correctly: Marie Schilli.
6 The Jewish staff at the hospital had been integrated into the UGIF in late 1942 and therefore held identity cards intended to protect them from arrest.
7 In the original: 'Youpins', a pejorative French term for Jews.

We ask you, Commandant, since misdemeanours were committed, to make the Jews pay, as they are the only ones at fault and the only ones responsible.

We appeal once again, Commandant, to your strong sense of justice, and we place our trust in the actions that you will take.

Yours sincerely,

DOC. 310
On 4 September 1943 Heinz Röthke outlines the plans of the Security Police for measures against Jews in the Italian-occupied zone[1]

Record (marked 'secret') by Section IV B, Office of the Senior Commander of the Security Police in France,[2] SA 225a (Rö./Ne.), signed p.p. Röthke, Paris, dated 4 September 1943 (copy)

Re: preparations for implementing measures against the Jews in Italian-occupied territory[3]
Case file: in progress

1. *Memorandum*:
A) *Implementation of the operation without exceptions*
If the planned operation in the Italian-occupied territory is to have a satisfactory outcome, it must be carried out without exceptions. Aside from the fact that the vast majority of the available police are not qualified to determine whether any specific Jew, depending on his largely coincidental nationality, should or should not be included in the anti-Jewish measures, it would also be highly detrimental to us in propaganda terms if we were to make a whole range of exceptions with regard to individual nationalities or to whether, for example, a Jew with French nationality had been naturalized only after 10 August 1927 or whether he had already held French nationality before this date.[4] Moreover, it should be noted that it is precisely the wealthy and influential Jews who as a rule have French nationality through birth rather than acquiring it after 1927. Even Frenchmen who are not anti-Jewish would not understand if we did not intern first precisely the most harmful of the Jews, that is, the wealthy and influential Jews. Indeed even if it turns out later on for political reasons not to be possible to deport some or all of these Jews, internment still appears to be a particularly urgent measure. Furthermore, with regard to internment, it will not be possible for the time being to make allowances

1 Mémorial de la Shoah, XXVa-338. Published in French translation in Klarsfeld, *Calendrier*, pp. 1650–1652. This document has been translated from German.
2 Helmut Knochen.
3 Following the Allied landings on Sicily and the removal of Mussolini, in late July 1943 the new Italian prime minister, Marshal Badoglio, initiated secret negotiations with the Allies for an armistice. The Wehrmacht began preparations to seize control of the Italian zone in France and occupied this territory on 8 Sept. 1943, immediately after the proclamation of the armistice between Italy and the Allies. Against this background, Alois Brunner and Heinz Röthke planned a large-scale operation for the roundup of the Jewish population in this zone.
4 The law of 10 August 1927 had made it easier for foreigners in France to become naturalized. Here Röthke refers indirectly to the failed attempts to revoke such naturalizations for Jews: see Introduction, pp. 77–78.

for nationals of friendly, neutral, or allied states. All of these states were already asked six months to a year ago to take back their Jews into their sovereign territories. Most states have already complied with this request and have by now completed the repatriation. Only Turkey can still carry out repatriations on an appreciable scale. Therefore, no exceptions are to be made for the Jewish subjects of any of the states in question. Interventions could be directed subsequently to IV B, Office of the Senior Commander of the Security Police and the SD, and would be processed further from here after detailed examination of the nationality circumstances.

The Jewish subjects of enemy states must also be interned at once because for these persons to remain free would be even less defensible than for the other Jews. These Jews would be transferred to internment camps for Englishmen, Americans, etc.

The main target areas of the operation are envisaged as being the Côte d'Azur, the départements of Savoie and Haute-Savoie, Grenoble, as well as places on the border or on the boundary of our sphere of interest. To prevent an exodus of Jews during the operation, it will be absolutely necessary to start in places on the border and to comb the entire territory in question from east to west.

The Jews will be apprehended together with their families. They can take with them the most essential items of clothing as well as everyday items, unless for particular reasons their immediate transport to provisional reception camps appears necessary.

The commandos of Lyons and Marseilles will set up provisional reception camps (in Jewish schools, disused factories or similar premises) in these two cities. Hauptsturmführer Brunner will travel over the course of the 5th or the 6th to Lyons and Marseilles with Hauptscharführer Brückler[5] in order to make all the preparations unobtrusively on site and to get a sense of the local situation.

Once the Jews have been taken into custody, they will be transferred from the provisional reception camps in transport trains with 1,000 to 2,000 persons on each train to Drancy camp for Jews, where their nationality status will be thoroughly investigated, they will be divided up and – insofar as they meet the deportation criteria – evacuated to the East.

It is imperative to completely cleanse the former Italian zone of influence of Jews not only in the interest of the final solution to the Jewish question in France, but also for the safety of the German troops. Opinion locally is that this argument could also be used with the French government should it decide to intervene on behalf of Jews who already possessed French nationality before 1927, or should it – as can be expected – intervene on behalf of all Jews of French nationality in general.

Since the Italians prohibited the stamping of the identity and food ration cards of all Jews in their zone of influence, it is even more difficult here to determine whether individual suspicious elements are members of the Jewish race than it is in the formerly occupied territory of France, where at least the Jew registries can be consulted. French enemies of the Jews are therefore to be enlisted for the operation and are to track down and report Jews living in disguise or in hiding. Money is no object. (Recommendation: 100 francs per Jew.)

5 Ernst Brückler (b. 1912), joiner; joined the SS in 1932; worked under Eichmann in Vienna from 1938; had assignments in Slovakia, Greece, and France; officially declared dead in 1950 by the Bremerhaven municipal court.

B) *Implementing the operation with exceptions*
If the French government wants to stoop to providing protection for certain categories of Jews from our planned measures against Jews, then they can at most have an interest in the Jews of French nationality and here once again only in the Jews who were already naturalized before 10 August 1927 or in the Jews who acquired French nationality through birth, and their spouses and children. Since a general cleansing of the territory is necessary, it is proposed that any difference in treatment should be applied only after arrival at Drancy camp for Jews. Exceptions for Jews who already held French nationality before 10 August 1927 could only be made locally if the French police were available for the operation. In that case, French police stations, as well as other French administrative offices, would have to ascertain for each French Jew individually whether or not internment is an option. Although the review could be monitored to a certain extent by our forces, this process would allow for all sorts of sharp practices and fraudulent manoeuvres. However, insufficient forces are available on the German side for naturalized and non-naturalized Jews to be separated during the operation itself. Additionally, it can be assumed that the French government itself will lose interest in a considerable portion of the non-naturalized French Jews and will not intervene on their behalf. Besides, it could be pointed out to the French government that in the past it repeatedly expressed regret that the Italian military and civil authorities gave the Jews every form of support. The French government should therefore be pleased that this protection is now gone and that it is finally possible to take effective action against the Jews. Should the French government thus wish for a generous ruling on exemptions for Jews of French nationality, such requests could be rejected also with reference to the explicit order of the Reichsführer SS.

Recommendation: exemptions for the Jews of French nationality in whom the French government has an interest to be granted at the earliest by means of release from Drancy.

2- Senior Commander of the Security Police and the SD – for the attention of SS-Sturmbannführer Hagen.

DOC. 311

On 15 September 1943 the Military Commander issues a regulation that transfers the assets of Polish and Czech Jews in France to the Reich[1]

1.
Regulation on the Forfeiture to the Greater German Reich of the Assets of Jews who were Subjects of the Former Polish State
15 September 1943

By virtue of the authority vested in me by the Führer and the Commander-in-Chief of the Wehrmacht, I hereby decree the following:

1 *VOBl-F*, no. 97, 27 Sept. 1943, pp. 553–555. This document has been translated from German.

§ 1

(1) In the territory of the Military Commander in France the assets of Jews who on 1 September 1939 were
  a. subjects of the former Polish state or
  b. stateless but most recently subjects of the former Polish state

  shall be forfeited to the Reich.

(2) The Military Commander in France reserves the right to make other provisions in individual cases.

§ 2

Sections 3, 4, and 5 of the Regulation of 2 December 1942 on the Forfeiture to the German Reich of the Assets of Jews holding German Nationality or having held German Nationality (*VOBl-F*, p. 451) shall apply accordingly.

§ 3

This regulation comes into force upon its promulgation.

The Military Commander in France[2]

2.

Regulation on the Forfeiture to the Greater German Reich of the Assets of Jews who were Subjects of the Protectorate of Bohemia and Moravia

15 September 1943

By virtue of the authority vested in me by the Führer and the Commander-in-Chief of the Wehrmacht, I hereby decree the following:

§ 1

(1) The assets of Jews who lost or will lose the citizenship of the Protectorate of Bohemia and Moravia pursuant to § 2 of the Regulation of 2 November 1942 on the Loss of Protectorate Citizenship (*Reichsgesetzblatt* I, p. 637) (1)[3] shall be forfeited to the Reich upon loss of Protectorate citizenship.

(2) Additionally, the assets of Jews who when the Regulation of 2 November 1942 came into force, that is, on 11 November 1942, were stateless and had most recently held Protectorate or Czechoslovak citizenship and who at this date were resident abroad or subsequently took up residence abroad are forfeited to the Reich.

(3) The Military Commander in France reserves the right to make other provisions in individual cases.

§ 2

Sections 3, 4, and 5 of the Regulation of 2 December 1942 on the Forfeiture to the German Reich of the Assets of Jews holding German Nationality or having held German Nationality (*VOBl-F*, p. 451) shall apply accordingly.

§ 3

This regulation comes into force upon its promulgation.

The Military Commander in France

2 Carl Heinrich von Stülpnagel.

3 Footnote in the original document: '§ 2 of the Regulation of 2 November 1942 reads: "A Jew loses Protectorate citizenship, a) if at the time this regulation comes into force he is resident abroad, b) if he subsequently takes up residence abroad."

DOC. 312

On 6 October 1943, hours before his execution, Chuna Bajtsztok writes a farewell letter to his teacher[1]

Letter from Chuna Henri Bajtsztok,[2] Fresnes prison, to his teacher and tutor, Mr Peyreigne dated 6 October 1943, 1 p.m. (copy)

Dear Mr Peyreigne, my devoted teacher,

I could never have imagined that one day I would be writing to you in such a situation and addressing such words to you! The fact is that I am going to be executed in three hours' time. I was arrested on 1 June for terrorism (an act committed as a partisan)[3] and I was condemned along with twenty-five of my brothers in arms on 1 October, the day the new school year started. I am taking the liberty of addressing one of my three final letters to you.

First of all and once again I have to thank you for the good school year 1941/42, which I owe in large part to you. I want to thank you for trying, in vain obviously, to turn me away from this path, which I could see that you sensed I was going to take.

But, my dear friend, I always felt myself to be somewhat different from most other young people, and I have always wanted to be true to my word once my decisions had been made. I therefore have no regrets except for causing grief to my friends and comrades, my parents, and my brother.

I may perhaps be taking advantage of your kindness, but I would like to ask you if you would write to my former French teacher, Mr Bouquet, who is now the headmaster of the Thiers Boys' School in Le Rainey (S. & O.),[4] to express my thanks also to him and to ask him to do all he can to look after my younger brother, who is at present a pupil at his school.

I would also like to ask you to let my other teachers know what has happened to me, as well as Mr Rousson, and the caretaker of the school, who will be able to tell Mr Plaud.

That is more or less all I had to tell you. You will be able to guess what I am thinking. I regret nothing, and I do not feel I should be pitied. I believe that my death will be worthy of my life. I know what I have lived for and for which I perish.

I embrace you most sincerely and thank you in advance.

Goodbye, my dear teacher.

1 Mémorial de la Shoah, CCXVI-70. Published in Guy Krivopissko, *La Vie à en mourir: Lettres de fusillés (1941–1944)* (Paris: Tallandier, 2003), pp. 253–254. This document has been translated from French.

2 Chuna Henri Bajtsztok (1923–1943), student; joined the communist resistance at the beginning of the occupation; joined the youth organization of the far-right collaborationist party Rassemblement National Populaire under a false name; arrested in an armed operation in early June 1943; sentenced to death on 1 Oct. 1943; executed by firing squad five days later at Mont Valérien, Suresnes.

3 In the original: 'acte de franc-tireur-partisan'. 'Francs-tireurs et partisans' was the name of a communist resistance group.

4 Seine-et-Oise département.

DOC. 313

On 25 October 1943 Maurice Schwaitzer informs his family of his impending departure from Drancy[1]

Letter from Maurice Schwaitzer,[2] Drancy, to his wife and daughter,[3] dated 25 October 1943 (copy)

My dear wife and dear daughter,

It is with great joy that I read your letter, and I am happy to know that you are in good health. I am in excellent health too.

The parcel which was announced has not yet arrived, but I hope I won't have to wait long to receive it. And I would like to have it, because it contains things that will greatly help me. Morale is still good here. We are hoping that the war will end quite soon, that we'll all return home, and that life will continue as it did before. Although I do not want you to worry, I have to tell you that we will be leaving this week, probably on Thursday morning. We will leave in railway wagons, 50 people per wagon. We will of course be given enough food for several days. We are going to Metz, and we don't know where we'll be going from there. Don't trouble yourselves over me. I am not the only one, and I am sharing this fate with my comrades. I think about you a great deal, and I would like you to be spared this fate. At least I hope that you will be able to make the best of it. My darling, please forgive me for asking you to pass on several messages for others. You must know that they are as unfortunate as me, and it makes them very happy to know that their families will have news of them. Such things are of inestimable value, and I hope that you will not be annoyed with me for that. It is true that we are leaving on Thursday, but it may be useful if you go and see Mr Lecroux.[4] You can talk to him about me, and perhaps he can do something for me, if it's not already too late. In any case, I want to say goodbye to you. And to my dearest daughter: your father is always thinking of you, and he asks you to continue to work hard, so that one day I will be proud of you. In my thoughts, across all the barbed wire fences around me, I am coming back to you all, to you, my only and dearest daughter. Have courage, lots of courage and patience. Evil cannot last forever, and I firmly believe that we will see each other again. One day, a bright sun will light up the world again, and we will all be together once more. Goodbye my darling, and goodbye my dear daughter. With love from the depths of my heart!

1 The original is privately owned. Copy in Mémorial de la Shoah, CMLXXVI(4)-11. This document has been translated from French.

2 Maurice (Moïse Aron) Schwaitzer (1887–1943), tailor; emigrated to France from Russia; naturalized in 1930; arrested at home by the French police in early Oct. 1943 following an anonymous allegation that he was forging identity papers; interned in Drancy camp and deported to Auschwitz on 28 Oct. 1943.

3 Marguerite Schwaitzer, née Wiener (1900–1976), housewife and seamstress; Monique Schwaitzer (b. 1929), later manager at a pharmaceutical company. Mother and daughter escaped arrest in exchange for payment, but both were forced out of their rented apartment, which was confiscated. They went underground until 1944, living in a hotel under assumed names; following a court decision, they were able to return to their ransacked apartment in 1946.

4 Presumably an acquaintance of Maurice Schwaitzer's who worked at the Paris Police Prefecture and had previously been able to warn him of roundups.

Your husband and father,
Maurice

Give my best to Mr and Mrs Mangin,[5] as well to all the family.

DOC. 314
On 25 October 1943 Georges Edinger opens the first joint board meeting of the General Union of French Jews in Paris[1]

Address by Georges Edinger[2] to the board of the UGIF in Paris on 25 October 1943 (copy)

Ladies and Gentlemen,

Before we proceed to today's agenda, I would like to extend a warm welcome to our colleagues and associates from the southern zone on behalf of the board of the northern zone.

Firstly, I want to assure our friends and colleagues who have been prevented from being present at this meeting, our dear presidents *Lambert* and *Baur*, our colleagues *Stora* and *Musnick*,[3] our associates *Katz* and *Israelowicz*, that all of our thoughts have constantly been with them, and all of our efforts have been directed towards them.[4]

Right up to the last minute, we had hoped that Raymond and André[5] would be seated at this table, in the place which is theirs by right; unfortunately a setback, and let us hope that it is only a setback, has prevented them from being here.

Our thoughts equally turn to our associates from Paris, from Lyons, from Marseilles, from Nice, and to others as well, who have had to pay with their liberty for the unceasing commitment with which they have tried to help relieve the increasing misery we see all around us; this is the central role of the UGIF.

I am happy that today – after almost two years of existence – the board can finally come together in its entirety,[6] although alas incomplete.

We are going to be called to discuss serious questions, questions of structure, questions of organization, questions of centralization; I sincerely believe that the UGIF will

5 Schwaitzer may here have been identifying the suspected authors of the anonymous denunciation which led to his arrest.

1 Archives du Consistoire central de Paris, CC-24. This document has been translated from French.
2 Georges (Alexandre-Gompel-Georges) Edinger (b. 1890), businessman; co-owner of a chain of lingerie shops; supporter of Jewish charitable institutions; appointed treasurer and board member of the UGIF North in early 1942; president of the UGIF from Nov. 1943; seized by members of the Jewish resistance in August 1944 and interned in Drancy.
3 Fernand Musnik (1915–1945), milliner; head of the UGIF's youth and occupational retraining department from 1942; arrested in early Sept. 1943; interned in Drancy; deported to Auschwitz on 17 Dec. 1943; died in Dachau in early March 1945.
4 André Baur and Leo Israelowicz were held in Drancy from 21 July 1943; Marcel Stora and Fernand Musnik were interned there from early Sept. 1943. Raymond-Raoul Lambert and other leading members of the UGIF South were transferred to Drancy in late August 1943: see Doc. 294. Georges Edinger himself had been detained for 24 hours in July 1943: see Doc. 307.
5 Raymond-Raoul Lambert and André Baur.
6 With the establishment of a joint board for the UGIF North and the UGIF South, some of the reforms proposed by André Baur at the beginning of the year were implemented: see Doc. 294.

emerge strengthened from these negotiations. If our thoughts are turned towards the future, this will not be to the detriment of the present, which is onerous and uncertain, as much for our co-religionists as for the institutions that the UGIF has the responsibility and the duty to maintain.

I also sincerely believe that the positive results of our work give us hope that the UGIF and its personnel will be allowed to work in peace, and that our friends will be able to take up their places among us again.

I regret that your necessarily short stay here will not give you the time to visit all of our institutions. We would nevertheless be pleased if some among them were to have the honour of your visit, and each and every one of us will see it as their duty to show you around.

DOC. 315

On 15 November 1943 the Marseilles office of the General Union of French Jews informs the head office in Paris that the members of the former Camps Commission have been arrested[1]

Letter from the director general of the UGIF South (GK/MK No. 8802),[2] Marseilles, to the interim director general of the UGIF,[3] Paris, dated 15 November 1943 (copy)

We regret to inform you that the staff from the third section (formerly the Camps Commission)[4] of our fifth directorate, which is based in *Sisteron* (Hautes-Alpes département), led by secretary general Mr Edgard *Dreyfus*,[5] were arrested on 4 November and transferred to *Nice*.

We have just learned that the secretary general of our fifth directorate, Mr *Guckenheimer*,[6] who had only recently been released, suffered the same fate on Wednesday the 10th of this month, along with all of his staff. He not only headed the secretariat general of the fifth directorate, but also ran the operations of the local office in Nice.

You will not fail to realize how difficult it is becoming for us to guarantee the smooth running of the UGIF in the southern zone under these conditions.[7]

1 YVA, O.9/28. This document has been translated from French.
2 Gaston Kahn, member of the CAR refugee aid organization in the 1930s; board member of the UGIF South in 1942; head of the UGIF office in the town of Gap and the fifth directorate (formerly CAR) in 1943; interim director of the UGIF South from Sept. to Dec. 1943; then went underground.
3 Georges Edinger.
4 The Commission des camps was founded in Toulouse in 1941 to coordinate and support the work of the Jewish relief organizations (OSE, ORT, and HICEM) in the camps and to distribute the funds, which primarily came from the American Jewish Joint Distribution Committee (JDC).
5 Edgard Dreyfus (1902–1944), office clerk; sent to Drancy on 19 Nov. 1943 and deported the following day to Auschwitz, where he perished.
6 Ernst Guckenheimer (b. 1905), born in Frankfurt am Main; naturalized citizen of France; office clerk; arrested in Nice along with his wife, Herta, and deported on 20 Nov. 1943 to Auschwitz, where he perished.
7 In late Oct. 1943 Alois Brunner had demanded that the UGIF leadership provide a map indicating the locations of the UGIF offices. This map was used in the roundups of Nov. 1943, when numerous UGIF sites, including those in Sisteron, Marseilles, Chambéry, Brive, Limoges, Périgueux, and Toulouse, were searched.

As it was agreed during our last meeting in *Paris* that you would be in charge of liaison with the central occupying authorities, we entreat you to direct their attention to this state of affairs, which is liable to compromise the UGIF's mission. Intervening on the local level appears to us unlikely to be effective.

Please keep us informed of the steps you are taking. Thank you in advance,

DOC. 316

On 15 November 1943 the French Ministry of the Interior's representative in Paris criticizes the French police for handing over French Jews to the Germans[1]

Memorandum (JPI/SP) from the prefect and representative of the French Ministry of the Interior, signed Ingrand,[2] to the secretary general of the French police,[3] Vichy, dated 15 November 1943[4]

Memorandum

The procedure followed by the police prefecture remained defensible only as long as Drancy camp was still managed by the French administration[5] and with respect to those Jews who were found to be in breach of French law.

Following a conversation I had with Mr Permilleux,[6] the content of which is confirmed by the attached note,[7] it has become clear that the situation has changed significantly. The German authorities are sending the police prefecture lists of people to be arrested with no reasons for the arrests and without allowing the police to verify not only whether the Jew has committed any kind of offence, but even whether the person concerned really is a Jew.

This procedure means that French citizens are being handed over to the German authorities without any justification to be interned in a German camp.[8]

It is important that we put an immediate stop to such inadmissible divergences from correct procedure. Only the government can and must take a clear position on this question by forbidding all the police services, including the prefecture of police, from arresting French Jews if it has not been proved that they have broken French law. And even when the latter is the case, it seems impossible to then order internment in a German

1 AN, F7, vol. 14 887. Published in Klarsfeld, *Calendrier*, p. 1703. This document has been translated from French.

2 Jean-Pierre Ingrand (1905–1992), lawyer; born in Tunis; studied in Paris; master of petitions (*maître des requêtes*) in the French Council of State; worked in various ministries from 1933 to 1936; representative of the Ministry of the Interior in Paris; resigned in Jan. 1944; fled in 1947 to Argentina, where he worked for the railways; president of the Alliance française in Buenos Aires, 1964.

3 René Bousquet.

4 The original contains a handwritten note.

5 This refers to the practice of imprisoning in Drancy camp Jews who had been arrested by the French police for violating antisemitic regulations. Drancy internment camp was under French administration until the arrival of Alois Brunner: see Introduction, p. 82.

6 Charles Permilleux (b. 1896), police commissioner; head of the Service spécial des affaires juives, a special branch of the Paris Criminal Police created to prosecute violations of antisemitic regulations.

7 This is not in the file.

8 The German camp referred to here is Drancy.

camp, because this represents an obstruction of the normal course of French justice. Such a measure is all the more extreme since most of those concerned are deported to Germany.

If the government were to continue to allow such procedures, it would be morally liable to a significant degree, not only for its own actions but above all for those of the officials implementing the measures, who are receiving instructions of a threatening nature from the German authorities.

DOC. 317

On 20 November 1943 the Senior Commander of the Security Police requests that Chief of Police Bousquet grant access to the lists of French Jews maintained by the prefectures[1]

Letter from the Senior Commander of the Security Police and the SD in the sector of the Military Commander in France (B.Nr. II pol 1–106/1), signed Knochen, Paris, to the secretary general of the French police, René Bousquet, Vichy, dated 20 November 1943

Re: inspection by German police officials of the lists of Jews maintained by the prefects in the southern part of France.
During police investigations it is often important to determine whether certain persons are Jews. In many cases this information can only be ascertained by consulting the lists of Jews maintained by the prefectures.

The Einsatzkommando of the Security Police and SD in Limoges has therefore asked the regional prefect in Limoges[2] for permission to consult the list of local Jews. The regional prefect turned down the request of the Einsatzkommando of the Security Police and SD on the grounds that, according to the French governmental authorities concerned, German agencies may be granted access to the lists of foreign Jews, but not to the lists of French Jews.[3] This is supposedly in accordance with an agreement reached between the secretary general of the French Police and the Higher SS and Police Leader.[4]

I am not aware of any such agreement. Since the inspection of the lists of Jews is undertaken only to establish conclusively and clearly whether certain persons are Jews, I cannot understand what reasons there might be for not allowing German police officers to do this. I therefore ask that the prefects in southern France be immediately in-

1 AN, F7, vol. 14 887. Published in French translation in Klarsfeld, *Calendrier*, pp. 1707–1708. This document has been translated from German.

2 René Rivière (b. 1900), lawyer; born in Algeria; sub-prefect in Paris in 1933; chef de cabinet of the governor general of Algeria, 1935; prefect of the Hautes-Alpes département, 1937; prefect of the Haute-Vienne département and regional prefect in Limoges, 1943; suspended from duty in Oct. 1944.

3 The Commander of the Security Police and the SD for Limoges asked the prefect in Limoges for the list of all Jews registered in the département. The prefect declined this request, citing orders from Vichy.

4 This is a reference to the agreement between Bousquet and Oberg: see Doc. 239.

structed to comply unconditionally with requests by German police officers to consult the lists of Jews.

I await confirmation that arrangements have been put in place.[5]

DOC. 318

A German police officer in Strasbourg reports that Drancy tunnel diggers are among those who escaped from a transport to Auschwitz on 20 November 1943[1]

Report by Friedrich Köhnlein, police officer,[2] 5./P I.Wachbatl. V., Strasbourg, to SS-Obersturmführer Rötke,[3] Feldpost no. 03 069 o.V.i.V.,[4] Paris, dated 3 December 1943 (copy)

Re: report on the transport of Jews on 20 November 1943.[5]

The transport left Paris-Bobigny railway station at 12.10 p.m. and made a stop in Leroville[6] at 8.30 p.m. During the inspection of the wagons, it was discovered that the struts on the ventilation hatches in wagon no. 6 had been torn off. The inspection revealed that the wagon elder and another 18 men had escaped (as was immediately reported by telex from Neuburg Novéant[7] to the Senior Commander of the Security Police and the SD).

The nineteen men escaped on the steep gradient near Leroville, where the train travels at only walking pace, although several warning shots were fired from the last guard wagon. Because of the darkness and the thick fog in the area, the escape could not be detected until the train came to a standstill. I at once gave orders for all male prisoners, except for the sick and elderly, to remove their shoes, which were stowed in an empty car and returned only at Auschwitz. After this, the journey proceeded without further incident.

Enclosed are a list of the escapees' names and two of their identity documents, as well as a number of letters and cards, which were thrown out of the train during the journey. Also enclosed are three unused Wehrmacht tickets.

5 In his reply, dated 26 Nov. 1943, René Bousquet refused to grant access to the lists. A few weeks later he was removed from his position as chief of police as a result of German pressure.

1 YIVO, Occ 19. Copy in Mémorial de la Shoah, XXVc-249. This document has been translated from German.

2 Friedrich Köhnlein (b. 1902), police officer; joined the Württemberg Urban Police in 1923; promoted in 1926 and 1928; joined the NSDAP in 1933; served in the Strasbourg Urban Police during the occupation; served in the 5th Volunteer Police Regiment in Croatia in 1944; captured by Western Allied forces in 1945.

3 Correctly: Röthke.

4 The meaning of the abbreviation could not be ascertained.

5 The transport to Auschwitz with 1,181 Jews was guarded by an Urban Police unit which had been transferred from Strasbourg to Paris the day before. Köhnlein was the head of the guard unit on the train.

6 Correctly: Lérouville (Meuse département).

7 Located on the Franco-German border, Novéant-sur-Moselle was renamed Neuburg in Lothringen by the Germans in 1940. Most of the deportation trains from Drancy and Compiègne passed through the station here on the way into the Reich and further east.

I would like to note that most of the escapees were the tunnel diggers of Dracy camp.[8] If these men, as discussed before departure, had been segregated and loaded into the cars without clothes, they would certainly not have escaped.

DOC. 319
In December 1943 the Jewish resistance organization Armée juive in Nice describes its activities since September[1]

Report, signed Henri and H. P.,[2] Nice, undated (carbon copy)

Armand[3] – Nice
From the start of September 1943 until the start of December 1943.
September 1943: when the Nice catastrophe struck (10 September 1943),[4] Armand had only just been organized. Training sessions up to September 1943: 2.

Contact was constantly maintained during the upheavals but the Armands had to hide; in other words, no action was possible.
Cause of Armand's weakness in September and October 1943 in Nice:
Although Armand should have intervened against certain notorious informers, it was unable to do so due to:

a) lack of training
b) lack of arms
c) insufficient numbers of men
d) some of the Armands being in hiding with their relatives: relatives are always a decisive handicap for an Armand –
e) the Armands who stayed by themselves having become immersed in social activities, information-gathering, and other activities …

8 Correctly: Drancy. Twelve of the nineteen escapees were 'tunnel diggers' from Drancy camp. The tunnel out of the camp, which approximately forty prisoners had begun digging in Sept. 1943, was discovered by the SS in early Nov., shortly before it would have been completed. Several of the tunnel diggers worked in the Jewish camp administration. These men were replaced and assigned to the next deportation train. They managed to smuggle a small saw and a screwdriver onto the train before it departed.

1 AIU, AP 5/52, Fonds Henri Hertz. This document has been translated from French.
2 Henry Pohorylès (b. 1920), born in Strasbourg; head of the Armée juive in the Nice region, autumn 1943–July 1944; arrested in Paris along with members of the Westerweel Group in July 1944 (see Doc. 335); initially held in the prison in Fresnes, then in Drancy camp; deported on 17 August 1944; during the journey, he managed to escape from the train with several of his comrades.
3 Armand is the code name for the Jewish resistance organization Armée juive, renamed Organisation juive de combat in 1944: see Introduction, p. 80.
4 This refers to the mass arrest of Jews in the Nice area. Almost 2,000 Jews were arrested in this operation under the command of Alois Brunner and transferred to Drancy camp between mid Sept. and mid Dec.: see Doc. 310. After the Italian zone was occupied by German troops, almost 25,000 Jews, 15,000 of whom were not French citizens, had moved to the Côte d'Azur, which was still under Italian occupation, in the hope that they would be evacuated or would be able to escape to Italy.

Countermeasures starting in mid October:
1) new recruits
2) purchase of arms (see appendices)[5]
3) training in different terrain every Saturday morning and live shooting. Training in the city with simulated targets.

Intelligence service:
An intelligence service has been established. All of the Armands gather intelligence at their posts, which is then collated centrally. Observations are also carried out in cooperation with the Resistance.

Current targets:
The former police inspector Boina, who sold out two leaders of the Resistance who had been of great service to us (a target of general importance). The highly valued notorious woman informer Merry Seidlitz (a specific target for Jews).

Long-term targets:
Alice,[6] a female Gestapo agent, a specialist in hunting Jews, probably responsible for the arrest of Mr Jacques Wister.[7]

Current weaknesses:
Absolute secrecy, and yet the Armands are still too active socially, and the work of an Armand requires total autonomy.

This question will be resolved upon my return. Similarly, Zionism often overly sentimental.

Armand lacks high-capacity automatic weapons.

Links with the Resistance:
a) Links exist with the Jewish FTP.[8] We briefly considered sharing an instructor, but in the end we realized how weak they were in Nice. Contact is being maintained, but quite loosely.
b) Gaullists: in contact with the Resistance Council *in Nice,*[9] which has no shock troops. We are doing our best to regroup 'Combat'.[10]

The only result: they produced some papers.[11] They are probably also going to lend us one or two machine guns.

Upon my departure, we negotiated sharing weapons dropped by parachute, which we would collect together. A lot of fuss but few positive results.

5 Not in the file.
6 The secretary to SS-Hauptsturmführer Helmuth Retzek, who headed the Security Police and the SD office in Nice.
7 Jankiel Waintrob, known as Jacques Wister; head of the Zionist youth movement in Nice and a prominent member of the Armée juive until autumn 1943; organized escape routes to Switzerland and hiding places for children and adults after the Brunner operation started in Nice; murdered in Oct. 1943.
8 Francs-tireurs et partisans, communist resistance movement.
9 This refers to the Conseil national de la Résistance, founded in mid 1943 by Jean Moulin, a representative of General de Gaulle, to coordinate the activities of the various French resistance organizations.
10 Gaullist resistance movement in the southern zone, founded in 1940 by Henri Frenay and Berty Albrecht as the Mouvement de libération nationale.
11 This refers to false identity documents.

Contact in Marseilles with what is left of 'Combat':[12] will procure arms for us.
Conclusion: In Nice, without being over-optimistic, we can say that Armand constitutes the only real combat force in place. Its men are determined and are prepared to act.
Henri

Crossing into Spain: Given the serious situation we are facing, we thought we should broaden the field in our search for candidates, notably where age limits are concerned. We have also dispatched some candidates.

Departure from Nice: approximately twenty.

For the future: Only admit young people and introduce stricter selection.
H. P.

DOC. 320

On 6 January 1944 the prefect in Amiens asks the Vichy government to intervene with the German authorities to obtain the release of Jews from his département who have been arrested[1]

Letter (hd/1d) from the prefect of the Somme département,[2] signature illegible, Amiens, to the head of government,[3] the minister and permanent secretary of the interior,[4] and the Directorate General of the French Police, Vichy, dated 6 January 1944[5]

Re: arrests of Israelites
I would like to inform you that on 4 January the local German authorities arrested all the Israelites of French nationality residing in my département, irrespective of their age or state of health.[6]

In the course of this operation, Mr (Lucien) Aaron, 66 years of age, veteran of the 1914–1918 war, decorated with the Croix de Guerre and the Verdun Medal, *almost blind,* married to an Aryan residing at 44 rue des Trois Cailloux in Amiens, and Mrs Ponthieu, née Louria (Renée), 22 years of age, married to an Aryan and *pregnant,* were apprehended.[7]

12 Presumably this refers to other resistance organizations in Marseilles.

1 AN, F7, vol. 14 887. Published in Klarsfeld, *Calendrier,* pp. 1734–1736. This document has been translated from French.

2 Charles Daupeyroux (1890–1959), lawyer; practised law from 1912 to 1919; sub-prefect in 1922; prefect of the Lozère département in 1939; prefect of the Somme département, August 1943–Jan. 1944; suspended from duty on 24 Jan. 1944; forced to retire in Jan. 1945.

3 Pierre Laval.

4 Antoine Lemoine.

5 The letter was sent via the prefect and representative of the French Ministry of the Interior in Paris and, for information only, to the regional prefect of the Laon region in Saint-Quentin.

6 This was one of the first roundups undertaken by the German police that targeted French Jews outside the Paris metropolitan area. The number of these roundups subsequently increased greatly. The French government decided not to intervene and raised no objections to the French police's involvement in them.

7 Lucien Aaron (b. 1878), born in Constantine, businessman; admitted to the Rothschild Hospital on 31 Jan. 1944 and not deported. Renée Ponthieu (1921–1984), a nurse, deported on 20 Jan. 1944 to Auschwitz; returned in May 1945 to France; activist in the post-war peace movement.

Also arrested were two children who had been in state care:
– (Georges) Hirsch, born on 14 June 1934 in Vienna, residing at 14 rue Albéric de Calonne in Amiens,
– (Cécile) Redlich, born on 29 April 1929 in Paris, residing at 9 rue Cottrel-Maisant in Amiens, as well as the young boy
– (Jean-Louis) Wajnberg, born on 24 April 1935 in Amiens, residing with his parents in Rosières-en-Santerre.[8]

Others seem to have been arrested by mistake.

They are:
– Mr (Raymond) Schulhof, veteran, born on 25 March 1898 in Paris, residing at 14 rue Albéric de Calonne in Amiens, as well as his wife, née Levy (Fleurette), born on 2 April 1901 in Verdun, and his mother-in-law (Louise) Levy, born on 26 February 1873 in Thionville.[9]

Mr Schulhof held identity card no. 800, which was valid until 29 February 1944, a photographic reproduction of which I have attached to this letter.[10]

As this document states, Mr Schulhof, who held the position of delegate to the General Union of French Jews, must be 'exempt from all internment measures' and the same protection extended to any members of his family who live with him.

Finally, the following two people of Aryan race were also subject to an internment measure:
– Mr (Vladimir) Kasmine, born on 24 December 1900 in Voronezh, of French nationality, veteran of the 1939/1940 war, decorated with the Military Cross, employee of an electricity company, and resident of Amiens, 131 rue Delpech, for over 25 years.

The above-named was arrested at his home, as was his wife, who is of Jewish race.[11]
– Mr (André) Lehmann,[12] shirt-maker, born on 1 November 1893 in Besançon, residing at 118 rue Lemerchier in Amiens.

The latter was forcibly registered and then kept on the Somme département s list of Israelites at the express request of the Commissioner General for Jewish Affairs.

However, the president of the Civil Court of Amiens issued a definitive ruling on 4 June 1943, according to which Lehmann should not be considered as belonging to the Jewish race.

8 Correctly: Georg Hirsch, born in Vienna; hidden in a small village in the Pyrenees; taken to Amiens by the Gestapo in early 1943 and housed there with the Schulhof family. Cécile Redlich, born in Paris; cared for by the French welfare system following her parents' deportations in July and Nov. 1942. Jean-Louis Wajnberg, born in Amiens; arrested along with his family. All of these children were deported on 20 Jan. 1944 to Auschwitz, where they were murdered.

9 Raymond Schulhof, an estate agent, and his relatives were deported on 20 Jan. 1944 to Auschwitz and murdered there. The Schulhofs' three children survived the war in hiding: see Ginette Hirtz, *Les Hortillonnages sous la grêle* (Paris: Mercure de France, 1982).

10 This is not in the file.

11 Vladimir Kasmine was interned in Drancy in Jan. 1944 and released in late Feb. 1944. Nadine (Dvoira) Kasmine, née Sobol (b. 1901); born in Brest-Litovsk; became a French citizen in 1938; deported on 20 Jan. 1944 from Drancy to Auschwitz, where she was murdered.

12 André Lehmann, a 'half-Jew', is thought to have been held in Drancy until summer 1944 and liberated by Allied troops.

All of these persons were sent to Drancy camp on the day of their arrest; I informed the office of the French ambassador,[13] delegate general of the French Government in the Occupied Territories, of this by telephone, so that an urgent intervention with the senior German authorities would be undertaken to obtain the release of the people indicated above.

I also note that I will be sending on to you later the complete list of persons arrested over the course of the day on 4 January.

DOC. 321

On 17 January 1944 Georg Halpern writes a letter to his mother in which he describes his life in the Izieu children's home[1]

Letter from Georg Halpern,[2] Izieu, to his mother[3] in Hauteville, dated 17 January 1944

Dear Mama,

I received your postcard, which made me very happy. I am well. I'm having fun. At Christmas we celebrated and put on plays, and we ate well. We ate gingerbread, chocolate, quince jam, a bag of sweets, we drank Ovaltine, and we were given toys.

I received a paint box and a pad of drawing paper.

Are you in good health? The little New Year's postcard was very nice. I already replied to Papa.[4]

No snow has fallen yet. I am eating well, I am well. We go for walks on Thursdays and Sundays. We get up at 7 o'clock in the morning, we have coffee, a slice of bread and jam, at noon sometimes soup or vegetables, dessert. For our afternoon snack, we have bread with chocolate and milk, and for dinner soup, vegetables, and soft cheese. I'm sending you 1,000,000,000,000 (a thousand million) kisses, your son who loves you very much.

13 Fernand de Brinon.

1 Imperial War Museum, London, private papers of Georges Halpern. Published in facsimile in Georges Halpern, *En souvenir de Georgy: Lettres de la Maison d'Izieu, 1935–1944*, ed. Serge Klarsfeld (Paris: Aperture, 2002), p. 21. This document has been translated from French.

2 Georg Halpern (1935–1944), fled with his parents from Vienna to France in 1938; from 1940 in various children's homes run by the OSE welfare organization; in the Maison d'Izieu (Ain département) from April 1943; arrested there by the German police in early April 1944 (see Doc. 327); transferred to Drancy the next day; deported to Auschwitz, where he was murdered on 13 April 1944.

3 Serafine Halpern, née Friedmann (1907–1989); interned in St-Louis Hospital in Perpignan in 1940; subsequently stayed in the De l'Espérance sanatorium in Hauteville (Ain département), not far from Izieu; emigrated to Israel after the war.

4 Julius Halpern (1905–1989), dentist; born in Lwów; assigned to one of the Foreign Labourer Groups (GTE) established by the Vichy government during the occupation period; emigrated to Israel after the war.

DOC. 322

On 28 January 1944 the Paris Police Prefecture informs the representative of the Vichy government's Ministry of the Interior about the arrest of 643 foreign Jews[1]

Letter from the Paris police prefect[2] (Criminal Police Department, subdivision for Jewish affairs), signed Misset, to the prefect and representative of the minister and state secretary of the interior in the occupied territories,[3] Paris, dated 28 January 1944

I am writing to inform you that the occupying authorities have just issued a written order, of which I have attached a copy,[4] ordering a new roundup of all foreign Jews who had their identity checked between 1 and 8 December 1943, with the exception of Argentinians, Poles, and Turks.

The same authorities considered it necessary that the French (and Jewish) wives and children of targeted foreign Israelites should also be arrested, and that the fate of the head of the family should decide that of the other members of the family.

These roundups, which took place during the night of 21–22 January 1944, resulted in the arrest of 643 persons, including 135 who had been hospitalized at the Rothschild, out of a total of 1,679 wanted Israelites.[5]

DOC. 323

On 23 February 1944 the Security Police complains that premature inspections of apartments by the Rosenberg Task Force confiscation squad have prompted Jews to go into hiding[1]

Report by Section IV B, Office of the Senior Commander of the Security Police in France, signed SS-Sturmscharführer (initials illegible), Paris, dated 23 February 1944 (excerpt)[2]

d. Jews

In collaboration with the relevant departments within the French police during the reporting period, 220 cases were processed. In total, 129 Jews were arrested and interned. These arrests were made mainly for the usual violations of the regulations pertaining to Jews. As a result of a meeting with the French police, arrests have increased slightly.

1 AN, F7, vol. 14 887. This document has been translated from French.
2 Amédée Bussière (1886–1943), civil servant; sub-prefect in 1918; prefect in 1929; police prefect in Paris from 1942; suspended from duty in August 1944; dismissed in 1945; sentenced to lifelong hard labour as well as loss of civil rights and confiscation of assets; released on probation in 1951.
3 Presumably Jean-Pierre Ingrand.
4 This is not in the file.
5 During a further roundup conducted by the Paris municipal police on 4 Feb. 1944, which primarily targeted Polish Jews, 485 people were arrested. In the first three months of 1944, in the Paris metropolitan area alone, approximately 2,000 Jews were arrested in this way and taken to Drancy.

1 AN, F7, vol. 14887. This document has been translated from French.
2 Extract from the general situation report by the Security Police and the SD. The file does not contain the whole report.

It must be pointed out that the Western Office[3] began locating Jews' residences, and their personnel turning up caused the Jews to become suspicious, prompting them to leave their residences. These Jews then procure false documents, and can be found again only with great difficulty. This complicates local work immensely. Furthermore, conspicuously large numbers of Jews have recently been picked up with forged or false documents on them.

No other exceptional incidents have come to our attention during the reporting period.

As always, we received a large number of tip-offs, which for the most part were made anonymously.

DOC. 324

In February 1944 Cécile Klein-Hechel gives an account of how she escaped from Alsace to Switzerland via Vichy and Grenoble[1]

Letter from Cécile Klein-Hechel,[2] temporarily residing in Baden, 51 Zürcherstrasse, to the Swiss Refugee Relief,[3] Pastor Paul Vogt,[4] dated February 1944

Application for subsistence aid for the undersigned and her four-year-old boy
My life in Switzerland, 1910–1927
My stay in Alsace, 1927–1939
My experiences during the war in France, 1939–1943.
Residing with my family in Switzerland since 9 September 1943 as an emigrant.

I, Cezile Klein, was born on 24 November 1905 in *Ustrzky*[5] (Poland), the daughter of Israel and Anna Hechel, née Warscher. In 1910 I came with my parents to Switzerland, where we settled in Baden, where my 80-year-old mother still lives today. My parents were Orthodox Jews and I was raised accordingly. We led a modest life and strove at all times to live in peace with everyone and not to be a burden on anyone, which we always succeeded in doing.

3 This is a reference to the Western Office (Dienststelle Westen) of the Rosenberg Task Force. On the confiscation of household goods, see also Doc. 325.

1 AfZ-ETH Zürich, IB VSJF-Archiv, K.457. Published in French translation in Claude Klein, 'Un témoignage des années d'Occupation: De Grenoble à la Suisse', *Esprit*, no. 349 (Nov. 2008), pp. 183–196. This document has been translated from German.

2 Sluwe Cescha (Cécile) Klein, née Hechel (1905–1988), seamstress; born in Galicia; lived in Baden (Switzerland), 1910–1927; married to Charles Klein (1899–1979), retailer; in Sélestat (Alsace) from 1927; mother of Berthe (b. 1928) and Claude (b. 1939); escaped to Vichy via Dijon in 1940; fled to Grenoble in 1941 and to Switzerland in Sept. 1943; privately interned in Baden, Dec. 1943–Dec. 1944; initially returned to Grenoble, then to Sélestat; emigrated to Israel in 1979.

3 The Swiss Refugee Relief was founded in 1936 as an umbrella association of 13 aid organizations under the official name of the Swiss Central Office for Refugee Relief.

4 Paul Vogt (1900–1984), pastor; headed the Swiss Protestant Relief Agency for the Confessing Church in Germany in 1936; co-founder of the Swiss Central Office for Refugee Relief; directed the Protestant refugee parish in Zurich, 1943–1947; during the war initiated the Protestant 'free places' campaign (*Freiplatzaktion*) that aimed to find private accommodation for refugees from the labour camps; founded the Working Group of Christians and Jews in 1945.

5 Probably Ustrzyki Dolne (Galicia).

In Baden I attended primary school, the commercial secondary school, and the technical school of the Aarau Trade Museum. After finishing school, I served an apprenticeship as a boy's tailor in the local workshop of Mrs H. Flury-Maag and completed my apprenticeship to her complete satisfaction. In the Aargau [canton] apprenticeship examination in Aarau I was placed fourth among seventy-two female apprentices in my trade and obtained the certificate of apprenticeship. I continued to work for some time for the woman who taught me my trade and also for myself until getting married.

In 1927 I married Charles Klein, born 20 April 1899 in *Brzsko*[6] (Poland). We are both naturalized French subjects. From 1927 to 1939 we lived in Sélestat in Alsace, where we were, through hard work and prudence, widely known for running a ready-made clothing store (Maison 'Jägert'), which we purchased after several years. We led a respectable middle-class life. I was active in various welfare organizations, regardless of their religious affiliation, and provided accommodation to many refugees from Germany and Vienna without suspecting that my family and I would later get a full taste of this horrible fate in turn.

When the war broke out in 1939, my husband enlisted in the military and I was left alone with my twelve-year-old daughter. In November 1939 I gave birth to my second child.

Alsace was occupied by German forces in June 1940. Taking a few belongings in a rucksack and two woollen blankets, I fled with my two children to Dijon, where we arrived in the night. But here I was overcome by a new fear. The city had been evacuated. The relatives whom I had planned to call on were no longer here. They had already fled on the night I arrived. For hours I stood, miserable and distraught, with my children in the streets of this city among thousands of refugees. Droves of refugees passed by us, like a mass migration. The whole thing reminded me of the exodus from Egypt. With my son in my arms and my daughter next to me, I looked into the terrified faces of these wailing, hounded, and hunted people. Countless aeroplanes flew above our heads in this turmoil and shots rang out, such that the ground, on which all kinds of vehicles loaded down with all manner of things were travelling, trembled as if the end of the world had begun. I trudged to the train station, which was packed with people and cars – people who appeared to have lost everything, including their minds. It seemed as if everyone had questions for everyone else, while at the same time everyone wanted to be the first to arrange departure. Without purchasing a ticket, people pushed their way onto the train that was ready to depart, and no one could say where it was heading. Only away from here, for the Germans are coming! We travelled for three days and three nights without knowing the destination. Our meagre provisions were soon exhausted. From the second day on, we had nothing left to eat or drink and no milk for my seven-month-old son. On the fourth morning the train stopped. We were in Vichy. I thought we must be close to starving to death, and we were parched with thirst. A young lady from the Red Cross tenderly took my son out of my arms and led us to the second-class waiting room. Here my little boy was given a bottle of milk, and my daughter and I each a bowl of soup. Once we had recovered a bit and decided to go into the city, we realized, to my

6 Probably Brzesko (Galicia). Charles Klein emigrated from there to France in 1922, settling in the town of Sélestat.

horror, that here, too, everything was caught up in a wild exodus. The same dismal and dramatic picture as in Dijon! I wanted to take my children back to the train station and flee further. But I was not allowed to go as far as the train station. I had to stay in Vichy. We were able to stay for a while in an apartment abandoned by refugees. The refugees returned, however, and I began to search for an apartment, which I furnished with only the bare essentials. After several days, the tremendous ebb and flow of refugees subsided. Great floods of people back and forth: from Vichy they fled to Bordeaux and from Bordeaux to Vichy. It was enough to make you lose your mind, this hapless frenzy of being pursued and hunted, and indeed it almost drove me to despair. After the dramatic days and nights on the train, I was happy to finally be able to lie in bed with my children, for we were unspeakably exhausted.

The Germans then occupied Vichy. This brought quiet to the city. Then came the ceasefire, and the Germans withdrew again.[7] I still knew nothing of the whereabouts of my husband. I set off to the Red Cross office to enquire about this. To my surprise they were able to locate him. After France had collapsed, he had fled just like everyone else and made his way to Vichy. We were reunited in our hopeless situation and we could see clearly: we were ruined! We had lost all of our worldly possessions overnight. Being religious by upbringing, I had always tried not to succumb to Mammon.[8] But all the same I felt more clearly than ever before that it was impossible to get by without money. We were able to stay in our primitively furnished two-room apartment for about eight months. Then came the order to evacuate Vichy within a few days. This order was issued to all Jews! All the streets were filled again with a frantic rush.[9] After a lengthy back and forth and various setbacks, we were able to find out that Mont-Fleury near Grenoble was open to Jewish refugees. We set off with new hope in our hearts and we fled with our children to our new place of sojourn. New concerns and problems weighed down on us. The apartment had no gas supply, and everything else was hard to come by, not to even mention food. All sorts of vexations were the order of the day when it came to taking care of legal formalities.[10] Each day brought new refugees, and each day it was necessary to get our documents stamped, etc.

The 26 August 1942 will remain a horrifying memory for everyone affected! Over the course of three days the French gendarmerie, on order from the highest German authority, had to round up all Jews still present in France.[11] This veritable manhunt got under way at 5 o'clock in the morning. These unfortunates were picked up from their apartments, loaded on to open trucks and taken to the assembly points in the barrack square, etc. Here they stood all day long, gathered together as they were, mostly women and children, but

7 The ceasefire was signed on 22 Jun. 1940. After the Wehrmacht withdrew, the French government established itself a few days later in the spa town of Vichy.

8 'Mammon' is an Aramaic word that refers to avarice and the idol of money.

9 A decree of 3 June 1941 mandated the expulsion of Jews from the département of Allier. This was followed by a police operation in the early morning of 12 June, during which the police searched hotels, guesthouses, and furnished rented apartments for Jewish refugees, who were ordered to leave the département within four days.

10 Through its second Statute on Jews, enacted in early June 1941, the Vichy government required Jews in the southern zone to also register with the authorities: see PMJ 5/271. The law also stipulated that food ration cards had to be renewed every month – a rule that applied to the entire population.

11 See Introduction, p. 70, and Doc. 262.

also elderly people. None of them had fled into the forests, nor did they go into hiding at acquaintances, for they did not believe the pursuers to be so terrible, reckoning that they would take pity on them, of all people, and not deport them. No weeping and lamenting was heard. The sun beat down relentlessly the entire day on these masses of rounded-up people, who, forsaken by God, awaited their fate with petrified faces. According to accounts, the unfortunates were taken at night in trucks to Lyons and then from here to Drancy. There were fresh victims every day. Many had actually gone into hiding at the homes of Christian acquaintances; many others, however, hid in the forests in order to elude the pursuers. The latter were, of course, soon driven back to civilization by hunger, and then fell into the hands of the gendarmerie. We experienced at first hand this frightening and terrifying hunt for human prey on several occasions in other cities. One glance out of the window was enough to send a terrible shiver of fright through your entire body. We, as French Jews,[12] were not supposed to be in danger of deportation here in Mont-Fleury/Grenoble. Out on the streets you were bawled at by Gestapo officials, and time and time again we had to have our rationing documents and all other necessary documents stamped with the large Jewish stamp 'Juif'.[13] We were exposed to the contempt and ridicule of the entire world. We had to 'declare' ourselves over and over again and were questioned about the most outrageous things and sent away, only shortly thereafter to be called back and dismissed again, as if they wanted you to get tired of the process and give up. This combination of horror and insanity that was unleashed back then on the many oppressed and hounded unfortunates had tormented me so much that my entire inner self threatened to dissolve into madness. Soon I no longer knew who I really was and whether I was awake or dreaming. A bundle of uncontrollable, agitated nerves raged inside me and threatened to engulf my consciousness! 'What do these people want from us?' we asked ourselves a hundred times over. It wasn't long before I could no longer speak at all. Then I saw things which baffled me, and I feared I was going blind. In my shattered state I heard things which made me think I was losing both my hearing and my sanity. I didn't know what would become of me, for existence seemed to have become unbearable to me.

All these horrible things, and certainly my own condition as well, had a detrimental impact on my 16-year-old daughter, who also had to endure a considerable share of the general indignities. I tried to devise a way for her to escape. Finally, a liberating thought came to me through the Christian Scouts organization. I heard accounts of how children had illegally fled to Switzerland this way.[14] Amidst all sorts of hardships and difficulties, my daughter finally made it – albeit illegally – across the Swiss border with such a Scout group led by a knowledgeable Christian Scout. Today she is in a Zionist camp, where she is being trained in agricultural and practical work to prepare her for emigrating to Palestine as a working Zionist after the war.[15] And that makes her happy, and it makes me content.

12 Meaning Jews of French nationality.

13 The law of 11 Dec. 1942 mandated the use of a special stamp to identify Jews' documents and food ration cards; *Journal officiel*, 12 Dec. 1942, p. 4058.

14 From autumn 1942 onwards, members of the French Protestant Scout movement (Éclaireurs unionistes) worked in cooperation with the refugee aid organization Cimade to accompany Jewish refugees to the Swiss border.

15 In early Dec. 1942 Berthe (Bracha) Klein reached Switzerland, where she lived at the children's home in Versoix on Lake Geneva that was run by the Zionist organization Hehalutz. She emigrated to Palestine in Feb. 1945.

The day came when Grenoble was occupied by the Italians.[16] This improved the lot of the Israelites. We were no longer hounded, and even as strangers without a home, we did again feel like we were human beings among other human beings. Co-religionists now poured in here from all parts of the German-occupied territories and sought protection and safety here from their pursuers. You understood these poor people only too well! Hounded and fearful, the unfortunates asked again and again if it were really true that you would be left alone here and that you would actually receive a 'permi sejour'.[17] It must indeed be acknowledged that the Italians were very good to us hunted Jews. Despite all our hardship and deprivation, we enjoyed a respite that allowed us to recover from the strain inflicted on our nerves in the preceding period. But it wasn't to last long.

Italy soon collapsed. Grenoble was reoccupied by the Germans. The streets were simply teeming with Germans and again you saw the notorious Gestapo officials, the sight of whom was enough to send a jolt of pain through your body.[18] The looting of apartments was a daily occurrence. It was said that some of the looting was being carried out by people posing as Gestapo officials, but apartments were being looted nonetheless and you stood there powerless against everything. It no longer felt safe to go on the streets, for it meant taking the risk of never coming home again, and it was likely that your apartment would be ransacked while you were away. The situation became untenable and we decided to leave everything and try to cross the Swiss border illegally. My husband and I and our child (our three-year-old son) got ready to flee. We took our bags, we locked up our apartment and gave the key to a neighbour, who promised to send essential items of clothing to Switzerland if we lived to see that day. And we actually did see that day on account of this generous Catholic family. We had to leave for Evian at 6 o'clock in the morning. We had torn up all of our Jewish documents, because the Germans were aggressively hunting for Jews in the trains. Anyone suspicious-looking was mercilessly pulled off the train! These persons were then deported to Drancy. Unfortunately, the furthest our train was able to go was Aix-les-Bains, because the line was blown up the night before in an act of sabotage. Everyone had to get off in Aix-les-Bains. It was 9 o'clock in the morning, which was a dangerous time for us. We hastily made off in search of a secluded park, where we were beset by a thousand fears that we would eventually be taken away after all. For the Gestapo was zealously carrying out its inglorious activities everywhere. When nightfall came, we risked returning to the train station in order to scout out the situation. We bought tickets to Evian, but we got off a station earlier to reduce the chance of being snared in the Gestapo's nets. It was midnight when we set out along the railway tracks, with me carrying the child in my arms. To our surprise, more and more refugees gathered on what we thought would be a deserted path. There were around 70 people, including many orphaned children whose parents had been deported. Each of these refugees was wearing Catholic emblems, crucifixes, etc. or the popular Catholic Scout insignia. Most were German Jews, including some from Vienna, who had torn up their documents in the forests. Groups then hired trucks for transportation to our common destination. And off we drove towards our unknown fate. The journey was made almost in silence with its quiet cargo,

16 After the landing of the Allies in North Africa, German and Italian troops occupied the previously unoccupied southern zone on 11 Nov.; the Italian zone now stretched all the way to the Rhône.

17 Correctly: *permis de séjour*, French for 'residence permit'.

18 See Doc. 310.

each and every one looking petrified. These were people who were held to be fair game and were trying to save their bare lives. The journey proceeded further and further into the unknown, for no one knew where we were going. But what was that? Suddenly a searchlight illuminated our truck, which got waved down. It seemed to us all that something terrible was in the offing; we awaited what was to come. The drivers took off at once! We had fallen into the gendarmerie's hands. '*Papiers!*'[19] they yelled! Everyone in the lorry was speechless with fright. The gendarmes wasted no time in pulling the people out of the truck, brusquely shouting questions at them. The orphaned children desperately called out for their parents and frail women experienced a nervous shock. Everyone who could do so fled into the forest that stretched out on both sides of the road. As the officers ran after them, the refugees who had already been apprehended took flight, and so that's how it happened that they couldn't arrest everyone. I was captured while fleeing. I was reunited with my husband, who was carrying our son, at the nearby police station, but my handbag, which contained just my most essential things, had been lost. The officers had to leave us alone to chase after the others. We took the opportunity to escape again, but soon they were pursuing us once more. A woman fleeing with a swaddled baby in her arms fell to the ground and the gendarme had to deal with her, which kept our pursuer at bay, allowing us to flee into the forest as he lost sight of us. We found a place to hide in an old wooden cabin, where we concealed ourselves as best we could, for outside we could hear the screams of those being hunted and the groans of the unfortunate ones who were being taken away. The gendarmes used flashlights to search for the refugees, and even passed by our hiding place. We crouched together and it slowly became quiet outside, for those who could be caught had been taken away. We took turns standing and crouching to better withstand the cold until dawn arrived, which we experienced while freezing and shivering. What were we to do? If we were to venture out, we would be doomed. That's what we said to ourselves. Every so often we glanced out into the dawn and around the unfamiliar area. I sighted a church spire some distance away, close to a village. An old farmer was walking past our hiding place with a milk churn on his back. With tears in my eyes, I spoke to the old man, confiding in him our predicament. 'Come with me, I'll take you to the pastor in the village,' he replied. 'Don't be afraid; the gendarmes aren't in our village.' We entrusted ourselves to the old man, put on our rucksacks and followed him, with the child in my arms who had long gone without the bare necessities. We were warmly received by the old pastor and were able to tell him of our sad experience. The 80-year-old village pastor seemed to have already heard about the night-time incident and the manhunt, for people had already brought him rucksacks and suitcases which those fleeing had abandoned to avoid capture. The pastor had apparently already experienced such drama several times before, and this wasn't the first time that refugees had found the shelter they had been seeking through him. He discussed the matter of our accommodation with friends of his in the village. We were by no means to return to Grenoble, for street fighting was already occurring there between the Germans and the Italians – this was something we had already experienced first-hand.[20] A very kind farmer's family warmly granted us a place to stay during the day, and were happy to be able to feel human again among other humans

19 French in the original: 'identity documents'.

20 On 8 Sept. 1943, while taking over the Italian-occupied zone, the Wehrmacht disarmed the Italian soldiers and took them prisoner.

after the ordeals we had been through; yes, we regarded these kind-hearted people as our merciful Samaritans, to whom we will be eternally grateful. They not only gave us good food and drink, but they also consoled us. Yes, the kind family even organized a smuggler for us; his fields run along the Swiss border and he promised to take us there. – After we bid farewell to our dear hosts, we set out for the second time towards the Swiss border. –

We marched 25 kilometres that night to the barbed wire along the actual Swiss border. We gave our all because we had to escape our tormentors. We were so physically exhausted and distressed that our legs barely held us up. Our thoughts were out of control, everything was running wildly through our heads, everything was a muddle. We reached the barbed wire barrier, but now we had to somehow break through it! We were still accompanied by our smuggler. My husband, who was carrying our son, had already managed to break through. I was having a harder time of it, as I wasn't able to press my body close enough to the ground since I constantly kept getting stuck. Yet it was imperative to take advantage of every minute, because everything could depend on it. A cold sweat came over me; my husband looked on petrified and stricken from the other side of the barbed wire, watching my futile efforts to do the impossible by pulling this way and that. I realized that my clothes were what made it impossible and without further ado decided to strip down to my underwear. I finally managed it, and, dazed by my successful breakthrough, I continued running forward, for we had not yet crossed the actual border, which we were told was still about another 40 metres further. Our escort called me back to tell me to get dressed and this I did in great haste. Reunited on the other side of the barbed wire, we continued ahead towards the longed-for Swiss border. Rough scree-strewn slopes and ravines that were exhausting to scramble up and down made our night-time hike more difficult as we fled through enemy territory. Horrifying precipices appeared to open up in front of us, and the woods even seemed to be an impenetrable primeval forest, for we were wearied and fatigued beyond endurance, nearing the point of utter exhaustion. We then reached an open field. Lights appeared, and strengthened by new hope, we forged ahead towards the lights. To our dismay, we realized that during the night we had wandered around in a circle, for we once again stood in front of the barbed wire barrier. Then, if that wasn't enough, shots suddenly rang out! As if pursued by the Furies, we fled at once back into the forest, where, on the verge of passing out, we sat down on the damp scree and rested. We were intent on remaining here until the morning. My brain was working feverishly, exhausted by what we had just experienced and muddled by all the horrors that the recent past had caused us to endure. We heard shots ring out every so often, and we spent the night, until the dawn of a new day, in this agitated state of mind, our thoughts obsessively churning, while alternately pacing back and forth with my child in my arms, and then crouched down until my shaking made it impossible. In the distance we could hear Swiss drum beats and every so often bugle calls as well. After we had trekked about a quarter of an hour, we had an encounter with a Swiss soldier. He greeted us in a friendly manner as he approached and guided us to the next sentry.[21] After providing all necessary information, we were given something to eat. A group of soldiers led us gently down to the first reception camp in Charmille,[22] near

21 After crossing the border on 9 Sept. 1943, the family was taken to the Swiss customs frontier office in Hermance, and from there handed over to the Swiss gendarmerie.

22 Correctly: Les Charmilles. It served as a reception camp for refugees from Sept. 1942.

Geneva, where we joined around 400 other fellow sufferers. Everyone here told each other the terrible things they had experienced. I realized that I was far from the only one with a tale of woe. We stayed in Charmille for 14 days, before being taken to Champel[23] refugee camp and then to Belmont.[24] From here, my husband was taken to Sierre labour camp and later to Birmensdorf/Zurich.[25] My son was sent to Carleton children's camp near Geneva. I remained alone in Belmont camp.

All the terrible experiences weighed heavily on me, and because of the entire dismal situation of camp life and my broken self, I nearly lost my grip on who I actually was and thought I would never be able to calm my nerves and recuperate. I was a broken person, a reject from human society, a destroyed being. I felt that I was nothing. But yet there I was. –

There awoke in me, with elementary force, a longing for my beloved mother[26] in Baden, who is getting on in years. And a homesickness for Baden itself, where I spent my early years. Old dear memories from my youth in Baden came back to me. I yearned to see my former employer in Baden, Mrs Flury, under whose care and kind influence I had spent one of the most pleasant times of my life. And it's been four and a half years already since I last saw my 80-year-old mother. I knew only too well that my dear mother was without means and unable to support a refugee like me. The situation in the camp at the time was almost too much to bear, knowing that here I was so close to my beloved Baden, my actual home. In my distress I wrote to Mrs Flury, and asked her to seek ways and means for my release so that I could return home to Baden.

Mrs Flury wrote back right away and began by consoling me in motherly fashion. She also promised that she would furnish me and my son with meals for a temporary period of three months. This met the conditions for my provisional release from the camp. A formal request was written and approved shortly thereafter. And so I have been back in old Baden since 3 December 1943. My son was subsequently released from the children's camp near Geneva and returned to me. The Flury family always lovingly comfort me in my predicament when I visit them each day. I am living with my mother, whose carer I became after a short while, for she suffered a broken arm shortly after I came to Baden and could now not do without me. Today I feel like a human being again, even if, depending on my state of mind, the horror I experienced takes hold of me like an inescapable nightmare. Again and again my thoughts also return to the home we left behind in Alsace, the birthplace of our two children. And here comfort and consolation are vitally important given the insanity of our times. –

On 1 March it will be three months since my benefactor took me on. The provisioning I have been granted will therefore soon end. That is why, with this letter to the esteemed Refugee Relief, I kindly ask to be granted subsistence aid from this date on. In early

23 Champel camp was located in the metropolitan area of Geneva, as was Charmilles camp.

24 This is a reference to the Belmont refugee shelter in Montreux, a town in the canton of Vaud.

25 Both camps – Siders (French: Sierre) in the canton of Valais and Birmensdorf in the canton of Zurich – were set up in 1940 as internment camps for members of the Polish army who had fled from France to Switzerland, before being converted into labour and training camps for refugees in 1943. The couple were interned from Oct. 1943 by a police order; Charles Klein remained in Birmensdorf until Nov. 1944.

26 Anna Hechel, née Varcher (1863?–1952); Polish national; emigrated from Galicia to Switzerland; moved to Sélestat after 1945.

February I received, for the first time, support of 30 francs from the Children's Aid Organization. My husband, who, as I mentioned, is in the Birmensdorf/Zurich camp, comes to Baden on weekly leave every Saturday around noon and stays to Sunday evening.

In welcome anticipation that you will approve my application to the best of your ability, I would like to heartily thank you for your kind efforts in advance and am pleased to look forward to your gracious kindness.

Most respectfully,[27]

DOC. 325

On 21 March 1944 the Commissioner General for Jewish Affairs speaks out against French participation in the theft of household effects in the South of France[1]

Note from the French Commissioner General for Jewish Affairs, signed Paty de Clam,[2] Paris, dated 21 March 1944

Note

on the subject of the seizure of Jewish furniture and household effects in the southern zone.

- On Tuesday, 21 March, at 3.15 p.m., I had a meeting with Mr von Behr.[3] Also present were Mr Roethke of the SS, Mr Klingenfuss,[4] and Mr Classen[5] from the German embassy.
- Mr von Behr informed me that the German authorities want to seize all Jewish household belongings and furniture in the southern zone.
- This applies to all movable property belonging to Jews in houses and apartments which are *unoccupied*, either because the Jews have been deported to Germany or because they have fled.
- The German authorities will arrange for the confiscated property to be taken to Paris and redistributed among people, both German and French, who have suffered war-related losses. Mr von Behr did not give me any details about what percentage would be allocated to French recipients; according to Mr von Behr, the allocation and distribution of the portion intended for French victims of war damage would be carried out *by the Milice*.

27 Her request was granted; Cécile Klein-Hechel, who had also sought aid from other relief organizations, received monthly support from the Protestant 'free places' campaign.

1 AN, F7, vol. 14 887. This document has been translated from French.

2 Charles du Paty de Clam (1895–1948), lawyer; worked for the French high commissioner of the Levant (Aleppo, Damascus, Beirut), 1920–1940; head of the Vichy government's Office for the Levant from 1941; Commissioner General for Jewish Affairs from Feb. 1944; resigned in late May 1944.

3 Kurt von Behr (1890–1945), retailer; joined the NSDAP in 1933; worked for the Rosenberg Task Force in France; head of the Western Office (Dienststelle Westen) of the Task Force in 1944.

4 Karl Otto Klingenfuss, also Klingenfuß.

5 Correctly: Peter Klassen (1903–1989), diplomat; in charge of antisemitic propaganda in the information service department at the German embassy in Paris, 1941–1944.

- The German authorities demand that the French police cooperate in the confiscations, at the very least by maintaining order during the operation.
- Mr von Behr declared himself to be in complete agreement with Mr Darnand,[6] who was to speak about this planned measure to the head of government.
- It seems obvious that this operation is only the first stage, and the second stage will consist in confiscating the furniture and other moveable property in apartments inhabited by Jews.
- It remains to be seen whether it is appropriate for the police or the *Milice* to participate in the operation.[7]

1) The seizure of household effects by the Germans will be exploited by Gaullist radio, which will allege that we are stealing the furniture of French people; they will make very sure not to mention that this concerns Jews.
2) In addition, it is certain that the Germans will reserve most of the seized furniture for themselves. The operation will therefore appear to be confiscation carried out by the police or the *Milice* on behalf of the Germans and exclusively for their benefit.
3) Finally, this operation will result in the removal of goods of considerable value from France.[8]

DOC. 326

On 28 March 1944 the board of the General Union of French Jews discusses the repatriation of Romanian and Turkish Jews and the organization's financial situation[1]

Minutes of the plenary meeting of the UGIF's administrative board in Paris on 28 March 1944, undated[2]

Present: Messrs *Carcassonne*, *Gamzon*, *Geissmann*, *Hemardinquer*, and *Katz*, for the southern zone;
Mr *Edinger*, Dr *Morali* and Dr *Weill-Hallé*, Mrs *Scheid-Hass* and Mrs *Stern*, Mr Albert *Weil*, Dr Didier *Hesse*, Mr Marcel *Lévy*, and Mr Robert *Lévy*.
Absent: Mr *Rudnansky* and Mr *Schah*, excused.
Reading and approval of the minutes of the previous plenary meeting of the administrative board on 26 January 1944.
Opening the meeting, Mr *Edinger* expressed his satisfaction at seeing both sections of the UGIF's administrative board assembled once again in Paris. The meeting was in

6 Joseph Darnand (1897–1945), politician; founder and member of radical right-wing organizations; appointed secretary general for public order in Dec. 1943; escaped to Germany in August 1944; arrested in Italy, 1945; condemned to death in Paris in Oct. 1945 and executed.
7 From May 1942, the French government repeatedly but unsuccessfully protested against the activities of the Western Office of the Rosenberg Task Force.
8 In view of Paty's hostile stance, the German authorities subsequently approached Laval directly. The head of government did indeed agree to French participation in the theft of furniture, but the preparations dragged on and a joint operation never took place.

1 Archives du Consistoire central de Paris, CC-24. This document has been translated from French.
2 Parts of the document have been underlined by hand.

keeping with the decisions taken during the plenary meeting, which set out the terms and conditions of the reorganization and stipulated that the board should meet in Paris at least once every two months.

The president reminded everyone that he had attended the meeting of the board of the southern zone in Lyons and that he had, on that occasion, met the regional directors of the southern zone. He told Director General Mr *Geissmann*[3] that he was extremely satisfied with the way he had implemented the reorganization and the centralization of services in the southern zone. In the not too distant future, in spite of the difficulties created by the evacuation of the coastal regions, we will be able to consider the reorganization complete.

Northern zone report

Mr *Edinger* informed the meeting of the events which had taken place in the northern zone since the last meeting, following numerous arrests that had occurred in the various départements in our zone. We had to dissolve all of our provincial delegations, except the one in Seine-et-Oise.

A new Dienststelle[4] has been created in rue de Bassano, of which the UGIF will take charge in the same manner as it did with Lévitan and Austerlitz[5] – in addition to the supplementary needs in Drancy camp, which will make up a large part of our activities.

There have been a number of releases from Drancy camp of inmates of Romanian, Turkish, Spanish, and Swiss nationalities, who are to be handed over to the UGIF for repatriation. In accordance with the most recent decisions taken, the costs of repatriation for the Turks and Romanians would be covered by the budget for the southern zone.[6]

The president indicated that as of today:

172 people have been repatriated to Turkey, at a cost of 868,500 francs;

15 people have been repatriated to Romania, at a cost of 45,000 francs.

The costs of their stay were covered by the northern zone.

We have, moreover, also taken on the costs of the repatriations to Switzerland and Spain.

The different services in the UGIF's northern zone (children's homes, boarding schools, homes for the elderly, cafeterias, social centres) have been operating normally.

Mr *Edinger* invited his colleagues to take advantage of their stay to visit some of these centres, particularly the Guy-Patin Centre, which is currently supplying more than 1,500 meals per day to the various Dienststellen.

3 Raymond Geissmann, lawyer; regional representative of the General Union of French Jews (UGIF) in Lyons in 1942; simultaneously deputy secretary general of the Israelite Consistory and the Jewish Scouts of France (EIF); director general of the UGIF South from Dec. 1943; testified at Klaus Barbie's trial in 1978.

4 Here and below, German in the original: 'office(s)'.

5 This refers to three Drancy subcamps located in Paris where hundreds of Jews were held between July 1943 and August 1944. These Jews, who were deemed 'not deportable' – because they were married to non-Jews, for example – had to undertake forced labour related to the theft of furniture from Jews' homes. The UGIF was responsible for providing meals to the internees.

6 In autumn 1942 foreign governments that had protested against the arrest of their Jewish citizens in France were urged to repatriate these individuals. Most of the countries did not take this opportunity and ceased their protests. In some countries, particularly Turkey, the process was protracted. The travel costs associated with repatriation were primarily covered by the UGIF.

Mr *Geissmann* and Mr *Katz* will hold a special meeting with the directorate of the Social Welfare Service to examine practices in the northern and southern zones with a view to harmonizing them.

Southern zone report

Mr *Geissmann* informed the meeting of the situation in the southern zone. He described the UGIF's social activities in the southern zone, where the financial difficulties are great: only the sale of Alliance stocks fills the coffers.[7] Other difficulties arise from the dispersal of the Israelites in this zone.

Mr *Geissmann* detailed the situation in Lyons, Grenoble, and Chambéry, as well as his contacts with the occupying authorities.

He reminded everyone that the UGIF in the southern zone currently comprises a directorate general and a social welfare central office, with 20 welfare offices run by regional directors, headed by Mr *Katz*.

Following the evacuation of the Montpellier region, the regional directorate had to be recalled.[8]

Staff salaries

Mr *Edinger* remarked that, in contrast to the southern zone, the UGIF in the northern zone had not obtained authorization to raise its staff salaries, in spite of the numerous steps that it had taken since November.

Mr *Edinger* indicated that he had sent another report to the Commissariat General for Jewish Affairs.

Stock sales

In accordance with the decision taken at the meeting of the board of the southern zone, the following resolutions were made:

Considering:

1) that the law of 29 November 1941,[9] Article 3, stipulates that the UGIF's resources will be drawn particularly from the assets of dissolved Jewish associations,
2) that the successive orders from the Commissariat General for Jewish Affairs have allocated the assets of several different dissolved associations to the Union,[10]
3) that some resources are indispensable to the Union in order for it to accomplish its mission,

it has been decided:

to sell the transferable securities that belonged to the Alliance israélite universelle and to the École normale israélite orientale[11] for around 10,000,000 (ten million) francs as registered securities, including the following: […][12]

7 This refers to the Alliance israélite universelle (AIU). Founded in France in 1860 as a Jewish charitable society, it established a network of schools in Central Europe and the Mediterranean at the end of the nineteenth century, with the support of the French authorities. It became part of the UGIF in 1942. Its offices and archives in the northern zone had already been confiscated in 1940.

8 The French Mediterranean coastal region had been evacuated in early 1944 in anticipation of an imminent Allied landing.

9 See PMJ 5/295.

10 This could not be found.

11 A school founded in Paris by the AIU in 1868 to train select graduates of AIU schools as teachers.

12 A detailed list of securities follows.

It was specified that these items are not earmarked for any special purpose. The administrative board fully consents that in order to bring about the sales, transfers, and conversions, Mr *Couturier*, the accountant, will be responsible for all the necessary signatures, thereby giving him full powers to sell the above-mentioned securities, to receive the money, and to issue the relevant receipts.

A lengthy exchange of views then took place regarding the financial situation, particularly in the southern zone.[13]

At one of the next meetings of the administrative board of the southern zone, the conditions under which it would be possible to draw upon the solidarity fund will be examined.[14]

Administrative board

Mr *Edinger* updated the administrative board regarding a measure taken in the northern zone with a view to bringing the number of members in the section up to nine, through the nomination of deputy members.[15]

To this end, it nominated Mr Robert *Lévy*, secretary general of the presidency; Mr Marcel *Lévy*, head of group 7 (provisioning); and Mr Didier *Hesse*, assistant head of group 4 (youth and professional retraining).

The administrative board approved these nominations.

DOC. 327
On 6 April 1944 the French gendarmerie learns of the German roundup targeting the Izieu children's colony[1]

Report from the French gendarmerie (Légion du Lyonnais, Compagnie de l'Ain, Section de Belley, Brigade de Brégnier-Cordon, no. 61), signed Marcel Fontaine, dated 6 April 1944[2]

Today, 6 April 1944, at twelve o'clock,

I, the undersigned Marcel *Fontaine*, sergeant major of the gendarmerie at the Brégnier-Cordon post in the Ain département, was in the barracks in uniform, in accordance with the orders of my superiors, when a German officer appeared. After informing me that the director of the children's refugee colony in Izieu, Ain,[3] had been absent for several days, he asked us to arrest her as soon as she returned and then to detain her pending further orders. This officer also told us that he had given the order to the post-

13 From summer 1943 the UGIF was required to collect compulsory membership fees. In the southern zone, these dues were paid only in part; moreover, the number of exemptions was very high.

14 Under the law of 22 July 1941, the surplus of the proceeds from sales carried out in the course of the Aryanization proceedings went into a so-called solidarity fund for impoverished Jews: see PMJ 5/273, Article 22. Initially, this fund was used to pay for the administrative activities of the UGIF as well as most of the expenditures for those in need in the occupied zone. Due to the dwindling number of Aryanizations, the fund could only be used to a limited extent in 1944.

15 The purpose of this step was to replace the three board members who were deported to Auschwitz in Dec. 1943: see Doc. 314.

1 AD de l'Ain, AD38 3U6. This document has been translated from French.

2 The original contains handwritten administrative notes.

master to hold all post addressed to the camp and to deliver it to the brigade office, so that the brigade office can inform the Belley barracks immediately by telephone.

In possession of these initial pieces of information, I went to the village of Izieu, where we learned from the neighbours that the Germans had already arrested everybody from the colony, which is to say four staff members and 32 children,[4] who were taken away in two lorries to an unknown destination, probably Lyons.[5]

Since no resident of the colony remained behind, it was very difficult to obtain any precise information about the identities of those arrested, since there is considerable fluctuation among the resident staff and children. After examining the list of food ration cards issued for the village, we were able to establish that there were:

1) the finance officer. – 2) the female physician. – 3) two maids who had recently arrived and whose identities are unknown, and 32 children, namely:

17 French from North Africa,	including	5 Jews
6 Polish	–	1 –
2 Slovaks	–	2 –
2 Germans	–	2 –
1 Spanish	–	1 –
1 Siamese	–	1 –
1 Palestinian		
1 Belgian		
1 Austrian		

The record forms attached have been filled in with what little information could be obtained.

We know of no reason for the arrests, but they are likely due to the Jewish religion of the majority of those arrested.[6]

In witness whereof, we have made three copies of this document, the first to be sent to the prefect of the Ain département in *Bourg*, the second to the public prosecutor in *Belley*, and the third to the archives.

Signed and concluded in Brégnier-Cordon, on the day, month, and year as above.

3 The Maison d'Izieu children's home was established in the Italian occupation zone by Sabina and Miron Zlatin in May 1943, with the support of the OSE children's welfare organization; until Jan. 1944, a total of 105 Jewish children were housed there, usually temporarily. Sabina Zlatin, née Chwast (1907–1996), a welfare worker, managed to get many Jewish children out of the French internment camps in the unoccupied zone and place them in families or children's colonies. In early April 1944 she was in Montpellier looking for a new and safer place for the children to stay.

4 Seven adults and 45 children were arrested.

5 The arrests took place under the direction of Klaus Barbie, head of Section IV B, Office of the Commander of the Security Police in Lyons. Barbie himself was present on this occasion.

6 Contrary to the impression given by the numbers presented in the document, all but one of these children were Jewish; the non-Jewish child was released in Brégnier-Cordon. The other 51 prisoners were interned and interrogated at Fort Montluc in Lyons; the next day, they were taken to Drancy. Of the 44 children, 34 were deported on 13 April 1944 to Auschwitz and murdered there upon arrival. None of the other prisoners survived.

DOC. 328
On 10 April 1944 the Swiss police record the Dreyfus family's illegal border crossing[1]

Completed record form issued by the police division of the federal Swiss Justice and Police Department, signed G. A. Hermann, Geneva, dated 10 April 1944

1. Surname: Dreyfuss[2]
2. First name: Gaston
3. Nationality: French
4. Former nationality (in case of statelessness): –
5. Father's first name: Joseph
6. Mother's first and maiden name: Reine Bloch
7. Date of birth: 24 May 1897
8. Place of birth: Marmoutier
9. Former address: Naves near Annecy[3]
10. Profession: industrialist
11. Marital status: married
12. Religion: Israelite
13. Accompanying family members: *his wife:* Jeanne, née Kahn, b. 7 December 1909, French, Israelite. *His children: Gérard*, b. 16 October 1933, French, Israelite, single; *Huguette*, b. 30 November 1938, French, Israelite, single. *His father:* Joseph Dreyfuss, b. 30 August 1869, French, Israelite, married; *his mother:* Reine, née Bloch, b. 16 August 1872, French, Israelite.[4]
14. Identity documents: 1 French service record – 1 French passport – 4 French identity cards – 1 driving licence – 3 certificates of residence – numerous French papers.
15. Military service: 20th Nancy Corps, 2nd class soldier (regular discharge)
16. Motives for and circumstances of flight, route followed:

Born in 1897 in Marmoutier (Alsace), I lived there until 1912 and received primary and secondary education there. Between 1912 and 1916 I continued my studies in Strasbourg. From 1916 until 1918 I was a soldier in the German army. From 1918 until 1939 I again lived in Strasbourg. I got married in 1932. In Strasbourg, I owned a wholesale trading business and a tannery on the outskirts of the city. In 1939, I was subject to labour conscription and deployed in my own factory. From 1940, I was in Limoges until 1943, then in St Joriod,[5] and then in Naves, near Annecy. My parents, who were still living in Marmoutier in 1939, sought refuge in several different places and rejoined us in Limoges in 1941.

We have come to Switzerland to avoid the measures taken by the German authorities against the Israelites, in particular those of Alsatian origin.

1 Archives d'état de Genève, dossier Dreyfus. This document has been translated from French.
2 Correctly: Gaston Dreyfus (1897–1986), leather dealer; established a company in Strasbourg in 1919; fled to Limoges in 1940; moved to the Italian occupation zone in April 1943; fled to Switzerland in April 1944; returned to Strasbourg after the war.
3 Correctly: Nâves. Today the village is part of the municipality of La Léchère (Savoie).
4 Jeanne Dreyfus, née Kahn (1909–1983), housewife; Gérard Dreyfus (1933–2009), leather dealer; Huguette Dreyfus (b. 1938), teacher; Joseph Dreyfus (1869–1962), butcher; Reine Dreyfus, née Bloch (1872–1953), housewife.
5 Correctly: Saint-Jorioz (Haute-Savoie).

We found a smuggler who was introduced to us by someone named *Albert* in Annemasse. We do not know the name of the smuggler himself. I paid 75,000 French francs for all of the family.

17. Place and date of border crossing: Fossard, on 9 April 1944 at 10 p.m. We were stopped at a customs post and taken to the Cropettes holding centre.[6]
18. State of health: a medical examination will be carried out today.
19. Family and acquaintances in Switzerland: one sister: Mrs Ed. Picard, 86 rue d'Argovie. Good friends: Mr Jean Wild, 84 Pirsigstrasse, Basel; Mrs Gaby Weil, 12 rue Juste Olivier, Lausanne; Mr Paul Picard, 6 rue du Mt Blanc, Geneva.
20. Possible guarantors in Switzerland: the above
21. Detailed list of assets in Switzerland and abroad: we own buildings and factories in France.
22. Has the 'information for refugees' been communicated to the refugee? – It will be, during their transfer to Charmilles.[7]

Interrogated by:
Corporal G. A. Hermann
The refugee: [signed]

DOC. 329

On 14 April 1944 the Senior Commander of the Security Police and the SD in France issues detailed instructions for increasing the number of arrests of Jews[1]

Instructions (marked 'secret!') from the Senior Commander of the Security Police in France (IV B 4), signed SS-Standartenführer and Colonel of the Police Dr Knochen and (p.p.) SS-Hauptsturmführer Brunner (IV B 4), dated 14 April 1944 (copy)[2]

Instructions
about an increase in the number of arrests of Jews in the territory under the jurisdiction of the Senior Commander of the Security Police and the SD in France.

1. *The category of Jews to be arrested*

a) All persons considered to be Jews in accordance with the laws are to be arrested irrespective of their nationality or other circumstances.
b) When Jews are arrested, the whole family must be included. In the event that family members of the person arrested are located outside the jurisdiction of the SD commando, the relevant commando or field office responsible is to be notified immediately by telex – failing that, by phone – to arrange for the arrest to be carried out at that location.

6 A reception camp in Geneva.
7 Charmilles reception camp was in the metropolitan area of Geneva.

1 BArch, SS HO 1478. Published in French translation in Klarsfeld, *Calendrier*, pp. 1815–1819. This document has been translated from German.
2 The original contains handwritten underlining.

c) The entire network of relatives is to be considered part of the family: parents, children, married children, siblings, married siblings; young children accommodated in children's homes must also be included in the operation. In the case of a removal from a children's home, a Jewish parent, if available, should be taken there so as to be present when the removal takes place. Should members of the Jewish family not be found in residence at an apartment, it is recommended that the apartment be occupied until the return of the missing Jews.
d) When carrying out arrests in cities, particularly in buildings with multiple residential units, in each case the entire building must be searched for Jews. In order to save labour and fuel, the arrest operation is to be prepared such that officers not only arrest one Jew, but always cleanse a specific area (an entire village in rural areas, or a block of houses) in one go.

2. *Jews in French labour camps, penitentiaries, and prisons*

a) In addition to Jews living freely or in hiding, all Jews interned in labour camps for foreigners as well as in penitentiaries and prisons are to be removed from these facilities. The removal from penitentiaries and prisons is important because foreign Jews have a predilection to let themselves be convicted of smaller crimes in order to evade German measures until any invasion takes place.

However, removing Jews from camps, penitentiaries, and prisons should proceed such that the officials dealing with Jewish affairs appear at these facilities unannounced and ascertain the number of Jews present. In the case of the labour camps, it is best to do this at night.

The transfer of the Jews cannot be accomplished through a written order, because in this case the French will release the Jews beforehand or transfer them to another prison or work site.
b) All Jews are also to be removed from the OT labour camps.[3] In the event that the construction sites require replacements, Jews living in mixed marriages can be made available from Drancy camp. These Jews, however, may be deployed only in contained and guarded areas, and also only at construction sites where this can be justified on grounds of secrecy.
c) Jews residing in care homes or establishments disguised as sanatoriums are also to be removed from these facilities and transferred to Drancy, provided that they are not too old and they are fit for transport.

3. *Jews exempted from the measures:*

a) Jews living in genuine mixed marriages are for the time being exempted from the measures, provided that they are not engaged in activities which are prejudicial to the occupying force.
b) This will prevent an intervention by French people who have contact with the Jews through the mixed marriage. Moreover, the provisions laid down by the RSHA do not permit the evacuation of these Jews to the East.
c) Jewish mixed marriages which took place after July 1940 are to be regarded as nonexistent and the Jewish partner is to be arrested. Children from the marriage are to

3 These were labour camps run by Organization Todt in order to construct military facilities, primarily on the Atlantic coast.

remain with the non-Jewish parent. However, if this parent wants the Jewish parent to take custody of the children, they are to be taken to Drancy.

4. *Belongings and assets to be brought to Drancy camp – assets remaining behind*

a) The following are eligible for evacuation to the East:
Jews of French nationality
Jews with the nationality of the former Czechoslovakia (what is now Bohemia, Moravia, and Slovakia)
Poland
Norway
Holland
Belgium
Luxembourg
Yugoslavia (Serbia and Croatia)
Greece
Baltic States (Lithuania, Latvia, Estonia)
Albania
Italy
and all stateless Jews (including those who emigrated from the territory of the Reich).

At the time of arrest, these Jews are to be told to bring all of their cash, foreign exchange, gold coins, jewellery, securities, and deposit certificates with them. In addition, they are to bring all necessary items (clothes, underwear, bedlinen, shoes, etc.) with them.

b) Radio sets belonging to Jews are to be seized and handed over, against a receipt voucher, to the Wehrmacht command for use by the troops, unless the commander issues other instructions.

c) Apartment keys of subtenants are to be given to the apartment owner or the caretaker. If the furniture or the building belongs to the Jew and there is a branch of the Western Office of the Reich Ministry for the Occupied Eastern Territories in the city, the keys are to be given to this office. If there is no local branch of this office, the keys are to be given to the Commissariat General for Jewish Affairs and in villages to the mayors. The local Wehrmacht billeting office is to be left to decide about the furniture and apartments, insofar as they are needed for billets.

d) Jews of foreign nationality (but this only applies if they are in possession of a valid passport) are also to bring money and assets with monetary value as well as clothes with them. If the Jew is the owner of his own apartment, house, property, or shop, he must hand over the keys to a trustee of his choosing. Handling things this way will prevent the confiscation of any assets from Jews transferred from Drancy to an internment camp or from subjects of neutral states who are returning to their home country. This will eliminate from the outset unnecessary extra work as well as interventions by foreign diplomatic missions. Moreover, such an approach does not give the Jews and the foreign diplomatic missions occasion for atrocity propaganda.

e) When arresting Jewish partners in mixed marriages, assets are always to be handed over to the non-Jewish partner, unless there are special circumstances. The Jew must, however, take with him the items needed for his labour deployment.

5. *Transfer to Drancy camp for Jews*

a) The transfer of arrested Jews who are detained at the individual Security Police and SD offices must be completely escape-proof. In most transports, one to two Jews are missing upon arrival at Drancy camp. If there is no other way to secure them, they are to be bound together by the hands with a length of rope.

b) The Jew transports are to be reported by telex promptly to IV B 4 - BdS, for the attention of SS-Obersturmführer Röthke. The telex should include the number of Jews, the number of escorts, and the scheduled arrival time of the train insofar as this can be determined. If there is no telex connection, the departure of the transport is to be communicated by telephone at PAS[4] 0150, extension 236–238, or FAS 3894, and outside office hours to the duty officer, at PAS 0150, extension 154. In the event that the telex or telephone message fails to arrive on time, the transport leader is to be given a sheet of paper containing the telephone number PAS 0150, extension 236–238, or PAS 3894, in order to prevent the transports from waiting unnecessarily at the train station. The bus can be at the station within 20 minutes of the transport leader telephoning.

c) Based on this information, the transports will be collected on arrival from the train station by two buses intended specifically for this purpose. Moreover, each bus has four Jewish stewards who attend to the luggage at the train station so that the escorts need deal only with the Jews, thus eliminating any possibility for escape on arrival at the train station.

d) The transports are to be sent to Drancy with a list in duplicate (serial number, name, and date of birth). One list, with a brief note confirming the route and receipt of the transport, is to return with the escorts. The index cards as well as the Jews' other personal documents are to be sent along to Drancy in a sealed envelope or package with the transport list.

e) The correct personal documents are to be taken from the Jews and enclosed with the index cards, along with any forged identity cards, food ration cards, clothes ration cards and tobacco ration cards.

6. *Simplification of record-keeping – completion of an arrest index card*

a) The arresting official is to fill out an index card for each arrested Jewish family. This is necessary because it makes it possible to identify the entire group of relatives as well as assets and further details.

b) If the arrested Jew is known to have committed any offences, these are to be recorded on the index card under 'Reason'. In particular, in the case of mixed marriages or uncertain Jewish descent, the column 'related to an Aryan' is to be completed in detail.

c) Assets found on the Jews are to be recorded on the card. All assets (item 4a) are to be left with the Jews, that is, they are to be brought to Drancy. Cash, jewellery, foreign exchange, and other assets with monetary value are not to be taken from them.

d) The pre-printed index cards are to be collected as needed during the handover of the Jewish transports in Drancy and given to the transport escorts for delivery to the requisite office.

7. *Accommodation for arrested Jews until their transfer to Drancy*

[a)] After their arrest and until being transported to Drancy, Jews are as a rule to be taken to the prison customarily available to the office carrying out the arrest. In order not to put too much of a burden on prison operations, a wing should be set up specific-

4 The meaning of PAS here and FAS below could not be ascertained.

ally for Jews, because older Jews as well as Jewish women with young children must also be accommodated.

b) If, in the case of larger operations, the available facilities are insufficient for accommodation, other accommodation options, such as hotels, should be used as assembly camps. Obviously in such cases appropriate arrangements must be made for guarding the prisoners.

c) Detained Jews accommodated in hotels are responsible for the cost of their board (soup).

8. *Payment of a bounty for information regarding Jews in hiding and in disguise*

a) According to instructions issued by the RSHA, bounties may be paid for Jews in hiding and in disguise. Each case will be handled individually. The bounties should not be too high but, on the other hand, must offer sufficient incentive. The commander shall determine the amount of the bounty. The bounty cannot be the same amount in all areas. In most cases, it must be larger in urban areas than in rural areas.

b) The bounties may be paid out only after the Jews have been arrested. After the arrest, the amount of cash possessed by the Jew is determined during processing and recorded on the index card. Using this money, the bounty is to be taken from the Jew and paid to the confidential informant. The officials dealing with Jewish affairs and the local office head must sign off the payments. If a Jew arrested on the basis of information provided by a confidential informant has no money, the bounty shall be paid out from another Jew's money. A note must of course be appended to both index cards. The confidential informant's exact address or identification code is to be recorded on the index card, so that verification is always possible.

c) In the case of Jews who hold a valid foreign nationality, the bounty is to be paid out of intelligence service funds.

d) The payment of bounties eliminates extra administrative work. Confidential informants can be paid as soon as their information proves useful. This is necessary because as many private individuals as possible will have to be utilized if an area really is to be cleansed of Jews.

e) All asset-related matters and bounty payments are to be handled properly and correctly. Any failure in this respect will be punished.

DOC. 330
On 15 April 1944 Mrs Salm van Brussel asks the General Union of French Jews for help in looking for her husband[1]

Letter from Mrs J. F. Salm van Brussel, 19 rue de Cronstadt, Nice, to the president of the UGIF,[2] 120 boulevard de Belleville, Paris 20, dated 15 April 1944

Dear Mr President,

I am taking the liberty of asking for your association's kind help in the sad situation in which I find myself.

1 Mémorial de la Shoah, CDXXIII-9. This document has been translated from French.
2 Georges Edinger.

My husband, Alfred Salm,[3] a Dutch citizen born in Maastricht on 10 May 1875, was arrested by the German police in Nice on 3 February this year. His only crime was to be born an Israelite.

Since then, I have done my best to obtain news of him. I successively approached the German authorities, the local German police, the Ministry of Foreign Affairs in Vichy, the Dutch affairs office in Paris, and the International Red Cross in Geneva. Everywhere the answer has been the same: we cannot find anything out, and there is nothing we can do for the Jews.

What is important to me above all is to know whether or not my husband is still in Drancy camp, if he is in good health, and if I can be granted permission to receive news from him at least once and to send him a package of clothing or supplies.

Between 1905 and 1934, my husband was a wholesale grain merchant in Rotterdam, where he was known as a very honourable tradesman; he had the best reputation, always only did good and never harmed anybody.

We were married by a registrar in Rotterdam on 17 September 1908. Because I am a Catholic and an Aryan, my husband later arranged a religious marriage ceremony for us in the Catholic cathedral in The Hague, out of respect for my beliefs.

I always hoped that my Aryan descent and my Catholic beliefs would lead the German authorities to treat my husband more considerately. Unfortunately, I have not heard a word from him for the 72 days since his arrest, and I am beginning to wonder if he is still alive. My anxiety is even greater since he is of an advanced age and in delicate health, which was why we left the Netherlands in 1934 and settled in Nice. I am sure you will understand that I very much need to be reassured about his current fate.

I would also like to beg you to attempt to find information about where he can be found at the moment, about his health, and about the possibilities of communicating with him, even if it is only once.

All of my hope rests on you. I am only writing to your association so late because I was not aware of its existence. I found out about it from a good friend, also an Aryan, whose Israelite husband was also arrested. She confirmed to me that she was able to receive three postcards from her husband and she had twice been able to send him packages with supplies thanks to your dedicated assistance. I can add that this Russian-born Israelite has been a naturalized French citizen for 32 years.

I would like to express my eternal gratitude to you in advance for anything that you might be able to do to help my poor husband. And while I await your response with the greatest impatience, Mr President, I remain gratefully yours,

Signed

I would like to add that if you were to incur any expenses for your efforts, I would be very happy to reimburse you.[4]

3 Alfred Salm (1875–1944), interned in Drancy camp in early Feb. 1944 and deported to Auschwitz four days later.

4 In his reply, dated 21 April 1944, the secretary general of the UGIF informed Mrs Salm that written confirmation that she was not Jewish issued by the Commissariat General could have saved her husband from deportation. However, he added, it was not possible for the UGIF to establish contact with deported persons or to provide information on their whereabouts: Mémorial de la Shoah, CDXXIII-9.

DOC. 331

A French intelligence officer records acts of desperation among Jews before their deportation from Vittel on 18 April 1944[1]

Letter from the prefect of the Vosges département,[2] Epinal, to the state secretary of the interior,[3] Secretariat General for Public Order, Vichy, dated 26 April 1944[4]

I hereby send you the attached copy of a memorandum from the commissioner of the general intelligence service of the Vosges département about incidents which happened at Vittel internment camp,[5] where Jewish inmates have taken their own lives.

The Prefect

Memorandum

250 Jews who had been interned in the Beau-Site Hotel in Vittel[6] left the internment camp to be sent to the Paris area. The departure took place on 18 April at 7.59 p.m.[7] Five special carriages were added to the train for Langres. The windows of the carriages were barred with wooden rods to make sure they could not be opened.

During the train's departure and the inmates' arrival at the station, a German security detail checked papers and prevented people from entering the station.

Several incidents took place at the internment camp on the day before and the day of the departure. Several people tried to kill themselves; some women threw themselves out of windows along with their children, others slit their wrists. The number of attempted suicides was estimated at about a dozen. The wounded are being treated at the German hospital in Vittel.

Up to now three deaths have regrettably taken place:

1) Tamar Benjacob, 58 years old, Costa Rican national since 16 April 1941, formerly Polish;
2) Joel Bauminger, 38 years old, Paraguayan national since 17 April 1941, formerly Polish, physician;

1 AN, F7, vol. 14 887. This document has been translated from French.
2 Albert Daudonnet (1897–1962), administrative official; pursued an administrative career from 1914; became a prefect in 1922; prefect of the Vosges département from Sept. 1942; arrested by the German police in May 1944 and taken to the Tyrol region via Compiègne camp; returned to France in May 1945; pensioned off in 1946; his application for reinstatement in the civil service was turned down in 1951.
3 Antoine Lemoine.
4 The document was also sent to the prefect and delegate of the Ministry of the Interior in Paris and to the regional prefect in Nancy. Parts of the original have been underlined by hand.
5 This German internment camp for citizens of enemy nations located in the restricted zone consisted of several adjacent hotels surrounded by barbed wire. It was established in spring 1941. The camp inmates were held as hostages for a potential exchange for German citizens held by enemy states.
6 In fact, 166 persons, including 40 children, left Vittel. Most of them were Polish Jews who had been brought to France from the Warsaw ghetto in Jan. and May 1943 because they had either British or American passports or immigration papers. The negotiations for an exchange broke down in late 1943 because many countries did not accept the papers, many of which had been bought.
7 The train took the internees to Drancy; the group was deported to Auschwitz on 29 April 1944.

3) Bluma Cohen, wife of the above-named, 26 years old, Paraguayan by marriage since 21 June 1942, formerly Polish.

These three people died following an injection that was administered to them by Dr *Bauminger.*

On the morning of 18 April, several Germans who reportedly belong to the SD service requisitioned a number of bicycles in the street with nothing but the simple promise to their owners that the bicycles would be returned at 7 p.m. However, the owners retrieved their bicycles when they saw them parked in the street.

Five bicycles were 'requisitioned' in this manner.

The night before the Jews' departure, a certain Lucien *Mougin*, a self-employed plumber, was arrested by the Feldgendarmerie, along with his wife and his brother. The latter two were released some time afterwards.

Mougin is charged with helping two Jews escape.[8] *Mougin*, who worked in the camp at the hotel where the Jews were housed, was very well known to the inmates as 'Lucien'.

He was transferred to the Prison de la Vierge in Epinal.

All of this happening on the same day caused a degree of agitation among the population.

General *Giraud's* family, interned in Vittel, left the city on Friday, 14 April, on the 5.40 p.m. train for Nancy; a 2nd class compartment had been reserved.

According to what we heard in Vittel, the family is currently still in the Nancy area.[9]

DOC. 332

In a letter to his fiancée dated 17 May 1944, Max Scher informs her of his transfer from Marseilles to Drancy[1]

Handwritten letter from Max Scher,[2] Les Baumettes prison, Marseilles, to Jeannette Sarre, 12 rue de Baignoir, Marseilles, dated 17 May 1944

My dear darling,

I am glad that I can still write these few lines in secret before my departure, because I have just been told that I will be leaving for Drancy. I can tell you right away that I am feeling fine, I'm in excellent spirits. I have no worries about the future and the next few weeks, because (I have a premonition about this) events are going to come to a head. We will be free, and I will once again be with you to cherish you as in the past. The wonderful hours that we spent together are not dead; they are revived daily inside me,

8 The two Jews in question are thought to be Felix Aizenstadt and Sluzim Dudelzak.

9 The wife of General Henri Giraud and six other members of his family had been taken hostage by the German police in Oct. 1943. From Vittel they were taken to Friedrichroda in Thuringia. General Giraud had served as the commander of the French troops in North Africa until early April 1944.

1 The original is privately owned. Copy in Mémorial de la Shoah, CMLXXXVI(13)-14. This document has been translated from French.

2 Max Scher (1913–1986), tailor; born in Warsaw; emigrated to Paris with his parents; lived in the Old Port quarter of Marseilles from 1941; arrested there and transported to Drancy; deported from Drancy to Auschwitz on 30 May 1944; escaped from the camp in late Jan. 1945; deputy mayor of the 3rd arrondissement of Paris in 1963; made a Knight of the National Order of Merit.

and I remember all the little flaws that make your character so charming and make me forget the sad place in which I find myself. My dear, be brave. Our separation will be brief, and I hope that my love will be powerful enough to make you wait for my return.

I leave tonight for Drancy, where I will be fine according to what one hears. If you get no news, then I beg you to be brave and to have confidence, because I don't think I'll be able to write to you before the liberation. My dear, I am thinking of you night and day. I would like my belief in the future to take root in you as well, so that you cease worrying and get back to enjoying normal life once again. Think about me often, but do not be upset about me, because I am really not suffering (except from our separation), neither morally nor physically, and after my return I will spoil you more than I ever have. But you will also spoil me as you never have before. And to see the modest life we had, so pleasant, before me again gives me courage that no one [...][3] and around me, because I know that I [...]. My dear little Jeannette [...] I left her, just as she will find me again [...] was (in my good moments) and that she will forget [...] the bad moments that were caused by my current situation. Get in touch with Adolphe, his sister, and their mother,[4] give them all my best, and tell them that [...] they should have courage and confidence.

Embrace your mother for me,

My love to Roger and Mireille.

Say hello to everyone. And to you, my only reason to live, my most tender kisses.

My associate Heftman[5] owes me two pieces of lining and several metres of white cloth that he should give to you as my share. Say hello to everyone. Max.

Mr Léon, the boarder at the Bonnardets in Monestiers, and his wife and child are here with me. Take courage. [...]

DOC. 333

On 30 June 1944 Maurice Bensignor writes a farewell letter to his son from Drancy[1]

Handwritten letter from Maurice Bensignor,[2] Drancy, to his son Sam, dated 30 June 1944

My dearest boy,

How happy the brief messages that I was able to read from you made me! Some details were superfluous because I know of what you can be capable. What is essential for me to know is that you redouble your efforts to be careful and that you are even more careful and that you do nothing that might attract attention to yourself. If only you knew how

3 Several words are missing or illegible in this passage.

4 Scher's brother Adolphe, his sister Odette, and his mother, Feiga Scher, had gone into hiding, with the help of non-Jewish acquaintances.

5 Presumably Joseph Heftman (b. 1910), tailor; born in Łuków (Poland); arrested in Marseilles; taken to Drancy camp before Max Scher arrived; later deported to Auschwitz; survived.

1 Mémorial de la Shoah, CMLXXXVI(6)-15. This document has been translated from French.

2 Maurice (Moise) Bensignor (1893–1945), retailer; born in Aydın (Turkey); attended the Alliance israélite universelle (AIU) school there; lived in Paris before 1914; worked as a retailer in Versailles; arrested at his home in late May 1944 and interned in Drancy; deported to Auschwitz on 30 June 1944.

many diverse cases there are among those who arrive here, and the regrets they have about diverging slightly from their usual conduct, at the last minute, which has ended up in them being arrested and then brought here. And yet they had God knows how many guarantees. So, my dear boy, think carefully about what I am telling you. There are already enough of us who are suffering here and who will continue to suffer. Keep yourself safe, for the love of your father and for the duties that you still have to fulfil.

I find nothing of what you tell me about your friends' attitudes surprising because I know how you chose them and how greatly they value you. They have all proved it most eloquently. As for the family you are living with, I am sure your praise is more than just vain words to console and calm me. Their initial gesture and their general attitude are the best proof of their sincerity, their goodness, and the nobility of their hearts. I could never make it up to them, and even less would I know how to find the words to express my gratitude to them. Not that they expect this of me, I am sure, because they are too good-hearted. Nevertheless, I hope they know that during my long sleepless nights, I think of them and of all they are doing for you. Without having had the pleasure of meeting them all, I hope they will allow me to tell them that I count them among my own and that I have taken them to my heart.

My dear boy, the departure has now definitively been set for tomorrow.[3] After the stress and uncertainty of the last few days, we must now resign ourselves and accept our sad fate. We are leaving for an unknown destination for an indefinite period of time. They have given us provisions for five days, and sufficient supplies will be following us. We are allowed to take some of our luggage with us, just with the essential things, so that our luggage does not take up too much space in the wagon. Because there will be sixty of us in each. The rest of our things will follow in a special wagon. I was able to get everything into the suitcases and bags that I was given, and I was able to divide everything up in such a way that I will lack nothing in case any piece of luggage goes missing or is damaged.

We have an abundance of food supplies. We may not know exactly what they are or the precise amounts, but you should know that we will lack nothing. We have copious amounts of preserves, jam, honey, sugar, and meat, as well as plenty of other things, all perfectly good; there is no shortage of clothing or linen. The selection and variety of the rare foodstuffs shows us that each and every one around you has made such a great effort to make our lives easier.

I would like to thank them all from the bottom of my heart; they have no idea how they have eased my pain by giving me the means to care for my four dear children's health.[4] This was the cruellest thing for me at the start of our internment, not being able to feed them properly: faced with the threat of an imminent departure I was too afraid to use up our provisions that I had been saving up. If by bad luck we had arrived in the early afternoon, we would undoubtedly have left the next day.[5] Since then, there have

3 The train left for Auschwitz the same day. Maurice Bensignor's two daughters, Reine (b. 1923) and Jeannine (b. 1926), had been arrested with him. Only Reine Bensignor survived; she was liberated by British troops at the Altona Hospital in Hamburg in 1945. His wife, Rachel (née Houly), and son Sam (b. 1921) escaped arrest.

4 In addition to his two daughters, Reine and Jeannine, this is thought to refer to his nieces Jacqueline (b. 1930) and Marcelle Houly (b. 1932).

been fewer new arrivals, which meant they were unable to put together a new transport for quite a while. Given the way things are going, it will perhaps be the last one.[6] Unfortunately, we have been included. All the efforts and activities I undertook to avoid this have come to nothing. Therefore we must resign ourselves and accept this with courage and the confidence that we will soon be liberated.

I am staying strong for myself and for the children in my care. The parents of the little ones need not worry, because I am looking out for them even more than for my own children. All of them are in relatively good health, and our morale is also good. Have just as much courage as we do and let's hope that we will all meet again as soon as possible.

I will not be able to fill the entire page, however much I would have liked to prolong this delightful correspondence, of which this letter will be the last for a while.

Tell everyone who is worried about us and suffering with us that I will not forget them. Embrace them all tenderly from all of us. I would have liked to ask all the others to add some words, but that would have been too imprudent, because I am already doing something pretty dangerous. I kept myself from appearing on the balcony to see Miss D. because of the potential consequences. To her and to all our friends, my most affectionate thoughts, and to all the family, and to you my dearest boy, my warmest embrace. I am sending love to all of you with all my heart.

Have courage and confidence, I will see you again soon.

Your father who loves you,

M

Please give Z's friends our news.

DOC. 334

On 8 August 1944 Charles de Gaulle's provisional French government receives a report about Drancy and Auschwitz by an escaped prisoner[1]

Memorandum (marked 'confidential') from the Free France Commissariat for Internal Affairs (Documentation Department, no. 6374) containing a report by an Auschwitz prisoner who had escaped (information received on 3 August 1944), dated 8 August 1944[2]

Drancy Camp and Deportation to Poland
Account of an Escape
Arrived at *Drancy*, 26 February 1943
Left for Beaune-la-Rolande, 20 March 1943
Returned to Drancy, 19 June 1943
Left for Poland, 18 July 1943

5 The previous transport had left Drancy on 30 May 1944.

6 In early June 1944, Allied troops landed in Normandy and established a bridgehead that the Wehrmacht could not break. However, three more transports left France before the liberation of Paris in August 1944, carrying 1,781 Jews in all. Two of these transports left from Drancy.

1 AN, F60, vol. 1678. This document has been translated from French.

2 The original contains handwritten notes. Several parts of the text have been blanked out.

When Captain *Brunner*[3] and his deputy *Bruckner*[4] arrived at Drancy and sent the French police away, the prisoners were interrogated, mainly regarding their families.[5] [...]

It was after Brunner's arrival that we witnessed beatings in the camp for the first time. He had all the prisoners assembled in the courtyard to show them how a Jew who does not obey the rules was to be punished. Two days later a staircase elder,[6] who had wanted to pass on a letter in secret, was abused and forced to crawl across the camp courtyard. To make him go faster, Brunner kicked him and fired his gun behind him to scare him. The man was thrown into the prison and beaten so severely that he had to be treated by doctors, who gave him stitches.

At Drancy, we wore tags attached to our buttonholes. They bore the number 1 for those who were not to be deported, 2 for those awaiting their families, 3 for the wives of prisoners of war (a category that was merged with that of spouses of Aryans, i.e. not to be deported), 4 for French nationals, 5 for the spouses of Aryans, and 6 for prisoners who were shortly going to be released.[7] Our prisoner numbers also featured on the tags.

Captain Brunner, upon arriving at the camp, put an end to the searches that preceded the deportations, saying: 'Whatever it costs me, I want to tell you that this isn't a deportation any more; it is an evacuation. We are sending you to labour camps, where you will live with your families, and you will be paid for the work you do.'

The deportees left with their families and their luggage. Their heads were no longer shaved.

My turn came on Friday, 17 July. We went to the departure staircase at midnight.[8] [...]

The departure took place on Saturday, 18 July, at 5.30 a.m. from Bobigny station, because the station at Bourget had been demolished in an air raid on 14 July. Germans were guarding the streets the whole way. We boarded very quickly because the Germans hit those who weren't moving quickly enough on their own with their batons.

Like my trip from Beaune-la-Rolande to Drancy, this one also took place in a livestock wagon. We were fifty to a wagon. The wagons were locked, and a skylight was left open at each end. There were three buckets of water and one bucket for waste. No straw on the floor.

We left around midday in sweltering heat. We rationed the water because we did not know if there would be any more later. As we were not searched, we were able to bring our clothes, provisions, and blankets. Very few people touched their provisions; we did not know how long the trip would take and were afraid of not having enough.

3 In the original 'Le Cap. Brunner': Alois Brunner.

4 Correctly: Ernst Brückler.

5 See Docs. 304 and 307. The subsequent passage has been blanked out.

6 *Chef d'escalier*, a prisoner functionary in charge of the prisoners accommodated on a particular staircase.

7 Under Brunner's command letters were used to categorize prisoners: A, B, C1–C5. 'A' referred to the 'Western workers' (mainly spouses of 'Aryans' and 'half-Jews') who had been called up for forced labour in France working for Organization Todt, the 'furniture operation' (Möbelaktion), etc.; 'B' stood for 'Eastern workers', who could be deported. All the others were among the groups of internees who could not be immediately deported (members of the camp administration, Jewish citizens of neutral or allied countries, family members of prisoners of war, etc.).

8 The prisoners selected for the next deportation train were assembled a few hours before departure in a specific stairwell in the camp complex. The subsequent passage has been blacked out.

Under guard by Reichswehr[9] soldiers, we went as far as Metz, where they refilled our water buckets. The train stopped for about an hour, and then we set off again. During the trip, some fell ill, and overall there were eleven deaths on the transport. The dead had to remain in the wagons.

The train made two more stops, one of which was long enough to allow us to take care of our needs and wash ourselves at a pump.

In Breslau, the Reichswehr soldiers were replaced by SS men. The former, even though they'd felt sorry for us, had already asked us to give them our jewellery. We didn't believe what they were saying, and so we didn't hand over anything … When we arrived at the freight station in Auschwitz, we received the order to get out of the wagons without touching our suitcases or bags. Everything had to remain behind.

My wife and my little daughter got off, along with all of our companions: men to the left, women and children to the right. I saw the head of the SS guards tear handbags away from women and toss them carelessly to the ground, and also take off women's and children's coats. It was five o'clock in the evening. We were beginning to understand …

Two German commanding officers arrived, accompanied by a third – this one I took to be a physician. A sorting process began: about 330 able-bodied young men and women were put to one side. The elderly, the infirm, and the women holding children in their arms or by the hand got into trucks. The 350[10] – I was among their number – marched about two kilometres and arrived at the *Birkenau* camp. There the women and men were separated.[11]

Then we were no longer being ordered about by Germans, but by (Aryan) Poles. Upon our arrival, they made us go into a barrack, where we had to undress completely and leave all of our papers, money, and jewellery in the pockets of our clothes. Once we were naked, they made us leave the barrack, and two Germans at the door examined us – *even our private parts* – to make sure we hadn't hidden anything. It was around 11 in the evening, and the night was cold. We were led into another room, and there we were *shaved all over.*

They did the same thing to the women; I saw it the next day, when the women were lining up to go to the washroom.

At 1.30 a.m.: a cold shower. Nothing to dry yourself with. None of our clothing or personal items would ever be returned to us. We were then given some clothing, consisting of an old shirt, an old pair of trousers, and a jacket, with no regard for size. No shoes, no clogs – we were barefoot.

At around 4 a.m., overwhelmed with exhaustion, we were led into another barrack. An SS man entered, followed by two Poles. The first one picked out one of us who had to sing, and we were forced to remain standing until 7 a.m., while the poor man sang himself hoarse …

Then we were interrogated. They asked us our surnames, given names, marriage status, our parents' address (no one responded to this question), what we had studied, what our occupations were. (Perhaps we thereby put our signature, not at the bottom of any

9 As in the original. Correctly: Wehrmacht.

10 Mismatched numbers in the original.

11 Of the 1,000 persons on the transport, 369 men and 191 women were selected for labour upon arrival; all the others were murdered immediately. Fifty-two prisoners survived until 1945.

declaration, but on a so-called 'correspondence card', which some received from the Birkenau camp …)

Then they tattooed an identification number with a Star of David on our forearms and led us to a barrack inside the camp, where I can say that around 50,000 deportees were being held, because I made some comparisons and inquiries.

When I asked one of the camp heads when I would again see my wife and my daughter, who had been deported at the same time as me and had left Auschwitz aboard a truck, he led me outside the camp and showed me an enormous chimney in the distance, from which white smoke was rising. He said these simple words: 'Your wife and your daughter are going up in that smoke …'

I did not want to believe it, and I asked other people in the camp. Unfortunately, it was true: all the sick, the elderly, the people who could not provide any labour, they had been sent to a shower room where, instead of water, gas was released. After that it was the cremation ovens. Everybody who left on the trucks had taken that route …

As for us, we began to submit to the camp schedule: reveille at 4 a.m., roll call at 5 a.m., departure for work at 6 a.m. We were not yet going to work because it took us four days to learn to obey the commands. For example, to line up in rows at the moment of roll call in short, precise movements. This instruction was accompanied with baton blows and punches.

Nothing to eat until midday. Then soup: a ladleful of water with a cabbage leaf and potato peelings floating around in it.

From 1 p.m., we are ordered about again until 5.30 p.m.[12] Roll call at 6 p.m. At 7 p.m., bread is distributed. We are supposed to receive 500 grams, but the Poles (some of whom are Jews) steal part of our ration. We also receive a slice of sausage – made out of who knows what … We go to bed in a barrack where there are 600 of us (5 or 6 to a bed made of boards, with no straw and three blankets).

One day we were assigned to work levelling the ground. We transported soil on wooden barrows. Every 10 metres, we were automatically hit with a baton. I saw workers who were nothing but skin and bones, actual walking skeletons, their bodies entirely covered in wounds. And one was not allowed to stop working under any circumstances for the entire day. Nothing to drink, there is no drinking water in the camp – all under the glaring sun. When one of us falls and does not get up again, we take him back with us in the evening, because the dead also need to be 'present' at the roll call …

If you make a mistake, the punishment is 25 blows. But often it just means one more for the crematorium.

The camp is entirely surrounded by electrified barbed wire, and we admire the courage of those who willingly go to their deaths. One of them, […],[13] 23 years old, died this way on 27 July at 11 o'clock in the evening.

What I saw at Birkenau included …

I saw a Jew laid on his back, a baton placed across his throat, and a German, spreading his legs, put one foot on either end of the baton and rocked back and forth until the poor man gave up the ghost. This was done for no reason.

12 Change of tense as in the original.
13 Passage (presumably the name) blacked out.

For not folding our sheets properly, we were forced to remain in a half crouch on the balls of our feet for half an hour, our arms stretched out in front. Seeing as this position is impossible to maintain, we tottered or fell, and the blows from the baton made us take up the exercise again.

If a prisoner is 'found to be ill' during the men's medical examination, he is sent to the crematorium. If he is not 'found to be ill', he has the right to a beating and returns to work. Most of the sick prefer to die rather than complain.

When a prisoner does not perform his tasks, he is sent to the penal detail, where he is snuffed out within a fortnight.

Three men were forced to do 'duck jumps' for an hour inside the barrack for having talked to each other in the column on the way back from work. They were about 40 years old. The exercise was too difficult for them, and so they were so severely beaten that one of them died.

One Sunday, a German came back drunk. When he spotted a group of five prisoners, he ordered them to run around a barrack. On every lap, he shot dead the prisoner bringing up the rear.

I spoke to a young Pole, 23 years old, who had been castrated in the course of a medical experiment. He told me that a few other young women and young men before him had also been subjected to these sterilization experiments …

Jaworzno

One day a special commission selected a certain number of us to be transferred to Jaworzno camp (General Government of Poland).[14] There were around 500 of us, 200 of whom were going to work in a coal mine, while the others were to stay behind to dig a canal in fine sand. This was gruelling work, which meant that at the end of several months our fellow prisoners no longer looked like human beings.

We were assigned to three mines: Dachsgrube, Rudolfsgrube, Leopoldgrube, located 1, 3, and 5 kilometres from Jaworzno camp. No matter the weather, we made our way from the camp to the work site and back on foot. We set off chained together in groups of five by five, all connected to a central chain, surrounded by SS men with machine guns in their hands and two men from the Wehrschutz (territorial army), accompanied by four dogs.[15]

Once a prisoner is assigned to work, he is given a prisoner's uniform. This uniform is striped vertically in blue and white, and consists of a pair of trousers, a jacket, and a

14 Jaworzno lies between Cracow and Katowice in what was then Regierungsbezirk Kattowitz (province of Upper Silesia), around 20 km north of Auschwitz, in a heavily industrialized area with coal and sand mines. From June 1943 to April 1945 it was the location of Neu-Dachs SS labour camp, a satellite camp of Auschwitz. The camp provided prisoner labour for the coal mines Dachsgrube, Rudolfsgrube, Friedrich-August-Grube, Richardgrube, and Leopoldgrube, operated by the coal-mining company Jaworznower Steinkohlegruben AG. In August 1943 a total of 1,600 prisoners from Auschwitz were forced to work there; in early 1945 the number had risen to 3,664. By 1945 more than 13,000 prisoners, 80 per cent of them Jews, had passed through the camp.

15 The labour camp was guarded by SS-Obersturmführer Bruno Pfütze's 4th Guard Company. Many Volksdeutsche (ethnic Germans) from Eastern and South-eastern Europe were among the 200 to 300 SS men in this unit.

cap. Every item of clothing must have the prisoner's identification number sewn onto it, written in ink upon a white background. The Jewish star appears in red. The women are dressed in men's overalls, blue in colour, which have a wide red stripe painted on the back.

Dressed in these prisoner's uniforms, we would pass in front of a camp for English prisoners. On several occasions, they tossed us cigarettes and pieces of bread, but when we tried to pick them up, fights broke out and we were beaten with the baton. After that, the English did not try again … My team was made up of three prisoners led by two Polish Aryan miners. We had to load thirty-five tonnes of coal onto wagons in the space of eight hours. The temperature in the mine was +2 degrees. There was a constant drip of water, and we had to wade through the mud in clunky shoes that did not fit and seriously injured us.

What I saw at Jaworzno included …
Reveille was at 4 a.m. and roll call at 5 a.m. A prisoner who had left the barrack to go to the lavatory had fallen asleep. Because he was not at roll call, the Germans let loose their Great Danes, which obviously found the man. They did not bite him, but they tore off all of his clothes. The Germans then took a baton and beat him to death.

Coming back from the mine one day, I was reeling from the toxic gases, and I went to the infirmary to ask for an aspirin tablet. The doctor, an Aryan Pole, asked me why, and I told him that I had a terrible headache. So he took a great swing with his fist straight at my face, saying, 'This should cure you.'

I. J.[…],[16] one of my fellow prisoners, around thirty years old, suffered from colic. He died next to me in the lavatory because he never wanted to undergo the medical exams for fear of being sent to the crematorium …

The escape
The working hours at the mine are: 7 a.m.–3 p.m., 3 p.m.–11 p.m., 11 p.m.–7 a.m.

I waited five weeks to be on the night shift to be able to escape. On 6 September I went down into the mine at 10.45 p.m. to begin my work. But I only pretended to make the descent. I dirtied my face, I put on a cap I had stolen eight days previously, and I hid. I covered my prisoner's uniform with another one, a uniform from which I had scraped the paint off the back during the nights at the camp. I also covered the traces of paint with coal taken from the mine.

I waited until 11.15 p.m. so I could blend in with the civilian workers leaving the mine. They had gathered at 11 p.m. behind the gate, which did not open until 11.15 p.m. As soon as this door opened, I squeezed in and, in the middle of the group, was able to get past the guards and their dogs without being recognized. Those were the ten most frightening seconds of my escape …

Unhurriedly I reached the main gate of the mine yard, and I found myself on the road. I did not know where to go, as I did not know the topography of the area, but I knew that France was to the west, and I had noted the direction of the sunset.

16 Name blacked out.

I had to walk the length of the camp and, when I had left it 500 metres behind me, I went deeper into the forest, which is very thick … For three nights and two days I wandered on aimlessly, walking during the night, resting during the day. I had no food except a few raw potatoes I dug up from a field. The second night, at around 4 a.m., I had to swim across the river that marks the General Government border.

On the third morning, I came to a farm and approached it, but the farmers could not give me anything to eat because they were very frightened of the large numbers of police in the area. I learned that I was very close to Katowice, and that a group of free French workers could be found at a construction site about 500 metres away. I approached the site with extreme caution and told them that I was an escaped prisoner – without giving any other details. They immediately helped me by giving me food, but these workers could not do much for me, as they themselves were very afraid.

So I went to the Deutsche Arbeitsfront (Arbeitsamt),[17] where I declared that, having come from Nice on a worker transport, I had got drunk on the train, and that others had taken advantage of this to steal my papers and my money. I presented them with a made-up identity and was immediately employed as a cook in a hotel. I received the Ausweis[18] and all the necessary identity documents.

[…][19]

17 German in the original for the two (in fact distinct) institutions: 'German Labour Front' and 'employment office'.
18 German in the original: 'identity card'.
19 The rest of the passage is missing.

DOC. 335
On 10 October 1944 the Resistance fighter Meta Lande tells a friend about the arrest of fellow resisters in Paris[1]

Letter from Meta Lande,[2] Paris, to a friend, dated 10 October 1944 (copy)[3]

Dear friend,

You're finally hearing from me after a long time, since I was unable to write sooner. A lot has happened in the meantime, so much that I don't know where to begin.

You've probably heard already how Nano,[4] Lolly,[5] and others (friends from Holland) were caught.[6] Enclosed is another letter from Cor (Max Windmüller)[7] in which he wrote to you in great detail about everything. His letter was written back in June but then went unsent, and much of the information in it is now outdated. You know Nano, Cor, and Willi[8] were working in France, that is, they *brought friends from Holland* here and where possible sent them onward to Spain. Lolly and Betti did the technical work required for organizing *provisions* and so forth. This all went well until 24 April. It is still not certain how and by whom we were *betrayed*.[9] On that day, Nano, Willi, and Zippy[10] (who had just returned *from Italy*, where he made contact with *Jews who had gone into hiding*), as well as Lolly and Susi, who just happened to be together in Lolly's room, were arrested.

1 JDC, SM 39/50 no. 24. This document has been translated from German.

2 Meta Lande, later Shulamit Roethler (1924–2017); after her father was interned in Dachau in 1938, she was taken on a children's transport from Vienna to the Netherlands, where she was put into a hachsharah (an agricultural training school) in Loosdrecht, a town in the province of Utrecht. From May 1942 to Jan. 1944 she was a member of the Dutch-led Westerweel Group, initially in Toulouse and later in Paris. Lande emigrated to Israel after the war.

3 The copy of the letter was made on the stationery of Hehalutz's main headquarters: Hehalutz Geneva Office, 53 rue des Paquis, Geneva.

4 Kurt Reilinger (1917–1945); involved in the production of forged documents; deported to Buchenwald on 17 August 1944; freed when the camp was liberated in 1945 and returned to the Netherlands, where he died in a car accident.

5 Lolly Ekart (b. 1923), nurse; joined the Armée juive resistance organization in 1943; served as deputy leader of the Paris branch of the Westerweel Group; on 9 August 1944 sent to Drancy, from where she was freed when the camp was liberated.

6 They belonged to the Westerweel Group, which was named after the non-Jewish Dutch teacher Joop Westerweel. Its members, mostly young Jewish émigrés from Germany or Austria, along with non-Jewish Dutch citizens, attempted to save young people from the Netherlands from deportation by taking them to Spain via Belgium and France. The refugees were supplied with forged documents in Paris that identified them as members of the Wehrmacht, thus making their journey through occupied France much easier.

7 Max Windmüller (1920–1945); co-founded the Westerweel Group in 1942 and served as its liaison in occupied France from 1943; became the leader of the Dutch section of the Armée juive/Organisation juive de Combat (OJC) in Paris in April 1944; imprisoned first in Fresnes and later in Drancy in mid July 1944; taken to Buchenwald on 17 August 1944; killed in April 1945 by an SS officer while on a death march.

8 Ernest Hirsch (1916–1945); fled from Aachen to the Netherlands in 1937; joined the Westerweel Group in 1942 and organized a network in France; had contact with the Armée juive/OJC in Toulouse and formed a Dutch section; arrested and taken to Buchenwald in mid August 1944.

9 The caretaker of the tenement building where the Group was living in Paris had denounced them.

10 Alfred Fraenkel (b. 1920); active in the Westerweel Group, 1942–1944; had contact with the Armée juive/OJC in Toulouse; deported to Buchenwald in mid August 1944; liberated in April 1945.

Cor was in Holland at the time, and Betti was in the south. I had returned to Paris from the south several days before. I see that I'm going into too much detail; all the memories resurface as I write. After a few months we received the important news that every single one of them was in a prison near Paris,[11] naturally detained as non-Jews. Cor was busy at the time here in Paris trying to get the five of them free, and Els,[12] who has *worked* for the *Gestapo* in order to copy plans and so forth at night. She did a great deal of useful work, and I took over all the technical matters although everything had changed a lot.

Most of those who went to Spain went via the South. Friends who were here only had to be supplied; they worked during the day. Back then we were in very close contact with our French friends. Cor made the necessary documents for them. Some of our friends joined the *French Resistance* during this time. Cor came into contact with people who worked for the Intelligence Service[13] but were playing a double role. We had all had great trust in these people, who were also Jews (as they claimed) and you can just imagine the catastrophe. We appeared to be very close to freeing Nano and Willi; everything had been arranged. We even succeeded in smuggling a letter into the prison, which Nano himself answered.

The Resistance, including Cor, had planned to enter the prison in 'real' uniforms with the aid of forged papers and pick up individual 'cases' for interrogation. That same week about thirty friends, of whom twelve were Dutch, were caught. Everything, and I mean everything, was betrayed by the so-called Intelligence Service. They had waited long enough, and were in possession of Gestapo plans as well as those of [Dept.] VI which had to be sent to England (and so we had them doing something else against our 'five'). Well, what should I tell you, I can barely continue so matter-of-factly, because everything is still so fresh and also concerns me personally. I was the only one who remained. I had just happened to leave half an hour before they came. I shouldn't say this, but sometimes I think I would have rather been caught. Every one of them was caught. Cor, Els, Leen,[14] (who you probably know) and then all the lads who belonged to the *Resistance*. After that I stayed in contact with the French, and we combed all the prisons in order to find out where they were. But it wasn't until a few days before Paris was liberated that our lads in the Resistance (*the Jewish group*) went to Drancy and returned with Lolly and Susi and one of our French friends. *They, together with the Croix Rouge,*[15] *liberated the camp, about 1,500 people, Jews.* We had never thought the Germans would leave without taking the Jews with them or at least dropping a bomb on the camp.

We now learned from the two of them that in the final weeks the Gestapo already knew everything and that almost all our lads had been sent to Drancy. You can't imagine how happy we all were, because that meant that they hadn't been shot dead yet, which for some of them was pretty much what was expected. It was their and our good fortune

11 This is a reference to Fresnes prison.

12 Paula Kaufman (b. 1920), nurse; active in the Westerweel Group, 1943–1944; arrested in mid July 1944; deported to Buchenwald on 17 August 1944; liberated by Allied forces in 1945.

13 'Intelligence Service' in English in the original.

14 Probably Hans Erlich (b. 1919); member of Hehalutz; joined the Westerweel Group in late 1943; worked for the German Luftwaffe under the name of 'Leendert Van der Meyde', during which time he smuggled documents to the Allies; arrested and taken to Buchenwald in mid August 1944; liberated by Allied forces in May 1945.

15 French in the original: 'Red Cross'.

that everything came to an end for the Germans and that they could therefore no longer bring the 'case' involving our French friends to a complete close. But our friends still had to endure enough: *ice baths, 24 knee bends, blows to the body, and all their techniques.* One of our French friends, who was carrying a code but after 24 hours of being beaten still refused to say anything, was beaten to death by them. Everyone held up so *remarkably well*; nearly everyone who made the greatest sacrifices for the others had worked *day and night* for them.

Now you will ask yourself whether everyone was set free. That, unfortunately, is *not* the case. The Germans didn't have room to transport the entire Drancy camp and so they took with them only 50 of those who were being held as criminals in the prison at Drancy awaiting punishment – all the lads and several girls, including Els.

On 17 July,[16] a week before the Americans arrived here, they were added to a German transport and left in the direction of Belgium.[17] But about three weeks later all our French friends and only one Dutchman returned one after another. They *jumped out of the moving train,* which had to travel rather slowly due to sabotage. Every day we waited for our other friends. They would certainly also have jumped if they saw any chance at all. But after fourteen days of waiting, no one else arrived. So I went to look for our friends with two haverim[18] and a non-Jewish lieutenant in the Resistance. We had a car from the FFI.[19] We followed the train's entire route, from one village to the next, speaking with all the 'Chefs de Gare'[20] and so forth. We got as far as Liège, which is still a combat zone. From there, they probably travelled to Germany via Aachen. –

While on the road we heard, among other things, that the train had to stop because of sabotage just a few kilometres from where the first group had jumped off.[21] So the Germans discovered everything that had happened and completely locked the train wagon and placed it between the Gestapo and the Green Police;[22] the prisoners had previously been in the last wagon. All of them were certainly guarded so closely that it would have been impossible to attempt an escape. In any case, 27 of the 50 have returned. None of them were recaptured; the only bad thing for us is that all our haverim are still being held in the train.[23]

This is the story of our Dutch group here in France. *Everything was certainly worth our efforts,* for without them all our friends would not be in *Spain*.

I haven't heard anything at all from Holland since early June. Many of our friends who had been living in hiding were denounced. Many of them were sent to Celle. It was not possible afterwards to stay in contact with them by post nor was it possible to travel.

16 Correctly: 17 August 1944.

17 This last transport from Drancy, which consisted of three wagons, was also carrying Alois Brunner. Among the prisoners were 51 Jews, most of them resistance fighters, as well as well-known personalities who were to be used as hostages.

18 Plural of haver, Hebrew for 'friend'; in Zionist discourse also 'member', 'comrade'.

19 Forces françaises de l'intérieur (French Forces of the Interior). In early Feb. 1944 the most important factions of the military resistance within France came together to create a unified armed force.

20 French in the original: 'station managers'.

21 At least 21 people were able to escape from the train in this manner. The breakout took place near Morcourt, in the département of Somme, during the night of 20 to 21 August.

22 This is a reference to the German Order Police.

23 The train reached Buchenwald on 25 August 1944. Only ten of the deportees survived.

At the moment I'm trying to put my papers in order to travel to Maastricht. Perhaps the transport passed by there and perhaps it might be possible to make contact with our friends in the area.

As of now, I can't leave here until I know what happened to our friends. I have certainly considered emigrating to Palestine at the first opportunity that arises, but I just can't yet. No matter how things turn out, I will never have any regrets despite how difficult it all was. The sacrifices we made weren't in vain. We must continue doing our work even if sometimes we don't know if it's doing any good.

DOC. 336
On 12 March 1945 Max Scher writes a postcard to his girlfriend as a free man[1]

Postcard from Max Scher, Regroupement des Français, 14 Aleja Maria Panny, Częstochowa, Poland, to Madame Jeannette Boy,[2] Hotel Idéal, 12 rue du Baignoir, Marseilles, dated 12 March 1945.

My sweetest darling, I wrote you on the 9th to give you news of me, after so many months of silence.[3] I cannot express to you my joy at being able to write you these few lines because, ever since our forced separation, I have not stopped thinking about you, and what haunted me most was that I was leaving you without news. But it was *impossible* because in the concentration camp[4] no escape was possible; we were dealing with SS men who were unbelievably savage and utterly devoid of humanity. I must be one of the few who managed to escape their clutches, since here I am, free for the last five weeks, and hoping to be near you very soon to take up the life we knew, which was so happy, and which I am sure will be even more beautiful after these months of separation. I would love to have your news as soon as you receive these words; write to me at the address indicated on the other side. Give my news to my family, since I do not know where to write to them, and reassure them regarding my situation because now I want for nothing, except for you, France, and my family. I'm sending hugs to Roger, Mireille, your mother, in fact everyone, and for you the most affectionate and tender kisses.

1 The original is privately owned. Copy in Mémorial de la Shoah, CMLXXXVI(13)-14. This document has been translated from French.
2 In an earlier letter to his fiancée (Doc. 332), sent to the same address, Max Scher had written her name as Jeannette Sarre. It is not known why in this postcard he wrote her name as Jeannette Boy.
3 In his first postcard, Max Scher told her briefly that he had succeeded in escaping to the zone controlled by the Red Army on 23 Jan. 1944: Mémorial de la Shoah, CMLXXXVI(13)-14.
4 This is a reference to Auschwitz.

Glossary

American Jewish Joint Distribution Committee (JDC, Joint)

Committee founded in the United States in 1914 to coordinate the relief efforts of American Jewish aid organizations. It provided funding and aid to Jews and Jewish organizations, especially in Eastern Europe. Following the outbreak of the Second World War, its efforts extended to Nazi-occupied and Nazi-controlled territories, including the ghettos, where it supported schools, orphanages, cultural institutions, and other important areas of Jewish life.

Amitié chrétienne

Ecumenical relief organization founded in 1942 in Lyons by Abbé Alexandre Glasberg. It provided aid to Jewish prisoners in the internment camps in Vichy France and sought to rescue prisoners from the camps. The organization's most notable operation was the liberation of 108 children from Vénissieux camp outside Lyons just before they were due to be deported to Drancy. The children were hidden with French families; most of them survived the war.

Arrondissement

In France: administrative district in Paris, Marseilles, and Lyons; in Belgium: administrative, judicial, and electoral district below the provincial level.

Aryan (*Arier*)

Term used to describe the peoples supposedly descended from the Indo-Europeans. It was used in Nazi Germany to support the thesis of the inequality of human races and the superiority of those with 'German and related blood' over 'non-Aryan races', above all Jews.

Aryanization (*Arisierung*)

The process of expropriating Jews and excluding them from a 'racially purified' economy. It involved the confiscation or liquidation of Jewish property, assets, and businesses, and the forced transfer of these to individual non-Jews or to the Reich.

Association of Jews in Belgium (Association des Juifs en Belgique / Vereeniging van Joden in België, AJB/VJB)

Countrywide association imposed by the German occupation regime in November 1941, merging together all Jewish organizations in Belgium. Membership was compulsory for Jews. It had the task of implementing German anti-Jewish measures, assisting with preparations for emigration, dealing with healthcare provision and social welfare, and setting up Jewish schools. The association was also made to register Belgium's Jews for forced labour and deportation.

Blocked account (*Sperrkonto*)

Special account holding the liquid assets of Jews who had emigrated. The accounts were set up because German financial policy prohibited Reichsmarks from being removed from Germany without heavy penalties.

Brussels Trust Company (Brüsseler Treuhandgesellschaft)

Corporation founded by the German military administration in Belgium in October 1940. It acted as a front for the seizure, centralization, liquidation, and administration of the assets of Jews and other 'enemies of the Reich'.

Central Office for Jewish Emigration (Zentralstelle für jüdische Auswanderung)
Institution established first in Vienna in August 1938 by the Security Police and SS Security Service to expedite the emigration of Jews from Nazi-controlled territories. There were four such offices, set up in Vienna (1938), Prague (1939), Berlin (Reich Central Office for Jewish Emigration, 1939), and Amsterdam (1941). Adolf Eichmann headed the offices in Vienna and Prague.

Chief of the Military Administration (Militärverwaltungschef)
A rank and a function within the military government. Used to designate the official in charge of the administrative staff within the military government in Belgium and northern France, who reported to the Military Commander (Militärbefehlshaber). The same role also existed within the military government in France.

Comité de Nîmes (Comité de coordination pour l'assistance dans les camps)
Committee founded in late 1940 to coordinate the work of approximately thirty non-Jewish and Jewish relief organizations. It provided aid and support to prisoners in the internment camps of Vichy France. Member organizations included the YMCA, the Quakers, and HICEM. It was usually referred to as the Comité de Nîmes after the town in southern France where its meetings were held.

Commissariat General for Jewish Affairs (Commissariat général aux questions juives)
Agency established by the Vichy government in March 1941 to centralize France's anti-Jewish legislation, oversee the implementation of further anti-Jewish measures, and manage Aryanization policies. It was initially headed by Xavier Vallat and from May 1942 by Louis Darquier de Pellepoix. The Commissariat General for Jewish Affairs was dissolved on 17 August 1944, two days before the liberation of Paris.

Committee for Jewish Refugees (Comité voor Joodsche Vluchtelingen, CJV)
Dutch welfare organization that aided Jewish refugees from Germany. It was founded in 1933 as a subcommittee of the Committee for Special Jewish Interests (Comité voor Bijzondere Joodsche Belangen). It was chaired by Prof. David Cohen and its most influential administrators were Raphaël Henri Eitje and Gertrude van Tijn-Cohn. In March 1941 the CJV was banned by order of the German occupiers; its infrastructure formed the basis of the Jewish Council, which also took over its responsibilities.

Commune (French administrative district)
The smallest territorial and administrative division in France. Each commune has a mayor and an elected council.

Criminal Police (Kriminalpolizei, Kripo)
Criminal investigation force that, together with the Gestapo, constituted the Security Police (Sipo). The Criminal Police mainly dealt with non-political crimes including offences against the war economy (black market activity, slaughtering animals without permit, contravention of the rationing regulations), rape, murder, and arson. It was also heavily involved in the persecution of groups such as Sinti and Roma and homosexuals.

Dagmar House (Dagmarhus)
Premises on Rådhuspladsen (Town Hall Square) in Copenhagen used by the German occupation administration. From September 1943 Dagmar House served as the headquarters of the German civil administration and the German Security Police.

Département
Main administrative division in France and its overseas territories, each governed by a council and a prefect (*préfet*).

Dutch SS (Nederlandsche SS)
Dutch branch of the Allgemeine-SS founded on 11 September 1940 by Anton Mussert, leader of the Dutch National Socialist Movement (NSB), and headed by Johannes H. Feldmeijer. Officially part of the NSB, it was under the command of Heinrich Himmler; from November 1942 it was known as the Germanic SS in the Netherlands (Germaansche SS in Nederland). At its peak it had approximately 7,000 members.

Einsatzkommando
Task force of the Security Police (from 1940: of the Security Police and the SD) deployed at local level in parts of occupied Europe against supposed political or racial enemies.

Expositur
Section of the Jewish Council in Amsterdam headed by Edwin Sluzker. Established in 1941 on the orders of the German authorities, its initial purpose was to assist Jews with filling out emigration applications. From summer 1942 it acted as a liaison with the Central Office for Jewish Emigration. The Expositur also processed summonses for deportation and applications for exemption.

Feldgendarmerie
Military police units of the Wehrmacht, established in 1938. The units were mainly in charge of policing duties within the German army, but were also active in the occupied territories.

Feldkommandantur (FK)
District headquarters of the German military administration, responsible for military security, law and order, and the administration of an occupied region.

Foreign Exchange Protection Commando (Devisenschutzkommando, DSK)
Office of the Reich Finance Administration. By order of the Plenipotentiary for the Four-Year Plan, Hermann Göring, it was responsible for confiscating foreign currency, gold, and other valuables in the occupied territories to benefit the German war economy. In occupied Belgium, it was particularly involved in identifying Jews and informing the Gestapo about them, thus facilitating deportation.

Four-Year Plan
A series of economic measures initiated by Hitler in 1936 and managed by the Office of the Four-Year Plan under the leadership of Plenipotentiary Hermann Göring. The plan aimed to prepare Germany for war within four years. It focused on the rearmament of Germany and the mobilization of the economy, and aimed to make the country more self-sufficient in raw materials.

Free France (France libre)
Resistance organization and government in exile established by General Charles de Gaulle in London on 25 June 1940, one week after his appeal for resistance was broadcast to France by the British Broadcasting Corporation (BBC). It had strong links with the resistance inside occupied France and saw itself as its external counterpart. Its armed forces, the Forces françaises libres (Free French Forces), were made up of soldiers from metropolitan France as well as troops from the French

colonies. The organization was renamed Fighting France (France combattante) in July 1942.

Gauleiter ('Gau leader')
Head of an NSDAP Gau (region).

General Union of French Jews (Union générale des israélites de France, UGIF)
Administrative body established in November 1941 by the Vichy government's Commissariat General for Jewish Affairs after extreme pressure from the German authorities. It incorporated all Jewish organizations in France and their assets, with the exception of the Central Consistory of French Jews and religious associations, which continued to operate separately. Membership of the UGIF was mandatory for all Jews. The UGIF had two autonomous branches: one in the occupied zone and one in unoccupied Vichy France.

Germanic SS (Germanische SS)
Collective name for the SS units in occupied Western Europe (Norway, Denmark, Belgium, and the Netherlands) that were centralized under Himmler's authority in 1942. The units were modelled on the Allgemeine-SS in Germany.

Gestapo (abbreviation for Geheime Staatspolizei; Secret State Police)
Secret State Police in Nazi Germany and German-occupied Europe, established by Hermann Göring in 1933 with the aim of combating internal 'enemies of the state'. From 1934 it was led by Heinrich Himmler and in 1936 it became part of Reinhard Heydrich's Security Police. In 1939 the Security Police merged with the SD to form the Reich Security Main Office (RSHA). Thereafter the Gestapo became known as RSHA Amt IV, though the term Gestapo often continued to be used, and was headed by Heinrich Müller. It was divided into five departments: (a) Political Opponents, (b) Sects and Churches, (c) Administration and Party Affairs, (d) Occupied Territories, and (e) Security and Counter-intelligence. By the end of 1944 the Gestapo had a staff of 32,000.

Green Police (German: Grüne Polizei, Dutch: groene politie)
Colloquial term for the German Order Police due to the colour of their uniforms.

Haute Cour de justice (High Court of Justice)
Court constituted by France's provisional government in November 1944 to try approximately 100 Vichy government ministers and officials. The trials took place between 1945 and 1960 and were presided over by magistrates and a jury composed of parliamentarians and members of the public, both groups selected on the basis of their political affiliation as detractors of the Vichy regime. The trials resulted in three executions; a further fifteen death sentences were issued but not put into effect.

Hehalutz (Hebrew for 'the pioneer')
International umbrella organization, dating from before the First World War, for Zionist youth movements seeking to prepare *halutzim* (pioneers) for agricultural settlement in Palestine.

HICEM
Acronym for three Jewish advocacy organizations that merged in 1927: the Hebrew Immigrant Aid Society (HIAS), the Jewish Colonization Association (JCA, ICA), and Emigdirect (EM). HICEM was based in Paris until Germany's invasion of France in mid 1940, and subsequently in Lisbon. Its purpose was to organize Jewish

emigration and to financially support emigrants in the destination countries; it enabled approximately 90,000 Jews to escape persecution.

Higher SS and Police Leaders (Höhere SS- und Polizeiführer, HSSPF)

Officials appointed by Himmler from 1937 onwards to act as his deputies, responsible for ensuring police control and coordinating the activities of the Security Police, the SD, the Order Police, the Waffen SS, and local auxiliary police units in all occupied territories and, to a limited extent, in the Reich.

Hird

Paramilitary unit of the Norwegian far-right party Nasjonal Samling. Founded in 1934 and led by Johan Bernhard Hjort, it obtained police powers in March 1941 and became part of the Norwegian armed forces in 1943.

Independence Front (Front de l'indépendance / Onafhankelijkheidsfront)

Belgian resistance organization set up by communists in March 1941 which sought to bring together Belgian resistance groups from across the political spectrum, combining civilian and armed resistance against the German occupiers.

Jewish Agency for Palestine ('Jewish Agency')

Agency founded in 1929 to represent Jewish interests in the British Mandate for Palestine. It cooperated with the British Mandate government and advised it on socio-economic issues. The Jewish Agency served as the political leadership of the Jewish community in Palestine until the establishment of the State of Israel in 1948. It also worked to help Jews emigrate to Palestine.

Jewish Coordination Committee (Joodsche Coördinatie Commissie, JCC)

Any of three distinct organizations of Dutch Jews that existed at different times under this name. The first was an umbrella network of Jewish organizations established in December 1940 in Amsterdam to represent Dutch Jews and to provide information and advice on anti-Jewish policies in the occupied Netherlands. Headed by Lodewijk Ernst Visser, the JCC provided assistance on legal and financial matters, and organized cultural events. It was critical of the Jewish Council for what it viewed as cooperation with the Germans. The committee was dissolved in October 1941 by the German authorities and from that point the Jewish Council was the only official representative of Dutch Jews. In autumn 1943 a second JCC was set up in Geneva by Mozes Heiman Gans, S. Isaac, and S. I. Troostwijk, with the aim of providing aid to persecuted Dutch Jews and gathering information about the deportations. A third committee, the Jewish Coordination Committee for the liberated Dutch territory, was established in 1945 and became in the aftermath of the war the most important point of contact for all Jews in the Netherlands.

Jewish Council (Judenrat)

Council within a Jewish community, often also called (Jewish) Council of Elders, established on German orders in Nazi-occupied Europe. In occupied Poland the councils were set up under a decree issued following the German invasion in September 1939. Their main purpose was to ensure the implementation of Nazi orders and regulations. Across occupied Western Europe the German occupiers sought to impose similar structures on Jewish communities. In France and Belgium countrywide Jewish Associations were set up, similar to the Reich Representation of German Jews. In the Netherlands, a Jewish Council was set up with that designation (Joodsche Raad). In Luxembourg the community representative body was forced to implement Nazi orders, and was later turned into a Council of Elders. In Norway and Denmark no councils were established.

Jewish Defence Committee (Comité de défense des Juifs / Joods Verdedigingscomité, CDJ/JVC)
Organization founded in Belgium by Jewish communists and Zionists in September 1942 on the initiative of the Independence Front. Together with non-Jewish helpers, it supported Jews and resistance fighters, but its main task was to protect Jewish children from deportation. It placed Jewish children with non-Jewish families and Catholic institutions; more than 3,000 children were saved as a result.

Jewish Scouts (Éclaireurs israélites de France, EIF)
Jewish scout movement in France, founded in 1923 by Robert Gamzon. It sought to attract both French and immigrant Jewish youth to Judaism and supported Jewish refugees in France. After being dissolved in 1943 the movement went underground.

Joodsche Schouwburg
Dutch theatre founded as the Hollandsche Schouwburg in Amsterdam in 1892. In 1941 the name was changed to Joodsche Schouwburg and only Jewish artists were allowed to perform there for Jewish audiences. From 1942 it served as a detention point for Jews before their deportation to Westerbork and Vught camps. The last transport from the theatre took place on 19 November 1943. It became a memorial site in 1958.

Jøssing
Norwegian term for an opponent of Nasjonal Samling. The term came into use after an incident in the Jøssing fjord in February 1940, when British troops captured a German ship without opposition from the Norwegian navy. Opponents of Nasjonal Samling claimed the label as meaning 'Norwegian patriot'.

Keren Kayemeth LeIsraël (Jewish National Fund)
Fund founded in 1901 in Basel to purchase land in Palestine for Jewish settlements. It had branches in many countries, including in Western Europe.

Kreisleiter
Head of an NSDAP Kreis (territorial subdivision of a Gau).

Kriegsverwaltungsrat ('war administration counsellor', KVRat)
Senior rank in the military administration with responsibility for a range of key areas of occupation policy.

Lippmann, Rosenthal & Co. Bank
Jewish-owned bank in the Netherlands, established in 1859 on Nieuwe Spiegelstraat in Amsterdam. The bank initially dealt only with the accounts of affluent Jews, but later also managed the accounts of small savers. To facilitate the expropriation and looting of Jewish property, the German authorities established a counterpart on Sarphatistraat, using the same name as a front in the attempt to gain the trust of the Jewish population. The original bank was later liquidated and all its assets transferred to the Sarphatistraat bank. Funds from the latter were also used to finance the Westerbork transit camp and deportations.

Marechaussee (Koninklijke Marechaussee, KMar; Royal Dutch Marechaussee)
Branch of the Dutch armed forces, established in 1814, that performs military police duties and supports the civilian police. During the occupation of the Netherlands it lost its military function and operated as a gendarmerie.

Milice française

Paramilitary organization established on 20 January 1943 by the Vichy regime to suppress French resistance. It had approximately 30,000 members and quickly became the political police of Vichy, playing a key role in implementing anti-Jewish measures. The organization was placed under the command of Head of Government Pierre Laval, but its de facto head was Joseph Darnand.

Military Commander (Militärbefehlshaber, MilBfh)

Military head of a German-occupied country, in charge of occupation policy and administration. Subordinate to the commander-in-chief of the army (Oberbefehlshaber des Heeres).

Mischling ('half-caste' or person of 'mixed blood')

Classification under Nazi racial law to describe an individual of combined Aryan and non-Aryan, particularly Jewish, descent. The First Regulation (14 November 1935) to the Reich Citizenship Law (one of the Nuremberg Laws of 1935) categorized *Mischlinge* according to the number of Jewish grandparents: *Mischlinge* of the first degree ('half Jewish' – one Jewish parent or two Jewish grandparents) and *Mischlinge* of the second degree ('quarter Jewish' – one Jewish grandparent). In order to prevent the birth of children of 'mixed blood', marriage was effectively prohibited between Aryans and '*Mischlinge* of the first degree' (those with two Jewish grandparents).

Mobile Reserve Group (Groupe mobile de réserve)

Paramilitary group affiliated with the police and deployed against resistance fighters in the southern zone of France.

Nansen Relief (Nansen Hjelp)

Norwegian relief organization founded in 1936 and headed by Odd Nansen, son of polar explorer and Nobel Peace laureate Fridtjof Nansen. It brought more than 500 Jewish refugees from Czechoslovakia and Austria to safety in Norway. After the German invasion of Norway in April 1940, the organization focused on supporting refugees in the country. Its activities ceased in late 1942.

Nasjonal Samling (Norwegian for 'National Union', NS)

Norwegian far-right party oriented towards National Socialism and Italian Fascism, founded in 1933 by Vidkun Quisling. It gained approximately 2 per cent of the votes in the Norwegian parliamentary elections in the 1930s. After the German occupation of Norway, it was the only authorized political party in the country. In 1943 it had around 44,000 members.

National Socialist Movement (Nationaal-Socialistische Beweging, NSB)

Movement founded in the Netherlands by Anton Mussert and Cees van Geelkerken in 1931. It was initially oriented towards Italian Fascism rather than to German National Socialism, but in the second half of the 1930s its antisemitic and pro-German tendencies intensified. After the occupation of the Netherlands, it aligned itself with the Germans and promoted a Greater Netherlands within a Germanic confederation under German leadership. It had approximately 50,000 members in 1940.

National Socialist People's Welfare Organization (Nationalsozialistische Volkswohlfahrt, NSV)

A National Socialist social welfare organization founded in Berlin in 1933. Its welfare work was restricted to 'valuable' members of the *Volksgemeinschaft* and included annual charity drives for the poor, funding holidays for mothers and children, food distribution to large families, the evacuation of children from urban areas, and assistance to bombing victims during the war.

Nuremberg Laws
: Laws proclaimed at the annual Nazi Party rally in Nuremberg in September 1935. They comprised three pieces of legislation: the Flag Law, the Reich Citizenship Law and the Law for the Protection of German Blood and German Honour. The latter two laws excluded German Jews from Reich citizenship and prohibited them from marrying or having extramarital relations with persons of 'German or related blood'.

Oberfeldkommandantur (OFK)
: Regional headquarters of the military administration, here specifically in occupied France and occupied Belgium, under the command of the Military Commander (Militärbefehlshaber).

Oberregierungsrat
: Senior civil service rank in a ministry or other government agency. It was more senior than Regierungsrat, often the head of a department.

Œuvre de secours aux enfants (OSE) (Children's Aid Society)
: Jewish welfare organization established by Jewish physicians in 1912 in Russia. After the Russian Revolution the organization expanded into other European countries with significant Jewish populations and focused on caring for children (medical services and distribution of clothing and food). In 1933 it relocated its headquarters from Berlin to Paris. It ran several orphanages (*maisons d'enfants*) in France for Jewish refugee children, especially from Germany and Austria, and brought children to safety in neutral countries.

Old Reich (Altreich)
: Germany within its 1937 borders, prior to the annexation of Austria in March 1938 and of the Sudetenland in October of the same year.

Order Police (Ordnungspolizei, Orpo)
: German uniformed police between 1936 and 1945. Its branches included the urban police (Schutzpolizei), municipal police (Gemeindepolizei), and the rural police (Gendarmerie). The Order Police was initially administered by the Interior Ministry; it was merged with the SS in 1936. During the war, it was in charge of policing the civilian population in the occupied territories and in Eastern Europe it was also directly involved in killing operations as part of the 'final solution'.

Organization Todt (OT)
: Organization for large-scale infrastructure projects established in 1938 by engineer and later minister for armaments and munitions Fritz Todt. It undertook military infrastructure and fortification projects across occupied Europe, including the Atlantic Wall (an extensive system of fortifications along the coast of continental Europe and Scandinavia against an anticipated Allied invasion) and launch sites for V-1 and V-2 missiles. The OT relied on forced labour and employed approximately 2 million workers, including prisoners of war, camp inmates, and Jewish forced labourers. Albert Speer became head of the OT after the death of Fritz Todt in 1942.

Parti Populaire Français (PPF) (French Popular Party)
: Extreme right-wing party in France, founded by the former communist politician Jacques Doriot in 1936. From 1941, along with other collaborationist parties, it was

authorized by the German authorities to also operate in the occupied zone. Its members actively participated in the persecution of Jews, especially in the roundups overseen by Alois Brunner in the southern zone from autumn 1943.

Radio Oranje

The radio service of the Dutch government in exile in London, which broadcast to the occupied Netherlands during the Second World War. From July 1940 it aired daily Dutch-language programmes via the airwaves of the BBC, which were received secretly in the Netherlands. Anti-Jewish measures were addressed on many occasions, and reference was repeatedly made to the unity of the Dutch people.

Regierungspräsident

Civil service official in charge of a Regierungsbezirk (administrative subdivision approximately equivalent to a British county).

Reich Citizenship Law (*Reichsbürgergesetz*)

One of the Nuremberg Laws proclaimed in September 1935. The Reich Citizenship Law introduced a new distinction between 'subject of the state' (*Staatsangehörige*) and 'Reich citizen' (*Reichsbürger*); only those with 'German or related blood' could be the latter.

Reich Commissariat (Reichskommissariat)

Civilian regime set up by the German government in a number of occupied countries. In Western Europe these included the Reich Commissariat for the Occupied Dutch Territories, the Reich Commissariat for the Occupied Norwegian Territories, and (from July 1944) the Reich Commissariat for Belgium and Northern France. Each commissariat was administered by a Reich commissioner, who reported directly to Hitler.

Reich Germans (*Reichsdeutsche*)

Designation commonly used during the National Socialist period to distinguish Reich citizens who were residents of the German Reich from Reich citizens who were resident abroad (*Auslandsdeutsche*) and from foreign citizens with German ethnicity (*Volksdeutsche*, ethnic Germans). After the annexation of Austria in March 1938, Austrian citizens also acquired the status of *Reichsdeutsche*.

Reich Security Main Office (Reichssicherheitshauptamt, RSHA)

Office created by Heinrich Himmler on 27 September 1939 by merging the SD and the Security Police, and headed by Reinhard Heydrich. The RSHA played an important role in the regime's policies of persecution and extermination. It was responsible for intelligence gathering and criminal investigation. Through the work of Section IV D 4 (later IV B 4), run by Adolf Eichmann, it was instrumental in the implementation of the 'final solution'.

Reichsgesetzblatt (Reich Law Gazette, *RGBl*)

Official gazette of the German Reich between 1871 and 1945, which published laws and regulations.

Rexist Party of Belgium (Parti Rexiste)

Far-right political party, based predominantly in French-speaking areas of Belgium, founded by Léon Degrelle in 1936 as a breakaway faction of the ruling Catholic Party. The Rexist Party won 11 per cent of the vote in the 1936 general election. Between 1940 and 1944 the Rexists openly supported the German occupiers and established a volunteer force which fought in the war against the Soviet Union.

Rosenberg Task Force for the Occupied Territories (Einsatzstab Reichsleiter Rosenberg, ERR)

Agency founded on Hitler's orders at the beginning of 1940 and headed by Alfred Rosenberg. Its purpose was to confiscate pieces of art and cultural assets, libraries and archives, and furniture and household goods owned by Jews and other 'enemies of the Reich', starting in Western Europe. Its activities began in France in September 1940 and were subsequently extended to Belgium and the Netherlands, and to the occupied eastern territories. A renewed authorization for ERR operations was issued by Hitler on 1 March 1942. This gave the ERR the right to seize material thought to be useful for the ideological objectives of the Nazi Party and the future research of the Advanced School (Hohe Schule) of the NSDAP.

Rue de Ruysbroeck Committee

Reference to the Hilfswerk der Arbeitsgemeinschaft von Juden aus Deutschland (Hidag), which was established by German Jewish refugees in autumn 1940 and based at rue de Ruysbroeck in Brussels. In March 1942 the relief committee, which provided support for Jews from the German Reich wishing to settle in Belgium, was incorporated into the Association of Jews in Belgium (AJB/VJB).

SD (abbreviation for Sicherheitsdienst; SS Security Service)

Intelligence service of the SS, founded in 1931 by Heinrich Himmler and headed by Reinhard Heydrich. Served initially as an internal intelligence service for the NSDAP. Its tasks included the detection and surveillance of those classed as political and ideological enemies, especially Jews, communists, Social Democrats, and Freemasons. In 1939 it was incorporated into the Reich Security Main Office (RSHA) along with the Security Police (Gestapo and Criminal Police). It played an instrumental role in the planning and implementation of the 'final solution'.

Secretary general (secretaris-generaal, secrétaire général)

Most senior civil service rank in a ministerial department in Belgium or the Netherlands, second only to the minister. During the occupation, the secretaries general were given the task of administering the respective ministries and running day-to-day government business while the Dutch and Belgian governments were in exile in London.

Security Police (Sicherheitspolizei, Sipo)

One of the two police branches after Himmler's reorganization of the entire police apparatus in 1936 (the other being the Order Police). The Security Police was headed by Reinhard Heydrich between 1936 and 1942 and consisted of the Gestapo and the Criminal Police. It was incorporated into the Reich Security Main Office in 1939.

Senior Commander of the Security Police (Befehlshaber der Sicherheitspolizei und des SD, BdS)

Head of a Reich Security Main Office field office in an occupied territory during the war; also subordinate to the Higher SS and Police Leaders.

Sonderkommando

Subunit of the Einsatzgruppen operating in the rear of the German armies.

Sperrstempel ('exemption stamp')

Stamp inserted by the German occupation authorities in the Netherlands in the passports held by those Jews who were temporarily exempt from deportation, for example because they worked for the Jewish Council or were considered economically useful to the Germans.

SS (abbreviation for Schutzstaffel; 'protection squadron')
: Paramilitary force established in 1925, under the leadership of Heinrich Himmler from 1929. The SS apparatus was responsible from 1934 for running the concentration camps and from 1941 for the extermination camps. Other branches of the SS included the Waffen SS and the Allgemeine SS (membership organization).

State Inspectorate of the Population Register (Rijksinspectie van de Bevolkingsregisters)
: Population register in The Hague headed by Jacob Lentz, who developed a system of registration and identity cards to track the population in the Netherlands. The inspectorate compiled lists of what were thought to be Jewish family names and sought out unregistered Jews by the same names. In 1942 it created the so-called dot maps which indicated the density of Jews by district. The German occupiers used these lists to assist in rounding up Jews and preparing deportation lists.

State Police (Statspolitiet, STAPO), Norway
: Norwegian state police established in July 1941 as a political police force, based on the German Gestapo, and headed by Karl A. Marthinsen. It assisted the German authorities in suppressing Norwegian resistance, combating political crimes, espionage, sabotage, and persecuting Jews. All its members were in Nasjonal Samling.

State secretary (Staatssekretär)
: The most senior rank of permanent civil service official in a Reich ministry. There were sometimes several state secretaries in one ministry.

Swiss Children's Aid (Secours suisse aux enfants)
: Offshoot of the Swiss Aid Association for Child War Victims, created in 1940 to help care for children displaced during the war. It was under the supervision of Hugo Remund, chief physician at the Swiss Red Cross.

Undersecretary (Unterstaatssekretär)
: Civil service official within a Reich ministry; rank below state secretary.

Vélodrome d'Hiver (Vél d'Hiv)
: Indoor sports arena in Paris used as a holding centre for around 8,000 Jews arrested in the roundups in Greater Paris in mid July 1942. Jewish families were interned in the stadium in appalling conditions before being sent to camps at Pithiviers or Beaune-la-Rolande, from where deportations to the East took place.

Verordnungsblatt (*VOBl*)
: Gazette that published legislation, regulations, and decrees, including anti-Jewish ones, issued by the German authorities in the occupied territories: Belgium and Northern France (*VOBl-BNF*), Netherlands (*VOBl-NL*), Luxembourg (*VOBl-L*), and France (*VOBl-F*).

Volkskörper ('people's body' or 'body politic')
: The notion of a biologically defined collective body of the German people under National Socialism. The concept distinguished between individual bodies deemed to be of (hereditary) 'value' or 'non-value', and provided Nazi functionaries with a framework for determining policies to cultivate certain elements within society and to eradicate others.

Weerbaarheidsafdeling (National Socialist Defence Section, WA)
Paramilitary arm of the Dutch National Socialist Movement (NSB), comparable to the SA. It was established in 1932 by Anton Mussert. Banned in 1935, it resumed activities after the German occupation of the Netherlands in 1940. It was known for its violence, directed particularly against Jews and critics of the new regime.

Wehrmacht
Collective term for the German armed forces – army, air force (Luftwaffe), and navy – from 1935 to 1945. The Wehrmacht was the successor to the Reichswehr (1919–1935). The Armed Forces High Command (Oberkommando der Wehrmacht, OKW) under Wilhelm Keitel coordinated military activities, although each of the three military branches had their respective high command: OKH (army), OKM (navy), and OKL (air force).

Western Office (Dienststelle Westen)
The operations of the Rosenberg Task Force (ERR) in Western Europe were reorganized in 1942 when a Western Office was set up by Alfred Rosenberg as a field office of the Reich Ministry for the Occupied Eastern Territories; from November 1944 it was reassigned to the ERR. The Western Office confiscated the furniture of Jews in Western Europe who had fled or been deported (*Möbelaktion*, 'furniture operation').

Westerweel Group
Dutch resistance group formed in summer 1942 and named after the Dutch teacher Johan Gerard (Joop) Westerweel. It organized support for Jewish refugees living in the Netherlands, as well as false papers and routes through German-occupied France for groups of young Jewish refugees. It saved between 200 and 300 young Jews, most of whom were pioneers preparing to settle in Palestine. In spring 1944 Germans infiltrated the group and its leading members were arrested. Westerweel was executed in Vught concentration camp in August 1944.

White Buses
Rescue effort for concentration camp prisoners during the last months of the Second World War, organized by the Swedish and Danish Red Cross and initially restricted to Scandinavian inmates. The rescuers later negotiated the release of thousands of prisoners from other nations, among them many Jews. The evacuations from the concentration camps at Neuengamme and Ravensbrück to Denmark and Sweden were carried out mostly on the white buses that gave the operation its name.

World Jewish Congress (WJC)
International organization founded in Geneva in August 1936 with the backing of the American Jewish Congress (AJC). It was set up with the aim of promoting Jewish unity, supporting the establishment of a Jewish national home in Palestine, campaigning for political and economic equality for Jews across Europe, and combating Nazism and antisemitism. The organization is still in operation today.

YMCA (Young Men's Christian Association)
Christian youth organization founded by George Williams in London in 1844 to provide urban youth with recreation. By the twentieth century it had established centres worldwide. During the war the organization gave support to civilians and soldiers alike. From spring 1940 the YMCA in France aided women and children in

the internment camps in south-western France, where it also coordinated the activities of the various relief organizations.

Zionism

Movement that originated in Central and Eastern Europe in the late nineteenth century and advocated the re-establishment of a Jewish state in Eretz-Israel (Land of Israel – Palestine).

Approximate Rank and Hierarchy Equivalents

NSDAP and Civil Service

NSDAP	Civil Service
Reichsleiter	Staatssekretär
–	Oberpräsident (only in Prussia)
Gauleiter	Unterstaatssekretär
Hauptbefehlsleiter	Ministerialdirektor
Oberbefehlsleiter	Regierungspräsident
Befehlsleiter	–
Hauptdienstleiter	Ministerialdirigent
Oberdienstleiter	–
Hauptbereichsleiter	Ministerialrat
Kreisleiter	
Oberbereichsleiter	Regierungsdirektor
Bereichsleiter	–
Hauptgemeinschaftsleiter	Amtsrat
Ortsgruppenleiter	
Obergemeinschaftsleiter	Oberinspektor
Gemeinschaftsleiter	Inspektor
Haupteinsatzleiter	–
Einsatzleiter	–
Hauptbereitschaftsleiter	Obersekretär
Oberbereitschaftsleiter	Sekretär
–	Verwaltungsassistent
Bereitschaftsleiter	–
–	Assistent
Hauptarbeitsleiter	Assistent
Oberarbeitsleiter	Amtsgehilfe
Arbeitsleiter	–
Oberhelfer	–
Helfer	–
Polit. Leiter-Anwärter	–

Source: Michael Buddrus, *Totale Erziehung für den totalen Krieg: Hitlerjugend und nationalsozialistische Jugendpolitik* (Munich: De Gruyter, 2003).

SS, Wehrmacht, British Army, US Army

SS	Wehrmacht	British Army	US Army
–	Reichsmarschall	–	–
Reichsführer-SS	Generalfeldmarschall	Field Marshal	General of the Army
SS-Oberstgruppenführer	Generaloberst	–	General
SS-Obergruppenführer	General der Waffengattung (Infanterie, Artillerie, etc.)	General	Lieutenant General
SS-Gruppenführer	Generalleutnant	Lieutenant General	Major General
SS-Brigadeführer	Generalmajor	Major General	Brigadier General
SS-Oberführer	–	Brigadier	–
SS-Standartenführer	Oberst	Colonel	Colonel
SS-Obersturmbannführer	Oberstleutnant	Lieutenant Colonel	Lieutenant Colonel
SS-Sturmbannführer	Major	Major	Major
SS-Hauptsturmführer	Hauptmann	Captain	Captain
SS-Obersturmführer	Oberleutnant	First Lieutenant	First Lieutenant
SS-Untersturmführer	Leutnant	Second Lieutenant	Second Lieutenant
SS-Sturmscharführer	Stabsoberfeldwebel	Regimental Sergeant Major (Warrant Officer Class 1)	Sergeant Major
–	Oberfähnrich	–	Senior Officer Candidate
SS-Hauptscharführer	Oberfeldwebel	Staff Sergeant Major (Warrant Officer Class 1)	Master Sergeant
SS-Oberscharführer	Feldwebel	Warrant Officer Class 2	Technical Sergeant
–	Fähnrich	Ensign	Officer Candidate
SS-Scharführer	Unterfeldwebel	Staff Sergeant	Staff Sergeant
SS-Unterscharführer	Unteroffizier	Sergeant	Sergeant
–	Stabsgefreiter	Corporal (senior)	–
–	Obergefreiter	Corporal	Corporal

SS, Wehrmacht, British Army, US Army

SS	Wehrmacht	British Army	US Army
SS-Rottenführer	Gefreiter	Lance Corporal	Acting Corporal
SS-Sturmmann	Obersoldat	Private (senior)	Private First Class
SS-Mann	Soldat	Private	Private
SS-Anwärter	–	–	–

Sources: SS/Wehrmacht ranks: Heinz Antzt, *Mörder in Uniform: Organisationen, die zu Vollstreckern nationalsozialistischer Verbrechen wurden* (Munich: Kindler, 1979). Wehrmacht/US army ranks: Tim Ripley, *The German Army in World War II, 1939–1945* (Hoboken: Taylor and Francis, 2014). Wehrmacht/British army ranks: Ben H. Shepherd, *Hitler's Soldiers: The German Army in the Third Reich* (New Haven: Yale University Press, 2017).

Security Police (SIPO)
Sicherheitspolizei (SIPO)
Chef der deutschen Polizei / Chief of the German Police
Chef der SIPO / Chief of the SIPO
Kriminaldirigent
Reichskriminaldirektor
Regierungs- und Kriminaldirektor
Oberregierungs- und Kriminalrat
Regierungs- und Kriminalrat
Kriminaldirektor
Kriminalrat / detective chief superintendent
Kriminalkommissar / detective superintendent
Kriminalinspektor / detective inspector
Kriminalobersekretär / detective chief sergeant
Kriminalsekretär / detective sergeant
Kriminaloberassistent / detective chief constable
Kriminalassistent / detective constable
Kriminalassistentenanwärter / detective constable candidate

Source: Hans-Christian Harten, *Die weltanschauliche Schulung der Polizei im Nationalsozialismus* (Paderborn: Ferdinand Schöningh, 2018).

Chronology

Date	General	Denmark	Norway
January–May 1942	**20 January** At the Wannsee Conference German officials discuss the coordination and implementation of the murder of the European Jews.	**15 January** The Reich Foreign Office demands the introduction of anti-Jewish laws in Denmark based on the German model. The Reich Plenipotentiary refuses to comply and points out the Danes' readiness to cooperate with the Germans.	
June 1942	**11 June** The officials in charge of Jewish affairs for Paris, Brussels, and The Hague meet to plan deportations from Western Europe. The deportation figures decided on at the meeting are revised on 22 June.		

Netherlands	Belgium	Luxembourg	France
		23 April 24 Jews are deported from Luxembourg to Lublin via Trier and Stuttgart.	**27 March** The first deportation train from the Compiègne and Drancy camps takes 1,112 persons to Auschwitz. **6 May** Heydrich announces in Paris that stateless Jews will be removed from the occupied zone and transported to the East.
26 June The Central Office for Jewish Emigration in Amsterdam announces the conscription of Jews 'for labour deployment in Germany'.	**13 June–12 September** More than 2,250 Jews are deported to northern France for forced labour.		**5 June** The second transport to Auschwitz leaves Compiègne camp with 1,000 persons on board. **16 June** German-French negotiations on the deportation of 10,000 stateless Jews from the unoccupied zone begin. **22–28 June** More than 3,000 people from the Drancy, Pithiviers, and Beaune-La-Rolande camps are deported to Auschwitz.

Date	General	Denmark	Norway
July 1942			
August 1942	**13 August** Switzerland closes its borders because of the growing numbers of refugees from France.		**13 August–2 September** The Security Police arrest 11 Jews, including the chief rabbi of Oslo, from their holiday locations.

Netherlands	Belgium	Luxembourg	France
1 July Westerbork becomes a German-controlled transit camp. **14 July** 500 Jews are taken hostage in the course of a round-up in Amsterdam to force others to comply with the deportation orders. **15 July** The first deportation train leaves Westerbork. **25 July** From exile, Prime Minister Gerbrandy condemns the beginning of the deportations. **26 July** An open letter protesting against the deportation of Jews is read from the pulpits in Dutch churches.	**15 July** The Association of Jews in Belgium is tasked with initiating 'labour deployment to Germany' by issuing summonses. Mechelen transit camp is established. **25 July** Resistance fighters raid the office of the Association of Jews in Belgium to burn registration cards.	**12 July** A third transport from Luxembourg with 24 Jews on board passes through Chemnitz, presumably on its way to Auschwitz. **26–28 July** Two transports with a total of 181 Jews from Cinqfontaines/Fünfbrunnen on board leave Luxembourg for Theresienstadt.	**1 July** Eichmann briefly visits Paris. **16–17 July** The French police arrest almost 13,000 stateless Jews in Paris. More than 8,000 of them are confined in the Vélodrome d'Hiver sports stadium; the others are deported to Auschwitz on 19 July.
	4 August The first deportation train leaves Mechelen for Auschwitz.	**Late August** The German occupiers violently quell strikes protesting against the conscription of young Luxembourgers into the Wehrmacht.	**7–13 August** 3,472 stateless Jews held in internment camps in the unoccupied zone are handed over to the Germans.

Date	General	Denmark	Norway
September 1942	**September 1942–February 1943** Battle of Stalingrad.	**Late September–early October** Renthe-Fink is dismissed as Reich plenipotentiary and replaced by Werner Best.	
October 1942			**6–7 October** In Trondheim and the surrounding area all male Jews over the age of 15 are arrested.

Netherlands	Belgium	Luxembourg	France
	15 August–October Large-scale roundups in Antwerp, Brussels, and Liège. **29 August** Robert Holzinger of the Association of Jews in Belgium is assassinated by Jewish communists.		**23 August** The Roman Catholic Archbishop of Toulouse orders a letter to be read aloud in churches which condemns the handing over of the Jews. **26 August** The French police arrest 6,600 stateless Jews in the unoccupied zone.
	September The Jewish Defence Committee is established. **24 September–3 October** Leading members of the Association of Jews in Belgium are imprisoned in Breendonk. **30 September** Reeder bans Belgian police units from taking part in roundups of Jews.		**2 September** The handing over of Jews from the unoccupied zone leads to growing unrest in the French population.
2–3 October The Jewish labour camps in the Netherlands are disbanded; inmates and their families are deported.	**6 October** The Military Commander announces the conscription of adult Belgian men and women for forced labour in Germany.		

Date	General	Denmark	Norway
			26 October All male Jews over the age of 15 are arrested by the Norwegian State Police by order of the occupation authorities. The Law on the Confiscation of Assets of Jews is promulgated.
November 1942	**8 November** Allied troops land in Morocco and Algeria.		**17 November** The Law on the Compulsory Registration of Jews defines the term 'Jew'. **26 November** Mass arrests throughout Norway; 532 Jews are deported to Auschwitz.
December 1942	**17 December** Twelve Allied governments issue a joint declaration condemning the extermination of the Jewish population in Europe.		**14 December** Jewish spouses in 'mixed marriages' are arrested.
January 1943			

Netherlands	Belgium	Luxembourg	France
	30 October 240 Jews escape from deportation trains to Auschwitz.		
			11 November German and Italian troops occupy southern France. **Mid November** The French border with Spain is closed and subsequently guarded by German police, Feldgendarmerie, and customs officials.
16 December The process of moving 500 ‘protected Jews’ to Barneveld camp begins.			**12 December** Identity cards of Jews in the southern zone are marked with a special stamp.
5 January Vught camp is established.	**15 January** Deportations are resumed after being suspended since 31 October.		**22–27 January** Thousands of people are arrested in Marseilles, transferred to the occupied zone, and interned there.

Date	General	Denmark	Norway
February 1943			**24 February** 158 Jews previously interned in Norway are deported.

Netherlands	Belgium	Luxembourg	France
21 January The Jewish psychiatric institution Het Apeldoornsche Bosch is closed down and around 1,000 inmates and staff are deported to Auschwitz.			The Jews among them are deported to occupied Eastern Europe in late March 1943. The city's port area is destroyed soon afterwards.
17 February The Catholic bishops publish a pastoral letter which condemns the general introduction of forced labour and the deportation of the Jews.	**18 February** In exile in Portugal, Maurice Benedictus writes two detailed reports for the Belgian government in exile about the persecution of the Jewish population in Belgium since 1940.		**9 February** Deportations from France to Auschwitz are resumed. **10 February** The French police arrest 1,549 stateless Jews in the mistaken belief that this will prevent the deportation of French Jews to the East. **16 February** The Vichy government orders the conscription of non-Jewish Frenchmen for forced labour in Germany. **20–24 February** The French police arrest around 1,800 foreign Jewish men in the southern zone; they are taken to Drancy for deportation to the East.

Date	General	Denmark	Norway
March 1943	**2 March** On the instructions of Foreign Minister Ribbentrop, 30,000 foreign Jews, most of them from Western Europe, are to be temporarily exempted from deportation so that they can be exchanged for interned Germans.	**23 March** In the only democratic elections in a German-occupied country, the great majority vote for a policy of negotiation with the Germans.	
April 1943			

Netherlands	Belgium	Luxembourg	France
2 March–20 July Sobibor extermination camp becomes the main destination for deportation trains from the Netherlands. **27 March** A resistance group attacks the office of the Amsterdam population register. **30 March** Jews are required to leave the provinces of Friesland, Groningen, Drenthe, Overijssel, Gelderland, Limburg, North Brabant, and Zeeland.	**March** The Independence Front distributes the first underground newspapers. The German police set up an office for issuing 'Aryan certificates'.		**4, 6, 23, and 25 March** More than 4,000 people are deported to Sobibor on four transports. All other deportation trains go to Auschwitz.
13 April Jews are now permitted to live only in Amsterdam or in Westerbork or Vught camps. **29 April–4 May** The announcement by the German occupiers that all former Dutch soldiers will be recaptured and made to perform forced labour results in a strike.	**19 April** Members of different resistance groups attack the 20th deportation train. More than 200 Jews manage to escape from the transport before the train reaches the German border.	**6 April** 99 Jews from Luxembourg are deported to Theresienstadt on the last of the larger transports.	**3 April** Himmler meets with police chief Bousquet in Paris.

Date	General	Denmark	Norway
May 1943			
June 1943			
July 1943	**10 July** Allied troops land in Sicily.		
August 1943		A wave of strikes sweeps the country and resistance groups intensify their sabotage activities.	

Netherlands	Belgium	Luxembourg	France
21 May The Jewish Council receives the order that around half of its employees are to be deported. **25/26 May** 3,000 Jews are arrested during a roundup in Amsterdam and taken to Westerbork.			**9 May** Alois Brunner is named head of a Sonderkommando tasked with organizing the deportation of Jews to the East.
6–7 June A transport of children leaves Vught camp for Sobibor via Westerbork.	**28–29 June** Some Jews with Belgian citizenship are released from Mechelen transit camp.	**17 June** The head of the Council of Elders and his family are deported to Theresienstadt. The only Jews left in the country are those who are in 'mixed marriages' or have gone underground.	
	26 July The Military Commander agrees to have Belgian Jews included in the deportations.		**21 July** André Baur is the first of a number of leading figures of the UGIF to be interned in Drancy.
			Early August Head of Government Laval refuses to strip Jews naturalized in France since 1927 of their citizenship.

Date	General	Denmark	Norway
		28 August Best gives the government an ultimatum and demands the death penalty for saboteurs. **29 August** The government resigns and the leading state secretaries take over the administration. The leaders of the Copenhagen Jewish Community are arrested.	
September 1943	**3 September** Italy signs an armistice with the Allies, which is made public on 8 September.	**17 September** Hitler decides that the Danish Jews will also be deported; German police seize the membership lists of the Jewish Community in Copenhagen. **28 September** The attaché at the German legation alerts leading politicians to the impending deportation. They inform the Jewish Community.	
October 1943		**1 October** Arrests in Denmark begin at 9 p.m. The Swedish government declares that it will allow Danish Jews to enter Sweden.	

Netherlands	Belgium	Luxembourg	France
			In response, the German police decide that they will no longer differentiate between French and foreign Jews.
29 September Last major roundup in Amsterdam. The Jewish Council is dissolved and Barneveld camp is closed.	**3/4 September** Belgian Jews are arrested in the course of roundups in Brussels and Antwerp. Nine people suffocate during the transport from Antwerp to Mechelen.		**8 September** Wehrmacht units occupy what was the Italian-occupied zone. **10 September** Alois Brunner and his Sonderkommando arrive in Nice and begin a planned operation to arrest Jews.
	9 October The Belgian secretaries general lodge a protest with the Military Commander against the arrests in early September 1943,		**5 October** Corsica, occupied by the Wehrmacht since early September, is liberated by resistance groups, Free French Forces, and Italian soldiers.

Date	General	Denmark	Norway
		3 October The Lutheran bishop of Copenhagen issues a pastoral letter condemning the persecution of the Jews which is read aloud in all churches. **13 October** A further 175 Jews are deported.	
November 1943	**28 November–1 December** Tehran Conference of Allied leaders on military strategy and plans for the post-war world order.	**2 November** Eichmann visits Copenhagen; it is agreed that persons over 60 will be spared, deported 'half-Jews' and Jewish spouses in 'mixed marriages' will be returned, and those deported from Denmark will stay in Theresienstadt.	
December 1943			
January 1944			

Netherlands	Belgium	Luxembourg	France
	the treatment of the victims, and the confiscation of the residences of arrested Jews.		
15 November Jewish prisoners are deported from Vught camp to Auschwitz and to Westerbork.			**13 November** After the Germans block his radio broadcast, Head of State Marshal Pétain embarks on a 'strike'.
			Late December The French government in Vichy is restructured under German pressure.
January–September Deportation transports to Auschwitz, Theresienstadt, and Bergen-Belsen.			**4 January** The German police arrest French Jews who had previously been spared in Laon, Saint-Quentin, and Amiens.

Date	General	Denmark	Norway
February 1944		**End of February** The first food parcels for the Danish prisoners in Theresienstadt are dispatched.	
June 1944	**6 June** Allied troops land in Normandy.	**21 June** A Red Cross delegation and Danish representatives visit Theresienstadt.	
July 1944	**20 July** Stauffenberg assassination attempt on Hitler.		

Netherlands	Belgium	Luxembourg	France
			Early January Bousquet is replaced by Joseph Darnand as police chief and by Antoine Lemoine as state secretary of the Ministry of the Interior.
3 June The last inmates of Vught camp (the Philips work detail) are deported. **30 June–10 July** Dutch Jewish prisoners from Bergen-Belsen are taken to Palestine in exchange for interned German nationals.			
	5 July The German police conduct a last large-scale roundup of Jews with Belgian citizenship in Liège. **31 July** The last deportation train leaves Mechelen.		**21–25 July** Alois Brunner has 233 children from the UGIF homes sent to Drancy. Most are murdered in Auschwitz a few days later.

Date	General	Denmark	Norway
August 1944			
September 1944	**17–27 September** Allied troops fail to cross the Rhine.		
October 1944			
December 1944	**16 December** The Wehrmacht launches the offensive known as the Battle of the Bulge in the Ardennes. It collapses eight days later after Allied troops counter-attack.		

Netherlands	Belgium	Luxembourg	France
			17 August The last deportation train leaves Drancy for Buchenwald along with Alois Brunner's Sonderkommando. **19–26 August** Liberation of Paris.
13 September Last transport from Westerbork. **Mid–late September** The southern part of the Netherlands is liberated.	**Early September** Liberation of Antwerp and Brussels. **8 September** The Belgian government returns from exile.		
19 September–May 1945 Dutch railway workers go on strike. In response, the German occupiers stop food and fuel deliveries to the West until December.			
December 1944–April 1945 'Hunger Winter' famine.			

Date	General	Denmark	Norway
January 1945	**27 January** Soviet troops liberate Auschwitz.		
February 1945	**4–12 February** At the Yalta conference, the Allied leaders decide on an outline for a peace settlement in Europe.		
April 1945		**15 April** The White Buses take Danish prisoners from Theresienstadt to Sweden.	
May 1945	**5 May** German troops surrender in north-western Germany, Denmark, and the Netherlands. **8 May** The German Reich surrenders.		**2 May** Interned Jews from 'mixed marriages' are able to leave Norway and go to Sweden.

Netherlands	Belgium	Luxembourg	France
5 February 433 Dutch Jews are taken from Theresienstadt to Switzerland. **12 February** Westerbork camp is liberated.			

Abbreviations

§	section (of a German law, code, or regulation)
§§	sections (of a German law, code, or regulation)
AA	Auswärtiges Amt (German Federal Foreign Office)
AD	Archives départementales
AfZ-ETH Zürich	Archiv für Zeitgeschichte, ETH (Eidgenössische Technische Hochschule) Zürich (Archives of Contemporary History, ETH Zurich)
AG	Aktiengesellschaft (public limited company)
AHAP	Archives historiques de l'archevêché de Paris (Historical Archives of the Archdiocese of Paris)
AIU	Alliance israélite universelle
AJ	Armée juive (Jewish Army)
AJA	American Jewish Archives
AJB/VJB, A.J.B./V.J.B.	Association des Juifs en Belgique / Vereeniging van Joden in België (Association of Jews in Belgium)
AN	Archives nationales, Paris
ANLux	Archives nationales de Luxembourg
ANOM	Archives nationales d'outre-mer (Overseas Territories Archives)
ARP	Anti-Revolutionaire Partij (Anti-Revolutionary Party)
Art.	article (of a law, code, or regulation)
BA-MA	Bundesarchiv-Militärarchiv (German Federal Archives/Military Archives), Freiburg
BArch	Bundesarchiv (German Federal Archives), Berlin
BBC	British Broadcasting Corporation
BCRA	Bureau central de renseignements et d'action (Central Bureau of Intelligence and Operations)
Bd.	Band (volume)
BdS	Befehlshaber der Sicherheitspolizei (Senior Commander of the Security Police)
CAR	Comité d'assistance aux réfugiés (Committee for Assistance to Refugees), France
CBJB	Comité voor Bijzondere Joodsche Belangen (Committee for Special Jewish Interests), Netherlands
CC	carbon copy
CDJ/JVC, C.D.J./J.V.C.	Comité de défense des juifs / Joods Verdedigingscomité (Jewish Defence Committee), Belgium
CegeSoma	Centre d'étude guerre et société / Studie- en Documentatiecentrum Oorlog en Hedendaagse Maatschappij (Study and Documentation Centre for War and Contemporary Society), Brussels
CHF	currency symbol for Swiss francs
CIE	Centre d'information et d'études (Centre for Research and Intelligence), Algiers
CJV	Comité voor Joodsche Vluchtelingen (Committee for Jewish Refugees), Amsterdam
CNI	Commissariat national à l'intérieur (National Commissariat of the Interior)
CPN	Communistische Partij van Nederland (Communist Party of the Netherlands)

CSU	Christlich-Soziale Union (Christian Social Union)
DJM	Dansk Jødisk Museum (The Danish Jewish Museum)
DNB	Deutsches Nachrichtenbüro (German News Agency)
DSK	Devisenschutzkommando (Foreign Exchange Protection Commando)
EIF	Éclaireurs israélites de France (Jewish Scouts)
Emigdirect	Emigrationsdirektorium (Emigration Directorate), Berlin
ETRA	Eisenbahntransportabteilung (Wehrmacht Railway Transport Department)
FK	Feldkommandantur (district headquarters of the German military administration)
Fl.	currency symbol for Dutch guilders
fol.	folio (of an archival source)
FPF	Fédération protestante de France (French Protestant Federation)
Fr., Frs.	currency symbols for French or Belgian francs
Fr. b.	currency symbol for Belgian francs
FSJF	Fédération des sociétés juives de France (Federation of Jewish Societies in France)
FTP-MOI	Francs-tireurs et partisans – Main-d'œuvre immigrée (French partisan organization)
Gestapa	Geheimes Staatspolizeiamt (Gestapo Central Office)
Gestapo	Geheime Staatspolizei (Secret State Police)
GGD	Gemeentelijke gezondheidsdienst (Municipal Health Service), Netherlands
GmbH	Gesellschaft mit beschränkter Haftung (private limited company)
GTE	Groupements de travailleurs étrangers (Foreign Labourer Groups)
HIAS	Hebrew Immigrant Aid Society
HICEM	acronym for three Jewish advocacy organizations: *HI*AS, *IC*A, and *EM*igdirect
HL-senteret	Senter for studier av Holocaust og livssynsminoriteter (Norwegian Centre for Holocaust and Minority Studies)
HSSPF	Höherer SS und Polizeiführer (Higher SS and Police Leader)
ICA/JCA	Jewish Colonization Association, Paris
ICRC	International Committee of the Red Cross
IfZ-Archives	Archiv des Instituts für Zeitgeschichte München-Berlin (Archives of the Leibniz Institute for Contemporary History)
JCC	Joodsche Coördinatie Commissie (Jewish Coordination Committee), Netherlands
JDC, J.D.C.	American Jewish Joint Distribution Committee
JHM	Joods Historisch Museum (Jewish Historical Museum), Amsterdam
JO	*Journal officiel de la République française* (law gazette of the French government)
JTA	Jewish Telegraphic Agency
KdS	Kommandeur der Sicherheitspolizei und des SD (Commander of the Security Police and the SD)
KJV	King James Version
KKL	Keren Kayemeth LeIsraël (Jewish National Fund)
LBIJMB	Leo Baeck Institut Archiv, Jüdisches Museum Berlin (Leo Baeck Institute Archives at the Jewish Museum Berlin)
LVF	Légion des volontaires français contre le bolchévisme (Legion of French Volunteers Against Bolshevism)
MBF	Militärbefehlshaber in Belgien und Nordfrankreich (Military Commander in Belgium and Northern France)

MJB/JMB	Musée juif de Belgique / Joods Museum van België (Jewish Museum of Belgium), Brussels
NATO	North Atlantic Treaty Organization
NB	*nota bene* (take note)
NCO	non-commissioned officer
NIOD	Nederlands Instituut voor oorloogs-, holocaust- en genocidestudies (Netherlands Institute for War, Holocaust and Genocide Studies), Amsterdam
NOU	*Norges Offentlige Utredninger* (Official Norwegian Reports)
NRA	Riksarkivet (National Archives of Norway), Oslo
NS	Nasjonal Samling (National Union), Norway
NSB	Nationaal-Socialistische Beweging (National Socialist Movement), Netherlands
NSDAP	Nationalsozialistische Deutsche Arbeiterpartei (National Socialist German Workers' Party)
NSNAP	Nationaal-Socialistische Nederlandsche Arbeiderspartij (National Socialist Dutch Workers' Party)
NSV	Nationalsozialistische Volkswohlfahrt (National Socialist People's Welfare Organization)
N.V.	Naamloze vennootschap (public limited company in the Netherlands and Belgium)
OCCI	Comité d'organisation des industries chimiques (Organizing Committee for the Chemical Industry), Paris
OCIS	Œuvre centrale israélite de secours (Central Jewish Welfare Organization)
OFK	Oberfeldkommandantur (regional headquarters of the military administration)
OJC	Organisation juive de combat (Jewish Army)
OKW	Oberkommando der Wehrmacht (Wehrmacht High Command)
ORT	Russian acronym for the 'Society for Trades and Agricultural Labour'
OSE	Œuvre de secours aux enfants (Children's Aid Society)
OT	Organization Todt
PA AA	Politisches Archiv des Auswärtigen Amtes (Political Archive of the German Federal Foreign Office)
PCF	Parti Communiste Français (French Communist Party)
PMJ	*The Persecution and Murder of the European Jews by Nazi Germany, 1933–1945*
p.p.	*per procurationem* (by proxy)
PPA	Parti du Peuple Algérien (Algerian People's Party)
PPF	Parti Populaire Français (French Popular Party)
PQJ	Police aux questions juives (Police for Jewish Affairs), France
RAF	Royal Air Force
RC	Reichskommissar (Reich Commissioner)
RM	currency symbol for Reichsmark
RNP	Rassemblement national populaire (National Popular Rally), France
RSHA	Reichssicherheitshauptamt (Reich Security Main Office)
SA	Sturmabteilung (Storm Troopers)
SD	Sicherheitsdienst (SS Security Service)
SDAP	Sociaal-Democratische Arbeiderspartij (Social Democratic Workers' Party), Netherlands
SFIO	Section française de l'Internationale ouvrière (French Section of the Workers' International)

SHPF	Bibliothèque de la Société de l'histoire du protestantisme français (Library of the Society for the History of French Protestantism), Paris
SNCF	Société Nationale des Chemins de Fer (French National Railways)
SPRL	Société privée à responsabilité limitée (Belgian equivalent to a private limited company)
SS	Schutzstaffel (Protection Squadron)
STO	service du travail obligatoire (mandatory labour service)
Str.	Straße (street)
trans.	translated by
UGIF	Union générale des Israélites de France (General Union of French Jews)
UN	United Nations
USHMM	United States Holocaust Memorial Museum
VdB	Volksdeutsche Bewegung (Ethnic German Movement)
VOBl	*Verordnungsblatt* (law gazette)
VOBl-BNF	*Verordnungsblatt des Militärbefehlshabers in Belgien und Nordfrankreich* (Law Gazette of the Military Commander in Belgium and Northern France)
VOBl-F	*Verordnungsblatt des Militärbefehlshabers in Frankreich* (Law Gazette of the Military Commander in France)
VOBl-L	*Verordnungsblatt für Luxemburg* (Law Gazette for Luxembourg)
VOBl-NL	*Verordnungsblatt für die besetzten niederländischen Gebiete* (Law Gazette for the Occupied Dutch Territories)
VNV	Vlaams Nationaal Verbond (Flemish National Association)
WA	Weerbaarheidsafdeling (National Socialist Defence Section), Netherlands
WHO	World Health Organization
WJC	World Jewish Congress
WVHA	Wirtschafts-Verwaltungshauptamt (SS Business and Administration Main Office)
YIVO	Institute for Jewish Research, New York
YMCA	Young Men's Christian Association
YVA	Yad Vashem Archives
YWCA	Young Women's Christian Association

List of Archives, Sources, and Literature Cited

Primary Sources

Archives

American Jewish Archives (AJA), Cincinnati
American Jewish Joint Distribution Committee (JDC) Archives, New York
Archief Sint-Sixtusabdij (Archive of St Sixtus Abbey), Westvleteren
Archiv des Instituts für Zeitgeschichte München – Berlin (IfZ-Archives, Archives of the Leibniz Institute for Contemporary History), Munich
Archiv für Zeitgeschichte, ETH (Eidgenössische Technische Hochschule) Zürich (AfZ-ETH, Archives of Contemporary History, ETH Zurich)
Archive of the Royal Palace, Brussels
Archives de l'Alliance israélite universelle (AIU), Paris
Archives du Consistoire Central (Archives of the Central Consistory), Paris
Archives départementales (AD) de l'Ain (Archives of the Ain département), Bourg-en-Bresse
Archives départementales (AD) des Bouches-du-Rhône (Archives of the Bouches-du-Rhône département), Marseilles
Archives départementales (AD) de la Charente-Maritime (Archives of the Charente-Maritime département), La Rochelle
Archives départementales (AD) du Nord (Archives of the Nord département), Lille
Archives d'État de Genève (State Archives of Geneva), Geneva
Archives générales du Royaume / Algemeen Rijksarchief (National Archives of Belgium), Brussels
Archives historiques de l'archevêché de Paris (AHAP, Historical Archives of the Archdiocese of Paris)
Archives nationales (AN), Paris
Archives nationales de Luxembourg (ANLux)
Archives nationales d'outre-mer (ANOM, Overseas Territories Archives), Aix-en-Provence
Archives de l'Œuvre de secours aux enfants (OSE, Children's Aid Society), Paris
Bestuursarchief Gemeente Beilen (Administrative Archives of the Municipality of Beilen), Midden-Drenthe
Bibliotheca Rosenthaliana, Amsterdam
Bibliothèque de la Société de l'histoire du protestantisme français (SHPF, Library of the Society for the History of French Protestantism), Paris
Bundesarchiv (BArch, German Federal Archives), Berlin
Bundesarchiv-Militärarchiv (BA-MA, German Federal Archives/Military Archives), Freiburg
Central Zionist Archives (CZA), Jerusalem
Centre d'Étude Guerre et Société / Studie- en Documentatiecentrum Oorlog en Hedendaagse Maatschappij (CegeSoma, Study and Documentation Centre for War and Contemporary Society), Brussels
Dansk Jødisk Museum (DJM, The Danish Jewish Museum), Copenhagen
Directie-generaal Oorlogsslachtoffers / Direction générale victimes de guerre (Directorate-General for War Victims), Brussels
Felix-Nussbaum-Haus, Osnabrück
Fondation Paul-Henri Spaak / Paul-Henri Spaak Stichting (Paul-Henri Spaak Foundation), Brussels
Frihedsmuseets Dokumentarkiv (Document Archives of the Museum of Danish Resistance), Copenhagen
Herinneringscentrum Kamp Westerbork (Westerbork Memorial Centre), Hooghalen
Het Utrechts Archief (The Utrecht Archives), Utrecht
Imperial War Museum, London

Joods Historisch Museum (JHM, Jewish Historical Museum), Amsterdam

Kazerne Dossin, Memorial, Museum and Research Centre on Holocaust and Human Rights, Mechelen

Københavns Stadsarkiv (Copenhagen City Archives)

La Contemporaine: Bibliothèque, archives, musée des mondes contemporaines (La Contemporaine: Library, Archives, Museum of Contemporary History), Nanterre

Landeshauptarchiv Schwerin (Schwerin Regional Main Archive)

Lavon Institute, Tel Aviv

Leo Baeck Institute Archives at the Jewish Museum Berlin (LBIJMB)

Mémorial de la Shoah, Paris

Musée Juif de Belgique / Joods Museum van België (MJB/JMB, Jewish Museum of Belgium), Brussels

Nationaal Archief (National Archives of the Netherlands), The Hague

National Archives and Records Administration (NARA), Washington, DC

Nederlands Instituut voor oorlogs-, holocaust- en genocidestudies (NIOD, Netherlands Institute for War, Holocaust and Genocide Studies), Amsterdam

Norges Hjemmefrontmuseum (NHM, Resistance Museum), Oslo

Politisches Archiv des Auswärtigen Amts (PA AA, Political Archives of the German Federal Foreign Office), Berlin

Rigsarkivet (Danish National Archives), Copenhagen

Riksarkivet (NRA, National Archives of Norway), Oslo

Riksarkivet (Swedish National Archives), Stockholm

Royal Archives, Windsor

Sammlung Mahn- und Gedenkstätte Düsseldorf (Memorial to Victims of the Nazi Regime, Düsseldorf)

Schweizerisches Bundesarchiv (BAR, Swiss Federal Archives), Bern

Senter for studier av Holocaust og livssynsminoriteter (HL-senteret, Norwegian Centre for Holocaust and Minority Studies), Oslo

Simon Wiesenthal Center Library and Archives, Los Angeles

Wiener Library, London

United States Holocaust Memorial Museum (USHMM), Washington, DC

Yad Vashem Archives (YVA), Jerusalem

YIVO Institute for Jewish Research, New York

Newspapers, Magazines, and Official Bulletins

Algemeen Handelsblad

Aufbau

België Vrij

Brüsseler Zeitung

Bulletin de la Fédération des sociétés juives d'Algérie

Bulletin du Front de l'Indépendance

Bulletin de l'Union générale des Israélites de France

Dagens Nyheter

De frie Danske

De Telegraaf

De Vrije Gedachte

De Waarheid

De Zwarte Soldaat

Deutsche Zeitung in den Niederlanden

Fraternité: Organe du Mouvement national contre le racisme (zone Sud)

Fritt Folk

Gringoire

Het Joodsche Weekblad

Het Parool

Israelitisches Wochenblatt

Je suis partout

Jewish Bulletin

Jewish Chronicle

Jewish Echo

Journal officiel

Krakauer Zeitung

La Gerbe

L'Action française

L'Ami du peuple

Le Drapeau rouge

Le Matin

Le Pays réel

Le Petit Parisien

Luxembourg Bulletin
Manchester Guardian
Nederlands Algemeen Politieblad
New York Times
Norsk Lovtidend
Norsk Tidend
Notre voix
Reichsgesetzblatt
Storm SS: Blad der Nederlandsche SS
The Times
Trouw
Unzer Wort
Verordnungsblatt des Militärbefehlhabers für Belgien und Nordfrankreich (VOBl-BNF)
Verordnungsblatt für die besetzten niederländischen Gebiete (VOBl-NL)
Verordnungsblatt des Militärbefehlshabers für Frankreich (VOBl-F)
Verordnungsblatt für Luxemburg (VOBl-L)
Vrijheid, Orgaan van de VBJ, Vrije Belgische Jeugd / Jeunesse belge libre
Vrij Nederland – je maintiendrai: Onafhankelijk weekblad voor alle Nederlanders

Diaries, Letters, and Memoirs

Berr, Hélène, *The Journal of Hélène Berr*, trans. David Bellos (London: MacLehose Press, 2008).

Blüdnikow, Bent, *Min fars flugt: Jødiske skæbner i oktober 1943* (Copenhagen: Gyldendals Bogklubber, 2013).

Bolle, Mirjam, *Letters Never Sent: Amsterdam, Westerbork, Bergen-Belsen*, trans. Laura Vroomen (Jerusalem: Yad Vashem, 2014 [Dutch edn, 2003]).

Burger, Jaap, *Oorlogsdagboek*, ed. Chris van Esterik (Amsterdam: Bert Bakker, 1996).

Cahen, Bob, *Brieven uit de trein Westerbork – Auschwitz (enkele reis)* (Haarlem: Tuindorp, 1996).

Cahen, J., *Ergens in Nederland: Brief uit kamp Westerbork, 1 november 1942*, ed. Dirk Mulder (Hooghalen: Herinneringscentrum Kamp Westerbork, 1988).

Cohen, David, *Voorzitter van de Joodse Raad: De herinneringen van David Cohen (1941–1943)*, ed. Erik Somers (Zutphen: Walburg Pers, 2010).

Durlacher, Gerhard, *Stripes in the Sky* (London: Serpent's Tail, 1991).

Eberhard, Pascale (ed.), *Der Überlebenskampf jüdischer Deportierter aus Luxemburg und der Trierer Region im Getto Litzmannstadt: Briefe Mai 1942* (Saarbrücken: Blattlausverlag, 2012).

Frank, Anne, *The Diary of a Young Girl: The Definitive Edition*, ed. Otto H. Frank and Mirjam Pressler, trans. Susan Massotty (London: Penguin, 2007).

Flinker, Moses, *Young Moshe's Diary: The Spiritual Torment of a Jewish Boy in Nazi Europe* (Jerusalem: Yad Vashem, 1971).

Friediger, Max, *Theresienstadt* (Copenhagen: Clausen, 1947).

Friedländer, Saul, *When Memory Comes* (New York: Avon Books, 1980).

Gans Premsela, Jenny, *Vluchtweg: Aan de bezetter ontsnapt* (Baarn: Bosch en Keuning, 1990).

Gasquet, Frédéric, *La Lettre de mon père: Une famille de Tunis dans l'enfer nazi* (Paris: Le Félin, 2006).

Gronowski, Simon, *L'Enfant du 20e convoi* (Brussels: Pire, 2005).

Halpern, Georges, *En souvenir de Georgy: Lettres de la Maison d'Izieu, 1935–1944*, ed. Serge Klarsfeld (Paris: Aperture, 2002).

Heumann, Hugo, *Erlebtes – Erlittenes: Von Mönchengladbach über Luxemburg nach Theresienstadt: Tagebuch eines deutsch-jüdischen Emigranten*, ed. Germaine Goetzinger and Marc Schoentgen (Mersch: Centre nationale de littérature, 2007).

Hillesum, Etty, *The Complete Works, 1941–1943*, ed. Klaas A. D. Smelik and Meins G. S. Coetsier, trans. from Dutch and German by Arnold J. Pomerans (Maastricht: Shaker, 2014).

Hirtz, Ginette, *Les Hortillonnages sous la grêle* (Paris: Mercure de France, 1982).

Jakobs, Rose, *De roos die nooit bloeide: Dagboek van een onderduikster, 1942–1944* (Amsterdam: Arbeiderspers, 1999).

Klein, Claude, 'Un témoignage des années d'Occupation: de Grenoble à la Suisse', *Esprit*, no. 349 (Nov. 2008), pp. 183–196.

Koker, David, *At the Edge of the Abyss: A Concentration Camp Diary, 1943–1944*, ed. Robert Jan van Pelt, trans. Michiel Horn (Evanston, IL: Northwestern University Press, 2012).

Koker, David, *Dagboek geschreven in Vught* (Amsterdam: G.A. van Oorschot, 1977).

Krivopissko, Guy, *La Vie à en mourir: Lettres de fusillés (1941–1944)* (Paris: Tallandier, 2003).

Liebman, Marcel, *Né Juif: Une enfance juive pendant la guerre* (Paris: Duculot, 1977).

Liempt, Ad van, *Frieda: Verslag van een gelijmd leven* (Hooghalen: Herinneringscentrum Kamp Westerbork, 2007).

Maier, Ruth, *'Das Leben könnte gut sein': Tagebücher von 1933 bis 1942*, ed. Jan Erik Vold (Munich: Deutsche Verlags-Anstalt, 2008).

Maier, Ruth, *Ruth Maier's Diary: A Jewish Girl's Life in Nazi Europe*, ed. Jan Erik Vold (London: Vintage Books, 2008).

Manen, Henry, *Au fond de l'abîme: Journal du Camp des Milles*, ed. Philippe Joutard (Maisons-Laffitte: Éditions Ampelos, 2013).

Mechanicus, Philip, *In Dépôt: Dagboek uit Westerbork* (Amsterdam: Polak en Gennep, 1964).

Mechanicus, Philip, *Waiting for Death*, trans. Irene R. Gibbons (London: Calder and Boyars, 1968).

Nussbaum, Felix, *Fragezeichen an jeder Straßenecke: Zwölf Briefe*, ed. Peter Junk and Wendelin Zimmer (Bramsche: Rasch, 2003).

Oppenhejm, Ralph, *The Door of Death*, trans. Joyce Tufton (London: The Harvill Press, 1947 [Danish edn, 1945]).

Pinkhof, Detje, *Een dagboek met sprookjes uit Kamp Westerbork* (Haarlem: Tuindorp, 1998).

Rood, Coen, *Onze dagen: Herinneringen aan de jodenvervolging* (Amsterdam: Boom, 2011).

Schapira, Charlotte, *Il faudra que je me souvienne: La déportation des enfants de l'Union générale des Israélites de France* (Paris: L'Harmattan, 1994).

Schelvis, Jules, *Er reed een trein naar Sobibor* (Hooghalen: Herinneringscentrum Kamp Westerbork, 2012).

Schelvis, Jules, *Inside the Gates: An Authentic Story of Two Years in German Concentration Camps, 1943–1945*, trans. Senta Kushkulei-Engelstein and Gerda Baardman (Tricht: Elzenhorst, 1990 [Dutch edn, 1982]).

Schroeter, Kurt, *Tage, die so quälend sind: Aufzeichnungen eines jüdischen Bürgers aus Gröbenzell im besetzten Amsterdam, September 1942–Januar 1943*, ed. Kurt Lehnstaedt (Munich: R. Kovar, 1993).

Silber, Salomon, *Een joods gezin in onderduik: Dagboek* (Kampen: Kok, 1997).

Taieb, Karen (ed.), *Je vous écris du Vél' d'Hiv: Les lettres retrouvées* (Paris: Laffont, 2011).

Vidal-Naquet, Pierre, *Mémoires*, vol. 1: *La brisure et l'attente, 1930–1955* (Paris: Seuil, 2007 [1995]).

Wright, Myrtle, *Norwegian Diary, 1940–1945* (London: Friends Peace and International Relations Committee, 1974).

Wyers, Suzette (ed.), *Als ik wil kan ik duiken … Brieven van Claartje van Aals, verpleegster in de joods psychiatrische inrichting Het Apeldoornsche Bosch* (Amsterdam: Thomas Rap, 1995).

Ziekenoppasser, Hans, 'Stem uit het verleden', *Nieuw Israëlietisch Weekblad*, 147, no. 27 (2012) pp. 68–71.

Zuckermann, Paul, *Berthe chérie: Correspondance clandestine de Paul Zuckermann à sa fiancée. Drancy, août 1941–septembre 1942*, ed. Michel Laffitte (Paris: Éditions du Retour, 2014).

Works Published before 1945

Comité d'information interallié, *La Persécution des juifs: Les conditions de vie dans les territoires occupés* (His Majesty's Stationery Office: London, 1942).

Friediger, Max, *Jødernes historie* (Copenhagen: P. Haase, 1934).

Goudsmit, Sam, *Simcha, de knaap uit Worms* (Amsterdam: Querido, 1936).

Hakker, Joseph, *La Mystérieuse caserne Dossin à Malines: Le camp de déportation des Juifs* (Anvers: Éditions 'Ontwikkeling', 1944).

Verne, Jules, *Hector Servadac*, trans. Ellen E. Frewer (New York: C. Scribner's Sons, 1905 [French edn, 1877]).

Primary Source Collections

Akten zur deutschen auswärtigen Politik 1918–1945 [ADAP], series E: *1941–1945*, vol. 3: *16. Juni bis 30. September 1942* (Göttingen: Vandenhoeck & Ruprecht, 1974).

Akten zur deutschen auswärtigen Politik 1918–1945 [ADAP], series E: 1941–1945, vol. 6: *1. Mai bis 30. September 1943* (Göttingen: Vandenhoeck & Ruprecht, 1974).

Cerf, Paul, *Longtemps j'aurai mémoire: Documents et témoignages sur les Juifs du Grand-Duché de Luxembourg durant la Seconde Guerre mondiale* (Luxembourg: Editions du Letzeburger Land, 1974).

De koningin sprak: Proclamaties en radio-toespraken van H. M. Koningin Wilhelmina 1940–1945, ed. M. G. Schenk and J. B. Th. Spaan (Driebergen: Christelijk Lektuurkontakt, 1985).

Dijkstra, G. J. (ed.), *Gemeente Beilen 1940 bis 1945*, vol. 3 (Beilen: publisher unspecified, 2001).

Documents diplomatiques suisses / Diplomatische Dokumente der Schweiz 1848–1945, vol. 14 (Bern: Chronos, 1997).

Enquêtecommissie Regeringsbeleid 1940–1945: Verslag houdende de uitkomsten van het onderzoek, vol. 6ab ('s-Gravenhage: Staatsdrukkerij- en Uitgeverijbedrijf, 1952).

Foreign Relations of the United States: Diplomatic Papers, 1942, vol. 2, *Europe* (Washington, DC: United States Department of State, 1962).

Foreign Relations of the United States: Diplomatic Papers, 1943, vol. 2, *Europe* (Washington, DC: United States Department of State, 1964).

Friedman, Tôviyyā, *Dokumentensammlung über 'Die Deportierung der Juden aus Norwegen nach Auschwitz'* (Ramat Gan: City Council, 1963).

Het Joodsche Weekblad: Volledige uitgave van alle nummers verschenen van 11/4/1941–28/9/1943 (The Hague: Omniboek, 1979).

Himmler, Heinrich, *Der Dienstkalender Heinrich Himmlers 1941/42*, ed. Peter Witte, Michael Wildt, and Martina Voigt (Hamburg: Christians, 1999).

'Inndragning av jødisk eiendom i Norge under den 2. verdenskrig', *Norges Offentlige Utredninger* [NOU] 1997: 22 (Oslo: Statens forvaltningstjeneste, 1997).

In Memoriam (The Hague: Sdu Publishers, 1995).

Joods Historisch Museum Amsterdam, *Documents of the Persecution of the Dutch Jewry* (Amsterdam: Athenaeum Polak & Van Gennep, 1969).

Klarsfeld, Serge, *Le Calendrier de la persécution des Juifs de France*, vol. 1: *Juillet 1940–août 1942* (Paris: Fayard, 2001).

Klarsfeld, Serge, *Vichy–Auschwitz: Die 'Endlösung der Judenfrage in Frankreich'*, trans. Ahlrich Meyer (Darmstadt: Wissenschaftliche Buchgesellschaft, 2007 [French edn, 2001]).

Klarsfeld, Serge and Maxime Steinberg (eds.), *Die Endlösung der Judenfrage in Belgien: Dokumente* (New York: Klarsfeld Foundation, 1980).

Le Drapeau rouge clandestine: Pages glorieuses de l'histoire du Parti Communiste de Belgique (Brussels: Jacquemotte Foundation, 1971).

Monneray, Henri, *La Persécution des Juifs en France et dans les autres pays de l'Ouest, présentée par la France à Nuremberg* (Paris: Éditions du centre, 1947).

Nationale Kommission für die Veröffentlichung Diplomatischer Dokumente der Schweiz, *Diplomatische Dokumente der Schweiz*, vol. 14 (Bern: Benteli, 1997).

Pope Pius XII, *Discorsi e radiomessaggi di Sua Santità Pio XII*, vol. 4: *Quarto anno di pontificato 2 marzo 1942–1 marzo 1943* (Vatican City: Tipografia Poliglotta Vaticana, 1955).

Veld, N. K. C. A. in 't, *De SS en Nederland: Documenten uit SS-archieven, 1935–1945* (Amsterdam: Nijhof, 1987).

Secondary Literature

Aalders, Gerard, *Nazi Looting: The Plunder of Dutch Jewry during the Second World War* (Oxford: Berg, 2004).

Abitbol, Michel, *The Jews of North Africa during the Second World War* (Detroit: Wayne State University Press, 1989).

Abuys, Guido, *Het eerste transport 15 juli 1942 vanuit kamp Westerbork* (Hooghalen: Herinneringscentrum Kamp Westerbork, 2012).

Abuys, Guido and Dirk Mulder (eds.), *Genezen verklaard voor … Een ziekenhuis in kamp Westerbork, 1939–1945* (Hooghalen: Herinneringscentrum Kamp Westerbork, 2006).

Adler, H. G., *Theresienstadt 1941–1945: The Face of a Coerced Community*, trans. Belinda Cooper (New York: Cambridge University Press, 2017 [German edn, 1955]).

Adriaens, Ward, et al., *Mecheln – Auschwitz 1942–1944: De vernietiging van de Joden en zigeuners van België / La destruction des Juifs et des Tsiganes de Belgique / The Destruction of the Jews and Gypsies from Belgium*, vol. 1 (Brussels: VUBPRESS, 2009).

Alary, Eric, *La Ligne de démarcation* (Paris: Perrin, 2003).

Alberts, Klaus, *Theodor Steltzer: Szenarien seines Lebens. Eine Biographie* (Heide: Boyens, 2009).

Allouche, Murielle and Jean-Yves Masson, *Ce qu'il reste de nous: Les déportés et leurs familles témoignent* (Paris: Michel Lafon, 2005).

Åmark, Klas, *Att bo granne med ondskan: Sveriges förhållande till nazismen, Nazitysklad og Förintelsen* (Stockholm: Albert Bonniers, 2011).

Améry, Jean, 'Die Tortur', *Merkur*, 208, no. 2 (July 1965), pp. 623–638.

Améry, Jean, 'Verfemt und verbannt: Vor dreißig Jahren – Erinnerungen an die Emigration. Manuskript für den Deutschlandfunk 1968/69', in Jean Améry, *Werke*, vol. 2 (Stuttgart: Klett-Cotta, 2002).

Andenaes, Johannes, Olav Riste, and Magne Skodvin, *Norway and the Second World War* (Oslo: Tanum, 1966).

Andersen, Palle, *Det moralske dilemma: Den illegale presse og den tyske jødeaktion oktober 1943* (Esbjerg: Historisk Samling fra Besaettelsestiden 1940–1945, 2003).

Arnaud, Patrice, *Les STO: Histoire des Français requis en Allemagne nazie, 1942–1945* (Paris: CNRS Éditions, 2010).

Arndt, Ino, 'Luxemburg: Deutsche Besetzung und Ausgrenzung der Juden', in Wolfgang Benz (ed.), *Dimension des Völkermords: Die Zahl der jüdischen Opfer des Nationalsozialismus* (Munich: Oldenbourg, 1991), pp. 103–104.

As, Aad van, *In het hol van de leeuw* (Hooghalen: Herinneringscentrum Kamp Westerbork, 2004).

Bachmann, Martin, *Geliebtes Volk Israel – fremde Juden: Die Nederlandse Hervormde Kerk und die 'Judenfrage', 1933–1945* (Münster: Lit, 1997).

Bak, Sofie Lene, *Dansk antisemitisme 1930–1945* (Copenhagen: Aschehoug, 2004).

Bak, Sofie Lene, *Nothing to Speak of: Wartime Experiences of the Danish Jews, 1943–1945* (Copenhagen: Danish Jewish Museum, 2013).

Bar-Efrat, Pinchas, *Denunciation and Rescue: Dutch Society and the Holocaust* (Jerusalem: Yad Vashem, 2017).

Becker, Jean-Jacques, *Un soir de l'été 1942 … Souvenirs d'un historien* (Paris: Larousse, 2009).

Belot, Robert, *Aux frontières de la liberté: Vichy-Madrid-Alger-Londres. S'évader de France sous l'Occupation* (Paris: Fayard, 1998).

Benjamin, Igal, *Faithful to Their Destiny and to Themselves: The Zionist Pioneers' Underground in the Netherlands in War and Holocaust* (Jerusalem: Yad Tabenkin and Ghetto Fighters' House, 1988) (in Hebrew).

Benz, Wolfgang (ed.), *Dimension des Völkermords: Die Zahl der jüdischen Opfer des Nationalsozialismus* (Munich: Oldenbourg, 1991).

Benz, Wolfgang and Barbara Distel (eds.), *Der Ort des Terrors*, vol. 7: *Niederhagen/*

Wewelsburg, Lublin-Majdanek, Arbeitsdorf, Herzogenbusch (Vught), Bergen-Belsen, Mittelbau-Dora (Munich: Beck, 2008).

Berg-van Cleeff, Jeanne van den, 'Verpleegster uit nood', in Guido Abuys and Dirk Mulder (eds.), *Genezen verklaard voor ... Een ziekenhuis in kamp Westerbork 1939–1945* (Hooghalen: Herinneringscentrum Kamp Westerbork, 2006).

Berlière, Jean-Marc, *Policiers français sous l'Occupation* (Paris: Tempus Perrin, 2009).

Bernay, Sylvie, *L'Église de France face à la persécution des Juifs, 1940–1944* (Paris: CNRS Éditions, 2012).

Beuys, Barbara, *Leben mit dem Feind: Amsterdam unter deutscher Besatzung, Mai 1940–Mai 1945* (Munich: DTV, 2012).

Billig, Joseph, *Le Commissariat général aux questions juives (1941–1944)*, vol. 1 (Paris: Centre de documentation juive contemporaine, 1955).

Blom, Hans, *In de ban van goed en fout: Geschiedschrijving over de bezettingstijd in Nederland* (Amsterdam: Boom, 2007).

Blom, J. C. H., 'The Persecution of the Jews in the Netherlands in a Comparative International Perspective', in Jozeph Michman (ed.), *Dutch Jewish History: Proceedings of the Fifth Symposium on the History of the Jews in the Netherlands* (Jerusalem: Hebrew University of Jerusalem, Institute for Research on Dutch Jewry, 1993), pp. 273–290.

Blüdnikow, Bent, 'Stille diplomati og flygtningehjælp: Den jødiske menigheds ledelse 1933–1943', in Hans Sode-Madsen, *'Føreren har befalet!' Jødeaktionen oktober 1943* (Copenhagen: Samleren, 1993), pp. 137–173.

Bohn, Robert, *Reichskommissariat Norwegen: 'Nationalsozialistische Neuordnung' und Kriegswirtschaft* (Munich: Oldenbourg, 2000).

Boom, Bart van der, 'Ordinary Dutchmen and the Holocaust: A Summary of Findings', in Peter Romijn et al., *The Persecution of the Jews in the Netherlands, 1940–1945: New Perspectives* (Amsterdam: Vossiuspers UvA, 2012), pp. 29–55.

Boom, Bart van der, *Wij leven nog: De stemming in bezet Nederland* (Amsterdam: Boom, 2003).

Boom, Bert van der, *'We weten niets van hun lot': Gewone Nederlanders en de Holocaust* (Amsterdam: Boom, 2012).

Bornstein, Heini, *Insel Schweiz: Hilfs- und Rettungsaktionen sozialistisch-zionistischer Jugendorganisationen 1939–1945* (Zurich: Chronos, 2000).

Boterman, Frits, *Duitse daders: De Jodenvervolging en de nazificatie van Nederland (1940–1945)* (Amsterdam and Antwerp: Arbeiderspers, 2015).

Brachfeld, Sylvain, *Ze hebben het overleefd* (Brussels: VUBPRESS, 1997) [French edition: *Ils ont survécu: Le sauvetage des Juifs en Belgique occupée* (Brussels: Racine, 2001)].

Brasz, Chaya, 'Rescue Attempts by the Dutch Jewish Community in Palestine, 1940–1945', in Jozeph Michman (ed.), *Dutch Jewish History: Proceedings of the Fifth Symposium on the History of the Jews in the Netherlands* (Jerusalem: Hebrew University of Jerusalem, Institute for Research on Dutch Jewry, 1993), pp. 339–352.

Broder, Pierre, *Des Juifs debout contre le nazisme* (Brussels: EPO, 1994).

Bruland, Bjarte, *Det norske Holocaust: Forsøket på å tilintetgjøre de norske jødene* (Oslo: HL-senteret, 2008).

Bruland, Bjarte, *Forsøket på å tilintetgjøre jødene i Norge* (Bergen: B. Bruland, 1995).

Bundgård Christensen, Claus, Niels Bo Paulsen, and Peter Scharff Smith, *Dagboek fra Østfronten: En dansker i Waffen-SS 1941–1944* (Copenhagen: Aschehoug, 2005).

Bundgård Christensen, Claus, et al., *Danmark besat: Krig og hverdag 1940–45* (Copenhagen: Høst, 2005).

Bundgård Christensen, Claus, Niels Bo Poulsen, and Peter Scharff Smith, 'Germanic Volunteers from Northern Europe,' in Jochen Böhler and Robert Gerwarth (eds.), *The Waffen-SS: A European History* (Oxford: Oxford University Press, 2017), pp. 42–75.

Cabanel, Patrick, *Histoire des Justes en France* (Paris: A. Colin, 2012).

Caestecker, Frank, *Ongewenste gasten: Joodse vluchtelingen en migranten in de dertiger jaren in België* (Brussels: VUBPRESS, 1993).

Carpi, Daniel, *Between Mussolini and Hitler: The Jews and the Italian Authorities in France and Tunisia* (Hanover, NH: University Press of New England, 1994).

Cohen, A. E., *Het proces Rauter* ('s Gravenhage: Nijhoff, 1952).

Cohen, Elie Aron and Aad Nuis, *De negentien treinen naar Sobibor* (Amsterdam: Elsevier, 1979).

Cohen, Jaap, *De onontkoombare afkomst van Eli d'Oliveira: Een Portugees-Joodse familiegeschiedenis* (Amsterdam and Antwerp: Querido, 2015).

Commission spéciale pour l'étude des spoliations des biens juifs au Luxembourg pendant les années de guerre, 1940–1945, *La Spoliation des biens juifs au Luxembourg 1940–1945: Rapport final* (Luxembourg: La Commission, 2009).

Conze, Eckhart, Norbert Frei, Peter Hayes, and Moshe Zimmermann, *Das Amt und die Vergangenheit: Deutsche Diplomaten im Dritten Reich und in der Bundesrepublik* (Munich: Pantheon, 2010).

Croes, Marnix, 'The Dutch Police Force and the Persecution of the Jews in the Netherlands during the German Occupation, 1940–1945', in Bruno De Wever, Herman Van Goethen, and Nico Wouters (eds.), *Local Government in Occupied Europe (1939–1945)* (Ghent: Academia Press, 2006), pp. 67–82.

Croes, Marnix, 'The Holocaust in the Netherlands and the Rate of Jewish Survival', *Holocaust and Genocide Studies*, vol. 20, issue 3 (2006), pp. 474–499.

Croes, Marnix, 'The Netherlands 1942–1945: Survival in Hiding and the Hunt for Hidden Jews,' in Beate Kosmala and Feliks Tych (eds.), *Facing the Nazi Genocide: Non-Jews and Jews in Europe, 1941–1945* (Berlin: Metropol, 2004), pp. 41–72.

Croes, Marnix and Pieter Tammes, *'Gif laten wij niet voortbestaan': Een onderzoek naar de overlevingskansen van joden in de Nederlandse gemeenten, 1940–1945* (Amsterdam: Aksant, 2004).

Croes, Marnix and Beate Kosmala, 'Facing Deportation in Germany and the Netherlands: Survival in Hiding', in Beate Kosmala and Georgi Verbeeck (eds.), *Facing the Catastrophe: Jews and Non-Jews in Europe during World War II* (Oxford: Berg, 2011), pp. 97–158.

Cüppers, Martin, *Walther Rauff – in deutschen Diensten: Vom Naziverbrecher zum BND-Spion* (Darmstadt: Wissenschaftliche Buchgesellschaft, 2013).

Czech, Danuta, *Kalendarium der Ereignisse im Konzentrationslager Auschwitz-Birkenau, 1939–1945* (Reinbek: Rowohlt, 1989).

Dahl, Hans Fredrik, *Quisling: A Study in Treachery* (Cambridge: Cambridge University Press, 1999).

De Dijn, Rosine, *'Du darfst nie sagen, dass du Rachmil heißt': Die Geschichte von Laja Menen und ihrem Sohn Rudi* (Munich: Deutsche Verlagsanstalt, 2005).

Dean, Martin, *Robbing the Jews: The Confiscation of Jewish Property in the Holocaust, 1933–1945* (Cambridge: Cambridge University Press, 2010).

Debruyne, Emmanuel, 'The Belgian Government-in-Exile facing the Persecution and Extermination of the Jews', in Jan Láníček and James Jordan (eds.), *Governments-in-Exile and the Jews during the Second World War* (London: Vallentine Mitchell, 2013), pp. 197–212.

Deen, James M., *The Prisoners of Breendonk: Personal Histories from a World War II Concentration Camp* (New York: Houghton Mifflin Harcourt, 2015).

Dellemann, Th., *Opdat wij niet vergeten: De bijdrage van de Gereformeerde Kerken, van haar voorgangers en leden, in het verzet tegen het nationaal-socialisme en de Duitse tyrannie* (Kampen: Drukkerij J. H. Kok, 1950).

Delmaire, Danielle, 'The Fate of the Jewish Communities in the North of France during World War II', in Dan Michman (ed.), *Belgium and the Holocaust: Jews, Belgians,*

Germans (Jerusalem: Yad Vashem, 1998), pp. 337–338.

Doorslaer, Rudi van, 'Conclusion finale', in Rudi van Doorslaer, Emmanuel Debruyne, Frank Seberechts, and Nico Wouters (eds.), *La Belgique docile: Les autorités belges et la persécution des Juifs en Belgique pendant la Seconde Guerre mondiale* (Brussels: CEGES, 2007), pp. 1060–1084.

Doorslaer, Rudi van, 'Eindconclusie', in Rudi van Doorslaer, Emmanuel Debruyne, Frank Seberechts, and Nico Wouters (eds.), *Gewillig België: Overheid en Jodenvervolging in België tijdens de Tweede Wereldoorlog* (Brussels: SOMA, 2007), pp. 1062–1086.

Doorslaer, Rudi van, 'Jewish Immigration and Communism in Belgium, 1925–1939', in Dan Michman (ed.), *Belgium and the Holocaust: Jews, Belgians, Germans* (Jerusalem: Yad Vashem, 1998), pp. 63–82.

Doorslaer, Rudi van, 'Les enfants du ghetto: L'immigration juive communiste en Belgique et la quête de la modernité (1925–1940)', in Rudi van Doorslaer (ed.), *Les Juifs de Belgique: De l'immigration au génocide, 1925–1945* (Brussels: Centre de recherches et d'études historiques de la Seconde Guerre mondiale, 1994), pp. 59–78.

Doorslaer, Rudi van, Emmanuel Debruyne, Frank Seberechts, and Nico Wouters (eds.), *Gewillig België: Overheid en Jodenvervolging in België tijdens de Tweede Wereldoorlog* (Brussels: SOMA, 2007).

Doorslaer, Rudi van, Emmanuel Debruyne, Frank Seberechts, and Nico Wouters (eds.), *La Belgique docile: Les autorités belges et la persécution des Juifs en Belgique pendant la Seconde Guerre mondiale* (Brussels: CEGES, 2007).

Dostert, Paul, 'La Déportation des Juifs à partir du territoire luxembourgeois (1941–1943)', in Thorsten Fuchshuber and Renée Wagner (eds.), *Émancipation, éclosion, persécution: Le développement de la communauté juive luxembourgeoise de la Révolution française à la Seconde Guerre mondiale* (Brussels: EME, 2014), pp. 210–211.

Dostert, Paul, *Luxemburg zwischen Selbstbehauptung und nationaler Selbstaufgabe: Die deutsche Besatzungspolitik und die Volksdeutsche Bewegung, 1940–1945* (Luxembourg: Imprimerie Saint-Paul, 1985).

Eismann, Gaël, *Hôtel Majestic: Ordre et sécurité en France occupée (1940–1944)* (Paris: Tallandier, 2010).

Eismann, Gaël, 'The "Militärbefehlshaber in Frankreich" and Order and Security at the Local Level in Occupied France', in Bruno De Wever, Herman Van Goethem, and Nico Wouters (eds.), *Local Government in Occupied Europe (1939–1945)* (Ghent: Academia Press, 2006), pp. 147–177.

Fivaz-Silbermann, Ruth, *Le Refoulement de réfugiés civils juifs à la frontière franco-genevoise durant la Seconde Guerre mondiale, suivi du mémorial de ceux parmi eux qui ont été déportés ou fusillés* (Paris: Klarsfeld Foundation, 2000), pp. 9–10.

Fivaz-Silbermann, Ruth, 'Refoulement, accueil, filières: Les fugitifs juifs à la frontière franco-genevoise entre 1942 et 1944', in *Schweizerische Zeitschrift für Geschichte*, 51 (2001), pp. 296–317.

Fivaz-Silbermann, Ruth, 'Une migration urgente et transitoire: La fuite des Juifs de France en Suisse au temps de la "solution finale"', *Diasporas*, 20 (2013), pp. 103–108.

Flim, Bert-Jan, *Saving the Children: History of the Organized Effort to Rescue Jewish Children in the Netherlands, 1942–1945*, trans. Jeanette Ringold (Bethesda, MD: CDL Press, 2005 [Dutch edn, 1996]).

Foray, Jennifer L., *Visions of Empire in the Nazi-Occupied Netherlands* (Cambridge: Cambridge University Press, 2014).

Fransecky, Tanja von, *Flucht von Juden aus Deportationszügen in Frankreich, Belgien und den Niederlanden* (Berlin: Metropol, 2014).

Friedländer, Saul, *Nazi Germany and the Jews*, vol. 2: *The Years of Extermination, 1939–1945* (New York: HarperCollins, 2007).

Friis, Erik J., 'The Norwegian Government-in-Exile, 1940–45', in Carl F. Bayerschmidt and Erik J. Friis (eds.), *Scandinavian Studies: Essays Presented to Dr. Henry Goddard Leach on the Occasion of His Eighty-fifth Birthday* (Seattle: University of Washington Press, 1965), pp. 422–444.

Frijtag Drabbe Künzel, Geraldien von, *Het geval Calmeyer* (Amsterdam: Mets & Schilt, 2008).

Gaida, Peter, *Camps de travail sous Vichy: Les 'Groupes de travailleurs étrangers' (GTE) en France et en Afrique du nord, 1940–1944* (Morrisville, NC: Lulu Press, 2018), pp. 199–216.

Gerdes, Uta, *Ökumenische Solidarität mit christlichen und jüdischen Verfolgten: Die Cimade in Vichy-Frankreich 1940–1944* (Göttingen: Vandenhoeck & Ruprecht, 2005).

Goldbaum Tarabini Fracapane, Silvia, *The Jews of Denmark in the Holocaust: Life and Death in Theresienstadt Ghetto* (London: Routledge, 2021).

Goldberger, Leo (ed.), *The Rescue of the Danish Jews: Moral Courage under Stress* (New York: New York University Press, 1987).

Gotovitch, José, *Du rouge au tricolore: Les communistes belges de 1939 à 1944: un aspect de l'histoire de la Résistance* (Brussels: Labor, 1992).

Gotovitch, José, 'Résistances et question juive', in Rudi van Doorslaer (ed.), *Les Juifs de Belgique: De l'immigration au génocide, 1925–1945* (Brussels: Centre de recherches et d'études historiques de la Seconde Guerre mondiale, 1994), pp. 129–136.

Griffioen, Pim and Ron Zeller, 'Comparing the Persecution of the Jews in the Netherlands, France and Belgium, 1940–1945: Similarities, Differences, Causes', in Peter Romijn et al., *The Persecution of the Jews in the Netherlands, 1940–1945: New Perspectives* (Amsterdam: Vossiuspers UvA, 2012), pp. 55–92.

Griffioen, Pim and Ron Zeller, *Jodenvervolging in Nederland, Frankrijk en België: Overeenkomsten, verschillen, oorzaken* (Amsterdam: Boom, 2010).

Grimnes, Ole Kristian, *Norge under okkupasjonen* (Oslo: Aschehoug, 1983).

Gryglewski, Elke, Hans-Christian Rasch, and David Zolldan (eds.), *The Meeting at Wannsee and the Murder of the European Jews: Exhibition Catalogue*, trans. Caroline Pearce (Berlin: House of the Wannsee Conference, 2020 [German edn, 2020]).

Grynberg, Anne, *Les Camps de la honte: Les internés juifs des camps français 1939–1944* (Paris: La Découverte, 1991).

Hæstrup, Jørgen, *... til landets bedste: Hovedtræk af departementschefsstyrets virke 1943–1945*, vol. 1 (Copenhagen: Gyldendal, 1966).

Hájková, Anna, 'Das Polizeiliche Durchgangslager Westerbork', in Wolfgang Benz and Barbara Distel (eds.), *Terror im Westen: Nationalsozialistische Lager in den Niederlanden, Belgien und Luxemburg 1940–1945* (Berlin: Metropol, 2004), pp. 217–248.

Hansson, Svante, *Flykt och överlevnad: Flyktingverksamhet i Mosaiska församlingen i Stockholm 1933–1950* (Stockholm: Hillelförlaget, 2004).

Happe, Katja, *Viele falsche Hoffnungen: Judenverfolgung in den Niederlanden 1940–1945* (Paderborn: Ferdinand Schöningh, 2017).

Have, Wichert ten (ed.), *The Persecution of the Jews in the Netherlands, 1940–1945* (Amsterdam: Amsterdam University Press, 2012).

Heijden, Chris van der, *Grijs verleden: Nederland en de Tweede Wereldoorlog* (Amsterdam: Contact, 2001).

Helstrup, Søren, 'Besættelsen 9. April 1940', in Hans Kirchhoff, John T. Lauridsen, and Aage Trommer (eds.), *Gads leksikon om dansk besættelsesrid 1940–1945* (Copenhagen: GAD, 2002), pp. 42–47.

Herbert, Ulrich, *Best: Biographische Studien über Radikalismus, Weltanschauung und Vernunft 1903–1989* (Bonn: Dietz, 1996).

Herzberg, Abel Jacob, *Amor Fati: Seven Essays on Bergen-Belsen*, trans. Jack Santcross (Göttingen: Wallstein Verlag, 2016 [Dutch edn, 1980]).

Herzberg, Abel, *Kroniek der Jodenvervolging, 1940–1945* (Amsterdam: Querido, 1985).

Heymans, Albert, *Jood zonder ster* (Westervoort: Van Gruting, 1999).

Hirschfeld, Gerhard, *Nazi Rule and Dutch Collaboration: The Netherlands under German Occupation* (Oxford and New York: Berg, 1988).

Hirschfeld, Gerhard, 'Niederlande', in Wolfgang Benz (ed.), *Dimension des Völkermords: Die Zahl der jüdischen Opfer des Nationalsozialismus* (Munich: Oldenbourg, 1991), pp. 137–165.

Hoffmann, Christhard, 'Fluchthilfe als Widerstand: Verfolgung und Rettung der Juden in Norwegen', in Wolfgang Benz and Juliane Wetzel (eds.), *Solidarität und Hilfe für Juden während der NS-Zeit*, vol. 1: *Polen, Rumänien, Griechenland, Luxemburg, Norwegen, Schweiz* (Berlin: Metropol, 1999).

Holbraad, Carsten, *Danish Reactions to German Occupation: History and Historiography* (London: UCL Press, 2017).

Hollander, Ethan J., *Hegemony and the Holocaust: State Power and Jewish Survival in Occupied Europe* (London: Palgrave Macmillan, 2017).

Houwink ten Cate, Johannes, 'Die moralische Debatte über den Amsterdamer Judenrat', in Norbert Fasse, Johannes Houwink ten Cate, and Horst Lademacher (eds.), *Nationalsozialistische Herrschaft und Besatzungszeit: Historische Erfahrung und Verarbeitung aus niederländischer und deutscher Sicht* (Münster: Waxmann, 2000), pp. 211–216.

Jäckel, Eberhard, *Frankreich in Hitlers Europa: Die deutsche Frankreichpolitik im Zweiten Weltkrieg* (Stuttgart: Deutsche Verlags-Anstalt, 1966).

Jasch, Hans-Christian and Christoph Kreutzmüller, *The Participants: The Men of the Wannsee Conference*, trans. Charlotte Kreutzmüller and Jane Paulick (New York: Berghahn, 2017 [German edn, 2017]).

Joly, Laurent, *Vichy dans la 'solution finale': Histoire du Commissariat général aux questions juives, 1941–1944* (Paris: Grasset, 2006).

Jong, Loe de, *Jodenvervolging in Nederland 1940–1945*, 2 vols. (Amsterdam: Verbum and NIOD, 2018).

Jong, L. de, *Het Koninkrijk der Nederlanden in de Tweede Wereldoorlog*, 12 vols. (The Hague: Nijhoff, 1969–1986).

Jørgensen, Harald (ed.), *Indenfor murene: Jødisk liv i Danmark 1684–1984* (Copenhagen: Reitzel, 1984).

Jørgensen, Rasmus, *Deporteret: Beretningen om de danske kz-fanger* (Copenhagen: Jyllands-Postens Forlag, 2005).

Kampe, Norbert, and Peter Klein (eds.), *Die 'Wannsee-Konferenz' am 20. Januar 1942: Eine Einführung* (Berlin: Metropol, 2017).

Kaspi, André, *Les Juifs pendant l'Occupation* (Paris: Seuil, 1997).

Kasten, Bernd, *'Gute Franzosen': Die französische Polizei und die deutsche Besatzungsmacht im besetzten Frankreich, 1940–1944* (Sigmaringen: Thorbecke, 1993).

Katz, Per, *Jøderne i Danmark i det 17. århundrede* (Copenhagen: Reitzel, 1981).

Keizer, Madelon de, *Het Parool. 1940–1945: Verzetsblad in oorlogstijd* (Amsterdam: Otto Cramwinckel, 1991).

Kirchhoff, Hans, *Augustoprøret 1943: Samarbejdspolitikkens fald – Forudsætninger og forløb: En studie i kollaboration og modstand*, vol. 1 (Copenhagen: Gyldendal, 1979).

Kirchhoff, Hans, *Den gode tysker: G. F. Duckwitz – De danske jøders redningsmand* (Copenhagen: Gyldendal, 2013).

Kirchhoff, Hans, 'Endlösung over Danmark', in Hans Sode-Madsen (ed.), *I Hitler-Tysklands skygge: Dramaet om de danske jøder 1933–1945* (Copenhagen: Aschehoug, 2003).

Kirchhoff, Hans, *Et menneske uden pas er ikke noget menneske: Danmark i den internationale flygtningepolitik 1933–1939* (Odense: Syddansk Universitetsforlag, 2005).

Kirchhoff, Hans and Lone Rünitz, *Udsendt til Tyskland: Dansk flygtningepolitik under besættelsen* (Odense: Syddansk Universitetsforlag, 2007).

Klein, P. W. and Justus van de Kamp, *Het Philips-Kommando in Kamp Vught* (Amsterdam: Contact, 2003).

Klempner, Mark, *The Heart Has Reasons: Dutch Rescuers of Jewish Children during the*

Holocaust (Amsterdam/New York: Night Stand Books, 2012).

Knoop, Hans, *De Joodsche Raad: Het drama van Abraham Asscher en David Cohen* (Amsterdam: Elsevier, 1983).

Koblik, Steven, *The Stones Cry Out: Sweden's Response to the Persecution of the Jews, 1933–1945* (New York: Holocaust Library, 1988).

Kolb, Eberhard, *Bergen-Belsen: Vom 'Aufenthaltslager' zum Konzentrationslager 1943–1945* (Göttingen: Vandenhoeck & Ruprecht, 2002).

Komissar, Vera, *Nådetid: Norske Jøder på flukt* (Oslo: Aschehoug, 1992).

Komissar, Vera and Sverre M. Nyrønning, *På tross av alt: Julius Paltiel, norsk jøde i Auschwitz* (Oslo: Aschehoug, 1995).

Kosmala, Beate and Feliks Tych (eds.), *Facing the Nazi Genocide: Non-Jews and Jews in Europe, 1941–1945* (Berlin: Metropol, 2004).

Kreis, Georg (ed.), *Switzerland and the Second World War* (London: Routledge, 2014).

Kreth, Rasmus and Michael Mogensen, *Flugten til Sverige: Aktionen mod de danske jøder oktober 1943* (Copenhagen: Gyldendal, 1995).

Kreutzmüller, Christoph, 'Contested Dispossession: The Netherlands', in: Christoph Kreutzmüller and Jonathan R. Zatlin (eds.), *Dispossession: Plundering German Jewry, 1933–1953* (Ann Arbor, MI: University of Michigan Press, 2020), pp. 216–235.

Kreutzmüller, Christoph, 'Eichmanns Zahlen für die Niederlande', in Norbert Kampe and Peter Klein (eds.), *Die Wannsee-Konferenz am 20. Januar 1942 – Dokumente, Forschungsstand, Kontroversen* (Vienna, Böhlau, 2013), pp. 357–378.

Kreutzmüller, Christoph, *Händler und Handlungsgehilfen: Der Finanzplatz Amsterdam und die deutschen Großbanken (1918–1945)* (Stuttgart: Steiner, 2005).

Kreutzmüller, Christoph and Jonathan R. Zatlin (eds.), *Dispossession: Plundering German Jewry, 1933–1953* (Ann Arbor, MI: University of Michigan Press, 2020).

Kühn, Volker (ed.), *Deutschlands Erwachen: Kabarett unterm Hakenkreuz 1933–1945* (Weinheim: Quadriga, 1989).

Kvist Geverts, Karin, 'Ett främmande element i nationen: Svensk flyktingpolitik och de judiska flyktingarna 1938–1944', *Acta Universitatis Upsaliensis, Studia Historica Upsaliensa*, 233 (Uppsala: Universitets-biblioteket, 2008), pp. 184–194.

Laffitte, Michel, *Juif dans la France allemande: Institutions, dirigeants et communautés au temps de la Shoah* (Paris: Tallandier, 2006).

Lambauer, Barbara, *Otto Abetz et les français ou l'envers de la Collaboration* (Paris: Fayard, 2001).

Landsberger, L., A. de Haas, and K. Selowsky, *Auschwitz*, vol. 2: *De deportatietransporten van 15 juli tot en met 24 augustus 1942* (The Hague: Nederlandsche Roode Kruis, 1948).

Landsberger, L., A. de Haas, and K. Selowsky, *Auschwitz*, vol. 4: *De deportatietransporten in 1943* (The Hague: Nederlandsche Roode Kruis, 1953).

Lazarus, Jacques, 'Juifs au combat', in Marek Halter (ed.), *Les Révoltés de la Shoah: Témoignages et récits* (Paris: Omnibus, 2010).

Lee, Daniel, *Pétain's Jewish Children: French Jewish Youth and the Vichy Regime, 1940–1942* (Oxford: Oxford University Press, 2014).

Leshem, Peretz, *Strasse zur Rettung: 1933–1939 aus Deutschland vertrieben – bereitet sich jüdische Jugend auf Palästina vor* (Tel Aviv: Verband der Freunde der Histadrut, 1973).

Levin, Irene, 'Det jødiske barnehjemmet og Nic Waal', *Tidsskrift for Norsk psykologforening*, vol. 46, issue 1 (2009), pp. 76–80.

Levine, Paul A., *From Indifference to Activism: Swedish Diplomacy and the Holocaust, 1938–1944* (Uppsala: Ubsaliensis S. Academiae, 1996).

Liempt, Ad van, *Hitler's Bounty Hunters: The Betrayal of the Jews* (Oxford: Berg, 2005).

Liempt, Ad van and Jan H. Kompagnie (eds.), *Jodenjacht: De onthutsende rol van de Nederlandse politie in de Tweede Wereldoorlog* (Amsterdam: Balans, 2011).

Lindwer, Willy, *Het fatale dilemma: De Joodsche Raad voor Amsterdam 1941–1943* (The Hague: Sdu Uitgeverij Koninginnegracht, 1995).

Longerich, Peter, *Wannseekonferenz: Der Weg zur 'Endlösung'* (Munich: Pantheon, 2016).

Loock, Hans-Dietrich, *Quisling, Rosenberg und Terboven: Zur Vorgeschichte und Geschichte der nationalsozialistischen Revolution in Norwegen* (Stuttgart: Deutsche Verlags-Anstalt, 1970).

Lothe, Jakob and Anette Storeide (eds.), *Tidsvitner: Fortellinger fra Auschwitz og Sachsenhausen* (Oslo: Gyldendal, 2006).

Lundtofte, Henrik, 'Den store undtagelse – Gestapo og jødeaktionen', in Hans Sode-Madsen (ed.), *I Hitler-Tysklands skygge: Dramaet om de danske jøder 1933–1945* (Copenhagen: Aschehoug, 2003).

Lustiger, Arno, *Rettungswiderstand: Über die Judenretter in Europa während der NS-Zeit* (Göttingen: Wallstein, 2011).

Markham Walsh, Ann, *Dancing Through Darkness: When Love and Dreams Survived a Nazi Death Camp* (Nashville: Dunham Books, 2012).

Marrus, Michael R. and Robert O. Paxton, *Vichy France and the Jews* (Stanford: Stanford University Press, 1996).

Meckl, Markus, 'Unter zweifacher Hoheit: Das Auffanglager Breendonk zwischen Militärverwaltung und SD', in Wolfgang Benz and Barbara Distel (eds.), *Terror im Westen: Nationalsozialistische Lager in den Niederlanden, Belgien und Luxemburg 1940–1945* (Berlin: Metropol, 2004), pp. 25–38.

Meershoek, Guus, *Dienaren van het gezag: De Amsterdamse politie tijdens de bezetting* (Amsterdam: Van Gennep, 1999).

Meershoek, Guus, 'Onder nationaalsocialistisch bewind', in Doeko Bosscher, Augustinus J. J. Meershoek, and Piet de Rooy (eds.), *Geschiedenis van Amsterdam. Tweestrijd om de hoofdstad 1900–2000* (Amsterdam: Sun, 2007), pp. 235–335.

Meinen, Insa, 'Die Deportation der Juden aus Belgien und das Devisenschutzkommando', in Johannes Hürter and Jürgen Zarusky (eds.), *Besatzung, Kollaboration, Holocaust: Neue Studien zur Verfolgung und Ermordung der europäischen Juden* (Munich: Oldenbourg, 2008), pp. 45–79.

Meinen, Insa, *Die Shoah in Belgien* (Darmstadt: Wissenschaftliche Buchgesellschaft, 2009).

Meinen, Insa, 'Facing Deportation: How Jews Were Arrested in Belgium,' *Yad Vashem Studies*, 36:1 (2008), pp. 39–72.

Meinen, Insa and Ahlrich Meyer, *Verfolgt von Land zu Land: Jüdische Flüchtlinge in Westeuropa 1938–1944* (Paderborn: Schöningh, 2013).

Melkman-de Paauw, Fré, *Hoe het verder gaat, weet niemand: Naoorlogse brieven uit Amsterdam naar Palestina* (Amsterdam: Contact, 2002).

Mendelsohn, Oskar, *Jødenes historie i Norge gjennom 300 år*, vol. 2: *1940–1985* (Oslo: Universitetsforlaget, 1987).

Mendelsohn, Oskar, 'Norwegen', in Wolfgang Benz (ed.), *Dimension des Völkermords: Die Zahl der jüdischen Opfer des Nationalsozialismus* (Munich: Oldenbourg, 1991), pp. 187–197.

Mendelsohn, Oskar, *The Persecution of the Norwegian Jews in WW II* (Oslo: Norges Hjemmefrontmuseum, 2000).

Meyer, Ahlrich, *Täter im Verhör: Die 'Endlösung der Judenfrage' in Frankreich 1940–1944* (Darmstadt: Wissenschaftliche Buchgesellschaft, 2005).

Meyer, Ahlrich (ed.), *Der Blick des Besatzers: Propagandaphotographie der Wehrmacht aus Marseille 1942–1944 – Le regard de l'occupant* (Bremen: Edition Temmen, 1999).

Meyer, Ahlrich and Insa Meinen, 'Transitland Belgien: Jüdische Flüchtlinge in Westeuropa während der Zeit der Deportationen 1942', *Theresienstädter Studien und Dokumente*, 14 (2007), pp. 378–431.

Michman, Dan, 'De oprichting van de VJB in internationaal perspectief', in Rudi van Doorslaer and Jean-Philippe Schreiber (eds.), *De curatoren van het ghetto: De vereniging van de joden in België tijdens de nazi-bezetting* (Tielt: Lannoo, 2004), pp. 25–45.

Michman, Dan, 'La fondation de l'AJB dans une perspective internationale', in Jean-Philippe Schreiber and Rudi van Doorslaer (eds.), *Les Curateurs du ghetto: L'Association des Juifs en Belgique sous l'occupation nazie* (Brussels: Labor, 2004), pp. 29–56.

Michman, Dan (ed.), *The Encyclopedia of the Righteous Among the Nations – Rescuers of Jews during the Holocaust: Belgium* (Jerusalem: Yad Vashem, 2005).

Michman, Jozeph and Bert-Jan Flim, *The Encyclopedia of the Righteous Among the Nations – Rescuers of Jews during the Holocaust: The Netherlands* (Jerusalem: Yad Vashem, 2004).

Michman, Jozeph, Hartog Beem, and Dan Michman, *Pinkas: Geschiedenis van de joodse gemeenschap in Nederland* (Amsterdam: Contact, 1999).

Mogensen, Michael, 'October 1943 – The Rescue of the Danish Jews', in Mette Bastholm Jensen and Steven L. B. Jensen (eds.), *Denmark and the Holocaust* (Copenhagen: Danish Center for Holocaust and Genocide Studies, 2003), pp. 33–61.

Møller, Per and Knud Secher, *De danske flygtninge i Sverige* (Stockholm: Gyldendal, 1945).

Moore, Bob, *Survivors: Jewish Self-help and Rescue in Nazi-Occupied Western Europe* (Oxford: Oxford University Press, 2010).

Moore, Bob, *Victims and Survivors: The Nazi Persecution of the Jews in the Netherlands 1940–1945* (London: Arnold, 1997).

Moore, Bob, 'Warum fielen dem Holocaust so viele niederländische Juden zum Opfer? Ein Erklärungsversuch', in Norbert Fasse, Johannes Houwink ten Cate and Horst Lademacher (eds.), *Nationalsozialistische Herrschaft und Besatzungszeit: Historische Erfahrung und Verarbeitung aus niederländischer und deutscher Sicht* (Münster: Waxmann, 2000), pp. 191–210.

Morina, Christina, 'The "Bystander" in Recent Dutch Historiography', *German History*, 32:1 (2014), pp. 101–111.

Nataf, Claude, (ed.), *Les Juifs de Tunisie sous le joug nazi, 9 novembre 1942–8 mai 1943* (Paris: Manuscrit, 2012).

Nefors, Patrick, *Breendonk, 1940–1945: De geschiedenis* (Antwerp: Standaard, 2004) [French edn: *Breendonk, 1940–1945*, trans. Walter Hilgers (Brussels: Racine, 2006)].

Nøkleby, Berit, *Holdningskamp* (*Norge i krig: Fremmedåk og frihetskamp 1940–1945*, ed. Magne Skodvin, vol. 4) (Oslo: Aschehoug, 1986).

Obschernitzki, Doris, *Letzte Hoffnung – Ausreise: die Ziegelei von Les Milles 1939–1942. Vom Lager für unerwünschte Ausländer zum Deportationszentrum* (Berlin: Hentrich & Hentrich, 1999).

Ottmer, Hans-Martin, *'Weserübung': Der deutsche Angriff auf Dänemark und Norwegen im April 1940* (Munich: Oldenbourg, 1994).

Panicacci, Jean-Louis, *L'Occupation italienne: Sud-Est de la France, juin 1940–septembre 1943* (Rennes: Presses universitaires de Rennes, 2010).

Pennewaard, Aline, 'Lists and Human Beings: The Deportation of Dutch Jewry, viewed from Within and Without, 1942–1943', PhD dissertation, University of Haifa (2021).

Persson, Sune, *'Vi åker till Sverige': De vita bussarna 1945* (Rimbo: Fischer & Co, 2002).

Peschanski, Denis, *La France des camps: L'internement 1938–1946* (Paris: Gallimard, 2002).

Petrow, Richard, *The Bitter Years: The Invasion and Occupation of Denmark and Norway, April 1940–May 1945* (London: Hodder & Stoughton, 1975).

Petrucci, Filippo, *Gli ebrei in Algeria e in Tunisia 1940–1943* (Florence: Giuntina, 2011).

Pezechkian, Johanna, 'La "Möbelaktion" en Belgique', *Bijdragen tot de Eigentijdse Geschiedenis / Cahiers d'histoire du temps présent*, 10 (2002).

Plard, Henri, 'J'ai porté l'étoile en solidarité avec les Juifs', in Brigitte Leblanc and Christelle Chevallier (eds.), *Mémoires de la Shoah, 1933 à 1946: Photographies et témoignages* (Paris: Editions du Chêne, 2005), p. 66.

Pollmann, Dorlies and Edith Laudowicz (eds.), *Weil ich das Leben liebe: Persönliches und Politisches aus dem Leben engagierter Frauen* (Cologne: Pahl-Rugenstein, 1981).

Poser, Norman, *Escape: A Jewish Scandinavian Family in the Second World War* (New York: Sareve Press, 2006).

Poznanski, Renée, *Jews in France during World War II*, trans. Nathan Bracher (Hanover, NH: University Press of New England, 2001 [French edn, 1997]).

Presser, Jacques, *Ondergang: De vervolging en verdelging van het Nederlandse Jodendom 1940–1945* (The Hague: Staatsuitgeverij, 1965) (abridged English edn: *Ashes in the Wind: The Destruction of Dutch Jewry*, trans. Arnold Pomerans [London: Souvenir Press, 2010]).

Pundik, Herbert, *In Denmark It Could not Happen: The Flight of the Jews to Sweden* (Jerusalem: Gefen Publishing, 1998).

Rayski, Adam, *Nos illusions perdues* (Paris: Balland, 1985).

Reilly, Jo, David Cesarani, Tony Kushner, and Colin Richmond (eds.), *Belsen in History and Memory* (London: Frank Cass, 1997).

Rens, Herman van and Annelies Wilms, *Tussenstation Cosel: Joodse mannen uit West-Europa naar dwangarbeiderskampen in Silezië, 1942–1945* (Hilversum: Verloren, 2020).

Riste, Olav and Berit Nøkleby, *Norway 1940–45: The Resistance Movement* (Oslo: Aschehoug, 1994 [1970]).

Romijn, Peter, et al., *The Persecution of the Jews in the Netherlands, 1940–1945: New Perspectives* (Amsterdam: Vossiuspers UvA, 2012).

Roseman, Mark, *The Villa, the Lake, the Meeting: Wannsee and the Final Solution* (London: Penguin, 2002).

Rozenblum, Thierry, *Une cité si ardente: Les Juifs de Liège sous l'Occupation (1940–1944)* (Brussels: Pire, 2010).

Rünitz, Lone, 'Danish Refugee Policy, 1933–1939', in Marc Dujardin (ed.), *Refugees from Nazi-Germany in West-European Border States, 1933–1939/1940: Similarities and Differences in Granting Asylum between European Liberal States and Societies. Causes and Consequences of the Distinct Refugee Politics in Europe in the 1930s* (Brussels: Koninklijke Vlaamse Academie van België voor Wetenschappen en Kunsten, 2004), pp. 55–60.

Rünitz, Lone, *Danmark og de jødiske flygtninge 1933–1940: En bog om flygtninge og menneskerettigheder* (Copenhagen: Museum Tusculanum, 2000).

Sæland, Frode, *Herman Beckers krig: Historien om familien Becker og jødene i Rogaland under andre verdenskrig* (Oslo: Aschehoug, 2009).

Saerens, Lieven, 'De Jodenvervolging in België in cijfers', *Bijdragen tot de Eigentijdse Geschiedenis / Cahiers d'histoire du temps présent*, 17 (2006), pp. 199–235.

Saerens, Lieven, 'Die Hilfe für Juden in Belgien', in Wolfgang Benz and Juliane Wetzel (eds.), *Solidarität und Hilfe für Juden während der NS-Zeit*, vol. 4: *Slowakei, Bulgarien, Serbien, Kroatien mit Bosnien und Herzegowina, Belgien, Italien* (Berlin: Metropol, 2004), pp. 193–280.

Saerens, Lieven, *Étrangers dans la cité: Anvers et ses Juifs (1880–1944)* (Brussels: Labor, 2005).

Saerens, Lieven, *Onwillig Brussel: Een verhaal over Jodenvervolging en verzet* (Leuven: Davidsfonds, 2014).

Saerens, Lieven, *Vreemdelingen in een wereldstad: Een geschiedenis van Antwerpen en zijn joodse bevolking (1880–1944)* (Tielt: Lannoo, 2000).

Safrian, Hans, *Eichmann's Men*, trans. Ute Stargardt (Cambridge: Cambridge University Press, 2010 [German edn, 1993]).

Schaap, Jord, *Het recht om te waarschuwen: Jodenvervolging en vernieuwing in de Radio Oranje-toespraken van Wilhelmina* (Groningen: Wolters-Noordhoff, 2005).

Schelvis, Jules, *Sobibor: A History of a Nazi Death Camp* (London: Bloomsbury, 2014).

Schoentgen, Marc, 'Das "Jüdische Altersheim" in Fünfbrunnen', in Wolfgang Benz and Barbara Distel (eds.), *Terror im Westen: Nationalsozialistische Lager in den Niederlanden, Belgien und Luxemburg 1940–1945* (Berlin: Metropol, 2004), pp. 49–70.

Schoentgen, Marc, 'Luxembourg', in Wolf Gruner and Jörg Osterloh (eds.), *The Greater German Reich and the Jews: Nazi Persecution Policies in the Annexed Territories, 1935–1945*, trans. Bernard Heise (New York: Berghahn Books, 2015 [German edn, 2010]), pp. 290–315.

Schoentgen, Marc, 'Luxemburger und Juden im Zweiten Weltkrieg: Zwischen Solidarität und Schweigen', in Marie-Paule Jungblut (ed.), *Et wor alles net esou einfach: Questions sur le Luxembourg et la Deuxième Guerre mondiale: Contributions historiques accompagnant l'exposition* (Luxembourg: Musée d'Histoire de la Ville, 2002), pp. 150–163.

Schram, Laurence, 'La Caserne Dossin à Malines, 1942–1944', *Les Cahiers de la mémoire contemporaine / Bijdragen tot de Eigentijdse Herinnering*, no. 12 (2016), pp. 99–117.

Schreiber, Jean-Philippe (ed.), *Hertz Jospa: Juif, résistant, communiste* (Brussels: Labor, 1997).

Schreiber, Marion, *Stille Rebellen: Der Überfall auf den 20. Deportationszug nach Auschwitz* (Berlin: Aufbau, 2001).

Schroeter, Daniel J., 'Between Metropole and French North Africa: Vichy's Anti-Semitic Legislation and Colonialism's Racial Hierarchies', in Aomar Boum and Sarah Abrevaya Stein (eds.), *The Holocaust and North Africa* (Stanford: Stanford University Press, 2019), pp. 19–49.

Schwarz Lausten, Martin, *Folkekirken og jøderne: Forholdet mellem kristne og jøder i Danmark fra 1849 til begyndelsen af det 20. århundrede* (Copenhagen: Anis, 2007).

Schwarz Lausten, Martin, *Jews and Christians in Denmark: From the Middle Ages to Recent Times, ca. 1100–1948*, trans. Margaret Ryan Hellman (Boston: Brill, 2015 [Danish edn, 2007]).

Schwarz Lausten, Martin, *Jødesympati og jødehad i Folkekirken: Forholdet mellem kristne og jøder i Danmark fra begyndelsen af det 20. århundrede til 1948* (Copenhagen: Anis, 2007).

Seberechts, Frank, 'De Joden in België in het Interbellum', in Rudi van Doorslaer, Emmanuel Debruyne, Frank Seberechts, and Nico Wouters (eds.), *Gewillig België: Overheid en Jodenvervolging tijdens de Tweede Wereldoorlog* (Brussels: SOMA, 2007), pp. 44–52.

Seberechts, Frank, 'Les Juifs en Belgique durant l'entre-deux-guerres', in Rudi van Doorslaer, Emmanuel Debruyne, Frank Seberechts, and Nico Wouters (eds.), *La Belgique docile: Les autorités belges et la persécution des Juifs en Belgique durant la Seconde Guerre mondiale* (Brussels: CEGES, 2007), pp. 45–53.

Seberechts, Frank, 'Spoliatie en verplichte tewerkstelling', in Rudi van Doorslaer, Emmanuel Debruyne, Frank Seberechts, and Nico Wouters (eds.), *Gewillig België: Overheid en Jodenvervolging tijdens de Tweede Wereldoorlog* (Brussels: SOMA, 2007), pp. 374–453.

Seberechts, Frank, 'Spoliation et travail obligatoire', in Rudi van Doorslaer, Emmanuel Debruyne, Frank Seberechts, and Nico Wouters (eds.), *La Belgique docile: Les autorités belges et la persécution des Juifs en Belgique durant la Seconde Guerre mondiale* (Brussels: CEGES, 2007), pp. 370–450.

Semelin, Jacques, *Persécution et entraides dans la France occupée: Comment 75 % des Juifs en France ont échappé à la mort* (Paris: Les Arènes, 2013).

Semelin, Jacques, *The Survival of the Jews in France, 1940–44*, trans. Cynthia Schoch and Natasha Lehrer (Oxford: Oxford University Press, 2018).

Sijes, B. A., *De Arbeidsinzet: De gedwongen arbeid van Nederlanders in Duitsland 1940–1945* (The Hague: Nijhoff, 1966).

Sinke, Onno, *Verzet vanuit de verte: De behoedzame koers van Radio Oranje* (Amsterdam: Augustus, 2009).

Sjoerds Gerbrandy, Pieter, *Landgenoten! De radiotoespraken van Minister-president Prof. Mr. P. S. Gerbrandy in de jaren 1940–1945 gehouden voor Radio Oranje en De Brandaris* (Franeker: Wever, 1985).

Snoek, Johan Martinus, *De nederlandse kerken en de joden 1940–1945: De protesten bij Seyss-Inquart, hulp aan joodse onderduikers, de motieven voor hulpverlening* (Kampen: Kok, 1990).

Sode-Madsen, Hans, '"Her er livets lov egoisme": De danske jøder i Theresienstadt', in Hans Sode-Madsen (ed.), *'Føreren har befalet!' Jødeaktionen oktober 1943* (Copenhagen: Samleren, 1993), pp. 174–219.

Sode-Madsen, Hans, 'The Perfect Deception: The Danish Jews and Theresienstadt 1940–1945', *Leo Baeck Institute Year Book*, 38 (1993), pp. 263–290.

Sode-Madsen, Hans, *Reddet fra Hitlers helvede: Danmark og de Hvide Busser 1941–45* (Copenhagen: Aschehoug, 2005).

Spina, Raphaël, *Histoire du STO* (Paris: Perrin, 2017).

Steinberg, Maxime, *L'Étoile et le fusil*, vol. 2: *1942: Les cent jours de la déportation des Juifs de Belgique* (Brussels: Vie Ouvrière, 1984).

Steinberg, Maxime, *L'Étoile et le fusil*, vol. 3: *La Traque des Juifs, 1942–1944* (Brussels: Vie Ouvrière, 1986).

Steinberg, Maxime, 'The *Judenpolitik* in Belgium within the West European Context: Comparative Observations', in Dan Michman (ed.), *Belgium and the Holocaust: Jews, Belgians, Germans* (Jerusalem: Yad Vashem, 1998), pp. 199–221.

Steinberg, Maxime, *La Persécution des Juifs de Belgique (1940–1945)* (Brussels: Vie Ouvrière, 2004).

Steinberg, Maxime and Laurence Schram, *Transport XX Malines – Auschwitz* (Brussels: VUBPRESS, 2008).

Stephenson, Jill and John Gilmour (eds.), *Hitler's Scandinavian Legacy* (London: Bloomsbury, 2014).

Stokman, Siegfried, *Het verzet van de Nederlandsche bisschoppen tegen nationaal-socialisme en Duitsche tyrannie* (Utrecht: Het Spectrum, 1945).

Stræde, Therkel, 'Deutsche Besatzungspolitik in Dänemark 1940–1945', in Oliver von Wrochem (ed.), *Skandinavien im Zweiten Weltkrieg und die Rettungsaktion Weiße Busse: Ereignisse und Erinnerung* (Berlin: Metropol, 2012), pp. 21–30.

Struye, Paul and Guillaume Jacquemyns, *La Belgique sous l'Occupation allemande (1940–1944)* (Brussels: Éditions Complexe, 2002).

Stuldreher, Coen, *De legale rest: Gemengd gehuwde Joden onder de Duitse bezetting* (Amsterdam: Boom, 2007).

Tangestuen, Mats, *Fredriksens Transport: Krigens største redningsbragd* (Oslo: URO/KORO, 2012).

Thijn, Ed van, *Achttien adressen* (Amsterdam: Augustus, 2004).

Thing, Morten, *De russiske jøder i København 1882–1943* (Copenhagen: Gyldendal, 2008).

Thomsen, Erich, *Deutsche Besatzungspolitik in Dänemark, 1940–1945* (Düsseldorf: Bertelsmann, 1971).

Ugelvik Larsen, Stein, Beatrice Sandberg, and Volker Dahm, *Meldungen aus Norwegen 1940–1945: Die geheimen Lageberichte des Befehlshabers der Sicherheitspolizei und des SD in Norwegen*, vol. 1 (Munich: Oldenbourg, 2008).

Ulstein, Ragnar, *Svensketrafikken*, vol. 1, *Flyktningar til Sverige 1940–43* (Oslo: Det Norske Samlaget, 1974).

Ulstein, Ragnar, *Jødar på flukt* (Oslo: Det Norske Samlaget, 1995).

Umbreit, Hans, *Der Militärbefehlshaber in Frankreich* (Boppard am Rhein: Harald Boldt, 1968).

Unabhängige Expertenkommission Schweiz – Zweiter Weltkrieg, *Die Schweiz, der Nationalsozialismus und der Zweite Weltkrieg: Schlussbericht* (Zurich: Pendo, 2002).

Unabhängige Expertenkommission Schweiz – Zweiter Weltkrieg, *Die Schweiz und die Flüchtlinge zur Zeit des Nationalsozialismus* (Bern: Unabhängige Expertenkommission Schweiz – Zweiter Weltkrieg, 1999).

Vandepontseele, Sophie, 'De veplichte tewerkstelling van joden in België en Noord-Frankrijk,' in Rudi van Doorslaer and Jean-Philippe Schreiber (eds.), *De curatoren van het getto: De vereniging van de joden in België tijdens de nazi-bezetting* (Tielt: Lannoo, 2004), pp. 149–181.

Vandepontseele, Sophie, 'Le travail obligatoire des Juifs en Belgique et dans le nord de la France', in Jean-Philippe Schreiber and Rudi van Doorslaer (eds.), *Les Curateurs du ghetto: L'Association des Juifs en Belgique sous l'occupation Nazie* (Brussels: Labor, 2004), pp. 189–231.

Vries, Hans de, 'Konzentrationslager Herzogenbusch (Vught)', in Wolfgang Benz and Barbara Distel (eds.), *Der Ort des Terrors*, vol 7: *Niederhagen/Wewelsburg, Lublin-Majdanek, Arbeitsdorf, Herzogenbusch (Vught), Bergen-Belsen, Mittelbau-Dora* (Munich: Beck, 2008), pp. 153–184.

Wallerang, Mathias, *Luxemburg unter nationalsozialistischer Besatzung: Luxemburger berichten* (Mainz: Gesellschaft für Volkskunde in Rheinland-Pfalz, 1997).

Warmbrunn, Werner, *The Dutch under German Occupation, 1940–1945* (Stanford: Stanford University Press, 1963).

Warmbrunn, Werner, *The German Occupation of Belgium, 1940–1944* (New York: Peter Lang, 1993).

Wasserstein, Bernard, *The Ambiguity of Virtue: Gertrude van Tijn and the Fate of the Dutch Jews* (Cambridge, Mass.: Harvard University Press, 2014).

Weill, Joseph, *Contribution à l'histoire des camps d'internement dans l'anti-France* (Paris: Éditions du centre, 1946).

Weiss, Peter, 'Die Rettung der Juden in Dänemark während der deutschen Besetzung 1940–1945', in Wolfgang Benz and Juliane Wetzel (eds.), *Solidarität und Hilfe für Juden während der NS-Zeit*, vol. 3: *Dänemark, Niederlande, Spanien, Portugal, Ungarn, Albanien, Weißrußland* (Berlin: Metropol, 1996), pp. 11–86.

Wenck, Alexandra-Eileen, *Zwischen Menschenhandel und 'Endlösung': Das Konzentrationslager Bergen-Belsen* (Paderborn: Schöningh, 2000).

Wieviorka, Annette and Michel Laffitte, *À l'intérieur du camp de Drancy* (Paris: Perrin, 2012).

Wijngaert, Mark van den, 'The Belgian Catholics and the Jews during the German Occupation, 1940–1944', in Dan Michman (ed.), *Belgium and the Holocaust: Jews, Belgians, Germans* (Jerusalem: Yad Vashem, 1998), pp. 228–233.

Wijngaert, Mark van den, *Het beleid van het comité van de secretarissen-generaal in België tijdens de Duitse bezetting 1940–1944* (Brussels: K.A.W.L.S.K., 1975).

Wouters, Nico, 'De jacht op de Joden, 1942–1944', in Rudi van Doorslaer, Emmanuel Debruyne, Frank Seberechts, and Nico Wouters (eds.), *Gewillig België: Overheid en Jodenvervolging tijdens de Tweede Wereldoorlog* (Brussels: SOMA, 2007), pp. 517–612.

Wouters, Nico, 'La chasse aux Juifs, 1942–1944', in Rudi van Doorslaer, Emmanuel Debruyne, Frank Seberechts, and Nico Wouters (eds.), *La Belgique docile: Les autorités belges et la persécution des Juifs en Belgique durant la Seconde Guerre mondiale* (Brussels: CEGES, 2007), pp. 514–611.

Yahil, Leni, *The Rescue of Danish Jewry: Test of a Democracy* (Philadelphia: Jewish Publication Society of America, 1969).

Zee, Henri van der, *De Hongerwinter: Van Dolle Dinsdag tot Bevrijding* (The Hague: BZZToH, 1989).

Zee, Nanda van der, *Westerbork: Het doorgangskamp en zijn commandant* (Soesterberg: Aspekt, 2006).

Zee, Sytze van der, *25,000 landverraders: De SS in Nederland: Nederland in de SS* (The Hague: Kruseman, 1967).

Zee, Sytze van der, *Vogelvrij: De jacht op de Joodse onderduiker* (Amsterdam: De Bezige Bij, 2010).

Zeitoun, Sabine, *L'Œuvre de secours aux enfants (OSE) sous l'Occupation en France* (Paris: L'Harmattan, 2012).

Zomeren, Dick van, *Geschiedenis van de joodse gemeenschap in Weesp: ze waren gewoon ineens weg* (Weesp: Ark/Heureka, 1983).

Index

Newspapers and periodicals are included in the index only if the text contains information about them (e.g. publication period, editors), and not if they are merely mentioned or cited as a source. For ease of reference, the categories 'antisemitic and nationalist parties and movements', 'Jewish organizations and welfare associations', 'legislation', and 'Minister/Ministry' group together entries for the countries covered in this volume.

Europe, late 1942
Faroe Islands
Shetland
REICH COMMISSARIAT NORWAY
Oslo
SWEDEN
Skagerrak
Kattegat
North Sea
DENMARK
Copenhagen
Baltic
Northern Ireland
Dublin
IRELAND
BRITAIN
London
REICH COMMISSARIAT NETHERLANDS
Amsterdam
Hamburg
Berlin
Chelmno
GERMAN REICH
English Channel
Brussels
BELGIUM
Channel Islands
(Occupied by Germany in 1940)
Luxembourg
Protectorate of Bohemia and Moravia
Prague
Atlantic Ocean
Paris
FRANCE
Vienna
Ostmark
SWITZERLAND
Vichy
ÉTAT FRANÇAIS
VICHY FRANCE
(from 10 July 1940)
Occupied by Germany on 11 Nov. 1942
Zagreb
Venice
Marseilles
ITALY
PORTUGAL
Madrid
SPAIN
Corsica
Adriatic Sea
Rome
Vatican
Sardinia
Tyrrhenian Sea
Balearic Islands
Mediterranean Sea
Gibraltar (British)
Spanish Protectorate in Morocco
Algiers
Tunis
Sicily
Malta (British)
Morocco (French)
Algeria (French)
Tunisia (French)
0 100 200 300 km